The Preobrazhensky Papers

Historical Materialism Book Series

The Historical Materialism Book Series is a major publishing initiative of the radical left. The capitalist crisis of the twenty-first century has been met by a resurgence of interest in critical Marxist theory. At the same time, the publishing institutions committed to Marxism have contracted markedly since the high point of the 1970s. The Historical Materialism Book Series is dedicated to addressing this situation by making available important works of Marxist theory. The aim of the series is to publish important theoretical contributions as the basis for vigorous intellectual debate and exchange on the left.

The peer-reviewed series publishes original monographs, translated texts, and reprints of classics across the bounds of academic disciplinary agendas and across the divisions of the left. The series is particularly concerned to encourage the internationalization of Marxist debate and aims to translate significant studies from beyond the English-speaking world.

For a full list of titles in the Historical Materialism Book Series available in paperback from Haymarket Books, visit:
www.haymarketbooks.org/category/hm-series

The Preobrazhensky Papers

Archival Documents and Materials
Volume I: 1886–1920

Edited by
Richard B. Day and Mikhail M. Gorinov

Translated by
Richard B. Day

Haymarket Books
Chicago, IL

First published in 2014 by Brill Academic Publishers, the Netherlands
© 2014 Koninklijke Brill NV, Leiden, the Netherlands

Published in paperback in 2015 by
Haymarket Books
P.O. Box 180165
Chicago, IL 60618
773-583-7884
www.haymarketbooks.org

ISBN: 978-1-60846-373-2

Trade distribution:
In the US, Consortium Book Sales, www.cbsd.com
In Canada, Publishers Group Canada, www.pgcbooks.ca
In the UK, Turnaround Publisher Services, www.turnaround-psl.com
In all other countries, Publishers Group Worldwide, www.pgw.com

Cover design by Ragina Johnson.

This book was published with the generous support of
Lannan Foundation and the Wallace Global Fund.

Printed in Canada by union labor.

10 9 8 7 6 5 4 3 2 1

Library of Congress Cataloging-in-Publication data is available.

Dedicated with Love and Gratitude to Judi

Contents

Foreword by Mikhail M. Gorinov xvii
Preface by Richard B. Day xlix

Part I. The Beginning of the Road: 1886–1917

1. From the *Autobiography* (1886–1916) 3
2. From 'My Memories of Ya.M. Sverdlov' and Revolutionary
   Activity in the Urals during 1906–1907 13
3. '...A Page from Revolutionary Memories'
   (March 1908–February 1917) 23
4–5. Articles Published in the Newspaper *Ural'skii rabochii* in
   October and December 1907 36
       4. 'On the Present Moment', 15 October 1907 36
       5. 'The Task of the Moment', 1 December 1907 43
6. 'A Grandiose Expropriation', An Article Published in the
   Newspaper *Proletarii*, 29 (16) April 1908 50
7. Report from the Gendarmerie-Administration of Perm Province
   to the Director of the Department of Police, M.I. Trusevich,
   on the Discovery during a Search of E.A. Preobrazhensky of a
   Manuscript Written by him 'To Members of the Duma-Fraction',
   26 August 1908 54
8. From a Report by the Gendarmerie-Administration of Perm
   Province to the Director of the Department of Police, N.P. Zuev,
   on Determination of E.A. Preobrazhensky's Authorship of the
   Letters that were Seized in the Ekaterinburg Post and
   Telegraph-Office, and on his Arrest, 12 December 1911 58
9–73. Articles Published in the Newspaper *Obskaya zhizn'* from
   January to August 1912 62
       9. 'The Coming Election-Campaign', 8 January 1912 62
       10. 'The Parliamentary Elections in Germany', 12 January 1912 ... 66
       11. 'A Grievous Misunderstanding', 12 January 1912 69

12.	'Again On the Question of the Rising Price of Foodstuffs', 13 January 1912	71
13.	'The Harvest-Failure and Russian Industry', 15 January 1912	74
14.	'The English Guests in Russia', 17 January 1912	77
15.	'Then and Now', 19 January 1912	79
16.	'A New Newspaper', 20 January 1912	81
17.	'It's All in Vain, Vanya…', 25 January 1912	84
18.	'In a Rut', 26 January 1912	87
19.	'Alexander Sergeevich Pushkin (Born 20 May 1799, Died 29 January 1837)', 29 January 1912	89
20.	'Incomparables', 8 February 1912	92
21.	'On Grain-Prices', 9 February 1912	94
22.	Review of the Book by O. Schreiner, *Woman and Labour* (Published by S. Dorovatovsky and A. Charushnikov, Moscow), 10 February 1912	97
23.	'On Grain-Prices', 12 February 1912	99
24.	'Economic Essays', 14 February 1912	102
25.	'A Siberian *Zemstvo* and the Siberian Press', 19 February 1912	105
26.	Review of the Journals *Russkoe bogatstvo* (January) and *Sovremennyi mir* (February), 26 February 1912	109
27.	'A Benefit-Performance by a Renegade', 26 February 1912	114
28.	'Postscript', 29 February 1912	116
29.	'A Grandiose Strike', 6 March 1912	117
30.	'The Workers' Movement in February', 9 March 1912	121
31.	Survey of the Journals *Russkoe bogatstvo* (February), *Nasha zarya* Nos. 1–2, and *Mir* (January), 11 March 1912	122
32.	'Reply to Mr. Lyubosh', 14 March 1912	126
33.	'Once Again on a Siberian *Zemstvo*', 15 March 1912	128
34.	'A Little Pamphlet: "Poetry of the Yellow House"', 16 March 1912	130
35.	'The Price of a Cadet's Conscience', 18 March 1912	133
36.	'In Memory of A.I. Herzen (born 25 March 1812 – died 9 January 1870)', 25 March 1912	136
37.	'On the News of the Day', 6 April 1912	142
38.	'Manilovism in Siberia', 8 April 1912	144
39.	A Review of the Journals *Sovremennyi mir* and *Russkoe bogatstvo* (March), 8 April 1912	147
40.	'The Workers' Movement in March', 12 April 1912	152
41.	'An Instructive Lesson', 15 April 1912	153

42.	'A Little Pamphlet', 22 April 1912	155
43.	Review of the Journal *Vestnik Evropy* (April), 25 April 1912	157
44.	'The Incurably Ill', 29 April 1912	159
45.	'A Duel and Deputies' Immunity', 6 May 1912	164
46.	'The Workers' Movement in April', 11 May 1912	166
47.	Review of A. Bykova's Book *The Time of Troubles in Russia* (Published by S. Dorovatovsky and A. Charushnikov, Moscow), 11 May 1912	168
48.	Review of the Journals *Russkoe bogatstvo* and *Sovremennyi mir* (April), 13 May 1912	170
49.	'They Married Me without Me', 18 May 1912	175
50.	'To the Congress of Members of the Bourse in Siberia', 20 May 1912	177
51.	'Amongst the Journals', 23 May 1912	180
52.	'Prospects for the Harvest and Grain-Prices', 24 May 1912	182
53.	'On the Cadet Party-Conference', 29 May 1912	184
54.	'The Poor Industrialists!', 6 June 1912	187
55.	'The Workers' Movement in May', 9 June 1912	191
56.	Review of the Journals *Russkoe bogatstvo* and *Sovremennyi mir* (May), 10 June 1912	193
57.	'The Right to Suicide' (I), 17 June 1912	198
58.	Review of the Journal *Vestnik Evropy* (June), 19 June 1912	203
59.	'On Professor Zhakov's Lecture' (A Letter to the Editor), 24 June 1912	205
60.	'The Right to Suicide' (II), 24 June 1912	208
61.	'On Professor Zhakov's Lectures' (A Letter to the Editor)', 29 June 1912	213
62.	'On the Events in Turkey', 29 June 1912	215
63.	'On Professor Zhakov's Lectures', 1 July 1912	217
64.	'On Professor Zhakov's Lectures', 3 July 1912	220
65.	Review of the Journals *Sovremennyi mir* and *Russkoe bogatstvo* (June), 8 July 1912	223
66.	'The Workers' Movement in June', 12 July 1912	227
67.	'The "Democrats" from *Zaprosy zhizni*', 18 July 1912	229
68.	Review of the Journals *Vestnik Evropy* (July) and *Zavety* (June), 20 July 1912	232
69.	'The Far-Eastern Question', 22 July 1912	236
70.	'A Question that Needs an Answer', 27 July 1912	238
71.	Review of the Brochure by Ya. Borin, 'For Home and Hearth (The War of 1812)' (Published by S. Dorovatovsky and A. Charushnikov, Moscow), 28 July 1912	240

72. 'The Right to Suicide' (III), 29 July 1912 241
73. Review of the Journal *Russkoe bogatstvo* (July),
    5 August 1912 245
74. Report of the Yenisei Provincial Gendarmerie-Administration
    to the Director of the Police-Department G.G. Mollov on the
    Impossibility of Determining the Author of a Letter Addressed
    to the Exile I.S. Shvarts, 11 September 1915 247
75–6. Articles Published in the newspaper *Zabaikal'skoe obozrenie* in
    March 1916 250
    75. 'Quo Vadis', 14 March 1916 250
    76. 'Our Defencists', 21 March 1916 254

Part II: In the Years of Revolution and Civil War: 1917–20

1. From the *Autobiography* (for February 1917–20), 1925 263
2. From 'My Memories of Ya.M. Sverdlov' (for the Period from 1917
   to 1919), 1926 266
3–5. Articles Published in the Newspaper *Zabaikal'skii rabochii* in
    March–April 1917 270
    3. 'On our Party's Programme', 22 March 1917 270
    4. 'Dual Power, Dual Soul and Cowardice' (I), 31 March 1917 ... 273
    5. 'Dual Power, Dual Soul and Cowardice' (II), 9 April 1917 275
6–7. Speeches at the First All-Russian Congress of Soviets of Workers'
    and Soldiers' Deputies, 6–22 June 1917 277
    6. 'On Relations with the Provisional Government', Session
       of 6 June 1917 (Evening) 277
    7. 'On the Struggle Against Anti-Semitism', Session of
       22 June 1917 (Evening) 280
8–12. Speeches at the Sixth Congress of the RSDRP(B), 28 July
    (10 August)–3 (16) August 1917 283
    8. Report on the Work of the Social-Democratic Party in the
       Urals, 28 July (10 August) 6th Session 283
    9. Speech Concerning the Resolution 'The Current Moment
       and the War', 30 July (12 August), 9th Session 286
    10. Speech Concerning the Resolution 'The Current Moment
        and the War', 2 (15) August, 13th Session 288
    11. Discussion of the Question of Elections to the Constituent
        Assembly, 3 (16) August, 14th Session (Morning) 289
    12. Speech on the Resolution 'On the Political Situation',
        3 (16) August, 15th Session 291

13.	The Pamphlet 'What the Urals Workers Need' September–October 1917	292
14.	'We Must Not Wait', An Article Published in the Newspaper *Ural'skii rabochii*, 15 November 1917	308
15.	From the Protocols of a Session of the Moscow City-Wide Conference of the RSDRP(B) on the Question of War and Peace, 13 January 1918	311
16.	'A Constituent Assembly of the Soviets', An Article Published in the Newspaper *Pravda*, 25 January 1918	313
17–23.	Articles Published in the Newspaper *Ural'skii rabochii* in March–May 1918	318
	17. 'War or Peace?' (I), 3 March (17 February) 1918	318
	18. 'Peace and War' (II), 6 March (21 February) 1918	322
	19. 'Peace or War?' (III), 7 March (22 February) 1918	326
	20. 'Peace or War?' (IV), 9 March (24 February) 1918	329
	21. 'The Anniversary of the Revolution' 12 March (27 February) 1918	332
	22. 'Peace is Signed', 19 (6) March 1918	339
	23. 'The Great Apostle of Socialism (In Memory of Karl Marx. Born 4 April 1918, Died 14 March 1888)', 5 May (22 April) 1918	341
24.	The Article 'A Congress is Necessary', Published in the Journal *Kommunist*, June 1918	346
25–6.	Articles on 'The Urals Counter-Revolution', Published in the Newspaper *Pravda*, 29 (16)–30 (17) June 1918	355
	25. 'The Urals Counter-Revolution' (I), 29 (16) June 1918	355
	26. 'The Urals Counter-Revolution' (II), 30 (17) June 1918	358
27–36.	Articles and a Report, Published in the Newspaper *Ural'skii rabochii* in August–December 1918	361
	27. 'Tedious Work', 13 August 1918	361
	28. 'Worldwide Bolshevism', 11 October 1918	365
	29. 'No Privileges', 27 October 1918	367
	30. 'To the Provincial Conference of the RKP', 15 November 1918	369
	31. 'Report to the Perm Provincial Conference of the RKP', 21 November 1918	371
	32. Concluding Remarks at the Perm Conference of the RKP, 23 November 1918	375
	33. 'Two Congresses', 27 November 1918	382
	34. 'From Congress Impressions' (I), 30 November 1918	384

	35. 'From Congress Impressions' (II), 3 December 1918	387
	36. The Union of Oppressed Peoples, 8 December 1918	390
37.	A Letter from the Presidium of the Ural Oblast Committee of Communes to V.I. Lenin Concerning the Critical Position of Sections of the Red Army on the Eastern Front and the Possibility of Surrender of Perm to the White Guards, no later than 24 December 1918	391
38–42.	Articles Published in the Newspaper and in the Weekly *Pravda* in December 1918–March 1919	402
	38. 'The Gentlemen of Tashkent', 26 December 1918	402
	39. 'On Forms of Proletarian Dictatorship', 9 February 1919 ...	405
	40. 'Once Again on Military Specialists' (From the Pre-Congress Discussion), 16 February 1919	411
	41. 'On Forms of Proletarian Dictatorship', 2 March 1919	415
	42. 'On Forms of Proletarian Dictatorship. The Shortcomings of Soviet Power', 16 March 1919	421
43–4.	Reports for 10–16 May 1919 from the Plenipotentiary of the VTsIK and Responsible Representative of the Central Committee of the RKP(B) in Orel Province E.A. Preobrazhensky to the Central Committee of the RKP(B) on Assisting the Local Authority in Mobilisation of the Population for the Struggle against Denikin	426
	43. A Short Report of Four Days of Central-Committee Plenipotentiary Preobrazhensky, 10–13 May 1919	426
	44. Second Regular Report from Plenipotentiary Preobrazhensky, 13–16 May 1919	429
45–6.	Articles Published in the Newspaper *Pravda* at the Beginning of June 1919	431
	45. 'Islands of Socialism' (I), 1 June 1919	431
	46. 'Islands of Socialism' (II), 5 June 1919	435
47.	Report of the Plenipotentiary of the VTsIK and Responsible Representative of the Central Committee of the RKP(B) in Orel Province E.A. Preobrazhensky Concerning Mobilisation of the Population of the Province for the Struggle against Denikin, 6 June 1919	438
48–56.	Articles Published in the Newspaper *Pravda* in June–August 1919	443
	48. 'Islands of Socialism' (III), 19 June 1919	443
	49. Obituary 'Memories of Comrade Tolmachev', 22 June 1919	446
	50. 'Islands of Socialism' (IV), 26 June 1919	448
	51. 'The Management of Soviet Estates', 29 June 1919	451
	52. 'Who Will Hold Out Longer?', 27 July 1919	454

53.	Notes on the Red Army (I): 'The Struggle against Spontaneous Decomposition', 29 July 1919	458
54.	Notes on the Red Army (II): 'The Struggle against Spontaneous Decomposition', 1 August 1919	463
55.	Notes on the Red Army (III): 'Cementing the Army', 14 August 1919	466
56.	Notes on the Red Army (IV), 24 August 1919	470
57.	Protocol No. 57 of a Meeting of the Committee of the Bolkhov Organisation of the RKP(B) of Orel Province Concerning Implementation of the Party's Policy with Regard to Middle-Peasants and Reasons for the Collapse of Party-Cells in the Parishes, 30 August 1919 (6 o'clock in the evening)	474
58.	Protocol No. 37 of a Session of Members of the General Meeting of the Bolkhov Organisation of the RKP(B) of Orel Province Concerning Tasks Facing the Communists of Town and Country, 30 August 1919 (11 o'clock in the evening)	477
59.	Protocol No. 58 of the Session of the Committee of the Bolkhov Organisation of the RKP(B) of Orel Province in Connection with Murder of the Communist Makarin, 30 August 1919 (11 pm)	480
60.	Letter by E.A. Preobrazhensky to V.I. Lenin with a Proposal to Change Tactics in Relation to the Don Cossacks, August 1919	483
61–2.	Articles Published in the Newspaper *Pravda* in September–October 1919	485
61.	'The Lessons of Mamontov', 18 September 1919	485
62.	'When Will the Revolution Begin in Europe?', 12 October 1919	489
63.	Resolution of the First All-Bashkir Conference of the RKP(B) on the Tasks Facing the Communists of Bashkiria in the Period of Civil War, 8 November 1919	492
64.	Address by the Representative of the VTsIK E.A. Preobrazhensky at a Session of Responsible Party-Workers of the Ufa Provincial Organisation of the RKP(B) Concerning Failure of the Putsch Mounted by Bourgeois Nationalists, 25 January 1920	495
65.	Address by the Representative of the VTsIk E.A. Preobrazhensky at a Session of the Plenum of the Ufa Provincial Committee of the RKP(B) Concerning the Work of the Provincial Committee in Conditions of Conflict Between the Centre and the Bashkir Republic, 11 February 1920	497
66.	From the Address by E.A. Preobrazhensky at the Sixth Ufa Provincial Conference of the RKP(B) Concerning Economic Construction and a Federal Constitution, 3 March 1920	500

67. E.A. Preobrazhensky's Address to a Meeting of Responsible Workers of Ufa Province Concerning Conditions in the Bashkir Republic and the Tasks Facing Communists as a Result of the Uprising Mounted by Bashkir Nationalists, 13 March 1920 503

68–9. Addresses of the Central Committee of the RKP(B) to Party-Organisations and the Provincial Committee of Bashkiria, April 1920 509

    68. To the Party Organisations of Bashkiria – Concerning Wide Involvement of the Toiling Masses of the Republic in the Communist Party, April 1920 509

    69. To the Provincial Committees of Kazan, Simbirsk, Samara, Ufa, Chelyabinsk and Orenburg – Concerning the Inadmissibility of any Development of National Animosity towards the Tatar and Bashkir Press, April 1920 512

70. An article 'Concerning the Mobilisation of Unskilled Labour-Power', published in the newspaper *Pravda*, 30 March 1920 514

71. E.A. Preobrazhensky's Diary with Notes on Questions Discussed at Meetings of the Politburo and the Plenum of the Central Committee of the RKP(B), 4 May–24 September 1920 517

72. Letter to V.I. Lenin concerning K.B. Radek's Speeches on the War with Poland and its Press-Coverage, 6 May 1920 526

73. Response from Secretary of the Central Committee of the RKP(B) E.A. Preobrazhensky to the 'First Draft of Theses on the National Question', prepared by V.I. Lenin for a Report to the Second Congress of the Comintern, not earlier than 5 June, no later than 19 July 1920 528

74. Resolution taken by the Politburo of the Central Committee of the RKP(B) Concerning the Case of Oskar Blum, 29 July 1920 532

75–7. Articles published in the newspaper *Pravda* in July–August 1920 30 July–15 August 1920 534

    75. 'A Very Promising Experiment', 30 July 1920 534

    76. 'Comrade Larin's Next "Project"', 11 August 1920 537

    77. 'On a New Book by N.I. Bukharin', 15 August 1920 540

78. Report by E.A. Preobrazhensky to the Commission of the Central Committee of the RKP(B) on the Question of Eliminating Inequality in the Ranks of the RKP(B), no later than 24 August 1920 546

79. From a Draft Circular-Letter of the Central Committee of the RKP(B), Prepared by E.A. Preobrazhensky, Concerning the Question of Struggle Against Bureaucratism and Material Inequality in the Party, no later than 24 August 1920 550

80–3. Articles Published in the Newspaper *Pravda* in September–
December 1920 555
    80. 'The Average Communist' (I), 19 September 1920 555
    81. 'The Average Communist' (II), 21 September 1920 557
    82. 'The Social Basis of the October Revolution',
        7 November 1920 560
    83. 'A Straw for the Drowning White Guards',
        12 December 1920 563

Part III: *The ABC of Communism*: 1917–1920

1. E.A. Preobrazhensky's Pamphlet *Peasant Russia and Socialism (Towards a Review of Our Agrarian Programme)*, 1918 569
2. E.A. Preobrazhensky's Book *Anarchism and Communism*, 1918 592
3. E.A. Preobrazhensky's Chapters from the Book *The ABC of Communism* (Co-authored with N.I. Bukharin), 1919 646
4. E.A. Preobrazhensky's Book *Paper Money in the Epoch of Proletarian Dictatorship*, 1920 732

Biographical Notes 799
References 850
Index of Names 853

Foreword
Mikhail M. Gorinov

Evgeny Alekseevich Preobrazhensky was one of those 'unlucky' historical figures. In *The Ugly Duchess*, Lion Feuchtwanger provided the unforgettable literary characterisation of such figures who are unjustly treated by a thankless humanity.[1] In our recent past, there are many such persons who are both genuine and real. Take Leon Trotsky... During the Civil War, he led the victorious Red Army, with whose bayonets Great Russia was restored in a new form from practically nothing. Yet up to this day, his name is anathematised by both 'Red' and 'White' segments of the Russian political spectrum. Joseph Stalin really 'took Russia from the plough to the atomic bomb'; under his leadership, our country acquired perhaps its greatest world-influence in all of its history and, in a literal sense, became the hope of humanity, but, even half-a-century later, the mass media paint him exclusively in black.

But at least these politicians are remembered – unlike Evgeny Preobrazhensky, who is now totally and unjustifiably forgotten.[2] Most people today associate the surname Preobrazhensky exclusively with the Professor Preobrazhensky who was a character in Bulgakov's *Heart of a Dog*.[3] Even those who know the person in question are still perplexed: at a time of liberalism's 'triumph' in Russia, why publish the works of a 'Trotskyist theorist' (the indelible cliché bestowed upon Preobrazhensky by his political opponents)?

Just who is Evgeny Alekseevich Preobrazhensky, and why is his work so important today?

The biography of E.A. Preobrazhensky (1886–1937) is noteworthy even when compared with the destinies of the brightest stars of Bolshevism. During the Revolution of 1905–7, he took part in the December armed insurrection in Moscow

---

1. The reference is to Lion Feuchtwanger's historical novel concerning Margaret Maultasch, Duchess of Tyrol.
2. In the West, of course, Preobrazhensky is far better-known than he is in Russia. Several of his works have been translated into English, and he is generally recognised as one of the foremost participants in the Soviet industrialisation-debates of the 1920s.
3. The reference is to Mikhail A. Bulgakov's comic satire on pseudo-science.

and became one of the leading Bolsheviks in the Urals, being arrested several times. Following the defeat of the revolution, he went underground, was arrested, served a prison-sentence, and hurried back from exile. In 1917, he participated in key revolutionary forums in Moscow and the Urals, including the First All-Russian Congress of Soviets and the Sixth Congress of the Russian Communist Party (Bolsheviks). In 1918, he led the Bolshevik organisation in the Urals region. In 1919, E.A. Preobrazhensky fought for Soviet power in the south and east of the country, and, at the same time, wrote (together with his co-author N.I. Bukharin) the famous *ABC of Communism*, which familiarised not only citizens of Soviet Russia and the USSR but also the rest of the world with communist doctrine during the first decade of Soviet power (the book was translated into all major languages). In 1920, Preobrazhensky was elected as one of three secretaries of the CC of the RKP(B);[4] in other words, he stood at the peak of the Bolshevik political Olympus. During the first half of the 1920s, he became one of the leaders of the (Trotskyist) Left Opposition and wrote a number of works in which he predicted the crisis of the NEP-economy of the 1920s, including its details and timing, and proposed the way out (which was actually implemented, although in a crude and rigid manner, along the lines of 'Stalinist industrialisation'). During the same years he published probably the only Bolshevik work specifically devoted to the ethical problem (*On Morals and Class Norms*). In the mid-1920s, he produced perhaps the most fundamental of all theoretical works from the Bolshevik camp, giving an innovative analysis of the Soviet economy and its prospects (*The New Economics*). From the 1920s to 1930s, he developed the 'theory of a collapsing currency' (the title of a book in which he gave a model of how a market-economy functions in conditions of inflation). In the early 1930s, he provided a deeper theoretical analysis of the cycle of expanded capitalist reproduction that appeared in Karl Marx's *Capital*. And in 1937, E.A. Preobrazhensky was one of the very few people who betrayed no-one while he was under interrogation in the torture-chambers of the NKVD.

By answering the first question – as to who Preobrazhensky was – we have already touched upon the second: why publish his works today? At the very least, they must be published for the sake of restoring historical justice.

But this is only one part of the phenomenon of 'Preobrazhensky's relevance'. The other is historical and cognitive. In the person of E.A. Preobrazhensky, we see the 'ideal Bolshevik'. Through his life and works, we can gain an understanding of the 'people of a special mould, cut from a special material' (Stalin's expression), who, after completing the Great October Socialist Revolution, literally 'elevated' humanity, compelling it for the next sixty years to develop according

---

4. Central Committee of the Russian Communist Party (Bolsheviks).

to new and more just laws. And today, following the disappearance of the Soviet Union, every rational person sees how inhumane the world has become in the absence of this 'restraint'. Preobrazhensky is the 'ideal Bolshevik'; in his works, when they are taken apart from political circumstances, we see the Bolshevik Revolution in 'a chemically-pure form': with its achievements and shortcomings, its advances and reverses, its truth and its lies. And if you wish to understand the history of the Russian Revolution, which means the history of Russia during the first third of the twentieth century, and thus the history of the world during this period, then you should read Preobrazhensky.

But the works of E.A. Preobrazhensky are of more than academic interest. Inflationary processes, whenever and wherever they have occurred – whether in 'war-communist' or post-communist Russia, in the Weimar Republic or in modern Argentina – develop 'according to Preobrazhensky'; that is, according to the laws he discovered in the 1920s. The leaders of any country who aim to overcome backwardness and achieve genuine emancipation find in the works of E.A. Preobrazhensky even today a formula for such a dash towards the 'realm of freedom'. It was no coincidence that a Spanish translation of his *New Economics* appeared in the 1960s in revolutionary Cuba. And, however much our home-grown 'liberals' today dismiss the planned economy, the development of a modern and sophisticated world-economy is, nevertheless, itself being planned, although it is true that the decision-making centres are no longer to be found in the 'Old Square'.[5] In the works of this same E.A. Preobrazhensky, we find an unsurpassed analysis of the mechanisms for securing the dynamic equilibrium of an economic system.

And finally today, in an epoch when the cult of the 'golden calf' shamelessly prevails – a time of the all-pervading (and truly 'totalitarian'!) propaganda of vulgarity, meanness and immorality; in this currently-graceless era predicted by Jack London, when the all-destroying 'Iron Heel'[6] triumphs and is destroying even the slightest expression of spirituality in the human soul, every yearning for the ideal, every attempt to transform earthly life on the patterns of celestial harmony – we find in the character and works of this same Evgeny Alekseevich Preobrazhensky, in the images of the 'Old Bolsheviks' he forever embodies, in his self-sacrifice, unselfishness and self-denial reminiscent of the early Christians, a hope for man's noble destiny, a faith in his better future, and a love for all who are 'humiliated and offended'.

---

5. *Staraya ploshchad'* [Old Square] was formerly the central headquarters of the Soviet Communist Party.
6. See London 2006.

The 'popovich'

Thus E.A. Preobrazhensky[7] is of interest to the researcher not simply as a personality of the early twentieth century, but also as a kind of 'ideal type' (or more precisely, as one of the 'sub-types') of a Russian revolutionary.

L. Haimson rightly identifies three major social sources in the formation of Russia's revolutionary intelligentsia: the provincial service-nobility, the *'popovichy'*, and the non-Russian (non-Orthodox) national minorities. In his opinion, the representatives of each of these strata made a specific impression on the shape of the counter-élite that was destined to shake the structure of Russian statehood to its foundations in 1917.[8]

Evgeny Preobrazhensky was a typical *'popovich'*. According to Haimson, those who came from that milieu (V.G. Belinsky, N.A. Dobrolyubov, N.G. Chernyshevsky, B.I. Nikolaevsky and others) brought to the ranks of the revolutionary intelligentsia: 1) an acute sense of duty towards the people; 2) a steadfast attention to moral questions, even to the point of assigning them a quasi-religious quality (the intensive working out of this problematic within the limits of political and social programmes, a commitment to consistent personal embodiment of the norms of revolutionary ethics); and 3) an intellectual need to find a replacement for the Russian-Orthodox 'cosmology' (its conception of the universe and the principles and laws that govern it).[9]

Thus a study of the early period of E.A. Preobrazhensky's life, of the time that shaped him as a revolutionary from the *'popovichy'*, is completely in order. Without an analysis of the mentality of one of these people – in Stalin's words, 'people of a special mould'[10] (Stalin, incidentally, was not a *'popovich'* in the strict sense, although he did graduate from a spiritual academy and Orthodox seminary) – one cannot fully understand the peculiarities of the Russian Revolution and its subsequent transformation.

The 'little homeland' and the family

Evgeny Alekseevich Preobrazhensky was born on 15 February 1886 (this and subsequent dates are given in the old style) in the town of Bolkhov, the district-centre of Orel province, located 55 *versts*[11] north of the city of Orel. Towering

---

7. For a bibliography of the major works on E.A. Preobrazhensky see Gorinov and Tsakunov 1991; 1992.
8. Leopold Haimson uses the term *'popovichy'* to refer to 'the descendants of the representatives of Orthodox clergy and the graduates of its spiritual academies and seminaries'. See Haimson 1995.
9. Haimson 1995, pp. 123, 125.
10. Stalin 1951, p. 46.
11. [One *verst* is the equivalent of 1.0668 kilometres.]

above the steep bank of the Nugr River, and crowned by the cupolas of 18 churches and high bell-towers, this ancient trading town seemed like a miraculous vision from an enchanted Russian fairy-tale. It was often called, and is today still called, the 'second Suzdal'.

On both the maternal and the paternal side, Evgeny Preobrazhensky was born into an environment of hereditary Orthodox priests. His father, Aleksei Aleksandrovich, was also born to the family of a priest on 8 March 1853, in the village of Uporie, in the Trubchevsky district of Orel province.[12] He was an extraordinary man, distinguished by a pronounced commitment to spiritual enlightenment. His fate was to provide convincing evidence of how correct S.N. Bulgakov was when he claimed that 'In Russian history the "spiritual estate", with all its infirmities, truly was also the most "spiritual"'.[13]

Graduating from the Orel theological seminary, A.A. Preobrazhensky taught pre-school for two years at the same seminary. Then he spent the next seven years at the *zemstvo* public school in the village of Zhipriyatino, also in Trubchevsky district. He was, it seems, an extraordinary teacher. Evidence of this can be seen in the monetary rewards that he repeatedly received from the *zemstvo* and from the Ministry of Public Education. On 15 August 1983, A.A. Preobrazhensky was ordained as a priest of the Pokrovsky church in Bolkhov. In that same year, he used his own resources to open a grammar-school, and two years later a Sunday-school in Pokrovsky parish. In 1886, the year of his son Evgeny's birth, Father Aleksy, again using his own resources, opened a parish-school: 'there he himself taught and preached [namely, taught the Law of God]. From 1890 to 1894, he was a member of the Bolkhov branch of the diocesan school council (the institution that governed all local Church-schools). At the same time, from 1884 to 5 November 1894, Preobrazhensky senior taught God's Law 'in the third-level private school of Lady Bankovsky' and later preached for many years at the Bolkhov city-school for men.

On 17 February 1895 (two days after Evgeny celebrated his ninth birthday), A.A. Preobrazhensky, at his own request, was transferred from the Pokrovskaya to the Troitskaya church (built in the late seventeenth and early eighteenth centuries). His parish-school also moved here, and it is precisely this temple, perhaps the most beautiful in Bolkhov, that is associated with the most memorable childhood, adolescent and youthful religious experiences of the future revolutionary.

The scant information from A.A. Preobrazhensky's service-record confirms and supplements the memories of his grandson, Leonid Evgenyevich Preobrazhensky, the son of E.A. Preobrazhensky from his first marriage with Rosa

---

12. *Formulyar svyashchennika Troitskoi g. Bolkhova tserkvi Alekseya Preobrazhenskovo, 1 July, 1906*. TsIAM. F.418. op 321. D. 1496. L. 16–16 ob.
13. Bulgakov 1946, p. 25. Bulgakov was himself the grandson of priests on both sides of his family.

Abramovna Nevel'son (1898–1980).[14] 'According to my mother's stories' – writes Leonid Evgenyevich – 'the Preobrazhenskys, as far back as she could trace the history of their family, were clergymen, but only Aleksei Aleksandrovich received the honour of being ordained as an Archpriest, after graduating from the seminary and putting in long service as a parish-priest'. Talking about his father's library, L.E. Preobrazhensky recalled a very interesting detail, characterising A.A. Preobrazhensky as an educated man who was quite tolerant of dissenting views: 'This library was collected with my father from the time when he was a student in the gymnasium, and despite his travelling across Russia at the beginning of the twentieth century, additions were made continuously to the Bolkhov library not only by my father but also by Aleksei Aleksandrovich. One can certainly assume that he was the only Archpriest who kept a large volume of literature that contradicted religious views'.[15] Evgeny Preobrazhensky's father was one of the finest representatives of Orthodox parish-priests, those 'little fathers', as they were affectionately known among the people, who over the course of centuries baptised and married, raised and taught, admonished and buried numerous generations of the Russian people, mentoring them spiritually as well as hearing their confessions.

Unfortunately, we know very little concerning the other members of the Preobrazhensky family. As of 1906, it included six members in addition to A.A. Preobrazhensky (and after that point it did not change): his wife, Varvara Alekseevna (born Levitskaya) – in 1906 she was 42 years old – was the daughter of an Archpriest and was educated at the Zhizdrinsky boarding school, as well as the five children. Having graduated from the Orel diocesan school for women, the daughter Lyudmila, 22 years old, assumed 'the duties of a teacher in the village of Khotetov in Bolkhov district'; the son Viktor, 21 years old, was studying 'in the sixth class of the Orel ecclesiastical seminary'; daughter Olga, 18 years old, was studying 'in the eighth grade of Mrs. Gitterman's Orel girls' gymnasium'; the daughter Aleksandra, 11 years old, attended the second class of the Bolkhov girls' pregymnasium; and Evgeny, the third child in the family, was then 20 years old.[16]

---

14. M.M. Gorinov has the text of the recollections. The citations come from the manuscript prepared for publication by the Press of the Main Archive of Moscow (hereafter, L.E. Preobrazhensky n.d.).

15. L.E. Preobrazhensky n.d., pp. 1, 8. Later, A.A. Preobrazhensky was known as a participant in the renewal-movement in the Russian-Orthodox Church. In 1922, in particular, he was elected to the renewal-leadership of the Bolkhov diocese by representatives of the 'Living Church' with the support of local authorities. See Osipova 1998, p. 217.

16. *Formulyar svyashchennika Troitskoi g. Bolkhova tserkvi Alekseya Preobrazhenskovo*: TsIAM. F. 418. Op. 321. D. 1946. L. 16–16 ob.

With many children, the family was typical of the Russian-Orthodox clergy at the time. However, unlike in former times, there was already division in this family. There was a growing undercurrent, so characteristic of that tragic epoch, of differing world-views; of the five children, two received a spiritual education and three, including our hero, a secular education.

The lives of E.A. Preobrazhensky's parents ended tragically: 'By 1932, the Preobrazhenskys were twice subject to de-kulakisation, and in 1936 Aleksei Aleksandrovich was arrested and died in prison. Varvara Alekseevna did not long survive him. In addition to the trauma of her loneliness, there was also a physical trauma: after falling from a porch, she lay on the ground for a long time without any assistance, fell ill and soon died'.[17] But at the time when Evgeny, the third child, was born to the Preobrazhensky family in 1886, these dramatic events were still far-off.

Childhood

What happened during the childhood of this *'popovich'*, and what were the origins of his ardent revolutionism? In an autobiography written for the *Granat* encyclopaedic dictionary, E.A. Preobrazhensky specified three qualities that characterised him in childhood: a developed intellect, religiosity, and a loathing of material inequality.

The role of his intellectual gifts ('I learned to read very early and already at four years of age read the stories in the ABC of Tolstoy') is clear enough in the life of this revolutionary: they were precisely the precondition for his later innovative research in the field of economic theory. But this feature of personality does little to help us in understanding the genesis of social radicalism in our hero: it is far from the case that every intellectual becomes a revolutionary.

The revolutionary vector in the destiny of this *'popovich'* from Bolkhov is more readily-explained by the other aspects of his childhood-view of the world: religiosity and an inclination towards egalitarianism. 'In my childhood I was very religious', E.A. Preobrazhensky recalled in his autobiography. 'I spent a great deal of time in the bell-towers of the two churches where my father served: I caught pigeons, ruined crows' nests and did rather well at ringing the small bells'.[18]

To understand better his earnest religiosity during childhood, let us turn to the method of historical analogy. On 16 June 1871 – that is, fifteen years before the birth of E.A. Preobrazhensky – a son was born to another hereditary Orthodox priest's family, in Livnakh, another small town in the same province, Orel.

---

17. L.E. Preobrazhensky n.d., p. 1.
18. Preobrazhensky 1989, p. 120.

He was given the name Sergei in honour of the revered Sergei Radonezhsky. This Russian boy was destined to travel an extremely complex road of spiritual development: from religious conviction in childhood to uncompromising atheism, and then to become one of the most educated Marxists of his era, and still later, having abandoned Marxism, to return to the bosom of the Russian-Orthodox Church. We are talking about the brilliant Orthodox philosopher and theologian S.N. Bulgakov.

In the autobiographical essay *My Homeland*, written in the autumn of his life, Father Sergei reconstructs his childhood religious experiences and recalls for us the 'aura' of Orthodoxy that so pervaded the family life of a priest. 'Our home' – recalled Bulgakov – 'was not far from the mountainous part over the river and five minutes from the Sergievskaya church. It was made of wood, with five rooms and large porches'.[19] It was in just about the same kind of home, likewise situated over the river, that the Preobrazhensky family also lived.[20] 'The holy cradle. Everything inside it was poor and simple (although better than the average standard of living in Livnakh), with modest wooden furniture but also a "divan" and two "armchairs" in the "living room". With icons everywhere and burning icon-lamps, it was like a church'.[21] By analogy, one can imagine the interior-fittings of the Preobrazhensky family-home, whose level of material well-being was likewise relatively high. 'Father once said – L.E. Preobrazhensky remembers – that his parents were very wealthy people, and even after two confiscations[22] they were still the most well-to-do people in town'.[23] But it is important to emphasise that the Preobrazhenskys probably began to appear rich at the beginning of the 1930s (they faced a second confiscation in 1932). By that time, the merchant-stratum had been eliminated, and compared with people sitting on a starvation ration-card, a Bolkhov Archpriest might really look like Croesus.

I think there is no risk of stretching the truth in supposing that the young Evgeny Preobrazhensky, 'very religious' in his childhood, had about the same relation to the Church as did the young Sergei Bulgakov, who wrote in the twilight of his life:

> ... Homeland my homeland, its sacred place was the Sergievskaya church... For us it was something just as given and self-explanatory as... nature herself. It was beautiful, like nature, with a quiet and humble beauty... How we loved

---

19. Bulgakov 1996, pp. 5, 13.
20. The approximate location of the Preobrazhenskys' home was pointed out to M.M. Gorinov by a student of local lore, A.E. Benediktov, during a visit to the town of Bolkhov in the early 1990s.
21. Bulgakov 1996, p. 14.
22. ['De-kulakisations']
23. L.E. Preobrazhensky n.d., p. 2.

> this temple – as we loved our mother, our homeland, and God – with a singular love, and how we were inspired by it. For us it was both a sanctuary and a place of rapturous beauty – there was nothing more for us, but this was enough... In childhood we knew nothing more of the realm of 'culture': neither music nor any other art for which the soul thirsted. But it was complete, because the Church provided everything, truth through beauty and beauty in the truth.[24]

Church-regulations determined the entire daily life of a priest's family, and in this regard the Preobrazhenskys were no exception. As Bulgakov wrote:

> Both of them – father and mother – were completely imbued with a simple and naïve church-faith that allowed no questioning and no doubt, nor any liberties or privileges. The *Tipikon*[25] set out our domestic rules concerning fasting and celebrations, worship and prayer. The order of our life breathed this atmosphere, and we could not imagine anything different. Thus it was self-evident to us, as with the laws of nature, that fasting days, and especially the severe régime of Lent, could not fail to be observed; that morning and even evening-attendance at services, regardless of time of year or weather, were imperative; and there could not even be any question of human weakness, health-conditions, and so on. Such questions never arose, and for us children such questions could never arise, for we were so dedicated ourselves and so loved the temple and the beauty of its services.[26]

The Church set alight in the souls of the young '*popovichy*' an aspiration to high ideals, to finding an inconceivable harmony in a sinful earthly life; it made them complicit in the fate of the people. Consider again the words of Father Sergei:

> Together with the Church, I absorbed the Russian people into my soul, not externally, as some sort of object of veneration or reason, but from within, as my own essence, at one with myself. There is no more popular and, so to speak, popularising and unifying element than the Church, precisely because within it there are no 'people' but only the Church, the one for all and rendering all as one.[27]

And it was precisely the Orthodox Church that gave rise to the first social experiences in the vulnerable souls of children: inadvertently, it made them feel the prevalent social injustice and become aware of the poverty and sufferings of

---

24. Bulgakov 1996, pp. 15–16, 18.
25. The regulations were a liturgical-church collection of daily instructions on the order and manner in which Christians were to perform services and prepare food.
26. Bulgakov 1996, pp. 19–20.
27. Bulgakov 1996, p. 18.

the people; it awakened within them a sense of penitence towards the 'peasant'. For the Easter-festival, S.N. Bulgakov recalls, children would receive new clothes. But they were also aware that some child whom they knew would have to come to church in old clothing:

> Showing off in church in my new clothes, I timidly searched with my eyes and found him – in his ugliness. It is true that he would hardly be so aware of his own wretchedness, and I adjusted perfectly-well to a certain spiritual discomfort and readily forgot any reproaches of conscience. But they always occurred, those reproaches.[28]

Indeed the psychology of the 'repentant intellectual' – which he could not distinguish from Christian repentance – along with his '*narodnichestvo*', originated precisely thus.

Compare this with Preobrazhensky: 'My loathing of material inequality arose from social sentiments that awakened in me at a very early age. I remember that when I was eight years old, I demonstratively threw aside new boots that mother had bought for Easter on the grounds that poverty forced Mishka Uspensky, my childhood-playmate and the son of a shoemaker, to dress for Easter in boots that had holes'.[29] To be sure, Preobrazhensky was more radical in his egalitarianism than Bulgakov, but this egalitarianism, this sense of penitence in relation to the people, grew from one-and-the-same common source – the 'popularising' element of the Russian-Orthodox Church.

The revolt against God

His further spiritual evolution was typical of many '*popovichy*' of the nineteenth century, beginning with V.G. Belinsky, N.G. Chernyshevsky, and N.A. Dobrolyubov.[30] Preobrazhensky's sincere religiosity during childhood did not survive confrontation with the flow of atheistic-denunciatory literature that dissolved the foundations of Russian society's world-view at the time: God was overthrown.

'At first, I studied in the private school of my father and then, before entering the gymnasium, I spent two years at the Bolkhov city-school. During the first two to three years in the Orel gymnasium, I did well and was the second-best

---

28. Ibid.
29. Preobrazhensky 1989, p. 120.
30. The seminarist Dobrolyubov, for example, was 'one of the most devout people in Nizhnii Novgorod, considering it sinful to have tea with a bun before mass on a festive day and assiduously making the sign of the cross before each church during walks'; later he became a vehement atheist. See Smirnov 1984, p. 10.

student in the class, but then I lost interest in the gymnasium-subjects because I was distracted by reading newspapers and journals with a liberal-populist leaning, novels by our classical writers, and textbooks on history'.[31] In 1897, Evgeny Preobrazhensky entered the Orel classical men's gymnasium, where the Decembrist P.I. Yakushkin was educated along with the writers N.S. Leskov and L.N. Andreev, the brothers Petr and Aleksandr Stolypin, and other notable personalities of Russian history and culture.[32] 'In my fourteenth year' – Preobrazhensky continues – 'I arrived independently at the conviction that God does not exist'.[33]

How did this turnabout in Evgeny's soul occur? S.N. Bulgakov again helps us to understand better the causes, circumstances, and the actual process of transition from the religiosity of childhood to atheism, for at just about the same age (in one place he speaks of being 12 to 13 years of age, elsewhere of 14 to 15) he experienced something similar:

> I was born and grew up under the shelter of the Church, and this always determined my nature...I always lived in the faith and by the faith. How could it happen that this faith of mine became disbelief...? How did it happen? Somehow unexpectedly, almost as if it were self-evident, the prose of the seminarists and the seminary began to displace the poetry of childhood.[34]

For Preobrazhensky, the role of 'the seminarists and the seminary' was apparently played by the 'prose' of life at the gymnasium and by 'an inside view of what went on in the religious kitchen'.[35] Doubts and questions began. 'Once it appeared, the internal dissonance deepened and passed over into a religious crisis'.

It is possible that the latter might have been resolved relatively painlessly had there not been added to the typically-critical attitude of young people, with their scepticism and non-conformism, the influence of another very powerful factor: the culture of the Russian intelligentsia, which at the time was literally saturated with atheism. 'I knew no culture other than that of the intelligentsia', Bulgakov acknowledged, 'I did not know...[The result was my] adolescent helplessness when confronting my lack of faith, and my *naïveté* allowed me to think...that it was the only possible form of world-outlook that existed for "sensible" people'.[36]

---

31. Preobrazhensky 1989, p. 120.
32. Information concerning the Orel gymnasium was kindly provided to M.M. Gorinov during the early 1990s by the Orel historian E.I. Chapkevich.
33. Preobrazhensky 1989, p. 120.
34. Bulgakov 1946, pp. 25–6.
35. Preobrazhensky 1989, p. 120.
36. Bulgakov 1946, pp. 27–32.

Compare this with Lev Tikhomirov, who developed along a path that was parallel in many ways to Bulgakov's:

> Everything I heard as a youth systematically undermined my childhood religious beliefs. I saw around me the practice of religious rites, but they were either insincere or shameful. An educated man either did not believe, or else he believed in contradiction with his own convictions. *The things a youth, a lad, had to hear or read about religion!* The books said nothing of Orthodoxy. They spoke of the superstition of Catholicism, the inconsistencies of Protestantism, the fanatical cruelty of the Clericals, even adding that none of this applies to Orthodoxy. The mocking reservation was all too clear, especially as materialism was preached openly. Yet if there is no God, if Christ was a man, then, of course, it is easy to judge what Orthodoxy is. I began very early to read Pisarev [also one of the *maîtres à penser* for the young Preobrazhensky]... At his prompting the matter occupied me endlessly. At 15, I believed in all possible 'arbitrary origins' [of life], in Pouchet, Joli, Mussi and so forth just as firmly as in the roundness of the Earth or in the ignorance of Pasteur, the emptiness of Pushkin and the 'obscurantism' of the Slavophiles.[37]

Among the literature that strengthened his atheistic views, E.A. Preobrazhensky recalls two volumes on the *History of Culture* by Kolb: 'This superficial work had such a strong influence upon me precisely because the author consistently exposes all religious superstitions and religious ignorance without, however, any understanding of the historical laws involved'.[38] The reference is to *The History of Human Culture* by the well-known German statistician F. Kolb, a man of quite radical views (he was a deputy in the Frankfurt Parliament during the Revolution of 1848), who considered that 'religions arose due to fear resulting from the weakness and ignorance of man'.[39]

In his 'religious nihilism' (S.N. Bulgakov's expression)[40] E.A. Preobrazhensky showed the consistency that so characterised him (remember how he threw away the new boots that his mother gave him as an Easter-gift). In his autobiography he recalls the 'aversion to religion' that seized him, and that 'what interested me at the time was not so much the explanation of religion as its absolute denial'. Evgeny's rebellion against God led to sharp conflict in the Preobrazhensky family. The youth's 'stubborn struggle' began 'within the family against church-attendance and other religious practices'.[41]

---

37. Tikhomirov 1997b, pp. 72–5.
38. Preobrazhensky 1989, p. 120.
39. See Kolb 1872, p. xi.
40. Bulgakov 1946, p. 30.
41. Preobrazhensky 1989, p. 120.

What was it like for the truly and deeply faithful father and mother to observe all this? It was especially difficult, it seems, for the father. On 1 March 1899, he was confirmed as chairman of the Bolkhov branch of the Diocesan school-council, and in 1900 he was elected as representative from the priesthood to the Bolkhov *zemstvo*. These events occurred in the very same year as Evgeny's rebellion against God. Within the family there was a stubborn struggle with the faithless son. In 1902, when the rebellious young man was 16, his father was appointed dean of all the churches in Bolkhov. Henceforth A.A. Preobrazhensky was called upon to manage the Bolkov parish Church-schools, to monitor decorum in the city's temples, and to oversee the behaviour of students at religious institutions, but he could not wrest his own son from the embrace of atheistic temptations. Apparently, after one of the family's domestic quarrels, Preobrazhensky senior could not bear such an ambiguous position. In 1903 he submitted a request to be relieved of his duties as dean.[42]

The conflict between father and son would last for decades. Echoes of it can be seen in the reminiscences of L.E. Preobrazhensky: '... Mama, sister and I visited Bolkhov [the reference is to the 1920s and 1930s] inexcusably rarely. Father [E.A. Preobrazhensky] went there quite often, but each time returned upset and very quiet'.[43]

The mother, Varvara Alekseevna, also found it hard to endure the son's withdrawal from God. L.E. Preobrazhensky recalls the circumstances of his father's first arrest, which came in 1906:

> I hesitate to imagine how distressed this woman [Varvara Alekseevna] must have been, learning from a certain 'well-wisher' that her twenty year-old son was imprisoned, and somewhere in Perm, so far away. One can imagine what titanic energy this woman expended upon her son when he returned some time later.[44] How irrefutably she demonstrated to the convinced atheist the need to take up and wear a cross. And she prevailed. This story was told to me by father in the early 1930s, when in my presence a small golden cross accidentally fell from his wallet. But the strange thing is that receipt #5096, from 20 December 1936, the time of father's last arrest, lists the confiscated contents of the wallet but not the cross. I suppose that father put it back on when he was arrested. On the other hand, anything is possible if the person doing the search characterises a library by the number of its books.[45]

---

42. *Formulyar svyashchennika Troitskoi g. Bolkhova tserkvi Alekseya Preobrazhenskovo*: TsIAM. F. 418. Op. 321. D. 1946. L. 16–16 ob.
43. L.E. Preobrazhensky n.d., p. 1.
44. After five months, Preobrazhensky and his comrades were released from prison under police-supervision following a four-day hunger-strike (Preobrazhensky 1989, p. 127).
45. L.E. Preobrazhensky n.d., pp. 3–4.

The die is cast

What happened in Evgeny's soul after his renunciation of God? Apparently, as with S.N. Bulgakov, he experienced 'a transition not from faith to disbelief, but from one faith to another, strange and empty but nevertheless a faith with its own sacred objects'. '...The very character of my disbelief' – Bulgakov recalled – 'was not a condition of religious emptiness and indifference, but faith in human "progress" and the like'.[46]

The plausibility of such an analogy is partly confirmed by the reminiscences of Akhmed-Zaki Validov (Validi) – a historian, student of Turkey, and one of the leaders of the Bashkir Republic in 1919–20, who was close to Preobrazhensky during that period. According to his observations, Preobrazhensky's atheism (lack of faith) gave others the impression of a religious feeling:

> Preobrazhensky was a sincere atheist. He saw atheism as the source of all science, as reflected in *The ABC of Communism*. During a conversation I once said: 'Can we really speak so categorically about all of these metaphysical premises: you, my friend Preobrazhensky, should have become a priest, you must have chosen this communist way by mistake'. Later I spoke of this with Lenin, who replied: 'Validov was quite correct'.[47]

What was the new faith that Preobrazhensky adopted, or more correctly, gradually adopted in place of the Orthodoxy he rejected? It seems that initially it was just as unconscious and vague as his earlier religiosity in childhood, a kind of amorphous revolutionism: more an attitude than a conviction, a feeling rather than a doctrine. Preobrazhensky wrote of 'a state of undefined and formless revolutionism'[48] in which he found himself for a long time. Most likely the new 'creed' initially had more of a negative than a positive character and consisted of a notorious 'nihilism' – a profound alienation from historical Russia and its total rejection.

Atheism – alienation from traditional Russia – revolutionism. At the time, these milestones in the spiritual evolution of a Russian intellectual almost inevitably followed one after the other: the loss of religious conviction inevitably led to finding revolutionary commitment. '...Together with the loss of religious faith – observes S.N. Bulgakov – I naturally, almost automatically, adopted the prevailing revolutionary attitude of the intelligentsia, without reference to any particular party'.[49]

---

46. Bulgakov 1946, pp. 31–2.
47. Validi 1997, pp. 238–9.
48. Preobrazhensky 1989, p. 123.
49. Bulgakov 1996, p. 92.

In the minds of Russians at the time, Orthodoxy was inextricably connected with autocracy: the tsar was anointed by God; during the coronation-ceremony he was informed of the mystical grace of God, before whom he henceforth took full responsibility for the country and the people. But in order to be responsible for all, he must have unlimited authority in the state and autocratic power. Having lost their faith in Orthodox mysticism, the Russian intelligentsia looked upon autocracy as nothing more than a despotic dictatorship, and the entire system of state and legal relations in the Russian Empire was deprived of any legitimacy.[50]

Having rejected Orthodoxy, however, the Russian intelligentsia did not lose the sense, cultivated by the Church, of their blood-ties to the people (a unique kind of unconscious and spontaneous democratism). As a result, the social contrasts that previously seemed natural (even though they accepted them with some spiritual discomfort), together with the poverty of a section of the people, now became, in the eyes of the 'suddenly-enlightened' intellectuals, an unnatural condition. The veil was lifted, as it were, and spontaneous democratism broke through from the unconscious sphere to the level of consciousness, clashing with the living reality of autocratic and gentry-ruled Russia and taking the form of an uncontrollable urge to revolutionary action. Russian life – they had only a vague, somewhat 'bookish' impression of life abroad; ideas that arose in the West were usually carried over uncritically to Russian soil, serving as one of the sources of the social utopianism of the Russian intelligentsia[51] – suddenly seemed monstrously unjust and was transformed by the pen of the radical '*popovichy*' (Belinsky, Chernyshevsky, Dobrolyubov) into an object of merciless scorn, the force of which was only slightly mitigated by the 'Aesopian language' of censorship. 'Even before the first underground-literature came into my hands' –

---

50. 'It was perfectly natural – recalled S.N. Bulgakov – that with the loss of religious faith, the idea of sacred imperial power, with a special reverence for God's anointed, evaporated for me and, worst of all, took on a disgusting, intolerable taste of officialdom, hypocrisy, servility. Sharing the view of the entire Russian revolution, I hated it and the extent to which I share all its sins against Russia' (Bulgakov 1946, p. 28).

51. 'The real source of the weakness of our political programmes is that they are too theoretical, too remote from the nation, too little adapted to the conditions of our country. The fledgling culture of our homeland has not yet had time to accumulate enough political and social observations, drawn from the life of the country itself. The man from our intelligentsia forms his mind mainly according to foreign books. He thus creates a world-view that is purely deductive, based purely upon logic, in which everything is very orderly except for the base, which is very weak. Due to that sort of world-view, with us people are able stubbornly to demand "implementation of what is unattainable and even not of any serious importance, while simultaneously neglecting matters of capital importance"' (Tikhomirov 1997c, pp. 25–6). An uncritical attitude to the latest 'last word' of Western sociology, in turn, was the result of 'losing an Orthodox sense': the resulting ideological vacuum, coupled with alienation from historical Russia, inevitably turned inquiring Russian minds to the works of foreign thinkers.

recalled Preobrazhensky – 'I was already quite radically inclined under the influence of reading *Russkoe bogatstvo, Russkie vedemosti, Otechestvennye zapiski*, Saltykov-Shchedrin and especially Dobrolyubov and Pisarev'.[52]

A single desire arose in the ecstatic minds of young people upon reading such works: to 'renounce the old world' and 'shake its ashes from our feet'. For example, this is exactly what Dobrolyubov called for in his uncensored 'Letter from the Province' (addressed to A.I. Herzen), in which he claimed that the source of Russia's centuries-old poverty was the 'miserable idolatry of the tsar...Our condition is horrible, intolerable, and only the axe – can save us, nothing but the axe will do...Russia is summoned to take up the axe'.[53]

The same attitudes, evoked by reading the works of revolutionary democrats, were fuelled in E.A. Preobrazhensky by his observations of the dark side of Russian reality, which, as in any other country, was not idyllic: '...during vacations I constantly observed the distress, poverty and oppression of the peasantry in the villages of Bolkhov, Mtsensk and Bryansk districts, where I often spent my vacations'.[54]

In the soul of the Bolkhov *'popovich'*, who had rejected God, a sense of wholeness, embracing all of mankind and including the sinners ('love the sinner and hate the sin'),[55] a Christian love, gradually separated out into love for the 'people' and hatred for 'their oppressors'.

Preobrazhensky's revolutionary education was completed when he became acquainted with illegal revolutionary literature: 'The first illegal literature came into my hands when I was in the fifth class at the gymnasium. Among these first works I remember a hectographed feuilleton from Amfiteatrov's *Deceived Gentlemen*, which had previously been published in the newspaper *Rossiya*; a proclamation from a revolutionary committee of students at the Ekaterinoslav Mining Institute; an account of the beating of students by Cossacks; and a few revolutionary verses such as the *Marseillaise, Dubinushka*, and *Boldly, Friends, Do Not Falter*, among others'.[56]

Finally the hour came for his ultimate choice of a revolutionary destiny, as E.A. Preobrazhensky emotionally wrote some years later:

> I remember, as if it were today, one very important moment of my biography. It was during summer-vacation when I went home to Bolkhov and settled into the darkest corner of our garden. Behind the bath-house there was a small bench amid the lilacs, and I began to re-read all my illegal possessions, both

---

52. Preobrazhensky 1989, p. 121.
53. Dobroyubov 1984, pp. 284, 288.
54. Preobrazhensky 1989, p. 121.
55. See Kuraev 1997, p. 80.
56. Preobrazhensky 1989, p. 121.

old ones and those recently acquired, including a hand-written notebook with various student-proclamations, humorous and lyrical poetry as well as certain facts from a revolutionary chronicle. At a certain moment I was confronted by a purely practical question in its complete enormity: What should I do? Was I willing to join the ranks of the revolutionaries, with all the ensuing consequences, such as expulsion from the gymnasium, rupture with my family, prison, exile and so forth? At that moment I made a decision and said firmly to myself: yes, I am going to join the revolutionaries, no matter what may happen.[57]

The moment of the decisive step, of the final 'betrothal with the Revolution', frequently took the form of an oath and was an important landmark in the destiny of each of our revolutionaries. Recall the famous oath of Herzen and Ogarev, sworn on Moscow's Sparrow Hills:

We...ran up to the Sparrow Hills at the spot where the first stone of Vitberg's temple was laid. Flushed and breathless, we stood there mopping our faces. The sun was setting, the cupolas glittered, beneath the hill the city extended farther than the eye could reach, a fresh breeze blew on our faces. We stood leaning against each other and, suddenly embracing, vowed in sight of all Moscow to sacrifice our lives to the struggle we had chosen. This scene may strike others as very affected and theatrical, and yet twenty-six years afterwards I am moved to tears as I recall it; there was a sacred sincerity in it, and our whole life has proved this.[58]

And likewise, Evgeny Preobrazhensky decided to follow a path of uncompromising struggle for the revolutionary transformation of Russia.

Revolution and morality

The new revolutionary faith infused Evgeny's life with great meaning. But 'faith without action is dead'. And the first oppositional action became a kind of 'playing

---

57. Ibid.
58. Herzen 1962, p. 87. Compare this with the remark by Vera Figner: 'On one poetic Swiss evening, during a secluded walk in the vineyards, my sister put some highly moving questions to me: had I decided to devote all my energies to the revolutionary cause? Would I be able, if necessary, to sever all relations [which were rather traditional in nature] with my husband? Would I give up science for the cause, and my career? I answered enthusiastically. After that I learned that an organised secret revolutionary society was planning to act in Russia; I read the charter and programme of this society, and after I agreed to all points I was accepted as a member. At the time I was 21 years old'. (Figner 1964, p. 124). M.M. Gorinov is grateful to A.S. Pokrovsky for proposing the idea of using the memoirs of V.N. Figner to reconstruct the compelling motives behind Preobrazhensky's choice of a revolutionary destiny.

at revolution', in which the participants practised, as it were, being revolutionaries and tried on the clothes of 'a fighter against the autocracy'. Preobrazhensky recalled how, when vacationing with Vanya Anisimov – a childhood-friend and son of a merchant in Bolkhov – they often set out 'together for the most remote places outside of the city and expressed our protest against autocracy by singing the *Marseillaise*, but in such a way that we alone could hear it. When we passed by the Bolkhov city-jail – a miserable, old-fashioned building that usually held a couple of dozen petty thieves and horse-rustlers – our thoughts turned to Kresty and Butyrka, where fighters against the autocratic régime, who were so dear to us, were languishing'.[59]

The ardent revolutionism, which Preobrazhensky was brimming with, gave birth to a vague wish to share the new-found truth with those around him:

> After returning from vacation to the gymnasium, I decided to devote a minimum of time to the gymnasium's subjects, just enough to get a third grade in my courses, and to transfer the focus of my activity to evenings of avidly reading foreign works on rice-paper while devoting all my time during the days to reading books on the history of culture, on history in general, especially the history of revolution, and also on the basic elements of political economy. In addition, Ivan Anisimov and I began to broaden our propaganda among the students, started a couple of circles, and entered into contact with people who were under surveillance in the city of Orel.[60]

Revolutionary proselytising gradually led from 'playing at revolution' to the level of real revolutionary activity. During this period Preobrazhensky developed 'a mystical passion to reproduce illegal literature'.[61] In the conditions of a censored press, this was precisely the way in which the young insurgent manifested the inclination towards spiritual enlightenment that he inherited from his father. The hand-written journal *Shkol'nye dosugi*, founded by Evgeny and the poet Aleksandr Tinyakov, no longer satisfied him – it was too apolitical. Nor was he content with printing 'a few small things' on the hectograph – a simple means of reprinting text and illustrations, invented in Russia in 1869 by M.I. Alysov and capable of yielding up to a hundred copies of the original.

> I dreamed of a printing press, and by the next vacation I prepared 'a technological advance' in order to make my dream come true. Among the revolutionary young people in our Orel circle of that time were the children of Aleksin, who owned the local print-works. At my insistence, Sasha Aleksin stole from his father's type-cabinet five pounds of type, which I intended to use for a

---

59. Preobrazhensky 1989, pp. 121–2.
60. Preobrazhensky 1989, p. 122.
61. Ibid.

more perfect reproduction of a 'Collection of Revolutionary Songs': the *Marseillaise* and others. During vacation I went home with the type and 'opened' a print-works in the bath-house of my father's garden. I made the cases, set out the type and began the compositing work for 'We Renounce the Old World'. In order that my solitary work in the bath-house should not become a matter of suspicion to the family, I convinced father that it was physically good for me to rise at dawn and to go and bathe in the local river Nugr. Of course, I did not go to bathe but spent the entire time in the bath-house trying to master the publishing trade. Nothing came of my type-setting: the letters fell out and some were missing... After tormenting myself for two weeks in this undertaking, I decided to 'shut down' the print-works, buried the type in the ground, and in the autumn returned it to Aleksin's print-works. We had to continue at the technological level of the hectograph and later to adopt the mimeograph [a rotator], on which we printed various proclamations on instruction from the Orel Committee.[62]

Did Evgeny realise in those years that the 'revolutionary struggle' would not only alienate him from family and friends but also continuously pose moral-ethical questions and require violations of moral precepts? In order to 'open a print-works' he had to convince a comrade to steal type from his father, and now he was constantly deceiving his own parents.

Whatever the case, several years later the theme of 'revolution and morality' became for him a subject of intensive reflection. F.V. Vinogradov, who in 1910 spent some time with E.A. Preobrazhensky in the Aleksandrovsk transit-prison near Irkutsk, recalled:

One of comrade Preobrazhensky's reports [which he gave in the prison], on 'Ethics and the Materialist Conception of History', dealt with the pressing need to clarify what are the ethical demands on a revolutionary. The report began with a fundamental proposition: 'The good of the revolution is the highest law'. Two evenings were spent on discussion of this report.[63]

In August 1918 Preobrazhensky stated more concretely the thesis he expressed in 1910:

Soviet power defends the proletarian revolution. 'And with what means', asks the Left S-R? We reply: 'For such a high purpose all means are appropriate that serve the end, and they can only be judged in terms of expediency'.[64]

---

62. Preobrazhensky 1989, pp. 122–3.
63. Vinogradov 1934, p. 32.
64. E.A. Preobrazhensky, 'Skuchnoe zanyatie', *Ural'skii rabochii*, 31 August 1918.

Still later, in 1923, Preobrazhensky would devote a special work to the moral-ethical problematic, *Morals and Class Norms*, the basic idea of which would be the same: 'The good of the revolution is the highest law'; with representatives of one's own camp one must be honest, decent and sympathetic; when dealing with enemies of the revolution, 'everything is permitted'.[65] Thus the splintering of a love for all of humanity led, in the final analysis, to a divided ethics and a dual morality.[66]

'Dear God, this is what has happened everywhere!', I.A. Bunin, E.A. Preobrazhensky's great compatriot, despairingly exclaimed at the height of the Civil War. 'What horribly unnatural things have been done by entire generations of boys and girls who have memorised Ivanyukov and Marx, gone about with their secret printing presses, collecting for the "Red Cross" and distributing "literature", shamelessly pretending that they are dying for their love of the Pakhoms and Sidors while every minute stirring up hatred for the landowner, the manufacturer and the Philistine for all these "blood-suckers, spiders, oppressors, despots, satraps, members of the bourgeoisie, obscurantists, and the knights of darkness and violence"!'[67] Bunin, it appears, was correct except for one thing: the compassion for 'the Pakhoms and Sidors' was no 'shameless pretence'. S.N. Bulgakov revealed its deep Christian origins.

Discovery of the truth

For some time, it seems, it was the negative side of revolutionism that prevailed in Preobrazhensky's consciousness. But the positive revolutionary ideal was so amorphous that he soon experienced spiritual discomfort, as he recalled in his autobiography:

> When I entered the seventh class at the gymnasium, I could no longer remain in a state of undefined and formless revolutionism. I had to choose between the Socialist-Revolutionaries and the Social-Democrats. At that time the decisive influence in working out my world-view came from two works: *The Communist Manifesto* and *The Development of Scientific Socialism* by Engels. Pondering these two works for a long time, I decided that the Narodnik worldview was bankrupt and *unscientific* [italics added] and that Marxism alone could show me the proper path.[68]

---

65. Preobrazhensky 1923.
66. On the problem of revolutionary amorality see Tikhomirov 1997c, pp. 108–13.
67. Bunin 1990, p. 99.
68. Preobrazhensky 1989, p. 123. It is probable that an important role in Preobrazhensky's wavering between populism and Marxism was played by Georg Friedrich Kolb,

Why, of the numerous revolutionary teachings of that time, did Preobrazhensky and so many others choose Marxism? The 'triumphal procession' of Karl Marx's teachings amongst the Russian intelligentsia of the period, I believe, was the result of a very complex social-psychological phenomenon, the core of which was 'withdrawal from Orthodoxy' on the part of feelings and consciousness, which deserves further attention.

What do we mean by this? The spiritual nature of someone raised in the bosom of the Orthodox Church is, in our view, distinguished by three main characteristics: 1) in the sphere of emotions, by a dominant feeling of true love and suffering for one's fellow man; 2) in terms of rationality, by an optimistic dualism: a realisation that the world and its history are a constant struggle between the forces of light and darkness, which is destined to end with victory for the forces of light with the affirmation, by a consciously-chosen part of humanity, of the Kingdom of God;[69] 3) in the routine of daily life – by an endeavour (expressed much more clearly than in other confessions) for orderliness through the cyclical movement of everyday living: every believer is included in the daily, weekly and annual cycle of prayers and rituals, days of feasting and days of fasting.

The Orthodox believer, having lost his faith, did not lose along with it the storehouse of his soul that was formed by Orthodoxy: it remained pervaded by a love for man, it still understood the world through the paradigm of optimistic dualism, and it strove for order in daily life. And we believe that of all the revolutionary teachings of the time – we have already spoken of why the loss of faith almost automatically led to revolutionism – it was precisely Marxism that answered to the highest degree the spiritual aspirations of 'believers who had lost their faith'. Its social imperative – struggle for the happiness of the disadvantaged and the toilers – satisfied the need to love the Pakhoms and Sidors. Its philosophy – dialectical and historical materialism, crowned by a communist eschatology – easily 'docked' with the dualistic optimism of the Orthodox ideological doctrine. Its political-economic ideal – a planned economy – promised the believer who had abandoned Orthodoxy a return to the lost orderliness of life. Its emphatic objectivism also played an enormous role in Marxism's contagious attractiveness – its 'scientism' and technicism, which so readily lived up to the spirit of a rationalistic epoch. Altogether, 'Marxism presented to Russian young people a scientifically based social idealism, a true path on which to serve the people, and a certain guarantee of progress and prosperity'.[70]

---

whom he so esteemed in his youth. Kolb's view of the 'factors of progress' was close to that of the Narodniks.

69. See, for example, Tikhomirov 1997d, p. 31.
70. Zander 1989, p. 6.

Coming to Marxism, the best representatives of Russian youth regained, as it were, their spiritual equilibrium. The spiritual evolution of G.M. Krzhizhanovsky was typical in this regard:

> The initial searches by the *raznochinsty* [non-gentry intellectuals], which have come down to us in the aging pages of *Sovremennik* and *Otcehstvennye zapiski*, the accusing words of Saltykov-Shchedrin, the freedom-loving brilliance of the publicist Mikhailovsky, the ponderous preaching by Lavrov, the various brochures and publications by the members of *Zemlya i volya* and *Narodnaya volya*, and finally, the remarkable tolling in the springtime of our lives that we heard in the publications of the *Ozvobozhdenie truda* group – this is the literary chain whose links we followed in our conversion from indeterminate lovers of the people into fully determined Marxists. And upon completing this turn of the road, there stood the great work of Marx, his *Capital*, solid like a rock...! Thinking through the pages of that book, for the first time we began to feel solid ground under our feet...[71]

E.A. Preobrazhensky followed an analogous route. In the autumn of 1903 his Marxist choice took on a formal-organisational aspect: Evgeny Preobrazhensky, Ivan Anisimov and Aleksandr Litkens, who constituted the Social-Democratic troika at the gymnasium, began intensive work in the educational institutions of Orel, acting in the capacity of a cell of the Orel Committee of the Russian Social-Democratic Workers' Party. 'As a matter of fact, I consider myself to have been a member of the Party from the end of 1903, although my formal acceptance into the Party, with Litkens and Anisimov, only took place two to three months later'.[72]

The apostle of revolution

At the close of 1903 Evgeny was just 17 years old. Finally acquiring a coherent world-view, the revolutionary neophyte, with truly apostolic passion, devoted himself to Social-Democratic propaganda, trying to convert as many of the uninitiated as possible to the Marxist faith:

> At the beginning of 1904, when the Russo-Japanese War began, the Orel Party-Committee issued a proclamation against the War and assigned the three of us to distribute a large number of copies in the gymnasium. We did this as follows. During one lesson all three of us simultaneously left our different classes and went to the cloakroom, where the coats of all the students were hanging,

---

71. Krzhizhanovsky 1984, pp. 11–12.
72. Preobrazhensky 1989, pp. 123–4.

and seizing the opportune moment we distributed 150–200 proclamations in the pockets of all the students of the upper classes. The operation went splendidly, and when the students put on their coats and left for home they were all surprised to find in their pockets the publication of the Orel Committee. There was an enormous scandal, the administration rushed about in search of the people responsible, and the gendarmerie conducted an investigation but did not find the culprits. After this, our first organised action, the Orel Committee decided it could accept us formally into the Committee's group of propagandists, and this was done after a brief colloquium in February 1904. In the spring of that year, I received a small study-group of two workers from the Khrushchevsky mechanical-works and gave them a long but not very persuasive explanation of the Party's programme.[73]

With characteristic modesty, Preobrazhensky underestimated his abilities as a propagandist. In any event, the next episode of his biography reveals him to be a talented agitator and conspirator:

In the summer of that same year, I passed into the eighth class of the gymnasium and, on the advice of the Committee, took on summer-tutoring in the centre of the Maltsevsky factories,[74] at the Dyatkovo factory in Bryansk district, with the son of Zolotov, the district's superintendent of police. I converted Nikolai Mikhailovich Zolotov, my pupil... to the Social-Democratic faith. Officially working with him on Latin, we spent most of our efforts on propaganda amongst the workers of Dyatkovo, Ivot and the other Maltsevsky factories... Police-superintendent Zolotov, my pupil's father, put in a great effort to catch our organisation's Dyatkovo cell, which was distributing illegal literature and putting out proclamations by mimeograph. We protected this mimeograph and the illegal literature in quite a unique way. My pupil complained to his father that he had no place to keep his books and notes and asked to use one of the drawers of his father's desk that could be locked with a key. The father willingly provided the drawer and key, and it was in that drawer that we kept both the mimeograph and the illegal literature while the father, Zolotov, was scouring Dyatkovo in pursuit of the pernicious distribution-apparatus. Similarly, when we had to hold large meetings in the forest for individual factories, we asked the police-superintendent for his two horses in order to go hunting, and the completely unsuspecting superintendent gave us

---

73. Preobrazhensky 1989, pp. 124–5.
74. The Maltsevsky (more correctly, Maltsovsky) factories were a group of machine-building works, iron-foundries, glass and cement-works – the largest being the Lyudinovsk iron-foundry, steel-smelter and engineering works; the Dyatkovo crystal-works; and the Ivot, Chernotinsk and Bytoshevsk glass-works, among others – located around the city of Bryansk (in the Maltsovsky factory-region).

his horses with bells on, and we made the round of organisations in our area. This whole story came to light only a year later.[75]

Within a year the revolutionary whirlwind was already storming over Russia. And if previously his revolutionary enthusiasm left Preobrazhensky with little time for studies, what could be expected in 1905, the first year of the first Russian revolution?

> ...An attitude of tense expectation, a nerve-racking impatience and hope prevailed in...Orel, [recalls A. Golubkov] where I lived from May [1905] while continuing...my work in the Central Technical Bureau of the Party.[76]...I became involved with a circle consisting of the local young people. I remember that, among others, comrade E.A. Preobrazhensky worked in that circle, at the time having just completed or else being in the process of completing his studies at the gymnasium and already being actively involved in party-activity.[77]

'In 1905 – writes Preobrazhensky – our group conducted a general strike in the educational institutions of Orel during April and May, and despite all this – despite my public appearances at student-meetings where we adopted our academic demands – I was not arrested and I even received my certificate of matriculation'.[78]

The certificate of matriculation

Those in charge of the Orel gymnasium (the first Orel gymnasium after 1 July 1904),[79] apparently had some quite liberal views. At least, the administration tolerated the anti-government passion of its student. Thus in his 'conduct-book', which Preobrazhensky later submitted upon entering Moscow University, the paragraph headed 'Misdeeds and other noteworthy matters concerning the student' contained merely 'streamlined' language and did not list the most impressive of his sins.[80]

---

75. Preobrazhensky 1989, pp. 125–6.
76. This was the structure designed to manage the 'technical' functions of the Social-Democratic Party, including transportation of party-literature from abroad and delivering it to the field, the production of passports, and deployment of illegal print-works: from the spring of 1903, it was located in Orel.
77. Golubkov 1931, p. 9.
78. Preobrazhensky 1989, p. 126.
79. GA OO. F. 64. Op. 1. D. 606. L. 18.
80. TsIAM. F. 418. Op. 321. D. 1469. L. 22 ob.

On 8 April 1905, there was a meeting of the 'Class-commission of the First Orel gymnasium concerning approval of students in the eighth class for graduation-examinations', which was attended by the honorary trustee, the director, the school-inspector and all teachers of the eighth-year graduating class. 'In discussing the moral maturity of the students, the commission determined to award a grade of five for conduct to all students in both sections of the eighth class [including the young rebel-atheist E.A. Preobrazhensky]... In a detailed discussion of all the information entered with the list of names, the commission determined to admit all students of the current 1904/05 school-year, in both the first eighth-year class (of 29 students) and the second (of 23 students), to try the final examinations [Preobrazhensky was in the second eighth-year class]'.[81]

Thus Evgeny had to pass the final examinations, which began on 2 May, at the same time as he was appearing at meetings regarding the general strike at the Orel educational institutions. For an essay on the question 'How important is poetry for the mind and the heart?', Evgeny received a grade of four.[82] On 3 May those who were graduating sat a test in Algebra, and on 4 May in Geometry. The average grade that Evgeny received for the written work in Mathematics was three. On 19 May he passed the examination on the Law of God. His answer received a grade of four. On 22 May Evgeny passed in Latin, also with a four. On 27 May he received three in Greek; on 30 May, for an oral examination in Mathematics, four; on 1 June, for History, four; on 2 June, for French, four; and for the final examination in German (for which the date is not available), five.[83] Preobrazhensky's certificate also contains another grade of five for logic (there was no final examination for this subject). The certificate also shows a grade of three for Mathematical Geography, Physics, and Geography (there were also no 'tests' for these subjects).[84]

In the gymnasium's archive there is an interesting document concerning the future plans of students in the graduating class. Under a heading 'Wishes to continue education', beside the surname Preobrazhensky is the entry 'abroad'[85] – the only such entry out of 52 graduates. Did Evgeny really plan to go abroad, and with what purpose – to continue his studies or on party-business? Whatever the case, he did not go abroad.

---

81. GA OO. F. 64. Op. 1. D. 606. L. 3, 6–6 ob., 7.
82. GA OO. F. 64. Op. 1. D. 627. L. 13.
83. GA OO. F. 64. Op. 1. D. 627. L. 15, 17, 20, 21, 22 ob., 24, 25, 29, 30, 33, 37, 41 ob., 42, 42 ob., 45–45 ob., 47, 48.
84. TsIAM. F. 418. Op. 321. D. 1496. L. 21.
85. GA OO. F. 64. Op. 1. D. 618. L. 3.

Baptism in battle

> In the summer of 1905 [E.A. Preobrazhensky recalls] I went to Bryansk on party-work; and there, together with two other comrades, I led the work of the Bryansk Party-Committee. I lived at Bryansk station. With no bed in my room, I slept on two newspapers spread out on the floor; I ate only sausage and bread, spending no more than twenty *kopeks* a day; and every evening I walked to and from Bezhitsu, that is, 18 *versts*, in order to conduct workers' circles at the Bryansk locomotive-building factory.[86]

It should be noted that Bryansk district was the only industrial centre in the predominantly-agricultural province of Orel, and it was here that the workers' movement made itself heard in 1905. The historical records show that during that year there were strikes

> in almost every plant and factory of the district... The panic was enormous, and the government deployed all its forces to put down the growing number of strikes. The meetings, which were called in the factories and attended by thousands of workers, were dispersed by armed force. The factory-towns were flooded with Cossacks and soldiers.[87]

The local Social-Democratic organisation played a significant role in the rise of the workers' movement.

> The party-members here were many times more numerous than in any other cities of the province, for in many factories the Party already had illegal factory- and works-committees (in Maltsev and Bryansk)... At the head of the Bryansk Social-Democratic Committee were: N. Konyukov, Ignat Fokin, E.A. Preobrazhensky, Vera Slutskaya and others.[88]

His period of work in Bryansk was an important landmark in Evgeny Preobrazhensky's biography: for the first time he was honoured with the attention of officials from the gendarmerie-office – at the time the main collectors of materials concerning the history of the Russian revolutionary movement. From the first 'case' in which the surname Preobrazhensky appeared, it turns out that in the village of Ivot, in the Dyatkovo district of Bryansk, he led the work of a Social-Democratic circle. The details of this reached the local police-officer, who decided to question the daughters of Ivot's village-priest, Anna Pavlovna and Olga Pavlovna of the Krasnikov family. But the young '*popovny*' either feigned ignorance in order to shield their Social-Democratic acquaintances or else they

---

86. Preobrazhensky 1989, p. 126.
87. VKP(B) 1926, p. 80.
88. VKP(B) 1926, p. 101.

really did know very little. Whatever the case, the police received only trivial information from them. Meanwhile, they are very interesting to us, for on the fragile pages of the archived case we encounter the names of people we know well: Evgeny Preobrazhensky and Nikolai Zolotov, the same Zolotov whose father was the police superintendent, the one who a year earlier provided the desk-drawer in which the friends contrived to store their cache of illegal literature together with the mimeograph. The '*popovny*' gave the following account:

> 1) that they, the Krasnikovas, know by rumour that in the village of Ivot there is a Social-Democratic circle, but they do not know who has organised it or anyone who belongs to it, and 2) that they, the Krasnikovas, are being visited by students Mikhail Yakovlevich **Fenomenov** and Dmitry Ivanovich **Azbukin**, and that on 7 August they were joined by **Evgeny Alekseevich Preobrazhensky** from Dyatkovo [original emphasis] and Nikolai Mikhailovich Zolotov, who together took an early-evening walk in the woods and invited them, the Krasnikovas, to join them. When they came to a gate, four *versts* from Ivot, they saw sitting at the side of the railway-tracks about forty people, workmen from Stary and Ivot, whom Fenomenov, Azbukin, Preobrazhensky and Zolotov approached, followed by them, the Krasnikovas and... that a conversation began among them about something they, the Kranikovas, did not understand, and then this company sang revolutionary songs: 'The Red Banner', 'Let us Renounce the Old World', 'Dubinushka' and others, but they, the Krasnikovas, took no part in the singing...[89]

Could it be that the 'police-officer of the second station in the Bryansk district', who investigated this matter – unfortunately, his surname is not recorded in the case – was the same Zolotov, 'the local police-superintendent' of the Dyatkovo factory in the Bryansk district, about whom Preobrazhensky wrote in his autobiography? Was this why, of the four surnames of those who accompanied the '*popovny*' during the walk in the woods – Fenomenov, Azbukin, Preobrazhensky and Zolotov – only the surname Zolotov is not emphasised? The police-superintendent could not fail to recognise his own 'wayward' son! And was this why, as distinct from Fenomenov and Azbukin, the records emphasise not only the surname but also the patronymic of Preobrazhensky? Did the police-officer remember his son's 'teacher' from a year earlier? And was it this investigation that uncovered the dirty tricks of the previous year by Preobrazhensky and Zolotov? Remember the sentence in Preobrazhensky's autobiography: 'This whole story came to light only a year later'.

---

89. GA OO. F. 883. Op. 1. D. 210. L. 510.

But the Preobrazhensky matter did not go to court. While the investigation was underway (the last entry dates from 14 October 1905)[90] stormy political events erupted throughout Russia, including Orel province. In October 1905, an all-Russian political strike broke out. The telegraph-workers, switchmen and office-staff of Orel station were all involved, along with the railwaymen of Bryansk and Elts. The strike began to spread to other branches and enveloped the entire province. Strike-committees were formed in Verkhov, Bryansk and on the rail-line from Orel to Gryaz.[91]

During these turbulent days, Evgeny went briefly from Bryansk to Orel.

> In October...1905, I was co-opted at the suggestion of Olympii Kvitkin onto the Orel Committee. At the time, the Orel Committee was taking a compromising attitude. Ponomarev, the Committee's leader after Olympii Kvitkin left, laughingly said to other members of the Committee that 'We have two solid Bolsheviks: 20 year-old Mikhail Ekaterinoslavsky and 19 year-old Evgeny Preobrazhensky'. Despite such jokes, I stuck firmly to my views and defended the position of our Party's Third Congress... In October, following publication of the famous manifesto, I participated in the struggle against pogromists in Orel and was then sent to work at Bryansk factory.[92]

Preobrazhensky ended up being drawn into the most important events of the revolutionary movement in the autumn of 1905. Let us recall the sequence of events. On 17 October, the Emperor put out the manifesto bestowing political freedom and promising to summon a legislative Duma. The Bolsheviks regarded this announcement as a ruse intended to weaken the revolution. On 18 October, the Orel-Bryansk Social-Democratic Committee decided to intensify preparation of the masses for armed struggle. On that day in Orel there was a demonstration of print-workers in which several plants took part. Singing the *Marseillaise*, the demonstrators moved through the streets of Bolkhov. They headed for the jail to free the political prisoners, but their route was blocked by a large group of Cossacks and Black Hundreds. A battle began (remember the *Autobiography*: 'I participated in the struggle against pogromists in Orel'). The following day a fighting detachment was created in Orel, headed by O.A. Kvitkin. On 19–20 October, in the Raditsa and Bezhitsa settlements of Bryansk district (precisely the areas where Preobrazhensky worked before going to Orel) a soviet of workers' deputies was organised, which lasted until the end of 1905. The soviet demanded

---

90. GA OO. F. 883. Op. 1. D. 210. L. 519.
91. Stroev et al. 1987, p. 33.
92. Preobrazhensky 1989, p. 126.

that the authorities withdraw the troops and recognise the workers as responsible for maintaining social order.[93]

During these tense days the revolutionary 'career' of Evgeny Preobrazhensky took meteoric flight. In mid-October 1905, at the suggestion of N.M. Mikheev – his comrade in the Orel students' revolutionary organisation who was now working in Moscow – and with the approval of the Moscow Committee, he travelled to Moscow, where the culminating events of the first Russian Revolution were approaching. It fell to E.A. Preobrazhensky to be at their epicentre: he was appointed chief-propagandist for the Presnensky district.[94] Virtually unknown until then, the 19 year-old graduate of the Orel gymnasium now entered the all-Russian political arena.

Knowing E.A. Preobrazhensky as a person, we can now turn to his creative works. In this volume, we are publishing the works by E.A. Preobrazhensky that characterise his life and activities from his birth up to 1920. Essentially, this involves the years 1917–20: including letters from the archives, his notes, and the text of speeches; articles in the periodical-journals *Ural'skii rabochii*, *Ural'skaya pravda*, *Proletarii*, *Obskaya zhizn'*, *Zabaikal'skoe obozrenie*, *Pravda*, *Ezhenedel'nik pravdy* and *Kommunist*, together with published speeches, brochures and books. Also included are the reminiscences of E.A. Preobrazhensky from the 1920s to 1930s concerning the early years of his biography. All these materials are either archival documents that are being published for the first time or else they are re-publications of items long-forgotten over the years (apart from the autobiography).

It was a particularly complicated matter to find Preobrazhensky's articles in the newspaper *Obskaya zhizn'* (published in Novonikolaevsk from January to August 1912) and in *Zabaikal'skoe obozrenie* (Chita, March 1916). The point is that they were not published under his usual pseudonym 'Leonid' (or 'L'), but under the names 'M. Leonov' ('M.L.') and 'E. Iduchansky'. These works were at first identified by indirect means, and then direct confirmation was obtained indicating that they belonged to the pen of E.A. Preobrazhensky. The Russian researcher S.D. Garnyuk discovered in Moscow's Central Archive of Social-Political History a previously-unknown autobiography of E.A. Preobrazhensky, which revealed the pseudonyms under which he published in *Obskaya zhizn'* and *Zabaikal'skoe obozrenie*.[95] As a result of our research-work, we are able to make available for study about seventy previously-unknown articles by E.A. Preobrazhensky devoted to a very wide range of questions: the most important Russian and international political events of the day, fluctuations in the price of grain,

---

93. Stroev et al. 1987, p. 33; VKP(B) 1926, p. 101.
94. Preobrazhensky 1989, p. 126.
95. TsAOPIM. F. 685. Op. 1. D. 11. Kor. 2. L. 52–52 ob.

lectures on the literature and philosophy of Professor Zhakov, on the novelties of contemporary *belles-lettres*, on the classics of Russian literature by A.S. Pushkin and A.I. Herzen, on the issue of suicide and on the prospective development of human civilisation. We believe that there must be other articles by E.A. Preobrazhensky scattered throughout the pages of other periodical-publications that are likewise virtually-unknown to researchers, let alone to general readers.

This book consists of three parts: Part I, The Beginning of the Road, 1886–1917; Part II, The Years of Revolution and Civil War, 1917–20; and Part III, *The ABC of Communism*.

Parts I and II begin with the memoirs of E.A. Preobrazhensky, in which a general characterisation of the corresponding stage of his biography is provided, and then the works of our hero are set out in strictly-chronological order. Moreover, all of Preobrazhensky's known articles and letters are published in Part I; and in Part II, all the known archival documents and speeches in party- and soviet-forums; the newspaper-articles are abbreviated, and we omit most of the numerous responses by Preobrazhensky in *Ural'skii rabochii* to international events during 1918.

In Part III are published E.A. Preobrazhensky's major works: *Peasant Russia and Socialism (Towards a Review of Our Agrarian Programme)*, a brochure published in 1918 that includes articles written at the end of 1917 and published in *Pravda* along with a number of additional pages written specifically for the brochure; [the book] *Anarchism and Communism*, published in 1918 after appearing earlier that year in the form of essays in *Ural'skii rabochii*; [Preobrazhensky's chapters in] the 1920 edition of the book *The ABC of Communism: A Popular Exposition of the Programme of the Russian Communist Party-Bolsheviks*, written jointly with N.I. Bukharin and first published in 1919; and [the book] *Paper-Money in the Epoch of Proletarian Dictatorship*, published in 1920 as E.A. Preobrazhensky's first major work devoted specifically to financial questions. We do not include a number of popularising works by E.A. Preobrazhensky that essentially repeat the content of the books and brochures that we do include: among those left out are *On Peasant-Communes (A discussion between a Communist-Bolshevik and a Peasant)*, published in 1918 in Moscow and Petrograd; *Do We Need a Grain-Monopoly?* (Moscow, 1918); *Why Turn to the Poor Peasants?* (Petrograd, 1918); *The Organisation of Agriculture* (a publication by the agricultural department of the Elizavetgrad Party-Committee of the Communist Party (Bolsheviks) of Ukraine; and *Three years of the October Revolution* (Moscow, 1920).

The archeographical preparation of the documents was done according to the 1990 'Rules for Publication of Historical Documents'. Typographical and grammatical errors in the original texts have been corrected without reservation and there are several clarifications indicated in square brackets.

The scientific background-apparatus includes a preface, notes...and biographical notes.[96]

For their assistance in preparing this publication, the author wishes to thank V.A. Kozlov, Deputy Director of the State-Archive of the Russian Federation; E.L. Garanenkova, Director of the Scientific Library of the State-Archive of the Russian Federation; A.A. Fedyukhin, researcher at the State-Archive of the Russian Federation; L.P. Kosheleva, A.S. Masal'skaya, L.A. Rogovaya, E.P. Karavaeva and A.A. Oshchepkova, all at the Russian State-Archive of Social and Political History; M.D. Afanasyev, Director of the State Public Historical Library of Russia; M.D. Dvorkina and I.B. Tsvetkova, at the State Social-Political Library (formerly the IMEL library); and Acting Director of the State-Archive of Sverdlovsk district, A.G. Saposhnikov. Special recognition goes to the editor of the volume, Yu.B. Zhivtsov; to N.A. Tesemnikova for the archeography and for compiling the name-index; to M.Yu. Morukov, Deputy Director of the Centre for Scientific Use and Publication of the Archival Collection at the Main Archive of Moscow, and also to all those at the Centre who helped with work on the book. For his assistance with all aspects of the work, my thanks go to my co-author, S.V. Tsakunov, who discovered a number of the most interesting documents we have included and financed the typographical work. This publication would not be possible without the interest and participation of the English journalist Simon Pirani. The compiler of this work is especially grateful to Professor Richard B. Day, at the University of Toronto, who, in fact, initiated this project and has supported the compiler and the authors' collective at every stage in bringing it to publication.

---

96. [The Russian version of this book also contains a list of acronyms and abbreviated names of various governmental and economic institutions. In this edition, we have included the full names in the texts.]

Preface
Richard B. Day

In his foreword to this volume, which I have translated from the Russian edition, the Moscow archivist Mikhail M. Gorinov spoke of Evgeny Alekseevich Preobrazhensky as 'one of those "unlucky" historical figures' whose accomplishments have been forgotten by a 'thankless humanity'. This description was certainly appropriate when introducing Preobrazhensky's work to Russian readers; after the purges of the 1930s, the Stalinist machine of repression all but eliminated any memory within the USSR of the countless Old Bolsheviks who were consumed in the purge-trials of the 1930s. In other countries, however, many of these revolutionaries are far better remembered than in their own homeland. The most prominent among them – Leon Trotsky, Evgeny Preobrazhensky and Nikolai Bukharin – have been the subject of countless studies by historians and activists, and some of their works are as familiar to historians as those of Vladimir Lenin. In Trotsky's case, the great biographical trilogy by Isaac Deutscher portrayed Trotsky as a 'prophet' of revolutionary redemption and one of the heroic figures of the twentieth century.[1]

There has been no biographer of Isaac Deutscher's stature to dramatise the life of Evgeny Preobrazhensky. But since Alexander Erlich's pioneering study on *The Soviet Industrialization Debate*,[2] published in 1960, Preobrazhensky has become widely-acknowledged as one of the foremost Russian economists of his generation. Following Erlich's book, several of Preobrazhensky's major works were translated into English. These included *The New Economics* (in 1965),[3] *From N.E.P. to Socialism* (in 1973),[4] *The Crisis of Soviet Industrialization* (in 1979)[5] and *The Decline of Capitalism* (in 1985).[6] Even decades before these

---

1. Deutscher 1954; 1959; 1963.
2. Erlich 1960.
3. Preobrazhensky 1965.
4. Preobrazhensky 1973.
5. Preobrazhensky 1979.
6. Preobrazhensky 1985.

writings on economic theory were translated, Preobrazhensky was already well-known in the West for co-authoring, together with N.I. Bukharin, *The ABC of Communism*,[7] a manual on the Bolshevik party-programme that was translated into several languages in the early 1920s and has since been republished many times in English.

My own familiarity with Preobrazhensky arose from my early study of Leon Trotsky's views on economic policy during the decade-and-a-half following the Russian Revolution.[8] I found that while Trotsky and Preobrazhensky agreed on many key issues, including the need for 'primitive socialist accumulation' in order to finance industrialisation, they also differed on the role of foreign trade: Trotsky believed socialism could not be built in a country that deliberately shut itself off from imports of advanced technology and even from foreign capital-investments, whereas Preobrazhensky was more committed to import-substitution and averse to foreign investment – at least until the revolution came in the West and made possible international socialist planning. It was this difference, I believe, that led Preobrazhensky to reconcile himself reluctantly with Stalin's industrialisation drive by the late 1920s, although he never endorsed the extremes of forced collectivisation or the reckless pace of the First and Second Five-Year Plans, with their deadly cost in terms of millions of lives during the great famine that Stalin precipitated in order to crush peasant resistance. But since the second volume of *The Preobrazhensky Papers* will have much more to say about economics than the current one, these issues are best left for detailed commentary in that context.

What does need to be emphasised, for present purposes, is that the Preobrazhensky who is revealed in this first volume of *The Preobrazhensky Papers* does in fact turn out to be equally as unknown to Western readers as to his own compatriots in the former Soviet Union. To those of us who have studied Preobrazhensky as an economist – a technical economist with a unique facility for translating macroeconomic policy-issues into the mathematical formulae of Marx's reproduction-schemes – the Preobrazhensky whom we meet here seems almost to be a different person. Often the participants in the Soviet-industrialisation debates of the 1920s have been criticised for ignoring the humanistic ambitions of Marxism and for reducing Marxist discourse to quarrels over production-targets. Thanks to the research-efforts of my colleague, Mikhail M. Gorinov, these new documents reveal a Preobrazhensky whose interests were strikingly wide-reaching – far-more extensive than we ever imagined – and who rarely turned to economic themes until the Revolution of 1917 brought them directly to the forefront of the Party's concerns.

---

7. Bukharin and Preobrazhensky 1922.
8. Day 1973.

In this collection of documents, many of which could only be attributed to Preobrazhensky after extensive archival research, the reader discovers Preobrazhensky in a personal way that was hitherto impossible. Through historical analogies, Mikhail M. Gorinov elaborates this new insight in his foreword, hypothesising the sort of life-trajectory that led the son of a respected priest from his first questioning of God to his final revolutionary commitment. This volume includes a remarkable series of documents that elaborate the sweeping range of Preobrazhensky's interests in Russian history and culture, in political events of the day, in wide-ranging philosophical and social questions, in political and social institutions, and most particularly in the lives and concerns of Russian workers and peasants. The story is one of a young man awakening to a history of tsarist repression and forsaking his own rather privileged social position in order to commit his life to the pursuit of justice and human dignity.

Most striking, in this context, is the scope of Preobrazhensky's familiarity both with Russia's cultural heritage and with many of the original philosophical concerns that prompted Marx's own inquiries into the science of economics. In this volume Preobrazhensky confidently makes reference to Herzen, Pushkin, Lomonosov, Belinksy, Chernyshevsky and numerous other luminaries of Russian history and culture, and he does so with the same facility as when commenting on the works of philosophers such as Hegel, Kant, Feuerbach, J.S. Mill, Nietzsche, Spinoza or Schopenhauer. The Preobrazhensky of this volume was clearly much more than a technical economist: he was a prototypical member of the Russian intelligentsia at the turn of the twentieth century. And like so many others of his generation, he became a Marxist in order that the achievements of human culture might ultimately become accessible to those classes whose toil made cultural achievements possible in the first place.

The Preobrazhensky with whom most of us have been familiar was tirelessly accused by Stalinists during the 1920s of antagonism towards the peasantry and of attempting to destroy the *smychka*, the alliance of workers and peasants proclaimed by Lenin to be the foundation of the new Soviet Republic. Yet in this volume there are several documents that demonstrate exactly the opposite: a passionate commitment to improving the well-being of the peasantry. Preobrazhensky's accounts of his personal visits to newly-formed communes and *artels* in 1919 (see, for example, Documents 2:45–6, 2:48 and 2:50–1), combined with his frequent observations regarding the peasants' interest in supporting the Revolution for the sake of acquiring land and access to a better life, make it perfectly clear that he regarded improvement of peasant-life as one of the fundamental purposes of the Revolution and a precondition for improving the lot of Russian workers. No-one will read such documents without being struck by the absurdity of Stalinist charges that Preobrazhensky always wished to 'exploit' the peasantry as some new form of 'internal colony' in order to finance industrialisation.

Although Preobrazhensky, in his role as economist, has often been criticised for ignoring the human dimension of Russia's tribulations, readers familiar with that criticism will be struck by the fact that he was actually one of the first Bolsheviks to become seriously concerned with the re-emergence of a privileged bureaucracy within the Party and government after 1917. Time and again in the documents that we have included in this volume one encounters prescient denunciations of privilege and trenchant warnings of the consequences for the Revolution. In Document 2:42, for example, we read of 'an economically-privileged caste' and 'a new workers' bureaucracy' emerging within Soviet institutions. Condemning excessive centralisation, Preobrazhensky repeatedly linked his criticism of bureaucracy with calls for democratic workers' control from below to eliminate every form of privilege and abuse of power (among others, see Documents 2:29, 2:30, 2:38–42; 2:78–81).

At the close of this volume, the documents do become more directly concerned with economics, and we have included four such works: *Peasant-Russia and Socialism*, Preobrazhensky's critical review of the Socialist-Revolutionary agrarian programme and a proposal for a Bolshevik alternative; *Anarchism and Communism* a political-economic critique distinguishing anarchist localism from the requirements of socialist planning; the chapters that Preobrazhensky contributed to his joint publication with N.I. Bukharin, *The ABC of Communism*; and his first major work on monetary theory, *Paper-Money in the Epoch of Proletarian Dictatorship*, a completely original and now-classic work on the economic theory of inflation. Apart from the chapters from the *ABC*, which we have retranslated for this volume, these final works, like the other documents in this collection, appear here in English for the first time.

Thanks to the exhaustive research by Mikhail M. Gorinov, the 'story' recounted in this volume is not merely a biographical and intellectual documentary but also a human tale of hope and enthusiasm combined with moments of disappointment, apprehension, and even occasional despair. Frequently Preobrazhensky expressed his worry that without revolutionary assistance from Europe, Soviet Russia might not, and probably would not, survive – an issue on which he clashed with Stalin as early as August 1917 (Document 2:12; see also Documents 2:13, 2:17–20 on the need for revolutionary war, and Documents 2:21–2) and which subsequently led him to oppose Lenin on the choice between the Brest-Litovsk peace-treaty and revolutionary war. A particularly poignant moment of despair comes in Documents 1:75 and 1:76, written in March 1916, at the height of the imperialist War. In these essays, Preobrazhensky sought to sustain his flagging hope for ultimate human progress with a quotation from the great nineteenth-century revolutionary, Alexander Herzen:

When Herzen summarised the sad outcome of the 1848 movement in *My Past and Thoughts*, he was struck by the insignificance of the results achieved compared to the original goals and the efforts expended on their behalf, yet he still found consolation for himself and his contemporaries: 'The polyps die...serving the progress of the reef', he wrote, and 'We, too, shall serve something'.

In Document 1:36, Preobrazhensky also quoted Herzen at length, emphasising that even a failed revolution contributes to historical progress. This affinity with Herzen helps, I believe, to explain the inner conviction that sustained a man like Preobrazhensky through his many dark days of imprisonment, exile and persecution, including the darkest days that would come in the 1930s and culminate in his execution in 1937 on the order of Stalin. In his article on the imperialist War, Preobrazhensky revealed an element of his own personality that could never be expressed in his 'scientific' writings. He explained his own life's mission as follows:

> ...There is no fate, no predestination, only struggle, and we ourselves, in all our actions, are involved in the pattern of laws that define the course of history. While the question of civilisation's salvation remains a question of the elements struggling to that end, we do have a cause that is great in its consequences, capable of justifying all the sacrifices, and able to inspire great enthusiasm. That means we know what is good and what is criminal...There is no evil without good, even though the good in such circumstances is always too meagre. The good in the tragedy we are experiencing lies in the fact that it has made one thing perfectly obvious: civilisation and collectivism are henceforth synonyms; their destiny is just as inseparably connected as the life of an organism is connected with the integrity of the head and the heart....
>
> If only there were sufficient forces to save civilisation, if only the turning point would come and we would begin to see the dividends of victory! Oh, then we would find the elements of virtue in the crime; the rays of the sun, which today are blocked-off, would illuminate the darkness for us; we would find in the oceans of spilled blood the medicines to heal our wounds; in the pointless chaos of the tragedy we would behold the reason of history. Then all those who are now perishing in the various corners of the world as victims of the worldwide tragedy, all those confident of a future...[9] would be able to say with satisfaction before their death: *morituri te salutant, libertas!*[10]

---

9. [The source is damaged, making the next two words illegible.]
10. [We who are about to die salute you, freedom!]

This first volume of *The Preobrazhensky Papers* will be accompanied by four (and possibly five) further volumes, providing the most comprehensive collection of Preobrazhensky's works ever assembled. We have undertaken this effort in the interest of promoting historical scholarship, but also from the personal conviction that when historians 'know what is good and what is criminal' they also have a duty – indeed, a quite unique and solemn privilege – of helping to restore human dignity to good men who have been victimised by evil. Evgeny A. Preobrazhensky was such a man. In his foreword, Mikhail M. Gorinov poses the question of why Preobrazhensky's works should today be republished. Apart from the professional curiosity of historians, I believe his most compelling answer is that this work must be done 'for the sake of restoring historical justice'. It is with that conviction in mind that I have attempted to capture both the spirit and the substance of Evgeny Preobrazhensky's work in my efforts as translator of this volume.

Part I
The Beginning of the Road: 1886–1917

No. 1
From the *Autobiography* (1886–1916)[1]

1925

I was born in 1886 in the town of Bolkhov, in Orel province, into the family of a priest. I learned to read very early and at four years of age already read the stories in the ABC of Tolstoy. In my childhood I was very religious. I spent a great deal of time in the bell-towers of the two churches where my father served: I caught pigeons, ruined crows' nests and did rather well at ringing the small bells. My loathing of material inequality arose from social sentiments that awakened in me at a very early age. I remember that when I was eight years old, I demonstratively threw aside new boots that mother had bought for Easter on the grounds that poverty forced Mishka Uspensky, my childhood-playmate and the son of a shoemaker, to dress for Easter in boots that had holes. At first, I studied in the private school of my father and then, before entering the gymnasium, I spent two years at the Bolkhov city-school. During the first two to three years in the Orel gymnasium, I did well and was the second-best student in the class, but then I lost interest in the gymnasium's subjects because I was distracted by reading newspapers and journals with a liberal-populist leaning, novels by our classical writers, and textbooks on history. In my fourteenth year, I arrived independently at the conviction that God does not exist, and from that moment

---

1. [From Preobrazhensky 1989, pp. 588–9. The autobiography continues in Document 2:2.]

I began my stubborn struggle within the family against church-attendance and other religious rituals. This aversion to religion grew even more because I had an inside view of what went on in the religious kitchen. My atheistic views intensified still further when I read two volumes of the *History of Culture* by Kolb. This superficial work had such a strong influence upon me precisely because the author consistently exposes all religious superstitions and religious ignorance without, however, any understanding of the historical laws involved. But this was more of a plus than a minus for my subsequent development. What interested me at the time was not so much the explanation of religion as its absolute denial.

Even before the first underground-literature came into my hands, I was already quite radically inclined under the influence of reading *Russkoe bogatstvo, Russkie vedemosti, Otechestvennye zapiski*, Saltykov-Shchedrin and especially Dobrolyubov and Pisarev. Moreover, during vacations I constantly observed the distress, poverty and oppression of the peasantry in the villages of Bolkhov, Mtsensk and Bryansk districts, where I often spent my vacations.

The first illegal literature came into my hands when I was in the fifth class at the gymnasium. Among these first works I remember a hectographed feuilleton from Amfiteatrov's *Deceived Gentlemen*, which had previously been published in the newspaper *Rossiya*; a proclamation from a revolutionary committee of students at the Ekaterinoslav Mining Institute; an account of the beating of students by Cossacks; and a few revolutionary verses such as the *Marseillaise, Dubinushka*, and *Boldly, Friends, Do Not Falter*, among others. I remember, as if it were today, one very important moment of my biography. It was during summer-vacation when I went home to Bolkhov and settled into the darkest corner of our garden. Behind the bath-house, there was a small bench amid the lilacs, and I began to re-read all my illegal possessions, both old ones and those recently acquired, including a hand-written notebook with various student-proclamations, humorous and lyrical poetry as well as certain facts from a revolutionary chronicle. At a certain moment, I was confronted by a purely practical question in its complete enormity: What should I do? Was I willing to join the ranks of the revolutionaries, with all the ensuing consequences, such as expulsion from the gymnasium, rupture with my family, prison, exile and so forth? At that moment I made a decision and said firmly to myself: yes, I am going to join the revolutionaries, no matter what may happen.

During that summer, the only revolutionary 'cell' in our town apparently consisted of me and my childhood-comrade, Ivan Anisimov, the son of a local merchant who later became a Menshevik and emigrated, it seems, along with the Whites. We set out together for the most remote places outside of the city and expressed our protest against autocracy by singing the *Marseillaise*, but in such a way that we alone could hear it. When we passed by the Bolkhov city-jail – a miserable, old-fashioned building that usually held a couple of dozen petty thieves and horse-rustlers – our thoughts turned to Kresty and Butyrka,[2] where fighters against the autocratic regime, who were so dear to us, were languishing.

After returning from vacation to the gymnasium, I decided to devote a minimum of time to gymnasium-subjects, just enough to get a third grade in my courses, and to transfer the focus of my activity to evenings of avidly reading foreign works on rice-paper while devoting all my time during the days to reading books on the history of culture, on history in general, especially the history of revolution, and also on the basic elements of political economy. In addition, Ivan Anisimov and I began to broaden our propaganda among the students, started a couple of circles, and entered into contact with people who were under surveillance in the city of Orel. During that period I developed a mystical passion for reproducing illegal literature. By that time, I had abandoned the hand-copied journal *Shkol'nye dosugi*, which I had established and managed together with Aleksandr Tinyakov, a poet who later went mad, because it was politically irrelevant. Printing a few small things on a hectograph, likewise, did not satisfy me, although with a single print run we got a hundred copies. I dreamed of a printing press, and by the next vacation I prepared 'a technological advance' in order to make my dream come true. Among the revolutionary young people in our Orel circle of that time were the children of Aleksin, who owned the local print-works. At my insistence, Sasha Aleksin stole from his father's type-cabinet five pounds of type, which I intended to use for a more perfect reproduction of a 'Collection of Revolutionary Songs': the *Marseillaise* and others. During vacation I went home with the type and 'opened' a print-works in the bath-house of my father's garden. I made the cases, set out the type and began the compositing work for *We Renounce the Old World*. In order that my solitary work in the bath-house should not become a matter of suspicion to the family, I convinced father that it was physically good for me to rise at dawn and to go and bathe in the local river Nugr. Of course, I did not go to bathe but spent the entire time in the bath-house trying to master the publishing trade. Nothing came of my typesetting: the letters fell out and some were missing. When I finally set up the first verse after enormous effort, and with trepidation tried to print my first copy, all the letters were upside-down. When I finally had them properly arranged, there was not enough type for two verses. After tormenting myself for two weeks in this undertaking, I decided to 'shut down' the print-works, buried the type in the ground, and in the autumn returned it to Aleksin's print-works. We had to continue at the technological level of the hectograph and later to adopt the

---

2. [The reference is to Kresty prison in St. Petersburg and Butyrka prison in Moscow.]

mimeograph, on which we printed various proclamations on instruction from the Orel Committee.

When I entered the seventh class at the gymnasium, I could no longer remain in a state of undefined and formless revolutionism. I had to choose between the Socialist-Revolutionaries and the Social Democrats. At that time the decisive influence in working out my world-view came from two works: *The Communist Manifesto* and *The Development of Scientific Socialism* by Engels. Pondering these two works for a long time, I decided that the Narodnik world-view was bankrupt and unscientific and that Marxism alone could show me the proper path. This change in my world-view also had certain practical consequences. Up to that moment I was distributing among the students not only social-democratic literature that came to us from members of the Orel Committee of the Social-Democratic Party – Veleryan Shmidt and Petr Semenovich Bobrovsky (who later became Mensheviks) – but also S-R literature supplied to us by Nikkeleva, an S-R who was under surveillance. I remember how, with grim determination, one day I told Nikkeleva that I could no longer help her with the distribution of S-R literature because I had now become a Social Democrat.

Among the comrades who participated at that time in our student revolutionary organisation, I remember especially clearly Aleksandr and Evgraf Litkens, both of whom died tragically (Evgraf was later Deputy Commissar of Education), D. Kuzovkov, N. Mikheev, Ledovsky, and E.M. Kotina; among the seminarians, I remember Romanov, M. Fenomenov and others. I recall one particularly curious incident involving Anisimov – whom I have already mentioned – the older Litkens, and myself. We constituted the SD troika in the gymnasium and constantly had to store a significant quantity of illegal literature. In order to avoid amateurish methods – burying literature in the ground, stuffing it in the hollow of tree-trunks or the like – we decided to organise a small storehouse in the apartment of Barinov, who was under surveillance. For that purpose we decided to build a second brick-wall in the Russian stove[3] and to keep our illegal treasures behind that second wall, with one brick on the top that could easily be slid out. One Sunday, with enormous effort and care, we completed all this construction and solemnly placed all our illegal reserves in this new depository. But then a small misfortune occurred. The mistress of the house, who came from time to time to stoke the stove in Barinov's apartment, which was in another part of the building, got it burning well and then wanted to put the poker back under the fire-chamber, but now the poker would not go all the way in. The frightened mistress

---

3. [The text reads 'в подгрубке русской печки', referring to the flue, fire-chamber and chimney of a Russian stove, a highly-efficient device that directs the heat through a series of internal passageways built of brick so that the bricks absorb and radiate almost all of the heat rather than letting it escape through the chimney.]

went to tell the master, and with a lantern they investigated the opening but found nothing: the wall looked like a wall, but still the poker would not go in. This stove became a topic of conversation for the neighbours, and the following Sunday we wisely decided to eliminate our storehouse with the same care that went into it. We carried out the bricks at night and dumped them into the Orlik river. But when the mistress next came to heat the stove, the poker went all the way in just as it normally did before. The master came again, and with a lantern they investigated once more and found nothing. This time they were even more frightened than on the first occasion, and the master began talking about some kind of evil force connected with the fact that his tenant, Barinov, was under surveillance. Ultimately this incident ended without any particular consequences for us. In the autumn of that same year, 1903, we developed more intensive work in the educational institutions and acted as a Social-Democratic cell of the Orel Party-Committee.

As a matter of fact, I consider myself to have been a member of the Party from the end of 1903, although my formal acceptance into the Party, along with Litkens, and Anisimov, only took place two to three months later.

At the beginning of 1904, when the Russo-Japanese War began, the Orel Party-Committee issued a proclamation against the War and assigned the three of us to distribute a large number of copies in the gymnasium. We did this as follows. During one lesson, all three of us simultaneously left our different classes and went to the cloakroom, where the coats of all the students were hanging, and seizing the opportune moment we distributed one hundred and fifty to two hundred proclamations in the pockets of all the students of the upper classes. The operation went splendidly, and when the students put on their coats and left for home they were all surprised to find in their pockets the publication of the Orel Committee. There was an enormous scandal, the administration rushed about in search of the people responsible, and the gendarmerie conducted an investigation but did not find the culprits. After this, our first organised action, the Orel Committee decided it could accept us formally into the Committee's group of propagandists, and this was done after a brief colloquium in February 1904.

In the spring of that year I received a small study-group of two workers from the Khrushchevsky mechanical-works and gave them a long but not very persuasive explanation of the Party's programme. In the summer of that same year, I passed into the eighth class of the gymnasium and, on the advice of the Committee, took on summer-tutoring in the centre of the Maltsevsky factories,[4] at the Dyatkovo factory in Bryansk district, with the son of Zolotov, the district's

---

4. [The Maltsevsky (more correctly, Maltsovsky) factories were a group of machine-building works, iron-foundries, glass- and cement-works – the largest being the Lyudinovsk iron-foundry, steel-smelter and engineering works; the Dyatkovo crystal-works;

superintendent of police. I converted Nikolai Mikhailovich Zolotov, my pupil – who now lives in France – to the Social-Democratic faith. Officially working with him on Latin, we spent most of our efforts on propaganda amongst the workers of Dyatkovo, Ivot and the other Maltsevsky factories. This is where I first came to know Fokin, who later played a major role in building our organisations of Soviet power in the Bryansk district. Police-superintendent Zolotov, my pupil's father, put in a great effort to catch our organisation's Dyatkovo cell, which was distributing illegal literature and putting out proclamations by mimeograph. We protected this mimeograph and the illegal literature in quite a unique way. My pupil complained to his father that he had no place to keep his books and notes and asked to use one of the drawers of his father's desk that could be locked with a key. The father willingly provided the drawer and key, and it was in that drawer that we kept both the mimeograph and the illegal literature while the father, Zolotov, was scouring Dyatkovo in pursuit of the pernicious distribution-apparatus. Similarly, when we had to hold large meetings in the forest for individual factories, we asked the police-superintendent for his two horses in order to go hunting, and the completely unsuspecting superintendent gave us his horses with bells on, and we made the round of organisations in our area. This whole story came to light only a year later.

In 1905 our group conducted a general strike in the educational institutions of Orel during April and May, and despite all this – despite my public appearances at student-meetings where we adopted our academic demands – I was not arrested and I even received my certificate of matriculation. In the summer of 1905 I went to Bryansk on party-work; and there, together with two other comrades, I led the work of the Bryansk Party-Committee. I lived at Bryansk station. With no bed in my room, I slept on two newspapers spread out on the floor; I ate only sausage and bread, spending no more than twenty *kopeks* a day; and every evening I walked to and from Bezhitsa, that is, 18 *versts*, in order to conduct workers' circles at the Bryansk locomotive-building factory. In October of the same year, 1905, I was co-opted onto the Orel Committee, at the suggestion of Olympii Kvitkin. At the time, the Orel Committee was taking a compromising attitude. Ponomarev, the Committee's leader after Olympii Kvitkin left, laughingly said to other members of the Committee: 'We have two solid Bolsheviks: 20 year-old Mikhail Ekaterinoslavsky and 19 year-old Evgeny Preobrazhensky'. Despite such jokes, I stuck firmly to my views and defended the position of our Party's Third Congress. Before that time, one curious thing did happen at the Orel Committee. It sent Olympii Kvitkin to be its representative at the Third

---

and the Ivot, Chernotinsk and Bytoshevsk glass-works, among others – located around the city of Bryansk (in the Maltsovsky factory-region).]

Congress, but he went as a Menshevik and returned as a convinced Bolshevik, completely supporting me and Mikhail Ekaterinoslavsky in our Bolshevik views. In October, following publication of the famous manifesto, I participated in the struggle against pogromists in Orel and was then sent to work at a Bryansk factory. I stayed in Bryansk until mid-November and then, at the suggestion of N.M. Mikheev, who was then working in Moscow, and with the agreement of the Moscow Committee, I went to work in Moscow where I was appointed as propagandist responsible for the Presnensky district. I worked there during the whole time leading up to the uprising, and during the uprising I attended meetings of the District-Committee that led the insurrection in Presnensky, when Sedoi commanded our forces. My function at the time was mainly to conduct meetings at the striking factories, which were already coming under fire from artillery in the Vagankovsky cemetery. When Presnya was already surrounded by Semenov's forces and in flames, I hid my Browning in the water-closet of my apartment, made my way at night through a line of soldiers in the centre of the city, and left to spend several days in Orel, after which I returned to work for the bureau of our Central Committee in Moscow, which was led at the time by Rykov. A.I. Rykov suggested that I choose between two organisations where the most serious failures had occurred – Kostroma, and Perm in the Urals. I chose the Urals, and within five days I was already on the scene and was introduced to the Perm Committee.

At that time, Klavdiya Timofeevna Novgorodtseva was a regular worker in Perm, and Yakov Mikhailovich Sverdlov also came to knock together our party-association in the Urals after the January failure. I worked in Perm for about two-and-a-half months until, as a result of a provocation by Votinov, who was well known in Motovilikha, I was arrested along with other comrades on 18 March. This was my first time in prison. After about five months, and following a four-day hunger-strike, I was released from prison for lack of sufficient evidence, together with Bina Lobova, Liza Kin and other comrades and placed under police-supervision. When I left prison and walked about the city with a small bundle of belongings under my arm, in the street I met Aleksandr Minkin who informed me of the state of the organisation and suggested I that begin work. The next day I also had discussions with S-Rs on the other bank of the Kama, and the wheel of the usual underground-work began to turn once more. Given the collapse of the regional organisation, I was sent to Ekaterinburg, Chelyabinsk and Ufa to restore contacts, and in the autumn I arranged a local conference in the city of Vyatka in which I was unable to participate myself. Sent by the Perm Committee to procure Brownings in Petrograd for our Perm fighting detachment, I was arrested in Kazan station due to a provocation by Foma Lebedev (whom I later identified by chance in Orel in 1919 and who was subsequently shot in Perm).

I was then sent once more to Perm, where I sat for a second time in the Perm prison and subsequently in the famous Nikolaevsk[5] cells for about eight months. After that, when the case of our group went before the Kazan court, I was freed once more for lack of evidence.

Upon leaving prison, I went to the southern Urals where I worked mainly in Ufa at the Simsky factories and in Zlatoust. We succeeded in restoring the local Urals organisation, where one of the most prominent workers at the time was Nikolai Nikandrovich Nakoryakov (nicknamed 'Nazar'). With an excellent illegal print-works in Ufa, we resumed publication of our regional Urals organ, the *Ural'skii rabochii*, and also began publishing *Krestyanskaya gazeta* and *Soldatskaya gazeta*. In 1907 I was a delegate from the Urals to our Party's All-Russian Conference in Finland, where I first came to know Lenin. Until March 1908 my work in the Urals continued under steadily-deteriorating conditions, with an increasing number of failures and continuously-growing reaction. In March, I was arrested at the Chelyabinsk City-Conference, but I swallowed the agenda and the ciphered addresses and that same night successfully escaped from police-custody. Having failed completely in the Urals, I still could not give it up and fled from Chelyabinsk to Ufa, disguised as a typesetter. I was supposed to organise a Urals Conference, to take place in Zlatoust. I stayed in Ufa for a short while, but did not get to attend the Conference. I was arrested in the street by plain-clothes detectives at the end of April and immediately identified. In Ufa, before my arrest, I was involved in the following interesting incident. There was a search at Bryukhanov's home – he is now People's Commissar of Finance and was then a member of the Ufa Committee – in which the gendarmes expected to catch me since they had a description sent from Chelyabinsk. I met the gendarme-captain at the door, still in my disguise as a typesetter, and grasping what was going on I asked him if this was the home of the student Vernikovsky (he was the son of the person who owned two houses, in one of which Bryukhanov lived). The gendarme-captain, not suspecting the person he was dealing with, promptly pointed me to a large house next door, and I happily left in that direction. The gendarme only realised his mistake much later.

I spent some time in the Ufa prison and then was sent to Chelyabinsk. I was held in Chelyabinsk for trial in the autumn of 1909. At the time of the trial I was expecting a heavy sentence and attempted to escape from the convoy, but I failed and was badly beaten by the soldier-escorts. Meanwhile, the sentence turned out to be very light: we were all given exile to a settlement. After that, I was tried a second time in Perm under Statute 102 and received a second sentence of exile. We travelled by stages to the Aleksandrovsk transit-camp near Irkutsk and waited

---

5. [A prison located not far from Verkhnaya Tura.]

there until summer, when I was settled in rural Karapchansky in the Kirensky district. In exile we lived as a close-knit family in a commune that included the late Artem Sergeev, Petr Kovalenko, Anatoly Galkin and other comrades. Apart from daily work with the peasants I busied myself mainly with hunting. In the winter of 1911, the Ekaterinburg Committee of our Party suggested that I escape from exile, travel to Ekaterinburg, and then represent the Ekaterinburg organisation as a delegate to a party-conference being held abroad, which occurred a short while later in Prague in 1912. I happily accepted the proposal, especially since I had already corresponded with Nadezhda Konstantinovna Krupskaya about this conference and had received a short coded letter from Vladimir Il'ich. Not long before my flight from exile in the direction of Ekaterinburg, the Police-Department ordered that I be searched and for that purpose sent Treshchenkov, the famous gendarme-captain known for shooting down the workers in Lena. Because of the winter ice-flows on the Angara, Treshchenkov could not cross the river and turned back towards Kirensk having accomplished nothing. Somewhat later, on Christmas Day, the police-superintendent of Nizhny Ilimsk,[6] in whose jurisdiction we exiles were located at the time, received a telegram from the Department of Police ordering my immediate arrest because the Ekaterinburg organisation had already been arrested and my connection with that organisation had been established as a result. By coincidence, on Christmas Day the police-superintendent lay drunk, and his secretary, who opened the telegram, let slip its contents to our comrade-exiles in Nizhny Ilimsk. The comrades immediately sent a messenger to me, who galloped eighty *versts* in the night, and thirty minutes later I was already sitting in a peasant-cart and rushing towards the railway-station in Tulun. When the police-superintendent sobered up, read the telegram and set out to arrest me, I had already passed him by in Nizhny Ilimsk and was on my way to Tulun. From Tulun I went to Novonikolaevsk, where I began to work as a contributor to the legal Marxist newspaper *Obskaya zhizn'*. I published several articles in that newspaper, defending our Bolshevik position on the fundamental political questions of the day. By the way, that was also when I corresponded with Zinoviev, requested his cooperation with the newspaper and received one article that appeared with the initials G.Z. Vladimir Il'ich also promised to contribute but did not have time to send anything. In the autumn of 1912 our entire Novonikolaevsk organisation was arrested due to a provocation. Petr Kovalenko, who worked in that organisation, had been arrested even earlier. I was arrested one day before leaving to go abroad at the invitation of Nadezhda Konstantinovna Krupskaya to attend a meeting. From Novonikolaevsk I was sent

---

6. [The modern spelling is Nizhneilimsk.]

back to Ekaterinburg prison, meeting along the way with L. Serebryakov, Zelensky, Kuzmenko and others who were heading into exile.

In Ekaterinburg I was brought to trial along with Semen Shvarts, Evgeniya Bosh, A.V. Trubina, A. Paramonov and other comrades. Due to the stupidity of the procurator – who confused me in his indictment with some other Evgeny – and with the help of a defence that included N.D. Sokolov, A.F. Kerensky and N.M. Mikheev, I was acquitted, to everyone's surprise.

From Ekaterinburg prison I was again sent into exile, receiving a preliminary six months in prison for escaping. This time my stay in exile was brief, and in 1915 I was allowed to move to Irkutsk. In Irkutsk I joined the local party-organisation, which soon collapsed. After that, and in order to avoid another provocation, we organised a new group of the most 'trustworthy' comrades – including Zavadsky, Romm, Dzyarsky,[7] Krut, Samsonov and myself – acquired a printing press, and planned to begin work on publishing a proclamation that I had written in opposition to the War. It soon turned out that amongst us six 'trustworthy' people there was a provocateur. We dissolved our group, and it was only after the February Revolution, using the archive of the Irkutsk gendarmerie-administration, that we determined who it was that betrayed us. It was David Krut, who was brought to trial for this affair in Moscow in 1926. During my stay in Irkutsk I worked on the SD organ *Zabaikal'skoe obozrenie*, where I had two articles against the War published.

---

7. [This name was misprinted. The correct spelling is 'Zdzyarsky'.]

No. 2
'From My Memories of Ya.M. Sverdlov' and Revolutionary Activities in the Urals during 1906–1907

From 'My Memories of Ya.M. Sverdlov'[1]

1926[2]

In these recollections, I am reproducing only a small part of what I could say about Yakov Mikhailovich, especially regarding the underground-period of his activity. But in order to make the recollections more complete, I would have to draw upon a number of official party-documents from the corresponding period of our Party's history, read through all the memoirs of other people who participated in party-work and, with the help of these additional means, reconstruct in memory and by way of association much of what does not come to mind simply by an act of will. Unfortunately, I do not have the time for such detailed work, although I have not given up the hope of completing it some time in the future.

I briefly met Yakov Mikhailovich for the first time in Moscow in December 1905, when he was making his way to the Joint Party-Congress, which did not occur at that time, and was caught by a railway-strike in Moscow. At that time, he spoke to meetings of thousands of Moscow workers at the 'Aquarium' and distinguished himself by the great power of his voice. I have only a vague memory of him at this meeting in Moscow.

---

1. [From Preobrazhensky 1926, pp. 168–79.]
2. [This is the date when the memoirs were written.]

I came to know Yakov Mikhailovich better through my work in the Urals, where I arrived at the beginning of January 1906. The first time I met him was at a secret party-address in Perm, where he briefly informed me of the work that awaited me in the Perm organisation, which had been destroyed following the failure in December. My clearest memory is of a meeting of the Perm Party-Committee, which had to adopt a resolution on unifying our organisations in the Urals. At this meeting Yakov Mikhailovich gave a report on creating a Urals regional centre. In addition to Yakov Mikhailovich and several Perm workers, so far as I can remember the meeting was attended by Klavdiya Timofeevna Novgorodtseva, Liza Kin and others who worked in the Perm organisation. When discussion of the report ended, Yakov Mikhailovich whispered to me to present my resolution and added: 'You are, after all, a specialist in producing resolutions. So go ahead, propose what we need'. Although I did not regard myself as a specialist at resolutions, I drafted one on the spot and it was accepted by those present.

By that time, I had already formed an impression of Yakov Mikhailovich that changed little during my later meetings with him. I was most struck by the calm assuredness of this great organiser, who even at that time felt himself to be in his native element with all the most difficult organisational questions. Whenever difficulties arose concerning the combination of people and adoption of the necessary organisational measures for restoring our ruined organisations, he was extraordinarily quick, almost like lightning, to find the necessary solution and to implement it with little argumentation, as if it were the natural and only reasonable thing to do.

At that time, Yakov Mikhailovich did not work continuously in Perm because he had to travel throughout the entire Urals district. After assigning people to appropriate positions in the Perm organisation and giving all the necessary instructions, he would speed off to other cities in the Urals in order to do the same necessary organisational work there. It was largely thanks to his colossal organisational talent and inexhaustible energy that the Urals organisations were restored after the defeat in late 1905 and early 1906 and were able to send a Bolshevik representative to the so-called unification-congress.

Yakov Mikhailovich attached enormous importance to creating both a single association for all of our Urals organisations and a solid centre for regional leadership. This was necessary because of the distance of the Urals from the leading party-centres in Russia and abroad, and also because of the special features of life and the economy in the Urals. In historical terms, the correctness of this approach to the Urals party-association has been fully justified. After some wavering on the question of how useful it was to have regions, and a Urals region in particular, the Urals region became firmly-established earlier than others as a defined economic unit, and the Urals party-association was reconstructed.

The following example illustrates how unique the conditions always were for our work in the Urals, especially for propaganda-work. One agitator, who arrived in the Urals from either Moscow or St. Petersburg (this was in tsarist times) took great pains to lay out an eloquent case for workers to have an eight-hour day. His propaganda met with lively approval from the audience, but the workers who spoke after him remarked: 'The comrade-speaker quite rightly said that we need an eight-hour working day; we now work a six-hour day, and what can anyone earn in six hours?' (Because of overpopulation at the factories, the available work was usually divided up between all adult workers, resulting in an incomplete working week, a shortened workday and only partial wages.)

In part, Yakov Mikhailovich attracted certain new and valuable resources to the Urals, yet he was even more concerned with building up a leading cadre from among the local Urals workers. That was one reason why the Urals organisations, despite the colossal collapse, turned out to be most stable when a period of crisis brought complete disintegration and disappearance of organisations elsewhere.

In March 1906, as a result of efforts by the provocateur Votinov, who worked at the Motovilikha factory, and by other agents of the Okhranka, the reconstructed organisations in Perm and Motovilikha suffered an enormous setback. Arrests continued in April and May and all the most active elements in our ranks were rounded up. Yet despite the fact that more than two-thirds of our most active members were in the Perm prison, we were convinced that we could continue work on the outside. The guarantee of this was not merely the fact that lower levels quickly provided new workers to replace those who had been arrested, but also that 'Andrei' or 'Mikhalych' (two of the most common nicknames for Yakov Mikhailovich) remained at liberty and tirelessly continued his constructive work even in conditions of continuous shadowing and persecution by the gendarmes.

However, the days of freedom for Yakov Mikhailovich were also numbered. One fine day he was surrounded by detectives and subjected to the same treatment that normally comes when one is 'under arrest'. In these cases the detectives did not consider it necessary to hide their profession and brazenly followed a person waiting for the most opportune moment to make an arrest. Their task was to prevent the victim from disposing of or eating the documents, addresses and other papers that might be found on him. But, so far as I remember, Yakov Mikhailovich managed to swallow the ciphered addresses that were in his possession, and when the detectives grabbed him by both hands he was already 'clean', as we used to say in the underground. Following the arrest, 'Mikhalych' was put in a wagon and taken to the secret-police department, and then to Perm prison. Yakov Mikhailovich must have considered it fortunate that they arrested him in Perm and not in the territory of the Motovilikha factory. I should point out that in those days people arrested within the city of Perm were in a privileged position compared to those comrades arrested in the Motovilikha factory, for those arrested in the Motovilikha area were usually subjected to the most brutal beatings in an attempt to extract compromising information even prior to the judicial investigation.

Yakov Mikhailovich was arrested in the summer of 1906, in June I think, but at the moment I do not remember the exact date. However, I do remember very well the moment when all of us who knew him suddenly heard his familiar, powerful voice in the prison. We managed to exchange a few words before our outing period, for which almost all the cells of the political prisoners were opened simultaneously, and we had a more extensive conversation in the prison-yard. Yakov Mikhailovich told us about the conditions of party-work in Perm and other centres in the Urals and also about the circumstances of his arrest. The attitude amongst all of us at the time was firmly optimistic; we had no doubt concerning the victory of the revolution, and we did not expect to be detained for long behind prison-walls. I remember that during our first, or possibly our second, outing in the prison-yard, Yakov Mikhailovich measured the prison-wall and, after jumping on the shoulders of our tallest comrade, nicknamed 'Potap' (a worker from Tula with the surname Ivanov), calculated how much height would still be needed so that one might jump over the prison-wall.

His days in Perm prison passed, as they did for the rest of us, involving the following elements. First, relations with the outside-world and the continuation of party-work from behind prison-walls. In prison we discussed the state of things in the Party and tactical questions of the movement, and we worked out and sent resolutions to the outside world for the organisations to adopt. Yakov Mikhailovich sent his organisational directives through the prison-post, which at that time, under a comparatively free régime, made its way out and back by various routes. I remember writing, on his orders, some proclamation for the Perm organisation involving, if I am not mistaken, the elections for the Duma.

The second part of our work involved conducting propaganda within the prison among the younger and less-prepared comrades, mainly workers from Motovilikha and other Urals factories near Perm. There were several circles in the prison, organised mainly by Yakov Mikhailovich, in which we, the propagandists, did systematic work. Besides that, we read reports on various themes and held debates. I remember, in particular, that one of the persons who gave a report at the time was comrade Egor (the party-nickname of comrade Kanatchikov). Yakov Mikhailovich attached great importance to this work within the prison and followed it closely so that we might theoretically finish off the Mensheviks even behind the prison-walls; and we did have Mensheviks at the time because they had their organisations not only in Perm but also in a number of factories even though they were quite weak. We influenced the workers from these organisations and made Bolsheviks out of them.

The third part of our activity was preparation for escape. Although there was no particularly serious evidence against Yakov Mikhailovich, he had a feeling that the gendarmes would not set him free any time soon. On the outside things were boiling and seething at the time. There was such a shortage of workers, and he so wanted to get out of prison as quickly as possible to continue his interrupted work! Thus, soon after the arrest of Yakov Mikhailovich and at his insistence, we were sent thin steel-files from the outside, from Motovilikha, and we worked in full swing to file through the prison-bars, a task in which Ivan Chugurin, whose party-nickname in the Urals was 'Petr' or 'Petrukha', played an especially active part. We were also inspired to escape by the fact that, early in the spring, comrade Yakubov and several other comrades had escaped from the very corridor in which we were sitting (Yakubov was facing the death-penalty for armed resistance to the gendarmes), and they persuaded the prison-guard to flee with them.

Yakov Mikhailovich proposed following the same escape-plan a second time, that is, filing through the bars on the second floor, climbing down bed-sheets at night to meet the guard, with whom the organisation on the outside was to make a deal, and then running off together with him. At the same time, he also prepared another version of escape – during our exercise-outing, those who were not intending to flee were to 'get carried away' playing the elephant-game,[3] erecting an elephant of such size that it would be possible to jump over the prison-wall, and then, during the outing, we would run through the kitchen-garden past the guard, who at the time would be a member of our fighting organisation, and he would zealously open fire on the escapees but miss them.

Fourthly, we busied ourselves eagerly with reading. In prison we received much of the literature that we needed, and all of us, without wasting any time, greedily devoured it, beginning with such fundamentals as *Capital*. I forget who suggested that we introduce in our cells a so-called 'constitution', which forbade for a given time any talking, pranks or other disruptions of the silence. During this time, everyone was preoccupied. Conversations, mischief-making, tomfoolery and games were strictly regulated and assigned to a special time. Yakov Mikhailovich would read just like the rest of us, but his thinking, more than anyone else's, was directed to party-work on the outside.

Our outings in the prison-yard involved the following parts of a daily prison-routine: we played frantically at ball, billy-goat, and especially the elephant-game, whose significance for our prison-escape I have already mentioned. Besides that, during our outings and in the cells, especially after the evening roll-call, when the 'constitution' was not in force, we occupied ourselves with singing. Relatives

---

3. [The 'elephant-game' involves one person bending down and others climbing, one on top of the other, to see how tall the 'elephant' can become.]

or close friends of the prisoners would often come to the cemetery outside the prison, and we would greet them by singing revolutionary songs. Everyone knows that Yakov Mikhailovich had a voice like a trumpet. But his voice was not suited for singing, mainly because he did not hear well. But refusing to be daunted by this circumstance, he studied choral singing, and when, after a few tries he sang less and less out of tune, he laughingly said with satisfaction: 'Soon I'll have the deciding vote[4] in our singing'. We made use of Yakov Mikhailovich's voice whenever we had to communicate something over a long distance. That was necessary both for shouting in the direction of the cemetery and also, most frequently, for conversations with the women's yard, where they kept our female comrades. We communicated with them by prison-post and through the far window of the corridor that opened onto their yard. If the comrades from the women's yard could not distinguish what some speaker was saying from our corridor, they usually shouted: 'Send in "Mikhalych"'.

Following a hunger-strike in the summer of that year, I and a number of other comrades who were charged, along with Yakov Mikhailovich (the so-called 'Case No. 46 involving the Perm organisation'), managed to go to court under police-supervision, as the evidence against me and the others who were let out was weak. On the same day as my release, the late Bina (Lobova) and several men were also freed. From the assignments that were given to me while in prison, I began to carry out those involving escape; specifically, I was to make preparations for the second version of escape from the prison-yard. I had to find two guards from the Perm garrison who would agree to fire into the air during an escape over the prison-wall. The question of escape was urgent because, in addition to Yakov Mikhailovich, Chugurin and Savinov also had to flee since they faced trial in Nizhny Novgorod for the armed insurrection in Sormovsky. About three *versts* from the city, I had a forest-meeting with two soldiers who were sent by our military organiser. I became convinced that these soldiers were not up to the job. One of them immediately demanded to be paid a large sum of money, even before the operation, on the grounds that he might have to spend two to three years in a disciplinary battalion for not shooting accurately. But it was not simply a matter of the money. I profoundly disliked this type of person, and I suspected that he might take the money and then shoot not into the air but at our comrades. After consulting with other comrades in the organisation, we rejected this sort of guard. Unfortunately, there were no others who were more suitable. The escape-plan collapsed.

I was not outside for long – only a month. Of course, right after prison I took part in the work of the Perm organisation and, in particular, travelled about the

---

4. [The text reads: 'Скоро я уже начну принимать участие в пении с решающим голосом'. Sverdlov's joke was that the word 'голос' means both 'voice' and 'vote'.]

Urals organisations for convocation of the second Urals conference.[5] A month passed and I was arrested at the station in Kazan, through a provocation by Foma (Lebedev),[6] as I was setting out for Piter to purchase Brownings for the Perm fighting detachment of our Party. From Kazan I was taken back to Perm prison. As far as I can recall, Yakov Mikhailovich was no longer being held in the common cells, but in the so-called 'tower', in solitary. I must point out that sitting in solitary in those days was not punishment, and all the comrades, with few exceptions, went there in turn (more wanted to go than there was space for in solitary) in order to have time alone, not to worry about others in the room, and to have peaceful circumstances for more serious reading.

Soon afterwards, because of the terrible overcrowding of Perm prison, a great many prisoners were sent in the autumn of that year to the famous Nikolaevsk cells, which were situated not far from Verkhnaya Tura. Whether it was in this first group or in another, 'Mikhalych' was also sent to Nikolaevsk and placed there in a one-storey building of solitary-cells. The cells were dark with narrow windows facing the prison-yard. Soon after his arrival 'Mikhalych' began to work on another escape-project. From prison-stories we already knew about all the escapes that had occurred from the Nikolaevsk jail and in particular from the solitary-cells in which we were held. The most recent escape from this solitary confinement involved the famous Mikhail Vilonov, one of the most remarkable worker-Bolsheviks of our Party, who afterwards took part in Gorky's school in Capri, then joined Lenin in Paris and died from consumption during the period of reaction. The escape was accomplished by digging a tunnel from the solitary-cell to the street. This same version was again now considered, and we also worked out a plan to file the bars, get to the yard at night and escape over the prison-walls.

In Nikolaevsk we led just about the same kind of life as in Perm prison but with the one difference that there was neither a large city nor a large organisation nearby, and dealings with the outside were more difficult. Yakov Mikhailovich was the head of our corridor and looked after our material supplies. Every evening he came up to the 'grate' (a small opening in the cell-door) of each person in solitary and asked what to write down for the next day's meal. He urged everyone to ask for more, but since resources were scarce our commune mainly asked for boiled potatoes and sauerkraut. Here, too, the prison-day was spent mainly in reading and various political and theoretical debates. After the evening

---

5. This conference was scheduled for Vyatka, but I did not attend it myself because I was arrested beforehand. Artem and Nazar (Nakoryakov) played prominent roles at the conference.

6. I happened to meet this provocateur Lebedev in Orel in 1919, just before he was to be sent to one of the divisions on the southern front as head of the political department. I ordered his arrest. He was shot in Perm after confessing to his crime.

roll-call, as I remember, disputes would begin in our cells that usually involved other prisoners in solitary besides the Bolsheviks and S-Rs. Usually everyone in solitary would put his ear to the 'grate' and listen to whatever person was speaking. Yakov Mikhailovich broke the silence more than anyone else, for he could not speak quietly and always made the guard on duty nervous, fearing that an administrator might come by and punish him for the disorder. The S-Rs who were imprisoned with us were very weak when it came to theory, and picking them apart in a dispute was easy for us. We also played chess – each player had a board with figures made from black prison-bread, or what the Motovilikha workers called *nekalimka* (a special kind of steel). Among those held in solitary at the time, I remember A.N. Sokolov and Verbov.

All the prisoners in solitary were taken together for our outing. So long as there was no snow and it was not yet cold, we mainly played ball, while in winter our favourite game was the 'cow', as it was called. The feature of this game is that a player tried to fling a small wooden stick or snowball at someone else's feet; if he managed to hit the mark, the other players would pummel that person on the back from both sides and often throw him into the deep snow. Despite his physical weakness, 'Mikhalych' was most adroit at this game and rarely managed to get hit while he quite often thrashed less-agile companions.

Most of the political prisoners were not in solitary but in common cells at Nikolaevsk. The prison-régime was deteriorating from day to day. On one occasion two of our prisoners from the common cells were dragged to the punishment-cell and beaten for no serious reason. The organisers of this incident and of subsequent beatings were the well-known Urals prison-executioners: Kalachev, who was killed in Perm, and the chief warder I. Ustyunin, who was tried even in a tsarist court for the terrible beatings of political prisoners in the punishment cell that ended in the death of one of our comrades.

I witnessed only the beginning of this period, when we answered the first attack on our comrades with a general hunger-strike. The strike lasted exactly a week, from one Sunday to the next, and all of the prisoners were terribly exhausted, including Yakov Mikhailovich. The hunger-strike ended in some sort of compromise with the administration. At that time I was no longer in solitary but in a common cell. By the third or fourth day of the hunger-strike there were voices calling for an end to it. But the majority firmly resolved to continue. In the agitation to continue the strike, Yakov Mikhailovich took the most active part despite his poor health. He usually tied a towel around his stomach and for most of the time lay motionless on the bed, smoking a great deal of tobacco. His health began to decline as a result of sitting in the dark in solitary-cells and from lack of food and fresh air. He had all the signs of tuberculosis. His face became quite yellow and took on a brown tint. In terms of morale he remained totally invulnerable and strong as a rock with firm hope for the future. He recalled at the time that his tuberculosis began during his first confinement in the Nizhegorod prison; because of one his protests, the guards dragged him to a damp punishment-cell and beat him badly about the stomach and chest. In Nikolaevsk the tuberculosis became worse, and we all became very concerned about his fate.

It is interesting to note that even in prison Yakov Mikhailovich was somehow automatically at the head of everything connected with organisational work. Although he was only the senior person amongst those in solitary, in reality he was in charge of all our prison-organisations, and the senior man for the common cells, nicknamed 'Potapych' (Pletnev), always consulted him concerning all the basic questions of our prison-life.

In April 1907, the case involving our Perm organisation went to the Kazan judicial chamber. My case, in particular, was dismissed by the procurator on the grounds of insufficient evidence, and I was freed on exactly the evening before Easter. The comrades on the outside attempted to raise the question of freeing Yakov Mikhailovich on bail pending his trial, but these efforts failed. The gendarmes and procurator knew that although there was no serious evidence against Yakov Mikhailovich from a judicial point of view, he was the spirit of all the Urals organisations, not just the one in Perm, and he must be condemned no matter what, even if only on the basis of intelligence-information. Along with other comrades involved in our case, Yakov Mikhailovich was condemned by the Kazan assize-court and sentenced to two years in a fortress. He served those two years in Ekaterinburg prison.

I know very little of this period of his life, when he was earnestly involved with theoretical work, in particular with a thorough study of all the volumes of *Capital*, because at that time I was working on the outside in the southern Urals or else doing time in other Urals prisons. This period of his life has to be illuminated by those who were imprisoned at the time in Ekaterinburg.

It is well-known that upon leaving prison Yakov Mikhailovich, despite all the effects prison had on his health, continued party-work with even greater energy than before and soon found himself exiled to the Turukhansk territory. I did not meet him during this period, but I did re-establish correspondence. That was a very difficult time in the life of our Party. All the waverers, all the elements who were tired and had lost faith in the revolution, left the Party. Many of those who were in the front ranks of the movement during the period 1905–7 were no longer there during the ensuing period of reaction. Some abandoned work completely and forever, while others flirted with liquidationist leanings. Amongst formerly-close comrades there were very difficult encounters during this time, very difficult conversations, and often people upon whom we counted were no longer involved in any movement at all. All the old Bolsheviks, who never abandoned the Party, remember this difficult period of its history very well.

I wrote a letter during this time to Yakov Mikhailovich, stating my creed and asking about the prospects. I received a reply from him very quickly, in which he expressed his deepest pleasure at the fact that we were thinking alike and said he hoped that we would meet again in our work. During this period I nearly chanced to meet Yakov Mikhailovich in the Tomsk transit-prison; I was sent through the Tomsk 'shipping point' to Ekaterinburg, to my last trial, and I learned from the prison-public that a few days earlier Yakov had been at this 'shipping point'...[7]

---

7. [The autobiography continues in Document 2:2.]

No. 3
'...A Page from Revolutionary Memories' (March 1908–February 1917)[1]

January 1934

In 1908, I was brought to trial under Article 102 in three cities: in Chelyabinsk, where I was arrested at the party-conference in the spring of that year and was returned again to that city's prison after fleeing the police-administration; then in Perm, where our Perm organisation collapsed and documents were found that established my link with that organisation as a member of the Urals Regional Committee of the Bolsheviks; and finally, I was tried again in Ufa, where I was arrested on the street with articles for *Ural'skii rabochii*.[2] In Chelyabinsk, I was sentenced to exile by the Saratov court in the autumn of 1909, in the winter of that year I was sentenced to exile a second time in Perm by the Kazan court,[3] and after that my case in Ufa under the same article was dropped.

In the winter, our entire group was sent to a settlement in Irkutsk province, which first of all meant being shipped to Irkutsk prison. In Irkutsk prison, I met Artem (Sergeev), and we did not part until his flight from exile. From Irkutsk prison, we were sent in one enormous party to Aleksandrovsk transit-prison,

---

1. [From GA RF. F. 533. OP. 1. D. 1032. L. 45–163. Original. Typewritten.]
2. [See Documents 1:7 and 1:8.]
3. [According to Police-Department documents, E.A. Preobrazhensky was convicted on 5–7 May 1909 in Chelyabinsk by the Saratov court and on 14 September 1909 in Perm by the Kazan court. (GA RF. F. 102. OO. 1911. D. 5. Ch. 27 A. L. 50.)]

including all who were leaving either for the Yakutsk region or for the further parts of Kirensky district after the waters of the Lena opened.

In 1910, a great many revolutionaries were collected in the Aleksandrovsk transit-prison, expecting to be sent to the so-called Lena detachment. Among the deportees awaiting shipment were representatives from the most diverse revolutionary parties and groups. Even before being shipped into exile, the different groups of Bolsheviks joined together in order to continue political activity both in exile and after fleeing from exile.

Among the common mass of exiles in Aleksandrovsk, a group of Bolsheviks stood out who shared certain positions in terms of a political appraisal of things and in the sense of future prospects they anticipated. This group consisted mainly of Bolshevik cadres and also a certain number of Menshevik party-members who at this time broke with the liquidators. Those who thought alike recognised each other during the numerous political speeches that took place in the transit-prison, together with briefs, discussions and so forth. From the group of comrades who made their way together along the one road from Ust-Kut, namely to rural Karabchevsk[4] and Nizhneilimsk in Irkutsk province, there emerged a solid group of Bolsheviks who agreed on certain political positions and shared the same political mission.

In addition to me, this group included: the late Artem Sergeev, Petr Kovalenko, Anatoly Galkin, Vasily Shamshin and several others. After arriving in Karabchevsk parish, this group of Bolsheviks organised a unique commune, not simply a commune in our old sense of a settlement, but also a commune that was simultaneously the kernel of a political organisation.[5]

From the very beginning, this party-commune adopted its own rule that only party-members could join the commune. Once we were all in exile in Karabchevsk, then along with the hard struggle imposed by the material conditions of our existence we simultaneously adopted specific tasks for continuing revolutionary work. Those of us who still had ties with party-organisations *made preparations*[6] for a speedy escape from exile in order to return to party-work. Others postponed escape until a more favourable time if they could not immediately restore contacts with comrades in the organisation and return to active work in the underground. A third group, including those such as the late comrade Artem, aimed to return to political activity by way of emigrating.

---

4. [This should read 'Karapchevsk'.]
5. [For more detail, see Vinogradov 1925; 1934.]
6. [Here and in what follows, italics are used for the words that Preobrazhensky wrote above the lines with a purple pencil. The words 'made preparations' are written in to replace the crossed-out phrase 'dreams of a quick escape'.]

The first thing that had to be considered was creation of a certain fund of material resources to assist comrades who were escaping from exile to get back to party-work; then, the acquisition of passports for them and the establishment of contact with those colonies that lay along the escape-route, such as the Bratsk Stockade, Tulun and others. And finally, we took on the task of organising party-groups in all the exile areas of Kirensky district and made connections for that purpose with comrades *from other districts*. The first member of our commune to leave was the late Artem Sergeev. We provided him with a small sum of money for the road, a very poorly-forged passport, and personal letters to the comrades in Bratsk Stockade and Tulun in order to ensure his further passage. As we know from Artem's biography, he emigrated first to Shanghai, from there to the United States, and finally to Australia, where he participated in political activity as a Bolshevik, established contact with Lenin, and expended enormous energy in the campaign to defeat the proposal by Hughes to have Australia enter the War on the side of the Entente.

Of the remaining comrades, the next to flee back to party-work after Artem was P. Kovalenko. I will not deal with the details of his escape, and since P. Kovalenko is still among the living[7] he can speak for himself in more detail.

Before discussing subsequent events, I should note here that we managed to create something of an underground party-committee that was very restricted in membership and immediately assumed the task of organising the escapes of our party-group. Later, as I will mention below, we also established contact with our Bolshevik centres abroad.

After P. Kovalenko, Ana[toly] Galkin fled. Then, at the end of 1911,[8] I fled from exile on the day after Christmas.

The circumstances connected with my escape were as follows. In approximately mid-November, when the ice flows were at their height in the Angara, the famous Captain Treshchenko[9] was sent by the Police-Department to the village of Vorobyevo in Karabchevsk district, where we were living, to search me. Because of the ice-flows, he could not cross the Angara, waited there in a boatmen's log-hut for two days, and then turned back. Some time before that I had corresponded with Lenin, and I proposed the following to Lenin in connection with a Bolshevik conference that was being planned at the time to convene abroad and then later convened in Krakow.[10] In view of the fact that there were more than a hundred people among us exiles in the party-groups in Karabchevsk

---

7. [The document says: 'поскольку П. Коваленко является в живых'.]
8. [Preobrazhensky crossed out: 'as I remember'.]
9. [Captain Treshchenkov participated in the Lena massacre in 1912. His surname is spelt incorrectly in the document.]
10. [Apparently Preobrazhensky had in mind the Prague conference of the RSDRP in 1912. See Preobrazhensky 1989, p. 129.]

and Nizhneilimsk parishes, as well as in several parishes in the Kirensky district, I suggested sending one representative of Bolshevik exiles to the Bolshevik party-conference that was to be held abroad. I received a reply in which N.K. Krupskaya indicated the immediate plans of our Bolshevik centre abroad, and Lenin responded to my proposal approximately as follows: we have discussed your suggestion and it will probably be useful to send a representative, but you must remember that this representative must take a position supporting a break with the compromisers.

In 1921, while rabbit-hunting with Lenin[11] in Samarinsky woods, I reminded him of this letter and all the circumstances of the time. I told him that when we received the letter we could not understand what compromisers he had in mind, and it was only later, when we became familiar with the party-press, that we understood how a break with the compromisers was exactly the most vital question.

'Yes, that was the whole point', said Lenin.

Somewhat later, after I sent my response to the letter from Lenin and N.K. Krupskaya, which they received while abroad – as I later learned from private conversations with Nadezhda Konstantinovna – I received a letter from the Ekaterinburg Committee of our Party in which the Committee's secretary, the late Marusya Cherepanova, wife of the Bolshevik Cherepanov who was shot in Tomsk, suggested to me on behalf of the Ekaterinburg organisation that I represent them at the Bolshevik conference abroad and that, in the event of my agreement, I answer by telegram. Of course, I was delighted to accept this proposal and communicated my agreement by telegram. Some time later, in any case very soon after I sent my telegram, our Party's Ekaterinburg organisation was arrested and my telegram was among the evidence discovered in the search. The gendarmes established my connection with the Ekaterinburg organisation, and on that basis the Police-Department telegraphed an order to the Nizhneilimsk superintendent of police to go quickly to Vorobyevo, arrest me, and send me by convoy to Irkutsk. This telegram arrived on Christmas-Day, when the gentleman police-officer lay dead-drunk. The officer's secretary spoke about the content of the telegram with our comrades in exile in Nizhneilimsk, and they quickly sent a messenger to me in Vorobyevo. The comrade raced over eighty *versts* from Nizhneilimsk to Vorobyevo in a temperature of minus forty degrees and arrived in Vorobyevo at dawn on 26 December. He awoke me, told me what was up, and we decided immediately to arrange my flight. About an hour later, with all my belongings packed into a small pillow-case, I was ready to leave. The only

---

11. [In the Soviet period, V.I. Lenin and E.A. Preobrazhensky often hunted together. Planning a hunt in April 1921, Lenin wrote to Preobrazhensky: 'How are you at grouses? Can you go for one or two days on Saturday?' (Golikov et al. 1970–82, Vol. 10, pp. 370–1).]

problem was finding a horse since all the peasants in the village of Vorobyevo were drunk, in accordance with the custom of the time, and no-one wanted to travel to Nizhneilimsk even for a high price because of the holiday. By chance we found a horse belonging to one of the drunken peasants, but he did not go himself and Stepan Litvinov went with me as driver (as far as I know, he now works in Kharkov and is a communist). I was anxious when covering the eighty *versts* from Vorobyevo to Nizhneilimsk because every hour I expected to meet with the police-superintendent who was supposed to arrest me.

I still remember this trip from Vorobyevo to Nizhneilimsk as vividly as if it were yesterday. A small and very shaggy Siberian horse ran briskly along the taiga-road, and no-one else was there that morning on account of the holiday. The temperature was still forty degrees below zero. The taiga was completely silent, there was no wind, and frosty 'shots' could sometimes be heard from the frozen trees. Near one bridge over a taiga-creek, on two large and bent over birches, sat about a dozen heath-cocks. They allowed us to approach much more closely than they ever would have done had we been hunting. Litvinov and I were avid hunters, and Litvinov regretted terribly that he had no rifle with him. They took off with a loud noise, flew to the nearby woods, and sat cooing in the large pine-trees. This was about twenty *versts from Vorobyevo*, that is, one-quarter of the way. I made a mental note that I already had a twenty-five percent chance of avoiding prison and penal servitude (exiles who were sentenced for a second time under Article 102 received a minimum of six to eight years of servitude as recidivists, and that was precisely my situation). For one-half of the way, or forty *versts*, we travelled over empty taiga without a single house. The first stop we could make was halfway with the merchant Kuklin, which is where we headed. Upon entering his cottage, I said to myself: I'm already fifty percent of the way to freedom. After having tea and giving the horse a chance to rest, we set out again. By now the most difficult and deserted part of the route, from which there was nowhere to turn, lay behind us. But on the other hand, the rest of the way was precisely the most dangerous for us. The chief of police could not have slept through the entire day. He probably awoke by mid-day, read the telegram and, cursing like a wagon-driver, was already on his sleigh with a troika of horses with bells and heading towards us. We continued for another two to three hours, the sun began to go down, and there were about seven *versts* left to reach Nizneilimsk. But we did not meet anyone on our way except for a single horse harnessed to a sleigh with a half-drunk driver. Twice we stopped and listened for any bells ringing so that we might turn off in time onto some side-road into the woods. But everything was silent. Finally we approached the first houses of Nizhneilimsk, passed by the police-officer's residence, and hurried on to the apartment of a comrade who had prepared a reception for us. The comrades joyfully greeted the fugitive, recounting with hearty laughter that, according to the latest and most credible reports from secret agents, the police-officer was still snoring in his apartment. This meant that the greatest danger was past and the road was open for me to push on towards Tulun.

In Nizhneilimsk, our organisation had already prepared a passport for me, money, a fur-coat and a horse that a young lad was supposed to use to rush to a holiday drinking party with friends in the countryside where the first station was located.[12] From there I would pass through the small town of Ilimsk and gallop on to Tulun. And I remember that part of the trip most distinctly. I worried above all that the police-officer, once he awoke and travelled to Vorobyevo, would be smart enough to send a telegram with my description up the road to Tulun, and his colleague would catch me. That meant everything depended on speed. Among Siberian peasants on the main routes there is a custom that if they receive some passenger, they forward him to their friend, who responds with passengers coming the other way. If you are taken, for example, to Ivanov in the one village, then Ivanov would pass you on to his friend Petrov at the next station, who would send you only to Sidorov at the following station, and so forth. And returning passengers follow the same line. For me, this had the benefit that I did not have to look for horses at a station. The coachman took me immediately to his friend, his companion in the carriage-business, and I at once had a cart and driver to get me to the next station and so on. Since I told them everywhere that I was rushing to the Irbit fair and could not stay overnight, I was only at each station long enough to take tea and harness up the horse. After eating, I generously treated my next driver with vodka, which was a matter of good form and also kept my companion warm. I also added some fuel along the way, referring to the fact that I was cold. On two occasions I arrived at houses where my driver, along with a crowd of guests, was dead-drunk, climbed to kiss me, treated me to vodka and all kinds of Siberian snacks, and would not hear of travelling without first spending the night. In that case my driver *himself* got involved in the matter and negotiated with the hostess. They provided me with a horse and some lad, and we raced onwards. At one station there was no-one to be found at the home of my coachman's friend, *to whom he had sent me*, except for the pregnant hostess, and absolutely no-one else to send, such that I was entrusted personally with a horse, provided that when I reached the station I would go to their partner in the carriage-business. They warned me that the horse was tame and ran well, but that just about mid-way along the road a bear had left its winter-den and been spotted for a second day. I asked the woman to give me an

---

12. [The reference is to a station for changing horses.]

axe, paid her in advance for the 'drive', and left for the next station across the taiga-ridge. The sense of freedom was wonderful. It was gratifying that someone had entrusted a horse to me, as if I were one of them, and it was so uplifting to race alone through the stern beauty of the taiga-winter that I sang *a song* to myself on the winter-road like someone just released from prison. About an hour-and-a-half after crossing the ridge, I saw the tracks of a large bear that had crossed the road, and the tracks crossed again in the other direction about half a *verst* further on. Just in case, I checked the handle of my axe, my only weapon apart from a small Finnish knife, but I immediately felt ashamed of my precautions. It was about forty degrees below zero, and the bear had quite likely already buried itself somewhere in the snow and posed no threat to anyone.

When I arrived at the station, there was no need even to ask where the godfather of my horse's mistress lived. Without breaking its trot, the horse went right up to a house and stopped there on its own. It turned out that it knew the address perfectly well: this was the home of Godfather Vasily. When I began to pump him with some fuel, Godfather Vasily responded with such a 'greeting' from his own resources that in order to maintain my senses I had to say that I was feeling ill. When we were already seated in the sleigh, one of Vasily's friends came and told us that a local policeman was asking to travel with us to the constabulary on an urgent matter. That was the worst moment of my entire journey. My teeth began to ache terribly, and I covered up just about my whole face with my hood. Along the entire road I was quiet as if I were ill. In my position, silence was golden. But my fears were for nothing. The officer, who turned out to be a taciturn and gloomy blockhead, said not a word all the way, and when we reached the village he quickly headed off to meet his superiors and took no interest in where we were going. That point was as dangerous for me as the residence of the police-chief. Every year many people fled from exile along this route, both politicals and criminals. Travellers were watched, and my ridiculous forged papers, given to me by the comrades in Nizhneilimsk, had not a single residence-permit, making it very difficult for me to play the role of a merchant on his way to Irbit. When we got past the residence of the police-chief, I more than once listened in the night for the bells of an approaching troika. But this time, too, all went well.

I raced the whole way from the village of Vorobyevo to Tulun without a pause, a distance of about five hundred *versts*. I did not stop even once for a night's sleep along the route. I only slept in fits and starts in the sleighs. Even at the last station before Tulun, which I reached in the middle of the night, I did not allow myself the *luxury* of a few hours sleep. Then, in the fading starlight of dawn, I greeted with a sense of inexpressible delight the music of the distant locomotive-whistles that came from the railway-station in Tulun and welcomed me with victory and emancipation. My link with the Party, with the cultured world and revolutionary activity, which had been severed by the taiga, was now restored.

After the stress of this miraculous flight, after five sleepless nights, I finally had a healthy sleep and awoke that day, *I dare say*, in a far better frame of mind than the head of police did in Nizhneilimsk.

In Tulun I went to see Arseny Zaikov, my Urals comrade and co-defendent in the trial of the Perm organisation (the business involving Ya.M. Sverdlov, K. Novgorodtseva, *Chugurin* and others). There, together with a group of exiled comrades, I finished celebrating the New Year and then left for Novonikolaevsk. But the police-chief, after sleeping off his drunkenness and opening the telegram, had set out to arrest me in Vorobyevo. There he searched my apartment and asked the comrades where I had gone. They told him that, as far as they knew, I was heading for Shamansky, that is, they pointed him in a direction completely different from my real route. He followed that direction for the length of the Angara and beyond, all the way to Tulun, still hoping to catch me, while I was already seated in a railway-carriage.

It was no coincidence that I chose Novonikolaevsk. In the first place, Petr Kovalenko, a member of our Bolshevik commune, was already there; secondly, the family of Vasily Shamshin, who was still in exile after my escape, lived there; and thirdly, there was a party-organisation there headed by comrade Kovalenko, whose work I had already heard about while in exile. In Novonikolaevsk I began working as secretary for the *semi*-Marxist and *semi-philistine* newspaper *Obskaya zhizn'* and at the same time joined the Novonikolaevsk organisation of our Party in which P. Kovalenko, Sophia Kovalenko, Vas. Shamshin's father (Ivan Shamshin), brother (I. Shamshin), and sister (Dunya Shamshina), along with Mikhail Galunov and other comrades were already working. As a contributor to *Obskaya zhizn'* I managed to place several articles that were Bolshevik in character, among which I especially remember one that was connected with our platform for elections to the Fourth State-Duma. I communicated with our centre abroad and received from comrade Zinoviev one article for *Obskaya zhizn'*, which was published with the initials 'G.Z', and I also received a letter from him. Comrade Zinoviev wrote to me that they immediately saw in my articles a like-minded person, and that they were counting not only on the possibility of appearing legally *in print*, but also on some material results from our collaboration in the newspaper. Lenin, as comrade Zinoviev wrote, also promised to contribute to the newspaper. To my great disappointment, after discussing it with the publisher I was convinced that the chances of receiving any kind of decent honorarium for our comrades abroad were extremely small; in short, the publisher Litvinov would not promise to pay any more than three *kopeks* per line. Nevertheless, considerations of a political character would have secured our cooperation had my arrest soon afterwards not halted this communication on literary matters. I was arrested half a year after my arrival in Novonikolaevsk[13] and just a few days before leaving to go abroad. *What happened is that* not long before my arrest I received a letter from N.K. Krupskaya inviting me to a party-meeting that, as I later learned, did not occur. *Before this proposed trip* abroad,[14] I went to Barnaul and established contact with the Barnaul party-organisation. Although I was using a 'solid' passport and not a forgery, I could not long conceal my real name *after my arrest* because lieutenant Khristich, whose name and passport I was using, was found by the gendarme administration to have been killed in the Russo-Japanese war, and for that reason I was discovered. In the Novonikolaevsk gendarme headquarters, they already had my name in a card-file of those under investigation, and the gendarme Captain, finding that the Police-Department was looking for me, *rubbed his hands with delight and* very quickly, *without even questioning me*, first sent me to Tomsk prison and then to Ekaterinburg, where my co-accused were already imprisoned. I sat in Ekaterinburg for one and a half years awaiting trial together with my comrades Semen Shvarts, Evgeniya Bosh, Sergei and Mariya Cherepanov, Paramonov and a number of other Bolsheviks who were arrested and tried in the case of the Ekaterinburg organisation.[15] N.K. Krupskaya was also involved in our case because some of her letters and other documents were used as evidence, and the fact that she wrote them was established by an old passport, issued to her in Ufa, that identified her.

I was acquitted in court because of a blunder in the procurator's indictment. Relying on my telegram from Karabchansky parish, signed Evgeny, he confused me with another Evgeny, a member of the Ekaterinburg organisation, who worked in Tyumen on instruction from the same Ekaterinburg organisation but was a completely different person. By comparing the date of my letter to the Ekaterinburg organisation with that on my telegram, it was established that if I had been the same Evgeny as the one in Tyumen, then I must have been simultaneously in Tyumen and Karabchansky parish, which is impossible by the laws of physics. Despite the evidence they had against me, which the procurator did not manage to use very well, the court was obliged to release me, after which I was sent to Novonikolaevsk, quickly sentenced to six months for escaping from exile, and then returned to Karabchansky parish. This time I was in prison for about two years.

---

13. [E.A. Preobrazhensky was arrested on 6 August 1912. See GA RF. F. 102. 7 d-vo. 1912. D. 1942. L. 22 ob.]

14. [The original text, which Preobrazhensky crossed out, reads 'not long before'.]

15. [Among counsels for the defence in this case were A.F. Kerensky, N.M. Mikheev, and N.D. Sokolov. See Preobrazhensky 1989, p. 130.]

By the time I arrived in Karabchansky parish, mobilisation had already been declared. The only member of our old commune that I found in Karabchansky parish was Vasily Shamshin. After a time we two were joined by another roommate, the provocateur Krut, who was subsequently shot. From Vorobyevo I went to Nizhneilimsk, where there was a large colony of exiles, including several Bolsheviks.

Among the group of Bolsheviks in Nizhneilimsk, I remember the following comrades: M. Samsonov; P. Kovalenko, who by that time had already completed a round trip from Novosibirsk back into exile; his wife, S. Kovalenko; Bakinovsky; Bustrem; Vovchinsky and Pestkovsky among others. Political life in Nizhneilimsk was quite important. The colony there had many more members than the one in Vorobyevo. During 1910–11, we read essays and arranged debates as the Party's struggle was in full swing. Among the documentary evidence of our literary-political creativity at that time, I can cite two issues of *Lishennyi prav*, a *handwritten* journal put together by M. Samsonov.

Taking advantage of the right to move about within Siberia, which all exiles received at the time, in the spring of 1915 Samsonov and I left for Irkutsk, where both of us had many friends with whom we rapidly re-established ties. First we had to look after material arrangements. I made myself busy giving lessons, and M. Samsonov, having nothing better to do, worked in a painters' *artel*. Once we had a look around Irkutsk, we began creating a Bolshevik organisation from among the exiles. Among the members of that group I remember Babushkin, Bruno, Shmidt, M. Samsonov, N.N. Romm, Zavadsky, Petr Kovalenko, Sophia Kovalenko, Krut and Zdzyarsky, who was later a member of the Polish Central Committee, and we had contact with Iosif Kosior, who worked at the tannery. *We were in contact with comrades* Yanson, Vel'man and others.

While we were in Irkutsk, there were two underground Bolshevik groups and one amorphous illegal literary organisation that included both Bolsheviks and Mensheviks. The first underground group was the Vasil'chenko-Zhakov group. If I remember correctly, the second group included Bruno, Babushkin, Vel'man and several others. After a series of meetings and negotiations with a number of comrades, we managed to create an organisation that included eighteen to twenty members. Our organisation was constantly in touch with the Zhakov-Vasil'chenko group. Some of our members attended meetings of both organisations. At some point the question arose in both organisations of a merger. The Zhakov group accused ours of delaying a merger, and our organisation did delay the merger because there was no clarity regarding the terms on which unification might occur. *Some members of our group also warned of shades of 'syndicalism' in the Zhakov group.* As far as I can recall, there were no serious political disagreements between our groups apart from a certain caution concerning the *above-mentioned* anti-intelligentsia attitudes of Zhakov's group. It was only due to the absence of any political differences that it proved possible in preliminary negotiations to resolve the question of a complete merger of the two organisations. The merger was to occur on a certain date, although I do not remember precisely *when it was* except that it was a Sunday in the summer. It was agreed that in Zvezdochka, on the other side of the Angar, the Zhakov-Vasil'chenko group and our group would organise meetings separately to pass a resolution for merger, after which the two would merge into a single organisation that would then elect its executive organ. The meetings took place in Zvezdochka, *as did the joint meeting*. At that meeting, it was resolved that an organisational committee would be formed by agreement among a group of people who were leaders in the two organisations, and after that the meeting ended. *I was empowered to negotiate on behalf of our group*.[16] But on that very evening the major part of the Zhakov-Vasil'chenko group was arrested, together with their print-works.

Before the merger our group conducted all the party-work in Irkutsk. Apart from regular meetings of our organisation, where we discussed general political questions, this work involved creating and directing a number of circles. We had one circle in the railway-shops and several among the students, in two of which I was personally involved as a propagandist. I. Kosior had contacts with workers at the tannery where he himself worked.

Our organisation did not have a print-works because we were planning to merge with the Zhakov-Vasil'chenko group and we did not consider this to be an issue at the time.

Due to the War, my personal contact with Lenin and N. Krupskaya was severed during this period. We only rarely and by chance received some scattered issues of our *Sotsial-Demokrat*, and among the major organisations we had only sporadic contact with St. Petersburg and Moscow.

As for contacts with the literary group, I can say the following. Amongst the exiles there was a group headed on the Menshevik side by Tsereteli, while among former Bolsheviks there were Voitinsky, Rozhkov and others who subsequently became defencists. *So far as I remember*, comrade Karakhan was also in this group. I was not in this group, although I was in touch with Voitinsky and had one conversation with Tsereteli. It was agreed during my talks with Tsereteli in Usolye that the literary group would make room in its publications for articles by Bolsheviks, despite the fact that most of the editors disagreed with them – the Bolsheviks sided with Lenin and opposed taking a *pacifist* position against the War. On the basis of this agreement, I personally managed to place two articles in *Zabaikal'skoe obozrenie*, the first of which was entitled 'Quo Vadis?' (*Kamo gryadeshi?*),[17] while the second was a feuilleton whose title I cannot

---

16. [The word 'empowered' is written in to replace 'appointed'.]
17. [See Document 1:75.]

remember now, but which *I hope*[18] to find in the archives.[19] In this second article I succeeded – and this was probably the only such instance in our legal press – in fully and literally repeating Lenin's formula concerning *transformation of the imperialist War into a civil war*.[20]

Following the arrest of the Zhakov-Vasil'chenko group, and given the fact that it undoubtedly involved provocateurs from within the organisation, a small group from our own organisation resolved to renew work, but with very specific conditions. It was decided that this group would include only a small number of comrades who had absolute trust in each other. This group included M. Samsonov, N. Romm, Zavadsky, Zdzyarsky, Preobrazhensky and Krut. It was decided that this group would organise a print-works and issue proclamations, but it would have no technical periphery. At one meeting of the group a draft was read for leaflets against the War, written *by me*,[21] which was later handed over to the gendarme authorities by the provocateur Krut.[22]

We acquired the type and set about organising a printing press, while Krut prepared the cases and other wooden parts in the carpentry-shop where he worked. But somehow the first proclamation written by our organisation 'disappeared' from the cellar where Krut had put it for safe-keeping.

Shortly after our group was organised,[23] comrade Zdzyarsky learned through a contact he had made with a typist in the gendarme administration that they knew of our group's existence and that we were *soon* to be arrested. When Zdzyarsky discussed this fact with me, I asked him whom he suspected out of our five. He said that in his opinion the provocateur was Krut. I personally had no suspicion of Samsonov, Romm or Zavadsky. I did not know Zdzyarsky very well, and I was not *particularly* confident about Krut. In my personal opinion, the provocateur could only be one of *those* two.[24] I was never quite certain right

---

18. [This was written above the line, and the word 'can' was crossed out.]
19. [The article referred to was 'Our Defencists'. See Document 1:76.]
20. [This was underlined by E.A. Preobrazhensky.]
21. [Preobrazhensky wrote this above the line to replace 'by Preobrazhensky'.]
22. [For the activities of D. Krut, see Lipkin 1926.]
23. [For the activities of Irkutsk exiles see Lipkin 1927; Nikolaev 1928.]
24. [In the archives, there are rich and dramatic recollections by M. Zdzyarsky, whom many suspected was the traitor. They include, in particular, an account of the final meeting of the Irkutsk Committee: 'On the appointed day, we met at Krut's (to try to "determine" who was the provocateur – ed.). In addition to Krut, those present included Preobrazhensky, Romm and myself, the entire final committee. Zavadsky was suffering from a prolonged illness. (It turned out that the Okhranka knew the details of a discussion of the anti-war declaration in which only four members of the Committee were involved – ed.). There was a heavy silence, interrupted by Preobrazhensky. His words were terrible, nightmarish: "Among us four there is a provocateur! Who?" The terrible question of "who among us is the provocateur?" passed from person to person... The oppressive silence was broken by Preobrazhensky: "It is difficult, and we will not resolve this question here. I suggest dissolving our Committee and putting out the word that

up to the 1917 Revolution as to who the provocateur was, and the whole thing was only clarified for us after the Revolution in a telegram that we received *in Chita* from the Irkutsk comrades saying that Krut was the provocateur.

That was the end of our second underground-cell, which never got down to work.

After that failure, and expecting to be arrested for the affair at any time, I went from Irkutsk to Chita, where I remained until the February Revolution.[25]

January 1934
E. Preobrazhensky

---

we have no immediate plan to be involved in any illegal work"'. (GA RF. F. 533. Op. 1. D. 1047. L. 18–19).]

25. [E.A. Preobrazhensky moved to Chita in the spring of 1916 (GA RF. F. 102. OO. 1916. D. 5. Ch. 27 B.L. 46–7).]

Nos. 4–5
Articles Published in the Newspaper *Ural'skii rabochii* in October and December 1907

No. 4

'On the Present Moment'[1]

15 October 1907

Every new day takes us further from our glorious October Revolution,[2] and every new day brings us closer... to what? To a repetition of the October Revolution in the near future on a grander scale, or to a final consolidation of the Stolypin constitution?[3] This question, of whether the Russian Revolution ended in December with defeat of the proletariat,[4] taking us into a period of 'constitutional' routine, to use Lenin's expression, or whether the Revolution continues after experiencing only a temporary setback – this is a question that persistently confronts every Social

---

1. [From *Ural'skii rabochii* (Ekaterinburg), 15 October 1907.]
2. [The reference is to the Tsar's Manifesto of 17 October 1905, which announced a programme of democratisation for the country. The Manifesto was adopted in response to the revolutionary movement and was the high-point in development of the Revolution of 1905–7.]
3. [The reference is to the *coup d'état* of 3 June 1907. The basis for the coup was a charge, fabricated by the Okhranka, that the Social-Democratic fraction was involved with a military organisation and preparing an armed insurrection. On 1 June 1907, the head of the government, P.A. Stolypin, demanded that the fraction be excluded from work in the Duma and that its 16 members be arrested. The majority of the fraction's members were arrested, and the Duma was dissolved on 3 June. A new electoral law was simultaneously issued without being approved by the State-Duma.]
4. [The reference is to the armed uprising in Moscow.]

Democrat. And this is not surprising: on the answer to that question depends the kind of tactics that Soc[ial] Dem[ocracy] must adopt at the current moment.

But in order to answer the question that has been posed, we must turn from the political surface of what has occurred to a deeper economic analysis of the country: on its own, a study of political events on the surface will not help us to predict the future; it often happens that in the heat of a widespread movement, which creates room for great expectations, there are forces deep within the economic organism of the country that are invisible to the superficial observer, but are preparing a speedy death for that movement; and often, in the moment when a revolutionary wave is receding and taking faith in the revolution along with it, those same forces are preparing a revolutionary explosion that comes as a surprise to those uninitiated in the secrets of historical materialism. What occurs on the political surface is fleeting and does not repeat itself, but what is new and has appeared in the economic relations will inevitably have political consequences: these political consequences can, in appropriate circumstances, be predicted. The economic analysis, which must provide us with an answer to the question we have raised, can be one of two kinds: a general economic analysis of the country, or an analysis of the economic relations of the present moment. There is no dispute within our ranks about the fact that a general economic analysis provides irrefutable proof of the enormous potential force of revolution.

The development of Russia's productive forces on the basis of capitalist society depended directly on a radical resolution of the agrarian question. The development of industry cannot make any advance without an increase in the purchasing power of the rural population. An increase of that purchasing power cannot move ahead without an increase in the area of peasant land-holdings – not an increase along Stolypin lines, through a peasant bank[5] that does not increase the purchasing power of the countryside – but only through expropriating the lands of the gentry and the treasury to the benefit of the peasantry. The political gains of the October Revolution are so negligible, compared to the demands of developing capitalism, that it is truly ridiculous to suppose that there has occurred in the political superstructure an adaptation that corresponds, in the form of the Stolypin constitution, to the existing economic relations. In a word, a general economic analysis of the country indicates the inevitability of further development of the Revolution and its complete victory. Whether this victory will be total, whether the Revolution will be carried through to the end, whether Russia will be a republic or the Revolution will end with a partial victory over the old

---

5. [From 1882 to 1917 the Peasant-Bank (Peasant Land-Bank) of the Russian Empire gave loans on the security of lands being bought by peasants. The Stolypin reform involved purchasing some landlords' holdings and selling them in small parcels to the peasants.]

régime – these are not things that can be considered with absolute certainty. But one thing is clear – too little has been won for the rising movement to die out at its beginning.

Those are the conclusions to which a general economic analysis leads. But it appears that an analysis of the economic relations and tendencies of the current moment says something completely different. Russian industry is now, without doubt, passing through an expansion. From a mass of numerical data that has appeared in the *Torgovo-promyshlennaya gazeta* and in newspaper and journal-articles for the past three months, it is evident that an expansion of industry can be seen in the Central district, in Poland, in the Don Basin and even in the Urals. It is evident that there has been a rapid increase in the process of capital-accumulation, together with a perceptible reduction of unemployment compared to the summer of last year.

Every Marxist knows the enormous importance of the fact of industrial expansion. But the fact of industrial expansion can only be an enormous trump-card in the hands of those who talk about the end of the Revolution if it could also be demonstrated that the evident industrial expansion means the onset of normal conditions for the capitalist development of Russia. And it is precisely an investigation of the causes and very character of the current expansion that leads us to quite the opposite conclusions. That investigation shows that just as some industrial crises do not entail a revolutionary outburst, not every industrial expansion signals an end to revolution.

Let us look at the causes that enabled the expansion and the changes it must entail in the political situation of the country.

It has already been shown in the Social-Democratic press that the main cause of the expansion is an increase in purchasing power on the part of the peasantry and the proletariat, which is a direct result of the economic achievements of the Revolution.

The stubborn struggle of the peasantry and the rural proletariat against the landlords, which was evident in 1905 and part of 1906, has led to a significant reduction in rent and an increase in wages for agricultural workers, and the same results occurred because of the economic struggle of urban workers with their employers. An increase in the annual budget of the peasantry and the proletariat, and the corresponding increase of their purchasing power – that is the main cause of the current revival in industry. Especially characteristic, from this point of view, is the expansion of the textile-industry, whose fate is so closely tied to the economic position of the peasantry. The expansion of Western-European industry is also important in this regard, but only as a secondary cause.

But can the expansion that has begun in such conditions be a lasting one if we take into account that the position of the peasantry, along with the recent decline of the Revolution, has significantly deteriorated rather than improved, and that the same can be seen amongst the proletariat, who have retreated step by step since the December defeat in face of the organised force of capital and the autocracy, losing many of the things they had achieved? The answer will be perfectly obvious. Since the causes that stimulated the industrial expansion have ceased to operate, the curtailed market will not support this expansion, and an intensive industrial crisis will be its logical outcome.

Thus the current industrial expansion is a temporary improvement against the background of a deep depression of the entire economic organism of the country, a depression that will not end until the agrarian question is resolved in a sense favourable to the peasantry. A radical resolution of the agrarian question is closely tied up with carrying through to the end the Revolution that has begun.

But whatever the consequences of the industrial expansion for the immediate future, how will it affect the relation of social forces in the country? The first result of expansion must be development of the strike-struggle of the working class, which in part has already begun. In this struggle the proletariat will be in much better conditions than it was a year ago, during the period of crisis: the position of industry will favour this struggle. A successful economic struggle by the proletariat will have enormous political importance. From the experience of the Russian Revolution and the pre-revolutionary struggle of the working class we may draw this conclusion: successful economic actions by the proletariat are always preceded by successful political actions and vice-versa. The political actions of the proletariat, beginning in 1901, preceded the successful economic strikes by the workers. The successful economic struggle, beginning on 9 January, gave an impulse to the strike-struggle throughout all of Russia and preceded the victorious October movement. And the reverse is also true: the economic defeat of the St. Petersburg proletariat, for example, involving unsuccessful attempts to establish the eight-hour working day, served as the immediate cause of the political weakness of the St. Petersburg proletariat during the December days. Furthermore, the crisis of 1906, which caused the workers to experience systematic defeat by the capitalist class in their economic struggle, condemned the proletariat to political weakness at a time when the Duma-epoch gave only rare occasions for joint action by the Russian proletariat.

The general deterioration in the position of the proletariat, which followed the December defeat of the Revolution, is now driving the proletariat into struggle. The industrial expansion guarantees the success of this struggle, at least in the beginning, while the mere expansion of the economic struggle, in connection with an inevitable crisis, creates the necessary preconditions for massive political actions by the proletariat.

The expansion is changing the relationship of social forces in favour of the proletariat and thus in favour of the Revolution. On the other hand, the inevitable crisis will cause it to oppose the old system of the bourgeois classes. But especially important is the fact that the future action of the proletariat will not be an isolated one, and the guarantee of this is the growing consciousness of the peasantry. Those prophets who foresee an end to the Russian Revolution on the grounds of an industrial expansion are judging the Russian Revolution in terms of the West-European pattern. A stereotyped understanding of the Russian Revolution, and intemperate analogies with Western Europe, can only distort understanding of its future fate. Kautsky, in his remarkable brochure on the perspectives and moving forces of the Russian revolution,[6] showed comrade Plekhanov how to judge the Russian revolution. The inevitably-approaching industrial crisis will teach those who prophesy an end of the Revolution to be more attentive in analysing the peculiarities of economic relations in Russia compared to those in the West during the epoch when revolutions were occurring there. For those prophets, the fact of an expansion alone is sufficient reason to speak about the end of the Revolution. They do not understand the unique economic circumstances in which the Russian Revolution is occurring, nor do they understand that just as not every industrial crisis necessarily gives the impulse for a political revolution, not every industrial expansion signifies an end of the Revolution.

Thus, the essence of the present moment can be characterised as follows: fragmentation of active revolutionary forces on the political surface, together with concentration of potential forces of revolution in the economic depths.

L-d

---

6. [The reference is to Kautsky's 'The Driving Forces of the Russian Revolution and its Prospects', published in St. Petersburg in 1907. The article was written by Kautsky in November 1906 in response to an inquiry from G.V. Plekhanov, and appears in translation in Day and Gaido (eds.) 2009, pp. 567–607.]

Appendix

'On the Election-Campaign'[7]

15 October 1907

The first stage of the election-campaign is already over. The results for choosing electors in the workers' curia are already known. In Ufa province, all three workers' electors at the provincial convention are Social Democrats – candidate-members of the organisation. All five workers' electors from Perm province, and all four from Vyatka province, are party-members. As it turned out, not only are all the Urals electors Social Democrats, but also the majority of the representatives. There is no accurate information yet concerning elections to the peasant-curia, but the majority of the peasants' electors are leftists and Social Democrats. Because of the law concerning the urban curia, Social Democrats did not nominate candidates; in this curia the Cadets prevailed almost everywhere, while in the second curia, in all the large cities of the Urals, Social Democrats and leftists won and the Cadets suffered complete defeat. In the second curia in Vyatka, leftists won; in Perm, a Trudovik and a Popular Socialist; in Ekaterinburg, Chelyabinsk, Zlatoust and Ufa, Social Democrats.

The Urals proletariat is going for Social Democracy – this is the first conclusion to be drawn from the election results. The large and medium bourgeoisie is going for the Cadets, and urban democrats for Social Democracy and extreme leftists – this is the second instructive result of the elections. Apart from the Cadets themselves, who seriously call themselves a 'people's party', even in sections of our Party there are still people with the view that the Cadets are, for the most part, a party of urban democrats. The elections in the Urals refute this view.

In the recent elections, Social Democracy enjoyed an undoubted success and, wherever possible, the Party's electors were chosen.

In the Urals, Social Democracy was the only party that displayed energy in the elections and developed intensive agitation. And this was despite the sentiment in favour of a boycott amongst the broad masses, despite the sentiment favouring a boycott in our own ranks, and, finally, despite a complete lack of confidence in the Duma as an instrument for the emancipation of Russia. The conscious proletariat of the Urals expressed itself at the all-Russian conference

---

7. [An editorial article, most likely written in its entirety by E.A. Preobrazhensky. For a contemporary account of the original provisions and subsequent revisions of Russian law governing Duma-elections, see Harper 1908.]

in favour of a boycott of the Duma, but in compliance with the Party's decision it took part in the elections. The success in the election-campaign is for us simultaneously a triumph of party-discipline within the Party itself.

A party that has received mandates from hundreds of thousands of proletarians and peasants, a party that has demonstrated its internal strength and unity – that kind of party can boldly anticipate its future.

No. 5

'The Task of the Moment'[1]

1 December 1907

I consider the main task of the Party at the present moment to be the creation of strong, mass proletarian organisations. Of course, the organisation of the proletariat, as well as the strengthening of our ideological influence on the masses, is generally the basic task of Social-Democracy not only in Russia, and not only at the present time, but for worldwide Social-Democracy and for all times. In this article, I would like to outline why we must pay special attention to organisational work precisely now, and why we must place it in the foreground of our work among proletarians.

If the main task of Social Democracy in the nineties[2] was propaganda and agitation – leaving organisational activity in the background because there was nothing from which to build an organisation and there were not sufficient numbers of workers who had been touched by SD propaganda – the situation today is the opposite: the proletariat has been seized *en masse* by the ideological influence of Social Democracy, yet our organisational influence is very weak by comparison with our ideological influence. Leaving aside those with Social-Democratic leanings, even the mass of convinced Social-Democratic workers are beyond the narrow limits of our Party's organisation. In Germany, with three and a quarter million voters, there are more than five hundred and thirty thousand party-members and more than one and a half million workers are organised in trade-unions. Our ideological influence on the proletariat, in the sense of breadth, is scarcely inferior to that of German Social Democracy on the German proletariat; with universal suffrage, we would probably also receive about three million votes in elections.[3] Meanwhile, we have no more than a hundred and fifty thousand party-members; and in the trade-unions at the present moment, after the mass repression by the authorities, there is no doubt that we have fewer than the two hundred and fifty thousand recently shown in our statistics on the trade-union movement. If we take into account the German relation between the number voting for the party and the number who are organised, and compare it with our own relation in this regard, the weakness of our organisation is striking.

---

1. [From *Ural'skii rabochii* (Ekaterinburg), 1 December 1907.]
2. [The reference is to the 1890s.]
3. This figure takes into account the number of proletarians in Russia and our influence upon them if we also consider the results of the elections to the Second State-Duma.

By itself, this discrepancy between our ideological influence on the proletariat and our organisational influence must be enough to convince the Party to concentrate its work on strengthening proletarian organisations. But there are also other reasons that lead to this conclusion – the political position of the country on the one hand, and the economic position of the proletariat on the other.

The political position of the country is presently characterised by fragmentation of the revolutionary forces of the proletariat and peasantry at one pole, and concentration of the forces of the reactionary bourgeoisie and the nobility on the other. The relation of social forces, with this kind of grouping, is developing most unfavourably for those classes interested in the victory of the revolution, and for the proletariat above all. The reaction is growing stronger and forcing a retreat of the revolution, and it appears ready to smooth away all the consequences of the October movement if only it were objectively possible to do so. The proletariat faces the task of strengthening the position of the Revolution and forestalling the current advance of bourgeois reaction. And for the proletariat, strengthening the position of the Revolution will mean strengthening our own forces.

The Russian Revolution, like any revolution, has depended upon the spontaneous outburst of a popular movement, upon spontaneous upsurges of the revolutionary wave conditioned by disturbances in the area of economic relations. During moments of upsurge, such as we lived through in 1905, organisation of the masses does not play a major role, and the strength of the blows that the Revolution strikes against reaction depends almost entirely on the force of the economic factors that gave the impulse for the movement. It is another matter during an epoch when the revolutionary wave is receding, when the attack on reaction is replaced by defence against reaction. The extent to which the gains of the Revolution can be maintained against counter-revolutionary efforts will, in large measure, depend on conscious resistance to reactionary efforts, based upon the strength of organisation.

From the tactical point of view, since the December uprising our proletariat has had irreplaceable opportunities for mass political action, such as the dispersal of two Dumas in connection with the counter-revolutionary Act of 3 June.[4] These moments were missed, even though they were suitable for actions, because they did not coincide with a time in which such mass actions were objectively possible. They were objectively impossible not merely because there was no rising revolutionary wave at the time, with the corresponding attitude among the working masses, but also because our organisational influence was so very weak that any action would not just fail in every respect, but would actually be impossible. The objective possibility for a revolutionary offensive against reaction

---

4. [The reference is to dissolution of the Second State-Duma and changes in the election-procedures.]

exists in the presence of a spontaneously-rising revolutionary wave. And the objective possibility for action with a defensive character also exists when there are sufficiently stable and broad organisations of the revolutionary masses. After all, defence always requires fewer forces than offence. And at this moment, a moment of wild reaction, how far we can strengthen and extend proletarian organisation is a matter of enormous importance for Social Democracy, so that when the revolutionary wave is generally receding we might organise resistance to reaction on the part of the conscious proletariat, a resistance that will rely not on revolutionary attitudes – for which we may still have to wait a long time – but solely on the force of consciousness and the degree to which the masses are organised. It is not in our power to call forth a spontaneous upsurge such as the one that spoiled us in 1905, but the strengthening of our organisation amongst the proletarian masses does depend in large measure upon us. Of course, no degree of proletarian organisation can consolidate revolutionary gains that have been entirely lost due to the nature of the country's economic conditions, but preserving many other gains will depend wholly upon the proletariat, its consciousness and the degree to which it is organised.

This is the political motive that speaks for the urgency of energetic organisational work by the Party. An analysis of the current economic position of the Russian proletariat leads us to the same conclusion. Loss of the political gains of the Revolution has proceeded in parallel with the loss of the economic gains. Generally speaking, the economic position of the working class resembles its position in the pre-October days. The working class now faces the task of regaining what has been lost since the December defeat. This particularly urgent task looms before the working class precisely now, when the deterioration of its economic position has reached the extreme. On the other hand, the evident industrial expansion guarantees success in the struggle with capital.

Now that it has begun, the expansion makes it possible for the proletariat to go over from defence to offence. But if, in a political struggle, the force of the organised masses is overshadowed by the mighty spontaneous force of a revolutionary wave, then in the economic struggle with the organised force of the capitalists that our workers are facing, the very fact of an industrial expansion, however advantageous it may be to the workers, does not yet guarantee success; a strong organisation is needed, and the proof is strikingly evident in the failure of the summer textile-strike in the Central Industrial District.

Thus, the organisation must be strengthened. But the reader may ask: What kind of organisation are you talking about, trade-union or political? My answer is proletarian organisation, and it makes no difference whether it is trade-union or political. With us in Russia, strengthening our workers' trade-union organisation is identical with strengthening our Party's organisation and vice-versa. Our unions have always assisted the Party, doing the same work that the Party did or should have been doing, while on the other hand the Party has always led the economic struggle of the proletariat, fulfilling functions that, by the established pattern, are usually assigned to the trade-union department. This is the origin of the quest for a single class-organisation of the proletariat, which is everywhere growing in our Party. But for now the main task, of course, is not to create some particular form of organisation: whether it be a monistic organisation of the proletariat or a dualistic one – although the form does have enormous significance – the main task is organisation in general. If I speak in what follows of the economic organisation of the proletariat, that is only because a strengthening of proletarian organisation is, at the present moment, only possible on the basis of leading its economic struggle.

In what form is this strengthening of proletarian organisation conceivable, and what must be the character of our organisational work? Here, we come to the question of Party or non-Party trade-unions, and of their legality or illegality. I will not dwell on the question of whether they belong to the Party or are neutral, which has already been clarified in fractional discussions in the press and at congresses. For us Bolsheviks, it is clearly necessary to have the closest ideological and organisational links between the Party and the unions. As far as the legality or illegality of unions is concerned, the changed conditions, namely, the sharp deterioration in the legal position of the unions, making their legal existence impossible, compels the Party to adopt a certain position on this question. At the current moment, two immutable points of view are becoming evident on this question – the Bolshevik and the Menshevik. At the last conference of party-organisations of the Central Industrial District, a resolution was introduced on the question of the trade-union movement, recommending the organisation of illegal unions in view of the impossibility for trade-unions to exist legally, with the proposed basis of the union being party-cells around which members of the union must be grouped. The St. Petersburg Mensheviks proposed a resolution on this question that was exactly the opposite. Calling in the old way for the broadest possible neutrality, they recommended a semi-legal existence for the unions if a legal one was impossible.

The Bolsheviks, as is known, have no particular predilection for illegal existence; if they are defending the organisation of illegal unions, that only applies where the legal existence of unions is impossible without curtailing their tasks and distorting their essence as fighting organisations. Comrades are aware that in Moscow alone, for example, a single stroke of Reinbot's pompadour-pen eliminated more than twenty trade-unions, and similar events are occurring throughout Russia. Of course, there is no advantage in organising illegal unions where the possibility of their legal existence still remains. But that possibility is steadily being curtailed, and apparently it will continue to be curtailed. Up to now the administrative harassment of trade-unions has assumed an unorganised and chaotic character, depending almost entirely on the personality of one pompadour or another. But now, judging by newspaper reports, the government is preparing to put an end to trade-unions using legislative means. The semi-legal existence that Menshevik comrades are recommending to the unions is a singular misunderstanding. Essentially, our unions have always been in a semi-legal position. When trade-unions will be forbidden by legislation, or when they are already forbidden in many places by administrative means, what forms must this semi-legal existence take? The organisation of mutual-aid societies and an extension of their tasks? But does this not mean, in the final analysis, just squeezing the juice from a dried lemon? Of course, mutual-aid societies can be used, and in some places such use can be very successful, but it would be ridiculous to counterpoise these societies to trade-unions as a whole, even to illegal unions.

I believe the main task of the moment in the sphere of the trade-union movement lies not in making use of any remaining possibilities for the legal existence of unions, but rather in winning new possibilities. This task can be accomplished by the expansion of illegal trade-union organisations as far as possible. We must make the trade-union movement a broad, mass movement, and work to expand its activity so far that governmental repression will be helpless in face of the spontaneous demands of the masses in the organisation. And then the juridically illegal unions will in fact become legal.

But is it possible for illegal trade-unions to become mass organisations if they include only our party-members? Experience provides the answer to this question. It is evident from the practice of the trade-union movement in Moscow and the Central Industrial District that the transfer of the unions from a legal to an illegal existence at first brought a sharp reduction in members, after which a gradual and steady growth of the unions could be observed. Moreover, it should be noted that after the unions became illegal they stood on their own feet much more firmly than when they were in a legal position and subject to constant harassment.

Finally, there are theoretical considerations that speak against the impossibility of the illegal existence of unions in Russia today. Failure of an illegal trade-union movement, in the absence of legal possibilities for its development, would mean the impossibility of any trade-union movement in a country of developing and already strongly developed capitalism, a country with a proletariat numbering several millions. From the instructive history of the Western-European workers' movement, we know that this cannot happen.

The industrial expansion that we see at the present moment must not only guarantee the success of illegal unions, but it can also create a spontaneous and irresistible striving by the working masses for organisation, in the face of which government-bans on unions will be helpless, and that striving will make the unions legal in fact.

The resolution of the Moscow conference not only resolves the question of the party-affiliation and illegality of unions but also points to a certain type of party-organisation: it recommends making party-cells the skeleton of future illegal trade-unions. This form of organisation in the unions leads to a direct merger of the Party's organisation with the trade-union organisation, and it promises to achieve the monism of ideas and organisation towards which the Western-European workers' movement is inevitably heading in spite of deeply-rooted prejudices and a dualistic pattern. In our organ there will probably be more than one article dealing with how important it is for us to strive for a single class-organisation of the proletariat, how possible it is for us to approach this ideal at the level of capitalist development and of the workers' movement that we are now passing through, and, finally, how far the form of organisation proposed by the Moscow conference leads towards this goal.

Parodying the famous saying of Danton, on one occasion comrade Plekhanov finished his article in *Zarya* with the words: 'Organisation, organisation, and again organisation'. I must now simply repeat those words.[5]

L-d

Appendix

'Zlatoust'[6]

The conditions for work in Zlatoust are generally favourable. In the city itself there is the Zlatoust armaments-factory in which, together with the blast-furnace that is attached to the factory, up to five thousand people work; another six hundred at the depot-station, which together with the beer- and leather-factories and the railway-shops comes to about one thousand, five hundred workers. Social-Democratic work only began here very recently. Prior to the election-campaign for the Congress, Zlatoust was part of the Ufa region, and only

---

5. The present article appears over the signature of the author, because while the majority of the Joint Committee shares the views expressed here concerning the relation of the Party to the trade-unions, the views of the author are far from the prevailing ones within the Party and are subject to debate within the Bolshevik fraction. The editors invite comrades to express themselves in the pages of *Ural'skii rabochii* on the question dealt with in this article. The editors.

6. [From *Ural'skii rabochii* (Ufa), 1 December 1907. This article is unsigned but was apparently written by E.A. Preobrazhensky.]

since the spring of this year has it been considered an independent organisation. For a long time Zlatoust was considered, and is probably still considered, a stronghold of S-R influence in the Urals. The influence of the S-Rs remains strong in the factory even though it has recently been shaken, and the S-Rs themselves know that Social-Democratic influence is growing. At the station, our Party dominates completely. During the summer, work at Zlatoust was conducted quite vigorously, with study-circles and frequent mass meetings. But an unsuccessful strike at the depot disorganised all work at the station and, with the departure of several comrades, work at the factory and in the city almost came to a halt. At the present moment, the work is recovering. Links have been restored with the station-district. A large number of lower-level circles have begun to function, three more advanced circles have been organised for the preparation of propagandists, lectures are being given and discussions have begun with the S-Rs. The Committee has a print-works in which leaflets are published on the topic of the day. The newspaper *Zlatoustovskii rabochii* will soon begin to appear. In the factory there is an effort to organise a trade-union, which, unfortunately, can only be illegal since the factory is owned by the state.

In Zlatoust there is a small district, including Miass, where the Miass group is located and includes thirty members, and there are also links with the Satkinsk and Kusinsk factories. The Satkinsk organisation has requested a full-time [party-]worker, promising to maintain him, but the Zlatoust organisation cannot send such a worker because it has a need for such workers itself.

There are contacts with the peasants, but they are weak and undeveloped. The economic position of the peasants does not favour work among them, because the peasantry is prosperous and its attitude is conservative.

The election-campaign in Zlatoust went well. Despite opposition and strong counter-agitation from the S-Rs, the elections took place in the factory and all three Social Democrats were chosen as representatives. In the second election-curia the organisation also had its own candidate.

An unusual rise in food-prices is taking place in the city, which is especially disturbing for the working masses. The organisation plans to begin a struggle for the reduction of food-prices.

In conclusion, there is one curious thing. It is said that the S-Rs at one meeting adopted a resolution saying that since the S-R Party boycotted elections to the Duma, all those chosen as electors and as members of the Duma are traitors to the people.

No. 6
'A Grandiose Expropriation', An Article Published in the Newspaper *Proletarii*[1]

29 (16) April 1908

The Russian telegraph-agency accurately informs the Russian citizen of whenever a petty shop is robbed, of how many roubles are stolen and of just how many expropriators are hanged for the crime – yet this agency uttered not a single word about the grandiose expropriation conducted by the owners of Urals possessional factories[2] a year and a half ago. And as with every expropriation from the pockets of the people, this one was conducted with the help of secret and other advisors behind 'closed doors', without any bombs and revolver-shots. Behind the closed doors of cabinet-ministers, the Urals factory-owners were graciously permitted to mortgage possessional lands with private banks; and they mortgaged 2.5 million parcels with the private banks worth 8 million roubles.

Possessional lands are treasury-lands given to factory-owners with a temporary right of use. The factory-owners use these lands while they are operating factory-enterprises. When the latter shut down, they are deprived of the right to use the lands. Of course, factory-owners do not have the right either to

---

1. [From *Proletarii* of 16 April 1908. *Proletarii* was an illegal Bolshevik weekly newspaper. An organ of the St. Petersburg and Moscow committees of the RSDRP from 21 August (3 September) 1906 to 28 November (11 December) 1909), it was, in fact, the central Bolshevik organ. It was published in Vyborg (Nos. 1–20), Geneva (Nos. 21–40), and Paris (Nos. 41–50). The editor of the paper was V.I. Lenin.]

2. [For an explanation of possessional property in the Urals, see Document 2:13.]

sell or mortgage these lands, just as a bureaucrat does not have the right to sell a home that belongs to the treasury but is given to him to live in. Having allowed the mortgaging of possessional lands, the behind-the-scenes arbiters of Russia's fate have also recognised the factory-owners' right of private property in those lands. In other words, the secret gentlemen-advisors gave to the owners of possessional factories an enormous area of state-lands. How large this gift is can be seen from the following calculation. The total of possessional lands in the Urals is presently 2,264,000 *desyatins*.[3] These lands include the richest deposits of various minerals, and excellent stands of timber. If we take the value of a *desyatin* to be fifty roubles at a minimum, then the gift to the Urals factory-owners must be worth more than a hundred million roubles. It is possible that the noise being raised in the press and in the Duma, together with the protest of the working masses against the mortgaging of possessional lands, will prevent our expropriators from stuffing their pockets with further millions, but even what has occurred thus far is fraught with great consequences. The most characteristic aspect of this entire story is the fact that the whole matter was conducted in a most conspiratorial manner. The mortgaging operation occurred a year and a half ago, and meanwhile all this plunder only became known quite recently. The gentlemen-expropriators apparently foresaw all the noise and protests that are now occurring *post factum*, but it was important to them that this noise should not prevent the business that was being done at the time. No protests can now have any direct practical significance: the money has been expropriated and will not be returned, although the robbers have not gone into hiding and continue to live in high esteem and bliss in their old neighbourhoods.

The lands have been mortgaged with private banks. The private banks, of course, are perfectly familiar with possessional relations and knew very well that treasury-lands cannot be mortgaged by private persons. If they agreed to the operation, there can be no doubt that they did so after government-representatives took the great expropriators under their wing and promised the banks a guarantee for the millions they gave out; in other words, they recognised the expropriators' property-rights in the mortgaged land. And the latter circumstance has enormous importance for workers in possessional factories and for the peasants. Everyone knows that many possessional factories incur losses for their owners. If the latter do not close them down, it is because the profit from predatory forestry on these lands exceeds all the losses incurred by the factories. To close those factories would mean loss of the right to exploit the enormous forest-area along with the profits from that exploitation. But the factory-owners now have a different setup: having acquired the millions, they can boldly shut

---

3. [A *desyatin* is equal to 2.7 acres or 1.1 hectare.]

down the factories and deprive tens of thousands of workers of their income. On the other hand, in allotting land to the workers of the closed factories, the government will now operate not with its own possessional lands, but with lands that will legally belong to the private banks. The latter would be legally within their rights if they prevented any allotment of land to the workers. In the final analysis, the entire operation entails enormous disadvantages for the possessional workers and must evoke a most decisive protest on their part.

The liquidation of possessional relations in the Urals will inevitably involve the closure of enterprises that are hopeless from an economic point of view; this finale, with all its agonising consequences for the workers, cannot be avoided and is desirable from the point of view of the general interests of the Urals workers. But in the present case, enormous importance attaches to the question of how possessional relations will be liquidated. A handful of factory-owners, together with the autocratic clique, is attempting to liquidate the possessional remnants in such a manner that the workers will be left with neither an income nor land. Indeed, to make allotments to the workers according to the 1861 norm is the same as leaving them with no land. The allotments made according to the 1861 regulations are so small, given the conditions in the Urals, that they will not be able to ensure for the workers even the most beggarly existence and will condemn them to death by starvation.

The government, on the contrary, is preparing a most profitable withdrawal for the factory-owners, with millions in their hands, even though such withdrawal has violated all the laws on possessional rights and inflicted enormous loss on the state. In such conditions, the task of our Party in the Urals consists of defending at all costs, even with arms in hand, a *proletarian* resolution of the possessional question in the Urals. The question of what slogans we should put out in this case is one that we must discuss in a subsequent article, which will be especially devoted to this issue.

How must we protest against the robbery that has occurred in the Urals? Our fraction introduced a question on this matter in the Duma. There is no doubt that the question will, at best, have only agitational significance and will bring no practical results. Nor will any protest whatsoever have practical results, because the stolen millions will not be returned. And if the circumstances are such that the practical significance of protest can lie only in its agitational effect, then it would be better to pose the entire question differently in the Duma. Besides asking the question, in the name of the Urals workers our fraction must demand recovery from the factory-owners of the millions they have received, even if by auction of all their assets and termination of the transactions that have been made, even if the banks do not receive back the total sum they have given to the factory-owners and incur losses for their conscious participation in the robbery. Moreover, we will conduct agitation among the workers in support of our fraction's demand, taking the form of a strike and mass-resolutions at meetings and local gatherings, which will no doubt lead to a desirable outcome if we take into account the interest that the Urals workers have in a resolution of the land-question in the localities.

In essence, the 'Panama of the Urals'[4] is simply one part of an entire system of transferring the people's money and the people's assets into the pockets of the big capitalists, which is widely practised in our country in the form of orders from the treasury, subsidies, monopolies of all kinds, and so on. But in the present case, the robbery is so obvious that no fig-leaf can cover it up: with their 'performance', the robbers have put themselves in the dock. Our position on this question is quite advantageous, and we must make every effort so that the campaign will lead to the greatest possible discrediting of our gang of expropriators – and of their protectors 'by the grace of God' – in the eyes of the people of Europe, and will illuminate for Russia the predatory policy of the capitalists and the 'constitutional government'.

Leonid[5]

---

4. [The figurative reference to 'Panama' suggests the magnitude of the financial fraud. The board of the Panama company, created in France in 1879 to construct a Panama canal, bribed French ministers, senators, deputies and newspaper-editors in order to hide its plunder, abuses, and grave financial position. The collapse of the company in 1888 ruined tens of thousands of small shareholders.]

5. [A pseudonym of E.A. Preobrazhensky.]

No. 7
Report from the Gendarmerie-Administration of Perm Province to the Director of the Department of Police, M.I. Trusevich, on the Discovery during a Search of E.A. Preobrazhensky of a Typescript Written by him 'To Members of the Duma-Fraction'[1]

No. 410   26 August 1908

Secret

During a search made under the personal detention in Ufa of a student of the Imperial Moscow University, Evgeny Alekseevich PREOBRAZHENSKY, son of a priest, who said he was the nobleman Aleksandr Ivanov GORELOV, a manuscript was seized, 'To Members of the Duma-Fraction', a copy of which is herewith submitted.

Available information indicates that the person named PREOBRAZHENSKY, known in the organisation as 'Leonid', and who was summoned by a member of the Perm regional court in an investigation of the case of the Perm Committee of the RSDRP, was a member of the Regional Committee and a correspondent of *Proletarii*.

The Regional Conference of 11 May of this year, in Zlatoust, took place under his leadership.

I am informing Your Excellency of this matter in addition to my submission of 18 August, No. 360.

---

1. [From GA RF. F. 102. OO. 1908. D. 5. Ch. 42. L. 117–19. Ob. The report is the original. Typed. The article is a copy.]

Appendix: Copy of the manuscript 'To Members of the Duma-Fraction'.
For the Head of the Administration
District-assistant[2]

Appendix

'To Members of the Duma-Fraction'

No later than 29 April 1908[3]

Questions concerning the Duma-fraction are becoming the topic of the day in party-circles. The wretched representation that the RSD[4] has in its Duma-fraction threatens to do enormous damage to the Party's authority amongst the wide popular masses, and the Party is more and more persistently facing the question of what to do with its unfortunate offspring.

We never expected that the activity of a fraction that entered the Duma through the sieve of the new electoral law might fully satisfy the Party and the working masses. But we did think, and we had to think, that the fraction would do its utmost in this regard, and place itself at the complete disposal of the Party. In reality, we have seen something different. From the first steps in its activity, the fraction has occupied a ridiculous position in relation to the Party and its representative, the C[entral] C[ommittee]. We know that the fraction refused from the outset even to call itself the Social-Democratic fraction, and preferred to be called the Social-Democratic group, and it was only a unanimous resolution of the All-Russian Conference that forced it to renounce this step, which was dictated by a purely philistine fear of 'going to prison'. It seemed that the shackling of deputies in the Second Duma[5] would compel the fraction to declare itself the pre-eminent defender of proletarian interests in the Third Duma, and inspire it to be ready to share their fate in defending the cause of revolution. In reality, those shackles inspired them to renounce the party that sent them to the Duma.

---

2. [The signature is illegible.]
3. [On 29 April 1908, E.A. Preobrazhensky was arrested with a hand-written copy of 'To Members of the Duma-Fraction' in his possession.]
4. [Russian Social Democracy.]
5. [The reference is to the arrest of the Social-Democratic fraction in the Second Duma on 3 June 1907, and the ensuing trial.]

According to the resolution of the London Conference,[6] the Duma fraction is part of the Party and subordinate to the leadership of the CC. In its activity, the fraction in the Third Duma is attempting to separate itself from the Party; it has exchanged the leadership of the CC for the leadership of such people as Prokopovich and Kuskova. Not all comrades know,[7] for example, that the fraction directly refused to subordinate itself to the decision of the CC on the question of electing someone other than Meyendorff as deputy chairman of the Duma.[8]

The prevailing view in the fraction is that they are answerable not to the Party but to their voters, and starting from that view they are shunning the leadership of the CC. This view is, of course, a complete absurdity. The majority of the deputies entered the Duma under the Party's flag. The fraction's electors are the Party itself, from which our deputies now wish to detach themselves. Finally, if Social Democracy could now do a survey of all the fraction's electors, there can be no doubt that they would have an unconditionally negative view of the position taken by the fraction in relation to the Party, and of all the activities of the fraction itself. The fraction knows full-well, of course, that control by the electors over deputies is almost completely impossible. To shun responsibility to the Party in the name of responsibility to the electors in fact means an attempt to rid oneself of any responsibility to anyone at all. Being further from the Party means being further from going to prison for revolutionary speeches from the Duma-tribune – these are considerations that were foreign to the fraction in the first two Dumas, but they are now guiding the fraction in the Third Duma.

Furthermore, the fraction violated the resolution of the London Congress when it attended a meeting of the Duma-opposition that included representatives of the Polish *Narodowci*.[9]

But the main point is that the entire activity of the fraction in the Duma is completely unsatisfactory. Remember the miserable declaration that discarded and concealed our most important slogans and demands, and remember a whole series of other lame performances.

And however weak the fraction may be, it could still be very useful to the Party if it were not afraid to defend our position in the Duma completely and clearly, if it were simply a mechanism of the Party, completely following the directions

---

6. [The Fifth Congress of the Russian Social-Democratic Workers' Party met in London from 30 April (13 May) to 19 May (1 June) and adopted a resolution on relations with the bourgeois parties, the bourgeoisie and the State-Duma.]

7. [The original said 'известен' (it is known).]

8. Despite the resolution of the Central Committee, the fraction decided to vote for the peaceful reformer L'vov if his selection were to depend on SD votes.

9. [The resolution on popular democracy, adopted at the Fifth (London) Conference of the RSDLRP, declared: '...the Polish national-democratic fraction must be included among the Duma-groups with whom the S[ocial]-D[emocratic] fraction must enter into no discussions or agreements whatsoever' (KPSS 1983, p. 260).]

of the CC. This is not what we see in reality, and the Party must resolve this question, but how?

We believe that the Party must try all peaceful means, if I may use that expression, to direct[10] the fraction onto the proper course. We must remember that it is enormously important for the working class to have representation in the Duma at the present moment, when a number of questions are to be raised that deeply affect the interests of the proletarian masses: the question of persecution of the trade-unions, of the Urals settlements, and so on. Even more such questions lie ahead that could arise from certain[11] activities of the proletariat. For that reason, the Party, rather than deciding to withdraw the fraction from the Duma should it refuse party-supervision, should issue to the deputies a clear ultimatum.

And only when this ultimatum is rejected, when the fraction wishes to remain independent, must the Party decide upon withdrawal of the fraction. We have seen too much parliamentary debauchery in the West, which is so closely connected with the autonomy of a fraction from the socialist parties, to re-create such a product on Russian soil. The Party must demand subordination of the fraction, and let responsibility for the rupture fall upon those to whom a philistine life and a guarantee against prison and shackles is more dear than struggling and suffering for the cause of the revolution.

But the CC cannot issue an ultimatum to the fraction without securing the consent of the party-majority. Let the Urals organisation discuss the question presented here, and inform[12] the CC of any decisions taken.[13]

---

10. [The original said 'to correct' (исправить) rather than 'to direct' (направить).]
11. [The original said 'definitions' or 'determinations' (определениями) rather than 'defined' or 'certain' (определенными).]
12. [The text says 'известен' (known) rather than 'известит' (inform, notify, or make known).]
13. [There is no signature on the document.]

No. 8
From a Report by the Gendarmerie-Administration of Perm Province to the Director of the Department of Police, N.P. Zuev, on Determination of E.A. Preobrazhensky's Authorship of the Letters that were Seized in the Ekaterinburg Post and Telegraph-Office, and on his Arrest[1]

No. 4363

12 December 1911
Absolutely secret

In presenting copies of two letters from 4 and 15 November of this year signed 'L', seized in the Ekaterinburg post- and telegraph-office on 10 November and this 18 December, according to Article 1035 of the Regulations on Criminal Proceedings, addressed to the Kungur citizen, mechanic Sergei Aleksandrov CHEREPANOV, who was arrested on the night of 30 October this year in the matter of liquidating the Ekaterinburg group of the Russian Social-Democratic Workers' Party and who was a subject of the formal inquiry into evidence of crime, according to Section 1 of Article 102 of the Articles of Criminal Law, I hereby report to Your Excellency that their author is without any doubt comrade 'Leonid' – the priest's son Evgeny Alekseev PREOBRAZHENSKY who is involved in the inquiry entrusted to me by the Provincial Gendarmerie-Administration as an accused in the case of the group of members of the Perm organisation of the Russian Social-Democratic

---

1. [From GA RF. F. 102. 7 d-vo. 1911. D. 2349. L. 63–5 ob. The report is original. Typed. The letters are copies.]

Workers' Party and who was convicted by verdict of the Kazan court, held on 14 September, 1909, to exile in a settlement with deprivation of all rights and status, and with consequences according to provisions 28–30, 34, and 35 of the Articles of Criminal Law. The sentence concerning Preobrazhensky was addressed to the procurator of the Troitsky regional court for implementation.

The 'Semen' and 'S' mentioned in the letters...[2] refer to Itsko Srulev SHVARTS.[3]

In view of the evidence we have from agents that 'Leonid'-Preobrazhensky was to be a delegate of the Urals organisation at the forthcoming party-conference, and of the current possibility of his being summoned to the formal inquiry into evidence of a crime under Section 1 of Article 102 of the Articles of Criminal Law, I have sent on this 19 December telegram No. 2825 to the head of the Irkutsk Provincial Gendarmerie-Administration requesting the search and arrest of Evgeny Preobrazhensky, resident of the settlement of Nizhne-Ilimsk.

The subsequent result will be reported to Your Excellency in a supplementary.

A copy of this report is being sent with attachments by No. 4364 to the head of the Irkutsk Provincial Gendarmerie-Administration.

Appended are copies of the two letters signed 'L'.

Colonel[4]

---

2. [The section of the text dealing with the articles of Criminal Law under which Itsko Shvarts was convicted is omitted.]

3. [Although he was to be a delegate from the Ekaterinburg organisation of the RSDRP, I.I. Shvarts was unable to attend the Prague Conference because he was arrested in St. Petersburg. The delegate from the Ufa organisation, E.A. Preobrazhensky, was in Siberian exile, and was evidently unable to flee abroad.]

4. [The signature is illegible.]

Appendix 1

Copy of a Letter Taken during a Seizure on 10 November 1911 in Ekaterinburg Post-Office, According to Article 1035 of the Articles of Criminal Justice, Addressed to 'Ekaterinburg, Siberian Bank Building, Urals Technical-Industrial Company, e.v.b. to Sergei Aleksandrovich Cherepanov'. Post-Marked 'Nizhne-Ilimsk,[5] Irkutsk Province, 4.X–11'[6]

Dear Comrade,
    Immediately after receiving your letter I replied to you, as requested, saying that I am very pleased to accept your proposal. How am I to understand your current silence? I am beginning to make the worst assumptions, which are all-too possible in our situation. I am not certain that you will receive this letter, and for that reason I shall neither say much about my life nor raise the many questions that I have. I shall write in the event that everything finally becomes clear. Perhaps you did not receive the telegram that you requested and are drawing the wrong conclusions.
    I am extremely grateful for what you have done for me. Write or send me a telegram in order to relieve me of my bewilderment.

L.

Appendix 2

Copy of a Letter Taken During a Seizure on 18 December of this Year in Ekaterinburg Post-Office, According to Article 1035 of the Articles of Criminal Justice, Addressed to 'Ekaterinburg, Urals Technical-Industrial Company, e.v.b. to Sergei Aleksandrovich Cherepanov'. Post-Marked 'Nizhne-Ilimsk, Irkutsk Province, 15/XI–11'

Dear Comrade,
    I received your letter of 16 October and am hurrying to respond. I am very pleased that my telegram, expressing my agreement, was received in time. Prior to this I sent to you a letter for S, where I expressed my confusion concerning

---

5. [Now known as the city of Nizhneilimsk.]
6. [Under the letter there is a note: on the back 'For Semen' and below that 'For Semen' again.]

the silence on his part. I see now that at least the explanation for that circumstance is not so pessimistic in nature. But I am still unclear about some things. The thing is that S. wrote to me in a positive sense concerning the favourable outcome of his financial quests...[7] Now, I ask: did you not fully inform S. of the state of affairs or are his hopes carrying him too far ahead of reality? You ask what my plans are. My answer can be brief: I have decided to change my former address, in the first place, and secondly, not to mope while abroad. There is nothing more I can say. After all, just receiving the kind of suggestion that S. made to me is enough to make me feel as if I were in places and situations that today are merely a futile dream. If I received the same kind of suggestion from the other end of Russia, I would agree to accept it at once. Essentially, I understand your question very well concerning the plans. More concretely, you probably want to know if I can be of use for the Urals. I repeat that I am prepared to accept your proposal, if it will not be conspiratorial nonsense.

I understand your question about my health as a debt of decency owed to all those who are sitting in prison or living in exile. Since it would be improper to leave the question without an answer, let me say that I am feeling well, but could be incomparably better if I were somewhere further away from the place where I currently find myself. I am not corresponding with anyone else in our audience. I do not have an address for Nikanorych. Artem got stuck in Shanghai and has written nothing for months. Perhaps he has been involved in our matter. I have received one letter from Marki.[8] He is now an American citizen and a member of the Socialist Party. It is difficult to entice him with the prospect of participating in Russia, now that he may become President of the United States. I have my eye on some valuable people who might be useful in the case of a shortage of 'working hands'.

Best wishes.

With comradely greetings, L.
12 November 1911

---

7. [Part of the text is missing because it could not be read by the police-copyists.]
8. [The identities of the persons using the pseudonyms 'Nikanorych' and 'Marki' cannot be determined.]

Nos. 9–73
Articles Published in the Newspaper *Obskaya zhizn'*[1] from January to August 1912

No. 9

'The Coming Election-Campaign'[2]

8 January 1912

The beginning of elections to the Fourth Duma is not far-off,[3] and the democratic voter, whose progressive aspirations are not protected by the powers-that-be, and who has no particular enthusiasm for the 'popular representation' resulting from 3 June,[4] faces a serious task: to extract from the minimal rights that remain to him a maximum-effect that might in some measure change the face of the current State-Duma through strengthening its left-flank of consistent democrats. The average citizen has to cross himself before the thunder breaks. And to that end, he must first consider all the possibilities he has before him: on the one hand, there is the social recovery that is under way; on the other, all the forms of organised participation in the elections; and finally, the existence of weak points in

---

1. [The newspaper *Obskaya Zhizn'* dealt with social, political-economic and literary themes.]
2. [From *Obskaya zhizn'*, 8 January 1912.]
3. [The Fourth State-Duma functioned from 15 November 1912, until 6 (19) October 1917.]
4. [The Russian electoral law of 1907, which governed elections to the Fourth Duma, was extremely complex. Goldenweiser 1914 explained it in some detail, particularly the summary on p. 417.]

the existing electoral law that must be especially utilised in order to provide an opening for growing political activity in the country. The election-law of 3 June and democratic possibilities – to mention them side-by-side may seem ironic, if one recalls the origin of this law, which could more-readily be called a law of democratic impossibilities. However, we must not forget what miracles can result from the activity of the popular masses, who wish to have their say no matter what; and moreover, despite all our negative attitudes to the existing electoral law, we cannot and must not miss the opportunity to avail ourselves of its weak points, as I have mentioned. The fact that these weak points exist can be seen in the experience of the last election-campaign, which occurred in conditions worse than those for the coming elections to the Fourth Duma. Those conditions involved social reaction, an inclination towards boycott amongst an important section of the popular masses and the intelligentsia, and finally, the fact that elections were occurring for the first time under the new law.

What possibilities are there for a democratically-inclined voter to send the kind of candidates he wants to the Fourth Duma?

The most hopeful support for democracy comes, of course, from the workers' curia, which unfortunately sends only six deputies, in all, to the assembly of provincial electors. One can hardly doubt that in the coming election-campaign, too, all the electors from the workers' curia will turn out to be conscious defenders of the interests of the proletariat, or that the provincial assembly of electors, whatever its composition in political terms, will *volens nolens* have to send its class-opponents to the Duma.[5]

After the workers' curia, there is the peasant-curia. This curia did not justify itself in the last elections. Indeed, it was enough for there to be a single reactionary among the peasant-electors in order for the majority of the provincial assembly of electors to send him to be a member of the Duma. Moreover, the peasant-curiae exist precisely in those provinces where the *muzhik* is least enlightened, where he is downtrodden and under the influence of the reactionary gentry. Nevertheless, the peasant retains the possibility of sending a supporter of the compulsory alienation of the land from the hands of the die-hards and the servile spongers of nationalism. This was done by the workers' curia in the last election, and if the peasant does not do the same, it will be his own fault. The peasantry is dispersed and divided in political terms, and due to its economic position it is difficult to subject it to any organising force. It is difficult to expect it to be independent in the sense that interests us. A wider field of activity is opening here for the democratic intelligentsia, who are in touch with

---

5. As we know, according to the existing election-law the electors from the workers' and peasants' curia, where they exist, do not elect deputies themselves: rather, this right belongs to the general assembly of provincial electors.

the peasantry in various fields of activity on behalf of residents, as agronomists, medical attendants, land-surveyors, and so on.

There are also important chances for democracy in the second curia of those six cities that directly elect deputies to the Duma (St. Petersburg, Moscow, Riga, Odessa, Lodz and Warsaw). It is true that, apart from Riga, which sent the Social Democrat Predkal'n to the Third Duma, the others sent Cadets. But the balance of forces between democratic and Cadet voters in those cities is by no means such that the latter can reliably triumph over the former. For instance, in the supplementary election in St. Petersburg to replace Kolyubakin,[6] the Social Democrat N.D. Sokolov received up to five thousand votes, that is, approximately one-third of the votes cast for the Cadet Kutler. The elections in Moscow yielded less favourable results. But we must not forget that the only democratic candidate, I.I. Skvortsov, was 'interpreted'[7] and exiled, which led to the triumph of the Cadet Teslenko. Because of their socio-economic position, many elements that were drawn to the Cadets in the city's second curia will not be able to give their votes and their sympathies to liberal chatterboxes, rather than to representatives of the democratic cause, for long.

There are invisible changes occurring in the balance of social forces that even now promise quite tangible changes in the political situation, and a change in the winds will compel many of those who defected from democracy to liberalism to turn back again from liberalism to democracy. To win over the potentially democratic elements from the Cadets, leaving them with the strata of the middle-bourgeoisie and the bourgeois intelligentsia, would in many localities mean winning new deputies' positions from them.

In the second curia of the cities that do not have direct elections to the Duma, but rather elect delegates to choose electors at their provincial congress, this is exactly what happened. The only difference is that in the small country-towns of central Russia, the ordinary citizen is to the right of the Cadets, while in the outskirts the masses are to the left of the Cadets. We shall now see how much difference might come from sending even five to six democratic electors from the cities.

In the Third State-Duma, an enormous majority of the provinces sent either all oppositionists, or else all reactionary deputies, depending upon whatever majority formed in the provincial assembly of electors: either the Octobrist Right or the Cadet Left. There were cases where a few votes from Social Democrats

---

6. [September 21 (October 4), 1909, was the date fixed for the by-election to the Third Duma to replace the St. Petersburg deputy, the Cadet A.M. Kolyubakin, who had been expelled from the Duma.]

7. [A by-election to the Third Duma was held in Moscow on March 20 (April 2), 1911. The Social-Democratic candidate was I. I. Skvortsov-Stepanov, who was arrested in February and exiled for three years to Astrakhan province around the time of the elections]

and non-party leftists determined whether the majority went to the Cadets or to the rightists. In such circumstances, the Cadets, like it or not, were forced to concede [one] or two positions to Social Democrats and groups to the left of them. And conversely, when the Cadets had an independent majority, they had neither the need nor the wish to share places with the left. It is clear from this that, for democrats, who can count almost nowhere on an independent majority, the best position is one in which neither the Cadets nor the rightists have an independent majority. Thus, in the provinces that gave an independent majority to the Cadets in the last elections, democrats must work to eliminate that majority. A strengthening of the rightists, in that case, can be advantageous, since this makes leftists the masters of the situation, and the more right-wing the general composition of the provincial assembly of electors, the more left-wing will be the composition of the deputies it elects.[8] In the majority of provinces in the last election-campaign, the Octobrists and rightists were masters of the situation at the provincial congress of electors. Here the task of democrats is mainly to eliminate the Octobrist-rightist majority – not, of course, with the objective of creating a Cadet majority, from which nothing can be expected, but rather to achieve the kind of equilibrium between rightists and the Cadets that would, as mentioned above, put leftists in control of the situation.

Hence, the main task of the democratic strata of our society in the coming elections is to form a unified group of electors at the provincial assembly, opposed to both the rightists and the Cadets. And for that purpose, the workers must choose now the persons to elect as delegates and electors. The peasants must do the same in the election of delegates in the parishes. In the second urban curia, it is necessary to begin work now with the goal of counting the democratic voters, and they must be put in contact with one another to determine in advance the most desirable candidates.

M. Leonov[9]

---

8. This is [not] meant to suggest, of course, that in such cases one should vote for the rightists. That is inadmissible whatever the circumstances. I am also assuming that the leftists will enter into a technical agreement with the Cadets regarding the division of deputies' positions.

9. [One of E.A. Preobrazhensky's pseudonyms.]

No. 10

'The Parliamentary Elections in Germany'[1]

12 January 1912

As one would expect, the elections to the German Reichstag, which took place on 1 January (old style), ended with a brilliant victory for Social Democracy, a weakening of the reactionary bloc of conservatives and the centre, and a defeat for liberals of various shades, at least in the first round of voting. The Social Democrats, who had 43 seats following the 1907 elections (in by-elections over the next five years, that number grew to 53) now have 66 deputies already, and are taking part in second-round balloting for another 112. The number of votes that they received has grown to four million. Social Democracy has enjoyed such enormous success despite the government's pressure on the elections, such as instructing bureaucrats to vote for the government-parties, and despite a number of restrictions on agitation in the press and at meetings, especially in the rural areas of East Prussia, the kingdom of the Junkers.

What are the causes of this victory, and what will its immediate consequences be? The causes are primarily organic in character; they are the causes that are facilitating steady growth of the international socialist army, which is following at the heels of world-capitalism and, with every success of the latter, seeing its ranks increase by hundreds of thousands, even millions. The growth of socialism in Germany is connected, above all, with the successes of German capitalism, with the rapid and steady growth of the army of the proletariat, with sharpening class-contradictions between the working class and the employers. German Social Democracy successfully combines defence of the vital interests of the worker with struggle against the entire capitalist system as a whole, and this is the cause of its unshakeable and ever-growing success amongst the German proletariat. The new conquests by Social Democracy in the elections are a consequence, or more accurately, a partial manifestation, of the conquests that it is making amongst the workers, attracting to itself ever-newer strata of the German proletariat.

But in addition to these long-term causes, the success of German Social Democracy is also due to temporary causes, connected with the fact that various intermediate and mainly petty-bourgeois strata of society are being drawn to it. In Germany, there is no strong democratic party that, while not adopting socialist tasks, would work for a democratic reconstruction of the state and defend the

---

1. [From *Obskaya zhizn'*, 12 January 1912.]

economic interests of the peasantry and the urban petty-bourgeoisie within the limits of bourgeois society. Thus, when the weight of Junker-domination and the shameless robbery of the popular masses to the benefit of a gang of privileged people become particularly unbearable, the democratically-minded citizen turns to Social Democracy as the principal force that is struggling against the domination of the Junkers and big capital, and with his vote he takes revenge on the government for ignoring his interests. Analysis of the social composition of the army of voters for Social Democracy has shown that it includes hundreds of thousands of non-proletarian votes. From time to time, a section of these non-proletarian voters will not be faithful to Social Democracy, but at other times the number of these temporary fellow-travellers, *Die Mitloifer* as they are called in Germany, strongly increases in number. Thus, the striking success of Social Democracy in the 1903 elections, along with the fundamental causes of the growth of Social Democracy, was due to the influx of votes from petty-bourgeois groups of the population. At that time the Social Democrats received three million votes and won 78 deputies. But already in the 'Hottentot' elections of 1907, the gentlemen-*Mitloifer* abandoned them. A bloc was formed of all the bourgeois parties, and while Social Democracy won three and a quarter million votes, its number of deputies fell by about three dozen. On that occasion, the petty-bourgeois strata rushed to emphasise that they were hostile to socialism. Now the Social Democrats have collected more than four million votes, and in the first round have already won 66 seats. It is difficult to say how many of these votes came from the bourgeoisie. But there can be no doubt that the current victory of Social Democracy is connected not only with its successes as a class-party of the German proletariat, but also with the fact that the petty-bourgeois voters, distressed with the policy of the right-bloc, turned once more to Social Democracy. As we know, the Reichstag that recently came to an end introduced tariff-policies that increased taxes on the people's pockets by hundreds of millions to the benefit of the agrarians, raised indirect taxes, and threw hundreds of millions into a naval programme to expand the fleet. On the other hand, the rising cost of living, resulting from artificial as well as natural causes, still further intensified the discontent of the popular masses and adjacent strata of the population. The result of both these fundamental and temporary causes was the striking victory of Social Democracy.

Let us turn to the consequences of that victory. If the black-blue bloc is defeated in the second round of balloting by the joint efforts of Social Democrats and liberals, this will lead to formation of a left-leaning parliamentary majority that, in turn, will entail either dissolution of the Reichstag or an essential change in the entire policy of the government.

Their millions-strong army, ranged against Prussian reaction, is simultaneously a threat to Russian reaction and lends powerful support to the strivings of the working class of Russia for emancipation. Finally, the victory of Social Democracy provides an enormous opportunity to all the nations of the world who are threatened, precisely by Germany, with the greatest danger. Indeed, that danger is inversely proportional to the strength and successes of the international workers' movement.

M. Leonov

No. 11

'A Grievous Misunderstanding'[1]

12 January 1912

Markov and Zamyslovsky have to be congratulated on their great success. I am not thinking of how Markov successfully recovered from the bruising he took in the Russian assembly from his co-patriot Nikol'sky, nor of the new appropriation for patriotism that Zamyslovsky acquired without photographing receipts. I am talking about an even greater success – about the uproar of protest and indignation that arose in society in response to the patriot's accusation of Jews being involved in ritual-murders.[2] Hundreds of writers and scholars, both Russian and European, have lent the weight of their names to the protest against the wild accusations, and at St. Petersburg's factories signatures were collected among workers to protest. The press has been dealing with the issue continuously. It was only a few days ago that Leroy-Beaulieu, in a personal letter to *Rech'*, added his voice to the signatures of protest and declared that his long years of studying the question of ritual-murders have convinced him of the absurdity of the entire legend.

I would not add my signature to the protests by writers and scholars, or stand and collect signatures from the workers, nor would I spend many years of research into the history of the Middle-Ages. And the reason is not that I believe in the existence of a Hasidic sect that practices ritual-murders. And even if I did believe that, would two or three Christian boys really equal the thousands of Jewish corpses, women with their stomachs ripped open, murdered old people and children, and the sea of bloodless horror and suffering on the part of the nation selected for the patriotic exercises undertaken by the pogrom-instigators?

Imagine, dear reader, that some 'character' accuses you of the theft of a handkerchief, when you know [and] everyone around you knows that the accusation is absurd, when the accuser himself knows it and it can be seen in his face, and when, finally, he never even had a handkerchief in the first place. You do not begin seriously to justify yourself, to bring legal and factual evidence of your innocence, or to call in witnesses. You react quite differently...

But are they acting differently, those who publicly protest against the accusation of ritual-murder by the Jews and then submit historical and other kinds of

---

1. [From *Obskaya zhizn'*, 12 January 1912.]
2. [The reference is to the famous Beilis case, which created uproar throughout the country. An interpellation in the Duma was signed by forty deputies. For more detail, see Reznik et al. 1999.]

argument? Those who react in that way elevate the notorious lie by the Markovs and Zamyslovskys into a belief that some people may share while others reject it. This gives too much honour to the pogromists! Is it worth wasting words on expressions of outrage and indignation, is it worth being outraged and indignant, when what is needed is to show, with cold calculation, that the political domination of the 'die-hards' cannot exist without patriotic sensations and anti-Semitism, that if there were no legends of ritual-murders, they would have to be invented retrospectively and extracted from history, that without ritual-murders they would have to be feigned?

The existing social-political system, in its naked form, is too big a temptation to the exploited masses. It has to be painted up. We have an entire profession of such political painters, with the Markovs and Purishkeviches in the lead. We must understand that speculation on ritual-murders, and anti-Semitism in general, is a kind of food-campaign or a form of social works for the starving patriots. Otherwise they could not justify the shady money spent on them. What the Markovs and Zamyslovskys need are greater patriotic sensations to muffle the cry of children who are dying from starvation and the heavy sighs of the working proletariat who are protecting their right to life with a 12-hour day. And when these gentlemen, with their poverty of ideas, are unable to think up anything new and original, and in their dull-witted stubbornness again and again raise the cry of ritual-murders, it is enough, if we cannot simply treat them with scornful silence, to say: 'That is your profession, gentlemen'. To do otherwise is to fulfil the wish of the pogrom-makers, and to help in elevating the noise, which is the reason why the patriots launched the entire campaign.

No, I did not add my signature to the protest by the writers and scholars.

M.L.

No. 12

'Again On the Question of the Rising Price of Foodstuffs'[1]

13 January 1912

As we have noted in previous articles,[2] the unusually sharp increase in the prices for products, especially for products of mass-consumption, has provoked a widespread movement in Western Europe and will, no doubt, agitate the popular masses and prompt them more than once to action.

In Russia the high price of food-products has become a chronic phenomenon, and though we do not presently see the kind of movement that arose in the Central Industrial District during 1907 due to rising prices, the evil continues to be felt no less acutely, especially among the lower groups of the popular masses, for whom the loss of an additional *kopek* frequently means blood and tears.

Not long ago, it was reported in the newspapers that the frightful rise of prices on foodstuffs in Warsaw caused rumours of a possible general strike as a reaction to this increase in the cost of living. It seems that there is no other phenomenon that gives rise to so many prejudices and illusions as high prices and the attempt to struggle against them. For that reason, it is worthwhile and timely to clarify the question of high prices with regard to their causes and the most realistic means of struggling against them.

Prices for products can rise, in the first place, because of a change of conditions in the international market. For instance, if there is a reduction of grain-exports from the United States or a harvest-failure in Argentina, the demand for Russian grain can rise sharply; in connection with this, prices must rise in the West and, to a corresponding degree, after the deduction of costs for shipping, also for us in Russia. With other products that we import or export, for instance meat, cotton and so forth, the same thing can be repeated.

Additionally, the prices on products can rise within national borders because of tariff-policy and monopolies. If English swine eat Russian sugar but a Russian man drinks unsweetened tea, if we overpay monstrous sums for tobacco or tea, if we have to pay almost three times more for a bottle of vodka than it is worth, we owe all of this to tariff- and taxation-policy. To the same tariff-policy we owe the fact that almost all the products of Russian manufacturing industry, all of the calicos, cloths, footwear, and so on are of lower quality and cost more than in Europe. Because of the absence of foreign competition, our manufacturers are masters of the situation on the domestic market and, whether by agreement

---

1. [From *Obskaya zhizn'*, 13 January 1912.]
2. [The articles mentioned could not be located.]

or not, their only concerns with regard to the consumer's pockets are their own limitless appetites.

Finally, a rise in prices can have a local character, affecting only a single city, district, province or region, being associated with speculation by merchants who have monopolised the purchase and sale of products.

Depending on these three different causes of high prices, the means of struggle against them must also differ. The scapegoat for the agitated purchaser is usually the seller, whoever he may be. From what we have said, however, it is obvious that the seller may serve only as a transmission-mechanism, and the indignation of the robbed customers should not be addressed at him. If the rise in product-prices is connected with conditions in the international market, any struggle with him is useless. If, let us say, a *pood* of Russian wheat costs one-and-a-half roubles on the English market, and shipping costs twenty *kopeks*, then no allusions to patriotism can compel the grain-exporter to sell wheat in Russia for one rouble, even if fellow citizens are starving to death.

Patriotism is a source of profit, but not of losses. True, a prohibitive tariff could be levied on grain exported from Russia. But that would not only overturn the whole prevailing economic policy of the ruling classes, but would also delay our economic development. Finally, it would be disadvantageous for the popular masses in terms of their essential long-term interests, and inadmissible in principle. Indeed, the most beneficial tariff-policy for the people is no tariff-policy, meaning completely free trade.

Insofar as high prices are connected with tariff- and taxation-policy, it is possible to struggle against them only in a broad national context, only in the form of political struggle. The financial and economic policy of the government is linked with the whole nature of its power and with the class-interests of the social groups on which it relies. A struggle for partial improvement is inexpedient and pointless in terms of results; moreover, it displays a misunderstanding of the general causes of the evil to be fought against. We must not struggle with the consequences, leaving the causes untouched. That is why a strike by the workers of Warsaw, as a means of struggle against high prices, would be inappropriate insofar as the aim, of course, would be to achieve immediate practical results. And on the contrary, the demonstration by Vienna workers, who demanded from the government the elimination of duties on meat and protested in general against the entire tariff-policy of the government, was perfectly sensible.

The causes of high prices, as I have said, can also have a local character. In such cases, the struggle against them is easy and can be fruitful in terms of results. The most effective means is to organise the consumers into unions, which is being done successfully in all corners of Russia. But we must not spread illusions of solving everything by such means. This instrument is effective only within narrow limits, and the maximum that can be achieved in the event of success is to keep in the consumers' pockets sums that would otherwise remain with the small and large-scale merchants, while also getting a better quality of products. It is also possible to act on the municipalities and compel them to impose obligatory regulations on the price of baked bread; in general terms, to the extent that self-governing municipalities have the right to do anything in this regard, they should be forced to act in a desirable direction. Mass-purchases could be made, and the products could be resold to consumers in cases where prices are artificially inflated by merchants. Finally, merchants who are raising prices could be boycotted, if such a boycott does not already take place through the natural action of the buyer, who is looking to purchase wherever prices are cheaper. But none of these measures can shake the foundations of the existing tariff-policy, or economic policy in general, through which the interests of the broad popular masses are sacrificed to big capital. Only the transition to a people's economic policy can change things essentially.

M. Leonov

No. 13

'The Harvest-Failure and Russian Industry'[1]

15 January 1912

For the past two years, Russian industry has been in a condition of recovery. An increase of production can be seen in almost all branches, sometimes reaching fifteen to twenty percent above the production of the previous year. Demand is growing even more quickly than production, and cannot be satisfied in a timely manner. One need only recall the iron-shortage, which resulted in privileged terms for the import of iron from abroad, or the cement-shortage that resulted from the fever in construction. In terms of the volume of production, the past year set a record compared with all previous years, and significantly exceeded the volume of the preceding year, which was also one of expansion. The revitalisation has affected all the main branches of our industry except for oil, where, despite good prices and increased demand, production declined due to the natural exhaustion of oil-deposits in the Baku region.

Here are some figures to illustrate what I have been saying:

Extraction of bituminous coal in Russia over nine months:
1910 – 975 million *poods*[2]
1911 – 1,147 million *poods*

Iron smelted during the same period:
1910 – 135 million *poods*
1911 – 160 million *poods*

Iron and steel marketed over nine months:
1909 – 102 million *poods*
1910 – 115 million *poods*
1911 – 123 million *poods*

Smelted copper in the same period:
1910 – 1,035 thousand *poods*
1911 – 1,121 thousand *poods*

The oil extracted in all of Russia in 1910 was 528 million *poods*; the likely total for 1911 is 554 million *poods*.

---

1. [From *Obskaya zhizn'*, 15 January 1912.]
2. [One *pood* was equal to forty *funts* (Russian pounds) or approximately 16.38 kilogrammes (36.11 pounds). The *pood* was officially abolished as a unit of measurement in the mid-1920s.]

The textile-industry has also felt the influence of expansion. Thus in European Russia, according to the *Torgovo-promyshlennaya gazeta*, operating spindles and twiners numbered:

Spinners:
1908 – 8,044,684
1911 – 8,671,664

Twiners:
1908 – 364,941
1911 – 643,486

Expansion can be seen in the chemical-industry, but it was especially pronounced in construction and the branches associated with it.

A similar advance is also expected for the coming year. At any rate, that is how the industrialists are thinking. Not only are they projecting a significant expansion of production in the metallurgical industry for the next year, but they are even predicting the extent of an expected new shortage of iron.

In connection with all of this, the question naturally arises as to whether last year's poor harvest, which affected an enormous area over more than ten provinces and resulted in a grain-crop that was 258 million *poods* smaller than the average for 1906–10, will have an effect on conditions in industry. Tugan-Baranovsky thinks it will not, having on several occasions expressed the idea that expansions and crises in Russian industry are connected with analogous phenomena on the part of world-capitalism, not with the condition of our domestic market, and that the whole issue depends on available supplies of capital that can be invested in industry. The theoretical constructions of Tugan-Baranovsky have been adequately refuted in the economic literature. As for his most recent article devoted to this question in No. ___[3] of *Rech'*, the position taken there, that the current harvest-failure will not affect conditions in industry, is already beginning to be refuted by the facts of life. It is common knowledge that the Nizhegorod fair went very badly last year in connection with poor harvest-expectations. Recently, the newspapers have reported a series of bankruptcies in Lodz, a drop in production, and growth in unemployment. The same phenomenon can be seen in the Central Industrial District. Inventories of manufactured commodities are growing, industrialists are beginning to cut prices, and there is less work in the factories. The *Moskovskie vedomosti* reports from Ivanovo-Voznesensk that things are deteriorating in the textile-industry, and in that connection, prices for manufacturers are declining. The state of affairs in the

---

3. [The number is not given in the text.]

distilling industry is typical. For example, in 1910 the supplies of spirits came to 44,634,939 *vedros*, and in 1911, 52,913,333 *vedros*.[4]

Thus, the branches of industry most closely connected with conditions in the domestic market are already experiencing the effect of the harvest-failure. How great that effect will be in the future is difficult to say. It is also difficult to say how much the harvest-failure will affect expansion in the metallurgical industry. But there is no doubt that demand for agricultural machinery must see a relative decline – just as years of harvest-failure bring a decline in demand, or in the normal growth of demand, for printed cottons and manufactured commodities in general. Of course, the branch of production that produces means of production, which in most cases means metallurgy, does not depend directly on the condition of the peasantry or on a harvest-failure in particular, but only indirectly. However, such dependence does exist all the same, and there can be no doubt of that fact. For that reason, it may happen that not all of the industrialists' optimistic calculations for 1912 will be fulfilled in reality.

M. Leonov

---

4. [One *vedro* was equal to 3.249 gallons of the US standard-measure, or 2.706 imperial gallons. The *vedro* was also abolished in the mid-1920s when the USSR adopted the metric system.]

No. 14

'The English Guests in Russia'[1]

17 January 1912

In 1909 the Duma-Cadets, playing the part of a 'liveried opposition',[2] went to England as representatives of the Russian State-Duma. Although the English were bemused by a 'parliamentary opposition' coming from a country where, 'by the grace of God, there is no parliament', and were therefore dealing with people travelling on someone else's passport, the visit from the State-Duma was, nevertheless, treated as a visit from one representative institution to another. The English House of Commons thus owed a return visit to the Duma. And when there was talk, not so long ago, of an impending return-visit by the English, it seemed, and everyone expected, that this would be an official visit from the House of Commons and that the free citizens of England would not have to resort to counterfeit political documents. But it turns out that, in a certain sense, it is impossible either to enter or leave Russia according to form. It seems that in response to the 'parliamentary' visit of 1909, a group of financiers are travelling here with the project of acquiring profitable concessions in Russia and Persia, that the composition of the delegation was subject in advance to the Russian censor Mr. Rodzyanko – which must account for its pathetic composition – and that prominent Members of Parliament, such as Primrose, refused to join a trip that was organised somewhere behind the scenes, while others expressed amazement that they were not even invited. What an unexpected turn of events! Imagine, dear reader, that you pay a visit to some respectable family and you are impatiently expecting a return-visit. But, instead, they send their coachman to offer a good price for your horse. The visit by the Englishmen is an eloquent response to the comedy played out by the Cadets two years ago.

The newspapers are reporting that the government has expressed its wish that there should be no speeches on political themes at the reception for the English guests. A political visit without speeches on political themes – that would be rather strange. Yet it is completely natural if we are dealing not with a parliamentary visit, but with people 'on a trade-mission', some of whom just happen to be in Parliament. In that case, there is no need for pompous phrases, since, after all, business-questions concerning the pocketbook are not decided at public meetings and receptions, and they do not use the language of Mirabeau and Gladstone.

---

1. [From *Obskaya zhizn'*, 17 January 1912.]
2. [A servants' opposition.]

Liberalism, the common good, national friendship, and so on and so forth, have never been simply ideological concepts. But in the past, they completely covered up the economic essence, class-interests and monetary appetites that were hiding behind them. Today – when the values of liberalism and conservatism for the corresponding social classes have long been calculated and converted into gold, when men of affairs in the leading capitalist countries can only speak and hear of such high matters with an augur's smile,[3] when it is only in backward countries such as Russia that liberalism is still not sufficiently developed for its class-lineage to become clear to everyone who wishes to see – the representatives of a nation for whom time is money get straight to the point. And that is precisely why they forgo ideological ceremonies, which to us still seem necessary, and adopt such a casual capitalist attitude. It is also precisely why they commit such an indelicacy with regard to Russian liberalism: they are reminding everyone of just how backward it is.

M. Leonov

---

3. [In ancient Rome, the augury was a college of priests who interpreted the will of the gods through the actions of birds.]

No. 15

'Then and Now'[1]

19 January 1912

General D.F. Trepov stood for the compulsory alienation of part of the gentry's lands to the benefit of the peasantry, and for a Cadet ministry.[2] According to Count Witte, Admiral Dubasov, who put down the Moscow uprising, leaned towards the same measures. That was in 1906.

In that same year, following dissolution of the Duma, the government found it opportune under Article 87 – that is, as an extraordinary measure brooking no delay – to issue a law concerning the normal rest-period for shop-clerks, thus introducing essential improvements in existing labour-conditions. After passing through the State-Duma, a draft-law went for discussion to the State-Council, and a commission of the latter distorted it beyond recognition, in fact proposing through legislation to worsen the already abnormal circumstances of clerks and employees.

On 2 December 1905, an Imperial decree abolished the articles of the 1858 Penal Code by which workers were punishable for strikes. Once the workers were collectively freed from punishment, it logically made no sense to punish them individually for leaving work of their own accord. Consequently, Article 51 of the Penal Code became automatically void when the above-mentioned articles were repealed. For more than four years, this article has not been enforced. And yet when the government introduced a proposal to abolish Article 51 and it was accepted by the Duma, a corresponding proposal then went to the State-Council, where the majority of the joint commission on legislative proposals decided to retain Article 51.

This remarkable decision, which was at odds not only with the decision of the Duma and the government, but even with the Imperial decree of 2 December 1905, was promoted by a reporter for the commission-majority at the general meeting of the State-Council, on the grounds that abolition of the article in question was not 'timely'. Directness and candour are important. Legislation that benefits some workers, or at least does not worsen the actual state of affairs, is considered not 'timely' in 1911, that is, in an epoch when there is no widespread mass movement. Yet the same legislation was recognised as 'timely' in 1905–6, in the presence of such a movement. At that time, even General Trepov thought

---

1. [From *Obskaya zhizn'*, 19 January 1912.]
2. [In June 1906 D.F. Trepov, together with P.A. Stolypin and A.P. Izvol'sky, conducted negotiations with the Cadet leaders on the subject of Cadets entering a future responsible ministry. There were no concrete results from the negotiations.]

it 'timely' to defend compulsory alienation [of land] and a Cadet ministry. It was then thought timely to have the decree of 17 June 1905, establishing the autonomy of universities, which Mr. Kasso considers untimely in 1911, using his power to appoint professors and violating the law in other ways.

But there is no rule without exceptions. Apparently, Baron Tizengausen is such an exception, proposing to undertake labour-legislation not under the influence of mass strikes, as was always the case previously, but to make use of the current calm and thereby demonstrate his good intentions towards the workers. But alas! Looking over the results of the legislative creativity of the Baron and his co-thinkers in the Duma and the State-Council, we are convinced that all the government's draft-laws, published in 1905–6 and even earlier, go further and were more beneficial to the workers than the laws of the employers now sitting in the government-institutions. Tizengausen and his co-thinkers attempted to defeat the government's bill on insurance for workers and employees in enterprises belonging to the Ministry of Finance; they tried to make worse the existing laws on insurance for workers in general; and they did make worse the government's bill on shop-clerks. It turns out that they have used the political calm not to improve the position of workers, but to worsen it and to consolidate that deterioration through legislation.

Thus, there are no exceptions, and only one rule remains in force: the extent and intensity of reformist activity by the ruling classes is proportional to the extent and intensity of the workers' movement. And the government itself, in the person of Count Witte and many other government-representatives, has acknowledged this truth.

M. Leonov

No. 16

'A New Newspaper'[1]

20 January 1912

Issue No. 1 of a big new newspaper has appeared, *Golos zemli*, published by Mr. Sazonov. Clarifying its political position, the first article of the paper says: '*Golos zemli* is the natural successor to *Rossiya*, which was closed by the authorities in 1902, and to *Russkaya zemlya*, closed in 1904, and takes on the task of serving Russia – the great Russian land. If, during an epoch of gloomy bureaucratic absolutism, we boldly put forth the ideas of the people's rights and the people's freedom (*Russkaya zemlya* was closed, among other reasons, for promoting the need for a *zemsky sobor*), today, when this absolutism is to an important extent already undermined, when the press has a certain freedom and we have a popular government, our free voice will sound forth all the more loudly and boldly'.

Further on – after complaints about the intolerance of 'radical circles' that are suppressing freedom of opinion, hackneyed discussions of 'creative tasks', and a new complaint about excessive 'criticism' – the 'free voice' of the new newspaper turned to the First Duma.

'When the people were summoned to constructive work and the First State-Duma gathered, creativity was running low and the popular representatives launched a fierce criticism of the outdated and obsolescent system. This inability to formulate and attempt to resolve creative economic and social tasks firmly and clearly, this inability to reconcile separate opinions and find their points of contact in a common programme to save the country from collapse, rather than producing total disagreement, was one of the main reasons causing the First and Second State-Dumas to vanish without a trace'.

Not bad for defenders of 'the people's rights'. But the newspaper is not content with the Third Duma either, and as we shall see below, it is dissatisfied with everyone except itself.

In an article headed 'Under the Banner of Progressive Non-Partisanship'[2] we read: 'Before the Revolution, the Russian community was never so divided between parties, and we spoke with the people in the name of a single social and state-truth that prevailed over all private, group- and class-interests. In the revolutionary period, the community immediately divided into sharply defined political parties, each with its own god, its own sacred objects and ethics, along with the fragmentation of any single social conscience'.

---

1. [From *Obskaya zhizn'*, 20 January 1912.]
2. [Literally, 'Progressive Non-Partyness'.]

One would think this should be celebrated as sure evidence of progress. But no!

'Not a single one of the political party-programmes proved to be justified, the formulae turned out to be false, the entire course turned out to be bankrupt, and the parties lost the confidence of thinking people'.

But there must be one sure answer – patriotism. Yet Purishkevich is a patriot *par excellence*, Guchkov considers himself no less of a patriot, and Milyukov thinks the true patriots are the Cadets. Those on the extreme left are also patriots, if by patriotism we understand love of the fatherland, and if by fatherland we do not mean a group of exploiters. And the same holds for freedom, which every class understands and values in its own way. What is it that you gentlemen plan to defend? When we read in the leading article that 'the task of *Golos zemlyi* is to help society to sort out the formidable tasks of the present historical moment', we have to reply: 'First, sort out yourself and decide whom you intend to travel with'.

In 1902–4, when all cats were grey in the twilight of reaction, even the most doubtful liberal seemed to be a revolutionary. But eight years have passed since then. Those writing for the new newspaper appear to have slept during that entire time. And now we must recognise that the 'progressive non-partisanship' of the new newspaper is deeply reactionary, and even its appearance is a symptom of deep reaction. In the normal circumstance of political freedom, where there is even a relative space for class-struggle, every class reveals its own features in relation to other classes and finds its own political party. Non-partisanship – it makes no difference whether it is progressive or reactionary – is the lot of weak and intermediate groups who do not know whom to join in the ongoing struggle and who have no influence on its outcome. Freedom for classes and the resulting party-struggle, whatever sharp forms it might assume in both words and practice, is the powerful motive force of genuine social progress. The opposite is also true: wherever it happens, as in Russia following the defeat of the mass-movement of 1905 and 1906, that the class-struggle of all social groups is prevented from emerging under the levelling pressure of reaction, what we find is stagnation. And it is only in such a stagnant bog that flowers like *Golos zemlyi* can bloom. Is it not typical that a newspaper that was closed in 1902–4 is reborn only now, in 1912, rather than five-to-six years ago, when considerable freedom of the press existed and, despite great difficulties and restrictions, every class of our society could mount a defence of its own interests in the press? In those days, there was nothing for this paper to do. Now, on the contrary, when conditions are highly reminiscent of the pre-revolutionary years, and when we are far from having every class in a position to defend its interests in the press – it is precisely now that the people who had nothing to say in 1905–6 are beginning to speak up.

The time has come for empty stereotyped slogans and non-partisanship without principle, which has grown up in a dead field of suppressed initiative and now considers itself more progressive than class-clarity.

We take a different view. We see the 'progressive non-partisanship' of *Golos zemlyi* as a deeply reactionary development, and for that reason we cannot respond to the appearance of this newspaper with the usual 'welcome brother', just as we cannot welcome the conditions that have brought it to life.

M. Leonov

No. 17

'It's All in Vain, Vanya...'[1]

25 January 1912

The Cadet Vanya has already come out for the unification of all liberal and democratic groups during the coming election-campaign, under the flag of the Progressives.[2] An echo of this slogan, given out to all of Russia, can be heard in the leading article of No. 15 of *Sibirskaya zhizn'*. The ideas expressed in the article cannot be left without a response.

Pointing to the unfavourable conditions expected for opposition-groups in conducting the election-campaign, the author of the leading article writes:

> A characteristic of the coming election-campaign will be the absence of both Cadets and leftists – all of them, for 'reasons beyond their control', are planning to 'take cover' under the vague and ambiguous term 'Progressives'. And, to the extent that the campaign has already started among leftist groups, it is only this vague term that is appearing. In conditions where things cannot be called by their own names, there can be no talk of disagreements that characterise the different groups of our opposition... Moreover, life has moved ahead so far that these disagreements are hardly pertinent at the present moment.

What an amazing thought! Provided that we can call what the author says in the last two sentences a thought. Does the newspaper really think that once one social group or another is unable to defend its demands, the disagreements between them will be liquidated of their own accord or, at the very least, will become inappropriate? That would mean that external pressure alone is enough to make these disagreements, which are rooted in differences of class-interest, disappear, such that all groups might find themselves under a single flag. In the present case, it would be enough to deny all democratic groups the opportunity to speak in order to turn them all into liberals! If that were the case, the Cadets would have no reason to complain about reaction.

Let us read a little further. Now we hear talk of achieving such elementary rights and such simple public goods that everyone who has not made the idea of restoration the basis for a career must unite under their banner. Here, all party- and class-differences are receding into the background, and everything that in the slightest degree ignores sad reality is futile.

---

1. [From *Obskaya zhizn'*, 25 January 1912.]
2. [A group of moderate liberals organised in 1908, with 28 deputies in the Third Duma and 48 in the Fourth Duma.]

The sad reality must not be ignored. And not wishing to ignore it, we cannot forget that among the facts of this sad reality is the pathetic role of our Cadet liberalism, whose wretchedness stands out all the more clearly the less we are inclined to forget the recent past of those same Cadets: their behaviour in discussing questions of foreign policy; Maklakov's speech for three days concerning dismissal of the Duma and the council, during which he competed with P.A. Stolypin for the title of 'monarchist'; the behaviour of the same deputy in discussing the inquiry from the SD fraction concerning the convicted deputies of the Second Duma, when he prompted the Octobrists as to how to avoid obstruction from the Cadets; Milyukov's address in connection with the exclusion of Voiloshnikov; the proposal for a bloc with the Left-Octobrists, and so on and so forth. And we have yet to mention the Cadet press: its position in connection with the rumours of a 'new course' that it thought up by itself; the corrupting influence of this cult of hope in the 'charity of the victors'; the support for *Vekhi*, led by Izgoev and promoted feverishly, among other places, in the columns of this same *Sibirskaya zhizn'*, and on and on it goes. And it is precisely for these reasons that a steadfast defence of a genuinely democratic point of view on all questions of Russian life is so vitally important. The difference between the class-interests of the groups that support Russian liberalism and the interests of the popular strata on whom democracy rests, and thus the disagreements between Cadets and leftists, are so profound that to speak of them being inappropriate means either to be politically naïve concerning the first category, or else deliberately to throw dust in the eyes of ordinary citizens who have not understood the essence of the matter. The Cadets and leftists not only have programmes and tactics that are completely different, but they also have different attitudes even to such 'elementary rights' as, shall we say, freedom of assembly. Anyone who needs to be convinced of this can recall the Cadet draft-legislation on freedom of assembly introduced in the First Duma, and the reaction to it from those on the left.

But let us suppose for the moment that the disagreements can be viewed as inappropriate and can be liquidated. But there must then be a common point of view for eliminating disagreements, and where would one find it? Would the democrats become temporary liberals, or the liberals temporary democrats?

Of course, the Cadets have the latter in mind; otherwise there would be no sense to all the talk about 'reconciliation'. But a democrat might ask: why not the opposite? All one has to do is pose the question in order to be convinced of how naïve the author of the article is, or how naïve he imagines his audience to be.

But the newspaper mistakes its hopes for reality, claiming that the leftists are planning to 'take cover' behind the vague and undefined term 'Progressives'. 'Where did you learn that?' we ask. 'You can only be speaking for yourselves'.

If leftists were to be mixed up in a single group with liberals in the election-campaign, then participation in the election-campaign would lose half of its meaning for them. For leftists, coming out against the Cadets and their unprincipled liberalism is no less important than the struggle against 'restorationists'. Indeed, the movement to the right by the Cadets is also one of the restorationist consequences against which we must fight. For the consistent democrat, a Cadet is not much better than an Octobrist; the Cadets themselves have acknowledged this with their proposal for a bloc with the Octobrists. To merge with the Cadets in the pre-election campaign would mean declining one of the rare occasions, repeated only every five years, to show the masses the truest route to Russia's democratic renewal. And who would agree to such political suicide for the sake of the problematic benefit of seeing an extra dozen liberals of dubious merit in the Duma?

But perhaps it would be beneficial for leftists to conclude a long-term agreement with liberals, without altering their own slogans and undertaking only to support each other at every stage of the elections? To this we must answer – No. Given the existing electoral law, the leftists gain most from a balance of forces between Cadets and rightists. To give the Cadets a majority, and thus to make achievement of our own share of deputies dependent on their good will, would mean deliberately depriving ourselves of the possibility of putting our own candidates in the Duma. If the basis of an agreement between leftists and Cadets were the obligation for the latter, after achieving a majority at the provincial electoral assembly, to select a corresponding number of leftists as deputies, then at the decisive moment this obligation may not be fulfilled. An agreement presupposes the existence of party-discipline to guarantee that it will be observed. And can people give such a guarantee when they themselves presuppose and recommend dissolution into a formless mass of Progressives, particularly in view of the impetuous pursuit of deputies' arm-chairs that is so characteristic of our Cadets? We have yet even to mention a whole list of other considerations that speak against an agreement, but we intend to deal with those on another occasion.

Regarding the present moment, the author says: 'Here all party- and class-differences are receding into the background'. As far as the article under discussion goes, we can say that it is concealing party- and class-interests for the sake of certain specific party- and class-interests, and to agree to this would be both naïve and foolish.

M. Leonov

No. 18

'In a Rut'[1]

26 January 1912

The French say that appetite comes with eating. After the government set in motion Gololobov's complaint, accusing deputy Kuznetsov of slander from the Duma-tribune, Gololobov issued a statement about indicting all 33 leftist deputies who signed the inquiry concerning the murder of Karavayev. This is completely logical. Once 'A' is said, 'B' follows. The case of the complaint against the 33 deputies must go ahead after the precedent with Kuznetsov. The circumstances must quickly be clarified. Either what we see is a deliberately-contrived plan to exclude leftists from the Duma, in which case Gololobov's move was inspired by the purpose of implementing this plan; or else, tempted by the prospect of removing one SD deputy, the ruling spheres did not take into account the consequences, above all the fact that entry upon this slippery slope could lead to a situation in which Gololobov's second complaint must be satisfied, to be followed by a third and a fourth, and not only from the rightist side, but also from the opposition. Purishkevich alone could be charged twenty times over with slander. Guchkov and other Octobrists face the same prospect, to say nothing of leftists and the opposition. The predictions by deputy Pokrovsky are beginning to be justified, and soon Azef will institute a proceeding, in the corresponding instances, concerning the slander of his good name on the part of the Duma-majority. If the government continues along the path it has entered under Article 68, Paragraph 4, concerning the establishment of the Duma, while ignoring Article 14, then the Duma will risk having no-one left except people who never say a word and never raise a question.

And that is what would happen, if the only concern were exact application of the law and nothing else. But it is common knowledge that such cases do not demand the absolute rigour of justice. Indeed, when Purishkevich was similarly accused of slander in his day, the matter was terminated. Hence, the exact same article that left the right-wing Purishkevich free also provides the opportunity, in similar circumstances, to bring the SD Kuznetsov to the dock. No doubt, if what we are seeing is the implementation of a deliberate plan, then the complaints of rightists against leftists will proceed, but not the complaints against rightists.

Freedom of speech is coming to an end for the deputies. It is true that the Octobrists, according to some people, are worried and plan to protest 'energetically'. But we know what can be expected from these caricatures of protest.

---

1. [From *Obskaya zhizn'*, 26 January 1912.]

Even when these gentlemen are protecting their own bloody rights against the encroachments of reaction, they always remain loyal students of Kuropatkin.

That is the prospect, unless the situation is changed at the point where the existing balance of forces is formed and where the foundation of a real constitution lies.

M. Leonov

No. 19

'Alexander Sergeevich Pushkin (Born 20 May 1799, Died 29 January 1837)'[1]

29 January 1912

Today marks seventy-five years from the day, so memorable for Russia, when the life of our great poet ended after he was struck by the bullet of a high-society rogue.

It would be redundant to reproduce here the poet's biography: every literate Russian knows it well enough, and the things that do not need to be repeated in an obituary are the best monument to his genius. But every anniversary is an occasion for summarising the results, and in this case the summary involves the treasure of words with which the poet enriched Russian literature and, above all, Russian poetry. But this theme is inexhaustible, and the columns of a note in a newspaper are short. A few letters in a few lines are all that we can place on the altar of Pushkin-memories.

In the person of Pushkin, Russian poetry reached a height it has not surpassed. As a youth he had already absorbed the entire past of our poetry, which for him was the 'point he surpassed' when he completed his *Ruslan and Lyudmila*. If Lermontov wrote few works of poetic value before reaching the age of majority, the opposite was true of Pushkin: as a 16 year-old he wrote poetry that already showed signs of a free and natural talent, and many of these works retain their charm to the present day. In his *Fountain of Bakhchisarai* and *The Robber Brothers*, the poet's talent took a great step forwards; in *The Gypsies* and *Poltava*, written over a period of five days as a precious treasure of inspiration, he soars already to unparalleled heights. Finally, the talent of Pushkin unfolds in *Onegin*, an *unicum* in his own poetry and in all of Russian literature. Towards the end of his life, the poet wrote fewer lyrical works, and increasingly rose in his creations to objective contemplation and the embodiment of life. The poet's own personality became less visible, the master was less evident in the mastery, and he rose to Shakespearean heights where, as Heine remarked, art gave way to the expression of truth itself. That is the Pushkin who wrote *Feast in a Time of Plague, Mozart and Salieri* and *The Miserly Knight*.

Pushkin's prose is brilliant, and it represented an epoch in Russian literature that pointed it towards the true path of realism. Despite the eight decades that separate us from the appearance of *The Captain's Daughter* and *Peter the Great's Blackamoor*, they are still read with delight. But Pushkin was a master of words

---

1. [From *Obskaya zhizn'*, 29 January 1912.]

not only in Russian literature. According to French literary writers, all the prose that he wrote in French would do honour to the best masters of the word in France.

Pushkin's critical articles and commentaries are profound in terms of wisdom and artistic taste. Recall his notes on Shakespeare, where in a few lines he characterised with ingenious depth the very essence of Shakespearean creativity. Think of his reviews of French literature and, in particular, his response to Alfred de Musset, in which our poet immediately saw a true talent among the pretentious declamations of the French literature of the day. Among the world's geniuses, Pushkin was at home among equals.

Pushkin's personal life was tragic. He experienced everything that a genius must experience during the dark reign of Nicholas. He was driven out to Odessa and the Caucasus, locked up in a provincial backwater and deprived of the right to enter the capital. It was only by chance that he was not involved in the trial of the Decembrists, with all the possible consequences of that misfortune. True, he received considerable assistance from the government in his financial difficulties. But he was weighed down by these heavy chains that fettered his free talent, by humiliating dependence on people hostile to him whom he in turn despised. The savage censorship bore most heavily upon him, as the brightest star of Russian literature, and hindered the expression of his genius. In this regard, the poet exclaimed in one of his letters: 'Why was it my fate to be born in Russia with a soul and talent?'[2] The society that surrounded the poet regarded him mainly as a worldly person, as Pushkin the chamber-aristocrat and not the ingenious poet. Is it surprising that the company of high-society aunties, seeking diverse sensations in varying degrees of banality and ignorance, drove him to turn to the revolver in family-difficulties and to die at the hand of a womaniser?

Russian poetry is not rich with blossoms. Since Pushkin we have had many poets, but they are not his equal in terms of richness of imagination, involuntary and spontaneous inspiration, breadth of view and depth of thought, all expressed in plastic form. The form of verse has taken great steps since Pushkin, but with all the elegance of form that, like a children's pastime, must seem like decadent experiments on the part of today's poets in light of Pushkin's creative works. The most talented among them, such as V. Bryusov, manages in his best works to be only a pale copy of Pushkin's genius.

Pushkin emerged from a social context in which an insignificant group of people could devote themselves to learning, to 'dreams and passions', on the basis of the labour of the remaining mass of the population. The brilliant light of his

---

2. [The quotation is inaccurate. It should read: 'The devil prompted my being born in Russia with a soul and talent!' ('Черт догадал меня родиться в России с душою и талантом!').]

poetic genius is, indeed, a manifestation of the 'dark' labour of the *muzhik*-serf and the worker. The aristocratic inheritance belongs, by right, to democrats. The creative works of Pushkin are part of that inheritance, in whose contemplation those who are exploited might temper their verdict on a system that is already condemned by history.

M.L.

No. 20

'Incomparables'[1]

8 February 1912

A man would surely seem very eccentric to you, dear reader, if he took it in mind today to spread the word concerning the usefulness of glass by writing lines such as these:

> Wrong they are who think, Shuvalov,
> That glass is worth less than minerals.[2]

Today, one cannot read these lines by Lomonosov without a smile. But the fisherman from Archangel, who wrote them three hundred years ago, demonstrated the value of education. Can we still smile today after hearing recent debates? I raise this question because I am under the fresh impression (if the spirit of the Middle-Ages can be fresh) of speeches by right-wing deputies of the State-Council at the sitting of 26 January (1912) concerning the question of universal education.

For example, Petr Nikolaevich Durnovo most definitely thinks 'glass is worth less than minerals'. In a lengthy speech against the introduction of universal education and popular enlightenment in general, he says: 'Instead of building barracks for soldiers and means of communication, the government has thrown five hundred and fifty million roubles over ten years into so-called popular education, which is of doubtful benefit to the Russian people'.

Bishop Nikolai was so touched by the profundity of this truth, propagated by Durnovo, that he kissed him three times following the speech. The right-wing deputies almost gave the speaker a standing ovation.

Mr. Kokovtsov spoke in vain for the government, while Witte and many others tried to convince Petr Nikolaevich and his co-thinkers that glass 'is worth more than minerals' and that the draft-legislation deserved to be adopted. The rightists were firm in their convictions and voted against the legislation. For a long time I thought about an appropriate comparison for these ideologues of popular ignorance. By force of habit, I turned to Turkey. 'Worse than the Turks', I was inclined to say, but then I checked myself in time. After all, since 1908 the obscurantists in Turkey have been driven underground, and opposition to public education is no longer a qualification for high state-office.

---

1. [From *Obskaya zhizn'*, 8 February 1912.]
2. [From Lomonosov's 'Letter on the Usefulness of Glass'.]

I then turned to neighbouring Persia; but alas, here too the comparison was out of date.

Finally, I thought of settling on China, where the comparison might be clear and forceful. No such luck. Exactly three days ago China finally declared itself a republic, and there is no longer any need in that country to write, either in prose or in poetry, of the value of education.

My excursion through Asia ended badly, and now I lament wasting my time. Why did the thought not occur to me immediately that henceforth the Turks, Persians and Chinese will be comparing their own compatriots – those who decide, with no fear of popular ridicule, to raise their voice against education – with the rightists of our State-Council? Why did I not see that the most extreme rightists cannot be compared to anyone without giving an undeserved insult to the Asian peoples?

Indeed, they are incomparable.

M.L.

No. 21

'On Grain-Prices'[1]

9 February 1912

The question of the level of grain-prices on the world-market is enormously important for Russia. The level of these prices decides not only the prices on our internal market, and thus the budget of our popular masses as purchasers of bread, thereby affecting the interests of the entire agricultural population, but also the stability of our trade-balance in general, which is connected with these prices. For these reasons, a study of the question of grain-prices has both theoretical and, above all, enormous practical interest.

America establishes the prices on the world-market. Although Russia also exports a large volume of grain, it generally has to accept the established prices, like it or not, because this export is vitally necessary to it. It is true that, as time passes, Russia will increasingly emerge as one of the determiners of prices. But for now, in any case, the question of what determines a given level of grain-prices can only be fully explained if we first clarify the question of what causes a rise or fall of prices in the United States and Argentina. People who have looked into this question usually turn first in this direction.

In his articles in Nos. 7–8 of *Nasha zarya*, P. Maslov explains the rise of grain-prices in America by starting with his theory that he explained in Vol. 1 of *The Agrarian Question*. His view is the following. The most profitable agricultural economy is an extensive one, which yields a maximum product for a minimal expenditure of labour. An intensive economy, which demands supplementary expenditures of capital on artificial fertiliser, irrigation, drainage and so forth, provides an increase of the grain-harvest that is not proportional to the expenditures incurred; and for that reason, a unit of output from an intensive economy is more expensive (even though the absolute quantity of grain coming from each unit of land is greater than in an extensive economy). Since the supply of free land has been exhausted in the United States, while the demand for grain is continuously rising due to growth of the industrial population, it is necessary to make a transition to more intensive forms of farming in order to meet the unsatisfied demand. And since such a transition leads to increased production-costs per unit of output, the result is that grain-prices have necessarily risen and will continue to rise in coming years.

---

1. [From *Obskaya zhizn'*, 9 February 1912.]

There is no doubt that P. Maslov is fundamentally correct. The explanation that he provides for rising grain-prices is founded on the weighty arguments set out in his book *The Agrarian Question*, which apply to the general characteristics of intensive and extensive farming. On the other hand, this explanation fully harmonises with the labour-theory of value. But we cannot agree with Maslov insofar as his explanation ignores the phenomenon of rising absolute rent. As we know, P. Maslov denies the existence of absolute rent in general, and on this point he diverges from the theory of Karl Marx. On this matter he is mistaken. I will only note that it is precisely the rising price of grain in the United States in recent times that provides a brilliant illustration of K. Marx's theory of absolute rent.

Relatively slow processes, such as the transition from an extensive to an intensive economy, cannot lead to a sharp increase in prices similar to those we have seen during recent years in America. It is obvious that the rise in prices is not proportional to the rise in costs of production per unit of output. In addition to this basic factor, there is a further cause at work in America.

In reality, the rising price of grain in America is determined not only by an increase of expenditures on production, but also by the circumstance that the entire class of farmers is beginning to use its right to the land as a monopoly. And like any other monopoly, a monopoly of land-ownership excludes freedom of competition and is a means for burdening the entire non-farming population with a special kind of tax that the latter must pay in the form of a level of grain-prices that has risen above normal, that is, above the level of the costs of production. To express this in terms of the labour-theory of value, it means that a *pood* of grain will exchange for a quantity of other products in whose production more labour is involved than in the production of each *pood* of grain.

We are living at a time when the reduction of free land in America, given the enormous growth of the industrial population in both parts of the world, must make us particularly aware not just of the existence of absolute rent but also of its intensive growth. While Europe was being flooded with a mass of cheap American grain, this evil did not make itself felt. But in recent years, on the contrary, the circumstances have sharply changed.

The rise of grain-prices on the world-market is being determined, therefore, by profound causes. We are facing a long-term phenomenon. To count today on a significant fall in prices is just as impossible as it would be to hope for the opening of a sixth part of the world that might, as America did in its time, provide new agricultural areas for extensive farming.

This means that, in future, the development of Russian agriculture will take place in the presence of this favourable conjuncture.

At another time, we will have more to say regarding the consequences that must result from all these circumstances for the economic life of Russia, which interests of the different strata of the population will be affected, and by how much.

M. Leonov

No. 22

Review of the Book by O. Schreiner, *Woman and Labour*[1] (Published by S. Dorovatovsky and A. Charushnikov, Moscow)[2]

10 February 1912

The book by O. Schreiner, translated from English, holds a special place in the literature on the woman-question. It is not to be associated with the literature by bourgeois feminists, who try to establish their right to equality by lowering and dethroning the male half of humankind and who, in most cases, only do so to defend the emancipation of a privileged group of women. This book is above such literature. But it also does not belong with such literature as Bebel's famous book *The Woman and Socialism* or the brochure by K. Zetkin. On some points, the author expresses thoughts that are close to the position that Marxists defend on the question under discussion, but in the main she parts ways with them on the question of the roads to, and the possibilities for, women's emancipation.

In a few words, the author's point of view runs as follows. At earlier times women were the comrades of men in the struggle to exist. They were responsible for no less of the necessary work, and possibly for more. As the division of labour and the progress of technique deprived women's domestic work of its usefulness, and as the professions, being occupied by men, were not accessible to them, women were left only with sexual functions, and the woman began to turn into a parasite upon society. The parasitism of the woman leads to a decline in her mental activity and physical strength and, through the laws of inheritance, is threatening the whole of humanity with degeneration. The struggle against female parasitism is a struggle for the integrity of the race. The woman cannot wait for the female question to be solved through resolution of the labour-question in general. It will scarcely be solved by that route, because the economic progress of society and the increase in the well-being of the masses threaten to make the woman a parasite even among the working masses. In accordance with that general tendency, the increase in wealth leads to the conversion of the woman into an instrument of male sexual enjoyment. The instinct of the self-preservation of the race must involve not only women but men as well, and the idea of women's emancipation must prevail.

The author sets aside the fact that the parasitism of the woman is a phenomenon seen only in the highest classes of society, where the parasitism of men cutting coupons is no better. Among the working masses, the woman was long-ago

---

1. [See Schreiner 1911; 1912.]
2. [From *Obskaya zhizn'*, 10 February 1912.]

drawn into factory-work, and in the most important branches, the textile-industry, for example, the woman works no less than the man. The woman-worker does not say 'give us work', but rather 'exploit us less in our work'.

The instinct of motherhood, which is to guarantee the victory of emancipation, is also treated rather strangely. Why is it, given this instinct, that the woman still falls into parasitism and dependence upon the man? The author writes: 'Where there is a general attempt on the part of the women of any society to readjust their position in it, a close analysis will always show that the changed or changing conditions of that society have made woman's acquiescence no longer necessary or desirable'.[3] This is a perfectly true thought, but it does not go far enough. When does this 'general attempt' occur? Why is it precisely now that the instinct of motherhood must save the woman and the race from degeneration? Here, the author provides no answer. In reality, the enslavement of the woman, resulting from economic causes, will be liquidated by those same causes, insofar as it has not already been liquidated in the economic sphere by the participation of women-workers in productive activity alongside men.

The author is correct in explaining the opposition of men to female emancipation in terms of the fear of competition, rather than a negative attitude towards women as such.[4] But this in itself implies the conclusion that the opposition will end in a society where competition amongst the toilers will not take place.

Notwithstanding these shortcomings, this book can be recommended to all those interested in the woman-question.

The translation is excellently done.

M.L.

---

3. Schreiner 1912, p. 13.
4. Schreiner 1912, p. 190.

No. 23

'On Grain-Prices'[1]

12 February 1912

Before turning to the consequences that a rise of grain-prices on the world-market must have for the different classes of Russian society and for our economic development, I must first mention the conditions in which Russia must export its grain.

Russia's indebtedness has reached enormous figures. For the obligatory payments on debts and the accompanying interest we must pay out four hundred million roubles annually (the picture for 1912 is 404.5 million). Thus, we must export more commodities than we import in order to have the sums necessary for payments on the state-debt. And our exports actually exceeded imports in 1909 by 522 million roubles, and in 1910 by 363 million, while countries with developed industry, such as England and Germany, import more than they export. Since the main item that we export is grain, amounting to 847 million *poods* in 1910 for a sum of 746 million roubles, and about 680 million *poods* up to 10 December 1911, it is precisely in the sale of grain that extremely unfavourable conditions are forming for Russia. It [will be] forced to sell grain, however low the price and however advantageous it might be to hold back for a while and avoid reducing the price through competition with American exporters. Extremely characteristic in this respect are the following figures: in 1909, 760.7 million *poods* of grain were exported for the sum of 748.3 million roubles; subsequently, although we exported 847 million *poods* in 1910, as mentioned above, that is, about 87 million *poods* more, the total receipts came to 2.2 million fewer roubles. Attempts by the government to hold back grain in Russia cannot succeed, because taxes continue to be strictly collected, and the need to pay four hundred million on the state-debts drives a mass of grain from Russia, regardless of any artificial attempts to slow down exports. And, as with the hope that our exports, and above all grain-exports, might not have to occur under pressure of the need to pay interest on foreign debts, there are also no grounds for thinking that in the near future Russia might be able to dictate conditions on the world-market instead of accepting them, whatever they may be. Whether or not we have a famine, and whether or not sales at prices offered by the world-market justify the costs of production, we are compelled to sell grain. In a certain sense, freedom of competition does not exist for us. Naturally, there is one thing that we can count on in present conditions, and that is a rise in prices on the international market thanks to a relative

---

1. [From *Obskaya zhizn'*, 12 February 1912.]

decline of grain-exports from America. That such a price increase, determined by fundamental causes, is occurring and will occur, is something we discussed in a previous article.[2] This process may be interrupted from time to time, thanks to especially good harvests in the United States and Argentina. And given the volume of our grain-exports, a price increase of ten to fifteen percent means the possibility of receiving an additional hundred million roubles.

A rise in prices must affect the different classes of society differently. The greatest benefit goes to the large agrarians, who have access to credit and the opportunity, on the one hand, to avoid the clutches of the grain-dealers, and on the other hand, to wait for a rise in prices. For that reason, the past three years have significantly strengthened large- and medium-scale land-ownership. The circumstances are different for small-peasant farms. In the first place, on top of the peasant sit two, and sometimes more, levels of resellers. Even with normal conditions for the sale of grain, our peasant must leave enormous sums of profit in their hands. However, conditions for the sale of grain are never normal for our peasantry. The need to pay taxes forces them to rush ahead, without paying any regard to actual prices and the possibility that they might rise. In anticipation of the harvest they often take money from the landowners and kulaks even in the spring of the year. Small credits to help with a more advantageous sale of grain are almost completely lacking (and for a significant group of landlords, it is not beneficial to have the peasants using such credit). As a result, the lion's share of the profit from a rise of grain-prices on the world-market, and from a corresponding rise on the domestic market, falls to the resellers and exporters. The grain-merchants gain more than the grain-producers. For instance, it is now clear that sale of the 1910 harvest only partially benefited the agricultural economy, while a large part of the hundreds of millions that Russia received went to players on the bourse. Yet agriculture still gains considerably from a rise in prices, even in spite of these unfavourable conditions. With a further rise in prices, Western Siberia in particular, which now benefits only from a harvest-failure in Russia and only then enjoys an expanding grain-trade, will find it profitable to export grain abroad, even in the presence of an unfavourable tariff and the distance of shipment.

As for the urban population who purchase bread, a rise in prices will, of course, hit them in the pocket. But it would be incorrect to say that high prices on the world-market are disadvantageous to the non-agricultural population of Russia. There is one stratum for whom they are unconditionally disadvantageous. That is the stratum of the petty bourgeoisie, who can scarcely sustain competition with large-scale machine-production and are only surviving thanks to the 'sweat-shop

---

2. [See Document 1:21.]

system'. For certain members of these strata, a rise in prices could prove fatal and could facilitate the final triumph of large-scale capital over those branches of production that still remain in the small-scale economy.

As for the big and medium-bourgeoisie, in their role as consumers these classes scarcely feel the consequences of a rise in the price of grain. However, as merchants and employers they gain a great deal. A price-rise, bringing new millions into our agricultural economy from abroad, increases the purchasing power of the agricultural population, the main market for Russian industry, and fine days are coming for the factory-owners and merchants.

As regards the working class, it suffers immediately from a rise in prices because bread plays an enormous role in its budget. But the further consequences of a price-rise give it the opportunity to turn misfortune into advantage. An expansion of industry, connected with the rise in the purchasing power of the agricultural population, guarantees its success in the economic struggle, such that what it loses on bread can be more than compensated by a rise in wages.

In general and on the whole, a rise in grain-prices on the world-market means for Russia an inflow of new millions into agriculture, trade and industry. It facilitates the strengthening of capitalism and the accelerated economic development of the country.

M. Leonov

No. 24

'Economic Essays'[1]

14 February 1912

A few days ago, the State-Duma discussed an inquiry made to the government concerning the formation of a metallurgical trust in our country. The request was already submitted to a commission three years ago and is only now being discussed in the general assembly of the Duma. Providing an explanation, the government's representative said that the question regarding the formation of a trust by metallurgical manufacturers was actually raised in 1908, but the government knew nothing about it. The Duma postponed discussion of the explanation offered by the government: their attitude will become clear in a few days' time. We, however, would like to offer a few words on the issue.

The government's representative was correct when he declared that no-one has any knowledge of the trust's existence. In the proper sense of the word, there is no such trust in our country. All we have is the metallurgical syndicate '*Prodameta*',[2] that is, an agreement by the majority of metallurgical works involving the allocation of orders and establishment of the most profitable prices for the owners. But that does not make the situation any easier for the consumer. True, a trust is worse than a syndicate for the consumer: he is weaker when facing it because he is dealing, as it were, with a single owner who rules completely over the market and dictates prices. But it is already clear that the society of factory-owners, which calls itself the '*Prodameta*' syndicate and aims to pick the pocket of the consumer, is an undoubted evil. The reader can see that from the following figures.[3]

Of the three main products of the metallurgical industry throughout the whole empire, the share coming from the 'Prodameta' syndicate was approximately the following:

---

1. [From *Obskaya zhizn'*, 14 February 1912.]
2. ['*Prodameta*' was the largest industrial monopoly in pre-revolutionary Russia. The syndicate emerged in 1902. By 1914 it included ninety percent of metallurgical factories in the country and controlled eighty-five percent of all sales of ferrous metals.]
3. I have taken all the figures from the article by E. Vulekh in No. 30 of *Torgovo-promyshlennaya gazeta*.

	1909	1910	1911
		(first half-year)	
Merchant-iron %	80	80	89
Sheet and multi-purpose iron %	75	82	80
Girders and channels %	81	88	96

The syndicate, therefore, almost monopolised output of the main iron-products and could consequently dictate prices on the market. The effect of this circumstance on prices can be seen in the following figures for merchant-iron, which is the main product in demand by the broad masses. In *kopeks*, a *pood* of iron sold for

1900–1	165	1906–7	119
1901–2	145	1907–8	114
1902–3	127	1908–9	103
1903–4	128	1909–10	115
1904–5	124	1910 (up to December)	135
1905–6	121	1911	145–50

Prices began to rise quickly from 1909, namely, from the time when '*Prodameta*' syndicated the output of merchant-iron. Despite significant technical improvements and significant reductions in production-costs, the prices rose. Of course, another important consideration here is the growing demand, which prompted expansion of the industry. But the growth in demand could not have raised prices so quickly had the factories been competing among themselves. This is evident, among other things, in the example of the '*Krovlya*' syndicate of Urals factory-owners.[4] In 1909, this syndicate was responsible for 50 percent of sales in the empire, and in 1910 for only 38.5 percent. Since the syndicate was unable to monopolise the sale of roofing metal, the prices for it continued to fall at exactly the same time as the '*Prodameta*' syndicate managed to raise them significantly on its own types of iron. Thus prices for roofing metal fell by about 25 percent from 1909 to 1911. The '*Krovlya*' syndicate has not given up hope of uniting a majority of the Urals factory-owners, and if it reaches that goal, of course, it will succeed in raising prices. Then the consumer will be the loser here, too.

---

4. [The '*Krovlya*' syndicate, which controlled more than fifty percent of the total Russian production of roofing iron, was organised in the Urals in 1907.]

We must hope that the syndicate's calculations do not work out, not only in the interests of the mass of consumers but also for another reason that is no less important. The point is that the majority of factories in the Urals use backward technology and are not in a position to withstand competition from better equipped, purely capitalist enterprises. Backward factories must either cease to exist or else raise their technique to the required level. If the majority of backward Urals factories are still managing to survive, it is only thanks to starvation wages, various state-subsidies and, primarily, the predatory destruction of forests on factory-lands. A successful unification of the factories into a syndicate, an end to competition between the leading and the backward factories, and an increase of the price, will reinforce the position of the backward enterprises and become a serious obstacle to the reconstruction of Urals industry on capitalist principles. The success of the syndicate, as a result, will be an impediment on the road to economic progress.

We do not support having the ruling spheres influence economic organisation, be they an organisation of industrialists, workers or consumers. We are only opposed to their influence on one side along with benevolent neutrality or direct assistance (the syndicate of sugar-factories) on the other. As a result, the Russian consumer turns out to be defenceless against a unified industry, which, not being satisfied with a limit to competition from foreign industry through high tariffs, additionally tries to eliminate domestic competition among its members. Meanwhile, this domestic competition, given high tariff-barriers, is the principal stimulus for technical progress and the sole guarantee of the interests of the consumer.

M. Leonov

No. 25

'A Siberian *Zemstvo* and the Siberian Press'[1]

19 February 1912

As readers will already know, the State-Duma at its sitting of 30 January adopted draft-legislation from a commission on self-government concerning extension of the 1890 *zemstvo*-regulations to Siberia. The Siberian press had diverse reactions to this fact, but the responses that we have read generally reveal a complete misunderstanding. Here, for example, is what *Dumy Zabaikal'ya* writes in its 2 February issue:

> The date 30 January 1911 must be marked in the chronicles of Siberian life. On that day the State-Duma adopted draft-legislation on the introduction of *zemstvos* in the regions and provinces of Siberia.
>
> The draft has been adopted – the first step towards the goal has been taken – but this still does not mean that we are closer to reaching the end. And the short time remaining to the Third Duma's authority, together with the faint hope of the Council agreeing to the Duma's decision, will postpone any final resolution of the question, which is the most acute of all 'questions' for our region.
>
> Nevertheless, 30 January will remain a memorable day for Siberia and will be very instructive for the Siberian electors to the Fourth Duma.

This enthusiasm makes a comical impression if one recalls the essence of what is being discussed. The State-Duma spoke in favour of the 1890 *zemstvo*-regulations. What a wondrous event! As if the Duma of 3 June could speak in favour of anything else. Take note, dear reader, that the draft did not become law and that there is a 99 percent chance that it will not do so. So what is all the noise about just now?

The *Zabaikal'skaya nov'* was less enthusiastic on 2 February. Pointing to the difficulties the bill will have in getting through the State-Council and higher levels, the paper comments:

> It is difficult to expect in such conditions that the question of a Siberian *zemstvo* will become a reality in the near future. And for Siberia, as in the past, there remains only one moral consolation. We Siberians, as in the past, must repeat the excellent words of the artist: the lights are as close as they are

---

1. [From *Obskaya zhizn'*, 19 February 1912.]

far away. We would consider ourselves most fortunate if on this occasion our scepticism deceived us.

But here, too, there is not a word of criticism for the draft-legislation itself. The 'scepticism' refers to the chances of it being implemented, not to its provisions. In its 1 February issue, *Sibirskaya zhizn'* speaks more carefully:

> This draft is far from resembling those that were put together in Siberia in 1904–5. But it is, at any rate, a project for a zemstvo, and its basis is the idea of self-government, however restricted.
>
> We have said that the fate of the *zemstvo* is being decided in a desirable manner. We must understand those words in a conditional sense. One essential reservation must be made. The projected regulations for a Siberian *zemstvo*, which were worked out by a special commission of the State-Duma and have now been accepted by an enormous majority, are far from corresponding to those that people have wanted and still want for Siberia, and which are necessary in order to satisfy its needs and requirements.

The newspaper takes the view that anything is better than nothing, forgetting that in the present case the 'anything' may not happen (and we believe it will not happen), whereas a negative effect for the whole question of achieving self-government in Siberia is beyond any doubt. It is not difficult to convince oneself of this fact.

It is well known that the *zemstvo*-regulations of 1864 were based on those provinces with developed private ownership of land. The election of councillors took place at a congress of large and medium-sized landowners, and peasant and urban communities were created later. The law of 1890 gave preponderance in the overwhelming majority of provinces to the stratum of noble landowners; the participation of peasants in self-government was eliminated; and the parishes could only elect candidates, with the governor appointing councillors from among them. Then, the law strictly limited the competence of *zemstvos* and strengthened control by the provincial administration. The obvious question is: What might be expected from this law for Siberia, where genuine self-government is one of the most vital questions?

To expect something better would be just as impossible as making clothes for an adult from a child's jacket. Given the nearly complete absence of private landownership here, application of the *zemstvo*-law of 1890 to Siberia would lead to a situation in which the enormous majority of councillors would be chosen through the governor selecting them from candidates from the parishes. Such a prospect alarmed the initiators of the bill, however complaisant they generally were in making concessions to the opponents of self-government and in their diplomatic opportunism. The result is not the application of the law of 1890 to Siberia, but rather a new law, since it was necessary to reduce the census-criterion for private land-ownership to 10 *desyatins*,[2] to give representation to Cossacks and non-Russians and, in place of the leaders of the gentry, who are missing in Siberia, to give the chairmanship of the assembly to someone elected from the assembly, and so on. But if it was in fact necessary to introduce almost a new law, then why introduce the kind of law that deliberately does not answer the quest for genuine self-government and that contains the most negative features of the reactionary law of 1890?

The project's initiators give the following answers. The government, whose attitude in recent years has been opposed to introduction of a *zemstvo* in Siberia, especially since the well-known trip here by P.A. Stolypin and Krivoshein, refused to provide the necessary official materials for drafting the legislation. Secondly, the compromise-character of the project must facilitate its passage through the corresponding instances beyond the Duma. That was the explanation, at any rate, from the Tomsk deputy Nekrasov in his speech to the Duma-session of 30 January.

In the first place, however, the lack of official materials is a technical difficulty that it would not be difficult to get around, and which is by no means sufficient to warrant restricting oneself to repairing the old reactionary law rather than working out a democratic legislative project. Next, there is an internal contradiction between the first and second arguments. Once the government has expressed its negative view of introducing self-government to Siberia, then no law, not even a compromise, can count on implementation. At one time Nekrasov, the very person who reported for the commission on self-government, spoke in that spirit. Even if a compromise cannot be justified, at least it can be explained in the event that its practical results are obvious. But in the present case, not even the initiators believe in any practical results. Why, then, take the road of compromise? Apparently there remains only one justification, and that is the view that having the Duma accept the draft-legislation puts introduction of the *zemstvo* in Siberia on the agenda. But if we look at the matter from that perspective, can we then agree that the law of 1890 formulates Siberia's needs on the question of self-government?

The speech from a government-representative in the Duma-discussion of the law clarified the matter completely. Mr. Lykoshin declared that the government is totally avoiding any joint discussion of the law, and this is a sufficient guarantee that the draft will be buried. As a result, the policy of compromise received, and will continue to receive, the blow it deserves.

---

2. [A *desyatin* is equal to 2.7 acres or 1.1 hectare.]

The *Dumy Zabaikal'ya* in Chita says that 30 January will be very 'instructive for the Siberian electors to the Fourth Duma'. It is perfectly true, say we, that the voters of Siberia will remember 30 January as the day when the Siberian liberal deputies in the Third Duma traded their birthright not even for a mess of pottage, but simply for nothing.

Those Siberian deputies who are not infected by the spirit of compromise in face of reaction, which is so common among the Cadets, should have acted differently. They should have worked out and introduced legislation for a democratic and fully-fledged *zemstvo*. The project would not have passed, of course, just as the work of the Nekrasovs will not go any further. But it would have expressed the needs of Siberia on the *zemstvo*-question, and even if buried in the Duma, such a draft would have been of more significance. Only the politically blind can think that Siberia is not impatiently waiting for genuine self-government. And when the time came to introduce it in Siberia, the draft-law would serve as a starting point for fulfilling Siberia's long-standing aspirations. On the contrary, those who oppose and wish to restrict self-government are trying to escape with the minimum, and will put forth the work of Mr. Nekrasov and Co. They will say: in the persons of its deputies, Siberia has found possible satisfaction with the law of 1890, and so that is what it will now get.

The positions taken by many organs of the Siberian press are, therefore, more than strange when they fail to take any sort of negative view of the activity of those who initiated the draft-legislation. One must be very short-sighted not to see the perfectly simple truth: acceptance by the Duma of the project for restricted self-government merely weakens the position of future defenders of a truly democratic *zemstvo*, which is so badly needed and for which Siberia will impatiently wait until it finally comes.

M. Leonov

No. 26

Review of the Journals *Russkoe bogatstvo* (January) and *Sovremennyi mir* (February)[1]

26 February 1912

The *belles-lettres* of *Russkoe bogatstvo* have a long and well-established reputation: in general and on the whole, they always satisfy the censorship. This is both a negative and a positive achievement. It is negative because the result of special literary selection is a triumph of sameness, of monotony, and a cult of tendency that is incompatible with true artistic creativity. The positive aspect is that you know what you will find and what you probably will not find in the journal's pages. You do not risk an encounter here with Mr. Sanin,[2] whom the 'Marxist' *Sovremennyi mir* at one time so obligingly rushed to introduce to the reading public. Nor will you encounter either foolish novels *à la* Rukavishnikov or Kamensky, or the 'purple silence' of decadents. Here, realism always rules, and it is a chaste realism that knows where to place an ellipsis so that literature does not pass over into pornography.

The *belles-lettres* of the January issue are no different from the usual *belles-lettres* of the journal. Attention is drawn particularly to the story by Iulia Bezrodnaya, 'The Life has Left', in which she provides an essay on the psychology of disillusioned revolutionaries. On one side there is the attraction of purely personal interests in which the question of sex predominates (Rita, Duvanov), while on the other there is detachment from personal life, leading from revolution to the monastery (Gal'ka). Alone looms the figure of the revolutionary Andrei, who remains true to his old banner. The story is part of a still-unfinished novel of a stepdaughter and her stepfather.

The tale by F. Kryukov, 'Worldly Network', is written in soft tones with a shade of light melancholy concerning irrevocable circumstances. It describes an elderly monk, downtrodden and good-natured, who has travelled to see his aged mother, also a nun, and on the way back ends up in a wagon with a cheerful company of students who query him about the 'heretic Tolstoy'. Completely opposite worldviews do not prevent the monk from seeing good fellows in the students, or the students from seeing a simple man in the monk.

---

1. [From *Obskaya zhizn'*, 26 February 1912.]
2. [In the novel *Sanin*, by Mikhail Artsybashev (published in 1907), Sanin is an attractive, clever, powerful, life-loving man who is, at the same time, an amoral and carnal animal, bored both by politics and by religion. The novel's sexual preoccupations scandalised readers, apparently including Preobrazhensky.]

There is an interesting essay by E. Bakunina, 'Coney Island', portraying the life of Russian emigrants in New York.

As for the *belles-lettres* of *Sovremennyi mir*, there is little to say about them. They continue publication of the interesting novel by A. Sefarimovich, 'City on the Steppes', which we wrote about in our last review of journals and which we will have occasion to return to. The other *belles-lettres* do not deserve mention.

The journalistic section of both journals is very informative. In *Russkoe bogatstvo* one must mention, above all, the historical essay by V. Korolenko, 'Russian Torture'. Let us look at some short excerpts. Here, for instance, is the famous Kotoshikhin narrating the methods of torture used during the reign of Aleksei Mikhailovich:[3]

> There were tortures designed for all types of thieves: The criminal's shirt is removed and his hands are tied behind his back, by the wrists, with a rope, and that rope is covered with felt, and he is lifted up to a place constructed like a gallows, and his feet are tied with a strap; and one man, the executioner, places his foot on the strap between his feet and pulls him down, so that the criminal's arms are pulled straight above his head and are torn out from their sockets; and then, from behind, the hangman will begin whipping his back: thirty or forty strokes per hour...And if he will not confess the first time, within a week they will torture him a second and a third time. They will burn him with fire, tie his hands and feet together and place a burning log between them, and for others they heat iron-tongs until they are red-hot – and break the ribs...They also tortured with a heated steel-bar that was slowly moved over the human body, causing it to bubble, crackle and heave up.[4]

Peter the Great forbade torture in minor cases. Under Peter III, the Secret Chancellery was abolished, and he ordered avoidance of 'torture as much as possible'. Under Catherine, torture was finally abolished in 1774, although the order was sent secretly to the governors so that the people would not think they could indulge in unrest. Abolished on paper, torture in fact continued. It was only Alexander I who openly declared torture to be illegal.

The essay ends there, but it is to continue at a later time.

In 'Ritual Slanders in Jewish Popular Art', S. An-sky provides an essay on Jewish popular stories in which legendary figures, such as the detective Goilem, destroy intrigues by enemies of the Jews who attempt to create situations in which to accuse the Jews of ritual-crimes. The author finishes his essay, which clearly portrays the dismal position of the Jewish people, persecuted everywhere

---

3. [Tsar Aleksei Mikhailovich Romanov (1629–76).]
4. *Russkoe bogatstvo*, January 1912, pp. 127–9.

over a period of centuries, with the following lines: 'If, in order to expose slander and celebrate truth and justice, the popular imagination must resort to creating Goilem, to supernatural assistance from angels, to the voice of Heaven, to revelations in dreams, to secret pious men and miracle workers – this is evidence of the fact that the people have lost faith in ordinary terrestrial justice. And it is truly difficult to say where the greater tragedy lies: whether in the mournful annals of persecution of the Jewish people or in these exultant fairy tales of 'miraculous deliverance"'.[5]

The author of the article 'Sovereigns of the Land in Altai' provides interesting facts that are closely related to the interests of our region. The article supplies documentary evidence to show that the Cabinet has recently avoided making land available to the Resettlement-Department, land that is vacant and suitable for allotment to new settlers. They try to keep an enormous fund of land for themselves, which by law must be used for resettlement, and instead to lease their own land to peasants whose allotments are too small.

The most interesting article in the publicist section of *Sovremennyi mir*, as in the previous issue, is the one by Yu. Steklov on the secret police and provocateurs in France. Here, we get a picture of secret-police activity throughout the republican period of French history.

Even A. Herzen pointed out that a partiality towards the police, and particularly towards espionage, is a national weakness of the French. I think it more likely that this is an international weakness, as will become apparent when the whole of international police-activity someday finds its historian. Domination by a numerically small and privileged group over the masses of the population and the centralisation of authority – this is the soil in which various secret-police agencies flourish. This must be the explanation of why we see in the French republic things that have never occurred in constitutional England.

In Yu. Steklov's article, a panorama of amazing facts unfolds before the reader, which might be taken for the product of malicious fantasy on the part of those who are enemies of the police and criminal investigators, were it not for the fact that they are recounted by the participants themselves, by representatives of the police and by the investigators in their memoirs, for instance, by the police prefect André, the lead detective Rossignol and others. The facts are all the more amazing because they relate to the republican period. If the French monarchy resorted to detectives, terrorist-provocations and other such activities to frighten the cowardly bourgeoisie and thus show them its *raison d'être*, that is one thing. It is also understandable when the secret police organise fictitious attempts on the monarch's life to show him their own *raison d'être*, just as he does in relation

---

5. *Russkoe bogatstvo*, January 1912, p. 92.

to society as a whole. But it is different with a republic, with its transparency and freedom of organisation for the ruling groups, where it would seem redundant to resort to Bonapartist ways of ruling and sufficient to rely on the natural strength of its social authority in the country. Yet, in the example of France, we see something else.

The republican opportunists make use of the entire apparatus and all the techniques of the Napoleonic police to the extent that they survived after the Commune. While the Radicals were in opposition, they fulminated against opportunists for retaining all of the police-devices that helped them to stay in power. But as soon as the Radicals were at the helm of government, they availed themselves of the entire police-apparatus used by their predecessors. An example is the police prefect André. Using secret-police methods he published an anarchist newspaper, *La Révolution Sociale*, and through his agents, who were the editors, he called for a social war, expropriation of the capitalists' property, terrorist-assassinations and, among other things, the murder of André himself. He organised an international congress of anarchists who met at a police-address. Almost all the anarchist assassination-attempts in France during the nineties were organised with police-participation. The attack on President Loubet[6] was the work of a police-agent. The famous bomb-explosion in the French parliament in 1893 was prepared by the police and financed with their money. The facts go on endlessly. To conclude, we will provide one comical scene. Anti-government disturbances were expected when the president of the Republic was passing through Paris, and thus the prefect decided to arrest the most active anarchists. For that purpose, all the heads of detectives were brought in.

> All the heads were sitting in a semi-circle, each with a list in his hands. And then the following curious scene begins. The prefect calls the name of an active anarchist who is to be arrested, and an officer, looking at his list responds.
>
> 'Dupont?' – asks the prefect.
>
> 'No', says the head of the first team, 'he mustn't be touched, he is my man'.
>
> 'Durant?'
>
> 'Durant? Yes, his name is on my list', says the head of the second team.
>
> 'Dubois?'
>
> 'It's true that I haven't met with him for a couple of months now, but he is not worth going after'.
>
> 'Dupin?'

---

6. [Émile Loubet was President of France from 1899 to 1906.]

At this point, there is no response. At last they've found one anarchist whose name is not on their lists of provocateurs. They telephone the Ministry of Internal Affairs.

'Can we arrest Dupin?'

'What are you up to, for goodness sake?' is the reply. 'By no means, not Dupin, he is one of ours'.

And so it continues. An inspector who was not privy to the secrets of the police could understand nothing of this comedy. And ultimately, for the sake of form, a few arrest-orders were issued.[7]

M.L.

---

7. *Sovremennyi mir*, February 1912, p. 229.

No. 27

'A Benefit-Performance by a Renegade'[1]

26 February 1912

Five years ago, a small but cosy gathering of former democrats issued the sensational collection *Vekhi*[2] in which they bitterly attacked the Russian intelligentsia. In this campaign against their own past, Messrs. Izgoev and Struve were in the forefront, in accordance with the law that the further a man goes to the left in his better days, the harder he moves to the right after hitting the bottom in liberalism.

The Russian intelligentsia are accused of hundreds of sins: lack of patriotism, irreligiosity, idleness, destruction of the family, debauchery, and so on and so forth. Even their most positive qualities turn out to be negatives; even their capacity for self-sacrifice – this most precious attribute of man as a social being, which is as necessary as it is irreplaceable in the struggle of all social classes – even this comes in for debunking and mockery. The intelligentsia were revolutionary, and that is enough for renegades who have passed the examination for patriotism and loyalty to foam at the mouth while pouncing upon them.

I do not know whether Mr. Izgoev, who attacks the intelligentsia's lack of faith, goes to Mass, or whether he keeps birch-rods at home to maintain the 'principles of the family' and to establish 'ties between parents and children'. But the fact that Mr. Struve is more than just a patriot in words is apparent from his article in the January issue of *Russkaya mysl'*, entitled 'All-Russian Culture and Ukrainian Particularism'. In this article, Mr. Struve comes out as a Russifier in the spirit of Count Bobrinsky, and lays an ideological foundation for administrative repression against the cultural-educational activities of the Ukrainian intelligentsia. Evidently the blessing of Antonii Volynsky,[3] who instructed the authors of *Vekhi*, was of some use to him.

Mr. Izgoev works in the spirit of counter-revolutionary liberalism on the pages of *Russkaya mysl'*, *Rech'*, and ... *Siberskaya zhizn'*. Among other things, he wrote a series of articles on P.A. Stolypin in which he portrays the evolution accomplished by the latter over five years. Mr. Izgoev was careless. The example is

---

1. [From *Obskaya zhizn'*, 26 February 1912.]
2. [*Vekhi* was a collection of articles on the Russian intelligentsia, published in Moscow in 1909. Put out by a group of journalists and philosophers with a religious-idealistic bent, who were close to the Cadets, the work attacked revolutionary-democratic traditions and Marxism. The group included N. Berdyaev, S. Bulgakov, M. Gershenzon, A. Izgoev, P. Struve and others.]
3. [Antonius Volynsky (1863–1936) was an ultra-reactionary priest, a prominent political figure, and a member of the Holy Synod.]

infectious, and someone might write about his own literary biography in the same way as he wrote about the political biography of Stolypin. What if such a biographer directly confronted Izgoev – as collaborator in the Marxist journals *Zhizn'* and *Obrazovanie* – with Izgoev the right-wing Cadet? That this has not happened is simply due to the fact that no-one has been willing to take up the task: Izgoev was trivial as a Marxist and he remains trivial as a renegade.

But be that as it may, he is beginning to find the recognition he so fully deserves. The telegraph informs us that Purishkevich, in his latest Duma-speech to defend the policy of Mr. Kasso, and in his dirty attacks on young people, referred to Izgoev and his article on Russian students. Finally, the true essence of Mr. Izgoev's work is getting the appreciation it deserves from those in whose interest he worked and continues to work. For six years now, both Izgoev and Struve have been ideologically arming the reaction. The only surprise is that their labours are being applied only in the seventh year. The Russian reactionaries are rich in all things except ideological baggage. Their squalid thought does not go beyond pogrom-ideology and fairy-tales about Finnish and Japanese millions[4] that expose, above all, their own venal nature. Only professional inertia can explain why such precious jewels for the reaction as are scattered about in the works of Messrs. Izgoev and Struve are being recognised and appreciated after such delay.

But justice always prevails. Izgoev fully deserves the kiss he has received from Purishkevich. And we have to hope it will not be the last one. However, it would be unjust to say that this is all Mr. Izgoev deserves. May he now also receive the spitting contempt due to him from those who do not see their task in flinging mud at the liberation-movement, at its representatives and those who have sacrificed for it.

M. Leonov

---

4. [The Japanese spy Akami, and the leader of the Finnish party of active resistance, Zilliacus, had the idea of providing financial assistance to separatist-circles in order to promote armed action against the tsarist régime. There were plans to purchase weapons for the Revolution in 1905. For what was done in this connection, see Pogonii, Sobolev et al. 2001, pp. 133–7.]

No. 28

'Postscript'[1]

29 February 1912

My article 'A Benefit-Performance by a Renegade', which appeared in No. 45 of *Obskaya zhizn'*, had already been accepted when I happened to read in No. 47 of *Rech'* the note by A. Izgoev in which he protests in print against 'the Purishkevich kisses that are worse than any slander'.

There is no doubting the fact that kisses from Purishkevich are worse than any slander. The only surprise is that Mr. Izgoev did not foresee them when he wrote his article in the notorious *Vekhi*. The kisses addressed to Izgoev from the reactionaries follow from the entire content of his article, as do all the conclusions that Purishkevich and Co. are drawing and, one hopes, will continue to draw in the future.

But in his note, Mr. Izgoev himself gives documentary confirmation that he worked for the benefit of reaction. Here is what he writes, among other things, in *Vekhi*: 'We have openly pointed out their shortcomings to the young people. But our work, of course, can only lead to practical results with the establishment of a genuine legal system in Russian life... This did not happen. Reaction won out'.

And consequently? Consequently, the 'practical result' of the work by Mr. Izgoev amounted merely to providing ideological armament for reactionaries.

For Mr. Izgoev to protest and be shocked by the kisses of Purishkevich can only be hypocrisy or *sancta simplicitas*.[2]

But Mr. Izgoev is not naïve. Consequently, Mr. Izgoev requests that the newspaper that printed the information about Purishkevich's Duma-speech also familiarise its readers with the contents of his note.

We are not able to do so, because in a free rendition we would risk detracting from the pearls of this counter-revolutionary liberal's confession. Let the reader familiarise himself with the original.

M. Leonov

---

1. [From *Obskaya zhizn'*, 29 February 1912.]
2. Holy simplicity (naïveté).

No. 29

'A Grandiose Strike'[1]

6 March 1912

For a whole week, the attention of the world has been focused on a conflict, unprecedented in numbers, between the million-strong army of English coal-miners and a group of coal-industrialists. Compared to this conflict, the war between Italy and Turkey[2] seems like a minor episode. And that is not surprising. Old dame Europe has witnessed many wars between peoples, and in that regard nothing surprises her, but this is only the first time that the war between classes and the great social question of our day have appeared fully-developed in the bloodless clash between the miners and the mine-owners.

The immediate reason for the confrontation is already clear enough. The coal-miners work in three eight-hour shifts, and in that regard they have achieved something for which workers in other branches and other countries are still striving. But given the piece-rate practised in the coal-regions of England, the miners' wages are far from uniform, because rich seams are worked along with the poor ones. Those working in poor seams often do not manage to earn eighty *kopeks* a day, and with the cost of living in England, that is not enough to survive. But even the average earnings of a coal-miner are not high. The coal-miners therefore demanded a minimum-wage, that is, a wage below which no owner can pay even a single worker. They specified the minimum as five shillings a day. The owners refused to meet the miners' demands, and the latter voted for a strike with a majority of five-hundred thousand votes against (just over) one-hundred thousand. They gave a warning period of one month, according to the conditions of the mine-owners, and after the deadline passed they refused to work.

From an economic point of view, the owners had good reasons for refusing the coal-miners' demand. According to their declaration, the rate of profit on capital invested in the coal-industry does not exceed 3.5 percent on average, less than the interest on our government-securities. If these are true figures, which of course cannot be verified, then satisfying the demand of the miners must significantly reduce the rate of profit and consequently put it below the normal average rate in England. In those conditions, the industrialists can invest their

---

1. [From *Obskaya zhizn'*, 6 March 1912.]
2. [The reference is to Italy's war against Turkey in 1911–12 with the aim of seizing the Turkish possessions of Tripolitania and Cyrenaica (modern Libya) in North Africa. The war ended in the defeat of Turkey and surrender of these territories to Italy by the Treaty of Lausanne in 1912.]

capital in some other branch. In any case, the stubbornness of the owners is quite understandable, and so is that of the workers who wish to survive.

The strike has begun. More than a million miners are on strike, eight-hundred thousand in the mines and more than two-hundred thousand above ground. In addition to their extraordinary solidarity, organisation and confidence of victory, together with the twenty million roubles the trade-union has in its treasury, the coal-miners have one enormous advantage on their side – the dependence of England's entire industrial and commercial life on the coal-industry. The strike is depriving England's capitalist organism of its sustenance and imposing a hunger-strike upon it, which it cannot long endure any more than the living organism of a man can survive without food. For the time being, England is living on inventories of coal, but they will soon be exhausted. The industries most closely connected with the coal-industry are already closing down. In addition to the coal-miners, about half a million men in other industries are already without work. According to rough calculations, two weeks of the strike impose a loss on England as a whole of up to one billion, two-hundred million roubles. The railways have already cut shipments by half. And the fleet, despite the supplies it has stored, also risks eventually running out of coal.

That is how matters stand. The workers are declaring that they can hold out for one and a half months. But the situation cannot go on that long. The blow to the economic organism of England caused by this strike is so great that both the government and the coal-industrialists are already prepared to make concessions. The government has accepted that the miners' demands are just, and it is trying to convince the owners to accept them by promising to pay for their losses out of state-funds in the case of a pay-increase for the workers. The question has even arisen, if the coal-owners are stubborn, of nationalising the mines. Two-thirds of the owners have already agreed in principle to the main demand of the miners for a minimum-wage. There can be no doubt of the workers' victory.

The miners' strike is not limited just to England. In America, one-hundred-and-sixty thousand miners went on strike demanding a wage-increase of 40 percent; in Germany's Ruhr coal-basin, about two-hundred thousand have struck; coal-miners in France are preparing a one-day demonstration-strike with the demand for an eight-hour working day and a minimum daily wage of five francs; the mine-workers' union of Austria has presented a demand to the coal-industrialists for a pay increase of 15 percent; even in Spain, unrest is spreading amongst the coal-miners; and in Russia twelve thousand went on strike in the Dombrovsky region. The strike-movement among coal-miners is thus becoming international.

Let us turn to the main causes of the strike and its importance. The cause of the strike lies only partly in the immediate factor that provoked it, whose significance was minor, and its consequence will only be to improve the material position of the coal-miners in accordance with their demands. But there are other causes that are deeper, and whose consequences will be incomparably greater.

The main cause both of the present strike and of last year's strike by dock- and rail-workers in England, together with the enormous mass movement in all countries against the rising cost of living, is precisely the rise in prices on products consumed by the popular masses. A rising cost of living, with a constant wage-level, is equivalent to a reduction of the latter. Although wages have risen everywhere, they have lagged far behind the rise in the prices on products. As a result, the English coal-miners have had to attack the profits of the owners in order to have wages commensurate with higher living costs.

But there is also another cause at work. It is natural to ask why living has become so expensive and is affecting the working masses of all countries; why, for instance, the workers of Austria and Germany are affected to an even greater extent, thanks to the tariffs that exist in those countries on grain and meat, than the workers in England, with its free trade; and why it is precisely in England that the high cost of living has driven the proletarian masses, numbering in the millions, to rush into the strike-struggle for a second year.

All this will become clear to us if we recall the specific character of the evolution that England is now living through in terms of its economic relations.

When England was the most advanced industrial country and had undivided dominion over the world-market, when its industry was beyond any competition, naturally the profits of the capitalists were high and English employers were more willing than those on the continent to make concessions to their workers. As a result, the economic position of the English proletariat was incomparably better than the state of affairs on the continent. But when England's monopoly position ended on the world-market; when German industry overtook English industry; when industry developed and strengthened in other countries, including Russia, and especially in America; when England began to be squeezed from all sides on the world-market and had to recognise the superiority of Germany, if only because it began to import more and more German manufactured goods, the position abruptly changed. The rate of profit declined, English employers began stubbornly to resist attempts by the workers to improve their position – and the typical result is that the workers' wages in the past decade have fallen not only relatively, namely, in comparison with the total profits of the entire class of capitalists, but, in many branches, also absolutely. And this has occurred along with an incredible rise in the cost of living! Is it any surprise that as a result of all these causes we are witnessing a development of the strike-movement that is unprecedented in the history of the West?[3]

---

3. The general strike throughout Russia in the days of October and December is not included here, since it had a different character.

As for the immediate consequences of the strike, they will entail first of all an improvement in the material position of the coal-miners. But this will be the least important consequence of the strike. We must not forget that the above-listed causes will continue to operate, and the coal-miners will not be able to hold onto their gains for long. The rising cost of living will undermine the budget of the proletariat, and new strikes are inevitable, both by the miners themselves and by workers in other branches of industry. But if the owners are already talking about the disadvantage of doing business in the coal-industry should the miners' demands be met, they will have even more reason to oppose any further rise in wages, which, however, is inevitable; otherwise, given the rise in prices, all the gains from the strike will be reduced to nothing. But on the other hand, it is impossible to throw away the coal-industry on the grounds that it is unprofitable. If a rise in the price of coal does not follow, there can be only one other way out: transfer of the coal-mines to the state, namely, the nationalisation of the coal-industry. The same fate is expected first and foremost in the other most important branches of industry. And where this might lead can be seen in the fact that the proletariat in England constitutes an enormous majority of the population, and with universal suffrage can easily win a government-majority. It is difficult to say what route the further development of England will take. Only one thing is beyond doubt: the productive forces of England are already outgrowing the existing production-relations, to express things in Marxist terms, and what this leads to is known well enough from world-history.

M. Leonov

No. 30

'The Workers' Movement in February'[1]

9 March 1912

Compared to the previous month, the workers' movement in February may not have strengthened, but it has also not weakened. As far as one can judge by information available in the press – and that information is always incomplete – there were more than thirty strikes in February. The number of strike-participants is not always given in newspaper-telegrams and chronicles. But to the extent that we have such information, we can say that the number of strikers exceeded twenty thousand. The biggest strike was by the coal-miners in the 'Saturn' mines in Poland, which ended favourably for the workers. The highest percentage of the other strikes, as could be expected, was in metallurgical enterprises. There were eleven of these, of which six ended in a full or partial victory for the workers, two failed, and there is no information on the other three. The growth of the strike movement in mechanised factories and the comparatively high percentage of successes for the workers are explained, of course, by the fact that the metallurgical industry is currently going through an expansion, and all the factories, in particular those working for the treasury, are flooded with orders.

As regards strikes in other industries, we have information about the outcome only in eight cases, of which five ended unsuccessfully and three successfully.

There is no information in the press concerning a whole number of strikes in small shops, of which there have been many. For instance, with regard to St. Petersburg, we read in *Stolichnaya molva* that 'There have recently been a number of strikes among workers in the tailoring industry. The strikes were brief and usually ended successfully for the workers. The only demands yet to be met are those by Jakobsen's workers, who have been striking for five days for a rise in wages'. The press reports a number of strikes by masons in Poland, but they have been brief and involved few workers, for that reason not attracting much press-attention.

In general, the industrial revival continues to find expression everywhere in a revival of the workers' movement.

M.L.

---

1. [From *Obskaya zhizn'*, 9 March 1912.]

No. 31

Survey of the Journals *Russkoe bogatstvo* (February), *Nasha zarya* Nos. 1–2, and *Mir* (January)[1]

11 March 1912

Of all the material published in the February issue of *Russkoe bogatstvo*, the most remarkable is a fragment from an unfinished work by Tolstoy, 'Posthumous Papers of the Old Man Fedor Kuzmich'. When Emperor Alexander I suddenly died in Taganrog in 1825, the most diverse legends began to circulate concerning his death. Among the people, the most popular legend said that the emperor did not die, but rather fled from the vanities of court-life, and a soldier of the guards who looked like him was buried in his place. On the other hand, there was much guessing in corresponding circles concerning the following quite unusual fact. In 1836, near Krasnoufimsk, the authorities detained an unknown rider who was dressed in peasant-clothing but by all indications belonged to a completely different social circle. Upon being arrested, the unknown man said his name was Fedor Kuzmich, a tramp who could not remember his relatives. According to the law, he received twenty blows with a rod and was given a sentence of hard labour that he served in Tomsk province.

In exile, he became famous as a seer and saint, and many people went to him for different sorts of advice. From his manner and habits, all who knew him concluded that the old man previously belonged to high society. The old man died in 1864. And then the legend took root in the popular consciousness that the former prisoner and tramp was none other than Alexander I, who had exchanged the imperial crown and palace for a pilgrim's staff and a hermit's hovel.

Lev Nikolaevich was very interested in the legend, so much so that he decided to take it as the starting point for a work that he began to write, a biography of Alexander I, supposedly written by the latter in the person of the old man Fedor Kuzmich in the twilight of his years. And even after the legend was finally dispelled by Grand Duke Nikolai Mikhailovich on the basis of research in archival documents, L.N. Tolstoy did not consider that a sufficient reason to put aside the work he had begun. Only illness and death prevented him from completing it. And even if it was not historically true, this was understandable if one recalls how close and familiar to him the departure of Alexander I must have seemed, since one week before his own long life ended in death, he too disappeared.

All of the merits in the works of this incomparable artist are evident in this unfortunately brief fragment. The psychology of the child who was to be tsar, his

---

1. [From *Obskaya zhizn'*, 11 March 1912.]

first steps on life's road, the situation in the palace – they are all provided with remarkable clarity in a few pages. These things cannot be retold here, and we can only recommend to readers that they read the original for themselves.

After this small fragment from the great writer, one hesitates to say anything further regarding the other *belles-lettres* in this issue, and we will pass over them to look at the publicist section.

In this section the most substantial and interesting items are the article by Professor I. Luchitsky on 'The Alienation of National Assets in France at the end of the XVIII Century' and an article by A. Gornfel'd 'On the Interpretation of Artistic Works'.

The article by I. Luchitsky deals with a most important moment in the history of the first French Revolution – the sale of lands confiscated from the Church and the aristocracy. Strange though it may be, this question has not been sufficiently illuminated in the historical literature, and even today it provokes debates among historians of the French Revolution. Some have the opinion that small peasant-agriculture was the main beneficiary from sale of the confiscated lands, while others think the opposite – most of the land went to the bourgeoisie. I. Luchitsky gives an interesting summary of the resolutions of the National Assembly, the Legislative Assembly and the Convention on the agrarian question, in which there is continuous indecision on the part of these institutions between a policy of selling the land to the highest bidder, and a policy of keeping the land for small-peasant property-owners in order to tie their interests to the interests of the revolution.

As for the interesting article by A. Gornfel'd, the basic ideas are approximately as follows. The history of every artistic work only begins, rather than ending, when it first makes its appearance. Every generation has its own understanding of the author's thinking and the character of the people involved.

Griboedov's Chatsky, and Chatsky as he is understood by people in the twentieth century, are two different people. Shakespeare's heroes are also regarded differently in different periods of history. An artistic work is a form, an algebraic formula, into which each epoch injects its own content. Just as a word in a language can completely change its original meaning over the course of a century, so an artistic work changes its meaning compared with what the author himself intended to express. But the starting point for creating the history of any work of art must be the author's thought and his own understanding of the characters he creates, not the arbitrary guesses of people from a later period.

The author objects to the distorted understanding of artistic works and to a so-called subjective interpretation. But he has not shown how one interpretation of an author's intentions is more legitimate than another. Where is the line that separates 'subjective' from 'objective'? He cites the general spirit of the work, which must preclude arbitrary interpretations. But the general spirit, after all, is also understood differently by different generations. Essentially, the author is struggling against subjectivism, yet he remains on the ground of subjectivism himself. The legitimacy of my interpretation, as opposed to yours, cannot possibly be established: both are legitimate by the fact that they both exist.

The author leaves out the fact that artistic works are interpreted differently not only by different generations but also by the different groups of a single generation. And this is inevitable in class-society, with its different ways of thinking on the part of each class. Yet it would be incorrect to think that there are as many Hamlets as there are people who have read the famous work by Shakespeare, although A. Gornfel'd, taking the position that he does, cannot prove the opposite. There are definite ways of understanding works of art, corresponding to the position and ideology of definite social classes and groups. The details of possible disagreements within these typical interpretations have no essential significance. These typical interpretations do not occur by accident but, to the contrary, are the product of social necessity. From this point of view, the history of an artistic work following its appearance can be scientifically grounded. To the ideologues of 'subjective sociology', on the contrary, no such ground can be discovered in a chaos of opinions, such that the author's own understanding is not a point of convergence but rather of disagreements.

———

In *Nasha zarya*, E. Smirnov touches upon an important question in the article on 'Election-Rights of Deputies of the Second Curia'. As we know, one of the articles on the composition of the Duma provides for losing the title of Duma-Deputy as a consequence of losing the qualification. But every person who is elected by residence or public-service qualification, or in the workers' curia, loses the right to be a Deputy after arriving in the Duma and giving up official public service, one's residence, or work in the factory. The Senate has recognised that a logical interpretation of this article contradicts the very existence of the State-Duma, and a clarification, as it were, has acknowledged the right of members of the Duma who have been elected on the residential or public-service qualification to stand for re-election to the next Duma. It is a different matter with the workers' curia. Those elected to be deputies from the workers' curia cease to be workers of the enterprise in which they previously worked, and they cannot participate in the next election from factory-enterprises. For that reason, the author of the article suggests a correction to the existing law on the Duma's composition, according to which the deputies elected in the workers' curia might again take part in elections in the enterprise where they worked before being elected to the Duma.

There is a substantial article by Ermansky, characterising our big bourgeoisie and its forms of organisation.

We should also make note of a witty article devoted to the famous 'English guests' and explaining the ridiculous role that the Cadets played in that entire affair.

The other articles are of a party-political nature, and are directed against the tendency of Marxism represented by the journal *Prosveshchenie* and the newspaper *Zvezda*.

———

In the journal *Mir* there are numerous rich illustrations that capture one's attention. The journal's main merits, it seems, are to be found in its illustrations. The atlas of illustrations that accompanies the work published in the journal by Konrad Gyunter, on 'The Origin of Man', is especially valuable. The *belles-lettres* of the journal are not brilliant, but they are diverse.

Among other things, there is an interesting essay on the relations between Frederick III, when he was still Crown-Prince, and Bismarck.

Whereas the current Crown-Prince of Germany is discontented with Bethmann-Hollweg and his own father, being unhappy over the latter's 'peaceful disposition and liberalism', Wilhelm's father was liberally disposed and expressed dissatisfaction with Bismarck and the grandfather of the German Emperor. He even had one secret meeting with Richter, the late leader of the Free-minded People's Party.[2]

The journal conveniently provides a section of scientific reviews, where the reader can pick up all the news from the world of the natural and other sciences.

M.L.

———

2. [*Freisinnige Volkspartei*]

No. 32

'Reply to Mr. Lyubosh'[1]

14 March 1912

Intending to take a stab at our newspaper, S. Lyubosh writes in *Sovremennoe slovo*:

> The people who live in Siberia are blissful optimists.
>
> Reports on the timeliness of introducing a *zemstvo* in Siberia are being stubbornly banned by the local administration, yet *Obskaya zhizn'* credulously informs us: 'Strong rumours are circulating regarding the departure of L.A. Kasso, Minister of Popular Education. His deputy, Maksim Kovalevsky, has been summoned, but he has declared that he would only agree to take up the portfolio on the condition that the Cabinet of Ministers should be answerable to representative institutions'.
>
> Perhaps the editor of *Obskaya zhizn'* would agree to a cabinet led by M.M. Kovalevsky as head of the main department on press-matters.

No, Mr. Lyubosh, he would not agree. But you would probably do so, if not in Kovalevsky's ministry then in Milyukov's – and if not as head of the main department on press-matters, then as head of the main prison-administration. A journalist, after all, carries a heavy responsibility. There are so many provincial newspapers to read in order to collect material for a feuilleton, and one does occasionally end up in a mess...

Our note [cited by S. Lyubosh] came directly from the capital-telegrams of *Ural'skaya zhizn'*. Therefore, we are not responsible for it. But we are pleased with this formal objection. Sometimes reports are knowingly absurd, and we do not print them. Thus we did not print, for example, the report of a 'change of course' which *Rech'* and *Sovremennoe slovo* flooded their columns with. We knew that the method of liberal propaganda consists, among other things, of attributing liberal intentions to the reactionaries who are in power. We knew that nothing has happened that might really change the course, apart from the eager wish of a frightened Cadet to see 'movement on the waters'.

But what is there that is impossible in principle, if one might use that expression, in a report that M. Kovalevsky was invited to take the post of Minister of Popular Education? If a liberal becomes a minister, does that mean he will be a liberal minister? After all, we know that in France M. Kovalevsky was a republican, but in Russia he is a monarchist. If you read his pre-election feuilleton in

---

1. [From *Obskaya zhizn'*, 14 March 1912.]

Russkoe slovo, does the author differ much from an Octobrist? In our opinion, Mr. Kokovtsov would risk nothing if he invited Mr. Kovalevsky to take up a ministerial post. Indeed, there was a time when the Cadet Kutler was Minister of Agriculture, and Prince Urusov was Assistant Minister of Foreign Affairs. And did Milyukov agree to enter a single ministry with Stolypin?

We have no reason to believe in the onset of a 'new course'; we do not believe that Milyukov has once and for all renounced his dream of a portfolio; we do not believe that Maklakov delivered a genuinely liberal speech; we do not believe that Izgoev has stopped throwing mud at the liberation-movement, or that P. Struve has completed his evolution from Left to Right.

But why should we believe that cooperation between Mr. Kokovtsov and Kovalevsky is impossible? And if the rumours mentioned above have no factual basis (which we had no way of establishing), the basis for such rumours has been fully established both by previous examples of Cadets' cooperation with the bureaucracy and by the evolution that they have recently undergone. After all, Mr. Kovalevsky is not a Cadet; he is further to the right than the Cadets.

Therefore, Mr. Lyubosh, we wish to you and your Party the realisation of your long-standing desires, and we will not be competing against you...

M.L.

No. 33

'Once Again on a Siberian *Zemstvo*'[1]

15 March 1912

In the 1 March edition of *Zabaikal'skaya nov'* there is a response to my article 'A Siberian *Zemstvo* and the Siberian Press', in which I mentioned, among other things, the Chita newspaper's position on that issue.

Quoting my article, in which I demonstrate the inapplicability of the statute of 1890 to Siberia, not to mention how incompatible it is with genuine self-government in general, the author writes: 'The newspaper apparently forgets that in the draft-legislation[2] there is an article that extends voting rights in elections to the provincial and district-boards to people who do not qualify on the basis of the property-census but have been educated to the second class in school and have lived in the electoral region for a year. Given this aspect of the law, there is no need to be distressed over the absence in Siberia of census-qualified private landowners'.

We certainly are not forgetting either this extension of the population's voting rights in the new draft, by comparison with the 1890 statute, or the other improvements it includes. And it is not we – the opponents of the census-based system as it applies in general to local self-government or elections to state-institutions – who are 'distressed over the absence in Siberia of census-qualified private landowners'. What must 'distress' us in the draft-legislation is the absence of voting rights for the entire population, without reference to differences on the basis of property or education. We must be 'distressed' by the fact that the proposed *zemstvo* will have fewer rights than the *zemstvo* that already exists in Russia, where the interpretive activity of the provincial administration is constrained by the authority and weight of the governing landowner-class in the *zemstvo* and in the country as a whole. Finally, we are 'distressed' because the mutilated bill is being presented to Siberia by people who pledged in the Duma-elections to defend a democratic *zemstvo* for Siberia and had no mandate just to repaint the building of 3 June.

The newspaper further comments: 'We can affirm that only a politically blind person would count upon early arrival of the time when Siberia will have a democratic *zemstvo*'. To speak that way, one must be very frightened by the reaction and firmly believe in the stability of the 3 June bloc. We do not share that confidence with the newspaper and, even if we did share it, we would

---

1. [From *Obskaya zhizn'*, 15 March 1912.]
2. That is, the draft-legislation that was passed in the Duma.

be recommending a renovation of the 3 June building to the people who live in it. For that reason, I can only regret that the final lines of my article were misinterpreted and that my opponent thought they were pessimistic. To the contrary, one could not be a greater pessimist than the people who agree to be satisfied with such legislation, or even more, whose hands were involved in the draft with which they plan to make Siberia happy.

The newspaper is convinced, as we are, that Siberia is waiting for a democratic *zemstvo*. 'Someday that time must come. But when? Is it not better to get a bird in the hand now and forget about the crane in the sky?'

Alas! The whole point is that the question cannot be posed that way. The legislation has passed the Duma, but not yet the Council. There is a very good chance that the State-Council will reject it entirely, or, maintaining its tactics of recent months, will make unacceptable amendments to it. So where is the bird in the hand? There is no such bird, so the question is: Which is better, a bird in the sky or the crane in the sky? And once it is expressed that way, we prefer the crane.

It is only at first glance that opportunism appears to be 'reasonable'. But in reality it is the least promising tactic, and in that regard it can be compared with cheap goods that, according to the German proverb, are simultaneously the most expensive.

Those who mistake a bird in the sky for a bird in the hand will have to learn this fact and remember the simple political rule that in order to seize a bird in the hand, one must strive for the crane in the sky.

M. Leonov

No. 34

'A Little Pamphlet: "Poetry of the Yellow House"'[1]

16 March 1912

'Here, could you write a review', said the editor, handing me a half-page with five short verses; on the sheet there is a note: 'For review by the editors of *Obskaya zhizn*".

I took the sheet and began to read: 'Konstantin Olimpov: Airplane-Poems. Nerve-Centre I. "Blood I"'.

What is this, what blood, and what does blood have to do with anything? And to the side it says 'Window of Europe' with 'ego' in the middle, in Latin.[2]

---

1. [From *Obskaya zhizn'*, 16 March 1912.]
2. [The poems by Konstantin Olimpov, as indicated by Preobrazhensky's reaction, did not make any literal sense in Russian. Still less do they have any literal meaning in English. It is not possible to give an 'accurate' translation because at least half of the words used do not exist in Russian. Markov 1968, p. 75 reproduces the diagram to which Preobrazhensky refers.

      Airplane Poesas
Nerve Centre I [*nervnik*]   Window of Europe
      Ego
Blood I   1912, Spring
    The origin of the River
    Universal Ego-Futurism

Markov refers to this as 'a typically Olimpovian quasi-cabalistic chart'. He adds that 'Judging by the statements of those who knew him and by much of his poetry, he was a madman... In fact, he may be the most typical ego-futurist poet. In his poetry Olimpov expresses a desire for madness, proclaims himself a genius... and glorifies aviation (for instance, the poem "Shmeli" ["Bumble-bees"]). His diction is characterised... by a wide use of neologisms and foreign words.... [H]is work becomes nothing but a chaotic verbal conglomeration echoing his occult erudition, as in... "Interlyudia" [Interlude]'.

In Terra (ed.) 1985, p. 161, the poetic 'programme' of ego-futurists is described in terms of creating 'an "irrational poetry" to understand "the unclarity of the earth"... Poetry was seen as an apotheosis of the ego, a quest for self-revelation'. We have attempted to translate Olimpov's work, but given the difficulties involved, we also include below the full Russian text from Preobrazhensky's article:

Интерлюдия
Эмпиреи – эмблема феургий,
Силуэт сабеизма фетиша.
В роднике вдохновенных вальпургий
Ищет лунное сердце финиша.
Электрический пламень миража
Обескрайнил кудрявые спазмы
И волна вольной волною виража
Метит путь из огня протоплазмы.
Искрострунный безгрезия крензель
Тки, шутя, экзотичную гибель.
Позвони, литургийных бурь вензель,

I began to read the poetry and could not contain my laughter. Here is the first poem:

INTERLUDE

Empyreans are the emblem of theurgies,
A silhouette of the Sabaism of a fetish.
In a spring of inspired walpurgies
The lunar heart looks for a finish.
The electrical fire of a mirage
Brings closer the curly spasms
And wave by wave it turns
Marking a path out of the protoplasmic fire.
A sparkle-stringed innocent krenzel[3]
Weave, joking, an exotic death.
Ring, a monogram of liturgical storms
And bleach it with light of the sun.
Gonfalons of musical religions
They are nuanced in a radiant scale.
We – poets, prophets, surgeons –
Like lightning we play gods.

Or here is the ending of the poem 'Bumble-bees'.

The nerves of the fliers tire – the pilots are terribly restless,
They fly to earth. Applauding wolfhounds greet them.[4]

A splendid epithet on hunting with hounds; but why wolfhounds and not fox-hounds or gun-dogs? It is insulting to many hunters.

И себя светом солнечно выбель.
Музыкальных религий хоругви
Нюансируют в радужной гамме.
Мы – поэты, пророки, хирурги –
Мольненосно играем богами!']

3. [The *mezinke tanz*, or *krenzel*, is a special dance by Ashkenazi Jews at a wedding to honour parents who have just married off their last child. The *krenzel*, or crown, is the wreath of flowers traditionally placed on the mother's head during the dance. The parents sit on chairs in the middle of the dance-floor, as friends and family dance around them in a circle, with each person kissing them as they pass.]

4. [Ослаби нервы летные, – пилоты жутко ёрзают,
Летят к земле. Встречайте их, рукоплесканья борзые!]

And here is the beginning of another poem:

AMOURETTE

Dance ceremoniously, prophet,
Sing praise to the Sorcerer's excesses.
With the flaming express,
Of ecstatic magpies.[5]

I read through all the poems, all of them written in the spirit of these excerpts, and I said to the editor:

'It is a witty caricature, though'.
   'What caricature? These were written seriously!'
   'Impossible', I answered, 'what is there serious about them?'
   'Yes, I assure you, they are serious; this is not the first time I have read works by this poet'.

So I begin to wonder: what if they really are serious? And even now I cannot decide.

Try to write a review after that.

Write that the poems are a witty caricature of our decadents, and then it will suddenly turn out that all of this was written seriously.

Write that the relatives of this poet must arrange a private hospital-room for him – and then it will turn out that all of this is, indeed, a caricature.

M.L.

---

5. Танцуй торжественней, пророк,
Воспой Кудесному эксцессы,
Воспламеняющим экспрессом
Экзальтированных сорок.

No. 35

'The Price of a Cadet's Conscience'[1]

18 March 1912

About two years ago, a grandiose scandal broke out in Baku. There was a mighty Baku millionaire named Tagiev – the owner of several enormous stores, oilfields, his own newspaper and the Tiflis governor, whom he had lured into his service – and at the age of 75 this wealthy man married a 15 year-old beauty. One fine day, he learned of his wife's feelings for one of his employees, the engineer Bebutov.

The Asiatic imagination of Tagiev led him to devise a reprisal against his rival in which disdain for humanity and a savage tyranny worthy of Genghis Khan were combined with his own sense of being above the law and of the omnipotence of gold, which can purchase anything.

Together with the captain of the border-guards, Mamed-Bekov, and a senior officer for special assignments under the Baku municipal governor, Tagiev lured Bebutov to his palace and there tied him to a stake. In the presence of women, they subjected the unfortunate engineer to such shameless humiliations that the victim refused to speak of them because of his shame.

After the company of barbarians finished their mockery of the victim, Tagiev telephoned the police and ordered them to beat Bebutov, who was now subjected to further assaults.

Overcoming the difficulties involved, the victim managed to institute legal proceedings against the 'master' of Baku, and now the omnipotent millionaire finds himself on the defendant's bench.

But Tagiev is not going to prison without a fight, especially when he himself built the prison and donated it to the government. He has resolved to defend himself. But on his own, of course, he cannot tie three words together. His eloquence is in his gold, and he will have famous attorneys do his talking. And does the reader know that the man who came to serve the high-handed Croesus is the same one who for five years has been singing so beautifully in the Duma about the inviolability of personality, respect for human dignity and other such wonderful things? Does he know that Tagiev's defender is Maklakov, one of the leaders of the Party of 'popular freedom'?

Some say Tagiev purchased Maklakov for twenty-five thousand, others say for a hundred thousand. In the State-Duma they made jokes about this, saying this sum is fair for an advocate, but too little for a deputy – still less for a liberal deputy and a party-leader. Maklakov did sell himself too cheaply, especially if we

---

1. [From *Obskaya zhizn'*, 18 March 1912.]

remember that he sold not just a few speeches, but his entire reputation, everything he has done in the past and, like a clown beating himself up for money, has exposed his own liberal hypocrisy.

But it is not Maklakov alone who is defending Tagiev. His colleague in the defence is the Duma-member Zamyslovsky, the same Zamyslovsky whose name is so often raised whenever there is talk of 'black money'. In the Tagiev case, Zamyslovsky is in his element, and we expect that he will share his experience with his colleague in the defence.

I would give a great deal for the opportunity to hear Maklakov's speech. Indeed, what can he say in Tagiev's defence? Will he show that there was no stake and no 'candle', and that if the victim is too ashamed even to speak of all the revolting humiliations he endured, then that fact alone is sufficient reason to consider the incident legally non-existent? Or will he be talented enough to find some other way and mount a defence in the way Bulatsel' did when he defended the pogromists in Kiev?

'Are the people before you really Black Hundreds and thugs' – he said, addressing the judges – 'they are "glorious Zaporozhian Cossacks"'.

It seems that the 'glorious Zaporozhian Cossacks', after receiving a fifty-*kopek* slap on the snout 'for the affair', were quite happy with their attorney. Perhaps Maklakov will also roll out before the judges a picture of how our 'grandfathers lived in olden times', showing that Tagiev is simply a brilliant page from a glorious past, squeezed into the little grey book of our own day, where everything has become shallow and people do not even know how to sell themselves, and where such great figures as Tagiev cannot even turn around without cracking the ribs of some 'neighbour'. And perhaps he will show that love for far-off people, as Friedrich Nietzsche said, is higher than love for a neighbour, and that 'we sing our praises to the madness of the strong'. And who knows, perhaps he will infect the judges with his attitude and even persuade the victim to regard his unhealed wounds and outraged feelings as something small and trivial in the face of eternity.

Yes, I would love to listen to Maklakov.

Moreover, he is no novice in such matters. Not so long ago he, along with Teslenko, another Cadet leader, defended some thieving Moscow quartermasters. After his thunderous speeches against embezzlement in the Duma and in the newspaper *Rech'* comes his defence of those quartermasters in a trial! A government-representative, the procurator, lays the charges, and the representatives of liberalism provide the defence against them. What a touching picture!

Of course, the leaders of liberalism did not provide a defence for nothing, but rather for the same money that they knew very well originated in the state-treasury. Whose role is more humiliating and shameful: that of the people who, with epic calmness, 'steal a soldier's boots' and go to the convict battalions in consequence, or that of the people who defend these thieves for money that was acquired through the same robbery, and then return in good conscience to the Tauride Palace to inveigh against bribery and embezzlement? Can one possibly be surprised now by the latest behaviour of Maklakov? Is there really any infamy, to put it mildly, of which such people are not capable?

There is a pitiful sophism, originating among professional lawyers, holding that political convictions cannot be an obstacle to defending cases such as those of the quartermasters. The wretchedness of that argument is all too obvious. The trials of the quartermasters, like that of Tagiev, are political trials in the broadest sense of the word, and any liberal who traded places with the procurator in such a trial might justifiably be called an Azef[2] of justice.

M. Leonov

---

2. [Evno Azef (1869–1918) was a Socialist-Revolutionary provocateur who worked for the secret police in organising the assassinations of other members of the Socialist-Revolutionary Party.]

No. 36

'In Memory of A.I. Herzen (born 25 March 1812 – died 9 January 1870)'[1]

25 March 1912

Today marks the centenary of the birth of Alexander Ivanovich Herzen, the great Russian publicist and social figure of the epoch of the peasants' emancipation. If, on the occasion of honouring Pushkin, it would have been redundant and insulting to the reader to provide a biographical essay on Russia's greatest poet, unfortunately the same cannot be said regarding our great publicist, a large part of whose life was spent in voluntary exile and whose collected works are still not published in full in Russia.

A.I. Herzen was the illegitimate son of a wealthy Russian landowner, Ivan Alekseevich Yakovlev, and a German woman whom he brought from abroad. As so often happens, the union of the two races bore excellent fruit. Herzen was raised in the spirit of the century and the surroundings in which he spent his childhood. He learned three languages, taught to him by foreign tutors, and hungrily read everything that he found in his father's quite abundant library. Already in his early youth, he developed strong social instincts, a thirst for adventure, thoughtful tendencies and the aspiration to write – characteristics that accompanied Herzen throughout his life. Already at 17 years of age, he wrote a philosophical discussion of Schiller's *Wallenstein*. At 20, Herzen entered Moscow University, where a circle of youths was forming at the time with an interest in social and political questions. In 1834, Herzen was banished along with other members of the circle to Perm and Vyatka, whence he was transferred to Vladimir by special petition of the adviser to the provincial administration. There, he married N.A. Zakhar'ina and had a son, Aleksandr, who subsequently became a well-known scholar and physiologist. In 1840, Herzen received permission to return to Moscow, where he joined the Stankevich circle, which was famous for nurturing the remarkable Russian writers of the forties. Herzen joined a social-literary group of people who called themselves 'Westernisers'. Study of Hegel and other philosophers enriched Herzen's theoretical thought and had a strong influence on his entire world-view. In 1842, Herzen was again banished to Novgorod, but within a year left his post and returned to Moscow. In 1847, following his father's death, he left to go abroad permanently.

From that moment the second period of his life began. At first Herzen's mood was joyful, as can be seen from letters of the time. But the events of 1848, that is, above all, the ferocious suppression of the workers' uprising in Paris, and the

---

1. [From *Obskaya zhizn'*, 25 March 1912.]

triumph everywhere of reaction over the European revolutionary movement during the following years, caused Herzen to have a profound spiritual crisis and become totally disillusioned with the present and future of Europe. But this newborn loss of faith in Europe led, with a psychological inevitability, to faith in Russia. This hope for Russia became the final refuge for Herzen's thought and the focus for all this future practical activities. Banished from Paris, Herzen took Swiss citizenship and then moved for good to London, where he established a famous free-Russian publishing house, and in 1857 began to publish the illegal journal *Kolokol*, which had enormous influence on the leading strata of Russian society and was even read by Emperor Alexander II himself. The enormous role that Herzen played in the Emancipation of the peasants is well known.

It is also well known that in the fifties and sixties he was the main focus of the entire Russian-emancipation movement of that epoch. On the other hand, he actively supported the international movement, especially in Italy; he contributed to French socialist newspapers such as the Proudhonist *La Voix du Peuple*, for example, which he supported financially and in which he headed a Russian department; and finally, he provided numerous services to emigrants from all countries who had come to London after the victory of reaction. His sympathies for the Polish movement in 1863 repelled a significant part of Russian liberal society, but, on the other hand, the young generation, grouped around Chernyshevsky and Dobrolyubov, considered him not sufficiently radical, such that he travelled his own road to the end of his life.

Herzen died in Paris on 9 January 1870, of pneumonia.

As a political activist Herzen played an enormous role in the social movement in Russia. But in this activity, his remarkably original point of view concerning the bourgeois civilisation of Europe had no essential significance. The struggle for all those principles that he defended in practice could be based elsewhere. It is interesting, at this point, to compare the views of Herzen and Marx, with whom, so to speak, his relations were completely rotten. Very soon after the July Days of 1848, Herzen understood that the Revolution had come to an end, and he looked with irony and regret upon those of its participants who did not understand the meaning of what had transpired and stubbornly awaited repetition of the movement, even composing in advance lists of members for provisional governments. Marx, too, as early as 1849, and decisively by 1850, became convinced that the period of bourgeois revolutions had ended, and he caustically laughed at those who had learned and understood nothing of what had happened. Herzen's remarkable characterisation of the bourgeois and petty-bourgeois way of life that triumphed after 1848 in Europe, and in France above all, corresponded in many ways with what Marx wrote on this theme in *The Communist Manifesto* and other works. Here are a few examples of how Herzen characterised the petty bourgeoisie compared to the knighthood of feudal times.

> The knight was more *himself*, more of a *person*, and kept up his dignity, as he understood it, whence he was in essence not dependent either on wealth or on position; his personality was what mattered. In the petty bourgeois the personality is concealed or does not stand out because it is not what matters; what matters is the commodity, the business, affairs, and above all *property*.[2]
>
> Under the influence of the petty bourgeoisie, everything was changed in Europe. Chivalrous honour was replaced by the honesty of the book-keeper, elegant manners by propriety, courtesy by affectation, pride by a readiness to take offence, parks by kitchen-gardens, palaces by hotels open to *all* (that is, all who have money).[3]

Herzen agreed with Marx not only in his negative view of the ruling bourgeoisie, but also in his belief that deliverance from the petty bourgeoisie, and the further progress of mankind, were possible only with the triumph of the 'fourth estate'. But at this point their disagreements began.

It is true that in his article 'On Liberty'[4] – which, even without exaggeration, on the occasion of an anniversary can be called a work of genius and, in terms of form, an unattainable perfection of prose – Herzen wrote: 'If the people should also be defeated in England, as in Germany during the peasant-wars, as in France in the July Days, then the China foretold by John Stuart Mill[5] is not far off. The transition to it will take place imperceptibly... Timid and sensitive people say this is impossible. I desire nothing better than to agree with them, but I see no reason to do so. The tragic inevitably consists in just this: the idea that might

---

2. Herzen 1905, p. 103.
3. Ibid.
4. Herzen 1905.
5. It is a question of achieving such a level of well-being and, at the same time, social peace, that any further movement is impossible because there is no need for it.
[Mill wrote: 'We have a warning example in China – a nation of much talent, and, in some respects, even wisdom, owing to the rare good fortune of having been provided at an early period with a particularly good set of customs, the work, in some measure, of men to whom even the most enlightened European must accord, under certain limitations, the title of sages and philosophers. They are remarkable, too, in the excellence of their apparatus for impressing, as far as possible, the best wisdom they possess upon every mind in the community, and securing that those who have appropriated most of it shall occupy the posts of honour and power. Surely the people who did this have discovered the secret of human progressiveness, and must have kept themselves steadily at the head of the movement of the world. On the contrary, they have become stationary – have remained so for thousands of years; and if they are ever to be farther improved, it must be by foreigners. They have succeeded beyond all hope in what English philanthropists are so industriously working at – in making a people all alike, all governing their thoughts and conduct by the same maxims and rules; and these are the fruits. The modern regime of public opinion is, in an unorganised form, what the Chinese educational and political systems are in an organised; and unless individuality shall be able successfully to assert itself against this yoke, Europe, notwithstanding its noble antecedents and its professed Christianity, will tend to become another China'. See Mill 1955, pp. 104–5)]

rescue the people and steer Europe towards new destinies is *unprofitable* for the ruling class; and for this class, if it were consistent and bold, the only thing that is profitable would be a state with American slavery!'.[6]

As can be seen from these lines, Herzen allowed for the possibility that history might proceed along two lines and that defeat of the popular masses, together with the ascendance of a bourgeois replica of China, was just as possible as further progress through victory over the ruling classes. For Marx, no such alternatives existed. He saw that the victory of the fourth estate is inevitable and that it follows from the very fact of the stabilisation and full development of bourgeois society. Marx proved to be correct, and his faith has been justified by the entire course of the international workers' movement.

We also see that Herzen speaks of the fourth estate not in the proper sense, but rather as the people in general. For Marx, on the contrary, a comparison of the peasant-movement of sixteenth-century Germany with the July uprising of the proletariat was impossible. Finally, Herzen believed the German period of civilisation would be replaced by a Slavic period, and he thought that the motive power of progress in this direction was the Russian people, united in their village-commune.[7] History has not justified his faith. Russia is moving forward on the path of civilisation not thanks to, but rather in spite of the village-commune, and it is doing so only to the extent that it is developing a capitalist mode of production and the class that is the genuine force of progress in the capitalist stage of development. On this point, too, Marx has been proven correct, not Herzen.

Although Herzen was destined to play the role of a major political figure, by his own recognition he was, above, all a writer and principally a publicist. In terms of quality and quantity, Herzen's literary inheritance can be divided into three parts: his *belles-lettres*, his philosophical articles, and his works as a publicist.

A remarkable master of the word, Herzen was not born to be an artistic writer of *belles-lettres*. It is true that such works as 'Who is Guilty' and 'The Magpie Thief' are also noteworthy as *belles-lettres*. But Belinsky was correct when he observed that in Herzen, as the author of *belles-lettres*, a profound mind

---

6. Herzen 1905, p. 338.
7. Travelling about Russian cities to give lectures on Herzen, the Cadet Rodichev found no better way to honour the memory of the great publicist and socialist than to present him as some sort of right-wing Cadet of our own time. It is all the easier to inflict such a terrible insult on Herzen because he is dead and cannot protest. The reader will see from the few lines that we have already quoted – and there are many more such passages in the body of Herzen's work – that Herzen linked the future of civilisation with the triumph of the popular masses, whereas the gentlemen-Cadets strive to ensure the triumph of the liberal bourgeoisie over the masses of the people, and they fear any movement by the people just as much as the reactionaries do.

overshadows talent. It is characteristic that in the period when he reached the height of his talent, Herzen abandoned *belles-lettres* as a creative form.

Nor was Herzen a philosopher *par excellence*. This did not prevent his articles from being a model for clarity to the point of transparency or a graphic account of different philosophical systems. 'Letters on the Study of Nature' can serve to this day as an excellent guide in this area. For Herzen, the last word in philosophy was Hegel's system. But he did not accept it as a matter of faith. Dogmatism was alien to his inquisitive and critical mind, and Hegel's dialectical philosophy was itself not disposed to dogmatism. As distinct from Belinsky, for example, who with linear passion carried to the extreme any position he adopted, Herzen had a great capacity to see, so to speak, the pros and cons of every thought, every theory, and the limits of its significance. Thus, having adopted Hegel's dialectical method of thinking, the most valuable part of Hegelian philosophy, he did not become a blind Hegelian. Generally speaking, in his mature years Herzen did practically no philosophical work, as in the case of *belles-lettres*. At that time he advanced and worked in the area where his talent developed in all its breadth – social commentary.

Herzen is not only the most significant of Russian publicists, but he also stands in the first rank among world-famous writers of this sort. His amazingly lustrous style, and the graphic form of his prose, can stand alongside the best works of Lessing, Heine, and perhaps even Berne. The truth is that anyone who has not read Herzen has not come to know all the flexibility, wealth and beauty of the Russian language. His works have to be studied in schools along with the creations of Pushkin and Tolstoy. Here, for good luck, is a small excerpt from *My Past and Thoughts* in which Herzen thinks through his disappointment and spiritual drama after the shooting down of the Paris proletariat during the July Days.

> Our historical vocation, our work, consists in this: that by our disillusionment, by our sufferings, we reach resignation and humility in the face of truth and spare following generations from these afflictions. By means of us humanity is regaining sobriety; we are its headache the next morning; we are its birth-pangs. If the delivery ends well, then everything will serve its purpose; but we must not forget that the child or mother, or perhaps both may die, and then – well then history, with its Mormonism, will start a new pregnancy. *E sempre bene*,[8] gentlemen!
>
> We know how nature disposes of individuals; sooner or later, either with no victims or on heaps of corpses – to her it matters not – she goes her own way or continues whatever may occur. Tens of thousands of years produce a

---

8. All is well.

coral-reef, abandoning to their death, every spring, the ranks that have run too far ahead. The polyps die without ever suspecting that they are serving the progress of *the reef*.

We, too, shall serve something. To enter into the future as one of its elements does not mean that the future will fulfil our own ideals. Rome did not complete Plato's Republic or fulfil the Greek ideal in general. And the Middle-Ages were not the development of Rome. Modern western thought will pass into history and be incorporated into it, will have its influence and its place, just as our body will pass into the composition of grass, sheep, cutlets and men. We do not like this kind of immortality, but what is to be done about it?

Now that I am accustomed to these thoughts, they no longer frighten me. But at the end of 1849, they astonished me, and despite the fact that every event, every encounter, every skirmish and every face – all were vying with each other as the last leaves of summer – I still stubbornly and feverishly searched for *a way out*.

That is why I now value so much of Byron's courageous thought. He saw that *there is no way out* and proudly said so.[9]

In this excerpt, where Herzen's nerves, so to say, are exposed to the iron laws of history, we see all the merit of his artistic prose come to the fore. And such pearls are scattered throughout his works. He draws images of Mazzini, Garibaldi and Bakunin that rise 'to their full height as if they were alive'.

We must thank fate for allowing Herzen to live the final part of his life in exile. No censor could lay a heavy hand on his freedom of speech, and he could develop all of his brilliant talent without any obstacles, even if only for a narrow audience. For that, he is guaranteed a readership among future generations.

An anniversary gives us the occasion to express the things for which we wish. As far as Herzen is concerned, they are twofold. First, that in our country there will finally appear a more complete collection of his works than the ten-volume Geneva edition of 1875–80. And second, that the remains of our great publicist and fighter will finally be transferred from Paris back to the country into whose history he has entered with all of his being, and which will utilise the results of his work, because his hopes for his own country were, in the end, the last refuge of his thought, disillusioned as he was with Western civilisation.

M.L.

---

9. Herzen 1905, pp. 100–1.

No. 37

'The Issue of the Day'[1]

6 April 1912

The best criticism of the Cadet Party is its own history. True, there has not been much time for such a history because the Party has only existed for a little longer than six years. However... not much experience, yet much experienced. The Cadets could already, with full justification, speak of themselves in the words of one of Fet's poems:

> Past hopes are
> Far off, like evening-reflections.[2]

The evening-reflections appear to be the demands that were set out at the Founding Conference of the Cadet Party as well as their speeches in the First Duma, which are now so foreign to the spirit of today's Cadet speeches, and especially to speeches that prospective deputies are giving to their voters.

> But memory of the past
> Lurks anxiously in the heart.

However, the reader should not think that 'memory of the past' always embarrasses a Cadet's heart. No, this happens only before elections. For five years the Cadets have behaved in the Third Duma as if they never had a programme and as if the one adopted at their October Congress belonged to some other party.

After following the Duma-activity of the Cadets over five years, and noting that their entire practice contradicts their programme and their pre-election promises, I have to admit that I have more than once asked myself a naïve question: 'Why don't the Cadets change their programme, since it only gets in their way, or else abolish it entirely, for they operate perfectly well (in an anti-democratic spirit) even without a programme?'

Now, I confess my naïveté. To advise the Cadets to reject their programme would be the same as advising some 'German tailor Ivanov', who has never been outside of his home-town, to write a poster revealing the one truth. Once in every five years the Cadets need a programme – when elections are approaching.

---

1. [From *Obskaya zhizn'*, 6 April 1912.]
2. [The quotation by Preobrazhensky is not correct. It reads:
   'Былое стремленье
   Далеко, как отблеск вечерний.
   Fet's verse says:
   Былое стремленье
   Далеко, как выстрел вечерний'.]

That is when it needs to be taken out, cleaned up with commentary, presented to the electors, fooling as many naïve souls as possible, and then hidden away again until the next election. As the reader will see, the Cadets' platform is not dead weight, but valuable capital; even though it is put away for safekeeping in the archive for five years, once in every five-year period it pays solid interest.

The current pre-election airing of the platform has already begun. The lead article in issue No. 84 of *Rech'*, devoted to the Trudovik conference, can be regarded as the first step. Regarding the demands posed by the latter, the newspaper writes:

> With the exception of very hazy references to past 'extra-Duma activities' in the revolution, and also references to the agrarian programme of the Trudoviks, which was set out during the First and Second State-Dumas, in all the rest of it there is hardly a single line that could not just as easily be repeated in pronouncements by the Party of national freedom [the Cadets]. This Party, of course, has always been no less of a 'steadfast defender of the toiling rural and urban strata of the population', and has always 'put the economic interests of the toiling people, and especially the peasants, in the forefront'. Likewise, it is striving to 'repeal the act of 3 June' and to 'develop widespread local self-government'.

And on it goes. When the Cadets bring out their programme 'for the festival', people go and debate with them. We are for the eight-hour working day – so are we – reply the Cadets. We are for allotting land to the peasants – and so are we. We are for freedom – we are too. We represent the popular masses – and so do we.

And when you point out to a 'steadfast defender of the toiling people' that voting for a 12-hour working day is not the same as struggling for an eight-hour day; that 'widespread local self-government' is one thing and a margarine *zemstvo* for Siberia another; that chauvinism in questions of foreign policy has nothing in common with defence of 'the toiling strata of the population', and that the same applies to voting for a strengthened militarism, and so on, you will get one melancholy answer: Ah, gentlemen, a programme is one thing, a programme concerns ideals, but reality is something else!

But if that is the case, our response is to ask why the Octobrists could not sign on to all of your demands and continue doing in practice what they have been doing all along?

The Cadet will say to himself – they cannot do this, for they have their own methods of fooling the voters, and we have ours.

M. Leonov

No. 38

'Manilovism[1] in Siberia'[2]

8 April 1912

The departure of the Irkutsk deputy Belousov from the Social-Democratic fraction has not only raised the extremely important question of deputies' responsibility to their voters, but has also posed the timely issue for Siberia of possible methods with which to defend local Siberian interests in relation to common Russian ones. The lead article in No. 310 of the Chita newspaper *Dumy Zabaikal'ya* is devoted to this question. The nonsense defended in this article and the political illiteracy of its author are too typical to be left unanswered.

It is not difficult to guess that the newspaper defends Belousov. But how does it defend him? Here are the actual words: 'Even if, in the action under review, the Irkutsk deputy was pulling a pre-election trick, one must still regard it as indisputably proper and reasonable'.

Is there any point in diluting these words with commentary? It seems that more than one respectable newspaper has adopted renegade behaviour as a principle, but here pursuit of a mandate, renouncing one's own past, and ignoring protests from the voters (see the letter of an elector in *Sibir'*, the protest from Cheremkhovsk workers, and declarations by the Irkustk newspapers *Sibir'* and *Irkutskoe slovo*) turns out to be 'indisputably proper and reasonable'.

With this sort of a start, one can judge what will follow. Further on in the article we read the following:

> We have had to speak out before, but we do not consider it redundant to reaffirm our staunch and definite conviction that the Siberian deputies in the Duma must constitute a group that is strongly united in Siberia's interests, and that any splintering among those elected by Siberia into political factions must be regarded as a most unfortunate event that is ruinous for Siberia.
>
> Of course, with regard to questions that arise in the Duma and affect the entire empire, every Siberian deputy is free to act according to his own social-political views; the voters knew, or should have known, whom they were choosing; this is the only way in which to measure the deputy's responsibility, in general state-matters, to those who sent him to the Duma.

---

1. [From the name Manilov, a character in Gogol's *Dead Souls*, represented as a type of easygoing, sentimental landowner whose name became a synonym for an idle, weak-willed dreamer and blowhard.]
2. [From *Obskaya zhizn'*, 8 April 1912.]

But as soon as talk turns to Siberia, its needs and the reforms being planned for it, and so on, there is no room even for mention of individual party-platforms. On such matters the group of Siberian deputies in the Duma must act in harmony and unanimity for the good of our native territory.

Ridiculing philistines, Heine said their heads are divided into drawers, and every question has its own drawer. The Chita newspaper likewise suggests to deputies that in their head they should have two drawers – one for all-Russian questions and another for Siberian ones. One can imagine where that could lead. For instance, the national drawer in any country votes against the budget in general, giving nothing whatever to the régime, in which case one region or another can get nothing whatsoever of the reforms it requires. But when the part of the budget that contains appropriations for regional needs comes to a vote, the regional drawer votes to support them. And there is no contradiction. But for heads that are not partitioned, for non-philistine heads that have the misfortune to think logically, there is indeed a contradiction here. But we, thank God, have drawers. Or here is another example: the question of introducing a *zemstvo* is under discussion. The all-Russian drawer stands for a democratic *zemstvo*. The Siberian replies: The snail is moving, but who knows when it will arrive? Margarine will do for us. Vote for margarine! In reality, it takes no particularly deep insight to understand that that there are not, and cannot be, any kind of Siberian needs whose satisfaction would not be tied up in the closest way with the successful democratic transformation of Russia. Mikhail Sadko quite correctly pointed out in *Irkutskoe slovo* that all attempts by Shilo and Chilikin to defend some Siberian point of view in the Duma have ended in a miserable fiasco. And it could not be otherwise. There can be no special Siberian point of view, just as there cannot be one for Chernigov or Tula.

The Chita newspaper's wish to see some sort of group-dance by Siberian deputies in the Duma is a senseless and harmful utopia. Siberia, like Russia, is divided into different classes with different interests. Disagreements are inevitable, both on the question of what Siberia needs and on the issue of the best ways to struggle for the achievement of necessary reforms. Even if Siberia's conditions are worse than those of any province in European Russia, that is still not enough to make all Siberian questions non-partisan and all Siberians like-minded.

We are told that Belousov's letter clearly underlines the incompatibility between a principled defence of common Russian interests and the regional interests of Siberia. In our opinion, this letter clearly underlines the fact that the political horizon of Mr. Belousov does not extend beyond the level of the average Siberian philistine; and the moral that follows from his letter is that in coming elections to the Fourth Duma one should not vote for philistines, who are so richly represented in the newspaper *Dumy Zabaikal'ya*, but should give a mandate to citizens who are politically conscious.

Consider the fact that three Siberian deputies have already split from the Social-Democratic faction, in each case because of Siberian questions. This proves once again that it is easy to be a radical in words. But any radical is worthless who cannot withstand the first taste of practical opportunism and, while remaining a Social Democrat for Russia, turns into an Octobrist for Siberia.[3]

The Chita newspaper's attempt to heat up regional patriotism[4] must be met with a decisive rebuff on the part of the Siberian press, regardless of differences. One may be a Cadet or a leftist. But if they are politically literate people, neither a Cadet nor a leftist can separate Siberian tasks from common Russian ones, or create a Siberian group-dance along with other parties or within them.

The Siberian newspapers must speak out on this question. If they keep silent about such questions, then what else is there to talk about?

M. Leonov

---

3. On the question of a Siberian *zemstvo*, our deputies have completely adopted the Octobrist point of view.

4. We are supporters of broad regional self-government and, for that reason, we are obviously speaking of the kind of local patriotism that contradicts the progressive tasks of our time involving the entire state. That kind of patriotism is ridiculous and harmful.

No. 39

A Review of the Journals *Sovremennyi mir* and *Russkoe bogatstvo* (March)[1]

8 April 1912

Leaving aside the novel by A. Sefarimovich, *City on the Steppes*, which continues in the March issue of *Sovremennyi mir*, in the *belles-lettres* section one must look above all at the posthumous notes of I.A. Konovalov in 'Diary of an Agitator'. The author of the notes – a prominent activist in the Social-Democratic Party – enjoyed great popularity in St. Petersburg as an agitator and not long ago took his own life. Although the notes take the form of *belles-lettres*, the autobiographical character of everything written in them is beyond doubt. We see, here, something in the nature of a 'human document' from a revolutionary life, one of those documents whose enormous significance, as raw material for a future *War and Peace*, can in this regard hardly be exaggerated. The activists of the Russian revolutionary movement are still awaiting their artist, who will give an objective picture of their internal world, their life and their struggle. All attempts in this direction have thus far been unsuccessful. *Andrei Kozhukhov* and *Little House on the Volga* by Stepnyak are lyrical works similar in spirit to French novels. Brandes was quite mistaken when he likened them to the creations of the world's great artists. Gorky's *Mother* mixes deeply truthful scenes with sentimental declarations. Ropshin's *Pale Horse* is an illustrated appendix to prejudices and is decadent in its thinking... In such conditions, documents such as Konovalov's notes are even more valuable, particularly if one takes into account that the truth they communicate, as in this case, is to a significant extent guaranteed by the tragic death of their author. The advantage of 'Notes of an Agitator'[2] also lies in the fact that the circumstances of life and the internal emotional experiences of revolutionary figures are sketched in a far from rosy light and are foreign to those renegade distortions of the truth that comprise the main content of most recent stories and tales of revolutionary life. These 'artistic' lampoons are much more a description of the moral decline of their authors than a portrayal of what they wish to describe.

---

1. [From *Obskaya zhizn'*, 8 April 1912.]
2. [The correct title is the one that Preobrazhensky first gave, namely 'Diary of an Agitator' (Дневник агитатора), which was published posthumously in book-form in St. Petersburg in 1913.]

In the published section of 'Diary of an Agitator' (the conclusion will follow), the question of love is bluntly posed along with family life in general within the context of party-work. We will have further occasion to talk about the content of the notes.

In *Russkoe bogatstvo*, our attention is drawn to a story in S. Pod'yachev's posthumous notes on 'Life and Death' that strikingly describes the hopeless position of one 'conscious' peasant, pressured by need and family quarrels, who has decided to kill for the purpose of a robbery but did not rob the local kulak. The real culprit ends his own life by suicide under the impression of the horrible deed that he has just committed.

An historical story by S. Kondurushkin, 'Descendants of the King of the Jews', proves once more that travelling through modern Syria does not qualify one to write on historical subjects from the first centuries of Christianity.

―――

The publicist sections of *Sovremennyi mir* and *Russkoe bogatstvo* are very substantial.

Sovremennyi mir publishes the conclusion of a most interesting article, which we have frequently cited, concerning the secret police and provocation in France. Here is one curious fact. In 1867, there was an international fair in Paris, attended by Emperor Alexander II and Bismarck along with police-chief Shtiber.

> While meeting with his secret Parisian agents – who moved in Polish circles as well – Shtiber learned from them that a young Polish worker-patriot, Berezovsky, planned to assassinate the Russian emperor in order to protest before the whole world against the cruelties of Murav'ev and the policy of the Russian government in Poland. Shocked by this news, Shtiber immediately headed for the prefect of the Paris police, Pietry, in order to warn him of the coming assassination and thereby to do his professional colleague a friendly service.
>
> But Shtiber could not find Pietry and left with his report to see Bismarck. After listening to his subordinate, Bismarck quickly decided that it was in the interests of Prussia to see the assassination take place. Even then, Prussia was preparing for war against France, and it needed to create hostile relations between Russia and France. The chance had unexpectedly arisen, and Bismarck strictly forbade Shtiber to interfere in the affairs of Russian political émigrés. Thus Pietry did not learn of the plot, and Berezovsky took his shot at Emperor Alexander II even with the indirect involvement of Prussian *agents-provocateurs*. It is understandable that Alexander II immediately left Paris in a state of extreme irritation after the attempted assassination. In that way Bismarck at least partially achieved his goal: a chill set in between the Russian and French governments.
>
> The French government subsequently expended great efforts to achieve a Franco-Russian alliance.

Other details are interesting concerning the Landezen affair, that is, the very provocateur who brought a group of Russian revolutionaries to court in France, received five years in prison himself, fled, and five years later was posted in Paris by the Russian government, in the guise of General Harting, for secret-police work. Yu. Steklov notes, with a number of facts, the French government's obsequiousness in relation to Russia in secret-police matters, which prepared the ground for a Franco-Russian alliance, and he therefore comments that 'the secret-police alliance preceded the diplomatic one and even partly caused it'.[3] When the Radicals came to power, naturally things did not change. Clemenceau, Briand and Caillaux all used the services of provocateurs, who committed all their energy to destroying the organisations of the French proletariat – the syndicalists. It is enough to point to the provocateur Métivier, who was considered to be a prominent syndicalist and was in the service of the secret police. At the time of the railway-strike, he placed a bomb at the home of the nationalist Missar, and Briand made use of this fact as one of his arguments for putting down the strike by force and preventing the railway-workers from organising into unions.

There is an interesting article here by G.V. Plekhanov, written with his usual mastery, on 'The Philosophical Views of Herzen'. The part that is published deals with Herzen's world-view during the Moscow period of his life. One can consider Plekhanov's assertion to be exaggerated when he refers to the idealistic character of Herzen's world-view at the time of 'Letters on the Study of Nature'; and it may be historically more accurate to note that it was precisely Herzen's dissatisfaction with Hegel's philosophical idealism, and his attempts to go beyond its limits, that made the work all the more valuable since it was undertaken as early as the forties by a Russian who, by his own recognition, was not a philosopher; nevertheless, future biographers and researchers of Herzen's works will not be able to ignore the views that G.V. Plekhanov expresses on this question (although they contradict the accepted ones).

The publicist section of *Russkoe bogatstvo* is especially rich this time. It is enough to mention that here we find a new article by Herzen, 'A New Phase of Russian Literature', which was never previously published and is translated into Russian from French; V. Figner's memoirs, 'With a Handful of Gold Amongst Beggars'; letters by G.I. Uspensky; the essay by V. Korolenko on 'Russian Torture in the Nineteenth Century'; and finally, Lev Deutsch's prison-recollections of Yakubovich.

In her memoirs, V.N. Figner tells how, after a twenty-year imprisonment in Shlisselburg and a year and a half of her life spent at her sister's in Nizhny, she was administratively exiled to her brother's estate in Kazan province, where she managed to renew her connection with the people's cause by providing

---

3. *Sovremennyi mir*, March 1912, p. 212.

assistance to those who were hungry. The result was dismal. The peasants treated the philanthropic work of this elderly Russian Narodnik as if it were a lordly escapade, and they wanted only one thing: to snatch as much as possible for themselves from the 'fine lady' through various cunning machinations and deceptions. And even the 'conscious' peasants fell in with the rest when it was a matter of possibly acquiring a few 'lordly' roubles. Disappointed, V.N. Figner ended her activity; the peasants turned out to be 'chocolate'.[4] But she did not lose hope of finding a true path to useful social activity. But where does it lead? In his article 'A Speech', A. Izgoev suggests that this path leads to finding 'true democracy', and with characteristic modesty he refrains from saying that this means the Constitutional-Democratic Party [the Cadets]. We have a different opinion on this matter. If the Narodniks (not only in the seventies but also quite recently) embraced a fantasy of the 'chocolate' peasant, and then in practice bitterly convinced themselves that the real peasant did not in any way resemble the product of their imagination, the fault does not lie with the peasant, and the essential point is that he has by no means ceased to be one of the points of support for democracy. The sorrowful history recounted by V. Figner can be seen in a great many cases; and if the peasant looks distrustfully upon attempts by the 'lord' to establish 'personal contact' with him – even if the 'lord' is kindly disposed towards him – and if he smiles ironically to himself at the help proffered to him, this is no expression of 'village-idiocy'[5] but rather a perfectly healthy class-instinct. Translated into the language of consciousness, it says: philanthropy will not help our situation because it does not get to the basic causes that are ruining the countryside.

The letters by Uspensky demonstrate with total clarity the abnormal conditions in which this remarkable talent had to work and why he did not give all that he might have. Upon reading his letters, every one of them expressing despair over money, one can imagine that throughout his entire life his creditors were standing at his window and peering in. Here are examples: 'With all my desire to lighten our lot, the truth is that I could not get ten francs anywhere....'.[6] 'We have literally no money and are indebted to the charcoal-dealer and the

---

4. [In her memoirs, Vera Figner accused Gleb Uspensky of a one-sided depiction of the peasantry as a 'human herd' driven by material interests: 'Why portray the peasant in such colours that... everyone will find repulsive?' Uspensky ironically replied that he was being asked to portray a 'chocolate peasant'.]

5. Of course, we have 'village-idiocy' in abundance. But one can only use that term when the peasant, unassisted, fails to link his immediate economic demands with political demands for democracy.

6. *Russkoe bogatstvo*, March 1912, p. 190.

laundress'.⁷ 'Money, for God's sake, they don't trust us in shops, I assure you'.⁸ And so it continues endlessly. What a fine atmosphere for artistic creativity!

Lev Deutsch's recollections of Yakubovich surpass other literature of the kind in that they contain neither sentimental sugar-coating of personality nor any exaggeration of the less than modest talent of one writer or another. With us, there is a deeply rooted philistine principle – 'speak well of the dead or remain silent' – which strikingly expresses an individualistic point of view both of the writer and of a man in general, attributing things to him rather than to the society that fed him and whose hands did his share of the socially necessary work. Deutsch has nothing bad to say about Yakubovich, but neither does he exaggerate the good. The work smacks of truthfulness, and that is its essential feature.

The historical essay by V. Korolenko discusses torture in the nineteenth century. The author here establishes a certain 'law', namely, that a resurgence of torture in practice, and the wish for a torturing ideology, are always connected with the victory or intensification of reaction. There appears to be no difficulty in predicting what the author will say in his next essay, which is dedicated to our own time.

M.L.

---

7. *Russkoe bogatstvo*, March 1912, p. 191.
8. *Russkoe bogatstvo*, March 1912, p. 187.

No. 40

'The Workers' Movement in March'[1]

12 April 1912

Judging by newspaper-reports, altogether there were 34 workers' strikes in Russia during March. In addition, there were a number of strikes in small handicraft-shops that we have not included. We know the number who participated in 19 of the strikes. It comes to 15,707 people. If we take into account the fact that we do not have the numbers of participants for several large enterprises, for instance, two mines in Dombrov, the Hartman plant, the Mytishchinsky factory and others, we can conclude that the number of participants in the strike-movement for March significantly exceeded twenty thousand men. (Last month it was about twenty thousand.)

As for the outcome of the strikes, in 17 cases we do not know. One case involved a protest, in 10 cases the strikes succeeded fully or in part, and in six cases they produced no results.

The most strikes occurred in St. Petersburg, namely, 11 out of the total; in the Baltic territory seven, and in Poland four; the remainder occurred in other parts of Russia.

The most significant was the strike at the Lena goldfields-company. Readers already know of the tragic episode in this strike. There was also a clash with police during the strike at the Aizert factory in Warsaw. The other strikes proceeded peacefully.

It is interesting to note that in cotton-textiles, the main branch of our industry, there have been almost no strikes for the past two months, whereas last year, according to recently published official reports, in one Moscow industrial district alone more than ninety thousand workers went on strike, mainly weavers. This circumstance can be explained by deteriorating conditions in the textile-industry resulting from the poor harvest.

It is also interesting to note that during the past two months the number of strikers reached a total approximately equal to that for all of 1909.

Generally speaking, the revival of activity among the workers is continuing and expanding.

M.L.

---

1. [From *Obskaya zhizn'*, 12 April 1912.]

No. 41

'An Instructive Lesson'[1]

15 April 1912

The telegraph has brought news that the commission of the State-Council decided to reject the Duma's legislative project for introducing a *zemstvo* in Siberia and expressed a preference for the Ministry of Internal Affairs to look into improving the existing local economy in Siberia.

The commission has rejected the legislation for the time being. But it is perfectly clear to anyone familiar with the general working of the State Council and its decisions with regard to introducing a *zemstvo* in Tavrichesky, the Donsky Voiska and Astrakhan province, in particular, that rejection of the project for a Siberian *zemstvo* is an established fact.

We shall have further occasion to discuss the consequences of this rejection for the people of Siberia, and particularly the conclusions that Siberians must draw in terms of waging the electoral campaign for the Fourth Duma with specific slogans. For now, it is enough to say that our prediction of the project's failure is beginning to be validated, and all of our arguments against the unprincipled and short-sighted opportunism of such gentlemen as the Nekrasovs and Belousovs are being fully confirmed. There is also no doubt that the entire section of the Siberian press that supported the margarine *zemstvo* has suffered a moral defeat. With its method of visual instruction, the commission of the State-Council is drumming into the heads of the political schoolboys, who incomprehensibly carry the title of deputies from Siberia, the fact that the fate of reforms in Siberia is intimately connected with the fate of Russia's democratic transformation as a whole, and that the time for the latter is not brought any nearer when groups striving for such transformation repudiate their own programmes.

Quite the opposite is true.

We can still understand Judas, who sold Christ for thirty pieces of silver. We can understand Isaiah, who sold his birthright for a mess of pottage. But where is the pottage for which the Siberian deputies, and those who express Siberian social opinion, sold their right to a democratic *zemstvo* that the people of Siberia have always demanded? Where is there any sign of even the crumbs of real benefit that opportunists always speak of when they continuously lose a rouble for the sake of a ten-*kopek* coin? Where are the ten *kopeks*? They do not exist. And the reason why they do not exist is because we do not even have opportunism, only a caricature of opportunism.

---

1. [From *Obskaya zhizn'*, 15 April 1912.]

The guilty parties, whose first response to the rejection was retreat, may say there is a real result from the 'struggle for a Siberian *zemstvo*' waged by Siberian deputies: the expressed wish by the commission of the State-Council for an improvement of Siberia's existing local economy. I agree that the wish expressed by the Council's commission is a very witty mockery of the Siberian deputies. But the question is: do they get the joke?

Perhaps some of them will draw a different conclusion from the lesson they have received. They will explain their failure by saying they did not bow low enough.

With such gentlemen, of course, there is nothing more to discuss.

M. Leonov

No. 42

'A Little Pamphlet'[1]

22 April 1912

Every Duma-speech at the tribune of the Tauride Palace by the Minister of Foreign Affairs is invariably followed by the Cadet party's own Minister of Internal Affairs, Pavel Nikolaevich Milyukov, who sets out to express the 'country's view' by condemning and approving. Bow to the left, bow to the right: one bow to the left and nine to the right.

Newspaper proof-readers are so accustomed to this 'daily occurrence' in our 'parliamentary' life that after making exhausting corrections to agency-telegrams of speeches by the Minister of Foreign Affairs they still cannot heave a sigh of relief.

No, after all, there is still a long speech by Milyukov!

'If only he got sick, God willing... But no, there is no escaping the proof-reading. He would sooner be carried to the Duma in his bed than skip a speech'.

The proof-reader turns out to be right. Not even twenty minutes pass and a courier enters the editorial room with a sinister stack of telegrams in hand. The proof-reader signs for them and begins reading with an expression of concentrated anguish.

After all, a diplomatic speech is not a lampoon by some Gegechkori.[2] He says to the right, for instance, 'you're a cosy bunch' while the text says 'a shady bunch'. So, settle for shady, which is perfectly true.

And thus the diplomats themselves have no understanding of what one actually said to the other and intended to say. Everything falls on the proof-reader. He leaves out a comma, and it turns out that no-one has any need for the Franco-Russian alliance; he omits the particle 'not', and it turns out that we have important interests in Persia and Mongolia.

'So, is it a fairly good speech?' I ask the proof-reader.

'Limitless in length, limitless in breadth'.

'And in depth?'

'That's for you to decide', replies the proof-reader.

Yes, that's for me to decide, but my work is not difficult. Just as the proof-reader knows that Sazonov's speech will be followed by Milyukov's, so I know, without reading the Minister's speech, what the Cadet leader has to say. The

---

1. [From *Obskaya zhizn'*, 22 April 1912.]
2. [Evgeny Gegechkori was a Menshevik from Georgia who served in the Third State-Duma.]

motif of the speech is always the same. After paying a 'tribute of respect' to the work of the Minister of Foreign Affairs, thus giving a stamp of approval from the 'society' of 3 June (which is a respectable organisation, not some group of boors and *Faterlandlose gesellen*),³ Milyukov will nevertheless make his bow to the left. This is all very good, he will say to Minister Sazonov, but still:

> 'Tis pity you don't know our rooster:
> You'd become less dim,
> Were you to learn a bit from him.⁴

In every phrase of Milyukov's speech, just as in every article by the Milyukovist *Rech'*, one hears this secret dream of getting the portfolio. Aye, just let us come to power and we'll do everything better. 'We'll not play that kind of music, we'll have the forest and mountains dancing'.⁵

I seriously doubt that the Cadet music will ever have the forest and mountains dancing. To the contrary, I am convinced that, once they get the portfolio, they will be dancing themselves to the music of those who will benefit from discrediting liberalism in practice.

The Minister of Foreign Affairs will be quite justified in taking a sceptical view of Milyukov's preaching: first, because the difference between their views is only a matter of detail; and second, mainly because our Minister of Foreign Affairs, while he has met with a number of diplomatic failures, at least has some experience. The Cadets have only a number of diplomatic speeches, and all are of questionable value.

M.L.

---

3. [People without kith or kin, or without roots.]
4. [The quotation is incorrect. The correct version is:
   "Tis pity you don't know our rooster:
   You'd become less dim,
   When learning a bit from him'.]
5. [This quotation is also incorrect. The correct version is:
   'And then the music will be different:
   We'll have the forest and mountains dancing!']

No. 43

Review of the Journal *Vestnik Evropy* (April)[1]

25 April 1912

The substantial April issue of this journal is quite rich in terms of both *belles-lettres* and the publicist section. Here we find a story by I. Bunin, 'A Waterless Valley', with all of the merits and shortcomings of this writer's countryside-tales. But the main attraction in the *belles-lettres* section goes to Gorky's story 'Three Days', half of which is published in this issue. The tale is pleasantly surprising with its absolute truthfulness and consistent spirit of realism, along with the complete absence of embellishment, pretentiousness and artificiality that have so often spoiled Gorky's works during his most recent creative period. If the tale 'Three Days' is not an accident, but rather characterises the start of a whole new period of Gorky's talent, then it would be a pleasure to say that the writer has finally found his niche, which, as Belinsky said, every writer is destined to do sooner or later.

There are very interesting recollections by the famous Narodnik Frolenko of his departure from the Shlisselburg fortress during the October Days.

In this issue there are also recollections by P.A. Tverskoi, 'Historical Material Concerning the Late Stolypin', which were a topic of discussion in the press for an entire week and provide an extremely valuable characterisation of P.A. Stolypin himself as well as shedding special light on the ruling group and the influences that make the music of governance in Russia.

In his short note 'Naïve Cynicism', M. Kovalevsky focuses on the activity of the State-Council in the famous bill on state purchase-orders and the one on construction. In the first, the interests of a million-strong army of vendors fell victim to the interests of capital even against the wishes of the latter, while in the second the interests of a wide circle of homeowners, mainly people of few means who built their houses on privately owned land, are sacrificed to the owners of that land. In the final analysis, the author remarks: 'The longer I live, and the more closely I watch what is happening before my eyes, the more I am struck by the naïve cynicism of the methods used by the powers that be to impress their subjects with how much they care for them. In the final analysis, it seems one must agree with the definition that one English judge gave of the law when he said 'It is an order given by the strong to the weak'.

---

1. [From *Obskaya zhizn'*, 25 April 1912.]

It is surprising that the honourable professor is so late in grasping the truth. It is all the more surprising since we are talking about the author of *The Origin of Modern Democracy*, every page of which is an illustration of the English judge's opinion.

But better late than never.

M.L.

No. 44

'The Incurably Ill'[1]

29 April 1912

There are two types of Narodniks in Russia. The first type includes those who have tasted from the Marxist tree of knowledge. They are quite taken with the Marxist critique, to which they give their own interpretation, and they have no aversion to calling themselves the true Marxists. (Marx, after all, has been dead for a long time and cannot protest.) But the main point is that such Narodniks are more-or-less familiar with Marx's theory and, in a polemic with the views of Marxists on one point or another, they do not make particularly gross distortions in their 'free interpretation'.

It is quite another matter with the second type of Narodnik. These people have never understood and, apparently, will not understand 'to their dying day' the main nerve of Marxist theory. They are destined forever to be a model of the kind of primitive psychological organisation that always confuses the desirable with the possible and the real, the objectively inevitable with the morally obligatory. If, for example, Marxists say that proletarianisation is inevitable in a country that has taken the path of capitalist development, and that it is an agonising and burdensome consequence of a generally progressive economic process, the simple-minded Narodnik of the second type comes to the conclusion that Marxists *aspire* to see the proletarianisation of the masses. If Marxists, for example, declare that the development of capitalism is a progressive phenomenon, the genial Narodnik considers it merely an inconsistency if they are not themselves participating in the process of capital-accumulation and are organising trade-unions rather than opening taverns and commercial enterprises.

It is true that after more than twenty years of drumming their theory into the heads of the Narodniks, Marxists have reduced the representatives of this second type to a small number. But all the same, these kinds of die-hard Narodniks still raise their voice in one place or another, and especially in the provinces where the reader is not as discriminating as in the capital.

To the list of Narodniks of this second type we must now add F. Sibirsky, author of an article published in No. 881 of *Golos Sibiri* with the title 'Proletarianisation and the Law of 9 November'.

We draw the reader's attention to this article.

---

1. [From *Obskaya zhizn'*, 29 April 1912.]

The essential ideas that F. Sibirsky expresses in this article amount to the following. Enacting the law of 9 November reinforced the proletarianisation of the peasantry, and the sale of land-allotments is taking place at an even faster tempo because of their hunger. Since the expansion of Russian industry has not followed in proportion to proletarianisation of the peasant-masses, the new strata of the proletariat, who are cut off from the village, cannot find their place in the city and are condemned to extinction. Not only has expansion of Russian industry not followed but, to the contrary, it is threatened with a curtailment of production as a result of the contraction of the domestic market connected with pauperisation of the peasant-masses. The aspirations of the rural proletariat in the countryside are reducing the price for working hands paid to the urban proletariat, and reducing to nothing all the achievements of the latter. There is only one moral that follows from all of this: Marxists have nothing to be happy about in the current proletarianisation of the peasantry because the process is holding back the development of industry and causing direct harm to the urban working class.

A reader who is the least bit familiar with the content of the debates that Narodniks have conducted with Marxists will see that Mr. Sibirsky is saying nothing new. On the contrary, it is all as old as Grandpa's bathrobe. The only thing that is new and surprising in the article is that it is written in the form of an attack on Marxists. And this is all the more surprising since the attacker is one of those who have suffered a cruel defeat in the most important of their own demands – their agrarian programme.

As the Germans say, the best defence is an offence. Mr. Sibirsky has followed this approach: an attack on the Marxists must divert attention from his own failure and from the desperate situation in which our Narodniks currently find themselves. Now isn't that truly strange? The author has painted a grim picture of the state of the village in connection with proletarianisation. The question necessarily arises: What is to be done? But instead of answering a direct question, the author turns to the Marxists and says: you, gentlemen, have nothing to be happy about in proletarianisation.

Whether Marxists are happy or not is a different question and has no relation to the matter at hand. The straightforward question is: What do you Narodniks propose to do? Instead of illuminating the consciousness of Marxists, have you, in your own consciousness, comprehended everything that is going on around you? Some provident people in your own midst have already begun to demonstrate that the *obshchina*[2] has not served as a foundation for your agrarian programme. Given the ongoing destruction of the *obshchina*, others, who are

---

2. [The village-commune.]

more honest, bluntly acknowledge that it is worthless. So, what is our opinion on this matter?

Let us now turn to the essence of the questions raised by Mr. Sibirsky. Given the current state of affairs, in Mr. Sibirsky's opinion Russian industry is not only unable to develop intensively, but also risks finding itself in an even narrower domestic market. He says:

> Thus, a consumer must be found for this expanded industry, if it has expanded. The foreign market will yield no such consumer, and industry cannot create consumers for itself. That leaves the agricultural economy. Can anyone hope that land-management activities will raise agricultural productivity in Russia so much that it can absorb up to another one and a half billion worth of commodities?

After giving a negative answer to this question and pointing out that large land-ownership cannot provide a market for industry, the author adds:

> But if the lack of a foreign and domestic market will not allow industry to absorb the proletarianised peasantry, then there can be no doubt that even the market that has been at industry's disposal will contract. For better or worse, the peasant, who has been proletarianised and ejected from the economic life of the country, was involved previously, did create value and was a consumer, if only a miserly one. If he joins the army of the unemployed, then this consumer practically disappears from the market, and industry's factories and shops will have to reduce production rather than dreaming about its increase.

The author is correct in focusing on the question of markets, but he goes about solving that question in a totally incorrect way. In the immediate future, our industry cannot count on foreign markets (but this may not always be the case. Take the example of Germany, which every year exports more and more manufactured goods to Britain) and its main support must be the domestic market. So what are the prospects here?

First of all, Mr. Sibirsky is completely mistaken when he claims that proletarianisation of the peasantry undermines the domestic market. The question should be posed this way: are the productive forces contracting or expanding in our agricultural economy? Indeed, this is the only way we can clarify the volume of products that will be created in agriculture and that will make it possible for those who produce them, after exchanging them for money, to acquire products from urban industry. Mr. Sibirsky did not ask this question, and thus arrived at the conclusion that our industry must contract, which contradicts all the real facts. In recent years our agriculture has experienced rather intensive progress, and this holds true both for large- and small-scale peasant-farming.

Rent-payments in kind are being quickly squeezed out by capitalist payments; and land-prices are rising, which, given the decline of rent-payments in kind, means rising income from independent cultivation of the land. In many places a transition can be seen from the three-field system of crop-rotation, and during recent years there has been an enormous increase in imports of artificial fertiliser and agricultural machinery. The area of cultivated land is itself expanding, due to clearing of the taiga and drainage. Contraction of the market could only occur if the productive forces of the village declined, if the peasants abandoned their allotments, and if more lands were left idle. That was the case, for example, in the French countryside during the years prior to the first Revolution. But here we are not seeing any such phenomenon.

The second important circumstance is the favourable world-conjuncture for our agriculture. I have already discussed this question in the pages of *Obskaya zhizn'*.[3] Here I will simply note that the rise in the price of grain on the world-market, for which there are profound causes, has already influenced and will continue to have a growing influence on the expansion of our agricultural economy and thereby also on the expansion of our internal market, for it means the inflow into it of additional hundreds of millions.

Finally, we must take into account the fact that of the more than a billion worth of imports into Russia, we could produce two-thirds of the imported manufactures ourselves. If this is not occurring now, it is due to a lack of national capital. In our country, merchant capital still predominates over industrial capital, as P. Maslov has quite obviously shown, and our industry is far from expanding to the limits that are possible with our present market.

Setting aside a whole number of particulars from the article by Mr. Sibirsky, I will deal with the relation of Marxists to the law of 9 November and the *obshchina*. There is no need to say that they are opponents of this law, which is impeding normal stratification of the countryside and its adaptation to developing capitalist relations. But they would also protest just as much against legislative protection for the *obshchina* if the Narodniks took it into their heads to implement this measure in conditions favourable to them. Marxists are not opponents of the *obshchina* in any and all circumstances, any more than they are supporters of large-scale agriculture always and everywhere. For them, the essence of the matter is the character of farming, not the forms of land-tenure. In every case, Marxists will stand for the form of land-tenure that guarantees the greatest development of the productive forces. If the *obshchina* could secure such development, they would stand for the *obshchina*, and there may be practical cases where that happens. It is theoretically possible that Marxists may speak

---

3. 'On Grain-Prices', I, No. 30, II, No. 33. [See Documents 1:21 and 1:23.]

out on behalf of small-scale land-tenure and against large-scale. Since we in Russia are facing a choice between backward feudal land-ownership by the gentry, and ownership by the small peasantry, everyone knows what choice Marxists have made. To think that all questions concerning forms of land-ownership have been decided once and for all by Marxists in favour of large-scale farming, and that everything comes down to expecting a *Zusammenbruch*[4] on the basis of concentration, would mean a vulgar understanding of their point of view just like the one given by Mr. Sibirsky.

At the end of his article, after pointing to the need for radical measures (which ones?) to prevent extinction of the proletarianised peasants, the author writes:

> But in order to take those measures, it is necessary to adopt a point of view that is different in principle from the one that is guiding the masters of Russian life on the one hand, and from the Marxists on the other. I am not saying and have no wish to say that the masters of Russian life – the gentlemen-nationalists, rightists and Octobrists – share the same platform with the Marxists. No, their platforms are diametrically opposed, but despite that fact neither platform, if it manages to be implemented, will save millions of Russian peasants from extinction.

What is it in the Marxists' platform that, if implemented, will not prevent extinction? Why is it that you, Mr. Sibirsky, having spoken of its worthlessness, do not find it possible to say just why it is worthless? Perhaps there are extrinsic reasons for this. But then, it is dishonest even to mention its worth or lack of worth, for no proof is being offered.

The Marxists have set out their agrarian programme. They are convinced that it will prevent extinction and guarantee the most rapid development of the productive forces of the country and the city. They are still sticking to those demands.

Can the Narodniks say the same thing for themselves?

M. Leonov

---

4. [Collapse.]

No. 45

'A Duel and Deputies' Immunity'[1]

6 May 1912

The duel between Guchkov and Myasoedov[2] has placed on the order of the day the question of how a deputy should react to a challenge to a duel that might be issued by someone whose affairs have been exposed from the Duma-tribune. Essentially, the answer to the question logically follows from the very idea of popular representation. The immunity that is guaranteed to a parliamentary deputy by the whole of society cannot be infringed upon by individual members of society, even if the infringement takes the form of a challenge to a duel. In general terms, there can be differing views concerning a duel: one may regard it as a pointless relic of the Middle-Ages that does not solve any questions; or, to the contrary, one may see it as the inevitable outcome of certain situations in which life places us. But it takes no great power of logic to convince even the most ardent proponent of the duel that this kind of reaction to parliamentary denunciations is generally quite senseless. The sole method of vindication for people who are denounced is clarification of the truth in a court and in the press. In such circumstances, a duel must be regarded only as a means for diverting attention from the essence of the matter that provided the material for the denunciations, and for transferring it to the level of a personal vendetta with the culprit.

But the deputy who comes out with a denunciation is serving a definite social function, and if there is any logic in him being challenged by those who are exposed, it would be just as logical, if not more so, if all those accused in a court were to challenge the prosecutor to a duel, and this would apply especially to those found innocent by the court.

Furthermore, in modern society the contradictory class-interests are so profound that even clarification and appraisal of the objectively established facts of life for one stratum, as seen by representatives of another class, is often the

---

1. [From *Obskaya zhizn'*, 6 May 1912.]
2. [In 1912, A.I. Guchkov of the Octobrist party accused S.N. Myasoedov, an army-colonel, of espionage. Myasoedov issued the challenge to a duel, which took place in April. Myasoedov fired first but missed, whereupon Guchkov fired into the air. A subsequent investigation found no grounds to support Guchkov's claims. In 1915, however, Myasoedov was again charged with espionage on behalf of Germany and was hanged, although many historians still doubt the validity of the charges and suspect that Myasoedov was made a scapegoat for Russian military failures in the First World-War. See Fuller 2006. Preobrazhensky, on the other hand, evidently though Myasoedov was guilty. See Document 2:7 in this volume.]

equivalent of a harsh insult. Every speech from a Social Democrat on the theme of exploitation of the workers is invariably an insult to the entire class of employers; and the same party's view of militarism, though freely developed in all its points, may be seen by the officer-corps as an insult to the army and the military uniform. But does all this mean that every employer and every officer in the country may challenge members of the Social-Democratic parliamentary fraction, along with its publicists and speakers at public meetings, to a duel? The sharp antagonism of views is a consequence of the class-structure of society, and this antagonism cannot be resolved through a clash between particular individuals from one class of society or another. This kind of question is decided by the encounter in which one class comes out against another class.

Guchkov's duel with Myasoedov did not decide any question whatsoever. It will only add another brush-stroke to the picture of the Octobrist party's super-clown, who has behaved in his usual role of comedian in this masquerade-duel. Its negative results are perfectly obvious. By accepting the challenge, Guchkov acknowledges in principle the propriety of challenging deputies to a duel in all such cases, and thus he overturns all notions of popular representation as a social function and converts the deputies into a group of private operators with their own private interests who are personally accountable for their activities as deputies and must settle their private accounts with other individuals in the country.

It may be that the Octobrists do look upon themselves as such a group of operators, and that view would not contradict reality. But all those deputies who enjoy moral support from the broad masses of the people must decisively fence themselves off from the Octobrist gentlemen and reject, once and for all, any attempt to impose upon deputies a new responsibility for answering to those people who may find clarification of the truth from the Duma-tribune either unpleasant or insulting.

M.L.

No. 46

'The Workers' Movement in April'[1]

11 May 1912

In the past month, the workers' movement in Russia acquired a breadth not seen for a long time and was reminiscent of the dimensions of 1906. The centre of gravity in the workers' movement over the past month shifted from the economic sphere to the political, although the economic struggle in different areas of the country continued and is still going on. According to newspaper-reports for the month of April, there were altogether 37 economic strikes. There is no complete information on the number of participants. The numbers are available only for 18 enterprises, that is, for one-half of the total. In these 18 enterprises, more than ten thousand (ten thousand, three hundred) went on strike. Unfortunately, information concerning the outcomes is extremely scarce and provides only very dubious material for making a judgement as to the greater or lesser success of the struggle as compared with last year, or even with the first months of the current year. Of 35 strikes, we know the outcome of the conflict only in 12 cases, in eight of which the strikes ended in either complete or partial success, while four were a total defeat for the workers. As before, the greatest number of strikes occurred in St. Petersburg. Of the total number of strikes, St. Petersburg accounted for 18, the Baltic territory for seven, and the Western territory for six. Moreover, one must not forget that the relatively greater number of strikes in St. Petersburg must be explained not only by the intensity of the strike-movement in the capital, but also by better coverage of them in the newspapers. As for the provinces, far from all the strikes that take place here become known through the newspapers.

Let us turn now to the political strikes. The widest movement was precipitated by the events in Lena,[2] to which workers reacted right up to the end of the past month in all the various corners of Russia. Overall, there were strikes in more than twenty cities and factory-centres. The number of participants, judging by approximate and partial data, reached two hundred and twenty-five thousand people. If we add the 1 May strikes in Riga and the Western territory, then the

---

1. [From *Obskaya zhizn'*, 11 May 1912.]
2. [The Lena massacre occurred in April 1912 when troops fired on striking workers from the goldfields. The working conditions were particularly harsh, including extremely low wages and a fifteen to sixteen-hour day. The immediate cause of the strike was distribution of rotten meat by a company-store. Workers' demands included an eight-hour day and a 30 percent rise in wages. Under the command of Captain N.V. Treshchenkov, gendarmerie-troops opened fire and, according to local newspaper-reports, killed two hundred and seventy workers and wounded the same number.]

number who participated in political protest-strikes and demonstrations for the month of April comes to more than two hundred and fifty thousand. This does not include 1 May strikes based on the old calendar, which we will take into account at the end of the current month.

As we see, the workers' movement took an enormous leap forward; and this was due, moreover, to the increasingly political character of the movement. The economic struggle, if it has not contracted, did not in any case expand by comparison with the previous months of this year.

[M.L.][3]

---

3. [This article was not signed, but it has been included in this collection of documents because Preobrazhensky was responsible at the time for the newspaper's articles on 'The Workers' Movement'.]

No. 47

Review of A. Bykova's Book *The Time of Troubles in Russia* (Published by S. Dorovatovsky and A. Charushnikov, Moscow)[1]

11 May 1912

Bureaucratic patriotism has no love for historical truth and is prepared to see any truthful account of the history of the Russian state as a 'shock to the foundations'. This applies especially to a popular recent account of the Russian state. Students are still permitted to know the truth from the lectures of Klyuchevsky, and the same holds for readers – however few they may be by comparison – of Kostomarov, Zabelin, Platonov and other historians. But for the wide popular masses, historical truth continues to be regarded as a luxury, and readers from among the people, as well as those studying in elementary and secondary educational institutions, are still forced to consume literature written in the spirit of Ilovaisky, which can justifiably be called an absolute historical forgery. Accordingly, there are plenty of patriotic histories being encouraged, while you can count truthful historical narratives on your fingers.

For this reason, one can only welcome the book whose title we have mentioned and hope for its broadest possible circulation. Here we have no falsification of the history of the Time of Troubles, but rather an objective and truthful account presented in simple and popular language. The causes and full circumstances for the rise of serfdom are presented, the social-economic underpinnings of civil strife during the Time of Troubles are well set out, and there is a vivid outline of the self-interested and narrow class-policy of the Boyars, who were ready to hand over Russia to the Poles in order to preserve their historic privileges. Naturally, the only basis for criticising the author is the fact that she did not give a sufficiently clear outline of the opposing class-interests between groups that supported and opposed the impostor, nor did she adequately explain the superficial form of turning to an impostor, with all of the external twists and turns of events, by referring to the very essence of the class-struggle, the historical meaning of which is completely lost for many readers in the actions of these historical supernumeraries.

---

1. [From *Obskaya zhizn'*, 11 May 1912.]

In the most general terms, we can strongly recommend A. Bykova's book to all who wish to familiarise themselves, through a work written in generally accessible form and with not too many pages, with this most interesting period in the life of the Russian people – a period that, by the way, is marking its 300th anniversary.

M.L.

No. 48

Review of the Journals *Russkoe bogatstvo* and *Sovremennyi mir* (April)[1]

13 May 1912

The April issue of *Russkoe bogatstvo* is poor in terms of *belles-lettres*. One tale that attracts attention is F. Kryukov's 'The Officer's Wife', which is devoted to the life of the Don Cossacks. F. Kryukov has performed a great service insofar as he has succeeded, in a number of essays and stories that are partially brought together in the book *Cossack Motives*, in giving the Russian public an impression of the inner life of a section of the Russian people that we know of only in terms of its repressive activity. In Kryukov's stories, we see the heroes of the whip in their family-life, with their human emotions and everyday joys and sorrows in conditions of their daily struggle for existence. Especially valuable are Kryukov's tales that describe the change in consciousness and moods among the Cossack masses after 1905. In elections to all three Dumas, the Cossacks have proven themselves to be far from a reactionary element. The author himself, by the way, was elected to the First Duma as a delegate from the Don *oblast* and belonged to the Trudovik group. As in the case of Siberia, the area of the Don Cossacks is deprived of *zemstvo* self-government. The Cossacks are also being ruined by military conscription: they must outfit and arm the Cossack regiments at their own expense, and their villages are deprived of the most able-bodied youth. Memories of past liberties live on among the Cossacks, and the idea of regional autonomy is firmly grounded in the instincts of the masses and the consciousness of the Cossack intelligentsia, which, regrettably, is not especially numerous.

The story of 'The Officer's Wife' introduces us to the daily life of the Don Cossacks. Generally speaking, F. Kryukov is not one of the brightest and most exciting writers. His work is long, monotonous and pallid. But his characters are life-like and credible, and between the lines of his stories you can hear the quiet rustling of reeds along the banks of the Don, feel the scorching southern sun, and smell the aroma of the little-Russian steppe. All of this is present in the story we are discussing. He also adds new dimensions to his previous portrait of Cossack life and therefore deserves the reader's attention.

In the *belles-lettres* section of the April edition of *Sovremennyi mir*, one must first pause at the final instalment of Konovalov's story, 'Diary of an Agitator'. I have already had occasion to mention this 'human document'. Now, as the story

---

1. [From *Obskaya zhizn'*, 13 May 1912.]

comes to its end, all of its merits stand out in even greater relief. The lives of revolutionaries provide a wealth of material for an artist, and especially for a playwright. But a work of art is not the photograph of a moment. For its objective artistic representation to become possible, the kind of revolutionary period that we have recently experienced must take form as a kind of geological stratum in history. It is no coincidence that the year 1812 only found its Homer half-a-century later. It is also no coincidence that all attempts to portray the heroes and circumstances of the Revolution in artistic literature have been unsuccessful. The point is not lack of talent, but rather absence of the necessary historical and psychological preconditions for such a portrayal. It is no coincidence that the most successful drama from the life of active revolutionary participants was created, it seems, by the English playwright Baring, whose *Two Faced* was produced with such success a few days ago on the London stage. It is easier for an outside observer to capture the most characteristic moments of events and the most typical attributes of the persons involved.

And that is why, until such time as the Revolution can be reflected in the mirror of artistic creativity, works such as Konovalov's are destined to remain the only reliable source for familiarising the public with the revolutionary world. All the convincing power of intimate truthfulness, which penetrates this work throughout, must be felt even by those who have personally formed the most negative impression of the underground and its heroes.

The highlight of the work is the hero's attempt to satisfy the need for personal happiness through love for a woman. In itself, this aspiration is not a defining feature. In one form or another, it arises and is satisfied at various stages of the Revolution. But for Konovalov's hero, this question has an altogether different dimension. For him, the awakened need for love is the reverse side of subconscious disappointment, or more accurately, of a growing lack of faith in the Revolution's favourable outcome. In this case, it is an important subjective symptom of a purely objective fact that has not yet been fully revealed, namely, the receding of the revolutionary wave. The quest for personal happiness and re-emergence of the question of sex are only the subjective reflections of a dying mass-movement that has carried the heroes of the tale on its crest. And that is why, from a purely objective point of view, the concluding lines of the diary must seem lacking in truth and internal logic: 'The period of a new upsurge is beginning. Morale is perceptibly rising...Obviously, the time will soon come when none of us will want to rest'.

Alas, the author of those lines is now resting forever in a cemetery, and every page of his work proves all the more that at the time when he was writing there could be no further upsurge.

But does this mean that we are dealing with a false, rhetorical, didactic and tendentious cliché of hope? No, quite the opposite, for the lines that we have quoted are fully justified in internal psychological terms, and they harmonise with the entire psychology of the work's hero. Indeed, for him to have faith, in spite of objective inevitability, was a matter of life and death, and what is surprising is that the wish, as source of the thoughts, still provided him with hope as a final crumb from the table of life.

As for the rest of the original *belles-lettres* in both of these journals, they are not worth discussing.

―――

In the publicist section of *Russkoe bogatstvo*, the most substantial and interesting articles are by Dioneo and V. Maisky, both of which deal with the position of the coal-miners. Dioneo notes the extremely characteristic fact of steadily growing animosity and hatred amongst England's bourgeois classes towards the proletariat. Utopian novels, so beloved by the English, are appearing with descriptions of the disastrous consequences of a victory for the working class. Dioneo cites the example of a novel that has appeared by Ernest Bramah, *The Secret of the League*, which has enjoyed enormous success amongst the middle-classes. Here is the sort of material it contains. The workers gradually gain power in the state after winning a majority in parliament, and socialists are at the helm of government. A number of laws are passed which, although favourable to the working class, do not satisfy them. The entire tax-burden now falls on the middle-classes, who, driven to extreme animosity, decide not to submit to laws that they find ruinous, and they take up arms and fortify themselves in the cities. The workers send their army out against them, using machine-guns and all the most advanced means of exterminating people. In the end, the middle-classes win: they compel the workers to submit, and they impose their own English sort of 3 June, changing the electoral law so that a majority is guaranteed to those who meet an appropriate property-qualification.

It is a characteristic fact, noted by the author, that the workers have no such animosity towards the bourgeoisie as the latter do towards the workers. They have only a pervasive lack of trust in them, which is fully justified by all the facts, especially of late. It is also interesting, as Dioneo notes, that the recent coal-miners' strike, which cost the whole country so dearly, and above all the workers, yielded vast profits to the mine-owners.

V. Maisky's article introduces us to the position of the German coal-miners and explains the causes of their recent defeat. In his article, he provides some interesting figures. The average wage of coal-miners in the Ruhr basin was as follows:

in 1905 – 4.03 *marks*[2]
in 1907 – 4.87 *marks*
in 1909 – 4.49 *marks*
in 1911 – 4.69 *marks*

Compared to 1907, the coal-miners' wages have fallen – and this at a time when prices for essential goods have risen over a decade by thirty per cent and more!

And working conditions?

'In the Ruhr districts, for example, every year 61 out of every 100 workers end up in hospital. In Bavaria, there are years when, over the course of 12 months, ninety percent of all workers spend some time in a hospital bed'. The life-expectancy of coal-miners in the Ruhr basin is 41 years. In 1909 the number of accidents in German mining amounted on average to 134 out of every 1,000. In other words, in the course of a year almost every worker came to some sort of grief.[3] The facts speak vividly for themselves, and I have cited only a few of them.

In the publicist section of *Sovremennyi mir*, we will mention the article by P.Z., 'On the Way to a "Brainless" Press'. Noting the evolution of technology in the American newspaper-industry, the author predicts the same fate for Russia. In America today, 'brainless' newspapers are multiplying more and more, that is, ones in which half of the material arrives in a ready and printed format from the centre, while the other empty parts of the sheet are filled in on location with the local events, advertisements, and so on that account for the newspaper's name. The very same material is used by dozens of newspapers, making it possible for the material sent out to be both substantive and interesting. And all of this also costs less than operating the entire newspaper with local resources.

For something similar to happen in Russia, two things would be needed. First, in the capitals there would have to emerge correspondingly solid organisations to service the press; and second, the provincial press would have to fall far below its current level and be transformed into small shops that trade only in things for which there is a demand. As for 'press-bureau' organisations in the capitals, thankfully they have not yet become established. In our country, the following types of organisations have appeared and partially operated: the 'Capital Correspondents' Bureau', the 'Cadet Press-Bureau', the 'Russian-American Bureau of the Press', the 'Bureau of Foreign News', the 'All-Russian Correspondents' Bureau "Petrograd"', the 'St. Petersburg Journalist-Association', and the 'St. Petersburg Bureau of the Press'. Of all these organisations, only the first and the last have

---

2. One *mark* equals approximately fifty *kopeks*.
3. *Russkoe bogatstvo*, April 1912, p. 42.

survived. The first, according to its own statement, provides services to 45 publications, while the numbers turning to it are still increasing.

Regarding the second condition for making the provincial press capitalistic – its moral decline – in this respect, things are moving ahead quickly. In the capitals and in the provinces, we have recently seen a whole swarm of unprincipled sheets with only one purpose: to collect subscription-payments and make money from the advertisements. Blackmail and extortion are beginning to flourish, an eloquent example of which we saw recently in Barnaul with the advertising of suspicious deals even in the very text of the newspaper. It will be interesting for Novonikolaevsk readers if we quote one part of the article in question that speaks of the decay of today's provincial press.

> Recently, the newspaper *Obskii vestnik* appeared in the city of Petropavlovsk.[4] Its editor-publisher (and in fact the editor) is a certain Dii Efimovich Konteev, who previously traded in pornographic pictures and other such items in Kamyshlov. Then he declared bankruptcy and, finding himself out of work, used his spare time to organise a branch of the 'Union of the Russian People' in that same city.
>
> By the time the sources of dirty money started to dry up in the Union, Dii Efimovich abandoned this activity, too. Changing his place of residence, he began, as we see, to publish a newspaper, and a 'progressive' newspaper at that.[5]

There is nothing we can add to all of that.

M.L.

---

4. The author meant to say Novonikolaevsk.
5. *Sovremennyi mir*, April 1912, p. 197.

No. 49

'They Married Me without Me'[1]

18 May 1912

In one of the recent telegrams from the south of Russia, we read: 'In Ekaterinoslav many of the local officials turned out to be signed up with the Party of nationalists without their knowledge'.

Imagine, dear reader, some sort of titular councillor named Ivan Ivanovich Ivanov. He is a gentle and quiet man, a service-executive who has never been involved in politics, but has also never been anyone's lackey. One fine morning he gets up, not suspecting anything, smiles light-heartedly over his morning-tea, and it turns out that he is already 'signed up'. He is signed up because his Excellency, the department-head, being also the chairman or deputy chairman of the local club of nationalists, 'vouched' for him.

It is not difficult to imagine how this whole 'marriage'-procedure took place for Ivan Ivanovich and his colleagues.

'So, Andrei Petrovich, can our Party count on success in the city?'

'What a question. Certainly. There are 22 people in my department ... You can sign them all up'.

'And have they already agreed?'

'Well yes, once I say so it means you can sign them up ...'

And they were signed up. The telegraph-director signed up his people; the chairman of the treasury-department, his; the head of the immigration-administration, his; and so on and so forth.

The organisation grew not by the hour, but by the minute, and by the time his Excellency finished his third cup of tea, there was already a union of nationalists in the city with two thousand members.

Ivan Ivanovich, together with his party-colleagues, discussed the current situation. To declare a lack of sympathy for the nationalist party would mean setting oneself up for retirement. To say that one has no interest in politics is useless, because his Excellency will reply that such a position is unworthy, whoever is not with us is against us, and indifference towards the nationalists looks like negligence on the job. There is still one other way out: declare that you belong to the Union of the Russian People. Then they'll leave you alone. But will they believe it? That's the question.

As a result, the newly created members of the party decided to let events follow their natural course.

---

1. [From *Obskaya zhizn'*, 18 May 1912.]

So we signed up, oh well. It's a shame, of course, since we've never before reached the point of joining up with a party of political lackeys. But what can be done? Wife, children, a piece of bread... Let them have their fun: when the elections come, we'll still spite them by giving our votes to the leftists. After all, the voting is secret...

M.L.

No. 50

'To the Congress of Members of the Bourse in Siberia'[1]

20 May 1912

On 15 May, the congress of Siberian bourse-members gathered in Omsk. Readers can find details concerning this congress in several reports on the congress from our special correspondent. In this article, we wish to focus on the general significance of the activity of our Siberian bourse-committees and on the direction the congress must follow if its work is to reflect the interests of Siberian commerce as a whole and the closely associated interests of the general economic development of our outlying district.

Up to now, Siberia has been deprived of *zemstvo* self-government, which even in its stunted form has done so much to raise the cultural and economic level of the population in European Russia, which finds itself in much better conditions for development of its productive forces than Siberia does. The miserable condition of treasury-management of the local economy in Siberia is sufficiently well known. It is not difficult to understand how this circumstance is reflected in the condition of Siberian commerce. Indeed, the chaotic condition of the local economy in Siberia points, above all, to the fact that Siberia has practically no means of communication, the main nerve of commercial activity, no roads, and no bridges. For months at a time, many localities are cut off from communication with the rest of the world. Without roads, it is impossible to attract into the flow of commerce a massive number of villages that have hardly gone beyond the stage of natural economy. The lack of communications devalues agricultural labour and makes it a fruitless waste of effort to produce more grain than the norms of consumption require, for there is nowhere to sell whatever grain might be produced, or else transportation to the point of sale does not justify the expenditures on production. The rational use of land is discouraged, and organisation of large-scale farms, using agricultural machinery, is held back – on the one hand by lack of markets in which to sell the grain and, on the other hand, by the narrowness of these markets. As a result, the Siberian peasantry does not represent, even in the slightest, the purchasing power that it might do if there were orderly means of communication to give an impetus for agricultural expansion.

Need one mention the role that could be played by improvement of the existing means of communication and construction of new ones for utilising the natural riches of Siberia that now lie idle? Need one point out that only *zemstvo* self-government is in a position to manage school-affairs rationally,

---

1. [From *Obskaya zhizn'*, 20 May 1912.]

along with veterinary and medical assistance to the population, the creation of proper statistics, agronomy, and so on? The demand for *zemstvo* self-government must be one of the main points in the programme of desired reforms that have to be advocated from the point of view of commercial interests, which, in this context, correspond with the interests of the entire population.

More intensive railroad-construction in Siberia, using both private capital and treasury-resources, must be the other most important demand of the congress. But since the fate of new lines lies entirely in the hands of the bureaucracy, while the latter, when deciding to undertake construction of one line or another – whether with treasury-funds or through granting concessions to private capital – is not guided at all by the interests of the population or the economic development of the country, it follows that the question at issue leads to demands of a general, political character.

The third important demand of the congress must be a reduction of the tariff-rate on materials exported from Siberia in general and on grain-products in particular. The existing tariff – which impedes the access of Siberian grain to the domestic Russian market and to ports that export grain abroad – frees the grain of Russian owners from the unnecessary competition of cheap Siberian grain and is, in essence, a disguised duty in favour of the large landowners in European Russia.

The tariff-break on iron-products,[2] which favours Urals industry and protects it against competition from the south, hands the Siberian consumer over to the power of Urals factory-owners. And here, it is a handful of industrialists who benefit – industrialists, incidentally, in backward and artificially supported branches – while the entire population of a vast region suffers.

In general, the whole of current economic policy is based on principles of protecting Russian capital and Russian agriculture while disregarding the interests of Siberian capital and Siberian agriculture. And Rozhkov was correct when he noted that the gentlemen in control treat Siberians almost as if they were foreigners. That relation applies in nearly all spheres without exception, beginning with questions of the land, criminal courts and popular education and ending with questions of an economic character such as road-construction and the tariff-structure.

The Siberian merchants are the strongest economic class in Siberia, and the bourse-committees are their most important form of organisation. In the absence of *zemstvo* self-government, the bourse-committees often take upon themselves functions that in normal conditions would be fulfilled by municipalities, and they frequently take the initiative to defend one or another demand in the interests

---

2. [Перелом тарифа на железные продукты.]

of the entire population, which again, in normal conditions, must be put forth by other, more authoritative organs of social autonomy and self-government. If we recall at the same time that the interests of under-privileged Siberian capital in many respects correspond with the interests of our entire 'under-privileged' region, at least as far as its most pressing needs are concerned, then there are grounds for thinking that the representatives of Siberian commerce, in formulating their demands, might go further than the united Russian industrialists, who in all their speeches have nothing more in mind than an attack on the treasury-chest and the consumer's pocket.

The congress of Siberian bourse-participants will only fulfil the role of spokesman for the most urgent needs of the whole of Siberia, a role that falls to them because of a whole set of circumstances, if it does not get buried in particulars and details and rises to an understanding of the interests of commerce as a whole and its connection with the interests of Siberia's economic development. But if the congress takes this path, the only path worthy of the conscious representatives of the commercial-industrial class of the region, and not the path of private and local interests, then it must not only formulate Siberia's urgent demands, some of which we have just enumerated, but also express its views regarding the only conditions in which realisation of all the necessary reforms in Siberia might be possible.

M. Leonov

No. 51

'Amongst the Journals'[1]

23 May 1912

In the May issue of *Vestnik Evropy*, the most interesting item in the *belles-lettres* section is, of course, the conclusion of Gorky's tale 'Three Days'. What I said a month ago about the first part of the story remains fully applicable to the second. The story is told to the end in a strictly realist spirit. This is very welcome to all Gorky's well-wishers, who could not approve of his works during the second period of his literary activity, which were clearly tendentious and, in some places, bombastic and unnatural. The well-wishers, being people with aesthetic taste, could not disagree with much of what was said about Gorky by his bourgeois critics. Gorky has now taken the path of realism. But does this mean there are reasons to speak of the 'resurrection of Gorky'? We think not. Gorky's realism during the first period of his literary activity was a particularly romantic realism. Today, we do not see the romantic element. The story in question can serve as an example. But the realism itself is different from what went before. Now it is missing the colour and brightness found in the first works by Gorky. Today's realism is to the former as Indian summer is to actual summer. Perhaps the cause has nothing to do with talent itself, but with the separation of the author from Russian life. However, the fact remains a fact. But if Gorky today has not risen above the works from his first creative period, or even regained them, we still welcome and take joy in the step forwards he has taken by comparison with the second period of his literary activity, when there were clear grounds to speak of a decline of his talent.

There are interesting short sketches in 'From the Notes of an Advocate' by V. Berenshtam, who has the habit of sharing from time to time, in the form of *belles-lettres*, impressions from his law-practice. Here, for example, we get a picture of a military court trying participants in agrarian terror. The session is closed, and not even the closest relatives of the accused are admitted. But what is impossible for the relatives is fully possible for the wife of the prosecutor, who wants to listen to her 'George', and for whom doors open that are closed to relatives of those accused, who are expecting the death-penalty. George very eloquently proves the need to apply Article 279 to the accused, and the young wife delights in her husband's eloquence. But then she learns from the speech by a lady's defence-attorney that the prosecutor is asking the court to impose a death-sentence on those accused. Now, the scene changes. The young lady faints

---

1. [From *Obskaya zhizn'*, 23 May 1912.]

and, upon reviving, keeps repeating: 'I never thought my George could be so wicked'. The chairman of the court, a general, soothes her by assuring her that the court will look into mitigating the plight of the defendants.

The other two sketches by Berenshtam are also interesting.

In the scientific-publicist section it is worth noting first the article by D.S. Pasmanik, 'The Scientific Basis of Biblical Criticism', which is devoted to the question of the social and community-roots of the religious creativity of Judaism, a question that has recently attracted attention from many researchers: not only specialised theologians, but also historians and sociologists. One might cite, for example, the book by Kautsky that recently appeared, *The Ancient World, Judaism and Christianity*, which is devoted to this question.

There is an interesting article by Maksim Kovalevsky, 'Legislative Borrowing and Adaptations', establishing the fact that there are numerous cases of plagiarism in the legislative creations of various peoples.

Also interesting are the letters of Tchaikovsky and Balakirev that shed light on the conditions in which the former created some of his famous early compositions.

M.L.

No. 52

'Prospects for the Harvest and Grain-Prices'[1]

24 May 1912

Recently, prices on the Novonikolaevsk grain-market have moved sharply lower, and traders are complaining about a complete stagnation in their business. This phenomenon is explained by the expectation of a good harvest for Russia in general, and particularly for those regions that were struck last year by the crop-failure. As we know, last year the Priobsk area enjoyed exceptionally favourable conditions in terms of both the good harvest and very advantageous conditions for selling that harvest. Western Siberia, Orenburg province and the Urals were struck by harvest-failure, and thus the Priobsk region turned out to be a centre for major sales. Compared to the grain-campaign of 1910/11, prices in the current campaign rose by approximately forty percent.

The harvest-outlook is very good today in the regions just mentioned, and it is fully understandable that prices, which were elevated due to last year's crop-failure, have begun to fall rapidly in anticipation of the harvest and, by 15 May, had declined by twenty percent. Naturally, many people are now asking how far the price-decline might go, and whether there are chances that it might be brought to a halt.

We believe that insofar as the price-rise was caused by an exceptionally poor crop in neighbouring regions and was, therefore, temporary in character, it must be followed by a corresponding decline. But we must not forget that the rise in grain-prices on the Novonikolaevsk market was not just a consequence of the crop-failure in neighbouring provinces, but was also influenced by other causes. It is not possible, of course, to determine with arithmetic precision what proportion of the rise was due to the crop-failure and what proportion resulted from other causes, mainly meaning the conjuncture on the world-market. But, in any case, it is absolutely necessary to take that conjuncture into account in order to orient ourselves in the current situation. Likewise, in making predictions for the future we must take that conjuncture into account along with harvest-expectations in the United States and Canada.

As I have already shown in my previous articles,[2] the rise of grain-prices on the world-market is not an accidental phenomenon and, besides a good or bad harvest in America, there are other factors contributing to such a rise[3] that will

---

1. [From *Obskaya zhizn'*, 24 May 1912.]
2. See 'O khlebnik tsenakh' in *Obskaya zhizn'*, Nos. 30 and 33 [In this volume, Documents 1:21 and 1:23].
3. [There is an error in the text, where 'понижение' (decline) appears instead of 'повышение' (rise).]

continue to have an influence. The harvest can only weaken this tendency, but a failure might also intensify it.

According to reports coming from the United States, where, in contrast to Russia, the calculation of future harvests occurs with great precision and care, the coming grain-harvest is estimated to be 21 percent below the norm, and the shortfall of winter-wheat alone is projected to be four hundred million *poods*.[4] For Canada and India, the condition of the new crop is, likewise, not so good. And in Europe, because of unfavourable weather, the harvest-outlook has deteriorated somewhat in recent weeks.

In general, the conjuncture of the international grain-market is pointing towards a significant rise in grain-prices. At this moment, we are actually seeing a rather significant price-rise, which is being held back only by sizeable stocks left over from last year's harvest in America and partly in Russia. The rise in prices is enormously important for Russia, and makes it possible to sell the coming harvest on good terms. As for the latter, reports coming from various provinces indicate that the harvest will generally be average or above-average, and there are some places where it is expected to be outstanding. All of this, of course, depends on future meteorological conditions.

Since grain-prices on the Novonikolaevsk market are determined, apart from accidental causes such as a harvest-failure in neighbouring areas, by the level of world-prices, there are grounds for thinking that the currently observed negative[5] tendency may soon be halted, all the more so since in the district of Chelyabinsk-Petropavlovsk they are expecting a major shortfall this year in the sowing of spring-wheat due a seed-shortage.[6] And that district, because of the Chelyabinsk tariff-break,[7] exports grain mainly to the Baltic ports. Should the Chelyabinsk tariff on grain-shipments be removed this year, the effect will be to increase grain-exports from the Priobsk region and the harvest will be realised at good prices.

M. Leonov

---

4. *S-Pb. Vedomosti* of 16 May.

5. [The text says 'positive', but the meaning is clearly 'negative'; that is, the current decline of local prices might be reversed by high world-market prices and the possibility of expanded exports.]

6. According to newspaper-reports, the area sown with spring-wheat in many agricultural districts is significantly reduced.

7. [To protect central-Russian agriculture and discourage social unrest, in 1896 the government imposed a 'tariff-break' at Chelyabinsk ('Челябинский тарифный перелом'), discouraging shipment of cheaper Siberian grain to the west along the Trans-Siberian railway.]

No. 53

'On the Cadet Party-Conference'[1]

29 May 1912

The newspapers have been reporting on the Cadet party-conference that recently met in St. Petersburg, where the question of the coming election-campaign to the Fourth Duma was discussed. The basic questions for the conference to discuss were, naturally, those concerning the election-platform and electoral agreements. Since, according to a resolution by the Party's Central Committee, the election-platform will be published in the near future, we will postpone for now any appraisal of its points, as they have been reported in the press, in case of possible inaccuracies. As for the resolution on electoral agreements, it seems to have been reported accurately, and we can take some time to consider it.

According to this resolution, the Cadets are entering into electoral agreements to the right, mainly with the Progressives, and they also intend to support those Octobrists who 'have shown themselves to be sincere and consistent constitutionalists'. On the other hand, they will allow electoral agreements with all parties that stand to the left of the Cadets.

As far as an agreement with the Progressives is concerned, it is perfectly understandable. Indeed, it was not so long ago that the Cadets themselves planned to enter the election-campaign under the flag of the Progressives and thus to use the votes of the undecided Progressive elements in their own interests. It was only when the Progressives joined together as an independent party or, if you will, group, that the Cadets changed their original decision and *Rech'* solemnly announced that the Constitutional-Democratic Party cannot begin the election with its own self-destruction. Half a year ago, this operation still seemed possible and advantageous. In a word, an agreement with the Progressives is perfectly natural, especially if we remember that only one evolution is possible for the Cadets, an evolution to the right; that they are trying more than ever to become the voice of those same social groups on which the Progressives depend, that is, the play-liberals of the gentry and the discontented representatives of capital; and that, finally, the Progressives represent to the Cadets a picture of their own future.[2]

---

1. [From *Obskaya zhizn'*, 29 May 1912.]
2. On this basis a split is possible in the Cadet party, especially at a moment of social upsurge.

What looks incomprehensible at first sight is the decision by the conference to support Left-Octobrists on the one hand, and to enter into an agreement with leftists on the other.

The word 'constitutionalist' is quite compromised for us, thanks to the Cadets. Today, this word is used by every conservative to describe himself when giving liberal speeches and sulking against one or another expression of current state-policy, but not in opposing the social conditions that give rise to and support that policy. But that is minor. Now the word 'constitutionalist' is to be compromised still further by attaching it to several Octobrists, and even with the touching epithet 'sincere'. As biting mockery, this appellation is perfectly understandable. After all, whatever liberal speeches one or another Octobrist may deliver, and whatever disagreements and divisions may arise within that Party, in terms of what is most essential – their attitude towards the Act of 3 June – all Octobrists are of one mind. If we recall that the Act of 3 June was an actual *coup d'état*, then the sincere constitutionalism of the Party and of individual representatives of the Party that accepted that Act – and that became a social force on the basis of the Act and fed on its consequences – must stand out in all its caricatured glory. In reality, all Octobrists are reactionaries without exception, for the Act of 3 June was a step backwards. They demonstrated this in a perfectly obvious way when they 'manfully' closed the doors in discussing the inquiry concerning the S-D fraction in the Second Duma, when Meyendorff and Kapustin acted in complete agreement with Gololobov and Rodzyanko. It is true that the gentlemanly Kapustins can be called constitutionalists – if one has in view the constitution of 3 June, which these gentlemen have no interest in changing. But if the word 'constitutionalist' is taken in that sense, that is, simply to mean a conservative, then starting with this Lassallean understanding of a constitution even Pobedonostsev[3] can be considered a constitutionalist, for he, too, stood on the ground of the constitution (in a Lassallean sense) of pre-revolutionary Russia and was no less of a 'sincere' constitutionalist than those who are constitutionalists within the limits of the 3 June régime.

The decision by the Cadets to support certain Octobrists and to enter at the same time into agreements with leftists is internally contradictory and cannot, in fact, be implemented, because it distorts the entire political meaning of the election-campaign for the Left. Generally speaking, support for liberals against rightists is expedient and is practiced everywhere. But to support one group of reactionaries against another is nonsense. It is well-known that consistently democratic groups do not plan to enter into any agreement with the Cadets in

---

3. [Konstantin Petrovich Pobedonostsev (1827–1907) was the arch-reactionary Chief-Procurator of the Holy Synod, known for notorious anti-Semitism and for describing democracy as a 'dictatorship of the vulgar mob'.]

the first stage of the elections. But even if certain groups on the Left recently projected such agreements, they have become totally impossible following the conference-resolution to support left-wing Octobrists. One has to think that the only real result of the conference-resolution will be support for the Left-Octobrists and a rupture with leftists. In reality, the Cadets, with a little more insight, should have posed the question directly: either the Left-Octobrists or the Left. It is difficult to imagine that they did not think their way through such a simple thing, and one has to assume that what we are seeing here is a deliberate game on two fronts. From the Cadets' point of view, there is nothing contradictory in this double game. The Octobrists are closer to them, of course, than leftists are. But the Left can also be useful in defeating the Right, so there is no sense in alienating them. That is also true because when liberals enter into agreements with the Left, it is the liberals who gain the most, as demonstrated by a mass of facts from electoral practice in the West and especially by the recent elections to the German Reichstag. Finally, in view of the clear unwillingness of the extreme Left to enter into any sort of deals with Cadets during the first stage of the elections, a position that has been reinforced following the Cadets' decision to support Left-Octobrists, the Cadets can boldly lay the blame for defeats in one locality or another on the leftists who supposedly prevented combined forces from defeating the Right.

Thus, a seemingly contradictory decision to support the Left-Octobrists and to enter an agreement with the Left, answers in reality both to the psychology and the interests of our liberals.

The election-campaign will show whether the Party's decisions will be of more benefit to those who are to the left or to the right of the Cadets.

M. Leonov

No. 54

'The Poor Industrialists!'[1]

6 June 1912

Traditional Russian liberalism, having grown up on the basis of the gentry's opposition to absolutism, supported free trade from the very beginning. On the one hand, this position answered the material interests of the landowning class, who were interested in inexpensive agricultural machinery, while on the other hand it was a winner in terms of relations to the broad masses of the population, who were handed over to be fleeced by a small handful of industrialists. But the more our liberalism's centre of gravity moved towards the progressive part of the merchant-class and manufacturers, the more discontent was provoked by the traditional liberal commitment to free trade. At the present moment, the progressive section of our bourgeoisie is totally committed to protectionism. Represented by its organ *Utro Rossii*, it is waging a systematic campaign not only to preserve, but also to strengthen a protectionist system that has already assumed monstrous dimensions. We will deal with one such article from the newspaper.

In No. 122, a certain Shloss writes, among other things, that:

> A somewhat strange impression of purely-armchair reasoning results from this mechanical and artificial division of society into two supposedly disconnected castes – the producers and the consumers.
>
> In real life every consumer is a producer and, vice versa, every producer is a consumer. Any industrialist, factory-owner or manufacturer is simultaneously a consumer – of machines in the extractive industries, and of both machines and materials in the processing industries. He is also a consumer in everyday life.
>
> Therefore, we must speak of protecting industry, certainly not of protecting the industrialists.

What could be more convincing than this argument? In place of this author I have not mentioned any others, since they would only weaken the force of the present argument. Yet Mr. Shloss apparently senses for himself the absurdity of the idea he expresses, and he hastens to grasp at examples from the economic history of other countries. He says:

---

1. [From *Obskaya zhizn'*, 6 June 1912.]

Our free-traders want to take an example from England, the only country that has no protectionism. But what example is there for us in England, a country that had already conquered the world three-quarters of a century ago with its industry?

If we wish to turn to economic history and draw evidence from it, then rather than dealing with chronology we must look at corresponding stages. England began to turn away from protectionism only in the twenties of the last century, a time when the industry previously sheltered by protectionism was becoming so strong that no other country's industry could dream of competing against it.

The same can be seen in another modern industrial giant – Germany. Just fifty years ago its industry was still a dwarf, yet now it is a threatening competitor for England.

We leave aside the question of whether Germany today needs the protectionism to which it still clings; we leave that question aside because it presently has no significance for Russia.

Thus, the employer is also a consumer, and he, too, suffers from protectionism. But what an amazing misunderstanding of his interests! Why is it that he does not demand the end of protectionism? Mr. Ryabushinsky must realise that the 'hired' publicist he has working for him is not distinguished by any particularly sharp mind or ingenuity when it comes to defending the merchants' pockets. As a consumer, the industrialist may suffer a loss due to protectionism, amounting, let us say, to a thousand roubles, but as a producer he gains tens of thousands.

The author's references to England and Germany are particularly unconvincing. Political economy takes it as an established fact, based on the history of economic development in these and other countries in Western Europe, that protectionism is a necessary first stage for the development of a country's national industry, and becomes an obstacle to further development if it is maintained beyond a certain period. If one listens to our manufacturers when they complain about reproaches concerning the technological backwardness of Russian enterprises, one would think we had long ago reached the stage where protectionism becomes redundant and harmful. But one need only mention the timeliness of a removal of tariff-protection – if not complete removal, then a partial easing – and the jeremiads[2] start up about the weakness, youthfulness and technological backwardness of Russian industry, which will be killed by free trade. When England removed tariffs, a section of the manufacturers also raised a cry about the destruction of industry; and with removal of grain-tariffs the landowners raised

---

2. [Preobrazhensky uses the term 'jeremiad' to refer to a lengthy lamentation concerning the state of society.]

a cry about the destruction of agriculture. Yet free trade brought nothing but benefits, both to English industry and to the English people.

According to Mr. Shloss, 'In the economic sphere we are unfortunately now living through the same period as England did a hundred and fifty to a hundred years ago, or Germany fifty to sixty years ago. Therefore, if we want examples from the history of other countries to be useful for us, those are the epochs to which we must turn our gaze'.

If we follow the author's advice and 'turn our gaze' to the England of a hundred years ago (the publicist prudently adds a hundred and fifty years ago, having no idea that he is immediately speaking of two different economic periods), then what we will see there is an already strong free-trade movement. As early as 1820, the London merchants served up the famous petition for free trade, and Canning's ministry took a number of measures to weaken the protectionist system. It turns out that it is also time for us to consider liquidating the monstrous protectionism by eliminating the tariff on imported manufactures and ending the subsidies for our industrialists.

Yes, Mr. Ryabushinsky has taken on quite an inept publicist...

The fact that our protectionism really is monstrous can be seen by comparing the tariff-rates for identical commodities in Germany, France, Austria and Russia. Our tariff-rates exceed the corresponding ones in other countries several times over.

'Talk about the excessive enrichment of capitalists under protectionism should be moderated', says Mr. Shloss. His tone is very moderate. Evidently, Mr. Shloss sees for himself that there is something to discuss here. And really, if we turn to the numbers, we see that for just the 12 most important products, the Russian consumer overpays the gentlemen-industrialists, by the most moderate reckoning, by 230 million roubles every year. And all of the indirect damage caused by protectionism cannot, of course, be calculated.

'Protectionism is not at all the equivalent of monopolisation, which truly does place the consumer in the hands of the producer'.

But that depends on what kind of protectionism. The fate of our sugar-industry shows that our protectionism can turn individual branches of industry if not into a monopoly, then into something very close to it. With the existing tariff, our consumer has no guarantee at all against the possibility of finding himself facing a series of monopolies in the most important branches of industry, which even now are syndicalising more and more every year.

There is yet another excellent passage in the article that concerns us. Mr. Shloss writes: 'There is no denying that with protectionism the consumer must overpay somewhat. But really, apart from anarchism, is there any social or state-theory that denies the inevitable need for certain sacrifices on the part of individual persons, or even the entire current generation, in the name of certain state- or social goals?'

Therefore, good people, go ahead and sacrifice. Sacrifice in order to fill the heavy purses of the gentlemanly Krestovnikovs. Don't be anarchists. After all, it's a matter of state.

In reality, it is not the state's business to support millionaires at the expense of the poor, or industrialists at the cost of delaying Russia's industrial development.[3]

M. Leonov

---

3. [Readers familiar with Preobrazhensky's work in the 1920s, when he endorsed protectionism and a foreign-trade monopoly for the sake of 'primitive socialist accumulation', will recognise the irony of the present article.]

No. 55

'The Workers' Movement in May'[1]

9 June 1912

In the past month, the workers' movement assumed even broader dimensions than in April. On the first of the month, there was the enormous one-day demonstration-strike, which was most extensive in St. Petersburg but also occurred in the provinces. In 15 of the most important centres for which there were reports in the newspapers, 288,000 participated, including those involved in the 1 May strike and reports of delayed responses to the Lena events, mainly in Poland. If we take into account the fact that there were also reports of a 1 May strike in several other cities, without any indication of the numbers, then we can safely assume that the number celebrating 1 May was up to three-hundred thousand.

As for the economic struggle, in the past month it has especially intensified. According to data we have available, there were 124 strikes during May. In this context, one must remember that when strikes are waged in a number of enterprises by a single profession, for instance, in the Moscow leather-works or by construction-workers in several enterprises of the city, they are often counted as a single strike. We know the number of participants in 85 cases, but not for another 39. For the 85 enterprises, the number was 72,230. If we include an approximate figure for participants in the other 39 enterprises, and also remember that the press does not give reports of all strikes, especially in the provinces, then we can confidently say that the number of participants in the economic strike-movement for May exceeded one hundred thousand.

Unfortunately, the information that we have is quite inadequate for illuminating the outcome of the strikes, which is the most interesting question. Out of 124 strikes we know the outcome only in 62 cases, that is, exactly one-half of the affected enterprises. For the rest, the outcome is either unknown or the strikes are still continuing. Of the 62 strikes for which we have information, 45 ended fully or partially to the workers' benefit, while 17 were complete failures. Thus, the number of fully or partially successful strikes comes to 63 percent. It is difficult to say how far these data, which refer only to one-half of the enterprises, reflect the true state of affairs. But whatever the case may be, the result is extremely characteristic. We have evidently entered a period when strikes must end favourably for the workers in the majority of cases, even despite their lack of professional organisations and in the presence of a strong organisation among

---

1. [From *Obskaya zhizn'*, 9 June 1912.]

the class of employers. A favourable industrial conjuncture transforms the weak into the strong.

In terms of territory, the strikes were distributed as follows. The greatest number occurred in St. Petersburg (72 strikes), followed by the Baltic territory (15 strikes) and Poland (eight strikes). The other 29 strikes occurred in different areas of Russia.

M.L.

No. 56

Review of the Journals *Russkoe bogatstvo* and *Sovremennyi mir* (May)[1]

10 June 1912

In the section of original *belles-lettres* in the May issue of *Russkoe bogatstvo*, the only item worthy of attention is the conclusion to F. Kryukov's tale 'The Officer's Wife'. I have already spoken of the beginning of this tale in the last journal-review. Now, the reader gets a finished picture of the Cossack, who has ingratiated his way to an officer's rank and then returns home to the plough, followed by his short stay at home in a life he could not stand, and then his departure to a place where 'the collegiate governor offered the position of police-officer for 72 roubles in hard cash'. The tale clearly portrays the daily life of Cossacks, and the tales and stories by Kryukov are just about the only material available for that purpose.

The story by O.N. Ol'nem, 'The Unemployed', depicting the life of the upper-level provincial administration, is pale and dry and prompts only one wish: to see less of such tedious and tiresome time-wasting on the pages of the journal.

The conclusion of the novel by A. Sefarimovich, *City on the Steppes*, is published in *Sovremennyi mir*. The novel has both merits and defects. The defects include the improbable causes for the moral decline of the engineer Polynov. Is it believable that in real life an intelligent, sensitive and loving wife, with her groundless jealousy and suspicions, would drive her husband into becoming an alcoholic who is 'no longer human'? If sober people, who are not so strict with themselves, turn into alcoholics, it is for other reasons that are more severe. Let me also say a few words about the style. Before getting to the novel by Sefarimovich, the first pages of *Sovremennyi mir* are taken up by an endlessly boring novel written by Rukavishnikov in a style that has all the charm of the fashionable stylistic insanity that comes when a healthy man breathes the atmosphere of the yellow house. Reading the novel by Serafimovich, one sees in it a reflection of the same manner of writing – to be sure, only to a limited degree, but perceptible nevertheless. Sefarimovich's previous writing was simpler and better. Neither he nor Gusev-Orenburgsky has guarded himself against the influence of a fashionable style whose social-pathological origin is beyond any doubt and whose literary significance is nil. This imitation of youth, an assimilation of the ugliest legacy of reaction into literature, produces an impression that is both ridiculous and sad. The nerve-racking style of writing is as suitable to these writers as a fashionable tail-coat and top-hat is to a village-priest such as Gusev-Orenburgsky

---

1. [From *Obskaya zhizn'*, 10 June 1912.]

portrays in his works. As in many other places throughout the entire novel, the concluding lines of the work are written in this fashionable style and would have been better left out.

Regarding the merits of the novel, they include the importance and topicality of the theme and a number of truthful pictures and scenes from the life of workers and the intelligentsia who are closely associated with them. Essentially, the whole novel by Sefarimovich is a play with two acts. In the first act, the engineer Polynov is energetic and incorruptible, the ideal type for his profession, but he is also sceptical of any kind of propaganda amongst the workers and of revolutionary activity in general. His wife, on the whole, shares her husband's point of view. The wife's brother, Petya, is a student, propagandist and organiser of workers' circles together with a group of conscious workers – representatives of another realm and another generation. The years pass, the circumstances change, and the second act opens. The engineer Polynov has become an alcoholic, and the student Petya has 'smartened up' and stopped 'playing a fool', as the wise philistines of our day put it: now he gladly accepts a position as legal consultant to a grasping manufacturer, but when a strike begins in the factories and the young generation, represented by his niece Katya, calls upon him to be an ally in helping the strikers, he frowns and replies: 'I can't bear these philanthropic ventures'. His old comrades from among the workers have experienced a similar evolution, including Volkov, the former leader of the movement, about whom the tavern-owner says: 'They have sold their home, and they made a good profit at that'. But with the enthusiasm and faith of youth, the new generation of the intelligentsia, in the persons of Katya, Borshchov and other workers, carries on the cause that Petya and Volkov have abandoned.

We must note, however, that A. Sefarimovich commits a great sin against reality when he treats the change of generations among the intelligentsia and the workers in the same terms. Among workers, the problem of the old and the young assumes a completely different character by comparison with the state of affairs in the intelligentsia groups. Of course, one encounters the Volkovs, who are willing to sell their home and become philistines, yet they are the exception. The majority of old and young workers continue to be hired workers, and for all of them the questions arising from the very essence of proletarian existence neither age nor lose their burning interest. On the contrary, among the intelligentsia the exceptions are precisely those who do not follow Petya's all-too-familiar evolution.

The story by B. Ivinsky, 'Enemies', has an interesting subject. An accordion-player, Zakhar, and the girlfriend he lives with earn their bread in a tavern by harmonising and singing. A 'blind musician', also an accordionist, arrives with a boy and offers his services. The tavern owner arranges a competition between the musicians, which ends badly for Zakhar, but the blind man understands that he has won a piece of bread from someone just as impoverished as he is, and in conclusion the tavern resounds with his sobs rather than a celebration of victory.

The publicist section in *Russkoe bogatstvo* is quite substantial. Here, we find 'Outrage', an article by S. Elpat'evsky, the best publicist in the journal. Elpat'evsky notes a complete dissolution of old and traditional relations and habits not only in the sphere of the broad masses, but also in the ruling bureaucratic circles where, despite established respect for rank, people 'from another world', unknown to anyone, have begun to rule – people such as Rasputin, Iliodor, Countess Ignat'eva, and so on. The author also points to a growth of hooliganism in the highest ranks of society. In this connection he writes:

> There is a view that those bawdy tavern-words that fly from the right-wing benches of the State-Duma are uttered with a deliberate intention to befoul and cover the State-Duma with dirt, but it seems more appropriate to take into account the effect of the environment. The amazing alliance of the upper levels of society with not just the lowest, but also the most vile strata of the Russian population, cannot but be reflected in the psyche and its forms of expression, in the manners of those who have formed this alliance. And one can assume that the famous authors of obscene words in the State-Duma utter them not simply to befoul the very idea of the Duma, and not just because they want to make themselves understood and convincing to that element of their audience who find exactly such coarse tavern-language persuasive, but also because they have taken on the colouring of their environment and absorbed its vocabulary and forms of address...When Counts rent an apartment together with the lowest and most flagrantly corrupt people, with provocateurs and the instigators of murder, and when they go out together to eat and drink, the white gloves of the Counts cannot help but be stained with the filth and blood of those bloody and filthy hands that touch them.[2]

It is difficult to disagree with any of this.

In a substantial article entitled 'Home-Rule', Dioneo familiarises the reader with existing opinions in England for and against the bill on self-government in Ireland, which was recently introduced in Parliament, and also with some of the history of Ireland's subjugation by fire and sword. Pointing out that all previous attempts by the Liberals to implement a curtailed form of Home-Rule were opposed by the Irish themselves, whereas now, to the contrary, they stand united

---

2. *Russkoe bogatstvo*, May 1912, p. 89.

in support of Asquith's bill, Dioneo explains this phenomenon by the fact that the Englishmen have sincerely recognised the mistake of their policy of national oppression and now the Irish are meeting them halfway. He writes: 'An open and brave admission by the ruling nationality that their entire behaviour towards the defeated nationality is unjustified is producing amazing results'.[3] 'It is a joyous thing to observe an expression of state prudence that should lead to reconciliation of the nationalities and their merger into one family, a single people'.[4]

Dioneo's idealistic view does not withstand criticism even from the figures that he provides to characterise the past and present financial relations between Ireland and England. Since 1801, Ireland has overpaid England to the sum of hundreds of millions of roubles. Since the time when the landlords' estates were redeemed in Ireland – an operation that was profitable for the latter due to a fall in income from the land caused by competition from cheap American grain – the opposite picture has prevailed. According to Dioneo's data, the estimates for 1912–13 show that England's expenditures on Ireland come to approximately 12 million pounds sterling (120 million roubles), while its revenues from there are more than 10,000,640 pounds-sterling (101,000 roubles). Therefore, England must overpay by a significant sum, which is not in the interests of the English ruling classes. And if we recall that the proposed legislation on Home-Rule reduces the overpayment to Ireland to zero, then the change of front among the English bourgeoisie on the question of Ireland is fully understandable. The state-prudence, which Dioneo so admires and which has dawned so suspiciously late upon the ruling classes of England, is essentially a simple economic calculation.

M.B. Ratner's article, 'Materialistic and Idealistic Elements in the System of Karl Marx', which promises so much by its title, essentially belongs in a section of ruminant literature. Everything that Ratner operates with in his article has been repeated a thousand times over in polemics against Marxists. He conscientiously gathers up all the specimens of bourgeois misunderstanding, or distorted and perverted understandings, of Marxism. As an exhibition of bourgeois narrow-mindedness in the area of theory, the article makes some sense. That was hardly the author's goal when he wrote it.

The publicist section of *Sovremennyi mir* contains a substantial article by G.V. Plekhanov, 'An Unsuccessful History of the "*Narodnaya Volya*" Party', devoted to the historical work of Mr. Bogucharsky that was recently published as a separate book. Bogucharsky wrote his history of the *Narodnaya Volya* party from a liberal standpoint so that, according to his description, the *narodovolsty* were more astute than the Narodniks since they understood the whole importance of political freedom for Russia; and the liberals are more far-sighted than

---

3. *Russkoe bogatstvo*, May 1912, p. 2.
4. *Russkoe bogatstvo*, May 1912, p. 5.

the *narodovolsty* because, while knowing the necessity for political freedom, they have also understood the futility of the latter's attempt to seize power. In this regard Plekhanov quite justifiably notes that just as we have had representatives of utopian *narodnichestvo*, so there have also been representatives of utopian liberalism such as Mr. Petrunkevich, who have counted on the prudence of an all-powerful bureaucracy that at some fine moment would make Russia happy by 'crowning the building'. If we compare the Narodniks with the liberals in terms of their greater or lesser historical far-sightedness, then the Narodniks were most certainly superior; although they idealised the people, and to that extent were mistaken, they saw the source for a possible transformation of Russia's social-political system in the autonomous activity of the popular masses, in their struggle against the ruling classes, and thus they were right on the main point.

In Plekhanov's article there are a number of valuable observations on the history of the period, which Bogucharsky writes about on the basis of published documents, but which Plekhanov himself witnessed and in which he participated. Plekhanov's article is interesting not simply as a talented expression of the Marxists' view of this particular period of Russia's history, but also as a valuable historical document.

L'vov-Rogachevsky's article, 'Artist and Truth-Seeker', gives a characterisation of Gorky's literary individualism and outlines the evolution the writer has undergone up to the recent period of his creative work, which is marked by features of realism. L'vov-Rogachevsky thinks that critics, who announced the 'death of Gorky' following the appearance of his tendentious works such as *Mother*, along with his publicist *belles-lettres*, were opposing Gorky's democratic ideals, which have become foreign to those of the intelligentsia who have moved to the right and succumbed to the influence of *Vekhi*.

Meanwhile, somewhat further on in the same article, the author himself gives a damning characterisation of *Mother* precisely from the aesthetic point of view. The critic does a poor job of separating attacks on Gorky's political credo, masked as aesthetic arguments, from attacks by his political co-thinkers, whose evaluations were motivated purely by artistic concerns and who took a negative view of the writer's tendentious works on that basis alone. G.V. Plekhanov, incidentally, was among this latter group. It is true that the Gorky's most unsatisfactory works in artistic terms, such as *Mother*, enjoy the greatest success among workers. But that only shows the aesthetic semi-literacy even of the most advanced strata of the proletariat. One hardly needs to point out that anyone who becomes enraptured over *Mother* does not understand the depth of creativity in Shakespeare and Goethe or appropriately value the incomparable works of Tolstoy.

M.L.

No. 57

'The Right to Suicide'[1]

17 June 1912

I

Does a man have a right to suicide?

That question is beginning to be discussed in the press since publication of Leonid Andreev's letter on suicide.[2] L. Andreev answers the question in favour of the person committing suicide. The right to end one's own life is an inalienable right of every man and is much less open to doubt than the right to smoke a cigarette bought with one's own money. That is how, or approximately how, Andreev thinks, and there are many among us who think the same way. But most people are probably on the side of those who take the opposite view of the issue. There have been many protests in the press against L. Andreev's letter. They condemn him because they see in his letter an indirect encouragement of suicide.

But all these reproaches are lacking above all in logic, not to mention the fact that they express a complete misunderstanding of the essence of the suicide-problem, as we shall see below. After all, the question concerns the right to suicide, not its expediency and moral acceptability. Therefore all moral maxims, first and foremost, have nothing to do with the matter, and the question has to be put this way: Does the individual or the group have the right to decide the fate of an individual life? It is only on this level that one can either dispute Andreev's opinion or agree with him.

The question of right is a question of viewpoint. From the viewpoint of a conscious worker, the employer does not have a right to the product of his labour; from the employer's viewpoint, it is exactly the opposite. In terms of the bourgeois-individualistic world-view that prevails in modern society, the right to suicide is incontestable. To deny that right is to deny the fundamental principle of modern society – the right of ownership. It is perfectly obvious that if I have the

---

1. [From *Obskaya zhizn'*, 17 June 1912. This piece continues in Documents 1:60 and 1:72]

2. [Leonid Nikolaevich Andreev (1871–1919) was one of Russia's most prolific early nineteenth-century writers. His 1904 anti-war story *Red Laughter*, a response to the Russo-Japanese War, led to his imprisonment in 1905 and subsequent emigration to Europe, where he lived for a time in Capri as a guest of Maxim Gorky. Although Andreev was an enemy of the old régime in Russia, he also ultimately opposed the Bolshevik Revolution.]

right of disposal, at my own discretion, of the things that belong to me, then the first such thing is my own person. Manchester-style non-intervention in private life prevails even when it is a question of ending that life itself.

In reality, modern society is far from recognising its members' right to suicide. This shows yet again how hopelessly entangled it is in its own contradictions, of which the aforementioned is only one of many. A clear expression of such contradiction occurs in the press when they speak out against the right to suicide, yet on basic questions take the viewpoint of the existing bourgeois society.

According to the teachings of the Christian Church, suicide is a sin and the person who kills himself cannot be buried according to Christian rites. If one looks at religion in the way Ludwig Feuerbach did, as a mystical reflection of the real relations between people, then in Christianity's attitude to suicide we can see a vague recognition of society's right over the life of an individual person. The sin against God, which the person committing suicide does according to the Christian religion, is, when translated from mystical into real language, a sin against society, whose interests are violated to one degree or another by the fact of suicide when the individual crosses beyond the line of individual rights and personal interests. The element of community in the Christian world-view is expressed, as we see, much more sharply than in the bourgeois-individualistic understanding of human relations. And that is not surprising, if we remember the social roots from which ancient Christianity developed.

It seems to us that the question of a right to suicide must be presented in a completely different light: the focus must be shifted not to a moral appraisal but to determining the causes of the phenomenon. Before deciding the question of a right to suicide, it is first necessary to clarify whether in the enormous majority of cases we are dealing with murder.

Until now, the problem of suicide involved mainly psychologists and the authors of *belles-lettres*. Sociology came rather late to the subject, and although it assumes decisive importance in clarifying the causes of suicide, the results of sociological research in this direction are thus far not very great. True, the most important step has been taken. Work on the statistical data concerning suicide has managed to establish a certain pattern. The average number of suicides has been established for a certain age, gender, time of the year, and partially for social status. But up to now, the link has not been established between suicides and a certain level of society's economic development or the position of certain classes in society and their evolution. There is no doubt that every class has its own suicide-figures and its own patterns as to how they change, just as every social structure – slave-owning, feudal and capitalist – has its own law of suicide. What needs to be done is to clarify one fundamental cause of suicides, which applies in all cases, when the external causes of suicide are so astonishing in all their variations. Whether it is an unemployed person who ends his life in a state of malnutrition or a rich bourgeois in a state of satiety, a hopeless paralytic or a young person in the bloom of youth and good health – in all cases we need to disclose a single hidden cause. What is this cause? In time, sociology will have to provide an answer to the question, for all the current answers, which cite dozens of psychological, physiological, racial, social and numerous other kinds of causes, explain nothing precisely because they introduce a superfluity of causes. If, for example, we are dealing with some concrete instance of suicide, and both a doctor from a medical viewpoint and a psychiatrist from a psychological viewpoint determine corresponding causes for the act, that by no means implies that the facts have been explained. Indeed, the spiritual imbalance and psychological abnormality pointed out by the psychiatrist also need to be explained. And thus the sociologist's work only begins where that of the psychiatrist ends. The phenomenon of suicide will, no doubt, provide a wealth of material for future research in the matter of understanding the most complex mainsprings of modern society. The methods that society uses in adapting to the struggle with nature and in the class-struggle find their expression through suicides – and these methods change with the social structure of society and vary even between different classes of one and the same society during one and the same historical period.

I posed the question above as to whether suicide may be, if not always then in the majority of cases, simply murder.

It seems to me that all suicides in circumstances of hunger and need have the undoubted character of murder. In certain primitive societies, there was a custom of killing old people beyond a certain age. The burdensome struggle for existence left no surpluses for those incapable of working, and in the interest of preserving the group they must not be allowed to take bread from the healthy. This custom somewhat moderated later, and out of a sense of pity the members of the community brought food to those fated to live too long who attempted to take their own lives. Our civilised society takes a different approach. Possessing enough supplies of vital necessities to feed twice as many people as there now are on the entire Earth, and disposing of productive forces that are capable of increasing those supplies without limit, modern society nevertheless systematically condemns a mass of able-bodied and healthy members to death by starvation once they turn out to be redundant for the current stage of development of the existing mode of production. The cruelty of our civilised society far exceeds the unavoidable cruelty of savages. But this cruelty also has a disgusting shade of hypocrisy. Debates about the right to suicide must involve mocking hypocrisy or, at best, unconscious insolence, in a society that throws a rope of hunger around its victim's neck, kicks out the bench from underfoot, and then discusses the profound question: Does this victim have the right to die?

The case for suicide-as-murder is not so clear when we are dealing with people who commit suicide in circumstances of satiety and disappointment with life. But with some effort of thought, it is also not difficult to find here a complete analogy. Indeed, the deep sense of apathy, the consciousness of being useless and other such psychological conditions, which precede suicide, are essentially only a subjective reflection in consciousness of the social uselessness of the particular individual. Here, the psychological condition is not the cause, only an accompanying aspect of the suicide. Insofar as we can find an explanation in the midst of generally spontaneous processes, an individual only senses his uselessness when the society makes clear that it has no use for the given individual. In this case, self-destruction is only the most comfortable way for society to free itself of redundant members; it is a surgical operation in which the unneeded or harmful limb severs itself from the body.

Confirmation of this way of thinking can be found in the particularly large number of suicides that occur among satiated classes, whose role in history has been played out but who have yet to be eliminated 'by order of the class-struggle'. One need only recall the suicides among the Roman aristocracy at the time of the collapse of the Roman Empire, or the suicides among the feudal aristocracy. Here, we must also include suicides on the grounds of disillusionment with life, which have assumed such monstrous numbers among the Russian intelligentsia in the period of counter-revolution and are closely linked with the superfluity of the intelligentsia and the tragic position of this social group in a period of reaction. The point is that this group experienced defeat in its struggle for democratic ideals and cannot fully achieve its historic destiny: to dissolve among the different classes of modern society and die out as an independent political force. This natural death, as the result of a normal social process, is being held back due to an insufficiently rapid process of class-differentiation, which in the case of victory for the October movement would have proceeded more quickly. The result is that the normal process whereby this class would die out *en masse* as an intermediate social group, with an independent initiative to play in the political struggle, has degenerated into a process of individual suicides: here, we see something analogous to what happens when the mass-struggle degenerates into terror and partisan attacks. Here we must also include many expropriations as one of the forms of suicide.

On the contrary, it is useful to remember here that in periods when the need for people is most intense, when every force is crucial for work and defence of the country – among agricultural peoples and emerging classes with an expansive future ahead of them – there are virtually no suicides resulting from disappointment with life.

The considerable numbers of suicides on grounds of unrequited or disrupted love hold a special place. It is difficult to establish social roots for such suicides, which are analogous to the animal-kingdom: remember the suicides of swans, turtle-doves, and so on. Moreover, we must not forget that it is not this final form of settling accounts with life that has made the problem of suicide the topic of the day and one of the most cursed questions of our times.

The question of a right to suicide will only make sense in a future society, where no material motives for suicide will exist. Only in a society that has guaranteed to all its members the means of existence will the question be appropriate as to whether an individual has a personal right, which certainly belongs to the group, and that is where the right to life and death will have to be found.[3] Today, no such right exists, only the duty of a death that is dictated to the individual by society and does not flow from his own internal aspirations. Today, every suicide is a new act of indictment against the existing social relations. And there is deep meaning in the instinctive movement that makes every person try to prevent another from ending his life: behind the external form of suicide, he unconsciously senses a murder in which the trigger of the revolver, pointed at the temple, is pulled not by the solitary hand of the condemned, but by the collective hand of the entire society pushing its victim beyond the doors of life.

M. Leonov

---

3. This issue is discussed in *O morali i klassovykh normakh* [*On Morality and Class-Norms* – Preobrazhensky 1923].

No. 58

Review of the Journal *Vestnik Evropy* (June)[1]

19 June 1912

In the *belles-lettres* section of the June volume of *Vestnik Evropy* there is 'not a thing'. Strictly speaking, there are stories there, as one must expect, but they are boring, lifeless and mediocre stories. They appear there out of duty, just as officials do on an office-day. But an office-day for mediocrity is a non-office day for talent. And during recent years, there have been too many non-office days in our artistic literature generally, and especially in the thick journals.

In this volume there is a story by N. Oliger, 'Country Corner', which puts in its time, but is bleak and empty.

Just as bleak and empty are the essays of V.I. Dmitrieva that have begun to be published under the title 'Youth'.

In 'The Hungry Village' there are interesting essays of a *semi-belles-lettres* sort by Tan. Here, a whole gallery of provincial types come before the reader: the land-captains, die-hards, the third element, the village-priesthood and finally, of course, and most frequent of all, the starving peasant. In the part of the essays included in the June issue, the most interesting figure is that of the village-priest, who is struggling with famine along with female students from Moscow in a touching unity. As it is meant to be in our modern times, for his 'discovery' of famine the untiring priest is repeatedly relieved of his post, shut up in a monastery, and so on. As for the peasants, Tan's essays show us the familiar faces of Chekhov's peasants, who still have no faith in the selfless representatives of the intelligentsia who are helping them and, as before, continue to believe in a new redistribution of the land.

The publicist section of the journal is more substantial than the *belles-lettres*. There is an interesting article by Maxim Kovalevsky, 'Herzen and the Emancipation-Movement in the West'. The author, who knew Karl Marx personally, indicates the reasons why Marx sharply disagreed with Herzen. Those reasons were: Herzen's attraction to national movements, which Marx saw as the greatest impediment to the development of international working-class solidarity; the lordly conditions in which Herzen lived; his friendship with Marx's personal enemies, and so on. The following remark by Kovalevsky is interesting: 'I suggest that Herzen and Marx were far from having irreconcilable points of view, that Herzen was a communist in his own way', and so on. Yes, he was a communist.

---

1. [From *Obskaya zhizn'*, 19 June 1912.]

But we still have to keep in mind the Rodichevs and Milyukovs, who have turned Herzen into a right-wing Cadet.

At the conclusion of his article, the honourable professor cannot avoid a corresponding moral for our own day: the failure of the European revolution of 1848, which shocked Herzen so deeply, resulted from the inability of liberal and revolutionary elements to go forward together. Hence the conclusion: in the coming elections, liberals and leftists must for a time forget their differences and act together. One must recognise that Herzen understood the causes for the defeat of democracy in 1848 much better than Mr. Kovalevsky does. In his own day, he wrote that the Revolution was defeated and 'it had to be defeated'. He pointed to the irreconcilable contradiction between the classes that saw in a republic the possibility even of partially resolving the social question, and those that became republicans unwillingly and were prepared at any moment to sell out the cause of freedom for fear of the people. The moral that follows from a study of the events in 1848, *even in Herzen's interpretation* – which was imperfect, and we have since moved far beyond it in our understanding of the events – was directly the opposite of Kovalevsky's moral. It proclaims that there cannot be any kind of stable alliance between consistent defenders of freedom and those who are ready to betray it after the movement's first successes. The Cadets, who are close to the professor, have in their own way already followed Kovalevsky's advice on a union, having decided to join up with the Left-Octobrists and thus to break off with the leftists. So much for your *'viribus unitis'*.[2]

There is an interesting article by A. Yurovsky, 'Our Amur Region', in which he provides a sketch of the economic position of the Amur region and Primorsky *oblast*, together with certain interesting data.

M.L.

---

2. [Joint efforts.]

No. 59

'On Professor Zhakov's Lecture'[1] (A Letter to the Editor)

24 June 1912

Professor Zhakov's lecture on Leonid Andreev made a negative impression upon me. But that is a matter of one's convictions. The worst thing is that such lectures have a negative effect upon listeners: instead of shattering the public's traditional and fetishistic views on the history of human thought, they reinforce them. Add to this the fact that there is no opportunity for debates with the chair that might have presented a different point of view. While I shall postpone a more thorough objection to the lecturer until he completes all of his lectures, here I would like to note the most essential points of disagreement with him.

The basic idea that the lecturer attempted to prove is this: in nature there exists only one law that stands out most of all, and that is the law of rise and decline, the law of rhythm. This law also operates in philosophy and poetry. Periods of rising mood are replaced by periods of declining mood. When the declining mood reaches its extreme, a reverse upward movement begins. Andreev's service lies in the fact that in his works he completely exhausted the possible decline, he expressed a chasm of world-pessimism, submitting in his creativity to a law that has acted throughout the whole of history.

The lecturer had to turn to that history, and this is where we heard a work that could be called either an arbitrary attitude to historical facts or an entertaining historical stroll. The lecturer presented himself as a representative of science and called his construction an attempt at a scientific and objective review of the question. In reality, his construction was purely subjective and contained not a hint of science. But there are different kinds of subjectivity. There can be subjective constructions that still express the most essential phenomena in history. They may explain them differently, but they do not hush them up. Our esteemed lecturer hushed up at least half of the phenomena in the history of human thought that had to be mentioned. And the problem is that his entire construction must then collapse: it cannot withstand even a touch – not to speak of criticism – if it even comes into contact with a reference to the facts, it is killed by a breath of genuine historical reality. And what kind of criticism can be more damning than that? Can the law set out by the lecturer exist in *class*-society? It is enough just to pose the question in order to answer in the negative or at the very least to say that it must be formulated in a completely different way. Indeed,

---

1. [From *Obskaya zhizn'*, 24 June 1912. This essay continues in Documents 1:61, 1:63 and 1:64.]

while the most sensitive and talented representatives of one class understand music as melancholy and philosophy as pessimism, the other class hears only the music of struggle, understands only the philosophy of action, and revels only in the poetry of hope. These opposing moods are alive and flourishing side by side in modern society. What kind of conscientious scholar can dwell on the one and say nothing of the other? Yet that is precisely what the lecturer did throughout his entire lecture.

Speaking of the Buddhists, he said nothing of their opponents; speaking of the tragedians, he never mentioned the sophists; speaking of Kant, he forgot about the encyclopaedists; he enthusiastically quoted Schopenhauer yet never hinted at Feuerbach; treating L. Andreev as a genius, he made Gorky die for the listeners and resurrected Tolstoy by violating chronology. Mr. Zhakov's 'law' contradicts reality, and for it to be true it would have to be formulated this way: *every social class lives through periods of rise and decline, and a rising mood on the part of the advancing class corresponds with a declining mood among the dying class.* In places where civilisation perishes entirely, where the entire society disintegrates (Greece, Rome), this law also requires amendments. To ignore the position of different classes, and especially different social worlds, is something that can be done only by people who are suffering – including certain professors – from an incurable Russian disease: an exaggerated capacity for generalisation.

Aside from that, the lecturer was inaccurate in several places and made one serious error. The error is that he counted Plato among the representatives of optimistic philosophy. Plato is considered to be the father of idealism, and idealism is generally and on the whole a deeply pessimistic philosophy. When he had to do so, the gentleman lecturer proved this to be true. Schopenhauer, in his introduction to *The World as Will and Representation*, clearly indicated the role that Plato (and Kant) played in his philosophical construction. Plato was also the father of Christianity, as the lecturer justly noted. And is Christianity an optimistic teaching? The doctrine of Plato's ideas, as with any recourse to other-worldly hope, expresses a deep discontent with life in the real world and is deeply pessimistic.

Next, Kant cannot be regarded as one of the pessimistic philosophers. The author of the first edition of the *Critique of Pure Reason* and the *Prolegomena* was a bracing fighter against metaphysics and, to a somewhat lesser extent, did the same work as the Encyclopaedists did in France. Kant was an idealist, but a *critical* idealist. What is important in his teaching is not just that things in themselves are unknowable, but that they also exist, and thus the objective world exists. Kant's philosophy potentially includes not just Schopenhauer, Hartman and Fichte, but also Hegel and Feuerbach.

The lecturer's law, as we can see, is not true. However, that is not all. The pessimism and optimism that he mentions do not at all mean harmony or dissonance with the cosmos. We can leave the cosmos aside. After all, we are dealing with people, with a society, and thus what is real in this context includes only those laws of nature that become laws of society. And the gentleman professor evidently has a very confused understanding of these laws.[2]

A man's declining mood, his spiritual dissonance, is not dissonance with the cosmos, but with a society of people just like him. This truth can be demonstrated by a social analysis of any pessimistic mood in a concrete social group over the entire course of history.

A brief review does not give me the opportunity even to mention all that I would like to say about the lecture. Among a number of blunders by the lecturer, I shall mention just one more. In his opinion, the attraction of modern European society to fairy-tales, to the unreal, is the expression of an optimistic rise that is under way. This is profoundly wrong. In the first place, Europe is not a single entity. However, we have already seen that classes are not visible from the height adopted by the professor. That part of Europe (the bourgeoisie, of course) that chases after fairy-tales does so precisely because it has lost any taste for reality, because the latter promises nothing good for it in the future: the expectation or presentiment of defeat in the social struggle can hardly create a disposition towards optimism.

The reader must be lamenting the fact that I have said nothing about Andreev. I repent. What can I do, if there is no space? And I would like to say something about the lecturer's aesthetic views on Andreev. Let me leave it at this: if Dühring has been made into a philosophical genius and Andreev into an artistic genius, then all those in literature who are without talent should consider themselves talented. Otherwise, where is there any justice?

M. L-v

---

2. For example, sociological criticism, in his view, must be expressed through a calculation of how many people from one class or another are reading the writer in question.

No. 60

'The Right to Suicide'[1]

24 June 1912

II

The total number of suicides in Europe reaches sixty to seventy thousand each year. Thus, every three to four years more people die than in the bloodiest war of our time. Suicides have reached the proportions of a genuine social disaster, moreover, a disaster that is growing in scale every year with a horrifying progression. This can be seen in the following figures from several European countries.

For one million people, there were the following numbers of suicides per year:[2]

Country	1825–50	1850–75	1875–1900	1900–8/9
Saxony	166.8	220.0	286.7	321.0
France	74.8	122.0	205.7	221.5
Prussia	97.0	124.5	200.6	200.4
Britain		65.6	81.0	102.0
Russia		30.0	32.6	34.7[3]
Denmark	238.0	268.1	244.5	189.0

Out of twenty European countries, the number of suicides over the past eighty years declined only insignificantly in two of them (Denmark and Norway), and in the rest it grew with enormous rapidity.

Society is more and more concerned with the growth in suicides, which must attract greater theoretical interest to the suicide problem and a number of new studies into the question. But the issue is not limited just to the realm of theory. The growing disaster will produce, and is to some extent already producing, a host of recipes for curing this social illness of our time.

---

1. [From *Obskaya zhizn'*, 24 June 1912. This article begins with Document 1:57 and continues in 1:72.]

2. I have taken the data from the article by Dr. Gordon in No. 5 of *Russkaya Mysl'* for this year [1912] with the title 'Contemporary Suicides'.

3. The figures for Russia are incorrect because in the case of St. Petersburg, which in terms of the number of suicides has recently been the world-leader, one can see that the data provided are far below the real numbers.

Insofar as these recipes are recommending increased repression by the state and the Church, directed against the property and religious rites of the people committing suicide and their families, the pointlessness of such measures is too obvious to merit further attention.

But even the recipes of those who frown upon legislative repression will remain sorry palliatives if the battle against suicides is assumed to occur on the basis of the existing social relations, on the same basis that actually nourishes the evil. But all measures within the limits of the existing system, such as social policy in the interests of the poorest classes, a corresponding spiritual and physical upbringing of youth and public hygiene in general, the struggle against alcoholism (which, by the way, can presently by nothing but a palliative) – all these measures can only mitigate the evil to a very insignificant degree. Even if the number of suicides does not decline, it will be a good thing at least to curtail their increase.

However, we are not presently interested in these tangible material measures in the struggle against suicides. We are interested in the battle against suicides now being contemplated on a moral level, in the attempts morally to disarm the person inclined to suicide by acting upon the strongest instinct of *homo sapiens*, the social instinct. These attempts find expression, among other things, in the dispute over the right to suicide that several press organs are coming out with in response to Andreev's letter, a dispute that, in future, will no doubt be more precisely formulated and more soundly based. It is already easy to see the direction this work will take. People will attempt to show that suicide is a theft in which the thief is the person committing suicide and the victim is society, since the individual owes his origin to the group, to which also belongs the right to compel the termination of life. They will prove that suicide is a shameful flight from the battlefield, a refusal to participate in the struggle of life within the process of natural development; that life itself is a social affair regardless of its content; that a forced death is repudiation of the work of successive generations; and finally, that suicide is an egoistic act because this unlawful destruction of ancestral property almost always disrupts to one degree or another the interests of those closest to the suicide, while the person committing suicide benefits by freeing himself from life's sufferings.

Such a theory of anti-suicidal morality, if one may express it that way, will no doubt enjoy great success, for not only in the consciousness of the leading part of the working masses – which quite understandably corresponds to the psychology and interests of the proletariat – but also in the consciousness of the bourgeois classes, mainly the intelligentsia, despite their traditionally individualistic world-view, the idea of the social man is making increasing headway.

The understanding of society as a conglomeration of Robinson Crusoes, freely interacting according to internal motives and individually responsible for their actions, was long ago rejected, and now the corresponding conclusions are being drawn in all the branches of social science. Think of the new school of criminologists, who refuse to judge an individual offender while leaving aside the society that schooled him and gave him direction; remember also the newest tendencies in the other social sciences – in biology, sociology, philosophy, psychology, the theory of knowledge, the theory of creativity, of morality, and so on and so forth. But even if in some cases – as we shall see below, in the minority of cases – this construction of anti-suicidal morality may be appropriate to the circumstances and may have a certain practical result, in the majority of cases it will represent only an unconscious attempt by society to rehabilitate itself and evade the charge of murder. This will become perfectly clear to us if we estimate for ourselves what percentage of suicides are connected with social causes, particularly material causes, in which the person committing suicide fulfils in general terms an act that has been dictated to him by society.

In No. 122 of *Russkie vedomosti* there is a statistical article on 'Life's Outcasts' with interesting data on the motives for the 3,160 suicides occurring last year in Moscow and in St. Petersburg over the past two years. These data give us an approximate understanding of the causes that lead seventy thousand people every year to take their own lives.

Out of the number cited – 3,160 – 35.7 percent of the total ended life by suicide as a result of hunger, poverty, unemployment, unbearable oppression from the bosses and similar causes. These causes account for the greatest percentage of suicides. Suicides on the basis of disillusionment with life account for 18.2 percent of cases. Causes of a romantic character are involved in 9.9 percent of cases. Causes having to do with family: the cruelty of parents, tyranny of husbands, and so on – 13.3 percent; physical and psychological illnesses, mental imbalance and alcoholism – 15.8 percent. School- and work-related suicides account for 7 percent. Let us sort through these figures.

My previous article sufficiently clarified the role of the existing social system in suicides of the first kind, that is, on the basis of hunger and poverty. Let us now consider suicides of a romantic character. There is scarcely any doubt that a good one-half of these suicides are closely connected with the material circumstances of the victim. Who is not aware of how often a marriage cannot occur between two loving people due to the penury of one of them or inequality in their social status, in a word, because the true nature of marriage is distorted by the intrusion of material causes and, as a result, we have a whole number of suicides on these grounds.

Take also suicide on the basis of family-complications. Here, the main role is played either by poverty – which, as we know, is not conducive to concord – or by the material dependence of the wife upon the husband, which compels her to endure cohabitation with a man she despises, or, finally, by the dependence of both spouses, who have come to despise each other, upon children, who in the absence of social upbringing play the role of binding element in a family where the spiritual and sometimes the physical bond has been broken. Here, therefore, the existing social conditions also play the main role, imposing their heavy hand on all, and especially on the poorest classes of the population.

As far as the social foundations of suicide on the basis of disappointment in life are concerned, I spoke of that in my previous article.

Finally, the social-political character is perfectly obvious in school-suicides, which have become so frequent lately as the gentlemen in a case,[4] inspired by surrounding circumstances, have again been able to commit all kinds of bullying against a child's spirit. Here, we should also remember that in school-suicides an enormous role is played by the material position of those involved, or more correctly, of their families. Whereas for the son of wealthy parents failure in school affects only self-esteem, and aside from school he can prepare himself for whatever he wishes to achieve, for a poor student a diploma is the means to life, and failure in school deprives him and his family of the hope of escaping poverty. That is why the percentage of suicides among poor students is always higher than among those who are well-off.

Even in the 15.8 percent of cases where suicide is due to physical and psychological illnesses, alcoholism and mental imbalance, the social element of the causes cannot be ignored. In the first place, the link between alcoholism and certain social conditions is sufficiently well known. There are, for example, states that are interested for financial reasons in the spread of alcoholism among the population.[5] And 'mental imbalance' is not a sufficient explanation for the causes of suicide. The whole point is what causes the mental imbalance. After all, along with physical causes (for instance, illnesses of the brain), it can also be brought on by causes of a social character such as, for example, prolonged hunger and unemployment, exhaustion in the political struggle, and so on. This means that social causes are also responsible for a number of cases included under this rubric.

Overall, hardly more than one-quarter of suicides occur on the basis of non-social causes. Three-quarters of them are either directly or ultimately due to reasons of a social character.

However, the essential point is not that society is guilty in three-quarters of suicides but that *contemporary* society is guilty. It is only through replacing the

---

4. [The reference is to Chekhov's *Man in a Case*, a rule-bound bureaucratically-minded teacher who killed the imagination of everyone he encountered.]

5. [The reference is to states that derive revenues from taxing alcohol or even have a state-monopoly, such as tsarist Russia.]

existing social relations with others that the real means for putting an end to the calamity of suicide will be found along with many of the other plagues of contemporary society.

And that is why today's morality, in its condemnation of suicide, cannot produce much in the way of success. This morality has its own internal contradiction. It deprives the individual of the right to dispose of his own person and promotes something in the nature of socialisation of the person. But, on the other hand, it (morality) while remaining on the grounds of the existing society, sees in suicide the act of a freely acting individual will and, forgetting its own sins, society condemns only the person committing suicide. And that is why when the existing society turns to the person who is attempting suicide and says: 'Don't kill yourself' – he can reply 'with the bitter smile of a defrauded son': 'Don't you kill me'.

M. Leonov

No. 61

'On Professor Zhakov's Lectures'[1] (A Letter to the Editor)

29 June 1912

When speaking of Professor Zhakov's first lecture, I mentioned nothing in my letter concerning the aesthetic appraisal of Andreev's works given by the lecturer. Now I shall offer a few words on that theme.

In the lecturer's opinion, Andreev is an ingenious artist. He is ingenious because he has embodied in his works the entire depth of world-pessimism and exhaustively expressed the mood of decline. For that reason, he ranks with the greatest artists of Europe and Russia, and the internal content of his creativity is a continuation of the creative work of Milton, Byron and Dostoevsky.

Someone who has not read Andreev might believe the professor. After all, if the artist has expressed so much in his works, does he not deserve to be ranked with the most ingenious writers of Europe? But anyone who has read Andreev, and who has the least artistic taste and aesthetic sense, must consider that comparison of Andreev with Byron a blatant contradiction of the 'algebra of aesthetics'. I am not debating the fact that there is much pessimism in Andreev's works, or that his pessimism may be more hopeless than Byron's. But an artist does not only need to express some idea or other – he must embody it in poetic images. An artist must justify poetically what a philosopher must justify logically. And has Andreev given such artistic justification for many of his thoughts and for the basic pessimistic idea of his creativity? No, and no again. His abstractions are without artistic content and completely arid; like a skeleton, they lack bodily form, and like a skeleton, they are ugly from an artistic point of view. 'The Black Masks', of which the gentleman professor has such a high opinion – is Andreev's most characteristic work in this regard. This artistic absurdity is the best example of how not to write an artistic work. Here, we have a clutch of abstractions not justified by images, and a clutch of ideas not personified in character-types. It is the same with most of Andreev's works – they are a pharaoh's herd of skinny cows on the green field of real poetry. There are works by Andreev in which the idea does not devour the images, or at least does not deprive them totally of flesh and blood, such as 'The Life of Vasily Fiveisky', 'The Tale of the Seven Who were Hanged', 'My Notes' and 'Once Upon a Time' (the best work by Andreev to date). These works display a great and original talent. But such works by Andreev are few, and they do not give the lecturer grounds for transforming Andreev into a

---

1. [From *Obskaya zhizn'*, 29 June 1912. The document is the continuation of Document 1:59 and continues in Documents 1:63 and 1:64.]

world-genius. What in the lecturer's opinion is most noteworthy in Andreev is really a juggling with abstractions that is incompatible with true art.

Speaking of Andreev's works, Tolstoy said 'You are frightening, but I have no fear'. These few words by the great artist are a crushing and destructive criticism of Andreev. A talent that is frightening but provokes no fear is not a talent. On the contrary, a true work of art acts with irresistible force and, in any case, can never inspire such comical debates over its importance as have emerged concerning many of Andreev's works. If Andreev's 'The Wall' has been taken for absolutism, if the child in the short story 'The Giant' has been taken to be the Revolution – or Russia, or humanity, or God knows what – all of this is evidence not so much of the wretched limitations of our critics, who are ready to find the most profound thought in any senseless, fashionable writer, but rather of the poverty, the *testimonium paupertatis*[2] of the artist. A creative work is not a riddle, not an enigma, not a cunning construction, but real life condensed into images, a picture that is understandable to each in its true meaning.

The lecturer contended that all true genius and greatness is comprehensible even for children. In Andreev there is much that is incomprehensible even for adults. Now ask yourself: Is it the gentleman-professor's rule that does not hold up, or does he make an exception precisely for Andreev?

The gentleman-professor made a blasphemous comparison of one of Andreev's works with Goethe's immortal *Faust*. Of course, something tiny can be compared with something great, and to highlight the nonentity of a pitiful plucked bush it is sometimes useful to place it beside a mighty oak. But it is the oak that benefits from such a comparison. Yet the gentleman-professor intended to glorify the bush. Would Andreev not be within his rights, paraphrasing Krylov, to say 'God deliver me from obliging professors'?[3]

M. L-v

---

2. [Proof of poverty or admission of ignorance.]
3. [I.A. Krylov's aphorism was: 'God deliver me from fools!']

No. 62

'On the Events in Turkey'[1]

29 June 1912

The recent events in Turkey are attracting increased attention from Europe. This is not surprising, if we remember that Turkey has become the object of its neighbours' greedy desires and thus the focus of a tangle of coming events that could be the starting point for a European war. The uprising in Albania, together with the revolutionary movement within the army, which is threatening to become a revolution like that of 1908; the continuing war with Italy, which affects the commercial interests of the Great Powers; and finally, the ever-increasing spirit of conquest, manifested in the annexation of Bosnia and Herzegovina, Italy's attack on Tripoli and the French seizure of Morocco – all of these together threaten grave consequences.

In Europe's bourgeois press, the opinion is taking hold that Turkey, by the time that Abdul-Hamid's rule ended, was on the eve of breaking up, because the interests of peoples oppressed by the Turks – the Armenians, the Bulgarians in Macedonia, the Albanians, and so on – were persistently demanding a European intervention that would finally resolve the Eastern question, which, to borrow Marx's words, is 'the donkey-bridge of European diplomacy'.[2]

The revolution and transfer of power to the Young Turks raised the hope that the renovated Porta[3] would make it possible for all the peoples of the state to find their own *modus vivendi* such that European intervention would not be necessary. But the bankruptcy of the Young-Turk régime quickly became apparent. The Young Turks failed to resolve any of the questions left by Abdul-Hamid's Turkey and continued the old policy of oppressing the nationalities they ruled. As a result, the question of Turkey's partition is once again on the agenda.

This view involves a very flattering estimation of the humanitarian and philanthropic impulses of international diplomacy and of the ruling social groups of the 'Concert of Europe' in general. Nevertheless, this view is either a pleasant delusion or a deliberate deception of the naïve. Italy, headed by the most liberal king in Europe, condemns as criminals and shoots the Arabs who dare to take

---

1. [From *Obskaya zhizn'*, 29 June 1912.]
2. [There is no parallel in English for the German phrase 'donkey-bridge' (*Eselsbrücke*) or *'ослиный мост'* in Preobrazhensky's text. English speakers would refer to a 'mnemonic device' or 'memory-aid'. The meaning is that 'the Eastern Question' is a summary way of referring to a whole number of interrelated diplomatic issues.]
3. [The Porta Aurea, or Golden Gate, was historically the ceremonial entrance to the city of Constantinople.]

up arms to defend their homeland. The French government, while cultivating patriotism at home, hands over to a military court and hangs those Moroccans who have learned its lesson of patriotism and have no wish to surrender their country to a greedy enemy as cowards. England, while defending the Armenians from Turkish atrocities with its right hand, uses its left hand to commit English atrocities against the Indians and relies on a policy of repression to pacify Ireland... But enough of that. Here, we have civilised Hottentots who see good in everything that extends their possessions, and evil in everything that leaves them unchanged – yet in relation to Turkey and its people, they turn out to be the selfless knights and Don Quixotes of humanity.

In reality, the fate of Persia shows that transforming a country into a civilised constitutional state does not save its independence. And the Young-Turk Revolution in Turkey, even if it had the best possible consequences for the internal life of the country, would never save Turkey if the European powers were prepared for its division and all of the consequences – up to and including a world-war that could result from such a division. Indeed, Austria annexed Bosnia and Herzegovina from Turkey exactly at the time of the Revolution, which it expected would produce no favourable results. Turkey can be saved only by the success of the revolutionary movement, which has begun in the army and has adopted the motto of autonomy for all the nationalities of the empire. If the Revolution wins out, Turkey will grow stronger internally and become an impressive power whose very existence will be the best defence against European appetites. Moreover, it will then be able to enter one of the groupings of powers and receive collective support. But if the stupidity of Young-Turk nationalism prevails, the partition of Turkey will be inevitable, and it has, in fact, already begun at the initiative of Austria and Italy.

M. Leonov

No. 63

'On Professor Zhakov's Lectures'[1]

1 July 1912

My aim in this article is to look at the last two lectures by Professor Zhakov. As a preface to his account of a 'sunny utopia', the author undertook a historical review of myths and legends and then reviewed the utopias of a new age: those of Thomas More and Campanella, the ideas of the utopian socialists and, finally, the 'utopia' of Karl Marx.

As for the history of legends, I will only note the explanation of totemism (the classification of species by primitive peoples using the names of various animals and birds) as an illustration of what curiosities can result from flights of intuition. In the lecturer's opinion, totemism results from a consciousness of the internal link between man and his animal-ancestors, in other words, it is something in the nature of primitive Darwinism. The reality is that totemism has a completely different origin, a social origin.

The presentation of the utopias of Saint-Simon and Fourier were extremely incoherent and said virtually nothing about the essence of utopian socialism. Saint-Simon's utopia was presented to the audience as a dream of a great Catholic church, but the lecturer mentioned not a word about the real essence of Saint-Simon's teachings, a socialist system of society as an ideal social order.

As for Fourier, it turns out that he produced a theory of 'peasant-villages' (sounds like buttery-butter). That is how the professor translated the word *'phalanstère'* into Russian.

And now for the 'utopia' of Marx. In the lecturer's opinion, Marx was a student of Hegel, his entire system was based on Hegelianism, and it therefore collapses if the latter fails. From what has been said, one can conclude that the lecturer evidently has a very confused idea of the role that Hegel's doctrine played in Marxism. Had the lecturer read *Capital* (and there are good reasons to doubt that he has), then he would have seen that Marx's conclusions with regard to the inevitable socialisation of the means of production are not based on the empty idea of the Hegelian dialectic and the corresponding 'triad', but rather on a study of enormous material on the history of economic development and a profound analysis of the essence of the capitalist mode of production and its

---

1. [From *Obskaya zhizn'*, 3 July 1912. Documents 1:59 and 1:61 are the previous parts of this essay. The conclusion is Document 1:64.]

moving forces. Were the critic to disprove Hegel's entire doctrine,[2] this would only reflect upon Marx's system in the sense of making the terminology outdated. And that is not to mention the theory of historical materialism in particular, which relates to Hegelianism as materialism relates to idealism, that is, as its direct opposite. The lecturer's second objection to Marxism consists of saying that this teaching ignores everything not related to the economic activity of mankind.[3] From Marxism's point of view, there is no understanding of life and the tragic death of Christ, Hus, and so on. There is no understanding of how a man can speak the truth in spite of his material interests and solely according to the voice of conscience. To understand all of this, one must begin with a moral principle and turn to the 'algebra of morality'. We will say more about 'algebras' later, but here we note only that the appearances of Buddha, Christ and Hus are phenomena of conscience and are, perhaps, not explainable from the viewpoint of utilitarianism;[4] but then, Marxism is not utilitarianism. Marxism considers the moving force of history to be the class-struggle, and not the egoism of the individual. Classes do battle under the influence of economic interests, but individual people may selflessly die in the interests of the whole. History is full of such examples. Christ was crucified, and Hus was burned. But they have also inspired followers, meaning that they represented the battle of one part of society against another. The dedication and sacrifice of an individual is one of the methods of social struggle, and it is only from the viewpoint of Marxism that these phenomena can be explained. The voice of conscience is the voice of the group (in class-society, the voice of a class), which is stronger than personal fear or advantage, just as a million are stronger than one. This is a force beyond the individual, transcending his limitations and possessing him, especially in certain of the most dramatic periods of history, and it drives the individual to actions that are unnecessary and harmful to him yet imperative and useful to the class. To say that a moral principle is at work here is to substitute a new name for the subject, rather than explaining it. A moral principle, or a moral law existing in reality and formulated by Kant in his famous 'Metaphysics of Morals' (*Grundlegung zur Metaphisik der Sitten*), is not an explanation, but rather itself needs to be explained. A thinking man of the twentieth century (even if he adopts the bourgeois-idealistic point of view) cannot be content with the notion that this

---

2. The entire development of modern sciences, especially in physics and chemistry, perfectly concurs with the basic idea of the Hegelian teaching – the idea of the dialectical development of nature.

3. This is a completely misconceived formulation. Marxism does not ignore phenomena that are not directly related to economic activity, but rather gives an explanation that differs, for example, from idealism or eclecticism.

4. This does not mean, of course, that utilitarianism refuses to give an explanation of these facts. From its own point of view it also explains them, as Helvétius does in *De l'esprit*, for example, or in the works of Bentham and others.

is an other-worldly voice, the voice of things-in-themselves within the world of phenomena.

Let us look further. The lecturer has a negative attitude towards idealism and materialism in their pure forms and searches for some third option. This third option is nature and the cosmos, understood as a tree of seven branches with an inherent force that aspires to perfection. The branches are: space, time, matter, psychology, logic, aesthetics and morality. Each of these branches has its own laws that cannot be reduced to the others. Let us look more closely at this 'tree' of the professor.

The first thing we notice is that human thought has an aspiration towards unity that has deep social-biological roots. The most ingenious thinkers consciously or unconsciously strove towards monism, towards an understanding of existence beginning with a single basic principle. Democritus, Heraclitus, Pythagoras, Plato and Epicurus were monists. In a new era, the great Spinoza, an Encyclopaedist (with a materialist point of view), was a monist. In the idealist sense, Hegel, Fichte, Schelling and Schopenhauer were monists. Feuerbach, Marx and Engels were monists. Mach, Avenarius and Ostwald are all striving for monism. But professor Zhakov apparently does not have the slightest inclination towards monism and takes the superfluous wisdom of philosophy to be eclecticism. That, of course, is where the gentleman-professor finds his own happiness. Every mind that aspires to monism faces an awesome task – to overcome conceptually all the endless variations in the phenomena of nature and to embrace them with a single principle. To the contrary, the eclectic never loses his peace of mind and, for him, no confounding problems exist. If some new area of facts appears, it is immediately assigned to an eighth branch of the 'tree of nature' and, if necessary, to a ninth or tenth, and so on, depending on the eclectic's weakness of mind. The only misfortune is that if philosophy were subject to the undivided rule of complacent eclecticism, we would never witness those collective accomplishments of the human mind that we now possess. Eclecticism is poverty in philosophy, a collection of handouts from different philosophical systems, and, as poverty, it cannot live on its own account.

M. L-v

No. 64

'On Professor Zhakov's Lectures'[1]

3 July 1912

But is it really true that nature is a tree with seven branches? No, it would be simpler and closer to the truth to conceive of it as one. Otherwise it would have to have as many branches as there are 'algebras', or compartments, in the heads of the philosophers to whose investigations it has the misfortune to be subjected.

Space and time, says the professor, are not one and the same. Spinoza thought that matter and extension are one and the same, and he was correct. Space, empty space without matter, is an abstraction that, like all abstractions, belongs to the 'algebra of the psyche', to use the professor's expression (in Kant's terms, the form of sensual perception). The algebra of time belongs here, too. With God's help, that leaves us with five algebras. Let us proceed.

What is matter? Insofar as it is accessible to our experience, through the mediation of our senses, it is a combination of the elements of sensations.[2]

Then there is the algebra of logic. With what does logic operate? Concepts. And what is a concept? A psychological experience or sensation.

And the algebras of aesthetics and morals. With what do they operate? With experiences of the beautiful in art and the beautiful in action. All experience consists of sensations. What does that leave us with? There remains only the 'algebra of the psyche', not the psyche in the narrow sense, but rather in the sense of the totality of elements of sensation that comprise the single material of our experience. Everything that we know is in this world of sensations; beyond it is what we have not come to know, but still can know. In the world there is nothing but matter that is being sensed[3] (or energy, which is the same thing).

But can it be, asks the professor, that a book and the idea of a book are one and the same? We answer that they are not the same, but between them there is no difference in principle that excludes the possibility of a monist conception. A footprint is not the same as the foot that made it, nor is it the same as the mud in which it is imprinted. Yet the foot, the footprint and the mud are all parts of a single material world sensed in its parts by the brain. But what does that leave us with? What is a book? Matter. What is a brain? Matter. What is the idea of a

---

1. [From *Obskaya zhizn'*, 3 July 1912. Earlier sections of this essay are in Documents 1:59, 1:61 and 1:63.]

2. This does not deny the objectivity of things as the causes of our sensations, or of being that is independent of our consciousness, since being is the presupposition for all consciousness.

3. If we understand matter not in terms of a dualistic relation to spirit.

book? A certain condition of the matter of the brain, the study of which (namely, of the brain in the process of learning) is a subject for the near future. Between my sensation of the book and the idea of it, and the possible visual sensation of my neighbour who is observing my brain at this moment, there is the same difference as between, let us say, a tactile and a visual sensation.

But, after all, says the professor, the laws of psychology and those of, say, aesthetics, logic, and morality, are completely different. If he wishes to say that the different sciences have different methods, and thus their existing division is expedient, there is nothing to debate with him. If he wishes to say that the material studied by the sciences is in principle different, then, as we see, he is mistaken.

Let us note here, by the way, that in depicting a difference between mathematics and logic the lecturer made a gross blunder that I would have taken to be a slip of the tongue had he not repeated it. The lecturer said that, by Hegel's logic, A=A. By Aristotelian logic,[4] this A=A is the law of identity and is correct. According to Hegel, everything in the world is flowing, everything is changing by the minute and the second, and within a second that which is now A will not be A any longer, but something else: A plus a certain change. Relying on this error, the lecturer counterposed Hegel's philosophy to the modern theory of the infinitesimal. Meanwhile, the theory of the infinitesimal logically results from Hegel's teaching and is its philosophical foundation.

Let us turn now to the main point of the lecture, the teaching on 'potential'. What is potential? Nowhere does the lecturer give a precise definition of this concept in so many words. So far as I understood him, he sees potential as nature's inherent aspiration towards the ideal, which is realised through an eternal process of development. To use the professor's comparison, potential, in relation to the developing cosmos, is the force that compels the germ of man to develop into a mature organism. In the professor's opinion, the world is not entirely spontaneous and has within it a certain purposefulness, some sort of consciousness. A study of the evolution of the heavens compels one to assume that the world is developing in the direction of a greater unity, a greater solidarity. The value of the world is increasing, and the hope for immortality has a basis because life that has died is reborn anew at a higher level of world-evolution.

Is there any scientific basis for Professor Zhakov's utopia?[5] In my view there is none, or at least no more than there is for any of the pessimistic systems that

---

4. [In Aristotelian logic, truth involves non-contradiction, whereas for Hegel, contradiction is itself the truth that drives all development.]

5. In his lecture, the professor made no distinction between the scientific part of his presentation and utopia, such that the listener might think that his view of potential represents some astronomic scientific conclusion. Emphasising the relativity and approximate character of all scientific knowledge, the professor, in the final analysis, did not

rely upon the law of entropy.[6] Science relies upon facts and can only predict the future insofar as it studies identical or relatively similar processes whose results it wishes to predict. That is how it is with astronomy, with the social sciences, and so on. The realisation of potential is endless through time, and the entire experience of man, in the face of the universe, is less than a millionth of a second in a day of the cosmos. What predictions can he make regarding the future of the latter? He may guess, dream, and believe in anything he wishes to believe in, but to know anything of an infinitely distant future world, with even the slightest probability – that is something he cannot do. Professor Zhakov's 'potential' is based on faith. And where faith knocks at one door, science leaves through the other.

Such is the sunny utopia of the professor in which – alas! – the light that is available to dim minds is so weak, and whose morality – a Tolstoyan non-resistance to evil – happens to be the supreme evil in a world where struggle is the source of all progress.

M. L-v

---

elevate science at the expense of utopia – as every scholar must endeavour to do – but rather, elevated his own utopia by diminishing science.

6. [An irreversible loss of world-energy.]

No. 65

Review of the Journals *Sovremennyi mir* and *Russkoe bogatstvo* (June)[1]

8 July 1912

The first pages of *Sovremennyi mir* always begin with something lengthy. The lengthy novel by Sefarimovich has yielded its place to a story by Gusev-Orenburgsky, 'The Ghost', which is evidently also lengthy, because it is 'to be continued'. While preparing to read this story, I thought: I will probably have to deal again with something spiritual. And so it turned out. Recently, Amfiteatrov addressed a comment to Gusev-Orenburgsky, noting that he has written about a hundred popes and a hundred and one deacons, and now he is writing about the hundred-and-first pope and the hundred-and-second deacon. But even if Gusev-Orenburgsky is repeating himself, you will still read the account of the hundred-and-first pope with interest, since it presents living characters described by a man who knows the context well and does have talent.

In the publicist section of the journal, there is an interesting article by the Polish Marxist L. Krzhivitsky entitled 'Vagrants and Homebodies'. The author presents a whole number of thoughts and facts to prove, first of all, that vagrants are usually thought of as people from the lower ranks of society who are unwilling to work and who, rather than endure a few months of systematic labour, prefer to sit systematically in prison and voluntarily to forgo all kinds of things on the outside. In L. Krzhivitsky's opinion, many vagrants come from the upper classes on account of an illness – an inclination to move about and an aversion to systematic work. Among these he counts several famous travellers, Nansen,[2] for example. There are different degrees of vagrancy. Some types of vagrancy, such as abandoning a trade in our industrial provinces – Vladimir, Kostroma and others – are treated by the author as another form of vagrancy. L. Krzhivitsky tries to show that the cause of vagrancy is neither a neurosis nor some kind of psychological disorder, as some sociologists believe, but, instead, the opposite is true: the neurosis results from not fulfilling a natural, humanly inherited tendency to move about. The point he makes is that in the past mankind experienced a period of nomadic life that in previous conditions was, of course, completely normal and necessary. A settled life has not yet finally overcome man's nomadic interests, and now those interests, making themselves felt in many people, but

---

1. [From *Obskaya zhizn'*, 8 July 1912.]
2. [Fridtjof Nansen (1861–1930) was a famous Norwegian explorer and Nobel laureate who completed the first crossing of the interior of Greenland in 1888 and reached a record northern latitude during his polar expedition of 1893–6.]

not finding an outlet, have a negative effect upon the psyche just like any other unsatisfied need.

L. Krzhivitsky contrasts vagrants with homebodies. If the former have a fear of staying in one place, the latter have the opposite fear of moving about, a fear of anything new: new places, new people, and new conditions of living. The second type is the outcome of the settled period. On the whole, the article by L. Krzhivitsky sheds light on one of the most interesting aspects of modern social life and deserves attention.

In the article 'Berdyaev and my Grandmother', Ortodoks deals with an article by Berdyaev, published in *Russkaya mysl'*, on 'Nationalism and Anti-Semitism in the Court of Christian Conscience'. In this article, the former 'Marxist' believer wrote, among other things, that 'For every Christian there is a religious duty to be anti-Semitic and to oppose the anti-Christian idea of Jewry'. And further: 'Hatred for the Jews, in terms of race, everyday life, or politics is inadmissible for every Christian and just as sinful as any hatred for another man. But a religious hatred for the anti-Christian idea of Jewry is possible and, in the deepest sense of the word, inevitable'. True, Mr. Berdyaev attempts to disassociate himself from pogromists and from *Novoe vremya* and other such journals. But Ortodoks is fully justified when he notes that, in terms of principle, Mr. Berdyaev takes the same point of view and differs with them only on the question of the most expedient methods for struggling with Jewry and, therefore, only in questions of tactics. Essentially, he speaks as a very pious Christian, but he nevertheless remains a pogromist ideologue.

In his article 'Democracy without the People', St. Ivanovich deals with the fate of the Trudoviks, who in his opinion are presently a parliamentary group with no organisational and few ideological ties to the social classes that produced this tendency. According to St. Ivanovich, the Trudoviks have lost their class-basis – the middle-peasantry, who are striving for a solution to the agrarian question – because of the differentiation within this class and, in general, because of the complete chaos in the contemporary village. And although the Trudoviks will have some success in the coming elections due to 'inertia', they are fated to remain 'democrats without the people' unless they 'decisively take a stand in defence of the medium and petty bourgeoisie of the countryside and the town'.

The article by St. Ivanovich contains some valid ideas, but it is also contradictory. In the first place, it is odd to think that a single party can defend the interests of both the middle- and the petty bourgeoisie. The author can hardly claim that the interests of the middle-ranking manufacturer or merchant are identical with those of the poor urban dweller or the poor peasant. Furthermore, it is not clear who the author thinks comprise the rural petty bourgeoisie; are they only the kulaks and generally those who are economically 'strong', the people on whom the late Stolypin made his wager, or are they all those in private farming? In any event, it is not possible simultaneously to defend the interests of semi-proletarians, the middle-peasantry, and the well-to-do up to and including the kulak. It is also fanciful to think that one party can simultaneously express the interests of urban and rural classes. The author himself points out in his article that there is an insurmountable contradiction between the persons selling agricultural products and the urban consumer. In that case, he is arguing with himself.

A. Ermansky touches upon an interesting question in his article on 'The Commercial-Industrial Class before Elections to the State-Duma'. There has recently been a debate in Russia over the question of the political role of large-scale capital and its possible evolution either to the left or to the right. The same Ermansky wrote on this topic in No. 4 of *Nasha zarya*. V. Il'in[3] responded with objections in No. 5 of the Marxist journal *Prosveshchenie*, and now A. Ermansky is returning to the question. He shows in his article that the Russian big bourgeoisie gets along perfectly with the current political forms of the state and that its diversion to the side of liberalism has no serious significance, since on the main question of the protectionist system the Ryabushinskys are in complete agreement with the Krestovnikovs. Thus all 'schemes' suggesting that the big bourgeoisie will inevitably go over to the side of the opposition are unfounded (the author has in mind such 'schemes' as those of Martov, Dan and others).

He writes: 'The whole *root of the mistake* in such schemes is that the authors start out with *their own* views of what is needed for a normal and free development of the productive forces in bourgeois society, attributing these views to capitalist actors. The whole problem is that this *ignores* the basic fact of a fundamental *divergence* between their own views and the objective interests of industry and the interests of the industrialists, as they themselves understand them and will inevitably understand them in the existing state of affairs'.[4]

A. Ermansky is too unfair to his co-thinkers: L. Martov and F. Dan are not so naïve as to attribute their own views concerning the requirements of capitalist development in Russia to the industrialists. They only have a certain tendency to do so. The mistake on the part of these publicists is that they assign too much importance to the large (and medium) bourgeoisie in implementing the necessary reforms in Russia, and they do not believe that the objective requirements of capitalist development, in terms of political reforms, can be achieved not only with bourgeois indifference, but even despite the bourgeoisie. Finally, they do not

---

3. [Vladimir Lenin.]
4. *Sovremennyi mir*, June 1912, p. 315.

believe in, or they have too little confidence in, the inevitability of speedy implementation of such radical reforms by a workers' and peasants' democracy.

Leaving aside the *belles-lettres* section of *Russkoe bogatstvo*, which contains nothing worthy of attention, let us turn to the publicist section. What is most interesting, here, is the response by V.G. Korolenko to 'The Russian Invalid' under the title 'Who is Guilty?' We strongly recommend to readers this reply involving the topical issue of the relation between military and civilian ethics.

In his letter from England, Dioneo deals, among other things, with a new phenomenon in the life of the English proletariat – its quest for higher education. It is interesting that this quest is not connected with another – to cross over into the ranks of the middle-bourgeois classes after receiving a higher education – but rather the contrary is the case: the workers are hoping to keep the young people who have received a higher education in their own ranks to provide leadership to the workers' movement. Dioneo gives a description of two such workers' universities: the well-known Ruskin College, which brings together more moderate cadres of working youth, and the London Labour College, under the leadership of professor Hurd and with the support mainly of the coal-miners' union – the most revolutionary section of the English proletariat.

In an article on 'The Materialistic and Idealistic Elements in the System of Karl Marx', M.B. Ratner searches for idealistic moments in Marxism, and thinks he has found them. He writes: 'Since the final irreducible element, which Marx uses as the foundation of his entire social-historical building, is labour in the form of a certain sum of physical and *mental* energy, what basis can there be in such circumstances to erect an hypothesis concerning the materialistic character of this social-historical philosophy?' Mr. Ratner displays little understanding of the theory he has tried to analyse. In the first place, for a Marxist, there is no difference between the mental and physical energy of man, which are very difficult to separate. What exists is the expenditure of energy by the human body. Indeed, if it were shown that in the process of production mankind expends more mental than physical energy, historical materialism would not for this reason cease in the slightest to be *materialism*. The point is not what sort of energy is expended, either by a single man or by the entire class, but rather what motives compel the expenditure of such energy – motives of an idealistic or an economic character. If one takes Mr. Ratner's point of view, it turns out that there is an idealistic element at the basis of activities by the class of big capitalists or the landed aristocracy, who defend the interests of their own pockets through an expenditure of 'mental' energy. As we can see, Mr. Ratner crudely confuses 'mental' with 'idealistic', which is totally inadmissible.

M.L.

No. 66

'The Workers' Movement in June'[1]

12 July 1912

In June, the strike-movement had an exclusively economic character and thus, by comparison with the movement in May, naturally had to take on narrower dimensions. During the month there was only one strike that, if not political, was close in character to a political strike – at the Zotov factory in Kostroma, where workers demanded dismissal of three members of the Black Hundreds whose denunciations caused several workers to be arrested for the 1 May celebrations.

If we compare the dimensions of the purely economic movement in May and June, it turns out that in June there were more economic strikes. This can be seen in the following figures. In May there were 124 economic strikes with approximately one-hundred thousand participants. In June there were 131 strikes.[2] As for the number of participants in these strikes, as usual it is difficult to determine, since the majority of strikes are reported by newspapers without any indication of the number who participated; we have data only for 46 strikes, in which 52,495 men took part. If we remember that the number of participants is usually known for the largest factories, and thus two-thirds of the strikes with an unknown number of participants occurred in the smaller enterprises, then we must assume that proportionately fewer workers were involved in these strikes, but, in any case, the total would not be fewer than in the one-third mentioned. Overall, therefore, the numbers who went on strike in June were no fewer, and probably more, than one hundred thousand workers. I say 'who went on strike' because the calculation includes only the new strikes that broke out in June, not those workers who were continuing strikes from previous months.

As for the results of the strikes, in 81 cases they are not known. We do know the results of 59 strikes, including those begun in June proper as well as those continuing from previous months. 35 strikes ended in complete or partial victories, while 24 ended in total defeats. As we see, in general the struggle ends, in about sixty percent of cases, in a way favourable to the workers. It is also

---

1. [From *Obskaya zhizn'*, 12 July 1912.]
2. All my data come from adding up information contained in the newspapers. But since the press does not provide information on all strikes, the data understate what has actually occurred. This is also true because certain strikes waged in a number of enterprises, such as a general strike by construction-workers or all the tailors in a city, are counted as a single strike. Minor individual strikes in artisan-enterprises with fewer than twenty members are completely overlooked.

characteristic that, in the enormous majority of cases, the strikes have an aggressive rather than a defensive character.

The territorial distribution of strikes is as follows. In St. Petersburg there were 27; in Moscow and the Central Industrial District, 25 strikes; in the Baltic territory 17 strikes; in Poland, 16; in Siberia, six; in the Urals, two; and in the rest of Russia (mainly in the South), 37. By comparison with last month, the strike-movement in the provinces intensified.

As for the division of strikes between branches of production, the relative majority, as before, occurred in the metallurgical industry, namely, 32 strikes; but it is characteristic that this month saw a rapid growth of strikes in manufacturing industry, which has by no means seen the same kind of expansion as in the iron-making industry. In manufacturing enterprises there were 17 strikes. The fever in construction was reflected in a higher number of strikes among workers employed at building sites. There were 13 such strikes if we count the Libavsky and Rizhsky strikes as two, although they involved many enterprises. There were eight strikes in furniture-joiner facilities, seven in print-works, and five involving unskilled workers and loaders. The others came in various branches (glass-factories, brick- and cement-works, sawmills and others).

The unusual persistence of many of the strikers should be noted. Several strikes in St. Petersburg have been underway since April and have still not been liquidated. And this is happening in the absence of strong trade-unions and regular assistance.

M.L.

No. 67

The "Democrats" from *Zaprosy zhizni*[1]

18 July 1912

At one time, there was a hope that the weekly journal *Zaprosy zhizni* would become a Trudovik organ and thus, to the benefit of the democratic struggle, would fill the gap that has emerged between the Cadet press on the one side, headed by *Rech'*, and the organs of consistent democracy, *Zvezda* and *Pravda'* on the other. After reading No. 17 of *Zaprosy zhizni*, that hope has to be abandoned.

The point is that the St. Petersburg workers' newspapers, *Nevskaya zvezda* and *Pravda*, came out with a series of articles in which they invited the democratic elements in St. Petersburg to vote for representatives of workers' democracy and thereby to win the capital away from the Cadets. Worker-democrats have always followed such a tactic, namely in the elections to the Second and Third Dumas and in the supplementary elections of 1909. Up to now, nothing has happened that would require a change of this tactic. On the contrary, the general evolution of the Cadets to the right, and especially their decision to support Left-Octobrists in the elections – excluding any possibility of an agreement with leftists – makes it even more imperative to maintain the established tactic. It is clear even to blind people that on the central question, the question of attitudes towards the régime of 3 June, there is an implacable contradiction between the Cadets and democrats, by comparison with which the divergence between Cadets and Octobrists can be regarded as a domestic misunderstanding. The results of the 3 June régime and the balance of forces supporting it do not favour the Cadets and keep them from power. But they are also afraid of any social disturbances or spontaneous popular actions. They fear that the result of a too-rapid movement forward may be that they will find themselves to the right of power, just as they are now to the left of it. Ultimately, they want to achieve the reforms desirable to them (that is, a very modest step forward) by way of liberal diplomacy, that is, in a way that has never resolved a single such question throughout the whole of world-history. The fear of independent popular action rallies the Cadets much more strongly with the Octobrists than it unites them with leftists in the struggle against the 3 June bloc.

It follows that every true democrat who is even the least bit thoughtful can only welcome the independent appearance of worker-democrats in the elections and their attempt to win one position or another from the Cadets. In the

---

1. [From *Obskaya zhizn'*, 18 July 1912.]

event that this attempt fails, there still remains a plus in uniting the active part of the proletariat with urban democrats, while, on the other hand, there is not the slightest danger of seeing the existing Cadet representatives from St Petersburg replaced by people who are further to the right. There is no Black-Hundred threat in St. Petersburg. In the elections to the Third Duma, the number of votes cast for the Octobrists and their allies fell significantly compared to the elections to the Second Duma, in which those parties gathered quite a substantial number of votes. There are no grounds whatever for expecting any sharp changes in the opposite direction during elections to the Fourth Duma. Moreover, the existing law provides for a second ballot. If we remember that the left-democratic bloc fell short of defeating the Cadets by only about fifteen hundred votes in the elections to the Second Duma, then it becomes clear that such a victory is fully possible in the elections to the Fourth Duma. The conditions in St. Petersburg are such that any bourgeois democrat has to make a clear decision as to who is closer to him and who is dearer: a consistent democrat representing the workers, or a half-hearted liberal representing the bourgeois intelligentsia and the middle-bourgeoisie. The 'Trudoviks' from *Zaprosy zhizni* are resolutely grasping at liberal coat-tails and attempting to justify their betrayal of democracy with a lot of miserable and incoherent words. In the weekly section, we read: '*Honest democratism* will find a better way to deploy its forces than to support the ambitions of Mr. F.F. (author of an article in *Nevskaya zvezda* – M.L.). There is too much of a gap between honest democratism and Machiavellianism'.

Thus it is 'Machiavellianism' for democrats to come out independently, and when two lists appear in the election-struggle in St. Petersburg, those of the democrats and the Cadets, the honest 'democratic' gentlemen will find 'a better way to deploy their forces' and will cast their votes for Cadets.

Further on we read: 'The only possible result of the agitation by *Nevskaya zvezda* will be a deepening of internal strife among democrats – a split in the opposition. And that, apparently, is the chief objective of the undertaking'.

Thus workers' democracy is already guilty by virtue of its existence; once it exists, it has no alternative but to adopt an independent line in the election-struggle. How would it express its independent existence otherwise? Consistent democracy in St. Petersburg faces a Cadet threat. The Cadets face a democratic threat. The 'democrats' from *Zaprosy zhizni* also face a democratic threat from the working class and the urban poor. What fine democrats!

We have never had a high opinion of the democratic commitment of such gentlemen as the Vodovozovs and the Blanks. Now that they have come out openly against St. Petersburg's democrats, we must recognise, leaving aside all polemical exaggerations, that these gentlemen are masked liberals, Cadets in a 'discounted edition for the people'.

All readers of *Zaprosy zhizni* who come from the democratic strata will now surely turn away from an organ in which they had hoped to see their own views expressed. Even in our century of renegades and apostasy, not everyone favours the prospect of supporting Cadet clerks who are *Stimmenvieh* (voting livestock) for the gentlemen Milyukovs.

M. Leonov

No. 68

Review of the Journals *Vestnik Evropy* (July) and *Zavety* (June)[1]

20 July 1912

The July volume of *Vestnik Evropy* includes the conclusion of the interesting sketches by Tan entitled 'The Hungry Village'. The reader is presented with interesting peasant characters as the current moods of the village emerge. Here is a picture from one essay, 'The Searchers'.

> Knock, knock... A mysterious knock.
> 'Who is it now? Come in if you must!'
> Two people enter, one tall and one short, both in sandals and sheepskin-coats. They stand silently in the doorway, their hats under their arms, and peer about, frowning, with such a strange, questioning, almost conspiratorial gaze.
> 'Well, what do you have to say?'
> They remain silent.
> 'Well, what is it you need, speak up, don't drag it out'.
> 'Why don't you open up to us?' replies the tall one, pleading but with reproach in his voice.
> 'What do you mean, open up?' flares my companion. (The author and his companion were travelling throughout the famine-stricken provinces to give aid personally with money they had collected from society – M.L.)
> 'Who are you, where do you come from, and why?'
> 'We assume that you are generals', fires off the other one unexpectedly, 'from the highest level of government'.

Then come the questions: are we here about the twelfth year,[2] are we from the 'striking students', have we heard anything about land-allotments, and so on.

Another pair of intercessors for society's case. They are all looking for the truth, but do not know where to find it. After inquiring where they might turn if they lose their case in lower courts, and being told that they might then turn to the Chamber and Senate, the peasant Belyakov unexpectedly says:

> 'They say there are different rules abroad, can't we appeal abroad?'
> 'There is no appeal abroad', my companion assures them.
> 'And what if we appeal to universal brotherhood?' asks Belyakov.
> 'What universal brotherhood?'

---

1. [From *Obskaya zhizn'*, 20 July 1912.]
2. [The reference is to the practice of redividing communally-held land, which often occurred after a 12-year period.]

'We have heard a rumour that there is a growing peaceful brotherhood of all states on Earth and on high'.

That is the kind of picture the reader can find in Tan's interesting sketches.

The tireless L. Deutsch continues to publish his always substantial and lively memoirs. In this volume, we see his memoirs from the time in the seventies, after his famous escape from Kiev prison, when he and Stefanovich were preparing to go abroad and learned of new moods and plans among the revolutionary youth of the day. Even though much of what Deutsch reports is already known from other sources, and partly from his own previous reminiscences, his 'On the Borderline' will be read with interest by anyone interested in the history of our political thought and the history of political struggle.

The section of *belles-lettres* in the new Narodnik journal *Zavety* is generally quite rich. In the third issue, in particular, the reader will find six complete original stories and tales and, of course, yet to be completed novels.

Let us pause for a moment to look at one novel, *That Which Never Was*, by Ropshin, the author of the *The Pale Horse*, which was sensational in its time. The novel is yet to be completed, and one must suppose that in the three issues of the journal that have appeared only a small portion of it has yet been printed. Nevertheless, we will say a few words about it without waiting for the ending.

Every bias is incompatible with art and ruins an artistic work: this is an axiom of aesthetics that does not require proof. But besides crude and palpable bias, there is also toned-down bias that is better masked – if one may use that expression – a fixed idea that penetrates throughout the work, giving it a certain colouring that soaks into every page. There is just such a preconceived idea in the story *That Which Never Was*. Every line of this new novel by Ropshin says: revolutionary activity is useless, unnecessary, harmful and morally inadmissible. Ropshin discredits the revolutionary in the same way as Gorky glorifies him in his story *Mother*, whereas both of them, if they wished to remain artists, should have been only *portraying him*.

But every bias is an abuse of reality and, for that reason, a tendentious work always can and must come into confrontation with the truth. In Ropshin's new novel, such an abuse of the truth is at the very core of the novel – the spiritual state of Bolotov when he learns of the battle of Tsushima,[3] in which his brother was with the Russian squadron. A convinced revolutionary, when he learns of this he feels a familial sympathy for his brother that he never felt before because he was alienated from him by conviction and by the type of activity he was engaged in, and now he confronts a new question: the question of people's right

---

3. [In late May 1905, the Japanese destroyed two-thirds of the Russian fleet in the Battle of Tsushima.]

to kill each other. From this moment, Bolotov begins to experience a spiritual crisis that results in a growing coolness towards his revolutionary activity and loss of faith in its usefulness.

Let the reader note that the spiritual turning point for Bolotov took place in mid-1905, the year of the greatest rise in the revolutionary movement and the greatest faith in its successful outcome. Could what happened to Bolotov in Ropshin's novel also happen in real life? Of course, individual people can experience any kind of spiritual crisis at a time when the entire social condition affects the masses in a completely opposite direction. And out of thousands of revolutionaries in 1905, of course we might find one who felt something like what Ropshin's hero lived through. But art and chance are two completely incompatible things. Art reproduces what is most general, most typical – and only to that extent is it art. What Bolotov lived through, and what was typical for renegades in the years 1908–9, was an exception for the year 1905, and as such cannot be of interest to the artist.

Therefore, the core of the novel, if we place ourselves in the situation in which the author himself located the spiritual process that he reproduces, this core turns out to be contrived, false, and therefore anti-artistic.

We will return to the novel in future and deal with its other defects as well as certain merits. For now, we will mention only what E. Kolosov said in *Golos Siberi*, namely, that the author mimics Tolstoy's manner of writing. Of course, it is useful to learn from the great master of words; but it is one thing to learn and another to act as the curved mirror of a genius. And if the note of preaching that is so characteristic of Tolstoy – so typical of the great writer and found even in his purely artistic works – if that note is natural for Tolstoy, in Ropshin's case it is, to say the least, ridiculous. Tolstoy's style comes from the height from which he viewed the world, but Ropshin swims at too low a level for that. *Quod licet Jovi, non licet bovi*.[4]

In his essay 'The Moral Ideal without an Ideal', V. Chernov tries to show an affinity between Nietzsche's moral attitudes and the experiences of the toiling classes that are fighting for a better future. This is a comforting discovery, of course, and is not new to this sort of literature, but for V. Chernov it is clearly a step forward on the road to becoming a bourgeois ideologue. But it is better if we listen to him: 'Our unsatisfied moral needs, in terms of which a *son of the people*, who is awakening to conscious life, approaches everything – religion, a general view of nature and life, politics – must become the starting point for *birth of a new moral personality* in the toiling man of the factory and village, the proletarian and the cultivator'.[5] While it is a simple matter for the people to arrive at this

---

4. [What Jupiter can do is not permissible for an ox.]
5. *Zavety*, June 1912, pp. 118–19.

moral ideal, for us disoriented intellectuals it is more difficult; nevertheless, with the help of Nietzsche, and God willing, we will succeed. Yet what does Nietzsche have in common with the fighting proletariat?

> Under the strain of a nightmarish spiritual illness, Nietzsche, like a spring under pressure, was straining in the attempt to *straighten up* and freely press his eager lips to the full goblet of life. Under the pressure of the entire nightmare of our own life, of the heavy leaden cloud of oppression and exploitation of every kind that oppresses the labouring man, he too (the labouring man – M.L.) is like a coiled spring striving impetuously to reach his full height. And in Nietzsche's hymns he hears native, familiar motives – *the will to health, the will to life, the will to power, the will to victory*.[6]

Given Nietzsche's obvious disdain and contempt, all these attempts to enrol as his relatives produce a laughable and pitiful impression. Nietzsche had an acutely negative view of the struggle of the socialist proletariat, and this was no thoughtless notion on his part, no accident or slip of the tongue. It is nonsense to attempt a reconciliation of Nietzsche's individualistic philosophy and the individualistic times of his 'I', his superman, with the comradely spirit of workers' cooperation that is founded on the principle of subordinating the individual to the interests of the whole. Nietzsche's morally rebellious individual not only rises up against society and its confining traditions, but also rapidly develops an energy that repels all those who would struggle alongside him against that society and who wish to make the struggle more expeditious by subordinating the individual to the organisation. And if Mr. Chernov declares Nietzsche's philosophy to be close to the moral experiences of the fighting proletariat, all this shows is that he himself is far from the latter and, to the contrary, stands in close relation with the bourgeois-individualistic ideology of which Nietzsche's teaching is a variant.

M.L.

---

6. *Zavety*, June 1912, p. 120.

No. 69

'The Far-Eastern Question'[1]

22 July 1912

The arrival of Japanese Prince Katsura in St. Petersburg has again placed before Russian society the question of the future of our Far-Eastern region and our interests in the East. Among the quite diverse opinions on the best policy for Russia in the Far East, the one attracting the greatest attention in society and in diplomatic circles is the idea of an identity of Russian and Japanese interests on the question of China and the thought that it may be possible and desirable to have, if not an alliance, a Russo-Japanese agreement in the interest of 'demarcating spheres of influence in Manchuria and Mongolia', or, to drop the allegory, an alliance for an amicable division of China's northern provinces.

This opinion is short-sighted and can become just as ruinous for Russia as the fatal hope, some time ago, of scattering the Japanese by waving our caps at them. First of all, Japan's interests not only do not coincide with Russia's interests in the Far East, but are diametrically opposed to them. Japan's economic development is creating a powerful need to acquire ever newer markets for its developing provinces and land for its surplus-population. An expansion of territory is possible for Japan at the expense of either China or Russia. At the present moment, Japan's agenda is to expand its possessions at China's expense, namely by annexing part of Manchuria. But such an expansion can cause protests first from Russia and second from the European powers. Protests from the Great Powers will not be particularly insistent because they have no serious interests in Manchuria. A clash with Russia may end in war, but there is presently no need for Japan to follow that route. It is better for it to interest Russia in its enterprise with corresponding compensation in the form of Mongolia or part of Manchuria, acquiring an ally for a time, instead of an enemy. But once Manchuria is divided and Japan comes into direct contact with Russian territory, a further expansion of its possessions will be on the order of the day. Is there any need to demonstrate that this expansion will be easiest at the expense of Russia, including Russia's own territory and the part acquired from China? One need only look at the map to realise how natural and irreversible precisely that course of events is. And is there any further need to show that, as in the last war, Japan will turn out to be in a better position, that it has a stronger navy and army that can be mobilised very rapidly and dispatched against the scattered and poorly manned Russian garrisons? The result of acquiring part of China's territory will

---

1. [From *Obskaya zhizn'*, 22 July 1912.]

be a future threat to us of losing our own possessions, along with the numerous other calamities connected with an unsuccessful war.

Is it not obvious from what has been said just how short-sighted are those diplomats who are prepared to go along with Japan's plans and even to consider an alliance with her? They want to take the first step towards a turn of events that will be so unexpected as to horrify them. But then it will already be too late to retreat. After the first step, which we may take together with Japan in accordance with its cleverly developed plan, she will the take the second step against us, rather than with us.

But what are we to do if things develop that way?

The wisest and most far-sighted policy for Russia in the Far East would be a policy of protecting the integrity of China, a policy of allying with China for the purpose of self-defence against Japan, not a policy of partitioning China in alliance with Japan. True, this policy is alien to adventurism and alien to a policy of robbing a weak neighbour, to which our diplomatic patriots and stupid 'Bismarcks' from the Octobrists are inclined. But, then, this policy guarantees a balance of forces in the Far East, it guarantees peace and opens China's doors for the development of Russian trade. We can then gain much while losing nothing, whereas in the opposite case we appear to achieve much at the outset but then lose much more later on.

An alliance with China would be a formidable fortress erected against Japan's aggressive intentions and protecting our Amur region from the strongest of enemies.

Conversely, an alliance with Japan against China is a wide-open door for Japan's breakthrough into our Siberia and the first step towards a deafening blow which we are prepared to bring down upon our own head.

Is it not clear which course is most favourable to Russia's interests, to the world's interests, and to the interests of the broad popular masses, who always pay the heaviest price for a policy of adventurism?

M. Leonov

No. 70

'A Question that Needs an Answer'[1]

27 July 1912

The scandalous revelations concerning the municipality of Odessa,[2] where almost the entire administration was accused of receiving bribes from the Belgians in the sum of more than two hundred thousand for granting them a concession for a tramway and electrical lighting, places reform of our urban self-government on the agenda once more, for the thousand-and-first time. I say for the thousand-and-first time because the entire history of our self-government since 1870 is replete with embezzlement of public funds, corruption and general misuse of public functions for selfish purposes. The urban economy in its present form, that is, while it remains entirely in the hands of the largest property-owners and while the remaining mass of the urban population – homeowners and those who rent – are deprived of any influence over it, is not much better than a branch of the treasury. In place of quartermasters-by-appointment, swarms of quartermasters-by-election are appearing over the entire expanse of the Russian land. Is there any need to add that thieves 'invested with popular trust' are a much more negative phenomenon than officials convicted for embezzlement? The only consolation is that the elections here are but a comedy, and the scandalous facts that fill the newspapers are indications not of failures of the principle of self-government, as the reactionaries believe, but rather of the shortcomings of the current system of self-government, which excludes from participation in urban affairs the broad strata of the urban population who are most interested in rational management of the economy and most capable of exercising real control over those who are elected. Moreover, these facts also speak of the psychology of that upper stratum of the urban bourgeoisie who, in their everyday lives and professional occupations, know only one principle: Get rich, no matter what it takes.

But even in places where the upper stratum of the urban population turns out to be more cultured and succeeds in managing the urban economy more or less tolerably, there are still phenomena that are completely inadmissible in a democratic municipality. It is true that in these cases they do not steal public funds,

---

1. [From *Obskaya zhizn'*, 27 July 1912.]
2. There is no need to add that the municipal council convicted of corruption consists mainly of true Russians. All these gentlemen Pelikans and Moiseevs made such a noise under Tolmachev and have now confirmed once again that bribery and waste are truly a fundamental part of the Russian spirit. [General I.N. Tolmachev was prefect of Odessa 1907–11.]

that councillors and members of the administration do not give themselves contracts through their own nominees, and that they do not provide running water to their own homes and pave only the streets on which their own homes are located. But here, other inadmissible things occur. On the basic question, the question of urban taxation, the character of self-government by the big bourgeoisie becomes completely obvious. There is no progressive income-tax, but rather the opposite; those who are poorest pay relatively more. Evidently, it smells of socialism to collect taxes progressively as incomes increase. And to impose taxation on the petty bourgeoisie, who live from hand to mouth, on coachmen and the poor in general – this is the height of patriotism and the worthiest of causes. In general, those strata of the urban population who, in relative terms, pay the most from their income, are the ones who participate least of all in governing the urban economy.

The reform of urban self-government is long overdue. But this reform must be radical, and there must be complete democratisation of the electoral law. The experience of St. Petersburg demonstrates this clearly. Everyone knows that in St. Petersburg, even under Plehve, an experiment began that allowed not just homeowners but also the most prosperous renters to participate in the election of city-councillors. The latter constituted a group of new representatives who tried to introduce European order into the urban economy. But since this group was in the minority and the old elected officials had a majority, namely, those who supported the old system of economy, which has been practised since olden times in Russia with great success for the pockets of the city-fathers, it turned out that nothing changed in St. Petersburg. As the senate-review by Neidgard demonstrated, theft continues in the capital, the economy is managed chaotically, and the city's urgent needs, such as a sewage-system, are still not being met. Bribery and nepotism are flourishing everywhere, the only difference being that everything is now arranged without the kind of patriarchal simplicity that one sees in some remote Stupidtown or Nowhereland.

All of this points to the need to go beyond a partial extension of voting rights to the city-dumas and to attract participants into self-government not just from among homeowners, or even from all who rent accommodation, but from the entire population living in the particular city. Only a municipal authority elected on the basis of free and equal suffrage can manage urban affairs in the interests of the entire urban population. Only the city's entire population can control the municipality most effectively, and only their independent activity can provide a guarantee against abuse by elected officials.

M. Leonov

No. 71

Review of the Brochure by Ya. Borin, 'For Home and Hearth (The War of 1812)' (Published by S. Dorovatovsky and A. Charushnikov, Moscow)[1]

28 July 1912

This year, Russia celebrates the centenary of the Fatherland-War. The anniversary has prompted numerous publications devoted to the events of 1812. Among the mass of such literature, there are a great many, perhaps a majority, that are hoorah-patriotic publications giving a distorted picture of the famous campaign. There are also brochures that provide a more-or-less objective account of the events of 1812 and the preceding years. Ya. Borin's brochure belongs among the latter. It is not possible, of course, to give a complete description of the Fatherland-War in one hundred and sixty pages. The most important events can be found in the book, and for a person completely unfamiliar with Russian history, this brochure gives a sufficiently clear portrayal of 1812 in terms of the chronology of events. The brochure is written in popular language, making it accessible to school-age children and to the general mass of the people.

Among a number of flaws in the brochure, which are inadmissible even in a volume of one hundred and sixty pages, is the complete absence of any characterisation of social-communal relations in Russia in 1812. It is unclear to the reader just what kind of Russia was fighting against Napoleon. Was it like Russia today, or was it some other Russia, such as, shall we say, the one that planted Mikhail Alexeevich[2] Romanov on the throne? The author makes a proper effort to explain the cause of the Napoleonic Wars in terms of the rivalry between England and France for the world-market. But why are references to the economic relations of the last century omitted when it comes to Russia?

M.L.

---

1. [From *Obskaya zhizn'*, 28 July 1912.]
2. [There is an error in the text. The reference should be to Mikhail Fedorovich Romanov (1596–1645), first tsar from the Romanov house.]

No. 72

'The Right to Suicide'[1]

29 July 1912

III

The role of existing social conditions in the development of the suicide-epidemic will become even clearer to us if we understand the social circumstances that, more than anything else, contribute to the development of the psychological preconditions for suicide and if, conversely, we also clarify which social relations strengthen the vitality and stability of the individual.

When a doctor or a psychologist, often one and the same, undertakes to ascertain a single common cause of suicides, he is in a happy position, or at least a happier one than the sociologist. No doubt, there are certain basic psychological moments that impel a person to end his own life and are shared by all suicides despite all the differences of external motives. It is true that attempts by certain doctors concerned with the problem of suicide have failed to show that the fundamental cause is a psychological abnormality or some kind of madness on the part of the person committing suicide: according to some researchers, the number of psychologically abnormal persons committing suicide runs as high as sixty percent and more, while others say it is scarcely thirty percent. But if we reject the tempting idea of seeing psychological abnormality in all people who commit suicide, there still remain other psychological elements that certainly can be observed in all suicide-cases. The basic element is depression, loss of the taste for life,[2] and a mood that cannot sustain life. But we need not pose particularly profound theoretical questions in order to see that this moment is not sufficient for explaining the causes of suicide. The spiritual condition that precedes suicide is not the cause of the latter, but rather, together with the suicide itself, it is a consequence of the real cause of suicides that we are endeavouring to grasp at least in general terms. Of course, a doctor may be satisfied with some generalisation concerning the spiritual condition of the person committing suicide. But the sociologist must go further, and the same holds for the thoughts of any thinking person who has considered the problem at hand.

---

1. [From *Obskaya zhizn'*, 29 July 1912. This article continues the discussion in Documents 1:57 and 1:60.]

2. If not for life in general, then for the existing life or the one that is anticipated over a long period of years.

Where is the cause for losing the taste for life and for the alienation from people that precedes suicide? I must make the reservation that I am not speaking here of the spiritual depression that results from physiological causes.[3] The suicide of an incurable paralytic only accelerates the process of natural death. In three-quarters of his existence, the afflicted person is already dead, and the death of the remaining quarter only appears from the outside to be forced.

Every investigator of contemporary suicides has certainly been struck by the fact that the highest percentage of suicides comes in the major urban centres and in countries at the highest level of capitalist development. The highest percentage of suicides in the world comes in Saxony, the most industrial part of Germany. Here, the means that capitalism creates for discouraging suicide are evidently weaker than the tendencies it creates for multiplying them. But we shall say more of this later. In Russia as a whole, the annual rate of suicide is 34.7[4] per million of the population, in St. Petersburg during recent years it has been 780 a year, and in Moscow, about five hundred. The average for St. Petersburg and Moscow over the past ten years is half that rate, but the difference between the average rate of suicides in the capitals and in the country as a whole remains striking. It is also extraordinarily characteristic that in terms of professions the highest rate of suicides comes in the army; specifically, during the five-year period 1903–7 there were 33.4 suicides per million in the country, but 136 among the soldiers and 1,941.5 among the officers (the average for four years according to Dr. Novosel'sky's data). The highest percentage of suicides in the history of the country comes in post-revolutionary periods and in epochs of counter-revolution.

These facts already tell us a great deal. They tell us that the greater are the forces in society that separate the person from the community, the individual from the family, the individual member of a class or stratum from the stratum or class as a whole, the more notably the graph of suicides rises.

The patrimonial order of society, the contemporary peasant-'commune', the medieval shops and guilds and other such social groupings assured the persons involved material assistance when in need, moral support and advice, and finally, they forcibly intervened in the private life of the individual. The important point is that a man was not left alone; he was not torn from the social environment. Developing capitalism ruthlessly destroys old social groupings that do not satisfy the new demands of developing productive forces. A process occurs involving a new regrouping of individuals, but before the new system can create

---

3. The distinction between psychological and physiological causes is, of course, very conditional. Every spiritual condition of a man is connected with certain physiological processes.

4. We must note that this figure is deliberately lower than the real one.

its own characteristic forms of unifying people, it propels them through a stage of dissociation, of isolation from one another, through a Sahara of distrust and hatred in which *homo homini lupus est*.[5] And it is in this transition that the most deaths occur among the weakest or those most oppressed by the new conditions of life. A man then enters into contradiction with his own social nature, which has grown out of thousands of years of the collective struggle for existence. He cannot endure the role of Robinson, frequently deprived even of Friday, surrounded by a stormy ocean of men who are inexorably indifferent and incomprehensible. He loses his social centre of gravity, like a broken branch that becomes detached from the social tree and rapidly falls to its physical death. What is important in the phenomenon of suicide is not the moment of physical separation itself, but the preceding moment, when the threads are broken that tie the individual to society.

A person from the provinces, who finds himself in the capital for the first time with a population of millions, knows very well the alienation amongst a sea of people that capitalism creates. No-one needs him, no-one is interested in him, and no-one helps him unless he is a member of some union, party or mutual-aid society. In the form of workers' trade-unions, mutual-aid societies and the corporations of other strata, along with political parties, capitalism creates new forms of association that constitute a powerful antidote to suicides. But there is a certain intervening period, sometimes very long, before the ruined small shopkeeper, the proletarianised peasant or the independent handicraftsman becomes a member of a workers' union and, in new circumstances and with a new outlook and new feelings, with the support of thousands of comrades, begins to travel his life's road.

And why is it that the army contributes the highest percentage of suicides? After what has been said, it is not difficult to understand. The army is a collection of people who are artificially torn from different social groups and mechanically regrouped into military units. The social separation of the soldier is not reduced by the fact that he lives in a barracks; rather, it increases, because he is compelled to live together with strangers who cannot replace all the internal threads of a natural social union that binds all its members together.

The high percentage of suicides in an epoch of counter-revolution and social disorder is also easy to explain in terms of the point of view we have been discussing. During a buoyant epoch people rally more closely to achieve common goals, the isolation of the individual is reduced to a minimum, and the powerful forces of the collective support the individual in his life and struggle. A completely opposite picture prevails during an epoch of disintegration, when the

---

5. [A man is a wolf to his fellow man.]

old associations fall apart and the new have yet to emerge, when the centrifugal forces of society prevail over the centripetal. The powerless individual, when facing society, loses his equilibrium and perishes in the first encounter with adverse circumstances, which at a different time would have had no essential consequences for him.

Thus, as a result of our investigation of the problem of suicide, we come to the following conclusions.

1) Two-thirds of suicides are conditioned by social causes. 2) The question of a right to suicide in modern society cannot even be raised, because it is not a right that exists, only an obligation of suicide, and thus it is not suicide, but murder. 3) Since the common ground for almost all suicides is the dissociation and isolation of the person from society, it follows that the real means of struggling against suicides in modern society is the development of all accessible forms of association between people: trade-unions, societies, parties, and so on, and the only radical way of curtailing suicide in general is through transition of the existing society to a higher level of development.

M. Leonov

No. 73

Review of the Journal *Russkoe bogatstvo* (July)[1]

5 August 1912

In the *belles-lettres* section of the July issue of *Russkoe bogatstvo*, the story by P. Bulygin, 'Children', attracts one's attention. It is interesting not only on the artistic side, but also because of its subject and the questions it raises. It tells the story of one love, namely, the love between a schoolgirl and a schoolboy, which drives them both to suicide because the parents of both refused even to hear of a marriage between the underage boy and girl. The tale is quite topical, and clearly illustrates the discrepancy that exists in modern society between the sexual demands and the social-economic conditions of life for middle-bourgeois strata. The schoolboy in the eighth class can already love seriously, and in a sexual sense is mature to do so. But this does not mean that he can marry, since he must complete his higher education and acquire a position. There are two ways out: turn either to prostitution or celibacy. The practice of life resolves the question in favour of the former. But not everyone can overcome the feelings of love, and frequently it ends tragically.

The true nature of marriage is distorted in today's society by overriding economic conditions, and sexual attraction and love are quite rarely the only motives for a marriage. But the sexual instinct is strong, and no matter how strong in turn the economic factors with which it must collide, it yields only after a battle, and meanwhile the parents must pick up their children from the battlefield: morphine and bullets from a revolver give them a better way out than the route suggested by bourgeois prudence. Love must be assured an independent place in life, and marriage must be separated from the economy. However, one need hardly point out that modern society is not up to such an operation: what is required is a society built upon completely different foundations.

In the article 'Peasant-Unrest in the First Year of the Reign of Nicholas I', Ignatovich explains the causes for a number of instances of serf-unrest in 1826. Highlighting the economic conditions of life among the serfs who rose up during that year, and referring specifically to the Noinsky and Tsei estates, the Demidov estate in Ryazan, the Ponomarev estate in Tver, and the Gryazev estate in Kostroma province, the author comes to the following conclusion:

---

1. [From *Obskaya zhizn'*, 5 August 1912.]

In each of the cases described the basis of peasant-discontent could be found in economic conditions. These involved mainly the unbearable quit-rents, the means used in the struggle over quit-rent arrears, work in the factories and plants, and so on. In this respect, the turmoil of 1826, which flared under the influence of more frequent and specific rumours than were normal under serfdom, was no different from the disturbances of succeeding years, when there were no rumours to awaken peasant-activity, but the economic and other causes of peasant-discontent still existed and fed the continuous hostility of the peasants towards their 'father-landlords'.

One cannot disagree with the author's conclusions, which are confirmed by a number of other studies of the same question.

One reads with great interest a number of essays by Mr. S. entitled 'Behind the Iron-Bars'. Having himself spent several years in prison and shackles, the author provides a thoughtful and truthful essay concerning the moods and changing convictions experienced by most prison-inmates. Characters pass before the reader – some have moved 'to the right', others 'to the left'. In general and on the whole, movement 'to the left' is expressed by loss of faith in a mass movement and in hope for salvation through the action of 'a small, tightly-knit band of revolutionary fighters'. The characters of Senya and the old man Akim Grigor'evich, workers and former S-Ds, are in this respect extremely curious. Movement 'to the left' among the S-Rs is expressed in a transition to anarchism and denial of the political struggle (the Kiselev character); and among the anarchists, by a transition to ideological hooliganism and criminality (Samuil). Mr. S. provides an impartial portrayal of prison-experiences and of the evolution of imprisoned revolutionaries. Generally speaking, this will be interesting reading for anyone interested in the fate of people who have been forcibly detached from life, often after heading a revolutionary movement that has receded. The essays will be interesting both for students of social psychology and for psychologists in general.

M.L.

No. 74
Report of the Yenisei Provincial Gendarmerie-Administration to the Director of the Police-Department G.G. Mollov on the Impossibility of Determining the Author of a Letter Addressed to the Exile I.S. Shvarts[1]

No. 423   *11 September 1915*
Krasnoyarsk   *Top-Secret*

Presenting herewith the intelligence-reports for No. 259, I have the honour to report to Your Excellency that the addressee is the exile to Yenisei province, Itsek Srulev *Shvarts*, originating from the middle-class of the city of Nikolaev in Kherson province, condemned to an exile-settlement on 5 November 1913, by the Kazan appellate-court for a crime stipulated under Part 1, Article 102, of the Criminal Code. Currently, he resides in the Shalaevo parish of Kansk district.

---

1. [From GA RF. F. 102. OO. 1915. D. 5. Ch. 27B. L. 38–38 ob. The report is the typewritten original. The letter is a typewritten copy.]

The author of this item[2] and the people mentioned in it are impossible to determine.
Reported in Irkutsk No. 424.
Colonel.[3]

Attachment

No. 259
The village of Shelaevo in Yenisei province,
'Long Bridge' Post-Office

I.S. Shvarts

Dear Isaac...

Now let's chat about social themes. In my last letter, I wrote that George, as in Georgii Valentinovich,[4] has almost no supporters here. In disturbing the hot ashes, I intend no pain.[5] Who knows whether, in different circumstances, he would have a position of more respectable power such as Guesde[6] now occupies? Now, however, the mood has begun to change, and influenced by the successes of the impudent Germans, many anti-patriots[7] are half-seriously expressing a

---

2. [The fact that E.A. Preobrazhensky was the author is confirmed by a letter of 19 September 1915:
'Top Secret.
'The chief of the Irkutsk Provincial Gendarmerie-Administration. 19 September 1915. City of Irkutsk. In the police-department... I have the honour of reporting that the author of the secret document addressed 'village of Shelaevo...' is a resident of the city of Irkutsk, with permission from the local administration, and is an exile of the Karapchansky parish of Kirensky district of Irkutsk province, Evgeny Alekseev Preobrazhensky...
'The above-named Preobrazhensky is presently under the supervision of the administration as a member of the directorate (committee) of the Irkutsk organisation of the Russian Social-Democratic Workers' Party, and on 14 August of the current year in a public meeting of the members of the Irkutsk branch of the Union of Cities he proposed a resolution, compiled by the local Social Democrats, including a demand for abolishing the Pale of Settlement, amnesties for political exiles and implementation of the freedoms that were announced by the IMPERIAL Manifesto of 17 October, 1905, but such resolution was rejected by the chairman of the meeting... Colonel (signature)'. (GA RF.DP.OO. 1915. D. 5. Ch. 27B. L. 48).]
3. [The signature is not legible.]
4. [The reference is to G.V. Plekhanov.]
5. [The text is here and throughout reproduced literally, including all the errors committed by the copyists who opened and inspected Preobrazhensky's letter.]
6. [Jules Guesde, a former 'intransigent', accepted a position as a minister without portfolio in the French government in August 1914.]
7. [The word 'пользуются' ('enjoy' or 'use') is written above the line.]

wish to go and fight against these knights of a defensive war. Ideas are stirring in broad bourgeois circles, and meetings have already begun that bring back a blissful memory of the boycott of 1904 and 1905 that might be expected. Recently, there was a public report, here, from a delegate of the local branch of the Union of Cities who attended the Congress in Moscow. After the report, representatives of our 'public' took time for 'questions' of a kind that set out their own point of view. At a second public meeting of the branch, they dealt with[8] questions on the issue of refugees, and I, being commissioned by my comrades, read out a brief resolution on freedoms, and the public supported and applauded everything we said. We have decided in future to make more systematic appearances in all such cases. And the blues[9] are doing their normal work. Not very long ago, they arrested 40 people here, and our publishing works awaits trial under Article 102. In Cheremkov, 10 people were simultaneously arrested, and 12 in Manzurka. But we, thank God, are still free.[10] There is still no significant workers' movement here. There have been only two strikes (a bakers' strike long ago, and recently one by tailors). The mood among the masses is one of bitter expectation for the near future. We have to listen to such amazing explanations of our defeats, such information on palace-treason, on the role of the Tsaritsa and the like, that people can only throw up their hands. All this sounds like the delirium of madmen, but it is the kind of delirium that leads people to troubling practical conclusions. I cannot resist giving you a typical example about which I.D. wrote to us. The action occurs in the headquarters of the Commander-in-Chief; the Tsar arrives with a minister of the court and Nik[olai] Nik[olaevich] greets them: 'You', he says to the Tsar, 'come here with me, and you moth...fu...and so on', he says to Frederiks, 'stand here', and he orders a guard with a rifle to hold the minister under arrest throughout the entire conversation, and this is how court-etiquette translates into the vigorous language of democracy.

I give you our irresponsible minister. And as for the amnesty, whose freedoms we are now making use of, the impending shipment to the front of all those in administrative exile will put an end to that, but here it is necessary first to restore...

Well, for now I shake your hand. EVGENY.

---

8. [The text says 'посвящались' ('devoted themselves to') but the correct word appears to be 'освещались' ('dealt with' or 'took up').]

9. [The reference is to the dark blue uniforms of the Irkutsk provincial gendarmerie-administration.]

10. [The sentence in the text reads: 'Но мы пока слав. идет'.]

Nos. 75–6
Articles Published in the Newspaper *Zabaikal'skoe obozrenie* in March 1916

No. 75

'Quo Vadis'[1]

14 March 1916

When Herzen summarised the sad outcome of the 1848 movement in *My Past and Thoughts*, he was struck by the insignificance of the results achieved compared to the original goals and the efforts expended on their behalf, yet he still found consolation for himself and his contemporaries: 'The polyps die...serving the progress of the reef', he wrote, and 'We, too, shall serve something'. Remembering now the spiritual tragedy of our great publicist, and the small bandage with which he managed to dress the bloody wound of his unrealised hopes, we must face the question: Will we, as participants and witnesses of the greatest events of world-history – as contemporaries in an epoch that is deciding the question not only of the paths of peaceful development in the coming century, but perhaps also the question of the existence of modern civilisation in general, as we say today – when we summarise our own action or criminal inaction during these great days, will we at least have a right to that invalid's pension of moral satisfaction with which participants in the events of 1848 had to content themselves? A polyp

---

1. [From *Zabaikal'skoe obozrenie* (Chita), 14 March 1916.]

in the liberation-movement of 1848 struggled, suffered, died, and naturally, at least to the extent of its labours, served the progress of the reef. What is the reef whose progress will be served by our generation of world-democrats, when, for the past year and a half we have wiped out our entire heritage from the past and thrown into the abyss the capital carefully accumulated since the time of the famous 'Manifesto', the capital whose growth justifiably served to measure the degree of stability and the future of our civilisation? This is a time when capitalism, faltering on its inability to solve the problems resulting from its own development, has turned to eliminating the surplus-population and destroying its own productive forces, when it has imposed bloodletting on the sanguineous organism of existing society merely to save the constricting garments of bourgeois production-relations that are bursting at every seam – and it has found unexpected allies in this attempt at partial suicide. The entire horror of the existing situation lies in the fact that in this attempt, whose entire objective meaning is to preserve and immortalise the most barbarian and most backward aspects of the current social system, those aspects most hostile to progress, the elements of the future society have themselves been taking part. And what is the objective meaning of this participation? It is terrible even to think of one possibility, yet we must still have the courage to recognise it: this participation may mean the beginning of the disintegration of contemporary culture; it may be an expression, or symptom, of the impossibility of any future society and the beginning of mankind's backward-movement on the reverse-road of progress. What reef does this democracy serve, when it contributes so much passion and idealism to a reactionary cause and, through its participation, is lending crime the appearance of virtue? Is it not the progress of a reef on which the ship of human culture will break apart with its entire cargo of our unrealised hopes; is it not the progress of a reef that will shipwreck all future progress? Where is there any guarantee that this simulation of suicide, made by a bourgeois society to save itself through involving its antagonists, will not turn into the most authentic murder of all culture and social development? Is there any guarantee in the fact that the 'conscious' portion of mankind expresses no misgivings and contemplates the developing events with truly idiotic self-confidence? But after all, the calf that is being led to the butcher is also calm and happily bounds along the roadway...

And there are so many facts to confirm the most pessimistic expectations. From Russia, we hear not only of universal apathy, indifference and a deadening of public sentiments, but also of the sort of mood reminiscent of a feast before the plague; a dissipated life, mad prodigality and luxury, and a daily growing pursuit of pleasures. These harbingers of catastrophe, so clearly reminiscent of the last days of Rome, have reached even as far as Siberia. And you cannot help but think, looking at this pre-execution delight of the bipeds – that they have come to an operetta, that they are watching a merry comedy, that they have been possessed by the cancan. And no-one thinks of the fact that in this entire theatre, in their entire life, which is empty and insignificant, they are acting on another much broader stage. Indeed, a tragedy is now being performed on the stage of world-history, and people are behaving as if they were participants at the feast of Belshazzar.

And the real tragedy is that a terrible hand will write ominous words before the onlookers at the feast.[2] And then the gay amusement will end. If only the saving hand would appear! But we hear so little of this, almost nothing compared to the horrifying responsibility of the moment, with its truly colossal potential for extinction and degeneration. Were the hand to appear, it would be a blessing. And if it does not appear, and a common abyss opens up – into it will fly not only those who have long been heading in that direction, but also those who counted on a long life to come, who believed in unstoppable human progress, who were prepared to overcome the final obstacles to a rational reconstruction of social life such that, through the heroic effort of millions of calloused hands, they might smash open the doors, hitherto closed to them, to an earthly paradise and then, more confidently and amicably, move towards great victories over the spontaneous forces of nature. Is that really why we conquered space, why we flew in the air, why the noble polyps of social instinct built a roadway with their own bones for the gradual progress of humanity, so that we, calling ourselves children of the Sun, might prove bankrupt when facing the ulcer of existing society and then flee all the more towards our own animal past and begin to measure all future progress by how closely we resemble the monkey?

It is a horrible prospect to struggle, to think and be inspired by noble impulses, and still to end up merely as an element of decay, merely as one of the worms crawling about on the corpse of world-civilisation. But there is another possibility that is no less horrifying for mankind: to wake up alive after attempting suicide and, with the first flashes of consciousness, to see before oneself all the same cursed problems that led to taking up the revolver.

But there is also a third possibility, on which the sun in the sky has yet to set, and as long as it exists there is still reason to live. The choice between proximate paths of conscious development or the destruction of civilisation is one involving a balance of forces. There is no fate, no predestination, only struggle, and we ourselves, in all our actions, are involved in the pattern of laws that define the course of history. While the question of civilisation's salvation remains a question of the elements struggling to that end, we do have a cause that is great in its consequences, capable of justifying all the sacrifices, and able to inspire great

---

2. [Daniel interpreted the writing on the wall to say, 'Thou art weighed in the balances, and art found wanting'. On the night of Belzhazzar's feast, he was murdered and his kingdom fell to the Medes and Persians.]

enthusiasm. That means we know what is good and what is criminal, what we are creating as children of the Sun and what we are destroying as descendants of the gorilla and orang-utan. There is no evil without good, even though the good in such circumstances is always too meagre. The good in the tragedy we are experiencing lies in the fact that it has made one thing perfectly obvious: civilisation and collectivism are henceforth synonyms; their destiny is just as inseparably connected as the life of an organism is connected with the integrity of the head and the heart. The development, strengthening and victory of an international community of sobriety: the energetic action of all the vital forces of world-democracy to restore the former whole and return to the old positions, to use the bankruptcy of bourgeois capitalist society to resolve the impending problems of social development in order to pass the answers on to the historical heirs of bourgeois civilisation – this is the guarantee that we will not be hurled backwards to the starting points of human culture.

If only there were sufficient forces to save civilisation, if only the turning point would come and we would begin to see the dividends of victory! Oh, then we would find the elements of virtue in the crime; the rays of the Sun, which today are blocked off, would illuminate the darkness for us; we would find in the oceans of spilled blood the medicines to heal our wounds; in the pointless chaos of the tragedy we would behold the reason of history. Then all those who are now perishing in the various corners of the world as victims of the worldwide tragedy, all those confident of a future...[3] would be able to say with satisfaction before their death: *morituri te salutant, libertas!*[4]

E. Iduchansky[5]

---

3. [The newspaper is damaged, making the next two words illegible.]
4. [We who are about to die salute you, freedom!]
5. [In addition to the party-nickname Leonid (L-d), E.A. Preobrazhensky also signed articles with the pseudonyms M. Leonov, M.L., and E. Iduchansky (TsAODM. F. 685. Op. 1. D. 11. L. 52).]

No. 76

'Our Defencists'[1]

21 March 1916

Russia's annexation to Western Europe has been completed within the sphere of the socialist movement: we now have the kind of opportunism that is most extreme and alien to the spirit of international Marxism and most dangerous in terms of the support it may find in the dark nationalistic instincts of the working class. The pioneer and chief ideologist of this opportunism, through malicious irony, is G.V. Plekhanov, the same Plekhanov who proudly declared at international congresses that there are no opportunists in Russian Social Democracy. True, he himself objects to such a charge and believes, in full compliance with Hottentot-morality, that when German socialists are defending their homeland, this is fully consistent with the spirit of revolutionary Marxism.

The official declaration of this has come in two appeals by the Petrograd and Moscow defencists, while their theoretical foundation is Plekhanov's book *On the War* together with his articles in the journals *Nashe delo*, *Sovremennyi mir* and in the collection 'Self-Defence'. Our entire bourgeois chauvinistic press is the necessary guide for understanding what it is that the defencists want. Let us analyse the basic theses of the defencists as they have appeared in their declarations and are shared by all our social patriots.

1) Germany is on the side of the aggressors.
2) The Allies are fighting for the right of nations to self-determination.
3) Participation in the War on the side of the Allied Powers does not contradict the International.
4) Defeat of the Allies would mean destruction of the socialist movement in these countries.
5) 'Defence' is the fundamental slogan of the moment, and to realise it there must be 'domestic peace'. Modern wars are essentially imperialist wars. On this everyone agrees. All defencists agree that the current war is also an imperialist war, but with one solid exception: the Central Powers are waging an imperialist war, but the Allies are fighting for the self-determination of nations. The German social defencists claim the opposite.

---

1. [From *Zabaikal'skoe obozrenie* (Chita), 21 March 1916.]

Who is right?

Let us consider a bit of history. The Spanish-American War can be regarded as the first imperialist war.[2] The aggressor was America. In the Anglo-Boer War,[3] it was England that attacked. The Chinese War[4] was a joint attack by all the capitalist nations on a backward Asiatic country, in which the extortionate interests of capitalism were particularly evident with no distinction between nations, political systems and so forth. Then came the Russo-Japanese War.[5] Allah himself would probably have difficulty in sorting out who was the aggressor here and who was on the defensive side. But it is perfectly obvious that both of the clashing sides were conducting an identical policy of conquest in relation to defenceless China.

In the plunder of Tripolitania, Italy was the aggressor, although now, 'by the way', it has been regenerated in the space of two years and is currently fighting for the self-determination of nations.

In the First Balkan War[6] the aggressors were Serbia, Bulgaria, Greece and Montenegro, with Turkey on the defensive, and essentially the allies fought for the national liberation of areas still under the Turkish yoke. And here, the theorem for Allah is the same as in the case of the Second Balkan War,[7] where everybody was attacking and everybody was defending.

And finally, there is the current war. The official list of its participants is a mess. The bourgeoisie and the social patriots of the Entente, who adopt the bourgeois view, claim that Germany is the aggressor and that it regards the War as preventive and precautionary; that is, Germany predetermined the course of events without waiting for the attack that she expected from the Allies once their armed forces were raised to the necessary level. With equal justification,

---

2. [The Spanish-American War began in 1898 in the context of a Cuban Revolution (from 1895) and the insurrection by the Filipino people against Spanish colonial oppression. Nominally intervening in support of the struggle by these peoples, the United States used the opportunity for its own purposes.]

3. [Great Britain's war against the Boer republics of South Africa, the Orange Free State and Transvaal, in 1899–1902. As a result of the War, in 1902 both republics were made into English colonies.]

4. [The reference is to suppression in China of the Boxer Rebellion of 1899–1901 by the armies of Germany, Japan, Great Britain, the United States, France, Russia, Italy and Austria-Hungary.]

5. [The Russo-Japanese War of 1904–5 over control of northeast China and Korea. Launched by Japan, the War ended with the Treaty of Portsmouth in 1905.]

6. [In the First Balkan War (1912–13) the members of the Balkan alliance fought for liberation from Turkish national and feudal oppression and for creation of their own national states.]

7. [In the Second Balkan War (1913) Bulgaria fought against Serbia, Greece, Romania and Montenegro. Turkey also entered the War against Bulgaria. The War ended in Bulgaria's defeat, followed by its adhesion to the Austro-Hungarian bloc.]

the supporters of Germany and Austria assert that it was England that launched a preventive war to destroy Germany's naval forces before they could rival England's own. Who is right? It seems to us that a historical look at previous wars illustrates one thing: it is only in those cases where one of the warring sides is far along the road of capitalist development compared to the other that it is possible to determine which side attacked. And the side that attacks is always the one that is economically more developed. When the colliding countries are equally developed or undeveloped in the capitalist sense, there is no possibility of discovering who is responsible for the collision: the cause is the need for capitalist development on both sides. In the current war, the colliding coalitions of capitalist nations are on approximately the same level of capitalist development. And the guilty party, here, is everywhere the same, namely, the existing level of Europe's capitalist development. But perhaps we should undertake a study of the yellow, blue, and green books and the protocols of diplomatic meetings? Let us follow Plekhanov's example and, instead of propagating among the proletariat of all countries the ideas of solidarity, instead of summoning them to struggle for those common goals that arouse no doubt among the working class, whatever their nationality, instead of enlightening their consciousness in the spirit of Marxism, instead of summoning them to international unity of action at the most critical moment of world-history, so that the catastrophe continuously experienced by the proletariat might, given the fraternal efforts of proletarians in all countries, be transformed into a catastrophe for the entire exploiting system – instead of all this, we will zealously dig into the diplomatic archives in order, twenty years later, to make the happy discovery, from some document or other, as with Bismarck's Ems dispatch, that the war in which we participated and for which we summoned the proletarians of all countries to shoot each other down, was a war of aggression. Do you wish to know the causes of the War? It is not the blue, yellow or green books or the pre-war exchanges of diplomacy between the exploiters that you need to study.

Read the second volume of *Capital*, where Marx, on the basis of the laws of capitalist production themselves, establishes the need for overproduction and crises, and consequently the search for markets; read about the law of primitive capitalist accumulation, and then the causes of the current war will be clear to you.[8]

---

8. Of course, Plekhanov knows this. If this expert on Marx could not draw from his teachings the necessary conclusions at this most urgent moment, when such conclusions were a matter of honour for a Marxist, this only shows that for him the national instinct is stronger and deeper than theoretical conviction. The great scribe of Marxism has turned out in practice to be a Pharisee.

The only guilty party in the present war is the capitalist mode of production with its inherent drive for expansion, which at a certain stage of development, following a series of partial wars, had to lead to a general clash between the capitalist nations and thus to find, in the extermination of one part of the capitalist whole, the means for the existence and development of the other.

And from this perspective, the question of who started it is completely insignificant and redundant.

War, like an earthquake or flood, is a manifestation of spontaneity in the social sphere. The forces responsible for it are beyond the limits of human will and consciousness, and to search for guilty parties among the victims of this spontaneity, among the millions set in motion, rather than holding the laws of capitalist development responsible, means doing the same as those institutions, which it is not convenient to name, that search for agitators in spontaneous popular movements. And our defencists, indeed, have really lowered themselves to exactly that vulgar police-philosophy of history.

What are the warring coalitions fighting for, what are the objective goals of the confrontation? He would be a pitiful Marxist who took the arguments of the participants as the cause and the goal of the struggle.

Meanwhile, that is how Plekhanov and his co-thinkers proceed, caught by the bait of bourgeois lies about the War and beholding its causes in the liberal-chauvinist argumentation of the combatants. The Allies are fighting for the right of nations to self-determination – they tell us – and that is the meaning of their involvement in the War. There is evidently no more naïve illusion than this one. Before the War, we saw how Russia and England 'self-determined' Persia. We saw with our own eyes how Japan, one of the members of the coalition fighting for the 'self-determination' of nations, issued an ultimatum to China that was far more aggressive in its goals than the one Austria presented to Serbia, which provoked the War. Then all of the Allies jointly 'self-determined' Greece, to the point where it ceased to be an independent state. But even that is a trifle. Just look at the brilliant self-determination of nations within the warring coalitions. Austria and Bulgaria have been made into provinces of Germany, and Turkey into its reluctant colony. And among the Allies? The small states have piled up debts to England and France that they can never repay, and their future freedom, for which they are shedding their blood, will be the freedom for Anglo-French capital to squeeze the last juices from their populations to pay interest on the debt.

England and France are now discussing conditions for a future trade-agreement with them, which are meant to erase national frontiers for the sake of their commercial-economic unification.

As for Russia, in view of its twenty billion in debts, which consist largely of foreign loans, it is already open to the stream and plundering of finance capital and must pay more than a billion every year in interest alone as the sum steadily grows throughout every day of the War. Moreover, our allies want to reinforce this enslavement with a trade-agreement that will replace German domination with Anglo-French domination, which will be ten times more burdensome. What is Russia paying for with its millions of lives and the billions from its current and future income?

Is it in order that money from the peasant's horse and cow, sold for non-payment of taxes, might go to a French and English bank rather than to one in Berlin, that it might flow there in volumes that monstrously exceed all possible payments under 'German domination'?

The political freedom of nations is based on their economic independence, and where the latter is destroyed the former is a myth. Therefore, in the course of the present war the right to self-determination, which corresponded to the economic structure of Europe at its previous stage of development, is already being practically consigned to the archives by all the participants in the struggle.

This right has now become an illusion that is denied by the phase of capitalist development we have reached.

But, in the final analysis, it is not important whether illusion or truth motivates the activity of the combatants so long as the struggle itself, with its customary consequences, turns out to be a struggle for goals that are real and profitable to the combatants. And for the bourgeoisie of all the warring countries that is the nature of the current struggle.

Let the right of national self-determination be an illusion. But the right to pick the pockets of poor people is no illusion, and that is what the War will bring to the French and English capitalists in their relations with Russia, Serbia, Montenegro and Italy, and for the Germans – in their relations with Hungary, Bulgaria and Turkey.

And the economic territory, for whose expansion and exploitation the ruling classes of the Entente and the Central Powers are fighting, is also no illusion. But what are socialists fighting for if the right of nations to self-determination is a fiction?

They are fighting for the real goals *of others* and for their own illusions.

If the authors of *The Communist Manifesto* had the right to assert that the revolting proletarians of all countries have nothing to lose in their struggle but their chains, and a whole world to win, then the socialists who are participating in the present war can say with equal justification that they are winning nothing, but losing an entire world – the world in which the shattered Second International was so close to prevailing.

From the point of view of the International, is participation by socialists permissible in the current war on any side whatever? The answer is obvious from what has been said.

The War arose from the fact that the modern world, divided into nations with their economic fences, prevented a free exchange of commodities and became too confining for capitalism in its current phase of development – in the phase of finance capital. But if the world became too confining for capitalism, in the language of a socialist this means that capitalist relations became too confining for the world, and the world-economy requires different relations of production. From the present position, which has led to the War, there can be only two ways out. The elimination of national frontiers while preserving the capitalist mode of production, or their elimination together with the replacement of capitalist relations by socialist ones. The first way out means destruction of one part of the capitalist whole in order that the other part might exist and develop, or else curtailment of development of the productive forces in both. And in both cases the capitalist mode of production is preserved at the cost of halting progress, at the cost of stopping any development of the productive forces.

The second way is the way of socialising the world-economy, the way of opening doors for progress and social development, the way of saving mankind and its future. The method of realising the first prospect is world imperialist war. It excludes the other method of world socialist reconstruction; and for that reason, from the viewpoint of the International, any participation in the imperialist War is participation in the struggle to preserve the existing order, on whatever front it occurs and whatever the loud phrases used to cover it up.

The clear proof of this is not only the fact that Purishkevich and Plekhanov, Bethmann-Hollweg and Scheidemann, Guesde and Poincaré have found common language and mutually support each other, but also the fact that at the Zimmerwald socialist conference, which signifies the beginning of a concentration of all proletarian forces for resolving the question by the second method, not only were there and could there be no socialist-defencists from all the warring countries, but they furthermore reacted to it with open condemnation.

'The defeat of the Allies will be disastrous for the socialist movement in these countries', cry the defencists. We do not know what this defeat may entail, but we are inclined to believe it would be more dangerous to the governments of these countries than to their peoples. But what is incontrovertible is the fact that participation in the War by socialists had already buried the Second International.

And that is without mentioning the fact that a complete defeat of either of the warring sides is impossible, something recognised by all the participants and sufficiently revealed in the existing relation of forces.

The participation or non-participation of socialists has essentially changed nothing in the situation at hand. After all, socialism was not strong enough to prevent this war. And why would socialism be made stronger by participating in it? Is it because it goes against its own nature, is it because suicide makes the person committing suicide stronger?

Finally, we must not forget the main point. If the attempt to save capitalist society by way of partial suicide and the enforced destruction of redundant productive forces turns out to be successful, and the imperialist War does not end in civil war, that will mean the end of social development and the death of civilisation.

From that perspective, one need scarcely be concerned about how socialism will die as a force struggling for humanity's future – whatever the national frontiers may be, or the trade-agreements, and with or without indemnities. Does it make any difference to a corpse what coffin it is buried in? If the war of nations ends in a war of classes, in which the proletariat is victorious, does it make any difference to socialism, which plans to eliminate all national frontiers, what is the map of Europe on which it is destined to triumph? But one thing does make a difference to every genuine socialist. If we are facing the death of civilisation, then it is better to perish among those fighting for its salvation than to be one of the products of its decomposition in the bosom of 'self-determined' nations. If it is the destiny of the forces saving culture to win, we want to be participants in victory on the side of those who at the most critical moments, in the maddest revelry of chauvinistic passions, at a time when vandals are destroying the heritage of international socialism, never degraded themselves before the brutalised street and never lowered the banner of the International before the orang-utans of nationalism.

'The centre of life at the present moment is defence of country, and correspondingly the centre of our current practical policy must be defence of country, which is its starting point and regulating principle'. What is the practical meaning of this slogan for a Social Democrat?

Refusal to fight for our own goals – that is what the defencists' slogan means; and unable to stop halfway in his fall, Plekhanov has already drawn that conclusion, announcing that at the moment he considers the political struggle within Russia to be harmful. Perhaps not all the defencists agree with him, but none of them think this way: first freedom, then defence. None of them regards democratic transformation as a necessary ambition taking precedence over any participation in a war. And these gentlemen dare to refer to the great figures of the first French Revolution.

It is true that everything that is great in history the first time returns as farce. The figures of the first French Revolution decided from the outset the question of their state-structure, and then they went to give battle at the borders with the hands of free men. Our Dantons go against the Germans while leaving the homeland to drift and be plundered by the agents of reaction.

E. Iduchansky

Part II

In the Years of Revolution and Civil War: 1917–20

No. 1
From the *Autobiography* (for February 1917–1920)[1]

1925

After Irkutsk, I went to Chita, where the February Revolution found me.[2] I left Chita in April as a delegate to the First Congress of Soldiers' and Workers' Deputies, which met shortly afterwards, and before the Congress I stopped in the Urals, where I began work in Zlatoust with my old Urals friends.

After the First Congress of Soviets, I returned to the Urals, was elected as a member of the Urals Regional Committee, and attended the Sixth Party-Congress[3] as a delegate from the Urals, where I was elected as a candidate of the Central Committee.

In the city of Zlatoust, where I returned to work, our Party was in a minority among the workers even during the October Days. The majority of workers were for the Socialist-Revolutionaries. During the October Days, I took part in our Party's armed demonstration with the slogan 'All power to the soviets' and, until I lost my voice, I and other comrades persuaded the workers of the Zlatoust factory to support transfer of power to the soviets. We were only partly successful. Then, to the

---

1. [From Preobrazhensky 1989, pp. 589–90. For the beginning of the autobiography, see Document 1:1.]

2. [The periphery did not immediately react to the fact that in Petrograd, on 23 February 1917, the bourgeois-democratic February Revolution began. Thus its first echo in the Urals only came on 28 February, with more complete effects on 1–2 March.]

3. [The Sixth Congress of the RSDRP(B) met on 26 July–3 August (8–16 August) in Petrograd. V.I. Lenin did not attend the Congress because he was in hiding in Razliv. The Congress protested against Lenin's attendance at the Provisional Government's court and adopted the slogan 'All power to the soviets'.]

contrary, in Simsky district, where I went on 26 October, our organisation succeeded everywhere in taking power and nationalising the enterprises of the Simsky mining region. After the October Days, I and other comrades took part in building up Soviet power in the Urals and in strengthening our party-organisations.

From the spring of 1918, our Urals organisation had to withstand the attack by the Czechoslovaks and then create a front against Kolchak. As a Urals delegate at the Fourth Congress of Soviets,[4] in the summer of 1918 I took part in putting down the uprising by the Left S-Rs, was slightly wounded in the left temple during the attack on the Central Telegraph, which was occupied by the S-Rs, and then was posted by the revolutionary council to the Kursk district for several days in order to maintain the discipline of our troops stationed on the frontier with Ukraine. From Moscow, I left again for the Urals, where Ekaterinburg had already been taken by Kolchak and our forces had retreated to the north. At this time, I was Chairman of the Urals Regional Committee, which took upon itself the functions of political department of the Third Army and did all the corresponding work with the resources of our organisations. With the attack on Perm by Kolchak's people, our Revolutionary Committee, under fire from the Whites, evacuated from Perm with the last detachments of the Mrachkovsky division, after which we began to retreat with all our forces in the direction of Glazov and Vyatka. After that, when the Urals regional association in fact lost almost all of its territory, the Urals Regional Committee was dissolved by a decree of the Central Committee and I was recalled to Moscow, where I started to work in the editorial office of *Pravda*. I was a delegate at the Eighth Party-Congress[5] and participated in the commission on the party-programme. After that, I was sent as plenipotentiary from VTsIK to Orlov province.

Upon my return to Moscow, I was present at the explosion in Leontiev Lane.[6] Following the liberation of the Urals, I was sent again to do party- and soviet-work in Ufa. I was elected from the Ufa organisation to the Ninth Party-Congress.

---

4. [E.A. Preobrazhensky made an error in the *Autobiography*. In the summer of 1918 he was a delegate to the Fifth All-Russian Congress of Soviets, which opened in Moscow in the Grand Theatre on 4 July 1918. On 10 July the Congress adopted the first Soviet constitution for the RSFSR.]

5. [The Eighth Congress of the RKP(B) took place in Moscow from 18–23 March 1919. The Congress adopted the Programme of the Russian Communist Party (Bolsheviks).]

6. [The reference is to the attack against members of the Moscow-city party-organisation on 25 September, 1919. In the hall of the Party's Moscow Committee at 18 Leontiev Lane, where the meetings occurred, the assassins threw two bombs whose explosive force killed and wounded about forty people.]

At the Congress, I was elected to the Central Committee, and the Central Committee selected me as one of three secretaries.[7]

After the Tenth Party-Congress,[8] I was appointed as Chairman of the Financial Committee of the Central Committee and the Council of People's Commissars, whose work I directed in adjusting our monetary circulation and financial economy to the conditions of the New Economic Policy; I was then Chairman of *Glavproforba*,[9] I was one of the editors of *Pravda*, and I fulfilled several other functions that it would not be interesting to list.

Among my literary works, apart from some minor pamphlets and many articles in *Pravda* and in the journals, I will mention the following: *Anarchism and Communism*; *The ABC of Communism* written with N. Bukharin; *Paper-Money in the Epoch of Proletarian Dictatorship*; *Reasons for the Decline of our Rouble*; *From the NEP to Socialism*; *On Morals and Class-Norms*; *V.I. Lenin*; *The Economics and Finances of Contemporary France*; *On Economic Crises under the NEP* and, finally, the first volume of the yet-unfinished work *The New Economics*.

---

7. [The Ninth Congress of the RKP(B) occurred on 29 March–5 April, 1920, in Moscow. In addition to E.A. Preobrazhensky, N.N. Krestinsky and L.P. Serebryakov also became secretaries of the Central Committee.]

8. [The Tenth Congress of the RKP(B) met on 8–16 March 1921, in Moscow. The Congress took the decision to turn from the policy of 'War-Communism' to the 'NEP'.]

9. [The Main Administration for professional training at the People's Commissariat of Education of the Russian Soviet Federated Socialist Republic (Главное управление профессионального образования Наркомпроса РСФСР).]

No. 2
From 'My Memories of Ya.M. Sverdlov' (for the Period from 1917 to 1919)[1]

1926[2]

My next meeting with Yakov Mikhailovich happened as early as 1917, when he moved from the Urals to St. Petersburg and became Lenin's right-hand man in all the events of that time. I came to St. Petersburg for the First Congress of Soviets[3] and ran into him when he was hammering together the Bolshevik faction in Smolny for the upcoming speeches at the Soviet-Congress. I often had to turn to Yakov Mikhailovich for directions concerning what stand to take on this or that question at the Congress. When Il'ich himself was not there, Yakov Mikhailovich either transmitted a resolution to the bureau of our faction from Vladimir Il'ich, which had to be substantiated, or, if the matter concerned secondary questions, he issued brief instructions on what we were to do. He was wholly consumed by the colossal organisational work that fell to him both from the St. Petersburg organisation and from the all-Russian organisation of our Party. He did not have a minute of peace. No-one knew when he had time to eat or sleep in those turbulent times.

---

1. [This is a continuation of Document 1:2. From Preobrazhensky 1926, pp. 179–83.]
2. [The date when the memoirs were written.]
3. [The First All-Russian Congress of Soviets met in Petrograd from 3–24 June (16 June–7 July) 1917. E.A. Preobrazhensky read to the Congress a draft Bolshevik resolution on the War, which the Congress rejected in favour of an S-R-Menshevik resolution.]

I remember several conversations that Vladimir Il'ich had with Yakov Mikhailovich during those days in Smolny. Whenever Vladimir Il'ich outlined a necessary measure, Yakov Mikhailovich invariably replied that the necessary measures had already been taken, or else he explained why the measures adopted could not be successful. It almost always turned out that he himself had already thought about what Vladimir Il'ich intended to suggest. Yakov Mikhailovich and Vladimir Il'ich were always remarkably coordinated in their work. In everything that concerned general political or theoretical questions, Yakov Mikhailovich absolutely and unconditionally trusted comrade Lenin and almost never spent time thinking about what Vladimir Il'ich proposed; he accepted his instructions, directives and suggestions as absolute truth, any discussion of which would be a waste of time. Conversely, on organisational questions he was himself the greatest specialist, and in this area Vladimir Il'ich, who was himself a great organiser, trusted in him as he did no-one else and, as we all know, he made no mistake in that regard.

I also remember the amazing tact and the amazing skill that Yakov Mikhailovich showed in his negotiations with the Left S-Rs and in all those measures that had to be implemented at the time, no matter what the cost and despite the resistance and hysterics of bawlers and windbags from that Party. He often seemed to agree to great concessions, only then to follow essentially the line that Vladimir Il'ich intended.

Relations between the Urals people and Yakov Mikhailovich somewhat deteriorated in 1918 because the overwhelming majority of party-organisations in the Urals spoke out at the time against the Brest peace. But the temporary frostiness very quickly passed as soon as this question was put to rest. Despite the severity of past disagreements, Yakov Mikhailovich never subsequently held comrades' mistakes against them when it was a question of assigning them to work or using them according to their real abilities.

I also remember Yakov Mikhailovich during the harshest period of the Soviet Republic's existence, when Ekaterinburg fell in the Urals and the White Guards took Yaroslavl'. In a conversation with me, he gestured at the map of Soviet Russia and said: 'They have us surrounded on all sides; they are closing in and we will soon be drawing on our last reserves'. But there was not a shade of doubt or confusion in the metallic tone of his voice. He firmly knew what had to be done, and he tried to arrange things so that whatever must be done was done thoroughly. At the time of the Left S-Rs' uprising in Moscow, he did enormous work in organising our resources and, as I remember, it was he who orchestrated the amazing manoeuvre at the Congress of Soviets that we used on the Left S-Rs, quietly arresting all of them in the meeting room and then throwing all the Bolshevik forces from the Congress into the districts to suppress the uprising.

Among Yakov Mikhailovich's most prominent characteristics I must mention the following.

First, he had an excellent knowledge of how to approach people, and he very quickly determined what they might contribute to the matter at hand. But in addition to this, he had an extraordinary sense of how to approach the less conscious workers, and he managed very quickly to win their trust. We, the professional revolutionaries of that time, mostly intellectuals, often had to live in the workers' quarters or systematically spend nights there. It cannot be said that we were unfamiliar with the workers' life in those days. But we knew it mainly in terms of what was required for the success of our propaganda and agitation. We had much less interest in the daily and family lives of our worker-comrades. If I may say so, we were looking psychologically in another direction. On the contrary, Yakov Mikhailovich had the ability to enter into all the family- and everyday details of life of those workers with whom he was in contact, especially, for example, when he stayed overnight. I remember that he was staying overnight at the home of one Perm worker whose wife did not much approve of her husband's seditious orientation. During his overnight stays at this worker's home, 'Mikhalych' won her over by rocking her child in its crib and sympathetically inquiring about all her family-matters and concerns. Within two-to-three days of meeting some new party-worker, 'Mikhalych' already used the familiar form of address with him, established friendly relations and won his complete trust.

Another very important trait of Yakov Mikhailovich was his ability to ascertain what was most essential in people while, on the other hand, not overlooking all the peculiarities and concrete details of their character. Generally speaking, there are two methods of understanding people: one is to sort people into definitive categories, into specific types, and then in our imagination they figure as artificially standardised and abstractly simplified subjects. The other method occurs when the person is intuitively grasped right away, with all of his peculiarities. This latter ability is enormously important for the person who is an organiser and who must, on first impression, properly allocate people to different functions. Yakov Mikhailovich had this great aptitude for intuitively understanding comrades whom he encountered in his work. His remarkable memory and knowledge of the Party's personnel became almost legendary. He stored in memory an image of what people were really like without forgetting the smallest detail. This greatly facilitated his extremely difficult work of organising and distributing party-resources. Many times after his death, I (and I was probably not alone) heard complaints from party-comrades that they were not being properly used[4] and were not known as well as they should be. How often I heard such

---

4. [This is the expression in the text.]

expressions as: 'Ah, if only Yakov Mikhailovich were alive they would put me to better use!'

The next peculiarity of Yakov Mikhailovich was his extremely tactful abstention from meddling in those fields of work where he did not consider himself to be an expert. Theory, for example, was one such field. During his entire life Yakov Mikhailovich only one time made a mistake when it came to theory, having written in exile a small pamphlet about capitalism. He never again returned to this area of work but instead modestly concentrated on the activity for which he possessed a truly great talent and where he was really irreplaceable.

Finally, one should remember Yakov Mikhailovich's remarkable ability to guide the necessary resolutions through meetings, conferences, congresses and so on. He always firmly knew what had to be done, whether it was a matter of following some plan of his own or, as was more frequently the case, implementing instructions received from Vladimir Il'ich. Everyone knows how quickly things proceeded at all the meetings he chaired. Often comrades who did not agree with one or another of his suggestions did not have time to open their mouths before the decision was already taken. Yakov Mikhailovich managed to do this without infringing anyone's right to speak out, introduce their own suggestion, and such like. On the contrary, all constitutional guarantees were observed, although the motion that was passed was the one called for by the Central Committee. I remember that several times I had to be Yakov Mikhailovich's opponent over some practical decision or other, or else in opposing the accelerated methods of decision-making. On those occasions I represented resistance on the part of the human material, whereas he represented speed, pressure, and 'time is money'. Yet I do not remember a single instance when I had cause to complain about violation of my formal rights, rather than my own awkwardness.

Since the time of Yakov Mikhailovich's death, our Party has rapidly grown in all dimensions and its work has become enormously more complex. The task of selecting people, which Vladimir Il'ch wrote about in his famous articles on the Workers' and Peasants' Inspectorate, has taken on the greatest significance for success in our work. How often I regret now that we do not have Yakov Mikhailovich with us today; with his work in the area of organisation-building and assigning people he would curtail those mechanical methods of classification and assignment that can never replace the colossal personal knowledge of party-members, the lack of bias and great organisational talent, always combined with readiness to listen to and understand everyone, that our remarkable organiser took with him to the grave with his untimely passing.

Nos. 3–5
Articles Published in the Newspaper *Zabaikal'skii rabochii* in March–April 1917

22 March–9 April 1917

No. 3

'On our Party's Programme'[1]

22 March 1917

II[2]

In today's capitalist society, every person sells something and, by doing so, acquires the means for living. The peasant sells the grain he produces; the artisan, the commodity he makes by himself; the capitalist sells the commodity made for him by the worker; and the worker sells the only commodity he possesses – his labour-power. Everyone wants to sell his commodity at the best price, and in this respect the worker is no exception.

For the worker to sell his commodity at the best price means selling less of his labour-power and receiving more for it. To sell less means to work less. Therefore, the worker is interested in shortening the working day.

---

1. [From *Zabaikal'skii rabochii* (Chita). 22 March 1917]
2. [The first part of this article could not be found in the central libraries of the Russian Federation.]

To receive more for it means receiving a higher wage for the labour-power provided to the capitalist.

Thus, in defending the interests of the working class, the Russian Social-Democratic Workers' Party demands in its programme that the working day not exceed eight hours and that the workers be able to get from the capitalist the highest possible wage, which can only happen through struggle. However, the worker is interested not simply in shortening the working day and raising wages, but also in not having his labour-power prematurely depleted, so that he does not die before his time from consumption and other occupational illnesses, so that his wife, working with him at the factory, might bear healthy children, and so that young workers do not exhaust themselves in work beyond their capacities. Therefore, our Party demands[3] in its programme a number of measures to protect the worker during the labour-process and endeavours to extend the worker's life. It has been statistically established that the current lifetime of a worker is, on average, one and a half times shorter than among the propertied classes of society. This must not be.

We are beginning to strive for all of the above-mentioned demands in the near future, without fundamentally undermining the rule of capital and without depriving the capitalists of the right to property in the factories, plants and mines.

But after achieving all this, the worker cannot stop there. He is interested not only in selling his labour-power more dearly, but also, in the final analysis, in not selling it at all and in being the owner of the product of his labour. Even with an eight-hour day, the proletarian only receives in wages from the capitalist a part of the values that he creates. He has the right to all of the value created with his own hands.

Therefore, the Social-Democratic Party seeks, as its final goal, the complete emancipation of labour from the power of capital. It seeks to hand over all the factories, plants and shops to the state – but not to the current state, rather, to a future one in which supreme power will belong to the proletariat. Such an important matter as supplying the entire population with the necessary products must not be left to depend on the greed, incompetence and whims of individual capitalists. Production must become a matter for the state, and no-one must have the right to encroach on the product of the workers' labour and to convert a matter that concerns the entire people into a means for personal gain and speculation.

In our current revolution, we can achieve only the first part of our programme, only the most immediate demands.

---

3. See our programme, published by the Chita committee of the Russian Social-Democratic Workers' Party.

To achieve the second part, we need the working class to become the strongest class in the country so that, having emancipated itself from the capitalists, it will be able itself to manage the whole matter of production. And this requires not only a second revolution, this time a socialist one, but also that the development of our industry reach such a level that the abolition of capital may be completed easily and painlessly. For now, we are far from that point.

This is what our Party is struggling for, and this is why we have the right to say that the Russian Social-Democratic Workers' Party is the party of the working class.

E. Preobrazhensky

No. 4

'Dual Power, Dual Soul and Cowardice'[1]

31 March 1917

I

In recent times, the reader has probably often encountered, in telegrams issued in the name of the Provisional Government, vague mention of the harm resulting from dual power. Perhaps the reader has also noticed that not a single soviet of workers' and soldiers' deputies has mentioned dual power, that soldiers' meetings rarely mention it, and then only from the front, which has yet to be affected fully by the breath of the Revolution. Conversely, not a single greeting from the liberal-bourgeois groups of Russia's various cities gets by recently without a conclusion concerning the harmfulness of dual power.

One thing is already *characteristic*: if we know *who is worried*, we can also know immediately *what they are worried about*.

It is well known that the workers and soldiers of Petrograd, having overthrown the old order, handed power over to the liberal-bourgeois Executive Committee of the State-Duma on the condition that they implement a revolutionary programme and lead the revolutionary struggle against the old régime to its conclusion.

There was a moment when the soviet of workers' and soldiers' deputies almost took power into its own hands.

That was the moment when the liberal members of the Duma were inclined to replace Nikolai Romanov with his brother. But under pressure from the soviet, the attempt to save the monarchy failed, power remained in the hands of the bourgeois elements, and the soviet of workers' and soldiers' deputies remained in its former role as controller over the actions of the bourgeois Provisional Government. We owe to its intervention the fact that Russia was saved from the shame of seeing the Romanov dynasty once again on the tsarist throne.

What is it that we have now: dual power or single power? It seems that there is no doubt. As long as the country is ruled by the Provisional Government, fulfilling its obligations to the revolutionary forces that gave power to it, we have a single power based on a compromise between the bourgeoisie and the toiling masses. And just as a parliament with ten parties is not an organ of ten powers, but rather implements only a single resultant power, so with us the presence of

---

1. [From *Zabaikal'skii rabochii* (Chita), 31 March 1917.]

several classes, which have created a coalition-government, provides no grounds for talking about a multiplicity of powers.

What is it that the liberal groups who are sending their telegrams to the Provisional Government want, and what do they fear?

They do not want the government to find itself under the control of revolutionary forces united in the soviet and acting in agreement with them.

The single power that they dream about is not a political unity of powers, implementing a definite programme, but the single power of the bourgeoisie in ruling the country. In other words, the proletariat and the soldiers overthrew the old régime and handed over administration of the country to the bourgeoisie with the condition of controls. And now they are saying to the working class: you have done your part, and now you can leave. Now we are the real power, and you are only a hindrance. How helpless and cowardly the bourgeoisie was when it was a matter of struggling with the old power that is now overthrown, yet how grand its appetite and confidence when it has been given the governance of the country.

The working class will not, of course, give the bourgeoisie the pleasure of its leaving the scene and renouncing control over the power it created. This control has already saved Russia from the spectre of the monarchy, ensured the implementation of a number of important reforms, and guaranteed the summoning of a Constituent Assembly. And when the bourgeois circles go on about the danger of dual power, in fact what we are hearing is their fear that our Revolution will be more democratic than suits them.

In its 29 March issue, *Zabaikal'skaya nov'*, with the article by D.P., has joined the chorus of voices concerning dual power. The article displays a gross misunderstanding of the meaning of the resolution adopted by the soviet of workers' deputies in Chita on the question of creating a unifying all-Russian centre for all the soviets of workers' and peasants' deputies that are active throughout the country.

The article also lacks any understanding of the meaning of the present Revolution, which is bourgeois in its tasks but is being realised by the forces of the revolutionary proletariat and the peasantry.

We shall return to this article in the next edition.

E. Preobrazhensky

No. 5

'Dual Power, Dual Soul and Cowardice'[1]

9 April 1917

II

The interests of the working class

In the previous article we said that we currently have no dual power. And now, a few words on a dual soul and cowardice.

There are two souls living in our bourgeoisie (and not in ours alone): a hostile relation to the old régime and a fear of the revolutionary forces that overthrew the old régime. The ideal revolution for the bourgeoisie is one in which the revolutionary people rise up, overthrow the old system and then surrender power to the gentlemen-capitalists and quietly exit the stage. The working class of Russia rose up, overthrew the old power and gave bourgeois elements the opportunity to be in power, but it did not leave the stage and it continues to exercise influence over the Provisional Government. And that is what displeases all conscious and unconscious defenders of the bourgeoisie. Yet the guilty party is the bourgeoisie itself. Not only did it prove incapable of overthrowing the old power, with whom it tried to reach an agreement until the very last moment, but even then, once the old system was overthrown, in the person of Milyukov and others it searched for a way to replace one despot with another.

The contributor to *Zabaikal'skaya nov'* is preaching that the current revolution is bourgeois.

We have known that for a long time. But we also know something that the critic of resolutions by our soviet of workers' and soldiers' deputies neither knows nor, apparently, is capable of understanding. We know that, although our Revolution is bourgeois, the bourgeoisie proved incapable of realising this bourgeois transformation. It is being brought about mainly by the forces of the socialist proletariat. The working class is not only feeding the gentlemen-capitalists with its labour, but it is also implementing and completing the bourgeois revolution, which the capitalists themselves should have completed and which is creating conditions for the most complete development of all the productive forces of bourgeois society.

---

1. [From *Zabaikal'skii rabochii* (Chita), 9 April 1917.]

Thus the working class has to take upon itself the work of carrying the bourgeois revolution through to the end. But it would never have achieved this goal had it left the Provisional Government to its own devices, had it exited the stage after surrendering its organised pressure on the authorities. But this influence must not be exercised only by the forces of Petrograd or solely in the name of the garrison and the working class in the capital. The Provisional Government is recognised by all of Russia and gives directions to all of Russia, and control over it can only be exercised in the name of all the toiling revolutionary forces of Russia. Consequently, only an organisation created by all the soviets of workers', soldiers' and peasants' *deputies can* be sufficiently authoritative to express the strivings of the entire revolutionary people. The resolution by the Chita Soviet spoke precisely of the creation of such an organisation. It said that such an organisation will be a government of the workers, soldiers and peasants in the sense, of course, that it will be an organ uniting all the forces of the Revolution for pressure on the Provisional Government. But none of those who drafted the resolution and voted for it allowed for such silliness as suggesting that this organisation have its own ministers, appoint its own envoys to other countries, collect taxes, operate its own treasury, and so on. The resolution used the word 'government' in a moral, not a literal, sense.

The current revolution is bourgeois. Nevertheless, socialist forces could be in power now and have the necessary physical strength. But they want the bourgeoisie themselves to do everything that can be accomplished in this Revolution and to do so under the control and pressure of the proletariat.

And since the bourgeoisie has never been able to carry a bourgeois revolution through to the end anywhere without the participation of the proletariat, the proletariat can in no case give up its right of control over the bourgeois power. And let no-one try to dissuade it from realising the most important tasks of the moment with bluster about dual power.[2]

E. Preobrazhensky

---

2. An unsigned leading article in *Zabaikal'skii rabochii* on 3 May 1917 commented: 'It is not our business to defend Lenin and his tactics since we do not support him'.

Nos. 6–7

Speeches at the First All-Russian Congress of Soviets of Workers' and Soldiers' Deputies

6–22 June 1917

No. 6

'On Relations with the Provisional Government'[1]

Session of 6 June 1917
(Evening)

Comrades! A great deal has been said here about different anarchies, about various republics, our minister-socialists have spoken, and I would like to share a small historical recollection of the time when the current minister Tsereteli was not yet a minister, when he was in Irkutsk and was chairman of public organisations. At that time a government-commissar – with the same name as mine, Preobrazhensky – was on his way from here to Irkutsk, and today's minister Tsereteli took part in drafting a programme sent to the Provisional Government that said they had no need for a commissar and that they requested he be returned. When my namesake went there and understood what had happened, he returned to Petrograd. Comrades, in the language of today's minister Tsereteli, this is called anarchy. And I think, comrades, that minister Tsereteli

---

1. [From Rakhmetov (ed.) 1930, pp. 217–19.]

should have remembered this more frequently when he went to Kronstadt and there struggled against what he himself had done when he was not yet a minister.

But that is trivial. In that same Irkutsk, whose representative, comrade Troitsky, spoke here, the eight-hour working day was enacted by a decree of the public organisations in which the current minister Tsereteli participated as chairman. This measure was also upheld by comrade Nikol'sky, who has so criticised the unfortunate Bolsheviks here. This measure was implemented in all institutions, not only those working on defence, but the others too. It was implemented by way of a decree extending to the whole of Irkutsk province. There was a resolution passed to raise wages by 50 percent. This was done not on the scale of the state, but by local anarchy: it was done in the local Irkutsk Republic.

Comrades, you can judge what we are facing now on the basis of who did this. If people said of the previous government that we trust it 'insofar as', then let me tell you that there are many places in Russia where, even if they do not distrust the present ministry absolutely, they still say: 'No support and no trust'.

If in Tiflis, where comrade Zhordaniya is chairman of the soviet of workers' and soldiers' deputies, they say: we show this government support 'insofar as' – if there, out of local considerations, they find it necessary to implement a series of revolutionary measures, then how will the present government relate to them when this socialist screen of ministers shields it from pressure on the side of democracy? It will call this anarchy.

This historical recollection says a great deal. It says that maybe we are on the eve of a decisive moment, on the eve of that moment when there is a beginning of so-called calming, the calming, after which, sometime and somewhere, we were promised reforms. I think that we are on the eve of a turning point in the Russian Revolution and, perhaps, we will soon and definitively have to say that the Russian Revolution has ended, that the Russian Revolution has given the maximum that it can give. There is only the consolidation of isolated details, the nitpicking, as was said by one of the speakers, from which there is no moving forward. I am not a prophet and cannot make predictions, but on the basis of the situation that we see before us, I will say this: the threatening symptoms, this striving to direct all forces into a struggle against the Left, not paying attention to all that threatens from the Right – this circumstance worries me.

People referred, here, to the example of the Great French Revolution. If you will peer into the past, then I say: there was a decisive victory there for revolutionary democracy, but how did it happen, and upon whom did this revolutionary democracy depend in conducting its decisive measures? This revolutionary democracy was a genuinely revolutionary democracy, not the one that ministers are talking about in vain from this podium. This revolutionary democracy implemented its decisive measures both in domestic and in foreign policy, in the army and elsewhere, because there was a war; it led to a complete rupture with the bourgeoisie, from which Russia, standing at a much higher level of development, in the persons of our socialist ministers cannot tear itself away. Perhaps our tragedy is the Revolution, perhaps we have come to the final summation and we will go no further, but this is a fact, and nothing will shield us from this fact.

I say that if the Russian Revolution has come to an end, then our opposition is weak. Have we not entered a period of the organic building of a bourgeois society, and perhaps those who represent the silenced voice of the proletariat here are right? Here and now, when we see on the part of our socialist ministers no similar resolve to break with the State-Duma, to dissolve the Duma, which is continuing to destroy our national resources, which they tell us are so meagre, then I ask: 'You, minister-socialists, why don't you do this?' Why, when there is a unanimous demand coming from all the provinces in this regard, why can you not satisfy it? Why do you remain silent here when we hear applause from the entire Congress for comrade Lunacharsky's resolution? I ask you: 'Are you afraid even of this?' On this matter, comrade Tsereteli has answered: 'Only an idiot fears no-one'.

No. 7

'On the Struggle Against Anti-Semitism'[1]

Session of 22 June 1917
(Evening)

Comrades, the section on the national question, or rather the commission on the national question, authorised me to propose a resolution here on the question of the struggle against anti-Semitism. The resolution was unanimously passed in our commission. Before reading it, I want to say several words about its essence. All of you know, comrades, that tsarism used anti-Semitic baiting, the incitement of other nationalities against the Jews, as a method of struggling for its own survival. In this way it took its revenge on the people, among whom the working class was the first to stand under the banner of Social Democracy and to begin the struggle on a mass scale against tsarism, while at the same time tsarism used this method to fight against them for its own survival, to deflect the people's accumulated outrage against tsarism onto the entire Jewish people. The Jewish people lived through the horrors of the pogroms during the first Revolution, they lived through these horrors of the pogroms, and a vast amount of Jewish blood was spilt in the first days of freedom, in the first days of the Revolution. When the period of reaction arrived, the hounding of Jews continued: all possible mockeries, all possible administrative and other measures against them increased and continued to increase with every passing day. When the War began, this hounding took on an especially wild and scandalous character. Jews were accused of espionage, of selling out the Russian Army to the Germans at the front, and of other abominations that could only be thought up by some reactionary mind. By using the Jewish people, they wanted to shield the figures of Myasoedov, Sukhomlinov and other real traitors who are known to all of Russia. The Revolution that took place in the February Days groped for and found the real oppressors, the real reason for the destruction of the Russian people. Thus this wager on the Jews, this wager on anti-Semitism, collapsed completely. But this was not the end of anti-Semitic hounding; it was not the end of using all those methods that were practiced under tsarism. If previously, before the Revolution, the struggle with Jewry and setting other nationalities against them was a method of maintaining the existing order, after the Revolution, at the present moment, this method is being used to try to resurrect overthrown tsarism and to introduce strife into the midst of the Revolution.

---

1. [From Rakhmetov and Miamalin (eds.) 1931, pp. 239–41.]

Comrades, those of you who have read the illiterate proclamations that were distributed everywhere during the first days probably remember that two phrases usually stood out: 'Down with the Jew-traitors' and 'Long live the father-tsar'. In this way, they clearly connected anti-Semitic baiting with hope for the recovery of tsarism as its consequence. In these illiterate proclamations, in these illiterate appeals, could be seen the donkey-ears of the Black Hundreds, who did not have time to adjust to the revolutionary condition. But subsequently, the more the crisis developed in the sphere of industry and foodstuffs, and the more the popular masses became dissatisfied with the present condition, the better the conditions were for such hounding, which was used to palm off on the popular masses slogans that were sympathetically received by other parties that were protecting their own interests, along with slogans that promised bread, and so on. At the same time, slogans of a most anti-Semitic character were heard. There is no doubt that this more sophisticated hounding, adapting to the moment, is more dangerous than the illiterate proclamations that circulated during the first days of the Revolution. Right now, comrades, many of you must be coming across this phenomenon, and many of you have to struggle against it. That is why the All-Russian Congress cannot avoid this question, why it cannot fail to address a definite appeal to all democrats and cannot fail to propose a number of measures aimed at fulfilling our duty to the Jewish people and opening the eyes of the masses, who are being led by this anti-Semitic demagogy towards a resurrection of tsarism and destruction of the freedoms won by the Revolution. The Congress must speak out authoritatively and bring the misguided people, who are currently following these dark demagogues, back to a proper path. Of course, only the most decisive measures can bring them back to a proper path. But since we must do our duty as propagandists, we will fulfil this duty.

The resolution that is proposed to the Congress declares the following (*He reads*):

1. The centuries-old lack of rights and anti-Semitic persecution of Jews in Russia, which serves as one of tsarism's instruments in its struggle for power and has assumed a particularly savage character in time of war – all of this has released a poison of misanthropy, hostility and distrust of Jews amongst the broad masses of the people.

2. Being unable to achieve return of the old order through open struggle, the counter-revolution is trying to use these dark prejudices of the masses to divert their attention from the real causes of the crisis that the country is experiencing and to provide an outlet for the spontaneous resentment and smouldering ferment among the popular masses through a movement directed against the Jews.

3. This anti-Semitic agitation, frequently masking under radical slogans, represents an enormous danger both to the Jewish people and to the revolutionary movement in the country, for it threatens to drown in fraternal blood the whole cause of freeing the people and to cover the revolutionary popular movement with indelible shame.
4. For this reason, the direct interest of the popular masses and the cause of the Revolution's honour demand from all revolutionary democrats a most energetic struggle against all attempts at anti-Semitic persecution and the suppression in embryo of all anti-Semitic declarations.
5. The All-Russian Congress of Soviets of Workers' and Soldiers' Deputies calls upon all local soviets to be on the alert for any machinations by anti-Semitic groups and agitators, to conduct tireless agitation and educational work among the broadest popular masses with the aim of fighting against anti-Jewish persecution, and directs its own Central Committee to attend to publication of appropriate literature on the Jewish question.
6. Extending its fraternal greeting to the Jewish working class, who are struggling in common in the revolutionary ranks, the Congress summons them to instil among the Jewish popular masses a firm conviction that all organised revolutionary-democratic elements in the country will staunchly defend them against any attempts to launch any sort of violent actions against Jews.

Nos. 8–12
Speeches at the Sixth Congress of the RSDRP (B)

28 July (10 August)–3 (16) August 1917

No. 8

Report on the Work of the Social-Democratic Party in the Urals[1]

28 July (10 August)
6th Session

Chairman: The delegate from the Urals, comrade Preobrazhensky, has the floor.

Preobrazhensky: The work of Social Democracy in the Urals is taking place in special conditions. With the exception of Maltsevsky and a few other factories, the workers are not pure proletarians, but have ties to the land. This connection to the land leaves a special impression on the psychology of the Urals worker and on the form of his struggle with capital. Possessional right[2] exists to this day in the Urals, and factory-owners have 2.5 million *desyatins* of land. The economy is most backward. There is chronic unemployment in the Urals, including up to forty-five to fifty percent of all workers.

---

1. [From *Shestoi s'ezd RSDRP (Bol'shevikov). Avgust 1917 goda: Protokoly*, pp. 80–1.]
2. [For an explanation of possessional property in the Urals, see Document 2:13.]

In place of the proven methods of class-struggle, one has to put forth special methods and adapt to local conditions. In the Urals, Social Democrats have been forced to lay out a specific programme, which may may explain the success of our Party. Even during illegal times, the threat of death faced Urals industry and immediately demanded effective slogans; the land-relations demanded a special agrarian programme. We have land belonging to representatives of foreign capital, which means that the workers are compelled to turn their attention to the struggle with international capital, to international politics.

On the other hand, there is the backwardness of industry. The worker's connection to the land facilitates the success of the S-Rs and Mensheviks as parties of the petty bourgeoisie.

Before the revolution, the Urals was considered a bastion for Bolshevism. Presently, the Bolshevik influence has relatively weakened; there are strong S-R organisations; the Mensheviks have also become stronger but, being only an appendage of the S-Rs, they have surrendered all class-positions.

Before the Revolution, there were underground Bolshevik organisations in Ekaterinburg, Lysva and at other points. The strength of Bolshevik influence just now is yet to be established, although we are without question the most influential party. A few summary data will provide a clearer understanding of this matter. In the Urals there have already been two conferences.[3] At the first, fifteen thousand, five hundred party-members were represented; at the second – twenty-two thousand party-members; moreover, not all organisations had representatives, so, in reality, the Party included up to twenty-five thousand members. Bolshevik organisation would have been even stronger but for a number of reasons, such as sackings at the factories and the political conditions of work for our organisations – which led to some reduction of our members and the strengthening of Menshevik organisations. All the same, the number of Mensheviks does not exceed one-third of the membership of our Party.

Our work is conducted mainly among the workers. We have little influence on the peasants, except for those who are connected to the factories. It is interesting to note that there were delegates from the parishes at our conference looking for solutions to different questions.

Amongst the soldier-masses, the S-Rs have the predominant influence.

---

3. [The reference is to the first two regional conferences of the RSDRP(B), held in Ekaterinburg. The first 'free' conference took place on 14–15 (27–8) April, 1917. It was called 'free' because it was the first to take place in conditions of legality. There were more than sixty delegates present. The second conference convened on 14 (27) July, 1917, with 63 delegates.]

Our organ *Uralskaya pravda* is published in eight to ten thousand copies, twice weekly. We are now hoping to publish it daily, since we have purchased our own printing press.

Trade-unions have emerged only among those workers who work at developed capitalist industries; in backward industry there is no basis for them. Our influence is predominant in the unions.

The events of 3–5 July initially created a subdued mood, but in general there was no negative effect and they even served as a kind of filter, and when we completed our Second Congress it turned out that we stuck with our previous point of view. (*Applause.*)

No. 9

Speech Concerning the Resolution 'The Current Moment and the War'[1]

30 July (12 August)
9th Session

Preobrazhensky: Comrade Stalin and comrade Angarsky differ in their understanding of the role of Allied capital and the liberal bourgeoisie.[2] I hope that comrade Stalin will answer comrade Angarsky's objections, which were absolutely unprovoked. The liberal bourgeoisie was understood as a motive force, because it could either oppose the Revolution or remain neutral. In February-March, it was forced by special circumstances to play the role of an accomplice and to tolerate the Revolution. I now turn to the most fundamental question that is touched upon in comrade Stalin's resolution. Comrade Stalin defends this resolution, but not on all points. First of all, I will talk about the technical failings of the resolution: in essence this is not a resolution, and I would suggest turning it into a resolution. But my objection has to do not with the content; rather it involves a literary-technical issue. What I want to say in terms of content is that the main question before us is whether the first stage of the Revolution is finished or not. We will not argue over the depth of the counter-revolutionary upheaval that we are living through. That question will be resolved by an objective analysis of the forces involved in the counter-revolution and those that can be motive forces in the Revolution. I am not so bold as to answer that question

---

1. [From *Shestoi s'ezd RSDRP (Bol'shevikov). Avgust 1917 goda: Protokoly*, pp. 115–16. The resolution 'On the Present Moment and the War' said, in part: '1. The war has recently assumed the dimensions of a world-wide clash. A new giant of imperialism has appeared on the scene, a new claimant to world-hegemony – America... 2. The most dangerous event for the imperialists of all countries is the Russian Revolution...' (KPSS 1983, p. 578.)]

2. [J.V. Stalin said: 'What is the origin of the Revolution? A coalition of four forces: the proletariat, the peasantry, the liberal bourgeoisie and Allied capital... These four forces of the February Revolution, while advancing together, have different objectives. The liberal bourgeoisie and Allied capital wanted a minor revolution for a big war. But that is not why the mass of workers and peasants entered into the Revolution. They had other goals: 1) to put an end to the War and 2) to overpower the landlords and the bourgeoisie' (*Shestoi s'ezd RSDRP (Bol'shevikov). Avgust 1917 goda: Protokoly*, p. 110).

N.S. Angarsky said: 'I completely disagree with comrade Stalin's way of posing the question... I believe that the moving forces of our Revolution, as in 1905, are the proletariat and the peasantry' (*Shestoi s'ezd RSDRP (Bol'shevikov). Avgust 1917 goda: Protokoly*, p. 114).

Following Angarsky's speech, E.A. Preobrazhensky justifiably remarked that the complaint directed against Stalin was 'absolutely unprovoked' (*Shestoi s'ezd RSDRP (Bol'shevikov). Avgust 1917 goda: Protokoly*, p. 115).]

right now. The role of the petty bourgeoisie in the next stage of the Revolution is still not sufficiently clear to us. Its withdrawal to the right is explained in terms of two causes: the actions of the proletariat and the breakthrough at the front. The petty bourgeoisie faces a need to defend the country, but for that defence of the country they need the apparatus that is in the hands of the imperialists. One can fully understand the panic that has gripped the petty bourgeoisie and thrown them into the embrace of counter-revolutionaries. Thus a rapprochement of the petty bourgeoisie with the imperialists has begun under the influence of internal complications and failure at the front. This process of rapprochement means an inevitable surrender by the petty bourgeoisie of all their positions inside the country. It is possible that the victory of the counter-revolution may turn out to be more fundamental than we think, and then the Revolution within our national boundaries is finished. In that case, I cannot agree with the assertion that a new outbreak is inevitable. I consider an agreement between the counter-revolutionary bourgeoisie, the capitalists, the landlords and the peasants to be completely possible. You have read what Chernov has already said about buying up the landlords' estates. Possibly this is the beginning of the moment when, on the most important question – the agrarian question – the petty bourgeoisie will also surrender their positions. Thus the possibility of such an outcome cannot be excluded. But the opposite is also possible. Given the impossibility of solving all the conflicts between the petty bourgeoisie and the big bourgeoisie, together with a situation of military successes at the front, we may face a new outbreak of the revolution. But who will be its participants? What does comrade Stalin mean by 'the poorest strata of the peasantry'? Up to now, Marxist literature does not have any definite conception of the poorest peasantry who are mentioned in the resolution. If these are the farm-labourers or that stratum of the peasantry who, given enactment of a radical agrarian reform, either will not lose out or will actually gain, then I say: the role of the soviets is still not completed. Their composition may change. The slogan 'All power to the soviets!' must be retained in so far as the possibility of an agrarian revolution cannot be ruled out.

People have spoken, here, of new outbreaks. What outbreaks? If they are outbreaks in which the proletariat participates alone, without any support from broad popular strata, then we will have a repetition of 3–4 July. But if these actions resonate with the peasantry, they will be enormously significant. And in this sense I endorse these outbreaks, but as a subordinate means, not as the basic means of struggle. I believe that comrade Stalin will clarify the sense in which he used this word, here.

No. 10

Speech Concerning the Resolution 'The Current Moment and the War'[1]

2(15) August
13th Session

Bukharin reads Point 9:
'Liquidation of imperialist domination places before the working class of the first country to realise the dictatorship of proletarians and semi-proletarians the task of lending all support (up to and including armed support) to the struggling proletarians of other countries. In particular, such a task is on the agenda for Russia if, as seems very likely, a new and inevitable upsurge of the Russian Revolution puts the workers and poorest peasants in power before the revolution occurs in the capitalist countries of the West'.

Bosh: I suggest replacing the words 'if, as seems very likely' with the word 'when' in order to express our certainty of the inevitability of revolution.

Bukharin: I am opposed to that amendment because it suggests a guarantee that what is said in this point will occur, without fail. We hope for that, on the basis of the facts, but we can give no guarantee.

The amendment is rejected.

Preobrazhensky: I am not satisfied with the wording of the point. I would suggest restoring the original wording, which definitively spoke of revolutionary war in the event of a dictatorship of the proletariat.

Bukharin: I remind comrades of the history behind this point. In my formulation, nothing was said about a revolutionary war. After the first reading of the resolution, the Congress wished to enter mention of revolutionary war, which I did, but in the resolution commission the real question arose – will we have the power to conduct a revolutionary war – and we included a more modest formulation, since we cannot irrevocably state whether we will have the power to conduct a revolutionary war. For these reasons, I am against comrade Preobrazhensky's amendment.

The amendment is rejected.

---

1. [From *Shestoi s'ezd RSDRP (Bol'shevikov). Avgust 1917 goda. Protokoly*, p. 202.]

No. 11

Discussion of the Question of Elections to the Constituent Assembly[1]

3 (16) August
14th Session (morning)

Shumyatsky: Point 10 says:
'Agreements are also permissible with non-party revolutionary organisations (for example, soviets of deputies, land-committees, sowing committees, and so on) that *fully accept our programme*'.

Preobrazhensky: I consider this point totally unacceptable and suggest replacing it with the following: 'No electoral agreements or drawing up of joint lists of candidates with non-party revolutionary organisations is permitted'.

Dzhaparidze: I suggest totally excluding this point.

Skrypnik: The question being raised is extremely important, and I suggest opening a debate concerning the essence.

Chairman: No objections? The debate is open.

Preobrazhensky: I am against removing this point, but I do suggest replacing it with my wording. This question is extremely important and was already debated in *Pravda*. Acceptance of our platform by non-party organisations is not enough, since one may fear that in this way we will reach a block with very dubious 'internationalists'. Non-party peasant-organisations could follow us because of our agrarian programme, without completely sharing the rest of the platform. Such allies may do us serious harm on the day after the elections, because on other programmatic questions they may come out with a completely different opinion.

Another fact that speaks against an agreement with non-party peasants is that we only pick up votes, but we do not recruit real supporters. This paves the way for parliamentary cretinism, which is the complete opposite of our views as expressed in the preface to comrade Lenin's preface to the brochure: 'No Agreements, No Compromises'.

Besides, such blocs will not give us the opportunity to take count of our supporters. Will we be cut off from the peasantry; will we lose sympathetic votes there if we do not agree to a bloc? Absolutely not. With a system of proportional

---

1. [From *Shestoi s'ezd RSDRP (Bol'shevikov). Avgust 1917 goda. Protokoly*, pp. 225–6. B.Z. Shumyatsky gave a report to the Congress from the commission on elections to the Constituent Assembly that proposed a plan for 'the practical conduct of pre-election work'. The plan included the following points: 1. Pre-election organs; 2. Monetary resources; 3. Agitation; 4. Blocs and Agreements; 5. Candidate-lists (*Shetsoi s'ezd RSDRP(B). Avgust 1917 goda. Protokoly*, pp. 220–1).]

representation, not a single vote is wasted. To recruit our followers we must go into the countryside and organise the revolutionary peasantry. They can follow us, and this will be a more authentic success than five to ten more seats for deputies. Our relation to the Constituent Assembly is completely defined. We will go there as a small group and uphold a strictly principled line.

Chairman: A motion has been made to limit speakers' time to three minutes. No objections? I consider it passed.

Solov'ev: I asked for the floor to speak on the motives for voting. The question of blocs with non-party organisations was discussed at the Moscow regional conference, where we came to the conclusion that such blocs are necessary.

Chairman: Comrade Solov'ev, you are addressing the essence, not the motives for voting.

Shumyatsky: I too will speak on the motives for voting. If comrade Preobrazhensky recognises the possibility of a bloc with S-R Internationalists, then his wording speaks against him.

Chairman: There will be no more talk about motives for voting. I am voting on comrade Preobrazhensky's amendment. It is rejected.

No. 12

Speech on the Resolution 'On the Political Situation'[1]

3 (16) August
15th Session

Stalin reads Point 9 of the resolution:
'9. The task of these revolutionary classes, then, is to strain with all their might to take government-power into their own hands and to direct it, in alliance with the revolutionary proletariat of the leading countries, towards peace and towards the socialist reconstruction of society'.

Preobrazhensky: I propose a different wording for the end of the resolution: 'to direct it towards peace and, in the event of proletarian revolution in the West, towards socialism'.

If we accept the wording of the commission, then we will have a conflict with the resolution by Bukharin that was already accepted.

Stalin: I am against such a conclusion to the resolution. The possibility cannot be excluded that precisely Russia will be the country leading the way to socialism. Until now, not a single country has had such freedom as Russia or tried to realise workers' control over production. Furthermore, the base of our Revolution is broader than in Western Europe, where the proletariat is completely alone in facing the bourgeoisie. In our country the proletariat is supported by the poorest strata of the peasantry. Finally, in Germany the apparatus of state-power functions incomparably better than the flawed apparatus of our bourgeoisie, which is itself a tributary of European capital. It is necessary to discard the obsolete idea that only Europe can show us the way. There is a dogmatic Marxism and a creative Marxism. I stand for the latter.

Chairman: I am putting comrade Preobrazhensky's amendment to a vote. It is rejected.

---

1. [From *Shestoi s'ezd RSDRP (Bol'shevikov). Avgust 1917 goda. Protokoly*, pp. 250–1.]

No. 13
The Pamphlet 'What the Urals Workers Need'[1]

September–October 1917[2]

The time is approaching for elections to the Constituent Assembly.

Not a single worker must miss the chance to defend the interests of his class through voting. But when voting he must clearly understand whom he is voting for. Otherwise, he may vote for his enemies or for the kind of dubious friends who cannot fight courageously and to the end for his interests. And making this mistake is all the easier, the more skilfully the different parties occupy themselves with fishing for votes and promoting themselves as friends of the entire people. Someone truthfully said, and with good reason, that people never lie as much as during elections. Let every worker remember that a vote, correctly cast for his workers' party, is capital that will earn him interest. But a vote cast for someone else's party will be a whip that he makes for himself, and in future it will painfully lash him for his ignorance and failure to understand his own interests.

---

1. [From Preobrazhensky 1917, pp. 1–9.]
2. [A date has been assigned to this essay based on its content.]

What the Urals Workers Need

Unemployment in the Urals

It was only very recently that the terrible level of unemployment in the Urals, which strangled the working class and deprived it of its crumb of bread, came to an end. But it has ended only temporarily due to the industrial expansion and military orders. And there are already signs of its return.

All unemployment is inevitable so long as capital dominates society and the employers are in charge of the factories. When it is profitable to do so, they expand production and hire new staff; when it is unprofitable, they curtail production and get rid of redundant workers. Consequently, unemployment in general can only be eliminated when the capitalist system is eliminated and replaced by an economy that is public and belongs to the people, namely, by a socialist economy.

But unemployment in the Urals has its own specific causes. And, in terms of size, it cannot be compared to the customary unemployment that we see in Russia and other countries where capital rules.

Until recent years, an enormous majority of Urals workers lived under the constant threat of curtailed work and factory-closures. A number of factories, public and private, were closed. Some workers had to leave for other parts of Russia to look for work there. Many had to abandon household-economies that served to supplement a wage at the factories. Some stayed and had to search for some other kind of work, take up handicrafts, turn to agriculture, get a job in lumbering work, and so on.

All of these were types of work that could not adequately provide for the workers and forced them to drag out a miserable half-starving existence.

But things were no better even at factories that did not close, but rather cut back on production. There was less work, but there were more workers, because the population grew and the numbers of hungry mouths and working hands multiplied. In order that all should suffer alike, the workers usually insisted that the available work be divided equally amongst everyone. A worker had to work every other day, sometimes every third, or else six-hour shifts were introduced for daily work. These idle days or idle hours were a scourge for the workers, because everyone's earnings dropped.

In general, unemployment reached enormous proportions throughout the Urals. If you count not only the private[3] unemployed, who have finally been

---

3. [The reference is to workers in private factories.]

thrown out of the factories, but also those who were underemployed, those not working full days, then out of every hundred Urals workers there were up to forty unemployed. And this was the case all the time, for decades, not during some isolated and particularly miserable year.

Wages

There is a general rule that says the higher the unemployment, the lower the workers' wages. When industry is expanding, when the workers are all employed and even in short supply, then they have cause to celebrate. They can then seek higher wages from the employers. Conversely, when production is falling and there are many unemployed, the capitalist triumphs and compels the workers to work for a lower wage. The enormous unemployment in the Urals was the main reason for the incredibly low wages. First of all, since the work had to be divided between all the workers, the individual worker did not work a full day and obtained only part of what he would be paid for a full day's work. Idle days and an equal division of unemployment led to an equal division of wages that were already at starvation-level.

The income of workers fell so low that in many places mature workers and often family-members earned from eight to twelve roubles a month while masters earned from twenty-five to thirty. But it was not always possible for workers to get even this pittance. At some factories, for example in Tagil, Katav and elsewhere, the factory-management refused to pay workers their wages for whole months because they had no money. The workers were given coupons to obtain goods from factory-stores. But since these stores did not have all the necessary products, and what they did have were sold at prices set by the management, this state of affairs led to further enslavement of the Urals workers.

The workers could not live on their paltry earnings, and they naturally looked for supplementary incomes. The main support for workers was the household-economy. Having one's own vegetable-garden, a cow and other livestock and poultry, the worker had to purchase much less with money than did the pure proletarian in the city. Apart from the household-economy, others kept themselves busy as handicraftsmen. One would often encounter workers in the Urals who, after finishing their work at the factory, continued their working day at home making chests, tubs, baskets and other homemade products.

But if the household-economy supported workers with their low wages, it provided even greater support to the factory-owners in their endeavour to prevent any rise in labour-costs. Had they been pure proletarians in the Urals factories, with no ties to the land (or even just to their own gardens), they would have fled to avoid dying of starvation. But the Urals workers, attached to one place, were compelled to make do with a beggarly wage and preferred to get at least something from the factory rather than nothing. Only the young people of the Urals factories were more mobile and, after leaving the homes of their fathers, went out to seek better working conditions in other parts of Russia. Thus the Urals working class found itself enslaved by factory-owners and for long years endured its half-starving existence with no prospects for a better future.

The death of Urals industry

A reader of this brochure who is not familiar with the position of Urals industry might ask: Why did Urals workers not follow the example of their comrades in the rest of Russia and seek to improve their condition through strikes and other means of proletarian struggle?

Here, we come to the main point that explains the fundamental causes of the disastrous situation of the majority of Urals workers.

There are profound reasons why the Urals worker could not march in step with his worker-comrades throughout Russia in the struggle to improve his economic position. These reasons lie in the fact that the Urals industry itself is hopelessly ill, that it is dying, and that strikes in these conditions cannot bring such favourable results for the workers as in other regions of Russia.

The Urals produces iron and other metal-products. There was a time when it was master of the market, the main and almost the sole supplier of iron for the whole of Russia. At that time, prices on the market were determined by the costs of production in the Urals, and production could never be unprofitable.

But from the late eighties and early nineties the Urals met with strong competition from southern industry. In the south, industry developed with the assistance of foreign capital and was organised according to the last word in European technology. Labour-productivity in the south turned out to be incomparably higher than in the Urals, and the iron-products of southern industry could be sold on the market at a much lower price than those from the Urals.

The prices fell, and Urals industry suffered one blow after another, leaving it with two options: either to rebuild on the basis of new principles, raising technology to the level in the south, or else gradually to die off while responding to falling market-prices by reducing wages. Only a small number of Urals factories were reconstructed on new principles and could stand firmly on their own feet (Nadezhdensky Bogoslovsky, Lysvensky, Chusovkaya, Kyshtymsky). Most factory-owners chose the second path. In order to maintain profits in the face of lower iron-prices, they lowered workers' wages and thus reduced the costs of production. This is the main reason for low incomes in the Urals. In this sort of situation, strikes by workers were doomed in advance to failure, and in those places where they did occur they either led to factory-closures, or else the workers were defeated and agreed to work for a starvation-wage in order to have at least some kind of income.

Let us consider how matters stood at different Ural factories – that is, in publicly owned, possessional and private factories – under the influence of competition from the south.

Under the autocracy, the state-owned economy was always badly-run and wasteful, and state-owned factories in the Urals had extremely low labour-productivity. When cheap southern iron appeared on the market, it no longer made sense for the treasury to retain factories that made a more expensive product, and the treasury started to close down its loss-making enterprises. That left only well-equipped factories working on military contracts, such as Motovilikha or Zlatoust.

Things were different at the possessional factories, of which there are almost thirty in the Urals. Everyone knows that possessional lands are essentially treasury-lands. These lands, with their mining deposits and forests, are placed at the disposal of factory-owners for exploitation, and they remain with the factory-owners so long as they operate the factories. According to treasury-terms, the land reverts back to the treasury when the owner closes the factory, and he himself must then provide the workers of the closed factories with provisions for a year. This is possessional right, a relic of serfdom, and it creates the most unbearable conditions in these factories. Possessional industry has long been dying, yet it cannot die. The technology at these factories is the most primitive, the output is the lowest, and things are done uneconomically and absurdly. Yet the owners do not close the factories. They do not manage them properly, nor do they let others do so – people who could take over the land, the mining resources and the factories and manage things as they are managed in the south. They do not want to manage things properly themselves, because all of these gentlemen are the worst and most noxious parasites possible. In essence, every capitalist is a parasite because he lives off the labour of his workers. But a real capitalist does not spend away all of the profit created for him by the workers; instead, he uses a large part of it for the expansion and improvement of production. This makes his profits even bigger, but then society also gains some benefits as a result. Possessional factory-owners are parasites in the full sense of the word. All the resources that fell into their hands were squandered on life abroad, on sparkling at the Romanov court, or on purchasing titles, as the merchant Demidov did when he transformed himself at the expense of his workers into the Italian count San-Donato, and such like. These gentlemen not only wasted all the profits from factories and lands on champagne, but they also spent all the public subsidies that they begged from the treasury under the pretence of raising production and improving the workers' conditions. Finally, they contrived to mortgage with private banks the possessional lands that are, in essence, the treasury's lands; and with the same brilliance and knowledge of business they drank and ate away the people's property. Imagine, dear reader, that some forester in the treasury's forest-department mortgaged the state-forests entrusted to his supervision and drank away the money. This thief would be tried for this crime and put away in a company of convicts. Yet our possessional factory-owners performed all of these operations with impunity. They lived very well under the tsarist autocracy! But now it is also clear why possessional factory-owners did not close their factories even though they bitterly complained about how unprofitable their enterprises were. They did not get their main profits from the factories at all. On the contrary, the factories may have run a loss, but this loss was covered with interest out of other 'sinless' incomes. Besides the above-mentioned sources, one must furthermore point to the rapacious destruction of forests. Firewood and lumber became more expensive in Russia with every passing year, and factory-owners reduced enormous areas of timber, hitherto untouched by the axe, and floated it off in every direction. In addition, they rented out arable lands and fields and thus derived even further income.

That is how possessional factories reached the final stage of decline yet still could not die. Possessional right attached them to a handful of high-ranking parasites and condemned the workers to a semi-starvation existence. Production not only failed to expand, but even contracted, to the point where only one or two shops were working in an entire factory. The enterprise existed for show, for form's sake, in order that the treasury not have any grounds to take back the land and resources it had put at the disposal of the possessionaires. Just let the workers strike in such conditions: 'Strike, my dear fellows', the factory-owner would say, 'It's no loss to me'.

As far as private factories are concerned, of which there are up to sixty in the Urals, things are just as miserable in the majority of them as in the possessional ones: practically the same wretched technology, the same low labour-productivity, the same plundering of natural wealth and the same starvation-wage. But the superiority of private factories over possessional ones lies mainly in the fact that they are private, and while access to productive capital here is difficult, it is not absolutely foreclosed as it is in possessional factories. As a result, the majority of factory-owners, once they plundered the most valuable riches and had no further interest in operating a loss-making enterprise, re-sold their factories to other capitalists or to joint-stock companies in which they, too, became shareholders. Others did not hesitate to shut down the factories when it was to their advantage. As I mentioned previously, some of the factories were re-equipped after falling into the hands of productive capitalists, their labour-productivity rose, the workers had an opportunity to secure better working conditions, and ultimately these enterprises, although they were in the minority, stood on their own two feet. But other factories fell into different hands that turned out to be even more nimble in plundering the territory's riches, and production neither improved nor expanded, but rather contracted or else the factories were shut down completely. 'Our gallant allies', the French and English capitalists, who acquired many factories from the former owners, rebuilt some of them while simply closing others and undertaking everywhere an even more skilful and brazen destruction of natural wealth. In the final analysis, the condition of the workers improved in some of the rebuilt factories, that is, in the minority, while in the majority it deteriorated further and the burden of unemployment grew even more.

That is how Urals industry was dying until recent times; and in dying it put the entire burden and torment of its death on the shoulders of the working class.

Industrial expansion in the Urals

Up to 1911, the Russian iron-industry was in crisis. More was being produced than the market required, prices were low and falling, and for several years before 1911 there was heavy unemployment in the Urals. Production fell, several factories closed, and a whole series of other factories faced closure.

Conversely, after the excellent harvests of 1909–10, when all our industry began to expand, especially in mining – when cast iron, iron and steel were in short supply and there was a so-called 'cast-iron famine' – the affairs of Urals industrialists began to improve. Prices for cast iron and iron began to rise, and even loss-making enterprises in the region began to turn a profit. And that is not all. Factories that had been closed down began to re-open, a number of closed treasury-factories gradually came back into operation, and production in others expanded. The destruction of the dying Urals industry was temporarily deferred.

The first result of industrial expansion in the Urals was a reduction in unemployment. But wages remained, for the time being, at the old level, and all the profits from rising prices on cast iron and iron went to the factory-owners. The strikes that broke out in one place or another were not, it is true, condemned to defeat as they were previously, but far from all of them ended successfully, despite the commitment of the workers. For instance, in the Minyarsky factory of Ufa province, which is known in the Urals for its revolutionary attitude and solidarity among the working masses, the strike of 1914 lasted seven months and ended in failure for the workers.

When the War began, the majority of enterprises in the Urals went over to defence-work. The staffing expanded further, certain factories were newly re-equipped, and new shops were built in others. Unemployment ended, and even many immigrant-workers appeared at the biggest factories. If earlier, in the nineties, there were up to two hundred and sixty thousand workers employed in the Urals – and Urals statisticians thought this number was exaggerated – and if we recall that, from that time up to the industrial expansion and the War, the number of unemployed grew strongly, then just how far the number of employed workers in the Urals has grown in recent years can be seen in the fact that an average of four hundred and fifty to five hundred thousand workers were represented at the Urals congresses of soviets.

The main affliction of the Urals – unemployment – was temporarily eliminated. But the low wages continued, with the exception of a group of factories where immigrant-workers played a large role, were not bound to the locality and were not prepared to work for a beggarly wage. Under the autocracy, it was virtually impossible to struggle for a pay-increase by way of strikes. The workers, being liable to conscription, could be sent to the front in the event of a strike, and the factory-owners used this threat to force the Urals proletariat to tolerate the harsh conditions. Moreover, the cost of living grew terribly, money was devalued, and wherever there was a wage increase it lagged far behind rising prices.

The Revolution found the Urals workers in this position. Following the Revolution, the long-suppressed discontent with burdensome economic conditions burst forth. Wages sharply increased under pressure from the working masses, although not everywhere to the same extent. There were small backwater-factories where raises were so small that they could not keep pace with the rate of price increases. After the first more or less significant raises, the workers began to demand more, and that is when they encountered determined opposition from the owners. The most stubborn opponents of wage-increases turned out to be the owners of those same factories that prior to the War dragged out a miserable existence and, by virtue of their ancient technology, made the workers' labour quite unproductive. In addition, the workers who for years had watched with their own eyes the plundering of forest-wealth, now demanded the establishment of a ten-*verst* strip within which factory-management would not have the right to destroy the forest for factory-needs. The depredation of forests, if not completely halted, thereby became much more difficult. But after all forestry, or more correctly destruction of the forests, represented, as we mentioned above, an important source of income for factory-owners. Thus, under pressure from the working masses, and as a result of rising wages, the old wounds of backward Urals industry were again revealed. Even apart from their own wishes, many factory-owners could not increase pay, simply because a backward enterprise cannot sustain higher wages and must close down. If it were only a matter of factory-owners' malice and greed, then it would not be difficult to deal with their resistance. But the essential point is that things are far more serious than that. Many of our factory-comrades who are in control of all the affairs of the enterprise have come to the conclusion that, with their current technology, the productivity of the factories is so low that even with the workers managing things themselves they would not be able to raise their wages. In a word, the bankruptcy of the backward Urals industry, which was temporarily obscured by the industrial expansion and military orders, was again clearly revealed after the Revolution. Once again, the Urals workers faced all the horrors of unemployment and a starvation-wage that they have not yet had the proper opportunity to put behind them. That is how matters began to take shape already during the Revolution, when the workers were at their strongest, and during the War, when industry was guaranteed treasury-orders and even the most decrepit and good-for-nothing factories were utilised. So what will happen when the deluge of profitable treasury-orders comes to an end, when peaceful work will have to be done for the market, and when the formidable and victorious rival of the Urals – the mining and metallurgical industries of the south – will again appear on the scene?

Urals workers must anticipate the adversities coming their way. They must begin a decisive struggle today to ensure no return to the past. After clarifying the future dangers and all the reasons for their disastrous situation in the past, they must attain human living standards not merely in brief years of industrial expansion or war, not merely as a respite from the exhausting unemployment peculiar to the Urals, but as a solid improvement of their situation.

Our Party has answers to all these questions and knows the way that leads to stable improvement in the lives of Urals workers.

But before we can begin to put forth our Urals programme for the workers, we must deal with the land-question in the Urals, for which a proper solution is enormously important to the workers' interests.

The land-question in the Urals

The treasury has more than a million *desyatins* of land in the Urals, and possessional holdings account for up to 2.25 million *desyatins*. The remaining land (more than six million) is in private possession. As for workers at treasury-factories, they are allotted land, as are workers in the possessional factories, but the allotments are often such that it would be better to have nothing at all. Factory-owners choose the land for allotment for workers at their own discretion, and they have tried to allot sections that have lost all value to the factory-management. They have given the workers either marshes with scrub or bare hills with tree-stumps left after felling the timber. Sections far removed from the estates were also given out. The workers were not content with such 'allotments' and have waged endless court-cases against the factory-owners. These matters dragged out in the Senate and at other levels for years, and most cases were not resolved in favour of the workers. And when a court's decision did go against the factory-owners, it was not implemented. This was the response of the Perm governor, for instance, in the famous case involving allotments to workers in the factories of Perm province.

The workers at private factories in the Urals have no allotted lands of their own. They only have garden-parcels. For the most part, they have to rent meadow-lands from the factory management. It is also more difficult for them to acquire wood. It was to the advantage of factory-owners to give them access to gardens, because that tied the workers to the land and made them into a permanent 'industrial reserve-army' prepared to work for any low wage.

But the factory-owners were never interested in allotting enough land to the workers to enable them to feed themselves from agriculture alone. In that case it would be more difficult to force them to work for starvation-wages. Thus they did everything possible to prevent any extension of workers' agricultural activities, and this also applied to the land-allotments of factory-peasants. It was also to their advantage to ensure that there were people without land, or very little, who would always have to rent access to meadows and arable lands, generating additional income from the rents. One must also note that nearly all the best meadows remained in the hands of factory-management.

Urals workers, in general, have very little involvement in agriculture: they only gather hay for their cattle from the meadows and keep kitchen-gardens. But there are a large number of peasants in the Urals who live both from agriculture and from supplementary work for the factories (transporting ore, chopping firewood, mining coal, and so on), and there are many parishes throughout the Urals industrial districts where peasants receive a large portion of their income by working for factory-owners, rather than from agriculture. And just as the workers are more interested in the meadow-lands, the peasants are interested in expanding lands under their ploughs. There is generally little land suitable for farming in the Urals. But the factory-administrations retain all the land that is suitable firmly under their own control, and when they lease it to peasants they are very careful never to make any mistakes.

But there is no doubt that the most deprived and wretched groups of toiling people in the Urals are those workers whose factories have closed, along with the redundant mining and metallurgical workers who, even when the factories are operating, cannot count on finding any earnings. One must remember that there are some mines, and thus also the factories built around them, that may close or curtail work not simply because the owners neither wish nor know how to operate them properly, but also because of such unavoidable causes as exhaustion of the ores or lack of fuel where the forests have been almost entirely depleted. The situation of these workers and factory-peasants was, and still is, the most difficult. Special thought must be paid to them in resolving the labour- and land-question in the Urals. This section of the population faces two choices: either to abandon familiar surroundings, liquidate their households and search for a better life elsewhere, or else to turn completely to agriculture. But the latter requires allotment of enough arable land for these strata of the population to live from agriculture alone. They must be allotted lands at the expense of the factory-owners, where the latter actually have arable land, or else, where the land is not fit for agriculture, a great deal of work will have to be done to make it fit – clearing forests, draining swamps and so forth.

Finally, one must also keep in mind Bashkir tenure, which is also found in the mining districts of the Urals. Several Bashkir communities still retain considerable areas of land, lakes for fishing, meadows and forests. The Bashkirs use only that part of their lands needed for livestock-farming and lease out all the other lands and lakes. One must note that, among the Russian population, relations with the Bashkirs are far from normal on account of the land, and the Revolution must re-establish these relations on more equitable terms.

Our demands

We have already mentioned that the enormous scale of unemployment in the Urals and the low wages result from the fact that industry itself is sick and dying.

So how do we treat it?

Let us begin with the treasury-factories. If appropriate measures are not adopted right away, the workers of these factories are threatened in future with all the disasters of unemployment. The point is that the largest factories, such as those in Motovilikha or Zlatoust, are adapted to defence-contracts. When the military contracts end, they are threatened with closure for at least as long as it takes to adapt to civilian work. Consequently, our first demand with regard to these factories, along with all the treasury- and private factories, is the immediate adoption of measures to prepare for their transition to peaceful work without reducing the scale of production. Still more serious is the matter of the remaining treasury-factories, almost all of which were shut down before the 'cast-iron famine' and have the most primitive technology. When the War ends, they may again find themselves in a situation where it will be unprofitable for the treasury to continue production and more economical to secure products from private factories in the south. In order to prevent this, it is necessary to work out a plan now for completely re-equipping these factories according to the latest technical requirements. When these factories can be re-equipped, the workers will no longer live under the permanent threat of factory-closures and will not have to consider taking over these factories and operating them themselves. This would mean taking over bankrupted enterprises and sustaining the struggle against well-equipped southern industry by lengthening the working day and cutting wages for themselves as 'worker-owners'.

Regarding the possessional factories, we have already indicated that they have the most backward production-technology and the lowest productivity. When treasury-orders come to an end, unemployment and a semi-starvation existence will once again await the workers of those factories. We cannot leave these factories in their old conditions. There are two ways to change the situation: either to hand over possessional factories to the state, so that the treasury can re-equip them in the same way as its own factories, or else to leave such re-equipping to the factory-owners themselves. Of course, the factory-owners will attempt to secure the latter outcome, but it will hardly be in the interests of the working class or of the country as a whole. These gentlemen have already proven that they are completely incapable of properly managing their enterprises. If they now refuse to re-equip their factories, citing a lack of funds, then for this purpose they will obviously solicit new subsidies from the treasury. And since they can just as easily squander these subsidies as they did the previous ones, it is better for the state itself to re-equip the factories. This is why we demand confiscation of possessional factories and their transfer to the state.

'But after all, that will be theft' – so the factory-owners and their defenders will say. To those who will say this, we suggest counting up all the subsidies received by the factory-owners, together with the value of the destroyed forests, and then comparing the resulting figures with the value of the decrepit, half-ruined factories. It may turn out that the factory-owners will then be left with a balance owing to the treasury.

The private factories, as we have already said, can be divided into two groups: a minority that are well equipped and require no special measures, and the majority that are old and dilapidated and must be stripped to the foundations and replaced with new ones. Due to low labour-productivity, the workers in such factories, following the end of military orders, face a future that threatens unemployment and wages reduced to the former beggarly levels.

We demand that the owners be compelled to rebuild their factories and to ensure their workers normal working conditions that are no worse than in other parts of Russia. Owners who are unable or unwilling to fulfil these demands must be deprived of the right to operate their enterprises, and the factories and mines must either be turned over to the state or leased to such capitalists as can completely satisfy the demands listed above.

To implement this re-equipping of Urals industry will mean rescuing the working class of the Urals from starvation-wages and their complete lack of faith in the future.

It must also be added, here, that the expansion and further development of Urals industry requires a transfer from wood-fuel to coal. The coal in the Urals is of low quality and cannot be used for coke that might replace charcoal. On the other hand, further destruction of the forests for fuel may lead, and in some places has already led, to deforestation of the Urals. It is therefore imperative to link the industrial Urals with the Kuznetsk coal-basin of Siberia by a special railroad, and it is also necessary to reconstruct the whole network of railroads and siding tracks in the Urals proper.

The development of Urals industry has been hindered thus far by antiquated mining laws and lack of freedom for the mining industry. As a result, many resources of the territory have been left undeveloped. It is necessary to remove all bureaucratic and other constraints on the freedom of the mining industry and for the government, or all those who wish to do so under government-supervision, to develop all the known riches of the region.

On the land-question, our Party's goal is to defend the interests of Urals workers and peasants, to raise the productivity of agricultural labour, and to protect the territory's natural riches from being plundered. With these interests in mind, we demand, first of all, the elimination of possessional land-tenure and confiscation of the land-holdings of private factory-owners.

An area must be fashioned out of treasury-, possessional and confiscated private lands that will be of significance to the entire state and will be at its disposal. The remaining portion must be put at the disposal of local self-government in the Urals to constitute a reserve from which allotments can be made of meadows, forests, and arable land to the workers and peasants of the Urals. We simultaneously demand the establishment of a purely industrial area of mining and metallurgy in the Urals as a special province or region in which the purely agricultural and steppe-regions of Orenburg, Ufa, Perm and Vyatka will not be included. In these circumstances, local self-government in the Urals region will be in the hands of the mining and metallurgical population, and the Urals workers, together with the adjoining peasant-communities, will be masters of their region.

With regards to the Bashkirs and their land-tenure, three groups of Bashkirs must be differentiated. In the case of Bashkirs who have land, meadows and forests in excess of the norm required by their economy (that is, mainly cattle-breeding), and who rent out the surplus-land, these land-surpluses must also be handed over for management by local Urals self-government. Those Bashkirs who have exactly the allotments they need as cattle-breeders will be left with their present holdings. Finally, the poor among the Bashkirs, who do not have sufficient allotments – that is, those who have yet to turn to agriculture but do not have sufficient space for cattle-breeding – must acquire land consistent with the cattle-breeding norm (and this norm, as we know, is higher than for agriculture).

As was pointed out above, there will be cases when, like it or not, workers from mines that are closed because of their output, or factories that are shutting down for the same reason, will have to go into agriculture. In addition, the regional self-government in the Urals may, and probably will, have land that is presently unfit for agriculture, but may be rendered suitable following clearance, drainage and other improvements. In such cases, rather than split the land into small portions for separate households, we will strive to have a Urals regional *zemstvo* allocate large parcels of land and organise large-scale model farms supplied with machinery, fertiliser and agronomists. It will be better for the workers to work on such advanced undertakings than for each to acquire his own small farm.

These are the demands of our Party, that is, the Party of revolutionary social democrats (Bolsheviks and internationalists) concerning the labour- and land-question in the Urals.

When will we be victorious?

Implementation of our Urals programme on the labour- and land-question is beneficial and necessary, not merely for the workers and peasants but for the entire country. We will eliminate the semi-serf form of possessional right that has held back the development of Urals industry and condemned workers to the horrors of unemployment and poverty; remove obstacles to the development of Urals resources, which has been prevented by private property in land and the lack of freedom in mining; and reorganise land-relations in the interests of workers, peasants, and the state. But while all this is inevitable, above all for the sake of the entire country and its economic development, implementation of our programme is meeting with the strongest opposition from the class of capitalists. On their own, our barons in the Urals are neither so frightening nor so strong, but behind them stand the entire capitalist class and the banks, and behind the latter is the mighty force of world-capital. Just as it is difficult to confiscate land-lords' holdings in Russia without compensation, thus affecting the interests of the entire class of capitalists, so it is even more difficult to expropriate the barons of the Urals without affecting our own and foreign capitalists, along with the biggest banks in Russia, Paris and London. Everyone knows that much foreign capital is invested in Urals industry; and our banks, on which Urals industry depends, are essentially just the agents of foreign banks. Therefore, implementation of our programme is inconceivable without a rupture and the greatest of struggles against not only Russian, but also international capital. Both confiscation of landlord-holdings, which are mortgaged to the banks, and confiscation of the lands of Urals barons will amount to confiscation of a part of banking capital. Moreover, the compulsory reconstruction of backward Urals industry on the basis of new principles will amount to the destruction of the most sacred right of my lord, capital, in another area as well – in the area of the free disposal of the means of production. Both measures are impossible without a rupture with capital and a heavy blow being struck against it. Such a blow must be struck that capital will lose the ability to resist and will no longer be able to subordinate state-power to its own interests, instead itself being subordinated to control by a democratic authority.

Do the workers and poor peasants of Russia have the strength for this?

On our own, we will be weak. Only in alliance with the revolutionary proletariat of Western Europe can we count on victory in such a difficult struggle. For that reason, every worker in the Urals who wishes to achieve a better life by implementing the Urals labour-programme must be an internationalist, namely, a supporter of fraternity with all the workers in the West and their ally in the common struggle against capital.

And if that is the case, then not a single proletarian vote in Urals elections to the Constituent Assembly must be cast for the Menshevik and Socialist-Revolutionary parties, which do not support a resolute struggle against capital, but rather a compromise with it.

They have created and supported a coalition-ministry, that is, a division of power with the capitalists within the country. Such peaceful coexistence with the capitalists has required them to reject implementation of a number of urgent reforms in the interests of the toiling masses. With the coexistence that they also intend to observe in future, the Urals workers will not see implementation of all those demands that will resolve our labour- and land-question on proletarian terms. Therefore, if the Mensheviks and Socialist-Revolutionaries, namely, the compromisers with capitalists, have a majority in the Constituent Assembly, then it is not only the Urals labour-programme but all fundamental reforms in general that this Constituent Assembly will not provide for the people, because all of these reforms are offensive to capital. Such a Constituent Assembly will be a conciliation-chamber between the toiling masses and capital, to the benefit of capital and the disadvantage of the toilers, and it will not realise the hopes placed in it by all the common people of Russia.

And to the contrary, if a majority of resolute supporters of the struggle against capital is sent to the Constituent Assembly, then the cause of the working class and poor peasants will be in safe hands, and such representatives will courageously and fully implement the demands of workers and peasants. They have no fear of a rupture with international capital and the banking sharks. The Constituent Assembly, as supreme organ of the revolutionary people, will not draw back from armed struggle with capitalist Europe to defend the demands of the toiling masses, and in this struggle it will have beside it, as a powerful ally, the working class of the West – and then the Constituent Assembly will honourably fulfil its duty to revolutionary Russia and will bring to Urals workers, in particular, satisfaction of their most important demands.

For this reason, in elections to the Constituent Assembly the workers and peasants of the Urals must vote in a body for members of the Party of revolutionary social democrats – for Bolsheviks and internationalists. Not a single vote must be cast for those who compromise with capitalists, for the Mensheviks and Socialist-Revolutionaries, who in a coalition-ministry have given over to the capitalists the power won by the soldiers and workers; who also prepared, through their connivance with the capitalists, the Kornilov uprising that almost brought the Revolution to ruin; and who intend to live peacefully in future with the worst enemies of the toiling people.

In voting for the Bolsheviks, let every Urals worker say that we have had had enough of unemployment, enough of starvation-wages, and enough of rule by the factory-owners who exiled and flogged our grandfathers and great-grandfathers to death under serfdom and now want to force our own children to die of starvation. Only a resolute struggle against capital and victory over it will bring our emancipation!

No. 14
'We Must Not Wait', An Article Published in the Newspaper *Ural'skii rabochii*[1]

15 November, 1917

The authority created by the Congress of Soviets[2] can become stronger and hold its ground only in the event that the demands set forth by participants in the October Revolution are at least partially realised. The demand for bread is the most fundamental and pressing demand of the broad popular masses, and it is necessary to turn immediately to its implementation. It would be completely inadmissible and ruinous for our Party and for the Revolution if we postponed measures in this direction until after the final suppression of counter-revolution and the fortification of the new authority. This would amount to strengthening the new authority through the military-technical suppression of our opponent, while at the same time impairing it by not giving to the people those things for which the second revolution was accomplished.

What exactly are the measures that must be taken without delay?

Implementation of the decree on land and the actual transfer of landlord-holdings to the peasants will increase the supply of grain coming to the market from former estates.

---

1. [From *Ural'skii rabochii*, 15 November 1917.]
2. [The Second All-Russian Congress of Soviets took place in Petrograd from 25–7 October 1917. The Congress passed a decree on peace and another on land, proclaimed the establishment of Soviet power and created the first Soviet government.]

But this supply will not be sufficient. It is necessary to extract grain from that section of the peasantry that possesses large surpluses. But in the majority of cases, this means precisely those strata of the peasantry that are profiting less than other strata (those with little land or grain) from confiscation of the landlords' estates. Grain can be acquired from the well-to-do strata of the peasantry only in exchange for the products of manufacturing industry.

Consequently, it is necessary to turn to the demobilisation of industry and to do so speedily and without losing a moment. According to a declaration by one informed representative of the military department, as early as a month ago there was a supply of shells on hand sufficient for half a year of the most intensive firing.

It is possible, therefore, without the slightest risk to the country's defence, to turn at least to partial demobilisation.

I appeal to the Urals comrades and to all responsible members of factory- and works-committees, and of the soviets and of other workers' organisations, to take the most decisive and immediate measures in the matter of demobilising the Urals industry. There must be rapid organisation of a regional committee for demobilisation and preparation of a demobilisation plan, and in certain factories it is already possible to have a rapid transition to peacetime work. Of course, it is especially necessary to see that advances made on orders from the military department, orders whose completion can be postponed or cancelled (there are some orders that are based on a calculation of a war lasting two to three years), instead be used for peacetime work.

There are certain items (ramrods, for instance) that can go directly to the market, instead of senselessly being left for months to rust in commissariat-warehouses.

All iron-trimmings and small scraps of metal must be immediately put to use in preparing cramps, nails, clamps and other products necessary for the village.

There is no space in a short article to list everything that must now be done. The main thing is to be persuaded that what we need today is not simply to pass a resolution about what must be done, but actually to do what is required. What we need is feverish and urgent work. A pood of iron or steel committed to the village-market means a bag of flour for those who are starving, new support for the workers' and soldiers' authority, and the most well-aimed and accurate volley against our enemies in the counter-revolutionary camp.

Comrades! Long distances have prevented us from actively participating in battles against the troops of Kerensky and the counter-revolution. But here in the localities, we can lay down fire against the counter-revolution by putting out iron-products for the rural market.

Make haste, comrades! Let us all be concerned and anxious for the fate of the new authority, and let every conscious worker ask himself every night before sleeping: 'What have I done this day to strengthen my own authority, the authority of the workers?'

E. Preobrazhensky

No. 15
From the Protocols of a Session of the Moscow City-Wide Conference of the RSDRP(B) on the Question of War and Peace[1]

13 January 1918

From the speech by A.Ya. Arosev[2]

Comrade Arosev (co-rapporteur): Marxists have no fetishes – and nothing frightens us. We are never afraid of compromises if the place and time require them. In terms of place, we are in a backward country, an Asiatic country, and that is why the socialist Revolution could develop. The time is the final days of capitalism. Our socialist Revolution will prevail only with the support of the Western proletariat. In order to transfer the Revolution to the West, we must guard our Revolution in every way possible, deepen it and entrench it behind Chinese walls...

We do not reject a socialist war, but we need three to five months to organise a new socialist army. The army must be connected to a base, and the base must be socialist. The waging of a socialist war is a further advance of the Revolution, but for now it is impossible. We must move towards a compromise, for without compromises history cannot be made. Sometimes

---

1. [From TsAOPIM. F. 3. Op. 1. D. 17. L. 1–2. Original. Typewritten.]
2. [A.Ya. Arosev spoke following a report by E.M. Yaroslavsky.]

there is more revolutionism and more boldness in a compromise. We must conclude some kind of peace.³

Speech by E.A. Preobrazhensky

Comrade Preobrazhensky: Can it be that the compromise with the Junkers during the October Revolution taught Comrade Arosev nothing about how to proceed now, during the struggle against Kaledin, and so on.⁴ Within Chinese walls, we will not organise our economic life. Peace is precisely a permit for German capital as far as Vladivostok. If we are to strike at the parts, then it is necessary to strike now at Germany, and after Germany join up with England and all the rest. But in our country alone, in Russia, there is no discipline. The way out, of course – is demobilisation of the army and immediate creation of a new army. As for the second point of view – it is similar to Menshevism.⁵

R. Samoilovna
Secretary of the Moscow Committee

---

3. [Next came speeches by Ilyushin, Maksimov, Goncharov, Zemlyachka, Muralov and others.]

4. [On the night of 25–6 October 1917, the Moscow Military-Revolutionary Committee issued an order announcing the uprising in Petrograd and summoning workers and soldiers in Moscow to support the Revolution that had begun. At the same time, the counter-revolutionary Junkers of the Alekseevsky and Aleksandrovsky military colleges, with support from the regional military staff, from the 'Committee of Public Safety' formed by the City-Duma, and from others, occupied a number of important points in the centre of the city. The Moscow Military-Revolutionary Committee, in this situation, concluded a 24-hour truce with the 'Committee of Public Safety' starting from 12 a.m. on the night of 30 October. A.Ya Arosev was in the thick of these events and he, together with A.S. Vedernikov, led the Red Guards (Akademiya Nauk 1967 pp. 167–74). The Don military government, headed by Ataman A.M. Kaledin, waged a struggle against the Soviet authority from October 1917 to February 1918. His attempt ended in failure.]

5. [By majority-vote, the Conference adopted the Moscow Committee's resolution of 11 January 1918. This was followed by:
'*Comrade Sol'ts*: No comrades who disagree with the resolution have any right to oppose it.
'*Comrade Tikhomirov*: Although we oppose the resolution, of course we will always stick together.
'*Comrade Preobrazhensky*: It is a shame even to raise this question, since we do have party-discipline'.
The resolution is not included in the text of the protocol.]

No. 16
'A Constituent Assembly of the Soviets', An Article Published in the Newspaper *Pravda*[1]

25 January 1918

10 January, the opening day of the Third All-Russian Congress of Soviets,[2] will forever be indelibly imprinted in the memory of all participants in this historic assembly.

Within the walls of the Tauride Palace, which have so often resounded to the servile anthem of tsarism, for the first time the music of the *International* sounded forth not as music of the future, but as the solemn song of a victorious proletarian revolution.

And following the international anthem of the workers, like a historic memory of a path already travelled, the sounds of the *Marseillaise* rang out. The *International* succeeded the *Marseillaise*, just as the proletarian revolution leaves behind the bourgeois revolution and the grandson replaces the grandfather to take his place at the feast of life.

For a moment, the immortal shadows of Danton and Robespierre flashed before us as symbols of bourgeois heroism, and from the distance of a historic past, the stern Convention smiled at its worthy great-grandson – the Convention of the Republic of Soviets.

During the period when the State-Dumas dominated, or rather were in bondage, there were many

---

1. [From *Pravda*, 25 January 1918.]
2. [The Third All-Russian Congress of Soviets of Workers', Soldiers' and Peasants' Deputies met in Petrograd from 10–18 (23–31) January, 1918. The Congress affirmed the 'Declaration of the Rights of the Toiling and Exploited People', adopted basic resolutions on socialisation of the land, and approved the dissolution of the Constituent Assembly.]

occasions when the Tauride Palace and the bourgeois parliaments of all countries welcomed diplomatic lies with applause and underlined their solidarity with the bourgeois classes of other powers.

These signs of gratitude were either hypocritical and deceitful – because they were often followed the very next day by the animal-like chauvinistic howls of bankers quarrelling over markets – or else they were carefully weighed and expressed in pounds sterling when they represented the mutual curtseys of robbers who had reached an agreement on how to divide the booty. The bourgeois parliaments were making merchants' bows to each other, welcoming the ambassadors of capital from other countries.

The All-Russian Congress of Soviets also welcomed ambassadors. But breaking the etiquette of bourgeois hypocrisy, these ambassadors were submitting their credentials to the Congress not in the name of peoples, but on behalf of the revolutionary proletariat of their countries. They all welcomed the Great October Revolution, they all promised support for Soviet power from the workers of the Old and New Worlds, and when they departed amid burning applause from the excited Congress, along with the music of the *International* they carried away in their spirit the inaudible music of deepest feeling for the brotherhood of peoples, which the bourgeois world did not and could not know. Platten from the Swedish internationalists, comrade Petrov from the socialist party of England, Nissen from the Left-Social Democrats of Norway and Sweden, Williams from the American Socialist Party, Rakovsky from the Social Democrats of Romania – they all addressed the Congress on behalf of the workers of their countries.

But everyone felt someone was missing from the diplomatic corps of the international proletariat. We wanted to see comrade Liebknecht together with us and away from the prison-bed where he is languishing day in and day out with malicious consumption; we would have liked to carry him in the hands of the Revolution to a diplomatic bed in the Tauride Palace. We would have liked to hear comrade Friedrich Adler speaking from the rostrum as the herald of a revolution underway in Austria and to welcome his liberation as its first real victory.

They were not present. But the spirits of Liebknecht, Adler, and MacLean soared among us; they were chosen as honorary chairmen of the Congress, together with comrades Lenin and Trotsky, and they will remain with us in spirit and silently guide the work of the Third All-Russian Congress of Soviets.

The Third Congress has gathered under good omens. The proletariat of Austria and Hungary have embarked on a path of revolutionary struggle. We are beginning to build, whereas in the West they have only begun to break things down.

Let us hope that the time will soon come when the first congress of workers' and soldiers' deputies from the republics of Europe will gather in Petrograd.

E. Preobrazhensky

Appendix: Summary of E.A. Preobrazhensky's Speeches at the Third Congress of Soviets of Workers', Soldiers' and Peasants' Deputies[3]

Third Session, 25 (12) January 1918

Preobrazhensky deals at length with 'the especially fortunate position', in his words, that the united internationalists find themselves in and expresses the hope that they will remain in exactly that position. Then he speaks of the fact that the Revolution was not made by exhausted soldiers and land-greedy peasant-property-owners, as the united internationalists claim. It is equally untrue that only a few proletarians support the Bolsheviks. If that were true, then even the socialist revolution in the West, which the united internationalists are also calling for, could not possibly be of any help. But the whole question lies in the fact that this is another slander of the soldiers. As for the peasantry, the Bolsheviks are not closing their eyes to the fact that the peasantry are not yet sufficiently in favour of a socialist system, but further development of the Revolution will create objective conditions in which the peasantry will implement socialisation of the land.

Sixth Session, 28 January (15 January in the Old Style) 1918[4]

Following Martov, comrade Preobrazhensky speaks from the Bolshevik fraction.

He says that the national movement is only historically progressive when it is directed against the yoke of imperialism and when it occurs in a bourgeois-capitalist system.

Only in these circumstances – the speaker points out – is every national movement essentially directed against reaction, against the claims of imperialist states on small nationalities, and only then does it take on the character of a revolutionary struggle.

In these conditions, the national movement usually has the goal of creating new, independent state-units with strictly defined national-territorial boundaries. After that goal has been achieved, the basis for class-struggle is created within these tiny new states. The path in this direction is cleared thanks to the national-liberation struggle, thanks to deliverance from national oppression, which always leads to a weakening of class-animosities and class-contradictions.

---

3. [From *Pravda*, 25 January (12 January in the old style) 1918; *Tretii Vserossiiskii s'ezd Sovetov rabochikh, soldatskikh i krest'yanskikh deputatov*, p. 40.] St. Petersburg, 1918, p. 40

4. [From *Pravda*, 28 January (15 January in the old style) 1918; *Tretii Vserossiiskii s'ezd Sovetov rabochikh, soldatskikh i krest'yanskikh deputatov*, pp. 76–7.]

In the struggle against national oppression, experienced by one nationality or another that does not yet have independence, all classes of that nationality usually join together, and mutual class-tolerance, along with the national prejudices nourished by national oppression, remain in full force.

Therefore, to the extent that the national movement, following its victorious completion, eliminates the factors that blur class-partitions and weaken class-antagonisms, it is progressive and revolutionary in character.

The speaker deals at length with the case of Russia, which under tsarism united – by means of police-coercion and measures of the crudest repression – a multitude of nationalities into a compulsory union with the Great Russians. And the national movement, which in those days broke out at various moments among these nationalities, was essentially an anti-tsarist movement that naturally merged with the general current of revolutionary struggle by the entire people.

Comrade Preobrazhensky refers to the parallel between these positions and the situation that accompanied the struggle by Ukrainians for autonomy under the government of Kerensky.

The Bolsheviks sympathised with the movement headed by Ukrainian Socialist-Revolutionaries and Social Democrats, even though the latter were hardly different from the Russian social-compromisers, because their movement pursued a goal common both to them and to the toiling Russian people: to overthrow the bourgeois government of Kerensky.

But now, insofar as the Ukrainian bourgeoisie, by way of Mr. Vinninchenko, are disguising themselves with the tag of socialists, trying to use the principle of self-determination for a struggle against Soviet power both within and beyond the limits of Ukraine – to that extent, civil strife is objectively revolutionary and inevitable.

In general terms, so long as the bourgeoisie is injecting its chauvinist and bourgeois-imperialist content into the principle of self-determination, so long as it uses this slogan to dull the consciousness of the toiling masses of neighbouring nations by distracting them from the class-struggle, the Soviet authority will just as consistently, resolutely and mercilessly struggle against that way of applying the principle of self-determination in practice.

We are accused – says the speaker – of binding, forcibly binding, self-determining nationalities to a Soviet organisation of power within the frontiers of their own independent territories. We are told that in this respect we are violating our own principles. Comrade Martov is astonished because at the same time as we demand referenda – namely, a general vote as a means of expressing the people's will – for Poland, Lithuania, Courland and so on in face of Germany, we are also, within Russia, binding Ukraine, the Caucasus, Finland and so on to a Soviet federation based solely upon suffrage for the toiling masses, withholding this right from the bourgeois part of the population.

Yes, that is so, but whoever sees in this our duplicity or a contradiction of our own principles does not see, or does not wish to see, one very essential circumstance. While in Ukraine, the Caucasus and so on the bourgeois parliamentary principle has already outlived itself and is already a bygone stage of political development, in Courland, Poland and Lithuania the peoples not only have yet to win for themselves a democratic system, but also have yet to free themselves even from the yoke of tsarism.

In every region there are two periods of political development. Wherever in the western regions of Russia they have still not thrown off the chains of monarchical enslavement, it is impossible to demand of them a Soviet organisation of power, for they still have a purely democratic revolution ahead of them, whose result must be the fall of tsarism.

Nos. 17–23
Articles Published in the Newspaper *Ural'skii rabochii* in March–May 1918

3 March (17 February)–5 May 1918

No. 17

'War or Peace?'[1]

3 March (17 February) 1918

I

The agreement by the Government of People's Commissars to sign the new conditions of peace, which have worsened since Brest and are being dictated by the German counter-revolutionaries, has incited passionate protest among broad masses of the proletariat

---

1. [From *Ural'skii rabochii*, 3 March (17 February) 1918. For the continuation of this article, see Documents 2:18–20. The series of articles devoted to war and peace was written by E.A. Preobrazhensky during a period of sharp disputes within the Party: to sign or not to sign the annexationist and predatory peace-agreement pressed upon the Soviet state by the Central Powers. In opposition to Lenin and his supporters, who decided to sign the Brest peace at any price, the Left-Communists came out with N.I. Bukharin at their head (E.A. Preobrazhensky included), and the then People's Commissar of Foreign Affairs L.D. Trotsky. V.I. Lenin managed to prove the necessity and inevitability of signing the peace on 3 March 1918, in Brest-Litovsk. According to this peace, Russia lost approximately one million square kilometres of territory and was obliged to demobilise its army and fleet and pay six billion marks in gold. After using the interlude of peace needed to restore the country's economy, create the Red Army and stabilise the Soviet state, and also in connection with the Revolution in Germany, within eight months the Soviet government annulled the Brest treaty, on 13 November 1918.]

and caught the ranks of our Party completely unprepared for this decision. There exists an absolutely erroneous notion that the decision to sign the peace-pact was dictated by the German offensive, and that in this regard it is a product of confusion and panic in the leading circles of our Party and among members of the Central Executive Committee. This notion is fundamentally mistaken and can be explained by the complete lack of information among rank-and-file party-members concerning the internal struggle that, since the time of the Brest negotiations, has been waged inside our Party and also inside the Party of Left S-Rs on the question of peace at any price or socialist war. A far-reaching discussion was impossible in the press and at meetings for quite obvious reasons: this would have meant informing the ruling imperialists of Germany of the existence of such disagreements and would have weakened the position of our delegation at Brest, which up to the end defended the demand for a democratic peace without annexations.

Discussing the situation that had come about in connection with the exorbitant peace-conditions proposed by the German imperialists at Brest, three tendencies emerged in the Party that the reader will see below essentially came down to two: either for signing the annexationist peace or for socialist war.

From the very beginning, comrade Lenin and his group of supporters stood for signing the annexationist peace on the following two grounds. Although our worker-peasant Revolution was victorious within the country, it had not yet grown strong, and its fate in future depends completely upon a socialist revolution in Europe. Although the world proletarian revolution is maturing with every passing day, there are no guarantees that it will begin within the next few weeks. In such conditions, to enter into single combat with German imperialism and to wager all the achievements of the October Revolution would mean gambling with an enormous probability of defeat, for not only a socialist war, but even serious resistance, is out of the question at the moment. It is much more expedient, therefore, to buy our way out of imminent war by conceding Courland to the German imperialists and by accepting their other demands in order to strengthen Soviet power inside the country and eliminate all the consequences of the War, leaving the Austro-German alliance and the Entente imperialists to continue exterminating each other until the moment of a general European revolution. Meanwhile, the Soviet power could prepare its forces for a real revolutionary war, and enter at a moment when victory over imperialism would be assured both by our own onslaught from without and by the pressure of the working masses of Europe from within. Otherwise, our revolution will be strangled by a simultaneous onslaught by German imperialism and by the forces of bourgeois counter-revolution lurking within the country.

Comrade Trotsky defended a point of view that found expression in breaking off the Brest negotiations, that is, to stop the War but not sign a peace, which actually happened. All comrades know the motivation for this decision from the party-press, which explained in considerable detail and quite comprehensively the motives behind this solution to the question (if it is possible, here, to speak of a solution).

At one of the meetings of leading party-workers in Petrograd, where all tendencies in the Party surfaced concerning the question of war and peace, I characterised Trotsky's position as a one-week compromise. This was fully confirmed by the further course of events. The way out that he proposed gave a postponement in which to resolve the question, but it did not give any solution as such, which should have involved either signing a peace in the event of a German offensive or else revolutionary war. In either case, the question would have to be resolved under much worse conditions. Everyone knew that the peace-terms would then be more onerous, and those who supported Trotsky's position consciously accepted that fact. It was equally obvious to everyone that a revolutionary war, should it begin in such conditions, would initially be doomed to severe setbacks. This was especially clear to me personally when, at a meeting of the fraction of Bolshevik delegates to the Third All-Russian Congress of Soviets, my proposal – to put the Red Guard immediately in the trenches and declare a general mobilisation of the proletariat in all cities close to the front – was voted down by an enormous majority.

As for the position that we supporters of a revolutionary war took, with some disagreements over the particulars, the main motives for our point of view consisted of the following.

Conclusion of an annexationist peace with the German imperialists would inflict the most severe blow to the international workers' movement, because it would mean the beginning of an end to the War according to the imperialist method, with annexations and indemnities in the East, and the result would be to open up the possibility of peace in the West on the basis of a compromise between the bourgeoisies of Germany, England and France at the expense of Russia.

A paper-treaty with Germany that is not based on a real balance of forces represents no protection for Soviet power, leaving it under the constant threat of violence from the German counter-revolution and making its very existence dependent upon the favour of Wilhelm. Any preparation of a revolutionary war under such conditions would be out of the question; all socialist reforms would come to nothing through granting privileges to German capital and German industry; and in the East, a new war against former allies would be inevitable with either the occupation of the Amur district or the payment of debts that have been repudiated.

A retreat in the face of German imperialism would be only the beginning of a general retreat along the whole battle-front, and liquidation of the Revolution would occur in the worst possible form, in the form of the Soviet authority strangling the proletarian revolution with its own hands. A revolutionary war, no matter how badly we are prepared for it, is inevitable and has already begun with the struggle against Ukraine, Romania, the Polish legions and others allied with the German counter-revolution. This war will strengthen Soviet power within the country, and no defeats on the external front will be capable of overthrowing it. After being transformed from a national into a civil war, this war cannot be stopped with any artificial agreements that would be equally unreliable on both sides. It can only end with the defeat of one side, and if turns out to be the Revolution, then its liquidation in that way would be of the greatest benefit to the world proletarian movement and would rescue our Party from an inglorious death.

Such are the main outlines of the disagreements that took shape in the Party on the question of war and peace. I will return to a more detailed defence of the position in favour of revolutionary war in subsequent articles.

E. Preobrazhensky

No. 18

'Peace and War'[1]

6 March (21 February) 1918

II

In my previous article in *Ural'skii rabochii* No. 37, I set out the main arguments by those who supported signing the annexationist peace that was being dictated to us by the German counter-revolutionaries, and also the arguments of those who supported a socialist war.

Now I will examine in more detail the motives of those who supported signing the counter-revolutionary peace, and endeavour to demonstrate that, in the existing circumstances, this peace cannot be anything other than counter-revolutionary, both on an international scale and in terms of all its consequences for our Russian Revolution.

Here is the first argument. We are told that the Soviet authority, which has held on within the country by whatever means necessary, is the most important factor of the world proletarian revolution. One may pay for its existence with Courland and Estonia, with the self-determination of Lithuania and Poland, with reparations, with Ukrainian grain and with a temporary refusal to fight against German imperialism.

We fully agree that up to now the October Revolution and the Soviet socialist authority were the most important factors of the world proletarian movement. But why?

Precisely because this authority was worker-socialist not in words, but in deeds, because it waged an irreconcilable struggle against the imperialists of all countries, taking a direct path to its goal and not betraying its principles under any conditions, even the most unfavourable. *That* is the authority that has charmed and will continue to charm the proletariat of the West, and that is also the authority that was and will remain terrifying and hateful for the imperialists of the entire world.

It is not the structure of this authority, but rather the revolutionary content of its actions that serves as a factor of the European revolution. Take this content away from it, and even if it is headed, as before, by such revolutionaries as Lenin and Trotsky, in practice it will inevitably turn into a weapon of German imperialism; and no phrases about the preparation of a revolutionary war will be able to

---

1. [From *Ural'skii rabochii*, 6 March (21 February) 1918.]

extinguish its counter-revolutionary character in reality. In principle, the politics of this power will not differ significantly from the conciliatory policy of the soviets led by the Dans and Chernovs. The question then is: Was it worthwhile for the proletariat to make the October Revolution in order to replace a compromise with its own bourgeoisie, and with Anglo-French imperialism, by a compromise with Austro-German imperialism in even more humiliating and shameful conditions? If such a Soviet authority remained intact – and I consider that to be most unlikely – then it would do so because of its harmlessness to imperialism, and that is exactly why it would no longer inspire hope among the exhausted proletariat of the West. Such an authority would compromise the very idea of the dictatorship of the proletariat, showing that even the workers' power is capable of betraying its principles and surrendering its positions without a fight when threatened by the armoured fist of its enemies. Moreover, an annexationist peace would serve as a crushing blow to the revolutionary workers' movement in Austria and Germany, frustrating the struggle for a general democratic peace in these countries. Such a peace would give the German imperialists the opportunity to get out of the War on the Eastern Front with huge spoils, it would consolidate their position inside their own countries, and it would justify their policies and their existence in the eyes of the German people. This peace would undermine the hard work of our comrade-internationalists in England, France and Italy, and it would compel the proletariat of these countries to regard war with Germany as a war against the stranglers of the Russian Revolution.

As for the hopes held by supporters of a counter-revolutionary peace – that a suitable agreement with the Hoffmann super-robbers can be reached and, if concluded, will [not] remain just a non-binding scrap of paper for these scoundrels – the fact that the truce has already been breached is a menacing warning for the future. The recently-revealed and now-obvious unwillingness of the German aggressors to conclude any agreement whatever with the Soviet authority, even one that is most ruinous and humiliating for the Revolution and advantageous for the Prussian Junkers, proves that these gentlemen can teach many old Marxists how to protect the interests of one's class. Long ago, comrade Lenin taught us not to yield to constitutional illusions and to make all tactical calculations on the basis of the real relation of forces. Now he wants to protect Soviet Russia from the Germanic boot with a paper-agreement, under which the signature of Hoffmann will be enough to guarantee that it will be breached.

Thus, the signing of an agreement brings us no benefits even in the sense of the most short-lived respite before a new clash. Now, from the point of view of our internal position, let us look at what we lose simply through the fact of signing this document.

First of all, it is clear to everyone that no defeats on the front, even the most serious, are able to overthrow Soviet power within the country if this power stands at the head of the working masses in repelling the onslaught of German capital.

The first days of the German offensive were irrefutably persuasive in proving this. If there was panic, it was created first and foremost by the position of the Council of Peoples' Commissars, who agreed to sign a peace-pact and thus spread bewilderment and confusion among the proletarian masses.

Conversely, as soon as it became clear that there could be no salvation without a struggle, there appeared everywhere an unprecedented upsurge in mood and a desire to defend the Revolution to the last drop of blood. Our position immediately strengthened; conversely, the defeatist bourgeoisie turned out to be isolated in the position of a German agent awaiting the arrival of 'their people' in the form of the advancing German White Guards.

It cannot be otherwise. A defeat at the front is capable of overthrowing an authority that is not supported within the country. But when the authority symbolises protection of the Revolution against enemy-invasion, these defeats serve as the sturdiest cement in uniting it with the masses.

To the contrary, the signing of a counter-revolutionary peace, as well as any policy of vacillation and uncertainty, kills the enthusiasm of the masses and, in opposition to the top leaders of the Soviet authority that is conducting such policies, creates an unnatural but inevitable bloc of all the opponents of such a peace; the revolutionary masses, who support Soviet power but oppose its ruinous policies, turn out to be involuntary allies of all the opponents of Soviet power. In these conditions, the defence of Soviet power will prove an extremely difficult task, and it is precisely at this moment that its position will be shakier than ever before.

Let us now look at whether it is even possible to speak of a peaceful agreement with the German imperialists as something real, not a fantasy, when it comes to implementing it in real life. This agreement, as I have indicated, will be violated by the German counter-revolutionaries the moment it is to their benefit. But can the Soviet authority not also violate the agreement from the first day after its final signing?

On this point, of course, even the signatories entertain no illusions. To dissolve the Red Guard and the Red Army would not only mean the complete disarmament of the Revolution within the country, but it is also impossible in practice, because the armed masses will never hand over their rifles without a fight.

This means that the agreement will immediately be broken, and there will be a legal pretext for the Hoffmanns to continue a policy of invading our Republic. To discontinue government-sponsored agitation against German imperialism, as required by one point of the agreement, means prohibiting all soviets from writing anything in their press against the stranglers of our Revolution, for according to our constitution the soviets are the organs of governmental authority and their press is the official press. And that means that violation of the agreement is inevitable from the very first day. As far as non-interference in the affairs of Ukraine is concerned, we cannot even discuss that issue, since the current interference is by the Austro-Germans and the territory of Ukraine is not defined.

Therefore, the agreement is a fiction in every sense, an attempt by way of an ingenious plan to suspend the class-struggle against German capital. Such utopian plans have never been implemented in any revolution, even in those cases when they were advantageous for the revolution. In the present case, this plan to buy our way out of the struggle against German imperialists with territories, reparations, disarmament of the Revolution, betrayal of principles, and by handing over our republic's head to the Hoffmann executioners, is not merely a utopia – we should be so fortunate – but also a counter-revolutionary utopia.

Lenin's entire plan is essentially an attempt to save the life of the Soviet authority by committing suicide. It is possible for people to save their honour through suicide. But only a madman can count on a lasting and peaceful life by putting a bullet in his head.

E. Preobrazhensky

No. 19

'Peace or War?'[1]

7 March (22 February) 1918

III

As readers of the newspaper *Pravda* have now learned, comrade Lenin stood for an annexationist peace from the very beginning, when the German conditions first became known and the Rada had yet to conclude its treacherous secret peace with Austria and Germany. Some comrades may conclude from this that the latest severe trials, to which our socialist republic has been subjected as a result of the German invasion, have already confirmed the correctness of all of comrade Lenin's calculations and have again proven his perspicacity and ability to take into account all of the aggregate circumstances and conditions in which our struggle takes its course.

Such a conclusion would be fundamentally mistaken.

Of course, if in general terms there were no objectively possible way out of the situation other than signing a predatory peace, then, no doubt, the peace had to be signed when the conditions were more acceptable. But the point is that a peace between the Soviet Republic and imperialist Germany is, generally-speaking, impossible, even if it were signed ten times over by comrades Lenin and Trotsky on the one side and Kühlmann and Hoffmann on the other. And, of course, what has happened now would inevitably have occurred in some other form had a peace been signed in early January or December. The only possibility would have been slightly fewer losses of artillery, supplies, and so on, and even this is doubtful.

Here is the proof.

Our struggle with the Ukrainian Rada began independently of the negotiations with Germany, and our victory over it inevitably pushed it into an agreement with the Austro-German imperialists and only accelerated this process. But even if we had not defeated the Rada, being surrounded on all sides by enemies, it would have been compelled by its own bourgeois nature to look for an agreement with the imperialists of the Central Powers, not with Soviet Great-Russia. And since the struggle here would inevitably have continued, if only because of the indeterminacy of its frontiers with Great-Russia, we would thereby also have been drawn into a struggle with Austria and Germany...[2]

---

1. [From *Ural'skii rabochii*, 7 March (22 February) 1918.]
2. [There is a gap in the text because the original newspaper is damaged.]

In that case, too, it would have been inevitable, even if a peace had been signed. And then there would have been no way to avoid the inevitability of an armed clash with German imperialism, the only difference being that, by that time, no-one would have had any doubts, perhaps even including the most resolute supporters of peace at any price. In hindsight, therefore, it is necessary to recognise that the most correct position was that of the people who stood for delaying the negotiations for the sake of arousing the proletariat of the West while simultaneously using this time to adopt speedy and decisive steps to prepare for defence of the Revolution.

By now, it is even clearer that no agreements with the Hoffmanns can give even the least postponement for our Revolution to prepare 'a revolutionary war not in words, but in deeds', to use comrade Lenin's expression. From this perspective, an article in the bourgeois German newspaper *Norddeutsche Allgemeine Zeitung*[3] is typical, saying among other things: 'It is clear that the Bolsheviks are no more thinking of a stable peace nowadays than they did previously...This means that Germany, in concluding peace with Russia, must secure certain and lasting guarantees of the fulfilment of all obligations'. And since one of the points of the agreement obliges the Soviet authority to dissolve the Red Guard and the Red Army, which are especially hated by the German capitalists, one must assume that the gentlemen Hoffmanns will make certain that this point of the agreement does not remain only on paper.

The result is that instead of 'preparation for a revolutionary war not in words, but in deeds', according to the conditions proposed to us, peace ensures such preparation in words, but disarmament in practice. This peace will force us to exchange the worker's rifle, the sole real protection of Soviet power from the violence of German imperialists, for a paper-agreement that provides all the means for self-suffocation by the Soviet authority and to which, no doubt, guarantees will be added so that this suffocation will occur speedily enough to satisfy the German bandits and our own White Guards.

In ancient Greece, those condemned to death were themselves given the right to implement the death-sentence by taking poison. For the Soviet authority, signing a peaceful (what a mocking word!) agreement with Germany, and implementing it under the sharp eye of the Hoffmann executioners, will not mean the possibility of salvation, but simply execution by the Greek method.

But the working class has no wish to kill itself voluntarily, it will not surrender its rifles, and it will fire at the Hoffmann executioners until the last bullet while retreating inch-by-inch into the interior of the country. And if the Turkish *bachi-bouzouks*[4] want to arrange the 'self-determination' of Armenia in such a way as

---

3. [This newspaper was a government-organ in Berlin from 1861–1918.]
4. [Ottoman mercenaries.]

to commit their hundred and first massacre there, if their appetite is extending beyond the South Caucasus, then we can offer them only one response: try to take it yourself. And let the Austro-German gangs try to take grain from Ukraine. It will cost the bandits dearly, and they will not get it without being filled with lead.

Only the policy of the rifle, firing non-stop – this is now the only real policy and the only one worthy of the Soviet authority with regard to the bandits of German capital, and the Fourth Congress of Soviets in Moscow will no doubt confirm this.

E. Preobrazhensky

No. 20

'Peace or War?'[1]

9 March (24 February) 1918

IV

In his theses on peace, which were read at a party-meeting in Petrograd as early as the beginning of January and published recently in *Pravda*, comrade Lenin considered it necessary to sign a peace mainly because, in his opinion, we would benefit most from using that interval to fortify Soviet power in Russia while the imperialists of the Central Powers were settling scores with the Allied imperialists on the battlefields.

In one of my counter-theses, read out at another meeting, and in my speech against Lenin's position at that same meeting, I pointed out exactly the opposite: signing an annexationist peace with Germany would inevitably create the basis for a compromise in relations between England and Germany, because German imperialism's acquisition of spoils in the East would make it more compliant in the West. The result of such an agreement would be to create a common bloc of world-capital against the Russian Revolution.

Debates over tactics are resolved by the facts. And now the latest facts, touching upon just this question, are evidently beginning to justify the predictions made by those who opposed comrade Lenin's position.

At the last solemn session of the German Reichstag, where the successes of the German bandits in the East were summed up, Chancellor Hertling made a speech, parts of which were directly addressed to President Wilson and must be recognised as extremely significant. Everyone knows just now that in the struggle with Austria-Hungary, America is assuming the decisive role; President Wilson is the president not only of his own country, but also of the entire capitalist trust of the Allies, and that is why an address to him from the German chancellor can be regarded as the beginning of official negotiations on an agreement between the warring sides. Hertling not only expressed agreement with a whole series of positions put forward by Wilson in his recent speech, but also directly conveyed his hope that on the question of peace-terms 'the responsible representatives of the warring powers would come together in an intimate meeting for discussion'.

---

1. [From *Ural'skii rabochii*, 9 March (24 February) 1918.]

In other words, Hertling is suggesting to his enemies that they enter into formal peace-talks, thus considering for his own part that an agreement is possible.

Why is it that an agreement, which the German imperialists only yesterday considered impossible, has today become possible?

It is precisely because the gentlemen Hertlings and Hoffmanns consider their predatory enterprise in the East completed not only as a matter of fact but also formally, having in their pocket the agreement by the Government of Peoples' Commissars to accept their peace-terms. Now the moment has come for a deal with their main rivals, with people from 'their own circle', who are bourgeois to the core and with whom it will be even easier to reach an understanding given the fact that the Eastern spoils, if worst comes to worst, are sufficient, while the struggle in the West promises incredible losses of people and material values.

At the same time as Hertling is dragging Wilson to the stock-exchange, the prominent head of the trade-unions in Germany, Legien, who is one of the most cynical henchmen of Wilhelm and the imperialist policy of Germany's rulers, has made an offer to Gompers, likewise a social-patriot and henchman of the American billionaires, to come together in a neutral country for discussion of peace-terms.

This suggestion from Wilhelm's social-patriotic agent is, of course, intimately linked with Hertling's speech. What we have before us, then, is the undoubted fact of a clearly expressed wish from the side of the German imperialists to end the War in the West with a deal based on a number of concessions by the Germans.

It is also extremely characteristic that the most recent telegrams are relaying rumours that Germany has offered Alsace-Lorraine to France on condition that its right to all conquests in the East be recognised. Of course, this rumour will turn out to be false, but the truth that it does reveal is that the moment is now favourable for a deal, and the corresponding steps are already being taken to initiate negotiations.

We therefore see before us every indication that comrade Lenin's calculation has turned out to be mistaken and that Russia's exit from the War will not only fail to secure any interval for it but rather threatens to bring it face-to-face with a most powerful alliance of the whole of world-capital, whose first goal will be to liquidate all the conquests of the October Revolution.

The only conclusion, which is self-evident from all of this, is that, for the proletarian-peasant republic of Russia, all paths are closed to any agreement with one or the other coalition of imperialists. We can only keep for ourselves what we defend through deadly struggle. And everyone will agree that even if we exhausted our forces in the imperialist War up to the fall of tsarism, we have only begun to gather them for a defensive socialist war. These forces are growing with every passing day, while the forces of the German imperialists are every day dwindling further, and it is impossible to stop this inevitable process by any means. The end to which all this leads has already been demonstrated by Kerensky's adventure on 18 June.[2]

E. Preobrazhensky

---

2. [On 18 June (1 July), 1917, Kerensky announced a new Russian offensive against the Germans despite the disintegration of the Russian army. After brief initial successes, within three days the Russian offensive collapsed and a German counter-offensive was under way, pushing into Ukraine.]

No. 21

'The Anniversary of the Revolution'[1]

12 March (27 February) 1918

> 'The days of our lives are as fleeting as the waves'.

Today marks exactly one year since that unforgettable day when the colossus of Russian tsarism crashed to the ground under the blows of the revolutionary workers and soldiers of Petrograd to the deafening crackle of machine-guns that had been shooting down the revolutionary people.

12 March, the anniversary of the Revolution, is not just some incidental date when the calendar says we must take account of what has occurred. No, this will be the day for an *actual* accounting of the first two stages of the Revolution, and its supreme accountant will be the Fourth Extraordinary All-Russian Congress of Soviets, whose decisions will open a new stage in our Revolution. Whatever decision the Congress takes regarding the basic question of the moment, the question of war and peace, a historic line will be drawn precisely on the anniversary of the Revolution.

Let us look back today on the path we have travelled, take note of the most prominent events, and then try to understand the present and what will follow from the events that have already occurred.

The February Revolution, which began with the commotion of a hungry crowd, mostly women, grew on the fifth day into a worker-peasant rebellion that ended victoriously, mainly because the regiments of the Petrograd garrison went over to the side of the insurgents. The fall of tsarism, which astonished everyone with its swiftness and ease, was prepared by all the consequences of the protracted War, food-devastation, the ruin of the wide toiling masses, the exhaustion resulting from the War and the bitterness against its suspected culprits. Given the heavy burden imposed upon the popular masses, tsarist oppression and robbery by the bourgeois-landlord class became especially intolerable. The swiftness of the Revolution is explained not only by the complete isolation of the autocratic government from all classes of Russian society, even including part of the nobility, and not only by complete moral decay at the top and the contempt in which the ruling faction was held by the popular masses and the entire country in general, but also by the masses making use of the experience they gained during the unsuccessful first Revolution of 1905.

---

1. [From *Ural'skii rabochii*. 12 March (27 February) 1918.]

That Revolution showed that an upheaval cannot succeed without support from the army.

In 1917, the main forces of the Revolution were devoted to the army-organisation, and from the very first days soviets were created not only of workers', but also of soldiers' deputies. The February Revolution also inherited from the Revolution of 1905 the idea of soviets as mass organisations of the insurgent people that gradually extended beyond the workers to the army and into the villages.

Both the Revolution of 1905 and all the bourgeois upheavals in the West teach us to remember this truth in particular, that a revolution that fails to arm itself or allows itself to be disarmed inevitably culminates in defeat for the popular masses. That is why we held on to our rifles and those of the revolutionary soldiers with such compulsive determination from the first days of the upheaval, and why the bourgeoisie failed in all its attempts to convince the masses that their role had come to an end with the overthrow of tsarism and that they could disperse and leave control of the country completely to the Provisional Government. The armed masses remained in control of government-authority, and Russia was saved from a silent counter-revolution that would inevitably have occurred had the Revolution disarmed itself.

So far as it was a question of liquidating tsarism, the masses allowed themselves no mistakes; the conscious vanguard of the proletariat, having in its ranks the figures of 1905, acted resolutely and skilfully, and the entire structure of the autocracy was shattered in a few days. At the same time, every step of victory was consolidated by the formation of stable organisations that took upon themselves the functions of control and of leading the movement during the next period.

Even at the height of the struggle, amidst the thunder and crackle of gunshots, the workers of Petrograd turned to electing deputies to the soviet. On 28 February, the Petrograd Soviet of workers' deputies held its first meeting.

After the elections, the military units sent soldiers' deputies to join the workers' deputies.

At the first news of the upheaval in Petrograd, the same was done throughout the provinces as in the capital. Soviets were set up, local authorities were arrested, and communication was established with the revolutionary centres of the country.

Although the autocracy was broken by the power of the workers and soldiers, and all armed force was at the disposal of the Petrograd Soviet, it was still not this soviet, but rather the temporary committee of the State-Duma that planted itself in power and put forward the first provisional revolutionary government. This government was, indeed, quite temporary, and as far its revolutionism is concerned, the very mention of it now seems excessive.

Thus the Petrograd Soviet allowed the bourgeoisie to seize the helm of state in the persons of Prince L'vov, Milyukov and Guchkov, with the addition of Kerensky dressed up as a socialist. Was this a political mistake on the part of the Petrograd Soviet, or was it inevitable? Most likely it was the latter, for the worker- and soldier-masses had only begun to organise themselves throughout the country and the peasantry was still unaffected by the Revolution, while the bourgeoisie was fully prepared for power. All of the *zemstvos*, municipal self-governments, military-industrial committees, and the majority of the cultural and educational organisations were in its hands, and the immense majority of officials from all departments also stood for, or else now adopted, the viewpoint of bourgeois liberalism.

The Petrograd Soviet's caution will be quite understandable if we also remember that it had to decide the question of power in a moment of continuing warfare, when the attitude of an army of millions towards the Revolution was still unknown. At the same time, the Petrograd Soviet reserved to itself the right of control over the activity of the Provisional Government in spite of the cries about the pernicious nature of dual power that came from the direction of the bourgeoisie, who were seeking a unified authority – needless to say, a unified authority for themselves, and not for the popular masses.

As for the question of peace, which was of decisive importance for our Revolution, which originated above all as a protest against the protracted imperialist War, it too was placed on the waiting list.

Simply by virtue of the fact that the central authority, and especially control over the country's foreign policy, was in the hands of representatives of the bourgeoisie, it was self-evident that it would not be properly solved. The famous manifesto of the Petrograd Soviet to the peoples of the whole world, on 17 March, called upon the peoples to take the fate of peace into their own hands after freeing themselves of bourgeois governments, yet at home this soviet left the question of war and peace to Guchkov and Milyukov.

On the other hand, our bourgeoisie and the imperialists of the Allied countries made every effort not to stop the War but, on the contrary, to use the Russian Revolution in the interests of a war that tsarism had not waged with sufficient success. On the question of the War, there was a sharp clash between the interests of the workers and the soldier-peasant masses, on the one side, and the propertied class on the other.

Sharp protests arose against the foreign policy of Milyukov, who tried in this regard to keep everything as it was, even including preservation of Russia's obligations resulting from the secret predatory agreements concluded by tsarism with the Allied capitalists. The protest-demonstrations of 20–21 April were provoked by his famous note to the Allied governments, in which he cynically emphasised servile loyalty to Allied capital, in spite of the moods and wishes of the broad masses of workers and soldiers. The attempts by Kornilov, then commander of the Petrograd region, to call in artillery to suppress the movement, resulted in a humiliating failure, and all the troops declared their willingness to obey only those orders that were approved by the Petrograd Soviet. The bourgeois Provisional Government learned by experience that real power was not in its hands. The first governmental crisis had occurred, ending with formation of a coalition ministry.

The bourgeoisie found itself too weak to control the revolutionary country without the support of socialists, and the latter, represented at the time by the Mensheviks and Socialist-Revolutionaries, were, in turn, afraid to take power solely into their own hands without the bourgeoisie.

Thus emerged the notorious coalition, which in practice meant the triumph of bourgeois power, protected from the people by such 'socialist' figures as Tsereteli, Chernov, Skobelev and other social-carps who were reeled in by the savvy bourgeois bosses.

But development of the class-struggle was impossible to stop by any combinations of 'socialist' and Cadet portfolios, just as it was impossible to wriggle out of a revolutionary solution to all the fundamental questions posed by the Revolution: the questions of land, peace, workers' control and the right of nations to self-determination.

At the first all-Russian meeting of the soviets, the supporters of a rupture with the bourgeoisie, adopting the slogan of 'All power to the soviets!', numbered sixty persons out of four hundred. Petrograd was ahead of all the rest of Russia, and here, sooner than anywhere else, the worker- and soldier-masses were going over to the ranks of the Bolshevik Party. The first review of all the forces of an emerging new revolution, a revolution against domestic and world-capital, a revolution against the imperialist War, occurred early in July at the first All-Russian Congress of Soviets, where Bolsheviks, Internationalists and the Left Socialist-Revolutionaries, who announced themselves here for the first time, already numbered up to one hundred and eighty deputies. In the Petrograd demonstration of 18 July, which took place under the slogan of 'Down with the ten minister-capitalists, down with the imperialist War!', the St. Petersburg workers and soldiers were openly embarking on this new path before all of Russia.

Meanwhile, the compromisers in the provinces were still triumphant in most of the soviets; and Petrograd, which had run off ahead at the beginning of July, paid severely for its far-sightedness. The spontaneous half-rebellion and half-democracy of 3–5 July, occurring under the slogans 'Down with the coalition with the bourgeoisie!' and 'All power to the soviets!', ended in the movement's defeat. Democrats had sufficient forces to take state-power into their own hands, but at the time Russia would not have supported this enterprise, since it began too early. Meanwhile, the compromising Central Executive Committee of the soviets did all it could to evade the power offered to it by the workers and soldiers of Petrograd.

The liquidation of this outburst, which coincided with the defeat of our military at the front after Kerensky's adventure of 18 July, was accompanied by an enormous intensification of reaction. Then began the famous charges that the Bolsheviks were German hirelings and spies; the left-socialists' newspapers were closed; and hundreds of people were thrown into prison, both in the rear and at the front. The Kornilovites of all shades captured power with the social scoundrel Kerensky at their head. Next came the question of introducing a military dictatorship, dispersing the soviets, and forcibly introducing discipline into the soldiers' ranks under threat of shootings and the death-penalty. General Kornilov, who had hastened with the implementation of all of these measures, was defeated by the combined forces of all the soviets and abandoned at the decisive moment by the panic-stricken Kerensky. Kornilov's defeat abruptly shifted the relation of forces in the country to the left, in the direction of the worker- and soldier-masses; and the coalition with the bourgeoisie, who sympathised with Kornilov's action, clearly revealed itself as a coalition with explicit counter-revolution. The trust that all the compromisers had enjoyed among the broad masses of the toiling people was finally undermined. At the same time, the peasant-masses lost patience. Instead of the land promised to them by the Socialist-Revolutionaries, they were met with punitive detachments carrying orders, written by their ministers, for arrest of the land-committees, and they decided to put an end to the landlords' estates using their own methods. The wide agrarian movement began with devastation of the landlords' manors and seizure of the nobles' lands.

If the Kornilov mess dispersed all conciliatory illusions amongst the soldier-masses, comrades such as Avksent'ev, with their circulars aimed at protecting the landlords' holdings, cured all the landless and land-hungry peasantry of these illusions. A new revolution was brewing, a revolution against the bourgeois-landlord régime as a whole, and every attempt by the compromisers to force the toilers' gigantic class-conflict with capital and landed property into the narrow framework of a parliamentary struggle at the Constituent Assembly ended in a pitiful fiasco.

The October upheaval overthrew the bourgeois régime in Russia and buried along with it the compromising parties of Mensheviks and Socialist-Revolutionaries, who had exposed themselves as agents of capital preserving their supremacy under the flag of socialism. The slogan 'All power to the soviets!' came alive. The Second All-Russian Congress of Soviets, which turned out amid the thunder of guns aimed at the Winter Palace, proclaimed the triumph of the worker-peasant Revolution and took over all state-power.

The bourgeois-democratic February Revolution, which in words won all freedoms for the people but left the privileges to capital, including the privileges of state-power, had run its course. The October Revolution transferred power to the workers and peasants in fact; the promises of land were realised by transferring land to the peasants without redemption and without any delays, and workers' control over production was introduced and legalised. On the basis of the dictatorship of the workers and the poorest peasants, the intensified and rapid construction of a new life began. All state-machinery, from top to bottom, passed into the hands of the organised toiling masses. The nationalisation of banks and of the major industrial enterprises was carried out; the sabotage perpetrated by all the conscious and unconscious defenders of bourgeois supremacy was broken. Together with this destructive and constructive work, the Soviet power waged a deadly struggle with all the counter-revolutionary forces that had entrenched themselves on the Don, in Orenburg, and in Ukraine. The attempt by the collaborators to regain the power they lost in the October Days, under the flag of the Constituent Assembly, suffered a miserable collapse. All the centres of counter-revolution within the country were gradually liquidated and, by the end of the first year of the Revolution, worker-peasant power triumphed everywhere.

But the main battles still lay ahead. It was easy to break the resistance of the domestic bourgeoisie and its henchmen. It was a different matter with powerful external opponents – with world-capital.

Publication of the secret agreements, and refusal to pay the foreign loans concluded by tsarism, caused the imperialists of the Allied countries to take up arms against our Revolution. On the other hand, the truce on the Austro-German front could not continue indefinitely. The Soviet authority's refusal to sign the predatory peace-conditions offered by the German plunderers brought the White Guards of Hindenburg to our defenceless borders. In that way, our Revolution approached its natural limit. It was victorious within the country, but it ran into the blank wall of world-capital. Now the fate of all our conquests is being determined on the battlefields with world-capital. There cannot be the slightest doubt that with our own forces alone we will be defeated and crushed. Our Revolution must become a world proletarian revolution – otherwise, it will inevitably perish.

Today the Fourth Extraordinary Congress of Soviets of Workers', Soldiers', Peasants' and Cossacks' Deputies is gathering.[2] The Congress will decide the question of war and peace. It will sum up a year of revolution and declare firmly

---

2. [The Fourth All-Russian Extraordinary Congress of Soviets met in Moscow from 14–16 March 1918. The Congress ratified the Brest treaty and confirmed the decision of the VTsIK to move the capital of the Soviet Republic from Petrograd to Moscow.]

that in spite of severe trials at the front, the Soviet authority, which has entered into the flesh and blood of toiling Russia, indestructibly stands on its own feet inside the country and can only be uprooted within Russia along with the blood and flesh of the toiling people.

At the same time, if the Congress accepts the predatory conditions of German imperialism it will thereby say that the proletarian-peasant Revolution of Russia has been defeated by world-capital and that, following its parade of internal victories, it is entering an era of external defeats.

The Fourth Congress can reject the predatory conditions and declare a socialist war against German capital.

That will mean the struggle continues. But the struggle will also continue in the event that the pseudo-peace with German imperialism is signed; it will be postponed only by a few weeks, not more.

The workers and peasants of Russia will never voluntarily allow themselves to be strangled by the noose of an extortionate peace.

In this final fight, the outcome of the struggle will depend on the working class of Europe and, above all, on the proletariat of Austria and Germany. If we win support from them, our conquests will remain forever ours. If there is no such support, we will be defeated by the forces of the imperialists of all countries; and then woe betide the workers and peasants of Russia who woke up too early, and praise be to those who were decades ahead of the proletariat of the entire world in a mighty breakthrough to the ideal of socialism.

E. Preobrazhensky

No. 22

'Peace is Signed'[1]

19 (6) March 1918

In today's telegrams, the reader will find an announcement that the All-Russian Congress of Soviets in Moscow – by a vote of 724 to 276, with 118 abstentions – ratified the conditions for peace signed previously by our peace-delegation and by the organs of governmental power.

This decision by the Congress would have been shockingly unexpected in the first days of the German advance – if, from the very outset, it was precisely the Congress that had to address the question of whether to sign an onerous peace or to summon the toiling people of Russia for the most brutal resistance. But once the preliminary signing of the peace had already taken place, and the Congress, in this respect, was faced with a fact, the very question took on a different form, namely, the Congress had to decide whether to terminate the factually established armistice with the Germans or to declare war after refusing to ratify the preliminary peace-agreement. The Congress has decided in favour of signing the peace, and thus it has left to the German imperialists all the political disadvantages of a new declaration of war.

We have more than once indicated on the pages of our newspaper that we consider the policy of peace at any price a terrible blow to the world proletarian movement, which is the only source of our salvation – we think that German imperialism will not give us any breathing space because, having paused for now in their advance towards Petrograd from the south, they are beginning to approach it from the north by means of war with the Finnish Socialist Republic. In the East, as a result of peace with the Germans, we are on the eve of a new war, while the surrender without a fight is demoralising the forces of the revolutionary proletariat and killing the elation that seized the proletariat after the brazen violence of the German bandits. From this point of view, the decision of the Congress, which has surrendered toiling Russia to the executioners of imperialism – this decision will be disastrous unless the conscientious proletariat reverses it in practice.

But it can only reverse it through the most active and feverish preparation for impending and inevitable combat with the German predators. Only in this way is it possible partly to neutralise the ruinous decision, and only by utilising every minute of peace for the purpose of defence do we approach the moment of actually annulling its disastrous conditions. Otherwise, the interval of truce will

---

1. [From *Ural'skii rabochii*, 19 (6) March 1918.]

only give the German predators the opportunity to gather forces and to use this time better for the offence than we use it for the defence. As a result, it is not the victim, but the executioner who will benefit from the notorious 'breathing space', because, after all, the executioner also happens to need a certain 'breathing space' to strengthen the gallows and pull tight the rope.

Let the peace be signed. The war with imperialism continues, and woe betide those who are able calmly to doze off with a noose about their neck: those who slumber at such moments are fated not to wake up.

E. Preobrazhensky

No. 23

'The Great Apostle of Socialism (In Memory of Karl Marx.
Born 4 April, 1818, Died 14 March, 1888)'[1]

5 May (22 April) 1918

Today marks exactly one hundred years since the birth of the greatest leader of the worldwide proletariat and one of the most ingenious people in all of human history, Karl Marx. This name is sacred for every worker who knows what this man did for the proletariat and for the future. The working class of Russia is fortunate in having the opportunity to honour its great teacher at a moment when it is in power, when the goal for which Karl Marx lived and struggled is within reach of the proletariat, when the expropriation of the expropriators has already been carried out on the territory of Russia, and when we are able for the first time, on behalf of the whole proletarian government, to recognise the achievements of a great communist and to erect a majestic monument to him.

It is impossible, in few words, to cover all of the significance of the works of Karl Marx for the worldwide workers' movement. I must emphasise only what is most central and fundamental.

Karl Marx was not only the greatest tactician – that is, practical leader – of the workers' movement, but also, above all, an ingenious theorist and ideologist of the working class.

What does a theorist of the working class mean?

It refers to a person who studies the condition of the working class, studies the society in which the working class develops, studies the laws of development of human society in general, and thereby makes it possible for the working class to understand itself, to find its place among the other classes of society, to establish its goals and objectives and to struggle for their realisation with the least expenditure of forces, with the fewest blunders and the fewest losses. A theorist is like a person with a lantern who illuminates the path for the working class, warns of defeats when they are inevitable, and helps the working class to gain victories and take advantage of all their consequences.

As early as the *Communist Manifesto*, which was published seventy years ago, Karl Marx and his friend Friedrich Engels proclaimed the most fundamental points of their doctrine, the doctrine of scientific communism. Throughout the rest of their lives, they further developed and supplemented what was said in

---

1. [From *Ural'skii rabochii*, 5 May (22 April) 1918. The dates given in the title are not correct. Marx was born on 5 May 1818, and died on 4 March 1883.]

this brilliant work. In the *Communist Manifesto* every worker finds the symbol of his faith; it is a catechism, and it is the monumental book of the struggle of the proletariat.

Before Marx and before the publication of the *Communist Manifesto*, the ideas of socialism were, to a certain extent, in circulation, but what kind of socialism was it?

The best variant of this socialism was the utopian socialism of the Frenchmen, Fourier and Saint-Simon. These people proved all the advantages of socialism over capitalism, but their plans for implementation were pathetic and naïve. They thought they could convince the bourgeoisie to implement socialism because it is beneficial for the whole of mankind, but in response they met with complete indifference or mocking disdain. This was a bourgeois-nobleman's socialism that served only as a form of useless chatter after a copious dinner. Finally, there was also worker-socialism, which distinguished itself from the socialist chit-chat of the bourgeoisie by adopting the name of communism. Workers such as Weitling arrived independently at the idea of the necessity of socialism for the workers, but they dragged religion into socialism and could not break out onto the true pathway and abandon these infantile thoughts.

This kind of socialism did very little to help the working class to understand itself and forced it to pin all its hopes on the priests or the bourgeoisie, that is, on its class-enemies.

The *Communist Manifesto* demonstrated with the utmost clarity that socialism is not a contrivance of bourgeois daydreaming in the excessive heat, not a nebulous Christian outburst in the spirit of equality for the workers, not the dream of an astute academic, but a vital necessity for the working class, its class-goal, its fundamental task, which must be realised in order to emancipate the proletariat from the power of capital.

Moreover, the *Manifesto* proved that socialism is necessary for the emancipation not only of the working class, but also of the whole society, as a higher social order, and that this order is both necessary and inevitable if humanity is to have any prospect of advancing. It is inevitable because capital, in flourishing, prepares its own destruction. Every additional worker who comes to the factory from the ranks of the independent handicraftsmen, and every ruined peasant, means an extra spade to dig the grave for the entire bourgeois system.

Karl Marx not only proved the necessity and the inevitability of communism for the working class and the whole of mankind, but also outlined the way more clearly. He proclaimed the struggle for power as the immediate goal of the proletarian struggle, the struggle for the dictatorship of the proletariat, because only after conquering power can the proletariat suppress all sorts of counter-revolutionary attempts by the propertied classes to retrieve their lost supremacy; and only by possessing power will it achieve the elimination of classes and the transformation of former exploiters into rank-and-file members of a working socialist society.

With astounding insight, Karl Marx further proved that communism in one country cannot triumph, that a worldwide association of the proletariat is necessary (an International), and that a proletarian revolution is necessary in all the advanced countries of the world. It was precisely the *Communist Manifesto*, and precisely Karl Marx, who for the first time issued the summons to all the world's workers: 'Proletarians of all countries, unite!'

The reader might pause and say: 'Everything you have said about communism and the paths to it are things we have already known for a long time – there is nothing new here for us'.

I know that is true. But my task, comrades, is precisely to show how it is that you know all of this and who taught it to you.

Our great teacher, Karl Marx, has taught you to understand what socialism is and to fight for it. We live by his intellectual capital, his knowledge, his genius, and his talents as a great strategist of the class-struggle. Do not forget, comrades, that long before we implemented the dictatorship of the proletariat it took form seventy years [ago] in the brilliant mind of our teacher, and it is only thanks to this fact that we have gone firmly and confidently towards our goal, not stopping midway and not allowing ourselves to be confused by capital's collaborators.

Following the *Communist Manifesto*, the most remarkable work by Karl Marx came in his articles written for a democratic American newspaper and collected into a booklet with the title *The Eighteenth Brumaire of Louis Bonaparte*. In this booklet, Karl Marx not only reveals all the reasons for the defeat of the French Revolution in 1848, but also provides a model of how a worker must understand the most complex manifestations of class-struggle, how he must conduct himself in revolutions in order not to be made a fool by the bourgeoisie. The worker who reads and masters this brochure will never fall for bourgeois deception at a time of revolution.

In 1859, Marx published *A Contribution to the Critique of Political Economy*. This work is remarkable in two respects. In summary terms, the introduction provides the foundation for a new philosophy of history, the so-called theory of the materialist interpretation of history. Simply stated, it gives an understanding of the whole of human history from the proletarian point of view, from the point of view of the class that produces value, that knows the value of labour, knows how to cherish its results and is able to understand why the class-struggle constitutes the main content of history and why its goal is the struggle for power – for power and for the greatest possible share of the national income.

By means of this history, Karl Marx put into the hands of the working class a powerful weapon of struggle against bourgeois deception, against the opium of religion and other means with which the propertied classes plundered the toiling masses and imposed recognition of their robbery as legal and necessary. Now the worker knows full well that all kinds of matters, such as rights, justice, religion, morality, and so on, must first be reduced to their essence, to whose interest – which class-interest – they conceal, whose pocket they serve, and then decide how to treat them.

This work is also remarkable because in it Karl Marx gives a complete basis for the so-called labour-theory of value. Contrary to bourgeois economists from the camp of capital's ideological lackeys, he proves with ingenious simplicity and clarity that the value of every product is determined by the amount of labour-time required for its production. Yet, from this seemingly simple and 'peaceful' thought, he draws the inescapable revolutionary conclusion that the creator of values, the worker, has a right to the full product of his labour, that profit, rent, and such like, are only different kinds of robbery of the working class by the parasitical propertied classes.

In his *Capital*, which is Karl Marx's main work and which he did not live long enough to complete, he gives an amazingly precise, clear, strictly mathematical and scientific analysis of the entire capitalist economy as a whole. Capitalist society, in its grandest and most complicated form as well as in its developing mechanism-organism, is disassembled into small pieces, and all of its astonishing structure is studied to the last detail. Every worker who reads and, most importantly, *understands and appreciates* the great work of Marx, will at once be able to see and understand the most complex and entangled phenomena of economic life and will, above all, see with all clarity the conclusion to which Marx is led by his objective and sober study of capitalism. This conclusion is that capitalism is pregnant with socialism from its very beginnings and *nothing* can stop the birth-process of a new society. The process can only be delayed or accelerated.

Karl Marx attempted throughout his entire life to promote such acceleration. He stood at the head of the communist movement of all the countries of the world. He was the founder and leader of the First International, which arose in 1866,[2] and he headed it until its disintegration. He tried to lead the workers' movement in all countries and to warn it in advance of mistakes by way of letters, articles, and personal communication with the leaders of socialism. Karl Marx was a revolutionary to the core, a proletarian by virtue of his miserable half-starved life, and he passionately hated capital. He spitefully and maliciously mocked any deviations by the socialists of his time from the path of revolutionary struggle onto the path of moderation and reconciliation with the bourgeois classes. He stigmatised all the future Scheidemanns in German Social Democracy

---

2. [The First International was founded in 1864 in London, but held its first congress in Geneva in 1866.]

and the Hendersons in the English labour-movement. The quick instinct of a revolutionary never betrayed him. He has given us great models of how the passion of a revolutionary must be combined with the cold calculation of a politician and a skilful fighter.

The genius of Karl Marx, as leader of the proletariat, also became apparent, among other things, in the fact that he thoroughly studied, with profound and undivided attention, every step of the workers' movement and tried to draw lessons from the experience of individual proletarian detachments in separate countries for the sake of the most successful struggle of the entire working class. Thus he was the first to see, with brilliant insight, the Paris Commune of 1871 as the embryo of a new proletarian government, and on the basis of this experience he was able to portray the general features of the state of the future. Studying the Commune, Karl Marx in his conclusions predicted the appearance of our soviets as organs of the dictatorship of the proletariat.

The great apostle of communism did not live to see his life's goal accomplished, to see the socialist revolution, even though his revolutionary passion compelled him to count too much upon a revolution even during his own lifetime. We are more fortunate than our teacher. His ideals are already being implemented in our century in Russia.

Let us honour the great teacher, comrades, not only by erecting the first monument in the world to the fighter for proletarian power, not only by studying his great works, in which the spirit and brain of the proletariat have merged, but also by not breaking or allowing the greatest monument to our teacher to be broken – the monument that we have already erected in our own land to the creator of *Capital* and the author of *The Communist Manifesto*. Comrades! Protect Soviet power, because in this power the mighty spirit of Karl Marx is embodied, because there cannot be any better monument to him than the dictatorship of the worker and the expropriation of the expropriators.

E. Preobrazhensky

No. 24
The Article 'A Congress is Necessary', Published in the Journal *Kommunist*[1]

June 1918

The lively debates at the recently-concluded Urals Regional Conference of our Party[2] – which was distinguished by a large multitude of people (78 out of more than ninety organisations in the region, with a total of thirty-six thousand members, were represented by 136 delegates) – involved a discussion of the general policies of our Soviet centres and of economic policy in particular, which is the same thing as the policies of the Central Committee of the Party.

Here is the resolution that was accepted by everyone at the Conference with nine abstentions:

> The Fourth Urals Regional Conference of the Communist Party, having discussed the question of the direction of the general policies of the central Soviet authority in recent times and, in particular, the question of the relationship of this authority with the local regional authority, notes that:
> 1) the international, domestic and financial-economic policies of the central Soviet authority are clearly aimed at putting into effect the major points of the Brest agreement, whose implementation is gradually

---

1. [From *Kommunist* (organ of the group of Left-Communists) Moscow, June 1918, No. 4, pp. 13–14.]
2. [The Conference met from 25–9 April 1918 in Ekaterinburg.]

transforming the soviets into agents of the will of world-capital, leading to suspension of socialist construction and liquidation of a number of the most important achievements of the October Revolution;

2) the agreement with the cooperatives, annulling the entire programme of economic and political struggle against the rural bourgeoisie, who have rallied around these organisations; the replacement of workers' control by technical and commercial soviets; the attempted bureaucratic construction of socialism from the top-down at the hands of officialdom, together with rejection of mass-proletarian creativity from the bottom-up; the declaration of immunity for the capital and enterprises of foreigners, and for Russian capitalists who have sold off their banks and enterprises to foreigners, and so on – all these measures and a whole series of others most directly affect the Urals as an area with large investments of foreign capital before the Revolution, as a region that serves, by virtue of its natural resources, as the strongest bait for world-capital and, finally, as the region that is most organised and advanced in the work of socialist construction;

3) with regard to the Urals, the domestic policy of the central authority is characterised by disregard of the local Soviet authority in the region and distrust towards it, expressed in the dispatch of the centre's own commissars, with extraordinary powers, who are bringing chaos and disorganisation into the existing organisational structure of the Urals and, at best, are absolutely useless.

Noting all of the foregoing, the Conference resolves:

1) To bring to the attention of the Party's Central Committee and the Party as a whole the attitude of the organised Urals proletariat, as represented at the Conference, concerning the evident bias in the policies of the central authority, which are at odds with the Party's new programme and with the economic resolutions of the Party's Sixth Congress.

2) To propose to the Central Committee the speediest possible convening of an all-Russian party-congress on the basis of representation at the Sixth Congress, and to have it discuss all the questions that were first put on the agenda after the Seventh Party-Congress, with regard to which it is possible and probable that the policies of the Central Committee are at odds with the opinion of the party-majority.

3) To charge the Party's Regional Committee and the Bolshevik fraction of the Regional Council of Commissars with developing a draft-constitution for the Urals workers' commune that takes into account the economic and everyday characteristics of the region, and to have them submit this draft to the next congress of Urals soviets for implementation on

the basis of the constitution of the Federated Soviet Republic that was accepted at the Third All-Russian Congress of Soviets.

4) To endorse the policies of the Bolshevik fraction of the Regional Council of Commissars and to charge it with continuing its current and future work in a spirit of faithfulness to the party-programme and to the fundamental tasks of consistent socialist construction of the economic life of the territory.

I am not going to deal with all of the points in the present resolution, but I do want to discuss one of them concerning the demand for the prompt convocation of a broad party-congress.

I think that even those comrades who remain extremely pleased with the results of the Party's Seventh Congress[3] on the question of ratifying the peace-agreement will hardly consider this Congress to be particularly authoritative in terms either of the number of members represented or the number of delegates who attended. The Extraordinary Congress, which convened on the basis of a completely unanticipated standard of representation, with only some 35 deputies, could not even discuss the new draft-programme; moreover, after the Congress, the course of events raised the kind of tactical questions that the Central Committee of the Party cannot be recognised as having the authority to decide. Comrade Lenin long ago pointed out that the difference between a programme and tactics is not one of principle, but more of degree. And we have been dealing recently with exactly the kind of tactical error by the Central Committee, at least in questions concerning the economic construction of the country, that implies cancellation of our programme. Every person who is the least bit familiar with party-matters will agree that a programme of state-capitalism, imposed upon the dictatorship of the proletariat from above by 'the really-left' communists, and the retrospective formulation of state-capitalism as an inevitable stage of development for Russia – all of these are by no means questions of a tactical nature. Furthermore, the new course was not planned by the Congress, and apparently the Party will soon have to resolve the question of how far the dictatorship of particular individuals can extend from the railways and other branches of the economy into the Russian Communist Party.

I must note that the point about the immediate convocation of a congress was adopted at the last Urals Conference *unanimously*.

---

3. [The Seventh Congress of the RKP(B) took place from 6–8 March 1918, in Petrograd. The Congress adopted a resolution 'On War and Peace' that included the following comment on the Brest treaty: 'The Congress recognises the need to ratify the onerous peace-agreement with Germany that has been signed by the Soviet power in view our lack of an army, in view of the extremely unhealthy state of our demoralised units at the front, and in view of the need to use any breathing space, even the most brief, in advance of imperialism's coming attack on the Soviet Socialist Republic' (KPSS 1983, p. 26. An addendum to the resolution specified that it not be published (KPSS 1983, p. 27).

In his polemical feuilletons directed against the position of the Left-Communists – which contain some very grand discoveries or, to put it more precisely, inventions about state-capitalism in Soviet Russia – comrade Lenin refers to the publishers of *Kommunist*[4] as a tiny group. The publishers may be a tiny group, but the number of party-organisations that share the viewpoint of *Kommunist* currently represents an imposing magnitude. The majority of Urals organisations generally take the position of *Kommunist*. The proof of this can be seen not only in the resolution quoted above, but also in the resolution concerning international policy and the country's tasks in economic reconstruction. All three resolutions were adopted with absolutely no reference to the theses in the first issue of *Kommunist*, and even before they became known in the Urals.

In particular, the economic resolution is not a product of theorising, but instead results from practical experience in the matter of socialist reconstruction in the Urals. The Urals organisations will not repudiate their resolutions, whose validity is confirmed by life itself. And a congress becomes urgently necessary because of the sharp disagreement of an entire region with the party-centre – along with the fact that a number of organisations elsewhere in Russia share the platform of the Left-Communists – which gives grounds to think that the policy of the Party's Central Committee and its fractional membership, if one may use the term, absolutely does not correspond to the alignment of forces between tendencies in the Party.

But the Congress has to be inclusive, so that the entire Party will be fully represented and all of the questions subject to its decision can be thoroughly debated in the localities.

Appendix: Resolution of the Fourth Urals Regional Conference of the Communist Party Concerning Economic Reconstruction and the Party's Tasks[5]

9 May 1918

In terms of industry, the condition of the productive forces of the country is characterised at the present moment by the deterioration or complete absence of the

---

4. [The journal *Kommunist* was the organ of the Moscow *oblast*-bureau of the RKP(B). It reflected the viewpoint of Left-Communists and was published after March 1918, first as a newspaper and then as 'a daily journal of economics, politics, and social life'. The editorial collective consisted of N. Bukharin, V. Obolensky (Osinsky), K. Radek and V. Smirnov.

5. [From *Ural'skii rabochii*, 9 May 1918. It seems most probable that E.A. Preobrazhensky was the author of this resolution, since he was customarily author of the resolutions adopted at congresses or conferences that he attended as a delegate.]

most necessary machines and other instruments of production, by the absence or shortage of raw materials (coal, cotton, and so on), by insufficient means of consumption, which are prerequisites for the utilisation of labour-power, and by the unprecedented breakdown of transport, together with the availability within the country of a quantity of labour-power that is completely adequate for the normal functioning of the entire industrial organism.

In agriculture, many of the necessary machines and tools are missing, along with a reduction in numbers of the horned working livestock that is connected with the War, with the elimination or destruction of a number of intensively cultivated estates and, in a number of localities, with crop-failure and famine in these years. The necessary supplies of seeds for the 1918 agricultural season are lacking, at the same time as the rural bourgeoisie has in its hands the required quantity of seeds for sowing and they are available either locally or in nearby provinces. At the same time, the abundance of labour-power in agriculture, which in the previous years of warfare suffered from a shortage of hands, can now serve to alleviate the crisis.

In the sphere of exchange, the transition-period from capitalism to socialism is characterised by the restriction of private trade, by the widespread development of the direct exchange of commodities, which has a non-systematic and disorganised character, and by the gradual withering away of money-circulation. This period is marked by the paralysis and breaking down of the capitalist means of accounting for production and consumption, however imperfect they may be, at the same time as other methods, characteristic of the socialist system, are missing.

By and large, the transition period that we are experiencing from capitalism to socialism is characterised by the extreme collapse of the productive forces, by the lack of correspondence between production and consumption, and by the continuation of all of the disadvantages resulting from a socialist reconstruction that has only just begun.

The task of reconstructing society on new socialist principles, and of raising the productive forces, has to be accomplished in the context of the unfinished war with the Ukrainian bourgeoisie and German imperialism, and under the threat of a new war in conditions where the socialist republics of Russia are encircled by a ring of world-capital that is greedily striving to intervene in the economic life of the country and to transform Russia into a place for the investment of German capital's surpluses.

Under such conditions, there are only two objectively possible ways of raising the country's productive forces: one way is by admitting foreign capital into the country, allowing its organised intrusion into the country's economic life, subordinating to it our entire industry and agriculture, restoring the capitalist régime and gradually liquidating all the socialist reforms that have begun.

The second way is the development of the productive forces of the city and village and the reconstruction of industry by socialist Russia's own forces, using the foreign market only for purchasing, in the form of commodities, the instruments of production most indispensable to us, with the complete exclusion of foreign capital from the role of organiser of production, together with the final liquidation of bourgeois property in the instruments of production within Russia and the completion of the entire socialist reconstruction of our economy. There cannot be any middle-way between these two methods of economic reconstruction of the country; they are the only ones possible and, at the same time, they are mutually exclusive.

In full accord with the economic resolutions of the Sixth Party-Congress, with the party-programme, and with the entire spirit of Soviet economic policy before the recent twist towards conciliation with capital, the Regional Conference considers the only path possible for a proletarian communist party to be the economic reconstruction of the country based on steadfast, resolute and consistent construction of a socialist economy.

We presuppose that the essence of transition from an unorganised and state-capitalist economy to a communist one is expressed by the fact that the role of compulsory organisation of production and distribution, based on class-contradictions between labour and capital, is replaced by the conscious social organisation of all the forces and means of the national economy.

Whereas in capitalist society the centre of gravity was and is the subordination of social needs to the class-interests of capital and direct management by producers,[6] in the communist system, which is being organised, this centre of gravity must be social organisation and social regulation of production.

The Conference believes that the task of the present moment is the organisation of the entire social production and consumption under the direct control and leadership of workers' production-unions and of the corresponding economic associations of the peasant-poor, together with the merger of all branches of economic activity in the organs of the Soviet state (the economic departments of soviets and the soviets of national economy).

This organisation must include a fully specified policy of state-trustification of the major branches of industry and the establishment of their influence over the small and backward branches, along with the concentration of different types of production in specific economic areas set out in a comprehensive state-plan for the organisation of the productive forces.

Contrary to amalgamation of separate branches of industry based on capitalist rule, the socialist policy of trustification must be based on the conscious and

---

6. [In this context, the meaning of 'the producers' is apparently 'the owners' of individual enterprises.]

organised association of the producers for the purpose of the most expedient utilisation of all the forces and means of production,[7] which can only succeed in the specific circumstances of a resolute and consistent implementation of workers' control by workers' production-unions at every level of the organisation of production.

In the sphere of agriculture, the social organisation of production by the poorest peasantry must proceed by way of the development of communist land-tenure.

This development presupposes widespread use of large-scale agricultural techniques and takes complete nationalisation (socialisation) of agricultural production as its ultimate goal.

The planned organisation of social production as a whole is impossible apart from a proper organisation of appropriate product-exchange between industry and agriculture. The vitality of the new form of social production depends most directly upon the possibility of raising the productivity of social labour to a level higher than that established by the rule of capitalist oppression, and, from this point of view, the tariff-policy of the trade-unions leads to the development of labour-discipline among workers and must be based on the setting of precise norms of production with assistance from the organs of workers' control.

The currently existing free exchange of products serves to impede the proper organisation of product-exchange between city and village, while facilitating the process of primitive accumulation and, above all, the enrichment of the rural bourgeoisie.

From this follows the need to bring the exchange of products into an organised channel – exclusively through state-supply organs. If this exchange could not be established until now, one of the most important reasons has been the economic disorganisation of semi-proletarian strata of the village and the far-from-completed process of expropriating the rural bourgeoisie.

The gradual organisation of orderly product-exchange must inevitably lead to the displacement of monetary means of circulation. In the final analysis, all the products exchanged between private craftsmen must be merged with the social organisation of distribution.

The first step in this direction will be the organisation of consumer-communes, with mandatory registration of all consumers as members.

The worker-peasant Revolution in Russia has only just begun the inevitable and protracted process of expropriating the expropriators and has not yet affected the existence of a whole range of parasitical strata of the population

---

7. [There is an error in the text, which says 'of all the forces and means *by* production'.]

who are continuing to live by means of their accumulated assets and through speculation.

The effective system for undermining the existence of these parasitical strata and for bringing them into productive [labour] is the introduction of budgetary books for every person with an income in excess of the customary minimal standard of living.

The process of nationalising the banks must lead to a situation in which the entire monetary-trade turnover will be concentrated in these organs for state-distribution of monetary resources. The consequence of this must be the establishment of mandatory use of current-accounts in the banks by every person and institution involved in the circulation of money.

The establishment of mandatory use of current-accounts in branches of the state-bank and the introduction of budget-books require decentralisation of banking activities to the localities under direct control by the economic organs of the soviets.

In view of the fact that the socialist economy of Russia, surrounded by capitalist states, cannot exist as a self-sufficient[8] economic organism, between it and the latter there must develop exchange-relations that are inherently antagonistic and cannot possibly exist over the long term; only the complete nationalisation of foreign trade with the fullest possible nationalisation of production and exchange can temporarily guarantee that these relations will not lead to the disintegration of the socialist form of economy. Moreover, it must be emphasised that these very relations carry in themselves the embryo of that sort of disintegration, and the way out of this blind alley can only be an international communist revolution as a near-term prospect.

The threat of intensifying capitalist influence over the national economy of Russia prohibits any possibility of the socialist state cooperating with Russian or foreign capital in the sphere of organising production. At the same time, this organisation of production on a state-scale can only be accomplished by way of conscious organisation of the productive classes of the population, the establishment of iron labour-discipline in their ranks, and in no circumstances by way of artificially restoring the bourgeois-bureaucratic oligarchy.

Outlining the foregoing programme of economic policy, the Urals Regional Conference of the RKP believes that only its resolute and consistent implementation will correspond to the class-interests of the Russian and international proletariat and to the tasks of the international communist revolution, which is developing due to the natural course of events in all the countries dominated

---

8. [There is a typographical error in the text, which uses the word 'самоподавляющего' when it should say 'самодовлеющего'.]

by capitalism. Regardless of whatever ordeals may be in store for the Russian Revolution in the immediate future, only the consistent development of every aspect of class-self-determination and self-organisation at any given moment will be able to guarantee and accelerate the final victory of the workers' movement. The resolution is passed unanimously with two abstentions.[9]

---

9. [In the introduction to this resolution, Preobrazhensky mentioned nine abstentions, not two.]

Nos. 25–6
Articles on 'The Urals Counter-Revolution', Published in the Newspaper *Pravda*

29 (16)–30 (17) June 1918

No. 25

'The Urals Counter-Revolution'[1]

29 (16) June 1918

I

At the call of the regional military commissariat, the workers of the Urals factories sent their best forces to the front against the Czechoslovaks. When almost the entire local organisation of Communists, numbering three hundred persons, had left Nev'yansk factory under arms, the automobile-company [motorised company], which had evacuated to the factory from Luga and had always opposed the local soviet, began a counter-revolutionary uprising.[2] This company, consisting

---

1. [From *Pravda*, 29 (16) June 1918. This article continues in the next document.]
2. [The Nev'yansk uprising, or the uprising of the 'automobilists' as it was called, began on 12 June 1918. By 17 June, the insurgents had already been driven out of the city. The event occurred during the struggle of the Red Guards against the revolt by the Czechoslovak corps. In the spring of 1918, a mobilised detachment of two hundred and fifty men from the Petrograd area was in Nev'yansk and became the nucleus of the insurgency. The detachment was under the command of the former captain A. Eliseenko, a member of the S-R Party. The rebels took action under the slogans: 'All power to the Constituent Assembly!' and 'Power to the people, without the Bolshevik tyrants and traitors!'. The Nev'yansk uprising triggered a number of other anti-Bolshevik movements in the Urals.]

of various White-Guard elements, was to oversee repairs of motorised equipment, but, in fact, all of the equipment was used against the Soviet authority, including two armoured vehicles intended for the struggle against the Czechoslovaks. The revolt was led by one Eliseenko, who billed himself as an anarchist. Moreover, at the head of the movement there was a military staff that included, besides Eliseenko, the officer-Cadets: Melent'ev, Frolov, Miller (a pharmacist by profession), Khionin (a photographer), as well as the student Brodovsky, nephew of a millionaire, the Right S-R Vorob'ev, and the leader of the local Mensheviks, Bakhtin.

The insurrectionists arrested the local soviet, the commissars and those Bolsheviks who had not gone off to the front, numbering 22 people, and locked them in a detention-facility. During the arrest of the commission of inquiry, the chairman of the commission and his comrade were killed. A meeting was held of frontline-soldiers, and the former officers and soldiers from the kulaks joined the White Guards. At the meeting, one of the motorists, a sailor-White Guardsman, argued that after the overthrow of the Soviet power, things must be arranged so that the country would be ruled by a single person with fitting experience. Even though they were intimidated, a mass of residents at the meeting spoke out against shooting those arrested and for investigation of the affair by a commission of inquiry. It needs to be said that the counter-revolutionaries, who had interrupted communication with Ekaterinburg, assured the masses that Ekaterinburg had been taken and that all the commissars had scattered after plundering state-funds. They said Soviet authority had collapsed everywhere, and they insisted on executing the prisoners.

The Nev'yansk White Guards were surrounded by detachments sent almost simultaneously from Ekaterinburg and Perm, and with the support of armed workers from Kushva, Tagil and elsewhere. Soon the arrested comrades heard the crackle of machine-guns approaching closer-and-closer to the factory. The most horrific hours had come for the prisoners. One of those arrested, comrade Kaskovich,[3] had already been shot on the evening of 12–13 June. The rest were awaiting execution at the same time, but a decision by the meeting had saved their lives. Now the moment was approaching for the retreating White Guards to retaliate against the prisoners. The accursed murderers began shooting our comrades through the cell-windows and then hurled hand-grenades at them. When most of the comrades were scattered about the floor in pools of blood, with arms and legs torn off and dislocated entrails, a cry rang out, 'Whoever is alive, get up!' The survivors began to get up, the wounded began to moan, and the comrades thought the Red-Army men had arrived. But it was a base deception by the

---

3. [There is an error here. The correct name is S.F. Kos'kovich.]

executioners. Seeing that some of the prisoners were still alive, the White Guards again began to throw grenades into the cell to finish off the others.

Soon, however, our advancing forces compelled the White Guards to retreat from the prison, and the Red-Army men began to open the doors. The survivors and three individuals who were not wounded were about to defend themselves with bottles, thinking that the White Guards were again deceiving them, but this time there was no deception. When it became clear that comrades had come to free them, the wounded also began to stir. Some begged to be shot, since they did not have the strength to bear the torment any longer, while others asked to be bandaged. The three survivors grabbed rifles and, together with the newly arrived Red-Army men, rushed after the retreating executioners.

This is what I was told by a comrade from Nev'yansk, in the most concise and frank words, while *en route* to Moscow. He was one of the three who survived, one of those whose entrails were somehow miraculously not blown apart and whose arms were not severed by the grenades of White Guards.

In the Krasnoufimsk district, according to information obtained in Ekaterinburg, the counter-revolutionaries dispersed the soviets and resorted to other means of struggle for the Constituent Assembly. Our comrades there were buried alive, their ears, noses, and so on were cut off, and the children and wives of the poor peasants, who had defeated the kulaks, were murdered.

Many conclusions can be drawn from these facts. I want to stress only one circumstance.

Let the proletariat of Russia know that White Guards in the Urals eviscerated conscious workers and ripped off their legs, and that their leaders, along with the Cadets and the Black Hundreds, included one Menshevik and one Right S-R.

Let them know that the Constituent Assembly of the Skoropadskys and Chernovs is trying to build the foundation of its power on representatives of the village-poor who were buried alive, on the severed ears and noses of peasants, on the detached legs and arms of children and wives, and on the ashes of their wretched homes.

E. Preobrazhensky

No. 26

'The Urals Counter-Revolution'[1]

30 (17) June 1918

II

In the previous article, I spoke of one the strongest manifestations of counter-revolution in the Urals – the Nev'yansk uprising. Now I shall deal with other counter-revolutionary outbursts and then clarify the social basis on which the counter-revolution in the Urals relied and which it may rely on in future in its futile attempts to depose Soviet authority.

According to the reckoning of the conspirators, an uprising was to have occurred in Ekaterinburg itself, being led by the union of frontline-soldiers from the Verkh-Isetsk factory, simultaneously with the Nev'yansk action. (The factory is located within two *versts* of the city.)

The union of frontline-soldiers, earnestly supported by kulak-elements of the factory and with a former ensign, an avid defender of the Constituent Assembly, as its chairman, demanded that the military commissariat issue weapons to the union's members so that they, the old soldiers, could 'defeat the Czechoslovaks in a single day'. The demand was rejected, and it was suggested that anyone wishing to fight the Czechoslovaks should join the ranks of the Red Army on normal terms. The union refused, and at two successive meetings that it organised on 11 and 12 June at Verkh-Isetsk square, bringing together all the rural and urban counter-revolutionary elements, it waged agitation under the slogan 'Down with the soviet, it is not giving out weapons to fight the Czechoslovaks'. This slogan was a vile deception of the masses, whom the conspirators had not yet decided to call upon in support of the Czechoslovak uprising. This deception was exposed in documents a few days later when the chairman of the union of frontline-soldiers, the ensign who had eluded pursuit by our comrades, threw a note into the window of his apartment saying: 'Leaving Ekaterinburg, hope to be back soon with the Czechoslovaks'.

To obtain weapons, depose the soviet and join the Czechoslovaks – this was the real plan of the conspirators. When they failed to obtain weapons, the conspirators decided to plunder the armoury of the first railway-district. Meanwhile, Black-Hundred elements from the railwaymen and deputies of the Mounted Hundreds of Red-Army men attended the meeting and promised support,

---

1. [From *Pravda*, 30 (17) June 1918.]

whereupon they were quickly disarmed (the Hundreds consisted for the most part of hooligans and shady elements, and it had been planned to disarm them much sooner).

The first meeting dispersed of its own accord, and the armed forces that were sent to disperse and arrest the conspirators were late in showing up. The next day a meeting began, but the conspirators scattered with the approach of our forces. Only a small number of them were arrested, and one, who intended to throw a hand-grenade into our detachment, was shot immediately on the spot. At other places and on other occasions, several dozen conspirators were arrested, most of them armed.

Thus the attempt to organise an uprising in Ekaterinburg resulted in complete failure for the conspirators, although with very few losses on their part.

Here, it is necessary to mention and impress upon all the toiling masses of Russia that at the counter-revolutionary meeting in Verkh-Isetsk, the resolution demanding dispersal of the soviet was passed at the suggestion of a person who spoke on behalf of the Federation of Anarchists. It is true that the anarchist group later (and *later* is the point) repudiated this person in print, but this dissociation is not worth much. Prior to the Czechoslovak action, the anarchists joined with all the Black Hundreds in their speeches against Soviet power, and it comes as no surprise that all the shopkeepers, former gendarmes and White Guardsmen at the meeting raised their hands enthusiastically in support of the resolution proposed on behalf of the anarchist group. It is important for the counter-revolutionaries to implement the slogan 'Down with Soviet power' with the anarchists as allies, and as for what comes next, that is something only they know.

It is also interesting that at one secret night-time meeting of the conspirators in a forest, where, as luck would have it, one of our comrades was a silent observer, the question of who must take power after dispersing the soviets led to a typical argument between the conspirators that nearly resulted in hand-to-hand struggle. Some took the position that power [must be] transferred to the Constituent Assembly. Others were fiercely opposed, insisting that things would be even worse under the Constituent Assembly and that it would be better simply to remain without any authority (these people comprised a bloc of the criminal element and muddle-headed workers under the influence of anarchists). A third group said that there is no point in arguing now over who must take power – 'that will become obvious later' – the important thing now is to depose the current authority. This 'third group' are the real Black Hundreds and leaders of the counter-revolution who, for the moment, are keeping quiet about the monarchy. In essence, the meeting turned out exactly according to their recipe: it came to no decision on what must happen the day after the upheaval, and at the same time it remained committed to overthrowing Soviet power.

In addition to Nev'yansk, the soviets were dispersed in Verkh-Neivinsk and also in Polevsk factory, where a gang of frontline soldiers even dug trenches at the approach of Soviet forces. The insurgents were defeated within a few hours and many were arrested. There were also attempts to overthrow the soviets in other factories where the best workers' forces had left for the front and where previously organised groups of counter-revolutionaries remained behind.

At the present moment, when serious attention is being directed to our rear in the Urals, when dozens of agitators are being dispatched with literature from our Party and the purely military forces are being reinforced, one can hardly expect serious counter-revolutionary outbreaks. Where such outbreaks have occurred and been suppressed, the atmosphere cleared immediately and the worker masses clearly dissociated themselves from the bourgeois-kulak elements.

E. Preobrazhensky

Nos. 27–36
Articles and a Report, Published in the Newspaper *Ural'skii rabochii* in August–December 1918

13 August–8 December 1918

No. 27

'Tedious Work'[1]

13 August 1918

At a time when Soviet armies are straining every effort in order to return its capital to the Urals proletariat, when many of the workers and peasants who claim allegiance to the Party of Left S-Rs are simply and unpretentiously spilling their blood at the front in the struggle against the Czechoslovaks[2] and White Guards, the Perm *'litterateurs'* of that party, with a boyish zeal typical of political infants, are attacking the Communist Party with the kind of desperation that hitherto was seen only in the White-Guard press.

The leading article for 9 August in the Left S-R newspaper *Krest'yanin i rabochii*, published by the Motovilikha organisation of that party, can serve as a model of that sort of literature. In this article, where lies are blended with stupidity in one colourful pattern,

---

1. [From *Ural'skii rabochii*, 13 August 1918.]
2. [The Czechoslovak Legion was formed in Russia from prisoners taken from the Austro-Hungarian army – Czechs and Slovaks – during the First World-War to take part in the war against Germany. The uprising spread across the Volga region, the Urals and Siberia during May-August 1918. Ekaterinburg was taken on 25 July.]

every White Guard and Right-S-R will find for himself many fond ideas and arguments against Communists that he first made up as long ago as when the Kerensky ministry was baiting the Bolsheviks. It is tedious and difficult to respond to such articles, but it is necessary to do so at least for the sake of those Left S-R workers and peasants who are honestly fulfilling their duty by defending Soviet power with weapons in hand. The Motovilikha *litterateurs* of the Left S-Rs are evidently unable to understand that, by defending the position of the Central Committee of their Party, they are undermining the political meaning of the struggle by their own comrades at the front. Their comrades, who are also our comrades, are saying just one thing with their struggle: the Czechoslovak uprising is an attempt to draw Russia into imperialist war under the command of the Dutovs and must be crushed. Yet with their Moscow adventure, the Central Committee of the Left S-Rs were politically seeking the same thing as the Right S-Rs; namely, war with Germany, the kind of war that, occurring simultaneously with the current war against the Allies, implies smothering Soviet power from two directions. This is just the thing that the Savinkovs and Alekseevs want, and it is what the supporters of the Left S-R Central Committee are in fact striving for. But the Left S-Rs who are fighting at the Czechoslovak front are opposing this through their deeds. The Motovilikha *litterateurs* of their Party are striving to nullify this truly revolutionary struggle with their penmanship. Nevertheless, the benefits of this struggle will not be wasted for the worldwide revolution, just as the exercises of the Motovilikha '*litterateurs*' are not wasted for the counter-revolution.

Let us understand, however, the stupidity and lies of the aforementioned article. We will begin with the lies. The author of the article assures his readers that the Soviet authority is accepting 'the restoration of foreign debts and thereby the obligation of paying redemptions abroad, for landlord holdings, of up to thirty billion roubles, imposing the kind of yoke upon the toiling village that could not be imposed even by the Tsar "liberator" Alexander II, who delivered the peasants from captivity into economic slavery, a new kind of captivity...'

The naïve lie of this assertion is clear to everyone who knows that of the entire sum of our foreign debts, Germany's portion accounts for less than one-tenth, and no Bolshevik has ever offered to pay the repudiated debts to the Allies. All talk of the thirty billion amounts to silly inventions intended for the uninformed reader who also does not know that the Left S-Rs in their time firmly resisted when the Bolsheviks passed laws for repudiation of the debts and nationalisation of the banks.

Let us look further. The Motovilikha *litterateur* declares that 'The government of Russia delivered up to Germany, for execution, the partisans who rebelled in the Ukraine'.

Just who was delivered up, and when? If you do not give specifics, it means this, too, is a lie.

Next comes a new accusation: 'The government of Russia sent to Germany specially selected, healthy and fully outfitted soldiers, issued to them a higher food-ration compared to the Russians, and provided them with money'.

The French and English imperialists were very disturbed, because the exchange of prisoners is providing Germany with new divisions for the Western Front. The 'internationalist' who wrote the leading article in the Motovilikha newspaper is also infected with this worry. But here is how matters stand in reality: we very much want to recover our prisoners from Germany and Austria and to send back the German and Austrian prisoners who are now playing an enormous revolutionary role there. But the governments of Austria and Germany are delaying the exchange in every possible way; they very much need Russian prisoners for labour in the rear, and they fear the return of their prisoners from Russia like the plague.

Another accusation: 'Manufacturing equipment is being relocated to Germany'.

When this unworthy and false invention was repeated more than once at meetings in Moscow by Spiridonova and others, the assertion was labelled as slander from the rostrum of the All-Russian Congress and in our press, and our comrades suggested to the slanderers that they call up before a tribunal those who charged them with the slander. The Left S-Rs in Moscow have kept silent about this, and so the stamp of slanderers will remain on their forehead, as well as on the foreheads of their Party's Motovilikha *litterateurs*.

With regard to the defamatory lies from Left S-R agitators, at the All-Russian Congress of Soviets[3] comrade Lenin exclaimed: Isn't the Brest peace-agreement bad enough in itself, without embellishing this burden further with lies like that? A day or two before the Moscow adventure[4] he said that a party that resorts to such methods of public lying is a hopeless party. The words turned out to be prophetic, and now we are observing all across Russia a picture of the final disintegration of this 'hopeless party', which has broken up into separate and totally disconnected groups.

Let us turn now from the lies to the stupidity. In the article we read that

> A year ago, when Kerensky's policies found the dead end of the Revolution, the actions of 3 July[5] revealed the policy of the authorities. We remember that afterwards the authorities staged an offensive – the authorities could no longer hide their face behind a veil of bitter politicking while they were carefully

---

3. [The reference is apparently to the Fourth Congress of Soviets.]
4. [The murder of the German ambassador Mirbach.]
5. [Anti-government demonstrations by soldiers and workers occurred on 3 (16) July 1917. The cause had to do with events in late June and early July – the unsuccessful offensive at the front and the dissolution of military units.]

and gradually preparing a trap for the toiling people. The murder of Mirbach is likewise an act aimed at revealing the true face of the authorities.

The Motovilikha *litterateur* of the Left S-Rs is quite the historian. For him, Kerensky's June offensive[6] comes after 3 July. However, that is a minor point. He tells us that the aim of the Mirbach murder was to reveal 'the true face of the authorities'.

If that is the case, then the undertaking was pointless, because Soviet power had long ago revealed its face in the struggle against capital; nevertheless, the face of some other people was certainly revealed in the Moscow action. From behind the pale-pink mask of a Left S-R there suddenly appear, without any rouge, the real faces of Avksent'ev and Chernov, who support the petty kulak in domestic politics and the Allies' cause in foreign policy.

In conclusion, a couple of words on the comparison of the current policy of the Soviet authorities with the policy of Kerensky. How many times do we have to explain to the Left S-R schoolchildren – whom we ourselves at one time dragged away from Kerensky by their ears, saving them from the shameful fate of the Savinkovs and Avksent'evs – that the foreign policy of one or another government must be judged according to which class is in power and which goals it pursues.

Kerensky waged imperialist war with the corresponding means, and Soviet power is defending the proletarian Revolution.

'But with what means?' asks the Left S-R.

Here is our answer: With such a great objective, any means that attain the goal are good enough, and one can only discuss them from the point of view of expediency.

It is boring to refute inventions that have long ago been disproven, and just as boring to prove truths that were proven long ago. But we Communists are not responsible for the fact that the pathetic bumpkins of a party that was sick in the head from the time of its birth still exist and are fiercely attacking us.

E. Preobrazhensky

---

6. [The Russian offensive of July 1917 involved armies on the South-Western Front attacking the German and Austrian armies and was undertaken at the insistence of the Allies. The enemy launched a counter-attack, and the Russian armies were defeated.]

No. 28

'Worldwide Bolshevism'[1]

11 October 1918

It seems that the month of October, at the initiative of Russian workers, is destined to become the month of proletarian victories and of the death of the bourgeois order. In October 1905, the autocratic structure was shaken for the first time under the onslaught of the workers. In 1917, the October Revolution disposed of bourgeois power in our country. Finally, in October 1918, we can already note the Bulgarian Revolution[2] and the uprising in Ukraine. The month of October has not ended yet, and according to the old-style [calendar] it only begins in two days, and already the initiative has been taken in expanding the Russian Revolution to Europe. One can hardly doubt that the Ukrainian uprising will end with the restoration of Soviet power in Ukraine[3] and that the revolt by the soldiers in Berlin[4] will carry over into Austria-Hungary.

We have already been informed of the unusually rapid growth of Bolshevism in Germany. The uprising by German soldiers in Ukraine and Germany will bring a quick and decisive response.

One of today's telegrams speaks of the horrifying (from the point of view of the bourgeoisie) growth of Bolshevism in Poland and of the enormous success of Bolshevism in Italy. We have also noted more than once that the overwhelming majority of Italian socialists share the [Bolshevik] position. In America, half a million workers, united in the Industrial Workers of the World,[5] sympathise with the Bolsheviks. Even in Japan, the ruling clique sees with horror how sympathies for the Bolsheviks are growing among the most backward masses of workers and how their determination to begin a struggle along Russian lines is gathering momentum.

The four-year criminal war has prepared inexhaustible reserves of explosive material among the popular masses of the entire world. And just as in Ukraine,

---

1. [From *Ural'skii rabochii*, 11 October 1918.]
2. [In Bulgaria, the soldiers' Vladaya Uprising declared the overthrow of Tsar Ferdinand and the creation of a republic. Ferdinand abdicated in favour of his son Boris and fled the country.]
3. [The reference is to the rebel-movement in Ukraine, directed against the occupying Austro-German armies, that began in late September 1918 under the leadership of the Central Military-Revolutionary Committee that was established by the First Congress of the Communist Party (B) of Ukraine.]
4. [The Berlin uprising by workers and soldiers came on 9 November 1918.]
5. [The trade-union organisation 'Industrial Workers of the World', or IWW, was formed in the United States in 1905.]

where the first words of the rebellious soldiers were the cries 'Down with the War', 'Down with Wilhelm', and 'Long live the Bolsheviks', so everywhere else, throughout the entire world, the action of the popular masses against the War and imperialism is beginning with expression of the most passionate sympathy for Soviet power and our Party.

The period of triumphant imperialism is coming to an end. We are entering the Bolshevik period of history, in which the struggle for a Soviet Republic of Europe and then of the entire world is no longer the dream of a healthy Bolshevik appetite, but rather the immediate task of the day. We have already turned to realisation of this task.

No matter how we may have to move from victories to defeats and back again, one thing is clear: the conclusion of the epoch that has now begun will be the victory of worldwide Bolshevism and, as a result of that victory, worldwide Soviet power.

E. Preobrazhensky

No. 29

'No Privileges'[1]

27 October 1918

When the Government of People's Commissars was formed after the October Revolution, it resolved, mainly at comrade Lenin's insistence, that members of the highest organs of power in the Republic receive compensation no greater than that of a good skilled worker in the capital.[2]

This resolution, which was strictly implemented, had enormous principled importance and an enormous moral influence on the masses.

Since that time, unfortunately, we have steadily retreated from the rule of paying the highest soviet- and military workers according to the scale of trade-unions, and we are thereby violating one of the essential points of our programme.

It began with the fact that we started to hire engineering and military specialists for higher pay. The efficiency of those we attracted hardly rose because of the increased payments, and when the best part of the intelligentsia came over to the side of Soviet power, such a tactic of buying talent was rendered useless and politically humiliating for the intelligentsia.

Then higher rates of pay were recently confirmed for officers and civilian-employees of the Red Army in observance of the sort of traditions that recall bourgeois habits and are totally indecent in a worker-peasant republic.

Protests are already breaking out in the army against the new salaries, which are unjustified from the socialist point of view. The better and higher-minded officer-workers are refusing to accept the supplementary compensation.

That was the response, for example, of the Cossack officer Kashirin, a military comrade of Blücher and one of the most remarkable and idealistic Cossack Bolsheviks. That is also how many other of the best representatives of the Red Officer-Corps are inclined to react.

A most serious error has been committed that is already doing enormous damage to our cause.

This error, like its predecessors, must be corrected.

We must return to the former resolution of the Council of People's Commissars and implement always and everywhere this principle: in paying people in the highest positions, there can be no privileges that are not required by the job.

---

1. [From *Ural'skii rabochii*, 27 October 1918.]
2. [The question of the level of compensation for people's commissars and of reducing compensation for the highest employees and officials was taken up at a session of the Council of People's Commissars on 18 November (1 December) 1918. A corresponding resolution was adopted, written by V.I. Lenin.]

The Urals regional soviet of trade-unions must speak out against privileges in payment for the labour of the highest officials.
We have no need for a privileged soviet-bureaucracy.

E. Preobrazhensky

Appendix:

'To all Workers and Peasants of the Urals'[3]

23 October 1918

By the will of the working class and the poorest peasantry of Russia, the Party of Communists is the ruling party of the Soviet Republic. All the most important positions in soviet-organs are occupied by members of our Party. For this reason, the Party of Communists carries the total responsibility for the activity and behaviour of its members who occupy these or other posts.

Meanwhile, certain members of the Party, sometimes occupying responsible positions, have been exposed recently in a number of instances of improper behaviour, misuse of power and particularly of drunkenness, which is especially common in the districts where party-organs have the weakest control over members.

The Party of Communists has no intention of hiding or hushing up the misdeeds of its depraved members, but it does not have the resources to keep track of the activities of them all. The Urals Regional Committee thus turns to all the working population of the Urals and is giving them supervision and control over all Communists who are carrying out soviet-duties. Let the workers and peasants bring all abuses by party-members to the attention of the regional party-committee. The real culprits will be shown no mercy. They will be expelled from the Party, removed from their posts and, if appropriate, handed over to a revolutionary court.

It is obligatory for all party-organisations and Communist cells, without exception, to publish and post this declaration in all inhabited localities of the region.

The Urals Regional Committee of Communists

---

3. [From *Ural'skii rabochii*, 23 October 1918.]

No. 30

'To the Provincial Conference of the RKP'[1]

15 November 1918

Today, the Congress of the Communist organisations of Perm province must begin. The Congress is being convened at a time when the rallying of all Communist forces in the province is especially necessary, when every force must be accounted for and in its place.

The work of the Party is so infinitely great in scope and diverse in content that it is only through the special skill of squeezing from every Communist all that he can give to the Party that it might manage even partially all the tasks that it faces.

It is enough to point to the most important points on the congress-agenda in order to understand the important tasks that it faces.

Party-work in the province is in a deplorable state, with the exception of a few factory-centres. Things are especially bad as far as work in the village is concerned. Over the course of a year, work among the peasantry has been done so badly and is so insignificant that it is only now that the countryside is essentially beginning to live a conscious life. Here, a year of revolution has passed in vain. Things are also in a sad state in a number of small factories that have been abandoned by comrades and hardly visited from the centres.

Conditions are even worse in soviet-work, for which our Party, as the ruling party, is responsible to the toiling masses of the country. Many fine Communists, upon entering soviet-work, have turned into poor officials. But at times something much worse has happened. Many poor Communists, or people who have stuck to the Party for the advantages power brings, have landed in soviet-institutions in the districts and parishes and are committing the greatest outrages, using the apparatus of power for arranging their own private affairs. Embezzlement of soviet-property, drunkenness, ridicule and mockery of the defenceless population – these are crimes that one must frequently encounter in reviewing the activity of local soviets.

Only party-control can save Soviet power from dissolution and decay where there is no free control by the proletariat, where soviet-workers are suspended in the air and not accountable to the masses. Control by the Party means control by the proletariat in the form of its leading and organised section.

But control at the provincial level can only be accomplished by a provincial party-organisation that knows the composition of local workers. It has the

---

1. [From *Ural'skii rabochii*, 15 November 1918.]

responsibility to see that the soviets conduct policy in the spirit of communist construction so that soviet-institutions banish stagnation and the deadly spirit of state-offices.

It is necessary, therefore, to create a provincial party-committee or some analogous organisation that can control the provincial executive committee and all the district-executive committees. Until now, this control has been lacking, and from the moment when the regional committee of the Party arrived in Perm, such control has been only partly accomplished by a regional committee that does not possess the resources needed to complete all the work that should fall to provincial party-organisations.

That is only one aspect of the tasks that the Congress faces.

These tasks must be resolved by any and all means.

E. Preobrazhensky

No. 31

'Report to the Perm Provincial Conference of the RKP'[1]

21 November 1918

Comrade Preobrazhensky deals with the work of the *oblast*-committee since the evacuation from Ekaterinburg.

With the fall of the Red capital in the Urals, he says our Party has been at the head of a movement that has captivated the Urals proletariat, a movement aimed at organising the defence of the Urals.

The Party has mobilised its members and thrown them into the front. Courses have been created for training new party-members.

The diversion of party-forces into soviet-work has led to the erosion of party-work and contributed to the destruction of Soviet power.

Party-workers became bureaucrats. It was necessary to take preventive measures against this decay, to return to party-work, and thus to revive soviet-work.

The decisive blow by the Czechoslovak bands coincided exactly with the moment when we decided to bring back to the Party the soviet-workers who were buried in papers.

The interests of the Revolution demanded not merely improvement of soviet-work, but also that it be brought under party-control; but the whole impending danger required that workers be sent to the factories and villages in order to conduct revolutionary mobilisation there. Looking at the work we have done in that regard, we can say that we have coped with it, and we must add that it is only thanks to our Party's efforts that we have succeeded in creating a reliable barrier against the enemy's advance from beyond the Urals and even launched our own offensive against Ekaterinburg.

After the evacuation from Ekaterinburg, the Regional Committee was temporarily delayed in Kushva and then relocated to Perm.

The Regional Committee has focused its attention mainly on the press. The Committee's organ, *Ural'skii rabochii*, which a few months ago appeared in five to six thousand copies, is now being printed in seventeen to eighteen thousand copies, and in the next few days the print-run is intended to increase to twenty to twenty-five thousand.

We wanted to convert *Ural'skii rabochii* into a popular newspaper suitable for the widest masses of workers and peasants, but this idea was set aside and *Ural'skii rabochii* has remained a paper for leading workers, a serious leading

---

1. [From *Ural'skii rabochii*, 21 November 1918.]

party-organ. To serve the wider peasant-masses and the Red-Army men, *Krasnyi nabat*, *Okopnaya pravda* and others have been created. This has been done according to the Regional Committee's plan, but without its direct involvement.

As far as publication of brochures is concerned, several were published in Ekaterinburg. We have not managed to sort out the publishing house in Perm, because there is absolutely no-one available and no time to write brochures. All party-workers have so many tasks that there is hardly time here to eat.

Thus far the Regional Committee has published two pamphlets in Perm – my own and the one by comrade Safarov. Soon the *Ural'skii sbornik*[2] will appear, providing a survey of party- and soviet-work during the revolution. This collection will be our report, as it were, covering one and a half years of revolutionary work.

The Regional Committee has had enormous work to do in distributing resources. The point is that two hundred comrades were sent from the centre to the Urals for organisational-agitational work. They had to be assessed and assigned according to their abilities. In addition to them, we had to assign evacuated party-workers, who altogether numbered up to six hundred people.

There was a particularly big fuss with the evacuees. Often they were living serenely on soviet-money that was advanced to them during the evacuation and were not available for registration. We have taken strict measures against such Communists. We set up a control-apparatus and made an agreement with the soviet so that not a single Communist can leave Perm without permission from the Regional Party-Committee. That has enabled us to keep track of all evacuated workers, and we have assigned them to the front and the rear.

Our party-canteen played an important part in the search for Communists who were hiding in railway-cars and steamers, since anyone who wanted to eat was compelled to report to the Committee.

When we arrived here in Perm, no work at all was being done in the districts. When we began to hold big public meetings, following Moscow's example, they were attended by very few listeners since the masses were already forsaking the Party. Through tireless work, we have now managed, in some measure, to set things right.

After dealing with agitation in Perm, we organised extensive agitation in the districts, and for this purpose recruited all the forces we possibly could. The comrades from the localities know what we have accomplished in this regard.

We focused special attention on work in the Red Army, where we now have a very solid organisation of Communists.

---

2. [No information could be found concerning this publication.]

Is there any need to mention the enormous importance of our military work? The truth is that a very great many Communists, sitting in the soviets, failed to explain the purpose of revolutionary mobilisation to workers and peasants, and when they did make an announcement, they limited their effort merely to posting a decree on the doors of the soviet. The 46 organisations of our Party, which comrade Zarin[3] mentioned, likewise did nothing to help the masses to realise the mobilisation. The Regional Committee, through its agitators, had to take care of this work as well.

But carrying out the mobilisation was not enough. It was also necessary to work among the grey mass of the Red Army. In Perm, we are now setting up lectures, discussions and theatres for Red-Army men. Party-cells have been organised in every regiment and division, and their work is being directed through their representatives in the Political Department of the Regional Committee.

But however much political work our Party has done in the army, a great deal more still remains. And however many workers have come to us, they are still far too few to develop political work in the army as extensively as we would like to.

In order to make up for the shortage of party-resources, we have set up courses in Ekaterinburg. In Perm, we have used courses for military agitators to reach our goals.

To provide leadership for all the political work in the army and at the front, we have selected five people and entered into an agreement with the military council of the Third Army for our Party to monopolise all the agitational-organisational work.

Recently, we have faced the next question of work in the village. This is an issue of paramount importance because we are now making the transition to socialisation of the instruments of agricultural production, and for proper implementation of the law on organising the village, we need to create a network of rural party-organisations.

To provide leadership for work in the village, we have established a section under the Regional Committee and intend to create cadres of agrarian agitators for direct work in the localities...

Wherever there is no proper control on the part of the leading centres, dissolution of the party becomes evident. With the growing number of organisations, this control is becoming more-and-more difficult to achieve. This is why we are now handing that responsibility over to the masses themselves, by issuing an

---

3. [At the evening session of the Perm Provincial Conference of the RKP(B), on 16 November, Zarin spoke as leader of the Perm Regional Committee. He said, in particular, that since mid-May 1918 'forty-one parish-, eleven city-, and twenty-five factory-organisations were organised in the region' (*Ural'skii rabochii*, 20 November 1918).]

appeal to that effect to all the workers and peasants of the Urals. Furthermore, we have established a special investigative commission to examine any cases of Communists who are committing abuses. We hope that these measures will improve the health of the party. If not, then we will not hesitate even to shoot those comrades who are disgracing the party by their behaviour.

A summary of responses to the questionnaire distributed to conference-participants will be the best report on the work of our Party's Regional Committee.

The report by comrade Preobrazhensky concludes the evening-session of 16 November.

E. Preobrazhensky

No. 32

Concluding Remarks at the Perm Conference of the RKP[1]

23 November 1918

Russia is a federative republic, says the rapporteur, and this means that it can consist of separate Soviet Republics. Our Party has never rejected the possibility of a regional association. The Urals represents a single economic unit with its own peculiarities that differ from other parts of Russia. For this reason, the need for a regional association arises.

We are regionalists, but we are also centralists, because we consider ourselves tied to the centre even though we are taking a revolutionary path to unify the Urals as an economic unit.

Without waiting for a directive from above, we have nationalised a number of the largest regions at a time when the centre has still not decided to do so. Now we are implementing the nationalisation of peasant-inventory and, following the revolutionary path, we are building a communist economy in the countryside. True, the centre has not yet given instructions, but they say: give it a try, and if your plan succeeds we will follow your path and issue the corresponding decree.

The same comrade Lenin, whose name was here taken in vain, taught us that decrees are a cover, but to build life and find the way forward is something we must do for ourselves by the revolutionary path. And that is what our organisation is doing.

It is up to you to say whether the Urals region will live as a single unit, whether it will continue creating the communist revolution, or whether you will acknowledge the necessity of the old rotten partitions created by the pompadours.[2]

---

1. [From *Ural'skii rabochii*, 23 November 1918.]
2. [E.A. Preobrazhensky is polemicising with Sorokin, who presented a report at the morning-session of 17 November from the fraction of the Perm Provincial Executive Committee. Sorokin declared that in the area of economic construction, 'we are unwaveringly carrying out the principle of centralism, totally rejecting the principle of regionalism [*oblastnichestvo*]' (*Ural'skii rabochii*, No. 234, 20 November 1918). At the same morning-session of 17 November, delivering his concluding remarks, Sorokin, according to the newspaper-report, emphasised that 'the fraction of the Provincial Executive Committee has implemented the principle of centralism in its work, which the comrade-regionalists [*oblastniki*] reject, wanting to make the Urals into some kind of state within a state. The Central Executive Committee decided the question regarding a regional association, and did so in a disappointing way for the regionalists, who were fleeing from Ekaterinburg and apprehensively asking at each station: "Will we soon be in Perm?" The latter words from Sorokin [implying cowardice] provoked a storm of indignation. Demands came from all sides of the hall for the speaker to name names. The chairman had difficulty calming the meeting by promising that Sorokin will answer for this insult

In conclusion, comrade Preobrazhensky reads out a resolution on the reports of the Regional and District-Committee proposing a regional soviet.

In the name of the fraction from the Provincial Executive Committee, Comrade Sorokin introduces a counter-resolution.

The two resolutions are voted on consecutively, and the resolution presented by comrade Preobrazhensky (see No. 233 of *Ural'skii rabochii*)[3] is accepted by a majority of 126 to six

E. Preobrazhensky

Appendix 1: Letter from the Urals Regional Committee of the RKP(B) with a Request to Send a List of the Party-Workers who were Officially Sent to the Urals[4]

2 September 1918

Esteemed comrades!

The party-workers that you have sent to be at the disposal of the Urals Regional Committee of Communists for appointment to one or another task near to or at the front often refuse assignments, settling in wherever they please and not where they could be employed more usefully for the common effort. Several have been seen drunk, and other comrades have arrived here after extremely long delays. In response to our question: 'Why are you late?', we received the answer: 'Along the way we dropped in at home', and, as a result, they are a whole month late (that was the case with comrade Kurganov).

Bringing these matters to your attention, the Urals Regional Committee of the Russian Communist Party (Bolsheviks) requests that you provide a list of the workers you have sent so that it might be possible to clarify how many still have not arrived here.[5]

Chairman   E. Preobrazhensky
Secretary   Vl. Kosarev

---

to a party-court. Finishing his speech, and to the friendly laughter of part of the gathering, Sorokin said that even comrade Lenin shares their point of view concerning the need for provincial boundaries and is opposed to a regional association' (*Ural'skii rabochii*, 23 November 1918).]

3. [This issue is missing from the files.]

4. [From *Perepiska Sekretariata TsK RKP(B) s mestnymi partiinymi organizatsiyami. (avgust-oktyabr' 1918g.): Sb. dokumentov*, Vol. 4, 1969, Moscow, p. 214.]

5. [The letter was received by the Central Committee of the RKP(B) on 11 September 1918.]

Appendix 2: Letter from the Urals Regional Committee of the RKP(B) to the Central Committee of the RKP(B)[6]

4 October 1918

Dear comrades!

The Urals Regional Committee of the RKP considers it a duty in the present letter to provide a short account of its activity since the time of its election and to outline its party-work.

The Committee's work has taken place in the conditions of a rapidly changing situation characteristic of a period of the Great Revolution.

Having begun our activity on the basis of the resolutions of the Fourth Regional Conference (communist measures in production and distribution, in the city and in the village; building the Red Army; organic party-work and so forth), the Committee, driven by the storm of war, rapidly turned to mass organisation and agitation to mobilise the Red Army and subordinated all its work to the aims of revolutionary war. The disagreements that existed between committee-members at the March Conference over the question of the Brest peace were by this time forgotten. It became clear to us that in the current conditions we can, and we must, preserve the Soviet Republic and hold out as the home of world-revolution and its living example.

From the very beginning, we discerned in the Czechoslovak movement an attack against the Soviet Republic by Anglo-French robbers in alliance with the domestic counter-revolution. In precisely this spirit, we published a resolution that was subsequently developed in a number of articles in *Ural'skii rabochii*. We summoned the Urals proletariat to armed struggle and urged all soviet-organisations to adjust all their work to the aims of war – to be up to the requirements of war; we mobilised all agitators and organisers and subordinated them to the interests of revolutionary war. The Regional Committee's own resources were distributed as follows: comrades Malyshev, Mrachkovsky, Voikov, Tolmachev, and Akulov were sent to the front, and comrade Goloshchekin to frontline-headquarters; for soviet-work and the organisation of production – comrades Beloborodov and Kuz'min; for travelling work – comrades Safarov and Tolmachev; to the presidium of the Regional Committee for direction of all party-work as a whole – comrades Preobrazhensky, Safarov and Goloshchekin. An agitation-department was organised under the Committee, which put out a mass of agitation-leaflets and sent out agitators throughout the region. In connection with the retreat, a whole series of illegal party-cells was organised.

---

6. [From *Ural'skii rabochii*, 4 October 1918.]

In order to complete such extensive work, and in view of the loss of comrades Malyshev and Vainer, who fell heroically on the battlefield, the Regional Committee expanded its composition through co-optation to include more responsible and prominent workers.

After the evacuation from Ekaterinburg, an emergency-conference of active Urals workers was called in order to restore contacts with the localities.

At the present moment the activity of the Regional Committee consists of the following: 1. On the basis of need, the Committee is distributing and directing agitators and organisers to the front, to the countryside, and also sending candidates for soviet- and military duties. 2. A special troika has been selected to organise rural work. 3. A group of five has been established as the military bureau of the RKP, bringing together and directing all political work in the military units. 4. The newspaper *Ural'skii rabochii* is being published. 5. Control is being exercised over soviet-institutions. 6. An investigative commission and control-department have been created. 7. Regular tours of the front and extension of control over county-organisations.

Regarding the question of the Party's tasks at the current moment, the Regional Committee points out that it fully accepts and considers it necessary to implement the policy of the Central Committee. The five months that have passed since signing the Brest agreement have convinced us with sufficient clarity that our fundamental task and duty to the socialist revolution is to defend our positions in the form of a Soviet Republic that has established the dictatorship of the proletariat and is implementing socialist measures in economic life.

Experience has demonstrated that time is needed for the proletariat of Western Europe to learn about us and to understand us. But having established the power of the proletariat, in the present conditions we can only hold out and strengthen ourselves, and become a real state, by defending our existence with arms in hand against one group and making use of the contradictory interests of others. At the same time, we must always be prepared to change our tactics and relations abruptly, depending upon a changed relation of forces on the world-scale.

The international situation at the present moment is this: both groups of imperialist powers are implacably hostile to us. But if the hostility of Germany is determined mainly by the fact that we are a Soviet Republic, and that we are lighting the torch of international revolution, on the part of the 'Allied' states of England and France there is further hostility on the grounds of a rupture of the Allies' Eastern Front against Germany.

From a general and simultaneous attack against us on all sides – from the west, the south, the north and the east, from a simultaneous tightening of the circle by the robbers from all the imperialist powers – we are being saved by the implacable contradictions between the imperialist [powers].[1] During four years of the War, the victor was Germany, and it demanded a universal 'Brest', which would mean universal imperialist domination by Germany and would be tantamount to death for England and America, with the result that there could be no peace. In the fifth year, America entered the War with all its strength and wealth. The fortunes of war turned in favour of America and England, and now they are demanding a 'Brest' from Germany so that again there can be no peace. Thus, this hostility between the robbers gives protection against a simultaneous offensive against us, making it possible for us to become stronger as they – the group of predators – grow weaker and more demoralised, ultimately providing us with conditions for tacking and manoeuvring in order, at the opportune moment, to strike first at one and then at the other.

Of the two coalitions hostile to us, one – the Central Powers headed by Germany – have the greatest need, like it or not, not only to renounce an armed offensive against us, but even to make concessions. And it would make no sense, just now, for us to enter into an armed conflict with Germany. On the contrary, since Germany is now in the vice of a hellish war that it caused itself, we can make use of it, in individual instances, for our own struggle against the opposing side – England, France, and America.

For us, the most dangerous enemies at the present moment are England, France and America. They are now attacking us with armed force from the north and the east, and directly – with their own troops – from Archangel, after bribing the Czechoslovaks and White Guards in Siberia, the Urals and the Volga, and after landing troops in Vladivostok and penetrating to the heart of our Republic with their treacherous bribery: Yaroslavl', the Moscow plot, and so on. And the armed clash with these plunderers springs from the whole content of our Revolution. The substance of our Revolution was exit from the imperialist War, but by that same act we destroyed the Eastern Front, which is necessary to the Anglo-French robbers in their predatory interests. The substance of the Revolution was annulment of the loans and nationalisation of the plants and factories, but in that very act we struck mainly at the pocket of the Anglo-French bankers, since seventy percent of the loans and foreign capital in our country belonged to the Anglo-French. Our Revolution could not resolve a single question of war and social reconstruction without overthrowing our own bourgeoisie. But our bourgeoisie, with its economic ties, is mostly bound up with Allied capital, and the best ally for our bourgeoisie in suppressing Soviet power is, again, the Anglo-French. The conclusion is clear – it is only possible to save the Soviet Republic, to

---

1. [The word is unclear, but appears to be 'powers'.]

save the Revolution, through a bloody, life-and-death fight with the enemy who is attacking us – the imperialists of England, France and America.

The question necessarily arises: When the European powers are presently such giants compared to us, can we hold out in a fight against them? To this we respond with a decisive 'Yes!' Here are the objective facts. The War, which arose from a crisis of capitalist development within existing frontiers and multiplied that crisis many times over – this War is not only not coming to an end, but is entering an even more bitter period and thus is finally pushing the imperialist states over the precipice. On the other hand, the workers and toiling masses, driven to the extreme of exhaustion and destruction, are beginning to rise up. In the West, we are observing the gradual decomposition of state-organisms. Austria is already a sinking ship due to the War and the developing revolutionary movement. Germany, on the one hand, is suffering military defeats in the West, while on the other hand, it is choking on the Brest treaty, unable to cope with the uprising by the masses in the occupied regions. Its state-mechanism is shaken, the army is dissolving, the workers are rebelling, and Germany's ally, Bulgaria, has already entered a period of revolution. Thus, at the present moment we are guaranteed against a possible military offensive from this direction, and at the same time, the revolution is closer in these countries. The coalition of Entente-powers is subject to the same process, especially France, which has been totally bled. However serious the military campaign against us by England and France, we see that their army is decomposing by the day, while ours is becoming stronger. To defeat and occupy us solely with a foreign army, an army that is separated by thousands of *versts* from its main base in the rear, is absolutely impossible. Even to suggest that the Allied predators might succeed for long in organising an army out of Russian peasants and workers, who every day will become more convinced of the counter-revolutionary efforts of the White-Guard swine, is also a utopia. That is how matters stand in the camp of our opponents. On the contrary, our Soviet state-organism and our army are growing stronger every day.

These are the objective grounds of our tenacity. But I repeat that we can only become invincible through a bloody confrontation, for if we were defeated now by the Czechoslovaks,[2] that would mean being thrown back into the imperialist war with Germany; it would mean becoming irredeemable debtors to Anglo-French capital, and, in the final analysis, would strike a blow at the international revolution.

There is only one way out: either to wage revolutionary war and advance towards socialism, or else be forced to wage imperialist war and to throw

---

2. [The author apparently has in mind the alliance of the Czechoslovaks, the White Guards and the Entente.]

Russia and Europe back for many years to capitalist slavery. Our Party, the Party of communist revolution, must instill in the consciousness of the masses the inevitability of choosing between these two paths and lead the masses to revolutionary war.

Our Party must participate directly in the mobilisation of military forces, in securing the rear against counter-revolution, and in the political education of the mobilised masses.

We must remember that the basic character of our Revolution is communism. And for that reason, the only party-organisation worthy of calling itself communist is one that implements communist foundations in real life.

All the branches of production must be established on communist principles, with an increase in labour-productivity. In particular, our attention must be directed to the distribution of all products, taking into account the needs of the entire country as a whole.

Soviet-work in many localities is in an extremely pitiful state. In order to raise it to the required standard, it is imperative to establish active control over all soviet-work and soviet-workers. Every unfit element must be ruthlessly rejected and transferred into social labour or the trenches. Particular attention must be given to party-work in the village: to be victorious, the proletariat needs an ally, and the village-poor, with an interest in socialist revolution, are that kind of ally. But these poor people are still ignorant, oppressed and deceived. We must go to the neglected rural corners to agitate and organise the poor peasantry. Our programme must be the catechism of the poor peasants, who number in the millions. Our Party of class-struggle must also wage this class-struggle in the village and link the interests of the rural poor with the interests of urban workers. Only then will we be invincible.

At the present moment, the Regional Committee considers the immediate task of our party-cells to be one of purging the organisations of unfit elements who are alien to us and have entered our Party either for a career or else to corrupt it. The Regional Committee intends to implement strict control of the activity of all party-cells and their membership-personnel. Only pure, only committed, only genuine communists can be members of our Party. Let the others, who have not adopted the communist programme of our Party, remain in the ranks of our sympathisers. The criminal element that has penetrated into our Party must be not only driven out but also punished. In addition to the newspaper and travelling, the Regional Committee intends to direct future party-work by way of circular letters concerning all questions of practical work.

With comradely greetings.

Urals Regional Committee of the RKP(B)

No. 33

'Two Congresses'[1]

27 November 1918

Two important congresses have concluded in Vyatka: the Provincial Congress of Soviets and the Provincial Congress of Committees of the Poor.

At the Congress of Soviets, there were 226 voting delegates and six with an advisory role. In terms of parties, the distribution of delegates was: 126 Communists, 98 Communist-sympathisers, three Left S-Rs, one Left S-R sympathiser, one maximalist, and three non-party people.

At the Congress of Committees of the Poor, the enormous majority of delegates belonged to the Communists, and there were even more Communist-sympathisers.

The two congresses merged to discuss the most important common questions, including: 1) the current moment, 2) the report concerning the Sixth All-Russian Congress of Soviets, 3) the Red Army, 4) relations between soviets and committees of the poor, 5) the land-question and communist construction in agriculture. Subsequently, the congresses separated. The Congress of Soviets turned to reports from the Executive Committee and the Regional Soviet, and to elections for the new Executive Committee. The Congress of Poor People's Committees discussed their own questions concerning the construction of committees of the poor and their tasks, the food-question, and the Communist Party. Reports from the localities took a great deal of time.

All the resolutions suggested by the Bureau of the Communist fraction were accepted by the Congress, either unanimously or with four to five abstentions.

Among the resolutions that were accepted, one must note one point in the resolution concerning the Red Army, which was adopted from the report by comrade Anuchin. On this point, the Congress resolved to confiscate all the belongings of deserters from the Red Army. The resolution on communist agriculture, adopted from the report by comrade Preobrazhensky, has great significance. The resolution speaks of the need to eliminate private property in the agricultural equipment of the village, to concentrate it at rental stations, and to convince whole villages to go over to social working of the land as soon as the coming spring.

It is also necessary to note the resolution adopted at the Congress of Soviets following the report by comrade Goloshchekin, which condemned attempts to separate from the region and confirmed the decision of the Second Congress

---

1. [From *Ural'skii rabochii*, 27 November 1918.]

regarding the need for Vyatka province to remain in the Urals Regional Association.

The Provincial Executive Committee was elected partly from its former members and partly from new representatives, mainly workers from the localities.

The congresses demonstrated that Soviet power is stable in Vyatka province and that the rural poor in most places have already put down the kulaks.

E.P.

Appendix: From the Presidium of the Vyatka Provincial Congress of Soviets[2]

25 November, 1918
Moscow. Central Committee of Communists,
People's Commissar of Internal Affairs,
the editors of *Izvestiya* and *Pravda*

The Third Congress of Soviets in Vyatka province and the First Provincial Congress of Committees of the Village-Poor have concluded. The composition of the Congress of Soviets (with the exception of two Left S-Rs, one maximalist, and one anarchist) consisted of 126 Communists and 84 of their sympathisers. The Congress of Soviets adopted a resolution acknowledging the need for the Urals regional association and annulling the decision not to recognise the Urals regional association, and a new Provincial Executive Committee was elected. Both congresses completed a great deal of organisational work towards strengthening Soviet power in Vyatka province...

The Presidium of the Congress: Preobrazhensky, Akulov, Popov.

---

2. [From *Perepiska Sekretariata TsK RKP(B) s mestnymi partiinymi organizatsiyami. (noyabr'-dekabr' 1918 g.): Sb. dokumentov*, Vol. 5, 1970, Moscow, p. 175.]

No. 34

'From Congress Impressions'[1]

30 November 1918

I

From 20–5 November, two congresses took place in Vyatka: the Provincial Congress of Soviets and the Provincial Congress of Committees of the Poor. Both congresses consisted mainly of peasants, with just a few individual workers' representatives scattered about. The Ishevsky and Votkinsky factories, recently liberated from the White Guards, did not have time to send representatives. Elabuzhsky factory did not send representatives. All the other districts were more-or-less fully represented.

At sessions of the Communist fractions, it was decided in advance to merge both congresses for discussion of common questions. As a result, there were up to a thousand people, including guests, who could hardly get into the rather small theatre.

After the opening came the obligatory duties for our congresses – the *Internationale*, telegrams of greetings, the funeral-march for victims of the revolution; and after the inevitable discussion of the current situation, about which unanimous resolutions were adopted, the Joint Congress turned to discussing the question of the Red Army.

One thing interested me: whether there would be heated debates over this question, whether everyone would say what he really thought about the Civil War, about an army of three million, about the new call-ups, or whether a resolution, buttered-up with general hackneyed phrases by one speaker or another, would be adopted with formal unanimity and without any particular debate.

The resolution was adopted unanimously, or almost unanimously. But meanwhile, there was a point in the resolution concerning the obligatory handover by village-communities of deserters from the Red Army and the confiscation of their belongings.

Well, I think it was adopted unanimously because everyone seriously understands that words must lead to action, and this will be more difficult than raising a hand for the resolution. However, as we shall see below, the point concerning the struggle against desertion came to be thoroughly aired, even though the occasion was completely unexpected.

---

1. [From *Ural'skii rabochii*, 30 November 1918.]

The question of the relations between committees of poor peasants and the soviets was discussed. Heated debates occurred. In one district freed from the White Guards, the committees of poor peasants dispersed all the soviets, which were in the hands of kulaks, and themselves took over all of the soviets' functions. In another district, exactly the opposite occurred: the poor were occupying the soviets, and it was decided to dissolve the committees of the poor because they were superfluous. Some suggested declaring the committees of the poor to be the sole authority in the countryside, not suspecting that this would tear up our Soviet constitution.

This suggestion alone is clear proof that we are living in a revolutionary period when there is no time to cope with laws, even those that are most basic.

Others proposed to dissolve the committees of the poor entirely after re-election of soviets in a spirit that would favour the poor.

A third group suggested retaining the committees, whatever the circumstances, as economic and food-organs but not as political and administrative bodies.

A fourth group suggested dissolving the parish-committees of the poor in rural districts and also dissolving the rural and village-soviets where they exist, so that in the parishes there would be a parish-executive committee, and the committees of poor peasants would be their executive organs in rural areas and villages.

One had the feeling is that this is a new question for which life has yet to provide an answer. A resolution had to be adopted concerning new elections, under the control of poor-peasant committees, to those soviets that are dominated by kulaks. The acute question concerning the very existence of one organ or another remains open, until life itself indicates the proper course.

In discussing the point concerning relations between committees of the poor and the parish-soviets, the question came up as to who should be regarded as the rural poor. Lively debates began. These debates continued even more vigorously two days later at the Congress of Poor-Peasant Committees, when the two congresses separated to address their own specific issues.

In the opinion of some, the poor include all peasants who do not hire workers.

But that way of talking brought a clever response from another speaker: 'And what if a soldier's widow with children hires someone to harvest her strips of land: is she poor, or is she a kulak?'

Another said: 'The poor are horseless or one-horse peasants'.

And here, a speaker countered: 'We are five brothers working our land together, and we have three horses. Does that mean we are not poor?'

Some said: 'The poor are those with little land under cultivation'.

This brought a quick response: 'And what good is it, land, if it is so small that it produces nothing?'

Others discussed moveable and immoveable property and grain surpluses, and eventually people groped their way towards what had to be determined. Taking into account the number of cattle, the quantity of arable land, the productivity of the soil and the size of the family, surpluses or shortages of grain, moveable and immoveable property, as well as earnings on the side – they came to a definition of the poor in terms of a whole series of indicators.

But then, to our surprise, the question of the poor was carried over to an entirely different plane. One peasant stepped up and remarked: 'We know who the poor are, we crushed the kulak, and then new parasites appeared, new idlers. How should we fight against them?'

There were exclamations of support in the hall and protests at the same time. I was interested in the issue of who these idlers are, and I anxiously awaited the appearance of further speakers.

The issue was explained: the idlers are former prospectors who have returned from Siberia; some are returning soldiers and sailors who, following demobilisation, are not able to return to the routine of working life; others are gamblers and drunkards, together with all those who welcome the expropriation of kulaks as a way to stuff their own pockets.

This was a heated question, and the debate became intense. Some pointed out that not every idler is guilty, for some are unable to work. Others cautioned against the danger of finding oneself in the company of the kulaks, for whom all the village-poor are idlers. If you are not rich, then you are guilty and an idler.

One speaker came forth and protested against dividing the poor into idlers and toilers. He heatedly defended the former prospectors and showed the meeting the best way to deal with the kulak.

'What did you deal in?' we ask the kulak.
'Hides'.
'Then take his hide'.
'And you?'
'Fat'.
'Then squeeze every bit of fat out of him'.
'And what did you deal in?'
'Soap'.
'Then lather up his throat'.

The meeting broke into laughter and rewarded the speaker with applause. The idlers were forgotten for the moment and people turned to other questions.

E. Preobrazhensky

No. 35

'From Congress Impressions'[1]

3 December 1918

II

The land-question was discussed at the Congress, but not at all in terms of an equalising division of land, such as occurred at all the peasant-congresses where the tone was set by the S-Rs, although questions concerning the unequal distribution of land were raised in the debates by deputies, and I, as rapporteur, received several notes on this theme.

In my report, I dealt mainly with the advantages of communal farming, as compared with small independent farming, and demonstrated that our countryside has now encountered the need for social tillage, the need to liquidate the barbarism of small-scale agriculture. In the resolution that I proposed, a number of transitional measures towards communal farming were outlined: confiscation of the equipment of kulaks and White Guards and its concentration at rental stations; the distribution of all agricultural machinery going to the countryside solely to the rental stations, with a ban on selling it as private property; and registration of the entire peasant-inventory and also its gradual concentration at the rental stations for social usage. Finally, the need also for a timely transition to social tillage by whole villages, starting as early as the spring of 1919.

The report brought a considerable exchange of views. Some believed that working the land socially would be easy in their localities, if only there were enough machines. Others said that the poor peasants support communal farming but the middle-peasants will not go for it. A third group suggested that neither poor nor middle-peasants will go for social tillage, because there is not the unanimity required for working communally.

As for the registration of inventory and turning it over for social use, delegates from several places proudly pointed out that this had already been implemented where they came from.

Almost all complained of an enormous shortage of agricultural machinery and hardware.

In the pile of notes that I received, the most diverse questions were raised: 1) will the rental station take the machinery that is owned by an association of three farmsteads; 2) can a family with six brothers, working together on undivided

---

1. [From *Ural'skii rabochii*, 3 December 1918. For the beginning of this article, see Document 2:34.]

land, be considered a commune; 3) can the poor be resettled on kulak-parcels and the kulaks on the parcels of the poor; 4) will the land-department provide tractors to the communes and how much what will it cost to use this machinery; 5) should the forests not be released to the poor, free of charge, for building homes; 6) can large homes be constructed in the village for communal living; 7) will it be possible to keep a dog or cat in a commune, and who will feed them, and so on.

When my resolution was put to the vote and approved after a minute, suddenly another delegate introduced an amendment from his seat: on the point that spoke of transferring kulak- and White-Guard inventory to the rental station, he suggested adding 'and the confiscated inventory of deserters from the Red Army'.

The issue was clear. The resolution dealing with confiscation of the inventory of deserters had already been adopted earlier by the Congress in its resolution concerning the Red Army. Now the only issue was what to do with this confiscated inventory. It is perfectly appropriate to transfer it to the rental stations for social use, as the comrade who introduced the amendment suggested.

I spoke in favour of adopting the amendment, but among the congress-deputies it provoked a storm. A number of speakers took the floor, while from their seats people began to speak in twos and threes. And they all opposed the amendment.

'How', said one, 'can you confiscate the property of a deserter if he does not have title to it?'

'Why should the wife and children suffer if the husband is a deserter?'

'Introduce an amendment to the amendment: to confiscate the property that belongs to the deserter himself, while not involving the families'.

'Cancel the amendment, we are not toying at resolutions here. Everything must be considered properly'.

I took the floor and tried to explain that the immediate question had absolutely nothing to do with whether to confiscate all or only part of the belongings of a deserter. The question was what to do with the inventory once it had already been confiscated: should it go to the rental station, or somewhere else?

My explanation did not succeed. The noisy delegates did not understand that they had already decided the question yesterday and that there was no time to change the decision in a discussion of the land-question. Some of them, evidently, had suddenly thought about it when it was already too late.

Comrade Goloshchekin took the floor and posed the question briefly and to the point. If a deserter is concerned for his family, let him not forsake his comrades at the front. The fate of those spilling their blood at the front for Soviet power matters more than the fate of a deserter's family.

The Congress calmed down, and the resolution with the amendment was adopted, with several abstentions out of concern for all the deserters or those who are dreaming of desertion.

The reports from the localities, delivered at the Congress of Poor People's Committees, gave a detailed picture of the colossal work that these organisations have done. The countryside is being transformed. A new force has grown up there that is a powerful aid to Soviet power in carrying out all its decrees. What is the significance of some food-detachments or other forces sent from the outside, when compared to the organised strength of the countryside?

Tsar Nicholas I boasted that in the nobility he had forty thousand district police-officers to control the people.

What do these forty thousand die-hards amount to, when compared to the forty thousand committees of the poor that the Soviet authority already has in our countryside, along with the millions organised around them?

The dictatorship of poor peasants – this is no longer the phrase of some speaker at a meeting, but a living fact.

At the Congress of Soviets in Osinsk, one thoughtful and conscious peasant began his report with the words: 'In our village today, people do not look upon communism as some kind of serfdom'. This phrase stuck in my memory because it says so much. The petty property-owner is saying good-bye to his illusions of petty-bourgeois freedom, in order to replace this illusion with genuine freedom in the collective.

From both of the Vyatka congresses, I took away the impression that our countryside, which has survived a period of mass struggle and overpowered the kulaks, not only no longer looks upon communism as some form of 'serfdom', but has also stopped seeing it as some kind of fantasy.

With a few shining and successful examples of work in a commune, or even just successful experiences in working the land socially, the toilers of the countryside will have a real measure of the advantages of communal farming.

These are the slogans now for the countryside: 1) 'All inventory to the rental stations' and 2) 'Mass social tillage by entire villages for the coming spring!'

E. Preobrazhensky

No. 36

The Union of Oppressed Peoples[1]

8 December 1918

A revolutionary alliance of Soviet Russia with all the peoples of the East who are oppressed by imperialism is fated to play an enormous role. We do not know how quickly the English and French workers will begin to storm their imperialism from within, although there are reasons to think that the wait for this will not be long. But then, we do know that the toiling masses of India and China have already begun the struggle for their emancipation from foreign enslavers. The delegates from northern and southern China who visited comrade Lenin advised that the revolutionary movement in southern China has already become enormously intense, and the banks and customs-duties that were in the hands of English, American and Japanese predators have already been nationalised. As the delegates indicated, in order to suppress the revolution in southern China, Japan has had to send in its armies that had been readied for Siberia. The armies of northern China, which were to participate with their forces in supporting the Czechoslovak counter-revolution in Siberia, have also been diverted there.

Thus the Chinese Revolution has already done us enormous service and continues to do so, attracting to itself some of the forces of our enemies.

In India, according to Hindu revolutionaries, the uprising against British dominion can be expected very soon. By way of Central Asia, we may enter here into direct contact with liberated India and render it essential support. But India's support for us will be even greater simply because of fact that English imperialism, which is trying to put pressure on our Tashkent Soviet Republic from the direction of India, will be hurled back.

The recently concluded agreement by revolutionary representatives of the countries of the East, concerning a joint advance with Soviet Russia against their common enemies, marked the first step towards an alliance of all the victims of imperialism against their hangmen.

The Allied hangmen will be attacked simultaneously from two sides, Europe and Asia; and however our fortunes may change in this struggle, the final victory of hundreds of millions of the oppressed is perfectly obvious.

E. Preobrazhensky

---

1. [From *Ural'skii rabochii* 8 December 1918.]

No. 37
A Letter from the Presidium of the Ural Oblast Committee of Communes to V.I. Lenin[1] Concerning the Critical Position of Sections of the Red Army on the Eastern Front and the Possibility of Surrender of Perm to the White Guards[2]

No later than 24 December 1918[3]

Esteemed comrades,

Taking advantage of comrade Rozental's departure from here, we are sending you a brief communication concerning our affairs and, first and foremost, an account of the circumstances of the recent defeat on the northern section of our front, the result of which, in coming days, may be the surrender of Perm with all of the attendant consequences.

First of all, concerning the quality of the units that occupied the Kushva region. Out of 10 regiments that were located there, only one was in combat for less than a month. The others *were in uninterrupted combat*[4] for four to five months or longer, lost *from one-half to nine-tenths* of their personnel, were reinforced by totally unsuitable peasant-elements, and were physically so overstrained at the moment when the White-Guard attack began, that to demand steadfastness from them would have been to demand the impossible.

---

1. [The original letter was to the Central Committee of the RKP(B). The published version is addressed to V.I. Lenin.]
2. [From RGASPI. F. 5. Op.2. D.15. L. 5–7. Copy. Typewritten.]
3. [Perm was taken by Kolchak on 24 December 1918.]
4. [Here and throughout the document, the italicised parts were underlined by the author of the letter.]

The situation became catastrophic when a temporary but severe food-crisis arose before the attack, when the troops literally sat for days without any bread, receiving only half a herring, and when they finally had to fight at minus twenty five degrees without warm boots and clothing.

In a word, every unfavourable condition that was conceivable coincided with the moment of the attack, and there is almost no doubt that all these circumstances were known beforehand and taken into account by the enemy.

On the other hand, the enemy, as captured documents show, not only had a plan for attacking Perm, which was strictly implemented, but also enormous reserves (for each active regiment, it has two in reserve).

The catastrophic retreat from Kushva began when a single Communist peasant-regiment (which received the banner of the Central Executive Committee) held back the offensive. The retreat was complicated by the seizure of Lysva and then of Kalino, so that part of the army found itself cut-off and retreated to the north by the Lunevskaya[5] after blowing up the Chusovoi bridge. The units that were fighting in the direction of Lysva were also exhausted. Here is a small but clear example: the Lesnovsko-Vyborg regiment is now in the frontline with one hundred and twenty men, fifty of whom are regulars. This entire squadron had frozen feet, but accepted every order without question, though they were unable to carry them out. When Tolmachev, Safarov and Preobrazhensky went to the frontline, they found that the same Communist regiment was there, despite being deathly tired, that had succeeded a day earlier in destroying en entire enemy-regiment. As for the other units, they are demoralised by defeat and are worth absolutely nothing in terms of battle-readiness without a thorough rest in the rear and good reinforcements. With regard to the hastily formed reinforcements that were sent during these weeks to the front, in the majority of cases they only corrupted the units that were not yet completely demoralised. Without proper shoes, sheepskin-coats or felt-boots, and with half of the regiment lacking rifles (we do not have enough arms) – in such circumstances, the reinforcements either run away or flee to the Whites. An entire such battalion on our front surrendered to the enemy after opening fire on its own machine-gunners. In another company, it was necessary to purge every tenth man after an attempt to send a delegation to the brigade-commander with the declaration that this was a war against their own people. Forming a unit is treated as a matter of gathering the necessary quantity of boots, rifles and commissars, and the party-organisation is not managing to provide the units with a nucleus of Communists, which is the only true cement that makes a unit battle-ready.

---

5. [Written by hand in black ink by E.A. Preobrazhensky.]

At the present moment, the front is located seventy *versts* from Perm. Thanks to the currently proceeding transfer of three regiments from the southern section, where things are still not so bad for us, it is possible that the agony of Perm's fall will be delayed. However, to save Perm is just-about impossible without a rapid transfer of forces from other fronts in the country, and we already reported this to the high command of the Republic a week and a half ago.

The evacuation is going very badly. There is an enormous danger of leaving to the enemy much that is valuable. Up to four thousand railway cars have accumulated in Perm from the entire former front and from the factories. Half a million *poods* of metal, intended to be shipped by water, have to be loaded into the cars. Add to that something as bulky as the Motovilikha factory and others. The central collegium has turned out to be an ineffective, semi-bureaucratic establishment. There is not enough fuel, as a result of the railways being deprived of Kizel coal; the railway-workers are committing sabotage; part of the workers have scattered due to the food-shortage; others are complaining; most of the locomotives are completely worn-out; the roads are choked-up; and from Perm, the holdup extends beyond Vyatka. The plan of evacuation, worked out a month ago and reckoning on three days, has turned out to be useless.

As for the attitude of the worker- and peasant-masses, it varies. In Lysva, the workers accompanied the Red Army off with music, and for that the Whites arranged a slaughter in the factory. In Motovolikha, the attitude is not good, and it is even worse among the railway-workers. The most important reason is the food-crisis. Amongst the peasantry, the villages that have strangled their kulaks are for us; but where stratification has not occurred, they are against us.

If we succeed in conducting the evacuation, which is absorbing too many forces, we intend subsequently to transfer the focus of our work to the formation of reserves, to the creation in every military unit, *without exception*, of a tightly-knit nucleus of Communists, and to serious and protracted preparation for recapturing the Urals. All of this has been done before, but not to an extent that corresponds to the importance of the goal. We have committed more forces to work in the villages, counting on first creating there the material with which to build the army, uniting the poor, and economically improving their position. In many places this work is already completed.

We received your order concerning the registration of soviet-Communists at the height of the evacuation-commotion, and will possibly reply after a delay.

We have sent all the workers you requested except for one. If Perm should be surrendered, we will regroup forces and return a part of them to your disposal. As for Communists from the national sections, we are dispatching them every day and they already number nearly a hundred persons.

When the fate of Perm becomes clear, one way or the other, we will try to send one of our members to give you a personal and detailed report.

We are attaching a resolution adopted at the next-to-last session of the Regional Committee with the participation of Kharitonov, Zalutsky and Zof. With comradely greetings.

E. Preobrazhensky, G. Safarov, A. Beloborodov

Appendix 1: Resolution Adopted at a Meeting of the Regional Committee of the RKP with the Participation of Responsible Petrograd Party-Workers and Leading Workers from the Front Following Discussion of the Question of the Causes of the Latest Defeat of the Red Army on the Urals Front[6]

1. *It is necessary to implement real party-control over the entire military apparatus, its personnel-composition and its work.*
2. *It is necessary for Communists to be appointed to the most responsible duties, even if initially they are not fully prepared in a technical sense.*[7]
3. It is necessary to move the centre of gravity of political work in the army to the formations-department and to establish in each unit at least a small but solid nucleus of Communists.
4. It is necessary rapidly to create a lower-level commanding staff from Communists who have combat experience.
5. It is necessary to send to commanding-officer courses people who are neither randomly selected nor careerists, but Communists with combat-experience.
6. It is necessary, in view of the fact that the experience of using the old officers in the role of commanders, with certain exceptions, has in general and on the whole failed, to endeavour to create a single command out of Communists and to eliminate the institution of military commissars.

With regard to the Urals front, it is necessary to have:

1. A rapid creation of reserves.
2. Removal from combat of proletarian units that have been in battle continuously for several months and have lost all combat-readiness[8] – as the necessary cadre for future peasant-formations.

---

6. [From RGASPI. F.5. Op.2. D. 159. L.5–8. Copy of the original. Typewritten. The letter and the resolution carry the stamp of the Urals Regional Committee of the RKP(B).]
7. [The italicised parts were underlined in the document.]
8. [In the margin to the left of this point, there is a note in ink, apparently written by S. I. Gusev, member of the Revolutionary War-Council of the eastern front: '*The UOC*

3. An exchange of units that are being formed from peasants in the Urals for units being formed in other localities of Russia.
4. Centralisation of the accounting of all products located in the rear and their use as supplies for the army.

In addition, the meeting declares its support for summoning a party-congress for the resolution of a number of urgent questions, in particular the question of building the Red Army.

Appendix 2: Report of the Urals Regional Committee of the RKP(B)[9] to the Central Committee of the RKP(B) on the Causes of the Fall of Perm and the Need for an Investigation into the Circumstances of the Defeat of the Third Army[10]

No later than 30 December 1918

The catastrophe on the Urals front began with the battles in the vicinity of Kushva, where units of the 29th Division were deployed. The regiments of this division had been in combat continuously for five months, had lost the most combat-ready element of conscious Urals workers, had not received bread for five days up to the moment of the enemy-offensive and, with the onset of temperatures of minus twenty-five to thirty degrees, had neither felt boots nor warm clothing. These were the conditions when the enemy-attack began.

The defeat in the Kushva area already predetermined the fate of Perm, as we have already notified the Central Committee, but its catastrophically rapid and disgraceful fall, leaving to the enemy military equipment and enormous supplies of all kinds, was not due to the unfavourable balance of forces in which the defence of the city occurred.

[Urals Regional Committee] *especially insists on this*.

9. [The Urals Regional Committee of the RSDRP(B) was created in April 1917. By the Seventh (April) Conference of the RSDRP(B), the region's organisations included ten thousand party-members, by the Sixth Congress of the RSDRP(B) – twenty-five thousand, and by October – thirty thousand. At the Third Urals Regional Conference of the RSDRP(B), occurring on 15–18 January 1918, in Ekaterinburg, the regional organisation was represented by 69 voting delegates and 10 non-voting delegates from 52 party-organisations that included 35,069 party-members. At the Fourth Urals Regional Conference, held from 25–9 April 1918, 102 delegates participated from 57 organisations that included 30,278 party-members.]

10. [From *Perepiska Sekretariata TsK RKP(B) s mestnymi partiinymi organizatsiyami. (noyabr'-dekabr' 1918 g.)*, Vol. 5, pp. 312–18.]

The organisation of unit-formation

The formation of new units and reserve-companies by the Department of Special Formations and the Urals Regional Commissariat has become, essentially, a matter of gathering the necessary quantity of overcoats and boots and of putting together a completely random composition of people with a commanding staff that is in most cases unfit. These units were scarcely a fighting force and, more often than not, they deserted in their entirety to the side of the enemy. Reinforcements of that sort, when sent into older fighting regiments, often demoralised the battle-ready units rather than being assimilated into them. Political work among such formations did not succeed in producing the desired results, and the dispatch of units to the front often occurred despite categorical declarations from political workers that these units would defect to the enemy. The apparatus of unit-formation suffered and still suffers from the same flaw as the operational staff of the army (see below). Concretely: it has involved the dominance of mediocre old officers or explicit White Guards who, essentially, formed units for the 'people's army' (a few examples: the defection to the Whites during three weeks in the month of September of the 21st Company, which was formed in Perm; the defection at the time of Perm's fall by one soviet-regiment at full strength; the rebellion of the cavalry-regiment formed in the village of Ilyinsk; the need to arrest the entire commanding staff of the engineering battalion of the 10th Division, formed at the Ocher factory and numbering up to three thousand men, and such like).

Practice in the Urals has demonstrated that the old officers are completely unfit for combat and frontline-service in the Red Army.

They have introduced into the army the old methods of building on the basis of external subordination, and have demonstrated, on the whole, their complete inability to raise the combat-readiness of the army. With rare exceptions, they either shun combat-leadership at the front, or else go over to the Whites individually or with their units.

The work of the Third-Army staff

In the Third Army there was essentially no supreme command. All the division-commanders can confirm this fact. Members of the Urals Regional Committee had to be personally convinced of this by trips to the front, and it is a fact known by all the responsible St. Petersburg workers who, to one degree or another, have come into contact with military work.

The staff as such, during the entire campaign, showed no initiative in the leadership of military operations, either in the offensive or in the defensive, and if it happened on separate parts of the Third Army's front that the combat-initiative passed from the enemy to us, this was due to the private initiative of the staffs of individual divisions. The army's staff never attempted to develop action on the scale of its front, leaving combat-operations to take their natural course. To the extent that the staff did show initiative, apparently it took the ill-considered form, for example, of the attempt to establish around Perm a sector of 32 guns, without protecting them with a sufficient number of reliable infantry – the result of which was surrender of all these guns to the enemy. Elements alien to Soviet power came to dominate in the staff, with a habitually bureaucratic attitude to matters that were strange to them. As for the party-comrades who occupied responsible staff-positions, they dissolved and assimilated into an environment alien to them and lost their ties to the Party and their sense of party-responsibility for the matters entrusted to them.

Work at the staff usually lasted no more than a few hours per day. During the most tragic moments at the front, the commanders of divisions that were in action could not contact the command apparatus for a period of twenty-four hours or more, and unaccountable staff-workers responded instead. Over time, the staff of the Red Army adopted all the worst features and defects of the staff of the old army, up to and including drinking bouts and lewdness with a circle of women who had contacts with White-Guard organisations. This had a profound effect on the lower elements of command, forcing them to act as if they were the staff of the army. In the defence of Perm the results were catastrophic. Any effective defence-measures undertaken by the army's staff were systematically late. The required initiative was not shown in making use of all available resources, and the most obvious measures of protection were not taken, such as sending out parties to reconnoitre the enemy or establishing outposts at the exposed parts of the city's front (Motovilikha, the Sibirsky highway).

The supply of the army

One of the most important reasons for the defeat at the front was hunger and the inadequate supply of the army. The military supply-apparatus was organised in the same way as all the other military institutions.

Besides the usual bureaucratic-military spirit in such institutions, the supply of the army lacked any timely accounting of future requirements, there was no preparation for transition to a winter-campaign, and finally, there was criminal ignorance concerning the availability and place of storage of various kinds of supplies and products belonging to the army supply-department and available to the staff and the divisional staffs. Some examples:

1) reinforcements were not sent to the front because of the lack of arms for them; in order to equip the army-units, Communist squads were disarmed in

places where there had been, and were expected to be, White-Guard insurrections, while on a barge in Levshino, on the day before the enemy arrived, two hundred crates of rifles were accidentally discovered that were left to the White Guards;
2) at the same time as the 13th Division had enormous supplies of bread (up to fifty thousand *poods*), the 29th Division was starving and soldiers were being fed the raw meat of animals that had died;
3) likewise, there were instances when the army's warehouses had stocks of various kinds of supplies while a division lacked even those that were most essential.
4) the army supply[-department] had skis, but the skis were not used in organising formations, because no-one knew that the supply existed;
5) a great deal of fault for the inadequate supply of the army also lies with soviet supply-organs, which had no records of their supplies on hand and acted bureaucratically in a way that directly contradicted the interests of Soviet power in a civil war. While soldiers' feet were freezing at the front, the provincial supply had at its disposal seven thousand pairs of felt-boots that were only discovered during the evacuation. Whenever the Regional Committee of the RKP and the Regional Soviet struggled with bureaucracy in the provincial soviet-institutions, the latter opposed control in every way possible by appealing to the centre. (Things were just as abnormal with regard to foodstuffs.)

Transport

The fact that in the evacuation of Perm colossal stocks of various kinds of commodities and military equipment were left in the hands of the enemy must be attributed to disorganisation in the management of transport. Above all, the regional communications-authorities were unable and unwilling to adapt transport to the needs of wartime, showing in this respect a routine inclination to callous formalism under cover of so-called execution of orders coming from the centre.

On the other hand, the department of military communications operated the railway in the area of the front.

The department of military communications was not a separate and coherent organisation, extending its influence over the entire front, but rather a near-staff organisation headed by a certain Stogov, who was not a specialist in railroad-matters, was hostile to Soviet power, and was under no control whatever. The result was a large number of locomotives and rolling stock being left to the enemy at railroad-junctions (Kushva, Chusovoi and others) and the impossibility of organising shipment of necessary items to the front because of the rails being jammed. The catastrophe of the Perm evacuation was due to the same causes.

Just how bankrupt the organisation of transport-management was can be seen in the fact that on the day before the final surrender of Perm, with the transfer of control of the railroad-section to the 29th Division, up to twenty locomotives were discovered in the depot that were not used during the initial days of the evacuation.

Organic deficiencies of the Urals front

The main forces of the Urals front, formed as a result of revolutionary (voluntary) mobilisation of Urals workers, have been almost destroyed during five months of war.

The combat-ready regiments on the Urals front, because of the absence of reserves, have inevitably been used to the last man.

During five months of fighting, losses on the Urals front have reached fifteen-and-a-half thousand men, while the total reserves sent from the centre during this time have been five thousand men.

As for local reserves of mobilised peasants, their fighting quality has been sufficiently described above, in the point dealing with the organisation of formations.

This circumstance ultimately proved to be fatal in the days of the final enemy-attack on Kushva-Perm.

The role of the Urals Regional Committee

Responsibility for what happened lies not only with the Communists working in military institutions, but also with the Urals Regional Committee as a purely party-organ. Despite the fact that the Regional Committee did everything possible to strengthen party-work in the army and among the population, and to organise control over the work of military institutions within its proper limits, and often by exceeding its authority, the main and basic fault of the Regional Committee consists of the following: knowing all the circumstances described above, both before the catastrophe and at the moment when it developed, the Regional Committee did not resolve to break through formal obstacles and take a number of extraordinary measures for organising the defence of Perm on its own responsibility, and thus it did not fulfil its revolutionary Communist duty. The Regional Committee is all the more guilty in that it did not resolve to implement fully the plan it had outlined to subordinate all the activity of the military apparatus to party-control, insofar as such control is required by the basic tasks of building a strong army and by the peculiarities of the current war as a civil war. All political work in the army, by agreement with the Military Soviet of the army, was assumed by the Regional Committee on its own responsibility.

This created the possibility of developing enormous agitational and organisational work, of supplying the front with newspapers, of organising up to seven thousand Communists in the units, of raising the discipline and consciousness of the soldiers, and of liquidating by organisational measures the abuses of the commanding staff. What was required was to adapt the entire personnel of the army to the needs of civil war and to make the entire mechanism run properly. The Regional Committee understood its task to be continuation of the work that was to be done by Lashevich, a member of the Central Committee, but which he could not personally fulfil. His Central-Committee mandate, in the opinion of the Regional Committee, was to strengthen the Party's position and to facilitate its task of compelling the entire non-party – and often outright White-Guard – elements in the staff and various military institutions to serve our interests. In reality, something different happened. The Central-Committee mandate, with the passage of time, began to serve only as a barrier to every kind of party-control over military officials; party-comrades were excluded from all participation in deciding the most important questions concerning the front; they were shown out of the room when some 'responsible' semi-White Guard gave some report or other; and things became so disgraceful that members of the Regional Committee had to get the most important news from other people, even from the servants of the staff.

The Regional Committee is guilty of not warning the Central Committee of the emerging state of affairs and of stubbornly failing to implement the intended plan whatever the cost.

The need for a party-investigation

On the basis of everything that has been described, the Urals Regional Committee of the Party categorically insists that the Central Committee speedily appoint a party-investigation of all responsible Communists from the Military Soviet of the Third Army, an investigation of all the commanders, of the responsible workers in all military institutions, and of the Urals Regional Committee, in order to clarify all the circumstances of the defeat.

The Regional Committee of the RKP considers this investigation to be necessary not only for discovering and punishing the individual culprits responsible for the shameful defeat, but even more, to account for the bitter experiences during the defeats that have occurred and to initiate a radical party-reappraisal, on an all-Russian scale, of the methods of building the Red Army.

The Urals Regional Committee regards this matter as so important in party-terms that it considers it completely inadmissible to resolve it in a military-disciplinary manner without a serious party-investigation organised on the basis described above.

This document is signed by:[11]
The Chairman of the Urals Regional Committee of the RKP
Members
Workers from Petrograd

---

11. [The signatures are missing from the document.]

Nos. 38–42
Articles Published in the Newspaper and in the Weekly *Pravda* in December 1918–March 1919[1]

26 December 1918–16 March 1919

No. 38

'The Gentlemen of Tashkent'[2]

26 December 1918

One of the most essential points of our programme speaks of the elimination of privileged officialdom and of paying for the labour of people who perform social duties, even at the highest level, according to the norms established for skilled workers. The difference between skilled and unskilled labour – this is the only difference that the workers' and peasants' power can permit. And when the Council of People's Commissars, as it was first constituted following the October Revolution, established remuneration for its members at 500 roubles a month, that is, the same or even slightly less than was being earned at the time by the best metal-workers in Petrograd, this measure had enormous moral and political significance. In the point dealing with payment for labour in the highest positions, we implemented our programme on the

---

1. [The weekly was published in 1919 as a Sunday-supplement to *Pravda*.]
2. [From *Pravda*, 26 December 1918. The expression in the title originated with M.E. Saltykov-Shchedrin. In his *Gentlemen of Tashkent*, the author portrayed the tsarist empire seeking conquest and profit at the expense of culture and the common good.]

first day following the Revolution. Many of us know that this resolution, as propaganda on behalf of Soviet power, was worth thousands of our best speeches.

Unfortunately, since that time, and without sufficiently serious justifications, we have been making one retreat after another from our programme. This began, as is well known, with the notorious specialists, whom it was decided to recruit into work in the institutions and enterprises of Soviet power through especially high salaries. Enough time has passed since implementing that experiment to appraise its results objectively. The experiment has not succeeded. Those specialists, or so-called specialists, who had no wish to work for the Soviet authority, have mocked it through various types of the most sophisticated sabotage ***despite the increased salaries. And paying no regard to those increased salaries***, those who have wanted to work have done so. Only in a very few cases has additional compensation purchased greater energy or conscientiousness.

But let us assume that the experiment has succeeded, as many people think is the case. Today, there are absolutely no reasons to continue a policy of paying bribes for talent and knowledge. The intelligentsia has in part undergone, and in part is now undergoing, a change in its relation to Soviet power. This change is conditioned by the fact of the Soviet authority's stabilisation, and also by the fact of accelerated disintegration of the capitalist system in the greater part of Europe. In such conditions, privileges for specialists are unnecessary, harmful, and, in the final analysis, even fatal to the financial resources of the Soviet Republic. This is all the more true because these specialists generally have nowhere else to turn: there is no bourgeois demand for their labour, and no-one other than the Soviet authority is in a position to give them work.

Retreat from the principle of proletarian payment for the labour of specialists and of soviet-workers is often expressed in the most distorted forms. In many local soviets, the members of executive committees have awarded themselves high salaries, with absolutely no consideration of the rates established in the given locality for trade-union workers, and they have skilfully managed – and are still managing – to skip the queue and acquire all kinds of products beyond the established norms, thus actually doubling, if not tripling, the real wage; and finally, certain elements among the soviet-gentlemen of Tashkent have contrived to receive a salary in two or three different places simultaneously.

But the greatest blow to our principles for the payment of labour undoubtedly occurred not so long ago, with the rates established for the army and military institutions.

There are absolutely no rational reasons why the labour of a Red officer should be paid in the way that is now occurring. In terms of compensation, a Red officer must relate to the Red-Army man in the same way as a skilled worker relates to one who is unskilled. To increase this proportion by raising compensation, to establish a proportion that is reminiscent of the bourgeois-noble régime, is completely inadmissible. It is especially inadmissible to increase payment on the basis of holding a higher command-post. Why should the commander of an army receive more than the commander of a division, or the division-commander more than a regiment-commander? I would like to hear from any Communist who would undertake to answer that question.

The enormous harm resulting from the new rates introduced in the army is especially felt by those who are working near to the front or frequenting the front. The enormous and completely unjustified difference in payment demoralises the Red-Army man, provokes completely justifiable protests, and undermines the possibility of establishing comradely relations between rank-and-file Red-Army men and the commanding staff. I know of a number of concrete instances showing that under the influence of the new rates, the relation between the commanding staff and ordinary Red-Army men has sharply deteriorated. Certain officers have voluntarily forgone the pay-rise in order to preserve the former comradely relations with Red-Army men.

But most absurd of all is the fact that workers in the rear, under the staff-headquarters, are also now receiving the higher payments. A typist working for the staff is receiving almost one and a half times more than a typist in any other Soviet institution, and at times they are even housed in one-and-the-same building. And for what great feats and merits?

All this causes demoralisation among the toilers and creates a particularly rotten 'staff'-atmosphere in the Soviet Republic that is analogous to what prevailed in the good-old-days for the bourgeoisie. In the final analysis, one might ask: to whom are we obliged in carrying out such a rash and politically dangerous measure, which can only be welcomed by our enemies on the other side of the trenches?

The conclusions that we come to are the following.

All privileges in the area of payment for labour must be eliminated, and no retreats from our programme must any longer be permitted.

Determination of the compensation for all toilers of the Republic, beginning with the Chairman of the Council of People's Commissars and the Supreme War Council and ending with the last messenger-boy, must be done by the trade-unions according to a single common principle as declared by the October Revolution.

Anything beyond that originates in the evil bourgeois-gentry system, which it is unbecoming for Communists to imitate in the second year of the proletarian dictatorship.

E. Preobrazhensky

No. 39

'On Forms of Proletarian Dictatorship'[1]

9 February 1919

Comrade Osinsky's article 'New Tasks in Constructing the Soviet Republic', published in *Pravda* on 15 January, deserves serious discussion, regardless of how one appraises one or another of its author's contentions and conclusions. The question has two dimensions: theoretical and practical.

From the theoretical side, it is a matter of enormous interest to determine what forms the proletarian dictatorship can assume in general terms, and particularly what forms it must inevitably assume in mainly-peasant countries.

The practical side of the question concerns what form of dictatorship is most expedient at the present moment.

Comrade Osinsky is perfectly correct when he claims that we have yet to realise the commune-state as it appeared to comrade Lenin a year and a half ago. 'It has turned out', he adds, 'that the commune-state is not, in any case, the first transitional stage, the first form of the dictatorship of the proletariat and the poor'. The question then becomes: What is the 'first form' of the proletarian dictatorship? Is it what we have now?

It would be historically incorrect to make that claim. The first form of the dictatorship already lies in the past. It was the period in the life of the soviets when they possessed total power over virtually every question on both a local and state-wide scale; when their work, for the most part, was destructive with regard to the bourgeois-gentry system; when the masses in the localities could dictate their will to the soviets, and saw their wishes transformed into reality without coming into collision with the organised will of the proletariat, even in those cases when the interests of particular strata and local interests did not correspond with the interests of the toilers as a whole.

Comrade Lenin, of course, did not dream up the idea of the commune-state when he wrote about this type of state. He wrote mainly on the basis of the living experience of the Paris Commune and the first steps taken by our own soviets. But the Paris Commune was only the embryo of a proletarian state in its very beginning, not its centralised form.

Now we are experiencing a second, centralised form of proletarian dictatorship that often takes on quite an ugly expression, as comrade Osinsky points

---

1. [From *Ezhenedel'nik pravdy*, No. 3, 9 February 1919. This article continues in Documents 2:41 and 2:42. In the latter two documents, it was published as an article 'for discussion', implying that it represented the author's personal opinion.]

out and as we all recognise. And if even Engels, seeing only the single experience of the Paris Commune, could optimistically hope that the 'lumber of state-institutions' could already be liquidated by a new generation grown up after the revolution, then there is nothing surprising in the fact that comrade Lenin also did not give a picture of all the ulcers that might afflict the soviet-organism during a particular period of its life.

When we turn to an appraisal of this second stage of proletarian dictatorship, which in Russia, at least, is a fact, we must not overlook the following important conditions. Centralisation and the bureaucracy inevitably associated with it are spreading in our country, not only in the administrative-military institutions, whose temporary character is obvious, but also in the economic organisations, because socialism is a centralised social economy. Arbitrariness and lack of control on the part of individual soviet-bureaucrats has replaced the arbitrariness and lack of control of entire local organisations. All the same, we have a step forwards, here, because it is an easier matter to struggle against the bureaucratism and arbitrariness of separate individuals.

We also must not forget that Russia is a peasant-country, and our dictatorship is, for the most part, proletarian. We will probably know the enormous importance of this circumstance only after we become familiar with the form of proletarian dictatorship in mainly-proletarian countries, in Germany for example. It is very important to emphasise this circumstance when speaking of the length of the current stage of dictatorship in Russia, with its extremely harsh and often outwardly non-democratic forms of administration.

Comrade Osinsky suggests that 'we have entered a different period of development', that 'the methods and forms of administration can and must be changed. We must curtail the authoritarian elements in the workers' dictatorship and take steps towards a developed form of worker-peasant democracy, a commune-state'.

We fully agree with comrade Osinsky not only that many 'methods and forms of administration' can and must be changed, but also that they could have been completely avoided even in conditions of heavy fighting. However, we emphatically disagree with the view that the Soviet Republic has entered some kind of 'different period of development'. As of yet, there is no such different period. The external danger continues to be menacing. The danger of new outbreaks of domestic counter-revolution, on the basis of growing exhaustion from civil war and the growing fatigue of the struggling masses, remains undiminished from a year ago. Finally, the peasant-composition of our country and the difficulties of a workers' dictatorship in such conditions will remain for an extremely long time. To illustrate, I will give a real-life example. There is one district in the Urals where the proletarian dictatorship had to be introduced through violence on the part of a minority of newly arrived workers and a minority of the local poor against a kulak-majority together with the middle-peasants who follow the kulaks. The problem was crowned by the fact that the alien-worker 'dictators' themselves fell apart as a result of irresponsibility and distance from the major party-centres that had sent them. What will help with this misfortune? 'A developed form of worker-peasant dictatorship?' That would mean creating 'developed forms' for a kulak counter-revolution. A strengthening of party-control, a strengthening of dictatorship over the dictators? This is the only possible means, but it entails concentration rather than weakening of the dictatorship. Only after our final victory in the Civil War will it be possible to eliminate the harsh forms of dictatorship that are sometimes exerted by one person or by a narrow group, with all their attendant risks and instances of distortion and corruption of the soviet-organism in a given locality and, in analogous circumstances, throughout the whole of Russia. Following such a victory, or as victory is becoming clear, we can liquidate costly and dangerous forms of dictatorship after entering into definite contractual and business-like relations with petty-bourgeois elements who are unsympathetic to Soviet power on the basis, for instance, of this kind of conversation.

> 'You are opposed to Soviet power, opposed to communism?'
>
> 'Yes, we are opposed', is the answer, say, from the well-to-do peasantry and the Cossacks.
>
> 'But you do know that we have won, that we are a strong power, that through compulsion we can do whatever we have to do?'
>
> 'We know'.
>
> 'Is it not better for you, then, to do voluntarily what the Soviet Republic asks of you and thus free yourselves from our administrative and food-procurement agents, and such like, to whom you object?'

The discussants then scratch the back of their heads and, rather than fomenting counter-revolutionary conspiracies or conducting passive resistance, they prefer to accept our conditions.

I do not know whether the constitution of commune-states anticipates such mutual relations, or whether these relations can be embraced by some kind of 'developed form of proletarian dictatorship', but I do know one thing. We are already attempting to follow this road, and we are doing so with some success (grain-assessments[2] in place of stock-taking, imposing requisitions and sending

---

2. [разверстка хлеба]

out food-detachments); in line with our successes in the struggle against foreign and domestic enemies, we will certainly follow this road on an even greater scale, and thus largely resolve the question of the struggle against the decay of the soviet-organism in those places where soviet-organs are deprived of the invigorating proletarian nourishment of democratic mass-control from below.

Of course, we must decisively struggle against tendencies to replace the self-activity of the masses with bureaucratic tutelage wherever this tutelage is excessive, wherever it is harmful, and wherever the masses can manage one-or-another task better through their regularly re-elected organs. The policy of ignoring the plenums of soviets, or deviating from their regular meetings, as often happens in the provinces, and the policy of bureaucratic pressure from above on local organisations that are working efficiently, must be vigorously discouraged. But we must not fall into the opposite extreme. If, say, the dictatorship of particular individuals in the area of food can yield as much as one-eighth of a pound more bread than would be the case with the kind of elected organisation in which people are more concerned with babbling than with business, then every worker would prefer dictatorship with the extra eighth of a pound rather than the dubious right of 'democratically' electing the babblers. Every Marxist knows that the world has never yet seen a single revolution or counter-revolution that has taken place on the basis of struggle **for a different form of rule** while maintaining **essentially the same economic policy**. The worker and poor peasant will forgive us for any form of dictatorship if this dictatorship looks after **their** concerns and if, in the current circumstances, this dictatorship, even if it has degenerated into a dictatorship of particular individuals in certain institutions, is more successful in alleviating the food- and production-crisis.

To all these partial complaints, or more precisely, elaborations that I have made in reference to comrade Osinsky's article, I would like to add one further point that he missed. His characterisation of the shortcomings of Soviet power at its present stage of development is incomplete in the sense that he forgot to mention the emergence in our country of a privileged soviet-bureaucracy as a stratum that is **economically** better off. I consider this ulcer to be the most serious of all.

Without even mentioning the notorious 'specialists', whose salaries should never get through the doorways of a worker-peasant state, it is necessary openly and honestly to recognise that the soviet-bureaucracy and soviet-workers, including Communists, have a tendency to become a privileged caste, enjoying a number of advantages that are inaccessible to ordinary workers. We have stripped the bourgeoisie and for the most part replaced them in many provincial cities exclusively with soviet-workers and their wives, and not with rank-and-file workers. What is it that prevented a different kind of organisation?

We have moved the bourgeoisie out of their private residences, but have we settled many workers into them in this second year of the proletarian revolution?

Many comrades are inclined to think that the deep dissatisfaction of the masses with the privileges of soviet-workers and soviet-functionaries, with this philistinism, is a matter not worthy of consideration. This is a profound error, moreover, an error on the part of a self-interested party. In terms of this question we can unconditionally leave the decisive role to the broad toiling masses themselves, even including those who are opposed to Soviet power. What does the Soviet authority really lose if some commissar or other is deprived of an extra coat or of a leather-jacket that he does not need at a time when a Red-Army man does need it during a rainy autumn?

No privileges! That is the slogan that must be implemented – and it must be implemented **by the Soviet authority itself**. In this respect, it would be extremely useful to publish a special decree allowing any citizen of the toiling class to bring before a people's court, perhaps a court specially formed and elected for this purpose, any person in power who is exposed for creating his own privileged living conditions by way of his responsible position.

In conclusion, I would like to tell all comrades who fear that the Soviet power is sinning too grievously against the formality of worker-peasant democracy to acquire a more correct perspective by looking thoughtfully and more often at the other side of the front. How do matters stand with democracy in the camp of our enemies?

We will all agree that things there do not measure up. Half a year ago, all our opponents came out against us with the slogan of a Constituent Assembly. And where did they end up? Those who were hopelessly enamoured with democracy during an epoch of civil war ended up vanishing from the scene. And all of our remaining **serious** opponents ended up with personal despotism, because both Kolchak and Krasnov actually have, formally and in practice, greater powers in their own hands than Nicholas II had prior to February. Things have reached the point where, for example, the Cadet newspaper *Ufimskaya zhizn'*, in justifying the Kolchak insurrection, specifically declared in one of its lead-articles: 'Russia is not mature enough for an elected authority'. However, Soviet Russia, despite the monstrously difficult conditions of the struggle, has preserved an elected Soviet authority, no matter how significant one-or-another of our retreats from a democracy of the toilers in separate instances or in particular localities (for example, in the area close to the front).

We have no right to disregard the colossal importance of this fact.

Of course, in certain places it would be alluring even now to demonstrate the stability of Soviet power by giving our enemies from the S-Rs and Mensheviks not merely full freedom of speech, but also newsprint and printworks, at the treasury's expense, for a struggle against communism. But this struggle at Soviet expense on behalf of the bourgeoisie – which is what it is, in the final analysis – is a little premature. It is ridiculous to shake our fists after a fight is over, but to put one hand or even one finger in our pocket before the fight ends is more than ridiculous;, it is inadmissible from the point of view of those millions in whose name and for whose interests we must carry things through to a final victory in the shortest possible time. If, in place of Martov's articles, which he himself will be ashamed to re-read in five years time, we use the paper to publish a non-party textbook on arithmetic by Lunacharsky's department,[3] the working class will suffer no loss. The same applies to other freedoms for our opponents. A worker or peasant cannot live without bread. But they will be quite content to live without articles and speeches from the Martovs and Spiridonovas.

E. Preobrazhensky

---

3. [A.V. Lunacharsky was People's Commissar of Education.]

No. 40

'Once Again on Military Specialists' (From the Pre-Congress Discussion)[1]

16 February 1919

In his 'Letter to a Friend', placed in *Pravda* on 9 February, comrade Trotsky again raises the question of using military specialists in the Red Army. The policy of brushing aside this question, considering it to have been resolved by life, apparently has not succeeded, since this question has confronted us time-and-again and is actually posed by life itself. Likewise, it has proven far from sufficient, in convincing the other side, to call supporters of a different viewpoint if not directly fools, then people showing clear signs of sabotage of the brain.

The question demands discussion: it demands a fundamental discussion that takes into account the whole experience on all the fronts during the entire period of the Civil War. It must not be forgotten that, in the final analysis, the issue is, first and foremost, one of the least expenditure of forces, the least expenditure of worker-peasant blood.

Until now, certain supporters of the recruitment of specialists have attempted to present the whole dispute as if the issue were essentially one of whether to make use of military science in the Civil War, or whether it is possible to manage with our 'own means'. This way of posing the problem is very advantageous for comrade Trotsky and all those who agree with him, since it renders the position of the other side hopeless in advance. However, the whole problem with such a simplification of the question is that it appears in such proof-read form only on paper, in the process of a polemic, but that is not how it is in reality.

If there were responsible comrades in our midst who needed to be read a lecture on the benefit of education, this would degrade our Party first of all, not to mention the fact that the pages of our press should not be taken up by such a tedious and useless business.

Thus we reject at the outset the attempt to divide the disputing parties into those who support education, military science and technique and those who oppose such things. The dispute involves a different line of division, and the question must be put in a totally different way.

What is the question in reality?

Under the dictatorship of the proletariat, the working class is the organiser both of production and of state-power. No one else can do this work for it,

---

1. [From *Ezhenedel'nik pravda*, No. 4, 16 February 1919. A note from the editor of the weekly explained that 'The article is published for discussion-purposes'.]

regardless of whether the proletariat of a given country is or is not fully prepared to take possession of the entire mechanism of production and of the state. The Red Army is part of the mechanism of the Soviet state. The proletariat must take possession of the military apparatus or, more accurately, create its own military apparatus in the shortest possible time. No Communist doubts that it is now precisely the working class, just as it was once the militaristic nobility, that must be organiser of the military machine. The dispute only begins when the question arises as to what degree, or whether to any degree at all, the new class-organiser can utilise the technical resources of the old tsarist army in constructing a new class-army.

At the outset, this was a purely theoretical debate. The year-long experience of building the Red Army, together with the experience of the Civil War, makes it possible to keep the theoretical discussion to a minimum and to operate more with the facts.

What do the facts say?

The facts say that use of military specialists has turned out, in many instances, to be successful, and that many of these specialists even now bring substantial benefits to the Red Army. On the other hand, the facts say that on all the fronts we have had numerous instances of treason, treachery, and counter-revolutionary activities on the part of the former officer-corps. We have had, and we still have, an enormous volume of facts involving malicious sabotage by officers who have been brought in to instruct the Red Army but who do practically no work, despite the advantageous economic conditions of service. If on one side of the scale are placed all the cases of honest work by the old officers and of heroic deaths by their representatives in battles – and on the other, all the cases of treason and sabotage, no-one can undertake to say which will outweigh the other. But a general conclusion can still be drawn, and it will run approximately as follows: use of the old officers has been successful for the Soviet power to a rather limited degree, and there is no evidence sufficient to assert that the pluses from this use balance the minuses.

But this is not the only conclusion that we can draw. Use of the old officers has had a negative effect in that it has pushed our Party to follow the line of least resistance in the matter of constructing the Red Army. Too few schools were organised for Red officers; seventy percent of those attending turned out not to belong to our Party, and those who were sent to the schools were not first of all frontline or even rank-and-file Communists. This could have been avoided, of course, if from the very beginning we had based all our hopes in building the army on our own commanding staff of Communist workers.

There is more. In volunteer-regiments, comprising mainly workers, the old officers did not pose a danger to us as a politically alien force. From the moment that our army is transformed into a mainly peasant-army, a non-volunteer army, the creation of a commanding staff that is not our own threatens to convert the non-proletarian army into an instrument of a different class.

When whole battalions and regiments of this kind – units in which a commanding staff that is alien to us is joined with soldier-masses that are hostile or indifferent to Soviet power – go over to the side of our enemy, this is only an early warning of much greater misfortune. (Incidentally, the party-congress must know precisely how many cases of treachery and treason there have been on all the fronts.)

The use of old officers and military functionaries has a negative effect in that we automatically began to build, and we are continuing to build, all our military apparatus along the former lines. When the old officers enormously outnumber Communists, this is absolutely inevitable. All the habits and all the worst aspects of the tsarist army are automatically carried over to the Red Army. It is enough to point to the criminally negligent and bureaucratic-official work of a number of military institutions on whose conscience must weigh numerous bloody defeats at the front. If even half of the military institutions worked as our party-organisations do in feverish times, if the haemorrhoidal-bureaucratic heritage from the tsarist army had been absent from the very beginning in constructing various departments in the rear of the Red Army, if the entire apparatus had been constructed with the participation of worker-organisations, making use of their habits, methods and tempo of work, then we would, quite likely, now be nearer to an ideal type of Red Army.

Consider the work done by the departments for forming [military units]. The main part of this enormously important work cannot be done by the old officers, because it is class-political work. Taking account of those mobilised and sorting them according to class and property, and finally according to their political attitude, can be entrusted only to a Communist, and not just to any Communist. Where the old officers have had this responsibility, reducing their work to matching a certain number of overcoats, boots and rifles with a certain number of people, headed up by the first available commanders (in the tsarist army, this is what 'forming' [units] meant), the result on Soviet territory, if not a White army, is in any case not a victorious army.

In conclusion, it will not be redundant to point to yet another totally objectionable consequence of the mass-enlistment of military specialists; that is, the impossibility of the Soviet power digesting this whole element at once, with the consequence that it is not the Soviet authority that makes use of the cadres of specialists it incorporates but, on the contrary, it is the specialists who make use of the Soviet authority in their own interests. Recently there have been far too many of them who are specialists in obtaining salaries for wearing holes in the seats of chairs at public expense. The dominance of this element leads to a situation in which the Communists who are sprinkled into this milieu are either powerless to change anything or, even worse, they are imperceptibly assimilated into it. In his 'Letter to a Friend', comrade Trotsky notes the existence of a certain sort of very unattractive Communists who are opposed to specialists merely because they see in them more resourceful and capable workers who are able to push aside Communist ineptitude. I do not know whether comrade Trotsky has noticed the emergence among us of another sort of Communists, those who are hypnotised and whose vigilance is lulled to sleep by the magical 'yes sir', 'as you order' and 'the smell of flattery', and who consider servility more comfortable for their state of mind than severe criticism from party-comrades. There are different forms of laziness and unwillingness to learn. Among responsible Communists in military posts I have observed a kind of laziness that is fostered in our comrades by the exclusive environment of the old officers surrounding them. These comrades, having become accustomed to staff-offices, begin to think of themselves as virtual military people; and in complete harmony with the officers' spirit of 'the good-old-days' they begin to distinguish themselves from 'Communist *shpaks*' (in the contemptuous terminology of the officer-caste, *shpak* is the term for a civilian). The emergence of this type represents an unconditional victory over us, a bloodless moral victory of the old officers. The worst of it is that the victims in this case are old comrades who have been tested in battles and tempered by prison and exile, whom one would expect to be immune to all kinds of 'crafty courtiers' and to understand where they have been sent by the Party, why, and for how long they will be left at their posts.

For a complete and objective portrayal of this question, I would have to go beyond negatives and point also to the positive aspects of enlisting military specialists in the Red Army. I am not doing so because my task has been the following: I wanted to demonstrate that the opponents of enlisting specialists, and also the opponents of enlisting them in such numbers and so carelessly as we have been doing, are not confined to the group of personages against whom comrade Trotsky is polemicising, that the very question is more complicated, and that many circumstances are connected with it that are only now becoming clear.

We are building, we make mistakes, we measure things, we correct our mistakes, and then we build anew. No-one can claim that in the enlistment of old officers there have been no mistakes. We have to acknowledge and correct those mistakes. For that reason, it would be desirable to include in the congress-agenda not just a point referring to military policy, which is too general, but rather a special topic on the Red Army.

E. Preobrazhensky

No. 41

'On Forms of Proletarian Dictatorship'[1]

2 March 1919[2]

The question of studying the form of proletarian dictatorship that now exists in Soviet Russia is not so much one of theoretical interest as one of profound and vitally practical interest. Without a general analysis of this form, it is difficult to sort out particular issues or to separate what is essential from what is fleeting and incidental, what is unavoidable from what is easily overcome.

But this general analysis cannot be done without examining all the circumstances of the Civil War as a whole, both in the current period and during the first months of proletarian rule.

All of us frequently return in our thoughts from the present period of proletarian dictatorship to the first days of the October Revolution and the first days of the existence of the soviets in general. A comparison of the soviets' past with their present appears, on the surface, to be far from favourable to the present. Previously, each and every worker took part in electing the soviets; a decision of the soviet was considered to be law, which everyone implicitly obeyed without any external coercion; the masses were deeply interested in every question discussed in the soviets; and meetings of a soviet were attended by crowds of thousands wherever there was enough room. Every question was decided quickly, there was no domination by officials and no bureaucratism, and the masses were seemingly captivated by a new form of power in which authority was not regarded as an organ of coercion. At any given moment, everyone was prepared to rise up as one man in defence of the soviets, because defending them meant defending oneself.

That is how it was. Every one of us knows that things are different now, but not all of us are taking into account where the deterioration (one might even say – degeneration) of soviet-power lies, why this deterioration has occurred, or how long the current stage of proletarian dictatorship will last.

Let us consider these questions.

Those who yearn for the past often limit their criticism of the present form of dictatorship to a simple comparison of the work of today's soviets with that of soviets in the first months of the revolution, pointing out the enormous shortcomings of the present form but taking no account whatsoever of all the circum-

---
1. From *Ezhenedel'nik pravda*, No. 6, 2 March 1919. A note from the editor of the weekly explained that 'The article is published for discussion-purposes'.]
2. [This article begins in Document 2:39 and continues in Document 2:42.]

stances that conditioned the type of soviets and the tempo of their work a year or a year and a half ago. Meanwhile, the conditions that decisively determined things at that time were varied: they included the international, the domestic political, and the economic situations.

Our February Revolution occurred at the height of war between the European imperialists. From the moment of the Revolution up to February 1918, over the course of a year, what we essentially achieved was a breathing space from war, if we leave out the artificially provoked June offensive when the initiative for renewing military action did not come from German imperialism. In fact, the imperialist War on our front died away, and the army spontaneously demobilised without any government-orders, simply collapsing under the pressure of the mass of millions of workers and peasants who had been forcibly brought into it. The soviets of this period were organs for the organised dissolution of autocratic-gentry institutions and then of the bourgeois system. They restrained the passion from below, introduced a certain structure into the spontaneous process, were held back at certain points, particularly under the influence of social agents of the bourgeoisie, but in general and on the whole, just like the masses, they followed the path of least resistance in destroying the old fetters. And for a time, the international conditions were such that they had no need to replace the 'chains of serfdom' with any new ones.

The work of destruction – this is a merry and easy task, and during such periods there is no significant gap between the word and the deed. In the course of this work, the soviets could objectively be organs not only of the conscious, but also of the spontaneous will of the toilers. And regardless of how the bourgeois-noble upper classes raised an outcry over dangers and the destruction of the country (they quite correctly foresaw their own destruction), for the lower classes of the people, the mass of desertions, which led to a regular demobilisation and elimination of the officer-caste, along with party-discipline, brought enormous relief associated with the end of the slaughterhouse and the confidence of survival.

The same could be said of all of the soviets' activities, to the extent that the soviets took the lead in destroying all feudal-bourgeois relations and threw off every kind of bondage. In this destructive work, it would be difficult to say whether the soviets led the masses or the masses led the soviets. Probably, the latter is true.

Consider the economic sphere. Despite the enormous exhaustion caused by the War, the feudal-bourgeois system still had certain resources at its disposal for continuing its normal existence. The propertied classes had funds for personal consumption, as well as various types of fixed property. The work of redistribution, to the benefit of the toilers, was something the toilers found easy and festive. There was wide scope for the spontaneous activity of the masses, and the distance between a resolution and its implementation was also negligible here. This was all the more true because in the work of redistribution, the interests of individual groups of workers and peasants rarely ran up against the interests of all the toilers as a whole. The organisation of production was hardly beginning, while redistribution was in full swing. The workers demanded a rise in wages – and this measure was implemented, because there was still, in the final analysis, something available for the taking. The peasants demanded the state-forest – and they chopped away at it with the soviet's approval while no one thought of the state's interests. A food-train on its way to Petrograd had to be held up somewhere along the way because in some given locality there was a shortage of bread – it was held up, with no regard for the consequences.

In a word, it was all power to the local soviets and there was nothing more to be said. At the time, the working class could allow itself this luxury, and the activity of the masses was not for nothing: the energy they expended was always justified, in whole or in part, by acquiring what they needed.

Finally, let us recall the domestic political situation. The attempted counter-revolutionary coup, ventured by Kornilov, was suppressed by the workers and soldiers as a trifle. Even the October Revolution, thanks to the weakness of the bourgeoisie, occurred with minimal losses on the part of the proletariat. The bourgeoisie was so dumbfounded by the completed revolution and all its consequences that for several months it was unable to organise any resistance or attract to its side the upper strata in the countryside – if we leave aside insurrections on the periphery that were suppressed with little effort. With the Brest peace, we were also able to buy off their class-ally, German imperialism, in part because the war between the imperialists was still not finished.

In this way, favourable domestic and external conditions made it objectively possible for the soviets of the first period of proletarian dictatorship to emerge in the form they did.

Tolstoy wrote of the 'happy, irretrievable time of childhood'. The childhood of the soviets was just such a happy time, but what is most important for us now is the fact that it is an *irretrievable* time. When appraising the second period of proletarian dictatorship, we must begin by understanding this fact, not by restricting ourselves to sighing about the childhood period of the existence of Soviet power.

The current form of proletarian dictatorship came about because of the greater danger posed to the Soviet Republic from without. We suffer from the fact that our revolution began earlier than in other countries of the world. Had there been a simultaneous crash of capitalist relations in the leading countries, we would have no need for the incredible stress on the spiritual and physical resources of the people involved in building a regular army for civil war. Our domestic position deteriorated in connection with the organisation of counter-revolutionary forces that rely on the economically strong strata of the peasantry. In the economic sphere, we have to produce and build up supplies in extremely painful conditions, rather than distributing what has already been produced. Finally, we must build a socialist – and thus, inevitably, centralised – economy in an economically backward and mainly petty-bourgeois country.

It is perfectly obvious that with different international, domestic, political and economic conditions, and with more organic tasks of construction appropriate for a new level of development, the dictatorship of the proletariat would inevitably have taken forms different from those, say, at the end of 1917. All that remains is to examine which aspects of the dictatorship of the second period are more-or-less accidental, deformed, excessive and surmountable, and which are connected with the very essence of this period and with the very existence of Soviet power in general, given the existing conditions.

Let us begin with the fundamental question, the question of whether or not the dictatorship of the proletariat and poor peasants is presently the dictatorship of a majority or the dictatorship of a minority of the toiling population of Russia. Foaming at the mouth, our enemies try to prove precisely the latter, and claim that we do not have Soviet power at all, that what really exists is simply a régime of commissars. If you have the majority on your side, they say, then why is there any need for dictatorship?

If we do not have the majority, then perhaps the majority is for our enemies in the White-Guard camp, for Krasnov, Kolchak and Denikin?

Neither the Mensheviks nor the S-Rs make this claim, particularly those among them who have recently visited the kingdom of the White-Guard authority.

Perhaps the majority is for the Mensheviks and S-Rs, and generally for the defenders of democracy and the Constituent Assembly?

The Mensheviks and S-Rs flatter themselves with this hope, but then one can ask: If they have the majority, then why is it that Avksent'ev and company so vigorously defended the need for dictatorship precisely in the territory where the Constituent-Assembly supporters held power and where, in their opinion, they had the support of a majority?

The question, it turns out, is not as simple as our opponents imagine, and during a period of civil war there are, apparently, other ways of determining the will of the toiling masses besides voting, ways that over a period of just a few months can produce, and in fact have produced, entirely different results. One need only recall Belorussia and Ukraine before and after the overthrow there of Soviet power, or Siberia before the rule of Kolchak compared with today, and so forth.

The experience of civil war has demonstrated the complete failure of any struggle by petty-bourgeois elements against the bourgeois-monarchist dictatorship under the flag of a Constituent Assembly and with the implementation of the principles of bourgeois democracy. On the contrary, the same experience of civil war has demonstrated that it is fully possible for capital to struggle against labour under this exact same slogan, especially in the first phase. Thus, when answering the question of whether the majority does or does not stand for Soviet power, the contending possibilities are either the dictatorship of the bourgeoisie or the dictatorship of the proletariat – the petty-bourgeois strata, with all their dreams and illusions, are completely out of the picture.

There cannot be any dispute over which of these two dictatorships, the ones actually up for choice by the toilers, defends the interests of the majority. And once victory over the dictatorship of White Guards turns out to be necessary for the interests of the majority of the population, something that is recognised both by the Mensheviks and the S-Rs, then the natural question is whether victory over the dictatorship of capital is possible without recourse to dictatorship in general and to the form of dictatorship that we have today, which intensifies or moderates depending on the intensity of the struggle.

Recently the Mensheviks, like losing gamblers, are time-and-again burning with impatience to do battle with us in elections to the soviet in the hope that by speculating on hunger, the burdens of life and the abuses by various Soviet-Tashkent gentlemen they might win an *electoral* victory over us. Suppose, for the moment, that in elections to the soviets the Mensheviks and S-Rs did win out, and suppose, further, that as a result of this electoral victory they took power – just what would they do in our place? Under the slogan of the Constituent Assembly, and with their attempts to rely on general democratic organisations, they would be beaten from both the left and the right. In order not to be defeated by the right, by the Krasnovs and Denikins, they would have to adopt, generally and on the whole, the same methods of struggle as we have done, for no-one has yet thought up any other methods to guarantee a victory, nor has history provided any such examples. But in that case, all the howls from the right about Bolshevik dictatorship and violence against the masses turn out to be the simple and invariable demagogy of people who have suffered such a profound defeat that they think they are fully insured against the possibility of finding themselves in power and then demonstrating once again to the toiling masses their own complete infirmity.

But if the current form of proletarian dictatorship, which is being carried out in the interests of the enormous majority, is completely inevitable in the conditions of the moment, this by no means implies that everything is just fine with us, or that our existing form of Soviet power does not involve a whole series of deformities and distortions against which the most decisive struggle is required.

What these deformities are, and how we can struggle against them, even in the present conditions unfavourable to any normal construction, is the question we will turn to next.

E. Preobrazhensky

No. 42

'On Forms of Proletarian Dictatorship. The Shortcomings of Soviet Power'[1]

16 March 1919[2]

The previous article spoke of the inevitability in Russia of the current form of proletarian dictatorship, which is connected with increased centralisation and limits on the spontaneous activity of soviet-democracy. Now let us investigate those manifestations of distortion and corruption of Soviet power that, even though they are blooming in red during precisely this period of proletarian dictatorship, are, nevertheless, not absolutely inevitable and irrevocable accompaniments of this concentrated form of dictatorship.

As I have already mentioned, the decline in spontaneous activity of the labouring masses, as compared to the first weeks after the October Revolution and the first months after the February Revolution, is due to the general fatigue of the masses and also to the fact that in places the masses have lost the ability and the right to decide **all questions**, even general questions of state. It is perfectly clear that after losing somewhere in Sormova, Ivanovo-Voznesensk or Perm, the possibility of deciding the most important questions on the spot and often in terms of purely local interests, the masses must make the transition to **actively** deciding those same questions on an all-Russian scale and not fall into a philistine sleep, leaving it to those they have elected to trade-union and soviet-organisations to decide all the state-wide and even local questions without being subject to any control. Of course, a man who acts independently only where and when he smells a five-*kopek* coin – such a man is difficult to re-educate all at once, and the waning of mass-activity was inevitable. But together with this, we have also seen, and are still seeing, another menacing process. Those elected from among the masses are beginning to develop a taste for their new position, that is, for work not subject to any control, work that does not require referring every decision to the masses or expending any effort on objections, explanations, and so on. The result is to drowse off in soft bureaucratic armchairs (even if they are soviet-armchairs); and many very valuable workers, sent by the masses to responsible posts, do not even do what they can and should be doing to awaken mass-activity. It may be that involving the masses in state-wide work and training

---

1. [From *Ezhenedel'nik pravda*, No. 8, 16 March 1919. A note from the editor of the weekly explained that 'The article is published for discussion-purposes'.]
2. [For previous parts of this article, see Documents 2:39 and 2:41.]

them for state-work is a long process that will not be completed, perhaps, by our generation. However, the job must be undertaken now.

Besides the bureaucratisation of soviet-workers and the conversion of revolutionaries into functionaries who are completely detached from the masses and psychologically estranged from them, we are seeing on the part of this new worker-bureaucracy an unwillingness to do even what the letter of our constitution requires.

In a number of cities, for example, they have completely stopped calling plenums of the soviets, or else they do so extremely rarely. Reports are never delivered in front of the masses, and the soviets, absorbed in some work or other, have completely forgotten the good old habit our soviets once had of giving an account at each meeting to their electors. Not wishing to spend time on this, 'busy people' fail to understand that one of the most important matters in our republic is precisely the task of managing the state by way of the masses and with their active support. Even on questions that are vitally important and deeply troubling to the masses, such as the food-question, an account is rarely given to the masses, and the social opinion of hungry workers is beginning to be formed by some speculator from Okhotny Ryad[3] rather than by the Communist Party and the people it has sent into soviet-work.

However, we would not fully appraise the enormous danger of the separation of soviet-workers from the masses – who have lost all hope of improving their lives through 'independent action' – if we passed over in silence and failed to take account of a fact that, unfortunately, we do not like to discuss but which a party capable of surviving, a party of the future, must speak about publicly. I am talking about the fact that an enormous stratum of our soviet-workers, both elected and non-elected, are not merely threatening to become, but to some degree actually have become, an economically privileged caste. By comparison with the ordinary worker, these privileges are expressed in higher payment for labour, in more comfortable apartment- and food-conditions, in greater access to means of transportation, and in greater ease of acquiring necessities from various soviet-institutions. Of course, the excesses received by soviet-workers in terms of financial means and food-resources are, in general and on the whole, not great, despite all the philistine tales on this account. The introduction of equality throughout the entire Republic would not in the slightest degree alleviate the food-crisis or moderate the financial crisis. But here is what does matter. Those groups that have landed in privileged positions endeavour, as a rule, to

---

3. [Even at the beginning of the nineteenth century, Okhotny ryad was a commercial district with numerous shops, warehouses, taverns, and so on. The district was reconstructed in the 1930s and is now the site of an expansive underground shopping mall attached to the Moscow Metro.]

hold on to their positions. The result is creation not simply of a bureaucracy, but of a conservative bureaucracy, like the workers' bureaucracy of Germany and England, which smothers any embryo of new and fresh impulses on the part of the workers' movement in those countries. In order to retain his post, which is more profitable and **attractive than work at the bench**, an elected soviet-worker endeavours either to postpone the moment of new elections if he is threatened with losing, or else he employs every effort to succeed if new elections do occur. What this leads to is the fact that the composition of soviet-workers almost always remains the same, and the attempt by our Party to attract every worker without exception into the business of managing the country by turns, even if this involves minor functions and extends only so far as circumstances permit – this attempt encounters stubborn resistance from the new workers' bureaucracy.

There has already been much talk about a purge of the Communist Party, about eliminating from its ranks all kinds and degrees of hangers-on. When speaking of the proletarian dictatorship and the different processes connected with it, both healthy and unhealthy, we cannot avoid touching upon the inner condition and personal composition of the Party that is conducting this dictatorship.

The question of purging the Party is posed as a question of state, since cleansing the Party of its self-seeking, careerist and criminal element must also improve the health of our Soviet institutions. But it is obvious that there will be no genuine purge unless the main cause is eliminated, which compels every rogue to cling to us in the Party with the same annoying stubbornness of a fly clinging to honey. We must eliminate every economic privilege attached to being in our Party; more than that, we must make remaining in our Party even somewhat disadvantageous in economic terms.

On the other hand, removability and responsibility on the part of soviet-workers will help to make certain that power itself is less frequently converted into a means of profiteering.

For that reason, it is necessary to make special mention in our programme of the emergence, discernable among us, of a socialist, privileged, and rarely removable bureaucracy, together with the need for determined struggle against this evil.

The greatest misuse of power, the greatest embezzlement of public property, and the greatest outrage against the very idea of communism is being committed by the special 'service-class' of the Soviet régime, which is most strongly represented in the countryside. Every régime is surrounded by such a class. Though it may seem strange, the Soviet authority also has this element, which penetrates it through service in the form of those elected to different executive committees and congresses and also in the form of people who are ardent supporters of the

Communist Party. In the majority of cases, these are either semi-intellectuals or *déclassés* from the workers or peasants with no desire to return to their main profession. Of course, I am only speaking here of the worst part of this element, the criminals or semi-criminals.

How can we free the countryside of these 'Communists'?

In places where the population supports Soviet power, this element must be driven out from below and replaced by the uncorrupted, purely labouring element of the village, however badly prepared they may be for work in the executive committees.

In places where the population is opposed to Soviet power but thinks it is currently dangerous to oppose it openly, it is better simply to bypass the Soviet Constitution and govern through responsible plenipotentiaries of Soviet power. Least of all should we be confused in such cases by Menshevik and S-R howling about naked dictatorship and a régime of commissars. Wherever necessary, an authority that expresses the will of the majority is obliged to subordinate the minority by other means, even by non-democratic means. In either case the 'service element' that has attached itself to the Soviet authority for 'feeding' purposes will be rejected as useless.

In conclusion, I must add a few words concerning our economic and military spheres of construction.

Herzen spoke of his father in terms of clever uselessness. Our economic construction, in a period of the most extreme dictatorship over the economic sphere, is very often accompanied by clever uselessness. Comrades who are versed in the matter know just how many 'central boards' and 'centres' there are that represent such clever uselessness, having no real production base and being severed from control by trade-union organisations. It appears that the Tea-Centre, which has a solid staff of employees at a time when there has long been no trace of tea, is the most striking example. Production is organised 'according to plan', and frequently they begin by hiring an official and then look for some work he can do – not the reverse. As a result of centralisation, which is a general characteristic of socialist society, in our country we have wildly disfigured forms in certain areas. All these fatty deposits of bureaucratism must be pitilessly severed, and in future we must reject any construction of socialism that comes from Manilov-like[4] functionaries in the offices. Workers' production-organisations have only recently begun to be regularly involved in the creation of economic centres. But there was a period when even the trade-union centres themselves were starting to be converted into bureaucratic departments.

---

4. [*Manilov* was a character in Gogol's *Dead Souls*, whose name has become synonymous with lack of principle, sentimentality and day-dreaming.]

Economic construction can attract broad new strata of workers; all that is needed is to approach the matter in such a way that the creator and organiser of socialist forms of economy from top to bottom is the worker, so that we will have the skill and experience to elicit from below, from the toilers, the talents that have perished there along with the energy that has not yet been awakened by life.

If the dictatorship of the proletariat in the economic sphere has sometimes led to creation of clever and foolish uselessness, the same thing has also occurred in our military construction. In the construction of the Red Army, we can see a harmful inclination towards copying the old army, a copying that cannot be justified by considerations of the matter at hand nor by any other considerations. One has merely to read the recently affirmed regulations on garrison-duty or to recall efforts to introduce symbols of difference in command (communist ranks, and such like).

One of the tasks of the coming party-congress will be the following: to outline, by drawing upon the collective experience of all comrades who are working at the different ends of Russia and in different spheres of social activity, the means of struggle against the ugly distortions in the form of proletarian dictatorship that we now have and that is objectively necessary. Moreover, we must prepare now for the transition from this form to another one that anticipates the withering away of state-institutions in general, and this means that it is necessary to struggle decisively against all tendencies that facilitate the solidifying of existing forms and the conversion even of many Communists into members of some kind of conservative party.

E. Preobrazhensky

Nos. 43–44
Reports for 10–16 May 1919[1] from the Plenipotentiary of the VTsIK and Responsible Representative of the Central Committee of the RKP(B) to Orel Province E.A. Preobrazhensky[2] to the Central Committee of the RKP(B) on Assisting the Local Authority in Mobilisation of the Population for the Struggle against Denikin

No. 43

A Short Report of Four Days from Central-Committee Plenipotentiary Preobrazhensky

Orel Province   *10–13 May 1919*

10 May

Upon arrival, arranged a meeting of most active party-workers. Complete contact established. They selected a leading group of five to speed the work. Organised a bureau of complaints under the Department of State-Control, with Communists on duty for 24 hours. Spoke to the plenum of the city-soviet. Attended meeting of the elected bureau. Insisted on a trip about the province by several responsible local workers.

---

1. [The reports for 10–13 and 13–16 May were registered in the Secretariat of the Central Committee of the RKP(B) on 21 May 1919 with No. 5255.]

2. [E.A. Preobrazhensky was dispatched to Orel province in accordance with the following decision by the Central Committee of the RKP(B):

'Resolution of the Central Committee of the RKP(B) on the delegation of responsible plenipotentiaries to conduct mobilisation in the localities and look into party-work (April–May 1919).

'For the purposes of more successful mobilisation in the localities and familiarisation with the party-work of provincial organisations, the Central Committee of the RKP(B) has resolved to delegate the following responsible plenipotentiaries for temporary work:

11 May

Spent five hours in discussion with students. Familiarised them in detail with the coming work. To dispatch them quickly turned out to be impossible: 1) they must all, especially their leaders, be acquainted with the affairs of the district to which they are being sent; 2) need a minimum of two to three days to sort them all out according to their degree of preparedness. Decided to send them directly to districts where there are already reliable comrades and with leaders to the others.

From the report of the Cheka-inspector, assigned by the Supreme Cheka-Committee, received a disgraceful picture of the local Cheka. Meeting was convened of a small group of comrades on the question of how to liquidate this cesspool most carefully and usefully in terms of the business at hand. Incidentally, a fugitive from arrest, Ul'yanov, who is accused of various crimes, is now Chairman of the Chekists in Chernigov province.

Established that many convicted bandits and scoundrels, who were driven out of the Party, now occupy responsible positions in Ukraine. This is an important reason for peasant-disturbances there.

12 May

Began assigning the students to the districts.[3] This took the better part of two days. For now, sent three persons to each district. Unexpectedly received

---

to Vyatka province, comrade Steklov; Vladimir, comrade Krylenko; Voronezh, comrade Eremeev; Gomel, comrade Pravdin; Ivanovo-Voznesensk, comrade Ryazanov; Kaluga, comrade Yaroslavsky; Kostroma, comrade Lunacharsky; Kursk, comrade Bukharin; Minsk, comrade Dmitriev; Moscow, comrade Maksimovsky; Nizhegorod, comrade Semashko; Orel, comrade Preobrazhensky; Tambov, comrade Podbel'sky; Tver, comrade Sosnovsky; Tula, Kanatchikov and comrades from the Moscow organisation: Kryukov, Merkulov, Emel'yanov, Ilyushin, Osipov, Esinov, Ovsyannikov, Pisarev.

'Each of the above-listed comrades, as a responsible representative of the Central Committee of the RKP(B), is to head a group of students for courses established by the VTsIK and the proletarian university.

'On Monday 5 May, at 5 pm at the premises of the Secretariat of the Central Committee RKP (third floor, apartment 4, and in Moscow, No. 7, apartment 3) there is to be a meeting of the comrade-plenipotentiaries to discuss the work.

'Secretary of the Central Committee RKP

'Travelling-Inspection Department of the Secretariat of the Central Committee'.

(From GA RF. F. 1240–P. Op. 1. D. 1. L. 1. Original.)

E.A. Preobrazhensky sent back from Orel province a large collection of documents (reports, accounts, telegrams, and texts of resolutions sent from the parishes by the students), which subsequently constituted an entire fund in one of the most important archives of the country, TsGAOR USSR (the Central USSR State-Archive of the October Revolution, now GA RF, the State-Archive of the Russian Federation). See GA RF. F. 1240–P. Op. 1. D. 1.]

3. [Mobilisation was conducted in the parishes of Bolkhov, Bryansk, Dmitrov, Kroma, Livnensky, Orel and Trubchevsk.]

information that might have to provide also for four districts of Chernigov province that are attached for military purposes to Orel province. No party-contacts with these districts. Saved part of the students for these districts. Students are generally weak. Only about a quarter of them are effective workers.

In personal tour of hospitals, found no special disorders. The regional apartment-directorate is distinctly careless in work.

Approved arrest of the Cheka-collegium and removal of its chairman. The least of crimes by those arrested involved numerous bribes, hooliganism and constant drunkenness. New staff drawn from absolutely reliable comrades under chairmanship of comrade Komlev, sent from the supreme Cheka-committee.

13 May

Established contact with inspector of military supply. On the 15th will have a report of the investigation. Incidentally, the inspector found in one warehouse two thousand rifles that were never accounted for. Sent a commission to investigate political work in the army. Calling a meeting tomorrow for those managing agitation and propaganda.

Sent Volin to Bryansk because out of three thousand workers mobilised there, only seven hundred turned up, and they refused to go without the others. Out of five hundred Communists mobilised in the province, only half appeared by our arrival. Tomorrow, at a meeting of the organisations, will introduce a resolution for the arrest and handover to a military court of those who again fail, for the *last*[4] time, to appear by the appointed deadline. For two years, the general mobilisation has gone badly, although desertions are falling. With the coming completion of sowing, a further decline in number of deserters is inevitable.

Initiated an audit of the union of disabled soldiers. Decided with Ostrovskaya to re-examine all those exempted from mobilisation.

E. Preobrazhensky

---

4. [Underlined by E.A. Preobrazhensky.]

No. 44

Second Regular Report from Plenipotentiary Preobrazhensky[1]

Orel Province   *13–16 May 1919*

Received responses to my queries concerning the progress of local mobilisation. In not a single district did the mobilisation occur satisfactorily. In most cases, it had not even begun at the moment when they received my query. The matter is even further complicated by the announcement of general mobilisation for Orel province. In Trubchevsk parish, seventy percent did not turn up for general mobilisation. This number is now falling somewhat. The peasants in this parish are not volunteering for mobilisation. This information refers to the time prior to arrival of the students and my plenipotentiaries. One thing is clear: to implement parish-mobilisation, a most serious campaign is needed, which will require more than a month.

The trade-union mobilisation, with the exception of Bryansk, where an effort that started excellently was disrupted by Veisman's report and the centre's flippantly credulous attitude to it, is proceeding satisfactorily. So far as I can see, the workers' attitude is good. This is evident in resolutions by various workers' meetings and their organisations.

Of five hundred Communists mobilised, more than four hundred have appeared and the late comrades continue to arrive from the districts. Mobilisation uncovered several slackers.

With the end of field-work, desertion is falling throughout the province.

Party-work is going badly. In the Provincial Committee, there is currently not a single comrade dealing exclusively with party-work, which I brought to the organisation's attention. In Bryansk, at the Bezhetsk locomotive-building plant, *there is not a single worker from the bench* in the Communist organisation. This is out of eleven thousand workers! I urgently request that the Central Committee leave comrade Volin for one month in Bryansk region exclusively for party-work.

In view of the resolution by the trade-unions and committees of assistance regarding an increase in the percentage of draftees, and in view of the protest against this by the Provincial Economic Council, which fears a fall in the productivity of work for the military due to the proposed supplementary mobilisation, a meeting between the Economic Council and the trade-unions is scheduled for 22 May, when the question of supplementary mobilisation of workers will finally be clarified.

---

1. [From RGASPI. F. 17. Op. 66. D. 27. L. 130–2. Handwritten.]

The Chairman of the Provincial Economic Council told me that he has outfits and boots available for more than one and a half regiments, yet the local garrison and those being sent to the front are lacking much of what they require. The cause: centralisation in the distribution of supplies, together with incredible bureaucratism and paralysis of the entire apparatus. Incidentally, the March unrest among draftee-companies in Orel occurred because the soldiers were lacking outfits, while the economic council had everything that was needed but there was no order for the transfer of supplies to the Regional Commissariat. I bring this to comrade Stalin's attention. I will send detailed information with the next report. One more detail. The representative sent by the Provincial Economic Council to get coils of cloth (for work on the soldiers' linen), *has already been waiting for them for six weeks in Moscow.*[2]

According to information from the Provincial Land-Department, thirty percent of the land ploughed by peasants in the province is on soviet-estates. I will be able establish a detailed picture when I know the details myself, because the Provincial Land-Department blames everything on a certain letter from comrade Lenin to Sereda, whereas others blame the Provincial Land-Department, which allegedly does not temporarily allot for ploughing even the land that it cannot work itself. However, the inertia of the Main Sugar Directorate is an established fact: the beetroot plantations in Sevsk district may remain un-seeded. To clarify the matter, I sent the manager of the Provincial Land-Department to Sevsk district.

I have been faced with colossal work, and the need to put things right in Orel has prevented me from going to the districts and taking a look at the countryside. Today, however, I am leaving for Karachev and then to Eletsk and Livensk districts.

A complaints-bureau has been organised under control.[3] 15 complaints have been submitted and already considered. I suggested to the district-executive committees that they organise such bureaux.

Plenipotentiary for Orel Province
E. Preobrazhensky

---

2. [Underlined in the document.]
3. [The reference is to the Department of State-Control (see the report of 10 May).]

Nos. 45–6
Articles Published in the Newspaper *Pravda* at the Beginning of June 1919

No. 45

'Islands of Socialism'[1]

1 June 1919

I

From my many impressions of the provinces, I would like to say something about agricultural communes.

The village-commune, at the present moment, is the sort of multi-faceted unknown that will either cheer or disappoint us.

I will say a few words about those [communes] that will already be pleasing to the eye of every socialist. I have in mind the communes of the Karachev district in Orel province.

Six communes and 52 *artels* are registered with the district land-department. The large number of *artels* is explained by the fact that peasants do not like the word 'commune'; this word is not popular, and many *artels* that are not only production-associations, but also come close to practising communist distribution, avoid calling themselves 'communes'.

Of this number, 39 *artel*-communes have been subsidised by the land-department. All of the communes

---

1. [From *Pravda*, 1 June 1919. The article appeared under the heading 'In the Village' in four issues of the newspaper. For the continuation, see Documents 2:46, 2:48, and 2:50.]

and *artels* have been fully supplied with seed-grain and implements. At the time of my visit to Karachev district, almost all of the communes had finished spring-sowing at a time when many peasant communities, being preoccupied with quarrels and disputes over the allotment and repartition of land, had not even begun to sow.

What do these 58 commune-*artels* signify in economic terms?

The number of souls in them includes about three thousand five hundred persons, and the amount of land up to four thousand *desyatins*. In the largest commune, there are up to one hundred persons and one hundred and ten *desyatins* of land, while in the smallest there are about thirty persons and no more than forty *desyatins*. Thus, the communes are average in size or smaller, and cannot achieve all the advantages of large-scale agriculture. But the things they can accomplish are of colossal importance. First and foremost, all the communes have introduced the multiple-field system, although the land-department did not have sufficient seed for sowing clover and other grasses.

The distribution of land-sections under one crop or another has been supervised by an agronomist, as was the case in many other matters. The communist distribution of resources in field-work, and the success of the work itself, were quickly apparent in the fact that at ploughing time a part of the workforce of the *artels* and communes, without causing any loss to the farm, were not involved in agricultural work, but rather in the construction of new cottages, in repairing bridges, in road-improvements, in making various simple kinds of equipment, and in working fields belonging to Red-Army men.

This aspect of the matter is making a very strong impression on the peasants of surrounding villages. Nevertheless, there are only about sixty communes in the district, and the area that they work represents only three or four percent of the peasant land-area, while the grain that they will collect is only about five to six per cent of the total harvest in the district. Why is this so? Why does the peasantry stubbornly cling *en masse* to old and primitive ways of working the land?

The comrades from the Karachev district land-department pointed out all the following causes to me. The peasants have no confidence in the stability of Soviet power, they fear a victory by the Whites in the Civil War and the return of the landlords, and they are afraid that the first thing the landlords will do is mercilessly slaughter all the communards along with the Communists. Another cause is that not one commune has yet brought in a crop, and the current year – this year's harvest of spring-crops – will decide the matter. In the third place, one must recognise the enormously conservative influence of the women, a matter that I draw to the attention of all Communist women's organisations. In the villages, two of the most ardent opponents of the commune are the kulak and the woman, with the former having the most to lose from communism and the latter having the most to gain. The kulaks are propagating false and foolish rumours against the commune, and the women are spreading these rumours as if they were facts. (They say that upon joining the commune everyone must supposedly remove all crosses, that it is forbidden to christen children, that all icons must be removed from the commune 'by decree', and other such lies.) Once, let us suppose, ten or fifteen male heads of households have decided to form a commune, having themselves overcome thousands of inner doubts, the matter is still far from settled. It is still necessary to overcome a second line of trenches by convincing the wives to join the commune. In this regard, it is not persuasion that prevails as much as household-politics and the still-prevalent pattern in the village: 'Let the wife see that she fear her husband'.[2] In the first instance, the wife only joins the commune out of fear of her husband, and thus, by an irony of fate, the rigid patriarchal order turns out to benefit socialism.

Meanwhile, even in the comparatively small communes that have formed, the woman is already being emancipated from the kitchen and from family-servitude. Cooking for the *artel* falls mainly to the old women; they, together with adolescent girls, look after the youngsters, while adult women busy themselves exclusively with agricultural work, complete it more rapidly, and thus have more time for other matters or for leisure. There is no doubt that the woman will be converted from being the most stubborn opponent of the commune into its most committed, ardent and interested proponent.

I want to note one important fact. Despite the fact that Karachev district is not, for the most part, a producing district, and that the majority of its parishes are poor, it is not mainly the poor peasants who are joining the commune, but the middle-peasantry. This is explained by the fact that the middle-peasants, in the first place, are a more enterprising and economically progressive element than the poor, and also by the fact that the middle-peasants do not accept the poor in their midst when they can add nothing of value to the common effort. One often sees instances where the poor peasants do not enter the commune even when the land-department promises them all kinds of assistance, and not merely assistance in words. When one part of the rural community has formed a commune and things are going smoothly, the remaining members of the community take senseless and savage revenge on those who are succeeding: they threaten to burn and ruin the harvest, they mutilate the cattle, they look for a fight, and they steal and divide among themselves the seeds received by the communards, and so on. It is this attitude of 'neither me nor anyone else' – an obvious mark of our 'Russian' Asiatic character – that, together with kulak-intrigues, the religious stupidity of women and other charms of rural life, is smothering the young and still-tender shoots of socialist construction in agriculture.

---

2. ['Nevertheless do ye also severally love each one his own wife even as himself; and let the wife see that she fear her husband' (*Ephesians* 5:33).]

But life has many sides and many shades, and much that is unexpected will emerge from the wreckage of old foundations. As a rule, religion defends the viewpoint of an obsolete system that gave servants of the Church the place of honour at its dining table. But then, we have a monastic commune at Karachev. This is a model commune in terms of both its economic relations and its internal structure. In this commune, the division of labour has been implemented in a very original manner: the old people, who are unable to work in the fields, are assigned to pray both for themselves and for the others. Those capable of labour are working the land.

Is this example not symbolic? Does it not foreshadow the fate of religion, which is a property of the dying past and is hobbling to the grave along with it?

As for working together socially, this is something that comes about gradually, although a decree on the matter was at first misunderstood in the village. People thought that working socially was obligatory for all peasants. Already this spring, the peasants in certain communities divided themselves up into scores of teams according to a definite plan for working the land.

In conclusion, one must underline the fact that all of the communards, while not being party-members, are, nevertheless, the most committed supporters of Soviet power. They voluntarily give over all of their surpluses to food-organisations and conceal nothing. For instance, people from one commune made a special trip to the land-department to report that they had twenty carts of leftover straw that the land-department should take. Not a single deserter has been registered in the communes, and they voluntarily work the neighbouring fields of Red-Army men. In a word, the communes are genuine blockhouses of socialism in the countryside, and their participants are the most conscientious in implementing all measures of the soviet-authorities.

This is my impression after becoming familiar with affairs in this area within a single district. Observations of other localities will have to complete the picture and correct any mistakes. These observations will have to be made by other comrades in other provinces.

E. Preobrazhensky

No. 46

'Islands of Socialism'[1]

5 June 1919

II

Together with the manager of the District Land-Department and the agronomist, we went to the commune closest to the city. The commune received 48 *desyatins* of land from a landlord's estate or, more precisely, from a suburban cottage-site with an excellent location on the banks of a small, winding river.

On the way to the commune, the department-manager told me about its history. Unlike most other communes in the district, which have been formed by middle-peasants, this commune consists exclusively of the rural poor from neighbouring villages. Its present members wavered for a long time before entering the commune. Some of them spent many sleepless nights and wore themselves out with reflection and inner turmoil before finally coming to a decision. All this may seem incomprehensible to the reader, but one must not forget that the person who enters the commune makes a decisive break with his community and former way of life, and his indecision and agonising doubts are well founded.

Above all, the communards who were described to me doubted whether they would really be given the assistance that the Land-Department promised them and without which the very enterprise would be hopeless. When this help was provided, all doubts vanished, the attitude of the communards improved, and even the stubborn enemies of the commune – the women – gave up their opposition and also seemed to develop some confidence in the venture's success.

Touring the commune's property, we encountered a small herd of communal pigs, perhaps six or seven, that were rather thin and small. It turned out that this herd comprised the sum of all the pigs that the communards possessed before joining the collective, and the Land-Department had still not managed to provide the commune with any assistance in this respect. We passed sections of land sown with oats. The commune sowed 15 *desyatins* with oats, in addition to potatoes, peas, and such like. The oats, which were only sown in the spring, are the commune's main hope, and the intention is to gather winter-crops from all the old strips that were sown prior to the commune's formation. Young boys were keeping watch at the ends of the strips. In general terms, the commune's work was completed about a week sooner than in neighbouring communities.

---

1. [From *Pravda*, 5 June 1919.]

We approached the house. The wooden dacha was crammed with communards. Previously, a single landowner's family lived here. Now there are forty souls. In order to alleviate crowding, the communards have already begun to construct a new, additional house.

We go in. It is very crowded and sparse inside, but not dirty. I notice things that remind me of our Siberian exile-communes. Things are worse, no doubt, than they were under the landowner, but they are incomparably better than in any peasant-cottage. We pass a number of rooms occupied by different communards, and then we glance into the kitchen. We see a large common cooking pot. At the stove, on 'permanent duty', is an old woman who prefers cooking to any other work. The diet of the communards is very scant. There is almost no flour. They eat mainly oatmeal-porridge, sauerkraut and potato-remnants. Milk is important, and there is enough for more than the children. In this respect, things especially improved when the District-Executive Committee handed over to the commune a Simmental cow expropriated from a city-merchant.

On the upper level are single people and a pair of newlyweds. In the largest and brightest room, which serves as library, office and meeting place for the commune-committee and all the communards, there hang portraits of comrades Lenin, Trotsky and Liebknecht.

Liebknecht, now deceased, loved our Russian peasant-songs. Could he have imagined that the creators of those songs would so soon replace portraits of the tsar in their cottages with his photographs and with portraits of figures from the Third International?

Along the way, we learn that at general meetings of the commune the women, who were opposed to it in principle from the beginning, do not participate in voting and generally do not attend. They only send someone every half-hour to find out 'what the men have decided'.

The men of the commune live together very amicably, and during the commune's entire existence there has not been a single case when a work-assignment made by the commune-committee, was disobeyed by anyone. Even the thought of insubordination seems preposterous to the communards. The women live together less amicably, and frequently the committee has to sort out various female quarrels and conflicts.

There are numerous children in the commune. To ensure that they do not go without instruction, a teacher has been invited as a full-fledged member of the collective.

After seeing the house we go out to the veranda, which has been built on a steep bank of the river and is surrounded by enormous old linden-trees. The communards are discussing their plans and their hopes. They are already building the new house, and they have constructed a bridge across the river. They are thinking about whether they should reconstruct a water-mill that was once on the river, since there is no mill in the vicinity. From discussions with the department-manager they learn that one of the communes in the district, in a grain-area that has no forest, requires two-wheeled carts and is offering grain in exchange. Our communards are delighted. They have no grain, but they can provide as many two-wheeled carts as might be needed.

This is a small detail, but it also characterises the beginning of a new world of relations during the transition period – barter-exchange between the communes.

On the veranda, they bring us a huge jug of milk from the merchant's expropriated cow. On the other side of the river two nightingales sing profusely in a grove. The lindens and poplars have only begun to break into leaf, and the air carries the delicate aroma of 'nature's spirits'. Two of the communards, who are talking with us, are filled with bracing good cheer; they laugh, and their eyes sparkle even when they are serious, like nestling birds that are preparing to fly and are confident that they will not injure themselves.

Two springtimes are occurring simultaneously. The one comes every year, the other is initiating a new epoch in the history of mankind. Not long ago, there were other masters sitting on this veranda, holding different conversations and singing different songs. The beginning of their spring was beautifully described by Turgenev, who was enamoured of the system of the nobility and its heroes. The overture to its melancholy death came in the music of Tchaikovsky.

There is no music as socialism erects its first foundations, there is no singing by the hungry worker who is establishing the basis of a new society, and the only paint that covers the fields of civil war is too monochromatic for the artist. We are building. We have no time to portray just what we are building. But the time will come when a new society will also produce its own artists, who will lovingly describe the these young shoots of a new life that is springing up on the ruins of the old, and economists will write volumes on the embryology of socialist agriculture.

E. Preobrazhensky

No. 47
Report of the Plenipotentiary of the VTsIK and Responsible Representative of the Central Committee of the RKP(B) in Orel Province E.A. Preobrazhensky Concerning Mobilisation of the Population of the Province for the Struggle against Denikin

6 June 1919[1]

Owing to my departure to Eletsk and Livensk districts, I am late in writing this regular report.

With some exceptions, mobilisation of the parishes did not take place voluntarily, but it is generally occurring and in several places has already been completed. The numerical data of those appearing will be obtained in a couple of days. The shortfall will be significant. Much time was spent on preliminary agitation, when there were still hopes of conducting a purely voluntary recruitment.

Following receipt from me of the summary-data of the results, I request permission from the Central Committee to leave for Moscow, because everything humanly possible has been done, given the limited resources. After 10 June, it will hardly be possible to count on any increase of the number of those mobilised, and the organisation of political work among the volunteers is under way in each city-district.

---

1. [From RGASPI. F.17. Op. 66. D. 27. L. 133–6 ob. Handwritten; GA RF. F. 1240–P. Op. 1. D. 74. L. 1–1 ob. Copy: Typewritten.]
The document is not dated, but the text reports: 'Today, the 6th, the workers turned up at work'. The date of registration in the Central Committee of the RKP(B) is 13 June 1919, entry 6059.]

As for the trade-union mobilisation, to the extent of the first three percent it is fully completed everywhere. Increasing this figure to ten percent in relation to Orel would mean reducing to a minimum the work on preparing army-supplies...[2] the workers have a positive attitude, or mobilising elements with White-Guard sympathies, since they involve former proprietors who are now employed as simple workers or else similar elements of former office-employees. Mobilisation of such elements contradicts the foundations of the organisation of the Red Army. For that reason, the provincial soviet of trade-unions objected to increasing the percentage of trade-union mobilisation with respect to such petty-bourgeois cities as Orel and nearby towns.

The struggle against desertion is proceeding successfully. Our agitation was very important, but even more significant was the strengthening of detachments to catch deserters. It would be a good thing to make skilful use of the hostility in the village between that part of the peasantry whose children and relatives are at the front, and those who are hiding deserters. As for use of drastic measures – in particular, the demonstrative shooting of two to three deserters in each district, as others are suggesting – I say this: there is no certainty whether this means will lead to a speedy eradication of desertion or, on the contrary, will demonstrate our organisational weakness and merely cause deserters to abandon passive tactics, and instead actively oppose our organs of power. We have a small example from Trubchevsk district. A militiaman from a detachment to catch deserters shot one deserter. Then all six hundred deserters in the parish joined together and nearly beat to death two Communist-agitators, and in order to settle things it was necessary to send a detachment of a hundred men with the assistance of other agitators. I am inclined to think that so long as our position is not so critical as to require risky measures that might backfire, it is better to strengthen our organisational apparatus for the struggle against desertion and to work more systematically than in the past.

The mobilisation of thirty percent of Communist men, announced by the Central Committee, has not been implemented here due to events on the railroad and the need to have all forces under arms. But apart from that, I would venture to say that mobilisation to that extent is completely impossible to accomplish. Here are the reasons:

1) The numerical data that the Central Committee has concerning the number of party-members in Orel province (on the basis of representation at the Eighth Congress) are purely mythical. Following the mobilisation of five hundred men, and following the re-registration and flight from the Party of all the 'manorial'

---

2. [The following word is indecipherable because of damage to the text.]

Communists in connection with the change of policy in the village, the Party has been bled dry and has lost from half to two-thirds of its members. I personally know of one parish-cell where only seven men remained out of a hundred members.

2) If, by my approximate calculation, there are no more than twenty-five hundred Communists in Orel province, then, after deducting Red-Army Communists, women, those unable to serve and the absolutely essential cadre in the three main centres of Orel, Bryansk and Elets, where there are fewer than a hundred armed Communists in each city, on average in each district we have no more than a hundred men, which is political folly. In other words, we are already physically unable to have parish-executive committees made up of Communists in half of the province's parishes. If the Central Committee's intended mobilisation is fully implemented, then we will be consciously accepting the fact that power in two-thirds of the parishes will be organised on the basis of non-party members. Since I do not know whether the Central Committee is prepared to accept such a risk, I consider it my duty to warn of the possible consequences.

3) While Soviet power in the villages has recently gained in moral strength among the masses of the peasantry, in organisational terms it is badly shaken. As the food-personnel are warning, this could have fatal consequences in terms of realising the harvest. We must not forget that there are no committees of poor peasants at our disposal, and everything that we might acquire will come through our own thin stratum of rural Communists. But I have already encountered parishes where there is *not even a single*[3] Communist and where no-one was put forth as a candidate for re-election to parish-executive committees.

In view of all this, the Central Committee's hope for 'thousands of Communist fighters' for the southern front sounds like ironic mockery, and the telegram to that effect only shows that the Central Committee is completely in the dark concerning the real state of affairs in the localities.

But a directive from the Central Committee, even if it has no basis, is, for us, a military order. I and other comrades are obliged to fulfil it, but I warn that I will do so while taking into account the interests of the Revolution as a whole. I believe that we can provide from two to three hundred people, that is, a company of Communists, but if the Central Committee insists on recruiting more it will do so on its own responsibility, not mine.

I earnestly request that the Central Committee raise with the War-Commissariat the issue of being more deliberative in its actions. Such drastic measures as the deliberate mobilisation of self-interested elements among the railway-workers

---

3. [Underlined in the text.]

cannot be implemented without so much as warning party-centres in advance or allowing for political preparations for the operation. The railway-workers' strike, which very nearly ended in a great deal of bloodshed, was caused, in large measure, by this kind of carelessness, to put it mildly. The preceding directives for mobilisations were ordered to be implemented within time-limits that did not even allow for the simple *notification*[4] of outlying districts and rural areas. All the local workers likewise earnestly request that important decrees not be published without first making inquiries concerning how and whether they can be fulfilled locally. In particular, I will be making a personal report in Moscow concerning the land-decree of 9 April and the ruin that it caused.

For the purpose of replenishing the terribly depleted ranks of the Party, I consider it absolutely imperative to establish party-schools in each provincial city, mainly for[5] youth. This must be done at once. I will take the appropriate measures, here.

―――

Immediately after my arrival from Liven, I left for the railroad-meeting, where up to four thousand people were gathered. The mood of the masses was abominable. They would still listen to me and Purov, but our other people were not allowed to speak. They almost tore to pieces the chief of the railroad-militia, and we had to shield him from the crowd with our own bodies. At the meeting they adopted a resolution against mobilisation. On the 5th, the workers refused to work. We forbade meetings, posted draconian orders, gathered reliable military forces, and arrested ten active wreckers from the works and one big landlord who had been agitating against Soviet power. Some small groups provoked a soldier to fire. Machine-gun fire nearly broke out. At the same time, a campaign was waged in the city against self-seeking railroad-workers (all the factories passed a resolution against self-seeking railroad-workers). Today, the 6th, the workers turned up at work. An order to put an end to deferments and for a general call-up of all known strikers was effective. Seventy rifles and four thousand cartridges, which had been hidden for an armed action, were taken from a group of railroad-workers. The Communist organisation, especially the organisation of Communist armed forces, was on high alert. I believe that the movement has now been liquidated. Those mobilised are beginning to turn up.

The question of outrages on the part of food-security detachments and of these detachments in general is very acute. Objectively, they are playing an enormously counter-revolutionary role. We must quickly think of another means

---

4. [Underlined in the text.]
5. [The original version said '*peasant*-youth' but Preobrazhensky crossed out the word 'peasant'.]

of control on the railroad. This is particularly important in view of the general deterioration regarding the food-question. The activity of the detachments has a terribly demoralising influence on military units going to the front.

In conclusion, I recommend implementing the following measure that might partly replace those thousands of Communists that the Central Committee is counting on for the Ukrainian front. I recommend to Sklyansky that he issue an order that all those mobilised through the so-called voluntary mobilisation on no account be dispersed among various reserve-battalions. In each provincial city, they must be gathered into a single unit, subjected to especially intensive political work and be joined by a certain number of Communists, and then those already trained can be moved speedily to corresponding units at the front.

I ask that this report be read at the plenum of the Central Committee, because some of the questions addressed require a decision in principle.

E. Preobrazhensky

[In the upper right-hand corner of the report is a pencilled note: 'Telegraph that he may return to Moscow'. The signature and date are missing. In the upper left-hand corner there is another pencilled notation: 'Member Dim'; and below: 'For your information'.]

Nos. 48–56
Articles Published in the Newspaper *Pravda* in June–August 1919

19 June–24 August 1919

No. 48

'Islands of Socialism'[1]

19 June 1919

III

Besides communes, I also visited several soviet-estates.

One has to admit that, until recently, many comrades from the centre considered, and perhaps still do consider, the more than three thousand communes listed by *Narkomzem*[2] to be a myth, and those comrades are even more inclined to regard soviet-farms as mythical undertakings of no more than paper-significance.

However, such an opinion of soviet-farms is no less false than the opinion concerning communes. Soviet-estates are now a fact, a completely real and tangible fact.

The truth is that Orel province has made great progress in the matter of organising soviet-farms; there are 136 soviet-estates here, whereas in other provinces

---

1. [From *Pravda*, 19 June 1919. For earlier parts of this article, see Documents 2:45 and 2:46.]
2. [The People's Commissariat of Agriculture.]

there are a third, a quarter, or even a tenth that many. Orel province is not typical, and it would be a mistake on the basis of its soviet-farms to draw conclusions for the whole of Russia. But it will be perfectly appropriate to study the basic features of soviet-farming on soviet-estates in the province where their organisation has advanced furthest.

Within our Party, and especially among comrades interested in the agricultural question, there has been much debate over what form of socialisation is most advantageous, most attainable, and leads most quickly to the goal – a soviet-farm or a commune. In most cases, the debates have been abstract in nature; people have not known how to pose the question, and living practice has not provided the data needed to resolve the debate. Now much is already clear. I will first deal with some numerical data that I have collected.

Let us compare the communes of Eletsk district with soviet-estates in the same district. There are 30 communes and artels in the district and 26 soviet-farms. The communes (in what follows, I will treat artels under the same heading as communes, since they do not essentially differ from communes in terms of their production-relations) have at their disposal an area of 2,230 *desyatins*, that is, an average of 74 *desyatins* per commune. The soviet-estates have 7,953 *desyatins*, or an average of 306 *desyatins* per estate.

This leads to the first conclusion. The fact that communes are farms of average size, rather than being large, already means that they are deprived of the advantages of large-scale farming. In 30 communes, with a total of 2,216 communards, the actual workforce numbers 1,106. In other words, there are two *desyatins* of cultivated land per worker.

In the two soviet-estates for which I have detailed figures, there are 216 workers and employees on 990 *desyatins* of cultivated land. It is true that the amount of labour hired by the day could not be calculated, and something would have to be added to the figure that I have given. But on the other hand, this figure of 216 workers and employees includes the workers and employees of the watermill, the stud-farm and the breeding station, and their numbers exceed the day-labour that would have to be added. That matter aside, in the estates there are 4.6 *desyatins* of cultivated land per worker.

In other words, simply because the soviet-estates are larger, the productivity of labour is more than twice as high as in the communes.

Let us look further. In the communes of the district there are 8.1 *desyatins* of cultivated land per working horse, but in the above-mentioned two estates, one horse works 10.6 *desyatins* of land; and while the only functioning tractor in the district works on the largest of the communes, on the estates they plough exclusively with horses.

In the communes, one might say that there are two cultivated *desyatins* per worker merely because the communes allot the land according to the common peasant-norm. In reality, the communards could cultivate more than two *desyatins* per worker.

This is certainly true. But we are not speaking about what the case would be if the land-area of the communes could be arbitrarily increased (this would also increase the superiority of soviet-farms), but only of what actually exists. And the reality is that the communes are average farms with an excess of labour-power and with a lower productivity of *agricultural* labour than in the case of soviet-farms.

This entails one conclusion concerning the inevitable future of our communes. In view of the fact that the communes of the central agricultural region are surrounded by peasant-communities with either inadequate or barely adequate land-allotments, development of the productive forces in the communes cannot take the form of an increase of cultivated land with the present number of workers. There are only two ways in which such a development could occur: an increase in the intensity of farming within the limits of an average type of farm and diversion of part of the commune's labour-force into non-agricultural work – into processing farm-products (butter, cheese, milling and the like) – or else departure for the city-centres.

Of course, this does not apply to communes that are able to merge on a large scale, or to communes in regions where there is a surplus of land.

In economic terms, the average soviet-farm is more advanced than the average commune. But things are completely different in another area, in the area of psychological development, the degree of consciousness, and generally in the degree of preparation for socialist forms of organising the labour-power of the commune on the one hand, compared with soviet-farms on the other. From this point of view, my visit to soviet-farms left me with a most dismal impression. I shall have more to say on this subject later.

E. Preobrazhensky

No. 49

Obituary: 'Memories of Comrade Tolmachev'[1]

22 June 1919

Not long before the surrender of Perm, in a small circle of the most responsible comrades from the Urals Regional Committee, we joked about who among us would be the subject of an obituary and how many lines of obituary would be needed to evaluate the services by each of us to the Soviet Republic.

None of us thought at the time that the first obituary would be dedicated to the youngest among the most responsible Urals workers.

Comrade Tolmachev was known and loved by all conscious workers of the Urals. As a simple Red-Army man he accompanied the armed workers against Dutov, and during that campaign, he was always in the lead. He opposed any retreat by our forces, at a time when not retreating meant perishing in the midst of insurgent Cossack villages. When the Czechoslovak offensive began, comrade Tolmachev never left the front or the immediate rear and gave everything to the defence of the Red Urals. He participated with the forces of the late Malyshev in defending the approaches to Zlatoust; after the fall of Ekaterinburg, he led a revolutionary mobilisation of Urals workers that produced thousands of proletarian fighters; he travelled from one unit to the other serving as the living connection between the defenders in the frontlines and the leading organisations and the command in the immediate rear. During the period of long and stubborn battles in the northern Urals, comrade Tolmachev headed the political department of the N army,[2] doing colossal work in connection with army-organisation and agitation. Following the loss of Perm, comrade Tolmachev continued the same work in Glazov, never departing from the front and always visiting its weakest points. When failure at the front deeply distressed him, he responded to each communication regarding needs at the front by doubling his energy and doing everything he could to ensure that the Red-Army men received everything they needed.

Recalled from the Urals front by the Central Committee of the Party, comrade Tolmachev was moved to Petrograd and perished while defending the city of world proletarian revolution. Being surrounded by White Guards, and having fired all his ammunition at the enemy, he reserved the last shot for himself.

---

1. [From *Pravda*, 22 June 1919.]
2. [Use of the latin 'N' refers to the number of the army, which was, presumably, not disclosed for security-reasons. In English or modern Russian usage the reference might typically be to the 'X' army.]

Of the members of the Urals Regional Committee, we have lost comrades Malyshev and Vainer, and now we have the fresh grave of comrade Tolmachev.

These brief lines are not the obituary for the deceased. As participants in a great struggle of worldwide importance, we cannot, under the blows of our enemies, appraise even one-hundredth of the services of our dear comrades who have died in battle. The obituary for comrade Tolmachev, along with Malyshev, Vainer, Khokhryakov and thousands of workers in Sysertsk, Lysva and Ekaterinburg will be built by the Urals proletariat. In a free Urals, they will find a place to erect a great monument to their fighters, and they will teach their children to honour the memory of the heroes of the Red front.

But the workers of all Russia must also know whom they have lost. Comrade Tolmachev was only 24 years of age, he was an excellent agitator, a wise journalist and, despite his youth, an experienced political leader. It is merely a matter of chance that he was not known throughout Russia. Great workers often avoid the capital, staying close to the masses in the provinces and dying in obscurity.[3]

Comrade Tolmachev was modest, and he died when he was only beginning to reach the full stature that would have made him one of the recognised leaders of the proletarian revolution.

Speaking over Pisarev's grave, Nekrasov said that 'It is good to die young'.

Over the body of comrade Tolmachev, we say that it is difficult to bury the young who have not yet developed their full intellectual powers. Only those comrades who knew the deceased well can understand what a force our Party has lost on the Petrograd front.

E. Preobrazhensky

---

3. [There is an error in the obituary: 'в независимости' appears rather than 'в неизвестности'.]

No. 50

'Islands of Socialism'[1]

26 June 1919

IV

Of the soviet-estates in Orel province, I managed to visit mainly the estate of former minister Khvostov in Eletsk district and then the estate of the late Stakhovich. Here, in a few words, is what I saw there.

The spring-grains were sown on time, and generally much earlier than on the peasant-lands. Travelling about the fields with the management, I was personally convinced that the grain is in excellent condition and much better than in the peasants' fields. On the majority of state-farms in Orel province, the winter-crops could not be sown, because most farms were only organised after the end of last summer. But on these two estates, winter-wheat and rye were sown, and now they are promising an excellent harvest. The potato-planting was coming to an end and they had already begun to plough fallow land for the winter-crop. It turned out that there were not enough working horses on the estates to ship out an enormous quantity of stored manure. The practical conclusion: The Supreme Council of the National Economy must direct all provincial and district-councils of national economy to turn their lorries over in good time to the soviet-farms for transportation-work; and the War-Commissariat, in order to save fuel for productive purposes, must issue an order to halt all movement of passenger-vehicles that are being driven about with criminal indifference carrying commissars of various ranks. On both estates, there are excellent fruit-gardens, hot houses and vegetable-gardens, and all this is in proper order. The equipment and cattle are sufficient. There is a breeding station on each estate, and on the Stakhovich estate there is an entire stud-farm with excellent breeding horses, many of which are famous. The surrounding peasants highly value the services provided to them by the estate in improving livestock-breeding. There is a very long queue to use the breeding stallions.

I had the opportunity to inspect thoroughbred horses, two herds of cattle, mainly Shvits and Simmentals, and a pigsty. The stock were kept in relatively

---

1. [From *Pravda*, 26 June 1919. For previous sections of this essay, see Documents Nos. 2:45, 2:46, and 2:48.]

clean conditions and looked excellent. Other [conditions][2] on the estates were beyond criticism.

In general, I found things to be in very good order on the estates, and for the first year of farm-operation, following the storms and the onslaught of the peasant-movement, they were even strikingly successful.

The estates that I visited were among the best equipped and best organised in Orel province. On other estates that were smaller and less well organised, things were less satisfactory. But in general and on the whole, the state-farms in Orel province, despite being in existence for less than a year, appear to be among the very best, when their organisation is compared to the state of affairs elsewhere.

As for the direct results of the state-farms, in terms of spring-grain alone they will provide more than half a million *poods* to the province this year. And this is not to mention a whole list of other profitable activities that are of less significance or the improvements of the peasant-economy that the state-farms have already begun to bring about, although still on a very modest scale.

Let me turn, now, to the darkest side of the state-farms – their management. In all the estates that I saw, the workers were a completely forgotten and incidental element, like refugees who were completely indifferent to the interests of the enterprise of which they were the vital force. Our programme speaks of soviet-farms as major socialist economic undertakings. Our soviet-farms are economic undertakings, but it is difficult to speak of them as socialist. The workers' committees that exist on the soviet-farms are a miserable paper-copy of workers' control, because, with the current level of consciousness of the agricultural workers, or rather unconsciousness, no control on their part is conceivable. Wherever the workers do attempt to interfere with management, they do so with a single purpose – to snatch anything that might improve their situation. In general, all the threads of management are presently in the hands of the managers, and the workers' attitude towards them differs from relations under the old régime merely by being less harsh. If in the communes excellent human material is squeezed into the vice of small – and thus insufficiently productive – farms, on the large soviet-estates, to the contrary, where technical conditions are favourable, there is a workforce that serves, if I may use the expression, as hirelings of socialism. The thought occurred to me that only a combination of the vital force and consciousness of the communards with the technology of the soviet-farms can provide us with genuinely 'socialist economic undertakings' in the countryside.

But this is music of the future. For now there is an urgent need to insert five to ten factory-workers into each soviet-estate and gradually to change the whole

---

2. [The text says 'other degrees' (Другие степени).]

cadre of workers in order to turn soviet-estates into bases of the urban proletariat who are presently dispersed as individuals in the villages. There is even a need to send a minimum of one Communist into each estate to serve as the vital eyes of our Party and to exercise the control that must at least partially compensate for the absence of workers' control.

As for the management of soviet-farms as a whole, it will be necessary to deal with this important and pressing goal in a separate article.

E. Preobrazhensky

No. 51

'The Management of Soviet-Estates'[1]

29 June 1919

In view of the fact that this question will soon be resolved, or more accurately, will not soon be resolved in practice, I wish to offer a few facts and considerations in opposing the existing system of management of soviet-farms, although some of them come with a very significant 'but'.

In resolving the question one must always keep in view the following important circumstances:

1. The worker-element of the soviet-farms is at such a low level of consciousness that it is not only unable in the majority of cases to achieve workers' management of the soviet-farms, but has not even matured to the point of workers' control.

2. The so-called specialists in the soviet-farms consist of the former landlords' managers, a certain number of landlords, and agronomists from the so-called third element. They comprise four basic groups; a) clear opponents of Soviet power and completely mediocre, lazy, and very easily replaceable 'specialists'; b) 'middle-peasants' from the service-class who are indifferent to Soviet power and equally indifferent to their work (you give a tug and they work, you ease up and they laze about); c) those genuine specialists who are unsympathetic, neutral, or sometimes moderately sympathetic to Soviet power but, at the same time, deeply love their task and work without any compulsion and without needing any petty control; d) specialist-communists, or those who are gradually becoming communists in the course of their work as specialists, coming mainly from among the agronomists. (An agronomist, in fact, cannot fail to be a proponent of the large-scale socialist farm.)

3. Our provincial executive committees and agricultural departments understand the need for soviet-farms and, in the **majority of cases**, have already outgrown their prejudice against this **form of cultured socialist farm, which is for now the only one possible.** Our district-executive committees and agricultural departments, in the **majority of cases**, are still gripped by petty-bourgeois antipathy towards soviet-farms, and often take a tolerant attitude towards the peasant-struggle with soviet-farms. As for parish-executive committees, in most cases they not only oppose soviet-farms in their present form, but are in principle opposed to the very idea of large-scale soviet-farming in Russia.

We draw the following conclusions from all of these facts.

---

1. [From *Pravda*, 29 June 1919.]

Many defenders of the present system of management in the soviet-farms point to the low level of consciousness on the part of agricultural workers and say: 'Given this state of affairs, is it really possible to consider any management of soviet-farms other than management from the centre?'

My thinking is exactly the opposite. Decentralisation of management in soviet-farms is necessary precisely because of the absence and the factual impossibility of real workers' control. Otherwise, all manager-specialists and the whole establishment of employees will be free both from any control from below, and from any real control from above (even any paper-control) because *Narkomzem*[2] is, today, unable to implement such control, and any assurance to the contrary is simply frivolous boasting. The choice is clear. We need to subordinate soviet-farms to the provincial executive committees and, at the same time, have a representative from the centre in the provincial economic council in order to ensure that a common pattern for the construction of socialism in agriculture is adopted for the entire country. Only then will it be possible to realise genuine control over the soviet-farms which, when they are confronted with their own outrages and shortcomings in the localities, reply not by correcting them, but with the comment: 'It is none of your affair, we answer to the centre'. Incidentally, the provincial executive committees should also be in charge of, or at least have the right to exercise real control over, the lands and farms belonging to the most esteemed State-Committee for the Sugar-Industry, whose operation in the localities is simply scandalous.

Now consider the composition of specialists. Obviously, those who specialise in ridiculing Soviet power must immediately be driven out of soviet-farms without paying the slightest heed to all the screams and cries that will accompany such an operation. Average workers who are rather lazy have to be prodded and occasionally removed as an example. Genuine specialists and conscientious workers have to be encouraged in every way possible without being pestered by petty control, given the broadest initiative in practical work, and supervised only in general terms.

As for the district-executive committees and district-agricultural committees, it is completely impossible, at present, to hand over management of soviet-farms to them, but they must be given the right of control, in the sense of the right to receive necessary information from the farms, to familiarise themselves with the state of affairs on them and, in the case of noticeable abuses, to seek their elimination through the appropriate higher organs.

The current position, in which some executive committee sees one or another disorder in soviet-farms but can do nothing about it, is completely intolerable,

---

2. [The People's Commissariat of Agriculture.]

and the same applies to the opposite case: sometimes the district-agricultural committees are capable of giving timely assistance to one-or-another state-farm, but they do not do so, because they resent the fact that the soviet-estates are not within their jurisdiction.

Of course, one can think of numerous different concrete schemes for the management of soviet-farms. I am not recommending any single such scheme. To work out such a scheme is not difficult. All that matters is to avoid mistakes on the main issues, to avoid repeating the mistakes of VSNKh[3] in new construction, and not to propagate bureaucratic (as distinct from proletarian) centralism. It is important to know how to utilise local forces to the full and to limit the role of the centre to providing general leadership and all forms of assistance in cases where local forces cannot manage things on their own.

In conclusion, I want to point out the need to attract the surrounding peasants into the discussion of economic plans on one or another state-farm, even if only in an advisory role. The peasantry must be brought to the idea that, in the final analysis, the state-farms are not organising a force that is alien and hostile to the peasants, that state-farms are an achievement of the people, and that all labouring peasants must take an interest in their proper arrangement just as they are interested in their own affairs.

E. Preobrazhensky

---

3. [The Supreme Council of the National Economy.]

No. 52

'Who Will Hold Out Longer?'[1]

27 July 1919

The protracted Civil War, in which the Soviet Republic has been involved almost from the moment of its founding, has not led us to a decisive victory, because of causes that are international in character and because of peculiarities in the social structure of our country.

Let us first clarify these causes, and then pose and attempt to give a completely objective answer to the question of how long the opposing sides in the struggle are physically and materially capable of continuing the War.

Insofar as our front with Denikin and Kolchak is our own domestic front, the outcome of the War can be decided in Ekatorinodar, Rostov and Omsk. Insofar as that same front is a world-front on the part of imperialism, which is attempting to smother us, the outcome of the struggle will be decided in Paris, London and Berlin. Since the question can essentially be resolved in a world-context only by the transfer of power into the hands of the European proletariat, it follows that the basic cause for the length of our Civil War is the comparative slowness in development of the revolution in the West.

However, the European proletariat has already appeared on the scene; it is already partially determining the foreign policy of its governments and, like a heavy anchor, is preventing the imperialist ship of the Entente from sailing into Russian waters to assist Kolchak and Denikin. The general fatigue of war and the dissolution of the system of government in the Allied countries are leading in the same direction.

For that reason, it is not only possible, but perhaps even probable, that the following will occur. The proletarian movement in the West will strengthen even more, the openly bourgeois governments will be compelled to resign, and for a certain period the imperialists will be forced to rule with the assistance of social-patriots. From this perspective, there is nothing improbable in a recent news-bulletin to the effect that in France, following the conclusion of peace, a 'socialist' ministry will be formed with Briand at the head in place of the Clemenceau cabinet; that in Italy the social-patriot Bissolati will govern; and in England, Lloyd George will create a hotchpotch-government including MacDonald and other yellow-pink 'workers' leaders'.

---

1. [From *Ezhenedel'nik pravdy*. 27 July 1919.]

All of these 'socialist' governments, being an epilogue to the World-War and a prologue to world proletarian dictatorship, will be compelled [not only] to make a number of concessions to the proletariat in the domestic political and economic arena, but also to refrain from any interference in Russian affairs.

Therefore, the possibility is not excluded that in the near future the Soviet Republic will be waging war solely against its domestic enemies. And once that happens, enormous significance will be attached to the general question of whether we can wage the Civil War over a long period and which side will more quickly exhaust its material and vital forces.

At the moment, the vital force that the Allies are continuing to maintain in Russia to assist the White Guards is quite small. And we, it appears, have every basis for concluding that the reason why our White Guards continue to preserve their fronts and even seriously to threaten us, as Denikin is threatening us now, is because of our own disorganisation, because of the imperfection of our military mechanism, because of the peasant composition of our army and the weakness within it of experienced proletarian and Communist cadres, and because of inadequate political work by our organisations.

Let the Allies continue to provide support to the White Guards with weaponry and money, and let the White Guards enjoy all the purely moral benefits of the fact that the strongest powers of Europe, the destroyers of German imperialism, stand by their side. Even then, our resources remain incomparably more imposing than the resources of our enemies.

Let us begin with what is most decisive, the living force of the army. On the territory occupied by the Soviet Republic, the population is twice as large as that at the disposal of all our domestic enemies taken together. This superiority is essential unless the war is brief in character and one side greatly exceeds the other in terms of the perfection of its technology.

Our war is protracted in character, and our opponents do not have a technological advantage, apart from a few tanks in Denikin's army.

But we have enormous numerical superiority over our enemies not only in terms of living forces, but also in terms of the quality of these masses. The fundamental mass-basis of the Red Army is the peasantry of our central provinces, who have experienced serfdom and received the lands of the nobles from the Soviet power. This mass either knows perfectly clearly, or else vaguely realises, that a collapse of Soviet power will once more reduce the peasantry to poverty and a lack of any rights.

On the contrary, the peasants forcibly mobilised by the Kolchak army did not see the slightest sense for themselves in the Civil War, victory promises them nothing except the obligation to make payments on tsarism's foreign debts, and in this they see only a complete lack of any rights and the dictatorship of golden epaulettes.

As for the other important element of the army, its core and skeleton in the cadres and commanding staff, in this respect our opponents have had an undeniable advantage that they partly maintain even today.

Their commanding staff is reliable, it has always been more than sufficient, and foreign newspapers have had good reason to laugh at the fact that in Denikin's army there are sixty thousand officers for fifty thousand soldiers. It is true that many members of this officer-corps have already been slaughtered. In Kolchak's case, this applies even more, and his army has begun to experience a crisis in terms of its commanding staff. On the other hand, we are slowly but surely expanding our cadre of commanders with politically reliable Red officers. In this respect, the relation of forces is gradually changing to our benefit.

As for cadres in the wider sense, here the following situation prevails. The purely bourgeois cadre of the Kolchak army is rather sparse, that is, the sons of the bourgeoisie prefer to remain in the rear and call others to defence of the 'motherland' while they occupy themselves with speculation. Kolchak's kulak-cadres have enormously declined in number due to losses, on the one hand, but also as a result of losing parcels of territory, on the other.

The rout of Kolchak is due mainly to these cadres being reduced to a minimum, along with the enormous demoralisation among the mobilised middle-peasants and workers, who are coming over to our side *en masse*. In future, every newly won factory in the Urals will replenish our units with revolutionary-minded proletarian cadres, at the same time as the kulak and bourgeois cadres of the Kolchak units, who are being thrown into battle at the most dangerous points, will melt away with each passing day.

In these terms, things are not so favourable for us on the southern front. The well-to-do Cossacks, who are the basis of Denikin's army, still remain even though an enormous number of them have been killed in battles to date. Denikin's officer-corps is more than adequate.

On the other hand, the possibility is not excluded of a temporary bloc between Ukrainian kulaks and the Cossack kulaks in opposition to proletarian power. On the minus-side for Denikin is the fact that our peasantry, even the kulaks, have the greatest contempt for the reactionary Cossacks, while the abundance on Denikin's side of former guards-officers with famous family-names (famous for the massacre of peasants) makes perfectly obvious the landlord-bourgeois character of his campaign and of his dictatorship. In such circumstances, Denikin will not succeed in forcibly dragging the peasantry along with him even to the extent that Kolchak temporarily managed to do. Denikin's army risks surviving only in the form of its cadre, and then it will finally be smashed by the Red Army, given its enormous numerical superiority.

As far as the fatigue of war is concerned, it is as great with us as with our opponents, but with the difference that it is easier for us to mitigate fatigue by spreading the burdens of war over a greater number of people. Our opponents' advantage lies in the fact that almost all of them have seized areas with greater surpluses of grain, and they are not affected by fatigue arising among the masses on the basis of famine.

Both we and our opponents are seeing a common war-weariness and dissolution of the fighting armies. The whole question concerns the issue of who will experience this process more rapidly and who will be the first to retreat and then finally be destroyed.

Who will it be?

Krasnov and the entire counter-revolution on the Don already have one foot in the grave; they are one step from collapsing, and even Krasnov's officers, as we see from the diaries of those who have been killed, already considered their cause to be hopeless and planned to flee to Persia.

With the help of Denikin and of typhus in our army, and thanks to our complacent disorderliness as victors and our confidence in taking Rostov 'within two weeks', along with other causes connected with the peasant composition of our southern divisions, the hostile Don front has survived, grown in strength and now seriously threatens us.

Kolchak is already out of action, his troops have largely disintegrated and in many ways we are reminded of Kerensky's army prior to the Tarnopol'[2] catastrophe. One of our enemies, and the most important one at that, has collapsed before we have.

Now it is Denikin's turn. The collapse of Denikin will begin when our peasantry, in the provinces that are close to the front, sense a threat to their land. This will impart a new spirit of commitment and bitterness to the Red Army, it will bring dissolution in the ranks of those whom Denikin has forcibly mobilised, and it will determine the outcome of our war against the Don counter-revolution.

To what has already been said, we must add that the working class of Ukraine are only now becoming soldiers *en masse*.

This represents a new and fresh force, a force that has not taken part in the Civil War during the past year and can tip the scales strongly in our favour.

But if we are apparently finishing with Kolchak because he could not wage the contest to the point of exhaustion, in the case of Denikin, it is quite possible that the war will end in annihilation. In that kind of contest, the ultimate victor is the one who, other conditions being equal, has the greatest living physical strength.

It is we who have the greater strength.

E. Preobrazhensky

---

2. [This was the name of the city of Ternopol' up to 1944.]

No. 53

Notes on the Red Army

'The Struggle against Spontaneous Decomposition'[1]

29 July 1919

I

Our recent failures on the southern front time-and-again raise the issue of a close study of the causes of spontaneous disintegration at individual sections of the front, of the struggle against this disintegration once the illness has already set in, and of preventing the illness once it is first detected.

Preoccupied with the latest news, with our heads buried in practical issues and the short-sightedness that inevitably results, we do not have time even to conceive theoretically all that is occurring, we have not yet studied all that is occurring, and we still have not fully studied the military mechanism with which we are operating on our numerous fronts. But this is the time to do so. It is precisely our practice that is beginning to demand a theory. Russian revolutionary Marxism has never suffered from neglect of theory. It is always accused of the opposite, especially when theoretical discussions distract significant intellectual resources, on the basis of very modest practice.

Now, to the contrary, on the basis of colossal practice we have surprisingly little time or place for communications of any kind.

With the following remarks, I hope to encourage comrades who are more competent in the matter to draw some generalising conclusions on the question of the Civil War and the military instrument in this war. There is no doubt that some of our most responsible comrades, who have become involved in military work but never lost their capacity for the theoretical conclusions that are necessary in order to avoid serious errors – these comrades communicate virtually nothing of their conclusions in the press for the benefit of others, whose practical activity is not gaining from their experience and their reflections. Comrades Trotsky and Sokol'nikov have started to write some things, but being preoccupied with 'the present moment', they have not gone much further.

---

1. [From *Pravda*, 29 July 1919. This article continues in Documents 2:54–6.]

We need theoretical conclusions in order to minimise our expenditure of resources in the practical struggle and to avoid the luxury of mistakes that are too ruinous at the beginning of a civil war.

―――

There have been peoples for whom war was a craft and a state of war was natural. In order to preserve their martial spirit, the ancient Germans busied themselves only periodically with agriculture, regarding it as dull and unattractive but necessary work. Our Dnepr Cossacks of the seventeenth century and the mercenaries of Western Europe were demoralised not by the condition of war, but rather by the condition of peace.

In feudal society, with the existence of absolutism, a specific social class of knights was permanently on a military footing.

The warrior only gradually became the landowner, while still continuing for a long time to be his sovereign's soldier. The majority of society already lived in peaceful circumstances; only one class lived in military conditions, but it, too, gradually began to go over to peaceful living as a special type of military-agricultural class. Our Cossacks are a similar military-production association with only one difference, and that is that the Cossack is more closely and directly involved with agricultural production than is the case with the landlord. But such an organisation, however much the purely military association of particular groups of the population gradually diminishes within it, was (and, in the case of the Cossacks, still partly remains to this day) not an artificial, but a natural formation.

With the break-up of serfdom, with the liquidation of absolutism and of domination by the nobility, and with the strengthening of bourgeois society, only a small and insignificant cadre of professional officers remain on a permanent military footing with the top nobility at their head. Bourgeois society, as such, is not a society of warfare. But this society must always be prepared for war. On the basis of universal military conscription, it vigorously cultivates the system of a standing army that had already emerged under absolutism. But this army, based on the removal of hundreds of thousands of people from production, is no longer a natural, but rather an artificial and compulsory formation.

If one can put it in such terms, this is its fundamental and principal difference from an army of medieval knights, from the Dnepr and other Cossacks, and from the armed gentry and military people of our nobility. This artificial mechanism of a standing bourgeois army spontaneously tends towards dissolution. But during peacetime, bourgeois society quite successfully resists this tendency. On the one hand, it regulates the spontaneous attraction of home by designating a specific term of service, while on the other hand, it puts in motion established means of discipline, of moral influence, and an entire arsenal of punitive measures.

All of these measures, which are effective up to a certain point, prove much less successful during a time of actual war, especially during a prolonged and unsuccessful war, and they finally cease to be of any use when war overlaps with revolution.

A bourgeois army is not just artificial; it is also an artfully constructed mechanism. The Red Army is less artificial, but it is also a less artful mechanism. Above all, in the organisation of its reserves it begins to revert partly to a military-production, and thus a natural, formation. This applies to reserve-regiments, to special-purpose detachments, and to universal military training. The artificiality of the Red-Army formation is reduced by the unity of the class-composition of toilers in its ranks and also by the territorial character of a great part of its recruitment. But the Red Army is a less artful mechanism because of the class-diversity and technical imperfections of its commanding staff. In general and on the whole, the organism of the Red Army is also subject to spontaneous disintegration, and thus requires tireless application of all means to combat this decomposition.

This is something that we too-often forget.

If a particular unit is presently battle-worthy and internally strong, that stability is the result of a whole series of continuously acting causes. A combat-ready unit can be compared with filled vessels from which water flows out through one opening while flowing in through another. Equilibrium is established through a very complex interaction between the process of filling and the process of emptying. If the entry is blocked even a little, or the water-supply is decreased, then the vessel will gradually become empty. This comparison applies not only to reinforcement by reserves, but also to all the other factors that support combat-readiness.

Meanwhile, experience shows that while we have significant ability in building combat-effective units within a certain minimal period of time, that is, in the organised assembly, in appropriate proportions, all the factors that offset the elements of disintegration, we are also proving very unskilled at maintaining over time, at a constant level, what we have built. I am speaking here precisely of a lack of skill, not of the objective causes that sometimes make it necessary consciously to destroy a unit that is beyond repair.

However much we minimise the role of national character and its features in explaining one or another phenomenon of mass-historical significance, when it comes to building our armed forces, we must keep in mind our impetuosity, to use a harsh word, our mishmash of laziness and enthusiasm. It has already been mentioned that we stumble too-often, but then we rapidly raise ourselves up and recover from the blow. But in this regard, we expend a great deal more energy on the recovery than would be needed to avoid stumbling in the first place, if we adopted the requisite precautionary measures in a timely manner.

Consider a typical example. Following the experience of some severe shock, the front begins to be restored. The work, as always happens when we are struck by a blow, proceeds quickly and successfully. The shattered units are restored and revived, new ones are created, the position is stabilised, then an offensive begins and the enemy retreats.

All that is then needed is to preserve the established relation of forces, to avoid curtailing the scale of work, to maintain the heightened attentiveness and vigilance, and not to forget what happened yesterday. But no such luck! The impulse passes. Success demoralises those who organised the success; they rest on the laurels they have won; bit-by-bit, the force of disintegration methodically and imperceptibly ruins the whole structure; and then the influence often of a minor blow from the outside initiates a new crisis and collapse.

Then we labour again on a new building, again we organise a victory, and we organise it not only from all the elements that are at hand today, but also from those of yesterday. What was missing for the victory, if all the objective givens were on hand before the defeat? What was missing for the victory was the defeat – that is the only conclusion.

It is true that the defeat, especially if it is connected with loss of significant territory, not only has a productive effect in psychological terms on the organising elements of the army, but also provides new reserves from the toiling masses who are brought face-to-face with the possibility of a White-Guard invasion. In that case, the defeat ploughs a deeper furrow in the civil war and turns up forces hitherto unresponsive to our agitation. But the role of these reserves in districts not directly exposed to the danger is still limited, compared with the enormity of all the forces set in motion by our military and Soviet mechanism.

Just how are we to overcome those excellent characteristics of the Russian man that are such a dubious treasure precisely during a stubborn and protracted civil war? Just how, without recourse to the destructive prod of defeat, could we systematically and successfully overcome spontaneous processes of decomposition in the army and, without the assistance of a defeat, mobilise the enormous supplies of forces that we amazingly turn up only after our opponent has driven us to the wall?

As for our impressionism and lapses between ebbs and flows of energy – the best medicine remains the improvement of our existing military mechanism. For the most part, we took this mechanism from our class-enemies. This mechanism is adapted to a national war, but not to a civil war. That is its shortcoming. But it is not designed specifically for a Russian temperament. And that is its value.

In the same way, we cannot conceive any special means of struggle against decomposition other than perfecting our military and party-military mechanism. We only have to adapt the military machine to the specific characteristics of civil war at a stage of severe exhaustion of the masses, while simultaneously taking into account the great difference between circumstances at the different fronts in the struggle.

How the epidemic of disintegration begins, and how the mechanism must be perfected to struggle against it, is a matter to be taken up at another time.

E. Preobrazhensky

No. 54

Notes on the Red Army

'The Struggle against Spontaneous Decomposition'[1]

1 August 1919

II

Our misfortune lies in the fact that we are not only fated to realise socialism in a petty-bourgeois country, but are also compelled to wage socialist war with the hands of peasant-masses who are indifferent or hostile to it. There is no escaping this sad fact. But we can diminish the effect of this factor through a skilful distribution of proletarian forces in the army, and through skilfully grouping the peasant-masses according to their status in terms of property.

It is an unavoidable fact that the people are horribly exhausted as a result of two wars in a row. But much can be accomplished through a policy of evenly distributing the burdens of war among the greatest number of people, without leaving it to deserters, in the forests and ravines of our rear, to determine the question of creating reserves.

All of the above-mentioned objective causes, which are resulting in decomposition of the Red Army, act with spontaneous force; they act unwaveringly, implacably, and continuously. What can our military mechanism and the force of our Party do to resist this action?

I have spoken above of skilful and intensified propaganda. Although all the White-Guard newspapers are amazed and concerned by the enormous scale of our agitation and political work, we are, nevertheless, hardly doing a third of what we can and must do in this area.

We have militarised and bureaucratised our military-agitation apparatus. This is an enormous plus in the sense that our agitation and propaganda in the army do not depend on the attitude or wishes of the agitators; they have a systematic rather than a random character. But while benefiting from this systematic and persistent character, our agitation suffers enormously in terms of its quality.

First of all, the basic content of our agitation is often not what is required. Our younger comrades often forget one important thing. It is our peasantry, resting during mobilisation and deserting after being called up, who are still waging the Civil War.

---

1. [From *Pravda*, 1 August 1919. This article begins with Document 2:53.]

There are a million peasant-youths under arms. This is an enormously important historical fact from which we must draw all the conclusions.

The peculiarity of the socialist Russian Revolution consists not only in the fact that during October we seized power with the support of almost the entire peasantry – something that would be completely impossible for Europe with the possible exception of two or three Balkan states – but also in the fact that the struggle to defend the Revolution's conquests is taking place in our country with the actual participation of the enormous majority of the peasantry. However, the peasantry is taking part in this struggle to defend the land, not socialism.

The subjective motives that peasants and workers have for participating in the struggle are completely different. And that is why, in **agitation among peasant Red-Army men, we must put in the forefront not our own motives for the struggle, not the motives of workers, but their own motives, those of peasants**. In practice, it happens in many cases, if not the majority, that the opposite occurs. Some young agitator, having learned all the benefits that a communist economic system brings to humanity, yearns to share his Communist enthusiasm immediately with the peasant Red-Army man. But the middle-peasant, who represents the majority in our army, turns out to be stubbornly indifferent to Communist slogans; he carries the heavy burden of war against the Krasnovs, Denikins and 'cadets' **for his own** reasons, and not out of the same motives as a conscious worker-Communist. Because his 'class-consciousness' enlightens him in exactly the opposite direction, and people stubbornly impose upon him motives for struggle that are not his own, our unskilled propaganda has often inevitably had a counter-revolutionary significance. The enthusiastic Communist-agitator, not knowing how to adapt to his listeners, frequently achieves only one thing: he ultimately and officially, so to speak, in the name of Soviet power, convinces the peasant that he is waging the war for someone else's cause, and thus he leads the Red-Army man to the same conclusions as all the White-Guard leaflets are urging upon him.

Meanwhile, there are so many vital and business-like truths that are extraordinarily convincing for the peasant, yet are completely ignored in our agitation! Here are some examples. Under the tsar, the state-budget reached three billion in gold, of which almost two billion fell upon the peasantry in the form of direct and indirect taxes. Translated into the purchasing power of our paper-rouble, this amounts to two hundred billion in taxes every year. How much is the peasantry now paying in taxes?

Translated into the current rouble, how much would the peasantry have to pay on the foreign debts of tsarism and the Kerensky period, which climbed to nineteen billion roubles?

In terms of our current rouble, what is the value of the landlords' estates that the peasants are now acquiring and that the White Guards want to take from them while at the same imposing all the losses upon them?

I have not seen a single brochure, nor a single leaflet or poster that speaks in a comprehensible manner, **with figures to hand**, and not merely phrases, of these economic benefits that Soviet power brings to the peasantry. Speeches are being given that could just as well have been given a month, half a year, or a year ago. Witless appeals are written, made up of general phrases that in no way respond to the questions that are disturbing the masses **today**. Picture-posters are hung up that strikingly lack any ability to affect the observer through an artistic, popular, and simple idea.

The conclusion. Agitation in the matter of building the Red Army, in the struggle against spontaneous forces of decomposition, and in the matter of organising victories, is exceptionally important to us. It is an issue that deserves exceptional attention. We must use the colossal centralisation that we have achieved in our agitation apparatus in order, first of all, to say to Red-Army men throughout the whole of Russia **everything** that it is most important to say at the present moment, and secondly, to say it with all the talent that we can muster. It is imperative that the most prominent members of our Party, beginning with comrade Lenin, be obliged two or three times a month to provide personally authored popular brochures and appeals for the army.

It is a great skill to know how to speak to the masses, and not many people have it.

In the third place, it is necessary to change fundamentally the character of work by our agitators and educators, transforming them into organs of the Party, which in most cases has not been accomplished up to now, despite the resolutions taken in this regard.

Finally, we have hardly availed ourselves of the treasure, in the sense of agitation, provided by the deserters from Kolchak, who must be systematically assigned by a definite plan to all the agitational and educational points in the Republic.

E. Preobrazhensky

No. 55

Notes on the Red Army

'Cementing the Army'[1]

14 August 1919

III

We can never escape the peasant-composition of the Red Army. We can only bind it together with the comparatively scarce cement represented by cadres of conscious workers and communists. The fate of the Kolchak army indirectly demonstrates the enormous importance of such cadres in our own Red camp.

In the tsarist army, the cadre that connected the troops consisted exclusively of the commanding staff in both the lower and higher ranks. The entire mass of soldiers were so obedient as not to require any special sorting of rank-and-file soldiers, and it was not necessary to create in each company a connecting element from soldiers upon whom tsarism could particularly depend.

On the contrary, in a civil war that draws into the struggle the middle-peasantry, who spontaneously incline toward neutrality, and in which it is not reliable to mobilise the poor peasants and workers for the Whites, or the well-to-do peasantry for the Reds, the question of cadres in the lowest ranks of the army assumes an enormous and even decisive importance. In an examination of the headquarters of a division on the eastern front, documents that were recently seized in battle from the office of a defeated regiment of Kolchak's followers revealed that in each company there were from 13 to 26 officers serving as rank-and-file soldiers. They were the cadre that maintained the Kolchak army after the White-Guard command – as the result of a partially successful mobilisation of peasants, and following the extermination of a large number of officers who were attached to separate shock-units – undertook to cement together the mobilised masses by means of the available officer-cadre who were inserted into the units in the role of rank-and-file soldiers.

The annihilation of the larger part of the officers and kulak-volunteer elements of the Kolchak army led the Siberian army to catastrophe.

This lesson is also very instructive for the Red Army, even though we enjoy several extremely important advantages over our opponent. In the first place, the middle-peasant in general, and the middle-peasant of Great Russia in particular,

---

1. [From *Pravda*, 14 August 1919. This article begins with Documents 2:53–4.]

despite all his attempts to avoid taking any side in the Civil War, is much more willing, for a whole variety of well-known reasons, to fight in the Red Army than for the Whites. Then there is the fact that the kulak-Cossack cadre of the White Guards is much less numerous than the poor peasants and the proletariat, who comprise the cadre of our units. As a result of all this we, while using less compulsion and more agitation, are creating an army **whose mass** is more combat-ready than is the case with our opponents, and that is without mentioning the further fact that the number of heroic and purely-peasant regiments in the Red Army is quite significant. All the same, the presence of a permanent Communist and proletarian cadre has enormous importance, as a general rule, for the Red Army as a whole. Along with tested peasant-regiments that have honourably endured a year of civil war, we have a much larger number of regiments that were put together in a hurry without an adequate cadre and that are made up either of those taken prisoner or those who surrendered, or else their units were disbanded and reformed again from top to bottom while preserving only their regimental number.

From this point of view, it would be enormously interesting to do a study of the tested and steadfast units in the Civil War, on the one hand, and a statistical summary of the units that were taken out of service, that disintegrated, surrendered, and so on, along with the character of their internal composition, on the other. In any event, one thing is beyond dispute. In more than a year of the most intensive civil war, there has occurred a continuous natural selection of the most stable military units, those that have endured while sustaining the heaviest fighting and all kinds of deprivations along with colossal losses. The result is that the tested units that survived were those in which there was always preserved a definite proletarian and Communist cadre not only in the command but also among the ranks of ordinary Red-Army men, or, as was more rarely the case, there was a cadre of militant and conscious elements from the peasantry. On the contrary, the regiments that were formed exclusively out of mobilised peasants and provided with an number of also forcibly-mobilised officers, even when they had fine commissars, in the majority of cases turned out to be fragile and spineless formations that perished by the tens and were scattered like sand. The only exception involved those units that, despite all the inadequacies in their formation, were posted immediately to a front that was in a favourable condition, participated in victories for which they were not responsible, succeeded in distinguishing from among the peasant Red-Army men a stable fighting cadre, and thus acquired the kind of stable skeleton without which no unit can long survive in a civil war.

Such are the facts. These facts teach us a great deal, and above all, they teach us to treat with the greatest care the conscious and militant Red-Army cadres that have emerged during a year of warfare. These cadres have the miraculous ability to digest raw and fresh masses of reinforcements in the most improbable proportions. I know of one heroic regiment in which there remained in some companies only 6 to 15 of the original members, but nevertheless these handfuls of people were able to share and instill their fighting spirit and solidarity in hundreds and thousands of incoming reinforcements.

The fighting cadres of our units are more precious to us than territory, and territories are conquered more rapidly than such cadres can be created. It is, therefore, completely inadmissible to engage in unequal combat that leads to the physical destruction of these genuine standard-bearers of the Red Army. Our comrades at the front, of course, know full-well the value of our Red cadres, and if it turns out that they are forced to be inadmissibly extravagant with them, in most cases this results from conditions of struggle that are beyond their control. At times, there is no other way out.

In order for there to be another way, it is time to address on a practical basis not only the question of the expedient use of cadres, who are accumulated in civil war through a spontaneous process of natural selection, but also to go over to a planned and skilful selection of Red-Army cadres. We are now creating cadres of the Red officer-corps. We must apply the same planning and energy in creating Red-Army cadres.

Some army supply-battalions have already achieved much in this regard. The same work must be started everywhere in the rear. This is now becoming fully possible.

Kolchak has been smashed, the Denikin offensive has been halted and will perhaps quickly be followed by our own offensive, and thus organised and planned work in the rear can be started in the manner indicated without any delays. The goal can be reached, in practical terms, through the organisation under each provincial military committee of special cadre-companies. If each provincial military committee could organise up to five hundred selected Red-Army men, who could be posted in especially favourable conditions for political work, and if they could be prepared in accordance with a definite plan for their important role in the future, the question of Red-Army cadres would be put on a proper footing in the rear. Twenty thousand Red-Army cadres can cement together an army of half a million. Every comrade from the front is aware of this.

It is necessary to recall, here once more, the completely incorrect use of Communist cadres that continues to be practised. It would seem that there are enough Communists in our army and that they are sufficient to serve as the cement for the entire army-organisation. The reality is that there are extremely few companies with a sufficient number of Communists. The main mass of Communist cadres is employed somewhere near the front, but not in the frontlines.

All of this would be impossible if the presence of a sufficiently numerous cadre were recognised as being just as necessary in each unit as an established number of rifles, machine-guns, pieces of ordnance, and so on.

In a word, we must adopt the goal of creating steadfast army-personnel in the Red Army, and not entrust the matter exclusively to the spontaneity of civil war. To the main complaint that will be raised against what has been said, referring to the impermissibility of creating some kind of guards-element in the Red Army, there is a brief reply: never fear to draw all the conclusions arising from the fact that the proletariat comprises a minority in Soviet Russia and that it is also, simultaneously, the sole leader of the entire Revolution.

E. Preobrazhensky

No. 56

Notes on the Red Army[1]

24 August 1919

IV

Let us suppose that favourable conditions are created for our position in a certain sector of the front. The enemy is retreating; in the far rear, this retreat is already being interpreted as a final defeat; our military observers, ranging in advance of the cavalry, are already predicting the enemy's collapse at one point or another. But the attack is suddenly halted, then the summary reports speak of repelling the enemy's attacks, next, of stubborn fighting in which we have had to make some retreats, and finally, after several reports of a gradual, fighting retreat, we begin to get daily flashes of the names of stations and cities that are being abandoned with virtually no resistance. A full-blown catastrophe becomes evident.

What has happened at the front? When did the conditions form that led to the defeat, and what elements were involved in it?

For ordinary newspaper-readers, the defeat began at the moment of retreat. But for the comrades at the front, who are able to foresee the next day, the inevitability of defeat typically became clear even during the attack, especially in its latter stages, because even then the changes in circumstances began to appear.

How are these changes typically expressed?

The first and most important change occurs when over-stretched units reach their extreme limits. The disintegration of units as a result of incredible strain is the most typical occurrence in our Civil War. Strong, united and heroic units have disintegrated because they were physically unable to bear the burden of uninterrupted fighting any longer. I am reminded of the iron companies of Magyar internationalists on the Urals front, heroic worker-regiments that we ruined in the absence of reserves and that, in the final analysis, began to disintegrate from extraordinary fatigue. Even a brief rest, to the contrary, has made units that were losing their combat-effectiveness ready once more for battle. But if we were **forced** to operate without reserves during the first months of the War, or if we reduced them to ridiculously low numbers, the fact is that subsequently, once our entire military mechanism became organised and began to have at its disposal hundreds of thousands of mobilised Red-Army men, the problem of reserves should have been resolved much more rapidly and radically than was actually the case. Above all, it is imperative to establish, as a firm rule, a certain

---

1. [From *Pravda*, 24 August 1919. This article continues in Documents 2:53–5.]

definite time-limit beyond which it is **obligatory** for a unit involved in the fighting to go into reserve. That limit must be shortened according to the intensity of combat. Declarations by Red-Army men to the effect that they want to continue to advance must be ignored once a unit's posting on the battle-line has expired. Meanwhile, it is precisely in moments of successful attack that the inexorable law of the physical exhaustion of soldier-masses is ignored, and it is precisely during these moments that the ground is laid for a future defeat.

In this respect, there is no reason why we should not learn something from our opponents. When a certain army of ours found itself in catastrophic retreat from Kushva and Perm during the winter, we intercepted an order from the commander of the Kolchak front, saying that the operating division was to continue the offensive up to Kalino station. The further offensive on Perm would be conducted by a certain other division (the order mentioned one of our opponent's divisions that was being held in reserve). Despite the fact that we would have had to surrender Perm even to the forces of the division that was already waging the offensive against us, something that our adversary knew full well, and despite the fact that if two of our opponent's divisions participated in the battle the fall of Perm would be speeded up and the trophy would be all the greater for Kolchak's supporters, the White-Guard command was not enticed by this tempting prospect and continued, even in the face of such giddy success, to send into reserve the units that had been in combat for a specified time. Did we always do likewise during a period of successes?

A second important cause leading to the disintegration and defeat of units is insufficient reinforcements and their poor quality. Reinforcements of poor quality are especially harmful when they are inserted into units that are already weakened as a result of intensive fighting, but nevertheless remain at their positions. Then it often happens that it is not the old remaining cadres who work on the reinforcements and make them battle-ready, but, on the contrary, the sudden influx of a mass of reinforcements causes disintegration of the remaining combat-ready units. Our command has already drawn practical conclusions from this fact, and when fundamental reinforcements are involved, the units are sent into reserve and the reinforcements are worked over twice before battle; from within by the old cadre, and from without through agitational-political work. Unfortunately, conditions at the front do not always allow such an approach.

The result is that when all the above-mentioned causes begin to operate at once, when supply is unfortunately worsened for one reason or another, when incidents of treason occur more frequently among the officers (and they usually do occur more frequently in just such circumstances), and finally, when the enemy accumulates his strength – then all the conditions are at hand for defeat.

But really, the reader will ask, does all this accumulation of facts leading to defeat escape the attention of responsible comrades at the front?

Not at all. If one studies the reports in our military archives coming from the front in the period preceding a defeat, then in nine cases out of ten the reports that forewarned of defeat were submitted, and were usually submitted in good time. But if one simultaneously studies for the same period all the reports from all the fronts, then it turns out that there were more reports of inevitable catastrophes and defeats than actual catastrophes and defeats. In other words, all the reports cry out with a single voice, when referring to positions that are not equally grave. The conclusion that follows is that it is imperative to learn how to submit correct reports. Comrades should not think this is just a technical detail. Until such time as proper reports are submitted from the fronts, weighing every word, no planned and effective distribution of the Republic's military resources will be possible. But on the other hand, we all know that it is necessary to cry all the more shrilly from the front when there is a need to obtain something and to rouse the centre. The implication is that correct reports cannot be expected so long as the military centre retains all of its unwieldiness and inflexibility and does not carefully weigh every word in the same way as those making the reports.

We seem to have a vicious circle. However, there is a way out. I refer to something that is already evident.

Above all it is imperative to have decentralisation of the military apparatus. We are already encountering the need for such decentralisation in our general soviet- and production-apparatus. The opinion of all the plenipotentiaries of the Central Committee and the VTsIK was clearly expressed at a session of representatives held at the end of June. I am confident that if responsible party-comrades from the front were to gather in a meeting, they would call for the elimination of excessive centralisation in the military apparatus and for the independence of the various fronts on a number of questions, particularly questions concerning supply. The same must be said with regard to the rights of regional and provincial military commissariats.

However limited the free resources of people and supplies at the disposal of our military apparatus, these resources are still adequate to come to the assistance of the most threatened point at any given moment. But it is far from true that the assistance is always received by the most threatened point. The machine works too clumsily.

Besides eliminating excessive centralism, our military apparatus can become more flexible if it implements the resolution of the Eighth Party-Congress concerning regular congresses of military workers. **It is time to raise the question: why does this decision of the Congress still remain on paper?** It will be pointless to say that the military situation prevents such congresses. This objection does not stand up. During an offensive, you see, there is no time to get together because everything is going so well. During a retreat, there is no time to get together because things are going badly and everyone must remain at his post. Whether things are going well or badly, it appears that congresses are not possible in any circumstances. It is time that we finally implemented in real life the decision of the Congress. A gathering of military workers, where comrades come together who hitherto communicated with each other on questions of extreme importance only by means of telegraph, will have enormous practical significance; the common collective experience of military Communists will be put to use; many major inadequacies of the enormous mechanism will be alleviated; and the struggle against decomposition of individual sectors of the front will be waged more successfully.

E. Preobrazhensky

No. 57
Protocol No. 57 of a Meeting of the Committee of the Bolkhov Organisation of the RKP(B) of Orel Province Concerning Implementation of the Party's Policy with Regard to Middle-Peasants and Reasons for the Collapse of Party-Cells in the Parishes[1]

30 August 1919
6 o'clock in the evening

Meeting chaired by comrade Sleptsov. Secretary Zinoviev.
Present: Kutuzov, Simakov, Titov, Yudaev, Dreiman and Preobrazhensky.

Resolution:
1. On the character of work by the Bolkhov organisation of the RKP(B)

Comrade *Preobrazhensky* reported on the implementation of the policy of the Eighth Congress with regard to the middle-peasant, and also spoke of the city-workers. The question to be answered is why little attention is paid to the middle-peasantry and the city-workers, who are not supporting Soviet power, and also what is the cause of the collapse of Communist cells in the parishes.

Comrade *Sleptsov* says the reason for not being closer to the city-workers is that the worker here is very backward and, despite our repeated summons, they are not

---

1. [From RGASPI. F. 17. Op. 6. D. 198. L. 9–9 ob. Certified copy. Typewritten. Stamped by the committee of the Bolkhov organisation of the RKP(B).]

moving closer to us because they also do not stand for defending the interests of the proletariat. As for the [question] of attracting the middle-peasant to our side, comrade Smol'nikov tried to accomplish this, but unfortunately failed and irritated the poor peasants through an incorrect approach to this question. The parish-cells disintegrated in connection with the mobilisations – both party- and general mobilisations – and the best comrades were lost at the front; but matters are currently improving, the collapse of certain cells in the district must be regarded as temporary, and measures have already been taken by the district-Communist Party to organise them.

Comrade *Simakov* says that we failed to implement fully the theses of the Eighth Congress when comrade Smol'nikov was in charge because he made a very abrupt attempt. That this work is now improving is definitely shown by the last Bolkhov Congress of Soviets, where all members of the Executive Committee were Communists and all the proposals and resolutions of the Communist fraction were accepted without dispute. The reason why there are no cells in the city is because they were all merged under Smol'nikov into a single city-wide organisation; the collapse of parish-cells occurred because of mobilisation, and those who had supported us quickly left our ranks, but we hope that things will improve in this respect, and cell-organisers have been sent to the rural districts. As for the workers, he says that their indifferent relation to Soviet power results from the fact that their families are living reasonably well, and he adds: the district Communist Party and the entire organisation never deviate from the orders of the centre, but inadequacies and mistakes are typical and can happen not only at the lower levels, but also at the centre.

Comrade *Titov* observed that Smol'nikov, having a way with words and an oratorical talent, nevertheless did not succeed in winning the workers to the side of Soviet power, that it was he who dispersed the cells in the city, that he gave much encouragement to the well-to-do class, that the bourgeoisie always surrounded him with all kinds of petitions, and that under him the relation of the population to the Party of Communists was aggravated, especially in the villages.

Comrade *Dreiman* reported that Smol'nikov did not know how to conduct mobilisation among the workers because the worker here has his own home, has no particular needs, and is difficult to persuade. At one meeting of workers, Smol'nikov said that they should all be blacklisted as shirkers.

Comrade *Preobrazhenksy* says, in conclusion, that all the comrades' reports focused on Smol'nikov, and that the latter followed a correct line in relation to the workers and middle-peasants. He correctly merged the city-cells, as was also done in the centre. And it was thanks to our timely change in relation to the middle-peasant that there were not frequent uprisings at the front. He adds that for some reason a negative attitude is apparent here towards people from the centre, as in the case of Smol'nikov and Lobanov. In view of the undermining of certain comrades' reputations, which can be seen in every district, he proposes that, for the sake of more productive work, the best responsible comrades be relocated by the Provincial Party-Committee and other districts, and also that the resolution of the District Party-Committee be reviewed concerning the transfer of comrade Lobanov from the position of head of the Department of Administration to the Sub-Department for Information and Instruction.

Following all the reports and discussions, it was resolved:

1. To sort out the question of the Bolkhov organisation's work at today's general meeting of party-members.
2. To review the resolution of the district Communist Party concerning comrade Lobanov.

The session ended at 8 o'clock in the evening.

Original with the required signature[2]
Certified copy of the original:
Clerk of the district Communist Party
Podshchekoldin

---

2. [The document says: 'Подлинный за надлежащим подписом'.]

No. 58

Protocol No. 37 of a Session of Members of the General Meeting of the Bolkhov Organisation of the RKP(B) of Orel Province Concerning Tasks Facing the Communists of Town and Country[1]

30 August 1919
11 o'clock in the evening

Comrade Sleptsov in the chair, deputy chairman Simakov, secretary Zinoviev. Attended by 51 members.

Agenda:
1. The task of party-work both in the town and in the country.
2. Current matters.

Resolution:
1. The task of party-work both in the town and country.

Comrade *Preobrazhensky* pointed out that we are now close to liquidating Denikin's offensive. We are called upon to uphold the interests of the proletarian revolution consciously and firmly, and victory will be ours.

Concerning the countryside, he says that everyone there has now become a middle-peasant and we must seek out their best ideas. Our Party must base itself on the middle-peasantry. He adds that the last surviving great landowners are gone and this can be seen everywhere. We must work to organise the young people

---

1. [From RGASPI. F. 17. Op. 6. D. 198. L. 38–38 ob. Certified copy. Typewritten. Stamped by the committee of the Bolkhov organisation of the RKP(B).]

and the women in the countryside, who have been badly ignored. Moreover, our first task is to recruit members into the organisation, and that means the very best forces from the countryside; the second task is to explain to the middle-peasant what he can expect in the event of Denikin's victory. The cells that have disintegrated in the villages have to be resurrected.

Turning to the city-workers. He explains that the countryside is gaining the upper hand over the city and will strip the latter. Party-work in the city and the district must be strengthened.

Comrade *Kutuzov* speaks of the rural estate-owners, who first clung to us and then abandoned our ranks; he calls the middle-peasant a fine peasant. He recommends sending one comrade now to every parish for work in the countryside.

Comrade *Simakov* explains that there is no particular danger at the front and we will be able to protect and strengthen our Revolution. With regard to local party-work, he indicated that even if this work is not going well, at least it has improved by comparison with previous work. A union of young people has been established, instructors have been sent out to organise cells in the countryside, a petition has been submitted to the provincial Communist Party to reassign workers, in order to strengthen party-work comrades have been sent to courses in Moscow and Orel, and he also explained the causes of the disintegration of parish-cells.

Comrade *Sleptsov* calls upon comrades to work energetically and to embrace the slogan 'All in the Party'. We must move closer to the countryside, where we have sympathisers, and conduct wide and intensive work in the towns and villages.

Comrade *Lobanov* says that we must win the sympathy of the population in the city and in the countryside; we must send our best forces to the countryside to organise cells. Every member of the organisation must give an account of himself to the district Communist Party at least twice a month. We will work as the times require.

Comrade *Abramov*, speaking of the reason for the collapse of parish-cells and the complacent attitude of city-workers to Soviet power, asks comrade Preobrazhensky to explain the working intelligentsia.

Comrade *Preobrazhensky*, in conclusion, said that general improvement of party- and soviet-work requires a redistribution of political forces, wide agitation in the city and the countryside, and the attraction of workers into our party-ranks when we hold Party-Week. With regard to the working intelligentsia, he noted that they are timid and cautious and that we, through our own lack of tact and occasional coarseness, sometimes drive them away from us, and then at a difficult moment we cannot rely upon them. The debates end.

Resolved:
1) For the sake of more productive soviet-work in general, to ask the provincial Communist Party for a reassignment of responsible party-workers from one district to another.
2) To conduct the most extensive agitation on Sundays in the city and the villages to replenish the ranks of our party-family.
3) To commit party-workers for the sake of closely coordinating our work in the trade-unions and raising it to the required level.
4) To make every Communist responsible for giving an oral report of his party-activity twice a month at the general meeting.
5) In all the parish-executive committees, the chairmen must be party-comrades, Communists, and the executive committee must be notified to put this into effect.

The meeting ends at 11 o'clock in the evening.

Original with the required signature
Certified copy of the original:
Clerk of the district Communist Party
Podshchekoldin

No. 59
Protocol No. 58 of the Session of the Committee of the Bolkhov Organisation of the RKP(B) of Orel Province in Connection with the Murder of the Communist Makarin[1]

30 August 1919
11 pm
Not to be Released

Comrade Sleptsov chaired. Zinoviev was secretary. Present: Kutuzov, Simakov, Titov, Ivanov and candidate Dreiman, plenipotentiary Masterov of the provincial Cheka and Preobrazhensky.

Resolution:
Report by comrade Ivanov concerning his trip to the provincial Cheka in connection with murder of the Communist, comrade Makarin.

After making a brief report, comrade Ivanov reads the resolution of the provincial Cheka of this 29 August, which, after hearing the decision of the Bolkhov district Communist Party on 25 August, resolved: to shoot ten persons who are hostages from the bourgeois class, under the supervision of the district Communist Party, the District-Executive Committee and the plenipotentiary of the provincial Cheka. Debate was opened on this question.
Comrade *Ivanov* insisted on implementing the decision by the provincial Cheka and on sticking with our

1. [From RGASPI. F. 17. Op. 6. D. 198. L. 10. Certified copy. Typewritten.]

slogan 'For a single murdered Communist, we will respond by murdering hundreds from the bourgeoisie'.

Comrade *Preobrazhensky* says that until the investigation of the murder of comrade Makarin is finalised, the district Communist Party must set aside its resolution and request that sanctions come from the provincial Communist Party, otherwise he, as plenipotentiary from the TsIK, will revoke this resolution himself and the provincial Cheka will respond appropriately to any rash act.

Comrade *Simakov* makes a proposal: not to revoke the resolution of the district Communist Party and the district-Cheka, but to leave them in force until there is a detailed investigation and, if this murder was committed for political reasons, then to implement them.

Comrade *Slepkov* says he cannot agree with the opinion of comrade Preobrazhensky, who said that for the murder of a Communist the bourgeois must answer in the region where it occurred, since Communists must stick to the slogan of 'Class-struggle on a world-scale'; if we react leniently to the bourgeoisie's foul escapades, then we have no guarantee that another Communist will not be murdered tomorrow. Moreover, we are undermining our authority with the masses, in the form of the Red Army, whose speakers definitely declared at the time of comrade Makarin's funeral that for every Communist we must shoot ten bourgeois. Here are their words: 'You comrade-Communists do nothing but talk, and your words are empty'. Therefore, we must demonstrate that we are not just frivolous windbags.

Comrade *Ivanov*, insisting on his proposal, adds that we see things more clearly on the spot than they do in the centre, and there is no reason to be afraid of centralist comrades, particularly of comrade Preobrazhensky. This is the dictatorship of the proletariat, and we have no reason to sentimentalise with the bourgeoisie for as long as they survive, since we have no assurance that someone from our own family will not be killed today or tomorrow.

Comrade *Titov* added that this murder involved participation by the local bourgeoisie, and he proposes to shoot the hostages and not to revoke the previous resolution.

Comrade *Preobrazhensky*, replying to comrade Ivanov, says that we must be more restrained and keep our nerves about us. We must respect centralisation. We wage terror only at a moment when it is essentially necessary, not when a case has yet to be clarified or is criminal in nature. We are Communists – not anarchists.

The debates conclude.

Comrade Preobrazhensky's resolution is approved by three votes to one, with two abstentions: 'To revoke the district Communist Party's resolution of

25 August concerning hostages in the city of Bolkhov and, if the murder of Makarin was committed on political grounds, to turn to the provincial Communist Party for sanctions'.

The session ends at 12 o'clock at night.

Original with the required signature[2]
Certified copy of the original:
Secretary of the district Communist Party[3]

---

2. [The document says: 'Подлинный за надлежащим подписом'.]
3. [The signature is illegible.]

No. 60
Letter by E.A. Preobrazhensky to V.I. Lenin with a Proposal to Change Tactics in Relation to the Don Cossacks

August 1919[1]

Esteemed Vladimir Il'ich!

Excuse me for taking a few minutes of your time. First of all, I ask that you read the attached letter from the Kursk front. It partly explains why we were beaten despite having twice as many forces at our disposal as Denikin.

Secondly, I would like to say a few words concerning our military operations against the Don Cossacks.

At the time when we first occupied the region of the Don, as you know, an insurrection broke out that required a large force to put it down, and it has still not been suppressed.[2] Even the women and children took part in the insurrection. Now, whenever our units enter a Cossack village they are met by armed elements of the Cossack population who took no part in Denikin's recent operations. In other words, our entry into the Don region is not reducing the forces of our opponent, but expanding them, and this is tying up our best regiments. An offensive in the Don region,

---

1. [From RGASPI. F. 17. Op. 84. D. 33. L. 15–15 ob. Handwritten. The date for this document is given on the folder.]

2. [An armed struggle occurred in the Don region between the Don military government, headed by cavalry-general A.M. Kaledin, and the Don Cossack Military-Revolutionary Committee, headed by F.G. Podtelkov. On 24–5 February 1918, Podtelkov's forces took Rostov and Novocherkassk, and in March they proclaimed the Don Soviet Republic. A final White-Guard offensive, led by Denikin, was defeated in the summer of 1919.]

Denikin's main base, would only be fully justified and lead to a rapid and decisive victory if we had an overwhelming advantage in forces. The recent experience of our offensive along the entire southern front has shown that our forces are equal to Denikin's or slightly larger. In these circumstances, the projected plan for an offensive in the Don region can only benefit Denikin by providing him with new reserves.

I suggest the following. We must initiate a policy of dividing the Don Cossacks in an entirely different manner that might at first sight appear adventurous. We know from our comrades, who are arriving from underground-work in the Don, and also from the White-Guard newspapers, that the Don Cossacks are extremely tired of the War. Instead of conquering the Don, we must formally propose a peace, addressing, of course, the masses of rank-and-file Cossacks. We have to explain to them that we are only capturing Tsaritsyn, but we will not cross the Don and we will not intrude into their villages – in a word, that we are taking up a defensive position in relation to them. At the same time, we have to direct our main forces to the Kursk offensive and await the results. My proposal for taking a strong but defensive position along the line of the Don may have an enormously disintegrating influence on the Cossacks. This can be seen eloquently in the history of Krasnov's liquidation, when the mobilised Cossacks either scattered or came over to us in the hope of an end to the War.

If, in the near future, we manage to secure an armistice with the Baltic scoundrels, and if we make it widely known among the Cossacks, the absolutely inevitable result will be to divide them and create a party that will call for a 'breathing space'. And we, of course, will know how to use that breathing space.

That is the essence of my proposal. I would advise the same approach in relation to those parts of the territory of the Urals Cossacks that we have not defeated.

With comradely greetings.

E. Preobrazhensky

Nos. 61–2

Articles Published in the Newspaper *Pravda* in September–October 1919

18 September–12 October 1919

No. 61

'The Lessons of Mamontov'[1]

18 September 1919

Mamontov's cavalry has yet to be liquidated. After being driven out of Tambov province, it moved to Tula and the eastern part of Orel. Departing Orel and Tula, it began operating in Voronezh. From Voronezh, it will move wherever it has to, because our pursuing infantry cannot keep pace with it and is lagging some considerable distance behind. And even if Mamontov's force breaks through our frontlines in the near future and rejoins Denikin's main forces, we can expect the same or a similar detachment to reappear soon, because the enemy's first experience of a large-scale cavalry-attack

---

1. [From *Pravda*, 18 September 1919. The Russian-language title is: 'Уроки Мамонтовщины', There is no literal translation of this into English, but the term 'Mamantovshchina' evokes the sense of a 'terrible experience' with Mamontov. From 10 August to 19 September 1919, General Mamontov led a Cossack cavalry-raid in the rear of the Red Army's southern front with the aim of disrupting a counter-attack by Soviet forces. On 10 August, Mamontov broke through Soviet defensive lines in the region of Novokhopersk, and from 18–31 August, captured Tambov, Kozlov and Elets. Burdened with heavy wagons and losing manoeuvrability, Mamontov was surrounded and made a difficult retreat back to the frontlines to link up, on 18–19 September, with a force under General Shkuro, sent by Denikin to assist Mamontov.]

on our rear has been so completely successful. It would be odd to think that it will not be repeated. The Denikinites have found a new way of utilising their superiority in cavalry. We must quickly find some way of utilising our superiority in infantry, and of employing all our resources in general, in the struggle against future attempts to disrupt our rear with impunity.

What do the facts tell us?

Tambov, Kozlov and Elets were surrendered to the Cossacks almost without a fight. In places where the Cossacks did meet with more-or-less stubborn resistance, in Rannenburg[2] for example, they retreated and avoided any significant losses. This is understandable. A detachment that has broken through to the rear not only conserves its forces, which would otherwise melt away with every passing day, but also avoids becoming a large convoy, which is inevitable if it accumulates many wounded. The first conclusion to draw from these facts is the following. Behind our front, in the adjacent rear, we must create an uninterrupted line of large and small strongholds that will be able to mount major or minor resistance to the very end, to the last soldier and the last cartridge. Moreover, every narrow junction, all the large bridges, and generally every place that might be of interest to the robbers must be transformed into such a stronghold. All the garrisons of these reinforced positions must be more-or-less permanent forces, and every Red-Army man, along with every Communist in a reinforced position, must be especially accountable and subject to the most severe punishment for failing to show sufficient resistance to the enemy.

Next, we must quickly reinforce the organisation of partisan-detachments on foot and horseback, which we have already begun, and they must tirelessly remain on the enemy's heels without ever losing sight of him. All available automobiles and motorcycles must likewise be used for this purpose.

Further, it is necessary to establish assembly-points and the personnel for small partisan-detachments of Communists and sympathisers, who must remain in position without fail in the event of an enemy-attack and begin to operate exclusively in his rear.

Then we must fundamentally change the practice of pursuing cavalry with masses of our regular infantry. Up to now, almost all of our infantry forces that have encountered Mamontov's elusive supporters have, in fact, been useless and out of action, as if they did not even exist on the internal front. It is imperative to pursue the enemy with unbroken lines of infantry, however thin they may be. Only with such a system of pursuit can the latter assume a systematic character and, together with the lines of defensive strongholds, provide any essential result.

---

2. [In 1948, Rannenburg was renamed Chaplygin.]

A unified command of the internal front by means of telegraph-communications turned out, in fact, to be impossible. It is necessary to maintain live communications with all participants on the internal front and, in particular, to master...[3] On the other hand, the commanders of fighting detachments must be permitted much more initiative and independent action[4] by comparison with the practice on a normal integrated front.

Finally, the main thing we must do is speedily create new cadres of cavalry. On the one hand, our comrades in Orenburg province and the Urals region must apply every effort towards the most rapid formation of Red-Cossack regiments and, on the other hand, they must mobilise all the horses needed for cavalry. Additionally, every provincial military commissariat must be required, in the shortest possible time, to form at least a squadron of cavalry, ruthlessly gathering up all the riding horses, beginning with those belonging to the commissariat itself. If every provincial military committee rapidly forms at least a squadron, this will give us an entire cavalry-division.[5]

Mamontov's attack has succeeded as a military enterprise. But in political terms, it has been a complete failure. We can boldly claim that precisely this attack has demonstrated, in an especially striking and convincing way, the stability of Soviet power and the utter impotence of our domestic counter-revolution. Mamontov's supporters did not succeed anywhere in establishing an internal front. The bourgeois population of the cities and the kulak-upper stratum in the countryside remained totally inert when Soviet power temporarily disappeared, and they did not use the occasion to organise and consolidate themselves in the areas taken by the Cossacks. The stability of our rear was verified in a completely unexpected manner.

Whereas, in Kolchak's rear, the uprisings of peasants and workers are growing and intensifying spontaneously, without support from us, and while these uprisings are beginning to break out in Denikin's own rear, in our rear not even the appearance of a vital and organised White-Guard force was able to unify the counter-revolution of our internal enemies.

---

3. [There is a typographical error and part of the text is missing.]
4. [The text says 'самодеятельность'.]
5. [In these same days L.D. Trotsky, Chairman of the Revolutionary War-Council of the Republic, made a similar proposal. *Pravda* published his famous article 'Proletarians, to Horse!' in which he said in particular: 'The main defect of the Red Army is its lack of cavalry. Ours is a war of manoeuvre and demands the greatest mobility. This means a great role for cavalry. We have already felt our weakness in this respect: Kaledin, Krasnov and Dutov have always had superiority in terms of cavalry. Now the destructive attack by Mamontov has acutely posed the issue of creating numerous Red cavalry-units... The Soviet Republic needs cavalry. Red cavalrymen, forward! Proletarians to horse!' (*Pravda*, 20 September 1919)]

This fact is enormously important and demonstrates most convincingly the stability of the basis on which Soviet power rests, along with the complete hopelessness of attempts to overthrow it by any kind of cavalry-attack.

But an end must be put to these attacks. They may cost us far too much if they are repeated.

E. Preobrazhensky

No. 62

'When Will the Revolution Begin in Europe?'[1]

12 October 1919

We are already tired of asking such a question.

In this article, of course, I have no intention of making any prediction concerning the time within which the revolution must be completed in the capitalist countries of the West. I intend to answer a different question: How long is it possible for the revolution **not** to occur in the West?

Let us turn to an investigation of the economic basis of the strongest countries of the West, to production, distribution, and available inventories.

The central product of European capitalist industry, its grain, is coal. The most important coal-suppliers are England and Germany. Here is the position in England with regard to coal. At a meeting of the Allied Economic Council, Auckland Geddes gave the following information. It was expected that the current year would see 213 million tons of coal. 25 million tons were expected to be available for export, of which France was to receive 9 million. As a result of the disorder in production, and particularly the miners' strike in England, 183 million tons will be extracted. For this reason, not only is it impossible to export anything to France and Italy, who are trying to acquire English coal, but England itself will be forced to import 5 million tons for its own industry.

As for Germany, an unprecedented coal-famine has already set in there. Production has fallen to forty percent of what was extracted before the War. There is insufficient coal not only for export, but even for German railways, which have cut their work to a minimum.

As a result, Italian industry, which was sustained by English coal, is condemned to liquidation. In France, where mines have yet to be restored in the North, and for which English assistance is impossible, industry must experience a severe crash. Things are even worse in Austria. In Vienna, the trams have already come to a halt due to lack of coal.

As far as America is concerned, according to recent information, it is refusing to provide Europe with coal in response to the reduced production.

But the reduction in coal-output on such a dangerous scale means inevitable curtailment of all industry that functions with the use of coal, even if there were no other shortages.

Production of food-products has also been sharply curtailed. In England there was a crop-failure. The harvest was poor in Germany and France. As for American

---

1. [From *Ezhenedel'nik pravdy*, 18 September; 12 October 1919.]

grain, according to information from America the surpluses are not sufficient to satisfy European demands.

Moreover, in terms of materials and instruments of production, any and all inventories that were accumulated during the normal functioning of capitalist production, and which served the purpose of its expansion, have been totally exhausted during the years of war. Accordingly, production has contracted and is still contracting; the volume of food-products is inadequate; and even if they could be equally distributed, the commodity-reserve that is used for the normal operation of industry and for its expansion is lacking.

But the contraction of products subject to distribution in bourgeois society inevitably brings with it a rise in prices, especially if there is an enormous quantity of paper-money. The enormous rise in product-prices that we are seeing in the West is one of the forms of struggle in this society to reduce consumption. The real wage is falling. The paradise that was promised to the workers after the War, in return for their obedience and support for the War, is beginning to turn into a hell, not only for the defeated countries, but even for the victors.

The workers are trying to bring their real budget (that is, the quantity of products acquired for wages) to the pre-war level. But this cannot be done because the workers' pre-war volume of consumption also presupposed the pre-war scale of production. But production has now been reduced in some branches almost by half.

A widespread strike-movement is beginning. The first consequence of this movement is a still greater fall in production. The employers and bourgeois governments are making concessions. Almost without exception, the characteristic feature of mass-strikes in the West following the War is that they all end either with complete satisfaction of the workers' demands or in a compromise. But an even more typical feature is that they begin again in the same branches just a short while later. Why is that?

The answer is given by the example of the coal-miners' strike in England. The miners' demands were satisfied, the wage was raised and, at the same time, the selling price of coal was raised. But this means a rapid rise in prices for all other products whose production involves the consumption of coal, that is, almost all the products of industry. The concessions to the workers turn out to be a fiction; **for the purpose of consumption, bourgeois society gives to the workers what they had before, that is, an insufficient volume of products**; all that changes is the expression of wages in terms of money.

The strikes begin again, there are new concessions, the wage rises, but with no more success. The only real outcome of the new strikes is an even greater curtailment of production.

Assuming this is the case, what are the limits here to concessions by the capitalists?

Clearly, they can concede all that part of the surplus-value that now goes to them and is **currently being created**. However, according to information from English sources, for example, the coal-industry of England is already incurring an enormous loss, and the government, committed to maintaining the coal-industrialists, does not know how to pay them.

Thus, the capitalists in the major branches of industry already have **nothing** with which to make concessions to the workers, given the current disintegration of the industry. There is an objective limit to concessions, and the capitalists cannot defend themselves with concessions since the source of concessions – profit – turns out to be eaten up. They give no surplus-product to the workers. They are even lacking the means for reproduction of labour-power.

But perhaps the workers can lay their hands on the profit of previous years, on war-profits, and so on?

Alas, an enormous part of the war-profits are fictitious capital. They represent a right to acquire **future incomes from exploitation of the working class.** They are not evidence of products that already exist, but of those that have yet to be created. If all the state-debt obligations, all the loan-coupons, are taken out of bourgeois safes and given to the workers, the amount of bread consumed by the workers of London and Paris would not increase by a single pound. It is only now that the War, as a process of destroying **real values** and of accumulating **paper ones** in safes, is beginning to appear in all its dreadful consequences.

How long will the working class of the West try to find a way out of the resulting position by way of economic mass-strikes?

Clearly, the answer is as long as capital is still in a position to make **real** concessions to the workers (in this regard, resources are already coming to an end) and as long as the workers take fictitious concessions to be real ones.

The colossal strikes, which are continuing in the West, will very quickly bring the workers to a brick wall. Very soon, bourgeois society as a whole will have to reply to the workers: 'I can give no more'. The proletariat will then look for a way out, on the one hand, in complete expropriation of the bourgeois classes and consumption of their supplies (which are limited), but mainly – in the transition to socialist forms of production.

Any other outcome, namely, that the bourgeoisie will gradually restore production and pacify the workers somewhat with real concessions, is extremely improbable.

E. Preobrazhensky

No. 63

Resolution[1] of the First All-Bashkir Conference of the RKP(B)[2] on the Tasks Facing the Communists of Bashkiria in the Period of Civil War[3]

City of Sterlitamak 8 *November 1919*[4]

The conference of Communists of Soviet Bashkiria, meeting on the day after celebration of the second anniversary of the October Revolution, defines the international and domestic position that has emerged for the Soviet Republic, and its own tasks, as follows:

1. The disintegration of capitalism in the West and the collapse of the bourgeoisie's productive forces are continuing and intensifying. In all the countries of Europe, it is becoming evident that the bourgeois class is unable to manage the ruinous consequences of the World-War. The food-crisis is intensifying, inflation is growing, and working-class consumption is being curtailed.

2. On the basis of industrial collapse and hunger, a powerful strike-movement has begun in all the capitalist countries. This movement demonstrates in practice the impossibility of the workers improving their

---

1. [Adopted by the evening-session of the All-Bashkir Conference of the RKP(B) on the basis of a draft submitted by E.A. Preobrazhensky, representing the Central Committee of the RKP(B).]
2. [The report could not be found. The text of the resolution is published here according to the stenogram.]
3. [RGASPI. F. 17. Op. 6. D. 10. L. 4–4 ob. Original. Typewritten.]
4. [The beginning of the Conference was planned for 5 November, but 'in view of the absence of the CC representative, comrade Preobrazhensky, and of delegates from the majority of the cantonal conferences' the opening day was postponed to 8 November 1919.]

position within the limits of the capitalist system, and everywhere it is driving the proletariat to the path of seizing political power. Successes of the revolution in the West are being expressed in the formation of strong Communist Parties everywhere, in a number of strikes that are putting forth the demand for socialisation of industry, and in numerous actions by the European proletariat in defence of Soviet Russia. The successes of the revolutionary movement are also evident in America and recently in Japan.

3. The crisis of bourgeois society and the collapse of the predatory system of world-imperialism is also occurring through endless uprisings in the colonies, for whom the present moment is more favourable than ever-before to emancipate themselves from European oppression and thus to accelerate the crash of the entire capitalist system, which is founded on plunder of the oppressed peoples in the colonies.

4. In such conditions, the two-year existence of Soviet power and of Russia already represents, in itself, an enormous victory of the proletarian revolution. This victory will be even more decisive if the final stronghold of world-capitalism – the White-Guard army of Denikin – is defeated by the Red troops. A speedy destruction of Denikin is also imperative for Soviet Russia due to the enormous exhaustion of the country resulting from the prolonged Civil War that threatens to undermine all its vital forces.

5. The conference of Communists in Bashkiria places before the organisations in Bashkiria not only the common tasks of all Communists in Russia, but also special tasks in providing assistance to the Red front by conducting intensive Communist work among the backward Bashkir people, through political work in the Bashkir units that are being mobilised and through motivating all organisations in Bashkiria to succeed in the matter of supplying the starving centres with food-products.

Appendix

Note by V.I. Lenin Concerning the Policy of the RKP(B) Among the Eastern Peoples[5]

No earlier than 8 November, 1919[6]

If we merely 'fleece' the Eastern peoples, without giving them anything, then our *entire* international policy and the entire struggle 'for Asia' goes to the devil.

---

5. [From RGASPI. F. 2. Op. 1. D. 14810. L. 1–1 ob. Handwritten. Partially published in Struchkov 1985, p. 10; *Pravda*, 11 July 1956.]

6. [Golikov et al. 1970–82, Vol. 8, p. 7.]

It is better to leave the Bashkirs and Kirgiz entirely at peace, thus facilitating our policy of struggle for Asia. Otherwise, we accomplish nothing in Asia against English imperialism. We face a serious struggle for Persia, India and China, and for the sake of this struggle it is better to 'fleece' nothing from the small peoples of the East, or an absolute minimum that is stipulated quite precisely.

From each soviet- and party-worker, in Bashkiria and Kirgizia, demand a monthly account along something like the following lines:

1. What have we given to the Bashkirs, the Kirgiz, and others?
2. The results of educational work in general?
3. Especially – schools for Communists of the *given* nationality?
4. What have we taken? *Precisely*: grain? Cattle? And so on.
5. Incidents of conflict with the local Bashkir and Kirgiz authorities. An exact account of every incident.
6. How has the struggle gone against the khans, kulaks and bourgeoisie of each nationality?

No. 64
Address of the Representative of VTsIK E.A. Preobrazhensky[1] at a Session of Responsible Party-Workers of the Ufa Provincial Organisation of the RKP(B) Concerning Failure of the Putsch Mounted by Bourgeois Nationalists[2]

25 January 1920

Comrade Preobrazhensky: On the basis of personal impressions he says that Yumagulov's activity expresses opposition to the whole of Soviet economic policy by the kulak-part of the peasantry of Bashkiria, who are being pressed from two sides by the Communist Party of Bashkiria and by the peasant-poor, whom the Party is trying to promote in order to divide the Bashkir peasantry.

Subsequently, comrade Preobrazhensky portrays in general outline the events that preceded Yumagulov's activity, and he considers it necessary, in the event of possible further activities of a more serious character by the kulak-elements of Bashkiria, to prepare appropriate forces with which to repulse this danger. The experience of Yumagulov has shown us that we are prepared for such 'contingencies'.

The eastern sector, whose forces we counted on, was able to put forth a ridiculous number of armed

---

1. [Published according to the stenogram of the meeting of responsible party-workers of the Ufa provincial organisation of the RKP(B).]
2. [From RGASPI. F. 17. Op. 12. D. 710. L. 165. Copy. Typewritten]

forces at the moment when events developed. It is necessary to devote serious attention to increasing the military preparedness of the forces that the eastern sector has at its disposal and to strengthen its work.

Chairman
Secretary[3]

---

3. [The signatures are missing.]

No. 65
Address by the Representative of the VTsIk E.A. Preobrazhensky at a Session of the Plenum of the Ufa Provincial Committee of the RKP(B)[1] Concerning the Work of the Provincial Committee in Conditions of the Conflict Between the Centre and the Bashkir Republic[2]

11 February 1920

Report of the Presidium of the Provincial Committee

The report of comrade Preobrazhensky

Since the Plenum of the Provincial Committee ended, the Presidium has had to work in conditions that have been completely unfavourable in terms of the personal composition of the Presidium. Comrade Krivov fell seriously ill at the outset and had to be allowed to take leave, and a second member, comrade Yur'ev, only arrived in Ufa at the end of January. Guzakov never attended a single meeting, so the work of the Presidium stagnated; of course, with only one person, the work could not be done. It was only at the last moment that we were able to begin work and barely stick some departments together – that is how

---

1. [Published according to Protocol No. 1 of the Plenum of the Ufa Provincial Committee of the RKP(B).]
2. [From RGASPI. F. 17. Op. 12. D. 710. L. 3–3 ob., 5 ob.–6. Copy. Typewritten.]

we organised the Department of Agitation and Propaganda, whose management was assigned to comrade Stukov. Then, because almost no political work was done in the local garrison, resulting in numerous misunderstandings, we had *to think*[3] about creating a Military Department under the Provincial Committee that would follow and direct the work of the existing political organs under the military institutions. Comrade Kadomtsev was put in charge. We were not able to complete all of the tasks of the Provincial Conference and the Plenum, and some of them were only partially fulfilled. We can report complete satisfaction in relations between the Provincial Committee and the Presidium of the Provincial Executive Committee.

During this period, we more than once had to react to various misunderstandings in the districts: in one case, the requisitions were not conducted correctly, in another there was a delay in collecting grain or stagnation in party-work, and so on, but on a larger scale, the Provincial Committee has accomplished nothing. We also had to participate actively in settling the conflict that occurred in Bashkiria. Recently, because of our isolation from the centre and a complete lack of newspapers from the capital, we have had no news about party-work, nor even of the newly adopted regulations of our Party that are so essential for our work. On all the important questions of principle we have summoned meetings of senior workers, and four such meetings have occurred. Thus the resolution of major questions was not narrowly determined by the Presidium alone, but collectively. Matters that were not of principled importance were usually determined by the Presidium. As a result of the conditions that developed, we had to dissolve the urban district and declare a re-registration there: the causes for this will be discussed in detail by comrade Kadomtsev. Above all, the Presidium had to fritter away time on the details of urban work and negotiations with the Ukrainians, who regularly besieged us for entire days with requests to take leave in Ukraine.

The Department for Work among the Nationalities

The report of comrade Preobrazhensky

In place of the existing national sections, the Provincial Conference decided to create, under the Provincial Committee, a Department for Work among the Nationalities. It was resolved to achieve this as follows: to gather the chairmen of the sections – of the Chuvash-Mari, the Tatar-Bashkir, the Jewish, the Latvian and foreign groups – every week, under my chairmanship. Every sub-department

---

3. [Handwritten above the line.]

gives a report concerning its sub-department and receives direction from the chairman of the provincial committee. But thus far, separatism continues to occur in the activities of the sections, in the matter of accepting and excluding party-members, as well as in other matters. Things have improved somewhat in the Tatar-Bashkir Sub-Department, where comrades arrived from Sterlitamak. In the Sub-Department's work, we encountered one fact that also received attention from the Central Committee, namely, the resolution of their Congress concerning the existence of a Bureau of the Peoples of the East. That resolution provides the basis for creating a separate Muslim organisation in the districts and in the province, accountable to the Central Bureau, which even sent its own representative to us in Ufa for organisation of the Ufa Provincial Bureau. A meeting of responsible workers resolved that this question should be explored as a whole at the next All-Russian Party-Congress. In a word, the work of the Department of Nationalities is only at the conception-stage. Matters are going well in the Latvian Sub-Department. The Chuvash-Mari Sub-Department, in view of its small number of members, remains in embryo. The Jewish Sub-Department is only working in Ufa, since there is no Jewish population in the territory of the province. The foreign group, for the same reason, is working on a very minor scale. That is the general report. In future, we have to create a more complex apparatus out of these weekly meetings...[4]

Comrade Barbe: What is the attitude of the Tatar-Bashkir Sub-Department to the organisation of a Tatar-Bashkir republic and agitation for its creation?

Comrade Shamigulov provides information on the resolutions of the All-Russian Congress concerning this matter. A Tatar-Bashkir republic probably will not be established, but perhaps there will be only a Tatar one. Here in Ufa, we have received a Tatar newspaper in which the slogan 'Long live the Tatar-Bashkir republic' has already appeared. We have resolved that not a single Tatar Communist has the right to conduct any agitation for or against formation of this republic, but only to explain what the formation of such republics involves.

Comrade Preobrazhensky: We have acted in agreement with the centre. Once the question of a single economic and military policy was resolved, there was no longer any great danger in the organisation of national republics, but the experience with Bashkiria made us exercise caution and ask the Central Committee to pose the question at the Party-Congress. We have no final decisions on this question.

Chairman
Secretary[5]

---

4. [The speech by G.K. Shamigulov is omitted.]
5. [The signatures are missing.]

No. 66
From the Address by E.A. Preobrazhensky at the Sixth Ufa Provincial Conference of the RKP(B) Concerning Economic Construction and a Federal Constitution[1]

3 March 1920

Comrade Preobrazhensky gives a report on the question of economic construction. He reports on the practical steps outlined by the commission for implementing the decree on universal labour-duty for restoration of our ruined economy. Above all, the commission faced questions of how to overcome the ruin, how to take stock of the workforce and where to recruit it, and what organs will head up our economic apparatus.

Labour-power: 1) its basis is the proletariat directly connected with the factories and plants; 2) the proletariat that has been driven from the city by famine and is now dispersed in the countryside – it must be mobilised; and 3) the unskilled worker-peasants, who must also be drawn into building economic life by way of mobilisation. The remainder consists of the petty bourgeoisie, deserters, and citizens who have been jailed, all of whom must be mobilised and compelled to work.

Finally, there is the yet-to-be-demobilised Red Army, which has still to complete its military task.

It is imperative to resort precisely to mobilisation, to compulsory recruitment of citizens into economically creative labour, and to take into account the current

---

1. [From RGASPI. F. 17. Op. 12. D. 709. L. 7 ob. Copy. Typewritten]

truly exceptional moment – a tide resulting from plundering the organism of the entire people following the imperialist War.²

In order to implement this mobilisation, it is necessary, first of all, to think about supplying those who are mobilised with everything they require. Formation of a food-fund is far from solving the question of feeding all the mobilised citizens.

The commission concluded that it is not expedient to mobilise unskilled peasants, since that would result in such a colossal army, with such an enormous administrative apparatus, that Soviet Russia, with its presently ruined transportation, would not be able to supply it.

For that reason, the commission concluded that drawing peasants into labour should be done not through mobilisation, but by assigning one or another economic task.

The next issue is to raise labour-productivity. Here, there are two possibilities: on the one hand, the militarisation of labour and transferring the workers to barrack-conditions, on the other hand, the implementation of labour-discipline.

Here, there are two tendencies: 1) to adapt our entire economic apparatus and subordinate it to the military-economic apparatus, that is, the entire economic apparatus becomes infused with militarism; 2) or else the economic apparatus, with *Sovnarkhoz*³ and the trade-union at its head, subordinates the military-economic apparatus to itself. The commission takes the latter tendency as its starting point. We must adopt a military form of labour in implementing one or another economic task, that is, work out strict norms, functions and means of coordinating all possible economic institutions. We must place *Sovnarkhoz* at the head of our economic apparatus together with *Sovprofsoyuz*,⁴ and this means promoting conditions in which the statification of trade-unions continues and develops further, rather than having them return to their previous status. The militarisation of labour must be implemented in the sense of reconstructing our apparatus on a military footing, that is, so that every plan that is worked out is accomplished with the same persistence and speed as a military order.

Moreover, it is imperative to implement labour-discipline and personal responsibility through military-production courts, before which all workers and all economic and administrative institutions, from top to bottom, are equally accountable.

---

2. [The text says 'волна как результат расхищения организма всего населения после империалистической войны'.]
3. [The Council of National Economy.]
4. [The Council of Trade-Unions.]

A federal constitution

Comrade Preobrazhensky reports on relations with the Bashkir Republic and on the difficulties being encountered in practically implementing the federal constitution in view of its lacking a number of concrete and practical instructions, and he proposes the following resolution: the Ufa Provincial Conference proposes to the Party-Congress that it charge the Central Committee with working out a draft federal constitution on the basis of a single Red Army, a single production- and food-policy, and single state-wide control over all the resources of the RSFSR.

The resolution is unanimously adopted.

Chairman
Members of the Presidium
Secretary[5]

---

5. [The signatures are missing.]

No. 67
E.A. Preobrazhensky's Address to a Meeting of Responsible Workers of Ufa Province Concerning Conditions in the Bashkir Republic and the Tasks Facing Communists as a Result of the Uprising Mounted by Bashkir Nationalists[1]

13 March 1920

The uprising of the Muslim population. There are no special methods for Muslims to implement Soviet power. The difficulties are great, but the methods are the same as for Russians. To accept everything that is being said about minimising the economic tasks would result in the mullahs winning and the Communists surrendering. The practical conclusion – it is imperative to strengthen work among the Muslim population and to promote its internal stratification. There is no-one else to do the work, comrades, and no-one upon whom we might lean. The population is already stratified economically. We know that there are villages made up entirely of poor peasants on the one hand, but on the other hand there are rural districts where the kulak-population clearly predominates. We must gather Communists together, welcome Muslim comrades from other provinces, and create a school for study of the Tatar language. Physical measures must be taken against the mullahs. A conscious Muslim Communist detachment is needed to destroy the apparatus of the mullahs. But we have lost time.

---

1. [From RGASPI. F. 17. Op. 12. D. 710. L. 168–168 ob. Copy. Typewritten.]

All we can do is utilise the meagre Communist forces, point out to them their mistaken political views, and put them to work.

Congresses of the poor are impossible so long as the poor are not visible and the countryside is not yet stratified. For now, we need non-party conferences.

The following proposals are submitted:

1. To strengthen work in the countryside and send in our best party-forces.
2. To strengthen work towards stratification of the countryside in order to create a stable base for Soviet power.
3. To strengthen to the utmost our agitation amongst Muslims, relying primarily upon genuinely Communist Tatar and Bashkir forces that have not been contaminated with nationalist ideas or with a veneer of S-Rism or Menshevism. To create shock-groups from these forces to be sent primarily to localities that have experienced the insurrection and to the adjoining parishes.
4. To begin a merciless struggle against all negative manifestations of Soviet power in the form of behaviour that insults religious feelings, involves abuse, drunkenness, and such like.
5. To summon, in the near future, non-party conferences of the poorest peasants and middle-peasants from among the Muslim population.
6. To divide Ufa province into districts and to post responsible and tested party-workers in each of them for the purpose of agitation, for repair and organisation of Soviet apparatuses, and for control over their work.
7. To organise quickly a commission to review Soviet institutions in the province, to investigate [the causes of] the uprisings, and to receive and investigate complaints.

    This commission must be empowered to take various measures on the spot that are required by local conditions.
8. To conduct agitation urgently among the peasant-poor in order to put pressure on the kulaks and improve the conditions of the poor.
9. To conduct a purge of food-agitators and food-requisition detachments, getting rid of undesirable elements.
10. To conduct re-elections for the soviets and prevent any penetration by kulaks or White Guards.
11. To strengthen the province's administration-department with experienced workers.
12. To create a special department for work in the countryside under the Provincial Executive Committee.
13. To approve distribution of workers by districts (point 6) at the next session of responsible workers.

14. To request of the Central Committee that Communists at the front from Ufa province – Tatars, Bashkirs and Cheremis – be returned, by order of the Provincial Committee, for assignment by the Provincial Committee.
15. To create a specially designated Muslim Communist detachment from local forces and from comrades who are in the Kashirin unit in the Third and Fifth Armies.
16. To arm Communist cells in the province.
17. To subordinate food-agitators to the control of provincial and district party-committees.
18. To open party-schools quickly for the Tatar-Bashkirs.
19. To ask the Central Committee for urgent assignment of the best Muslim party-comrades from other provinces (5 to 6 comrades) to organise and conduct work amongst the Muslims.
20. To work to fulfil the lumbering- and transport-obligation completely, with this obligation being increased by one and a half times in the districts that rebelled, falling mainly on kulak-elements.
21. To establish discipline and responsibility from top to bottom in Soviet institutions, and permit no relaxation.

The proposals are accepted.

Comrades Artem and Preobrazhensky provide information concerning the Regional Conference in Bashkiria, where elections were held for delegates to the All-Russian Congress of the RKP[2] along with the selection of the Regional Committee.

The question of the Conference proceeded smoothly: there were frictions and rough encounters with Validov and others, who were opposed to the Conference, but the Central Committee ordered that the Conference must be held and that Shamigulov and Izmailov must attend and even be elected.

Stratification is beginning in Bashkiria. In places the poor are emerging, but the isolation of kulaks is also beginning, for the time being in the form of religious (sects).

There are about three thousand party-members in Bashkiria, including up to two thousand Russians. Those elected to the Congress are: Artem, candidate Dudnik, along with Said-Galiev and Akhmadulin.

The report by comrades Artem and Preobrazhensky is noted.

Chairman
Secretary[3]

---

2. [The Ninth Congress of the RKP(B) was held in March 1920.]
3. [The signatures are missing.]

Appendix 1

From a Cipher-Telegram from Chairman of the Revolutionary War-Council Trotsky to Secretary of the Central Committee of the RKP(B) N.N. Krestinsky[4]

No. 522   17 February 1920[5]
From Trotsky's train, Bashkiria   Secret

In determining our relation to the Bashkir Republic, the harmful attitudes of Ufa must be taken into account. They are openly speaking there of the Bashkir Republic as a temporary sop, which is extremely irritating to a Bashkir. At a party-meeting, Preobrazhensky spoke of the need to review the national programme at the Party-Congress and accused the Central Committee of making the Ufa workers victims of the eastern policy. The narrow-mindedness of Yeltsin, the hysteria of Artem, and the philosophy of Preobrazhensky are turning our Bashkir policy into its opposite.

Appendix 2

From a Cipher-Telegram from L.D. Trotsky to Secretary of the CC of the RKP(B) N.N. Krestinsky[6]

No. 544   2 March 1920[7]
                                                                                From Trotsky's train, Bashkiria
                                                                                                    Top Secret

Moscow. To Sklyansky for Krestinsky

1. I shall follow the course of the uprising. It is of no military significance. A scandal like the surrender of Belebey is explained by the unfitness of Vokhra.

2. The Bashkirs are not taking part in the uprising. The Bashkir units are holding up well. Of course, complications with the Bashkirs are possible. What is needed at the Revolutionary Committee is a comrade who can foresee complications,

---

4. [From RGASPI. F. 17. Op. 84. D. 63. L. 11. Copy. Typewritten.]
5. [Noted on the left margin of the telegram and on the top in black ink: 'From Trotsky's train 17/II/20'.]
6. [From RGASP. F. 17. Op. 84. D. 63. L. 17–18. Copy. Typewritten. Under the telegram is noted in black ink: 'Comrade Trotsky requests a prompt reply to this telegram'.]
7. [Received 3 March 1920.]

not provoke them. I believe Artem must be removed and Preobrazhensky transferred. Internal work is needed; the encouragement of political differentiation, the selection of suitable people, yet those in Ufa are replacing the class-question with the national question.

3. Yesterday, Validov was warned through direct contact about Bashkir units that might be attracted to a Muslim uprising. Validov answered with a long explanation in which he swore that not a single Bashkir will oppose Soviet power, and he proposed using Bashkir units for pacification...[8]

4. In order to resolve the Bashkir conflict, I must return via Ufa. Meanwhile [Validov] proposed taking the northern route in order to visit Perm and Vyatka, which are included in the First Labour-Army. If you think it is absolutely necessary, I can leave through Ufa. But unless Artem and Preobrazhensky are replaced by tactically firm people, who understand the meaning of our national policy, nothing will be accomplished in any event...[9]

Trotsky

Deciphered in the Secretariat of the Deputy Chairman of the Revolutionary War-Council of the Republic, 3 March 1920

Appendix 3

Resolution of the Presidium of VTsIK Concerning the Bashkir Revolutionary Committee[10]

4 May 1920[11]

The Presidium of the All-Russian Central Executive Committee resolved:

1. To recall from Bashkiria Yumagulov and Validov, members of the presidium of the Bashkir Revolutionary Committee, and also representatives of the VTsIK Artem (Sergeev), Preobrazhensky and Samoilov, since they have proven unable to pacify the groups struggling in Bashkiria.

---

8. [A quotation from a letter by A.Z. Validov is omitted concerning a parade and meeting conducted by the Bashkir Revolutionary Committee.]
9. [Paragraph 5 concerning the state of affairs in Poland is omitted.]
10. [From RGASPI. F. 17. Op. 84. D. 63. L. 117. Typewritten copy; GA RF. F. 1235. Op. 37. D. 2. L. 103. Typewritten copy. Published in *Dekrety sovetskoi vlasti*, Vol. IX, pp. 309–10.]
11. [The resolution was accepted at the meeting of the VTsIk Presidium on 7 June, 1920.]

2. Until the plenum of the All-Russian Central Executive Committee meets, to remove Yumagulov temporarily from membership of the All-Russian Central Executive Committee and to bring him to trial for the arrest of responsible Communists – members of the Bashkir Regional Committee – and for related criminal acts.

3. To appoint Malyutin to the Presidium of the Bashkir Revolutionary Committee as representative of the All-Russian Central Executive Committee. To appoint comrades Mostovenko and Vikman to represent the All-Russian Central Executive Committee on a five-member commission to summon the Bashkir Congress of Soviets and to conduct elections in the contested parishes.[12]

4. To include the city of Sterlitamak in the territory of the Bashkir Republic. The Sterlitamak District-Executive Committee must be guaranteed the ability to remain in the city together with its institutions, and they must be provided with all necessary accommodations. The protection of the city and responsibility for all measures necessitated by strategic considerations remain in the hands of the commandant appointed by the Trans-Volga Regional Commissariat. All questions involving transfer of the city to the Bashkir Republic, and all issues concerning the quartering of various institutions, are submitted for resolution to a special commission of three persons made up of one representative from the Bashkir Revolutionary Committee and one from the District-Executive Committee, under the chairmanship of the representative of the All-Russian Central Executive Committee in Bashkiria.

---

12. [In connection with the creation in November 1920 of a Bashkir regional party-organisation, the Central Committee of the RKP(B) sent a group of party-workers to Bashkiria: F.A. Sergeev (Artem), F.N. Samoilov, G.K. Shamigulov, P.M. Vikman and others.

They had to work under constant pressure from nationalist elements. In June 1919, the nationalist-leaning members of the Bashkir Revolutionary Committee ceased their work and attempted to create a political crisis in the Republic.

Just how complicated any attempt to resolve the question of leadership was in the Bashkir Republic can be seen in the documents: '27 September 1920 the *Orgburo* considers a request from Chairman of the Bashkir Central Executive Committee, comrade Shamigulov, for recall of comrade Mostovenko from Bashkiria' (RGASPI. F. 17. Op. 84. D. 63. L. 81). In turn, J.V. Stalin recommended to members of the Politburo that they 'recall from Bashkiria comrade Shamigulov, whom they absolutely cannot tolerate there, along with his faithful companion in arms, comrade Vikman'.

The comments on Stalin's letter were: 'Agreed. N.N. Krestinsky'. A second comment said: 'Categorically opposed to the question without discussions. I have another idea. I will propose it at the plenum. Preobrazhensky' (RGASPI. F. 17. Op. 84. D. 63. L. 82–3).

Nos. 68–9
Addresses from the Central Committee of the RKP(B) to the Party-Organisations and Provincial Committee of Bashkiria[1]

April 1920

No. 68

To the Party-Organisations of Bashkiria – Concerning Wide Involvement of the Toiling Masses of the Republic in the Communist Party[2]

April 1920

The age-old oppression of the Bashkir people by landlords and tsarist officials; the widespread and stubbornly disdainful attitude towards Bashkiria[3] that still persists among a significant element of the Russian population; the recent civil war, in which a majority of the Bashkir people were drawn by their White-Guard and nationalist elements into the counter-revolutionary camp and fought against the Russian peasants and Russian workers of Bashkiria, who remained loyal to the Soviet authority; and finally, a whole series of conflicts over land-relations between incoming Russians and the native Bashkir population – are making it extremely difficult to organise the Bashkir masses

---
1. [It appears that E.A. Preobrazhensky wrote these appeals shortly after his election as Secretary of the Central Committee of the RKP(B).]
2. [From RGASPI. F. 17. Op. 84. D. 63. L. 67–67 ob. Handwritten.]
3. [The text says 'к башкирину'.]

around the Communist Party, which first established itself among the Russian working population. The difficulty is made even worse by particular aspects of life among the masses of Muslim believers, by the force of religious prejudices and religious fanaticism in their midst, and finally, by agitation on the part of the nationalist-inclined bourgeois-intelligentsia upper stratum of the Bashkir people, who are doing everything possible to prevent poor Bashkirs from breaking with the well-to-do elements and becoming united in a single Communist Party (in deeds, not just words) together with the proletariat and the poor of other nationalities.

In these circumstances, recruitment of Bashkir Communists into our ranks is extremely important, for no one other than Bashkir Communists themselves can wage a successful struggle against the mullahs and their influence, on the one hand, and against young Muslim elements on the other. Every sincere and honest Bashkir Communist, and even every poor Bashkir peasant who merely sympathises with the Communists, is enormously important to our Party. The primary task of RKP organisations in Bashkiria is to attract the widest possible masses of poor Bashkirs into the Communist Party. Organising non-party conferences of the toiling masses of Bashkiria on the basis of cantons, supporting and developing unions of Bashkir Communist youths, organising study and reading rooms, discussions on political and religious themes...[4] organising volunteer Saturdays among Russian Communists to assist the families of Bashkirs in the Red Army, supporting organisations that are helping poor Bashkir peasants to survive, providing economic assistance to these poor people from their Russian comrades – all of these measures and more must be implemented in order to achieve our goal. Finally, it must be not only a duty, but also a matter of honour, for every genuine Communist in the Russian organisations to reinforce the struggle against remnants of great-Russian chauvinism and disdain towards the less cultured and economically weaker Bashkir population.

While opening wide the doors of our Party to the poor of Bashkiria, however, we must also make every effort to prevent penetration by careerist elements from the petty-bourgeois intelligentsia, who are striving for power and, in place of the class-struggle, waged jointly by the proletariat and the poor with no regard to nationality, are substituting chauvinist dreams about creating a Great Bashkir-Kirghiz state, about liberating the whole of the East under Bashkir leadership, and other such nationalistic fantasies. These fantasies are a crude mockery of the Bashkir poor, in circumstances where tens of thousands of people are dying of hunger within Bashkiria itself, have no roofs overhead, and lack even the most elementary ideas concerning the political life of the Republic at a time of

---

4. [An illegible insertion is written here, above the line.]

mass-ruin for the Bashkir population, who have received no guidance as to how to save themselves from extinction by taking the socialist road.

The Bashkir Republic will only become a genuinely socialist republic when the Communist organisations of Bashkiria succeed in raising up a sufficiently numerous cadre of Bashkir Communists, who will be able to deal with all the tasks of communist construction on their territory and who, instead of seeking autonomy from socialism, will look for salvation of their people in autonomy and the ways of achieving it.[5]

---

5. [There is no signature.]

No. 69

To the Provincial Committees of Kazan, Simbirsk, Samara, Ufa, Chelyabinsk and Orenburg – Concerning the Inadmissibility of any Development of National Animosity towards the Tatar and Bashkir Press[1]

April 1920

From the moment when the Autonomous Bashkir Republic emerged, and especially after meetings in Moscow clarified the negative attitude of Bashkir political figures to the idea of a Tatar-Bashkir republic, in the Tatar Communist press there have been several articles directed against the Bashkir Republic as a whole and against the Bashkir Revolutionary Committee, which has been treated as some kind of counter-revolutionary institution. The negative attitude in these articles towards the Bashkir Republic was often based upon motives that were by no means communist. These motives were frequently nationalistic in character, or at best they provoked suspicion that they were rooted in irritation with the Bashkirs because their form of self-determination diverged from that preferred by supporters of a Tatar-Bashkir republic. This kind of polemic not only offers no help in clarifying a communist consciousness among the toiling masses of the Tatar and Bashkir peoples, it not only fails to detach the poor of both peoples from their bourgeois-intelligentsia groups for the purpose of a fraternal alliance and struggle, but, on the contrary, it even promotes the ideological enslavement of the Tatar and Bashkir poor through nationalism, strengthens national hostility, and confuses all-the-more the already complicated and difficult national question in the East.

As for appraisals in the press of the Bashkir Revolutionary Committee as a completely counter-revolutionary organ, they are far more harmful to the central Soviet power than to the Bashkir Revolutionary Committee, which has become part of the common system of organs of the Federal Republic and exists in accordance with a specific decree of the VTsIK. Just as the presence in individual Soviet organs and institutions of people who are waging a non-Soviet policy, or who have deviated from Soviet policy, does not give anyone grounds for considering these organs themselves be non-Soviet and counter-revolutionary, so the fully admissible criticism of separate measures and individual members of the Bashkir Revolutionary Committee must not flow over into indiscriminate

---

1. [From RGASPI. F. 17. Op. 84. D. 63. L. 68. Handwritten.]

accusations that the organ as a whole is counter-revolutionary, when it includes representatives of the central Soviet authority.

Directing the attention of provincial committees bordering the Bashkir province, and of Tatar Communists, to this matter, the Central Committee of the RKP urges that they take the appropriate measures so that instructions[2] from the Central Committee, such as this one, will in future be redundant.

---

2. [The word 'instructions' is inserted below the line in place of 'address' or 'appeal' (обращение), which is crossed-out.]

No. 70

An Article 'Concerning the Mobilisation of Unskilled Labour-Power', Published in the Newspaper *Pravda*[1]

30 March 1920

Our pre-revolutionary economy employed a vast amount of crude labour-power that was redundant in peasant-agriculture. In terms of the volume and type of work that must be done by unskilled labour over the next year or two, there will be no essential change from pre-revolutionary years (seasonal agricultural labour for landowners has virtually ended, and the same can be said of work in capital-construction, but there is an increase in the volume of labour needed to procure timber and peat and to ensure the timely repair of transportation that has been destroyed in the Civil War). To avoid crude mistakes while mobilising unskilled labour in one form or another, we must start from the distribution of labour-power that prevailed in our economy immediately prior to the revolutionary years.

Before the Revolution, unskilled labour was mobilised by capitalism and by the state in two ways: either in the form of hiring unskilled workers who were completely or almost completely detached from the land, or else in the form of peasants who sold their labour during time freed from agriculture.

The Soviet authority can mobilise the main mass of crude manpower in these same two forms. It would be a mistake, however, to have any illusions concerning the possibility that a large part of the work could

---

1. [From *Pravda*, 30 March 1920.]

be done by a permanent army of workers completely detached from agriculture. There are even fewer grounds for thinking that the labour of a worker who is mobilised by the state and receiving rations and clothing from the state would be economically better than that of peasants who are enlisted for work but who still remain attached to their farms. An army of permanent workers is dependent on the state for food, but the state already lacks bread for skilled workers.

An army of seasonal workers and peasants depends, for the most part, on its own bread. An army of permanent workers requires clothing, the construction of housing, the organisation of an enormous supply-apparatus, and so on. An army of seasonally working peasants can make do with their own clothing, and often with their own tools. In a word, it would not be the least bit sensible for us to construct a permanent army of labour **in circumstances where the same work** might be done by assigning labour to the peasantry. Hence, the conclusion is to use the army for labour when it **already** lives at state-expense and **cannot, for military reasons, be disbanded**, but also to avoid any delay in demobilising peasants from the army when, on military grounds, their units can be disbanded. It is more advantageous to us to acquire the same volume of labour from this section of the peasantry through labour-assignments.[2]

In a backward country such as Russia, economic experiments must be undertaken with great care. By the same token, one must study very closely the experiments already undertaken. The outstanding success in procuring timber in Vyatka province both last year and this year (this year six hundred and twenty thousand cubic feet were collected, and four hundred thousand were shipped out) is a clear example of the enormous usefulness of the method of assignments (in this case, each labour-unit was assigned the task of procuring a specific quantity of wood). The peasantry prefer this method, saying to themselves that 'once the work is done, we're through with the treasury and we're free'. From this perspective, the third thesis of the Central Committee, concerning economic construction[3] and the mobilisation of unskilled labour, was not appropriately formulated. To begin with, it is necessary to distinguish between the two types of labour-mobilisation that I have mentioned above. Secondly, it must be emphasised that it is economically more important for our economy, in coming years, to have labour-conscription in the form of labour-assignments, not in the form of labour by standing armies. On the scale of our economy as a whole, only that portion of the work that, for one reason or another, cannot be assigned to the labour-force in the countryside – and

---

2. ['путем трудовой разверстки'].
3. [Apparently the reference is to the Ninth Congress of the RKP(B). An account of the opening of the Congress was published in the same issue of *Pravda*.]

that portion alone – will have to be done by a standing army of unskilled workers,[4] and only in these departments[5] does it make sense for this army to be assembled and fed by the Soviet state.

E.A. Preobrazhensky

---

4. According to my calculations, the procurement of wood alone, and the shipment and rafting, would require a labour-army of nearly half a million, working year-round.

5. [The text says 'в этих отделах'.]

No. 71

E.A. Preobrazhensky's Diary[1] with Notes on Questions Discussed at Meetings of the Politburo and the Plenum of the Central Committee of the RKP(B)[2]

4 May–24 September 1920

4 May

I was secretary for a meeting of the Politburo. Once again, a whole array of international questions. In connection with the Polish offensive, Trotsky suggested that a half-hour 'strike' be held at 1 o'clock throughout the entire country following news of the seizure of Kiev, which can be expected within a day. Prepare all provincial committees for this possibility now with encrypted telegrams. Preparations were rejected. Lenin commented: 'They will say that everything was fabricated in advance'. It was resolved to arrange a work-stoppage and meetings after the seizure of Kiev. All the while, Trotsky emphasised the lethargy of the press and the sluggishness of party-comrades despite the seriousness of the situation.

A general conviction that the Poles will be defeated and things will, in all probability end with the declaration of Soviet power in Warsaw.

---

1. [E.A. Preobrazhensky's diary was apparently seized by the NKVD organs at the time of his arrest. It is kept in the TsA FSB RF (Central Archive of the Federal Security-Service of the Russian Federation).]
2. [From TsA FSB RF. Handwritten.]

There were curious comments in connection with a discussion of Brusilov's[3] letter, read by Trotsky. Kamenev drew attention to the fact that the letter mentioned 'Orthodox' people, which might provoke scoffing and mockery on the part of workers. He suggested making it appear that the typist 'overlooked' this word and that it not appear in print. Il'ich supported the skulduggery, commenting that the workers [would notice][4] nothing else in the letter and would ridicule the fact that we want to rely upon the 'Orthodox'.[5] Trotsky insisted on the need to publish the letter in its entirety because this word is absolutely essential to Brusilov, who wants to say that he has not changed his views even while siding with Soviet power out of patriotic considerations. Stalin supported this approach: 'It is not our letter but Brusilov's, and he is the one who answers for it'. Radek also joined them. As a result, someone joked that the 'Orthodox' be replaced by the 'Jews'. It was decided to publish the entire letter.

In view of the possibility of all kinds of machinations on the part of patriotic officers, I suggested they be more carefully monitored by the VChK.[6] This was agreed without discussion.

There was an interesting exchange of opinions regarding the composition of the delegation being sent to England. Il'ich insisted that Krasin go to Germany, not to England. He expressed the thought that England, by way of Poland, is at war with us. A bloc with Germany, even if only tacit, already half exists; and in terms of the opportunity to order locomotives, it is precisely Germany that can provide us with something. In his opinion, our alliance with Germany is maturing in opposition to the Entente. Kamenev made some objection. The question was set aside.

The following decision was taken on Georgia: send a telegram to Sergo not to take Tiflis, which he promised to make Soviet within two weeks, and not to 'self-determine' Georgia at all. Several people laughed at the fact that the [Georgian][7] delegates signed an agreement by which they are obliged not only to hand over all the interned Denikinites, but also to expel the Entente from Georgia. Il'ich laughed aloud and remarked that it would be like walking a puppy around the Kremlin. Someone joked that the puppy may indeed 'do' what a badly behaved puppy is expected to do. It was agreed to leave the Georgian Mensheviks in

---

3. [Following the October Revolution, A.A. Brusilov remained in Soviet Russia. From May 1920, he was chairman of a special conference under the Commander in Chief of the Armed Forces of the Republic. The diary is referring to a letter from Brusilov to former Russian officers calling upon them to defend the homeland.]
4. [The original text is damaged and this word could not be read. 'Would notice' appears to be the most probable variant.]
5. [This word, too, is illegible.]
6. [The Cheka, or All-Russian Extraordinary Commission responsible for state-security.]
7. [The text is also damaged here.]

peace and deal with them later on the basis of their failure to fulfil points of the agreement that are clearly impossible.

We then self-determined the Tatar Republic. The supposed communists with Sultan Galiev[8] were demanding inclusion in their territory not only of Kazan (with a population that is one-fifth Tatar), but also Ufa and the whole of Ufa province. It was decided to give them Kazan, while guaranteeing the rights of the non-Tatar population, but not Ufa. There will be a lot to settle with these 'communists' in future.

The patience that comrade Lenin has for all these sorts of people is striking, since he knows very well their bourgeois nature.

There were jokes about the Turkish nationalists who 'agree' with communism. Soon, there will be nowhere to escape from all these people who agree with communism.

It is a pity that all these sessions are not being taken down in shorthand for the edification of posterity. Although I write things down as quickly as I can, it will all be forgotten later.

The most important issue at the plenary meeting was the question of Curzon's note. I was not personally prepared for a decision and had not thought through my own position. But it was perfectly clear to me that the issue was a war[9] with the whole of the Entente. Il'ich, who had considered the situation more thoroughly than anyone else, was also most prepared to reach a decision. He read out some brief theses that had been prepared very skilfully in advance. They began with the perfectly indisputable point that we must assist Polish workers to achieve the sovietisation of Poland, recommended rejection of mediation by the Entente and the League of Nations, and concluded with a directive to continue the offensive. Bukharchik noted long ago that Il'ich is 'preparing a new, new phase'[10] in world-politics, and this now became perfectly obvious.

The debates were very lively. I asked our Comintern-specialists, Zinoviev, Bukharin and Radek, whether the Comintern-representatives who had come for the Congress could give formal guarantees of support for Soviet Russia in a new war. Il'ich interrupted me with reproachful irony: 'Can there ever be **formal** guarantees?' Zinoviev answered that the representatives of other countries will do whatever we propose.

Trotsky presented the conclusions of the military command in the event of a new, general intervention: the left-flank is vulnerable from Romania, and the

---

8. [The text should read 'Said-Galiev'. Sakhib-Garei Said-Galiev was Chairman of the Revolutionary Committee of the Tatar ASSR in 1920–1.]

9. [This is how the text reads, but the apparent meaning is that 'the issue would lead to a war'.]

10. [The word 'new' is repeated in the text. 'Bukharchik' refers to N.I. Bukharin.]

necessary redeployments will take time. In the case of a Latvian offensive, the right flank is vulnerable. His general appraisal even of the Polish front was not entirely optimistic, pointing out that the Poles are not surrendering, that they are retreating in good order, and that there is no appreciable demoralisation among them.

In general and on the whole, two basic tendencies could be discerned in the ensuing discussion. The first [tendency]:

Il'ich: 1) We must reject mediation. Now is the time to do so. The Entente cannot move its troops against us, and our strong response will have an impressive influence on small states such as Romania, Latvia and Finland. 2) The proposal to conclude an armistice is an attempt to swindle us. 3) We must probe Poland with Red-Army bayonets to see whether it is ready for Soviet power. If not, we can always retreat under one pretext or another.

Zinoviev: We must attack, there is no other alternative.

Bukharin, Rudzutak and Kamenev spoke in support of Il'ich.

The second tendency:

Radek indicated that he, Markhlevsky and other Polish Communists *believe* that Poland is not ready for sovietisation. Our offensive will only provoke a wave of patriotism and drive the proletariat to side with the bourgeoisie. He also spoke of the fact that Europe in general has not matured[11] for social revolution.

Trotsky claimed it was not expedient to reject mediation. He said he had read recent French papers and was struck by how hostile their tone was towards England because of its compromising policy in relation to the Bolsheviks. He outlined the need to intensify the split between England and France, whereas rejection of mediation would strengthen the position of Millerand and compel Lloyd George to capitulate to the French. He said it is useful to have a delegation in England as permanent observers of the Entente's intentions, something we would be deprived of if mediation were rejected.

Rykov suggested that attempts to sovietise Europe by detachments such as Budenny's will only compromise us in the eyes of the European proletariat. The essential point is that we do not have sufficient equipment, shoes or clothing, there is not enough lead and nowhere to acquire it, and there is one strike after another in the factories working for defence. We cannot provide bread, yet we want the Red-Army men to march on Berlin. With such problems in the rear, it is unthinkable to confront the Entente.

---

11. ['Matured' is written in above 'not ready', which is crossed out.]

I wanted to say the same as Trotsky concerning the division between England and France. Furthermore, I mentioned that the English workers will not quickly absorb a change in our tactics. It is easy for us to change course, but it will be impossible to turn around the millions whom we have accustomed to thinking that we are only waging a defensive war and that we desire peace as soon as possible.

Kalinin said that our whole country wants peace and that we must be cautious in a year of famine, and so on. As usual, he did not speak very persuasively. Il'ich pounced on Rykov, saying that he was thinking in defeatist terms, that all the objective evidence indicates we are enjoying successes in industry and in providing foodstuffs. He objected to me that our delegation is advising against retreat, and they know the attitude of English workers better than we do. He also reported optimistic telegrams from Smilga.

When the vote was taken, everyone[12] unanimously accepted the theses of Il'ich as a basis. In voting on the individual points, everyone voted to continue the offensive, but on the point concerning mediation, Trotsky, Kalinin, Rykov, Radek and I voted against Il'ich.

Then Bukharchik said to me: 'See, traitor, surely you must be happy that we have shown our fist to the Entente'. I admit that I was not happy. I fear that we are miscalculating and heading for trouble. And at the same time I wondered whether I had made a mistake in opposing the Brest peace and was now mistaken again in opposing a rupture with the Entente. Such is the fate of a Left-Communist.

If only[13] Il'ich turns out to be right!

—

There were long debates over chairmanship of the embassy in England. The question was: Krasin or Kamenev. Krasin passed by one vote. After further arguments were made for Kamenev, I suggested another vote. In order to have a freer discussion, everyone left the meeting (Krasin, Chicherin, Brichkina) except for members of the Central Committee. After many expressions 'for' and 'against', Kamenev passed by a small majority of one or two votes. The main arguments: Kamenev, as a Central-Committee member, knows the spirit of our policy better and is generally a more prominent political figure than Krasin, especially in connection with the pressure on England resulting from our Eastern policy. Krasin was also vigorously defended. Chicherin favours Kamenev, since it is not possible to have Litvinov.

---

12. ['Against Trotsky, Kalinin, Radek and me' is crossed out.]
13. [Before these words the expression 'To hell with it' is crossed out.]

The Plenum was not fully represented. Smirnov was absent, as usual, but Rakovsky and Artem were also missing.

As usual, the so-called 'Chicherin' questions were discussed first. The main issue was the question of Polish negotiations. After the failure to 'sovietise Poland', Il'ich put forth the following plan of action: make maximum territorial concessions to the Poles, right up to the Hindenburg Line. 'Now all we can do is deceive them – he said – since our military affairs are going badly. Let's try to buy peace from them, even though there is little chance that they will go for it. Whatever happens, in the coming months we must finish with Wrangel. And once we have dealt with him, at the Congress of Soviets we can repudiate this peace and move all our forces against Poland if it seems appropriate. In order to appear truthful, at the VTsIK session we can order up patriotic speeches from Bukharin, Sosnovsky and others and have one-third vote against peace. We can say that the opposition became a majority at the Congress and then move again on Warsaw'.

Trotsky, who was ill and in a housecoat (the meeting was in his apartment) stood for all kinds of concessions to Poland and for peace. We desperately need a breathing space out of military considerations. He portrayed conditions at the fronts as dismal. It is difficult to expect any change for a month or three weeks. On the Wrangel [front] as well, concentration of our forces to give a three-to-one advantage for our side cannot be expected any sooner than twenty days hence.

There was complete unanimity concerning peace. Radek simply noted that we need not concede much to the Poles because they are anxious for peace whatever happens. He referred to recent Polish newspapers as well as to the fact that the Entente-papers are recommending to the Poles that they be moderate in their demands and conclude peace with us. He also said that the Poles will not believe in the sincerity of our peaceful intentions if we appear suspicious in giving them more than they are asking themselves.

Il'ich teased Karly for believing too-much in our enemies' newspapers, which are likely to say the opposite of whatever they want to hide.

The proposal for peace was accepted unanimously. Kamenev's draft address from the VTsIK to the Polish government was considered unsatisfactory and it was decided to revise it.

Concerning Persia the decision was: not to use a single soldier for the 'sovietisation of Persia' and to conclude peace with the Shah's government after securing Enzeli.[14] A proposal from the recently arrived Zinoviev to help the Persian revolutionaries with troops was rejected.

---

14. [The reference is to events in Iran (Persia) following the Enzeli operation, conducted by the Soviet Volga-Caspian naval flotilla on 17–18 May 1920. The operation was to secure the return to Soviet Russia of ships taken to Iran by the White Guards. The

Major debates resulted from my suggestion to appoint a commission to investigate our defeat at Warsaw.[15] Stalin had made this proposal earlier to the Politburo, but it was defeated. I said in its defence that the command of the western front, and especially Smilga, must have known the conditions at the front, and they were obliged to warn us if the directive to advance on Warsaw was threatened with catastrophe. My proposal was defeated.

Much time was spent on the question of what to do at the Party-Conference. I suggested opening a debate after Il'ich's political report and then having the organisational report follow. Trotsky, Bukharin, Stalin and others spoke against any debates. Trotsky suggested that by having debates at such a moment, when we require unanimity and must concentrate solely on how to secure victory, we would merely demoralise the Conference, focusing its attention on disputes over the failure at Warsaw, over who was right and who is guilty, and he finally asked how members of the Central Committee would themselves address this question.

Rykov supported me. I replied to Trotsky that the Conference is not some cell in an army-company that can be demoralised. And if it were, then our Party would not be worth much. Nothing should be kept from the Conference. Discussion does not demoralise, but rather strengthens a party that will know what happened and why it happened.

Il'ich supported me, and his comments were replete with deep faith in the Party. He pointed out that the kind of behaviour Trotsky was recommending at the Conference could destroy the Party, rather than cure it. We would be raising the question of leaders and followers and would ourselves be giving grounds for suspicion that the 'leaders' are hiding something. Everyone sensed that Lenin was speaking as the chief, as the father of the Party who knows how to guide it at a difficult moment.

My proposal passed the vote. At the same time, a heated argument developed over who is guilty for the Warsaw defeat, whether the time had come for offensive wars, and so on. Il'ich wanted the discussion because, in his opinion,

---

military-naval base in Enzeli Bay on the Iranian coast of the Caspian Sea was protected by elements of an English infantry-division and the White Guards. As a result of the successful operation, 23 ships and vessels carrying military property were returned to the Soviet Republic. As a result, Soviet ships could guarantee safe passage on the sea for economic cargoes, and this also facilitated the movement of troops for the final liberation of Transcaucasia and Turkestan. The Soviet government declared the Caspian Sea open for Iranian shipping, and Russian trade-institutions in Enzeli were turned over *gratis* to Iran.]

15. [The reference is to the Soviet-Polish War of 1920 (April–October), which was provoked by the Polish side. Launching a counter-attack, by 14 August Soviet forces had reached Warsaw. But having begun successfully, the operation turned into a defeat for the Soviet forces, because of mistakes in command.]

an exchange of views would make unnecessary any subsequent proposal for appointing an investigative commission.

In Il'ich's opinion, it was not the Central Committee that was guilty for giving the directive to advance and take Warsaw, but the military command. They should have called a halt if, for strategic reasons, it was dangerous to advance. Smilga telegraphed that we would take Warsaw on the 16th. And he had a better view of things than the Central Committee and the Politburo. It would have been possible to stop at the Bug and bring up reserves.

Trotsky pointed out that the military command had absolutely nothing to do with it. They received the order from the government to take Warsaw, and they had to do so. He pointed out that he had warned beforehand about overstretching our units and about the possibility of a counter-attack. The warnings were to no avail: as a result, we suffered defeat and lost the opportunity to have Kamenev be the signal-man for us in London.

I reminded Il'ich that on August...[16] he pointlessly attacked Rykov for defeatist talk. To take account of our forces and have regard for our rear is imperative if we do not want to be beaten. The command is guilty, especially Smilga, as the responsible political worker. But the Central Committee also erred in its calculations. I pointed out to Trotsky that at the decisive meeting he had voted with everyone else for continuing the attack, and it was precisely this that decided the matter and led to the defeat. In contrast, although five of us voted against Il'ich on the question of breaking with the Entente concerning its mediation in the War, on exactly this question it was Il'ich who turned out to be right. The rejection of mediation did not lead to intervention or to the defeat at the front. We five were right insofar as our votes said one thing: we must not overdo it, we must be careful, but we cast our votes on the wrong issue.

Trotsky commented that I can only speak for myself, not for him. He knows what he voted for. He pointed out that subsequently, when it was [still] not too late, he suggested giving instructions to Danishevsky to seek a solution in a conciliatory peace, which the Politburo rejected.

On the latter point, Trotsky is right. On this matter, he turned out, in my opinion, to be more far-sighted than the other members of the Politburo. But he was not right on the first point. If he knew what he was voting for at the decisive meeting, then that means he was voting for defeat. Indeed, if we had accepted mediation but still continued our attack on Warsaw, we would still have been defeated.

Bukharin insisted that there were no political mistakes. It was correct to adopt a general line of going from defence to offence, and the struggle is still not over.

---

16. [The date is missing from the text.]

Stalin contended that the mistake was strategic. The Central Committee does not answer for the concrete implementation of a directive. The command knew what they were doing. They could have responded to the order by saying they could not fulfil it.

---

24 September

The Plenum resumed yesterday evening. The VTsIK's declaration, written by Kamenev and addressed to the commission, was again revised. From Bukharin's suggestions, a proposal was accepted to note that Poland attacked Soviet Russia in the spring, after it had returned to peaceful labour, and another amendment was accepted concerning Russia's inexhaustible resources, which are sufficient, if necessary, to break the neck of the Polish landlords. Ioffe was given the right to propose corrections to the text if he should have any. Judging by Ioffe's telegram, he plans to bargain with the Polish landlords and has not understood our tactic. As he describes things, the Polish delegation is peacefully inclined and all the news from Poland points to their severe domestic circumstances. Ioffe planned to work in the diplomatic field, and we made the poor man unemployed by [condemning][17] him to wait silently for a negative response from Poland.

The conclusion of the *Glavkom*[18] was read out concerning the border. It proposed a border somewhat to the west of the Hindenburg Line. We accepted that and gave Ioffe instructions to make this line the limit for any territorial concessions.

As always in the Central Committee, vermicelli was discussed along with world-questions, namely, the Grzhebin publishing house, on whose behalf Gorky is a permanent petitioner. A commission was appointed and we gave 6 million to the publisher. There is but a single step between the great issues and the trifles.

Bukharin suggested that we send him to Germany. Zinoviev proposed himself. This rivalry over the question of who should sit in Moabit[19] or be ambushed by Prussian Junkers ended in a draw. In view of the Republic's difficult circumstances it was decided to send no-one. The Germans, including Levi, are complaining about dictators in Moscow but are themselves summoning them up in Berlin. Let the Independents split apart without any participation by 'agents of Lenin'.

---

17. [The text says 'осуждая' but it appears that it should say 'обрекая'.]
18. [The High Command.]
19. [A district in Berlin.]

No. 72

Letter to V.I. Lenin Concerning K.B. Radek's Speeches on the War with Poland and Its Press-Coverage[1]

6 May 1920[2]

Vladimir Il'ich!

Ganetsky can wait for Krestinsky's arrival. Not everything can be said over the telephone. The question of his transfer for foreign trade has already been discussed in the *Orgburo*, but not in the collegium.

The Shadrinsky peasants (of Ekaterinburg province) have provided the Central Committee with seven hundred *poods* of white flour. How do you suggest we distribute it? Shouldn't a large part go to the starving commissariats?

I suggest that we put an end to indecency on the matter of 'patriotism'. Radek has exaggerated 'national war' in his speeches. Today in Agitrosta,[3] Bergman included an indecent article about true Russian people who love the fatherland. What will they end up writing in Chukhlom? I ask your permission to give direction to newspaper-editors, especially those in the provinces.

E. Preobrazhensky

At the end of the second paragraph, Lenin noted: 'I am in full <u>support</u>' and at the end of the document is

---

1. [From RGASPI. F. 2. Op. 1. D. 13791. L. 1–1 ob. Handwritten.]
2. [Dated by reference to Golikov et al. 1970–82, Vol. 8, p. 527.]
3. [Agitation-Organisation of the Russian Telegraph-Agency. Its function was to issue bulletins to party-workers.]

his directive to the Secretariat of the Central Committee of the RKP(B): 'I propose a directive: all articles on Poland and the Polish war to be reviewed by responsible editors who are <u>personally</u> accountable. Do not overdo things, that is, do not fall into chauvinism, always distinguish landlords and capitalists from the workers and peasants of Poland. Lenin'.

No. 73
Response from Secretary of the Central Committee of the RKP(B) E.A. Preobrazhensky to the 'First Draft of Theses on the National Question', Prepared by V.I. Lenin for a Report to the Second Congress of the Comintern[1]

Not earlier than 5 June, no later than 19 July 1920[2]

Comments on the theses by V.I. Lenin concerning the national question

1. When defining the tasks of Communists in the area of the national question, a distinction must be made between the situation before the proletarian revolution and the situation after the proletariat comes to power. Prior to the proletarian revolution, the national question in the most important European countries is only a part of the general question of social revolution. After the revolution, solution of the national question must be *subordinated*[3] to the task of creating an

---

1. [From RGASPI. F. 2. Op. 1. D. 14355. L. 1–3. Original. Typewritten. In a note accompanying his 'First draft of theses on the national and colonial questions', V.I. Lenin invited 'all comrades, particularly comrades who have concrete knowledge concerning one or another of these very complex questions, to provide a response, or corrections, or additions, or concrete clarification' (Lenin 1958–65, Vol. 41, p. 161).]

2. [The document is not dated. The 'First draft…' was written by V.I. Lenin on 5 June 1920. The Second Congress of the Comintern began its work on 19 July 1920, in Petrograd.]

3. [V.I. Lenin received replies to the theses from G.V. Chicherin, N.N. Krestinsky, J.V. Stalin, M.G. Rafes, E.A. Preobrazhensky, P.L. Lapinsky and others. V.I. Lenin read them all, as is evident from his notes and comments, especially on E.A. Preobrazhensky's text. The word 'subordinated' is underlined by Lenin. In the upper right-hand corner of the page he made a note: "'Simply to subordinate' will not do: see my §12'.]

economic whole out of the resulting socialist republics. While there are no serious debates concerning the programme and tactics of the Third International in the conditions of the first situation, tactics in the conditions of a victorious proletarian revolution are not clear and are causing debates among Communists. In this respect, the RKP finds itself in a difficult *position*: since the European revolution has not yet been victorious, we need to support the national-revolutionary movement in the East, but since our proletarian revolution has already been victorious, we must turn to resolving the second task (partly at the expense of realising the first one).

2. The main difficulties concerning the national question, with which the Third International must deal and which it has already encountered to some degree, will lie not in the sphere of relations between today's leading capitalist countries, but rather in relations between tomorrow's leading communist countries of Europe.

The experience of Finland, Latvia, Ukraine and Azerbaijan, that is, former areas of the previous Russian state that are comparatively advanced in capitalist terms, makes this perfectly clear. There are no serious grounds for thinking that creation of a federation out of countries where the proletariat has been victorious, and restoration of their economy according to a single plan, will encounter serious obstacles. In this sense, the national question in Europe (with the possible exception of the backward eastern and south-eastern regions) is[4] part of the general question of the proletarian revolution and will be nine-tenths resolved by the very fact of its victory. The main difficulties lie in the relations between proletarian Soviet Republics and economically backward countries, *where there is no proletariat or it is just emerging, and where a commercial bourgeoisie and an upper stratum of intellectuals* exist as the only cultured elements of the people. These typical strata of capitalistically underdeveloped countries and colonies inevitably attempt to resolve the national question in approximately the same forms as occurred during the epoch when national-bourgeois states emerged; and thus, in conditions where Soviet unification of the world has begun, they turn into representatives of a degenerate[5] nationalism that is also condemned to die out without yet having created its gravediggers from amongst its own people. To prepare these gravediggers (where history allows the time), and to step forth itself in this capacity where there is no such time, will fall to – and in some measure is already falling to – the proletariat of the Soviet Republics. Hence the inevitable need not only to give all possible support to even a most insignificant minority of communist-inclined elements in these countries, up to and including their seizure of power in opposition to the majority, which is led

---

4. [The next word, 'only', is crossed out.]
5. [This word is handwritten above the line.]

by bourgeois nationalists, but also, where there is no such minority, to defeat the nationalist upper strata and establish direct relations with the lower elements of a backward people. It is an error to overestimate the revolutionary significance of national insurrections in the colonies. It would be all the more impermissible to overlook a moment when the position will change fundamentally, because,[6] from the moment when the proletarian revolution is victorious in London and Paris, the national-revolutionary movement in the East becomes a counter-revolutionary movement. On the territory of the RSFSR, the national movements in Turkestan, Bashkiria and Kirgizia are already counter-revolutionary movements, and it is exactly our experience in this area that shows just how misguided is any plan to use the movement in the East against European imperialism without taking care[7] today to create independent Communist groups in these countries. In view of the extreme wartime exhaustion of Europe in terms of materials, and the absolute need for the victorious proletariat to increase the flow of these materials from the colonies in order to sustain production, inclusion of the formal colonies in socialist Europe might become necessary before the time when these colonies mature and develop the forces needed for implementing a voluntary federation of the colonies with Europe. In this case, *if there is no possibility of an economic agreement with the leading national groups, their suppression by force inevitably becomes necessary, along with the enforced association of economically important regions with a union of European republics*,[8] during a period when the toiling lower strata of the people have been freed from the bourgeois upper strata, but have not yet put forth groups that are capable of taking power on the basis of a federation with Europe. Experience shows that it is easier for a proletarian state to deal with backward peoples, who are at the stage of a traditional way of life, and to enter into friendly relations with them, than with peoples embraced by commercial capitalism and whose bourgeois-intelligentsia upper strata stand in the way of direct relations with the lower strata.

Conclusions:

1. It would be better[9] in the theses to make a distinction in the spirit of what is said in the first point above. A corresponding distinction must be made in terms of practical[10] conclusions, otherwise what is basic in the one period becomes mixed up with what is secondary in the other, and vice versa, which makes any practical directives unclear.

---

6. [Inserted in place of 'since', which is crossed out.]
7. ['не заботясь' is crossed out and ' без заботы' is written above the line.]
8. [At the bottom of the page, Lenin noted: 'This is too much. Unproven and incorrect to use the terms 'inevitably' and 'suppression by force'. Fundamentally untrue'.]
9. [Written in above the line in place of 'it is necessary'.]
10. [Written by hand above the line.]

2. The following correction is needed in the eleventh thesis: either add 'young Muslims' to the third sub-point, following 'capitalism',[11] and in place of 'diplomatic'[12] and so on in the fourth line, say 'commercial bourgeoisie and chauvinistic upper strata of the intelligentsia'; or else merge the second point with the third (which is logically more correct), and under the rubric of the third formulate a new point concerning the need to struggle against the bourgeois uppers of backward countries insofar as they try to strengthen their oppressive position during the process of the liberation-struggle against foreign imperialism, while at the same time they implement imperialism in relation to even more backward indigenous peoples, hiding under the flag of assisting them and organising them for struggle against European capital.

Continue the fifth sub-point with the words 'being at any moment prepared to advance along the entire front against the bourgeois-national movement when it becomes objectively counter-revolutionary'.

3. In the fourth line of the twelfth thesis, after the words 'these prejudices', add 'to the extent that there is still time for such a tactic', and in the following fifth line, after the word 'concessions', add 'to the toiling lower strata of these countries'.

4. In the seventh line of the eleventh thesis, after 'these countries', add 'insofar as this movement does not become reactionary from the moment of the proletariat's victory'.

E. Preobrazhensky

---

11. [Lenin's notation: 'Pan-Islamism? The word "capitalism" is not even there'.]
12. [Lenin's notation: 'No such word is there!']

No. 74

Resolution Taken by the Politburo of the Central Committee of the RKP(B) Concerning the Case of Oskar Blum[1]

29 July 1920

To affirm the decision of the review-commission in the Blum case. To assign comrade Kursky to clarify the question of whether the sentence in the Blum case was published at the time; if not, to publish it now. Furthermore, to assign comrade Kursky to see that the sentence concerning Blum is strictly implemented. On 28 June 1920, the commission, consisting of comrades Preobrazhensky, Latsis and Kursky, which was appointed by the Politburo of the Central Committee of the RKP to address the question of whether there is any need to review the Blum case, after considering all the proceedings in the Blum case by the revolutionary tribunal under the VTsIK, together with the accompanying documents, and having also questioned comrades Bukharin and Radek and the Latvian comrades, came to the following conclusion:

1) Oskar Blum's guilt for being in the service of the Riga Okhrana-department in the role of a secret collaborator in 1908–10, up to and including his role in blackmailing, is established by the documents and is not refuted by Blum's diffuse and vague explanations.

---

1. [From RGASPI. F. 17. Op. 163. D. 76. L. 15–16 ob. The text of the resolution was written by E.A. Preobrazhensky (Protocol No. 23 of the sessions of the Politburo of the Central Committee of the RKP(B).]

2) There are no new grounds, either in his explanations or in the documents, for a review of the Blum case.

3) A review of the Blum case within the confines of the material already available could serve as a basis not for reducing but rather for increasing the norm of punishment, but in view of the necessity to preserve the integrity of the verdict of the Supreme Tribunal, which was carried out in the procedure established by the decree of the RSFSR, in observance with all the rules of practice, to accept the verdict as final.

Kursky
E. Preobrazhensky
Latsis

Original manuscript.

Nos. 75–7
Articles Published in the Newspaper *Pravda* in July–August 1920

30 July–15 August 1920

No. 75

'A Very Promising Experiment'[1]

30 July 1920

I wish to say a few words about the dramatisation of mass action with which your St. Petersburg comrades concluded the opening day of the Second Congress of the Third International.

Have you ever seen such a scene, in which several thousand artists and extras appeared?

On the square in front of the stock-exchange we saw such a scene.

Do you know of any theatre in which tens of thousands of spectators took part all at once?

According to the assurances of comrade Antselovich, on 19 June, there were up to eighty thousand spectators in the stock-exchange square.

That was outside. Just what was playing?

They were putting on 'The history of the most important moments of the workers' movement from 1848 to our own day'. That was precisely the weakest aspect of the very promising experiment in mass staging that was performed in St. Petersburg and must be

---

1. [From *Pravda*, 30 July 1920.]

regarded as a first attempt to create the theatre of proletarian revolution. 'He who proves too much, proves nothing', according to the proverb. And in St. Petersburg, an attempt was made to portray too much in the mass scene, and this weakened the impact of what was portrayed.

The St. Petersburg experiment demonstrates that mass dramatic scenes are the most successful and produce the greatest impression.

But the various symbols are less effective and less understood by the audience. The completely empty and dead moments on the stage were the transitions from one setting to another. Incidentally, even a very detailed programme is of little help, because only hundreds among the tens of thousands in the audience could read it.

The successful scenes included the rule of the bourgeoisie in the form of an enormous gold-coin, around which the bourgeoisie revelled; the uprising of the Communards, who drove the revellers from the throne of their merry-making, and the jovial song *La Carmagnole* and the dances of the proletarian fighters in the area cleansed of the bourgeoisie. Then came on stage the struggle by the defenders of the Commune against the White Guards of Thiers, the fall of the Commune, and the shooting of ranks of prisoners who, after the volley, fell from the side of the Neva.

Essentially, the events from the epoch of the Paris Commune would be sufficient to present in a most vivid way the most important moments in the history of the Commune and to provide the content for the entire spectacle, but the authors wanted to say too much, and for this they were punished with a number of scenes that were dull and not well understood by the audience. One empty part that was not understood was the peaceful period after the Commune. The portrayal of the Second International was not successful, apart from the moment when the former socialists divided into two opposing camps at the beginning of the World-War.

The portrayal of tsarism was a great success in the form of the two-headed eagle with the enormous figure of Nicholas in the crown and the whooping Cossacks who were carrying it through the street. The musicians played *God Save the Tsar*. Then the *Marseillaise* sounded and the collapse of the monarchy began. But the rest was quite unsuccessful: the period when Kerensky was in power was dull; the October Revolution only appeared on the stage in passing; and the whole period of the Civil War was a complete failure.

Some of the lighting effects were a great success, for instance the smoke above the corpses of the Communards who were shot, and so on.

The conclusion: a beginning has been made in mass proletarian theatre. Enormous work remains in terms of technical improvements. To this end must be directed some of the efforts that tried proletarian patience by preparing stage-representations of the rotten system for a small circle of the aesthetically developed public.

Such mass scenes as those in Petrograd make it possible, through characters and actions (provided the costumes, situations, and so on, are historically truthful), to familiarise wide strata of the proletariat with the most important moments of the class-struggle.

The experiment by those in St. Petersburg must on no account be left without development and further improvements.

E. Preobrazhensky

No. 76

'Comrade Larin's Next "Project"'[1]

11 August 1920

Not long ago, there appeared in *Ekonomicheskaya Zhizn'* a feuilleton by comrade Larin with the title 'The Laws of Monetary Circulation'. As for the 'laws of monetary circulation', even if they could be formulated like the laws of the criminal code, it would be extremely difficult to squeeze them into the space of two hundred and fifty lines. But comrade Larin is not really interested in the laws; what he needs is a lawful basis for presenting a particular practical suggestion. And like the majority of comrade Larin's new suggestions, this one is distinguished by clarity, simplicity, and important benefits for the state-treasury.

Here is the point. The Food-Commissariat (*Komprod*) is providing only forty percent of the bread needed by workers and employees. They have to buy the balance in the free market, throwing into it an enormous volume of paper-money. In turn, the state must put out an enormous volume of paper in the form of wages. Is it not possible to curtail this flow of paper?

'It is' – replies comrade Larin, on the basis of the 'laws of monetary circulation' that he has discovered. *Komprod* must procure more grain, and then workers will spend less in buying bread at the Sukharevka.[2]

This is not a particularly new idea. But how can we procure more than we are getting in current circumstances, how can we get more by relying on comrade Larin's 'laws'?

Let us listen to the author himself...

> Imagine that fixed prices double but grain-procurements rise only by one-tenth (the experience of recent years shows that with each significant rise in fixed money prices for flax, grain, and so on, the procurement of these products grew by more than ten percent even in central Russia, which has a wealth of Soviet money, and the increase was even greater in the outlying areas, which have a wealth of grain but are not saturated with paper-money). What will the results be for money-circulation and the country's requirements in terms of money-tokens? If *Komprod* procures not 220 million *poods*, paying 50 roubles for each, but rather 242 million at 100 roubles each, then 13 billion more would be needed to pay for the total procurement. But, then, the population would receive through state-supply approximately 20 million more *poods* of grain, and they could purchase 20 million fewer *poods* at all the '*sukharevkas*'. If we

---

1. [From *Pravda*, 11 August 1920.]
2. [A famous market in Moscow.]

take the average price of grain at markets in the consuming provinces and cities of Russia to be even 300 roubles a pound, this would mean for the toiling population an annual reduction in the need for money-tokens of 240 billion roubles.[3] In other words, a doubling of procurement-prices for grain would not only avoid any need to raise wages, or to increase the volume of paper-money being printed, and such like, but, on the contrary, would lead to an enormous reduction in such need. From the point of view of a meaningful 'political economy of the Soviet transition-period', a systematic and significant increase in the fixed procurement-prices for agricultural products is thus one of the most essential means of struggle against the accelerating accumulation of a mass of paper-money, together with its various undesirable consequences.

One can, of course, imagine anything. The only thing unexplained is why raising the fixed prices for grain from 50 roubles to 100 can yield 20 million more, rather than 200 million more or just 200 *poods* more. This is not clear from comrade Larin's 'laws', nor does it result from common sense. It is incomprehensible why the Ryazan peasant, in a region where a *pood* of flour on the free market costs ten thousand roubles, will surrender an extra *pood* to *Narkomprod* (if he has no need to do so), being tempted by a rise in price from 50 roubles to 100. It is incomprehensible why a Kuban Cossack or Siberian peasant, who sells grain on the free market at a price thirty to forty times higher than the fixed price, would likewise be tempted. The peasantry currently turns over grain to the Soviet authority in fulfilment of a certain obligation, but a 'payment' of 50 roubles, given a market-price that is from fifty to one hundred times higher, is of absolutely no interest to the peasants.

It is not the payment for the grain provided, which is totally detached from the price on the free market, that ensures the acquisition of grain and the possibility of increasing that acquisition, but rather compulsion on the part of the state-apparatus, improvements in the methods of this apparatus, together with the peasant's hope to get salt, kerosene and manufactures at fixed prices. But if we reason from the viewpoint of the real laws of paper-money circulation, then as a result of the state throwing 13 billion more roubles into procurement, there are not the slightest grounds for expecting an increase of procurements beyond the amount of grain that can be acquired for 13 billion on the free market. But, then, it is incomprehensible why the state must undertake such a 'profitable' purchase, rather than interested consumers or bag-men.

Raising fixed prices can only result in procurement of a greater quantity of product – greater by comparison with what can be purchased with an additional sum on the free market – when the fixed price does not deviate very far

---

3. [One *pood* = 40 Russian pounds]

from the free price. Meanwhile, such a condition no longer exists anywhere in Soviet Russia, except in the most remote areas. And we have yet to mention the fact that the increase in the present case also accelerates the rise of free prices, and thus has a negative effect on other aspects of economic relations. On the contrary, when the free price is completely detached from the fixed price, and when the peasants deliver to the state only such surpluses as can be secured through pressure from the state-apparatus of compulsion, a rise in the fixed prices risks failing to acquire even that additional quantity of grain that can be bought on the free market for an extra sum added to the sum of the previous fixed prices: the peasantry will pass by this extra sum, and not even notice it, since it is so insignificant.

I do not know whether comrade Larin's reasoning has influenced *Narkomprod*. If not, then that is to the honour of *Narkomprod*. I hope to show elsewhere that the laws of money-circulation, to which comrade Larin refers, say exactly the opposite of what he argues in his conclusions.

All comrade Larin's new suggestions usually fall into two groups: nut-shells that contain a nut, and nut-shells that are empty. His suggestions concerning the liquidation of internal money-accounting between parts of the Soviet state itself belong to the first category; the suggestion that we are presently considering belongs among the empty nut-shells.

E. Preobrazhensky

No. 77

'On a New Book by N.I. Bukharin'[1]

15 August 1920

A month ago, there came to light an extremely interesting book, *The Economics of the Transition Period*,[2] with deeply penetrating conclusions by comrade Bukharin. Reading this book makes one pleased to affirm, once again, that our Party not only displays remarkable practical skill in leading the great proletarian Revolution, but also retains the ability to comprehend in theoretical terms its every step forwards. The greatest practical importance of theory in a revolutionary epoch consists in the fact that having understood the beginning of any process and the direction of its development, you already have the keys to understanding its conclusion, and thus you know what you must do both today and tomorrow.

To those who have not found the time to read comrade Bukharin's book or do not intend to do so, I can recommend the review and summary given by Chlenov in *Ekonomicheskaya Zhizn'*. I am writing the present article for all those who have read the book already, and with whom I might discuss the pages they have read.

The first chapter of the book serves as an introduction for the chapters that follow, especially for the second one. There is little that is new in it compared with the author's previous works. But this introduction does serve as the starting point for chapters in which there are many new thoughts or older thoughts that are reformulated. My conclusion is that this chapter lacks even a brief description of an existing capitalist giant, whether Germany on the eve of the War or American capitalism. With such vital examples, it would have been possible more clearly to demonstrate the inevitability not only of the World-War, but also of the social-patriots' betrayal and the helplessness of every sort of petty-bourgeois pacifism, including the pacifism of the Second International, with its 1 May anti-militarism and its peaceful demonstrations at congresses.

What is most valuable in the second chapter is its scientific-Marxist definition of war as the struggle of classes, formed within the state, regardless of whether the state-capitalist trust of one country is waging war against the state-capitalist trust of another country, or whether one of the contestants is an entirely different class, such as the proletariat after it has seized power.

---

1. [From *Pravda*, 15 August 1920.]
2. [V.I. Lenin carefully studied N.I. Bukharin's book and doubted several of its conclusions, although he judged it to be generally excellent (Lenin 1929, pp. 348–403).]

What is important is the fact that war is a means of strengthening the mode of production that is the basis for the existence of the ruling class, and that war is not just a continuation of the policy of the ruling class by different means, but also the continuation of its economy by different means. Thus comrade Bukharin quite correctly says: 'Every type of production has its own corresponding type of state, and for every type of state there is a corresponding type of war'. We now know something more, not just in theoretical terms, but also through the living experience of Revolution: to every type of state, there corresponds a special type of army. Our Red Army has been cemented by the proletariat as the ruling class, and thus is suited to the Soviet type of state and to the entire structure of our internal relations. The army of feudal states either consisted entirely of the nobility (in the beginning) or had a cadre of nobles. The army of a capitalist state is cemented by the bourgeois-noble upper strata and by officers who are economically privileged.

In this same chapter there are a few lines with which I cannot personally agree. Comrade Bukharin writes:

> Socialist war is class-war, which must be distinguished from a simple civil war. The latter is not a war in the proper sense of the word, for it is not a war of two state-organisations. On the contrary, in a class-war, both sides are organised in the form of state-power: on one side there is the state of finance capital, on the other – the state of the proletariat.

It seems to me that this clever terminology is completely redundant in terms of the contents of the second chapter, and that it does not add any clarity to the general question being discussed.

What would we call our war with Poland? There is no doubt that this is both a socialist war and a class-war. The same applies generally to the war with the Entente. And what should we call our war with the late Kolchak or with the still-living Wrangel? This is where the difficulties begin. Usually, we call it a civil war. Of course, prevailing terminology is not obligatory for the purpose of scientific classification and might diverge from it. But there is not the slightest basis for refusing to consider or to call our war with Wrangel both a class-war and a socialist war. Comrade Bukharin says: indeed, this is not a war in the real sense; it is not a war between two state-organisations of different classes. Why not? Kolchak had his state, even if it was short-lived. We must hope that the noble-officer state of Wrangel will also turn out to be short-lived. But the fact is that Kolchak, Denikin and Wrangel headed up the remnants of a state that, by comparison with the Soviet state, has the advantage of existing for a hundred times longer or more – it is the remnant of the noble- and noble-capitalist state of the Russian Empire. But longevity and stability are not the point here at all.

To differentiate our war with White Poland from our war with Denikin, comrade Osinsky has attempted to introduce the term 'external civil war'. This attempt also fails completely. Why is the war with Wrangel an internal civil war, and that with Poland an external one? Is it because Crimea was part of the territory of the tsarist empire? But so were Poland, Estonia and Finland. Is it because people of Russian nationality fight for Wrangel? But were there not Russians with Yudenich in Estonia, and are there not Russians now in the Polish forces? And is it not possible for a single nation to dissolve into two states, headed by different classes, if there are grounds for this in the production-relations?

I think that in order to avoid all this confusion in the matter of scientific classification, it is quite enough to distinguish a war from an insurrection. From the very moment when the insurgent class succeeds in creating an army – which is the most important part of the state-apparatus – it is too late to speak of insurrection, and war takes its place. And there are no difficulties in classifying a war in class-terms. The French Republic at the end of the eighteenth century waged revolutionary-bourgeois war against the European monarchies. We are waging revolutionary-proletarian war against the bourgeois states of Europe and the remnants of our own bourgeois-landlord state. No special terminological changes are required, here. The term 'civil war', once the term class-war is introduced, can be abandoned completely. If there is some reason to keep it, then we might agree to do so with reference to the period during which the insurrection grows over into a class-war.

The central part of the book comes in the third and fourth chapters. The third chapter gives the real outlines of the capitalist system as a single entity in terms of political and economic relations prior to its crash. The crash is prepared by disruption of the process of expanded reproduction as a result of transferring a mass of forces and means to the service of war, that is, to the non-productive waste of material means, supplies and labour-power. In place of expanded reproduction, which characterises developing capitalism, there begins ever-increasing underproduction, which characterises disintegrating capitalism and is the condition for further disorganisation and collapse of the system.[3] The author traces the effect of this underproduction throughout the capitalist economic system: the social surplus-value – which is the necessary condition of reproduction – is consumed, the existing fixed capital wears out and is not replaced in timely fashion by new elements, the workforce is destroyed due to insufficient consumption,

---

3. For some unknown reason, the author insists on calling this increasing underproduction 'expanded negative reproduction', although this arch-scientific term involves nothing new in spirit when compared to 'growing underproduction', which fully express a process that is the opposite of 'expanded reproduction'.

and when it protests through strikes against insufficient consumption, the volume of production contracts even more, along with the quantity of consumer-products available for distribution in the society. The author probes the body of capitalism to see how the productive forces flow out through the bleeding wounds of war, how the bones of the capitalist skeleton begin to crack, how not only the cranium and spine but every bone breaks, along with every cartilage of the capitalist system's skeleton, under the blows of revolution. In his book on the state, comrade Lenin pointed out something that was later confirmed by the Russian proletariat in the practice of revolution: the state-apparatus of the bourgeoisie must be smashed to smithereens. Comrade Bukharin shows the same thing, in terms of social ties within the economic organisation of capitalism and how this was later confirmed by our proletariat through the revolutionary breaking up of capitalism's production-organisations. The analysis of this moment of social revolution is the most profound and valuable part of the book, although the conclusions are too generalised, insofar as they are drawn on the basis of the experience of our Revolution alone. Here, the author gives a completely new theoretical analysis, in light of which the previous ideas even of orthodox Social Democrats concerning the crash of capitalism must be regarded as futile daydreaming. This reassessment of our Social-Democratic sins is something that every Communist usually does 'for himself', in his own consciousness, insofar as the experience of proletarian revolution strikingly illustrates how inappropriate the old ideas were. Comrade Bukharin's service lies in the fact that he has finally, in the form of a scientific analysis of the proletarian revolution, said what each of us has thought out (and not always coherently) for himself. Educated by the 'Erfurt Programme', we imagined the socialisation of production quite differently from what has happened in practice. Ten years ago, hardly anyone among the most revolutionary Marxists conceived that in addition to destroying the bourgeois state, winning the dictatorship and expropriating the capitalist class, we must also finish the process of destroying the capitalist economy to its very foundations, dismiss almost all the technical personnel, from the foreman to the engineer, break their psychology through terror and hunger, and, only after this operation, absorb them anew into the socialist system of production.[4]

There is no doubt that, in the economic arena, our understanding of the crash of capitalism had nuances of opportunistic complacency and utopianism. It is probably a good thing that not every worker read the 'Erfurt Programme', and that

---

4. Just how vital were the remnants of our old ideas concerning the possibility of making the most extensive use of the capitalist production-apparatus can be seen in the fact that even in 1918, that is, half a year after the proletarian Revolution, someone (forgive me, Vladimir Il'ich) suggested that Soviet Russia would probably pass through a brief stage of state-capitalism.

recollections of that work did not prevent them from exercising the decisiveness that is required by the logic of revolution and proletarian instinct in driving out of production all the generals, officers and non-commissioned officers of capitalism. But once the process of ejecting them is completed and 'socialist accumulation' is beginning, then begins the process of using these dismissed technical forces on a new basis, and aversion to the specialist, if it reaches the point of general unwillingness to employ them in the socialist system of economy, takes on a reactionary character. It is a real pity that the rank-and-file worker cannot read the corresponding pages of comrade Bukharin's book due to his terrorising terminology and the terrifying Anglo-French-German quotations, which are only digestible for Professor Gredeskul's listeners.[5]

Exceptionally valuable in comrade Bukharin's book is his analysis of the mutual relations between town and country in the period of capitalism's crash. The town's violence against the country begins during a war even when capitalism dominates, for the products of consumption, which are necessary for the town and the army, must, given the disruption of natural commodity-exchange between industry and agriculture, be acquired by way of compulsion (the grain-monopoly) and limits on monopoly-incomes in agriculture (fixed prices). Under the proletarian dictatorship, this use of force is the only serious instrument for accumulating the means of consumption needed for production. With the imposition of grain-requisitions,[6] the small producers in the countryside are compelled to work for socialism and are partially included in the general system of socialist economy. Here, compulsion is essentially not an extra-economic factor, but rather a political and economic factor at the same time. It is difficult now to decide where the political coercion of the economic system begins and where the economic coercion of the political [system] ends. In place of the word 'coercion', which is connected with Manchesterian ideas, it would be better to speak of 'social discipline' or some other such term.

It seems to me that in the ninth chapter, the author goes too far in exaggerating the unsuitability of the basic categories of political economy for an analysis of the economic relations of the transition-period. It is difficult to say how matters will stand tomorrow in Germany, but today in Russia, for example, nine-tenths of all values are still created in the petty-commodity economy, and an enormous part of what is produced but not consumed by the producers themselves passes through the free market, rather than the distributive organs of the state. To say that the concept of value 'is least of all suited to the transition-period' is to allow

---

5. [Nikolai Andreevich Gredeskul (1864–1930) was professor and later Dean of the Kharkov Law-School. He helped to found the Party of Constitutional Democrats (the Cadets) and was elected as a Cadet to the First State-Duma in 1906.]

6. ['При проведении хлебной разверстки'.]

oneself to get somewhat carried away. It is also a little early to speak of the crash of the money-system. Metallic money continues to circulate without losing any of its value or significantly disturbing 'the economics of the transition-period', and in the area of paper-money circulation we will understand nothing unless we start from 'the fundamental categories of political economy'.

I have only touched upon a tenth of all the questions that are set out in this book and require discussion, but even at that point, my article is exceeding the norms of *Glavbum*.[7] Let us hope that that in the second edition, even if it results in being a little longer, comrade Bukharin's work will be translated from professorial language into that of the workers and peasants.

E. Preobrazhensky

---

7. [The Main Directorate of State-Enterprises in the Paper-Industry.]

No. 78
Report by E.A. Preobrazhensky to the Commission of the Central Committee of the RKP(B) on the Question of Eliminating Inequality in the Ranks of the RKP(B)[1]

No later than 24 August 1920[2]

Symptoms of demoralisation in our Party

At a whole series of provincial conferences that have taken place since the Ninth Congress (and in some cases, before the Congress) an intensive struggle has been revealed between the so-called lower and upper ranks of our Party. This struggle, which often gets mixed up with struggles of a different sort – for example, along the lines of a clash of Communists with peasant-sympathies with those from the cities, of workers from the trade-unions with the intelligentsia, of 'centrists' with local comrades, of civilian Communists with those in the military – has appeared to one degree or another in the Samara, Severodvinsk, Ufa, Ryazan, Don and Orenburg conferences, and to a lesser degree in those of Yaroslav, Tula, Bryansk and Orel. Often the struggle also takes other forms; for example, a mass exodus from the Party (two hundred people left the city-organisation of Velikii Ustyug), unwillingness of a number of worker-Communists to re-register (Samara), the demand for re-registration of members of provincial committees, and so on. Finally, the most

---

1. [From RGASPI. F. 17. Op. 86. D. 203. L. 3–3 ob. Copy. Typewritten.]
2. [Dated by reference to a letter from N.N. Krestinsky to V.I. Lenin (see the Appendix to Document 2:79).]

acute and dangerous expression of this struggle can be seen in the insurrection of Sapozhkov's division in Buzuluk,³ where a majority of the insurrectionary leaders were Communists (up to one hundred and thirty persons were implicated) some of whom had been in the Party since 1917 (six persons), and one worker, Osipov, even since 1916.⁴ After the city was occupied by the insurrectionists, some of the Communists and workers (mainly soviet-workers) retreated, while some stayed and, together with the trade-unions, organised a new executive committee.

Apart from the kulak- and anti-Semitic slogans of the Sapozhkov insurrection, it involved the same demands that are uniting the so-called lower ranks of our Party in the struggle against the upper ranks at the conferences already mentioned and within almost every organisation of the RKP ('Down with bourgeoisified false-Communist generals and self-seekers', with party-bureaucrats, 'Down with the privileged caste of Communist uppers'). One can certainly say that the latter slogans evoke sympathy amongst a large number of the rank-and-file members of our Party, and the split in our ranks along these lines is growing by the day. Even in Moscow itself, Communists in the districts pronounce the word 'Kremlin'⁵ with hostility and contempt.

In view of the fact that a diminished military threat on the fronts, and even more the end of warfare on the main fronts, is weakening many of the bonds that welded together all the Soviet ranks in the rear, in the army and the Party, we must expect a certain reaction against concentrated dictatorship, together with revelry in petty-bourgeois spontaneity. At this moment, the Party must be especially strong and united. Meanwhile, it is precisely the Party that is already displaying all the signs of internal division that might, at some fine moment, set Communists against Communists. For this reason, the attitude of the rank-and-file members of our Party must be studied more closely by the Central Committee of our Party, and it must meet halfway with the middle-ranks on matters where, as Communists and proletarians, they are perfectly correct. While continuing to struggle against such menaces as Makhno, against lack of discipline and petty-bourgeois decentralism in our ranks, in the interest of this very same struggle, we must adopt an entirely different attitude to the protest of rank-and-file Communists against their systematic exclusion from any influence over party-affairs, from real participation in party-life; and the same applies to protests against the rude behaviour of über-commissars and the insensitivity of some of the Party's

---

3. [The anti-Bolshevik uprising, headed by the Left S-R Sapozhkov, affected the Buzuluksky and Samarsky areas of Samara province in July-September 1920. The main slogan of the insurrectionists was 'Down with grain-requisitions, long live free trade!' The insurrection initially involved up to two and a half thousand people.]
4. [The text is not clear. It appears to say 1916.]
5. [That is, the adjective 'Kremlin' (кремлевский).]

upper ranks to the burdensome position of the proletarian masses, from whom they have become detached, as well as to protests against the immeasurable and mocking material inequality that exists among Communists themselves.

The Central Committee must steer a course in the direction of the middle-ranking Communist, who has only duties and practically no rights, and must pay more attention to his education, to attracting him into real participation in party-life, and to reducing the material privileges of the upper party-ranks for his benefit.

In concrete terms, I suggest the following:

1. Restore the importance and rights of general meetings of party-members in all organisations of the RKP and oblige responsible party-workers to spare no effort, together with all the members of the organisation, in a detailed analysis of all questions that have to be decided at these meetings. Also, to consider both local and state-wide questions at these meetings and to inform all party-members of the questions being decided by the Central Committee, as well as making the Central Committee aware of the attitude of the majority of party-members to the decisions it is taking.

2. Not only provincial conferences, but also plenary-meetings of provincial committees to be made public for all members of the Party.

3. Change the character of revision-commissions, giving them the right to review organisations in terms of their actual work, and also give them the right to act as courts of Communist honour in connection with the endless charges, in almost all organisations, against responsible Communists for abusing their position.

4. Require every responsible Communist, without exception, to be engaged in regular party-work, above all among the lower ranks of the proletariat, and make participation in *subbotniks*[6] absolutely obligatory for all, with no exceptions whatsoever.

5. To observe within the Central Committee itself the regulations concerning convocation of all-Russian party-conferences, and to declare war against a haughtily contemptuous and disdainful attitude toward such conferences and meetings with local workers, for without their convocation it is impossible to take into account the internal condition of the Party and the country or to avoid a mass of errors in the policy of the Central Committee and the government.

6. Reinforce the cadres of travelling instructors from the Central Committee and send Central-Committee members more frequently to exercise control of local work.

---

6. [Volunteer-work on Saturdays.]

7. With regard to responsible workers at the centre is it necessary to:
a) instruct the MK[7] to take them under special scrutiny, having each maintain a personal diary with the obligation to provide information concerning every day's work, b) instruct the MK to undertake a statistical investigation of the material living conditions and diet of Moscow Communists and of Communists associated with the Kremlin, and to curtail the latter to the benefit of the former, c) take away all personal automobiles, which in most cases serve mainly the personal needs of comrades, and send any extras to the front, to the Council of National Economy and to the Commissariat of Post and Telegraph, d) require every people's commissar and every member of the collegium to go to the localities at least twice a year, e) change the membership of the collegiums more frequently by attracting outstanding workers from the localities.

8. Create a special commission, with the participation of Central-Committee representatives, to work out in a timely manner all the measures necessary in the struggle against demoralisation in the ranks of our Party.

E. Preobrazhensky

---

7. [Moscow Committee.]

No. 79
From a Draft Circular-Letter of the Central Committee of the RKP(B), Prepared by E.A. Preobrazhensky, Concerning the Question of the Struggle Against Bureaucratism and Material Inequality in the Party[1]

Not later than 24 August 1920[2]

To all party-organisations and all members of the Party, concerning measures to strengthen party-discipline.

Draft-circular of the Central Committee

Recently, a growing alienation has been evident in the ranks of our Party between rank-and-file party-members and Communists in responsible positions.

This unhealthy phenomenon is rooted in the following causes:

1) Too-slow involvement in party-life of the enormous number of new party-members who joined us during Party-Week and for whose Communist education many organisations have put in a completely inadequate effort.

2) Transfer of the centre of gravity for party-decisions on the most important questions from general meetings to party-committees. Such a redistribution

---
 1. [From RGASPI. F. 17. Op. 112. D. 136. L. 3–4. Original. Typewritten.]
 2. [Dated by the response sent to V.I. Lenin by N.N. Krestinsky concerning the draft circular-letter.]

of party-functions, necessitated by conditions of the Civil War in its most acute period, are automatically continuing even today and causing party-life to wither at the lower levels of the organisation.

3) The extremely inadequate participation of all local party-organisations in discussion of general party- and political questions, and the attempt to focus attention mainly on fulfilling decisions taken at the centre.

4) The extensive material inequality amongst Communists.

For the sake of restoring healthy party-relations and more skilfully attracting young Communists into party-work, the Central Committee considers it necessary to implement the following measures:

I. As often as possible to summon general meetings of party-members, with the obligatory attendance of all responsible workers in the organisation. To pose at general meetings all the most important questions concerning general affairs of the Party, of politics and of local life. Concerning questions on which a decision has already been taken by the Central Committee and the central Soviet organs, an explanation[3] of the motives for such decisions should be given before all members of the Party. Questions being placed on the order of the day,[4] about which the party-centre has not yet taken any generally obligatory decisions, must be discussed at general meetings, and the opinion of the organisation must quickly be communicated to the provincial committees and to the Central Committee. Any resolutions adopted must be regarded as draft-decisions, because[5] resolutions of the party-centres, which must be implemented, may[6] differ from the decisions of one-or-another local organisation of the party. What is needed for regular discussion of questions having a local character, in addition to the reports of party-committees, is the introduction of regular reports from those who manage the departments of Soviet organs. In Moscow, there is being established a system of reports from party-committees to general meetings of party-members and to workers' meetings.

II. With the aim of attracting rank-and-file party-members into party-life, it is desirable that not only provincial conferences, but also all plenums of provincial committees, when dealing with questions that do not involve closed sessions, be made public for all members of the Party[7] and that corresponding

---

3. ['Выяснения' is hand-written above the line by E.A. Preobrazhensky in place of 'внесения', which is crossed out.]
4. ['На очередь дня' is written above the line.]
5. ['П.ч'. is written above the line.]
6. ['Могут' is written in to replace 'лишь', which is crossed-out.]
7. ['Партии' is written in above the line.]

measures be taken to increase attendance at the sessions, conferences and plenary-meetings.

III. The character of revision-commissions must be changed, giving them the right to review organisations in terms of their actual work (to review the implementation of circulars from the Central Committee and of resolutions by conferences, the speed with which business is conducted in party-committees, improvement of the bureaucratic apparatus, and so on.) The revision-committees are obliged to render account of any negligence both to the organs that selected them and directly to the Central Committee. Correspondingly, it is, therefore, necessary to select sufficiently responsible and effective comrades for the revision-commissions.

IV. In view of the endless complaints from rank-and-file Communists concerning various abuses by responsible comrades, and the impossibility of securing necessary party-countermeasures by any normal route, special party-commissions must be organised under all provincial committees, involving those comrades who are most impartial and widely trusted within the organisation, to consider all complaints lodged by one Communist against another.

Not a single complaint must be left without a justified response from the commission or a resolution by the provincial committee.

V. In view of the growing material inequality amongst Communists, and in order to eradicate it as quickly as possible, it is recommended to all provincial and party-committees that they conduct an investigation into the material living conditions of all the Communists of the given district, that they report the results of the investigation to the Central Committee and, in addition, that they take a variety of measures aimed at eliminating the privileged position of separate groups of Communists whenever they are not required by the business to hand.

VI. Require every responsible Communist, without exception, to be engaged in regular party-work, above all among the lower ranks of the proletariat and the Red Army, and make participation in *subbotniks* absolutely obligatory for all, in accordance with the resolution concerning *subbotniks*. The time spent on a *subbotnik* must be appraised not from the viewpoint of the direct results of the labour, but in terms of strengthening unity within the Party on the basis of fulfilment by every Communist, without exception, of all party-obligations.

VII. With regard to the central workers, the Central Committee deems it necessary to implement the following measures: a) require every people's commissar and every member of the collegium to go to the localities at least twice a year, b) change the membership of the collegiums more frequently by attracting outstanding workers from the localities, c) charge the Central Committee with special scrutiny of all responsible workers at the centre, and maintain a personal diary of each, with the obligation to provide information concerning every day's work, d) charge the Central Committee with undertaking a statistical investigation of the material circumstances and housing conditions of all Communists in the city of Moscow and in the province with the aim of establishing more uniform living conditions for them, e) charge the Central Committee with an investigation of conditions in the use of means of transportation on the part of responsible workers, with the aim of struggling against extravagance and lack of control in this area.

VIII. This circular must be read at all general meetings of party-members in all organisations of the RKP, and copies of the protocols of the meetings, together with the decisions taken, must be immediately sent to the Central Committee of the Party.

IX. In implementing this circular it is necessary to continue...[8]

Appendix[9]

The draft is accompanied by a note with the following comments:

24 August 1920

To Comrade Lenin

Esteemed Vladimir Il'ich!

As an attachment, I am sending you the draft circular-letter, written by comrade Preobrazhensky on the basis of his report concerning signs of demoralisation in the Party, together with the exchange of opinions among those of us who were at the commission (Preobrazhensky, myself and Minkov from the Moscow Committee). I would think that the reservation 'whenever they are not required by the business to hand', at the end of Point V, which speaks of the elimination of inequality in living conditions, should be developed in a separate point or even, perhaps, in a separate part of the circular.

The point is that the living conditions of provincial party- and soviet-workers are very difficult especially now, when we have made massive reassignments and are taking the majority of comrades away from the localities where they had all sorts of family-ties and connections with the countryside.

Our comrades are going hungry, and since they are also working under strain they frequently become exhausted and permanently fall by the wayside. It is imperative to make the mass members of the Party aware of the need to remedy

---

8. [The text ends here.]
9. [From RGASPI. F. 17. Op. 112. D. 136. L. 2–2 ob. To be sent. Typewritten.]

the hunger and to improve somewhat the living conditions of a small and active revolutionary cadre.

If the thought outlined above is sufficiently emphasised and developed in the circular, the last two lines of the draft, which carefully condemn demagogy on the grounds of inequality, but do so in a way not easily understood, will become redundant.

During the discussion in the commission, comrade Preobrazhensky did not deny the need to develop in the circular the idea of a certain unavoidable temporary inequality, but somehow he did not do so.

With comradely greetings.[10]

---

10. [The letter is unsigned. Judging by V.I. Lenin's note, addressed to the *Orgburo* of the Central Committee of the RKP(B) on 24 August 1920, its author is N.N. Krestinsky, Secretary of the Central Committee of the RKP(B). See Lenin 1958–65, Vol. 51, p. 268.]

Nos. 80–3
Articles Published in the Newspaper *Pravda* in September–December 1920

No. 80

'The Average Communist'[1]

19 September 1920

I

He numbers in the tens of thousands. He is the cement that strengthens our Red Army, which in its lower ranks is made up mainly of peasants. He carries all the burdens of life on the march, enjoying no rights and having more duties than the rank-and-file Red-Army man. The Red-Army man can withdraw – the Communist is obliged to be the last man on the battlefield. The Red-Army man can be taken prisoner and, perhaps, not be shot by the enemy. Communists are not taken prisoner. As comrade Trotsky excellently put it, he is part of our order of Red samurais, to whom the enemy shows no mercy and who never surrenders. In a moment when he is in acute need of food and clothing or fatigued from fighting, the Red-Army man can yield to despair or raise a protest. The Communist must be firm and indestructible, and, despite the suffering of his weary and tormented body, he must remain like iron, because he is a member of a great party that stands at the head of a great revolution, because he is a Communist.

---

1. [From *Pravda*, 19 September 1920.]

He numbers in the tens and hundreds of thousands, and stands at the forefront of the labour-battle. The non-party worker, suffering from malnutrition, can succumb, in a moment of weakness, to the agitation of Menshevik squawkers, and he can hurl bitter reproaches at the proletarian power for not providing him with what he needs. The non-party worker can become so carried away as to increase his own share by taking what rightfully belongs to another such worker at the opposite corner of the Republic. A Communist cannot do so. He must stand at his machine with the same determination as he stands with his rifle in the trenches at the most difficult moments. Tomorrow, every rank-and-file toiler will shower him with gratitude when victories come on the labour-front. But today, he must be as hard as flint in response to every reproach, to every attack, to the disappointment and desperation of the needy masses, to his own needs. He must not be shaken or take a single step backwards, for he is a Communist. The rank-and-file worker can rest on a Saturday, but a Saturday is precisely when a Communist must work more zealously than at any other time of the week. Indeed, it is precisely on a Saturday that he puts in those four hours of free, unpaid productive labour for all, whose rays shine forth into our life and must elevate mankind from the depths of capitalist disasters. Some people might go to rest, but not the person who carries in his hip-pocket a membership-book of the RKP, for he is a Communist.

When a truly scientific history of our Revolution and our Party is written, when every force is duly taken into account, the gigantic work performed for the world-revolution by the iron infantryman of our Party, our average Communist, will become perfectly clear.

The most thoughtful European Communists, who were here in our Soviet land during the recent congress of the International, enviously spoke of the fact that they have no such leaders as our Party has. Experience has convinced them of how important the brains of the foremost Communists are for the success of the proletarian revolution. But those among them who have known our Party longer (and their opinion is especially important to us), such as Bela Kun, were even more enthralled by the heroism of our proletariat and its Communist rank-and-file. At home, we hardly speak of them – partly because of the bad bourgeois habit of too-often repeating stereotyped phrases about leaders and tens of surnames even when this is not necessary and becomes sickening; partly because of the inability of the proletarian Revolution and the proletarian Party to photograph itself in its mass grandeur; and finally, partly because a healthy man has no reason to think and talk about his health.

But now we are told that there are signs of illness within the Party, that there are 'upper and lower strata' and antagonism between them.

What is this illness, and what is the cure for it?

E. Preobrazhensky

No. 81

'The Average Communist'[1]

21 September 1920

II

It would be incorrect and harmful to the Party to deny the fact that within our ranks we do not have the unanimity or comradely cohesion that we had in 1917–18. It is true that there are still organisations that have not changed in the least in this respect, but there are also those in which the psychological alienation of responsible comrades from rank-and-file Communists is an undeniable fact. In 1920, our Party is outwardly more disciplined and united than in 1918, but the voluntary and conscious discipline is less than it was then, and so is the comradely solidarity.

Let us turn to the causes.

Comparing the party-life of late 1917 and 1918 with party-life in 1920, one is struck by the way it has died out precisely among the party-masses. It is enough just to compare the agenda and the protocols of any randomly selected general meetings of two to three years ago with similar meetings this year. Previously, rank-and-file Communists felt they were not just implementing party-decisions, but were also originating them, that they themselves were forming the Party's collective will. Now they implement party-decisions taken by committees that often do not bother to submit decisions to general meetings. We know the causes: civil war, mortal danger, and the need to reach and implement decisions rapidly. However, we must acknowledge that, in this respect, the Party has gone too far in following the line of least resistance to the mechanics of the soviet- and military apparatuses. It is time to move to the next stage and to combine the current maximal centralisation, which enabled us to defeat our enemies, with the maximally active participation of all Communists in deciding all the most important questions concerning the Party and politics in general.

People are talking about bureaucratism. We do have bureaucratism – and here is a most graphic example of how it happens. Suppose that I, as secretary to the CC, have twenty visitors and forty papers to deal with in a day; this takes all the time that I can free from other duties. If the number of visitors increases to forty, and other matters to eighty, then either some of the visitors will systematically have to wait and the papers will lie idle for a long time (one form of

---

1. [From *Pravda*, 21 September 1920.]

bureaucratism), or else a decision will be taken on every question without my knowing the essential issue (another form of bureaucratism). In most cases, the source of bureaucratism within the Party is the same. A lack of correspondence between the volume of work and the number of workers – and this is an illness for which there is no serious treatment, other than educating and training ever-newer strata of workers. This kind of illness does not cure itself in a single month, and to think that there are any other cures is simply self-deception.

The psychological isolation of average Communists from the leading party-groups, and the isolation of leading groups from the proletarian masses – these are unquestionable facts. There are several causes. Besides what was said at the outset, it is necessary to point to the inattention of responsible comrades to the education of rank-and-file Communists, the difference in living conditions, the penetration into leading posts (mainly in the soviets) of careerist elements who are intrinsically alien to us, and the beginnings of psychological degeneration among a certain part of the old Communists.

Inattention to the education of party-reserves was at first due to responsible comrades being dragged by their ears into soviet-work. The Party's effort at the Eighth Congress to create better conditions for party-work by redistributing forces turned out to be inadequate. The party-schools have too few lecturers; there are too few responsible workers at general meetings of party-members; *subbotniks* are not attended under various pretexts, and so on. Here, the Party must make a new effort. A beginning has already been made with the letter from the Central Committee published in No. 21 of *Partiinye izvestiya*.

As for the differences in living conditions: here too, a decisive change is needed. Until now, we thought this was unimportant – but this issue has turned out to be important, because quantity is turning into quality, and a difference of living conditions is being reflected in the way we think and understand each other.

What is most of all causing the Party to fall out with the masses is the penetration of the Party by careerist and self-seeking elements. These elements can be divided into awkward and crude fools, who quickly depart and relieve the Party of their presence, and those who are smarter and more adroit at disguising themselves with their outwardly-Communist appearance. Given the extreme shortage of workers, these elements were, from time to time, forgiven a great deal. But when it is a question of driving honest workers from the Party and keeping Communist careerists, our decision must be clear. The workers are more precious to us. It is precisely these careerists who are trying to bring into the Party the spirit of a cold, callous and disdainful attitude towards rank-and-file Communists and workers in general; in their personal life, they attach no value to the Party's honour, to its sensitivity to proletarian need, or to its active engagement with every justifiable protest that originates from the working masses. Our average Communist does not always understand the great and important questions of international politics, but his proletarian senses are sound when it comes to appraising these elements. He senses that they are foreign to him; he insists upon it, and he is right.

Finally, there is the decay of proletarian psychology amongst certain old Communists, happily only a few. If a statistical study were done of the people with whom our stratum of senior Communists, five to six thousand of them, interact regularly in their daily lives and work, it would turn out that a certain percentage of them spend their whole lives honestly and industriously in virtually no contact with the working masses. Not a single Marxist would say that this has no consequences for such people, for their psychology and their habits. Meanwhile, time spent among the bourgeoisie and the bourgeois intelligentsia acts like a physical force – it may be slow and imperceptible, but it is real.

What must we do? What are the generally useful things we can do to preserve the proletarian spirit from top to bottom within the Party? It seems to me that we should begin with speedy implementation of the decision taken by the Eighth Party-Congress, having responsible worker-Communists periodically return to their [factory-]machinery. We have not implemented this decision because of our extreme shortage of resources, but experience has proven that we have lost more in this matter than we have saved. It also seems to me that it would be most useful and necessary to transfer responsible personnel – not workers – at least once a year to unskilled physical labour for a month to a month and a half. We have to try this. I am deeply convinced that these measures will on the whole prove justifiable. Finally, responsible comrades who are not fit for physical labour must be transferred temporarily to work at the provincial or district-level. In particular, it is necessary to begin by sending a third of the members of our collegiums in the central commissariats to the provinces and replacing them with workers from the localities.

The Party-Conference that is convening must discuss questions concerning the revitalisation of our Party. It must criticise with particular severity those organisations that have failed to retain in their ranks tens and hundreds of honest workers who joined us during Party-Week and were lost during re-registration.

In conclusion, I must point out that everything that I have said here was written not in my capacity as a member of the Central Committee, but as a contribution to party-discussion prior to the Conference.

E. Preobrazhensky

No. 82

'The Social Basis of the October Revolution'[1]

7 November 1920

When the October uprising occurred, all the opponents of Soviet power agreed that the Bolsheviks represented the interests of an insignificant minority of the population, that their success was temporary and accidental, and that the new power would not last even two weeks. The three-year existence of Soviet power is sufficiently convincing proof of the extreme superficiality and groundlessness of Cadet-Menshevik 'sociology'. It would be redundant now to refute the 'scientific analyses' of the Martovs, Chernovs and Kautskys, and the optimistic predictions of the Paris stockbrokers, who have already paid enough for their flippancy. But it is useful for us, for our own purposes, to have a clear understanding of those class-forces that gave us victory and ensured the destruction of all counter-revolutionary forces.

Besides the workers, the soldiers played the most active role in the October Revolution, that is, the peasantry that had been organised by the tsarist authority. The peasantry, at that time, was not yet internally divided. The entire mass of poor peasants, middle-peasants and kulaks supported not only the elimination of landlord rule in the countryside, but also the destruction of the urban bourgeoisie that occurred simultaneously. Accordingly, at the first and most crucial stage of the struggle, the Soviet authority relied upon not merely the entire proletariat, but also upon the entire peasantry. This gave the movement the powerful force of a hurricane that could not be resisted by all the organised elements of the bourgeois-landlord régime. This peculiar feature of the Russian Revolution will not be repeated in the West, where the peasantry will participate from the outbreak of the revolution as a force that is already stratified – with one wing supporting the advancing proletariat, and the other wing, probably larger, on the side of counter-revolution.

During the second stage of our struggle, in connection with grain-requisitions and the need to repel the pressure from Cossack generals and the Czechoslovaks, the stratum of well-to-do peasants separated from the Soviet power; and the middle-peasantry, the most numerous stratum of Russia's toiling population, found itself at a crossroads. The summer of 1918 was the most critical period in the life of the Soviet authority. The fate of the Revolution depended on who would be supported by the middle-peasant. The working class and poor peasants

---

1. [From *Pravda*, 7 November 1920.]

on the one side, and the kulaks, officers and bourgeoisie, with the support of foreign capital, on the other, were either equal in force, or else the latter were probably stronger than the former. An outcome in favour of the Revolution was decided when the middle-peasants, in our famine-stricken provinces and at the centre, came over to side with Soviet power, along with the middle-peasants of the Volga region and Siberia after their experience of the Kolchak régime convinced them that it was unacceptable. The subsequent defeat of Denikin demonstrated that the worker-peasant state, built upon an alliance of the proletariat with eighty percent of the peasantry, no longer faced any rivals for power within the borders of Russia.

If we look at the military force of the Revolution, the Red Army, it will be perfectly clear to us that it is built on the basis of a fighting alliance of the proletariat with the middle- and poor peasants, and on the leadership and supremacy of the proletariat within this alliance. It is true that in some districts we were able to use even well-to-do peasants against the counter-revolution (the peasantry on the Cossack borders, non-residents, the so-called toiling Cossacks, and the Siberian kulaks in the struggle against Kolchak), but, at the same time, there were occasions when the opposite occurred, and in some districts the poor were used against the Soviet power. But these exceptions do not alter the general picture.

For the past three years, this alliance with the middle-peasantry has also been an economic one. Without the peasants' grain, we would not have been able to defeat our enemies and would not be able now to restore our disorganised industry. Following the expropriation of the major portion of kulaks and the conversion of a significant part of the poor peasants into middle-peasants at kulak-expense, the source of our grain and other procurements, as well as of recruits for labour-duty, is the middle-peasant. The preservation of this alliance on economic grounds is a question of the utmost importance for Soviet power. And we have yet to mention the fact that without expansion of our agriculture, which can only occur on a mass scale during the coming decade as the expansion of middle-peasant farming, it will be impossible to fortify the workers' revolution in the West and to save the European proletariat from famine, since from the first day of their victory they will be subject to a 'grain'-boycott on the part of capitalist America. Hence there emerges the prospect of an economic bloc between our middle-peasantry and the whole of the European proletariat. This bloc will be all-the-more inevitable and beneficial for the peasantry because it is only with the rapid assistance of European technology that we can achieve a speedy revolution in the sphere of Russian agricultural production.

Throughout the entire Civil War, the middle-peasants always hesitated to follow the proletariat. More than once they wavered, especially in the face of new efforts and new sacrifices, and more than once they took a step in the direction of their class-enemies. It is enough to recall the mass desertions, which represented an attempt to burden the proletariat alone with the entire struggle for both the workers' and peasants' goals in the Revolution; it is enough to recall the surrender to the enemy without a fight on the part of several peasant-formations, or the resistance to grain-requisitions in several districts, especially during the first two years, and such like. And now, when we are on the verge of liquidating the last tsarist general who threatens the worker-peasant achievements, when the direct threat to the peasant's land is almost eliminated, there may be new wavering on the part of the middle-peasant. The military-economic alliance is turning mainly into an economic alliance, which, at the current stage, is less beneficial to the countryside. It is, therefore, important for us, at precisely this moment, to exert the greatest moral influence on the proletariat's ally on the one hand, and on the other, to use every possible means to provide the middle-peasant farm with maximal economic assistance from the city. It is no coincidence that the question of assistance to agriculture is one of the most important questions on the agenda of the Eighth All-Russian Congress of Soviets.

The inviolability of the alliance of workers and middle-peasants, which secured victory for Soviet power in the three-year Civil War, will also ensure the victory of the October Revolution on the economic front, where the main battles are yet to come. We know very well that the foreign capitalists, who have finally understood why our peasantry did not follow Kolchak, Denikin and Wrangel, will attempt to detach the middle-peasantry from the proletariat and to use the Right S-Rs, the Savinkovs and their other agents to create an alliance of the peasantry with European capital in the wake of Wrangel's defeat. These efforts are hopeless for one basic reason, and that is that given the disorganisation of our industry, such a combination would mean payment in gold of the sixteen billion in debts, which would fall upon the shoulders of that very same peasantry. The alliance with the proletariat protects the peasantry from this obligation, which would be the necessary consequence of any alliance with the S-Rs and European capital.

So long as capitalism rules in the countries of Europe and threatens to transform Russia into its colony, to plunder our grain and materials and to deprive the peasant of an income from his land, the October Revolution will have a sufficiently broad base in the worker-peasant alliance led by the proletariat.

E. Preobrazhensky

No. 83

'A Straw for the Drowning White Guards'[1]

12 December 1920

Had all the forces of Kolchak, Denikin, Yudenich, Miller, Petlyura, Horvat, and Semenov – in Finland, Estonia, Latvia, Lithuania, Poland, Romania, and Georgia – united in their day, and had they organised a single command for all these forces, then even without Entente-soldiers, all these forces would have been able to defeat the Soviet Republic.

But such a command was not created *and* **could never be created**. The White wolves, who threw themselves upon Soviet Russia, bared their fangs at each other and made it possible to defeat them separately.

With us, on the contrary, there was a single command and a single plan. We had iron discipline in the party that governed the country and led the defence of the Republic. The Communist Party was the victor in the Civil War, and it triumphed because of its energy, self-sacrifice, consciousness and, above all, its discipline and unity. Our enemies know this very well. It is not for nothing that the entire White-Guard press cited our Party as an example for the undisciplined S-Rs, who split into pieces and fragments, and for the Cadets, with their 'orientations' first to the Allies, then to Wilhelm, then back to the Allies, and then to some Allies in opposition to others; it was cited as an example for the White generals, who schemed against each other, and for the drunken officers who supported the 'prestige' of 'popular-democratic power' with drunken orgies at public houses.

The Whites learned to understand their enemy; they learned to understand the strength of the Communist Party, which was the cause of its glorious victories and of their own shameful defeats.

The counter-revolution has been smashed. In active struggle, the iron Communist Party turned out to be stronger than the various rabble of the bourgeois system. Our steely discipline neither broke nor bent; on the contrary, it hardened in open battle. Is it possible that it will rust more easily in a time of peace? Is it possible that the oak that could not be taken down by the hurricane of counter-revolution will be undermined at its roots by swarms of White worms?

This hope is the final comfort for the already-defeated enemies of the proletariat. For a long time, since the very beginning of the Civil War, they have been grinding their teeth over the civil peace within the Communist Party. As early as the Brest negotiations, they began to fabricate all kinds of silly rumours about

---

1. [From *Pravda*, 12 December 1920.]

a split in Bolshevik ranks, about a 'Bukharin fraction' forming to overthrow the Central Committee, about Trotsky having arrested Lenin, and other such nonsense. They systematically filled the White-Guard newspapers with such nonsense, and these fabricated stupidities expressed a genuine and real hope for a split in the Communist Party and for its self-destruction. And now, at the moment of the decisive military defeat of the counter-revolution, when one section of the defeated bourgeoisie is reverting to mysticism and investing all its hopes in the grace of God, while the other section remains Earth-bound and relies solely upon a split and disintegration within the Communist Party – at this very moment, we are openly revealing our illnesses and turning to cure them. One can imagine how this must delight and renew the hope among the most short-sighted of our enemies. The Bolsheviks have spoken of their illnesses, which must mean that, in reality, things are ten times worse for them than they are letting on. This is how they think of us – those who are accustomed in public always to represent **their own affairs** as ten times **better** than they are in fact. Our enemies have yet to understand that our tactic is not one of concealing or downplaying danger; we are more inclined to exaggerate danger, as we did during the attacks by Kolchak and Denikin, and perhaps that is the case now with regard to the question of the Party's illnesses. But those who were beaten in open battle are not giving up the hope of success, and along with other modes of struggle against communism, they are trying by secret and fraudulent means to take part in our inner-party affairs. Recently, we have turned up several letters that are being widely circulated among party-members, and are clearly of White-Guard or S-R origins. During the inspection of the People's Commissariat of Transportation, several letters of 'denunciation' turned up with false names. During the pre-election campaign, before the last Moscow conference, a letter circulated with my own name on it, in which extracts from one of my articles were mixed up with provocative additions from the friends of Savinkov. A letter of 'denunciation' also circulated from a battalion-commissar, a worker. It was written in the refined 'Chernov' style and proved, upon investigation, to be a fraud.

All of these facts show how eagerly interested the Whites are in following our inner-party disputes and how diligently they attempt to use them in their own interests. Our Party is a mighty organism with strong nerves, a clear mind, and acute senses. When, during our internal disputes, there appears on the horizon even the spectre of a 'third beneficiary', or when there is suspicion of elements hostile to us becoming involved in something, this is all it takes for all Communists to form a single steel-wall. In all our disagreements, every Communist must be clearly aware of the limits beyond which criticism within the Party, which clears out inner filth and awakens creative thought, becomes, instead, criticism directed against the Party as a whole and objectively helps our enemies.

We hope, and we are totally convinced, that the recently-confirmed attempts by our enemies to play the role of provocateurs in our domestic disputes will be swept away and will have no such consequences. Nor will they have the consequence of forcing us to end our struggle against our own shortcomings merely because the bankrupts of the counter-revolution are attempting to convert the remedy of freedom and criticism into a poison that will decompose the organism of the Party.

If every Communist has a sufficient sense of tact and care for the Party as a whole, we can confidently follow our road while unmasking all the machinations of our enemies along the way.

To their long list of defeats, they will then add one more: their unsuccessful attempt to speculate on our internal disagreements.

E. Preobrazhensky

Part III: *The ABC of Communism: 1917–1920*

No. 1

E.A. Preobrazhensky's Pamphlet *Peasant-Russia and Socialism (Towards a Review of Our Agrarian Programme)*[1]

1918

Towards a review of our agrarian programme

There are certain naïve Socialist-Revolutionaries who suggest that our Party, by issuing the Decree on Land at the All-Russian Congress of Soviets, renounced any intention of putting forth its own agrarian programme and limited itself to supporting the S-R version of socialisation of the land. Not only the Socialist-Revolutionaries, but even many of our own party-comrades, do not clearly understand how, in the final analysis, matters will stand with our agrarian programme. Although comrade Lenin took the floor as *rapporteur* at the Soviet-Congress and emphasised that accepting the S-R edition of the Decree on Land does not imply that we are abandoning our own agrarian programme, his address at the Peasant-Congress and his explanatory letter to *Pravda* concerning our view on socialisation of the land nevertheless failed to clarify this issue.

---

1. [From Preobrazhensky 1918a, pp. 1–23.] The present brochure consists partly of feuilletons published in *Pravda* at the end of 1917 and partly of pages that were specially written for this publication. The author's intention was, on the one hand, to propose a new draft of the agrarian programme for discussion at the Party-Congress and, on the other hand, to undertake a review of the new tasks that we face in our work in the countryside as a result of the October Revolution and the transfer of state-power into the hands of the proletariat and the poorest peasantry.

With regard to socialisation of the land, we must strictly differentiate between two sides of the question: that of principle, and that of tactics.

In tactical terms, our flexibility on this question can be quite far-reaching. Comrade Lenin was perfectly correct when he took the view that, in the extreme case, our Party can even vote to enact socialisation of the land should it happen that our abstention might lead to passage of some kind of bourgeois land-project.

In extreme circumstances, and out of tactical considerations, we can support socialisation of the land by going even further than just voting for it.

But it is another matter entirely when the question is one of assessing the S-R agrarian programme from the standpoint of principle. Here, there can be no room whatsoever for concessions. Even if socialisation of the land ceased being the programme of intelligentsia-groups and, instead, became the programme of the broad peasant-masses, this would still not provide the least grounds for revising our own views on this matter, unless we are also prepared to revise the very concept of socialism.

The fact is that we have criticised socialisation of the land from two points of view: both as a petty-bourgeois utopian measure, insofar as its implementation is supposed to strike a blow against capitalism; and also as a non-socialist measure, if what we have in mind is the socialist transformation of agriculture. Our objections on the first point have now receded, but not because the Socialist-Revolutionaries proved to be correct; on the contrary, it is precisely the revolutionary Social Democrats who have been proven correct. It is only the blow struck against capitalism in its vital centres, in the cities, that has made it possible in practical terms to regard the implementation of a number of measures as transitional steps in the direction of socialism. And this first victory over capital was won by the workers and soldiers not because of any 'socialisation of the land', but rather *despite* the opposition of a majority of members of the very party that takes socialisation of the land as the outstanding element of its programme.

As for our objections on the second point, they have not only retained all of their importance, but must also now be raised most forcefully against socialisation of the land. Socialism means conscious regulation of the economy on (at least) the national scale. The most important condition for socialism in agriculture (although by no means the only one) is that the working collective have not merely the right, but also the actual ability to dispose of a sufficient area of workable land. In this respect, a country with small-scale peasant-farming differs from one with large-scale farming only in terms of the greater difficulties it poses in the way of a socialist reconstruction of agriculture. This is why no genuine socialist can object in principle to nationalisation of all the land once power is in the hands of the toiling classes, which is exactly the case now in Russia. Nationalisation, in these circumstances, is the most genuine way of socialising the land, with no inverted commas.

Why is it that, in our Revolution, 'socialisation' (with inverted commas) has won out over socialisation (without inverted commas)? The answer is that the majority of peasants prefer things that way. And why do they have this preference? In comrade Lenin's view, the answer is that peasants consider the S-R socialisation of the land to be a transitional stage on the way to socialism, and they think that they will make their way to socialism along this peasant-path. Such optimism, however, is completely unfounded.

The peasants favour 'socialisation of the land' first because the transfer of confiscated manorial and other lands to the *obshchinas* means that a particular class acquires control over the land, rather than it being transferred to the entire people, as would be the case with nationalisation of the land. This means that the spoils of war, seized by the forces of both participants in the Civil War against the landlords, that is, by the proletariat and the peasantry, end up in the hands of the latter alone.

The peasants favour egalitarian use of the land not because it is a 'transitional measure on the way to socialism', but because it is the best way of achieving a fair division of the spoils.

But one can only speak of taking a step forwards if the break-up of land-relations in the village leads to the expansion of communal land-ownership at the expense of small-scale peasant-property.

Worker-proletarians have no connection with the land and no direct interest in it, and in this respect, the worker can have no quarrel with the peasant over how the spoils are divided. However, the worker does have an interest in raising the productivity of agricultural labour and thereby expanding the share of values available for distribution to all the workers in the republic of toilers. And since the greatest increase of productivity can only come from replacing small-scale individual farming with a common social effort, any expansion of 'socialisation of the land' (in inverted commas) at the expense of socialisation (without inverted commas) – that is, at the expense of nationalisation – simply means enhancing the position of small-scale farming at the expense of social farming.

The fact is that semi-proletarian and middle-peasants can only increase their labour-productivity through an *artel*, that is, through socialist farming, and they have just as much interest in that outcome as the worker. There is, so to speak, no potential conflict of interest between the labouring peasant and the worker as far as socialism is concerned. There is, however, an extremely long road of development and struggle that separates the present situation from the time when the independent petty farmer will become a full-fledged participant in a socialist collective. The worker, in the course of this struggle, will defend the higher form of socialist agriculture, whereas the peasant will take a stand on behalf of stagnant forms of small-scale independent farming. It is this kind of 'socialisation of the land' – that is, greater control of the land by small *obshchinas* – that will help to strengthen these stagnant forms, creating economic *Vendées*[2] throughout the whole expanse of agrarian Russia.

That is why our position concerning 'socialisation of the land' must be as follows. In those cases where the *only* choice is between small-scale individual peasant-holdings and tenure on the part of the *obshchina*, we are in favour of the latter. But in cases where 'socialisation of the land' interferes with nationalisation, we must make every possible effort to support nationalisation. In this regard, we must not forget that nationalisation has allies precisely amongst the poorest semi-proletarian elements of the peasantry – amongst all who have neither a horse nor equipment, amongst households where soldiers' widows have small children to raise – not to mention those peasants who are pure *batraks*.[3] Given their impoverished position, these groups of the peasantry can expect little benefit from the purely formal equality in land-distribution that is foreseen in the programme of the S-Rs. The fact is that these strata of the peasantry can make no use of the significant increment of land given to them by the Revolution, because they have no means with which to work it. State-assistance, given our financial position, cannot initially be very substantial, and since it is not substantial it can only be effective provided that it is not widely dispersed and if the recipients are complete *artels* of the organised poor, rather than individual holdings.

For these poor peasants, working the former landlord's holdings through an *artel* is an unavoidable economic necessity. 'Socialisation of the land', on the contrary, is the programme mainly of the better-off peasantry. With their fictitious and formal equality, they mask the real economic inequality between the better-off and semi-proletarian parts of the peasantry, transfer real control over the *obshchina's* land into the hands of those who can actually work it, and promote exclusion from the countryside of those who, because of their economic weakness, will be unable to use their land-allotments productively.

Many people have yet to realise the enormous extent to which the War has increased economic stratification in the countryside. The rise in fixed grain-prices benefited those with grain at their disposal. Today, they are still profiting from speculative grain-sales at prices of forty to fifty roubles per pood. Those who benefited most from the rout of the landlords are those who came in five wagons.[4] In the distribution of the landlords' cattle and equipment, those who gained most were those in charge, namely, the committees in which well-to-do

---

2. [Counter-revolutionary peasant-uprisings.]
3. [Landless agricultural labourers.]
4. [The reference is to the five covered wagons that carried the dowry at a well-to-do wedding: that is, the more prosperous peasants were already 'well-endowed' even before seizure of the landlords' estates.]

peasants predominated, as we hear in complaints everywhere. Who were the main people involved in working former landlord-holdings during the past sowing season? The answer, again, is those who had a horse and the labour-power required to work not only their own land, but other people's as well. Those strata of the peasantry who are buyers of grain, on the other hand, are quickly being ruined.

Very soon, there will be an acute struggle in the countryside amongst the peasants themselves – between the ruined poor and the strong peasants. We must see to it that this struggle does not take the form of a spontaneous rebellion, with a lumpen-proletarian tendency towards 'equalisation' and the plundering of household-treasures, but that it leads, instead, to an economic union of the poor so that, perhaps with state-support and at the expense of the stronger peasantry, they will be able to begin working their share of the former landlords' land through *artels*. Otherwise, that land will inevitably pass from their hands into those of the well-to-do peasant-strata.

In the process of breaking up land-relations in the countryside, we must try to ensure that the state of the working people retains as much land as possible so that it might be cultivated on a social basis. There is no doubt that most of the arable land will elude state-control and actually end up in small-peasant farming. Instead of taking a direct route to socialist reconstruction of agriculture, as would be possible in a country with large-scale farming, we must follow a long, difficult and roundabout path. In addition to the organisation of state-agriculture, which can only be accomplished after long preliminary work, we also have one other real means at our disposal: that is, state-control of exchange, which at some point leads to state-organisation of exchange. We should also keep in mind so-called Platonic ways of influencing stubborn individualists, including propaganda by word and deed in the form of organising showcase-examples of *artel*-farming and so forth.

II

The position of not having an agrarian programme, which currently applies to our Party, is no longer tolerable. We must have a congress as soon as possible, or else a plenipotentiary conference to review the programme. I would propose that this future congress or conference consider the following draft of an agrarian programme.

On the issue of the land, the party of revolutionary Social-Democrats, the Bolsheviks, aims for a complete reconstruction of agriculture based on socialist principles, and with this objective, it strives to implement measures that will either lead directly to this objective, following the transfer of central power into the hands of the toilers, or else will constitute transitional stages in the direction of socialist agriculture.

The Party advocates the following:

1) Complete eradication of all remnants of domination in the countryside by the nobility and the merchant-kulaks, including confiscation of all lands in the possession of landlords, merchants and wealthy peasants, together with all appanage-land, possessional land,[5] and monastery- and Church-land.

2) The elimination of private property in land, a ban on buying and selling land, and nationalisation of all land, that is, the transfer of ultimate control over the disposal of land into the hands of the state of the toilers, acting through the central power and local organs of self-government by the toiling popular masses.

3) Use of confiscated lands to form the greatest-possible number of large-scale model social farms, together with provision of the most extensive possible state-support to those peasants who possess neither a horse nor equipment, and to agricultural labourers and other proletarians and semi-proletarians in the countryside as they organise such farms to work the land on the basis of *artel*-principles.

4) The organisation of state-farming on treasury-lands and the most intensive efforts to reclaim non-workable land for purposes of farming and animal-husbandry.

5) A socialist resettlement-policy, that is, transfer of settlers not to small individual plots but, instead, to large-scale model farms that will be prepared and equipped in advance with all the necessary inventory, livestock, buildings and agronomists.

6) Exclusion of private merchants and speculators from the grain-trade, together with declaration of a state-monopoly in the purchase and sale of grain and in the sale of agricultural machinery and fertiliser as preliminary steps in the direction of state-regulation of all economic exchanges.

7) Gradual establishment of a system of state-control over agriculture and the use of all resources available to the state of the toilers in struggling against backward and stagnant economic forms, together with all possible support and encouragement for the transition from small-scale individual and unproductive farming to the most advanced forms of social farming.

8) Reallocation of the country's available resources from commerce into agriculture, and nationalisation of the banks for this purpose.

---

5. [For a discussion of possessional land, see Document 2:13.]

While striving to implement socialism in agriculture – as the only way to give a powerful impulse to the development of rural productive forces – in order to free rural toilers permanently from poverty and non-productive labour, and to protect not only rural proletarians and semi-proletarians but also small farmers themselves from the delusions associated with a system of small-scale farming, the Party will make every effort to ensure that all measures are taken during the transition from capitalism to socialism to safeguard the rights of rural hired labourers, who are subject to the most unrestrained and barbaric exploitation in every country whenever small-scale farming prevails.

The Party proclaims its unshakeable conviction that implementation of all the measures foreseen in its programme will demonstrate with the utmost clarity all the disadvantages associated with small-scale agriculture and all the superiorities of large-scale agriculture; and it relies upon experience to convince all the rural toilers that, following the transfer of state-power to the proletariat and the rural poor, there will be no higher rank or position than that of a full-fledged worker-manager of the socialist state, resulting in a mass-transition, on the part of individual small-scale farmers, to voluntary participation in the socialist army of labour.

―――

Now I wish to devote a few words to clarifying the above draft-programme. After the failure of our first agrarian programme, with its sad memories of the 'cut-offs', the Party concluded that, on the basis of the current or expected relation of forces in the Revolution, it should have a tactical revolution, but not a programme. Otherwise, an error in judging social forces (this kind of error is inevitable and happens frequently) would liquidate some, if not all, points of the programme. The basis of a programme must be a specific cycle of social development, not a relation of forces. There can be two such cycles: the period of breaking up feudal remnants in the name of capitalism's victory, and the period of breaking up capitalist relations in the name of victorious socialism.

With respect to the first cycle, comrade Lenin quite correctly put forth nationalisation of the land as the most progressive measure possible throughout the whole period of capitalist development. But our failures with regard to the agrarian question continued: the programme of nationalising the land was rejected at the Unity-Congress. And when our Party adopted nationalisation, virtually all the other points in the programme had become outdated; that is, we had entered a new cycle of social development, the period of liquidating capitalist relations.

The proposed draft of an agrarian programme begins with the proposition that, whatever victories or defeats may lie ahead of us, we have now entered the period of world socialist revolution. In this kind of period, an organic agrarian programme of revolutionary Marxism can only be a programme for the socialist reconstruction of agriculture.

This programme (not this particular programme, but any programme that begins with an account of the world's phase of development) must be one that we can stick to even in the event that the proletariat is defeated and, for some period or another, loses the positions it now holds. Even allowing for the unlikely possibility that capitalism in our country still has something of a future, we must recognise one thing, namely, that the most essential demands of the programme remain in full force and that others, while temporarily set aside, are not rejected as being inappropriate. That is how matters stand with nationalisation of the land, which can just as suitably be put forth as a progressive measure under capitalism and as the first condition for socialisation of agriculture. Development of an advanced system of state-agriculture is a measure that is equally progressive under capitalism and after its liquidation. The same is true of a resettlement-policy that leads to large farms and of a monopoly in the grain-trade.

The War has dealt such a heavy blow to the economy of the entire country that, no matter which class remains in power, we will not recover without a dramatic increase in agricultural productivity. Such a recovery cannot be expected without the organisation of a large-scale state-economy on the one hand, and state-control over peasant-agriculture on the other. If the big bourgeoisie or the petty bourgeoisie, or some bloc of these two classes, manages to consolidate power, this will mean payments on the entire state-debt and also on the lands taken from the nobility. Even if these classes taxed the proletariat all the more heavily, which they would surely do, it would still be necessary to make heroic efforts to raise agricultural profitability. Naturally, the national income would be redistributed in favour of the propertied classes, and every effort would be made to reduce consumption by the toiling masses, but none of this would solve the fundamental question. The petty bourgeois would have to establish large-scale farming. Whether any power other than that of the workers and poorest peasants will be able to deal with the tasks of revolutionary-economic creativity that will confront the country with objective inevitability after the conclusion of the War – that is a different question.

Wherever a country has embarked upon destroying capitalist relations, development of the productive forces in agriculture is conceivable only through forms of the socialist reconstruction of small-scale farming. However resistant the small-peasant farm, and whatever efforts might be made to raise its productivity, in the final analysis they will be futile unless the character of small farming is changed. Let this farm raise its productivity even to the level of the small-scale economy. The next task, in order that further progress might occur, is socialism, which is objectively the only solution.

Now I want to deal separately with each of the points in the proposed draft agrarian programme.

The first point concerns confiscation and requires no special explanation, since it is obvious and beyond dispute. In formulating this point and, to some extent, the two that follow, I have even attempted, as much as possible, to reproduce literally the resolution on the agrarian programme that was adopted by our party-conference in April. The second point is also not contentious when it speaks of nationalisation of *all* the land, since this demand is the ideal for our Party, however much life requires it to be curtailed in favour of petty property, group-holdings (the *obshchina*) or the kind of forgery of a socialist agrarian programme that we find in the S-R 'socialisation of the land'.

When I speak of organs of 'self-government by the toiling popular masses' implementing the agrarian programme locally, instead of referring directly to soviets, I do so only because this is a broader formulation that includes not only soviets, but also all other organisations with the same class-composition. This is particularly important with regard to associations of toilers among some of the nationalities, especially the smaller ones.

The third point has colossal importance for our programme. It was already included, with different wording, in the resolution of our April conference. It is *imperative* that economic associations of proletarians and semi-proletarians work the land in accordance with *artel*-principles and with the support of the toiling people's state; this is the form in which the process of transition will occur, from small-scale farming to large-scale social and capitalist farming, and then to socialist farming. These are the embryos of socialist agriculture that will prove, as early as the summer of 1918, to be facts rather than just pious wishes, especially in places such as Estonia and Latvia, where liquidation of capitalist agriculture has taken place under the leadership of soviets of farm labourers' [*batraks'*] deputies.

In order to understand why it is necessary to include in an agrarian programme the points concerning development of state-agriculture, a socialist resettlement-policy, and state-control of agriculture, we must keep in mind the conjuncture of the world grain-market after the War and the consequences of the War for our national economy. Implementation of these measures is essentially self-evident, whatever the circumstances, once central power passes into the hands of the socialist proletariat. I only want to emphasise that these measures are not merely desirable in the interests of expanding the area of socialist agriculture, but are also economically inevitable.

There are some economists in the West who expect, with perfectly good reasons, famine in Europe after the War. Because of the exhaustion of supplies during the war-years, the demand for imported grain in Germany, England, Italy and Austria must expand enormously by comparison with the pre-war period.

On the other hand, America will not be able to satisfy this demand to the same extent that it did previously, because of the shortage of commercial shipping caused by submarine-warfare and also because of expanding grain-consumption within America itself.[6] In postwar Europe, grain will be the most marketable and precious commodity. And to the extent that Western Europe will depend on Russian as well as American grain, the post-war conjuncture in the grain-market will be exceptionally, even extraordinarily, favourable for Russia.

To what extent will our agricultural economy be able to satisfy European demand for our grain?

In the first place, with us the War has also eliminated any disposable grain-surpluses that could be sent abroad quickly. The Revolution has increased the consuming capacity of the countryside. Under tsarism, there was underconsumption of grain, because it was necessary to sell it, whatever the circumstances, in order to pay taxes and, ultimately, to pay interest on foreign loans. Today, these conditions hardly exist.

On the other hand, there is a danger that grain-production will contract, for a variety of reasons. Inventories in agriculture have been depleted and are quite inadequate. The numbers of cattle and horses have fallen, and this is reflected in a contraction of land being worked and a declining quality (because of the reduction of imported fertiliser). Destruction of the most advanced landed estates, and the break-up of smaller capitalist farms, will lead to a decline of the productive forces in agriculture.

As a consequence, the condition of our agriculture immediately following the War will involve a tendency towards a fall in grain-production, together with a rise in domestic consumption. In these circumstances, the volume of grain-exports will have to contract, which, in turn, will mean even better conditions for us in the European grain-market, because the price of grain will rise dramatically compared to the cost of production.

Meanwhile, the economic condition of the country will be such that, for economic reasons, we shall have to export grain no matter what happens; if not a foreign-trade surplus, at the very least we shall need a balance of imports and exports with a very high volume of both. We need to replace worn-out assets both in our industry and, to some degree, in agriculture, at least that portion of assets that we cannot quickly produce within the country. We shall have to make enormous purchases of cotton, dyes, and other types of materials and fabricates that can only be acquired on foreign markets. We also have to remember that

---

6. It is necessary to point out, here, the enormous threat that Europe would face in the event of a war between America and Japan, which everyone on the shores of the Pacific Ocean considers to be inevitable. For Europe, as a consumer of American grain, this war would be catastrophic on a scale that is difficult to foresee.

annulment of the state-debt by decree is not the same thing as annulment in fact. Even if we have to negotiate this point not with bourgeois governments in the West, but instead with the victorious proletariat – in other words, assuming the very best conditions possible – it is still not clear to what extent Western workers will agree to the annulment, because this will involve our refusal to pay for values that they created and that belong to them. Small investors, no doubt, will have to be repaid; and as far as relations with America and Japan are concerned, in order to avoid an occupation of our Far-Eastern regions for non-payment of debts, it is perhaps best to remember Marx's words in another context to the effect that it would be 'cheapest if we could buy out the whole lot of them'.[7] It follows that we shall need money, and a great deal of it.

But since it will be impossible for us to export any industrial products, our trade-balance can only be active or, in the worst case, avoid being passive, if we can expand the export of grain and materials. Post-war conditions will be such that it will be impossible for us to afford the luxury of small-scale agricultural production for any length of time. In these circumstances, the utopian is not the person who supports the transition to social farming, but rather anyone who thinks small-scale farming will be viable. For this reason, the programme of our Party, as the party of social development, must have one main orientation, that is, upon socialist large-scale production.

What are the resources that will initially be available to us for a large-scale social economy?

Above all, the social economy will take over the large-scale model capitalist farms that have been preserved or rebuilt in the course of the Revolution or shortly following the transformation. In Estonia and Latvia, these embryos of socialism are already a fact, thanks to the energetic work by soviets of farm-labourers' deputies.

Then there are lands tilled by *artels*, to which the unions of rural semi-proletarians will have to resort with active support from the Soviet power. For the moment, it is difficult to predict how much land may be turned over to this kind of farming, which is not a pure form of socialist agriculture, although it will eventually become such. How successful this kind of land-usage will be depends upon how economically necessary it will be for the corresponding rural strata to band together, upon their level of consciousness, and upon the speed with which they abandon any illusions concerning the advantages of 'socialisation of the

---

7. [In *The Peasant Question in France and Germany* (Engels 1990), Engels cited Marx concerning the possibility of buying out large landed estates: 'We by no means consider compensation as impermissible in any event; Marx told me (and how many times!) that, in his opinion, we would get off cheapest if we could buy out the whole lot of them'.]

land', which can only be called a 'transitional measure on the way to socialism' if we stubbornly persist in paying undeserved compliments to the Left-SS-Rs.

As for state-agriculture, here vast opportunities are opening up for us. Tens of millions of *desyatins* of land are concentrated in state-hands, and with varying degrees of preparatory work, they can be made suitable for agriculture. With a good organisation of state-farming, a significant portion of the unemployed can be attracted into tilling this land, especially unskilled workers who will become available through the demobilisation of industry.

For the country as a whole, it would be difficult to imagine a more productive kind of public works.

A socialist resettlement-policy will initially contribute much less to social farming. With the liquidation of landlord-holdings, the movement to Siberia will be reduced to a minimum, or will perhaps disappear completely, and it will only be through internal migration, connected with the equalising effects of the redistribution of landed property, that the Soviet power might be successful in preparing certain areas of land for social utilisation. But in future, a socialist resettlement-policy will play an enormous role. We must keep in mind that a large portion of the arable land that is passing from the landlords to the peasants was already used by the peasants on a rental basis. The area of peasant land-use will expand, therefore, much less than the area of land in their possession. And if we consider the fact that the heroes of the day following the War will be the grain-growers, that agricultural work promises to be enormously profitable given the conditions of the world grain-market, and that the surplus-population of the countryside will no longer be moving to the city, then we see that the peasant will very soon encounter the spectre of land-shortages even if small-scale farming shows signs of improving labour-productivity compared to the pre-revolutionary period. At that point, resettlement will again become inevitable, and in those conditions, the state will be able to organise it on completely new principles, excluding any thought of propagating small-scale farming in outlying districts.

As for a state-monopoly of the grain-trade, consistent implementation of this measure will be of colossal importance for increasing the income from agriculture as a whole, particularly with a monopoly of foreign trade in grain, and will also serve the interests of achieving state-control over agriculture.

This measure: 1) frees the uncoordinated and unorganised producers of grain from a whole swarm of speculators, whose operations in grain have always been the most lucrative; 2) frees up part of the national capital for productive purposes, particularly in agriculture itself; 3) allows significant labour-savings in transportation, through the implementation of planned shipments; 4) concentrates sales in foreign markets and thus makes it possible to realise grain-surpluses in foreign markets in the best possible conditions; 5) prevents any tampering with the quality of Russian grain, something that private grain-merchants did extensively with the effect of lowering the price of Russian grain abroad; 6) opens up broad prospects for state-involvement in the process of agricultural production itself and, in particular, makes it possible to use premiums, price-increases, and so on, to support and develop production of the most profitable types of grain, while also encouraging the most progressive forms of land-use; 7) enables the state to lift the burden of indirect taxation from the poorest strata of the people through adding a mark-up on the price of bread sold to non-grain-producing strata of the urban population.

These, in brief, are all the most important arguments on behalf of the draft agrarian programme that I have proposed.

Now let us consider how practical the proposed programme is within the context of the Russian Revolution, and whether it is really fated to hang in the air, as certain pessimists are suggesting.

This question will lead us to another – the question of the stability of the bloc between the proletariat and the poorest peasants. In this regard, it must be said in advance that when mentioning the poorest peasants, we have in mind all the proletarians in the countryside, together with those peasants who have no horse, plus a significant number of those with only one horse, who are economically compelled to form a bloc with the urban proletariat and who, according to the old census of 1891, include up to five million out of a total of more than ten million households. These rural groups are compelled to go along with the proletariat not only prior to the liquidation of landlord-holdings, but also afterwards, because it is precisely now, in the period following the abolition of the nobility's property, that the next item on their agenda becomes the struggle with the upper stratum of kulaks in the countryside.

The worker and the poorest peasant in the Russian Revolution

In the foreword to his pamphlet *Material on the Agrarian Question*, comrade Lenin speaks of new content in our agitation among the peasantry – of a change in 'the basic line pursued by the worker in addressing the peasant' – which is connected with the way our Party posed the land-question in the course of the Revolution. Of course, changing the character of our agitation would not merit a more fundamental review if it were merely a question of one or two themes in our agitation being altered in response to circumstances, and if we were concerned only with agitational technique. The reality is that the relation we have adopted in practice with the poorest peasants essentially presupposes a review of the mutual relations between the proletariat and the small-holding peasants; and it is necessary to clarify whether this tacit review results from agitational enthusiasm and should therefore be considered 'incomplete' from the point of view of revolutionary Marxism, or whether, on the contrary, it rests on new facts that have come to light during the Revolution and have been created by the Revolution itself.

Comrades will surely agree that there are sufficient grounds for a review; what we must do is give it the proper basis, determine the limits within which it is to occur, and then anticipate all the possible distractions that might occur in the way of unprincipled demagogy or theoretical concessions to spontaneity.

It is obvious that however far-reaching the review of our relations with the poorest peasants may be, it must not alter the very concepts of 'class and class-struggle', for these are well-established in Marxist literature. On the contrary, it is only in light of these concepts that we can come to a better and clearer understanding of the changes occurring in the relation between the working class and the peasantry.

We normally understand the term social class to refer to a group of people who are joined: 1) by a common position in the process of production and, above all, by their relation to ownership of the means of production; 2) by an identical source of income and a common interest concerning distribution of the national income; and 3) by a common opposition between their interests and those of other social groups.

If we are dealing with an already-formed bourgeois society, whose fundamentals have not been affected by pressure coming from the proletarian revolution, then we are perfectly justified – and have been perfectly justified – in considering the proletariat and the peasantry to be different classes that (in most cases) have opposing interests.

Indeed, one of them owns means of production, while the other does not; one sells the products of its farm and is interested in raising their prices, while the other sells only labour-power and is interested in reducing agricultural prices. It is only with respect to a third point that the peasantry's position has always been contradictory. As a class of property-owners, it had interests in common with the big landowners and, together with them, defended the interests of the country against the city. But as a class of *petty* property-owners, who never shared the power of the bourgeoisie and the big landowners, it suffered, like the proletariat, from high taxation, from militarism and all its consequences and, finally, from all the various kinds of exploitation to which small peasants were exposed from the side of big capital and capitalist agriculture.

As a result, there were clearly sufficient economic reasons in capitalist society to explain why the peasantry was politically taken in tow by the possessing classes, why it adopted their ideology, and why, in revolutions where the proletariat intended to follow its own class-line, they played the role of a counter-revolutionary reserve in the hands of the bourgeoisie.

Now let us consider how far relations between the workers and the peasantry have changed during our Revolution, especially from the moment when central state-power passed into the hands of the proletariat and the poor peasants.

Consider the first point in our definition of the concept of class, that is, the relation to ownership of the means of production. Previously, there was a wide gap between the peasant and the worker in this respect. One was an owner of the means of production and an independent economic agent; the other, the proletarian, worked with other people's means of production. But now, with the transfer of power into the hands of the toiling masses of town and country, the worker is changing, with every step on the road to socialism, from a proletarian into a co-owner of the social means of production. The result is to erase and dissolve the fundamental difference that exists between the peasant and the worker in capitalist society. It is true that the worker gradually becomes owner of *social means of production*, while the peasant is no longer in a position to maintain the status of an individual and independent owner of the means of production. His range of 'independence' must contract with every step forwards on the road to organisation of the social economy.

The most important instrument for applying his labour, the land, is already not individual property once it is possessed by the *obshchina*, although it is also not collective on the scale of socialism. Nationalisation of the banks and credit, together with the state-monopoly of the grain-trade and use of agricultural machinery through *artels* – all of these have the effect of pruning the peasant's economic 'independence' and leaving him with very modest room to move.

On the other hand, an ever-growing bond develops between these two classes, insofar as they constitute a single bloc of working people, an alliance of those who create value against all those social groups who live off income that is not associated with labour.

In the circumstances of the Russian Revolution, this bloc of working people has enormous stability that goes far beyond anything seen in any of the revolutions we have known in the West. In our country, there are still many people belonging to that breed of Marxist pedants who affirm the truth of a contradiction between the interests of the peasantry and the proletariat, a truth that applied in the period of classical capitalism but has to be reviewed both in present-day Russia and in any other country that enters the epoch of the break-up of capitalist relations. These woeful Marxists snicker at the 'internationalism' of our soldiers who, in their opinion, are only internationalist as long as the War lasts; and they predict that, after the War, there will inevitably be a peasant counter-revolution. They learned all this from history-textbooks.

These gentlemen refuse to recognise the fact that it is not only the War, but more than anything else the struggle for land, that is driving our small-holding peasantry, that is, two-thirds of our entire peasantry, into an alliance not just with us, but with the entire international proletariat. Our peasantry is *economically* interested in the world proletarian revolution. This is obvious in the data showing the indebtedness of private agriculture to the banks. As early as 1915, this indebtedness amounted to three and a half billion roubles. During the War, the debts continued to grow, especially during the interval when the coalition-government temporarily suspended the law against land-transactions and lines of the gentry thronged to the banks in a mad rush to re-mortgage their land. If the indebtedness of private landholders to the banks is calculated in terms of the present value of our rouble, it must come to a total of approximately thirty billion.[8]

At the same time, we must keep in mind that the shares of our banks, including the land-banks, are quoted on all the European exchanges, and the 'interest' of foreign banks in the value of our banks is so great that most Russian banks can be viewed as mere agents of their elder brothers abroad. As a result, the transfer of the land to the peasants, without payment, represents a severe blow to the whole European bourse and brings our peasantry into a collision with the entire capitalist class of the West; and in this sense, every peasant from Orel or Kursk who is interested in the landlord's land, necessarily becomes an 'internationalist'.

We must also take into account the fact that our enormous state-debts can only be liquidated, for the most part, if there is a social revolution in the West; and if they are not liquidated in this way, it is mainly the peasantry, as the largest section of our population, that will have to pay them out of their own meagre incomes.

To put it crudely, therefore, the interest of our peasantry in the world proletarian revolution amounts to tens of billions of roubles. And since this sum could not possibly be raised even by a most punitive tax on the wages of our workers, it follows that the peasantry does not have, and objectively cannot have, any other way out of the existing situation except through an alliance and joint struggle, together with the proletariat, against world-capital.

Rather than showing any prospect for counter-revolution, these data demonstrate how deeply rooted is our worker-peasant Revolution, and it is only in this light that we can understand the failure of all the bourgeoisie's provocations aimed at turning the peasantry against the proletariat.

These attempts will also fail in future, so long as they speculate on a peasant counter-revolution under the leadership of the bourgeois class. Every counter-revolution in the West that involved participation by the peasantry took place in the presence of an economically powerful big bourgeoisie. With the transfer

---

8. This does not mean, of course, that in the event of paying off the debt it would be done with roubles at their old value, rather than in their current depreciated state.

of central power into the hands of the proletarian-peasant bloc, this condition no longer exists in our country.

Pseudo-Marxists, trying to frighten us with being trampled by a peasant counter-revolution, and at the same time protesting from a 'scientific-financial' point of view against our nationalisation of the banks, evidently do not understand the simple fact that by implementing these measures we reduce by half the possibility of any peasant counter-revolution led and organised by large-scale capital, assuming that such a possibility can exist in view of the above-mentioned peculiarities of our Revolution.

We have no intention, however, of proclaiming any complete harmony of interests between the Russian peasant and the worker. S-R assertions to this effect, proclaimed in absolute terms, are disproved by the very fact that their own party exists as a party mainly of the peasants. There does remain a contradiction of interests between the peasantry and the proletariat on the question of distribution of national income. Each class, quite naturally, wants to place a higher value on its own labour. In terms of the peasants, this takes the form of a struggle for higher grain-prices (not on the part of the entire peasantry, only of those with grain to sell), a struggle for lower prices on manufactured goods, attempts to evade state-taxes and so forth. In the case of the workers, we see the struggle to raise wages and shorten the working day. After the War, there will be a particularly serious contradiction between peasant- and worker-interests on the question of customs-duties on foreign goods, the removal of which will threaten the workers with terrible unemployment.

It is difficult to foresee what forms this class-struggle will take between the proletariat and peasantry on questions of income-distribution. There are reasons to expect that it will most likely have beneficial consequences in terms of the country's economic development as a whole. Under pressure from the peasantry, the worker will have to move beyond the backward technology and low labour-productivity that we see in our country by comparison with the West. The worker will be interested in raising the intensity of labour and improving the techniques of production in order to retain his economic gains without damaging the peasant, and also for the sake of developing the country's productive forces. On the other hand, he will also be interested in raising his real wages by reducing the price of bread, something that can only occur, if peasant-incomes are not to be reduced, on the basis of the socialisation of agriculture. In this regard, his pressure on the peasantry can have beneficial consequences in terms of agricultural progress. For these reasons, it may happen that a solution will take the form of both the peasantry and the proletariat looking for ways to increase their incomes not by moving values from the pockets of one class into those of the other, but rather by a general increase of labour-productivity throughout the entire country.

As a consequence, the contradictory interests that we have been considering are not objectively insurmountable to the extent that one class must strive for political dictatorship in order to suppress and economically exploit the other.

In any case, this contradiction, so long as the Revolution lasts, will be gradually overcome within the bloc of working people and will not disrupt that bloc as such, because it will be overshadowed by a far deeper and more severe contradiction between this bloc, on the one side, and world-capital on the other, with the result that the forces of unity will always be more powerful than tendencies of division.

In the event that our Revolution proves victorious (which presupposes, of course, that there will also be a victorious revolution in the West), it is true that the unifying cement, created by the conditions of a joint struggle against world-capital, will weaken, and conflicts of interest between the proletariat and peasantry over the distribution of national income will become more obvious and acute. But in addition to the fact that a peasant-movement cannot lead to counter-revolution on this basis without an economically dominant bourgeoisie, the accession to power by the proletariat and peasantry also creates entirely new possibilities for avoiding an acute class-struggle on these grounds. In capitalist society, the question of national income-distribution is decided through spontaneous class-struggle and the balance of power between the opposing classes. This way of resolving the matter is by no means inevitable in a society that finds itself on the road of socialist reconstruction, where it is possible to deal with income-distribution through a consciously implemented plan on the basis of a class-agreement. This is not the place to discuss how such a plan can be implemented without weakening the stimulus for developing the productive forces, but it is enough to point out that, in essence, we have already entered upon this road. The introduction of fixed prices on grain and industrial products, together with a minimum-wage, is essentially the first step towards conscious distribution of the national income. Because of the rapid decline of the rouble, these efforts have not fully achieved their goal, but that is a different question. A plan for the conscious distribution of national income, in conditions of agreement between classes that are represented by their parties and economic organisations, will be achievable for us in much more realistic form given certain necessary preconditions: these include a fundamental reform of the monetary system, a monopoly of the grain-trade, a monopoly of all foreign trade (including both exports and imports), the fixing of wages and minimal norms of output, and so on.

Of course, the effort to create a plan for conscious distribution of the national income does not preclude struggle between the sides over the principles of the plan itself, but that kind of struggle will be much more organised and systematic, and it will be easier to avoid the kinds of clashes in which the game itself will not be worth the candle, or in which there will be no assurance of victory for the side that is forcing the issue once all the conditions are taken into account.

Thus far, there has been an enormous effort to reach agreement between the proletariat and the peasantry on economic issues. At every congress of workers' and peasants' deputies, whenever the necessity arose, polemics between the two sides have been extremely acute and tense, but in the final analysis both have always come to the conclusion that there is no sense in the labouring classes tearing out each other's throats over the division of toilers' pennies, and a compromise-resolution has been unanimously agreed.

In the conditions of the Russian Revolution, there is only one circumstance in which a wide-based rural counter-revolutionary movement might occur against the proletariat. This might occur if *both the proletariat and the small-holding peasants*, acting together as a close bloc, are defeated by a third force, that is, by world-capital, which is supported within Russia by the bourgeois classes and the upper stratum of kulaks in the countryside.

That kind of defeat would lead to the restoration of the old economic positions of the bourgeois class, which the October Revolution has taken from them, and to a collapse of the proletarian-peasant bloc as a result of the most numerous element in the countryside, the middle-peasants, going over to the side of the peasant-bourgeoisie and politically isolating the proletarian forces of town and country.

The socio-economic basis for such a collapse would be an attempt by the middle-peasantry, after a losing campaign, to impose the greatest material costs of defeat on its former partner in the struggle. But it must be obvious to everyone that a peasant counter-revolution arising in these conditions would be the *consequence* of defeat, and not *its cause*.

Of course, the counter-revolutionary strata of the peasantry are not currently limited to the kulaks and shopkeepers or generally to a thin upper stratum in the countryside. The basis for counter-revolution among the peasantry has expanded to include part (a small part) of the middle-peasantry who have already succeeded in dividing up the landlords' livestock and inventory, together with the state-forests and that portion of the land that has fallen into their *de facto* possession during the months of Revolution, to an extent that exceeds all 'consumer'-norms or any other norms. This element of the peasantry is thirsting for the kind of order that would secure its acquisitions. It is opposed to any 'review' of what has occurred, and it is opposed to the Revolution because the Revolution is associated with instability in terms of land- and property-relations and does not provide any guarantee against unexpected and unpleasant surprises on that score.

But this makes the position of the peasant-poor all the more hopeless, for the poor can only realise all the opportunities created for them by the Revolution through alliance with the proletariat.

Thus far, the proletarian-peasant bloc has been consistently stable. It was stable during the compromising period of our Revolution, when it was more broadly based among the peasantry, and it is even more stable now that the well-to-do strata in the countryside have been excluded from the 'peasant-curia'. We have seen many examples in history of the proletariat and peasantry being used by the bourgeois classes, either in the form of 'civil peace' and 'national' unity during the imperialist War, or else in other ways, but this is the very first instance in world-history of a union of the proletariat and the poorest peasants being formed on the basis of implacable struggle against the entire bourgeois world. The political expression of this alliance in Russia is the bloc between the Bolshevik Party and the Party of Left Socialist-Revolutionaries, and the extraordinary significance of this alliance is that, for the very first time, the masses of the peasantry, numbering in the millions, have been *compelled* by all the international circumstances in which our Revolution is occurring to play the part of an *active* force for socialist transformation.

But these masses have little understanding of the final goals of the struggle into which they have been drawn, or of the new victories they have already won. It is of the greatest importance to demand from a political party of these masses that it undertake real work to guide the consciousness of the labouring peasantry in a direction that corresponds with the grandiose tasks and successes associated with this struggle. Unfortunately, however, the Left Socialist-Revolutionaries have evidently failed to realise that it is a profound misunderstanding on their part to insist, during a period of socialist transformation, on implementing a programme of 'socialisation of the land'; that is, the kind of programme in which the past prevails over the future, a programme that constantly lags behind the demands of the moment and, for exactly that reason, is most acceptable even to such active fighters against the October Revolution as the Messrs. Rudnevs[9] and the like.

Once we entered the period of combat against world-capital, once we confronted the bourgeois system with socialism, and once we found ourselves with no possible way out of the terrible consequences of the World-War other than socialism, it then turned out that whatever concessions we must make to the past *in practice*, under pressure from the unconscious masses, the agricultural programme of any real socialist can only be socialist reconstruction of the agricultural economy. Let no-one tell us that this can only be an immediate goal

---

9. [Vadim Viktorovich Rudnev (1874(9?)–1940) was a member of the Socialist-Revolutionary Party and a 'defencist' during the War. Following the February Revolution, he supported the Kerensky government. As a member of the S-R Central Committee, he headed that party's fraction in the Constituent Assembly. When the Constituent Assembly was dispersed in January 1918, Rudnev fled to the south of Russia and emigrated to Paris in 1919.]

for tomorrow. The issue will not be decided tomorrow. The question of what space we will create for social farming during the period of the break-up of land-relations in the countryside is being decided today. The struggle is being waged today between 'socialisation of the land' (with inverted commas) and genuine socialisation of the land, which means the transfer of all land in the country into the possession of the state of the toilers.

Nevertheless, there seems to be virtually no hope, at the present moment, that the Left Socialist-Revolutionaries will be capable of remaking their programme for 'socialisation of the land' into a genuinely socialist programme. This was demonstrated by the position that representatives of the Left S-Rs took on the land-question at the Third All-Russian Congress of Soviets, when even posing the question of a socialist reconstruction of agriculture as an immediate party-task in the countryside found no supporters, and when all such discussions were regarded not as a practical matter, but merely as expressions of an evil Bolshevik tone.

The following considerations will convince the reader of this conclusion.

'Socialisation of the land' in practice

The draft fundamental law on the land, which was presented to the Third All-Russian Congress by People's Commissar of Agriculture, comrade Kolegayev,[10] and was accepted in principle as the basis for the 19 articles of the first section, contained such odious points from the standpoint of a genuinely socialist land-programme that it is absolutely imperative to mention them here.

Item 3 of the general provisions of the law (Section I) is formulated as follows: 'The right to use of the land belongs only to the person who cultivates it with his own labour'.

It is clear to everyone that this kind of formulation is unacceptable from a socialist point of view. It completely overlooks the primary right of the state of the toilers to use the land in the interest of organising and developing socialist agriculture. It is apparent from Article 13 that this is not just some unfortunate formulation but is, instead, a declaration of the rights of small-scale farming. Article 13 says: 'Apart from personal labour, the right to use of agricultural land, as an exception to the general rule, includes the following: in cases where organs of local self-government (the *zemstvos*) or state-organs (the land-committees) find it necessary to create farms or exemplary fields for purposes of improving crops, they may make use of specific parts of the land-reserve (formerly belonging to

---

10. [Andrei Lukich Kolegayev (1887–1937) was a Left S-R and Commissar of Agriculture from December 1917 to March 1918. He broke with the Left S-Rs and joined the Bolsheviks in November 1918.]

monasteries, the treasury, appanages, the cabinet, and landlords) and work them with hired labour'.

Accordingly, the land-law, prepared by a representative of a party that considers itself to be socialist, graciously authorises – as an 'exception to the general rule' – state-use of the land in the interests of socialism in agriculture.

The law makes no mention whatsoever of avoiding the splintering of large-scale capitalist farms into tiny plots, or of putting them at the disposal of soviets of farm-labourers' deputies under state-control, such as has been done already in Estonia, Latvia and some parts of Russia. On the contrary, Article 22 of the third section says that land will be given, in the first place, to the local agricultural population, then to newly arriving agricultural settlers, with local farm-labourers only coming third. Even the terminology needs to be scrutinised. It appears that farm-labourers are not part of the agricultural population, but just some special kind of lower species in the countryside. What this point really means is that capitalist estates will be broken up to satisfy the land-requirements of local small-holding peasants; the remainder will go to newly-arriving small farmers; and farm-labourers will be as free as the birds to fly off to faraway places. And as a small landholder would understandably calculate, it will be all the easier for them to fly off if they have no inventory to carry with them...

Article 20 of Section II allows for state-use of the land only for cultural and educational purposes, not for social-economic ones. The state is assigned a role as propagandist on behalf of social farming, but it has no role as a powerful factor in the economic reconstruction of agriculture on the basis of social principles.

The character of the law's proposal on resettlement-policy is clearly apparent in Article 35 of Section VII, which says: 'For resettlement of farmers in new localities, *otrub*-holdings will be created'. A socialist state power that breeds small *otrub*-farms – even Stolypin would approve of such a resettlement-policy.[11]

With the assent of all citizens of the *obshchina*, those who wish to do so are to have the right to establish an *otrub* – but at the same time, it never entered the mind of the law's author to protect the rights of those members of the *obshchina* who may prefer, even without the assent of a majority of stagnant-minded supporters of small-holding farms, to begin working their share of the land on an *artel*-basis.

---

11. [Peter Arkad'evich Stolypin's agrarian policy aimed to establish a class of small property-owners by giving the peasant the right to leave the rural community (the *obshchina*) and to establish a single private holding, an *otrub* farm, that would be equivalent to the strips of land he had previously been allotted within the *obshchina*. If the peasant moved his domicile to the new holding, the result was a *khutor*, a fully-detached farmstead. By the end of 1916, some twenty percent of peasant-households had titles to their land, but only half that number had received consolidated plots. Another important element of the Stolypin reforms was a policy of resettling peasants from the central part of the country to its perimeter, including Siberia, Central Asia, and the North Caucasus.]

Article 19 of Section I provides for a state-monopoly only of the foreign trade in grain, and thus it tacitly implies that there is no need for a state-monopoly of the domestic grain-trade. This is an enormous step backwards by comparison with the current state of affairs. However imperfect our existing state grain-monopoly may be, and however unpopular it may be precisely among the peasants, everyone understands that all of its negative attributes are not due to the monopoly as such, but rather have been caused by the general circumstances of the country's economic disorganisation connected with the consequences of the War.

The parts of the law dealing with the rights of land-committees are also formulated in a completely unsatisfactory way, treating them merely as technical organs under the local soviets and the central Soviet power.

I have listed here only the most unacceptable and dangerous points in the Left Socialist-Revolutionaries' draft of land-legislation.

This law will have to be examined in more detail at our party-congress, where the amendments will have to be made that we consider minimally necessary in order that our representatives, speaking for a party that is changing neither the essentials of its agrarian programme nor the elementary principles of socialism, might vote in favour of the law in the Central Executive Committee of the Soviets.

No. 2
E.A. Preobrazhensky's Book *Anarchism and Communism*[1]

1918

Translated from the Greek language, the word 'anarchy' means 'without any ruler'. Anarchists, therefore, are people who strive for the kind of social order in which there will be neither rulers nor coercion, only the reign of total freedom.

Well then, a reader will ask, do Bolshevik-communists really think that life with coercion, regardless of its source, is better than total freedom?

No, reply the communists. Total freedom for the person and for human society is better than a life in which freedom is curtailed or anyone is coerced to act against his own will. But if one were to ask a bourgeois liberal, for example, what is the ultimate ideal of the liberal party, the liberal would also say that total freedom of the person and of all mankind is the most precious goal for which to struggle. In terms of the wish for 'total freedom', it seems that there is no way of distinguishing between a communist and an anarchist; indeed, the bourgeois liberal would have to be added to the same group, along with any other people, whether or not they belong to a party, who have a sound understanding of the benefits of freedom as compared with necessity and coercion.

This means we have to look elsewhere to find the main difference between anarchists and communists.

---

1. [Preobrazhensky 1918b.]

We might begin with the fact that anarchists are continuously repeating in their brochures, newspapers and speeches that they oppose any and all coercion along with any state-power as an organ of violence. If we accept this statement, then we have to ask the anarchist this question: What if the toiling masses are in control of state-power and use it to suppress their enemies? Are you also against that kind of power?

In this case, we will get different answers from the anarchists themselves. Some will say: 'We do not oppose such power as long as it fulfils tasks that benefit the toiling masses'. Others will reply: 'We are against all rulers and all authority, and we seek to destroy it in all circumstances'.

Here, we have a fundamental difference between Bolshevik-communists and anarchists concerning the attitude towards the state – not so much towards the state in general, as we shall see later, but towards the commune-state and rule by the workers and peasants.

We have to consider just what the state is and how it is regarded by communists. That the state is an organ of force and coercion is obvious to everyone who has faced the tax-collector, to every peasant whose samovar and cow have been sold for non-payment of taxes, and to every worker who has been locked up or shot for striking against capital. Even the bourgeoisie, whose banks, luxurious homes, factories and capital have been taken against their will by the Soviet authorities – even they, to their misfortune, now know that the state is an organ of compulsion.

The whole question is: Whose interests are served by organised force? Who controls these organs of compulsion? And how does it happen that not only all counter-revolutionaries and the entire bourgeoisie oppose the state-power of the workers and peasants, but also the anarchists, who, in this respect, turn out to be their allies?

The autocratic-landlord state

At one time, there was no state. That was a time when there were also no classes, when people were not divided into rich and poor, into those who lived by their own labour and those who exploited the labour of others. It is no coincidence that there was no state when people were not yet separated into classes. When, out of the primitive agricultural commune, in which all were equal, there began to emerge an upper stratum of the well-to-do; when this upper stratum headed the community's armed forces in time of war against its neighbours and was able to expand its possessions by plundering defeated peoples and then by plundering its own people – that is when the ground was prepared for the emergence of a state. The esteemed barons, counts and princes, as military leaders of the community and major landowners, began to create the institutions that represented the nucleus of a state. The prince became judge of his fellow tribesmen and, in his capacity as judge, he protected first and foremost his own interests and privileges against encroachment by his faithful followers. That was the origin of class-justice.

The rulings of this judge were left to his underlings to implement, and that was the origin of the police.

In the event of war, or in order to suppress major unrest within his own territory, the prince called upon his armed retinue. That was the origin of the soldiery that was to come.

Having accepted 'Christianity' and placated the representatives of religion with gifts and lands, the prince or count also came to dispose of the spiritual police and could support his exploitation through relying not merely on the sword and the whip, but also on the cross and the Gospel. This was the beginning of the merger of Church and state, which essentially meant conversion of the Church into an instrument of the ruling class for the spiritual enslavement of the people.

When the mutual struggle between different counts, barons and princes led to victory of the strongest, and when the strongest took the title of great prince, king or emperor and made himself supreme head of the country, then the rudiments of a state developed into a genuine and vast monarchical state. The barons, who had hitherto ruled over the peasants in their own districts, now joined with other barons, counts and princes, and together they clustered around the throne of the 'revered monarch', jointly ruling over the people, rather than each controlling his own locality. Out of this pooling of power by several minor boyars, barons and princes, together with the great landowners, the nobility established its power as an entire class of landed proprietors and aristocrats. The result was an entire joint-stock company of rulers united against the people, and every participant, upon entering this alliance, protected himself and was assured of support from all the other members of his class.

Now the prince or baron no longer made an appearance on his porch to judge the case against a peasant for destroying baronial property, non-payment of taxes or the like. Such matters were left to judges appointed by the state, that is, by the whole alliance of nobles and princes. When it came to enforcing the sentence and punishing a landless peasant who objected to being fleeced, this was left not to the old assistants and body-guards of the baron, but rather to the state-police, that is, to those who served the entire class of nobles and princes. As for the monarch, he considered himself an autocratic ruler, and in fact protected the autocratic rule of the landowners over all the rest of the people. This smokescreen was useful to the nobles, for it allowed the monarch to play the role of a just ruler before whom all were equal. He occasionally punished one-or-another upstart baron, in a modest show of justice, in order that the entire class of nobles might all the more easily extract millions in the form of rents, state-taxes and so on.

With this kind of noble-alliance, the class of plunderers clearly became stronger, while the toiling masses were dispersed and disorganised, rendering hopeless any sporadic uprisings by the oppressed. Previously, an individual peasant might have been protected by all the other peasants of the county against the violence of a count or baron; the baron's bodyguards might have been unable to put down the unrest, such that occasionally the barons and princes were driven out of the villages and towns, resulting in the creation of free towns and localities. Now this was impossible. If, for example, a peasant's cow trampled a noble's wheat, the court would levy a fine against him. If the peasant could not pay, or if he thought the fine was unjust, the court-bailiff would sell the peasant's cow to pay the fine. If the peasant resisted, the police would arrest him. If the whole village or rural district prevented the arrest, then more police or troops would arrive. If the entire district, province and region rose up, then the state of the nobles would send all available troops and police to put down the rising, and ultimately, at a cost of thousands of dead and wounded and millions in losses, they would compel the seditious peasant to pay a rouble-fine for the damage. Even in the slightest of matters, the entire state of the nobles would bristle with bayonets in total support of every individual noble against the peasant.

In this way, the organisation of the nobility into an autocratic state enormously strengthened this class, markedly weakened the toiling masses, and made them defenceless in the face of their plunderers.

All of this leads to two conclusions.

The first and most important is that the state, generally speaking, arises when the people are divided into classes, when property makes its appearance, when some own the property while others have nothing, when the entire class of owners has to defend this property, when a privileged class appears and has to defend its privileges against the ordinary people, and when the wealthy and noble-class must not only protect its wealth and privileges, but even extend them at the expense of the toiling people.

The second conclusion is that it is not the state that initiates the division of the people into classes or creates inequality between people and the exploitation of some by others; on the contrary, it is the emergence of classes and economic inequality that gives rise to the state as the organisation of the exploiters. But once it has appeared, the state strengthens the oppressing classes and even further intensifies economic inequality, the basis on which it arose.

The bourgeois state

But the state of the autocrat and the nobles (commonly called the feudal state) does not last forever, and the same holds for the economic force of the gentry's large-scale land-ownership on which it is built. Gradually, within the midst of the nobles' state, the class of the commercial and industrial bourgeoisie emerges and grows. Becoming greedier for pleasures and luxuries, the nobility begins to decline and the bourgeoisie starts to buy up landlords' properties. The bourgeoisie has control of the whole of industry, commerce, and even part of agriculture. It looks with envy at the incomes that the noble-class receives from land-rents, from various obligations of the peasant-serfs, and especially from government-taxes that are dispersed to the pockets of the nobility who rule the country. The bourgeoisie has to take the sources of income from the nobility and convert them into sources for extracting capital. In order to do so, to avoid being fleeced by the taxes and so forth levied by the gentry's state, and to transform the state to suit the capitalist mode of plunder rather than that of the nobility, the bourgeoisie must drive from power its competitor in stealing from the toiling people. This is accomplished through bourgeois revolutions that end either in the complete seizure of power by the bourgeois class, or else in a deal between the bourgeoisie and the nobility. In one way or another, the new state accommodates the interests of capital and capital-accumulation and protects it against any encroachments by the toiling masses.

From the point of view of the oppressed class, the proletariat, the bourgeois state does not differ essentially from the state of the autocrat and the nobility. Just as moving a captured bird from a small cage to a larger one does not mean its freedom, so, in the case of the working class, replacement of the autocratic-gentry state by the bourgeois state amounts only to a larger cage, not its elimination.

Consider, first, the differences between these two types of state. With the autocratic state of the nobles, it is the latter who rule the country, covering themselves up with the cloak of a monarch who supposedly stands above all classes and is equally benevolent towards all. The labouring masses must do what they are ordered to do without any questions. Here, the violence of a small group of plundering aristocrats against the majority of the toilers is perfectly obvious, undisguised, direct and brutal.

Under the bourgeoisie, on the contrary, the system of coercion imposed by the wealthy minority upon the majority of the people is wonderfully disguised, especially where state-power is focused in the hands of a parliament elected on the basis of universal suffrage or nearly-universal suffrage. In terms of managing its affairs in 'controlling' the toilers, the modern bourgeoisie does much better than the nobility, which hides behind goons and the police-superintendent.

Here, force is disguised by the appearance of formal freedom, just as the exploitation of the worker by capital is disguised in the economy. With serfdom, for instance, the peasant is directly compelled to work, let us say, three days a week for the nobleman, and it is perfectly obvious to everyone that the peasant owes half of his labour to the parasitic landlord. Under capitalism, the worker may 'freely' choose either to starve to death or to go and work for the capitalist at whatever wage the capitalist specifies. Here, the widespread fantasy of freedom masks not only the fact of exploitation, but also the portion of his labour that the worker contributes to the capitalist as unpaid labour, just like that of the serf for the landlord. The same is true of organised violence and the way in which it is manifested, or better, concealed in bourgeois society. Is it clear that parliament, elected by the majority of the people, is ultimately an organ that facilitates the suppression of the majority of toilers by a handful of capitalists? It is not so easy to make this clear, and only life itself teaches the working class to understand the whole cunning mechanism of capitalism and to evaluate properly the way in which the state answers to the interests and requirements of triumphant capital.

In bourgeois society, the supreme power belongs to parliament. Whereas in the autocratic-gentry system workers and peasants are simply ordered about and, in the case of opposition, are peremptorily seized by the scruff of the neck, here even the toiling classes are asked once every three or four years whom they wish to elect to parliament.

Just think of the honour, and of how difficult it is, then, to resist the temptation to think of oneself seriously as a free man!

True, the toilers are only consulted in an election every four years because everyone knows how they will answer. Everyone knows the peasants will choose either a landlord, a priest, or an 'enlightened' kulak, just as they have always done thus far in the West. And it is common knowledge that the workers send to parliament either lawyers who pretend to be socialists or else social-patriots and hangers-on of the bourgeoisie such as the Scheidemanns, and that only a minority of the proletariat will give their votes to genuinely revolutionary socialists.

The bourgeoisie knows all of this; and instead of directly employing violence against the masses or imposing a government from above, they count on the masses themselves to elect their own chiefs to whip them.

If there is any danger that ineffectual socialists might be in the majority, even if they are merely compromisers with the bourgeoisie, then the bourgeoisie has no misgivings about abolishing universal suffrage, as in the case of Saxony, or dispersing an inconvenient parliament, as Kerensky did with Finland's *Sejm*. In place of universal suffrage, in such circumstances a law is introduced to restrict the suffrage to those with deep pockets and property in general. The whole lie and fraud about parliament expressing the will of the people then vanishes like smoke. Parliament exists and is retained by the bourgeoisie only so long as it fully expresses the will of the bourgeoisie. If the right to vote now goes only to property-owners, and if the bourgeoisie thereby declares that power in capitalist society belongs to the deepest pockets, that does not mean that things are any different even when there is universal suffrage. Universal suffrage simply means that conditions have not yet compelled the bourgeoisie to admit that this is the case.

In reality, universal suffrage is rarely found even today in bourgeois society. After defeating the gentry or entering into a deal with them, the bourgeoisie considers even the present-day forgeries of universal suffrage to be a risky or completely redundant experiment. But later, the bourgeoisie becomes convinced that extending the right to vote to the toiling classes represents no threat and that the masses, who are in servitude to capital, can boldly be given the right every three or four years to choose between the lash and the whip, should they try to achieve this right by launching a struggle for electoral reform.

It is only in the years when the popular masses are awakening, in a pre-revolutionary period, that the bourgeoisie again becomes aware of its weakness and is compelled to do away with the democratic adornments of its state – either to convert parliament into an impotent talking shop, or else to put down the popular masses with the direct use of force.

In general terms, the bourgeoisie needs parliament not only to deceive the people (so long as it can serve that purpose), but also for several other reasons. The first is to demonstrate that the majority of the people oppose the gentry-class and thus to drive its former enemy, the landed aristocracy, over to the right-wing in parliament. And a second reason why parliament is important to the bourgeoisie is to serve as a political bourse for deals between the different groups of the propertied classes of capitalist society.

Indeed, the bourgeoisie is only united when it takes action against the proletariat.

Within the bourgeoisie itself, there are different groups with different interests: the financial bourgeoisie (who own the banks), the big industrial bourgeoisie, the middle-bourgeoisie, and that part of the petty bourgeoisie who are not close to the proletariat.

In face of their common enemy, the majority of the toiling and exploited people, it is important for all these groups not to allow their disputes to reach the point of an open fight, but to confine their struggle to parliamentary deal-making. Finally, parliament is a splendid means for diverting the attention of the masses from the predatory policy of the capitalist sharks, who are doing their real work of plundering the people beyond its walls while managing the majority in parliament as puppets. At the same time as the real work of finalising and implementing various robbers' plans is done outside of parliament, the unconscious masses listen with mouths-agape to the chatter of various orators in the parliamentary talking shop, thinking that the 'will of the people' is being accomplished there. This self-deception is reinforced all the more by the fact that within parliament the various Scheidemanns and other social-scoundrels play the part of implacable opponents of capital, and it seems to workers that their interests are being protected there. It is only when a real proletarian attack on capital begins, as happened with us in October, that the whole parliamentary fraud disintegrates and the rouge disappears from the faces of all the false socialists.

Accordingly, the difference between the gentry's state and the bourgeois state is simply that in the bourgeois state, violence against the masses of the people is better hidden.

Under the domination of the gentry and the autocracy, the workers and peasants are directly grabbed by the scruff of their necks while their pockets are turned inside-out – without all the talk – whereas in bourgeois parliamentarism they can 'express their agreement' with this operation.

The similarity between the two states lies in the fact that, apart from the upper layer of government (in one case, the hereditary monarch, in the other, an elected parliament), all the rest of the mechanism of rule, or to speak more correctly, of oppression, remains exactly the same.

The courts remain, and only the laws by which they judge are revised in the interests of capital.

The police and gendarmerie remain, only now they act in the spirit of their new masters.

The standing army remains, but the commanding staff is gradually, even if not in all cases, renovated with bourgeois officers and generals.

In the great majority of cases, the state-church remains, acting as the spiritual gendarme of capital and speedily adjusting to its demands. Even if the capitalists consider religion redundant for themselves, they use it quite successfully among the people.

The entire horde of bureaucratic appointees-from-above remains.

Secret diplomacy remains, the only difference being that foreign policy is conducted not so much in the personal interest of one or the other monarch as in the interest of the most influential groups of the bourgeoisie. The consequence is that war is declared in a bourgeois state, just as in the case of autocracy, without the consent of the people; and the greatest violence inflicted upon the millions of toilers, the violence of war, is caused by a small handful of capitalists using the entire bourgeois apparatus of power.

All of these similarities between the gentry-state and the bourgeois state are very easily explained. Each of them represents an apparatus for the oppression of the vast majority of the people by an insignificant minority. In any other circumstances, this oppression would not be necessary. This is why the bourgeoisie, understanding its own interests, asks which is more costly, parliament or the police, and the answer is always the police. Everyone will agree, for example, that in France the whole apparatus for oppressing the masses and supporting the bourgeois order under the Republic is much better suited to the protection of capital than it was to protecting the landed aristocracy and the priesthood prior to the Revolution. If the unemployed of today do not pay the landlord's rent for their apartment, then the entire judicial, police – and, if necessary, military – apparatus of power will be put into action in order to assure to the suffering bourgeois the inviolability of his property. It is easier for the worker, if he is supported by his unemployed comrades, to achieve an entire social revolution, than it is to repeal a penalty imposed by the judge.

Accordingly, the bourgeois state represents organised violence by the bourgeois class against the toiling masses. For the liberal bourgeois, there is a vast difference between the autocratic-gentry state and the bourgeois-parliamentary state. But for the worker, this difference can be expressed in just a few words: the cage is more spacious, the lash is not so harsh, and both are measured in accordance with the constitution.[2]

The proletarian state (I)

We have seen that the autocratic-gentry state is essentially the class of the nobility organised on the scale of the state. Beginning as the only strong and coherent military force, it later acquires the ability to make the toiling millions into its own instrument and comes to control enormous forces of oppression in the form of the police and standing army. The gentry-state is a sentry that stands on guard for the privileges of the nobility and defends them against any disturbance on the part of the toiling and exploited people, often using the people themselves for this purpose.

As for the bourgeois state, it is also an instrument for suppressing the toiling masses, but now in the interest of capital and the gentry, whose rights have been equalised with those of the entire bourgeoisie.

This apparatus, likewise, serves the interest of a minority, suppressing the resistance of the enormous majority of the population.

---

2. Even so, the party of the proletariat has always taken into account the difference between a less spacious and a more spacious cage: when the struggle was occurring between the monarchy and bourgeois parliamentarism, it supported bourgeois parliamentarism against the monarchy and made use of the parliamentary struggle, in order later to go beyond parliamentarism to the dictatorship of the proletariat and the poorest peasantry.

Now let us consider the proletarian state and how it differs from the previous two forms of state that belong to the plunderers and exploiters.

We will look at how the proletarian state emerges, how it is constructed, what its tasks are, and when this state might come to an end.

The proletarian state originates as a result of the victorious workers' revolution. The different elements of the proletariat, acting separately against the bourgeois state, inevitably meet with defeat because the bourgeois class, although it is an insignificant force on its own by comparison with the millions of the working masses, turns out to be strong enough to smash these detachments one-by-one with the help of the state-apparatus. This is very important to remember, for this fact alone – the enormous superiority of a class's state-organisation in the struggle against an opposing class – fundamentally repudiates all anarchist ravings concerning a struggle against the enemy by fighting squads that are not bound together by common discipline and led from a single centre with a single plan. If our worker-peasant October Revolution defeated bourgeois power in Russia, it is only because the proletariat displayed the utmost organisation and met the state-alliance of the bourgeois class with its own forces that were also organised on a state-wide scale in the form of the soviets and the all-Russian Bolshevik Party.

The bourgeois organisation clashed with proletarian organisation, and the latter was victorious.

The proletarian state, therefore, originates in the party that leads its struggle for power and in the mass-organisations of the proletariat, whose task from the outset is to bring self-control to the proletariat; that is, to help forge it into a class with definite goals and to subordinate every action by its different groups to those goals. When the proletariat, once unified as a class-determined fighting unit, defeats the bourgeoisie and takes power, then all of its class-organisations are simultaneously transformed into state-organisations.

This means that the soviets, as organs for proletarian self-unification, are transformed into organs to subordinate all other classes and groups in the country to proletarian power.

We see, therefore, that the proletarian state originates in battle on the fields of class-struggle, and we shall further find that it remains over time as the fighting organisation of the proletariat.

Now let us consider just what differentiates the proletarian state from the autocratic-gentry state and the bourgeois state, and how this difference in terms of goals is reflected in the very structure of proletarian state-power.

The gentry concentrates state-power in its own hands in order to protect its privileges as a class of big landowners, that is, its incomes and its domination over the masses.

The bourgeoisie seizes power after the bourgeois revolution in order to protect the privileges of capital and to help it in squeezing the greatest possible amount of unpaid labour from the working class.

Each of these states facilitates the plunder of the toiling masses and their suppression by a small handful of exploiters.

The proletarian state serves exactly the opposite purpose. Its task is to achieve what the Revolution cannot yet achieve, something that takes a certain period of time: namely, to take from the bourgeoisie, once and for all, the means of production, the factories and plants; to eliminate the division of society into classes; to end the exploitation of man by man; to introduce labour as a duty and to convert the whole of society into a single labour-army of comradely workers.

Before it can turn to speedy realisation of this programme, however, the proletarian state must still break the opposition of the property-owning classes. The propertied classes are only driven from power after a stubborn struggle, and once they are defeated in the centres, they provoke uprisings in different parts of the country. It has taken almost half a year for the proletarian power in Russia to suppress the main sites of counter-revolution on the Don, in the Urals region and in Siberia, and even in the seventh month of this struggle, the work has yet to be completed.

The proletarian state, therefore, is fundamentally different from the bourgeois-gentry types of state.

Whereas the bourgeois and autocratic states defend the privileges of the ruling classes, the goal of the proletarian state is to eliminate all privileges, all inequality and all exploitation. Once the proletariat takes power, it uses it not to transform itself into an oppressor and exploiter of other classes of the population, but to eliminate in future every form of exploitation in order to eliminate all classes and even the possibility of their emergence.

To eliminate classes, however, means eliminating the causes that lead to emergence of the state. In this sense, one can say that if communism is destined in general to triumph, the proletarian state is the final form of all possible states.

The proletarian state is the form of state in which the state in general dies away, being transformed from an organisation of a minority into the organisation of the toiling majority.

But does it make any sense, in that case, to speak of Soviet power as state-power?

Indeed, it does and it must.

Every state is an organisation of violence, and the proletarian state is also an organisation of violence.

But violence by whom, and towards whom?

The answer is: by the alliance of the exploited and the oppressed against the oppressors and the exploiters, by the toilers against the parasites, by the majority against the minority.

We see, therefore, that in terms of its goals the proletarian state differs, as Heaven differs from Earth, from the state of the nobility and the bourgeoisie. It also differs just as strikingly in terms of its construction.

The inscription on the doorway to the autocratic-gentry state declares that the only people who can be admitted to power are those who live by the labour of others and do not soil their own thoroughbred hands with crude labour – those who belong to the landed aristocracy and the landlord-class.

At the entrance to the bourgeois state, it says that the people who rule here are those who own capital and big property, who use hired labour for their own **enrichment**, who are certified to participate in power by virtue of having thousands and millions in capital and hundreds and thousands of workers employed in factories and workshops.

It is exactly the opposite in the case of the proletarian state. Here, the people excluded from power are those who live by the labour of others. Those who exploit others and enrich themselves by use of hired labour are excluded from power. In the proletarian state, the only people admitted to managing the state are those who toil, those who live by their own labour and not on incomes created by the hands of others.

Previously, the nobility were considered to be the upper class and the lower classes included all the others. Then the upper class was taken to include all the big landowners along with the whole of the big and middle-bourgeoisie and the bourgeois intelligentsia. In the proletarian state, the workers of town and country are the ruling class, and the classes that are deprived of state-rights are the landowners, the bourgeoisie and saboteurs from the bourgeois intelligentsia.

But having become the ruling class, the workers not only do not close the door to exclude anyone else from their ranks, but, to the contrary, they arrange things so that everyone will become a member of the working people and the whole of humanity will become privileged. In other words, power will belong to no-one as a special privilege.

In the autocratic-gentry state, the privileges of power were accessible only to a very small number of aristocrats. Those not born into the nobility were deprived of rights from birth and had no chance whatsoever of joining the ranks of the ruling class, with the exception of separate individuals who might acquire titles.

In the bourgeois order it is capital that rules.

True, when they paint the charms of the bourgeois system and its 'justice', the capitalists habitually point to the fact that everyone can grow rich. But this claim is obviously a mockery, because if everyone became bourgeois, where would there be any proletariat whose labour creates the wealth of the capitalists? Ivanov and Petrov, from the lower ranks, might grow to be rich and become millionaires, but that only means that Sidorov and Vasil'ev have been ruined and hurled out of the bourgeois class. And here, the privilege of being one of the capitalists and of the bigwigs in state-affairs is the lot of a very insignificant group of people.

In the proletarian state, to the contrary, everyone who works and does not belong to the class of exploiters can vote in the soviets, for example, and be elected there. And when the bourgeoisie, especially their lackeys from the Mensheviks and the Right-S-Rs, point out that the working class and the village-poor are excluding all other groups from power and are themselves becoming a privileged class, this claim, to say the very least, is absolutely untrue. Let the banker bring in a crop, mow the hay, clean rooms or work as a janitor or doorman in the bank that has been taken from him and nationalised, let him work even as a clerk, and then he will acquire the right to vote in elections to the soviet.

Abandoning idleness for work will not only give the banker an opportunity to participate in managing the state (should he have any wish to take part in the Soviet state!), but it will also be better for his health. His doctor, who treats the patient for obesity, will confirm this.

The worker-peasant state is beyond doubt a class-state, for a non-class-state exists thus far only in the fantasies of bourgeois scholars who make fools of the masses with their fables to the effect that the 'whole people' rule the country in the bourgeois-parliamentary system. But the proletarian class-state not only keeps the door open for anyone to take part in management; to some degree, it even makes this obligatory, because it introduces labour as a duty, eliminates the privileged propertied classes, and thus opens to all the possibility and the necessity to participate in deciding social issues. In the proletarian state, everyone who works also rules, and whether they acquire the right to participate in power will depend on the propertied classes themselves.

Let them give up their opposition to the proletarian state, acknowledge that they have been beaten, accept a position equivalent to that of workers and employees, and then they can also count on acquiring the rights that toiling people have in the workers' state. The bourgeois who wants to remain a bourgeois is depriving himself of voting rights.

The proletarian state in Russia is constructed as a republic of soviets elected by the toiling masses. Speaking in theoretical terms, however, there is no need to conclude that the proletarian state will always and everywhere take precisely the soviet-form. For instance, the Paris Commune was elected by universal suffrage. In Germany, for example, there is no absolute necessity for the dictatorship of the proletariat to emerge through soviets, although the intensification of class contradictions in the West makes any other route seem unlikely.

The dictatorship of the proletariat, especially at the early stages, can, and probably must, also emerge through other class-organs of the proletariat; it can come about through a parliament elected by genuinely universal suffrage once the bourgeois press is deprived of the opportunity to corrupt and poison the consciousness of the labouring people. A proletarian majority can drive the bourgeois minority from parliament and transform it into an organ of proletarian dictatorship. When the bourgeoisie established its own dictatorship, it used very different means to realise its power in different countries and different periods. The English bourgeoisie, in the epoch of the first English Revolution, used Parliament for this purpose and twice drove out the counter-revolutionary deputies. In the first three years of the Revolution of 1789, the French bourgeoisie operated elections with a property-based census and thus excluded the lower elements of the people from power.

Then, to the contrary, the excluders were themselves excluded from power by the revolutionary petty bourgeoisie when the Girondists, representing the provincial commercial bourgeoisie, were driven from the Convention. Subsequently, the bourgeoisie in France and all other countries openly created its class-dictatorship, allowing only property-owners to participate in elections to parliament – only the owners of significant property – and completely excluding the proletariat and the poor. Parliaments, elected on the basis of a census of property, were really soviets of bourgeois deputies. When the open and shameless triumph of those with the deepest pockets had to be covered up somehow, the bourgeoisie began to expand the voting rights of labouring people, proclaiming every such move to be an event of the greatest importance. In reality, however, the domination of the bourgeois class continued even under the cover of a parliament with a broader suffrage, and those things that were difficult or impossible to accomplish in parliament were simply accomplished backstage and kept secret from the people.

Thus, just as the dictatorship of the bourgeoisie assumed the most diverse forms without in any way ceasing to be a dictatorship, so the proletarian dictatorship can be implemented in a wide variety of ways, provided that one form of proletarian state or another ensures the most complete and rapid suppression of the propertied classes and achieves, as quickly as possible, the socialist reconstruction of society.

But for precisely these reasons, the proletarian power cannot in any circumstances make use of the state-machine left over from bourgeois society. As a minority in the country, the bourgeoisie had the kind of power-apparatus that was suited for suppressing the majority of the toiling people. Obviously, the workers and peasants have no need for such an apparatus, for their task now is to suppress a defeated minority of exploiters who are still in opposition.

In place of the police, who are trained in fulfilling the orders of a bourgeois government, there is the Red Guard, chosen, when possible, by the working population.

In place of the standing army, there is universal arming of the toiling classes; in wartime, there is a class-army, the army of workers and peasants. The bourgeoisie, wailing about the inadmissibility of a class-army and a class-militia, forget that they themselves – at the time of the French Revolution, for example, when they were threatened by their class-enemies – had their own class-based military and civilian force in the National Guard, not to mention the fact that the standing army, created through military conscription, remains a blind weapon in their hands right up to the moment of social revolution.

The court-apparatus must, likewise, be destroyed and replaced by a new one with elected judges. As for political courts, the proletariat, unlike the bourgeoisie, has no need for hypocritically hiding the fact that it judges its class-opponents and creates revolutionary tribunals for this purpose.

As far as the administrative apparatus is concerned, in place of a bureaucracy appointed from above, this work is done through locally-elected soviets, whose responsible members fulfil their task in roughly the same conditions as every worker in the factory, having no special privileges other than the need to work 16 hours a day instead of eight, as circumstances frequently require.

Election and the possibility of being recalled at any time – these are the foundations on which proletarian power is built.

As a result of the destruction of the bourgeois state-apparatus, the working class and the poorest of the peasantry are creating a special kind of state never seen in the world before, which in Russia is assuming the form of the Soviet Republic. This state turns its bayonets and prisons on the exploiting classes, and for them this state is organised coercion.

But as far as the workers and peasants themselves are concerned, for them the soviets are organs for clarifying and bringing to life the common interests of all the workers and peasants of Russia.

In the all-Russian congresses of soviets these common interests are ascertained and a plan of action is set out; if there are local soviets who disagree with this plan, they must submit to the will of the majority of the working people.

In this way, the Soviet authority is the organisation of coercion against the propertied classes and the organ of self-government for the toiling masses.

The proletarian state (II)

Is the proletarian state eternal and absolutely necessary throughout all stages in the development of communism, or will it become redundant with the achievement of full communism?

The great teachers of communism, Karl Marx and Friedrich Engels, more than once gave a definitive response to this question. Their answer comes to this: the proletarian state, like all previous forms of the state, is a temporary organisation. It will exist until it has fulfilled the tasks for which it is created; and it must cease to exist, it must become obsolete, when it is no longer required. Engels explicitly said that the state will be consigned to the museum, just as the stone-axe and other utensils of the Stone-Age were, once it has completed those tasks for which the state came into being.

However, the stone-axe obviously cannot be consigned to the museum so long as mankind has not yet advanced to the point where it knows how to make the steel-axe or to manage even more successfully without any axe at all. The proletarian state, likewise, can only die away once it has completed the work for which it is created, and in no circumstances any sooner.

What is it that the proletarian state must accomplish?

In the first place, it must finally suppress opposition from the propertied classes who are trying to regain power and control, and this includes not merely smashing the bourgeoisie in the form of the Kornilovs, Semenovs and Dutovs, and so on, within its own country, but also fundamentally destroying even the very idea of a return to the old order.

Until this task is completed, the proletarian state must remain in full possession of all its punitive instruments and means of compulsion. And anyone who comes forth at such a time in opposition to the existence of the proletarian state is, in fact, a counter-revolutionary and a comrade in the work of the Kornilovs and the Skoropadskys.

The proletarian state must, furthermore, crush not simply the armed opposition of the propertied classes, but also all of their opposition in the form of sabotage, disobeying decrees, and every kind of covert struggle. The proletarian state must continue to exist until society is no longer divided into classes, until all the former factory-owners, bankers, landlords and petty bourgeois have become working citizens of socialist society and have merged with the proletariat in a single army of labour. Everyone understands that, in this respect, the proletarian state faces enormous and prolonged work. First, it is necessary to eliminate the upper stratum of the bourgeoisie. This may proceed more or less smoothly. But it is much more difficult to liquidate all the intermediate bourgeois classes. Finally, the greatest difficulties will come in the struggle with the petty bourgeoisie of all shapes and colours, with the millions of handicraftsmen, merchants and village-kulaks. This struggle will be especially difficult in Russia, a country that is primarily petty-bourgeois. It will be no easy task to subordinate the small proprietor to accounting and control, for he is an anarchist by nature and distrusts the state, even the worker-peasant state. Producing cheaply and selling at a higher price – that is the programme of the petty bourgeois; and he will oppose any authority, even the socialist authority, that stands in his way, even if it does so in the interests of the entire toiling population.

The proletarian state will not attempt to expropriate small property-owners; all it must do is subordinate the small-scale economy to accounting. Later, the small proprietors will gradually liquidate themselves, for there will be no advantage to being a small proprietor under socialism, and there will be much more to gain from becoming a member of the socialist community with equal rights. To be a small proprietor, in such circumstances, could mean only one thing – working more and receiving less. And since no-one is his own enemy, the small owners will gradually, and without any measures of compulsion, melt away into the workers' state. It is obvious, however, that in the beginning the small property-owners will oppose accounting; and this is particularly true, for instance, in the case of real implementation of the grain-monopoly. During this time, the proletarian state must stand rock-solid at its post.

Any state arises in the presence of social classes. This means that the proletarian state must exist until such time as all classes are finally and irreversibly eliminated.

But the struggle of the proletarian power against the bourgeoisie of its own country cannot lead to final victory as long as this bourgeoisie receives support from foreign counter-revolutionary forces. The proletarian state is all the more necessary in a country such as Russia, which is surrounded on all sides by the hostile forces of world-capital that are trying to smother this base of the world proletarian revolution. But once the question of revolutionary defence and socialist war arises, it is perfectly obvious that such a war cannot be waged with any hope of success without a strong state-organisation. Where there is a war, there is also an army. And where there is an army, there is discipline and complete subordination of the soldiers to the proletarian government; that is, subordination to the entire working class as a whole. If the German imperialists beat us, this was only due to their iron-like state-organisation. And only an iron-like proletarian state is in a position to organise forces to oppose world-capital, to create a worker-peasant army and manage to defend the conquests of the socialist Revolution.

Therefore, the existence of the proletarian state will be necessary until the propertied classes are defeated within the country, until bourgeois forces are suppressed in other countries, and until the division of society into classes and all the privileged groups in society dissolve into a single labour-army of socialist society.

But suppose all of this is accomplished, that no-one can even dream of any return to the past, that the whole of society consists of citizens with identical rights and that the enormous benefits of a communist system are readily apparent by comparison with the capitalist system – will the state then be eliminated?

To this question we give the following answer: yes, it will be eliminated insofar as the proletarian state was the instrument for suppressing those classes and groups hostile to socialism, and there is no longer anyone to suppress.

Well then, what will happen in the event that capitalist relations within society have only been eliminated very recently? What if separate groups and a general minority disagree with the majority, strive for a privileged position and will generally be at odds with the interests of the majority and of society as a whole?

If voluntary agreement proves impossible, then of course the majority will have to implement its will by force. In those circumstances, one must acknowledge that for a time in the new classless society, which has yet to reach the stage of full communism but is rapidly approaching it, there will exist a certain remnant of the state in the form of organs that will implement the decision of the majority. Obviously, these remnants of proletarian state organs will not resemble the police of bourgeois society. What will probably happen is that the central workers' council will appoint one-or-another group of citizens at different times to implement its decisions that some particular groups refuse to obey.

The need for such compulsion will also disappear quickly, because the different social groups and society as a whole will learn through experience that it is hopeless for the minority to attempt to impose its will on the majority. Eventually, everyone will become accustomed to the fact that the majority's decision will always be implemented, and it will be enough for the majority to vote in order that a contentious decision will be put into effect even by those who disagree with it. The only way for a minority to implement its own decision will be through becoming a majority.

This subordination of the minority to the majority will be inevitable, of course, only if the question cannot voluntarily be decided to the mutual satisfaction of all sides. It is obvious to everyone that agreement is preferable to any kind of pressure and compulsion, even of the moral kind. When mankind reaches the point where it is so well-ordered and knowledgeable that it can manage without state-institutions as organs of political coercion, the state will then become a redundant institution that will be disadvantageous and even humiliating in the given stage of communism. This can be explained with a brief example. At a time when the mass of the population, thanks to the conditions of tsarism and capitalism, is indifferent and deeply corrupted by the spirit of cheating and petty thievery, our tramways, for instance, need both conductors, whose sole business is selling tickets, and controllers to supervise the conductors. This tax on the lack of social conscientiousness is economically useful and inevitable where the tramway-management spends, shall we say, one hundred thousand roubles per year on conductors and controllers to prevent public dishonesty from costing it three hundred thousand roubles. But if the enormous majority of the population is honest and can be trusted to deposit their tram-fares, and if the loss caused by a few remaining dishonest travellers should fall to ten to twenty thousand, then it would be better to do away with control, which would wither away as something redundant, unnecessary and insulting to the enormous majority of conscious and honest people. At some fine moment, the same thing will happen with the state, whose few lingering remnants will fall into disuse in an advanced communist society. This will be the moment when mankind has actually matured sufficiently for the full freedom of communism, when duties will be fulfilled simply because they are known to be socially necessary and not because society forcibly prevents its different groups from refusing to fulfil them.

In his introduction to *The Class Struggles in France*, Engels very clearly sketched the transitional character even of the workers' state as follows:

> ...[T]he state is nothing but a machine for the oppression of one class by another, and this refers to a democratic republic no less than to a monarchy. At best, the state is an evil, inherited by the proletariat after its victorious struggle for class-supremacy. As in the case of the Paris Commune, the proletariat will inevitably have to lop off at the earliest possible moment the worst aspects of this evil, until such time as a new generation, reared in new and free social conditions, will be able to throw away all this scrap from every state-institution whatsoever.[3]

During the period of struggle for communism, the proletarian state must and will exist, and its longevity will be determined by the strength of opposition from the propertied classes. Since it is already clear that the world-bourgeoisie is capable of mounting enormous forces of resistance, even the victory of proletarian revolution in Europe will not free the working class from the need to finish off bourgeois rule in America and Japan. At the outset, perhaps, it will even have to defend itself against these predators. This means we can confidently assert that

---

3. [Preobrazhensky mistakenly speaks of Engels' introduction to Marx's essay on *The Class Struggles in France*. The reference should be to Engels' introduction, written in 1891, to *The Civil War in France*. See Marx and Engels 1962, p. 485. The translation given here comes from Preobrazhensky's text and differs slightly from the standard English-language rendition of the passage.]

the proletarian state will still have to function for years, if not decades, in order to eliminate the rule of capital in all corners of the globe.

Now let us turn to what the anarchists think about the proletarian state and how they relate to it in practice.

Anarchists and the proletarian state

Anarchists are the opponents of every state-authority and every kind of organised coercion. For instance, this is what Peter Kropotkin writes concerning the state:

> We see in it an institution that has served, throughout the whole history of human societies, to hinder any form of voluntary association between people, to prevent the development of local initiative, to smother any liberties that already exist and to hinder the emergence of new ones. And we know that an institution that has already survived through several centuries and solidified into a certain form in order to perform a certain role in history cannot be adapted to serve the opposite role.[4]

Malatesta writes: 'The state creates nothing: even when it reaches its perfection it is a redundant institution that uselessly dissipates the people's strength'.[5]

Two thoughts need to be differentiated in the lines just cited. First, there is the objection to the state of the exploiters and emphasis on the complete impossibility of using this old apparatus of oppression to emancipate the toiling classes. On this point, there are no disputes between communists and anarchists. And second, there is the objection to any state whatsoever, including the proletarian state.

But when anarchist loathing for the state of the oppressors is carried over to the state of the toilers, to a state that arises as a fighting organisation of the oppressed masses, a vast chasm opens up between communists and anarchists. An anarchist who would follow Malatesta (who never saw a proletarian state) and greet the workers' state, which is waging a merciless struggle against world-capital, by repeating like a parrot that this state, too, is an institution that 'uselessly dissipates the people's strength' – that kind of anarchist would merely demonstrate that a condition of profound anarchy prevails in his own head. Every child knows that in an organised struggle, things go best for the side that is best organised. The state, as a class-organisation, is the highest possible form of organisation in class-society, and it multiples tenfold the forces of the class that can close ranks in this way. For exactly that reason, the proletariat, having

---

4. P. Kropotkin, *Gosudarstvo i evo istoricheskaya rol'.* [The excerpt comes from the beginning of Section X of Kropotkin's *The State: Its Historic Role.*]
5. Errico Malatesta, *Kratkaya sistema anarkhizma.*

organised its own state, does not 'uselessly dissipate the people's strength' but rather preserves its strength and strives for victory over the bourgeoisie with the least cost to its own forces. Conversely, an anarchistic method of struggle would guarantee much greater costs, but we shall say more on this later.

When anarchist theorists have had to answer the question of how they would regard a state of the toilers, should one arise, they have declined to respond on the grounds that a proletarian state of the toiling people cannot exist: the state has always been, is now, and will continue to be an organisation of the minority, and it can never happen in real life that the majority of the people will take power into their own hands. Were the toiling masses to defeat their oppressors in battle, these masses would have absolutely no use for a state. But life has given precise examples of the proletarian state, and it laughs mockingly at the anarchist theorists, demanding that they respond to the inescapable question.

This question, posed by life itself, is fatal for anarchism. It either requires recognition that not every state or every form of organised compulsion, only that of the exploiters, is harmful to the working class – in which case, anarchism would eviscerate the most essential point of its teaching and would have to descend from the clouds of categorical claims and dead phrases to the ground of real life – or else it would have to regard the workers' state, a state for suppression of the exploiters, a state of self-discipline among the toilers themselves, as a harmful organisation upon which they would have to declare war and thus find themselves in the company of the most embittered bourgeois counter-revolutionaries.

Let us consider how the anarchists have tried to escape this dilemma.

The first experience of the proletarian state came with the Paris Commune. Anarchism could not deny the emancipatory character of this remarkable organisation, and so we find that Peter Kropotkin, for instance, simply treats the Paris Commune as an anarchist commune. He recommends studying the Paris Commune as an example of how to make a social revolution, and he tries to avoid noticing, or perhaps he just fails to understand, how, on ground cleared by the Revolution, there began to emerge a new proletarian state with no historical precedent. In his brochure *Anarchy*, Peter Kropotkin writes:

> During a revolution, destruction is only a part of the revolutionary's work. Now he must also build. And this restructuring can be done either according to the old recipes, learned from books and imposed upon the people by all the defenders of the old order, by all those who are unable to conceive anything new; or else reconstruction can begin with new principles. That is, the autonomous construction of a socialist society begins in every village and every city under the influence of certain common principles that are adopted by the masses and will find practical expression in the localities and in the complex relationships that characterise every local area.

As an example of such construction, Kropotkin cites the experience of the Paris Commune and is most pleased by the fact that Paris declared itself at the time to be an 'independent city'. But Kropotkin is quiet about the fact that this independence was, first and foremost, independence from Thiers, from the counter-revolutionary bourgeois government at Versailles and the bumpkins of the Black Hundreds, and that precisely this fact made it revolutionary. In reality, the Commune strove to embrace the whole of France, to transform the entire country into an organisation of proletarian supremacy, and it perished because it failed in this effort.

In general and on the whole, the Paris Commune is not an example of an anarchist commune but rather the germ of the proletarian commune-state.

To anyone familiar with the history of the Paris Commune, anyone with no interest in distorting or misinterpreting its essential nature, it is clear that this was precisely a state-experience, albeit one of a new type.

The Commune prominently involved all the most important attributes of a state that the anarchists so despise. In the first place, it was a legislative organ and produced a series of decrees that were obligatory for all and were implemented with the threat of repression. It did not do away with courts; it simply made judges subject to election by the people. It did not eliminate the army and the military discipline that any army requires if it wants to avoid defeat; instead, it had an army built upon the general arming of the workers. And on it went.

In general terms, the Commune was a state adapted to the interests of the proletariat and to the need to put down the bourgeoisie; it was a state of the oppressed who had declared war on their oppressors.

Kropotkin could not understand, or else he had no wish to understand, the essence of the Paris Commune. To protect his bankrupt theory, he concealed the state-element of this socialist experiment by the Parisian workers. To the contrary, Marx and Engels, our teachers, defined the Commune with profound insight as the type of state created by the victorious proletariat. Here, for instance, is what Friedrich Engels wrote regarding the Paris Commune in his introduction to Karl Marx's *The Class Struggle in France*:

> Of late, the German philistine has once more been filled with wholesome terror at the words: Dictatorship of the Proletariat. Do you wish to know, Sirs, what this dictatorship looks like? Look at the Paris Commune. That was the Dictatorship of the Proletariat.[6]

---

6. [Preobrazhensky again gives the title as *The Class Struggles in France*, but the reference is to Engels' 1891 introduction to Marx's *The Civil War in France*. See Marx and Engels 1962, p. 485. Preobrazhensky also refers to 'the German philistine', whereas Engels spoke of 'the Social-Democratic philistine'.]

In the same brochure, Marx wrote of the Commune as follows: The 'true secret [of the Commune – E.P.] was this: It was essentially a working-class government …'

In another place, Marx again wrote of the Commune as a workers' government: 'The few but important functions which would still remain for a central government were not to be suppressed, as has been intentionally misstated by enemies of the Commune, but were to be discharged by communal and therefore responsible agents'.

A great many more such quotations could be cited from the works of our great teachers. And all these quotations would show not only that Marx and Engels considered the Paris Commune to be a working-class government, but also that they proved this truth with a whole series of facts drawn from the life and activity of this proletarian state-organisation.

The second example of the proletarian state has come with Soviet Russia following the October Revolution. How have the anarchists responded to this enormous experience of creating a worker-peasant state?

Through the very fact of its existence, Soviet Russia, as with the Paris Commune, is a most graphic repudiation of anarchist prejudice to the effect that **every power** belongs to an oppressive minority, that it is neither possible nor necessary for the majority of the toiling people to organise as a state in order to suppress the bourgeois minority. But whereas Kropotkin presumed to call the Paris Commune an anarchist commune, nothing of the kind has been possible concerning Soviet Russia. The October Revolution occurred under the slogan 'All power to the soviets'. The word 'power', so hated by the anarchists, was in the forefront, and this word became reality when the coalition-ministry was overthrown and the Soviet state-apparatus of proletarian dictatorship began to grow in strength. The anarchists took part in the October Revolution together with the Bolsheviks. Their efforts contributed to the victory. But they played a revolutionary role in the October movement not because of their anarchism, but rather in spite of it; it was **not rejection of any power in general, but rather struggle against the existing bourgeois power** that made them into allies of the proletariat, who were struggling not to eliminate power but to take power into their own hands. Of course, in their pronouncements the anarchists always emphasised that they were struggling against the bourgeoisie in the name of anarchy, but this did not change a thing, because in assisting the overthrow of bourgeois power, they helped the power of the proletariat to be victorious.

Since the October Revolution, three tendencies can be distinguished among Russian anarchists concerning their relation to Soviet power. One group of anarchists is speaking roughly this way: 'The Soviet power is fighting against the Russian and international bourgeoisie. For as long as this struggle lasts, it is necessary to support Soviet power even though anarchy would be a more perfect social system. To fight against Soviet power while the bourgeoisie is not yet defeated would mean helping the bourgeoisie'. That is how the smaller group of anarchists reasons.

A second group takes completely the opposite view. They suggest that Soviet power is, above all, power, and anarchists must destroy power in any form, whatever its consequences and in any and all circumstances. Hence: 'Down with all power including Soviet power, down with it immediately, and long live anarchy!'

Between these two extreme tendencies, there is a centrist group that wavers from one side to the other depending on the circumstances, all the while trying to emphasise that Soviet power is one thing but the soviets are something else entirely. This intermediate tendency, comprising a near-majority among Russian anarchists, takes an attitude towards Soviet power of 'so far, so good'. So long as the anarchists find that the policy of the Soviet power corresponds, for the moment, with the interests of anarchism, they ease their pressure on it and even support it. But should their deep thinkers conclude that this policy is not revolutionary, in those circumstances they turn not only against one or another measure but primarily against Soviet power in its entirety. Everyone understands that such an attitude towards Soviet power merely reveals utter confusion among the anarchists and their complete inability to relate to the proletarian state on the basis of any principled position.

The first of the anarchist groups that we mentioned honestly and openly supports Soviet power, which has yet to complete its work of suppressing the exploiter-classes, and they just as honestly and openly acknowledge in their deeds (even if not yet, perhaps, in their words) that the proletarian state can exist, that in the case of Soviet Russia it does, indeed, exist in practice, and that anarchism turned out to be mistaken on the most essential point of its teaching, the question of the state. This group is acting with a healthy revolutionary instinct in a revolutionary time, but that means it is also shelving the bookish reasoning of the Kropotkins.

Things are exactly the opposite with the group of anarchists who repeat like parrots what anarchist theorists wrote decades ago. The theorists of anarchism simplistically contemplate a transition from the exploiters' state to a community with no state: a social revolution begins, the bourgeois state is eliminated, and the reign of anarchist freedom results. But 'writing things on paper is easy because the ravines can be forgotten'. Real historical development has not followed the path predicted by Bakunin and Kropotkin, but rather that of the *Communist Manifesto* and its authors. The struggle of the proletariat to eliminate bourgeois domination has required the creation of the proletarian state; and between the state of the exploiting minority and the society of the future, which will be free of the state, there is the intervening period – the transitional state of the toiling majority. That is how matters have turned out in practice, in reality. But this genuine reality does not exist for the anarchist scribe. The prejudices and incoherent thoughts of anarchist theorists, strewn about on printed paper, are more precious to him than the lived experience of revolution. The anarchist scribes are oblivious to the **proletarian** state; more correctly, what they see in the proletarian state is just the hated **state**, and then they exclaim: 'Down with Soviet power' – at a time when the same cry is coming all the more loudly from the side of the bourgeoisie and the monarchist counter-revolutionaries. True, when the bourgeois and the monarchist cry 'Down with Soviet power', they put the stress on the word **Soviet**, while the anarchist stresses the word 'power', but the practical result is a genuine working alliance to overthrow the existing and concrete Soviet power that is finishing off, in real life, the domination of the bourgeoisie.

But the anarchist scribes, the 'consistent' anarchists, can take comfort on one point (there is no harm without some good!). To be precise, they are conserving to the end all the precepts of anarchism and they cannot be charged with abandoning even a single one of their 'truths' as far as the state is concerned. We cannot deny these anarchists their right to such 'comfort', especially when they have paid for it so dearly by allying with the counter-revolution.

As for the intermediate group of anarchists, who are balancing between the outdated book-wisdom of Kropotkin and the questions posed by the living reality of revolution, that group is essentially repudiating in practice the anarchist position that says all power everywhere merely oppresses the toiling people and can never serve them. Supporting in practice a number of measures by the Soviet power, measures directed against the bourgeoisie and imperialism, they acknowledge – with few words, but still quite eloquently – that there also exists a kind of power that suppresses the exploiters in the interest of the toilers. To come to that realisation, however, is the equivalent of suicide for the anarchist true-believer. Once he begins to differentiate between bourgeois power and the power of the toilers – he is as good as lost. He must then acknowledge that if the struggle is going on between two alternatives – between the power of the Skoropadskys and the Soviet power (and that is the case during May–June 1918) – then he can either abandon all struggle and forsake the Revolution, or else he must side with the power of the toilers against the power of the bourgeois hangmen. The possibility of such a choice was never anticipated by anarchist theorists, and their Russian followers must use 'their own heads' to decide how to address such a situation. Their responses differ, but ultimately they entail two choices: either to remain true to anarchist prejudices and serve the counter-revolution, or else to serve the Revolution but discard all prejudices to the effect that power always and everywhere has fatal consequences for the people.

As we have seen above, when Kropotkin found himself facing the fact of the emerging proletarian state in the Paris Commune, he found a Solomon-like solution for anarchism, so to speak, by expropriating the Paris Commune and claiming that it was an anarchist commune. History has given our own anarchists harder nuts to crack in the form of the soviets.

Just what are the soviets?

The bourgeois compromising parties and the anarchists have seen in the soviets mainly what they want to see. The compromising parties did not consider the soviets to be organs of proletarian rule, but declared them to be only trade-union and class-organisations that might, at best, exercise control over power, and they made every effort they could to confine them to that miserable role.

The anarchists generally answered the question in the following spirit: 'soviets are not organs of power, but rather organs expressing the will of the toiling people, and it is only the statist-Bolsheviks who are trying to pervert their nature and transform them into organs of power'.

This kind of miserable response demonstrates once more that the very fact of the soviets' existence is a living repudiation of all anarchist positions concerning the question of the state, and it renders them completely incapable of assessing these organs.

The attempt to avoid the word 'power' and replace it with 'the will of the toiling people' does nothing to save the anarchists, who are driven to the wall by the very course of our Revolution. We agree that the soviets are organs expressing the will of the toiling people. But is it really not possible for the will of the toiling people also to be the will to power?

In fact this is precisely what happened: the organs of the toiling people expressed their will to power and turned themselves into organs of power, which is what they had to do in order to guarantee the victory of the proletarian revolution. What does anarchism gain by declaring the soviets not to be organs of proletarian power but only of proletarian will?

It gains precisely nothing. The anarchists are only tying themselves up in words, often coming to conclusions that are amazing in their absurdity; for instance, some of them take the view that once the soviets become organs of power and create a central Soviet authority, they then cease to be soviets expressing the will of the people. In other words, once the soviets cease to follow the anarchists' recipes, they no longer express the will of the toiling people!

But is it really possible to tell a soviet, as a meeting of deputies elected by the toilers, how they should express the will of those same toilers? For the anarchist, this is a very serious question. The reader must remember that Malatesta and a number of other anarchist theorists always vigorously maintained that a person elected to one-or-another institution may express his own will, but can never express the will of hundreds and thousands of other people. A proper and consistent anarchist would also have to consider the soviets to be organs incapable of expressing the will of the masses. But at this point not even all of the anarchist bibliophiles are willing to slander the soviets by declaring them to be organs that are incapable of expressing the will of the proletariat. Hence the very fact of the soviets' existence, together with the work they are doing, has compelled the anarchists to disavow at least one of their prejudices.

But if a single soviet is an organ expressing the will of the toiling people, then how must anarchists assess a congress of soviets?

On this issue, a number of the anarchists reverse course and deny that the congress of soviets can express the will of the people.

When the congress of soviets elects a Central Committee and a Council of People's Commissars, all anarchists agree that the congress, and all the more so the institutions it elects, cannot express the will of the toilers.

In order to make perfectly clear the whole inconsistency and absurdity of the anarchists' point of view, let us take a brief example.

If some rural district in Ivanov has a grain-surplus, and the properly-elected district-soviet resolves not to send the surplus to the city, this will be an expression of the 'will of the toiling people'. But if the All-Russian Congress of Soviets, in order to save starving workers and peasants in a province where the crop has failed, resolves to collect all the grain-surpluses from the countryside, particularly those in the Ivanov district, this will not be an expression of the will of the toiling people but a manifestation of power and coercion.

Summarising what has been said concerning the relation of anarchists to the proletarian state, we therefore come to the following conclusion. Since the appearance of the proletarian state was completely unforeseen by anarchists, and since they imagined the course of the social revolution being completely different from what has actually happened, it turns out that the mere appearance of the soviets as the nucleus of proletarian power has compelled them to lose many of their prejudices that have been treated as truths for the past half-century. When the network of Soviets, following the October Revolution, came together in a single whole and constituted the framework of a proletarian-peasant power that had begun to fight for the elimination of classes, life itself then compelled the anarchists to face a dilemma: either to destroy the soviets as organs of power, or else to support them as instruments for destroying the bourgeois system.

As a result, the anarchists were unable to adopt any consistently principled position and presently find themselves in a condition of total theoretical chaos.

The communist economy and the anarchist economy

We have seen above that the anarchists' struggle against the proletarian state, at a time when this state has yet to complete its work of suppressing the resistance of the exploiters, has the inevitable effect, whatever their intention, of making them allies of the counter-revolutionaries. In the economic sphere, matters are even worse. The ultimate economic ideal of anarchism is simply a petty-bourgeois variant of capitalist commodity-economy and represents a step backwards even by comparison with developed capitalism.

In order to clarify differences between the communist and anarchist programmes for the economic reconstruction of society, let us first briefly sketch the tasks of communism in the realm of production and distribution.

In this connection, the reader must bear in mind that we have to speak throughout not only of an ideal communist society, which we anticipate as the final goal of the struggle, but also of relations during the transition-period that Russia has already entered and that Europe will also enter on the day after the proletarian seizure of power.

Communism is that social structure in which all means of production are the common property of the toilers, in which every worker contributes according to his ability and every member of society receives from the common supply a volume of products according to his needs. That is the most perfect and most ideal social system for every working person. But that system also presupposes perfect organisation, workers who are conscious and accustomed to social labour, and the kind of progress in technology that we are extremely far from enjoying at present. If every worker will consume according to his needs, and not according to some norm, that means the output of products must exceed the requirements of consumption.

The achievement of full communism therefore requires some time, perhaps a very long time, so that when the struggle against the exploiters ends and all persons are transformed into workers in the new society, there will then begin a long and stubborn struggle on the part of the toilers themselves for a more perfect type of social organisation, a struggle for a more advanced consciousness, for comradely discipline in labour and communist equality in consumption.

Generally speaking, communist reconstruction must occur in approximately the following sequence. The nationalisation of factories and plants, which is beginning today, must be completed with the transfer of all of the instruments of production to the toiling masses. When this task is completed, we shall have socialisation of the instruments of production and circulation (that is, of the railways, steamships, and so on).

Along with socialisation of the instruments of production (and nationalisation by the power of the toiling socialist workers is the most genuine form of socialisation), it is simultaneously necessary to implement strict accounting of all the workers in the country, of all the instruments and supplies, and also to calculate the quantity of products needed for consumption by the entire population. The volume of production will be adjusted to the volume of consumption. Every branch of industry must be assigned its task, which is calculated according to the whole country's need for its product, and the workers in this profession must fulfil this task no matter what happens, because on the fulfilment of tasks in each branch and each profession will depend the normal functioning of the whole enormous and complex industrial mechanism of the country. Leadership in the work of industry will be vested in a central council of the national economy that will operate through regional and provincial soviets, and the agent of this organisation and leader of production in each individual factory will be the factory-and-works committee or some other such organisation. No kind of planned communist economy is possible without perfectly prepared universal statistics and without central leadership in distributing the labour-force and the instruments of production.

Because of this kind of conscious leadership over the whole of industrial activity, in a communist system there cannot be overproduction of products to the extent that enormous surpluses spoil and the labour spent upon them turns out to be wasted, as often happens in the capitalist system. Conversely, it is also impossible to have enormous shortages of one product or another, because production will be based upon a more-or-less accurate calculation that accommodates the volume of consumption. For all of these reasons, there also cannot be any unemployment.

By comparison with communism, capitalism represents an economic system with no mind.

In the quest for profit, manufacturers produce some quantity or other of output at random. When overproduction of commodities occurs, the market sounds the alarm and prices fall. When there is a shortage of products, prices rise; and in the quest for profit, capital flows into these branches of industry, their production expands, and demand for the commodities that were scarce is now satisfied and even over-satisfied, because the clumsy capitalist mechanism cannot stop at the appropriate point and spontaneously replaces underproduction with overproduction. In the capitalist economy, production adjusts to consumption in a purely spontaneous way through the market.

That kind of adjustment is extremely costly to mankind and is accompanied by an enormous non-productive expenditure of labour. Under communism, there will be no such squandering of social labour because the role of the market, to the extent that the market contributes to redistributing labour according to the needs of expanding or contracting consumption, will be replaced by the work of statistics.

This means that the society of labouring people will consciously distribute its work among all members and will acquire, in the form of the central statistical bureau, the mind for its economic organism that is lacking in capitalism.

As we shall see later, anarchism prefers to leave society in the same mindless condition as capitalism, and it regards conscious regulation of production as an infringement on the individual freedom of the producers. From the point of view of the petty-bourgeois proprietor, this fear is fully justified!

The fact that ownership of the factories and plants on the basis of communist principles is more just than private property in the instruments of production is the least of the reasons why we are communists. This justice would hardly be worth anything to communism, were it not accompanied by an enormous advance over capitalism in terms of developing the forces of production. If, let us assume, an American worker in capitalist society normally produced more products in an eight-hour working day than he would under communism; if, despite the deduction going to the capitalist, he received more products in the form of wages than he would under communism, then communism would mean a decline in his living standard, not an improvement. In reality, of course, communism creates the possibility for an enormous rise in labour-productivity and consequently for an enormous increase in the worker's income compared to capitalism (with the same length of work-time).

But this increase in productivity is possible mainly as a result of the improvement of technology. Use of machinery means that the man does not directly produce, say, a needle, but rather approaches production in a roundabout way by first producing the machine that then makes the needle. The labour expended in producing the machine is less than the labour saved during the life of the machine. This is the whole rationale of technological progress and the basis for all of communism's hope for more rapid development of the productive forces than under capitalism. If some kind of labour-saving machine is invented under capitalism, it is very often not put to use. What matters to the entrepreneur is not whether the machine saves labour and is socially beneficial; for him, the whole issue is whether use of the machine brings profit and whether there is some advantage in acquiring it. As a result, labour-saving machines are frequently not put to use in capitalist society simply because the existence of low wages makes their purchase and use unprofitable in capitalist terms.

Communist society will not face such an obstacle, but will apply every labour-saving machine so that the entire focus of this type of economy will move to making the greatest possible improvements in technology. The masses, numbering in the millions, will share this interest; millions of people, not just the miserable tens or hundreds of today, will apply their creative skills in order to contribute, in one manner or another, to the common effort. As a result, a very extensive and extremely important kind of economic activity even under capitalism, the activity involved in producing machines and instruments of labour – or the production of means of production – will become more important than ever under communism and take on colossal significance. But still more important will be a correct distribution of labour, so that the production of means of production will occur in a proportion corresponding to the production of means of consumption. The difficulty of resolving this task becomes all the greater because this relation is continuously changing: one must take into account not only the needs of the current moment, but also the direction and speed of change. Capitalism dealt with this task, in one manner or another, by using the system of competition and market-prices. State-capitalism deals with the same task more successfully. But only communism, through years of practical experience, will perfect the ways of meeting this requirement. Just how anarchism would manage this job is completely incomprehensible. Moreover, the anarchists are so profoundly ignorant concerning the most important and difficult economic questions that they cannot even envisage the whole complexity of this matter and have never shown any interest in investigating it.

As far as the village-economy is concerned, we would describe the transition to communism in the countryside as follows. In those countries where large- and medium-scale agriculture already exists at the moment when the proletariat seizes power, organising a socialist economy will be no more difficult than organising large-scale industry in the cities. Making the transition to communist agriculture will be much more difficult for small-scale farming and for countries such as Russia, where small-peasant farming prevails.

In the beginning, socialist agriculture will occur only on state-lands worked under supervision of the proletarian state, on those advanced estates that have not been ransacked and divided and will be under the control of local soviets from the start, and finally, on those lands that will be worked by communes of the rural poor, which are now emerging in Russia and becoming increasingly numerous. In future, socialist agriculture, which in itself is more advantageous than independent farming, will have the powerful support of the workers' authority and will become more prevalent in the countryside with each passing year. Working the land through communes, under the leadership of soviet-agronomists and applying the most advanced machinery, fertilisers and farming methods, will mean less work and more output compared to independent farming. When all the peasants learn the advantages of socialist agriculture through experience, only individual eccentrics will stay on their small independent plots. Implementing the grain-monopoly will also accelerate this process. This will begin with the soviets calculating the whole grain-harvest in each village and rural area. After deducting the amount of grain that the village needs to consume until the next harvest, all of the remaining surplus will go to the state-granaries, and the village will receive in exchange, from the state food-authorities, a corresponding volume of all the products that the peasantry requires. Within the village itself, farming might presently be done entirely on the basis of *artel*-principles, some mixed form, or even private agriculture. In the future, every village will be transformed into a cell of *artel*-farming, while calculations by the central economic organs will mean that the whole commune will work together, rather than the parts operating independently.

In that way, the countryside will make the transition to communist working of the land, the borders between the land-holdings of separate villages will be erased, and the whole of the agricultural land will be redistributed and worked according to the scientific requirements of agronomy. Thus the separate village-communes will simultaneously merge into one vast Russian agricultural commune, and the village-commune will be fully integrated with the industrial commune of the cities as a single entity.

The distribution of labour between industry and agriculture must also satisfy a plan worked out consciously on the basis of statistics, and no particular groups of toilers will be able arbitrarily to remain in agriculture if it already has an oversupply of labour or vice versa. This is not the place for a detailed discussion of how, in a communist economy, there might be an alternation between factory- and agricultural labour. The important point is that labour will be distributed according to a definite plan. Every effort will be made to take into consideration the workers' own preferences in choosing their type of labour, but if personal desires conflict with the needs involved in implementing a definite plan of distribution, it is personal interests that must yield, not the interest that millions have in ensuring the normal course of production.

That is how production will be organised in the communist system. As for distribution, it will depend upon the character of production. Beginning with partial communism, it will culminate in full and unconditional communism.

Now let us consider the kind of economic system for which anarchism strives.

In this connection, one must, above all, keep in mind that whereas the goals of socialism and communism have long been fundamentally clarified in socialist literature, the same cannot be said concerning the goals of anarchists. This is an area where they enjoy complete 'freedom of opinion'. There are anarchist-individualists of the bourgeois type, anarchist-communists, anarchist-syndicalists, simple anarchists with no hyphens and so on. Each of these tendencies disagrees with the others in its understanding of what constitutes the most desirable kind of economic structure. There are anarchist groups for whom even the term 'economic organisation' seems offensive because it implies compulsion, discipline, or, at the very least, some kind of restriction of personal freedom. Others, the anarchist-syndicalists for example, have no fear of the word 'organisation' and even believe, to the contrary, that anarchism alone ensures the highest degree of organisation and stability in the economic structure of society. In view of this multiplicity of anarchist voices on the matter of the economic restructuring of society, we will single out from their discussions and theories only the most common themes on which almost all groups can agree. The common element consists in the fact that anarchists, denying any kind of state-authority, including proletarian power, favour distributing the instruments of production not to all the toilers as a whole, but to separate groups of comrades or *artels* of toilers. Next, the anarchists oppose any regulation of production from a special economic centre elected by the toilers because they confuse such a centre with the state that they hate. They call for *artel*-communes to exchange their products among themselves and, generally speaking, to determine their interrelations by mutual agreement. The worker freely joins the *artel*, and the *artel* freely enters into alliance with other *artels*. As for a whole series of the most significant questions concerning a proper distribution of the workforce, adjustment of the volume of production in separate branches to the volume of consumption, and so on – on all these questions, the enormous majority of anarchists converge in replying: 'Let us first destroy capitalism, and then life itself will show the way'.

This means that we must consider the inevitable consequences to which social organisation on the basis of anarchist principles would lead in step with the breakdown of capitalism. And where anarchists dismiss the questions they have not answered with the phrase that 'life itself will show the way', we will have to look at what 'life itself' shows us in Russia, at how anarchist ideals are transformed into reality and what remains of them.

Let us begin with our first fundamental disagreement with the anarchists: the matter of who will own and have disposal over the factories, and all the instruments of production in general, that are taken from the capitalists. We say: all the instruments of production must belong to and be at the disposal of all the toilers and all the workers of communist society. The Putilov factory, for example, belongs not to the thousands of workers employed there at any given moment, and not even to the hundreds of thousands who built it up over the course of two decades, but to every worker in the country. Conversely, every Putilov worker must know and feel himself to be master of the factories in Ivanovo-Voznesensk, of the coal-mines in Cheremkovo, of the Lena gold-mines and of all the instruments of labour throughout the Republic. The instruments of labour belong to everyone and to no-one in particular – and that is true communism. But in order for all the factories to belong to the entire working class, in order for this not to be simply an empty phrase, the workers must elect special organs of economic management; whether these be **departments in the soviets** or special soviets of the national economy elected by the workers is of no consequence. An all-Russian economic centre must also have the supreme right of disposal over all the instruments of production and the entire labour-force of the country. Every worker in a particular factory, and every factory- and workshop-committee, must regard itself as a plenipotentiary and agent of the entire working class as a whole – as an agent to which the particular enterprise is assigned. The all-Russian economic centre must have the right of general leadership and be subject to re-election if it does not satisfy the interests of the majority of workers.

The anarchists, on the contrary, stand for every factory, plant, workshop, and so on, constituting a unique, independent commune. The workers in this particular commune will also be its real masters. To become a member of the commune requires permission from the others, and the commune can only be merged with another commune through mutual agreement. In reality, this will mean breaking up the property of all the toilers in the instruments of production (if one can use the word 'property'), breaking up the right of collective disposal of all the instruments of production into separate elements, into separate little islands, and restricting the will of the toiling class as a whole in its disposal over all the instruments of labour. The workers of every factory will begin to regard themselves as the property-owners of their enterprise and, in fact, they will become petty bourgeois. Essentially, anarchism turns out to be capitalism without the capitalists, and in place of a single owner every enterprise will have a hundred or a thousand owners, but it will not be owned by all the toiling people of the entire country. Advocating this kind of anarchism does not kill off all the petty-bourgeois property-owning sentiments that the worker carries over from bourgeois society, but instead revitalises them. Typically, it is precisely the least conscious groups of workers who are attracted by anarchist slogans that oppose transferring ultimate management of the factories to the entire working class in the form of its central and regional organs.

The saying that 'we ourselves are the masters' is understood by unconscious workers to mean that they can exclude others from their factory should it somehow be convenient, that they need not do things in a way that suits the workers of the entire country, that in the case of less work they can exclude from the factory those workers who come from another locality – even if they have no expectation of joining another factory somewhere else, and even if the current workers could instead divide up the work equally among all.

The result is that actually implementing the slogan of the anarchists, and transferring disposal over each separate enterprise completely into the hands of the workers in that particular enterprise, amounts to dividing the single proletarian class into petty-bourgeois groups and *artels*, which then lead to feuds and internal strife in the ranks of the toiling people.

Let us now consider the results that would follow from introducing the anarchist economic system.

Suppose that every factory and every village constitutes a completely independent anarchist commune. Every commune works on whatever it chooses, however it chooses, and just as much as it chooses. Ask yourself just how any distribution of labour-power and of the instruments of production will be accomplished in such an economic system (if we can even use that word). We have seen how this goal is accomplished in capitalism, albeit with great difficulty and massive waste of resources, and how the same goal would be reached in communism much more readily and with no particular costs. With an anarchist economy, this goal simply cannot be reached. Just consider a brief example. Assume that the industrial consumption of coal is growing more quickly than it is being mined. With a capitalist economy, the looming shortage would be signalled in advance, albeit frequently later than is required, by the market-prices of coal, which would begin to rise sharply and would thus increase the price of shares in coal-enterprises. An influx of capital into the coal-industry will increase output, or else ways will be found to purchase coal abroad. With a communist system and universal accounting, the threatening shortage of coal will be known in advance and preventive measures can be taken much sooner than in the capitalist system. But what will happen with the anarchist management of separate communes?

What will happen is that the shortage of coal will become known when there is already no fuel for the furnaces. As a result, the enterprises that consume coal will come to halt, and at that point someone will have to take responsibility for expanding the coal-industry. But if expansion is only possible through opening new mines, and if new mines require special supplies of all the necessary implements as well as of technical personnel and workers, then the question arises as to what organisations are capable of fixing the whole business and whether, under anarchism, such organisations can even be permitted.

The same chaos will be happening in all the other branches of labour. Overproduction, together with unemployment, would be the eternal lot of an anarchist economy. For anarchism, there would only be two possible ways of overcoming the complete dissolution of the entire economy and avoiding a massively unproductive expenditure of resources. One is to preserve the whole commodity-economy and the market; that is, to have each commune sell its output in the market and purchase in the market what it requires. The other is to have an account of the required labour, needs and supplies of the entire country done by central and local organs that direct the economy and the distribution of resources and means – not according to the wishes of separate individuals or communes, but according to the interests of industry as a whole. There is no third alternative.

There are anarchists who, in the attempt to save the freedom of separate communes (a freedom that would prove, in future, to be worse than any necessity), do not oppose preserving the commodity-economy. Their teacher, in this respect, is the petty-bourgeois Proudhon. Others, the anarchist-syndicalists and anarchist-communists, for example, having learned something from socialists, are not alarmed by the word 'accounting'; they are for accounting, but only if the accounts are kept by individual trade-unions (or syndicates) and if they negotiate between themselves concerning the volume of products that have to be produced by each profession.

Of course, this is already a great step forwards, but it makes no sense without going further.

Above all, it is a matter of no consequence just who takes account of what volume of products is needed for production, of the scale of consumption, or who does the accounting of inventories, and so on. The whole point is the reason why there must be accounting to begin with. If accounting is done just so that the statistical tables will please some professor of political economy, then the task is not worth undertaking. Accounting is, first and foremost, needed for an **organised distribution of labour-power.**

But organised distribution certainly will not always mean the voluntary distribution that is of such concern to the anarchists. There is no doubt that some workers will be distributed to the professions they prefer, some will move out of a sense of duty to society, and some will be have to be compelled to move through the application of labour-discipline.

But might not the notorious compulsion be avoided if workers in those branches with a labour-shortage could be guaranteed more benefits and more products than workers receive in other professions, where there is a surplus of labour-power?

This could happen, but it would mean inequality in distribution and bribing one group at the expense of others – paying a sort of premium for lack of consciousness and for failure to understand the common interest.

This means that in the realm of production the anarchists face an insoluble task. They can have free trade between separate communes or, as they put it delicately, 'voluntary agreement' (buying and selling also means voluntary agreement), in which case the distribution of labour-power will take place just as in capitalism but at the cost of equality – long live the free competition so vividly defended by Proudhon. Or else there must be accounting and control over production on the scale first of the country and later of the entire world – away with the independence of each commune from the others as if they were baronial castles and medieval guilds; away with all the fears of any kind of organised distribution, even though in the first period it might occasionally be compulsory; and away with personal freedom in circumstances where it restricts the genuine freedom of all. But that would also mean forgetting about anarchism as its founders have hitherto understood it.

Under the capitalist system, distribution of the social income, or of all the values created by labour throughout the country, is designed primarily to satisfy the appetites of the ruling classes. Generally speaking, in any class-society the social groups that control production and possess state-power appropriate for themselves whatever share of the social product they can manage without fundamentally undermining the existence of the oppressed and toiling classes who are the foundation for creating all values. In any class-society, distribution of the national income is, first of all, based upon inequality. This distribution occurs chaotically and spontaneously. Every class acquires whatever it can grab from the total sum of created values following a cruel struggle with the other classes in which the final distribution depends upon the balance of forces between struggling parties. The stronger a class is economically, the more organised it is and the closer it is to possessing the apparatus of state-power, the bigger is the share of national income it can grab for itself.

But distribution of the national income in capitalist society involves not only class-struggle but also struggle within a single class. The class of capitalists and entrepreneurs wages a struggle not just against a general rise in the workers' wages; each separate manufacturer also strives to beat out the others in merciless market-competition. Moreover, the organisation of trusts, of syndicates and the system of state-capitalism, which has advanced so successfully during the period of World-War, already signifies transition to new forms of distribution, to more highly organised distribution of the national income. Centralisation within the trade-union movement and the system of wage-tariffs also introduce a certain organisation into distribution from the opposite corner, involving the sellers of labour-power.

Communism will mean not just equality in distribution, which is connected with the elimination of classes and the transformation of all into workers with equal rights; it will also mean conscious and organised distribution of the social income, without the use of force, as in the past, and according to completely different principles.

It would seem that the most just distribution of the social product would be according to the labour-expenditure that each contributes.

Suppose a worker has put in an eight-hour day and receives the corresponding right to a certain quantity of products whose production requires eight hours of labour. Every worker has his own record in a booklet, and on the basis of the labour-hours entered there, which he has contributed to society during a month, shall we say, he has the right to acquire back from society a corresponding volume of products from the social stores.

But the justice of such distribution is, in fact, still far from true communism. In this case, everyone receives what he contributes; he gets his labour back in another form and in an amount equal to what he gave.

This is still not communism in the sphere of distribution, but only a remnant of the petty-bourgeois habit of watching out for one's own and demarcating it from what is shared. People are not born equal in terms either of strength or abilities. An eight-hour working day is easier for some than it is for others.

One person needs to consume more, another less.

One has a family, the other is not married.

Moreover, the means of consumption will be distributed only on the abstract basis of labour-hours contributed, without taking into consideration other important circumstances connected with the scale of need and the physical strength of the worker.

Even less just would be distribution of products according to the volume of output provided by each worker. The natural differences of ability would stand out here all the more clearly, the inequality would be all the greater, and we would be even further from communism in distribution.

The most just and truly communist distribution occurs only when each member of society acquires products according to his needs – if the products are abundant – and if they are limited in quantity, on the basis of equality with all other members of society, with no regard to who worked how long and how much he produced.

Each must produce as much as his strength and talents permit without exhausting himself in work, but also consciously not working less than the minimum that is statistically established as a norm by the central council of the national economy (or some other such organisation), a minimum below which the level of output would entail a national economic crisis and inadequate consumption. But when the worker will no longer strictly calculate his hours above the norm, it will also be easier to overlook hours below the norm; that is, it will generally no longer be necessary to keep count of the hours of each worker. This will mean that each contributes to society according to his strength and abilities. These strengths and abilities will include a sense of selflessness and a desire to contribute as much benefit as possible, in other words, all the best instincts and impulses of man that can only be fully awakened in communism.

Whereas every small proprietor, after completing his work, say, sewing a pair of boots, not only does not sever the connection with his product, but, on the contrary, only now begins to calculate how much of **my** labour is invested in it and how much I can receive for this product, the communist worker loses all connection with the product of his labour following production. Already in large-scale capitalist production, the worker who contributes some small portion or other of the total labour involved in a locomotive, for example, can never envisage the whole object. The unskilled worker and the day-labourer are often even less able to see and perceive the fruits or their labour. The only record of the labour that remains is either in the proletarian's labour-book or else in the book of the factory-inspector. Still, there is a record of a certain amount of labour. The right that follows from this labour is the property of the worker, a part of his labour against which he can withdraw so much in the form of other products. With full communism, on the contrary, even this record will vanish. The worker, so to speak, pours his labour into an enormous social vat; this labour does not belong to him; but, from the other side of this vat, he opens a tap for the satisfaction of his needs. Millions pour in their labour and millions consume according to their needs, with no consideration given to whether someone gave more and consumes less or made less and consumes more.

The reader may say: 'All this is excellent, but we happen just now to be very far from true communism. Is it really possible to turn now to distribution on purely communist principles?'

We answer: no, we cannot decree a right to true communism; it must be earned, and we must grow towards it. And before reaching full communism, of course, mankind must still travel a certain preliminary and possibly quite long path. Given that bourgeois relations have yet to be broken up completely, given that we have advanced even less towards a finished structure of communist society, and given the numerous and profound bourgeois property-owning habits that have been developed over centuries among the working class itself, the only kind of distribution that is possible is one that corresponds to the existing level of development. It is not possible to leap over this stage; we must pass through it to a higher one. And we think that distribution will turn out to be a secondary matter once things are properly set up along correct communist lines within the sphere of production itself. Through lived experience, on the one hand, and as a result of rapid growth of the productive forces and a surplus of product-supply, on the other, communist distribution will inevitably be realised.

At the present moment, even if the non-labouring classes were eliminated, we would still not have [communist] economic distribution; on the contrary, we would still face the fact of class-struggle between workers and peasants for a greater share of the national income, that is, a struggle among the toilers themselves. It is not just the kulak who opposes the grain-monopoly and resists any accounting of his farm by state-organs, but also the simple well-to-do peasant who is trying to sell flour and other products of the countryside at the highest price possible. And why does he oppose accounting?

Leaving aside simple ignorance and the long-established and well-deserved hostility to the state that tsarism has created in the countryside, the average peasant opposes accounting because it is not beneficial to him, because it can reveal the inequality in income-distribution between the worker and the strong peasant to the disadvantage of the former, whereas the poor peasants can only benefit from conscious and (relatively) just distribution of this income. To distribute income justly, on labour-principles, between peasant and worker means establishing firm prices on all industrial products so that on average, let us say, an hour, a day, or a month of work of average intensity would be paid approximately the same.

At the present moment, therefore, we are still very far from truly communist distribution. In moving towards it, we must, first of all, eliminate without exception all sources of non-labour incomes that are holdovers from bourgeois society, while introducing a labour-duty for the former privileged classes. Then, we must transform the small proprietor into a worker of socialist society and tear out by the roots any possibility of class-struggle between the toilers over a greater share of the social income. Further, the masses will have to become convinced through experience of the superiority of truly communist consumption. In the beginning, for instance, people with families will receive additional compensation from the state. Then, the vast majority will see in reality that dividing the product between workers is not only unjust to those with families, and especially large families, but also pointless. Today's unmarried person is tomorrow's married person, and after that a person with a family. Whatever he gained in the past, while unmarried, he will now lose upon acquiring a family.

It turns out that the only winners in such a distributive system might be childless bachelors, that is, the group that does not return to nature what it has received from it – life itself. Already today, in many of the peasant-communes that have grown up, we see distribution on the basis of principles that are close to genuine communism. What is easy to introduce in a particular commune is difficult, but not impossible, to achieve in a state-commune. In the future, when there is no longer any need to encourage labour-productivity in particular communes and factories with special bonuses for production above the norm, when all members of communist society will be able, without counting hours of work, to provide a surplus of necessary products, and when accumulation of any kind of inventories will be absolutely pointless and even laughable – the time will come for truly communist distribution.

We see, therefore, that realisation of communist distribution will involve a certain natural process. Communist production will be perfected; in connection with this, distribution will also be perfected; and man himself will be perfected in the benevolent conditions of a society that has eliminated classes. And just as it is senseless, at the present moment, to dream of a rapid and thus coercive achievement of communist reconstruction throughout the entire economy, including even small-peasant farms, so it would be senseless to attempt, during the current transitional epoch, to apply the kind of distribution-system that is characteristic of a strong and mature communist society that has grown up on new principles and has possibly involved more than a single generation of people.

Anarchism, as represented by its most influential theorists such as Kropotkin, Jean Grave, Malatesta, Reclus and others, proclaims its support for communism on the same basis as communism does, that is, 'each contributes to society according to his abilities, and each receives from society according to his needs'.

But it is not difficult, of course, to express a good wish; the difficulty is in making it come to life. And it is here that anarchism tangles itself up in insoluble contradictions and turns out, in practice, to be a miserable plaything in the hands of petty-bourgeois spontaneity.

Communism does not simply proclaim equality in distribution; it also demonstrates, as we have seen above,[7] the conditions in which communist distribution can actually be realised. The anarchists consider it redundant to enter into any discussion of how, under what conditions, and through what kind of gradual process one or another point of their programme can be implemented.

Once the social revolution has begun, there must be an attempt to make every factory quickly into an independent commune and to make consumption immediately communist. Anarchists do not like to wait, and Kropotkin, for example, suggests beginning, first of all, with distribution according to communist principles, and then production will catch up with the scale of consumption. It is true that such a cautious anarchist as Malatesta warns against thinking that communist distribution can be achieved in any and all circumstances. He finds that, in order to have such distribution, people must grow, because it requires a high level of consciousness. But our Russian anarchists do not heed the warnings of Malatesta, because almost all of them belong to the party of 'immediate anarchists', a fact for which they have already been sufficiently and deservedly punished.

The question is: how can distribution on the basis of purely communist principles be realised when each factory is converted into an independent commune, when one commune will be in more advantageous and another in less advantageous conditions (for example, one factory with advanced and the other with backward technology), and when, finally, anarchism considers any compulsory equalisation of incomes to be inadmissible coercion?

Moreover, how can the masses be transferred immediately from capitalist into anarchist society at the low level of consciousness in which they are left by capitalism, which has corrupted and suffocated them?

The task is truly insoluble. Anarchism must either quickly acknowledge the unfeasibility of its ideal when the social revolution occurs and accept the inevitability of certain stages of development while society grows towards communist consumption, or else it must liquidate the emerging difficulties in the most expe-

---

7. [There is an error in the text, which says 'as we have seen below'.]

ditious way possible: that is, by declaring the people to be angels and by dismissing, as a malicious slander against the toiling people, every projection that individual groups, after becoming petty-bourgeois, will protect their own group-interests above all else.

The anarchists prefer, of course, the second way out, all the more so because it is convenient for purposes of propaganda: it offends no-one to declare that the masses are angels and super-conscious members of society.

In reality though, if the plants and factories became independent communes at the moment of social revolution, as in Russia following the October Revolution for example, then not only could there be no talk of communist distribution but the contrary would actually prevail: separate workers' groups would find themselves in conditions of the greatest inequality, and within the working class itself the ground would be prepared for a civil war of the worst possible type, a war between different groups of workers over dividing the products of their labour. The lived experience of our own Revolution, as we shall see below, provides a practical illustration of this.

Things cannot turn out otherwise. Life is what determines the consciousness of the people. If, under capitalism, the separate group-interests within the proletariat yielded to the general interests of the entire class, which was then under the pressure of capital, these group- and professional interests must begin to stir once more with the elimination of capital's power.

In communist society, separate groups of workers will have no possibility of growing rich at the expense of others, for distribution will be managed in the interests of the overwhelming majority of workers by organs that the majority have elected.

But this is not the case with anarchism. Every independent commune-factory can become a stronghold for protecting the narrow group-interests of that factory alone, instead of all the workers of society, and this will lead to such inequality in distribution that must horrify every honest anarchist.

Let us take an example. Suppose that after the Revolution we have an array of factory-communes in the South, in Petrograd, and also in the Urals. With the existing level of technology, most factories in the Urals will have labour-productivity two or three times lower than in the South. This means that, with the same number of workers and the same working day, every average factory-commune in the South will turn out two or three times more products. Suppose, in addition, that these factory-communes exchange their products with each other. Who will then receive more in exchange, the worker in the South, or in the Urals?

The Urals worker will be deprived not through any fault of his own, but because the factory owner-predators in the Urals did not care about improving the technology.

Hence, even in a single branch of industry there will be no equality in distribution. Whatever the factory, it has its own particular norms of output and income. And that is not all. The branches of industry that are most important for the economy of the whole country would have the opportunity to secure a privileged position at the expense of those that are less important. Consequently, it is not only a single miners' commune, with richer ore and better coal than another, that would provide a better income for its workers, but the entire coal-industry would be in a position to secure generally better conditions for its workers than would be the case in less important branches of labour.

The situation here would, in certain respects, be even worse than under capitalism. In capitalist society, the free capitals could flow into one or another branch of industry such that privileged monopolies on the part of the individual branches were almost impossible. With the existence of free anarchist factory-communes, it would be impossible to eliminate the privileged position of individual factories and branches of industry without coercion and the organised pressure of the majority who are being robbed. The only other way would be to open competing enterprises. But with what resources? Would taxes be introduced? Surely every anarchist would then sound the alarm, because a taxation-system presupposes a state-apparatus.

Could there be voluntary unions of communes with an interest in eliminating monopoly?

This is a possibility, but there would be no way of restraining coal-miners and railroad-workers from launching a struggle against any such unions that would weaken their monopoly-position. The struggle might lead to re-creation of the same sort of power that the anarchists would have just eliminated, which would then go to whichever side is stronger and would consolidate its victory. If the majority were afraid to impose its decision by means of organised pressure, then, in the best of circumstances, the monopolistic organisation would be able to defend its privileged position with bayonets and other such means. The result is that freedom for the minority would turn out to be compulsion and constraint for the majority. The one would be free to roam only because the other would be pinned down.

Anarcho-syndicalism in practice simply leads to the rise of privileged groups within the working class, to the robbing of some strata of workers by others, and to reinforcement of the habits associated with owning small property. This is plainly evident in the example of the Cheremkovo mines, where anarchists secured a majority and the results soon followed. The Cheremkovo workers declared the mines to be 'their own'; they opposed any nationalisation of the mines and introduced exactly the kind of 'communism' in distribution that makes the hair of every ideological anarchist stand on end. They set a price of sixty *kopeks* per *pood* for 'their' coal and refused to make deliveries for anything but cash, even though the Siberian railway was coming to a halt for want of coal. The importunities of the Cheremkovo anarchists had to be satisfied in order to keep the Siberian railway operating, and the result was that a Cheremkovo coalminer earned fifty roubles a day at the same time as the average wage in other types of labour and other localities was five times less.

Here you have an example of the sort of 'communist distribution' that results from conversion of separate factories and plants into independent communes. The predatory inclinations of the Cheremkovo workers even provoked protests from the anarchists themselves, although they were behaving exactly according to the recipe of their teachers. To begin with, they rapidly converted the mines into an independent 'commune' and threatened to blow them up should the workers' authority think of socialising them. Then they entered into a voluntary 'agreement' with the railway and set up 'communist distribution'. And when the anarchists became agitated with their dear students, who were simply implementing their programme, they then raised the same charge against the workers that is raised against anarchism. It is easy to declare a rapid transition to communist distribution. But it is silly to become annoyed when what actually happens is that the whole mass of the toilers are fleeced by a single group of workers. It is even more foolish to focus one's annoyance not on one's own mediocrity and inability to comprehend the connection between a mode of production and a mode of distribution, but instead on the workers, whom the anarchists themselves – certainly, through no fault of the workers – consider to be angels who are capable at any given moment of establishing anarchism.

In opposition to the anarchists, communists promote real communist distribution, but not by treating it as a trifling matter that the masses are fully prepared to implement. They begin by declaring that the task is difficult, they take the masses as they really are, and they set out the route that leads to the goal, without depending in any way on the pious wishes of separate groups of workers.

As an inevitable result of the higher stage of communist production, communist distribution can and must be realised. Then, it will not only be the best and most conscious groups who will be communists in distribution by their own choice, but the same will also apply out of necessity to people with pettybourgeois inclinations, if and when this inherited illness reappears.

The class-basis of anarchism

Every teaching and every theory remains relatively insignificant so long as it involves no more than a few people. When these few people increase the number of their supporters and become a more-or-less important party, then the teaching begins to look quite different. When the party that has formed begins to look for and finds support among the masses, then, in most cases, its programme changes beyond recognition in the course of being implemented. Strictly speaking, the leaflets on which the programme is printed may be reproduced without any change, but the Party's tactics, that is, its practical activity, rather than leading to the goal set out in the programme, will often lead it in another direction that is often completely the opposite. This happens because the Party's programme – or more often, certain of the slogans based upon it – are adopted and modified by the masses according to their own interests of the moment. From being the leader of the masses, the party turns into the source for ideas and arguments that justify the actions of the masses at the particular time. Those who imagine themselves to be the leaders end up taking orders from the masses, and often, for fear of being dethroned, become simply the blind instrument of their master, whose interests they serve.

This means that, with every teaching and every programme, a distinction must be made between two things: between what is on paper and for show and what is vital and real. In itself, for example, socialism is the programme of labour in its attempt to emancipate itself from capital. But socialism in the hands of the Scheidemanns, Sembats and Chernovs is a provocation for the proletariat to go to the slaughter-house in the interests of German imperialism on the one side and Anglo-French imperialism on the other; it is a matter of covering the baseness and brutality of capitalism with the red fabric of a socialist banner.

In itself and as a teaching, anarchism involves a number of wishes concerning the reconstruction of society on the basis of new principles, and the point about the liquidation of the state is quite compatible with the path that social development follows after capitalist domination is liquidated. But once anarchism falls into the sturdy hands of social strata that squeeze it like a lemon to get out of it what the present day requires, it is transformed into its own opposite.

When discussing anarchism, one must not simply criticise what is written in the brochures of the anarchists; one must also study how those brochures are subject to criticism by the masses who follow the anarchists, for there is no more harsh and destructive critic of a bankrupt teaching than the actual attempt to implement it.

We have looked at the main outlines of all the bookish hopes of the anarchists. In conclusion, we must look at the question of whom anarchism serves in practice, whose interests find protection in it and, in particular, which group-interests anarchism has had to defend in the course of our own Revolution.

It has long been noted in socialist literature that in Western Europe, anarchism is always most widespread in countries that are mainly petty-bourgeois – such as France, Italy, Switzerland and Russia – and it is least widespread in countries with large-scale capital and a factory-proletariat numbering in the millions, such as Germany, England or Belgium. In America, anarchism enjoys success mainly among European immigrants. Moreover, even in one-and-the-same country, anarchism usually enjoys more success among workers in the handicrafts and in small-scale industry and less success in large-scale capitalist enterprises. It has also been noted that anarchist attitudes always and everywhere grow during years of industrial crises and unemployment. It has been established that there was a strengthening of anarchism during the period when the revolution in Russia was demoralised and declining in 1906–8 and also during the decline of the October Revolution, around the time that followed the Brest peace.

These facts and observations are established beyond any doubt. And what do these facts tell us?

They point to some connection between anarchism and a petty-bourgeois foundation, between anarchism and those groups of the population that have been disoriented, such as the unemployed or the *déclassés*, that is, people who have lost their ties to a particular class, as in the case of the lumpenproletariat (the down-and-out proletariat) and especially in the case of the lumpenproletariat during a period of revolution.

But we cannot say on the basis of these observations that anarchists are the party of the petty-bourgeois class, of the lumpenproletariat, or of the unemployed. In fact, anarchism is not any one of these exclusively, although, in certain conditions, it is all three of them.

Why are there so many petty bourgeois in anarchism?

The answer is because anarchism is against every kind of state-power, and the petty bourgeois, especially when he is being ruined, is, likewise, opposed to the state. The petty bourgeoisie is a class incapable of establishing its own dictatorship. Power never stays for long in the hands of this class, and if it is grabbed from the hands of the gentry it becomes the booty of either the big bourgeoisie or the proletariat.

But when state-power is in the hands of big capital, it implements a policy that seizes the petty bourgeois by the scruff of his neck and accelerates his proletarianisation. On the other hand, proletarian power neither supports nor strengthens the small independent undertaking when it is being ruined, and when the petty bourgeois tries to profiteer at the expense of other toilers, it decisively repudiates him. With respect to state-power, the petty bourgeois is an anarchist by virtue of his class-position, especially in a period when the position of the small-scale economy is becoming completely hopeless.

Why is the lumpenproletariat inclined to anarchism? Because this social group strives for communism in the sphere of distribution (everything that is yours is mine) with no regard to production. Anarchism proposes to begin immediately with implementing equality in distribution. This is what the tramp needs, and during this interval of time he is a convinced anarchist; but when matters turn to production, then he will bid the anarchists farewell.

The inclination to anarchism grows in moments of acute unemployment for the same reasons. For the less conscious groups of the unemployed, who find themselves in critical circumstances, the question of how to improve their position **now**, of how to achieve redistribution of the country's food-supplies now, is much more interesting than having to ponder the task of eliminating the whole capitalist system and unemployment in general. This is why anarchism, with its emphasis on distribution, also finds supporters here. This is especially the case because anarchism is always willing to embrace adventurism in this regard, and has no misgivings about advising the masses to take from whatever source is to hand. In the meantime, it is clear that distribution of the existing supply of products is a small detail when it comes to resolving all the questions associated with the liquidation of capitalism; and no seizure or distribution of the supplies of capitalist society can occur without carrying the political part of the Revolution through to the end, that is, without wresting power from the hands of the bourgeoisie. In this respect, the temptation to find an easier way, the way that anarchists point to, is, in fact, an enticement to follow an even longer route that would never lead the masses to bread.

During the retreat of the first Russian Revolution, the successes of anarchism among certain parts of the proletariat, among the handicraftsmen and the proletarian intelligentsia, can be explained as follows. The struggle to overthrow tsarism ended in failure. The masses did not succeed in improving their position through an organised seizure of power. When people began to scatter in all directions, when everyone was trying to improve his own position after failing to improve that of the class as a whole, when the period of expropriations began, anarchism appeared to be an opportune justification for such actions. It seemed to those undertaking the expropriations that they were fighting against capital and tsarism, that they were attacking the enemy, when, in reality, these actions by small groups, in the interests of small groups, meant running away from the revolution: they might do harm to individual capitalists and agents of the autocracy, but they posed no threat to the class-domination of the capitalists and the gentry in general.

At the start of the Revolution of 1917–18, anarchism exercised no influence. It began to acquire strength as unemployment grew and as the difficulties of life increased for the toiling masses, while the possibility of quickly alleviating them in an organised way declined because of the attack on the Russian Revolution by world-capital. Following Brest, that is, the retreat of the Russian Revolution in the face of German imperialism, anarchism began to enjoy significant successes.

This was a time when the working masses had to come together, organise tightly around the soviets, introduce strict discipline and subordinate group interests to the general interests. Let us now take a look at which groups clung to anarchism – or more accurately, to particular anarchist slogans – during this period of revolutionary ebb and the beginning of organised construction.

The Soviet authority stands for nationalisation of the factories, namely, the transfer of the instruments of production into the hands of the producers, not those of separate groups within the class.

Anarchism came out for transfer of the factories and plants to the workers of those particular factories and plants. The least conscious groups of workers, those most contaminated by the habits of property-owners, supported anarchism in this connection not because they were interested in anarchist communism, but for exactly the opposite reason: they wanted to improve their own position at the expense of all the rest of the toiling masses. In this regard, anarchism relies upon the petty bourgeois within the workers' ranks, upon the property-owner and those with a petty-bourgeois psychology.

The Soviet power strives to introduce labour-discipline, whose rationale is the following: production is lagging far behind consumption, products are scarce, and productivity must be raised at any cost. There are two ways out of this position: either capital will be victorious, should we prove incapable of organising production and expanding the productive forces, or else we will raise production, introducing labour-discipline **ourselves**, and we will save the proletariat from the misfortune of having to increase production under the guns of the Skoropadskys, the whip of the Cossack and the lash of hunger. The struggle is between these two alternatives alone.

And which of them has anarchism supported?

With its demagogic struggle against labour-discipline, it has, in fact, supported the Skoropadskys and the Ryabushinskys; it has been an obstacle to the **communist path** of solving problems that can otherwise be solved in present circumstances only by the **whip of the Skoropadskys**. Anarchism has relied upon the least conscious groups among the workers who are trying to work less and receive more even in socialist enterprises.

To acquire values, without creating something of equal value in exchange, amounts to robbing those workers in other factories who are working conscientiously. In this connection, anarchism is the expression of petty-bourgeois interests and of backward groups within the working class, because, **in the final analysis, the entire class of the toilers consumes only what it produces and has no interest in lowering labour-productivity: the whole class cannot rob itself and, therefore, cannot protest against the labour-discipline that is increasing the quantity of products in the hands of the toiling people.**

We will go further. The Soviet power is trying to implement the grain-monopoly as a fact and to impose accounting on the economic activities of the petty bourgeois of the city and the village. This operation is very disadvantageous to the petty proprietor, because it deprives him of the opportunity to speculate on hunger and to profiteer at the expense of the rest of the toiling masses. (If every small proprietor had an average labour-income, he would have no reason to fear control.)

The anarchists, like the communists, are for a just and even distribution of the bread that is either not available in the country or else in very short supply. But there is only one way to undertake this distribution at present, and that is the state grain-monopoly. This measure cannot be implemented without the state-apparatus, and particularly without organised compulsion. The anarchists, who are rebelling against all power and Soviet power in particular, are receiving lively support from petty-bourgeois speculators who also oppose Soviet power because it deprives them of the opportunity to rob the starving and to bring their own supplies to market. Here too, therefore, the anarchists are receiving support from elements with the most vile and grasping interests.

The War and Revolution also created numerous groups of people who have been separated from their class and from productive labour, who either do not wish or are unable for some reason to return to the routine of working life. Confronted by the organised political force of the Soviet state, which is implementing all sorts of requisitions and confiscations according to a definite plan and in the interest of distributing to all of the needy according to a specific norm, these groups go into opposition and are defending their right to launch organised raids frequently under the flag of anarchism. Such 'anarchism' merely represents freedom to embezzle, and it is obviously connected with the wish to evade any control and restrictions on incomes, to evade productive labour, and this is perfectly obvious.

The ebbing of the Revolution has encouraged petty-bourgeois attempts to snatch as much as possible for oneself with no regard to what tomorrow will bring for the great army of toilers. This, too, is favourable soil for anarchism because the first obstacle to confront plunderers of all ranks and degrees is the proletarian power. What we face here is essentially desertion from the Revolution, just like the anarchist expropriations during the retreat of the first revolution.

Anarchism's deserting character[8] can be seen not only in the economic but also in the political sphere. Soviet Russia is under attack not by some disorganised

---

8. Desertion on the whole front of class-struggle by no means indicates personal bravery on the part of separate individuals and groups. An expropriation may be conducted very bravely, but this does not mean that expropriations cease to represent flight in all directions away from the fundamental tasks of the Revolution.

force, but by highly organised world-capital with a splendid military apparatus, even if it is in the first stages of decomposing. The resistance to this enemy must likewise be strictly organised. The struggle requires a disciplined army at the front and a disciplined army of producers in the rear. Everyone must do not **what he wants**, and not to **whatever extent he wants**, or just **how he wants**, but rather what must be done and in the way it must be done in the interests of the struggle as a whole. To protest against such organised struggle, and to claim the personal right to decide just how to struggle – for example, an anarchist detachment operating independently makes its own decisions not only about attack, but also **about retreat** – means deserting the difficulties of the struggle and putting oneself in the same privileged political position as the economic position asserted by the Cheremkovo worker when he claimed the mines for himself and 'freely' sought payment five times in excess of the norm, or in the same position as the petty bourgeois who wants control over **his** person and over shipment of **his** grain regardless of how it will hinder any improvement of food-conditions for millions of others and for the entire country.

Finally, another rich source of nourishment for anarchism is dissatisfaction with public authority, even on the part of genuine working people, if it takes over leadership of the country in conditions that are already deteriorating regardless of the will of anyone in power. The authorities turn out to be responsible for the consequences of tsarism's existence, for the effects of the War, for economic backwardness, and so on. When many average people, exhausted by the burdens of life that afflict the toilers, shout 'Down with Soviet power', what they are really shouting is 'down with the high cost of living, down with shortages of commodities, down with hunger, down with unemployment'. And to the great chagrin of the anarchists they are also the first to cry 'Long live Soviet power' if, partly due to its own efforts and partly for completely different reasons, commodities appear, bread appears, and prices come down.

The class-basis of anarchism is therefore extremely unreliable and unsteady, changing from one instance to another, and all the successes of anarchism are extremely superficial and fleeting. In any case, the petty-bourgeois element in anarchism almost always takes precedence, in reality, over the proletarian.

The tactics of anarchists

In conclusion, we must say a few words about the tactics of anarchists, that is, the means with which they are attempting to realise their goals.

During a revolutionary time, tactics are a matter of colossal importance. It often happens that a party's very democratic and socialist programme remains just an empty signboard and, in reality, the party directly or indirectly assists the counter-revolution or else reinforces the existing bourgeois-monarchist régime. Everyone is familiar with the examples of European and Russian social-patriots.

As for the anarchists, there is no correspondence between the goals they pose, together with all their good wishes, and the practical results of their activities. This holds especially true of Russian anarchists. The harm that they have done to the Russian Revolution, during its most difficult moments, exceeds that resulting from any of the blows they have struck against the bourgeois order.

In terms of tactics, all anarchists can be divided roughly into three groups: 1) peaceful anarchists who oppose any use of force in achieving their ends; 2) supporters of social revolution who recognise only mass-struggle and reject individual terror, separate attacks on capital, and every similar form of 'propaganda by the deed'; 3) and supporters of mass-revolutionary struggle who also acknowledge individual political and economic terror, expropriations, individual confiscations and so forth.

As for peaceful anarchists of the Tolstoyan type, anarchist mystics, and all those whose thinking inclines towards religion, the bourgeois-gentry and intelligentsia character of this kind of anarchism is so obvious that other anarchist tendencies set themselves apart from the non-resisters. It would, therefore, be pointless to talk about their tactics in this brochure, for this essay is not some scientific study of anarchism. In what follows we will speak only of those anarchists who acknowledge revolutionary means of struggle in pursuit of their goals.

It is characteristic of all anarchism to reject the political struggle and to attempt to focus all attention on the economic struggle.

That the basic goal of the struggle of the proletariat is precisely economic emancipation, that the struggle for economic reconstruction of society is the basic goal and the seizure of state-power only a means to that end – these are things that the founders of scientific communism, Karl Marx and Friedrich Engels, understood before the anarchists, and it was precisely from them that Bakunin learned (although not very well) the materialist understanding of history.

But having announced a profound truth, our great teachers warned against reducing it to a half-truth by recognising only part of it. The economic reconstruction of society on the basis of new principles, even anarchist principles, requires destruction of the state-power created by the exploiting classes and the proletariat's use of political power for the economic suppression of its enemies.

The organised struggle against capital, aiming for its destruction by the forces of the proletariat as a class, is also a political struggle, regardless of what forms it may assume.

When we had to deal, in the pre-revolutionary period, with a bourgeois parliament, we fought against the bourgeois system by using parliament, among other things, for the purpose of political struggle. We told the workers: If you are not strong enough to break up this institution, then you must get elected to it in order not to lose another opportunity to unite our forces and to use the parliamentary tribune for propaganda and organisation. While opportunists and pseudo-socialists of every variety tried at length to distort and misconstrue the true meaning of **our** participation in parliamentary struggle in the sense of **their own** parliamentary cretinism, and while they provided gratifying material for anarchist criticism, the results that we accomplished in this period for the sake of our own goals were not in any way diminished as a result. They are helping us now in our victories, and they will help the European workers in their victories because, along with other means, participation in the parliamentary struggle played a role in the work of the class-education of the proletariat and facilitated the growth of its socialist consciousness.

At the present moment, too, the participation of our comrades in European parliaments, however few they may be, is playing a great role in the work of agitation for proletarian revolution, and agitation from such tribunes supplements the work of underground-leaflets and secret meetings. For an illustration, it is enough to cite one example – the historic statement by comrade Liebknecht in opposition to the War in 1914, which made such an enormous impression on the working masses. In a completely unexpected way, the anarchists themselves indirectly recognised how correct we were in taking part in parliament **for the purpose of socialist propaganda** by entering the soviets and taking part in the All-Russian Congress of Soviets **for the purpose of anarchist propaganda**. They have carried their 'parliamentary enthusiasm' so far that at one time they even appeared in the Central Executive Committee of the soviets.

When the peaceful period ended in Russia and the political struggle assumed the form of direct struggle for proletarian power, the negative attitude of the anarchists to organised class-struggle and the dictatorship of the proletariat condemned them to a miserable role during the epoch of great transformation. After our two revolutions, it would be completely redundant to demonstrate the bankruptcy of anarchist tactics in terms of the political struggle. The proof is evident in the very fact of the victories of the February and October Revolutions. These revolutions triumphed precisely because of the seizure of power, in the first case by a bourgeois bloc, and in the second case by a bloc of the proletariat with the rural poor. If the masses in our Revolution had followed the anarchists even for a moment, if they had agreed to some Lenten sacrifice on the question of power, they would have suffered a cruel defeat in the struggle with the propertied classes. Facing an atomised mass, even if the exploiters' apparatus had been temporarily broken up, the bourgeoisie would have very quickly gathered its forces on a state-scale and, not having to face a similarly unified proletarian force, would have brought the toiling classes once again to their knees.

Now, every worker knows that the greatest blows to the economic domination of capital were struck not before October, but afterwards, that is, following the seizure of power by the proletariat. Having established its dictatorship, the proletariat acquired the possibility of smothering capital in an organised manner and the bourgeois system completely. Just as the anarchists' refusal to destroy and finish off the bourgeois system by using state-power condemned them to nibbling at it in pieces, through confiscating individual mansions, squeezing out individual contributions, and so on, so even earlier, in the first Revolution, their rejection of the struggle for power actually closed off the road to victory for the anarchists and drove them to the path of petty raids on separate capitalists and terror against individual agents of the autocratic régime. It is clear from the anarchists' actions in both the 1905 Revolution and the current revolution that such a tactic can, at most, frighten individual capitalists and dispose of individual government-agents, without shaking the exploitative system as a whole. But the anarchists, so long as they remain anarchists, have no other option. They are organically incapable of organising the toiling masses for victory, and there never has been, nor will there ever be, a case in history when anarchism proves capable of winning a major victory over capital.

The wretchedness of anarchist tactics becomes fully apparent whenever it is necessary to implement any measure that requires organised pressure on capital. Take, for example, labour-conscription for the bourgeoisie, a duty for which the anarchists have tried to agitate in a way that would appear to be even more leftist, even more radical than the Bolshevik-communists. If they were given complete freedom of action, would anarchism be able to accomplish this objective?

Even to pose such a question is laughable. It would be far easier for the anarchists to exterminate everyone with a bourgeois complexion, to exterminate the entire population of the bourgeois districts, than to implement a labour-obligation for the bourgeois **class**. To realise these measures at the current moment requires universal statistics of professions and skills; it requires comprehensive implementation of the grain-monopoly; and it requires a state-wide system of labour-books together with the organisation of the exchange of goods[9] and elimination of monetary tokens. All of these measures presuppose the existence of the proletarian state and its central economic organs, that is, of the kind of apparatus that anarchists avoid like the plague.

Take socialisation of housing. This measure has been partially implemented and can only be fully carried out in an organised manner by the organs of Soviet power. Could the anarchists accomplish it? By beginning with the requisitioning

---

9. [The term used is 'товарообмен'.]

of individual mansions they have shown in reality what their approach would be and just how brilliant the final result would be.

But anarchism not only represents no danger to capitalism as a system; by their tactics in our Revolution and the approach of their agitation, they have also frequently promoted definite successes for the counter-revolution. They have never been able to apportion their attacks on proletarian and on bourgeois power in such manner that their agitation would do more damage to the bourgeois system than to the Revolution and the Soviet authority. At the gravest moments for the Revolution, when the struggle was not between Soviet power and no power, but between the soviets' power and that of the Skoropadskys, the anarchists zealously incited the masses against Soviet organs and did part of the political work of the exploiters. During the Czechoslovak uprising, when counter-revolutionaries were preparing a number of insurrections behind the lines of Soviet troops and, to this end, working up the masses at meetings, the anarchists supported the general chorus of voices that were raising a howl against Soviet power and profoundly suggested that this meant victory for the idea of anarchism and not for the cause of the Dutovs.

It is no surprise that at one meeting of bourgeois politicians in Petrograd, according to newspapers of the time (see *Izvestiya TsIK*), the counter-revolutionaries vested great hope in the anarchists when it came to demoralising Soviet power and planned to use this destructive work for the final victory of a bourgeois dictatorship.

To summarise, it must be recognised that anarchism in Russia has played the role of a school for training workers in the art of defeat on all fronts in the struggle against capital. And the fact that they have so deeply bankrupted themselves in our great Revolution condemns them in future to having virtually no influence over the masses. Not a single group among the working class has any interest in repeating for a second time all their mistakes and ridiculous methods of struggle. Anarchism is not worth so much that anyone would pay that dearly for the right to be instructed in its bankruptcy.

E.A. Preobrazhensky

No. 3
E.A. Preobrazhensky's Chapters from the Book *The ABC of Communism* (Co-authored with N.I. Bukharin)[1]

1919

Chapter VII

The National Question and Communism

§ 55. *National oppression.* § 56. *The unity of the proletariat.* § 57. *The causes of national hatred.* § 58. *The equal rights of nations and the right to self-determination; federation.* § 59. *Who expresses the 'will of the nation'?* § 60. *Anti-Semitism and the proletariat.*

§ 55. National oppression

One of the types of oppression of man by man is national oppression. One of the partitions dividing mankind, apart from class-partitions, is national disunity, including national enmity and hatred.

One of the means of stupefying the proletariat and dulling its class-consciousness is national persecution,

---

1. [From Bukharin and Preobrazhensky 1920. *The ABC of Communism* was written by N.I. Bukharin and E.A. Preobrazhensky and was first published in 1919 to elaborate the new party-programme of the RKP adopted in March at the Eighth Party-Congress. This translation comes from the 1920 edition. The foreword to the book indicated which author contributed the particular chapters. Since the book has long been available in English translation, we have re-translated here only the chapters written by E.A. Preobrazhensky. This translation follows the Russian text more closely than does the one by Eden and Cedar Paul, first published in 1922.]

which the bourgeoisie knew how to use in its own interests.

Let us consider how the conscious proletarian must approach the national question and must resolve it in the interest of the speediest victory of communism.

A nation or nationality is a group of people who are united by a single language and who inhabit a particular territory. There are other indicators of nationality, but these are the most important and fundamental ones.[2]

The meaning of national oppression is best clarified by an example. The tsarist government persecuted the Jews, did not allow them to live throughout Russia, did not admit them into state-service, restricted their entry into schools, organised anti-Jewish pogroms, and so on. The same government did not allow Ukrainians to teach their children in schools using the Ukrainian language, they were forbidden to publish newspapers in their own language, and not a single nationality in the state was permitted freely to decide whether or not they wanted to live as a part of the Russian state.

The German government closed Polish schools; the Austrian government persecuted the Czech language and forcibly imposed German on the Czechs. The English bourgeoisie humiliated, and still humiliates, the indigenous people of Africa and Asia, subjugates the backward semi-savage peoples, plunders them and shoots them for attempts to free themselves from oppression.

In a word, when one nation in a state enjoys all the rights, and another only part of those rights; when a weaker nation is joined to a stronger one and is compelled by it to adopt a foreign language, customs and so forth against its will, so that it cannot live its own life – this is national oppression and national inequality.

§ 56. The unity of the proletariat

First of all, we must pose and resolve the most important and fundamental question: is the German, the Frenchman, the Englishman, the Jew, the Chinaman or the Tatar, regardless of which class he belongs to, an enemy of the Russian worker and peasant? Can he hate or be suspicious of a representative of another people simply because the latter speaks a different language, has skin that is black or yellow, or has different customs and morals? It is clear that he cannot and must not do so. The worker of Germany, the worker of France, or the Negro worker is a proletarian just like the Russian worker. Whatever language the

---

2. For instance, the Jews once had a territory and a common language, but now they have no territory and not all of them know the ancient Jewish language; the gypsies have their language, but they do not have a definite territory. The non-nomadic Tunguses in Siberia have a territory, but they have forgotten their language.

workers of different countries speak, the essence of their position is the fact that they are all exploited by capital and they are all comrades in poverty, oppression and lack of rights.

Can the Russian worker have greater love for his capitalist simply because the latter abuses him with genuinely Russian swearing, cuffs him with a Russian fist, or flogs strikers with a genuinely Russian whip? Of course he cannot, just as the German worker cannot love his capitalist merely because he ridicules him in the German language and in a German manner. The workers of all countries are class-brothers and enemies of the capitalists of all countries.

The same can be said of the poor peasants of all nations. The Hungarian semi-proletarian and the poor peasant of Sicily or Belgium are nearer and dearer to the Russian peasant – to the poor and middle-peasant – than his own wealthy kulak, and this applies all the more to such truly Russian skinflint-landlords as Purishkevich or Markov.

But the workers of the entire world must not merely recognise themselves as brothers by class and brothers in oppression and slavery. It would be a mistake if they each simply cursed their capitalists in their own language, if they only wiped each other's tears and waged the struggle against their enemies solely on their own behalf and within their own state. Brothers in oppression and slavery must be brothers in a single worldwide alliance for the struggle against capital. Forgetting all the national differences that stand in their way, they must unite in a single mighty league for the common struggle against capital. Only by uniting in such an international union can they defeat world-capital. This is why, more than seventy years ago, the founders of communism, Marx and Engels, issued the great slogan in their famous *Communist Manifesto*: 'Proletarians of all countries, unite!'

The working class has to overcome every national prejudice and hatred, not only for the sake of a worldwide attack on capital and complete victory over it, but also for the organisation of a single world-economy. Not only is it impossible for Soviet Russia to live without Donets coal, Baku oil or Turkestan cotton, but the whole of Europe also cannot manage without Russian wood, hemp, flax and platinum and American grain, or Italy without English coal, or England without Egyptian cotton, and so on and so forth. The bourgeoisie was incapable of organising the world-economy, and this is how it broke its own neck. Such an economy can be set right only by the proletariat. And for this it must proclaim the slogan: 'The entire world and all its riches belong to the entire world of labour'. But that kind of slogan means complete renunciation by German workers of their national wealth, and the same is true of English workers, and so on. If national prejudices and national greed stand in the way of the internationalisation of industry and agriculture, then down with them here, there, and everywhere, regardless of how they might be embellished!

§ 57. The causes of national hatred

But it is not enough for Communists to declare war on national oppression and national prejudices, to proclaim an international union in the struggle with capital and a worldwide economic union of the victorious proletariat. It is necessary to find a faster road for overcoming all forms of national chauvinism and egoism, of national stupidity and conceit, of national mistrust among the toiling masses. This heritage from a savage period of human life, and from the savage national persecution of the feudal-bourgeois epoch, continues to weigh like a mountain on the neck of the world-proletariat.

National discord and hostility have very ancient origins. There was a time when separate tribes not only fought each other for land and forests, but simply devoured their own kind from another tribe. The remnants of this savage mistrust and hostility of one people towards another, and even more of one race towards another, continue to survive amongst the workers and peasants of all countries. These remnants of tribal hostility gradually die out with the development of world-exchange, closer economic relations, population-movements and the inter-mixing of different nationalities who find themselves on a single territory, and especially on the basis of the joint class-struggle of the workers of different countries. Yet these remnants of national hostility are not only not diminishing, but are breaking out with new force when the contradiction of class-interest, or the appearance of such contradiction, is added to national hostility.

The bourgeoisie of every country exploits and oppresses its proletariat. But it makes every effort to convince its own proletariat that it is not the enemy, but rather the surrounding peoples. The German bourgeoisie cries to German workers: 'Beat the Frenchman, beat the Englishman'. The English bourgeoisie cries: 'Beat the German!' The bourgeoisie of all countries is beginning, especially in recent times, to cry: 'Beat the Jew!' All of this is done in order to transform the class-struggle of the working class against the oppressor-capitalists into a national struggle.

But the bourgeoisie is not content merely with national persecution as a means of distracting workers from the struggle for socialism. It is trying to interest them materially in the oppression of other peoples. During the recent war, when the German bourgeoisie bawled out 'Germany, Germany above all' (the German national anthem), the bourgeois economists of Germany endeavoured to convince their workers of how much they would benefit from a victory and thus from the oppression and plundering of workers in the defeated countries. Before the War, the bourgeoisie actually did bribe the upper stratum of the working class with its gains acquired from plundering the colonies and from oppressing backward and weak peoples. The workers of the leading European countries, in the form of their most highly-paid groups, yielded to the provocation by the capitalists and allowed the social-patriots to convince them that they, too, have a fatherland once they join in the plundering of colonies and semi-dependent peoples. The worker who is a patriot under capitalism is selling his real fatherland, socialism, for a pittance and is transforming himself into an oppressor of backward and weak nations.

§ 58. The equal rights of nations and the right to self-determination; federation

Declaring merciless war on all oppression of man by man, the Communist Party stands most decisively against national oppression, which is inevitable with the existence of the capitalist system. Even more decisively and mercilessly, it wages the struggle against the slightest complicity in this oppression on the part of the working class itself. But it is not enough for the proletariat of large and powerful states to renounce all attempts at oppression of the other peoples that its own bourgeoisie and aristocracy have crushed. It is also necessary that the proletariat of the oppressed nations harbour no mistrust of their comrades in the countries that were the oppressors. When the Czechs were oppressed by the German bourgeoisie of Austria, the Czech worker considered all Germans alike to be his oppressors. Our tsarism oppressed the Poles, but the Polish population retained its mistrust of all Russians, rather than simply of the Russian tsars, landlords and capitalists. In order to eradicate thoroughly all mistrust by the workers of oppressed nations towards the workers of oppressor-nations, it is necessary not merely to proclaim, but also to establish in fact, full national equality. This equality must be implemented in terms of equal rights of language, schools, religion, and so on. Moreover, the proletariat must be prepared to implement full national self-determination; that is, to allow complete freedom to the toiling majority of any nation to decide the question of whether that nation wants to live in a single state with another, whether it wants to enter into a close and voluntary state-union (a federation), or whether it wants to separate completely.

The reader may ask whether a Communist can really stand up for the separation of nations. What about the single world-proletarian state for which all Communists are striving? There seems to be a contradiction here.

We answer that there is no contradiction here. It is sometimes necessary, precisely in the interests of the most rapid achievement of complete unity of all the toilers of the world, to agree to a temporary separation of one nation from another.

Let us consider two instances that might be encountered.

Assume that in Bavaria, which is now part of a united Germany, a Soviet Republic is proclaimed, while in Berlin the bourgeois dictatorship of Noske and

Scheidemann prevails. Can the Bavarian Communists, in such an event, work for the independence of Bavaria? Not only Bavarian Communists, but also Communists from the rest of Germany must welcome the separation of Soviet Bavaria, for this separation will not be a separation from the German proletariat but only from the yoke of the ruling German bourgeoisie.

Take the reverse case. Throughout all of Germany, with the exception of Bavaria, Soviet power is proclaimed. The bourgeoisie of Bavaria is for separation from Soviet Germany, while the proletariat of Bavaria is for joining with it. How must Communists respond? It is clear that the Communists of Germany must support the Bavarian workers and put down with force of arms any attempt at separation by the Bavarian bourgeoisie. That would not be the suppression of Bavaria but rather suppression of the Bavarian bourgeoisie.

Suppose that Soviet power is proclaimed in both England and Ireland; that is, in the oppressor country and also in the oppressed country. Suppose, further, that the Irish workers do not trust the workers of England, the workers of the country that oppressed them over the course of entire centuries. Suppose they want complete separation from England. This separation is economically harmful. How must English Communists respond in such a case? Whatever happens, they must never respond *with force*, as the English bourgeoisie has done, to maintain the union with Ireland. They must grant it complete freedom to separate. For what purpose? First, in order to show the Irish workers once and for all that it is the English bourgeoisie and not the English workers who have oppressed Ireland, and thus to win their confidence.

Secondly, so that Irish workers may be convinced through experience that an independently existing small state is not beneficial to them. They must be convinced through experience that it is it is possible to organise production in the best way possible only through a close state- and economic union with proletarian England and other proletarian countries.

Let us suppose, further, that some nation with a bourgeois régime wants to separate from a nation with a proletarian régime, and that the working class of the nation that wants to separate, in its majority or at least in large proportion, favours the separation. We may additionally suppose that they are distrustful not only of the capitalists, but also of the workers belonging to the country whose bourgeoisie has oppressed them. In this case, too, it is best to allow the proletariat to deal directly with its own bourgeoisie, for otherwise the bourgeoisie will endlessly repeat: 'It is not we who are oppressing you, but some other country'. The working class will very quickly see that the bourgeoisie wants independence so that it might independently flay the hide of its own proletariat. It will also see that the proletariat of the neighbouring Soviet state calls upon it to form a union not so that it might be exploited or oppressed, but for the sake of joint emancipation from exploitation and oppression.

Thus Communists, being opposed to the separation of the proletariat of one country from another, especially when these countries have close economic ties, can, nevertheless, agree to a temporary separation. In the same way, a mother lets her child touch the fire once so that it will be ten times more anxious to avoid it.

§ 59. Who expresses the 'will of the nation'?

The Communist Party recognises the right of nations to self-determination right up to separation. But it considers that the toiling majority of the nation expresses the nation's will, not the bourgeoisie. Thus it would be correct to say that we recognise not the right of nations to self-determination, but rather the right of the toiling majority of a nation. As for the bourgeoisie, having deprived it during the period of the Civil War and proletarian dictatorship of all civil freedoms, we deprive it also of the right to a voice on the national question.

What can we say about the right of self-determination and separation for nations that are at a very low level, or at the lowest level, of development? What about nations that have no proletariat nor even a bourgeoisie, or else one that is at the very early stage of development? Take, for example, our Tunguses, Kalmyks, Buryats, or the numerous peoples of the colonies. What if these nations seek, shall we say, complete separation from more cultured nations and even from nations that have realised socialism? Would this not be a strengthening of barbarism at the expense of civilisation?

We think that if socialism will be realised in the leading countries of the world, the backward and semi-savage peoples will more readily enter into a general union of peoples precisely on a voluntary basis. The imperialist bourgeoisie, which plundered the colonies and forcibly annexed them, has reason to fear separation of the colonies. The proletariat, which has no intention of plundering the colonies, can acquire the materials it needs from these colonies by way of commodity-exchange, leaving the Tunguses and backward peoples to arrange their own domestic life as they please.

The Communist Party, therefore, in order to put an end to all types of national oppression and inequality, puts forth the demand for self-determination of nations.

The proletariat of all countries will avail themselves of this right in order to destroy nationalism and to enter voluntarily into a federal union.

When this federal union proves inadequate for the creation of a worldwide economy, and when the enormous majority are convinced by their own experience of this inadequacy, then a single worldwide socialist republic will be established.

If we examine the way in which the bourgeoisie posed and resolved (or complicated, as was more often the case) the national question, then we will see that in the epoch of its youth, the bourgeois class resolved the national question one way, but in the epoch of its old age and decay, it does so in a completely different way.

When the bourgeoisie was an oppressed class, when the aristocracy held power with a king or tsar at their head, when the tsars and kings gave away whole peoples to their daughters as marriage-dowries, at that time the bourgeoisie not only spoke fine words about the freedom of nations but even tried to realise this freedom, at least for their own nation. For instance, the Italian bourgeoisie, at the time when Italy was subordinated to the Austrian monarchy, stood at the head of their country's emancipation-movement and strove for the emancipation of Italy from foreign oppression and for unification into a single state. When Germany was divided into tens of petty principalities and was crushed beneath the boot of Napoleon, the German bourgeoisie strove for the unification of Germany into a single powerful state and for emancipation from the French enslavers. When France, having overthrown the autocracy of Louis XVI, was attacked by monarchist states in the rest of Europe, the radical French bourgeoisie led the defence of their country and created the anthem known as the *Marseillaise*. In a word, the bourgeoisie of oppressed nations everywhere stood at the head of their emancipation-struggle, created a very rich national literature, and produced ingenious writers, artists, poets and philosophers.

That happened in the past, when the bourgeoisie itself was an oppressed class. Why did the bourgeoisie of oppressed nations struggle for their emancipation? If one reads their poets and looks at the work of their artists, if one believes their words, it was because they opposed all national oppression and stood for the freedom and self-determination of every nationality, even the smallest. In fact, the bourgeoisie strove in its own day for emancipation from the foreign yoke in order to create *its own* bourgeois state, to plunder its own people *itself*, without any competitors, and to appropriate for *itself* the entire surplus-value created by the workers and toiling peasants of the particular country.

This is revealed in the history of any capitalist country. When the bourgeoisie is oppressed together with its own people, it raises a cry for the freedom of nations *in general* and declares the inadmissibility of *any and all* national oppression. But as soon as the capitalist class acquires power and drives out the foreign conquerors, whether they be a foreign aristocracy or a foreign bourgeoisie, it strives itself to subjugate any weak nationality whose subjugation might be profitable. The revolutionary French bourgeoisie, in the persons of Danton, Robespierre and the other great figures of their first revolution, summoned all the peoples of the world to emancipation from every tyranny; the *Marseillaise*, written by Rouget de Lisle and sung by the soldiers of the Revolution, was understood and cherished by every oppressed people. But that same French bourgeoisie (although represented by a different stratum), under the leadership of Napoleon and to the sound of that same *Marseillaise*, subjugated the peoples of Spain, Italy, Germany and Austria and plundered them throughout the entire period of the Napoleonic Wars. The oppressed German bourgeoisie, in the person of Schiller with his *William Tell*, voiced the struggle of peoples against their foreign tyrants. But that same bourgeoisie, in the persons of Bismarck and Moltke, seized and forcibly annexed the French province of Alsace-Lorraine, seized Schleswig from Denmark, subjugated the Poles of Poznan, and so on. Having emancipated themselves from the yoke of the Austrian aristocracy, the bourgeoisie of Italy began shooting the native Bedouins of Tripoli, the Albanians and Dalmatians on the Adriatic coast and the Turks in Anatolia.

Why did these things happen, and why are they still happening? Why is it that the bourgeoisie always and everywhere put forth the demand for national freedom and was never able to realise it anywhere?

This happens because every bourgeois state, once emancipated from national oppression, inevitably strives for its own expansion. The bourgeoisie of any capitalist country is never satisfied with exploitation solely of its own proletariat. It needs materials from diverse corners of the Earth, and it endeavours to acquire colonies in order that, having enslaved the natives, it might face no obstacles in supplying these materials for its factories. It needs markets for the sale of its commodities, and it endeavours to acquire them in the form of backward countries, with complete indifference to the attitude of the population and of the young and still-immature bourgeoisie of these countries. It needs countries to which it can export redundant capital and whence it can extract profit for itself from the local workers, and it enslaves these countries and disposes of them in the same way that it disposes of its own country. If it encounters a strong bourgeoisie that stands in the way of seizing colonies and economically enslaving other countries, then the question is decided by war, such as the World-War that has just ended in Europe. The result is that the colonies and backward countries find themselves in the same enslavement but merely with a different oppressor. But in addition to this, the list of enslaved countries now includes defeated Germany, Austria and Bulgaria, which before the War were free countries. In this way, development of the bourgeois system not only fails to shorten the list of countries finding themselves under the yoke of other countries and the bourgeoisie of those countries, but, instead, precisely the opposite happens: bourgeois domination leads to universal national oppression, and the entire world finds itself under the heel of the group of capitalist states that were victorious in the War.

§ 60. Anti-Semitism and the proletariat

One of the most dangerous forms of national persecution is anti-Semitism; that is, persecution of the Semitic race, which includes the Jews (together with the Arabs). The tsarist autocracy persecuted and victimised the Jews in the hope of saving itself from the worker-peasant Revolution. You are poor, said the Black Hundreds, because you are being fleeced by the Jews, and they attempted to direct the discontent of the oppressed workers and peasants not against the landlords and the bourgeoisie but against the entire Jewish nation. Meanwhile, the Jews, as with any nation, are divided into different classes, and it is only the bourgeois strata of Jews who plunder the people in the same way as the capitalists of other nations. The Jewish workers and artisans always lived within the Pale of Settlement in conditions of terrible deprivation and poverty, even greater poverty than that of workers in the rest of Russia.

The Russian bourgeoisie persecuted the Jews not only to divert from itself the anger of its own exploited workers, but also to rid itself of competitors in trade and industry.

Finally, we recently see in all countries the intensified persecution of Jews by the bourgeois classes. The bourgeoisie of various countries struggles in this way not only against one of its competitors in exploiting the proletariat, but also, after the manner of Nicholas II, against the approaching revolution. Until recently, anti-Semitism in Germany, England and America was relatively weak. Today, even English ministers are delivering anti-Semitic speeches. This is a clear sign that the bourgeois structure in the West is on the eve of collapse and that the bourgeoisie is attempting to buy its way out of the workers' revolution by serving up the Rothschilds and Mendelssohns for dinner. In Russia, anti-Semitism abated during the February Revolution and, to the contrary, began to grow all the more as the Civil War between the bourgeoisie and the proletariat intensified and as bourgeois efforts became increasingly hopeless.

All of this demonstrates that anti-Semitism is one of the forms of struggle against socialism, and it is tragic that any worker or peasant should allow himself to be played for a fool by his class-enemies.

Literature: Lenin, N., *O prave natsii na samoopredelenie* (articles in the journal *Prosveshchenie*); Stalin, J., *Natsional'nyi vopros i Marksizm*; Zalevsky, K., *Natsional'nyi vopros i Internatsional;* Petrov, S., *Pravda i lozh' o evrayakh*; Kautsky, K., *O evrayakh*; Bebel, A., *Antisemitizm i proletariat;* Steklov, Yu., *Poslednee slovo antisemitizma.*

Chapter VIII

The Programme of Communists and the Military Question

§ 61. Our former programme and the military question. § 62. The need for a Red Army and its class-composition. § 63. Universal military training of the toilers. § 64. The discipline of the whip or conscious discipline. § 65. Political commissars and Communist cells. § 66. The formation of the Red Army. § 67. The commanding staff of the Red Army. § 68. An elected or appointed commanding staff. § 69. The Red Army – as a provisional army.

§ 61. Our former programme and the military question

In Paragraph 12,[3] we discussed how the standing army of the bourgeois-landlord state was constructed and whom it served. It is perfectly understandable that the socialists of all countries, including Russian Social-Democracy, put forth the demand for elimination of the standing army. At the same time, socialists called for replacing the standing army with the armed people as a whole, eliminating the officer-caste and having the soldiers themselves elect the commanding staff.

Let us consider how Communists must relate to these demands.

Above all, the question arises: for what kind of society was the above-mentioned programme issued – was it for a bourgeois society, for a socialist society, or for the period of struggle against bourgeois society and for socialism?

It must be said that the socialist parties that adhered to the Second International had no clear idea themselves of the kind of society for which they were writing the programme. The majority assumed, however, that it was for a bourgeois society. All socialists customarily referred to the Swiss Republic, where no standing army existed but there was a universal people's militia.

It is perfectly obvious that the programme in question cannot be realised in a bourgeois society, especially during a period of steadily intensifying class-struggle. To eliminate the barracks means to eliminate the place where workers and peasants are drilled and transformed into the hangmen of their class-brothers. It means eliminating the only place where it is possible to create an army out of the toilers that will go to war against other peoples at any moment when the capitalists require it to do so. To eliminate the officer-caste means to eliminate the trainers who alone can enforce iron discipline and subordinate the armed people to the will of the bourgeois class. To allow elections for the commanding

---

3. [The reference is to § 12 ('The capitalist state') of Chapter One of *The ABC of Communism*. That chapter was written by N.I. Bukharin.]

staff means to allow the armed workers and peasants to elect their own, and not a bourgeois, set of commanders. This means that the bourgeoisie would help in building an army for the overthrow of its own state.

The history of capitalism in Europe has demonstrated, and continues to demonstrate, the impossibility of implementing the military programme set out by the socialist parties under a bourgeois system, where society is divided into classes and the class-struggle is intensifying. The more acute this struggle becomes, the more the bourgeoisie in power are disinclined to arm the entire people, instead doing the opposite and disarming the people while leaving weapons solely in the hands of trusted White-Guard detachments. The military programme of the socialists, if one wishes to implement it under the domination of the bourgeoisie, is, therefore, nothing but a miserable petty-bourgeois utopia.

But perhaps this programme would be appropriate precisely for the purpose of crushing bourgeois domination?

This also is not the case. It makes no sense for the bourgeoisie to try to protect itself against the working class, which wants to overthrow it, by arming the working class. The bourgeoisie introduced universal military conscription and entrusted a rifle to the worker-soldier only so long as it hoped to keep the soldier, drawn from the people, subordinated. As soon as the people rise up in struggle, they must immediately be disarmed. Every business-like politician from the bourgeois class knows this. Conversely, it also makes no sense for workers and peasants to demand universal arming of the people once they plan to arm themselves, disarm the bourgeoisie and deprive it of power. This means that the old socialist programme is also useless for the transition-period, for the period of the proletariat's struggle for power. It is fit only for the very brief interval of time when the existing bourgeois army is being dissolved. The only part of it that is appropriate is where it speaks of eliminating the officer-caste and having the soldiers themselves elect their commanders. In 1917, the Communist-Bolsheviks in fact made use of this demand in their old programme. By eliminating the top officers, they removed the sting from the army of the tsar and Kerensky and thus freed the army from subordination to the bourgeois-landlord class.

On the other hand, the old military programme is completely appropriate for a victorious socialist society. When the proletariat in several countries defeats the bourgeoisie and eliminates classes, it will then be possible to implement universal arming of the people. The entire toiling people will then be armed, for in a victorious socialist society everyone will be a toiler. Then it will possible to eliminate the barracks completely. It will also be possible to institute the election of commanders – something that cannot be helpful to a proletarian army, with certain fortunate exceptions, during an epoch of intensified civil war.

But here, another question naturally arises: exactly who, and what purpose, will be served by universal arming of the people in countries of victorious socialism? After all, the domestic bourgeoisie will have been defeated and transformed into toilers, and there can be no question of war between socialist states. But in this context, we must remember that socialism cannot triumph simultaneously in every country of the world. Some countries will naturally lag behind others in the matter of eliminating classes and realising socialism. The countries that have defeated their own bourgeoisie and transformed them into workers will have to wage war, or be prepared for war, against the bourgeoisie in those states where the proletarian dictatorship is yet to be proclaimed, or they may have to take up arms to assist the proletariat in countries where it has proclaimed its dictatorship but where the fighting against the bourgeoisie is yet to be concluded.

§ 62. The need for a Red Army and its class-composition

Most socialists who adhered to the Second International assumed that socialism can be achieved by winning a majority in parliaments. Lulling themselves with such peaceful-philistine and petty-bourgeois hopes, this majority naturally did not contemplate the possibility or the need for organising a proletarian army in the period of the struggle for socialism. However, another part of the socialists, who thought a forceful revolution with arms in hand was inevitable, did not foresee that this armed struggle may be quite protracted, that Europe may pass through a phase not only of socialist revolutions, but also of socialist wars. This is why not a single socialist programme raised the demand for organisation of a Red Army, that is, an army of armed workers and peasants. The Russian working class has been the first in the world to have to build this army,[4] since it is the first in the world to succeed in taking state-power firmly into its own hands and to have to defend it against attacks by its own bourgeoisie and by all the bourgeois states of the entire world. It is perfectly obvious that, without the Red Army, the workers and peasants of Russia could not have defended a single conquest of their revolution and would have been crushed by the forces of domestic and international reaction. A Red Army cannot be constructed on the basis of universal military service. During the epoch when the struggle is continuing, the proletariat cannot entrust rifles either to the bourgeois strata of the city or to the kulak upper stratum in the village; the only people who can join its army are representatives of the toiling classes, who do not exploit the labour of others and

---

4. We are speaking, here, of an army in the full sense of the word. As far as the beginnings of the Red Army are concerned, the army of the Paris Commune, which was created by the workers and urban poor of Paris in 1871, can be considered the precursor of our Red Army.

have an interest in the victory of the workers' revolution. Only the proletarians of the city and the poor peasants of the village can constitute the nucleus and foundation of the Red Army; and only adhesion to this nucleus by the masses of middle-peasants can make the Red Army, in terms of its composition, into an army of all the toilers. As for the bourgeoisie and the kulaks, they must fulfil their military obligations to the proletarian state through militia-duties in the rear. Of course, this does not mean that a sufficiently strong proletarian authority will refrain, in its turn, from compelling the exploiters to shoot at their White friends on the opposing front, just as the bourgeoisie, through its standing army, compelled proletarians to shoot down their own class-brothers.

Although it is formed on the basis of universal military service and appears to be an army of the whole people, the standing army of the bourgeoisie is in fact a class-army. Conversely, the proletariat has no reason to hide the class-character of its own army, just as it does not hide the class-character of its dictatorship. The Red Army is one of the apparatuses of the Soviet state. Generally speaking, it is constructed in the same way as the entire state-apparatus of proletarian dictatorship. And just as the right to vote in elections to the soviets is withheld by the Soviet constitution from those whom this constitution must economically and politically strangle, so the Red Army does not allow entry to those whom it must crush in the Civil War.

§ 63. Universal military training of the toilers

Universal military training of the toilers, which the Soviet Republic of Russia has undertaken, must, first of all, reduce barracks-training to a minimum. As far as possible, the worker and peasant must be instructed in military affairs without being withdrawn from production. This permits an enormous reduction in the costs of the army and forestalls any curtailment or disorganisation of production. Doing military training in their spare time, the workers and peasants are preparing to be soldiers 'of the Revolution' while continuing to be the producers of values.

The second important task of universal military training for the toilers is to create in every city and every rural district proletarian-peasant reserves that are able at any moment to take up arms with the approach of the enemy. The experience of civil war in Russia has demonstrated the enormous importance of these reserves for success in a socialist war. One need only recall the reserve-regiments of workers in Petrograd, who defended the Red capital from White robbers, the workers of the Urals or the Donetsk basin, or the workers and peasants of Orenburg, Uralsk, the Orenburg province, and so on.

§ 64. The discipline of the whip or conscious discipline

In an imperialist army, by its very nature, there can be no conscious discipline. Such an army consists of diverse class-groups. The workers and peasants, who have been forcibly driven into the barracks of a bourgeois army, are compelled, once they begin to understand their own interests, consciously to resist the discipline of their trainers, with their golden epaulettes, and consciously to destroy this discipline. This is why discipline in bourgeois armies must necessarily be imposed with a rod, why flogging and all kinds of torture and mass-shootings are not occasional events but the foundation of all order, discipline and 'military education'.

Conversely, in the Red Army, which is formed from the workers and peasants and defends the interests of workers and peasants, compulsion must gradually give way to voluntary acceptance by the toilers of the discipline of civil war. The higher the level of consciousness in the Red Army, the more the Red soldiers begin to understand that, in the final analysis, it is the entire class of toilers that commands them through their own state and its military command. Discipline in the Red Army is, therefore, subordination of the minority (the soldiers) to the interests of the toiling majority. Behind every reasonable order from the command stands not a commander and his own arbitrary will, not a bourgeois minority and its predatory interest, but the entire worker-peasant republic. This is why the political education of a soldier in the Red Army, why propaganda and agitation, are of completely exceptional importance.

§ 65. Political commissars and Communist cells

In the Soviet Republic of Russia, where all the toilers have the right to express their will through the soviets, the workers and peasants have already been electing Communists to the executive organs for two years. The party of Communists, to borrow a bourgeois expression, is the ruling party of the Republic due to the will of the masses, for no other party has proven capable of leading a victorious worker-peasant Revolution through to completion. As a result, our Party has become a kind of enormous executive committee of the proletarian dictatorship. In the Red Army, this leading role also falls to the Communists. The representatives of the proletariat's class-will in the army, the representatives mandated by the Party and by military centres, are the political commissars. This is what determines the relationship of the commissar both with the military staff and also with Communist cells in the units. The Communist cell is a part of the ruling party, and the commissar is the plenipotentiary of the Party as a whole. This is the source of his leading role both in the unit and in the unit's Communist cell. Likewise, it is the source of his right of supervision over the commander. He oversees the commanding staff, just as the political leader oversees a technical executive.

The task of the cell is to explain to the Red-Army man the meaning of the Civil War and the need to subordinate his own interests to the interests of all the toilers. The task of the cell is to demonstrate devotion to the Revolution by its own example and to inspire the same from its comrades in the unit. It is the right of every member of the cell to keep an eye on the Communist behaviour of its own commissar and other commissars, and to seek implementation of all necessary measures through a higher party-organisation or through more responsible comrades who are commissars. Only in this way will the Communist Party be in a position, without disrupting general military discipline on the part of Communist Red-Army men, to secure complete control over all its members and prevent any abuse of power on their part.

In addition to the cells and political commissars, the political education of the Red Army depends upon a whole network of political departments in the divisions, in the armies and at the fronts, and also on the departments of agitation and enlightenment of the military commissariats in the rear. Russia's proletarian state, in the form of these organisations, is creating a powerful apparatus of education and organisation for its army and is endeavouring to achieve the greatest possible results with the least possible expenditure of resources. Thanks to these apparatuses, the work of agitation and enlightenment in our army is not incidental but has a systematic and planned character. The newspaper, the spoken word at a meeting, and school-instruction are assured to every Red-Army man.

Unfortunately, however, the above-mentioned organisations have not avoided the common fate of almost every major organisation of the Soviet authority: they are subject to bureaucratism; they are inclined to become detached from the masses, on the one hand, and the Party, on the other; and, in practice, they are often transformed into a refuge for lazy and talentless military party-officials. A resolute struggle against such deviations is much more imperative and urgent for the Communist Party than the struggle against bureaucratism and parasitism in the general Soviet mechanism because, to a certain extent, the proximity of our victory in the Civil War depends on the successes of this struggle.

§ 66. The formation of the Red Army

Universal training must reduce barracks-training to a minimum, so that in future it will be possible to do away entirely with any Red barracks. The structure of the Red Army must gradually come to resemble a production-association of the toilers, thus doing away with the artificial character of an army-association. To put it more simply, the point is that the typical standing army of the tsar, or of a bourgeois-landlord state, consists of people who belong to the most diverse classes and who, through compulsory mobilisation, are torn from their natural base – the worker from the factory, the peasant from the plough, the employee from the enterprise, the merchant from his shop-counter. Those who are mobilised are then artificially assembled in a barracks and assigned to military units. For a bourgeois state, it was perfectly advantageous to eliminate any connection of the mobilised proletarian and peasant with his factory or village, in order to convert him all the more readily into a blind instrument for suppressing the toilers, and all the more easily to compel the workers and peasants of one province to shoot down the workers and peasants of another province.

In constructing the Red Army, the Communist Party endeavours to employ exactly the opposite method. Although the circumstances of civil war compel it sometimes to adopt the old methods of construction, essentially it is striving for something different. It aims to ensure that a military formation – for example, a company, battalion, regiment, or brigade – will correspond, when possible, with a factory, plant, village, hamlet, and so on. In other words, it is trying to replace the artificial military unit, existing on its own, with one based upon a natural production-association of the toilers and thus to reduce the artificiality. Proletarian units formed in this way are more united, and being disciplined by the mode of production itself, they require less recourse to compulsory discipline from above.

Creation of a solid and conscious proletarian cadre is enormously important for construction of the Red Army. The dictatorship of the proletariat, in such a predominantly-peasant country as Russia, means that the proletarian minority leads and organises the peasant-majority (the middle-peasants), who follow the organisational lead of the proletariat and have confidence in its political leadership and construction-activity. This applies especially to the Red Army, whose discipline and strength depend on the strength of its proletarian and Communist skeleton. To assemble this skeletal material, to distribute it properly, and to clothe it with a sufficient quantity of the dispersed, but much more abundant, peasant-material – that is the fundamental organisational task of the Communist Party in the work of constructing a victorious Red Army.

§ 67. The commanding staff of the Red Army

The building of the Red Army was begun on the ruins of the old tsarist army. Having been victorious in the October Revolution, the proletariat did not have its own Red proletarian officer-corps. There were only three ways in which the proletariat could adopt and apply the experience of the World-War to the Civil War, and for the purpose of the military training of its army could adopt and apply the accumulated military-technical experience of the régime that had been overthrown. These were: 1) to create its own Red commanders and permit them alone to take positions of command, leaving only the role of instructors to the old officer-corps; 2) to hand over command of the army to the old officers with appropriate supervision by commissars; 3) to use both methods together. Time was short, the Civil War had begun, and it was necessary to build the army rapidly and throw it into battle. For this reason, the proletarian authority was compelled to adopt the third method. Schools for Red officers began to be organised, which produced officers who, in general, were capable only of assuming lower levels of command. In addition, the old officer-corps was recruited as extensively as possible to construct the Red Army and take part in commanding it.

Use of the old officer-corps involved a number of very serious difficulties that have yet to be overcome. These officers turned out to consist of three groups: a minority who more-or-less sympathised with Soviet power; another minority who definitely supported and still support the class-enemies of the proletariat and actively assist them; and the majority, consisting of mid-level officers who support whichever side is strongest and serve the Soviet authority in the same way as a worker serves the capitalist – as hired labour-power. In these circumstances, the Communist Party had to make the greatest possible use of the sympathetic minority; to neutralise the White-Guard minority by using all measures of extraordinary repression; and to solidify support from the mid-level officers, who are politically neutral in the Civil War, by getting them to do honest work in the rear and to serve conscientiously at the front.

Use of the old officers has already yielded enormous results in the matter of building up the Red Army. In this regard, we quite profitably expropriated the bourgeois-landlord régime in terms of its military-technical knowledge. But this approach also proved extremely dangerous, because it entailed mass-treachery by the staff-officers and enormous losses on the part of Red-Army masses who were betrayed and delivered up to the enemy.

The principal task of the Communist Party, in this connection, is first to strengthen the preparation of real commanders of the worker-peasant army – Red commanders – while training Communists as rapidly as possible in the Red Academy of the General Staff that has been created by the Soviet authority. And secondly, we need to establish close unity amongst all commissar-Communists and all the Party's military workers to secure genuine control over all the non-Communist officers.

§ 68. An elected or appointed commanding staff

The army of a bourgeois state, created on the basis of universal military conscription, consists overwhelmingly of peasants and workers and is commanded by its officers, who belong to the aristocracy and the bourgeoisie. When we set out the demand for election of officers in our former programme, we had in mind taking command of the army out of the hands of the exploiter classes. This demand was based on the expectation that the army could be democratised while political power remained in bourgeois hands. Of course, this demand could not be implemented, because no bourgeoisie anywhere in the world would ever agree to surrender its military apparatus of oppression without a fight. But for the sake of the struggle against militarism, and for the struggle against the privileged officer-caste, the demand for election of officers was enormously important, since it would contribute to the destruction of imperialist armies in general.

The Red Army, conversely, is under proletarian control. The proletariat administers it through the central Soviet organs that it elects. It administers it at all levels of the army-hierarchy through commissar-Communists, the great majority of whom, both at the rear and at the front, are recruited from the workers. In such circumstances, the question of electing officers has only technical significance. The whole essence of the matter now concerns which procedure is most advantageous and makes the army, in current conditions, the most battle-ready: the election of commanders from below, or their appointment from above. As we keep in mind the mainly-peasant composition of our Red Army, the deprivations it must endure, its exhaustion due to two wars in succession, and the low level of consciousness in peasant army-units, it will be perfectly obvious to us that the election of officers could only cause our units to disintegrate. Of course, this does not exclude possible instances when, in individual volunteer-units and those that are tightly knit by revolutionary consciousness, the elective principle may cause no harm: the people elected would be just about the same as if they were appointed. But as a general rule, although election of officers is the ideal, at the present moment it is dangerous and harmful in practice. By the time the mass of the toilers, who now comprise the Red Army, reach the level where election will be both useful and necessary, it is quite likely that there will no longer be any armies left in the world.

§ 69. The Red Army – as a provisional army

The bourgeoisie considers the capitalist system to be the 'natural' order of human society and imagines its supremacy to be eternal. For that reason, the instrument of its supremacy, the army, is built solidly to last for years and years, if not forever. The proletariat looks upon its Red Army quite differently. The Red Army has been created by the toilers for the struggle against the White Army of capital. The Red Army arose from the Civil War and will disappear after final victory in that war, after the elimination of classes and the self-liquidation of the proletarian dictatorship. The bourgeoisie wants its army to be eternal, because this eternity would simply reflect the unchangeable bourgeois régime. On the contrary, the working class wishes a natural and glorious death for its offspring, since the moment when it will be possible to dissolve the Red Army will also be the moment of final triumph for the communist system.

The Communist Party must explain to Red-Army men that they are soldiers in the world's last army, provided that the Red Army will conquer the White Guards of capital. But it must also explain to all those involved in building the Red Army, to all its reinforced proletarian-peasant cadre, that the proletarian has become a warrior only temporarily and out of necessity, that the sphere of production alone is the natural location for his labour, and that participation in the Red Army must never lead to creation of some kind of stratum that will long be separated from industry and agriculture.

When construction of the Red Army began, growing out of the proletariat's Red Guards, the Mensheviks and S-Rs eagerly attacked Communists for betraying the slogan of arming the whole people, saying that they were creating a standing class-army. The fact that the Red Army will not be permanent is obvious in the fact that the Civil War cannot last forever. Ours is a class-army because the class-struggle has become extremely acute. Only a hopelessly dense petty-bourgeois utopian can acknowledge the class-struggle and speak out against a class-army. It is characteristic that the bourgeoisie itself thinks it is neither possible nor necessary to hide the class-character of its army during the epoch following liquidation of the World-War. The fate of standing armies in Germany, England and France is extremely instructive in this regard. The German constituent assembly was chosen through universal suffrage. Its support comes from the volunteer White-Guard detachments of Noske. An army created on the basis of universal military service can no longer provide support for bourgeois Germany given the intensification of class-struggle and the extent of bourgeois society's disintegration that Germany has experienced. In France and England, the support of the government comes not [only] from the army, which was created through universal conscription and took part in the World-War, but also from detachments of White-Guard volunteers, from the gendarmerie and the police. Thus not only Russia since the end of 1917, but also the whole of Europe since the end of 1918, are characterised by elimination of the system of universal military service and the transition to a system of class-armies. In these conditions, the Russian social-traitors – the Mensheviks and S-Rs – 'object' to the creation of the *Red Army of the proletariat*, while in the West their comrades, Noske and Scheidemann, are themselves organising *the White Army of the bourgeoisie*. Thus the struggle against the creation of the proletariat's class-army, in the name of universally arming the people and 'democracy', turns out, in practice, to be a struggle on behalf of the class-army of the bourgeoisie.

As for the people's militia, the example from the most democratic bourgeois republic in the world – Switzerland – has demonstrated just what this militia becomes at the moment when the class-struggle becomes more acute. With the bourgeoisie dominating the country, the 'popular' militia in Switzerland has turned into the same kind of instrument for oppressing the proletariat as any standing army in less democratic countries. Such will be the fate of any 'universally armed people', whenever and wherever it occurs under the political and economic domination of capital.

The Communist Party stands not for universally arming the people, but rather for universally arming the toilers. And it is only in a society consisting of none but the toilers, only in a classless society, that it is possible to have universal arming of the people.

Literature. There is almost no literature available. There are articles by Trotsky published in *Pravda* and *Izvestiya*; the collection *Revoyutsionnaya voina*, edited by Podvoisky and Pavlovich; Trotsky, L., *Mezhdunarodnoe polozhenie i Krasnaya armiya*; Trotsky, L., *Sovetskaya vlast' i mezhdunarodnyi imperializm*; Zinoviev, G., *Nashe polozhenie i zadachi sozdaniya Krasnoi armii*; Zinoviev, G., *Rech' o sozdanii Krasnoi armii*; Yaroslavsky, Em., *Novaya armiya*.

Chapter IX

The proletarian court

§ 70. The court in bourgeois society. § 71. election of judges by the toilers. § 72. The single people's court. § 73. Revolutionary tribunals. § 74. Punishments by a proletarian court. § 75. The future proletarian court.

§ 70. The court in bourgeois society

Among the institutions of the bourgeois state that serve to oppress and deceive the toiling masses, there is the bourgeois court.

In its sentencing activity, this esteemed institution is guided by laws that are compiled in the interests of the class of exploiters. Therefore, whatever the composition of the court, when making decisions it is constrained in advance by volumes of enactments in which all the privileges of capital and the lack of any rights for the toiling masses are summarised.

As far as organisation of the bourgeois court is concerned, it fully corresponds to the pattern of the bourgeois state. Where the bourgeois state operates more-or-less openly, where it has to reject hypocrisy in order to secure verdicts that are favourable to the ruling classes, the courts are appointed from above and, if they are elected, it is only by the privileged section of society. Conversely, to the extent that the masses are sufficiently disciplined by capital, sufficiently submissive to it and even consider its laws to be their own, to that extent the toilers, in some measure, are permitted to be judges themselves, just as they are permitted to elect their exploiters or their lackeys to parliament. That is how trial by jury came about and still operates, making it possible for verdicts in the interests of capital to be passed off as verdicts by 'the people themselves'.

§ 71. The election of judges by the toilers

In the programme of socialists who adhered to the Second International, the demand was set out for courts elected by the people. During the epoch of proletarian dictatorship, this demand is just as unrealisable and just as reactionary as the demand for universal suffrage or for arming the whole people. When the proletariat takes power, it cannot permit its class-enemies to be its judges. It cannot allow the representatives of capital or big landowners to be the guardians of its decrees, which are aimed at eliminating capital's domination. Finally, in the endless files of civil and criminal matters, court-pleadings must be conducted in the spirit of the new socialist society that is being built.

For these reasons the Soviet authority has not only abolished the entire apparatus of the old court, which served capital while hypocritically presenting itself as the voice of the people, but has also built a new court that makes no effort to conceal its class-character. In the form of the old court, the class-minority of exploiters judged the toiling majority. The court of the proletarian dictatorship is the court of the toiling majority over the exploiting minority. And that is how it is constructed. The judges are selected only by the toilers and from amongst the toilers. The only right that remains to the exploiters is that of being judged.

§ 72. The single people's court

Court-organisation in bourgeois society is extremely cumbersome. Bourgeois jurists are extremely proud of the fact that, due to a whole hierarchy of court-levels, complete justice is ensured and the number of legal errors is reduced to a minimum. In reality, the movement of a case through various instances always was, and still remains, most beneficial to the possessing classes. Having at their disposal a vast corpus of hired advocates, the wealthy strata of the population have full opportunity to seek favourable decisions from the higher courts, while the plaintiffs coming from the poor are compelled to give up pursuing their case because the costs are too high. Movement of a case from one instance to the other guarantees a 'just' decision only in the sense that it guarantees a decision in the interest of the exploiter-groups. The single people's court of the proletarian state reduces to a minimum the time taken from the moment when a case first appears in court to the final verdict. Judicial red tape is enormously reduced, and if it still exists, it is only due to the general imperfection of all Soviet institutions during the first months and years of the proletarian dictatorship. As a result, the court becomes accessible to the poorest and least educated strata of the population and will become even more accessible when the acute period of civil war ends and all relations between citizens of the Republic will acquire a more stable character. The Romans used to say that 'In time of war, the laws are silent'.[5] In a time of civil war, the laws serving the people are not silent and the people's courts are operating, but not all of the population have managed to become familiar with the essence of the new court or to appreciate all its advantages.

During a period when the old society is breaking apart and a new one is being constructed, the task of the people's courts is enormous. Soviet legislation is not keeping pace with life. The laws of the bourgeois-landlord system have been abolished; the laws of the proletarian state have been written only in general outlines and will never be fully written. The working class has no intention of perpetuating its dominion and has no need for endless volumes of different codes. Having expressed its will through some fundamental decrees, it can entrust interpretation and application of those decrees in particular cases to the people's courts that are elected by the toilers. All that matters is that the verdicts of these courts reflect a total break with the customs and psychology of the bourgeois system, so that the people's courts decide cases according to a proletarian conscience, a socialist conscience, rather than a bourgeois one. In the endless cases that arise with the breakup of old relations and the implementation of the rights of the proletariat, the people's courts have an opportunity to complete the transformation that began with the October Revolution of 1917 and that must extend to all relations between citizens of the Soviet Republic. On the other hand, in dealing with the vast number of cases arising independently of the conditions of a revolutionary epoch, cases of a common criminal character, the people's courts must manifest a completely new attitude to such crimes on the part of the revolutionary proletariat and produce an entire revolution in the character of the penal measures being established.

---

5. [*'Inter arma leges silent'*.]

§ 73. Revolutionary tribunals

A people's court that is elected and subject to recall by the electors, and in which each of the toilers must, in turn, exercise his right to be a judge – this is what the Communist Party regards as the normal court of a socialist state. But during an epoch of the most acute civil war, there is a need to organise revolutionary tribunals alongside the people's court. The task of revolutionary tribunals consists of speedily and mercilessly judging the enemies of the proletarian revolution. These courts are one of the instruments for suppressing the exploiters, and in that respect they are just as much organs of proletarian defence and attack as the Red Guards, the Red Army or extraordinary commissions. Accordingly, revolutionary tribunals are organised on less democratic principles than people's courts. They are appointed by the soviets and not directly elected by the toiling masses.

§ 74. Punishments by a proletarian court

In the bloody struggle against capital, the working class cannot refrain from imposing the most extreme measures of punishment upon its class-enemies. Abolition of the death-penalty is impossible so long as the Civil War lasts. But a purely objective comparison of the proletarian court with the court of bourgeois counter-revolution reveals how extraordinarily lenient workers' courts are when compared to the hangmen of bourgeois justice. Death-sentences are handed down only in the most extreme cases. This was especially characteristic of trials during the first months of the proletarian dictatorship. It is enough to recall, here, that the illustrious Purishkevich was sentenced in his day, by a revolutionary tribunal in Petrograd, to only two weeks in prison. In the practical activity of the proletarian court, the progressive classes of society, to whom the future belongs, show great generosity towards their enemies, whereas the dying classes are furious in their reprisals.

With regard to the punishments that are imposed by the proletarian court for crimes that have no counter-revolutionary character, they are fundamentally different from the punishments of a bourgeois court. This is perfectly understandable. The enormous majority of crimes committed in bourgeois society are either crimes against property-rights or crimes that, in one way or another, are connected with property. Naturally, the bourgeois state took revenge against the criminals, and the punishments of this society are different forms of the embittered owner's vengeance. The punishments for casual offenses were, and continue to be, just as senseless, and the same is true of crimes connected with the general imperfection of bourgeois relations as a whole (family-crimes, romantic crimes, those associated with alcoholism and degeneracy, or with ignorance and atrophy of social instincts, and such like). The proletarian court must continue to deal with crimes whose roots lie in bourgeois society, all of whose vestiges have yet to be liquidated. The proletarian court has acquired from the old régime a whole cadre of professional criminals created by that régime! Vengeance is absolutely alien to the proletarian court. It cannot take revenge against people for the fact that they lived in a bourgeois society. It is for this reason that the punishments of our proletarian courts are already reflecting a complete revolution in justice. Conditional sentences are applied with increasing frequency: this means punishment without punishment, and its main task is to warn against any repetition of the crime. Social censure is also used – a measure that can become real only in a classless society and that presupposes the growth of social consciousness and social responsibility. Imprisonment without labour – the kind of enforced parasitism so often employed by tsarism – is being replaced by social work. Generally speaking, the proletarian court endeavours to match the harm done to society by the offender with intensified labour. Finally, in cases where the court is dealing with a recidivist whose freedom, even after serving the sentence, would endanger the lives of other citizens, the criminal is isolated from society but still given full opportunity for moral regeneration. All of the above-listed measures, which amount to a complete transformation of the customary forms of punishment, have, for the most part, already been supported by the best of bourgeois jurists. However, these measures have remained merely in the realm of dreams for bourgeois society. They can only begin to be implemented in real life by the victorious proletariat.

§ 75. The future of the proletarian court

As far as the revolutionary tribunals are concerned, this form of proletarian court has no future, and the same applies to the Red Army once it has defeated the White Guards, as well as to the extraordinary commissions and all the other organs that have been created by the proletariat in a period of ongoing civil war. With the proletariat's victory over the bourgeois counter-revolution, these organs will pass away because there will be no use for them.

Conversely, the proletarian court, in the form of an elected people's court, will no doubt survive the end of the Civil War, and for a long time to come will have to use its sentences to mop up all the various fragmentary manifestations of bourgeois society. The elimination of classes does not immediately eliminate either class-psychology, which always outlives the social conditions that produced it, or class-instincts and habits. Besides, the very process of eliminating classes can drag out for quite a long time. Conversion of the bourgeoisie into a toiling group of people, and conversion of the peasants into workers of a socialist society – these are things that do not happen all at once. The latter process will be quite protracted and is threatened with many trials involving the courts. Likewise, private property in the means of consumption, which will precede purely communist distribution, will provide many occasions for misdemeanours and crimes. Finally, crimes against society, resulting from the personal egoism of individual members, and all sorts of offences against the common good, will, likewise, continue to be subject to court-deliberations. True, the court will then assume a different character; gradually, as the state dies away, it will be transformed into an organ for the expression of public opinion, approaching the character of a comradely court whose decisions are put into effect not by use of force, but, instead, will have only a moral significance.

Literature. There is almost no communist literature dealing with the bourgeois and proletarian court. The following items can be recommended from the traditional works: Marx, K., *Rech' pered sudom prisyazhnykh (Kel'nskii protsess kommunistov)*; Engels, *Proiskhozhdenie sem'i, chastnoi sobstvennosti i gosudarstva*; Lassalle, *Zashchitel'nye rechi* and also *Ideya rabochevo sosloviya. Programma rabotnikov* and other works from his *Sobraniya sochinenii*; Engels, *Anti-Dühring*, the sections dealing with the state; Kautsky K., *Priroda politicheskikh prestuplenii*; Van-Kon, *Ekonomicheskie factory prestupnosti*; Gernet, *Sotsial'nye factory prestupnosti*.

From the recent works: Stuchka, P., *Konstitutsiya RSFSR v voprosakh i otvetakh*; Stuchka, P., *Narodnyi sud i.t.d.*; Goikhbart A., *Kakoi sud nuzhen narodu. Dekrety o sude, izdanie Petrogradskovo Soveta*.

Chapter X

The School and Communism

§ 76. The school of bourgeois society. § 77. The destructive tasks of communism. § 78. The school as an instrument of communist education and enlightenment. § 79. Pre-school education. § 80. The single school of labour. § 81. Specialised education. § 82. The higher school. § 83. Soviet schools and party-schools. § 84. Non-school education. § 85. New educational workers. § 86. The treasures of art and science for the toilers. § 87. State-propaganda of communism. § 88. Popular enlightenment under tsarism and under Soviet power.

§ 76. The school of bourgeois society

In bourgeois society, the school fulfils three basic tasks: 1) it educates a young generation of toilers in the spirit of devotion to, and respect for, the capitalist régime; 2) it prepares the 'educated' trainers of the toiling people from the youth of the ruling classes; 3) it serves capitalist production, using science for technology and to increase capitalist profit.

The first task is accomplished in the school in the same way as in the bourgeois army, namely, first of all by the creation of a corresponding cadre of 'officers of popular enlightenment'. For a bourgeois school that is intended for the people, the teachers go through a specified course of instruction in which they are prepared for their role as animal-trainers. The only teaching personnel who are admitted to teaching in the schools are those who are trustworthy from the bourgeois point of view. This is overseen by the ministries of bourgeois education, and they ruthlessly drive out of teaching any persons who are dangerous, namely, the socialist element. Before the Revolution, the German elementary school served as a supplement to Wilhelm's barracks and was a striking example of how, through schools, the landlords and the bourgeoisie succeeded in manufacturing faithful and blind slaves of capital. Instruction in the lower bourgeois schools is carried out according to a specific programme that is entirely adapted to the task of the capitalist training of students. All of the textbooks were, likewise, written in the corresponding spirit. The same purpose was served by the whole of bourgeois literature, which was created by people who regarded the bourgeois system as natural, eternal, and the best of all possible régimes. In this way, the schoolchildren were imperceptibly imbued with bourgeois psychology and infected with enthusiasm for all the bourgeois virtues – with respect for wealth, glory, and an exalted station – and they were encouraged to strive for careerism and personal prosperity, and so on. The work of bourgeois teachers was completed by the servants of the Church, with their instruction in God's Law, which, thanks to the close ties of capital with the Church, always turned out to be the law of the propertied classes.[6]

The second objective is achieved in bourgeois society by the fact that middle- and higher education is deliberately made inaccessible to the toiling classes. Instruction in middle- and especially in higher educational institutions costs more than the toilers can afford.

---

6. Under tsarism, the popular masses in Russia were kept in subjection to the aristocratic state not so much by bourgeois-priestly-tsarist enlightenment, as by exclusion from any enlightenment whatsoever. In this respect, recall the theory of the famous obscurantist Pobedonostsev, who considered popular ignorance to be the main support of the autocracy.

This instruction lasts for a decade or more, and for that reason, it is inaccessible to the worker and peasant who, in order to feed the family, is compelled to drive his children into the factory, the field, or domestic work at a very early age. The middle- and upper schools in fact become educational institutions for bourgeois youth. Here, the young people of the ruling classes are prepared to replace their fathers in positions of exploitation or to become officials and technicians of the bourgeois state. The teaching in these schools also has a strictly-class character. While this may not be so obvious in the areas of mathematics, technology or the natural sciences, due to the very nature of these subjects, it is fully apparent in the social sciences, which essentially determine the world-view of the students. Bourgeois political economy is taught together with the most highly perfected ways 'to annihilate Marx'. Sociology and history are also taught in a purely bourgeois spirit. The history of law concludes with treatment of bourgeois law as the natural right of 'man and the citizen', and so on and so forth. As a result, the higher and middle-schools teach bourgeois sons everything required for the service of bourgeois society and for supporting the entire system of bourgeois exploitation. Should children of the toilers find themselves in the higher schools, they are generally the most talented, and in the enormous majority of cases the bourgeois school-apparatus successfully tears them away from their own class, inoculates them with bourgeois psychology and, in the final analysis, employs the talents of the toilers for suppression of those same toilers.

As for the third task, it is fulfilled in the bourgeois school as follows. In a class-society, science is divorced from labour. It is not only made the property of the possessing classes, but more than this, it is the profession of a specific and relatively narrow circle of people. Both scientific teaching and scientific research are detached from the labour-process. In order to use the facts of science for production, bourgeois society has to create a series of institutes for the corresponding utilisation of scientific knowledge for technical purposes, together with a number of technical schools that make it possible to keep production abreast of the successes in 'pure' science, that is, in science divorced from labour. At the same time, the polytechnic schools provide capitalist society not simply with knowledgeable technical personnel, but also with a cadre of supervisors and administrators of the working class. Furthermore, various trade-schools, commercial institutes, and so on, are created to serve the process of commodity-circulation. Those aspects of this entire organisation that are associated with production will remain. But those associated with *bourgeois* production must die away. Everything that promotes the development of science will be preserved – what will die away is the separation of science from labour. The teaching of scientific knowledge will be preserved – what will be eliminated is the manner of teaching it in detachment from physical labour. The use of science for production will be preserved and expanded – what will be eliminated are the limits imposed upon such use by the fact that capital only uses science insofar as it increases the rate of profit at any particular moment.

§ 77. The destructive tasks of communism

In the matter of the school, as in all other spheres, the Communist Party faces not only constructive tasks, but also destructive ones during the first period. Everything in bourgeois society's school-system that made the school into an instrument of bourgeois class-rule faces immediate destruction.

The higher-level school in bourgeois society was the domain of the exploiting classes. In the form of an endless series of gymnasia, real schools, institutes, cadet-corps, and so on, that kind of school must be destroyed.

The teaching personnel of the bourgeois school serve the purpose both of bourgeois enlightenment and also of deception. That section of the pedagogical personnel of the old school, who either cannot or have no wish to become instruments for communist enlightenment of the masses, must be banished without remorse from the proletarian school.

In the old school, textbooks were used that were written in the bourgeois spirit, and teaching methods served the class-purposes of the bourgeoisie. All this must be disposed of in the new school.

The old school had a tie to religion through obligatory instruction in God's Law, along with obligatory prayers and church-attendance. The new school achieves the obligatory exclusion of religion from within its walls, in whatever form it may attempt to enter and regardless of backward groups of parents who may want to drag some moderate form of it back in.

The old school at the higher level created a shut-in circle of professors, a scientific guild that prevented entry into the university by new teaching resources; this scientific guild of bourgeois professors must be dismissed, and the instructional departments must be made accessible to everyone with the ability to teach.

Under tsarism, instruction was forbidden in one's native language. Russian was the obligatory language in both the state and the schools. The new school eliminates all remnants of national oppression in the area of education, making instruction in the native language accessible to all nationalities.

§ 78. The school as an instrument of communist education and enlightenment

The bourgeoisie represents a very small minority of the population. But this did not prevent it from using the school, along with other means of class-repression, for educating and training millions of toilers in its own spirit, thereby imposing upon the majority of the population the outlook and morality of the insignificant minority. In capitalist countries, the proletariat and semi-proletariat comprise the majority of the population. The working class in Russia, although numerically a minority, is politically the leader and organiser of the struggle of *all the toilers*. It is thus natural that once it has taken the school into its own hands, it must employ it, above all, in order to raise all the backward strata of the toiling population to the required level of communist consciousness. The bourgeoisie used the school for enslavement of the toilers. The proletariat will use the school for their emancipation, for the elimination of all remnants of spiritual slavery in the consciousness of the toilers. The bourgeoisie, thanks to its school, brought up proletarian children in a bourgeois spirit. The task of the new communist school consists of raising bourgeois and petty-bourgeois children in a proletarian spirit. In the mentality and psychology of the people, the communist school must produce the same destruction and expropriation of bourgeois society as Soviet power has done in the economic sphere through nationalisation of the instruments of production. It is necessary to prepare the consciousness of the people for new social relations. It is difficult to build a communist society with masses who, in many areas of their spiritual life, continue to stand with both feet on the ground of bourgeois society and its prejudices. The task of the new school consists of adapting the consciousness of adults to the changed social relations and, most importantly, of rearing a young generation whose entire consciousness will be grounded in the new communist society.

With regard to the schools, this goal must be served by all of the following reforms, some of which have already been introduced, while others are intended for implementation.

§ 79. Pre-school education

In bourgeois society, the child is regarded, if not entirely then in large measure, as the property of the parents. When the parents say 'my daughter, my son', today this means not only the existence of parental relations, but also the right of parents to bring up their own children. From the socialist point of view, this right is completely without foundation. The individual person belongs not to himself, but to society – to the human family. It is only thanks to the existence of society that each separate individual is in a position to live and develop. A child, therefore, belongs to the society in which, and thanks to which, it has been born, and not simply to the 'society' of its parents. The most fundamental and basic right of educating children also belongs to society. From this point of view, the claim of the parents, through domestic upbringing, to stamp their children's psychology with their own limitations must not only be rejected, but also ridiculed in the most merciless manner. Society may entrust the raising of children to parents, but it may also choose not do so; and there is all the less reason for it to entrust child-rearing to the parents since the ability to educate children is encountered much more rarely than the ability to beget them. Out of a hundred mothers, perhaps one or two are capable of child-rearing. The future belongs to social upbringing. Social education makes it possible for socialist society to raise a future generation in the required manner, and to do so with the least cost and expenditure of resources.

But the social education of children is necessary not merely out of pedagogical considerations; it also has enormous economic benefits. Through the implementation of social education, hundreds of thousands and even millions of mothers will be liberated for production and for their own cultural development. They will be freed from mind-numbing household-work and from the endless number of petty tasks connected with child-rearing in the home.

That is why the Soviet authority is striving to create a series of institutions that will improve social education and gradually make it accessible to everyone. This is the case with the kindergartens, to which workers and employees engaged in labour can send their children and leave them in the charge of specialists in pre-school education. The same is true of residential kindergartens, where the children stay for a longer period, and also of children's colonies in which the children live and are educated either permanently or during a long period of detachment from their parents. Nurseries also belong to this category, that is, institutions for educating children younger than four years and for giving them shelter while their parents are at work.

The task of the Communist Party consists, on the one hand, of securing through Soviet organs an even more rapid development of pre-school institutions and improvement of the circumstances within them and, on the other hand, of using intensified propaganda among parents to overcome bourgeois and petty-bourgeois prejudices concerning the need for home-rearing and its advantages. This propaganda must be reinforced with examples of the very best educational institutions established by the Soviet authority. It is often the inadequate performance of residential schools, nurseries, kindergartens and so forth that discourages parents from sending their children there. The task of the Communist Party, and especially of its women's sections, is to persuade parents to work for *the improvement* of social education, not by *rejecting* it, but precisely by sending their children to the appropriate institutions and by establishing the most extensive control over them on the part of parents' organisations.

§ 80. The single school of labour

The pre-school institutions are established for children up to seven years of age. After that, education and instruction must occur in the school. Instruction must be compulsory, which marks an enormous step forwards compared with the time of tsarism. Instruction must be free of charge, which is an extremely important advance compared to what we see even in the leading bourgeois countries, where instruction is free only in the lower schools. Naturally, the instruction must be the same for all, which means eliminating all privileges in education and training for particular groups of the population. This universal instruction, equal and obligatory for all, must involve all young people from the age of eight up to seventeen years.

The school must be unified in nature. This means, in the first place, that the division between boys' and girls' schools must be eliminated and replaced by joint instruction of children of both sexes. It means eliminating the division between lower-, middle- and higher-level schools, which have no connections between them or affinities in terms of programmes. It means that the lower-, middle- and higher-level schools must not be divided in terms of general and specialised or professional education, and it also means eliminating the division between generally accessible schools and those reserved for specific classes and ranks. The single school entails a single progression that every student of the socialist republic can and must follow, beginning at the very lowest level – the kindergarten – and finishing at the highest, where all general and polytechnic education culminates, insofar as it is compulsory for all students.

It will be obvious to the reader not only that the single school represents the ideal for every advanced pedagogue, but also that it is the only possible type of school in a socialist, that is, a classless society or one that is striving to become classless. Socialism alone can achieve the single school, even though the desirability of such a school has already been set out by the pedagogues of bourgeois society.

The school of a socialist republic must be a labour-school. That means instruction and education must be unified with labour and be based upon labour. This is important for many reasons, in the first place for the success of teaching itself. A child absorbs most easily, willingly and thoroughly not what he learns from a book or from the words of his teacher, but rather what he experiences himself with his own hands. The easiest way to get to know the natural environment is through attempting to work upon it. The joining of instruction with labour has already begun in leading bourgeois schools. But it cannot be carried through to the end under the bourgeois system, which consciously rears the parasitic elements of society and separates physical labour from mental labour with an impassable gulf.

Labour is also necessary for the purely physical development of children and for the comprehensive development of all their abilities. Experience verifies and demonstrates that the time spent at labour in the school in no way curtails, but rather multiplies, the successes of children in absorbing the most diverse forms of knowledge.

Finally, for a communist society, the labour-school is absolutely essential. Every citizen of this society must, at the very least, know the general skills of all the professions. This society will not have any closed shops, ossified professions or congealed specialist groups. Even the most ingenious scientist must at the same time be a skilful physical worker. To the student who is completing the single labour-school, communist society says: 'You may or may not become a professor, but you must be a producer of values'. Having begun with children's games in the kindergarten, the child must pass to labour, as a continuation of play, in a completely imperceptible way, and must learn from the very beginning to see in labour not some unpleasant necessity or punishment, but rather the natural and voluntary manifestation of abilities. Labour must be a need, like the desire to drink and eat, and this need must be inculcated and developed in the communist school. In communist society, with its swift advance of technology, enormous and rapid transfers of labour-forces will be inevitable from some branches of production into others. For example, some discovery in the weaving and spinning industry may require a reduction in the number of weavers and spinners and an increase in the number of workers involved in producing cotton, and such like. In such cases, a new redistribution of forces between the professions is inevitable, something that can be accomplished only if every worker of communist society is familiar not merely with a single profession but with a whole variety. Bourgeois society was able to deal with such a state of affairs by using the industrial reserve-army, that is, the permanent cadre of the unemployed. In communist society, there will be no army of the unemployed; the reserve for any branch of industry that experiences a shortage of workers will lie in the ability of workers from another branch to make up this shortage. Only the single labour-school can prepare cadres of such workers who will be able to fulfil a variety of functions in communist society.

§ 81. Specialised education

Up to the age of seventeen years, all young people of the Republic must pass through the single labour-school and acquire there the sum of theoretical and practical knowledge that is necessary for every citizen of communist society. But instruction cannot end there. Besides general knowledge, specialised knowledge is also necessary. The scope of each of the most essential sciences is so great that there is no possibility of any single person mastering all of them. The single labour-school by no means excludes specialised education. It only postpones it to the final stage. Already at the second level of the single labour-school, that is, in the ages from fourteen to seventeen years, there must inevitably appear an inclination on the part of students to be captivated by one subject or another. It is not only possible, but necessary, even at this stage, to provide an outlet to these natural aptitudes for a more fundamental acquaintance with certain sciences and to do so without detriment to the general educational programme of the labour-school.

But genuine specialist education must begin only after the age of seventeen. This age marks an important distinction for other reasons as well. Up to the age of seventeen, the young people in labour-schools are more students than workers. The main task of the labour-processes in schools is educational, not to produce values and increase the state's budget. After seventeen years, the student becomes a worker. He must contribute his share of labour, his share of the products he has made, to the commune of humanity. He can only acquire specialised education after first fulfilling his fundamental duty to society. As a rule, therefore, after seventeen years of age the youth can only acquire specialised knowledge during non-labour time. With the development of technology, the working day will have to be shortened to even fewer than eight hours, and thus adequate time will be available to every member of communist society for specialised education. In certain cases of especially gifted people, an exception may be possible in the form of a temporary release from labour for several years for the purpose of education and scientific research, or else there may be a shortening of the working day by comparison with the general norm if all this is acknowledged to be socially necessary.

§ 82. The higher school

At the present moment, it is still not possible to foresee fully what will be the character of specialised higher schools under communism. Quite probably there will be many types, ranging from more or less brief courses up to polytechnics and laboratory-schools, where instruction will be conducted together with scientific research and all distinctions between the professors and their students will be effaced. But at present, we can already say with certainty that our universities in their current form, with their current professoriate, are obsolete institutions. They continue in the old spirit to provide the final schooling for young people who have completed the bourgeois middle-schools. For now, these universities can be reformed, renovating the professorial staff with people who perhaps have no qualification as 'doctors of bourgeois society', but who will be able successfully to implement a complete revolution in the teaching of social sciences and deprive bourgeois science of its last refuge. The composition of the audience can be changed by filling the university lecture-rooms primarily with workers, thereby making the natural and technical sciences accessible to the working class. But the attendance of workers inevitably poses the question of how to support them during their studies at the state's expense. All of this is discussed in Point 3 of our programme in the section dealing with popular education.

§ 83. Soviet-schools and party-schools

The Communist Party, having taken power, has destroyed the school apparatus of tsarism that survived virtually untouched during the time of Kerensky's government. On the ruins of the old class-school it has begun to build the single labour-school as *the embryo of the normal labour-school of the future communist society*. It is endeavouring to eradicate from the higher bourgeois school everything that was adapted to supporting the domination of capital and to make all the knowledge that was accumulated in the period of rule by the possessing classes accessible to the toilers, thereby beginning preparations for the *normal type* of higher school in communist society.

But among all the sciences familiar to bourgeois culture, there is none that would teach how to make the proletarian revolution. Among all the schools that the bourgeoisie built and that are now beginning to be built for the future communist society, there is none that would teach how to construct the proletarian state. The transition-period from capitalism to communism has brought to life a special type of school that must serve the ongoing revolution and construction of the soviet-apparatus. This is the goal that party-soviet schools are called upon to serve. Having arisen before our own eyes in the form of short-term and quite incidental courses, they have turned into and will continue to become permanent institutions for training party- and soviet-workers. This was inevitable.

Construction of the Soviet state – this is something totally new, with no examples in history. The work of soviet-institutions is developing and improving day by day, and every soviet-worker's success will necessarily depend on knowing the experience acquired by his predecessors. Self-instruction in state-administration, which occurs through participation of all workers in the soviets, is proving insufficient. It is necessary to gather up this experience, systematise and comprehend it and make it available to every worker who is participating in Soviet construction, so that every new cohort of workers who become involved in managing the state will not repeat the mistakes of their predecessors, so that they will learn not through their own mistakes but from those already committed by others and already paid for by the state. The school of soviet-work must also serve this purpose, and it is already doing so insofar as the Republic has a permanent central school of soviet-work under the All-Russian Central Executive Committee. There can be no doubt that corresponding soviet-schools will soon be established in every provincial capital-city.

As for the Communist party-schools, they are fundamentally changing their character during the period of actual transition to communism. From being the school of a particular party, relying upon the proletariat, and from being purely political schools, they are turning into schools for the communist reconstruction of society, and thus into state-schools. At the same time, they are becoming the military academies of the Civil War. It is only due to these schools that the proletariat is in a position to understand the meaning and the objective tasks of the Revolution that it made semi-spontaneously and semi-consciously, focusing only on narrow concrete goals and not having the opportunity to embrace the entire process of reconstruction as a whole. The party-schools are not only in the position to explain scientifically to the proletariat the nature and final goal of its revolution, but they also teach how to carry this revolution through to the end in the shortest time possible and with the least expenditure of forces.

§ 84. Non-school education

Tsarism consciously kept the majority of Russia's toiling people in a state of ignorance and illiteracy. Having inherited from the autocracy an enormous percentage of illiterates, the Soviet authority naturally must put in motion the most heroic measures to rid itself of this legacy. With this purpose in mind, the departments of popular education are opening schools for illiterate adults and are undertaking a number of other measures in the struggle against illiteracy. But besides using the school-apparatus of the Commissariat of Enlightenment, the Communist Party must employ all measures to ensure that the masses take part in the instruction of illiterates. The soviets of popular education must serve this end, being elected by the toiling masses who are interested in education. These same purposes are served by the mobilisation of all literate people for the instruction of all who are illiterate. This kind of mobilisation is beginning to occur in several localities of the Republic, and the Party must ensure that it is enacted everywhere according to a definite plan.

Besides the struggle against illiteracy, the Soviet authority must put great effort and resources into assisting the population, primarily the adult population, with self-instruction. For this purpose, a network of libraries is being organised that is satisfying the demands of the working reader, and everywhere possible, people's houses and clubs are being established along with the creation of people's universities. Cinematography, which in the past served as a means for promoting the depravity of the population and the enrichment of its owners, is gradually, but, to our regret, only very slowly, being transformed into the most powerful means of enlightening the masses and educating them in the spirit of socialism. All kinds of courses, free public lectures open to all, and so forth, thanks to a shortening working day, are becoming accessible to all the toilers. In the future, planned and organised holiday-excursions for the toilers will have enormous educational significance for the purpose of becoming acquainted with their own country and with the various countries of the world. These excursions will, in future, play an enormous role for purposes of contact between the toilers of all countries.

§ 85. New educational workers

The school-reforms undertaken by the Soviet authority have been more successful than any reforms and innovations in other areas. This cannot be explained simply by the fact that the Soviet state spends an incomparably larger part of its budget on popular education than even the most advanced of the bourgeois states.

Implementation of the idea of the single labour-school was, in large measure, already prepared by the leading pedagogues of bourgeois society. The best educators in Russia have been able under the Soviet régime to realise in part what they considered to be generally necessary from a purely pedagogical point of view. Among the school-workers who have come over to Soviet power from the bourgeois-landlord régime, there are many who were, and still are, opposed to the proletarian revolution in general, but who support the revolution in school-affairs that the proletariat has brought about.

But this fortunate circumstance by no means reduces the proletarian state's need for genuinely Communist school-workers. The number of Communists among teachers, as among all specialists in general, is an insignificant minority. The number of those opposed to communism is significantly greater. But an even greater number are workers with a bureaucratic attitude who are willing to serve any régime and follow any programme, but who have a special regard for what their fathers and grandfathers did. In this connection, the Communist Party faces two kinds of tasks: on the one hand, to mobilise all the best elements from amongst the teachers and, by way of intensive work in their midst, to make them over into a cadre of Communist workers; on the other hand, to create completely new cadres of educational workers from among the young people, who from the very beginning are being raised in the spirit of communism in general and in the spirit of a Communist school-programme in particular.

§ 86. The treasures of art and science for the toilers

Under the capitalist system, talent is looked upon as the property of its immediate possessor and as an instrument of enrichment. In that society, the product that results from the activity of talent is a commodity that can be sold for some price or other and thus can become the property of whoever will pay the most. A work of genius, with enormous social significance and representing essentially a collective creation, can be bought by any Russian Kolupaev or American Morgan and, with equal right, can be either altered or destroyed. If the famous Moscow merchant Tret'yakov had decided, at some fine moment, to burn his art-gallery, instead of giving it to the city of Moscow, he could not have been held accountable according to the laws of bourgeois society. As a result of the purchase and sale of art-works, rare books, manuscripts, and so on, an enormous number were not available for the broad strata of society to become familiar with them and they remained the privilege of the class of exploiters.

The Soviet Republic declares all art-works, collections, and so forth to be a social possession, and it is eliminating all barriers in the way of their enjoyment by society. This same purpose is served by all the orders aimed at eliminating private property in large book-depositories, which thereby also become a social possession.

The Communist Party must endeavour to see that state-power goes still further in this direction. Given the extreme shortage of books and the impossibility of rapidly expanding publication and the issue of reprints, it must limit private ownership even further in this area and concentrate books in public libraries, schools, and so forth.

Furthermore, in the interests of enlightenment and of providing the broad masses with the possibility of enjoying the theatre, it is necessary to nationalise all theatres and thus indirectly to achieve the socialisation of talent in areas of the stage, music and vocal art.

In this way all works of science and art, which were created on the basis of exploiting the toiling masses and represented an expense and a burden on their backs, are being returned once more to their real owners.

§ 87. State-propaganda of communism

As the bourgeois system is being destroyed and the new communist society is beginning to be assembled on its ruins, propaganda for the idea of communism cannot be left to the Communist Party alone, to be conducted only with its modest resources. Communist propaganda becomes a necessity for the entire society that is being transformed, and it must accelerate that inevitable process. For those building the new society, for those who often work without being aware, it must explain the meaning of their own efforts and of their work. Therefore, it is not just the proletarian school, but also the entire mechanism of the proletarian state in general that must serve the work of Communist propaganda. This propaganda must be waged by military-political organisations in the army and by all soviet-organs.

The strongest instrument for state-propaganda of communism is state publishing activity. Nationalisation of all supplies of paper and all printing houses makes it possible for the proletarian state, which faces tremendous shortages of paper, to publish millions of copies of materials that are most necessary to the masses at the current time. As a result, everything published by the state-presses becomes available to the masses at the lowest possible prices, and books, pamphlets, newspapers and posters are gradually becoming accessible to the masses completely free of charge. The state-propaganda of communism is ultimately becoming both a means for eliminating all remnants of bourgeois propaganda from the past, which poisoned the consciousness of the toilers, and also a powerful means for creating a new ideology, new habits of thought and a new understanding of the world among the workers of socialist society.

§ 88. Popular enlightenment under tsarism and under Soviet power

The following sums have been spent on popular enlightenment by the state:

	Roubles
1891	22,810,260
1911	27,883,000
1916	195,624,000
1917	339,831,687
1918	2,914,082,124
1919 (first half-year)	3,888,000,000

Thus, the transfer of power to the proletariat immediately led to an almost nine-fold increase of expenditures on popular education.

On 1 September 1917, there were 38,387 lower schools (in 26 provinces).

In the school year 1917–18, there were 52,274 elementary schools with 4,138,982 students.

In the school year 1918–19, there were approximately 62,238.

At the same time, during 1917–18, there were 1,830 second-level schools, and in 1918–19, 3,783.

There was absolutely no pre-school education under tsarism. Soviet power has had to organise everything from the start. Despite numerous unfavourable conditions, by 1 October 1919, there were 2,615 kindergartens, play-schools and homes in 31 provinces with 155,443 children. Altogether, about 2.5 percent of the children in ages from three to five years are being provided for. But in the cities, 10.1 per cent of the children are already being provided for, and this figure is rising continuously.

Literature on the question of the labour-school: 1) *Polozhenie o edinoi trudovoi shkole Rossiiskoi Sotsialist[icheskoi] Feder[ativnoi] Respubliki* (1918, izd. VTsIK, ts. 60 k.); 2) *Edinaya trudovaya shkola – doklad V.M. Poznera* (1919, izd. VTsIK); 3) *Trudovaya shkola. Byulleteni Otdela narodn[ovo] prosv[eshcheniya] MSRD*; 4) Blonsky, *Shkola i rabochii klass*; 5) Blonsky, *Trudovaya shkola*, chapters I and II; 6) Levitin, *Trudovaya shkola*; 7) Levitin, *Internatsional'nye problemy sotsial'n[oi] pedagogiki* (R. Zeidel', G. Kershenshteiner i dr.); 8) Krupskaya, *Narodnoe obrazovanie i demokratiya*; 9) Dyun, *Shkola i obshchestvo*; 10) Sharrel'man, *Trudovaya shkola*; 11) Same author, *V laboratorii narodn[ovo] uchitelya*; 12) Gansberg, *Pedagogika*; 13) Same author, *Tvorcheskaya rabota v shkole*; 14) *Ezhenedel'nik Narodn[ovo] komoss[ariata] prosveshch[eniya]* (appeared originally as a supplement to *Izvestiya VTsIK* and from number 18 was published independently (the latest number being 51–2). In the *Ezhenedel'nik*, a whole series of articles appeared on the Labour-School; 15) *Protokoly 1-vo Vserossiiskovo s'ezda po prosveshcheniyu* (izd. Otdela s'ezdov Narkomprosa, 1919).

In the non-communist literature can be included: Kershenshteiner, *Ponyatiya trudovoi shkoly*; Same author, *Trudovaya shkola* (izd. 4-e 'Zadrugi'. M. 1918); Gurlitt, *Problemy vseobshchei edinoi shkoly* (Gos. Izd.); Fer'er, *V novoi shkole*, izd. Gorb.-Pos; Vetekamp, *Samodeyatel'nost' i tvorchestvo* (izd. Gorb.-Pos); Shul'ts, *Shkolnaya reforma sotsial-demokratii* (Gos. Izd.); Fedorov-Hartvig, *Trudovoe shkola i kollektivizm*. M., 1918 (izd. Nar. uchit.); Yanzhul E.N., *Trudovoe nachalo v sholakh Evropy*. M., 1918 (izd. Nar. Uchit); Shatsky, *Bodraya zhizn'*; Myunkh, *Budushchaya shkola*.

Chapter XI

Religion and Communism

§ 89. Why religion and communism are incompatible. § 90. Separation of the Church from the state. § 91. Separation of the school from the Church. § 92. The struggle against the religious prejudices of the masses.

§ 89. Why religion and communism are incompatible

Karl Marx said 'Religion is the opium of the people'. The task of the Communist Party is to make this truth known to the broadest circles of the toiling masses. The Party's task is to see that all the toiling masses, including the most backward, firmly accept the truth that religion was previously, and continues to be, one of the mightiest instruments in the hands of the oppressors in support of inequality, exploitation and the slavish submissiveness of the toilers.

Certain rather poor Communists reason this way: 'Religion does not stop me from being a Communist – I believe in both God and communism at the same time. My faith in God does not prevent me from fighting for the cause of proletarian revolution'. Such reasoning is fundamentally untrue. Religion and communism are incompatible, both in theory and in practice.

Every Communist must regard social phenomena (the relations between people, revolutions, wars, and so forth) as things that occur according to definite laws. Scientific communism has fully established the laws of social development thanks to the theory of historical materialism created by our great teachers, Karl Marx and Friedrich Engels. According to this theory, there are no supernatural forces that act upon social development. And that is not all. The same theory establishes that the very concepts of God and other-worldly forces appeared at a certain stage of human history, and are also beginning to disappear at another stage, just as in the case of childish ideas that are not supported by practical life and by man's struggle against nature. And it is solely because it is convenient to the predatory classes to maintain the people's ignorance and childish faith in miracles (and the key to such miracles is in their pocket) that religious prejudices turn out to be so tenacious and confuse even very clever people.

Supernatural forces likewise have no influence on the changes that occur throughout nature as a whole. Man has achieved enormous successes in the struggle with nature: he acts upon it in his own interests and manages its forces, not thanks to faith in God and His help, but despite this faith and because, in the practical conduct of all serious matters, he is always an atheist. In its understanding of all the phenomena of nature, scientific communism relies on the facts of the natural sciences, which are implacably hostile to all religious fabrications.

But communism is also incompatible with religious faith in practice. The tactics of the Communist Party prescribe to its members a certain way of acting. The morals of every religion also prescribe certain behaviour to believers (for example, the Christian moral: 'Whosoever shall smite thee on thy right cheek, turn to him the other also'.)[7] In the vast majority of cases, there is an irreconcilable contradiction between the directives of Communist tactics and the

---

7. [*Matthew* 5:39].

commandments of religion. The Communist, rejecting the commandments of religion and acting according to party-instructions, ceases to be a believer. The believer, who also calls himself a Communist and infringes the Party's prescriptions in the name of religious commandments, ceases to be a Communist.

The struggle against religion has two aspects that every Communist must strictly distinguish. In the first place, there is the struggle against the Church as a special organisation for religious propaganda that is materially interested in the people's ignorance and their religious slavery. Secondly, there is the struggle against widespread and deeply rooted religious prejudices on the part of a majority of the toiling masses.

§ 90. Separation of the Church from the state

According to the Christian catechism, the Church is the community of believers, united by a single faith, by the sacraments, and so on. For a Communist, the Church is a society of people united by a particular source of income at the believers' expense, at the expense of their ignorance and lack of enlightenment. It is a society linked together with the society of other exploiters such as the landlords, the capitalists and their state, which it assists in oppressing the toilers while receiving help and support from it in exchange. The bond between the Church and the state has ancient origins. The bond between the Church and the feudal-landlord state was especially close. And this is understandable, if one remembers that the autocratic-aristocratic state depended on large-scale agricultural holdings, and that the Church itself was a great landowner possessing millions of *desyatins*. Both of these forces inevitably had to unite for the common struggle against the toiling masses and to strengthen their domination over them through their alliance. In the period of the urban bourgeoisie's struggle against the aristocracy, the bourgeoisie at one time furiously attacked the Church as the owner of lands that the bourgeoisie wanted to take over and as a property-owner and consumer of incomes collected from the toilers – incomes to which the bourgeoisie itself laid claim. In some countries, this struggle was very acute (France), while in others it was less so (England, Germany, Russia). Thus, the demand for separation of the Church from the state (which really meant transfer to the bourgeoisie of the resources that the state spent on the Church) was already put forth by the liberal bourgeoisie and by bourgeois democrats. But this demand was never implemented anywhere by the bourgeoisie. The reason is that the struggle of the working class against the capitalists began to strengthen everywhere, and the bourgeoisie discovered it was not beneficial to cast aside an ally. It considered that it was more advantageous to make peace with the Church, to purchase its prayers for the struggle against socialism, and to use its influence over the unenlightened masses to maintain their feeling of slavish submissiveness in relation to the exploiters' state ('There is no power but of God'.)[8]

What the bourgeoisie never finished in its struggle with the Church, the proletarian state has carried through to completion. One of the first decrees of the Soviet authority in Russia was the decree concerning separation of the Church from the state. All of the Church's lands were taken from it and turned over to the toilers, and all of its capital was made a possession of the toiling people. The Church was deprived of all the incomes that it received from tsarism and that it quite happily continued to receive during the epoch of the 'socialist' Kerensky's government. Religion was declared a personal matter for every citizen. At the same time, the Soviet power dismissed all thought of using the Church to strengthen proletarian dominion in any manner whatsoever.

§ 91. Separation of the school from the Church

Joining together religious propaganda with school-instruction is a second powerful instrument in the hands of the clergy for strengthening the Church's dominance and its influence over the masses. In this way, the future of mankind, its youth, is handed over to the priests. Under tsarism, support from religious fanaticism, stupidity and ignorance was regarded as a matter of state-importance. The Law of God was the most important subject taught in the school. The autocracy supported the Church in the school, while the Church supported the autocracy. Besides the obligatory Law of God in the schools and the equally obligatory attendance at services of worship, the Church acquired much more. It began to gather into its own hands all popular education and, for this purpose, the whole of Russia was covered with a network of parish-schools.

Thanks to the cohabitation of school and Church, young people from a very early age were either in the grip of religious superstitions or completely incapable of working out any coherent ways of thinking about the world. Religion and science give different answers to the same questions (for instance, the origin of the world), and the impressionable mind of the schoolchild becomes a battlefield between exact knowledge and the clumsy fabrications of obscurantists.

In many countries, the youth are raised not simply in a spirit of devotion to the existing régime, but often also in devotion to the already deposed autocratic-church-aristocratic system, as in France, for example. Such propaganda is counter-revolutionary even from the viewpoint of the bourgeois state.

Bourgeois liberalism has also included in its programmes the demand for separation of the school from the Church. It has struggled to replace the Law of

---

8. [*Romans* 13:1].

God in schools with the teaching of bourgeois morality, and to close the schools that are organised by religious societies and monasteries. But this struggle has nowhere been carried through to conclusion. An example is France, where all the bourgeois ministries have for two decades solemnly promised to dissolve all religious orders (Catholic religious societies), confiscate their capital and forbid them to teach in the schools, but have ended up reconciling and compromising with the Catholic clergy. Not long ago, Clemenceau gave a striking example of such conciliation towards religion and the Church, having at one time been an ardent enemy of the Church, yet ending up with an appeal to forget the hostility and personally handing out decorations for patriotism to representatives of the Catholic clergy. In the struggle to exploit other countries (the war with Germany) as well as in the domestic struggle with the working class, the state and Church have already entered a deal and mutually assist each other.

This reconciliation of the bourgeoisie with the Church finds expression not only in the fact that the bourgeoisie is putting under covers its old battle-slogans aimed at religion and is bringing its struggle with it to an end. This is nothing. The bourgeoisie itself is increasingly becoming a 'class of believers'. The great-grandfathers of today's European bourgeois were atheists, freethinkers and ardent enemies of priests and rule by priests. The fathers and children have taken a step backwards. Remaining atheists themselves, not believing in religious fabrications and privately laughing at them, they have, nevertheless, found it necessary to preserve these fabrications and to keep a religious bridle on the people. Ultimately, the sons of today not only consider a religious restraint necessary for the people, but are now prepared to apply it to themselves. After the October Revolution, we saw with our own eyes how the former liberal bourgeois and the bourgeois intellectuals thronged to the Church, and with what touching emotion they worshipped that which in better days they had ridiculed with laughter. Such is the fate of all dying classes that have no alternative but to find 'consolation' in religion.

Such a movement in favour of religion can be seen among the bourgeoisies of Europe that have yet to lose power. But if the bourgeois class is now beginning to believe in God and eternal life in Heaven, this only signifies that it senses that the hour of its death has arrived here on Earth.

Separation of the school from the Church has caused, and is still causing, protests from the most backward elements among workers and peasants. Many parents continue to insist that the teaching of 'God's Law' be admitted to the school as an optional subject for those who want it. The Communist Party is waging a most determined struggle against any such attempts to return to the past. To admit lessons of Church-obscurantism into the school, even as an optional subject, would mean giving *state-support for the strengthening of religious prejudices.*

The Church would then have at its disposal a ready audience of children (who are gathered at the school for a purpose that is exactly the opposite of religion); it would have at its disposal accommodations belonging to the state, and it would thus be in a position to spread religious poison among the youth almost to the same extent as prior to the separation of the school from the Church.

The decree concerning separation of the school from the Church must remain in full force, and the proletarian state must make no concessions whatsoever to the Middle-Ages. What has been done in this area is still inadequate, and ignorant parents are still completely free to mutilate their children's minds with religious fables. The Soviet power allows freedom of conscience to adults. But this freedom of conscience for the parents is being transformed into freedom for them to poison their children's minds with exactly the same opium with which the Church previously poisoned them. The parents are forcing upon their children their own stupidity and ignorance, and they are passing out as truth all kinds of rubbish that terribly complicates the work of the single labour-school. Liberating children from the reactionary influences of their parents is an important task of the proletarian state. The radical way is the full-scale social rearing of children. But for the immediate future, we must not limit ourselves to banishing religious propaganda from the school. The school has to take the offensive against religious propaganda in the family and see to it beforehand that the consciousness of children is immunised against all those religious fairy-tales that very adult people continue to believe in and give out as the truth.

§ 92. The struggle against the religious prejudices of the masses

If it has been comparatively easy, and almost painless, for the proletarian power to separate Church from state and school from Church, it will be an incomparably more difficult matter to struggle against the religious prejudices that have already taken deep root and are displaying enormous vitality in the consciousness of the masses. This struggle will be protracted and will require great persistence and patience. In this regard, our programme says: 'The RKP is guided by the conviction that only the realisation of purposiveness and awareness in all the social-economic activity of the masses will bring with it the complete dying out of religious prejudices'. What do these words mean?

Religious propaganda, faith in God and in all kinds of supernatural forces, find their most favourable soil where the consciousness of the masses is driven by all the conditions of social life in the direction of supernatural explanations for the surrounding phenomena in nature and society. The situation in the capitalist mode of production is most conducive to this. In bourgeois society, the production and exchange of products is not arranged consciously, according to a definite plan, but spontaneously. The market rules the producer. No-one knows whether too many commodities are produced or too few. It is not clear to the producer just how the whole enormous and complex mechanism of capitalist production works; why sudden crises and unemployment begin; why the prices of commodities rise at one time and fall at another; and so on. Not knowing how to explain the actual cause of social changes that are occurring, the rank-and-file worker turns to the 'will of God', which can explain everything.

In an organised communist society, to the contrary, the toilers will encounter no such mysteries in the spheres of production and distribution. Every worker will not only fulfil his assigned portion of social work, but will himself also participate in working out the general plan of production, and, at the very least, he will have a perfectly clear idea of it. There will be nothing mysterious, incomprehensible or unanticipated in the entire mechanism of social production, and no basis whatever for mystical explanations or superstitions. Just as it is clear to the joiner where the table he has made comes from, such that there is no need to look for its creator in Heaven, so it will be clear to all the toilers of communist society just what they are creating through their collective efforts and how.

For that reason, the very fact of organising and strengthening the socialist system strikes an irreparable blow against religion. And the transition from socialism to communism, that is, from the society that puts an end to capitalism to a society that is completely free from all relics of class-division and class-struggle, will lead to the natural death of all religion and every superstition.

But none of this means that we can be content with predicting the destruction of religion *in the future*.

It is especially necessary to wage a most serious and forceful struggle against religious prejudices precisely now, when the Church is emerging as a counter-revolutionary organisation that is attempting to use its religious influence over the masses to attract these masses into the political struggle against the dictatorship of the proletariat. The Orthodox faith, which is defended by the priests, is drawn towards alliance with the monarchy. This is why the Soviet authority must now develop the most extensive anti-religious propaganda. This is being accomplished through delivering special lectures, holding debates and publishing suitable literature, and also by the general spread of scientific knowledge, which little-by-little, slowly-but-surely, undermines the whole authority of religion. An excellent tool in the struggle against the Church was the recent opening, in many parts of the Republic, of the 'incorruptible' relics,[9] which demonstrated to the widest and, at the same time, most faithful masses, the base fraud upon which all religion in general is founded, and Russian Orthodoxy in particular.

---

9. [The remains of saints.]

However, the struggle against the religious backwardness of the masses has to be waged not merely with complete energy and persistence, but also with the necessary patience and caution. The faithful masses are very sensitive to any insults to their feelings, and the forceful introduction of atheism among them, along with violence and the mockery of religious rituals and cult-objects, rather than accelerating the struggle against religion will, in fact, impede it. A persecuted Church begins to enjoy even greater sympathy from the masses and awakens in them long-forgotten ties between religion and the defence of national freedom, reinforcing anti-Semitism and generally mobilising all the vestiges of an already half-dead ideology.

Let us provide some numbers showing how the tsarist government supported the Church with the people's money, how the people themselves supported this same Church by emptying their meagre pockets, and how much wealth the servants of Christ accumulated.

Every year, on average, the tsarist government, through the Synod and by other means, supplied the Church with up to fifty million roubles (that is, a hundred times more than that, in terms of today's rouble). The Synod kept up to seventy million roubles in the banks, and the churches and monasteries possessed vast tracts of land. In 1905, the Church owned 1,872,000 *desyatins* and the monasteries 740,000 *desyatins*. The six wealthiest monasteries had 182,000 *desyatins*. The Solovetsky monastery had 66,000 *desyatins*, the Sarovskaya hermitage 26,000, the Alexandro-Nevsky monastery 25,000, and so on. In St. Petersburg, in 1903, 266 income-earning properties belonged to the churches and monasteries in the form of houses, shops, building sites, and such like. In Moscow, there were 1,054 rental houses, not to mention 32 hotels. In Kiev, the churches owned 114 houses. And here are the evangelical incomes of the metropolitans and archbishops. The metropolitan of Petrograd received 300,000 roubles a year, the Moscow and Kiev metropolitans 100,000 roubles each, and the Novgorod archbishop 310,000 thousand roubles.

There were up to 30,000 Church-schools with up to one million in attendance. More than 20,000 religious instructors 'worked' in the lower schools of the Ministry of Education.

Everyone knows that the tsarist autocracy supported the Orthodox Church as the dominant and only true faith. Tens of millions of roubles were collected in the form of taxes from Muslims (the Tatars and Bashkirs), from the Catholics (Poles) and the Jews, and with this money the Orthodox clergy demonstrated how any faith other than Orthodoxy was false. Religious oppression under tsarism reached the most savage proportions. Meanwhile, the population of Russia was distributed in religious terms as follows: for every hundred persons there were nine Catholics, 11 Mohammedans, five Protestants, four Jews, and one of various other creeds.

As for the army of Orthodox clergy themselves, in 1909 it reached the following figures.

With 52,869 churches in Russia, there were:

Archpriests	2,912
Priests	46,370
Deacons	14,670
Psalm-Readers	43,518

With 455 monasteries for men:

Monks	9,987
Novices	9,582

With 418 monasteries for women:

Nuns	14,008
Novices	46,811

The total for the white and black clergy in Russia was 188,218.[10]

These are the numbers for the Orthodox clergy alone. But every people, professing other religions, has such a parasitic stratum. This entire mass, instead of receiving enormous sums of money from the population to support popular ignorance, on the contrary could have created an enormous sum of values through physical labour. With the perfection of its economic apparatus, the socialist state will introduce universal labour-duty for the clergy and other non-productive classes, turning them into workers or peasants.

Of the state-resources paid to the Church under the tsar, more than twelve million a year went to the urban and rural clergy (it is understandable why the reverend fathers oppose separation of the Church from the state, which is equivalent to separating tens of millions of roubles from their own pockets). But this is only part of the clergy's incomes; a far greater part of those incomes came from payments for religious rites, from leasing land and from interest on Church capital. No-one has established a precise figure of the clergy's incomes in Russia. The approximate annual income of the clergy was calculated to be up to 150 million roubles, that is, a hundred times more than that, in terms of our current rouble. Up to the present day, the clergy continues to receive an enormous part of these incomes from the people.

Literature: Kilchevsky, *Bogatstvo i dokhody dukhovenstva*; Lukin N.M. (Antonov I.), *Tserkov' i gosudarstvo v perekhodnoe vremya*; Minin S., *Religiya i kommunizm*;

---

10. [In the Russian-Orthodox Church, monk-priests, or hieromonks, wear black robes and conduct the liturgy in male or female monastic communities and also, if necessary, in parish-churches. Hieromonks are pledged to celibacy, while the white clergy – parish-, or secular priests (because they serve a lay community) – are expected to be married.]

Stepanov, I., *Proiskhozhdenie nashevo Boga*; Stepanov, I., *Dukhovenstvo, evo dokhody, evo motivy i proklyat'ya*; Kunov, G., *Proiskhozhdenie religii i very v Boga*; Kautsky, K., *Proiskhozhdenie pervobytnoi bibleiskoi istorii*; Kautsky, K., *Antichnyi mir, iudeistvo i khristianstvo*; Kautsky, K., *Katolicheskaya tserkov' i sotsial-demokratiya*; Bebel, A., *Khristianstvo i sotsializm*; Shtampfer and Vandervel'de, *Sotsial-demokratiya i religiya*; Lafargue, P., *Proiskhozhdenie religioznykh verovanii*; Danilov, S., *Chernoe voinstvo*; Kil'ver, R., *Sotsial-demokratiya i khristianstvo*; Bukharin, N., *Tserkov' i shkola v Sovetskoi respubliki*; Ya. Burov, *Chto oznachaet zakon o svobode sovesti?*; Lafargue, P., *Mif o neprochnom zachatii*; Nikol'sky, *Iisus i pervye khristianskie obshchiny*; Vipper, *Vozniknovenie khristianstva*; Pokrovsky, *Russkaya istoriya* (the article by Nikol'sky); Bednyi, D., *Otsy dukhovnye*.

Chapter XIII

The Organisation of Agriculture

§ 103. Land-relations in Russia before the Revolution. § 104. Land-relations after the Revolution. § 105. Why does the future belong to large-scale socialist agriculture? § 106. The soviet-farm. § 107. Urban agriculture. § 108. The commune and artels. § 109. Social cultivation of the land. § 110. Agricultural cooperation. § 111. State-sowing of idle land, the mobilisation of agronomists, hiring stations, land-improvement, and migration. § 112. Assistance to peasant-agriculture. § 113. Joining industry with agriculture. § 114. The tactic of the Communist Party in relation to the peasantry.

§ 103. Land-relations in Russia before the Revolution

Even before the Revolution, our agriculture was primarily peasant agriculture. Following the October Revolution and after the liquidation of the landlords' estates, our agriculture became almost exclusively peasant and involved almost exclusively small farms. In such conditions, the Communist Party must overcome quite unbelievable difficulties in the struggle for large-scale collective agriculture. But this struggle has begun, and even in this most difficult period, there are already certain results at the very beginning.

In order to clarify these circumstances and the conditions in which Communists must realise their programme in the Russian village, it is necessary to provide certain facts concerning our agriculture prior to the Revolution and the changes brought by the Revolution.

Before the Revolution, land-ownership in European Russia was distributed as follows:

	Desyatins
State-land	138,086,168
Peasant-allotments	138,767,587
Private property and land owned by institutions	118,338,688

Almost all of the state-land is either forested or generally not suited to agriculture in its present condition. As for the land owned by private people and institutions, it was distributed as follows:

	Desyatins
Landlords' land	101,735,343
Appanages	7,843,115
Church-land	1,871,858
Monasteries	733,777
Municipal	2,042,570
Cossack territories	3,459,240
Others	646,885

With regard to the allotment-land, according to the 1905 statistics, it was divided among 12,277,355 farmsteads, each with 11.37 *desyatins*. This average figure, however, conceals the meagre land of the majority of peasants in the central provinces because there were large allotments (although unsuitable for tillage) in the outlying areas. In reality, the former landlords' peasants, comprising the majority of our peasantry, had an average allotment of 6.7 *desyatins* per household. In several provinces and districts, the figure was less than half that size. By 1916, the number of peasant-households exceeded fifteen million (15,492,202), and the extent of peasant land-usage had increased very little. The land-shortage grew even further.

In view of the fact that only a small part of the treasury-lands are suitable for cultivation, the peasantry could expand their holdings [only] at the expense of the above-mentioned category of 'private property and land owned by institutions'.

Among private individuals, the first who had to be dispossessed were the landlords, with 53,169,008 *desyatins*, along with merchants, rich peasants, companies and agricultural associations of the bourgeois-kulak type. Altogether, the private owners with more than twenty *desyatins* had property of 82,841,413 *desyatins*. The agricultural associations had 15,778,677 *desyatins*. This was where the first blow of the peasant-revolution had to be struck. As regards the institutions, here the first land that could go to the peasants was that belonging to churches and monasteries together with part of the appanage-land.

§ 104. Land-relations after the Revolution

Private land-ownership, mainly in the form of the landlords' estates, was enormously indebted before the Revolution. More than sixty million *desyatins* were mortgaged for a total of 3,497,894,600 roubles. In other words, the real owners of the landed estates were Russian and foreign banks. This explains why various compromising parties, the S-Rs foremost among them, shouted so loudly for transfer of all land to the peasants without compensation and then retreated in cowardly fashion, rejecting confiscation when it had to be enacted in reality. Only the party of Communist-Bolsheviks, having no other connection with capital except through war to the death, only this party opposed the compromisers and supported carrying the peasant-revolution to completion against the landlords. This revolution found legal expression in the decree on the land that was introduced by the Communist Party and adopted by the Second Congress of Soviets.

According to this decree and the fundamental law on the land, adopted by the Third Congress, private property in land was declared to be eliminated; all the land of the Republic was made available to everyone who wants to work it with his own labour (use of the land was not restricted in terms of either nationality or citizenship). The land is being distributed equally on the basis of the number of family-members and in quantities regulated by labour-norms. Furthermore, and in accordance with the statute on socialist land-use, all lands of the Republic were declared to be the property of the worker-peasant state as a whole, which has the supreme right of disposal over all lands.

As a result of the land-revolution, reinforced by legislation, land-relations in Russia underwent a complete transformation and continue to experience numerous changes up to the present time.

Above all, both landed estates and large and medium land-ownership in general were completely abolished throughout Great Russia. The landed possessions of the kulaks are being levelled with those of the middle-peasants.

On the other hand, land-usage by the poor and by those peasants with the least land, after they acquired stock and inventory from the kulaks and from destruction of the estates, has expanded towards the norm based on family-size.

With regard to the equalisation of land-allotments by parishes, districts and provinces, it is still far from complete and will remain so for a long time.

It is still impossible, at present, to summarise the results of the revolution in land-relations, but, in the most general terms, almost all the arable land of the large and medium private owners has gone over to use by the peasants.

The landowners' land is now being ploughed. The Soviet authority has managed to retain in its own hands about two million *desyatins* in the form of soviet-farms. The peasants are also ploughing part of the municipal lands. They have acquired all Church- and monasterial land and part of the appanage-land. In general terms, about forty million *desyatins* of private land-holdings alone have been put at the peasantry's disposal.

In addition to the area reserved for Soviet estates and the lands of sugar-factories, the Soviet state retained almost all the former treasury-land and also the nationalised forests of the private landowners.

As a result, the Russian Communist Party must struggle for socialism in agriculture in the most unfavourable conditions. Most of the land-area that is actually at the state's disposal is not fit for cultivation. The major portion of the country's arable land is being used for small-scale, independent peasant-farming.

But regardless of how unfavourable conditions may be for the socialisation of agriculture in Russia, and no matter how stubborn the opposition from the petty-bourgeois economy, in peasant Russia the future still belongs entirely to large-scale socialist agriculture.

§ 105. Why does the future belong to large-scale socialist agriculture?

The large-scale capitalist undertaking beat down the small artisan and peasant-economy, and in industry it did so much more rapidly and noticeably than in agriculture. The communist economy is more advantageous and productive than the capitalist, and all the more so for the small peasant. Just as a pound is heavier than an ounce, so a *pood* is heavier than a pound and heavier still compared to an ounce.

At this point, we must demonstrate all of this as clearly as possible.

First of all, with socialist agriculture, all the land of the Republic must be demarcated in such a way that every district, region, field, and so on, in terms of the quality and features of the soil, is sown with the most appropriate grains, vegetables, grasses and technical crops (flax, hemp, sugar-beet, sunflowers and so forth). This must be determined by scientific agronomy. The opposite frequently occurs with our peasant-economy: grain is sown and yields a poor harvest in areas most suitable for flax, rye is sown where wheat should be grown, or even more often, the reverse occurs. With the implementation of a general scientific plan for all land-use, the productivity of the land would increase even if everything else remained unchanged.

It is only through medium- and large-scale farming (and more through the latter than the former) that a multi-field system of farming can be introduced. A system of field-rotation is enormously beneficial in agriculture. Meanwhile, with our peasant and his three-field system, approximately one-third of the land lies idle every year...[11] It is virtually impossible to lead the peasant to a proper field-rotation and a multi-field system when he is farming a *khutor*[12] (with little land), and this is all the more true when the rural community divides the land into strips.

With large-scale farming, there is no land wasted at the corners or boundaries of the fields. But with our peasant, to the contrary, hundreds of thousands of *desyatins* are wasted throughout the whole of Russia merely at the boundaries of the fields alone... By my calculation, simply because of the boundaries our peasant loses from sixty to eighty million *poods* of grain.

The main support of the soil's fertility is fertiliser. A large farm is in a position to maintain a larger herd of cattle (and also to manage with fewer horses), and thus can acquire more manure for fertiliser. It is more profitable for a large farm to acquire artificial fertiliser, or even to make various kinds for itself, something that is not so easy for a small-scale farm.

Most difficult of all is properly timed, deep and inexpensive ploughing (that is, requiring less labour-power). Here, the tiny farmer, compared to the large-scale socialist farmer (and even the large-scale capitalist one) is really a dwarf. The cheapest, most rapid and deep ploughing comes from using a tractor. It is impossible to work tiny peasant-strips with a tractor. And for that matter, a single tractor works less profitably than a tractor group of eight or ten employed in unison.

The same applies to other large labour-saving machinery. A steam-thresher and steam-harvester can only be used on a large-scale farm.

Finally, the fullest use of implements is, likewise, possible only on a large-scale farm.

For example, full usage occurs:
with a horse-drawn plough, on 21 desyatins of arable land;
with ordinary seeders, reapers and threshing machines, on 63 *desyatins*;
with steam threshers, on 225 *desyatins*;
with a steam plough, on 900 *desyatins*.

Meanwhile, simply using a steam-driven plough and a tractor raises the productivity of the soil by one-third, all other conditions being equal.

If a farm has to manage with horses, even here the superiority of large-scale farming is evident, because on a large farm every individual horse services more *desyatins*. It has been calculated that large farms require from one-half to one-third fewer horses to work the same area of land.

---

11. [This ellipsis and the one that follows are in the text by Preobrazhensky.]
12. [An independent farmstead fully detached from the periodically redistributed holdings of the rural community.]

Only on a large-scale farm can electricity be applied. Then, in place of a hundred small and badly constructed stables, there can be one large one; and in place of a hundred tiny kitchens, a single large one, and so on.

The most profitable dairy-farming can only be accomplished on a large farm.

But the greatest economy of all is the economy of labour-power, the possibility for mankind to reduce by one-half or one-third the labour-time required in agriculture, and to do so with no reduction in soil productivity, but even an increase by three or four times. Here is an example.

According to the last census in 1916, the entire sown area in Russia came to 71,430,800 *desyatins*. If we assume that this entire area is ploughed once a year (in fact, this is untrue, as every rural owner knows), then for all this ploughing, the peasantry would have to mobilise all the labour available, that is, up to twenty million men together with all the working cattle. To work this land with tractors (a tractor ploughs from eight to ten *desyatins* a day, and incomparably more if it works without interruption) only a million working hands would be needed.

A saving of nineteen-twentieths![13]

If, in place of a hundred meals prepared in a hundred separate kitchens, one large meal were prepared in a village's social kitchen, then ninety cooks out of a hundred would be redundant and could be employed in more useful work that would lighten the toil of others...[14]

The task of the Communist Party, therefore, is to struggle in every possible way for the most perfect economy in agriculture, that is, for a communist economy that is capable of freeing the countryside from a barbaric waste of resources on dwarf farms, from a barbaric exhaustion of the soil, from a barbaric Asiatic kind of livestock-farming and, finally, from a barbaric household-kitchen.

What are the ways in which the Communist Party intends to accomplish this great objective? There are several. Let us begin with the most rapid.

§ 106. The soviet-farm

When the peasants seized the landlords' holdings in 1917, many of them were cultured estates with model farming, using select thoroughbred cattle and complex agricultural machines, but the estates were destroyed. However, a portion of these estates managed to be saved when the soviets promptly recognised

---

13. It is true that, in addition to tractor-workers, we must take into account the labour-power of those employed in shops where the tractors are made, that spent on maintaining them, on oil, and so on, and calculate all this per *desyatin*. Then the advantage of work using tractors will be less, but it will still be enormous.

14. [The ellipsis is in Preobrazhensky's text.]

the need to protect them. The estates that were taken over by the soviets have come to be known as soviet-farms. In addition, the lands of other estates became soviet-farms when they could not be divided entirely among the peasants, because the latter already had allotments corresponding to the norm for all soviet-farming.

Soviet-farms are the only possible basis for creating large-scale model socialist agriculture, with all of its advantages. It is only through soviet-farms that we are actually in a position to show the peasants all the advantages of large-scale collective agriculture.

On them, we can introduce proper crop-rotation and demonstrate through experience all the shortcomings of the three-field system.

On them, we are in a position to put into motion all the agricultural machines, right up to the most complex.

Soviet-farms are the only points where thoroughbred cattle have been saved from destruction and are being bred. Only through the breeding operations on soviet-farms are we able gradually to improve the breed of cattle for the surrounding peasant-population.

With soviet-farms, it is easiest of all to create demonstration-fields for the peasants and also to improve the seeds by selective methods. Even now, sorting machines are not only selecting improved seeds from the grain of soviet-farms themselves, but they are also sorting seeds for the neighbouring population.

Agricultural schools are being organised under the soviet-farms, there are lectures on agronomy, and agricultural exhibitions are being arranged.

Workshops are being set up on soviet-farms to repair their own equipment first, and then to do the same for the neighbouring villages.

The task of the Communist Party consists of increasing the number of soviet-farms and the land at their disposal wherever possible (avoiding damage, whenever we can, to the interests of the peasant-farm). Gradually, we have to assemble here all the most valuable breeding cattle of the Republic. We must organise the technical processing of agricultural products according to the most advanced principles. We must eliminate bureaucratism and wasteful management of things as a result of certain soviet-farms coming to resemble monasteries for landlords, engaged only in supplying their own workers and employees but giving nothing back to the Soviet state. We must select a staff of skilled workers who are capable not only of exercising workers' control, but also of growing into workers' management of the estates, while also interesting the surrounding peasant-population in soviet-farms, drawing them into discussion of the soviet-farm's economic plans, and thus obliging them to look upon the soviet-farms as a matter of concern to the entire labouring population of the country. The number of soviet-farms by the autumn of 1919 was 3,536, and their cultivable land (excluding forests) was 2,170,000 *desyatins*.

§ 107. Urban agriculture

In view of the terrifying food-crisis that is a natural product of war and revolution, the proper arrangement of land-use in the cities has enormous significance for saving the urban proletariat from becoming extinct. This type of economy is beginning to be put in order, and it has an enormous future. The immediate task for municipal agriculture is to guarantee to every city a sufficient amount of land for a well-established large-scale farm. Before the Revolution, more than two million *desyatins* of land belonged to our cities. Most of this land is taken up by building sites, pastures, parks, and kitchen-gardens, and it still belongs to the cities. However, part of the arable area has gone to the peasantry and is now lost. This land must be returned to the cities; indeed, all of the land surrounding the cities must be expropriated to the extent necessary for proper and expansive farming.

Already in 1919, the land-departments of the soviets in several cities succeeded in taking over market-gardening and in securing an adequate supply of vegetables for feeding the whole working population of the city throughout the year. We must go further in this direction. We must see to it that every city has as much land under market-gardening as it requires in order to provide vegetables for the entire urban population. Every city must have a large farm supplying it with milk, at least for the children and all who are ill, which means having sufficient land for sowing fodder-grasses. With properly-established urban agriculture, it is also possible to supply the workers not only with potatoes and cabbage, but also with cereals (buckwheat, millet). With its own resources, it could support all of the city-horses, which would make it easier to implement nationalisation of the cartage-trade. With the exception of the capital cities, the programme outlined here (so long as it does not adopt the utopian goal of supplying the urban population with bread as well) can be put into practice for all the cities of the Republic during the coming year, and this is proven by experience.

But urban state-farms also have enormous significance in two further respects – in the first place, for the most complete utilisation of the colossal amount of fertiliser available to the city in the form of sewage, garbage and night-soil. To a great extent, this fertiliser is wasted. Secondly, they are important for the unification of industry with agriculture. Only if there is large-scale urban farming will it be possible, in coming years, for a certain part of the urban population to take part in agricultural work without any loss to industry.

Soviet-farms and urban agriculture must play a role as model undertakings, but they must also play the most decisive part in easing the food-crisis. Experience has shown that in the most difficult moment prior to collecting the new harvest, when the peasants have not yet begun, or are only beginning, to thresh the grain, it was the soviet-farms that saved the food-organs from a crisis. The first grain of the new harvest in 1918 and 1919 came from the soviet-farms. In future, this role of the soviet-farms must extend even further. Using all the lands of the soviet-farms, the Soviet Republic is in a position to receive from them approximately half of all the grain needed to feed the urban workers and employees, and thus will be able, in large measure, to reduce its dependence on peasant-agriculture.

§ 108. The commune and artels

In the future, soviet-farms can grow only at the expense of empty lands in the far reaches of the country, or else by using the former treasury-lands that can be brought under cultivation through melioration (that is, improvements, clearing and drainage). With regard to our agricultural economy as a whole, it can be converted into socialist form only when socialisation affects peasant-farming. Through the soviet-farms, the peasantry will learn the benefits of large-scale collective farming. They can only realise these benefits for themselves by associating in communes and *artels*. The transition from small-peasant farming to large farms usually occurred in capitalist society through the ruin and proletarianisation of the small owner. In socialist society, large-scale social farming can arise out of small farming mainly by joining together the many small farms.

Among the peasants, the words '*artel*' and 'commune' often have one-and-the-same meaning. Many communes are called *artels* because the peasant dislikes the word 'commune' and fears to use it, even when it is necessary to build a commune in practice. Generally speaking, the difference between a commune and an *artel* lies in the fact that the *artel* is simply a production-association (a fellowship in work), whereas a commune is both a production- and a consumption-association (that is, a fellowship in work as well as in distribution and consumption).

The number of *artels* and communes is growing rapidly in Soviet Russia. Here are the latest data on that account, relating to the autumn of 1919:

	Number	Area of Cultivable Land
Communes	1,901	approximately 150,000 *desyatins*
Artels	3,698	
Fellowships in social cultivation of the land	668	approximately 480,000 *desyatins*

These data indicate that the movement towards formation of communes and *artels* has a mass-character and will broaden and grow. But these figures show us the weak side of this form of association. Most importantly, the average size of the communes is quite small. What we are seeing is not a transition from small to large farms, but rather to a medium-sized farm or even something smaller. Consequently, the commune cannot demonstrate, either to its participants or to all the surrounding population, all the benefits specifically of a large-scale farm. In the area of a few *desyatins*, not all machines can be used to best advantage, nor is it always possible to organise crop-rotation. However, what is being achieved even by association in a mid-sized farm is extremely important. It enjoys advantages from the division of labour; some of the women are freed from work in the kitchen and can assist in completing all the agricultural work more quickly; there is the opportunity to make do with fewer horses; all the work can be done on time; the land is cultivated better; and the yield is consequently higher than on peasant-strips.

The economy of labour-power that is achieved in the commune is also expressed in the fact that the majority of communes undertake several kinds of non-agricultural work: they build mills, open handicraft-workshops, do repair-work and so on. The communes can only take the next step towards socialism by a further process of joining together.

This can occur either by the merger of two neighbouring communes, by increasing the size of a given commune through accepting tens of new members from nearby peasant-communities, or by the merger of one or several communes with a neighbouring soviet-farm.

At the present moment, the most important task of the Communist Party in the countryside is to raise all the small-peasant farms to a higher level, initially to the level of a mid-sized communal farm. There is every reason to think that this is precisely the road that will be followed, for the most part, in the further development of productive forces in the village. The proletarian state is able to accelerate this process not simply through consistent agitation by words and deeds (the soviet-farms), but also by providing the emerging communal farms with every advantage of a material kind (monetary support together with the supply of seeds, stock, implements and agronomic assistance).

§ 109. Social cultivation of the land

The commune is the closest association of peasants, not only for work but also for distribution and for a joint, comradely life. An *artel* is a permanent association only for work. Social cultivation of the land is an even less intimate association, one that is even freer and, one might say, casual, than an *artel*. A certain village-community that, due to its internal disagreements, is not able to form a commune, and that, for the same reason, is unable to join together in an *artel*, can, nevertheless, go so far as social ploughing without binding the participants in any other way. As a result, everything stays as it was, with the exception of one important condition: the community's land is not divided up into strips but will be cultivated as a single unit. Each household will retain its own vegetable-garden, every peasant will retain all of his personal property, and only the machines and horses will work for a certain period on behalf of the whole village.

The regulations on socialist land-management, which have been confirmed by the Central Executive Committee, foresee that this is the very first stage of collective farming. The benefits of this form of association lie in the fact that every peasant retains complete freedom of action in everything except the work-process itself and, for that reason, he finds it easier to join such an association without risk of losing his independence. Meanwhile, social cultivation also provides a mass of advantages: the elimination of strip-farming, the opportunity for a multi-field system, complete use of the implements, and a division of labour in the work-process that assists families who lack their own workers, implements, cattle and so on.

One can expect social cultivation of the land, as the first step towards collective farming, to become the most widespread form in our countryside. There are already figures showing that during the 1919 agricultural season, such cultivation occurred in a whole series of localities. Some very large communities divided themselves into teams and worked the land together. In certain cases, part of the common land of the village was cultivated in this way.

§ 110. Agricultural cooperation

Even before the Revolution, cooperation was widespread among the peasantry in processing various agricultural products. This includes butter- and cheese-making *artels*, which were particularly widespread mainly in the northern provinces and in the non-fertile provinces of the upper Volga. It also includes various kinds of *artels* and fellowships: for the initial processing of flax, for production of syrup, for drying vegetables and bundling hay, and so on. The Soviet authority is supporting all these associations in every way possible. The Communist Party's task is to encourage the toiling strata of the village to form such cooperatives, to expand them and perfect their work-methods, and, at the same time, to struggle against every attempt by small capital to entrench itself in such *artels* in order to fight against Soviet power and large-scale socialist farming.

§ 111. State-sowing of idle land, the mobilisation of agronomists, hiring stations, land-improvement, and migration

The enormous destruction of agriculture, caused by the War, has led to a great deal of land being permanently out of cultivation. The proletarian state cannot leave land to lie idle while at the same time an acute food-crisis prevails in the cities and in the non-fertile provinces. For this reason, the Soviet state is taking it upon itself to sow the idle land, regardless of to whom it may belong. This measure is especially important in the localities that have become an arena for the Civil War, because in those areas it very frequently happens that the entire kulak-population of the villages abandon their land and retreat with the enemy. It is just as important for the state to bring in the crops abandoned by their owners or that their owners cannot bring in on their own.

Russia's completely shattered agricultural economy can only be restored through a series of determined revolutionary measures. One such measure is *the mobilisation of agronomic forces*, that is, the military conscription of all agricultural experts. There have always been too-few agronomists in Russia. But currently this shortage is even greater, due to the enormous work that our countryside faces in order to rebuild agriculture and raise its productivity. The mobilisation of agricultural experts is essentially the socialisation of agronomic knowledge, which the state is in a position to use with the greatest effectiveness.

The imperialist War deprived Russia of the opportunity to acquire agricultural machinery from abroad. Our own production of agricultural machinery never satisfied the domestic demand, and we received many machines, including almost all the most valuable and complex ones, from Germany, Sweden and America. At the same time, because of the shortage of metal and fuel, among several other reasons, production in our machine-building factories has been reduced to a minimum. All of this has led to a colossal shortage of inventory in agriculture. Given the colossal need for machinery and the extremely short supply at the disposal of the proletarian state, a proper distribution of the inventory and its fullest possible utilisation is enormously important. Such utilisation is not possible with private property in agricultural instruments: part of the time, the machine is not being used by its owner, while his neighbours, at the same time, have no way to do their own ploughing or bring in their harvest.

In order to assist precisely those strata in the village that are most in need of inventory, and to ensure that the equipment is used to the fullest extent, it is imperative that it not be given out in the form of private property, but rather be used to supply the population in need of machines through hiring stations. In other words, the inventory intended for the peasants and allocated between different districts (small villages, parishes and regions), must not be sold to individual peasants, but must remain in depots where it can temporarily be put at the disposal of all who need it, for a certain payment to defer expenses. Such depots are called hiring stations. The equipment is stored there, cleaned up after the work and, in well-equipped stations, repaired. Hiring stations are already in existence and functioning, but they are very few in number. The task of the Soviet power must be to see that, wherever possible, all agricultural machinery intended for the countryside, and all complex machines without any exceptions, go only to the hiring stations. This ensures complete utilisation of inventory throughout the entire working life of the machine, not to mention the fact that it helps the poor, who have no way to purchase machinery for themselves. The inventory confiscated from kulaks must go to the hiring stations. Ultimately, a widely established system of supplying inventory through hiring stations can slowly-but-surely lead to nationalisation of the most important instruments of agricultural production and thus, besides giving direct assistance to the peasant-farm, will also facilitate its socialisation.

In the agrarian programme of the proletarian power in Russia, land-melioration must have one of the most important roles. There are several million *desyatins* at the disposal of the Soviet authority that are currently unfit for cultivation but can be made useful after minor work of clearing, removing roots, reclamation, drainage (drying out the soil with underground pipes and canals), artificial irrigation, and so on. However strict the limits for expanding the area for sovietfarms on stretches that are already under cultivation or were cultivated in the past, there are still broad opportunities that our young socialist agriculture can capture from nature through melioration.

Work on land-improvement – this is the most important of all types of social work that the Soviet power must organise and for which purpose, in the first place, all the parasitic strata of society must be employed.

Migration-policy. This point is not included in our programme, but we must consider it because the Soviet power will sooner-or-later have to give practical attention to the kind of migration-policy it should follow.

Notwithstanding the division of landlords' holdings, the lack of land is already very acutely felt in a number of provinces. At the same time, there are still vast expanses of free land in our outlying areas. Resettlement from the centre to the outlying areas is inevitable in the very near future. The task of the proletarian state will, then, not be to settle migrants in new localities on separate parcels for small-scale farming, but rather to prepare everything necessary for them to undertake large-scale communist agriculture (communal buildings, communal land with proper planning for multi-field farming, complex machinery, and so on).

§ 112. Assistance to peasant-agriculture

Soviet-farms, the communes and *artels*, and all the above-listed measures are capable of raising labour-productivity in agriculture and the fertility of the land through the organisation of large-scale collective farming. This is the only true and rapid way that leads directly to the goal. But whatever successes we enjoy in the area of organising soviet-farms and communes, the small peasant-farm will long exist, and, for a significant part of that time, it will remain *the prevailing form of agriculture in Russia*, in terms of both the extent of cultivated land and the resulting volume of products. The question arises as to how we might assist this kind of farming to raise the productivity of the land, even though it continues to marinate in its petty-bourgeois context.

Our programme cites several measures that the Soviet authority can implement for the purposes of assisting the petty-bourgeois farm. They are as follows.

In the first place, assistance with land-boundaries. The main evil of our village, which is becoming increasingly irritating to the peasants themselves, is farming on long and narrow strips. Too often, the lands of one community extend right up to the kitchen-gardens of the other, and vice versa. Some parcels lie seven to ten *versts* from the settlements and frequently remain uncultivated. To eliminate strip-farming and the long strips, the peasantry is spontaneously drawn towards the settlements, attempting to change the old land-allotment maps that, in the majority of cases, no longer correspond to the new distribution of land following the breakup of the landlords' estates. Insofar as this tendency towards the settlements is one of the forms of struggle against the long and narrow strips – and thus a precondition for more advanced farming – and insofar as the peasantry generally needs assistance with the boundaries, the Soviet authority must help them by providing land-surveyors and agricultural experts.

For the most part, the Russian peasant sows the land with the same seeds that he provides to the mill. Meanwhile, other conditions being equal, the harvest can be much-enlarged by sowing sorted seeds. The harvest can become even larger with use of improved seeds. The peasant can only acquire these seeds from the government, because it alone is in the position to purchase them abroad or to share with the peasantry the small supplies of improved seeds that have been saved from destruction on the soviet-farms.

The peasants' cattle are small and degenerate. An improvement in the strains of peasants' cattle is needed. Meanwhile, all the valuable breeding cattle that remain in Russia are currently gathered on soviet-estates and soviet-farms, or else they are registered with soviet-organs of animal-husbandry. By organising breeding stations on every soviet-farm that has breeding cattle, and through a planned allocation of bulls between district breeding stations, the state is in a position to provide enormous assistance to peasant livestock-farming.

The great majority of our peasantry are unfamiliar with a whole range of the most basic and extremely important kinds of agricultural expertise. In such circumstances, a wider diffusion of agricultural knowledge must in itself promote improvement in land-cultivation. In addition to giving lectures on agronomic themes, which are obligatory for soviet agricultural experts at the local agronomic stations, this can be done through providing a series of lectures at the soviet-farms, by establishing short courses, model fields, agricultural exhibitions, publishing popular agronomic literature, and so on.

Besides the diffusion of agronomic knowledge, the Soviet authority must provide direct agronomic assistance to the peasants. Given our poverty in terms of agricultural experts, mobilising them has already served a useful purpose insofar as those who previously served almost exclusively on the landlords' estates will now be working to benefit the peasant. Furthermore, among the peasantry itself, the Soviet authority must develop agricultural expertise as widely as possible. In addition to expanding the number of agricultural courses and schools, in the immediate future this can be most easily accomplished by having the most talented members of the communes and *artels* attend special courses, such that they can form a leading stratum of agronomically educated farmers who are recruited from among the peasants themselves.

At the present time, it is enormously important for the peasantry to be able to repair their worn-out implements. Given the current iron-shortage, there are no small, private handicraft-shops that are in a position to do all the necessary repair-work. Only the state can organise this work on a sufficient scale, both by expanding the repair-shops of soviet-farms and through planning an extensive network of shops specifically to do repairs for the peasantry.

Although there are millions of *desyatins* of peasant-land that is not fit for cultivation, at the same time it would be fully possible to convert it into suitable arable land. This is not being done, on the one hand, because such work is often beyond the resources of a single community, and on the other hand, because the peasantry does not know the methods of land-improvement. The proletarian state's assistance to the peasants in this regard can be especially valuable, and it is already being extended in a great number of localities, despite the Civil War.

In 1901–1910, the average yield per *desyatin* was:

	Rye	Wheat	Barley	Oats	Potatoes
Denmark	120	183	158	170	—
Holland	111	153	176	145	1,079
England	—	149	127	118	908
Belgium	145	157	179	161	1,042
Germany	109	130	127	122	900
Turkey	98	98	117	105	—
France	70	90	84	80	563
USA	67	64	93	74	421
Russia	50	45	51	50	410

Therefore, although the land in Russia is better than in the West, we are in last place in terms of land-productivity. Per *desyatin*, we get three-and-a-half times fewer oats than in Denmark and Holland; we get four times less wheat than in Denmark and three times less than in Germany and England; we get three times less rye than in Belgium; and even in Turkey, a *desyatin* of land provides twice as much of all grains as a *desyatin* ploughed by our peasant.

And to this must be still be added the fact that the yield on peasant-lands in Russia is even lower than shown in the table, because the average yield is calculated for all lands, including those of the landlords, where the harvest was from one-fifth to two-and-a-half times greater than on peasant-land.

It follows that even without increasing the amount of land, the peasantry has the possibility of collecting a harvest two to three times larger than today's if we abandon the ways of our grandfathers, and instead adopt new and improved agricultural methods.

§ 113. Joining industry with agriculture

During capitalism's final epoch, the development of cities assumed a completely deformed character due to the separation of industry from agriculture and industry's increased role in the whole economic process of society. All the best forces of the countryside systematically fled the village for the city. Not only did the urban population grow more quickly than the rural, but it also did so at the villages' expense. In a number of capitalist countries, the agricultural population has declined absolutely. On the other hand, some cities have grown to monstrous proportions. All of this has led to a number of the most harmful consequences for both the city and the countryside. Consider the most significant among them: the depopulation of the village and its relapse into a primitive state; its detachment from urban culture; the separation of the urban resident from nature and from healthy agricultural work, with the ensuing rapid physical degeneration of the urban population; the needless relocation to the city of several kinds of production involved in agricultural processing; the enormous exhaustion of the soil, due to the fact that the city does not give back to the village, in the form of fertiliser, what it takes from it in the form of food, and so on.

The rapprochement of city and village, bringing together industry and agriculture and attracting factory-workers into farming – these are the most immediate tasks of communist construction in this area. A beginning has been made by assigning several tens of thousands of *desyatins* of soviet-land to various plants, institutions and enterprises; by planning an organised transfer of urban workers to soviet-farms; by creating market-gardening at individual plants and factories;

by holding communist Saturdays for urban workers in suburban villages; by mobilising soviet-employees to harvest the market-gardens, and so on.

The Communist Party will be taking further steps in this same direction in the conviction that the future belongs to a coalescence of industry and agriculture, which will lead to the gigantically expanded and monstrously overpopulated cities being reabsorbed into the territory of the countryside.

§ 114. The tactic of the Communist Party in relation to the peasantry

In our agrarian programme, we speak of the goals we want to accomplish in agriculture. Let us now consider how we intend to implement our programme, which strata we intend to rely upon, and which methods we intend to use in order to attract the peasant-majority to our side or, at the very least, to ensure their neutrality.

In the struggle against landlord-agriculture, the urban proletariat had the entire peasantry behind it, including even the kulaks. This explains the rapid success of the October Revolution and the overthrow of the bourgeois provisional government that tried to postpone liquidation of the landlords' estates. But implementation of the law on so-called socialisation of the land and its equal division was already enough to drive the kulak into the camp of counter-revolution. The kulaks lost part of the land they had purchased before the Revolution, together with the land they had used by renting allotments from the poor. They have lost everything they managed to seize during the destruction of the landed estates. Finally, they were deprived of the opportunity to use hired labour. The kulaks are the class that would have replaced the landlords had our revolution remained within the confines of a bourgeois-democratic transformation. They are a class that is mortally hostile, by its very nature, to all attempts leading to the socialist organisation of agriculture. This class aspires, on the contrary, to move the development of our agriculture towards the kind of farm-economy that prevails in Denmark and America. Were it not for the proletarian power and its socialist policy, the soil of Russia, purged of the landlord, would have very quickly developed a typical bourgeois-farmer economy, using hired labour and improved methods of cultivation alongside an enormous stratum of the semi-proletarian peasantry. The kulak went into the Revolution inspired by the rosiest hopes and expectations, and he left it shorn even of a part of the property that he had before the Revolution. Until the kulak-class is fully liquidated, it must inevitably emerge as an implacable enemy of the proletarian state and its land-policy, and, in turn, it can expect from the Soviet authority only the most merciless struggle against all attempts at counter-revolution. The possibility also cannot be excluded that the Soviet authority will have to conduct a planned expropriation of the kulaks, mobilising them for public work and, above all, for work on improving the lands of the peasants and the state.

The main mass of the Russian peasantry consists of the middle-peasantry. The middle-peasant acquired the landlords' land with the help of the urban proletariat, and only with its help can he protect that land from the pressures of bourgeois-landlord counter-revolution. Likewise, it is only by allying with the proletariat and following its leadership that the middle-peasantry can save itself from the onslaught of world-capital, from robbery by the imperialist predators, from paying billions on the debts of tsarism and the Provisional Government. Finally, it is only the alliance with the socialist proletariat that will make it possible for it, without poverty, ruin and unbelievable torments, to move from petty farming, *which is condemned to disappear in any case*, to the most beneficial and productive form of large-scale comradely farming.

However, the spirit of the petty property-owner tempts the middle-peasant to ally with the kulaks, and he is driven in this direction especially by the need to share grain-surpluses with the urban proletariat in advance of any hope of receiving directly the products of urban industry in return. For this reason, the Communist Party must endeavour to separate the middle-peasantry from the kulak, who is essentially an agent of world-capital and is attempting to provoke the peasantry into losing everything it has won in the course of the Revolution. Furthermore, our Party must explain with particular clarity to the middle-peasantry that only temporary and transient interests can tempt it to join up with the kulaks and the bourgeoisie, whereas its longer-term, more important and fundamental interests dictate the need for it to ally, as a class of the toiling people, with the urban proletariat. Finally, in struggling for a socialist reconstruction of agriculture, we must avoid irritating the middle-peasant with the carelessness and hastiness of our own measures, and this means completely avoiding any attempt to force him into communes and *artels*. At the present moment, the fundamental task of communism in Russia is to see *that the workers and peasants, each for their own motives*, smash the counter-revolution. Once that happens, there will be no insurmountable barriers to the socialist reconstruction of agriculture. As for the rural poor, it is precisely this section of the village that remains the most consistent base for the proletarian dictatorship. This is true even though a significant portion of its proletarian and semi-proletarian strata, precisely due to the Revolution, have ceased to exist by raising themselves economically to the level of middle-peasants. Thanks to allies from the rural poor, the Soviet authority has succeeded in striking a number of serious blows against the kulaks and in separating them from the middle-peasant. Thanks to the communist attitudes of the poor peasants, we have succeeded in creating an apparatus of Soviet power in the countryside and in implementing the first, most important and decisive military mobilisations of the peasantry.[15] Finally, the poor have up till now contributed a large portion of the members in communes and *artels* and have helped to implement all the land-decrees – and not only the land-decrees – of the Soviet power.

The main task of the Communist Party in relation to the village-poor is to lead them out of the scattered condition in which they find themselves following the dissolution of the poor people's committees. The best way to rally the poor on a production-basis, and the soundest way to increase their influence in the village, is to make it possible for them to grow stronger on the basis of a more advanced mode of agriculture. This can be accomplished if all the poor peasants go over to working the land through *artels* or communes. The kulak is strong in the village because he is a good proprietor. The kulak-farm is the cream of the petty-bourgeois peasant-economy. By joining together in communes, the poor become representatives of a more perfect form of production than the usual peasant-production, and they make themselves economically stronger than the middle-peasant and even the kulak. And it is on this economic basis – on just this material superiority of the member of a commune over a petty owner – that the dictatorship of the poor can be built in the countryside. But this will already cease to be a dictatorship of the poor, in the proper sense of the word; it will not be the rule of 'beggars and freeloaders', as the kulaks complained (and sometimes with good reason) during the period of poor people's committees. It will be rule by the leading stratum of working people in the countryside, and they will be two centuries ahead of the majority.

But to rally all of the poor in communes is extremely difficult. Recently, it has been the middle-peasants who have joined the communes, and especially the *artels*, in large numbers. To the extent that poor peasants have yet to break with petty production, it is necessary to create a number of trade-unions specifically of the poor. These unions of the poor must continue the struggle against the kulak that was not completed by the poor people's committees. The poor must unite on the basis of mutual assistance. They must enter into economic relations with the state, insofar as they can accept certain kinds of work from it and receive in return various products on a preferred basis, together with economic support in general. There exist in Russia an enormous number of the most

---

15. In our agitation for the peasantry's active participation in the Civil War, it is necessary to underline precisely the peasantry's own motives for taking part in this war. The peasantry is not interested in the fact that we are struggling for socialism as such, but rather in the fact that we are denying imperialism the opportunity for barbarically exploiting the small property-owner, and we are preventing the landlord or the merchant from once-again throttling him.

diverse associations of the poor, but they all have a local character or are very temporary and fortuitous organisations. These organisations have to be united into larger bodies. A great future belongs to associations of the poor in the infertile provinces, where they are occupied in non-agricultural work (extracting tar and pitch, felling and storing lumber, different kinds of woodworking, and so forth).

A further task of the Communist Party in relation to the poor consists of merging them more closely with the urban proletariat, tearing them away from their petty-bourgeois habits and impossible hopes of individually having an independent and large-scale farm of their own and, wherever the poor are gathered, creating Communist cells and groups of sympathisers. Every poor peasant must become a communard, and every communard, a Communist.

Literature: Engels, F., *Krest'yanskii vopros vo Frantsii i Germanii*; Lenin, *Agrarnyi vopros i kritika Marksa*; Lenin, *Agrarnyi vopros v Rosii k kontsu XIX v.*

Of the popular pamphlets published after the Revolution: Zhegur, Ya., *Organizatsiya kommunisticheskikh khozyaistv v zemledelii*; Ky, *Sel'skaya kommuna*; Meshcheryakov N., *O sel'skokhozyaistvennykh kommunakh*; Preobrazhensky, E., *O sel'skokhozyaistvennykh kommunakh*; Larin, Yu., *Urbanizatsiya zemledeliya*; Meshcheryakov, N., *Natsionalizatsiya zemli*; Lenin, N., *Rech' ob otnoshenii k srednemu krest'yanstvu na 8-m s'ezde kommunisticheskoi partii*; Sumatokhin, M., *Davaite zhit' kommunoi*; Lenin, N., *Bor'ba za khleb*.

There are many brochures that are already out of date and not included here. A more detailed bibliography can be found in the brochure by V. Kerzhentsov, *Biblioteka kommunista*.

Chapter XIV

The Organisation of Distribution

§ 115. The Liquidation of private trade. § 116. Consumer-communes. § 117. Cooperatives in the past. § 118. Cooperatives today. § 119. Other organs of distribution.

§ 115. The liquidation of private trade

To every mode of production there corresponds a unique mode of distribution. With elimination of capitalist property in the instruments of production, the Soviet Republic inevitably came into collision with the capitalist apparatus of distribution, that is, with trade, and had to proceed with its gradual elimination.

First of all, the large commercial warehouses were confiscated. This was already imperative because of the acute food-crisis and the goods-famine. The goods that speculators had hidden away in the expectation of higher prices were distributed to the toiling masses, and this somewhat eased the crisis during the first weeks after the October Revolution.

But the nationalisation of the commercial warehouses was merely a first step. After that came nationalisation of large-scale trade. This was done for the purposes of the struggle against speculation and for making an account of all the commodities in the Republic, and also with the aim of distributing these commodities, primarily among the toiling classes. The Soviet authority introduced class-rationing not only for food, but also for manufactures and all household-articles.

But perhaps it would have been better for the Soviet authority to proceed this way: to confiscate all the supplies of commodities in the hands of private merchants and distribute them as class-rations – but to use the trade-apparatus and make it serve our own purposes, rather than destroy it.

In reality, this is, in large measure, exactly what happened. The commodities, unfortunately, were confiscated too late, when the larger portion of them had already been converted into cash that was hidden away by the owners. The entire apparatus of large shops went to the Soviet authority and began to function with the help of the shop-workers' trade-union. Only the upper stratum of the owners, who would now be a completely parasitic element, was removed. Indeed, in order to purchase the commodity, it was previously necessary to find it and then to do the deals. Once the main producer of commodities in the nationalised factories became the proletarian state itself, it would make no sense for it to sell the goods to itself through merchants whom it maintained at its own expense. Furthermore, with the establishment of the grain-monopoly, merchant-intermediaries are completely redundant between the peasant and the state, on the one hand, and the state and the consumer, on the other. They can play no part in tempting the peasants to deliver their grain to the state, nor is there any purpose in the peasants looking for purchasers of the grain, since there are none to be found.

Therefore, to the extent that the proletarian power has taken control of producing a number of the most important products, and since a significant portion of food is also being collected by its own organs, it needs its own apparatus of distribution. There is nothing left for private trade to do.

But how is it with the petty private trade that distributes the products of small-scale, independent handicraft-production? The Soviet authority has not taken control of this kind of production and still has not become a monopolistic buyer for its products. What is the situation with the petty trade that redistributes to the population (at exorbitant prices, of course) those products that the agents of Soviet power cannot provide at fixed prices?

This question, no doubt, is more complicated than the question of large-scale trade, whose elimination was foretold by the very fact of the expropriation of capital in general. It makes no sense for the Soviet power simply to forbid petty trade if it is in no position to replace this trade as a whole with the activities of its own distribution-organs. There were cases when local soviets and revolutionary committees, especially in the localities that had been cleared of White Guards, forbade free trade without having created their own food-apparatuses or, what is even more important, without having ensured any kind of proper supply for the population through these apparatuses. As a result, private trade was declared illegal, and prices rose many times over. Petty trade will only gradually be killed off as a larger and larger quantity of products for supplying the population pass through state-hands. If *Narkomprod*[16] now exists alongside the magnificently flourishing Sukharevka,[17] this means only one thing: the war between capitalism and socialism continues in the sphere of distribution, now involving the positions of petty trade, and it will only end when the state-authority becomes the main buyer of products from small-scale industry and subsequently transforms itself into the producer of these products. This does not apply, of course, to those instances when petty private trade puts into circulation products that had already been in the hands of the food-organs, when the issue is the struggle against thievery and other shortcomings on the part of the Soviet distribution-mechanism. In any case, petty trade will exist as long as large-scale production is not restored in the cities and as long as supplying the population with basic products of consumption has not yet been made a state-monopoly in practice.

Consequently, although elimination of every sort of private middleman from distribution is a goal of socialism that will gradually be reached, complete elimination of the apparatus of small-scale trade is impossible for the immediate future.

§ 116. Consumer-communes

Insofar as the main mass of products intended for the population passes or will pass through the state food-organs, there must be corresponding socialist organs of distribution. These organs must satisfy the following requirements. They must be centralised. This ensures the most just and equal distribution. It reduces the costs of maintaining the apparatus, which under socialism must, in

---

16. [The People's Commissariat of Food.]
17. [A famous market in Moscow.]

any case, require far fewer people and resources than a private trade-apparatus. The socialist distribution-apparatus must operate with the greatest speed. This is extremely important. It is necessary not simply that the apparatus itself require the minimum of resources from the state, but also that it not take up a minute of excess-time from the consumer. Otherwise, this will lead to an enormous non-productive expenditure of resources by the entire society. With the existence of private trade, the consumer who had money could, in the normal circumstances of capitalist society, acquire whatever he wished whenever he wished. In this respect, the socialist apparatus must be no worse than capitalist trade. Meanwhile, precisely because of the great centralisation of this apparatus, it can easily turn into a very bulky, bureaucratic and extremely slowly functioning machine, in which many commodities might rot before they reach the consumer. How must this apparatus be constructed?

The Soviet authority faced two alternatives: either to create an entire distribution-apparatus anew, or else to use all the organs of distribution created by capitalism that might be made to serve the goals of socialist distribution.

The Soviet authority took the second route. Creating its own organs where necessary, particularly during the first period of the breakdown of capitalist relations, it turned its attention to cooperation and adopted the goal of using the cooperative-apparatus for the distribution of products.

§ 117. Cooperatives in the past

Under the capitalist system, the primary task of cooperation was to free the consumer of the commercial middleman-speculator, leave the profit from trade in the hands of the associated consumers, and guarantee them high-quality products. Cooperatives achieved this end more-or-less successfully, but only for their own members, that is, only for a part of society. As for the childish dreams of cooperators concerning a peaceful renovation of capitalism with the aid of cooperation, in this regard, things stand as follows: with all of its successes, cooperation only noticeably squeezes out petty trade (more or less) but has hardly any effect on large-scale trade, and even uses its services. As far as cooperative-enterprises in production are concerned, they occupy a completely insignificant position within the overall system of capitalist production and have no influence whatsoever on the course and development of capitalist industry. In general, the gigantic organisation of capital never regarded cooperation as a serious competitor. Being perfectly capable in economic terms of strangling it like a kitten whenever necessary, it left it to the ideologues of cooperation to dream in peace of squeezing out capitalism, and to cooperative-bookkeepers to go into raptures over the profits taken from petty shopkeepers. Cooperation adapted itself fully to capitalism and occupied a certain place within its distribution-system. It was even beneficial to capitalism, reducing costs in the distribution-apparatus and thus squeezing a part of the redundant commercial capital into industry. On the other hand, by reducing the number of petty commercial intermediaries and bringing the consumer into closer contact with large-scale capitalist production, cooperation accelerated the trade-turnover, guaranteed the honest and timely payment of obligations and, in the final analysis, made even more hopeless the position of the industrial reserve-army from which a significant number of the unemployed customarily flowed into petty trade. Moreover, a number of studies have shown that, as far as peasant-cooperation is concerned, this kind of cooperation everywhere provided the greatest benefits to the strong and well-to-do peasantry while benefiting the poor hardly at all. In terms of its class-composition, consumer-cooperation can be divided into worker-cooperatives, those of the peasants, and those for the general urban population, that is, essentially the petty bourgeoisie and officials. Workers' cooperatives were always furthest to the left in the general network of cooperative-organisations, and furthest to the right among the class-organisations of the proletariat. In peasant-cooperatives, the tone was set by the big and sturdy peasantry. In urban cooperation, the petty-bourgeois intelligentsia played the leading role, emerging as the ideologists of cooperatives as a whole and promising them a great future through smashing capitalism with loaves of cooperative bread and potatoes.

The true nature of cooperation was revealed by the October Proletarian Revolution in Russia. With the exception of a part of the workers' cooperatives, all the rest of the cooperative-movement, especially in the person of its leaders from the intelligentsia and the kulaks, adopted an acutely hostile position with regard to socialist transformation. Indeed, Siberian cooperatives for buying and selling, together with other unions, sided openly with the White-Guard counter-revolution and supported crushing the Soviet Republic with the forces of world-imperialism.

On 1 October 1917, there were 612 united cooperative-associations in Russia. However, this figure appears to be lower than the actual number, for according to some data there were up to a thousand united associations in existence by 1 January 1918. On 1 January 1918, there were 281 associations in *Tsentrosoyuz*.[18] Among 269 of them there were 38,601 cooperatives with a membership of 13,694,196. But since a single cooperative was often a member of two or three associations simultaneously, apparently the number of cooperatives in Russia was lower than the figures suggest, and the same applies to the number of their members. As far as the industrial activity of Russian cooperatives goes, in 1918 all

---

18. [The Central Union of Cooperatives.]

the cooperatives and unions of cooperatives together had 469 enterprises, most of them tiny.

§ 118. Cooperatives today

Under the domination of capitalism, cooperation played a certain role within the system. With Soviet power, the cooperative-apparatus is fated either to die out gradually, along with all the rest of capitalism's apparatus for distribution, or else to enter into the system of proletarian socialist distribution, being elevated to the role of a state distribution apparatus. The former leaders of the cooperatives – Mensheviks, S-Rs and all kinds of other 'socialists' of the Kolchak variety – wanted to keep cooperation independent of the proletarian state, that is, to leave it free to die out. Conversely, taking into account the real interests of the enormous mass of toiling people, and particularly of the mass of cooperative-toilers, the Soviet power took a different path. Disregarding the opinions of the intellectuals leading the cooperatives, and refusing to reject the entire cooperative apparatus because of the counter-revolutionary proclivities of these leaders, the Soviet power continuously endeavoured to fuse cooperative-distribution gradually into its general system of distribution-organs. It tried not to compress, but rather to extend the range of cooperative-activity. In this connection, the practical tasks facing Soviet power and the Communist Party are, in general terms, as follows.

A normal cooperative of the bourgeois type is a voluntary association of citizens who contribute a certain sum to the association. As a rule, the cooperative serves only its own members, and it only sells products to the population as a whole when this causes no harm to its members. We consider it necessary for the entire population to participate in cooperatives, with every member of society signed up to one cooperative or another. Only then will distribution through cooperatives involve distribution amongst the entire population.

In a consumer-association, business is normally conducted on the basis of self-rule by all the members of the association. (If in practice a small number of administrators prevail, this is the fault of the members themselves. The constitution of a cooperative puts the members' general meeting in control.) When every citizen of the Republic is enrolled in cooperatives, they have every possibility of controlling the entire distribution-apparatus of the proletarian state from the bottom up. If the masses show enough independence, they can wage the most determined and successful struggle against any kind of abuses and bureaucratism in the work of distribution, and in that way achieve the necessary speed and accuracy in the work of the state-cooperative organisation. Thanks to this, and thanks to the participation of consumers themselves in the work of distribution, the distribution-organs will become organs of the masses themselves, instead of being suspended above their heads, and there is no doubt that this will promote the development of communist consciousness and of conscious, comradely discipline among the toilers, while also helping these masses to improve the work of the entire production- and distribution-mechanism of socialist society as a whole. It is further necessary, once the whole population is involved in cooperation, for proletarian strata of the population to play the leading role in the cooperatives. In the cities, this is being accomplished through the most active participation by urban workers in cooperative-activities, through electing a Communist proletarian majority to the management, and mainly by transforming the workers' own cooperatives, rather than general citizens' cooperatives, into urban consumer-communes. To the same end, it is necessary to work for a close bond between the cooperatives and the trade-unions, that is, between the organs of production and distribution. This bond has a great future. With time, the role of the state will become that of a central accounting office, and then the living bond between the organs of production and distribution will acquire especially great significance. Finally, Communists must participate as a unified group in the work of cooperative-construction and win for themselves the leading role.

In the countryside, the kulaks must be pushed out of managing the cooperatives. There must be an end to all privileged distribution in favour of the wealthy section of the village, by transferring the entire apparatus of rural cooperatives into the hands of the poor and of the conscious elements among the middle-peasantry.

§ 119. Other organs of distribution

From the moment of the October Revolution in Russia, there emerged a great variety of distribution-organs created by the Revolution itself. At their centre is the People's Commissariat of Food, with all its branches in the provinces and districts. The food-organs had, and still have, their own organs of distribution in the form of a network of food-shops and stores. At one time, the poor people's committees in the villages had a role in distribution as a counterweight to cooperative-distribution: while most cooperatives were distributing the products they acquired mainly in the interests of well-to-do peasants, the poor people's committees sought to distribute among the poor the larger and best part of the products acquired from the state. In the large cities, housing committees and housing communes are playing an important role in distribution. In addition, the trade-unions, and especially the factory- and plant-committees, have been involved in distribution.

The task of the Soviet power is to see that all these numerous organs of distribution are replaced by a single distribution-organ or that they are included as links in a single distribution-mechanism. In this connection, for example, the housing committees and housing communes serve a useful role, allowing consumers to acquire products without standing in queues for hours and even for whole days.

Chapter XV

The organisation of banks and monetary Circulation

§ 120. *Nationalisation of the banks and the single people's bank; the bank as a central bookkeeping department.* § 121. *Money and the withering away of the money-system.*

§ 120. Nationalisation of the banks and the single people's bank; the bank as a central bookkeeping department

Most workers have a quite vague idea of what banks are and what their role amounts to in capitalist society. The bank is some kind of enormous treasure-chest in which the wealthy deposit their capital. The worker who has savings in a bank also knows that interest is paid on deposited money, although sometimes deposits in a private bank go up the chimney and the depositors are ruined.

First of all, the bank is not a money-chest. At any given moment, the cash in a bank is completely insignificant. The essence of a bank's work is not at all to serve as a safe for people who have savings. It is true that hundreds of millions in savings pass through the bank, but they do not lie there idly. The money collected in the bank is continuously being put out into circulation. In the first place, it is given out as loans to entrepreneurs who open factories, exploit workers, and give back part of their profit to the bank for this loan (and the bank pays part of its own profit to the depositor). Secondly, the banks themselves open new businesses with the sums received from depositors, or else they finance those already existing. Finally, the banks lend out money to states[19] and collect interest from them, that is, through governments, they plunder the peoples of these states. And since the banks belong to a small handful of the biggest capitalists, the work of the banks ultimately amounts to extracting surplus-value by means of their own capital and the capitals deposited with them.

But the banks are not merely spiders sucking surplus-labour from workers and peasants. They also have a different kind of significance. If we suppose that

---

19. For example, foreign banks lent more than sixteen million roubles to our tsarist government and the government of Kerensky.

I have money and deposit in a bank, this means that I had some sort of commodities that I sold and converted into money. If a steady stream of money is passing through all the banks, and the amount of capital in society as a whole is growing, this means that a steady stream of new values is entering into circulation. Money is evidence of a product, a kind of passport for products. In general and on the whole, the movement of money gives an approximate estimate of the movement of products. Therefore, the banks inevitably become a type of accounting office for capitalist society.

From this, it is apparent what role banks can play in socialist society and what the proletariat must do with them after seizing power.

Following the socialist revolution, or more accurately, during the socialist revolution, the working class must seize all of the banks, and especially the Central State-Bank. This is imperative, first of all in order to confiscate all the monetary deposits of the bourgeoisie and all the securities and other monetary obligations of the capitalists. This seizure strikes a blow at the very heart of capitalist exploitation.

This is exactly what we did in the October Revolution and in November 1917, and thus we dealt a crushing blow to Russia's capitalist class.

What must the proletarian power do with the banks that it has seized? It must use everything of value in capital's banking organisation. That is to say, it must preserve the banks as an apparatus for registering production and for distributing financial resources. Above all, there must be full nationalisation of all banking activity. This means not only that all the banks taken from the bourgeoisie are converted into state-institutions of the proletariat, but also that all future banking operations are declared a state-monopoly. No-one except the state is permitted to open a bank.

Then all the banks must be integrated. The ones that are not needed are closed, and the only ones that remain are those required as branches of the single bank of the Soviet Republic.

In place of the most diverse methods of accounting and bank-operations that go on in bourgeois banks, in the single people's bank there will be uniformity and a simple system of accounting. As a result, the proletarian state will be in a position to have a complete picture of how much money the state is paying out and to whom, as well as how much it has received and from which sources.

But if all the incomes and expenditures of the state are recorded in the single bank of the Republic, what will become of the bank when the state itself more and more becomes the administrator of a single enormous economic apparatus encompassing the country?

It is clear that the bank will then play the same role as the bookkeeping office of any other economic enterprise. The bank, as such, will gradually be eliminated and will become, as it says in our programme, 'the central bookkeeping department of communist society'.

§ 121. Money and the withering away of the money-system

Communist society will know nothing of money. Every worker will prepare products for the common pot and will not receive any certificate of the fact that he gave so many products to society, that is, he will not receive any money. In precisely the same way, he will not pay any money to society when he needs to acquire something or other from the common pot. But it is another matter in the socialist system, which must be a transitional structure between capitalism and communism. Money necessarily appears and plays its role in a commodity-economy. When I, as a shoemaker, wish to acquire a coat, I convert my commodity, the shoes, first into money, that is, into a commodity through which I can acquire some other commodity in exchange, in this case the coat that interests me. And in socialist society, the commodity-economy will still continue to exist, at least in part.

Suppose that we have succeeded in putting down the bourgeoisie's opposition and have transformed the former ruling classes into working people. We would still have the peasantry who are not working for the common pot. Every peasant will endeavour to sell his surplus to the state and to receive, in exchange, the industrial product that he needs. The peasant will remain a commodity-producer. He will still need money to settle accounts with his neighbour and with the state, just as the state will need money to settle accounts with all the members of society who have not yet been included in a general producers' commune. It was all the more impossible to eliminate money immediately because an enormous volume of private trade, which the Soviet authority has not yet been strong enough to replace entirely with socialist distribution, is still being practised. Finally, it is not beneficial to eliminate money all at once insofar as the issue of paper-money replaces taxation and helps to sustain the proletarian state in unbelievably difficult circumstances.

But socialism is communism under construction, communism not yet completed. In line with successes in this construction, money must pass out of usage and, at some fine moment, the state will possibly have to put an end to the circulation of money, which will already be dying out. This is especially important for a genuine elimination of the relics of the bourgeois classes who are continuing to use their hidden money to consume values created by the toiling classes – and this in a society that has proclaimed the commandment: 'He who does not work, does not eat'.

Money gradually loses its importance from the very beginning of the socialist revolution. All of the nationalised enterprises, as with one enterprise belonging to a single great owner (in this case, the proletarian state), have a common cashbox, and thus no need for money in selling or buying between themselves. Gradually, moneyless accounting is being introduced. As a result, money is being squeezed out of an enormous sphere of the national economy. With regard to the peasantry, money is also increasingly losing its importance and direct commodity-exchange is coming to the fore. Even in private trade with the peasants, money is more and more receding into the background, and a purchaser can acquire grain only in exchange for some other sort of natural product such as clothing, fabric, utensils, furniture, and so on. The gradual elimination of money is also facilitated by the state's enormous issues of paper-money at a time when there is a great reduction in the circulation of commodities due to the disorder in state-industry. More and more, the spontaneous devaluation of money essentially amounts to its spontaneous annulment. But the strongest blow to money's existence will be struck by the introduction of budgetary booklets and payment for the workers' labour in products. In a labour-book will be entered how long he has worked, that is, how much he is owed by the state. And with the labour-book he will acquire products in a consumers' shop. In this system, those who do not work can acquire nothing for money. But this can only happen when the state is in a position to concentrate in its own hands such a quantity of products of consumption as will be adequate to supply all of the working members of socialist society. This is impossible without the restoration and expansion of our ruined industry.

In general terms, the process of eliminating money-circulation at the present time is taking the following form. At first, money is being expelled from the sphere of product-exchange within nationalised enterprises (factories, railways, the soviet-farm, and so on). Then money disappears from the sphere of accounting between the state and workers of the socialist state (that is, between the Soviet authority, employees, and the workers in soviet-enterprises). Next, money dies away and is replaced by the direct exchange of commodities in the transactions between the state and petty production (the peasants and artisans). Then money disappears in commodity-exchange within the small-scale economy, and will, perhaps, only finally disappear along with the disappearance of the small-scale economy as such.

Literature for Chapter XV: There is virtually no literature on this subject. The following can be recommended: Pyatakov, Yu., *Proletariat i banki*; Sokol'nikov, *K vorposu o natsionalizatsii bankov*. Also, a number of articles in *Ekonomicheskaya zhizn'* and *Narodnoe khozyaistvo*.

Chapter XVI

Finances in the Proletarian State

§ 122. The state as a parasitic apparatus. § 123. The proletarian state as a productive apparatus. § 124. The budget of the proletarian state.

§ 122. The state as a parasitic apparatus

As we have already mentioned above, the state is an organisation of oppression and domination by one class over another class or classes. If the entire bourgeois class, during capitalism's development, becomes more and more a class of parasites, who merely consume and contribute nothing to production, then what can be said of the bourgeois state that protects the peace and the incomes of these parasites from the exploited and indignant masses? The police and the gendarmerie, the standing army, the judicial apparatus and all the apparatuses in general for administering the country – they constitute an enormous mob of people, not one of whom has ever produced either a *pood* of bread, an *arshin*[20] of textiles, or even so much as a needle or a pin. This entire organisation lives at the expense of the surplus-product created by workers and peasants. This surplus-product is extorted by the state in the form of taxes, both direct and indirect. For example, this is how our tsarist government beat out of the workers and peasants more than three billion in gold. (If this sum is translated into current paper-money and its purchasing power, it comes to more than three hundred billion, that is, three times more than all the money currently in the whole of Russia). Only a small portion of the taxes went to production, for instance, to building railways and highways, steamships, bridges, state-factories, and so forth.

As for the proletarian state, so long as the Civil War lasts and the opposition of the bourgeoisie is not broken, this state, too, will partly have to be an organ that stands above production. The work of many of the organs of the proletarian state is not work that creates new values. On the contrary, a number of state-organs live at the expense of the products being created by workers and peasants. Such, for example, are our entire military apparatus and Red Army, the organs of administration, the organs for struggle against counter-revolution, and so on. But it is not the activities resembling the state of the exploiters that distinguish the proletarian state. What distinguishes the proletarian state is precisely the fact that this organisation gradually ceases to be a non-productive organism and becomes an organisation for administering the economy.

---

20. [1 pood = 16.38 kgm; 1 arshin = 0.71 m.]

§ 123. *The proletarian state as a productive apparatus*

Long before the conclusion of the Civil War, the major part of the proletarian state is already serving the production and distribution of products. This is clearly revealed just by listing the central and local commissariats. The largest of the Soviet organisations is the Supreme Council of the National Economy, with all its branches. This is exclusively a production-organisation. Then follow the Commissariats for Agriculture, Food, Communications, and Labour, all of which are, likewise, organisations involved in production, distribution or service to the working class. The same applies to the People's Commissariat of Enlightenment, which is being transformed into an organisation for creating an educated workforce through implementing the programme of the single labour-school. The Commissariat of Health-Care, in the proletarian state, is an organ to protect the health of the toilers; Social Security means security mainly for former toilers or future toilers (for instance, shelters and settlements). Even the Commissariat for Administration has been converted primarily into an organisation of assistance and leadership for local, mainly municipal, economic activities. In general and on the whole, the proletarian state-mechanism is becoming an enormous organisation that leads the national economy and serves it from different perspectives and in different spheres. This is perfectly obvious from an examination of the Soviet Republic's budget.

In terms of millions of roubles, the allocations for the first half of 1919 were as follows:

Supreme Council of the National Economy	10,976
People's Commissariat of Food	8,153
" " Communications	5,073
" " Enlightenment	3,888
" " Health	1,228
" " Social Security	1,619
" " Agriculture	533
" " Army-Affairs	12,150
" " Naval Affairs	521
" " Foreign Affairs	11
" " Nationality-Affairs	17
" " Justice	250
" " Internal Affairs	857
The Extraordinary Commission	348

We see from these figures that defence of the Republic still costs a great deal of resources. But set aside this expenditure, which is caused by extraordinary circumstances, and it will become perfectly clear that nine-tenths of the proletarian state's expenditures are expenditures on production, on its management, on securing its functioning in the future, on support for the workforce, and so forth, all of which are purely economic expenditures.

And that is not all. On communist Saturdays, the workers from production-organisations, the Red-Army men and the military commissars perform their duty to productive labour, although at the start, of course, on a modest scale. Until 1919, there was no state in the world whose officials regularly repaired locomotives and unloaded wood on the state's behalf.

§ 124. The budget of the proletarian state

We have seen that the further we proceed, the more the expenditures of the proletarian state will become productive ones. The question, now, concerns the sources from which the revenues must be drawn.

The finances of the Russian Soviet Republic provide some indication in this regard.

At the start of its existence, the Soviet authority had certain extraordinary revenues: these included the confiscated bank-accounts of the bourgeoisie; state-cash on hand, left over from the old government; sums coming from levies on the bourgeois class; sums acquired by selling supplies confiscated from private merchants and firms, and so on. But all these revenues turned out to be very small compared to the necessary expenditures. It is true that, for a certain period, levies on the capitalists were virtually the sole source ensuring the existence of local soviets, but these contributions could provide no essential support to the central authority. Ultimately, this source turned out to be much too short-lived, that is, the bourgeoisie was either completely fleeced or else, as happened most frequently, they scattered and hid their savings. A progressive income-tax also did not, and cannot, provide significant results. To the extent that it affects employees and workers, it makes no sense, since the state simply takes back in taxes a portion of what it pays out in salaries. And to the extent that it falls on the urban bourgeoisie, given the fact that this bourgeoisie has almost ceased to exist in official terms and is legally forbidden to carry on in its occupations, it is extremely difficult to collect, and such collections, in fact, turned out to be completely insignificant. This tax can be collected more successfully among the well-to-do peasantry, but to have a regular influx requires regular and systematic work by the taxation-organs, which are supported mainly by local organs of power and mainly in small rural districts. But this whole apparatus is still too inadequate to ensure success. With regard to the middle-peasant, to tax him while the Civil War continues is undesirable for political reasons, as he might be alienated from the proletariat. An attempt to collect ten billion as an extraordinary revolutionary tax failed, and a sum of less than two billion was collected after very great efforts. The basic source of state-revenues has remained the printing of paper-money. The issuing of paper-money, to the extent that it can still be used to buy anything, is essentially a special form of tax. This emission of money, leading to its devaluation, indirectly leads to expropriation of the bourgeoisie's money-capital by reducing purchasing power to a tiny fraction of what the bourgeoisie could buy with this money previously. Of course, the issuing of paper-money cannot long serve as a source of revenues for a state that is endeavouring to eliminate money altogether. The proletarian state now faces the question of how to build up its revenues on a more stable foundation.

Such a stable foundation is production itself. If the issuing of paper-money has been successful as a revenue-source, it is because this form of tax is collected without being noticed. In the same way, it is quite possible to collect invisible indirect taxes from state-monopolies. This form of state revenues is also profoundly fitting in its essence. After all, the cost of production for any product that issues from the state must also include the costs of administering production. And that administration is taken care of by the proletarian state-apparatus. In practical terms, this means that if passenger-transportation costs 1 billion roubles a year, the state must set travel-fares at a level that will provide 1 billion plus 200 million roubles from the movement of passengers. If all the manufactures that are produced cost 5 billion, they can be sold for 6 billion, and so on. The balance must go to maintaining the state. The revenues from monopolies can be collected not only in the form of money, but also indirectly, in the form of setting aside a certain quantity of products.

If the proletarian state becomes the organ for managing the entire socialist economy, then the question of supporting it, that is, our old question of the budget, becomes a great deal simpler. It will just be a matter of setting aside a specific quantity of resources for a specific economic expenditure.

But while the question of the state-budget becomes extraordinarily simplified, the matter is not so simple when it comes to clarifying what portion of the products can be consumed, that is, expended throughout the economy as a whole. The greatest skill will be required in calculating what quantity of products can be consumed without leaving any trace, and what quantity must be set aside as inventory that can serve expanded reproduction, for example.

Thus, the question of the state-budget, with the elimination of the state as a parasitic apparatus, is transformed into a general question concerning distribution of all the products of socialist society, for the state-budget becomes a component of the general budget of socialist society as a whole.

There is virtually no literature on this question. We can recommend Potyaev, A., *Finansovaya politika sovetskoi vlasti*.

Chapter XVII

The Communists' Programme on the Housing Question

§ 125. The housing question in capitalist society. § 126. The housing question in the proletarian state.

§ 125. The housing question in capitalist society

The privileges of the bourgeois class are nowhere as striking as in the sphere of housing. The best quarters of the cities are inhabited by the bourgeoisie. All of the best streets, in terms both of cleanliness and the abundance of gardens and trees, are inhabited by the propertied classes. Conversely, the working class in every country is resolutely driven to the outskirts. It is driven there not at all because the majority of factories are customarily situated on the outskirts of the city. If the factory is located in the city-centre, the workers of that factory still huddle in workers' settlements somewhere on the outskirts. And the factory-owners, even when their enterprises are built at the far ends of the city, still live in the centre.

Bourgeois families have entire houses to themselves, or apartments with more rooms than there are people living there, enjoying gardens, baths and all the conveniences of life.

Workers' families are crowded into cellars, single rooms and tiny apartments or, very often, into common barracks, just like prisoners sharing a cell. Inhaling factory-smoke, filings, wood-shavings and dust into his lungs throughout the working day, the worker must breathe all night in a room where five or six children are often sleeping.

It is not surprising that the statistics readily demonstrate how quickly people die in workers' quarters, where the working day is long but the hovels are small and life is short.

Here are the data. In England, for every thousand persons there is a mortality rate of 22 persons per year. In the bourgeois quarters, mortality falls to 17; in quarters specially reserved for the workers, it rises to 36; and in quarters inhabited by the very poorest sections of the workers, mortality rises to forty to fifty per thousand. In Brussels, the capital of Belgium, one person out of every 29 dies in the workers' quarters, while in the best bourgeois quarters, it is one out of every 53, that is, mortality in workers' quarters is almost twice as high as in those of the bourgeoisie.

The average lifespan for a bourgeois, living in brightly lit, warm and dry apartments, is one-and-a-half times longer than the lifespan of ordinary people in their basements and garrets on the outskirts.

In Budapest, the average lifespan of people living longer than five years is the following:

With one to two inhabitants per room	47.16 years
two to five " " "	39.51 "
five to ten " " "	37.10 "
more than ten " " "	32.03 "

Mortality rises even higher among workers' children when compared to the mortality of the bourgeoisie. In bourgeois quarters with no more than one inhabitant per room, child-mortality before the first year is four times lower than in quarters where there are more than three people per room. In ages from one to five years, mortality in bourgeois quarters is *twice as low* as among the workers.

But living in their rotten and stifling apartments, the workers not only have to die on average fifteen years sooner than the bourgeois, they are also compelled to pay the capitalist-landlord for this pleasure. Tribute must be paid to the landlords for every corner, every cellar and every attic, leaving aside any real room or apartment. Fail to pay and you will be driven out into the street. Paying for an apartment has always consumed a significant portion of the workers' income, from fifteen to twenty-five percent of his entire monthly income. This expenditure not only never declines, but is increasing in all the capitalist countries. For example, in Hamburg, for every hundred *marks* of income (a *mark* is about fifty *kopeks* at the pre-war rate) the following had to be paid out in apartment-rent:

	1868	1881	1900
For those with an income of:			
900–1,200 *marks*	19.8	24.1	24.7
1,200–1,800	19.9	18.9	23.2
1,800–2,400	20.3	19.5	21.6
6,000–9,000	16.5	15.7	15.1
30,000–60,000	6.7	8.1	6.0
more than 60,000	3.7	3.9	3.0

Thus, the smaller the income, the greater the percentage of it that is paid for an apartment and the more rapidly this portion rises every year. Conversely, for the bourgeoisie, the percentage of income paid for an apartment is nearly six times less for every hundred roubles of income, and this share, rather than rising, falls more rapidly.

§ 126. The housing question in the proletarian state

The proletarian revolution has brought a complete transformation in housing relations. The Soviet authority undertook nationalisation of bourgeois houses and abolished workers' arrears for apartments in some cases and reduced them in others. That is not all. Plans are in place, and are already partly implemented, to do away with all apartment-rents for workers living in nationalised houses. Next, in the largest cities a systematic resettlement of workers has begun, from basement-accommodations, semi-ruined houses and unhealthy quarters into the detached dwellings of the bourgeoisie and enormous homes in the central quarters. Additionally, there has begun a systematic supply to the workers of furniture and all the items of household-utensils.

The task of the Communist Party consists of continuing and extending this policy, perfecting the housing economy, struggling against neglect in the nationalised homes, preventing any deterioration in them as far as repair and cleanliness are concerned, and properly maintaining all the accommodations such as water-pipes, drains, steam-heating, and so on.

At the same time, while the Soviet authority is extensively nationalising large-scale capitalist property in houses, it does not have the slightest need to affect the interests of the small homeowner, including homeowners from the working class, employees and ordinary people. Attempts that have occurred in the provinces to implement the most extensive nationalisation even of small houses have simply led to a situation in which there was no-one to look after large and small nationalised homes, often leaving them to decay without anyone being willing to live in them. Meanwhile, among the small homeowners, this provoked grumbling and indignation against Soviet authority.

Facing the most serious housing crisis in the cities due to the halt of any new construction, the Soviet authority has put enormous work into a just allocation to all citizens of all the available housing. The apartment-branches of the soviets are registering all of the available apartments in the cities and placing lodgers in them according to a definite plan. At the same time, these branches are ascertaining the availability and location of all houses in every large city and reducing the space per person wherever there are families or individuals with more space than the norm allows.

Following the liquidation of the Civil War and the devastation in production, the urban population will begin to grow rapidly. Proletarians who have fled to the countryside will begin to return to the city, together with the excess-population of the villages. Soviet power will then face the question of new construction – the kind of construction that will satisfy the housing needs of a communist society. At the present moment, it is difficult to say what type of construction will be best: enormous homes with all the conveniences, gardens, common dining halls, and so forth, or well-built small homes for workers. Only one thing is clear: the housing programme must not conflict with the programme of bringing together industry and agriculture. It must facilitate the re-absorption of the city into its rural surroundings, rather than increasing the concentration in one locale of hundreds of thousands and millions of people who are deprived of any possibility to breathe fresh air, of people who are torn away from nature and condemned to a premature death.

Literature: Engels, F., *Zhilishchnyi vopros*; Fedorovich, *Zhilye pomeshcheniya rabochikh*; Dement'ev, E.A., *Fabrika, chto ona daet naseleniyu i chto ot nevo beret*; Svetlovsky, V., *Zhilishchnyi vopros na Zapade i v Rosii*; Pokrovskaya, M., *Uluchshenie rabochikh zhilishch v Anglii*.

No. 4
E.A. Preobrazhensky's Book *Paper Money in the Epoch of Proletarian Dictatorship*[1]

1920

Foreword

The question of our paper-money and its fate, as with the general question of money-circulation during the transition-period, is one of both theoretical and also enormous practical interest. In the completely new situation of a socialist economy, the problem of the withering away of paper-money circulation must be of interest to an economist. It is important for the average person to know the fate of the paper-currency he has in hand. The proletarian state must consider how long it can make use of paper-emissions together with natural taxes. The trade-unions have to know how to agree on wage-tariffs in conditions of a rapid fall in the exchange-value of the paper-currency. Meanwhile, in our press there are only a few newspaper-articles and a few pages in various brochures that address the theme of paper-money in the period of proletarian dictatorship. The purpose of the present work is to fill this gap.

---

1. [From Preobrazhensky 1920, pp. 3–84. This book gives a 'classic' description of Bolshevik thinking on monetary questions in the period prior to the New Economic Policy (NEP), which began in the spring of 1921. Its themes are developed in several subsequent works by Preobrazhensky.]

This brochure has all the flaws of a work written in a hurry, during moments and hours snatched from other duties that were often more urgent. The statistical material is inadequate, the literature on the question is not reviewed, not all aspects of the problem are elaborated, and the style is careless and ponderous. I was not able to do better. Either nothing would be published or else I had to publish this imperfect work. I preferred to do the latter. Shortage of free time also prevented the author from completing a brochure that would be easily read by every worker who may not be familiar with the elements of political economy. To those readers who find the beginning of the work difficult, I recommend starting at the middle or at the end; then it will also be easier to understand the first chapters.

Despite all of the inadequacies of this brochure, as author, I do not wish to forgo my right to make a dedication. I would like to dedicate this incomplete work to the instrument whose perfection and voluminous effort inspired the writing of these pages: to the printing press of the People's Commissariat of Finance. The revolutionary government of France was able to survive and wage war thanks to the issuing of paper-money; the *assignats* were what saved the Great French Revolution. The paper-money of the Soviet Republic has supported a new power during the most difficult period of its existence, when it was not possible to pay for the costs of a civil war through direct taxes. Glory to our printing press! True, it is not left with much longer to live, but it has already completed three-quarters of its work. In the archives of the great proletarian revolution, along with the cannons, rifles and machine-guns of our epoch, the mechanism of the *Narkomfin*[2] machine-gun will occupy the place of honour. This machine-gun shot up the bourgeois order in its rear, in its monetary system, and transformed the laws of monetary circulation in the bourgeois régime into a means for destroying that régime and a source for financing the Revolution.

I

Metallic and paper-money

To understand all of the phenomena in the sphere of paper-money circulation during the period of the dictatorship of the proletariat, that is, during the period of the withering away of the monetary system in general, it is first necessary to have a clear idea of the role of paper-money in the epoch when capitalist production exists in its normal condition. One cannot understand the laws of

---

2. [Finance-Commissariat]

a system's disintegration without first knowing the laws of that same system before the disintegration began. When a citizen of the Soviet Republic asks for the thousand-and-first time a naïve question as to whether the fall of the rouble will end soon, in order to answer even this very elementary question one must know what paper-money is, what its role is in the general system of capitalist economy, and what paper-money is in the period of capitalism's destruction. Only then, in the final analysis, can one say something about the fate of one or another paper-money system or of the value of one or another paper-money unit. In this work, therefore, we must begin with an account in the most general terms of what Karl Marx had to say about paper-money in the capitalist period.

Subsequently, we shall encounter the questions that could not even arise in the epoch when the author of *Capital* lived and worked. True, in the history of paper-money during the capitalist period it is a fact that one or another specific paper-money unit disappeared, and one has only to recall, for example, the liquidation of the *assignats* of the Great French Revolution. But all such facts, which provide most valuable material for understanding the laws of paper-money circulation in capitalist society, can only partly and indirectly throw any light on the dying spasms of the monetary system in the epoch of proletarian dictatorship. We are facing new questions insofar as the very function of paper-money is changing fundamentally. For these new questions, we can find no ready answers in quotations from Marx, but, instead, we must try to provide our own answers using Marx's *method*.

In view of the fact that not everyone who wishes to read this brochure has studied Marx, I must begin with certain elementary truths of political economy.

With the prevalence of commodity-production, that is, the sort of production in which the enormous majority of the values being produced are not consumed by the producers themselves, but are thrown onto the market for sale, there is a need for a type of commodity in which the value of all the circulating commodities can be expressed. Since the value of every commodity is determined by the amount of socially-necessary labour-time expended in its production, any commodity can essentially be the measure of value for other commodities. This commodity can be material of any sort – from silk to linen to cattle and the meat of cattle – as well as a volume of firewood or small bars of gold. Let us take one of the examples that Marx uses in Volume I of *Capital*:

$$\left.\begin{array}{l}\text{one frock-coat}\\ \text{ten pounds of tea}\\ \text{one quarter}^3\text{ of wheat}\\ \text{two ounces of gold}\\ \text{a half-tonne of iron}\\ \text{x of commodity A}\\ \text{and so on.}\end{array}\right\} = \text{twenty } \textit{arshins}^4 \text{ of linen}$$

In this case, all the commodities are equal to twenty *arshins* of linen. Despite all the variations of these commodities in terms of use, and despite differences in their measurements and weights, they are nevertheless all joined by an equal sign with twenty *arshins* of linen and, at the same time, with each other (any two magnitudes are equal, and each is equal to any third magnitude). What is common to all the commodities listed, despite the different magnitudes, is the amount of socially-necessary labour-time expended in their production. Consequently, in place of each commodity's name, we could list the identical number of labour-hours embodied in each commodity, say thirty hours of socially-necessary labour-time. These thirty hours, which are already expended in producing the amount of the listed commodity prior to its circulation, also make possible the equalisations. Thus one frock-coat equals twenty *arshins* of linen because the thirty hours of labour-time expended in its production are equal to the thirty hours of labour-time spent in producing the twenty *arshins* of linen. It is perfectly clear, therefore, that in place of twenty *arshins* of linen, we could just as legitimately put ten pounds of tea, one frock-coat, one quarter of wheat, and so forth. We know from the history of trade that the place of honour in measuring the value of other commodities in different epochs and at various ends of the earth has been assumed by various commodities: by precious minerals, cattle, furs, precious metals, salt, and so on. But history has confirmed one commodity as being suitable for this role in every respect:

> In proportion as exchange bursts its local limits, and the value of commodities more and more expands into a materialisation (embodiment) of human labour in general, the monetary form attaches to commodities that are, by their very nature, especially suited to fulfil the social function of a universal equivalent, namely, the precious metals.
>
> That money by nature is gold and silver, although gold and silver are not by nature money... is shown by the correspondence of the natural qualities of these metals with their social functions.

---

3. [A 'quarter' of wheat = eight bushels, or approximately one quarter-tonne.]
4. [1 *arshin* = 0.71m.]

> On the other hand, since the different magnitudes in terms of weight have a purely quantitative character, the money-commodity must be suitable for purely quantitative differences, that is, it must possess those characteristics that make it divisible at will into smaller parts that can be brought back together. Gold and silver by nature possess all of these properties.
>
> The use-value of the money-commodity becomes two-fold. Together with the special use-value that adheres to it as a given commodity – for example, gold serves to fill teeth, as the raw material for articles of luxury – it acquires a formal use-value that results from its specific social functions.[5]

In other words, the money-commodity, gold, is a use-value not only for the dentist's patients and for someone buying jewellery, but also for society, insofar as this society's spontaneous commodity-exchange uses gold in the function of money, in the role of universal equivalent of all other commodity-values.[6]

But gold is a product of labour, and as a product of labour, it has the same democratic origins as shoes, cloth, rye, and so on. It has its own independent value, created in the process of production, and it can measure its own value only in terms of other commodities:

> Like any other commodity, gold can express the magnitude of its own value only relatively, in terms of other commodities. Its own value is determined by the labour-time necessary for its production, and is expressed in the magnitude of any other commodity in which the same amount of labour-time is crystallised. Such determination of the relative value of some amount of gold in fact occurs at the place of its production through direct barter-trade. When it steps forth into circulation as money, its value is already given.[7]

In the equation that we have provided above, linen figures as the measure of values. But its place can be assumed by any other commodity listed in the first part of the equation that is identical to it in terms of value. Commodities are commensurable because they have an identical quality, the expenditure of human labour. The fact that money can serve as a measure of value is possible not because the Earth possesses gold as a precious metal, but because there is something in the commodities to be measured, because they emerge as commensurable from production itself, for each is a crystallisation of one or another quantity of human labour:

---

5. Marx 1907, p. 59. [Since there are some important differences between the standard English translation and the Russian one by I.I. Skvortsov-Stepanov that Preobrazhensky quotes, the translations given here are based on the latter, which, in many respects, is better at conveying Marx's thinking.]
6. The 'use' here is also partly physical, in the sense that gold-coins suffer from wear as a result of frequent and long usage.
7. Marx 1907, pp. 61–2.

It is not money that makes commodities commensurable. On the contrary, it is precisely because commodities, as value, represent embodied human labour and are, therefore, commensurable in themselves – it is precisely for this reason that they can measure their value in terms of one and the same particular commodity and thereby transform the latter into a common measure of their values, that is, into money. Money, as a measure of value, is merely a necessary form for the manifestation of the immanent (inherent) measure of value within commodities, labour-time.[8]

But while it possesses all of the attributes characteristic of any commodity, metallic money is lacking only in one – it has no price. If we speak of price as the money-expression of the value of commodities, then the money-expression of the value of money is a tautology, like oiled oil. Five roubles of gold can be worth neither four nor six roubles of gold. Five roubles is worth five roubles, which is the same thing as saying that money is money.

We have seen why gold can become the money material. In order to convert the money-material into coinage, it must be divided into certain units of weight:

> A given weight of precious metal, for example, an ounce of gold, is officially divided into particular parts that are baptised with particular legal names such as pound and *thaler*. Now the unit of monetary measurement, in the proper sense of the word, is any one of these parts, which are in turn subdivided into new parts, which from the mouth of the law acquire their own names: shilling, penny, and so on. In any case, a certain weight of metal, as before, remains the standard of metallic money. All that changes is the method of subdivision into its parts and the denomination of the latter.
>
> Instead of saying that a quarter of wheat is equal to one ounce of gold, the Englishman says it is equal to three pounds sterling, 17 shillings and 10½ pence.[9]

Gold, having been transformed into money-material and then into gold-money, serves as the means for measuring the value of commodities and, therefore, in the process of commodity-circulation, as the means of circulation.

Given the existence of a commodity-economy, every producer, whether a small shoemaker or the owner of a shoe-factory, whether an independent metal-craftsman or the owner of a factory producing locomotives, is the seller of the commodities he produces. At the same time, he is the buyer of other commodities produced for sale by other people. But in order to buy other commodities he must sell his own. To sell them means to convert them into money, in order

---

8. Marx 1907, p. 63.
9. Marx 1907, p. 90.

subsequently to convert the money into commodities. The market represents an eternal *quadrille*[10] in which one commodity is replaced by others in the course of circulation, and the role of permanent match-maker, the role of procuress between them, is played by money. The entire process is expressed in the brief formula C-M-C.

Upon entering into circulation, every separate commodity quickly leaves it through being exchanged for another commodity by means of money. Its subsequent fate has no connection with the market. It is either consumed by people directly, as in the case of bread, oil, shoes, and so on, or else it is consumed in industry, that is, worked up, as with a material such as iron, cotton, or flax. But money, insofar as it figures as the means of circulation, remains in circulation. True, a part of the money can flow abroad or be stored as treasure in depositories, but a certain minimum must remain in the channels of circulation, insofar as commodity-circulation always takes place.

What is this minimum, and how is the quantity of money that is necessary for circulation determined?

Here, we come to one of the most important questions of our study. Every commodity exchanges for money. But this by no means implies that a quantity of money is required for the circulation of commodities that equals the value of all the circulating commodities. One and the same sum of money over a certain interval of time, a month for instance, can turn over several times, even tens of times, and thus the value of commodities passing through circulation by means of money can exceed, and, in fact, exceeds by many times, the value of the monetary metal that plays the role of intermediary in this operation. The value of the money itself, its increase or decrease, and also the increase or decrease of the price-level of the circulating commodities, and finally, the speed at which money turns over – these are all magnitudes that determine the minimum-sum for circulation that we are looking for. Marx formulates the corresponding law of money-circulation as follows:

> For a given interval of time during the process of circulation, the quantity of money functioning as the circulating medium is equal to the sum of the prices of the commodities divided by the number of moves made by coins of the same denomination.[11]
>
> If the number of turnovers by coins increases, then their total number in circulation decreases. If the number of turnovers decreases, then their total number increases.[12]

---

10. [An historic dance and a precursor of square-dancing.]
11. Marx 1907, p. 90.
12. Marx 1907, p. 91.

With a general rise in the prices of commodities, the quantity of the circulating medium can remain constant if the volume of circulating commodities decreases in the same proportion as their price increases, or if the velocity of money increases in the same proportion as the prices rise, with the volume of the circulating commodities remaining constant. The quantity of the circulating medium may decrease if the volume of commodities decreases, or if the speed of the turnover increases more rapidly than the prices.

With a general fall in the prices of commodities, the quantity of the circulating medium can remain constant if the volume of commodities increases in the same proportion as their prices fall, or if the velocity of money declines in the same proportion as the prices fall. The quantity of the circulating medium may increase if the volume of commodities increases, or if the speed of the turnover decreases more rapidly than the commodity-prices fall.

The variations of the different factors may mutually compensate each other, so that, notwithstanding their continued instability, the general sum of the commodity-prices to be realised remains constant, and thus the quantity of money in circulation also remains constant. Consequently, we find, especially if we take comparatively long periods into consideration, that the volume of money circulating in each given country assumes a much more stable average level, and the deviations from this average level are much less significant than we would expect at first sight; exceptions occur in periods of strong disturbances that arise from industrial and commercial crises, or less frequently, from changes in the value of the money itself.[13]

The reader must understand that we are, thus far, speaking only of metallic money. We shall see below how the law formulated by Marx applies to the circulation of paper-money and all the possible changes that are involved.

We see, therefore, that commodity-circulation always requires a certain minimum-quantity of the medium of circulation. A reduction in the quantity of circulating money below this minimum creates difficulties in circulation and calls forth a number of measures to increase the quantity of money. On the other hand, an increase of money above the necessary quantity can easily be overcome by an outflow of money abroad or into different types of depositories, both private and social, or else by converting the metal into items of luxury.

From continuous use, the coins can wear. A gold-coin that weighs, shall we say, one *zolotnik*,[14] might lose half of the amount of metal stamped upon it because of long usage. But this does not prevent the worn coin from circulating at its full [nominal] value. When the purchaser takes this coin, he expects

---

13. Marx 1907, p. 93.
14. [4.26 grams]

to sell it in the same condition as he acquired it, with no intention of realising the gold contained in it as metal. The coin has significance only as a medium of circulation in the narrow sense, and in this function it can be replaced by a paper-banknote.

> If the very circulation of money effects a separation between the real content of coins and the nominal content, creating a distinction between their existence as metal and their functional existence, this implies the latent possibility of replacing metallic money, in its function as coinage, by tokens of some other material, or merely by symbols...[15]
>
> One commodity is quickly replaced by another commodity. Hence, in this process, which continually makes money pass from hand to hand, the mere symbolic existence of money suffices. The functional existence of money absorbs, so to speak, its material existence. Being in this case a transient and objective reflection of commodity-prices, it serves only as a symbol of itself and is, therefore, capable of being replaced by simple tokens. All that is required is that this symbol of money, as such, enjoy objective social recognition, and the paper-symbol achieves this by being given a fixed exchange-rate. This compulsory action by the state has force only within the borders of a given community or in the sphere of domestic circulation, but then it is also only within that sphere that money completely develops its function as the circulating medium, or as coins, and thus it can acquire the form of paper-money that is completely distinct from its metallic substance and has a purely functional form of existence.[16]

What is the quantity of paper-money that can be circulated without risk of depreciation? Marx gives an exhaustive answer to this question, and on this basis, one can understand not only all the phenomena of paper-money circulation in a normal capitalist epoch, but also the fundamental aspects of the depreciation of paper-currency in the period of the dictatorship of the proletariat.

> The state puts into circulation paper-symbols on which their various denominations, say £1 or £5, are printed. Insofar as they actually circulate in place of gold to the same amount, their movement reflects only the laws [that regulate] the circulation of money itself. A law peculiar to the circulation of paper-money can spring up only from its relation to gold and only from the fact that it represents the latter. Such a law, stated simply, provides as follows: the issue of paper-money must not exceed in amount the gold (or silver, as the case may be) that would actually circulate if not replaced by symbols. True, the quantity

---

15. Marx 1907, p. 97.
16. Marx 1907, pp. 100–1.

of gold that the sphere of circulation can absorb constantly fluctuates, now rising above and then falling below a certain average level. But the volume of the circulating medium never falls below a certain level that can be established through experience in any given country. The fact that this minimum continually undergoes changes in its constituent parts, or that the pieces of gold of which it consists are being constantly replaced by fresh ones, causes no change, of course, either in its amount or in the continuity of its functions in the sphere of circulation. Consequently, it can easily be replaced by paper-symbols. If, on the other hand, all the channels of circulation were today filled with paper-money to the full extent of their capacity for absorbing money, they might tomorrow be overflowing in consequence of a fluctuation in the circulation of commodities. There would no longer be any standard. But if the paper-money exceeds its proper limit, which is the amount in gold-coins of like denomination that can actually be in current circulation, it would then, apart from the danger of falling into general disrepute, represent in the commodity-world only that quantity of gold that it is generally capable of representing, that is, a quantity determined by the immanent laws of the commodity-world. If, for instance, a given amount of paper-money has a denomination as two ounces of gold but really only replaces one ounce, then, as a matter of fact, £1 would be the money-designation, say, not of the former 1/4 of an ounce, but of 1/8 of an ounce of gold. The effect would be the same as if an alteration had taken place in the function of gold as a standard of prices. Those same values that were previously expressed by the price of £1 would now be expressed by the price of £2.

Paper-money is a token representing gold or money. The relation between it and the values of commodities lies in the fact that the latter are ideally expressed in the same quantities of gold that are symbolically represented by the paper. Paper-money is only a token of value insofar as it represents a certain quantity of gold that, like any other mass of commodities, is at the same time a mass of values.[17]

The mistake of Hilferding

Before turning to the application of Marx's theory to concrete facts from the sphere of money-circulation, and to money-circulation in the epoch of proletarian dictatorship, we will consider, in passing, the attempt by Hilferding to 'deepen' Marx on the theory of paper-money circulation. In a footnote to a quotation from Volume III of *Capital*, Hilferding writes:

---

17. Marx 1907, pp. 98–9.

... [W]hen one reads Marx, certain passages dealing with monetary problems leave the impression that certain conclusions that follow from his theory of money clashed in his thinking with ideas suggested by the empirical facts of his day, a conflict that could not be reconciled satisfactorily in purely logical terms. The most recent experiences do, in fact, confirm the ultimate conclusions that are deducible from Marx's theory of the value of money.

Marx emphasises that there can be only as much paper in circulation as the amount of gold required. But in order to understand modern phenomena in this area, it is important to remember that this quantity of gold, once its value is defined, is at any moment determined by the value of the social circulation. If the latter falls, gold flows out of circulation, and vice versa. With a paper-money circulation and a non-convertible system in general [suspended coinage], these inflows and outflows could not occur, because the non-circulating paper-token would, indeed, be of little value. Here, one must revert to circulating value as the determining factor, and it does not suffice to regard a money-certificate simply as a symbol of gold, as Marx does in *Kritik der Politischen Oekonomie*.

It seems to me that Marx formulates the law of paper-currency (or any currency with suspended coinage) most correctly when he says: 'The worthless tokens are signs of value only insofar as they represent gold within the sphere of circulation, and they represent it only to the extent to which it would itself be absorbed as coin by the process of circulation; this quantity is determined by its own value, the exchange-value of the commodities and the rapidity of their metamorphosis being given' (*Zur Kritik*, p. 113). The detour by which Marx proceeds – first determining the value of the necessary quantity of coins and then, from that, the value of the paper-money – seems superfluous. The purely social character of that determination is far more clearly expressed if the value of paper-money is derived directly from the social value of circulation. The fact that, historically, paper-currency had its origin in metallic systems is not a reason for regarding it in this way theoretically. The value of paper-money must be deduced without reference to metallic money.[18]

Hilferding's mistake is quite apparent in the following example.

Assume that we have a state in which the minting of coins is forbidden, say Austria in 1870 or India in 1890 (the examples that convinced Hilferding of the 'inadequacy' of Marx's theory). Suppose that there are commodities in circulation worth 10 billion. This circulation is fully satisfied by the presence either of gold-coins worth 1 billion, by state-credit notes in the same amount, or by gold- and

---

18. Marx 1907, pp. 66–7. [See Footnote 32 of Chapter Two in Hilferding 1981, pp. 382–3.]

paper-money together coming to *the same amount*. Let us further assume that, because of an increase of production, the volume of circulating commodities increases by one-half, reaching 15 billion. If the velocity of money's circulation remains constant, and there is no possibility of non-monetary accounting, an additional sum of money is needed to provide for circulation and can be provided by the state in the form of paper-money. How much is this sum?

Marx would reply: a sum that corresponds to the sum of gold-coins that would be required to serve the expanded circulation.

The 'shorter answer' discovered by Hilferding would be: a sum that corresponds to the social value of circulation.

But we have to ask Hilferding: Please tell us how to determine the social value of circulation. If the volume of commodities has grown by one-half, and all other conditions have remained the same, does this mean that the state can expand paper-money by one-half, that is, by adding an additional half a billion to the billion already in circulation, without risking depreciation?

Of course, it does not. An increase of commodities by one-half does not mean that social value grows by one-half. Because of technological progress and other improvements, the social value of the commodities representing the increased circulation may be significantly lower than their volume. This will also determine the proportion in which the social value of circulation increases. How can this be measured?

Alas, we have to turn to gold for help, because in bourgeois society there is no system for accounting the socially-necessary hours of labour that we use in our theoretical analysis of capitalist production; and other values, with the partial exception of silver, are not authorised for use in the determination of prices. The socially-necessary value of circulation is:

the sum of commodity-values
the velocity of money-circulation

But the numerator of this fraction must, indeed, be expressed precisely in gold, and not in any Austrian *guildens* or Indian rupees: for the exchange-value of the latter, and how it changes, is exactly what has to be determined. Consequently, both the numerator and the quotient of dividing the numerator by the denominator will be a magnitude expressed in gold-currency. Thus, Hilferding also cannot manage without the scorned metal. What seems to him to be a shortcoming in Marx's system is precisely the fact that Marx bases all the laws of paper-money circulation on metallic circulation, and this is exactly Marx's merit. Marx's caution, which leads him by a 'detour', is explained not by the fact that his consciousness was influenced by empirical material in the sphere of money-circulation during his own time (in the way that Hilferding's consciousness is empirically influenced by the metamorphosis of the Austrian *guilden*), but by the fact that, in explaining the phenomena of paper-money circulation, Marx always has in view the entire economic system of bourgeois society as a whole. In explaining the laws of circulation, he does not for a moment lose sight of the conditions of production, which are the foundations of the entire building. The reference to gold means restoring the link that ties the fate of paper to the laws of commodity-production, because gold is not only the standard of value, but also has its own value, which it acquires through being produced on the basis of the general laws of labour-value.[19]

The shortcoming in Hilferding's construction lies exactly in the fact that where he departs from Marx, he also goes along with bourgeois economists, who usually regard money-circulation and its laws as some kind of world-in-itself, detached from the bases of production, and who, therefore, inevitably come to absurd conclusions.

As if anticipating the 'deepening' to which his theory of money might be exposed, in Note 90 to the second edition of Volume I of *Capital*, Marx wrote:

> The following passage from Fullarton shows how unclear even the best writers on money are about its different functions: 'That, as far as concerns our domestic exchanges, all the monetary functions which are usually performed by [gold- and] silver-coins may be performed as effectually by a circulation of inconvertible notes having no value but that fictitious and conventional value... they derive from the law, is a fact which admits, I conceive, of no denial. Value of this description may be made to answer all the purposes of intrinsic value, and supersede even the necessity for a standard, provided only the quantity of issues be kept under due limitation' (Fullarton: *Regulation of Currencies*', 2nd edn, London, 1845, p. 21.) [To this comment Marx replied] In other words, because the money-commodity is capable of being replaced in circulation by mere symbols of value, it is superfluous as a measure of value and a standard of prices![20]

True, Hilferding does not claim that paper-money can be the standard of value in bourgeois society, and he also underlines the 'impossibility of an absolutely paper-money system', but, in this way, he only demonstrates that he has not tied the ends together and clarified for himself just what might replace gold as the

---

19. In the present case, gold is important as a standard of value and as the spontaneous measure of commodities. In principle, this role could be played by any other commodity that has its own value. But in the practice of capitalist society, there is no commodity apart from gold, with the partial exception of silver, that fulfils this function in the process of exchange.
20. [Marx 1976, p. 225.]

thread that ties circulation to production and makes it possible to trace all the changes in circulation in light of the process of production.[21]

Instead of mimicking the inimitable style of Marx throughout his book, Hilferding would have done better had he tried to understand in the first chapters of his work the meaning of the Marxist theory of money-circulation. The facts concerning the history of the Austrian silver-*guilden* and the Indian rupee are fully explicable from the point of view of Marx's theory, provided that it is not subjected to any 'deepening'. And on the contrary, not a single fact concerning the history of the depreciation of paper-money can be fully understood unless the starting point and basis of the analysis are the laws of circulation of metallic money, that is, the laws of real commodity-exchange that also determine the fate of all paper-money systems.

II

Paper-money and its exchange-value

We have seen above that the issue of paper-money, as a rule, cannot lead to a fall in its exchange-value if it is issued in a sum that corresponds to the sum of gold-coins needed for circulation. The role of paper-money, in this case, is the role of a substitute for gold-coins. There are truly real values in circulation, commodity-values, and so long as every paper-money token is only a substitute for gold-money of the same value, which at any moment might make its appearance upon request, either from the bank-vaults, from private cash-boxes, or from abroad in exchange for commodity-values circulating in the market – so long as this is the case, the exchange-value of paper-money cannot significantly deviate from gold-currency. The golden circle that reveals its face in the price of one

---

21. Kautsky was perfectly correct when he reviewed Hilferding's book in 1911 (*Neue Zeit*. March 1911, pp. 771–2) and pointed out that Hilferding's construction breaches the labour-theory of value: it is not money that turns out to be the standard for measuring the value of commodities, but commodities that become the standard for the value of money. The 'academic quirk' (*akademische Schrulle*) of Hilferding, which is how Kautsky described his 'correction' of Marx, goes much further than even the author of *Finance Capital* would like. True, Hilferding emphasises that the laws of paper-money circulation and those of metallic circulation must not be confused. But he fails to show, and he should have shown, that by remaining on the ground of the laws he introduces concerning paper-money circulation, he also makes logically inevitable a revision of the laws of metallic circulation. Moreover, the reader will see below that without making 'reference' to gold, it is impossible, both theoretically and practically, to work through all the phenomena of paper-money circulation in the period of proletarian dictatorship. [Kautsky's review of Hilferding is available at the Marxists Internet Archive: see Kautsky 1911].

commodity or another is comparable to its paper-copy, and, in this case, it can only confirm that the copy and the original resemble each other as do two drops of water. With five roubles of gold, one can purchase the same shoes as with five roubles of paper-money.

However, we know from the history of money-circulation that the market-health of a paper-rouble, a *guilden, franc, mark*, crown, and so on is not always so robust. For citizens of the Soviet Republic, this is an especially well-known fact. In 1920, they have roubles that have less than one five-thousandth of their pre-war value. The history of money-circulation also knows of instances when the exchange-value of paper-money rose above that of its metallic originals.

In order to explain the most typical moments in the fluctuations of paper-money's exchange-value, let us look at all the main theoretical possibilities in the most simplified form.

Imagine a country whose entire commodity-fund in circulation is equal to 40 billion (in finished products, machines, factories, houses, land, railways, and such like).

A certain portion of these values can turn over several times in the course of a year, some even five times a year. Assume that for the circulation of these values, given certain kinds of non-monetary settlements, it suffices to have a money-circulation of 2 billion roubles, of which 1 billion is in gold and 1 billion in paper-money, and the paper-money is the equivalent of the metallic money. If we take as our starting point the situation typical for money-circulation in a capitalist country operating in normal circumstances, then a change in the exchange-value of the paper-currency can only occur because of a change in the quantity of circulating commodities, a change in the quantity of paper-money issued, or a change in the velocity of money.

Since the velocity of money is much less subject to fluctuations than the other two magnitudes, we can simplify by taking this rate as constant.

The first case. Our starting point is equilibrium with 40 billion of circulating values and 2 billion means of circulation, or money. In other words:

40 billion	C	— — —	2 billion	M
	(commodities)	(correspond to)		(money)

Let us suppose, to begin with, that changes occur in the magnitude of C, but M remains constant.

The second case. If, as a result of dislocation in production due to war, crisis, and so on, C falls, and in place of 40 billion we have only 30 billion, then the equilibrium will be destroyed. What will then happen with M? Once the sum of circulating commodities declines by one-quarter, then the demand for means of circulation also declines by one-quarter. How will this deduction from the sphere of money occur if the quantity of money remains the same? There is only one way, and that is through the depreciation of the total sum of money by one-quarter, or by 500 million. But gold cannot depreciate, because it has its own value, not simply as a standard for other values, but also as gold, as a precious commodity. Therefore, the blow of fate must fall upon the paper.

In the case that we have described, gold usually disappears from circulation without any state-involvement, or else the state stops the free exchange of paper for gold in view of the general attempt by the public and the commercial world to hold onto gold and to sell paper. In order to trace the influence of a reduction of C on the exchange-value of M, in this case, we must now suppose that we have in circulation not 2 billion in money, of which one half is gold and the other half paper, but rather 2 billion in paper.

This is the typical case in the history of paper-money circulation in bourgeois countries because – in time of war, for example – gold is locked away by the State-Bank, a fixed rate of exchange is imposed on paper, and its quantity is increased through new issues.

As a result, if the 2 billion of money in circulation entails an excess of 500 million, that is, an excess of one-quarter or 25 percent of the total, then the rate of the paper-rouble falls by 25 percent. In other words, the paper-rouble will be worth 75 *kopeks* when converted into the gold-rouble.

A panic in the paper-money market might break out that is so enormous, automatic and spontaneous (as it always is, in a bourgeois economy) as to cause a depreciation of paper-money that goes even further than is warranted by economic causes. But in the case that we are considering, a depreciation of paper-money by one-quarter provides the approximate axis around which fluctuations will occur in one direction or the other.

The other situation would be one in which the depreciation may not reach seventy-five percent in terms of gold,[22] which would occur when the fall of the exchange-rate is impeded by a number of causes (for example, the owners of paper-money, believing that the crisis is temporary, may not sell off paper in panic, but will accumulate it, and so on).

The third case. The number of commodities entering into circulation increases, but there are no additional forms of non-monetary transactions. The number of monetary tokens remains constant. Let us assume that this can be expressed in figures by saying that C = 50 billion, that is, one-quarter more than before. The means of circulation, as in the previous case, are 2 billion. To satisfy the requirements of circulation it is necessary to add 500 million roubles of money.

---

22. [That is, the depreciated paper may retain more than seventy-five percent of its value in terms of gold.]

What will happen if this additional money is not put into circulation by the state printing press? The necessary quantity of money may flow into the country from abroad, because the expansion of production and the increase of circulating commodities will mean, as a rule, that there is an expansion of foreign trade. A part of the money will come from depositories of all kinds, and there will be increased use of promissory notes, shares and other instruments as means of settling accounts. If all of this is not enough, then it may happen that in a country where the free issue of gold- and silver-coinage is forbidden, and where the government itself does not increase the coinage, that both the government's metallic coinage and the paper-money will rise above their normal rate. In our example, if 300 million of the 500 million comes from the greater use of promissory notes withdrawn from monetary depositories, and the need for 200 million is not satisfied by an inflow from abroad, then the rate of all the government's currency, including both paper- and metallic money, might temporarily rise proportionately, or by roughly ten percent. In this third case, we might include the rise in the rate of the Austrian *guilden* and the Indian silver-rupee that Hilferding analysed in his book.[23]

The fourth case. The quantity of circulating commodity-values remains unchanged at 40 billion, but the quantity of money in circulation falls by one-quarter. For example, the government decides at an inopportune moment to take 500 million of paper out of circulation in trying to go over exclusively to a gold-currency. The result will be exactly the same as in the third case, and this fourth case can essentially be regarded simply as a variant or different manifestation of the third.

The fifth case. The quantity of circulating commodity-values remains unchanged, and the quantity of paper-money increases because of new issues by 500 million. This case can be regarded as simply a variant of the second case, in which the commodities in circulation were 10 billion less than required. Here, the money is 500 million more than required. The result in both cases will be the same: an excess of money in circulation and a depreciation of paper-money.

Now let us consider examples in which the quantity of both the commodities and the money in circulation change.

The sixth case. The quantity of commodity-values in circulation increases from 40 to 50 billion, that is, by one-quarter. The quantity of money also increases by one-quarter through the issue of 500 million in paper. If we assume, for purposes of simplification, that the velocity of circulation remains constant and there are no additional means of non-monetary settlements,[24] then the paper-rouble does not fall if the government issues 500 million of new paper-money.

---

23. Hilferding 1918, pp. 39–48.
24. We can take an example that includes these facts. For instance, 800 million of paper is issued; instead, let 300 million be serviced by an increase in non-monetary

Countless practical examples of this case can be cited. In the history of the financial policy of our tsarism, it often happened that the ministry of finance issued a new series of paper-money in comparatively modest amounts in order to improve its revenues, and this did not cause any decline in the rate of the paper-rouble. This happened not because the circulating paper was no more than three times the size of the metallic reserves of the State-Bank, as the matter is explained by the financiers of the bourgeois world and by the financial 'theorists' of capitalism, but solely because an increase of the quantity of commodities in circulation made it possible to 'swallow' the paper-pills of the state without doing any damage to the rate of the rouble. If the gold-cover in the State-Bank had been significantly less than a third, the result, other conditions being equal, would have been just the same. And on the contrary, an issue of paper in excess of that required by the increased commodity-turnover would always lead to a fall in the rate of the rouble.

The seventh case. C increases and M increases, but C increases in greater proportion than M. Assume that the commodities in circulation are 50 billion, and the money is 3 billion rather than 2.5 billion. We have more paper-money than circulation requires. This is a variant of the second case. In its own financial practice, the tsarist government was long-familiar with this second case. Frequently in its history, the tsarist government rushed far ahead in its issue of paper-money than was permitted by an expanded commodity-circulation on the basis of developed commercial-industrial capitalism, and each time it was checked by a fall in the rate of the paper-rouble. For example, an increased issue of paper-banknotes under Alexander I led in 1810 to a fall of paper-money by 25.4 *kopeks* in terms of the silver-rouble. After numerous withdrawals of paper-money from circulation under Nicholas I and Alexander II, the rate rose and then catastrophically fell once again during the Russo-Turkish War because of an increased issue of credit-notes.

The eighth case. C increases more rapidly than M. Equilibrium is destroyed, in the sense that the money in circulation becomes insufficient. This is a variant of the third case.

The ninth case. C declines but M increases.

The ninth case is most typical for all periods of more-or-less profound revolutions, and especially for all prolonged and destructive wars, because all such moments involve a reduction or dislocation of industry and a decline of the quantity of commodities in circulation, at the same time as there is an enormous need for new taxes on the government's part and it is completely impossible to collect these taxes in the usual ways. This case includes the whole history of the *assignats* of the Great French Revolution, the Austrian paper-currency in

---

settlements and a higher velocity, and then there would need to be a 500 million increase in the means of circulation.

the period 1813–16, the paper-money system of almost all the participants in the World-War of 1914–18, and also the history of our own paper-rouble in the time from the beginning of the War up to the present.

Let us consider some of the most characteristic data.

The quantity of *assignats* issued in each year of the Great French Revolution and the speed of their depreciation are apparent in the table below, in which the rate of the *assignats* is given in the Hamburg (gold-) currency.[25]

Year and month	Quantity of *assignats* issued in *livres* (thousands)	The rate of *assignats* (of 100 *livres* in metal)
1 August 1789	120,000	98
1 October 1790	400,000	91
1 October 1791	1,154,000,000	84
1 August 1792	1,800,000,000	61
1 August 1793	3,775,816	22
1 August 1794	8,577,705	34
1 August 1795	17,466,553	three *livres* five *sous*
1 June 1796	45,578,809	three *sous* nine *deniers*[26]

Thus the *assignats* began to be boycotted in circulation after they fell in price by approximately six hundred times. (Our rouble, having approximately one five-thousandth of its pre-war value,[27] still continues in circulation.)

In Austria, the rate of the paper-currency (the so-called anticipation-coupons) changed as follows in connection with their increased issue:

	Sum	Rate (the price of 100 silver- *guildens* in paper)
December 1813	295,588,020	183
December 1814	475,612,790	228
December 1815	610,065,930	351
December 1816	638,715,920	328

---

25. Fal'kner 1919, pp. 189–91 [its title translates as 'Paper-Money in the French Revolution'.]

26. A *livre* contains 20 *sous*, a *sous* contains 12 *deniers*. [On 1 August 1789, 100 *livres* in *assignats* were worth 98 *livres* in metallic currency, falling to three *sous* nine *deniers* by 1 June 1796.]

27. [There is an error in the text, which says that the rouble in 1920 had *lost* a five-thousandth of its pre-war value.]

In other words, paper-money fell in price by approximately three times.[28]

The following figures show the extent of paper-money issues by European countries during the War, and in some cases after the War, together with the relation between the quantity of paper in circulation and the prices.

	Paper-money in circulation on 1 January 1919	In 1920
England	393 billion pounds	
Germany	32¼ billion *marks*	61.7 billion (April)
France	31,050 billion *francs*	
Austria	35,588 billion crowns	
Poland	5,267 billion *marks*	
Italy	18 billion lire (November)	20 billion (May)

According to calculations by the National Bank of New York, during the War the quantity of paper-money in the world-market increased by six hundred percent while the gold-supply grew by a total of forty percent. In 1914, the quantity of paper-money in circulation was 7,520 million dollars, by November 1918 it was already 40,000 million, and in December 1919 50,000 million. This figure does not include paper-money in Russia.

The growth in the quantity of paper-money in Poland was typical:

1 January	1919	5,267 million *marks*
1 March	1920	8,185 million *marks*
1 April	1920	11,000 million *marks*
31 May	1920	20,000 million *marks*
1 August	1920	28,000 million *marks*
20 September	1920	30,700 million *marks*

It is perfectly obvious that paper-money in Poland is heading for a catastrophe if the issues continue.

Besides Poland, the speed of paper-money growth is also catastrophic in Germany, Austria and Italy. In Italy at the beginning of the War, the paper-money in circulation reached 2.8 billion *lire*, but in November 1919 it was already 18 billion.

---

28. Silin 1913, p. 7.

The fall in the rate of paper-money can be judged by the rising price-level. It is true that the prices of products also rose during the War in terms of gold-currency, and this was especially striking in Sweden. Nevertheless, the figures given in the table below provide a clear idea of the growth of prices in connection with paper-issues.

If pre-war prices and the quantity of paper in circulation are taken as 100, then, in different months, the picture in different countries will be the following:

1919	Percentage-increase of paper	Percentage-rise in prices
United States (May)	173	181
England (August)	244	217
France (June)	365	293
Italy (April)	440	281
Switzerland (June)	230	250
Sweden (April)	275	336
Germany	875	1,000
Austria	3900	4,000

The following table gives an idea of the rise in prices by years:[29]

	England	France	United States	Sweden	Poland
July 1914	100	100	100	100	100
November 1918	233	237	249	320	–
January 1919	230	248	259	339	–
January 1920	236[29]	290	275	298	–
May 1920	374.2	–	–	–	4,000
1 August 1920	358	–	–	–	–

All of these figures are a real example for the ninth case that we looked at, when the issue of paper-money increases at the same time as production is curtailed and there is a decline of the commodity-fund in the market. But whereas the increase of circulating paper is easy to find in the corresponding information from the ministry of finance of one country or another, accurate information on the curtailment of production cannot be found for a single one of the bourgeois

---

29. According to the *Economist*, the figure for January 1920 is 334.7.

countries, and this is all the more true of the decline of the commodity-fund in the market. One could get an indirect idea of the extent of the decline of C only in countries where paper-money equivalent to gold-coin circulated before the wartime crisis and where the state did not increase the paper-circulation during the entire War. We would then have a constant M, and that would allow us indirectly to judge changes in C by changes in the value of M. Depreciation of the paper-currency would be a direct consequence of curtailment in the production and circulation of commodities.

Let us look more closely at the general characteristics of the ninth case.

When production falls, the quantity of commodity-values entering into the process of circulation falls, so that any new issue of paper-money is clearly not due to the needs of circulation; on the contrary, circulation requires a reduction of the existing quantity of paper-money, because this is the only possible way to stem a decline in its rate of exchange. Currency-issues result from the state's need to acquire necessary resources even at the expense of dislocating the state's entire monetary system. Since paper-money has no commodity-value – it can neither be eaten nor used as an instrument of production – the only rationale for increasing its issue is to use it for extracting from circulation the quantity of real values needed for the state, its employees, its workers and the army. The issue of paper-money is, therefore, a special form of tax imposed on society and collected without any tax-inspectors, militia or officers of the court. But this kind of tax has its own unique features, and without understanding them it is impossible to understand anything about the system of paper in a revolutionary period.

In order to get a clearer picture of the whole economic significance of paper-money issues in the current case and the progress of their depreciation, let us take our numerical example and subject it to the blows of industrial ruin, on the one hand, and increased issue of paper-money, on the other. Now, assume that our starting point is the first case, that is, in the process of circulation there are 40 billion in the commodity-market, and in the channels of monetary circulation there are 2 billion. For simplification, these 2 billion will consist entirely of paper, but it will be paper that is equivalent in purchasing power to gold-money. This can be portrayed as a diagram in the form of a rectangle where the white part portrays the commodity-circulation of 40 billion and the shaded area, 20 times smaller, the paper-money in the amount of 2 billion.

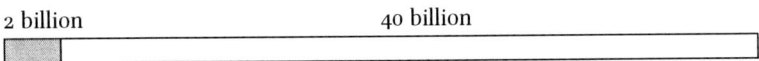

Now, let us suppose that the government issues 2 billion more in new paper and succeeds immediately in realising this sum, that is, in withdrawing from circulation the corresponding sum of commodities at the old, that is, the normal price (in the cases we are describing, this will never completely happen in practice, because the market very quickly responds to currency-issues with a rise in prices). For the purpose of simplification, let us also suppose for the moment that the sum of commodities in circulation remains the original 40 billion. Our diagram would then look different:

4 billion   38 billion
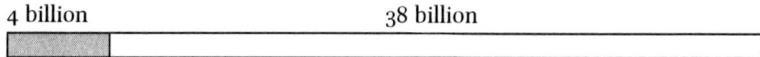

In other words, the issue of money in the amount of 2 billion, insofar as this sum is realised at full value in the market, takes out of circulation the sum of 2 billion in commodity-values. Consequently, the total paper-money grew, while the total commodity-values in circulation fell.

But this number must fall even further, because in the ninth case, which we are considering, we have a contraction of commodities due to yet another cause, and that is the dislocation in production. Let us represent this in figures as follows:

The paper-money is 4 billion, but the commodities in circulation are no longer 40 or even 38, but rather 30 billion.

How must all this be reflected in the falling exchange-rate of money?

The effect of a doubling in the amount of money is a halving of its exchange-rate. The effect of a decline of commodities in circulation by one-quarter is that the rate of money [must] fall even more. How far must the exchange-rate of the paper fall?

If there are 30 billion of commodities in circulation, then in order to maintain the full value of money, in accordance with the starting condition, only one-twentieth of this sum is required. Previously we had 40 / 20 = 2;[30] now we will have 30 / 20 = 1.5 billion.[31] But we already have 4 billion in circulation, which is 2.66 times larger. The rouble must fall in the same proportion. In other words, one full-valued rouble will equal 2.66 paper-roubles, or the paper-rouble will be worth about 37.6 *kopeks*.

This means that the next year begins with 30 billion worth of commodities in circulation, if they are priced in full-valued roubles. In terms of paper-roubles, these commodities will cost not 30 billion, but 30 × 2.66, that is, 79.8 billion. Suppose that in order to continue the War and all its other expenditures the government, in this next year, again needs 2 billion in taxes, which it cannot collect by normal means and must again extract by issuing paper. In order to withdraw from circulation values worth 2 billion in full-valued roubles, it must now issue not 2 billion, but rather 2 × 2.66 = 5.32 billion.

---

30. [40 billion in commodities was originally 20 times larger than the sum of money, which was 2 billion.]

31. [For the 30 billion in commodities to be 20 times larger than the money-supply, the latter must be 1.5 billion.]

Let us assume that this sum is issued, and by means of this 5.32 billion the commodity-values in circulation are cut by 2 billion. Suppose also that the disintegration of industry continues, that merchants begin to conceal commodities in order to avoid converting them into money whose exchange-rate is continuously falling, and that the volume of commodities in circulation contracts. Of the 30 billion, 2 billion are withdrawn through the government's paper-money, and let another 8 billion be withdrawn from circulation for the reasons just mentioned. At the end of the second year, we will then have circulating paper in the amount of 9.32 billion and commodities (in full-valued roubles) worth 20 billion. In these circumstances, with circulation requiring, as before, only one-twentieth, in this case 1 billion, we now have 9.32 billion. And this will mean that the paper-rouble will be worth approximately 10.7 *kopeks*.[32]

The third year begins, therefore, with the following situation. Paper in circulation comes to 9.32 billion, commodities in terms of full-valued roubles are 20 billion, but in paper-currency these twenty billion already cost 20 × 9.32 = 186.4 billion.

Suppose the government, as before, requires the issue of paper-money to acquire new revenues. In order to swindle out of circulation commodity-values in the amount of 2 billion in terms of full-valued roubles, that is, one-tenth of the entire commodity-circulation, it must issue paper to the amount of one-tenth of all the paper-money in circulation, that is, 186.4[33] / 10 = 18.64 billion. Assume that the government in the third year issues paper in this amount. Assume, further, that the total of commodity-values being withdrawn from circulation falls as a result of the dislocation of production from eight to three, that is, in this respect, there is a certain improvement. At the end of the year we will then have paper in circulation amounting to 18.64 + 9.32 = 27.96 billion and commodity-values in full-valued roubles of 15 billion. For the turnover of these 15 billion in circulation we require 15 / 20 billion full-valued roubles, or 750 million. We have in circulation 27.96 billion, that is, 27.96 × 20 / 15 times more, or approximately 37 times more than we need.

The rate of the rouble will be 2.7 *kopeks*.

Let us consider this further. From the theoretical analysis that we have given, we can see, even though we have used arbitrarily selected examples, all the main

---

32. As I have already indicated, with a panicky fall in the exchange-rate, this depreciation may go even further, or it may, on the contrary, slow down somewhat. For example, it is a fact beyond any doubt that our peasantry, who in the first years of the War accumulated money in the expectation that it would appreciate [that commodity-prices would revert to 'normal' levels], have now lost billions of roubles on this account even as they helped to slow the rate of depreciation.

33. [Preobrazhensky made an error here, giving the figure as 184.4 rather than 186.4. The appropriate corrections have been made for the following calculations.]

features of the entire mechanism involved in the depreciation of paper-currency, together with the main causes of that depreciation. Without encumbering matters with a further exposition of numerical examples, we can now already get a clear idea of how the process that has begun will continue in future. In this regard, there are a few possibilities that we must further consider.

1) If the issue of paper continues into the future, while the commodity-fund in circulation also continuously contracts, then the value of the paper-rouble will fall to zero. This could happen in a socialist society if it succeeded in rapidly taking control of the whole of commodity-exchange.

This could also happen in a unique way in bourgeois society, if money, having depreciated to the extreme, is simply driven out of circulation through the development of direct commodity-exchange and through the return to circulation of gold that was hidden away for bad times. This latter case can be studied in the history of the *assignats* of the Great French Revolution, when in 1796, with forty-four billion in circulation and after seven years of existence, the *assignats* began to be boycotted in the commodity-market and all paper-values turned out to be equal in value to the paper they were printed on.

2) After a more or less prolonged shock, bourgeois society begins once more to recover and, above all, let us suppose that the process of disintegration in production halts and then production begins to expand, which leads, at some fine moment, to circumstances in which C, having fallen, in our example, to 15 billion, now begins to increase. On the other hand, the bourgeois state, having freed itself of the extraordinary expenditures resulting from war, revolution, and so on, and having reinforced its power, is in a position to acquire taxes in the normal way without recourse to the issue of paper. Furthermore, under pressure from commercial-industrial circles, it makes desperate efforts to free the monetary circulation of its paper-ballast and begins to take paper out of circulation, buying it up with metal and then burning it. In these conditions, there begins in the sphere of money-circulation a movement that is the reverse of the one that led to 15 billion C, to 27.96 billion of paper-circulation, and to the fall of the rouble exchange-rate to 2.7 *kopeks*.

This reverse movement can continue to the point where equilibrium will be established between C and M, and the remaining paper-money in circulation will, again, become full-valued money. This case basically characterises (despite significant variations in the way the exchange-rate is raised) the money-circulation of bourgeois countries that are successfully surviving the crises in production and circulation.

3) The process of disintegration in industry comes to a halt, but the government has no intention of stopping the issue of paper-money. It prefers to take commodities from circulation, as long as it can do so without being troubled by

the most extreme increase in the issue of paper-money. In this case, we will witness the disappearance of the entire paper-money system of circulation. Such a situation characterises the transitional period from capitalism to communism. Then the greatest theoretical, and especially practical, interest will attach to the question of how long the agony of the paper-money circulation can go on. I suggest that it is clear for the reader that the most typical example of the situation we are describing is the paper-money circulation of the Soviet Republic in Russia. Below, we will discuss our paper-money circulation in more detail, with figures in hand and taking into account all the real circumstances that we cannot dwell upon in this general section. Here, we are interested only in the general features of the case under review, features that every country will encounter when entering the epoch of proletarian dictatorship and inheriting from the bourgeois period the apparatus of a paper-money circulation that is overburdened with paper from the time when management was in the hands of capitalist governments.

III

Paper-money after the proletarian revolution

First of all, it is perfectly clear that a class can only move towards destruction of the entire paper-money system of circulation if it is in power with a government that is assured of a different way of acquiring incomes on the basis of a completely different form of social distribution. If the health and strength of bourgeois society depend upon increasing the size of C, and if this increase of C is the thermometer that determines the healthy growth of such a society, then, for the transitional epoch from capitalism to communism, the thermometer that determines the success of the new society is the increase of a different magnitude, that of P, or the quantity of products[34] (and not commodities) that pass through the distributive organs of the socialist state.

The increase of P at the expense of C, the struggle of P with C, is the struggle of socialist distribution with the anarchic disorder of the market, which in Russian terms can be seen as the struggle of the *Komprod* with the Sukharevsky.[35] The more products that come into the hands of the proletarian state as a result of more and more nationalisation of enterprises and increased production in

---

34. [The reader will note that a 'product' is *distributed* for use, not *sold* for profit at market-determined prices.]
35. [The struggle of the People's Commissariat of Food (*Narkomprod*) with the open-air Sukharevsky market in Moscow.]

them, and also as a result of the successes of food-organs in acquiring supplies through a system of natural taxes on the peasantry, the more P will grow and the smaller will be the volume of C entering the free market. This leads to a whole series of conclusions that have enormous practical importance for the financial policy of the proletarian state, on the one hand, and for explaining a number of phenomena in the sphere of paper-money circulation, on the other.

In the first place, it is perfectly clear that growth of P at the expense of C must lead to an extremely rapid fall in the rate of paper-money, even if issues of paper by the state were to come to a halt. All of the billions in paper already issued, with the exception of a small portion received by the state in payment[36] for products at fixed prices, are being channelled into C, where they float with increasing difficulty on the drying swamps of the free market.

Secondly, the converse is also perfectly clear, namely, that the persistence and even expansion of petty commodity-production in countries with a proletarian régime delays a rapid decline in the sum of C. A situation is conceivable in which the systematic increase of P at the expense of C, or of systematic deductions from C, will only be equal to, or even less than, the growth of C on the basis of re-emerging petty production and its temporary expansion. In such conditions, a fall in the rate of paper-money will only occur under the influences of new issues, that is, we will have the seventh case mentioned above, albeit in a completely different situation.

Finally, we can also draw a third conclusion that might appear absurd, even though it is theoretically quite sound. If the socialist economy coexists over a long period with the petty-bourgeois economy, and if the free market is retained for a long time, then, for a significant part of the time in which the free market exists – if not for the whole time – the socialist state will have an opportunity to acquire a portion of the products of petty-bourgeois production through issues of paper that, each year, will add one or more zeros to their nominal value. That which costs one rouble today will cost ten the following year, then a hundred, then a thousand, and so on. If the printing press works well, then there is nothing to stop the government from adding zeros. Instead of 10 roubles, the paper can be printed as 10 million, and these 10 million can be exchanged for a pound of onions or a pair of boot-laces on the free market. This is no cause for alarm if workers' wages are four-fifths naturalised and the remaining fifth is adjusted so that rising pay-rates take into account the rate of paper. This prospect might horrify ordinary people, who still cannot forget the time when ten roubles would

---

36. The longer such payment continues, the more fictitious it must become, especially in connection with successes in the area of naturalising wages and the moneyless use of social enterprises such as trams, railways, the postal service, and so on.

buy ten pounds of flour or a pair of boots; it might distress people who live on money they have hidden away, or who are waiting for a rise in the rate on the paper that they are accumulating from day to day. But there is nothing terrible, here, for the socialist state, if it has a clear idea of the country's economy as a whole and is not subject to panic over the rise in prices. A fall in the value of money, given stability on the part of C, can be seen as a product of the state's own production, so to speak. The state can calculate more-or-less accurately the fall in the exchange-rate for each successive year, and then adjust its issuing apparatus accordingly. It must also adjust wage-rates with the aim of ensuring that the worker has enough money to acquire in the free market those products that remain in short supply until the full naturalisation of wages occurs.

There is only one prospect that might be dangerous to the Soviet state in the period of paper-money circulation, and that is that the crash of the entire system might occur not just before C disappears, but also before the volume of P in state-hands is adequate for naturalisation of the minimum-wage of workers. The fact that the *assignats* of the Great French Revolution ended up being used as rather poor wallpaper demonstrates that a boycott of paper on the free market may occur even before the market is itself prepared to wither away. But at what point does the crash occur? Does it come at some specific stage in the depreciation of paper-money, or is it affected by other factors? The collapse of the *assignat*-system began when the real purchasing power of *aasignats* fell to one five-hundredth of what it was originally. There has not yet been a collapse of the paper issued by Russia's Soviet government, even though the rate of paper has fallen (by November 1920) to approximately one five-thousandth. From this, we can apparently conclude that a boycott of paper by the market is not connected with the quantity of money that has been issued and its level of depreciation. In a country where a new cycle of bourgeois development has begun on the basis of ground cleared by a revolution, paper-money circulation has proven to be less stable than in one where the preconditions for any kind of bourgeois development have been eliminated and where, in particular, it is a matter of eliminating not just paper-money, but any kind of money-system whatever.

What does this mean?

We have now come to a very complex question that apparently cannot be resolved in the same way for the money-circulation of a bourgeois society as for a society in the transitional epoch from capitalism to communism.

The development of France's productive forces after the Revolution could only occur on the basis of capitalist relations. The economy, shaken by revolution and revolutionary wars and now facing a new cycle of development that presupposed a free market, could not become stabilised without a means of circulation with a stable value. Attempts to preserve some kind of stable unit in circulation became evident even before the collapse of the *assignats*, when the royal[37] (in our case, substitute tsarist) paper-currency managed to achieve a certain stabilisation and even appreciated in relation to the Convention's *assignats*. When the Revolution ended and the government of the Directorate, rather than initiating a withdrawal of paper from circulation, undertook colossal new issues, France's commodity-circulation responded with a boycott of the paper-rubbish, and the gold that had been hidden away during the Terror began to circulate once more. The collapse of France's paper-system occurred because there was no correspondence between the requirements of a new bourgeois cycle of development and a paper-system that had not adapted to the needs of the economy, but lagged behind it and stood in its way.

In Soviet Russia, where a significant and growing volume of products passes through the organs of socialist distribution, and where P is growing at the expense of C, that is, at the expense of the free market, it would seem that collapse of the paper-currency must come much sooner than in France. This would seem all the more true if we recall that in France, the *assignats* had real backing in the form of lands confiscated from the aristocracy and the Church, and they could be used to purchase a certain amount of land from the land-fund of the Republic. But, in fact, our paper-money circulation dates from the very beginning of the War, and a partial boycott of money can only be seen in certain outlying parts of the country, for example, in certain regions of the Ukrainian countryside. How do we explain the stability of our paper-money system when it has already been squeezed like a lemon?

It would be reckless to try to respond to this question with some kind of categorical answer.

The best place to look for an explanation, in this regard, is in the chief and fundamental difference between the bourgeois economic system and the system of socialist reconstruction. For the normal development of a commodity-capitalist economy, liquidation of means of circulation that have no stable rate is the prime condition for any forwards movement. A fall in the rate for money brings losses

---

37. The portrait of the King appeared on the *assignats* that were issued before the Republic was declared. After the Revolution, there was an ever-increasing issue of Republican *assignats*, and the royal *assignats*, since their number had not been increasing, enjoyed a privileged position and began to be quoted with a fifteen percent premium over Republican notes. The royal *assignats* were withdrawn from circulation, for the most part, by the financial decrees of the Convention. It would be naïve to think that the royal *assignats* had greater value, or that our 'tsarist' or Kerenskyite notes today have greater value because those who hold them hoped, or are now hoping, for a return of the old régime. The reason for a rising rate on the part of the more 'scarce' series of paper is not political, but economic. It is enough to recall that the first issues of Soviet money (for example, the yellow thousand-rouble note) still enjoy a higher rate in Ukraine.

and systematic ruin to thousands of commodity-producers and merchants, and for an enormous number of people it makes involvement in speculation more profitable than production. For a commodity-economy, either a rising rate of paper-money by any means possible, or else a boycott and expulsion from circulation, is urgently necessary.

On the contrary, for a society building socialism, the condition for its existence and a vital requirement in the sphere of distribution is not to raise the rate of paper-money, but to increase P at the expense of C. If the volume of products passing through the organs of socialist distribution is already large and growing, then to ensure the whole development of production, especially in its leading sector of nationalised enterprises, the growth of P is incomparably more important than any increase in the purchasing power of paper or the stability of its rate of exchange. For the commodity-economy that exists alongside socialist enterprises, the stability of the rate of paper-money is of primary importance, and the peasantry and handicraftsmen grasp for tsarist and Kerenskyite money, and so on, in order to have a somewhat stable unit for circulation – however, it is not the petty-bourgeois economy that makes the music of the transition-period, and it is not the petty undertaking that determines the fate of the entire society, including its future and the development of its productive forces as a whole.

But the growth of P at the expense of C is one of the most important of all the causes of paper's depreciation, and currency-issues will increasingly become only a secondary resource of the socialist state until it has secured for itself a sufficient volume of P for the naturalisation of workers' wages. *As a rule*, a bourgeois economy cannot bear the prolonged existence in circulation of paper that is depreciated and continuing to depreciate. But a socialist society under construction cannot bear a contraction of P, whereas it can patiently endure a fall in the rate of paper over a very long time. In this respect, it has stronger nerves than a bourgeois economic system does.

It seems to me that we must look for a second explanation, a more concrete one, in the difference between the surplus-products in the hands of the small peasant and handicraft-economy and the quantity that the state takes from circulation through issuing new paper. If these issues draw off only the surplus or a part of it, then no-matter how far the rate falls on paper, the real economic basis for possible further issues remains, because there is still the possibility of further reductions in commodity-circulation without destroying petty production itself, so long as the amounts withdrawn from it affect only the consumable surplus.

From what we have said, it is clear that the slow withering away of our paper-rouble is connected with the economic peculiarities of Russia. In countries of the West, when they become countries of proletarian dictatorship, paper-money might die out sooner, because they do not have the same widespread petty-bourgeois market that has prolonged and delayed the spontaneous liquidation of paper-money in Russia.

None of this means, of course, that paper can remain in circulation right up to the complete elimination of C. In every particular country that is entering upon the road of proletarian dictatorship, there may be a number of other causes, depending on economic conditions as a whole, that will lead to an earlier collapse of the paper-money system. It suffices for us to establish here that our experience with the stability of paper-money circulation during Soviet Russia's first years of existence can be quite satisfactorily explained on the basis of the general theoretical considerations given above.

There is one further conclusion, on the basis of the foregoing reasoning, that warrants consideration, because it arises of its own accord. Once the proletarian state has control over the lever of money's depreciation, once it understands the laws of paper-money circulation better than visitors to the Sukharevsky do, and once it can anticipate the consequences of its measures, can it not, then, consciously regulate both money-circulation and the price-level according to a definite plan?

As is known, every attempt of that sort on the part of bourgeois governments has inevitably ended in collapse; and in conditions where issues of paper continue and the economy is dislocated, all fixed prices have inevitably vanished into thin air. All withdrawals of commodities from circulation, and all taxes in the form of paper-issues, took place randomly, without the slightest confidence as to what quantity of real values would be acquired from the market or how far the rate must fall on the basis of the amount of paper already issued. In this respect, the proletarian state finds itself in better circumstances than any bourgeois state could do. The primary task of a bourgeois government, which, in difficult moments, has committed the sin of extraordinary paper-issues, is one of liquidating as quickly as possible the flow of paper and ensuring the appearance on the market of means of circulation in the form of real value, of gold, which alone is capable of providing an unorganised and mindless society with stability in commodity-circulation and of appropriately sorting out the claim that every commodity makes for a corresponding amount of some other commodity. A proletarian state, on the contrary, is an organised and conscious economic force. This state knows the laws both of the society it is replacing and of the remaining fragments that are tangled about its feet. To put the squeeze on petty-bourgeois spontaneity, to seize it with the apparatus of paper-money circulation and to subordinate this circulation to itself and to its own goals – this task is by no means beyond the reach of the proletarian dictatorship. The more firmly proletarian power stands on its own feet, the more products pass through its organs of distribution, the greater are the opportunities for it to manoeuvre freely and the easier it is for it to drive the free market and the free producer into a blind alley.

How is this to be done?

Consider, first, the matter of fixed prices. Clearly, it makes no sense to dream of establishing fixed prices when the issue of paper, and thus the major cause of their further decline, is continuing. Fixed prices can only be established if the government accepts as a basis the prices already established in the market, ends paper-issues, and begins to restore equilibrium to the process by withdrawing from circulation a corresponding quantity of paper that is proportional to the deductions from C that are occurring due to the disorder in production. But that kind of operation, while it may be very desirable for petty-bourgeois commodity-producers, brings no benefit to the proletarian state, which has no reason to play the part of a guardian or a kind mamma in protecting kulaks or would-be kulaks – with the exception, perhaps, of the theoretically-conceivable case when such a measure becomes temporarily acceptable as one of the transitional steps in the direction of purely socialist distribution. To be precise, this case may occur if P is close to ensuring the naturalisation of wages, but the cost of maintaining the apparatuses of state-distribution of products of secondary importance – those produced by the small-scale economy – outweighs the cost of the operation just mentioned. Here, we must only make the point that the establishment and maintenance of stable prices, on the basis of a scientifically grounded financial-economic policy, is fully possible for a sufficiently strong proletarian power, provided that support for the rate of paper is not made dependent solely on obligatory decrees written on paper.

But during the early period of a proletarian state's existence, an end to issues of paper-money is not only of no benefit, but is objectively impossible. The organs of distribution can only gradually acquire a sufficient volume of products, not to mention the fact that these organs are themselves being created virtually out of nothing and are conducting a totally novel kind of work for which capitalism has left no guidelines to the working class.

The author of these lines does not have the slightest doubt that the proletariat, in every country where it follows the workers of Russia and conquers power, will have to put the printing press into operation. If it is true that in the socialist revolution the proletariat retains some of the stones of capitalism's economic system – but not one of them unturned – as comrade Bukharin has convincingly demonstrated in his excellent book *Ekonomika perekhodnovo perioda*,[38] the one fortunate exception, at least for a certain period, is the circulation of paper-money.

---

38. ['The Economics of the Transition Period'.]

The system of issuing paper at a difficult moment, the apparatus for such issues, and the possibility of using them to extract a certain quantity of commodity-values from circulation – the victorious proletariat inherits all of this intact from the bourgeois régime. And to the extent that the proletariat will need to put the printing press into operation, it also has an interest in ensuring that the issue of paper not occur in a state of chaos, that the pace of decline in the exchange-rate be taken into account, that the depreciation of paper-money be coordinated with the wage-rate either prior to, or at the same time as currency-issues, and that there be at least an approximate understanding of how long the printing press can be used and of the time-limits imposed by objective conditions for replacement of this kind of taxation with the work of socialist organs of distribution. The experience of paper-money circulation in Soviet Russia is extremely instructive for the proletarian régimes of all countries that will put an end to bourgeois power and be compelled, for a certain period, to support their own existence by robbing the commodity-market through issuing new billions in paper-money.

In the matter of regulating prices, the proletarian power has the following possibilities. The prices that the victorious proletariat will find established on the free market can be taken as the basis for fixed prices. It can maintain these fixed prices for the portion of the product-turnover that occurs through its own organs of distribution. These prices soon become detached from market-prices, and will diverge from them all the more rapidly the longer the mass issues of new paper-money continue. The only sense in maintaining these fixed prices is that they differentiate between the values of products within P. For example, shoes are five to seven times more expensive than a pound of flour, a pound of flour is a hundred times more expensive than a sheet of paper, and so on. The value of a pound of flour within P becomes completely detached from its price on the free market, and any attempt to hold the prices of C subordinate to tables of fixed state-prices is completely futile. There is no need to verify this futility in practice, because it is established with irrefutable clarity by incontestable theoretical analysis. It would only be possible to regulate free-market prices by establishing a moving table of prices based on an approximate calculation of C and on the state's completely accurate knowledge of the quantity of paper-money that has been put into circulation.[39] Consider an example. Assume that the following market-prices have been established as a result of a long series of paper-issues by the state: 100 roubles for a pound of flour, 25 roubles for a pound of butter, 500 roubles for boots, and so on. Over a certain period, the state has to

---

39. It is difficult, of course, to calculate how much paper-money issued by other states is circulating within the country, but this sum cannot be particularly large.

issue several billions in paper. In order for the state, rather than the market, to establish future prices, immediately following the issue of a new series of paper, the state must itself raise all prices in a proportion that corresponds to the effect of the new issues. Then the price-schedules established by the state will not be merely a product of fantasy, but will be based on a calculation of the real relationship between C and M. Given the existence of a stable authority and the corresponding organs of repression, these prices will be sustainable until the next issue of paper, because they will be consciously introduced into the market at the same relative levels as would have been established spontaneously if the market had been master of its own fate. With succeeding issues, the state must proceed in the same way.

Only this kind of price-scheduling, in which commodity-prices in terms of paper are established on the basis of the relation between C and M, and where the state does not dictate prices, but prescribes them according to the dictates of the laws of the circulation of money – only this kind of scheduling is really achievable.

But why is it necessary?

That is already a different question. The main conclusion it would lead to is that, with prices leaping upwards over certain periods by anticipated amounts, even if these amounts can only be determined a year or six months in advance, it would be possible to create a proper schedule for rises in wage-rates. Instead of leaving workers to be eaten up by the free market, enduring continuous raids on their wages by speculators and peasants, and instead of wage-rates *following prices* with no hope of overtaking them and with worker-masses always being the losers, with the system of a moving price-schedule it would be possible to implement a moving schedule of wage-rates in such a way that prices would, essentially, be chasing after wages. Of course, one must not overestimate the benefits of realising such measures, and it would be senseless to dream of saving the workers from malnutrition in this way. It is only possible to protect the workers from exploitation by petty producers within rather narrow limits, because no price-schedule and no schedule of wage-rates can safeguard society against the fundamental evil of the transition-period, the reduction in consumption. If a country has 50 million consumers, but the annual volume of consumer-products at its disposal falls from the normal amount of 1 billion pounds to just 750 million, that is, 25 percent less, then no schedules of wage-rates and prices will save it from the inevitable malnutrition. Indeed, the depreciation of paper-money, or the decline of its purchasing power, depends not only on the quantity of M in circulation, as we have seen above, but also on the reduction of C under the impact of general ruin. If we regard rising prices from the point of view of the social distribution of products, then, in the final analysis, this rise is an instrument for curtailing consumption, either by certain strata of society or by society as a whole. Under the domination of market-spontaneity, this reduced consumption will fall primarily upon workers and state-employees. The task of the proletarian authority is to curtail consumption *for the whole of society*, and particularly for the parasitic classes. If the country is condemned to undernourishment to the extent of 25 percent, it is imperative that this undernourishment be distributed equally between workers and peasants and that it fall most heavily on the parasitic classes. With the system of a moving price-schedule and moving wage-rates, it may not be possible to achieve this equality in hunger, but at least distribution will tend in this direction under the influence of a deliberately conducted state-policy.

The system of a moving price-schedule may be useful to a proletarian state in those countries where, at the moment of the transfer of power to the working class, the monetary circulation will not yet be completely disorganised by previous paper-issues on the part of the bourgeois government (for instance, in the case of a revolution today in England, or, to some extent, in France). On the contrary, for the proletariat of more ruined countries, where the rate of exchange on paper is low to begin with, it might be more expedient to undertake an enormous issue of paper-money at the outset, to buy up everything possible on the free market (of course, this refers to everything that cannot be confiscated) and thereby, so to speak, to skim the cream from commodity-circulation before the stupefied market has the chance to cry 'thief' through a sharp leap in prices. To schedule prices, in those circumstances, would merely mean helping the free market to partially beat off the government's attack on its commodity-fund. Experience demonstrates that if the issue of paper continues over a long period, then the market, through its price-increases, will not only keep pace with issues, but will often even outstrip them and establish prices that represent a credit to itself because they are appropriate to a different proportion of M to C. On the contrary, when issues of paper are just beginning, the market is often so inflexible that prices are lower than would be appropriate to the quantity of paper; and the paper, instead of being spent as quickly as possible, is still being widely accumulated by different strata of people who have yet to learn through bitter experience the political economy of the 'transition-period'. In these cases, the proletariat has the opportunity essentially to rob the free market of its commodity-resources.

Once the terrorised market bestirs itself sufficiently, and through price-increases even rushes beyond what is warranted by the relation between C and M, then it makes sense for the workers' government either systematically to rein it in, or else to join the race against it. The first possibility would be realised through a moving price-schedule, the second by establishing wage-rates such that prices would be chasing wages, rather than wages chasing prices. It would hardly be possible to accomplish this completely, and such experiments (successful experiments) have yet to occur. But it is possible to set such a goal, and the proletarian state can, without doubt, consciously pursue at least a certain tendency in this direction. The least acceptable option is to leave everything to the will of market-spontaneity and not to turn knowledge of the market's own laws against that spontaneity. In any case, it is not at all difficult to construct a theoretical case in which wage-rates will determine prices, rather than the reverse. Imagine a country where workers' wages, after the proletariat seizes power, are only half-naturalised and the working class must acquire the other half from the free market, relying upon the purchasing power of paper-money. Let the two components of wages, expressed in gold-roubles, be 360 million plus 360 million, for a total of 720 million roubles a year. The worker will receive the first half of his wages without any difficulty from the state through its organs of distribution. But with the second half, an inevitable ordeal will begin. Suppose that the rouble has fallen by 100 times, so that in order to acquire products from the free market worth 360 million in gold, the workers must be given wages in the form of paper amounting to 36 billion a year. But these 36 billion will not spare the workers from ordeals and ruination, because prices, in the conditions that we have described, will continue to rise without interruption. It is necessary to establish, therefore, a graph of the increase in prices when commodities worth 30[40] million in gold are extracted on a monthly basis from the free market. Assume that our calculations lead us to conclude that prices must rise, on average, by 50 percent a month. In these conditions, it will already be necessary by the second month to pay the workers 4.5 billion in paper-money, rather than 3 billion, in order for them to acquire products worth 30 million in gold. In the following month, it will again be necessary to increase the payment by 50 percent, and so on. But that is not all. If the rouble falls by six times in the course of the year, that fall will not occur evenly over time. It will be necessary to take into account the different rates of decline in different parts of the year. All of the calculations will inevitably be approximate. But the only important thing is that the purchasing power of the total monetary portion of the wage is sufficient to guarantee, on average, that the workers can take from the free market a sum of values equal, when converted into gold, to 30 million full-valued roubles. That will mean increasing the wage-rates on a monthly basis; whether twice a month or once every two months is a purely technical question, but it is also extremely important in practical terms.

---

40. [The text gives the figure 36 billion, but 30 billion × 12 (months) yields the 360 billion in values.]

Of course, this theoretically conceivable example of wage-rates being adjusted to prices on the basis of a prior calculation of the rise in prices will only avoid becoming a utopian fantasy if the scale of the petty-bourgeois economy and the capacity of the free market are such as to permit systematic withdrawals in the proportions described. In other words, the case described here is only possible, generally speaking, if surplus-products worth 30 million in gold each month could be taken from the petty producer by way, for example, of direct natural taxes in the same amount. If this is not economically possible, then wage-schedules will never keep up with prices, and this will be the form in which the social necessity of curtailing consumption for the entire working class will become apparent in the transitional period.

IV

Paper-money as a form of taxation

In the normal circumstances of commodity-exchange in a capitalist society, money replaces the commodity and then, in turn, is replaced by another commodity. This is what happens when the seller is also a buyer, which is usually the case. The owner of money can buy the commodity because, at the other end, he sold something himself, and the money documents that sale. This is the case with metallic money. However, due to the issue of paper-money, a certain quantity of values is withdrawn from circulation without new commodity-values entering into the sphere of the commodity-turnover. The money enters into circulation, and the commodities are taken out of circulation. Leaving aside the case where paper-money is issued in a limited amount solely to serve an already expanded commodity-circulation,[41] the issue of paper by the state is designed to take commodities out of circulation without replacing them. But these operations of buying without selling can only continue because, in the majority of cases in the market, buying and selling nevertheless occur simultaneously. When it is a question of the free market in the period of proletarian dictatorship, the simultaneous sellers and buyers are, above all, the peasantry, followed by the artisans and handicraftsmen who own small enterprises that have not been nationalised, and finally, the owners of all kinds of property that was created before the Revolution and is now put up for exchange. True, the state itself can be a seller, insofar as it sells part of the products from its nationalised enterprises to the peasants. But these sales involve far smaller sums than the issues of

---

41. This is the typical position for capitalist society in the normal conditions of its existence.

paper-money. The result is that if the state issues 10 billion in paper, while selling commodities worth 1 billion to the peasants, the financial-economic effect is the same as if the state issued 9 billion in paper. So long as buying and selling occur between commodity-producers in the market on the basis of paper-money, the new series of paper-money that are entering into circulation from the state printing press do not have inscribed upon them that they are not matched by commodities correspondingly returning to the market. This new money is simply added to that previously in circulation, as if they were equal comrades sharing the same destiny. The whole affair can be visualised as one in which the state intervenes in commodity-exchange between the handicraftsman, the peasant and the owners of one kind or another of real values, injects its paper-poison into the channels of circulation, and, without bringing any commodity-values to the market, leaves the market taking commodity-values with it. Accordingly, from the viewpoint of the entire class of petty commodity-producers, who are coexisting with the proletarian state, the issue of paper-money by the proletarian state is always disadvantageous, always entails a deduction from the real commodity-fund of the small-scale economy, and is always a tax on petty independent production.[42]

Conversely, the matter must appear quite differently if we look at the entire process of production and distribution in the transitional epoch as a whole. The producers of real values are not simply the peasants and handicraftsmen, but also the workers in nationalised enterprises. During the transitional period, the workers of socialist enterprises are not so much involved in producing for mass consumption, as in restoring the very foundations of the economy: the instruments of production, transportation, the preparation of materials, and capital construction-projects whose full benefit only comes after several years. This reconstruction of the economy on the basis of new principles is of paramount importance for the entire society, and the whole future of the country depends upon successes in this area. The producers in this part of the economic organism must receive the necessary amount of consumer-products. If the state is only in a position to provide its workers with a part of their wages in kind, then they must acquire the other part in the free market. But if they are compelled to undertake this difficult and unpleasant operation on their own, the workers will be transformed from being the collectors of the tax in kind into those who are paying it, insofar as they cannot acquire on the market the necessary-minimum means of existence.

---

42. Provided that this tax is not replaced by an even-heavier direct tax in kind, which is even less advantageous for the petty producer.

Let us consider in more detail, therefore, how this kind of tax is shared between the different classes of society in the epoch of the dictatorship of the proletariat.

We will begin with those same workers in the nationalised enterprises. This is the most helpless group in society when it comes to the struggle that different classes wage against each other to avoid paying taxes. The product of the workers in the nationalised factories passes into the hands of the state. They have no possibility of selling what they produce as commodities or of raising their prices to the same level as prices must rise generally because of the issue into circulation of new masses of paper-money.[43] The workers continue to receive a wage, determined according to the schedule; or else they get an increase in the schedule, but it is inevitably lower than the price-level, so long as the schedule, as has been the case thus far in Soviet Russia, does not adjust to the new paper-issues. Going to the marketplace, the worker's wife can only curse and scold the peasant or the dairy-woman for the increase of prices, but she has no real way of restraining them if all she has in her hands is state paper-money. And when we see, every day in our markets, the figure of the suburban peasant, sitting on a cart of potatoes and, with Olympian calmness, calling out the price of the produce, while all about there is an agitated group of urban working women who are cursing the village-bandits while still buying at the announced 'village'-price, then what we have before us in full view is the relation of forces between the peasant and the worker. The peasant tries to dump his share of the taxes, which he incurs as a result of the issue of paper-money, onto the worker. The worker is powerless to avoid both his own share and the share that others pile upon him, by loading them onto someone else. The result is that the issue of paper-money, this special form of tax, has a tendency to fall mainly and in the greatest measure precisely on wages. The employees of state-institutions find themselves in exactly the same position as the workers of nationalised enterprises. For a very long time, ever since the second year of the World-War, there have been stories across Europe about the ruination of the middle-intelligentsia, the officials, and the office-workers. The greatest outcries about such ruination have come from Germany, where office-workers and officials were the first strata of society to be forced to begin curtailing their consumption and then to sell-off, to the benefit of the villages, the possessions they had accumulated in better times. The rise of prices on the free market, given the old rates paid to office-employees and officials, hit this group the worst of all because all the other strata of society knew how to avoid cutting consumption, at least during the early months. In view of

---

43. Strictly speaking, one should say '... to which prices must rise insofar as they are expressed in terms of depreciated paper-money'.

the enormous mobilisations and the elimination of the industrial reserve-army, unskilled workers were able to achieve a rise in wages. As for workers in the defence-sector, in all the belligerent countries they received higher wage-rates. But if you take the current position of workers and rank-and-file office-employees in Soviet Russia, it turns out that the latter, even more than the workers, have no way of resisting the 'tax' on their incomes. And this is not to mention the fact that workers with the highest priority in food-distribution, who are consequently somewhat less dependent on the free market, still retain, in numerous enterprises, the right to a premium in the form of a certain portion of the product that comes from their own enterprises. Thus, bakers in Moscow receive, in addition to their normal ration, several pounds of bread a day; the workers in perfumeries receive soap; the tobacco-workers get tobacco and cigarettes, and so on. The result is that a part of the workers are protected against price-increases by the rising prices on these products that they receive in excess of the norms, which they then exchange for the things they need on the free market. Office-employees have no such possibility; all they can do is resort to fair means or foul in order to increase their cash-resources through combining jobs, holding fictitious positions, accepting bribes, and so on.

The independent craftsmen and artisans of various sorts are in a different position insofar as they have no obligation to hand over the products of their labour to the state at fixed prices. They respond to the issue of paper-money with a corresponding rise in the prices of their products. If a tailor previously received 10 roubles for a coat, when prices rise by 100 times he gets 1,000 for this work; if they rise [again] by 1,000 times, he gets 10,000 for the coat, and so on. The same happens with the shoemaker, the maker of felt-boots, the metal-craftsman who repairs the peasants' equipment, and the representatives of tens of professions in small-scale handicraft-production. By raising prices above the level fixed by the state, they protect themselves against any reduction in their incomes.

They pursue the same end by their attempt to stick to the barter-exchange of commodities while boycotting the depreciating state-money. In any event, when the small craftsman begins to play with the peasant in contributing to the inflation of prices, he certainly is not helpless upon entering the struggle. In some districts and at certain moments, the peasant may turn out to be stronger, and this can be established through analysing the relationship between free-market prices for the products of agriculture and those of handicraft-industry. In other districts and at other moments, the outcome can be the opposite: in the contest between the handicraftsman and the peasant to evade a portion of the tax caused by the issue of money, the third parties who turn out to suffer the most are the urban worker and office-employee. At the cost of reducing the consumption of this group, the peasants and craftsmen (in the grain-producing provinces, for example) either maintain their consumption at the former level, or even consume more.

As for the peasantry – the most numerous class of the Soviet Republic – who still create the greater part of all the values produced in the country, their position in the struggle to evade the kind of tax we are considering is very strong. We will not speak, here, of the grain-monopoly, of the compulsory seizure of other products by *Narkomprod*, or of labour-conscription. Those issues will come later. For now, we will discuss only prices within the limits of the free market.

The peasantry has monopolistic ownership of almost all the food-products produced in the country. Whereas in a period of normal operation in the commodity-economy, products exchange, as a rule, according to their labour-value – that is, in accordance with the quantity of socially-necessary labour expended in their production – and deviations depend upon changes in supply and demand for one product or another, in a period when the whole of industrial activity is in disarray, it is precisely in the sphere of supply and demand that the important changes occur. A man can postpone the acquisition of material for a new suit of clothes as well as the acquisition of a whole range of other products that have no direct relation to satisfying the sensation of hunger. But it is a difficult matter to wait for one's dinner, and the demand for food-products inevitably relegates to secondary importance the demand for other products of consumption.

In a period of general economic disarray, together with a decline of the sown acreage and deterioration in the methods of land-cultivation, the peasant is in a privileged position with his products in the free market. The result is that the peasantry dictate their own prices, and the price-increase for grain, the most important product of the village, becomes the basis for all other prices in general. After accumulating an adequate supply of cash 'for any eventuality', the peasant either attempts to revert directly to barter, or else he sells his products only for such a sum of paper-money as will enable him to acquire real values in the free market. And since the sum of these values is limited and does not correspond with the value of the surpluses generated in agriculture, the inevitable result is consumption of these surpluses (apart from compulsory grain-deliveries) within agriculture itself, feeding wheat to cattle and fattening piglets with milk at a time when there is acute hunger in the cities and unbelievable prices for grain in the most productive grain-regions (the Ukraine).

On the other hand, being compelled to limit his need for urban commodities to those he can buy in the market or order from a craftsman, the peasant also has only a limited need for paper-money, beyond a certain sum. And since the depreciation of this money, which is predetermined by state-issues, begins with him, the peasant is the first to pass the burden of the tax we are considering onto other people's shoulders, and he has every opportunity to fend off all the counter-attacks by the craftsman, who responds, in turn, by increasing the prices of his commodities so that the urban worker and remnants of the bourgeoisie are ultimately driven to the wall and stripped clean.[44]

But if it is true that the peasantry is in exceptionally advantageous circumstances, in terms of freeing itself from the kind of tax we are considering, this by no means implies that the peasantry in general has not suffered, or is not still suffering a very great deal, because of the depreciation of money. We must not forget that the peasant is not only a producer of food-items (and also a seller, as long as the free market exists) with the ability to raise their prices; at the same time, he is also a person who holds money, a kind of cash-box, and the peasant did not instantaneously learn 'the economics of the transition-period'. During the first years of the War, when the depreciation of money occurred more slowly, the peasant kept hoping that depreciated money would regain its value. In the first year or two, he even entertained futile day-dreams to the effect that the tsarist ten-rouble note, for which he sold a *pood*[45] of grain and which carried the tempting words about convertibility into gold, would once again purchase ten *poods* of grain or the equivalent in other goods once 'normal conditions' returned. However, subsequent economic practice not only failed to confirm such hopes, but the red tsarist note could not now buy even two or three pounds of grain. And every peasant who was more-or-less sturdy and thrifty as far as 'tsarist' and 'Kerenskyite' money was concerned became increasingly worried about the fate of the jars he had stuffed with paper-money. The peasant might literally have repeated the words of Boris Godunov: 'Six years already (since 1915) have I reigned in peace (over the market); but joy dwells not within my soul'.[46] Everything that he accumulated in paper has turned into dust. Today, the peasant doubles the price of grain, but all this means is that the value of the money that he previously accumulated is half of what it was.

The issue of paper-money, in conditions where it is continuously depreciating, means, above all, the expropriation of money-capital that is lying idle. If, say,

---

44. The peaceful expropriation of the urban bourgeoisie by the peasantry is one of the most interesting pages in the transitional period from capitalism to socialism. Waging a stormy onslaught against the gentry class with the expropriation of the landlord's holdings, the peasantry gradually begins the expropriation of the urban bourgeoisie and its possessions insofar as the latter are forced to sell all the property that they have rescued from confiscation by soviet organs in exchange for products from the village: their coats of fox fur, their silk dresses, gold ornaments and so forth have all flowed out to the countryside. I know of a case where the peasantry in one district, satiated with all kinds of products collected from former merchants, agreed to sell grain only in exchange for silver-mounted icons.
45. [One *pood* = 16.38 kg or 36 pounds.]
46. [A line from Alexander Pushkin's *Boris Godunov*.]

during the year from January 1918 to January 1919, prices on products rose by ten times, then the person who in January 1918 owned capital worth 100,000 roubles in fact has only 10,000 in January 1919, and has lost 90,000. It is the same as if a tax had taken away nine-tenths of his fortune in cash. During the first years after the start of the War, the peasants continued to accumulate steadily-depreciating money, and were thereby exposed to continuous expropriation not simply of any new sums added by the monthly sale of products, but even of what they had previously saved in tsarist money before the Revolution. Moreover, in localities that passed from Soviet rule to the White Guards and back again, the peasantry saw their money annulled first by one side and then by the other, which also meant expropriation. In particular, to the extent that the peasantry maintained, or even increased their money-holdings, counting upon a return of the old régime, they thereby paid terribly for doubting the stability of Soviet power.

What applies to the peasant applies to everyone with savings in money – they were all systematically expropriated. No compulsory levies imposed by the soviets and no extraordinary tax could have cleaned out the secret money-vaults of the Kolupaevs and Razuvaevs[47] so thoroughly as the socialist state did with its expanding issues of paper-money. But the remnants of the capitalist class turned out to be more adept than the clumsy peasantry in resisting the depreciation of money that was hitting their pocket-books. These gentlemen understood very quickly that there was no sense in keeping money under wraps and being ruined by its depreciation. At a time when money is depreciating, the basic rule of speculation is to convert money into commodities and to hold the commodities in place of money. Speculators do this by storing up commodities that take little space and are less exposed to the threat of detection and confiscation. Since storage of large quantities is not technically feasible, the point is to turn over money as speedily as possible. If the speculator buys commodities for 100,000 roubles and sells them a week later for 150,000, his challenge is to minimise the time when this money-capital is in his hands, for today's profit of 50,000 will already represent a smaller sum tomorrow because of the continuous depreciation not merely of this profit, but of all money-capital in general. Given the constraints on hoarding a large volume of commodities, and the rapid depreciation of hoarded money, the best means of 'realising' profit, for the speculator, is consumption. Gluttony in place of accumulation – this is the law for tens of thousands of heroes of the Sukharevsky and Okhotny Ryad.[48] And to the extent that speculators are not successful in realising their profit through buying and concealing gold and other valuables, they can seize the moment for looking after

---

47. [Prototypical capitalist characters in the works of M.E. Satltykov-Schedrin (1826–89).]

48. [Traditional marketplaces in Moscow.]

their own self-supply. In general terms, this stratum of the population is successfully adjusting to the Soviet system and to the issue of paper-money and its depreciation, by evading taxes and passing them on either to the clumsy peasant or else to the worker and the office-employee.

We come to the conclusion, therefore, that an indirect tax, imposed by the Soviet power in the form of issuing paper-money, falls on those who hold money and on the peasantry, insofar as they are holders of a stock of cash; on the workers and employees, insofar as they are unable to realise the cash-part of their wages to acquire the necessary minimum of consumer-items and are thus compelled to go hungry; and also on the small producers, insofar as they lose values through the tax that are not compensated by any equivalent value. In the final analysis, the peasants and craftsmen turn out to be in a better position than workers and employees in terms of reducing their share of the tax, through the spontaneous struggle among all these classes in the arena of the free market.[49]

V

The paper-money of the Russian Soviet Republic

The October Revolution in Russia destroyed many of the old foundations, but the issuing of paper-money continued, and it remains the principal means for covering state-expenditures. The Soviet authority was fated to receive from Kerensky's

---

49. In his article 'Money', which appeared in No. 250 of *Ekonomicheskaya Zhizn'*, comrade Larin writes:

'It is better for the peasant if the state covers its general expenditures not by collecting taxes, but, instead, by issuing ever-newer sums of paper-money and thus driving up prices. High prices are much more of a blow to the worker and employees, who must buy everything and usually do not produce anything for sale. On the contrary, the peasant buys very little (especially in an epoch of war and revolution, when factory-production to serve the peasant-farm is steadily contracting). The peasant sells more than he buys, and thus he ultimately adjusts to the general rise in the country's prices, he hides away hundreds of thousands in jars in the ground, he acquires furniture, pillows, dresses, dishes, and so on from the cities. An end to covering state-expenditures with taxes... and the state's need to issue more and more paper-money – for the peasant, this is a means to transfer an important part of the state-burden from himself onto the shoulders of workers and employees'.

Comrade Larin is correct in pointing out that the issue of paper-money is more advantageous to the peasant than any direct taxes. But he is completely mistaken when he suggests that the peasant 'adjusts' when he fills up jars with paper-money. If, today, the peasant sells a bag of potatoes for 5,000 roubles and puts the money in a jar, and after half a year the value of the 5,000 roubles is 500 roubles, and after a year 50 roubles, then, God knows, no-one is 'adjusting'. It is precisely because the peasant sells more than he buys, returning from the market with paper, that, instead of adjusting, he is actually being ruined as the holder of money.

government a paper-money circulation in serious disarray. For its part, the government of Kerensky also received from tsarism a paper-rouble that was already significantly depreciated. Let us reconstruct, in basic figures, the main outlines of the history of our paper-money circulation since the start of the War.

At the moment when war was declared, that is, in July 1914, there was paper-money in circulation amounting to 1,700 million roubles. The gold-reserve of the state-treasury at that time, on 1 August 1914, was 1,604 million. Gold circulated at the beginning of the War on a par with paper, and the purchasing power of the paper-rouble within the country was the same as that of the gold-rouble. At the very outset of the War, as is well known, the tsarist government ended the free convertibility of paper into gold, fearing on very good grounds that all the paper, which was already about to expand, would rapidly end up in the state-treasury as a result of free convertibility, and all the gold would move from the state-treasury into private hands. The end of free convertibility and the *de facto* imposition of a fixed rate for paper immediately caused gold to disappear from circulation and created a gap between the price of the gold- and the paper-rouble. The rate of the paper-rouble began to fall. As far as the domestic market is concerned, this fall would hardly seem to be serious – provided, on the one hand, that the domestic commodity circulation did not contract and, on the other hand, that no new paper-issues were undertaken by the state. In reality, together with the contraction of commodity-circulation, which began with falling production, there also began a greater issue of paper in order to cover tsarism's military expenditures. If the sum of paper at the beginning of the War, as we have already said, was 1,700 million, by 1 January 1915, that is, only half a year after the declaration of war, the sum in circulation was already 3,125 million. By 1 January 1916, the sum of paper in circulation grew to 5,737 million; by 1 January 1917, to 9,225 million; and by 1 March 1917, that is, the moment of the February Revolution, the sum of paper-money in circulation was already 9,975 million. Thus the tsarist government, during the period of the War, increased the paper-money fund by more than five times. Specifically, it was the fate of the government to skim the best cream from the commodity-circulation at the time when the value of the paper-rouble remained relatively high.[50]

The Provisional Government that preceded the October Revolution sustained itself almost exclusively with revenues from issuing new billions in paper-

---

50. This necessarily leads to the conclusion that it is better for the revolutionary class to take power as soon as possible in order to acquire the greatest possible inheritance not only in terms of the country's resources in general, but also those that it can acquire in the first period of paper-money circulation, since paper-issues can enable the new authority to support itself at the beginning without any direct taxation.

money. Over the eight months of its existence, our bourgeois government issued 8,942 million in paper, and thus by 1 November 1917, the sum of paper in circulation had already reached 18,917 million.

The Soviet authority that replaced Kerensky's government likewise had no alternative at the outset but to draw its revenues from more and more issues of paper. But while each billion in paper that the tsarist government issued was, on average, equal in purchasing power to 300–350 million in gold, and each billion from Kerensky's government had a purchasing power of about half that amount, the purchasing power of the paper-rouble during the period of Soviet power fell sharply and with unbelievable speed. From the previous theoretical chapter, dealing with the rate of the paper-rouble, we know that in order to take the same values as before from the commodity-turnover, using paper-roubles, a progressively expanding volume of paper is required. This progression also continues to grow under the influence of a declining commodity-turnover, and rather than ending after the October Revolution, the decline steadily accelerated. The whole process of extracting values by issuing paper can be compared to getting wine from a barrel that is being refilled with water. To draw off the first bucket, all one has to do is fill the bucket; but to get a second bucket of pure wine, more than a bucketful of the mixture is required; and for a third, still more, and so on. The comparison will be complete if we imagine that the pure wine in the barrel is diminishing not simply because the mixture is being bailed out, but also because the wine is escaping through another opening (which corresponds to the reduction of C as a result of the economic disarray). The Soviet power had to draw values from the barrel of commodity-circulation that had already been considerably diluted with water, as a result of the very same operations on the part of tsarism and the Provisional Government. The result was that, despite the reduction of expenditures connected with the factual ending of the War, by 1 January 1918, the sum of paper in circulation was already 27,313 million; that is, during little more than two months of its existence, the Soviet power issued 8,396 million in paper-money, or somewhat more than the total issued throughout its entire life by the Provisional Government. By 1 January 1919, the sum of paper-money in circulation reached 61,265 million, a sum that must still be regarded as relatively modest, if one considers that the value of the paper-rouble, as shown below in a table of free prices, fell by the spring of 1919 to one five-hundredth of the gold-rouble, and that in place of expenditures on the imperialist War came new expenditures on the Civil War. However, one must also take into account the reduction of Soviet Russia's territory in 1918, when, for a time, we had lost Ukraine, Siberia, the Urals, the Don and the Caucasus. Because of the expansion of territory and depreciation of the rouble, among other causes, during 1919 there was an enormous increase in the issue of paper-money, with the total in circulation by 1 January 1920 reaching the astronomical figure of 225,016 million, which still does not include the paper-money issued in Turkestan.

If we consider the increase in the average monthly issue of paper-money during each year since 1915, we get the following picture:

	Year	Millions
New money issued per month	1915	217.6
	1916	281.6
	1917	1,507.6
	1918	2,829.3
	1919	13,645.9
In the first half of the year	1920	56,833.0

This flow of paper-billions is striking in terms of its unprecedented dimensions, but the real purchasing power of all these billions, and thus the real income of the Soviet government, is far more modest. The billions of paper turn out to be just paper-billions. This can be seen from the table of price-movements on the free markets. We provide below data concerning the most important food-products in the capital-cities and the provinces:

	Baked bread (one pound)					
	1913–14	June 1915	Autumn 1916	Spring 1918	Spring 1919	Spring 1920
Moscow	3.5 *kopeks*	4 *kopeks*	5 *kopeks*	3 roubles, 50 *kopeks* – 4 roubles	22–6 roubles	350–400 roubles
Petrograd	3.5 *kopeks*	4 *kopeks*	5 *kopeks*	4 roubles	30–35 roubles	500 roubles
Tver'	3 *kopeks*	5.8 *kopeks*	5 *kopeks*	3 roubles – 3 roubles, 50 *kopeks*	22–4 roubles	–
Saratov	2.1 *kopeks*	3 *kopeks*	–	70–90 *kopeks*	1 rouble 20 *kopeks* – 1 rouble, 50 *kopeks*	–

Rye-flour (one pound)						
	1913–14	June 1915	Autumn 1916	Spring 1918	Spring 1919	Spring 1920
Moscow	1 rouble, 1 kopek	1 rouble, 65 kopeks	2 roubles, 60 kopeks	150–180 roubles	800–1,000 roubles	–
Petrograd	1 rouble. 35 kopeks	1 rouble, 75 kopeks	2 roubles, 60 kopeks	300–400 roubles	1,400–1,800 roubles	–

Meat (one pound)						
	1913–14	June 1915	Autumn 1916	Spring 1918	Spring 1919	Spring 1920
Moscow	22 kopeks	34 kopeks	78 kopeks	8 roubles, 50 kopeks	45–60 roubles	300 roubles
Petrograd	22 kopeks	30–36 kopeks	80 kopeks	8 roubles, 40 kopeks – 9 roubles	50–70 roubles	–
Tver'	18 kopeks	–	–	–	15–20 roubles	–
Saratov	12 kopeks	20 kopeks	33 kopeks	–	16–18 roubles	–

The uneven rate of increase in free-market prices in the capitals and the provinces is clear from these tables, although recently the outlying areas have begun to catch up quickly with the capital-cities. But even with such sharp differences in prices between the capitals and the provincial cities, the rise in prices and the corresponding fall in the value of the rouble are striking.

In order to make perfectly clear the economic significance of issuing paper in non-depreciated and in fully depreciated currency, and to show, in particular, the real income (expressed in commodity-values) of the Soviet authority in 1919 coming from the issuing of paper-money, let us do a few calculations on the basis of the figures provided above. Take the average figures for the price of bread in Moscow and Saratov. In 1914, that is, at the beginning of the War, the average price of a pound of bread was 2.8 *kopeks*. The tsarist government, which issued paper-money in the amount of 1,425 million from the beginning of the War to 1 January 1915, was in a position to withdraw commodity-values just a little short of what could have been bought with the same sum of gold. If we take as the starting point for our calculation the price of 2.8 *kopeks* for a pound of bread, which corresponded to the price of bread in gold-currency, we will then be able to determine how much the issues of paper-money, when converted into gold-currency, brought in each year up to 1919. In that way we will get an approximate idea of the volume of commodity-values that could be taken from circulation.

In 1915, paper was issued in the amount of 2,612 million. The average price of bread was no longer 2.8 *kopeks*, but 3.5. The purchasing power of the rouble, measured by the price of bread, was 80 *kopeks* in gold. In other words, the tsarist government, with the issue of 2,612 million in paper in 1915, and with the rouble worth 80 *kopeks* (in terms of bread-prices), received commodity-values of 2,089.6 million.[51]

In 1916, 3,488 million was issued in paper. The average price of bread was 4.5 *kopeks*. (The exact figure in Saratov is unknown, but in the Volga area the average price was four *kopeks*.) The value of the rouble, with the price of a pound of bread beginning at 2.8 *kopeks* in gold in 1914 and rising to 4.5 *kopeks* in terms of paper-roubles in 1916, can be calculated as 62 *kopeks*. For the 3,488 million in paper, the tsarist government withdrew values approximately equivalent to 2,162 million in gold.

In 1918, the total of paper issued was 33,952 million, that is, about ten times more than took place under tsarism in 1916. The average price of bread was two roubles, 88 *kopeks*. The rate for the rouble was 1.1 *kopeks*. Having issued the enormous sum of 33,952 million in paper, the Soviet authority, with the rouble worth little more than a *kopek*, withdrew values from circulation of approximately 373 million. That was the real content of the flow of paper. Ten times more paper was issued, but six times less was withdrawn, in terms of value, than in 1916.

Let us consider how things stood just last year. The issue of paper was 163,751 million. The average price of bread was approximately twelve roubles. The value of the paper-rouble in terms of the price of bread was 0.23 *kopeks*, that is, a little more than one-fifth of a *kopek*. The enormous sum of 163,751 million roubles in paper, when this enormous sum is translated into gold-currency at the existing rate for the rouble, was equal to the comparatively modest sum of 383.5 million. Thus, while in 1919 we issued nearly five times more paper than in 1918, the real income of the proletarian state from this operation remained almost the same as in 1918.

If we verify these conclusions in terms of the average price of meat, the calculation will simply indicate a greater fall in the rouble and, therefore, even less purchasing power for the billions put into circulation, especially during the Soviet period. The years of revolution, except for 1920, were perfectly satisfactory

---

51. Prices for other products rose more quickly, especially for the products of industry. This means that calculating in terms of the average price of bread alone gives a higher total for real government-income than was actually the case.

in terms of the grain-yield in Russia. Consumption of grain by the producers was more stable, whereas the meat-shortage, connected with the sharp fall in meat-production, became apparent as early as the end of 1915. Furthermore, the consumption of meat in the peasant-economy was subject to sharper fluctuations. Thus, the best way to establish the rate of the rouble is by reference to bread-prices, not to mention the fact that bread is the most important, the most fundamental food-product in Russia and the main item traded on the free market.

The calculations that we have done are, of course, extremely approximate. In the first place, we used bread-prices in the spring, and not for the entire year. Then, for purposes of greater precision, it was necessary to take an average figure, based in turn on averages for all the regions of the country. Generally speaking, we should have established the rate of the rouble according to the average prices of all the most important products, in every district of the country and for every month of the year. Unfortunately, the author does not have the necessary material to make such a calculation. However, the figures and the calculations provided do give a rough outline and an approximate idea of both the rate of the rouble and the real revenues of the Soviet state as a result of the issues of paper-money.

A comparison of the quantity of paper issued in 1918 with the quantity issued in 1919, on the one hand (an increase by approximately five times), and a comparison of bread-prices in 1918–19 (also an increase by approximately five times) reveals a parallel in term of proportions. This correspondence is not fortuitous. In places where the commodity-market has already adapted to the endless issues of paper and rapidly expresses commodity-prices in terms of new amounts of paper as soon as they enter into circulation – in those places, a correspondence is necessarily established between the increase in price for the most important product being bought and sold, namely bread, and the increased quantity of paper in circulation. The figures for paper in circulation and for market-prices in 1918–19 are obvious confirmation of the theoretical conclusions that were drawn in the first two chapters on the basis of Marx's teaching concerning money-circulation.

Fine, the reader will say. But why did you not work with the corresponding figures for 1915 and 1916? Were things different them?

Yes, things were different, and they also correspond fully with the theoretical conclusions of the first chapters. If the price of bread in 1914 is taken as 100, then the rise in price in 1915 will be expressed as 125, and in 1916, 160. If the quantity of paper-money at the end of 1914 is taken as 100, then the growth of paper in circulation will be 183 in 1915 and 295 in 1916. The issue of new paper, if 1914, the moment of war, is taken as 100, will give the figure of 183 for 1915 and 244 for 1916. The whole table will look this way:

	Real price	As percent	Paper in circulation	New issues for the year
1914	2.8 *kopeks*	100	100	100
1915	3.5 *kopeks*	125	183	183
1916	4.5 *kopeks*	160	295	244

We see from this table that in the first two-and-a-half years of war, the rise in the price of bread lagged behind the quantity of circulating paper-money. It is precisely by means of this factual material that we can establish the enormous importance, for the rate of the paper-rouble in Russia, of the peasants' accumulation of money. There is not the slightest doubt that the comparatively slow decline of the rouble's rate in 1915–16 was connected with the circumstance that the peasantry, in the course of the War, accumulated an enormous quantity of paper in the hope that the rouble would return to its pre-war purchasing power, and thus the peasantry took billions in paper-money out of circulation. Our peasant, driven by his thriftiness and not expecting what happened, gambled on a rise first of the tsarist rouble and then of the Kerensky rouble, and he was ultimately ruined, of course, by this activity, which is anything but profitable during a revolutionary epoch. But already in 1917, the rise in prices began to converge with the growing issues of paper, and in 1918–9 the leap in prices strictly corresponded with leaps in the growing quantity of paper-money.[52]

If we were to attempt, on the basis of everything said above, to calculate how many billions in paper our Commissariat of Finances would have to issue in 1920 to acquire the same quantity of real values as in 1918–19, that is, 370–80 million in full-valued roubles, we would come to the following conclusion. In view of the rise in the price of bread by about ten times in 1920 (the average of Petrograd, Moscow and the non-producing provinces on the one hand, and the Volga region on the other, is about 200–250 roubles), it would be necessary to increase monetary emissions by the same amount, that is, to bring the issue of paper to the super-astronomical figure of 1,600,000 million, that is, 1,600 billion.

As we can see, the real revenues of the Soviet state from the issue of paper-money are exceedingly modest, but conversely the quantity of paper that is required not only each year, but even each month, is growing with unprecedented speed. In 1917, a *kopek* was still real, and you could still purchase something for fifty *kopeks*. By 1918, the role of the *kopek* was taken over by the rouble. In 1919,

---

52. In the first months of proletarian power [a slower depreciation] was also evident, which has to be explained in terms of the elimination of banks, credit, and non-cash transactions in general, and thus an increased demand for ready cash.

not only was the word *kopek* forgotten, but ten roubles replaced the rouble as the real unit of account. In 1920, the real unit of account was in hundreds and thousands, while single digits and tens disappeared the same way that the *kopek* did. In 1921, the real unit of account will remain a thousand.

The reader will ask: 'When will all of this end?'

Our Commissariat of Finances is asking: 'How are we still hanging on to our paper-system?'

And now we ask ourselves: 'When will the collapse of our paper-circulation occur?' It is perfectly obvious that a collapse cannot result just from adding zeros to our real paper-unit. Here, the difficulties are simply technical and involve merely the time and effort required to prepare the state-paper, nothing more. To reduce the number of zeros we might, for example, replace the number 1,000 with the letter T and print paper for 10T, 100T, 1000T and so on. Then 1000T could be replaced with the letter M (million) and we could print 10M, 100M, and so on. Eventually there would be no more numbers large enough and we would have to invent new ones.

In order to explain the persistence of our paper-money system despite the horrifying decline in the rate of the rouble, we must take into account the conditions and dimensions of the non-socialised parts of production in our country as a whole, and we especially have to establish, even if only approximately, what part of the values created and entering the market are withdrawn from circulation through our issues of paper. As we have seen, in 1918–19 we took out of circulation (basing the calculation on bread) 370–80 million. This sum is very modest and certainly nothing catastrophic. Recall that each year before the War, the tsarist government took from the country two to three billion roubles in taxes, of which half fell, in one form or another, on the peasant-economy and handicrafts. It is true that both the peasant-economy and handicrafts have suffered greatly from the War, but they have still suffered dramatically less than large-scale industry, without even mentioning the fact that the dimensions of peasant-farming have expanded extraordinarily at the expense of the landlords' lands. Our small-scale economy can withstand deductions of three to four hundred million roubles a year, even if we add to that figure the sum represented by natural taxation in the form of grain, meat and other monopolistic requisitions, of which we will speak further below.

It is another matter if the collapse should begin in a different way, on the basis of a saturation of circulation with older paper that has a more stable rate than newly-issued money, and especially on the basis of paper being squeezed out by natural commodity-exchange. It is a known fact that our tsarist and Duma-money has a more stable rate not only within the country, but also in some places abroad (Latvia, Estonia, Lithuania, Manchuria). The Kerensky-money also has a certain degree of stability. Finally, in Ukraine there has even appeared a premium on the Soviet yellow one-thousand notes in view of the issuing of new thousands of another more simplified and smaller specimen. This means that our new issues face a certain danger. However, paper-money with a more or less stable value usually goes into storage, while the channels of circulation fill up with continuously depreciating 'worse' forms of money that no-one is interested in holding. As for the prospect of cash being squeezed out by barter, this is a far more serious danger and is already far advanced in some regions, especially in Ukraine. The danger from this point of view is the following. The peasantry and the craftsmen now sell their products for money only if they can convert this money as rapidly as possible into a commodity that they need. What the state provides to these groups at fixed prices requires a completely insignificant amount of money as payment. The workers and employees of state-enterprises, being mainly recipients of paper-money and using it to purchase commodities, are usually not sellers of any kind of products, if we leave aside their sale of former possessions or of a portion of the products they receive either at fixed prices or in the form of a natural supplement to their wages (bakers get bread, weavers get textiles, soap-makers soap, and so on). Apart from the peasant, the main suppliers of commodities from their own undertakings are craftsmen and those employees of nationalised industries who have to do craft-work on the side (this group is especially numerous in the Urals, and is now growing in a number of other places). The gradual displacement of paper from trade involving cash, and the transition to a natural commodity-turnover, could put the workers and employees in a catastrophic position while scarcely affecting the peasantry and craftsmen, in terms of their mutual relations. It is true that both artisans and peasants suffer as large holders of money. But they can hardly lose much more than they have already lost. The Soviet authorities must prepare, without fail, to meet this possibility. If it is anticipated in advance, it may be possible not only to avoid a catastrophe for the most vulnerable in this respect, and also the most important element in building socialism, namely, the workers, but it is also possible, conversely, that a boycott of money, which is the equivalent of abolishing it, could become the starting point for a new financial policy based on new scientific foundations, perhaps involving a certain quantity of silver. We will speak more of this below.

Up to now, our financial policy has, certainly, not been based on any kind of scientific conclusions. This is partly clear from what has been said, and it is also well-known by every participant in Soviet construction in general, and particularly by everyone working in the area of Soviet finances. Our policy has been completely spontaneous in response to one or another circumstance and to the pressure arising from needs of the day; and it is mainly under the influence of an exorbitant demand for money and the impossibility of satisfying it in any timely manner that our policy is now groping its way towards the necessity of calculating even approximately how much paper-money is required for the immediate future,⁵³ and thus also towards posing the more general question concerning the system of paper-circulation during the transition-period. True, having committed a number of mistakes in the past, and, to some degree, continuing them even today, on one point – and an extremely important one at that – we have been absolutely correct: we have never begrudged the amount of paper needed for [printing] our money. However, now that we have looked backwards to the past, the time has now come to look forwards to tomorrow.

VI

Paper-money in the system of socialist production and distribution

At the present time, we can only study the paper-money circulation of the transition-period and its prospects on the basis of the three-year experience of the Russian Soviet Republic and partly on the basis of the very brief experience of Soviet Hungary.⁵⁴ Thus, in this chapter, as in the previous one, we will begin mainly with the facts and the economic relations of Soviet Russia; this is a major drawback, because the structure of the economy and the relative weights of different social groups in countries in the West, when they live through their own proletarian revolution, will be significantly different from the economic structure of Russia, a mainly-peasant country. Soviet Russia's experience with paper-money, and the conclusions based on that experience, can by no means be generalised for all countries with a proletarian dictatorship. This is all the more true because both the world economic conjuncture and the economic relations

---

53. Comrade Otto Schmidt, who has made this calculation using mathematics and working with factual material, came to conclusions that fundamentally correspond almost entirely to my own, which were reached mainly by a theoretical route.

54. On the experience of Soviet Hungary, see comrade Varga's very valuable brochure *Die wirtschaftspolitischen Probleme der proletarischen Diktatur* (Varga 1920), pp. 113–23, which is being translated into the Russian language. The Soviet government of Hungary was not able to print the paper-money formerly in circulation, which was issued in Vienna, and thus was not able to compel the peasantry to pay indirect taxes to the proletarian state. The peasantry boycotted the new money issued by the proletarian government and demanded, instead, the old money that originated from Vienna. The result was two paper-currencies in the country: the old currency, recognised by the countryside, and the new one, which circulated only in the cities where the new régime was economically in control. [The Hungarian Soviet Republic lasted for 133 days, from 21 March to 1 August 1919.]

between European countries after the revolution will probably be profoundly different from the conditions of existence in Soviet Russia, which has managed to survive for three years with its economy completely cut-off from economic relations with the entire world. Therefore, insofar as we encounter conclusions that might have importance for any country with a proletarian dictatorship, we will observe the greatest caution in making generalisations, all the while taking into account the peculiarities of Russian relations and making the appropriate corrections.

The proletariat is compelled to build its state and resurrect the economy on the ruins of capitalism. It is not the overproduction and full-blooded conditions of capitalism that made the socialist revolution inevitable but, on the contrary, its wasting condition and the ruin of the bourgeois economy, which was tangled up in its own contradictions and bled itself white as a result of the World-War. In different countries, the victorious proletariat will receive a different inheritance from capitalism. But, however much this inheritance may vary in dimensions and values, there is not a single country in which the proletariat will be able to avoid the kind of construction-period that, in the excellent expression of comrade V. Smirnov,[55] can be called the epoch of primitive socialist accumulation. It is necessary to gather together and take account of all the possessions expropriated from the bourgeoisie; to extend the expropriation to the enterprises; to assemble and put in position labour-power and technical leaders; to restore the technical equipment, especially in heavy industry but generally including everything that, in the bourgeois period, was called the *fixed* capital of production; to restore the means for acquiring material; and to extend natural taxes to all small-scale and mainly-peasant production to the benefit of the socialist economy that is being set up. If, in a country such as England, there is no protracted civil war accompanied by major destruction of the material base of the economy and the labour-force, and if the victorious English proletariat succeeds in quickly sorting out economic ties with the former colonies, then this period might be relatively brief. Conversely, in a country such as Russia, where capitalism left the proletariat a miserable inheritance; where primitive accumulation must, inevitably, be based on reduced consumption by the proletariat and on expropriation of a part of the surplus-product in petty production; a country where the redistribution of labour-power between the large- and small-scale economy in proportions reached long ago in Germany and England *on a capitalist basis* must now be achieved – after an enormous delay – during the *epoch of*

---

55. See Bukharin, *Ekonomika perekhodnovo perioda* [In English: Bukharin 1982, pp. 38–92].

socialist construction; where the three-year existence of proletarian power has been a period of cruel civil war and enormous expenditure of material forces for non-productive purposes – in that kind of country, the period of socialist accumulation stretches out over a long time and will inevitably assume the character of a difficult and agonising process.

In the present work, we are not directly interested in those aspects of socialist accumulation that involve assembling the dispersed labour-force, drawing the non-labouring elements into productive work, drawing office-employees into physical labour, or reducing the consumption of the proletariat for the sake of accumulating fixed capital for production; nor are we interested in the question of extending labour-conscription to petty producers for the benefit of the socialised economy. On the contrary, the main topics of our study are socialist accumulation in the form of a natural tax on petty production (requisitions of all types, as in the case of grain, and such like) and in the form of indirect taxation (through the issue of paper-money). At the present moment, the fate of our paper-rouble depends, above all, on the changing relation between the quantity of products that the proletarian state receives in natural form through its procurement-organs, and the amount that it takes from the free market through the apparatus of paper-emissions. Let us consider what these quantities amount to, and how the relations between them are changing.

Before the War, the annual product throughout the whole economy of Russia was valued at approximately eleven billion in gold.[56] In round numbers, industry, transportation and the whole of business accounted for 5,194 million of this sum, and agriculture for 5,360 million.

How far production in our industry has fallen, and how great the losses are that must be made good through socialist accumulation, in order to regain even the pre-war level, can be seen in a table that was compiled by comrade Larin and appeared in *Ekonomicheskaya Zhizn'*.

In view of the enormous interest that attaches to comrade Larin's calculation in general, and particularly in view of its interest for our investigation, we will reproduce this table here in full:

---

56. Prokopovich 1918, p. 64. The 'income' of 975–980,000 that Prokopovich calculated for trade must be excluded, because this is not essentially income, but rather the opposite – an expenditure by society on the bourgeois apparatus of distribution.

	Annual production 1913–14	Production in the first half of 1920	As a percentage of a half-year of peacetime-production
1. Paint, varnish, and such like. (Gla[va]nil[in], Gl[avko] kraslak)[57]	3 million *poods*	33,000 *poods*	2.2 percent
2. Paper and cardboard (*Glavbum*) with Ukr[aine]	13.5 million *poods*	1.03 million *poods*	15.2 percent
3. [Resin-products] *Glavresina*	1.84 million *poods*	34,000 *poods*	1.7 percent
4. Glass of all types (*Glavsteklo*); One case = 15 *poods*	440,000 cases	28,000 cases	13 percent
5. [Matches] *Glavspichka* One case = 1,000 boxes	3.65 million cases	310,000 cases	16 percent
6. Tobacco and low-grade tobacco (*Gl[av]tabak*)	4.3 million *poods*	380,000 *poods*	17.7 percent
7. Alcohol (*Ts[entro]spirt* 40° in barrels)	3.85 million barrels	1.93 million barrels (for 1919/20)	5 percent on a yearly basis
8. Sugar with Ukr[aine] (*Gl[av]sakhar*)	105 million *poods*	4.737 million *poods* (for 1919/20)	4.5 percent on a yearly basis
9. Raw starch (*Gl[av] krakhmal*)	13.2 million *poods*	1.042 million *poods* (for 1919/20)	7.8 percent on a yearly basis (for 1919/20)
10. [Coal] (*Gl[av]ugol'* with Ukr[aine] and Siberia)	1,800 million *poods*	225 million *poods*	25 percent
11. [Oil] *Gl[av]neft* (Cau[casus] and Em[ba])	600 million *poods*	100 million *poods*	33 percent
12. Copper (mining)	1.33 million *poods*	Less than 300,000 *poods*	Less than 50 percent
13. Manganese (with Ukr[aine])	17 million *poods*	–	–
14. Lead with Cauc[asus], Sib[eria]	100,000 *poods*	–	–

57. [Several of the references in this column are to the *Glavki* (Main Directorates) and *Centres* of the various industries listed.]

Table (*cont.*)

	Annual production 1913–14	Production in the first half of 1920	As a percentage of a half-year of peacetime-production
15. Zinc with Cau[casus]	200,000 *poods*	–	–
16. Platinum	300 *poods*	50 *poods*	33 percent
17. Gold from Sib[eria]	4,000 *poods*	240 *poods*	12 percent
18. Pyrite (sulphuric)	3.5 million *poods*	Less than 700,000 *poods*	Less than 40 percent
19. Magnesite	4 million *poods*	Above 1 million *poods*?[58]	Approximately 25 percent
20. Chromite	1.5 million *poods*	Approximately 500,000 *poods*	Approximately 30 percent
21. Iron-ore (without Crimea) with Ukr[aine]	530 million *poods*	32 million *poods*	12 percent
22. Cast iron with Ukr[aine]	257 million *poods*	30 million *poods*	2.4 percent
23. Iron and steel with Ukr[aine]	220 million *poods*	4.5 million *poods*	4 percent
24. Cotton (clean fibre, *Turk[meniya]*	20 million *poods* in 1915	4 million *poods* in 1919	20 percent
25. Cotton-fabrics (yarn)	19.8 million *poods*	330,000 *poods*	3.3 percent
26. Flax (sown area)	1.06 million *desyatins*	536,000 *desyatins* (in 1919)	50 percent
27. Flaxen fabrics (yarn)	3.24 million *poods*	540,000 *poods*	33 percent
28. Sulphuric acid	11 million *poods* for the entire Empire	1.25 million *poods* (for all of 1919)	11.4 percent
29. Soda (three-quarters Ukraine)	11.5 million *poods*	1.2 million *poods* Urals for all of 1919 – and Ukraine?	?
30. Potassium salts from Caucasus	1.6 million *poods*	Virtually nothing	–

---

58. [The figures are not clearly readable here or in item 29.]

Table (*cont.*)

	Annual production 1913–14	Production in the first half of 1920	As a percentage of a half-year of peacetime-production
31. Nitric acid	1.47 million *poods* for the entire Empire	nothing	0 percent
32. [Edible Oils] *Glavrasmaslo* with Ukr[aine], without Cau[casus], Don, Sib[eria]	23 million *poods*	500,000 *poods*	4.3 percent
33. All chemical products (including items 28, 29, 30, 31, 37)	32.62 million *poods*	1.7 million *poods*	10.4 percent
34. Portl[and] Cement (*Gl[av]cement*) with Ukr[aine], Cau[casus]	115 million *poods*	nothing	–
35. Wood[working] factories	–	45 million cubic feet of sawn lumber, 7 million pieces, 0.5 million cubic feet of plywood, and so on[59]	30 percent
36. [Flour] *Gl[av]muka* (industrial mills)	1,000[60] million *poods*	90 million *poods*	18 percent
37. Mineral fertiliser	10.03 million *poods*	(in 1916 = 4 million *poods*)	–
38. Tar-extraction (all products) without Belorussia	6 million *poods*	4.5 million *poods* (for 1920)	75 percent
39. Soap and candles (*Tsentrozhir*)	20.867 million *poods*	291,000 *poods*	2.8 percent
40. Pencils (Gross = 144 pieces)	500,000 gross	3,000 gross	1.2 percent

59. [The units of measurement are not entirely clear here. This seems to be the correct translation.]

60. [There is an error in the text here, giving the figure of 1 million rather than 1,000 million poods.]

Larin includes, here, the output from our enterprises for the first half of 1920. We are all aware that output increased in most of our industries during the second half of the year and, furthermore, that a number of previously-closed plants reopened. Nevertheless, the fall in production by comparison with the pre-war period is strikingly evident. Given that it is a matter of restoring very badly damaged industry, and that this must be done in a country with a mainly small-scale economy and little chance of any economic support from abroad, one can judge how great the need is to alienate[61] part of the incomes of small-scale production for a fund of '*socialist accumulation*'.

Now let us consider what resources there are in the very smallest, mainly-peasant operations. During the years of revolution, there has been an extreme decline in the productivity of agriculture. Because of the liquidation of landlord-agriculture, the yield on land where crops were cultivated in an advanced manner has fallen significantly. The sowing shortfall on peasant- and Cossack lands has reached an average of ten to twenty-five percent in the producing provinces. In a number of regions where the Civil War raged, the peasant-farm was badly ruined. We do not have figures to indicate the annual income of agriculture at the present time, but there cannot be the slightest doubt that this income, despite the fact that the peasants have acquired the land from the gentry, does not exceed the peasants' income in pre-war times and is far below the pre-war income of agriculture taken as a whole. We can get an approximate idea of the figure we are after, on the basis of indirect information concerning peasant-income before the War. From grain-farming, the peasantry in pre-war European Russia earned up to 2,450 million, from livestock 1,602 million, and from technical crops 540 million – altogether coming to about 4,592[62] million in agricultural work as a whole. The privately held farms (mainly owned by landlords and merchants) received, under the same headings, an income of 481 million roubles per year. If we deduct completely the income-figure for privately held agriculture, taking into account the general disorder in agriculture and also the increase of peasant-income due to the fact that the peasants have acquired 35 million of landlord-holdings, then the income of our peasantry, translated into gold at pre-war prices, can be estimated somewhere between the sums of 4 and 4.5 billion. As far as handicrafts are concerned, according to Prokopovich's figures, income here was calculated at approximately 611 million.

Before the War, the tsarist government and the nobility took values up to 1.5 billion a year from the peasants and handicrafts in direct and indirect taxes, land-taxes and rent-payments. The deductions that the Soviet authority has had to impose on peasant income are incomparably less. Accordingly, as a basis we

---

61. ['Alienate' in the sense of 'extract']
62. [There is an error in the text, giving the figure as 4,594 rather than 4,592.]

can take 4–4.5 billion as peasant-income, together with the 600 million of handicraftsmen, which has changed very little during the Revolution. Altogether, this gives a sum of 4.5–5 billion.

We have seen above that, for 1918 and 1919, the state, in very approximate numbers, used paper-issues to take from the commodity-market a sum of commodities worth about 380 million in gold. Part of these commodities came from craftsmen, and another part came from the owners of property acquired before the War. The main sum, of course, fell on the peasant-economy. Exactly how much is not something that can be established by any statistics. If we assume that, in the worst case, the peasant turned over products worth 300 million, then by adding this sum to the value of products received by the state through requisitions, we can come to a figure for the real deductions from the peasant's income. For the 1919–20[63] season, the peasant turned over to the state 265 million *poods* of grain, 43 million *poods* of potatoes, 6 million *poods* of meat, 920,000 *poods* of fats (butter, oils) for 1919 and the first eight months of 1920, 78 million *poods* of hay and 5.5 million *poods* of oilseeds. For the moment, we are leaving aside procurements of materials (flax, hemp, leather, and such like).

If we translate the value of all these products into gold at pre-war prices, we get about 315–20 million roubles. In other words, the Soviet state, to judge from all of these admittedly rough and approximate calculations, requires from the small peasants a minimum of products worth about 620–70 million roubles in gold each year. This is the minimum that sustains the Red Army and the workers and employees of the proletarian state. Procurements from state-enterprises, the fishing industry, for example, soviet-farms, and so on, are not included here, because these products go directly to the state's procurement-organs. As the army is reduced along with expenditures on the War, this sum will necessarily decline. At the same time, however, it must increase due to the opening of more and more new factories, expansion of work in existing organisations, and a whole number of new projects that are connected, for example, with the ultimate need to raise the general level of nourishment for the worker.

If we take this figure of 620 million as a basic figure that gives an approximate idea of the quantity of food-products that the state requires for the naturalisation of wages, then we reach one perfectly clear conclusion: the fate of the paper-rouble, and how much we need to rely on the printing press, depends, first and foremost, on how quickly state-procurements will grow in place of that portion of products that, until now, had to be taken from the market with paper-money. Already in the 1919–20 season, the food-products procured by socialist means amount to half, or a little more than half, of the products actually consumed

---

63. [The text says 'for the season 1913–20', but clearly the meaning is 1919–20.]

by workers, employees, and members of the Red Army. Now let us turn to the question of how close we are to liquidating the activity of *Narkomfin*'s printing press if the entire assessment levied by *Narkomprod* for 1920–21 (from August to August) should be completely fulfilled. For this year, *Narkomprod* has announced the following assessments: 454 million *poods* of grain, 24 million *poods* of meat, 3.3 million *poods* of butter, 117 million *poods* of potatoes, 29 million *poods* of oilseeds, about 500 millon eggs, and 75 million in requisitions of hay, about 50 million of which come from the peasants. Converted into gold-roubles, this gives a sum of about 650 million roubles. In other words, this means the following: if assessments for this year were completely fulfilled, the Soviet power would have a food-fund adequate for maintaining the army, the workers and the employees, and the issue of paper could be continued only for the purpose of acquiring commodity-values worth fifty to sixty million in gold, that is, for products of handicraft-production and those products from the peasant-economy that are not being procured by *Narkomprod*'s organs and that are not fundamentally important to the consumption of the mass of state-workers. If requisitioning were extended to these products also, and if a natural tax were levied on handicrafts, this sum could be reduced even further, and then the Soviet state would face the practical question: should the very costly system of paper-money be continued at all, and would it not be better to cease printing paper-money entirely?

That would be the question if assessments for 1920–21 were completely fulfilled.

But these assessments, according to *Narkomprod* itself, will not be completely fulfilled, especially if we take into account the enormous harvest-failure of 1920. Nevertheless, one thing that emerges very clearly from all the figures that we have cited is that we are moving quickly towards the liquidation of paper-issues, and if our paper-rouble were to be met with a complete boycott in 1921, we would face very serious difficulties, even a temporary crisis, but not a catastrophe.[64] This difficulty would only be of consequence during the interval when state-procurements had almost, but not quite, reached the level needed for naturalisation of wages, and we could overcome it through recourse to issuing silver-coins.[65] These coins could be issued in tens up to a couple of million, and full-valued paper-roubles, temporarily convertible into silver, could be

---

64. Things would have been very different had a universal boycott begun in 1918, when through procurements we acquired less than ten percent of the products we needed, or in 1919, when this figure hardly reached thirty percent. But now the critical period has passed.

65. We mention silver, here, because the Soviet authorities have a significant quantity of silver that is lying idle. Of course, there is no difference in principle between circulating silver or gold. I am speaking here only of what is most practical.

issued simultaneously. This convertibility would have to end soon, and then the new paper would again begin to fall in price, but by the time when the music of newly depreciating roubles commenced, we could have adapted all enterprises to a metallic basis.

This same undertaking might turn out to be worthwhile even in the event that the paper-rouble is not confronted with a boycott: when we are going over to the naturalisation of workers' wages, it may be necessary to continue issuing paper-money – but new money that has not already fallen to one five-thousandth in value – in order to acquire the necessary supplementary products of all kinds and articles from the craft-industry that the state is not yet able to supply to its workers. Once we have reached almost complete naturalisation of wages, and once the organs of socialist distribution are handling the greater portion, say, eighty percent of the surpluses from small-scale production, then the issue of silver-coins and paper on the basis of this 'silver-money' will be just another means for the socialist state to manage its accounts with the small-scale economy. At that point, all relations will take the following form.

In requisitions from the small producer, the Soviet authority will take an annual sum of products worth, let us say, 650 million in gold. A part of these values will be returned to the peasantry in the form of salt, kerosene, textiles, agricultural implements, nails, artificial fertiliser, equipment-repairs, and so on. For another portion, the state can issue special receipts that will be essentially a long-term state-obligation to the peasant and will have to be gradually discharged through industrial products as the plants and factories are restored. A third portion, representing rent from the peasants for land, will not be returned, but, instead, will be converted into a tax in kind.[66] Finally, the fourth portion of products from the small-scale economy, which are used to satisfy the secondary consumption-needs of workers in socialist industry, can be acquired using silver and a new paper-currency. Silver and the new paper can be distributed as a supplement to the basic pay-packet of the workers and can be used on the free market for various secondary purchases. In turn, the state can support the new currency and partially withdraw it from circulation back into the treasury by requiring the peasants to use silver or the new paper-roubles to pay for certain services that it provides that have not been made universally free (travel by rail or steamship, products not subject to planned distribution, occasional repairs, and so on, can be paid for with silver or the new roubles).

In the general system of socialist distribution as a whole, this would amount to the small change of the state's large accounts. The advantages of this method would be to make redundant any bulky supplementary apparatus for procuring

---

66. ['*Naturalnyi nalog*'].

and distributing secondary products and those that might spoil quickly, and it would eliminate red tape by allowing greater individualisation in the satisfaction of one consumer-need or another.

The disadvantage of this method is that it would create a certain possibility for the accumulation of money.

The point is that with the prevalence of commodity-economy, which presupposes the existence of gold or silver as the means of circulation, accumulation of these means of circulation amounts, essentially, to accumulation of commodity-values in the hands of a few. This accumulation transfers control over society's surplus-product to the wealthiest group. On the contrary, with an uninterrupted depreciation of paper-money, it is a senseless and losing proposition to accumulate paper-means of circulation, and from this perspective, the depreciation of money is simply one aspect of the dying out of the capitalist system in general. The issue of silver-coins creates the opportunity for such accumulation. But in general and on the whole, this danger is insignificant, not merely because the amount of silver-currency can be very limited, but also because part of the silver will be continuously returning back to the state. As for accumulation of the new paper-roubles, this operation represents no threat and can even be profitable to the Soviet authority: the accumulation of new paper-roubles will only make their exchange-rate more stable. Just as the accumulation of tsarist money by the peasantry delayed the process of its depreciation and increased the opportunity for the tsarist government to make new issues and to profit from them, so accumulation of the new paper by petty producers will only delay their depreciation and make it possible to liquidate them when such an operation can be properly prepared in economic terms. In the final analysis, the only people who lose from the accumulation of paper are those who hold on to it, while the state and society as a whole can only gain.

But suppose that the Soviet authority does not find it necessary to turn to issuing silver-coins, and can end the printing of paper at a time when naturalisation of wages has been achieved and secured, for the most part, and when the paper-rouble still has not lost *all* of its purchasing power. What will be the future fate of those thousands of billions (trillions) of paper-money that were put into circulation during the preceding years?

The answer to this question is not difficult, if we take into account the scale of the territory in which paper-money retains its importance as a means of circulation. This territory mainly includes the peasant's exchanges with the craftsman, involving that part of agricultural products that are do not go through *Narkomprod*, together with those products of the craftsman that are not controlled by organs of state-distribution. In the first period following the end of paper-money issues, their decline will automatically continue. Then, a turning point will come, and the rate of decline will either slow down markedly or come to a halt. This will quickly lead to a situation in which the holders of money will be in no particular rush to dispose of it, because holding it will not involve the same losses as before. As a result, billions worth of money from the channels of circulation will begin to be kept in money-boxes, which will decrease the weight of the mass of money on the market and then cause its further strengthening. Even a rise in the rate of paper-money is possible if the scale of petty production and, in particular, the quantity of values entering the free market, were to increase (on the basis of a temporary expansion of crafts, an improved harvest, and a rise in the peasant-economy). Moreover, an expansion of foreign trade might also raise the demand for Soviet paper-money. With the defeat of Wrangel, we already see a brisk decline in the rate for 'tsarist' money and better circumstances for Soviet money. This could have some influence on the rate of the Soviet rouble within the country, especially if there is a reduction in the issue of new billions. Thus, an end to paper-issues by the state not only will not finish off, but might even revive the paper-rouble in the free market, its native element, during the early years.[67]

A new cycle in the decline of paper – in this case, an irreversible and fatal decline – will be connected with the success of large-scale socialist industry at the expense of handicrafts. When the state gradually finds itself in a position

---

67. In his previously-cited article on money, comrade Larin writes, among other things, about money withering away:

'Money, as the sole measure of value, is already generally ceasing to exist. As the means of payment, money will complete its withering away when the Soviet state resolves the task of naturalising its relations with the peasantry in the area of procuring agricultural products... and when the actual increase of all rations to workers and employees relieves them of the need to turn to the Sukharevsky. We can foresee both of these things happening, and they might be resolved even in the coming years. And then money will also lose its importance as a store of value and will only remain as what it is in reality: coloured paper'.

To think that, with naturalisation of wages, money will become just paper throughout the whole country, is the same as expecting that within a few years commodity-exchange for money will also end between the peasant and the craftsman. This kind of optimism is completely without foundation. It will take more than *a few years* for socialist large-scale industry to squeeze out the craftsman, and this means that trade between the peasant and the craftsman will continue for a long interval of time. Perhaps Soviet money will be spontaneously squeezed out of use, but tsarist and Kerensky-notes, which are available in limited quantities, are far from becoming 'coloured paper', all the more so when we remember that, even with the naturalisation of wages, we can expect, for a certain period, a recovery of exchange between the worker and the peasant in connection with the need of urban dwellers to acquire agricultural products of secondary importance from the peasant, products that are not available through state-organs, insofar as they may be obtained from the peasants in exchange for part of the worker's pay. For example, the worker sells part of the calico he receives and purchases cream, cheese, and so on. All of these operations may require a supplementary increase in the quantity of money in circulation.

to serve the peasant better than the handicraftsman does, and can assure him better terms and better quality, the free market will then begin to die out, along with its declining importance for the peasant-farm and the squeezing out of the artisan by the socialist factory. And since this process will not just occur spontaneously, as it did under capitalism, but, instead, will be energetically promoted by the state's economic organs (for example, conscripting the artisans for work in large-scale industry after they have already become redundant in terms of a system of social economy), the dying out of the free market, the draining of this final swamp in which billions of paper-fish are already at death's door, will proceed very quickly. The rate on paper-money will fall precipitously, and at that point it will die once and for all.

The naturalisation of workers' wages and the introduction of workbooks, in accordance with which the employees and workers of the socialist state will receive from the state the products that they require, together with the introduction of record-books for the peasants, who turn over their surpluses to the state to acquire industrial products, will by no means rule out the possibility of introducing a special kind of short-term accounting unit such as cheques or coupons. Such tokens will probably have to be introduced for the convenience of distribution so that every worker-consumer might acquire the quantity of products he needs, taking into account his individual preferences. Suppose the state-cooperative warehouses have textiles, shoes, candy and toys for distribution, and suppose, on average, that each worker makes a monthly trip to the theatre, and so on. If coupons are distributed for all of these products and entertainments, then one person will prefer to get an extra pound of sugar; another an extra *arshin* of textiles; a third will prefer to go to the theatre twice rather than once, forgoing some food-product; a fourth will prefer to give up his turn at the theatre in favour of an extra dozen eggs; a fifth will want to get two *poods* of apples from the peasant instead of footwear, and so on. Use of coupons for such exchanges between consumers changes nothing in the system of distribution as a whole or in the quantity of products subject to distribution, but, at the same time, it does leave sufficient room for more complete satisfaction of individual wants. Consequently, the issue of such cheques or coupons, with a designation as to which products they can be used to buy, or else with no such designation, only an indication of the coupon's labour-value – there is such a mass of the most varied products that it would be neither possible nor sensible to designate what each coupon can buy – such issue will certainly be necessary throughout the whole prolonged period when socialist society will not yet be able to give every worker everything he requires in the way of consumption. This kind of coupons and their exchange will play an essential role as a certain corrective to the norms of socialist distribution.

Money, as a means of circulation and accumulation, will die out together with the commodity-economy, but its one positive aspect – the opportunity that it gives to each person to acquire first, and in greater measure, the things that he needs most (within certain limits, to be sure) – this aspect will be preserved through introducing a system of coupons in duly considered proportions.

E. Preobrazhensky

Biographical Notes

Abdul-Hamid II (1842–1918), Sultan of Turkey from 1876–1909; deposed by the Young Turks; known as the 'Bloody Sultan'.

Abramov, a member of the Bolkhov organisation of the RKP(B) in Orel province.

Adler, Victor (1852–1918), one of the leaders of the Austrian Social-Democratic Party; in 1918, Austrian Minister of Foreign Affairs.

Akhmadulin, delegate to the Ninth Congress of the RKP(B).

Akulov, Ivan Alekseevich (1888–1928), a Bolshevik participant in the revolutionary movement from 1907. From 1917–22, Secretary (and Chairman) of Bolshevik party-committees in the Urals, Vyatka, Orenburg, Kirghizia and the Crimea; in 1929, Secretary of the central Soviet trade-union organisation; from 1930, Deputy People's Commissar of the Worker-Peasant Inspectorate and first Deputy Chairman of the OGPU, Secretary of the Central Committee of the Communist Party of Ukraine; from 1933, procurator of the USSR; from 1935, Secretary of the Central Executive Committee of the USSR; purged.

Aleksei Mikhailovich (1629–76), Russian Tsar from 1645.

Aleksin, Sasha, childhood-friend of E.A. Preobrazhensky.

Alexander I (1777–1825), Russian Emperor from 1801.

Alexander II (1818–81), Russian Emperor from 1855.

Amfiteatrov, Aleksandr Valentinovich (1862–1938), writer and journalist; became well known after 1902 publication in the newspaper *Rossiya* of his feuilleton 'Deceived Gentlemen', a satire concerning the Tsar's family that led to his exile in Siberia (Minusinsk); in late 1917 and early 1918, editor of the newspaper *Russkaya volya*, in which he published a feuilleton concerning A.D. Protopopov, Minister of Foreign Affairs, leading to his being exiled to Irkutsk; emigrated in 1920.

Andreev, Leonid Nikolaevich (1871–1919), prose writer, dramatist and publicist.

Andrei, see Sverdlov, Ya.M.

Angarsky (*Klestov*), **Nikolai Semenovich** (1873–1943), political figure, writer and literary critic; participant in the revolutionary movement from 1902 and arrested several times by the tsarist Okhrana; in 1905, sent for five years to Turukhansk region; after fleeing exile, worked in the Moscow Bolshevik organisation; on instruction from the Moscow party, opened a bookstore to distribute legal and illegal Bolshevik publications; participated in the October Revolution; 1919–22, edited the literary journal *Tvorchestvo*; 1924–32, supervised publication of the *Nedra* press; author of several books. Purged.

Anisimov, Ivan, son of a merchant and childhood-friend of E.A. Preobrazhensky; later a Menshevik, apparently emigrated.

An-sky, Semen Akimovich (*Rapoport, Shloime Zeinvil*) (1863–1920), prose-writer, dramatist, publicist and public figure; wrote in Russian and Yiddish.

Antonii Volynsky (*Khrapovitsky, Aleksei Pavlovich*) (1862–1936), a Hierarch of the Russian-Orthodox Church and one of the candidates for the Patriarchy; from 1902, Bishop of Volhynia, later Archbishop of Kharkov; supported the Whites during the Civil War; subsequently emigrated and founded the Russian-Orthodox Church abroad.

Antselovich, Naum Markovich (1888–1952), member of the RSDRP from 1905; after the February Revolution in 1917, member of the Executive Committee of the Petrograd Soviet of Trade-Unions; one of the organisers of the Red Guard in Petrograd; member of the Petrograd Military-Revolutionary Committee; in November 1917, worked to supply grain for Petrograd; 1918–21, Chairman of the Petrograd Provincial Trade-Union Soviet, and in subsequent years, Deputy Chairman of the Worker-Peasant Inspectorate, People's Commissar of the Lumber-Industry, Deputy Minister of Trade for the RSFSR.

Anuchin, Sergei Andreevich (1889–1956), helped to organise the Red Army in the Urals. In 1917, he was delegate to the Constituent Assembly from the western front; at the end of 1917, Chairman of the Army-Soviet and Commander of the Third Army on the western front; from 1918, Commissar of the Urals District Army-Committee, Commissar of the Urals military district and member of the Revolutionary War-Council of the southern front; after the Civil War, Chairman of the Provincial Council of National Economy in Ekaterinburg province; involved afterwards in economic work in Moscow, and became an instructor at the Moscow Textile Institute.

Arosev, Aleksandr Yakovlevich (1890–1938), member of the RSDRP from 1907; conducted revolutionary work in Kazan, St. Petersburg and Moscow; arrested and exiled; after the February Revolution, Chairman of the Tver' Soviet; from 1917, member of the Moscow Military-Revolutionary Committee and commander of the Moscow military district; in 1918, Commissar of the General Directorate of the Workers' and Peasants' Red Air-Fleet; 1920, Chairman of the Supreme Revolutionary Tribunal of Ukraine; 1924–33, worked as a diplomat in France, Lithuania and Czechoslovakia; from 1934, Chairman of the All-Union Society for Cultural Contacts with Foreign Countries. Purged.

Artem (*Sergeev, Fedor Andreevich*) (1883–1921), member of the RSDRP from 1901; did revolutionary work in Ekaterinburg, Kharkov and in the Urals; following arrest in 1902, emigrated to Paris; returned to Russia to work as an *Iskra* agent; from 1905, headed the Kharkov Social-Democratic organisation and led an armed uprising in Kharkov; arrested in 1906; following imprisonment, member of the Urals and Ekaterinburg organisation of the RSDRP; arrested in 1909 and exiled to eastern Siberia; mid-1911, fled to Australia and participated actively in the labour-movement there; returned to Russia after the February Revolution and became Secretary of the Bureau of the Bolshevik District-Committee, supervising work in Donbass, Kharkov and Ekaterinburg provinces; elected to the Central Committee of the Party at the Sixth Congress; from November 1917 to 1919, held various posts on the Council of People's Commissars of Ukraine; in 1920, served as Plenipotentiary of the Central Committee of the RKP(B) and the All-Russian Central Executive Committee in Bashkiria; from November 1920, Secretary of the Moscow Committee of the RKP(B) and member of the All-Russian Central Executive Committee.

Asquith, Herbert Henry (1852–1928), British Foreign Secretary from 1892–5, Prime Minister from 1908–16.

Avenarius, Richard (1843–96), A Swiss idealist philosopher and one of the founders of 'empirio-criticism'.

Avksent'ev, Nikolai Dmitrievich (1878–1943), one of the leaders of the right wing of the S-R Party; during the First World-War, a social-chauvinist; after the February Revolution in 1917, a member of the Executive Committee of the Petrograd Soviet and Chairman of the Executive Committee of the All-Russian Soviet of Peasants' Deputies; from July to September, Minister of Internal Affairs of the Provisional Government; in October, Chairman of the pre-parliament; in 1918, participated in organising counter-revolution in the Volga region and in Siberia and became Chairman of the Ufa Directorate; arrested in November 1918 by Kolchak's forces in Omsk and sent to China.

Azef, Evno Fishelevich (1869–1918), a police-provocateur from 1892 and S-R leader of several terrorist-acts; died in Berlin in 1918.

Babushkin, Ivan Vasil'evich (1873–1906), a worker and revolutionary from 1893, when he was a member of a workers' circle led by V.I. Lenin; member of the 'Union of Struggle for the Emancipation of the Working Class' in St. Petersburg; one of the organisers and a correspondent of *Iskra*; frequently arrested; exiled to Verkhoyansk and then to Yakutsk; active participant in the Revolution of 1905–7; member of the Irkutsk and Chita committees of the RSDRP; shot in January 1906 when caught shipping weapons from Chita.

Bakhtin, member of the military staff that led the Nev'yansk uprising in the Urals in June 1918; a Menshevik.

Bakinovsky, Leon Vladislavovich (1884–?), began his revolutionary activity in Kostroma in 1902, and in 1904 joined the fighting organisation of the RSDRP; sentenced to exile in 1908 in Nizhneilimsk; in 1915 left party-work to serve on the Irkutsk city-council; rejoined the Bolsheviks in Irkutsk in 1918 as member of the Collegium of the local food-committee; subsequently, member of the board of the Union of Cooperatives in Omsk; further fate unknown.

Bakunin, Mikhail Aleksandrovich (1814–76), revolutionary, theorist of anarchy, one of the ideologists of revolutionary Narodism; in the 1830s, member of the circle of S.N. Stankevich; abroad from 1840 and participated in the 1848–9 revolution in Paris, Dresden and Prague; arrested by Austrian authorities and extradited to Russia in 1851; imprisoned in the Peter and Paul and then in Schlisselburg fortress; in 1857, sent into permanent exile in Siberia but escaped abroad in 1861; collaborated with A.I. Herzen and N.P. Ogarev; from 1864, a member of the First International, but opposed Marxism and denied the political struggle of the working class.

Bakunina, E., author of the essay 'Coney Island' dealing with the lives of Russian *émigrés* in New York.

Balakirev, Milii Alekseevich (1814–76), Russian-nationalist composer and pianist, leading figure in the group of nineteenth-century composers known as the 'Mighty Five' (including César Cui, Modest Mussorgsky, Nikolai Rimsky-Korsakov and Alexander Borodin).

Baranov, Mikhail Ivanovich (1888–1938), member of the RSDRP from 1905; in 1919–20, member of the Collegium of *Narkomzdrava*, head of the main Sanitation-directorate; in 1920–5, Deputy People's Commissar of Health for the Ukrainian SSR; in 1925–8, head of the Siberian territorial department of healthcare; Chairman of the Russian Red Cross; published in *Siberskaya meditsinskara zhurnal'*, *Profilakaticheskaya meditsina*, and *Byulleten' Nakomzdrava*. Purged.

Barbe, Antonina Kazimirovna (1897–1938), party-member from 1916; in 1919, Secretary of the Orel Provincial Committee and subsequently involved in economic work; in 1920, member of the Ufa Provincial Committee of the Communist Party; purged.

Baring, Maurice (1874–1945), English writer and critic, of aristocratic origins; in 1904–5 reported on the Russo-Japanese front; until 1912, Russian correspondent for the *Morning Post* and *Times* newspapers; translator of several works in Russian literature.

Bebel, August (1840–1913), one of the founders and leaders of the German Social-Democratic Party and the Second International, several times elected to the Reichstag.

Belinsky, Vissarion Grigor'evich (1811–48), Russian literary critic, publicist and revolutionary-democrat; editor for the literary magazines *Otechestvennye zapiski* ('Notes of the Fatherland') and *Sovremennik* ('The Contemporary') from 1839–48.

Beloborodov, Aleksandr Georgievich (1891–1937), member of the RSDRP from 1907; after the February Revolution, member of the Lysvensk Soviet and Party-Committee; after October, member of the Perm Regional Committee; from January 1918, Chairman of the Executive Committee of the Urals District-Soviet; in July 1918, signed the order for execution of Tsar Nicholas and his family; in 1919–20, member of the CC of the RKP(B); 1923–7, one of the leaders of the Trotskyist opposition; returned to government-work in 1930. Purged.

Belousov, Terentii Osipovich (1875–?), a Menshevik-liquidator and deputy in the Third Duma representing Irkutsk province; in February 1912 left the Social-Democratic faction in the Duma.

Bentham, Jeremy, English philosopher of utilitarianism.

Berdyaev, Nikolai Aleksandrovich (1874–1948), Russian religious philosopher; exiled abroad in 1922.

Berenshtam, Vladimir Vil'yamovich (1870–?), publicist and barrister.

Berezovsky, Anton Iosifovich (1847–1907), Polish revolutionary and participant in the uprising of 1863; subsequently fled abroad; lived in Paris from 1865, and in 1867 attempted to assassinate Alexander II in that city; sentenced to lifelong penal servitude, amnestied in 1906 but chose to remain in exile.

Bergman, (Portnoi, K.), (1872–1941), One of the leaders of the *Bund* and participated in the Social-Democratic movement from the 1890s; arrested in 1896 and sent to five years of exile in Siberia; delegate from the *Bund* to the Second Congress of the RSDRP; 1903–39, Chairman of the Central Committee of the *Bund* in Poland; in 1939, emigrated to the United States and abandoned political activity.

Berne, Ludwig (1786–1837), German publicist and literary critic who fought against feudal reaction and nationalism.

Bethmann-Hollweg, Theobald (1856–1921), in 1905–7 Prussian Minister of the Interior; 1907–9, Imperial State-Secretary for the Interior; 1909–17, Chancellor of the German Empire and Prussian Minister-President.

Bezrodnaya, Iulia Ivanovna (1858–1910), dramatist and prose-writer; her later works adopted social-critical themes in protest against all forms of oppression and the lack of spirituality in contemporary society.

Bismarck, Otto von (1815–98), first Chancellor of the German Empire from 1871–90.

Bissolati, Leonida (1857–1920), one of the leaders of the reformist wing of the Italian Socialist Party from 1892–1912, and then one of the founders of the Italian Reform-Socialist Party; a social-chauvinist during WWI and member of the Italian government from 1916–18.

Blank, Ruvim Mordkovich (1866–?), publicist and collaborator of the journal *Osvobozhdenie* (organ of the Russian liberal bourgeoisie); editor of *Nasha zhizn'*; editor of *Zaprosy zhizni*, a journal of Cadets, Trudoviks and Menshevik-liquidators.

Blücher, Vasilii Konstantinovich (1890–1938), member of the RSDRP (Bolsheviks) from 1916; decorated in WWI; worked for the revolution in Moscow and the Volga area; from November 1917, Commissar of the Red-Guard unit sent to Chelyabinsk to put down the uprising against Soviet power led by Ataman Dutov; Chairman of the Chelyabinsk Military-Revolutionary Committee, and chief of staff for the Red Guards in Chelyabinsk district; from July 1918, deputy commander and then commander of a partisan-army in the Urals and first to receive the Order of the Red Banner; held numerous other Soviet military offices; Marshall of the Soviet Union. Purged.

Blum, Oskar (?–1920), in 1908–10 a secret collaborator of the state-police in Riga.

Bobrinsky, Vladimir Alekseevich (1868–?), Count and major landowner; deputy to the Second, Third and Fourth Dumas; in the Second Duma, a leader of the moderate right; in the Third Duma, an active supporter of P.A. Stolypin; helped to organise a nationalist fraction in favour of Russification and an aggressive foreign policy; fought against Soviet power in the south of Russia after the October Revolution and emigrated in 1919.

Bobrovsky, Petr Semenovich (1881–?), active participant in the Orel Social-Democratic organisation in 1902 and member of the Orel Committee of the RSDRP; later a supporter of Plekhanov; in 1918–19, Minister of Labour in the White government of the Crimea.

Bogucharsky, V. (*Yakovlev, Vasily Yakovlevich*) (1861–1915), historian of the Russian revolutionary movement; exiled to Siberia in 1884 for links with *Narodnaya Volya*, and to Yakutia in 1890; moved from Narodism to Legal Marxism and then became an active figure in the liberal camp; most of his historical writings dealt with the revolutionary Narodniks of the 1860s–80s.

Borin, Ya. (*Borisov, Yakov Vasil'evich*) (1856–?), journalist and pedagogue from Stavropol province; Trudovik deputy to the First Duma.

Bosh, Evgeniya Bogdanovna (*Gotlibovna*) (1879–1952), member of the RSDRP from 1901; did party-work both in Kiev and abroad; arrested in 1912 and exiled to Irkutsk province; in 1914, fled to America and then to Norway; after the February Revolution of 1917, returned to Russia; became chair of the Kiev District Party-Committee, and in October 1917 of the Kiev Military-Revolutionary Council; following October, as a member of the first Ukrainian Soviet government, opposed the Brest treaty; joined the Trotskyist opposition in 1923; ended her life with suicide.

Brandes, Georg (1842–1927), Danish critic and scholar. In the early 1870s, formulated the principles of a new realism and naturalism; major work was *Major Currents in European Literature of the XIX Century*; thought literature should be an organ 'of the great thoughts of liberty and the progress of humanity'.

Briand, Aristide (1862–1932), French political figure and diplomat; in 1909, became Prime Minister of the 'cabinet of the three renegades' (Briand, Millerand, Viviani); Prime Minister in the years 1913, 1915–17, 1921–2; French representative to the League of Nations in 1924; 1926–31, Minister of Foreign Affairs.

Brichkina, Sof'ya Borisovna (1883–1967), member of the RSDRP from 1903; Secretary of the Moscow Military-Revolutionary Committee in October 1917; from May 1919, worked at the Council of People's Commissars and then as Secretary of the Council, Protocols-Secretary for the Politburo and for Central-Committee plenums; during the same period, deputy business-manager for the Central Committee; from 1921–35, worked for the Comintern, then as deputy head of the Secretariat of the All-Russian Central Executive Committee; in 1948–9, a Fellow of the Marx-Engels-Lenin Institute under the Central Committee of the RKP(B).

Brodovsky, student and member of the military staff leading the Nev'yansk uprising in the Urals in June 1918.

Bruno (*Pfafort-Bruno Genrikh Ivanovich*) (1890?), in 1906, participated in Riga circles linked to the RSDRP; 1908–13, worked in Dresden and Berlin, then in St. Petersburg; member of the St. Petersburg Party-Committee; arrested several times and sentenced to exile in 1913 to Irkutsk province, from which he escaped and lived in several different cities in Siberia.

Brusilov, Aleksei Alekseevich (1853–1926), aristocrat and cavalry-general; in 1916, commanded the south-eastern front and broke through the Austro-Hungarian defences; Supreme Commander of the Russian Army from May-July 1917 and supported continuing the War until victory; from 1919, with the Red Army; in 1920, appointed Chair of a Special Conference under the Commander-in-Chief of the Republic's armed forces; subsequently Inspector of Cavalry, and retired in 1924.

Bryukhanov, Nikolai Pavlovich (1878–1942), member of the RSDRP from 1902 and adherent of the Bolshevik faction; amnestied from exile in 1905 and sent to Ufa, where he became a member of the Party's Ufa Committee and member of the Urals District-Committee, taking part in publication of the newspaper *Ural'skii rabochii*; from March 1917, Chairman of the Ufa Soviet of Workers' Deputies; during the October Revolution, Food-Commissar for Ufa province; in 1921, People's Commissar for Food; in 1924–6, Deputy Commissar of Finance;

1926–30, USSR Commissar of Finance; from 1931, Deputy Commissar of Supplies; purged.

Bryusov, Valery Yakovlevich (1873–1924), founder of Russian symbolism, poet, prose-writer, dramatist, critic, teacher, translator; by shocking established literary tastes, earned a scandalous reputation; in 1917, regarded the October Revolution as a turning point in world-history and enthusiastically supported it; 1917–19, headed a committee for registration of the press; from 1920, member of the Communist Party; 1919–21, Chairman of the Presidium of the All-Russian Union of Poets; from 1921, rector of the Literary-Art Institute.

Bukharin, Nikolai Ivanovich (1888–1938), member of the RSDRP from 1906 and worked as a propagandist in Moscow; in 1915 worked for the journal *Kommunist*; after October, editor of *Pravda*; member of the Central Committee, the Politburo of the Central Committee, and the Executive Committee of the Comintern; in 1918, leader of the Left-Communists; in the 1920–1 trade-union dispute, led a 'buffer'-group and then sided with Trotsky; from 1923, opposed the Trotskyists and called for gradual 'growth into socialism'; author of several theoretical works; in 1928, leader of the 'Right-deviation'; expelled from the Politburo in 1929 and from the Party in 1937. Purged.

Bulatsel', Pavel Fedorovich (1867–1919), aristocrat, barrister, writer and a leader of the 'Union of the Russian People'; 1906–7 edited the newspaper *Russkoe znamya*; left politics after the February Revolution in 1917; shot by the Cheka.

Bulgakov, Sergei Nikolaevich (1871–1944), economist, philosopher and theologian; from 1923, lived in emigration; moved from Legal Marxism to religious philosophy and then to Orthodox theology.

Bulygin, Petr Pavlovich (1859–1914), nobleman, writer, member of the Cadets; literary activity began in the 1880s and dealt mainly with the moral flaws of the landlord-intelligentsia, generally ignoring the social problem.

Bunin, Ivan Alekseevich (1870–1953), from an ancient noble-family; poet, prose-writer and translator; did not fully accept the October Revolution and emigrated; Nobel laureate in 1933; buried in the Russian cemetery near Paris.

Bustrem, Vladimir Vladimirovich (1883–?), member of the RSDRP from 1905 working in Arkhangelsk, Tomsk, Nizhnyi Novgorod; member of the St. Petersburg garrison during the 1905 Revolution; arrested and sentenced in 1908 to six years' imprisonment; exiled to eastern Siberia, where he spent the last two years of exile in Irkutsk; from March 1917, member of the Executive Committee of the Arkhangelsk Soviet; a Menshevik-Internationalist, he later joined the RKP(B).

Bykova (*born Proskuryakova*), **Aleksandra Fedorovna** (1863–?), daughter of a senator and author of popular works on history.

Caillaux, Joseph (1863–1944), a leader of the bourgeois Radical party in France; Minister of Finance (1899–1902, 1906–9); Premier from June 1911–January 1912; opposed the War and was charged with treason but found not guilty; returned to active political life during the 1920s and 1930s.

Campanella, Tommaso (*Giovanni Domenico*) (1568–1639), Italian poet and advocate of utopian communism; portrayed an ideal society without private property in his *La città del sole* ('The City of the Sun'), written while he was a prisoner of the Spanish Inquisition (1599–1626).

Canning, George (1770–1827), Prime Minister of Great Britain in 1827; Foreign Secretary from 1807–9; Tory leader from 1822.

Catherine II Alekseevna (1729–96), Empress of Russia from June 1762.

Charushnikov, Akexander Petrovich (1852–1913), Narodnik; in 1879–81, sent to Vyatka to store underground-literature; 1898, created the Moscow publishing house of 'S. Dorovatovsky and A. Charushnikov' to produce democratic and revolutionary books; with Charushnikov's death, the publishing house ceased to exist.

Cherepanov, Sergei Aleksandrovich (1881–1918), member of the RSDRP from

1903; party-worker in Ufa, Samara, Ekaterinburg, Tagil and elsewhere; tried in 1911; after February 1917, one of the leaders of the military organisation of the Petrograd Bolshevik Committee; organised the newspaper *Soldatskaya pravda*; from June 1917, member of the All-Russian Bureau of Military Organisations under the Central Committee of the RSDRP(B); after October, member of the Tomsk Provincial Council of the National Economy; fought against the Czechs and White Guards at Tyumen' and then organised underground-activities in Tyumen'; August 1918, shot by the White Guards.

Cherepanova, Mariya A., Secretary of the Ekaterinburg organisation of the RSDRP; wife of S.A. Cherepanov; managed correspondence from the Urals with N.K. Krupskaya and V.I. Lenin in Paris.

Chernov, Viktor Mikhailovich (1873–1952), theorist and one of the founders of the S-R Party; in revolutionary movement from the late 1880s; in 1917, Minister of Agriculture in the Provisional Government; January 1918, Chairman of the Constituent Assembly; emigrated 1920.

Chernyshevsky, Nikolai Gavrilovich (1828–89), revolutionary-democrat and utopian-socialist, writer and literary critic; provided ideological inspiration for the Russian revolutionary-democratic movement of the 1860s.

Chicherin, Georgy Vasil'evich (1872–1936), nobleman; member of the RSDRP from 1905, Menshevik, internationalist during WWI; 1904–17, in emigration and supported the Bolsheviks; joined the RKP(B) in 1918; in 1917, helped to organise the return of political *émigrés* to Russia; member of the Soviet delegation at the Brest negotiations, at the Genoa Conference (1922) and at the Lausanne Conference (1922–3); 1918–30, People's Commissar of Foreign Affairs for the RSFSR and then for the USSR.

Chilikin, Feofilakt Nikolaevich (1876–?), deputy to the Third State-Duma from the Amur region; until 1909, a member of the Social-Democratic faction, but then not associated with any party.

Chlenov, Semen Borisovich (1890–1937), in 1905–7, one of the leaders of the revolutionary youth movement in Moscow; S-R; emigrated in 1910 and took part in the international student-movement; joined the RKP(B) during the Civil War; in the mid–1920s, worked at the People's Commissariat of Foreign Trade; 1930, instructor at the Institute of Red Professors and the Moscow Industrial-Economic Institute; subsequently worked at the Commissariat of Foreign Trade and as a professor of international law. Purged.

Chugurin, Ivan Dmitrievich (*Petr, Petrukha*) (1883–1947), member of the RSDRP from 1902; participated in the Revolution of 1905–7 in Sormovo; in 1911, attended the party-school in Longjumeau (France); from 1916, member of the St. Petersburg Committee; from 1917, Secretary of the Vyborg District-Committee of the RSDRP(B); during the October Days, member of the district-staff for leading the uprising; 1918–20, political worker in the Red Army and member of the Presidium of the Cheka; did economic work from 1921; director of the 'Krasnoe Sormovo' and 'Dvigatel' revolyutsii' factories in Nizhny Novgorod, of the Northern Shipyard in Leningrad, and Chairman of *Sibugol'*.

Clemenceau, Georges (1841–1929), Prime Minister of France 1906–9 and 1917–20.

Curzon, George (1859–1925), English lord, Conservative political figure and diplomat; 1919–24 served as Foreign Secretary; in July 1920, sent a note to the Soviet government demanding that it halt the advance of the Red Army at the eastern border of Poland.

Dan (*Gurvich*), **Fedor Il'ich** (1871–1947), one of the leaders of Menshevism; a Social Democrat from 1894 and a Menshevik from 1903; social-chauvinist in WWI; after February 1917, favoured coalition with the bourgeoisie; supported the Provisional Government; exiled abroad in 1922.

Danishevsky, Karl Khristianovich (1884–1938), member of the RSDRP from 1900 and a Bolshevik; from the end of 1906, member of the Central Committee of the RSDRP; 1909–11, worked in Moscow and sympathised with the compromisers; after February 1917, member of the Party's Moscow Committee and the Moscow Soviet; after October, member of the Revolutionary War-Council of the Republic and the Revolutionary War-Council of the eastern front, Chairman of the Revolutionary War-Tribunal of the Republic; Chairman of the Revolutionary War-Council of Latvia; from 1921, Secretary of the Siberian Bureau of the Central Committee, and thereafter involved in economic work. Purged.

Danton, Georges Jacques (1759–94), one of the Jacobin leaders in the French Revolution; helped in preparing the uprising of 1792 that overthrew the monarchy.

Demidov, Anatoly Nikolaevich (1812–70), spent nearly his entire life abroad at the Villa San Donato near Florence, receiving the title Prince of San Donato from the Grand Duke of Tuscany; in 1841, married Matilda Laetitia Bonaparte; contributed his father's collection of famous art-works to a gallery in St. Petersburg.

Democritus (*circa* 460–370 BC), Greek materialist philosopher and one of the founders of the atomic theory of the cosmos.

Denikin, Anton Ivanovich (1872–1947), lieutenant-general of the Russian Army and one of the leaders of the White movement in southern Russia during the Civil War; emigrated in 1920.

Deutsch, Lev Grigor'evich (1855–1941), Narodnik from the 1870s and then a Social Democrat, one of the leaders of Menshevism; arrested several times and fled abroad; social-chauvinist in WWI; after February 1917, returned to Petrograd as a right-wing Menshevik defencist; one of the editors of the Menshevik newspaper *Edinstvo*; following October, left politics and worked on the archive of G.V. Plekhanov.

Dioneo (*Shklovsky, Isaak Vladimirovich*) (1864–1935), journalist, critic and prose-writer; Narodnik during the 1870s, exiled to Siberia and then emigrated to London; 1896–1918, London correspondent for the Russian weekly *Russkoe bogatstvo* and the newspaper *Russkie vedomosti*; a liberal who took no part in the Russian revolution.

Dmitriev, Plenipotentiary of the Central Committee for Red-Army mobilisation in Minsk province.

Dmitrieva, Valentina Iovovna (1859–1947), teacher in the 1880s; in 1885, completed a medical course for women in St. Petersburg; arrested for possession of illegal literature; her main creative work dealt with personal impressions of the radicalism of village-teachers and a *zemstvo*-physician.

Dobrolyubov, Nikolai Aleksandrovich (1836–61), literary critic, publicist and revolutionary-democrat; contributed to the journal *Sovremennik*.

Dorovatovsky, Sergei Pavlovich (1854–1921), publisher of Maxim Gorky's books and financial backer of the journal 'Zhizn'.

Dostoyevsky, Fedor Mikhailovich (1821–81), one of Russia's most famous authors and member of the St. Petersburg Academy of Sciences.

Dreiman, Rudolf Ansovich (1887–1938), member of the RSDRP from 1905; after the February Revolution, member of the Executive Committee of the Tomsk Soviet; served in the Red Army following October, and then in the Soviet government of Latvia. Purged.

Dubasov, Fedor Vasil'evich (1845–1912), adjutant-general and admiral, graduate of the Naval Academy; fought in the Russo-Turkish War of 1877–8; 1897–9, commanded the Pacific-Ocean squadron; in 1905, suppressed the peasant-movement in Chernigorsk, Poltavsk and Kursk provinces; November 1905–July 1906, Governor-General of Moscow and led the suppression of the armed uprising in December; member of the State-Council from 1906; from 1907, member of the State Defence-Council.

Dudnik, Akim Minovich (1881–1934), party-member from 1917; in 1917–18, worked in food-supply in Ufa province; in 1919–20, Commissar for food in the Bashkir ASSR; subsequently worked in Ukraine.

Dühring, Eugen Karl (1833–1921), German philosopher and economist, Docent of the University of Berlin from 1863–77.

Durnovo, Petr Nikolaevich (1844–1915), Director of Police from 1884–93; senator from 1893; 1900–5, Deputy Minister and then Minister of Internal Affairs from April 1906 in the cabinet of Sergei Witte; in 1906, member of the State-Council and prominent on the right wing; sympathised with Germany in foreign affairs.

Dutov, Aleksandr Il'ich (1864–1921), Colonel of the Russian General Staff; in June 1917, elected as head of the All-Russian Cossack Conference; from September 1917, Ataman of the Orenburg Cossack army; led an anti-Bolshevik uprising in November 1917; in 1918–19, commanded the Orenburg section of the Cossack army in supporting Kolchak; fled to China in March 1920 and was murdered by Cossacks on his staff in the city of Suidun.

Dzhaparidze, Prokofy Aprasionovich (1880–1918), member of the RSDRP from 1898, doing party-work in Georgia and Azerbaijan; after February 1917, member of the Baku Party-Committee; elected candidate-member of the Central Committee at the Party's Sixth Congress; following October, Chairman of the Executive Committee of the Baku Soviet, Commissar of Internal Affairs, Commissar of Food for the Baku Council of the National Economy; one of 26 Baku commissars shot by the English after a temporary retreat of Soviet forces.

Egor, see Kanatchikov, S.I.

Ekaterina II Alekseevna (1729–96), Empress of Russia from June 1762.

Ekaterinoslavl'sky, Mikhail, in 1905 a member of the Orel Committee of the RSDRP.

Eliseenko, A., a former captain and S-R leader of the anti-Bolshevik Nev'yansk uprising in the Urals in June 1918.

Elpat'evsky, Sergei Yakovlevich (1854–1933), Russian writer and physician; sent to eastern Siberia for three years for being a member of The People's Will (*Narodnaya Volya*); later an editor of the journal *Russkie vedomosti*; in 1906, one of the organisers of the Trudovik Party.

Emel'yanov, Vasily Antonovich (1884–1961), member of the RSDRP from 1904, Bolshevik; participated in all three revolutions in Moscow; February-March 1917, member of the Presnensky Revolutionary Committee; after October, member of the Moscow Soviet of Workers' Deputies; during the Civil War, political worker in the Third Army on the eastern front; subsequently involved in soviet- and economic work; from 1937, recipient of a pension for merit.

Engels, Friedrich (1820–95), together with Karl Marx, founder of scientific communism.

Epicurus (341–270 BC), ancient-Greek materialist philosopher.

Eremeev, Konstantin Stepanovich (1874–1931), member of the RSDRP from 1896; after February 1917, member of the Central Committee; in October, member of the Petrograd Military-Revolutionary Committee and led the storming of the Winter Palace; led revolutionary troops in suppressing the uprising by Junkers and Kerensky-Krasnov; one of the organisers of the defence of Petrograd against Germany; in 1919–22, Plenipotentiary of the Central Committee in mobilising the population to support the Red Army; later a member of the Revolutionary War-Council and leader of the political department of the Baltic fleet.

Ermansky (*Kogan*) **Osip Arkad'evich** (1866–1941), Social Democrat, Menshevik; after 1907, a liquidator; contributor to the Menshevik journals *Sovremennyi mir*, *Nasha zarya* and *Sovremennik*; centrist during WWI; in 1917 a Menshevik-Internationalist; in 1918, member of the Menshevik Central Committee; left the Menshevik Party in 1921 to take up scientific work in Moscow.

F.F., see V.I. Lenin.

Fedor Kuzmich, see Alexander I.

Fenomenov, Mikhail, student at the Orel seminary.

Fet (*Shenshin*), **Afanasy Afanas'evich** (1820–92), poet and supporter of 'pure art'.

Feuerbach, Ludwig (1804–72), German-materialist philosopher and atheist, a forerunner of Marxism.

Feuchtwanger, Lion (1884–1958), German author of the historical novel *Die häßliche Herzogin Margarete Maultasch* (*The Ugly Duchess*), 1923.

Fichte, Johann Gottlieb (1762–1814), German-idealist philosopher.

Figner, Vera Nikolaevna (1852–1942), member of the Executive Committee of *Narodnaya Volya*; imprisoned for twenty years in the Shlisselburg fortress for involvement in the assassination of Alexander II; 1906–15, in emigration; author of *Memoirs of a Revolutionist*; died in Moscow.

Fokin, Ignatii Ivanovich (1889–1919), member of the RSDRP from 1906; conducted party-work in Bryansk, St. Petersburg and Saratov; after February 1917, one of the organisers of the Bryansk and Bezhetsk party-committees; from May 1917, Chairman of the Bryansk Committee and member of the Moscow District-Bureau of the Party; from October 1917, Chairman of the Bryansk Party-Committee and of the Military-Revolutionary Committee.

Foma, see Lebedev.

Fourier, Charles (1772–1837), French utopian-socialist.

Franz Ferdinand (1863–1914), Austrian Archduke whose assassination in Sarajevo contributed to triggering the First World-War.

Frederick-William III (1770–1840), King of Prussia after 1797.

Frolenko, Mikhail Fedorovich (1848–1938), revolutionary Narodnik; member of the Tchaikovsky circle; sent to the Urals in 1874 to organise Siberian fugitives into a fighting detachment; 1875–9, organised prison-escapes for Narodniks; member of *Narodnaya Volya*; involved in an attempt to assassinate Alexander II near Odessa and sentenced to death in 1881, with the sentence being commuted to life-imprisonment; amnestied in October 1905 and under police-supervision until 1917; member of the Communist Party from 1936.

Frolov, former lieutenant, member of the military staff that led the anti-Bolshevik Nev'yansk uprising in the Urals in June 1918; Cadet.

G.Z., see Zinoviev, G.E.

Galkin, Anatoly M., member of the RSDRP from mid-February 1910; member of the so-called Tomsk commune consisting of people who had served time in the Aleksandrovsk transit-prison (V.I. Shamshin, Artem Sergeev, E.A. Preobrazhensky, P. Kovalenko and others); subsequently exiled to Karapchansky parish of Kirensky district in Irkutsk province.

Galunov, Mikhail, member of the Novonikolaevsk organisation of the RSDRP.

Garibaldi, Giuseppe (1807–82), Italian national hero and participant in the Italian revolution of 1848–9; fought against Austria in 1848, 1859, and 1866 at the head of volunteer-forces; in 1860, headed the force that emancipated southern Italy and contributed to victory of the Italian revolution in 1859–60; in 1862 and 1867, fought to free Rome from papal rule; fought as a volunteer with the French against Prussia during the war of 1870–1 and supported the Paris Commune of 1871.

Gegechkori, Evgeny Petrovich (1881–1954), lawyer and a leader of Georgian Mensheviks; deputy to the Third Duma; from 1917, member of the Special Transcaucasia Committee of the Provisional Government, Chairman of the Transcaucasia Commissariat, minister of the Menshevik government of Georgia; emigrated in 1922.

George (Zhorzh), see Plekhanov, G.V.

Gladstone, William (1809–98), Prime Minister of Great Britain from 1868–74, 1880–6, 1892–4; leader of the Liberal Party from 1868.

Godunov, Boris (*circa* 1552–1605), Russian Regent and then Tsar.

Goethe, Johann Wolfgang von (1749–1832), one of Germany's most famous writers and an honorary member of the St. Petersburg Academy of Sciences; Goethe's tragedy *Faust* is regarded as one of the great works of world-literature.

Gololobov, Yakov Georgievich (1855–?), elected to the Third Duma in 1907 as an Octobrist; 1909, created a separate group of right-Octobrists; in December 1911, accused of involvement in organising the murder of Dr. Karavayev, a deputy of the Second Duma; the Duma found Gololobov innocent and he successfully sued his accusers.

Goloshchekin, Filipp (*Isai*) Isakovich (1876–1941), member of the RSDRP from 1903; did revolutionary work in St. Petersburg, Moscow, Kronstadt and the Urals; several times arrested and exiled; member of the Perm City-Committee and then Secretary of the Urals Regional Committee of the RSDRP; from 1917, regional Commissar of Justice and then Commissar of the Urals military region; member of the Executive Committee of the Regional Soviet and of the Regional Committee of the RKP(B); in July 1918, one of the organisers of the execution of the Tsar and his family; in 1918, main Political Commissar of the Third Army and member of the Revolutionary War-Council of the Turkestan commission of the All-Russian Central Executive Committee and the Council of People's Commissars of the RSFSR; from 1925, member of the Kazakh Territorial Committee of the RKP(B); from 1933, chief state-arbitrator under the Council of People's Commissars of the RSFSR. Purged.

Golubkov, A., leader of a Social-Democratic youth-circle in Orel.

Gompers, Samuel (1850–1924), trade-union leader in the USA; advocated political neutrality of unions and their involvement exclusively in economic struggle.

Goncharov, Nikolai Kuz'mich (1866–1970), member of the RSDRP from 1904; in 1917, Commissar of the Moscow Military-Revolutionary Committee; from April 1918, member of the Presidium of the Executive Committee of the Moscow Soviet; fought at the front in the Civil War; from March 1920, member of the Far-Eastern Bureau of the Central Committee of the RKP(B), member of the Siberian Bureau of the Central Committee of the RKP(B) and head of the political directorate for armed forces in Siberia; in subsequent years, involved in party- and economic work.

Gorky, Maxim (*Aleksei Maksimovich Peshkov*) (1868–1936), writer, publicist and first head of the Union of Soviet Writers in 1934.

Gornfel'd, Arkady Georgievich (1867–1941), literary critic, translator and correspondent of the journal *Russkoe bogatstvo*.

Grave, Jean (1854–1939), French socialist and theorist of anarchism and anarcho-syndicalism; social-chauvinist during WWI.

Gredeskul, Nikolai Andreevich (1864–?), jurist, professor, member of the Central Committee of the Cadet Party; deputy to the First Duma; left the Cadets in 1916; following October, adopted ideas similar to those of the Smenovekhovtsy.

Griboedov, Aleksandr Sergeevich (1795–1829), Russian playwright, composer and diplomat, suspected by the authorities of involvement with the Decembrists.

Guchkov, Aleksandr Ivanovich (1862–1936), leader of the Octobrist party; from 1910, Chairman of the Third Duma; 1915–17, Chairman of the Central Military-Industrial Committee; in 1917, War-Minister of the Provisional Government; one of the organisers of the coup-attempt by Kornilov, and then emigrated.

Guesde, Jules (1845–1922), one of the founders of the French Workers' Party and prominent in the Second International; a centrist in the pre-war years; a social-chauvinist during the War and minister in the French government, 1914–16.

Gusev, Sergei Ivanovich (*Drabkin, Yakov Davidovich*) (1874–1933), member of the RSDRP from 1896; participated in the revolutions of 1905–7 and 1917 in Petrograd; member of the Military-Revolutionary Committee; from 1918, one of the political leaders of the Red Army; from 1921, head of the political directorate of the Red Army and member of the Revolutionary War-Council; 1923–5, Secretary of the Central Control-Commission of the RKP(B), working in the Party's Central-Committee apparatus and the Executive Committee of the Communist International;

headed a military-historical commission of the Revolutionary War-Council of the Republic to study the lessons of WWI and the Civil War.

Gusev-Orenburgsky (*Gusev*) **Sergei Ivanovich** (1867–1963), prose-writer; studied at Orenburg and Ufa seminaries and became a teacher after leaving the seminary; published his first story in 1890 and became a professional writer in 1898; wrote mainly on the lives and attitudes of the Russian clergy.

Guzakov, Petr Vasil'evich (1889–1944), member of the RSDRP from 1905; participant in terrorist-operations in the southern Urals; from 1911, did illegal party-work in Vyatka, Kazan, Zlatoust and Ufa; arrested and sentenced to imprisonment and exile in Irkutsk province; following February 1917, Chairman of the Soviet of Workers' and Peasants' Deputies in Simsky region; following October, fought against Dutov's supporters as Military Commissar of the region; participated in transporting the Tsar and his family from Tobolsk to Ekaterinburg; 1920–3, head of the Cheka in Omsk and Bashkiria; 1923–5, Secretary of the Kursk Provincial Committee of the RKP(B); 1925–7, head of Soviet radio-broadcasting; from 1928, worked in the Supreme Council of the National Economy.

Gyunter, Konrad (1874–1955), German zoologist.

Haimson, Leopold (1927–2010), American historian of the Russian revolutionary movement.

Hartman, Eduard (1842–1906), German-idealist philosopher and predecessor of Schopenhauer.

Hegel, Georg Wilhelm Friedrich (1770–1831), German objective-idealist philosopher and foremost representative of classical German philosophy.

Heine, Heinrich (1797–1856), one of the most celebrated German romantic poets.

Helvétius, Claude Adrien (1715–71), French philosopher of the revolutionary bourgeoisie who considered human consciousness and passion to be the principal forces of social development; condemned by the Church as a proponent of atheism.

Heraclitus of Ephesus (late sixth and early fifth century BC), ancient philosopher of the Ionian school.

Hertling, Georg Friedrich Graf von (1843–1919), specialist in medieval philosophy and professor; from 1875, a deputy in the Reichstag for the Centre Party; from 1909, head of the centrist faction in the Reichstag; 1912–17, Bavarian Minister-President; Chancellor of the Reich in the autumn of 1918 and Prime Minister of Prussia; retired after Germany's defeat in WWI.

Herzen, Aleksandr Aleksandrovich (1839–1906), son of A.I. Herzen; studied medicine and natural sciences in Switzerland; from 1877, professor of physiology in Florence; from 1881, in Lausanne.

Herzen, Alexander Ivanovich (1812–70), revolutionary, writer and philosopher; became a revolutionary under the influence of the Decembrists while at Moscow University; arrested in 1834 and spent six years in exile; emigrated in 1847; gave up hope for Western revolutions after 1848 and turned to the idea of 'Russian socialism', which eventually encouraged the Narodniks; assisted in creating *Zemlya I Volya*; supported the Polish uprising in 1863–4; in his later years, became more attentive to the First International and the struggle of the working class.

Hilferding, Rudolf (1877–1941), one of the leading economic thinkers of Austrian and German Social Democracy in the Second International and author of *Finance Capital*; opposed Soviet power and the dictatorship of the proletariat; in 1923 and 1928–9, German Finance-Minister.

Hindenburg, Paul von (1847–1934), German Field-Marshal and President of Germany from 1925; commander of the Eastern Front during WWI; in 1933, appointed Hitler to form a government.

Hoffmann, Max (1869–1927), general of the German Army; during WWI, Quartermaster-General and Chief of Staff on the Eastern Front; *de facto* head of German negotiators for the Brest treaty with Soviet Russia.

Homer, legendary ancient-Greek author of the *Iliad* and the *Odyssey*.

Horvat, Dmitrii Leonidovich (1858–1937), lieutenant-general; 1902–18, head of the Chinese Eastern Railway, and in 1917, Commissar of the Provisional Government for the railway; summer 1918, declared himself to be 'Provisional Russian Supreme Ruler'; appointed by A.V. Kolchak as 'Supreme Plenipotentiary for the Far East'; from May 1918, commanded the forces of the Amur military region; emigrated to China and became adviser to the Mukden government on matters concerning the Chinese Eastern Railway; from 1924, Chairman of the Far-Eastern branch of the Russian All-Military Union (ROVS).

Hughes, William Morris (1862–1952), Prime Minister of Australia from 1915–23.

Hurd, Dennis, professor at the London Labour College.

Hus, Jan (1371–1415), Czech national hero and leader of the Czech Reformation; rector of Charles University in Prague; advocated return to early Christian principles and was burned at the stake as a heretic.

Ignatovich, Nina Ivanovna (1879–?), historian specialising in peasant-history during the first half of the nineteenth century.

Il'in, V., see V.I. Lenin

Iliodor (*Trufanov, Sergei Mikhailovich*) (1880–1952), a Russian monk and one of the founders of the 'Union of the Russian People'; a violent anti-Semite and, until 1911, a close associate of Rasputin; denounced Christianity in 1912; emigrated in 1914; author of *Svyatoi chert* (*The Holy Devil*) alleging an amorous relationship between Rasputin and the Empress Alexandra Feodorovna.

Ilovaisky, Dmitry Ivanovich (1832–1920), conservative historian and author of several history-textbooks for gymnasium-instructors.

Ilyushin, Fedor Nikolaevich (1892–?), member of the RSDRP from 1917; participated in the Moscow City-Conference of the RSDRP(B) on war and peace; Plenipotentiary of the Central Committee of the RKP(B) for the Moscow mobilisation for the Red Army.

Ioffe, Adolph Abramovich (1883–1927), in the Social-Democratic movement from the 1890s and a Bolshevik from 1917; in October 1917, a member of the Petrograd Military-Revolutionary Committee; in 1918 a Left-Communist; member of the Soviet delegation to the Brest peace-negotiations; from April to November 1918, RSFSR political representative in Berlin; 1919–20, member of the Defence-Council and Commissar of State-Control for the Ukrainian Soviet government; in 1920, Soviet representative in peace-talks with Estonia, Latvia, Lithuania and Poland; from 1921, Deputy Chairman of the Turk Commission of the All-Russian Central Executive Committee and the Council of People's Commissars of the RSFSR; Soviet participant at the Genoa Conference in 1922 and subsequently involved in diplomatic work; 1925–7, supported the Trotskyist opposition; ended his life by suicide.

Ivanovich, St. (*Portugeis, S.I.*), a Menshevik publicist and a liquidator after 1907; contributor to the newspaper *Golos sotsial-demokrata*, the journal *Nasha zarya* and other publications; social-chauvinist during WWI; after October, a contributor to the White-Guard press in southern Russia and then emigrated.

Ivanyukov, Ivan Ivanovich (1844–1912), Russian professor and historian whose works dealt mainly with the peasant-reforms.

Ivinsky, Boleslav (1879–1919), member of the Polish Socialist Party-Left; after February 1917, member of the Petrograd organisation of the PPS; at the end of 1917 sent to Ukraine; Commissar for Polish affairs in the first Soviet government of Ukraine; returned to Poland in 1919 and was a member of the Soviet of Workers' Deputies in Warsaw.

Izgoev, Aleksandr Solomonovich (*Lande Aron*) (1872–1935), originally a 'Legal Marxist', then a Social Democrat, before becoming a Cadet in 1905; worked for several Cadet publications, including the newspaper *Rech'* and the journals *Yuzhnye zapiski* and *Russkaya mysl'*; contributor to *Vekhi*; after October 1917, contributed to *Vetsnik literatury*; exiled in 1922 to Berlin and spent his later years in Estonia.

Izmailov, Abdrakhman Yu. (1889–1957), member of the RSDRP from 1907; in 1917 member of the Kazan Soviet; 1917–19, member of the Tatar Regional Committee of the RKP(B); in 1919–20, member of the Bashkir Regional Committee of the RKP(B) and Cheka-Chairman in Bashkiriya; in 1920, RSFSR representative to the Khorezm People's Soviet Republic.

Joli, associate of Louis Pasteur.

Kadomtsev, Erazm Samuilovich (1881–1965), a nobleman involved in the revolutionary movement from 1896 and member of the RSDRP from 1901; fought in the Russo-Japanese War; in 1906, organised armed workers' detachments in the southern and central Urals; in March 1906, member of the military-fighting centre under the Bolshevik Central Committee; emigrated in 1909; returned to Russia in 1914 to do revolutionary work in the army; participant in the October Revolution and the Civil War; subsequently involved in military, party- and economic positions.

Kaledin, Aleksei Maksimovich (1861–1918), general of the tsarist army and Ataman of the Don Cossacks; active supporter of the attempted putsch by Kornilov; one of the organisers of the White-Guard Volunteer-Army; shot himself following military defeat in January 1918.

Kalinin, Mikhail Ivanovich (1875–1946), member of the RSDRP from 1898; member of the St. Petersburg 'Union of Struggle for the Emancipation of the Working Class'; agent for *Iskra*; participated in the 1905–7 revolution in St. Petersburg; in 1912, member of the Russian Bureau of the Central Committee of the RSDRP; one of the organisers of *Pravda*; participated in the February and October revolutions in Petrograd; from 1919, Chairman of the All-Russian Central Executive Committee; from 1922, Chairman of the Central Executive Committee of the USSR; from 1938, Chairman of the Presidium of the Supreme Soviet of the USSR.

Kamenev (*Rozenfel'd*), **Lev Borisovich** (1883–1936), member of the RSDRP from 1901; did revolutionary work in Tiflis, Moscow and St. Petersburg; an editor of *Proletarii* and *Pravda*; in November 1917, supported a coalition-government with Mensheviks and S-Rs; after the October Revolution, Chairman of the Moscow Soviet, Deputy Chairman of the Council of People's Commissars, member of the Politburo of the Central Committee of the RKP(B); one of the organisers of the 'New Opposition' in 1925; in 1926, one of the leaders of the Trotsky-Zinoviev bloc. Purged.

Kamensky, Anatoly Pavlovich (1876–1941), nobleman; prose-writer, dramatist, fashionable writer of *belles-lettres* and contributor to the 'boulevard' press; after 1918, lived in Berlin, but returned to the USSR in 1924; emigrated in 1930 but returned in September 1935; died in the purges.

Kanatchikov, Semen Ivanovich (*Egor*) (1879–1940), member of the RSDRP from 1898; party-worker in Moscow, St. Petersburg, Saratov, Ekaterinburg and Nizhny Tagil; involved in trade-union work in Petrograd 1908–10; 1910–16, in prison and exile in Irkutsk province; in 1917, member of the RSDRP(B) party-committees in Novonikolaevsk and Tomsk; in 1918, Chairman of the Tomsk Military-Revolutionary Staff and Deputy Chairman of the Provincial Executive Committee; in 1919, served in Moscow as a member of the Collegium of the People's Commissariat of Internal Affairs, as member of the small *Sovnarkom* and one of the organisers of the Communist University named after Ya.M. Sverdlov; in 1920, member of the Siberian Revolutionary Committee and head of the Siberian department of public education, Chairman of the Tatar Regional Committee of the RKP(B); from 1921, rector of the Communist University in Petrograd; in 1924–6 head of a department of the Central Committee of the VKP(B); 1926–8 correspondent for TASS in Czechoslovakia; from 1928, involved with literary work.

Kant, Immanuel (1724–1804), renowned German-idealist philosopher and professor at Königsberg University from 1770.

Kapustin, Mikhail Yakovlevich (1847–?), hereditary aristocrat; Octobrist from 1905 and founder of the 'Union of 17 October' in Kazan province; deputy from Kazan to the Second and Third State-Dumas.

Karakhan, Lev Mikhailovich (1889–1937), member of the RSDRP from 1904; exiled to Tomsk in autumn 1915; after February 1917, member of the Presidium and Secretary of the Petrograd Soviet and member of the Military-Revolutionary Committee; from July 1917, a Bolshevik; in 1917–18, Secretary and member of the Bolshevik delegation to the Brest peace-talks; 1918–20, Deputy People's Commissar of Foreign Affairs; in 1921, political representative of the USSR in Poland; from August 1923, USSR representative in China; 1927–34, Deputy People's Commissar of Foreign Affairs, and subsequently ambassador to Turkey. Purged.

Karavaev, Aleksandr L'vovich (1855–1908), *zemstvo*-doctor and member of the Peasant-Union; elected in 1906 as deputy to the Second State-Duma from Ekaterinoslav; leader of the Trudovik group; author of works on the agrarian question; following dissolution of the Second Duma, devoted himself to medical practice; killed by the Black Hundreds in Ekaterinoslav on the eve of elections to the Third State-Duma.

Kasso, Lev Aristidovich (1865–1914), major landowner, professor of civil law at Khar'kov and later Moscow University; 1910–14, Minister of Popular Education; a radical conservative.

Katsura, Taro (1847–1913, Japanese soldier, politician and Prime Minister in 1901–5, 1908–11 and 1912–13; Katsuro's government waged war against Russia in 1904–5.

Kautsky, Karl (1854–1938), one of the major leaders and theoreticians of German Social Democracy and the Second International; a centrist whose theory of 'ultra-imperialism' implied a new stage of capitalism and indefinite postponement of proletarian revolution; opposed the October Revolution in Russia.

Kashirin, Nikolai Dmitrievich (1888–1938), Cossack by birth and a captain during WWI; one of the organisers of the Red Army in Verkhneural'sk; fought against Dutov's forces; in 1918, led a partisan-army in the southern Urals; after being wounded, served on the staff of V.K. Blücher; from September 1918, deputy commander and then commander of the 4th Urals Division; October–November 1919, commander of the 49th Rifle-Division; March–October 1920, Chairman of the Orenburg Provincial Executive Committee and commander of the Alexandrovsk army-group against Makhno; 1923–5 served on the staff of the Red Army; 1925–31, various military posts; 1931–7, commander of the North-Caucasus military region; from 1934, member of the Military Council of the USSR; in July-August 1937, commander of the Main Department for Military Preparations. Purged.

Kerensky, Aleksandr Fedorovich (1881–1970), member of the Trudovik Party; during the February Revolution of 1917, member and Deputy Chairman of the Executive Committee of the Petrograd Soviet (representing the S-R Party); member of the Provisional Government as Minister of Justice, Army- and Navy-Minister, Minister-Chairman and Supreme Commander; following the October Revolution, organised with Krasnov an unsuccessful attempt to retake the capital; supported neither the Whites nor the Bolsheviks during the Civil War.

Kharitonov, Moisei Markovich (1887–1948), member of the RSDRP from 1905; party-worker in Nikolaev and Odessa; 1912, emigrated to Switzerland; after February 1917, member of the Petrograd Committee of the RSDRP(B); did party-, economic and military work after October in Petrograd and Kiev; from 1921, Secretary of the Perm Provincial Committee of the RKP(B); from December 1923 to July 1925, Secretary of the Urals Regional Committee of the RKP(B);

member of the Trotsky-Zinoviev bloc; worked in the apparatus of the Central Control-Commission in 1928 and in the Commissariat of Foreign Trade. Purged.

Khionin, photographer and member of the military staff that led the anti-Bolshevik Nev'yansk uprising in the Urals in June 1918.

Khokhryakov, Pavel Danilovich (1893–1918), sailor and Bolshevik; in 1917, agitator on a frigate in Murmansk; in Ekaterinburg during the autumn of 1917 to assist local party-organisations in forming military units; head of the central staff of the Red Guards, head of the central staff of the Red-Army reserve in the Urals, and member of the Executive Committee of the Ekaterinburg Soviet and the Urals Regional Soviet; March 1918, Chairman of the Tobolsk Soviet in charge of moving the Tsar and his family from Tobolsk to Ekaterinburg; June 1918, formed an expeditionary force and a river-flotilla and commanded battle-operations on the Irtysh-Tura rivers; died fighting the White Guards.

Khristich, lieutenant, died in the Russo-Japanese War.

Khvostov, Aleksei Nikolaevich (1872–1918), Minister of Internal Affairs from 1915–16; right-wing leader in the Fourth State-Duma; executed by Soviet authorities.

Kin (*Orekhova*), **Aleksandra Petrovna** (*Liza*) (1879–1956), member of the RSDRP from 1904, doing party-work in Vyatka, Nizhnetigal', Perm and Zlatoust; arrested in Perm in 1906; worked in Samara 1907–10; in 1917 member of the Khar'kov City-Committee of the RSDRP(B); in 1918, Political Commissar of the medical administration of the Fifth Army; from 1920, member of the Khar'kov City-Soviet and worked for the Central Committee of the Communist Party of Ukraine; retired 1923.

Klyuchevsky, Vasily Osipovich (1841–1911), historian, professor at Moscow University and member of the Cadet Party; author of numerous publications, the most famous being his *Course of Russian History*.

Kokovtsov, Vladimir Nikolaevich (1853–1943), count, senator, member of the State-Council; Finance-Minister 1904–14 and Chairman of the Council of Ministers from 1911–14 following the assassination of P.A. Stolypin; prominent banker; emigrated 1918.

Kolb, Georg Friedrich (1808–84), sociologist, statistician and Bavarian political figure; author of the two-volume work *Culturgeschichte der Menschheit* (*History of Human Culture*).

Kolchak, Aleksandr Vasil'evich (1873–1920), polar explorer and admiral; 1916–17, commander of the Black-Sea fleet; 1918–20, leader of the White movement and 'Supreme Ruler of the Russian State'; shot by order of the Irkutsk Military-Revolutionary Committee.

Kolegaev, Andrei Lukich (1887–1937), one of the leaders of the Left S-Rs; participated in the October armed uprising in Petrograd; deputy to the Second All-Russian Congress of Soviets; member of the All-Russian Central Executive Committee; December 1917–March 1918, People's Commissar of Agriculture, but resigned in protest at the Brest peace; broke with the S-Rs after their attempted uprising and became one of the organisers of the Party of Revolutionary Communism; member of the RKP(B) from November 1918; 1918–20, Chairman of the special food-commission and member of the Revolutionary War-Council on the southern front; 1920–1, member of the Collegium of the Commissariat of Transportation; subsequently involved in economic work. Purged.

Kolosov, Evgeny Evgen'evich (1879–1937), writer; defencist during WWI; from early February 1917, leader of the S-Rs in Krasnoyarsk and editor of the newspaper *Nash golos*; published in the journal *Russkoe bogatstvo*, among others; Commissar for Kronstadt under the Provisional Government; supported intervention during the Civil War; relocated to Petrograd in 1922 and contributed to the journals *Byloe, Katorga i ssylka* and others; wrote on the Civil War in Siberia and the history of the revolutionary movement; arrested more than once from 1925. Purged.

Kolyubakin, Aleksandr Mikhailovich (1868–1915), *zemstvo*-figure and Cadet; 1905–6, Chairman of the Novgorod Provincial *Zemstvo*-Council; 1907, deputy to the Third Duma from St. Petersburg;

Secretary of the Cadet parliamentary group in the Third and Fourth Dumas; died in WWI.

Kondurushkin, Stepan Semenovich (1874–1919), prose-writer and journalist from a poor-peasant background; after graduating from the Kazan Teacher-Institute was invited by the Palestine Society to work in Syria, where he spent five years; published in *Russkoe bogatstvo* and other journals; war-correspondent during WWI for the Cadet newspaper *Rech'*; emigrated in 1918.

Konovalov, Ivan Andreevich (1884–1911), publicist involved in the revolutionary movement from 1902; arrested several times and exiled in 1906 to Tobolsk province; as correspondent for the journal *Russkoe bogatstvo* in 1909–10 researched the effects of Stolypin's reforms on the peasantry in Saratov, Kazan, Orel and other provinces.

Kornilov, Lavr Georgievich (1870–1918), infantry-general and Supreme Commander from July-August 1917; in late August and early September, led troops against St. Petersburg to restore order and was arrested; one of the organisers of the White-Guard Volunteer-Army in November-December 1917; died in battle.

Korolenko, Vladimir Galaktionovich (1853–1921), prose-writer, publicist and public figure; involved in the revolutionary movement from the 1870s as a Narodnik; spent many years in prison and exile; from 1894, shareholder in the journal *Russkoe bogatstvo* and member of its literary-editorial committee; from 1895, official publisher of the journal and its director from 1896–1918; defencist during WWI; after the October Revolution, protested against press-restrictions and repression by the Cheka, calling for 'the interests of the whole people' to be placed 'above the party-struggle'.

Kosarev, Vladimir Mikhailovich (1881–1945), member of the RSDRP from 1898; arrested more than once; in 1909 sent to the party-school on the island of Capri; upon return, arrested and sent to exile in Narym; after February 1917, Chairman of the Tomsk Soviet; participated in organising Soviet power in western Siberia; worked in the Urals following the Czechoslovak uprising; at the end of 1919, member of the Siberian Revolutionary Committee and Siberian Bureau of the Central Committee of the RKP(B); in 1921–2, Chairman of Novonikolaevsk City Executive Committee; 1923–8, member of the Central Control-Commission and its Presidium and also member of the Moscow Committee of the RKP(B).

Kosior, Iosif Vikent'evich (1893–1937), member of the RSDRP from 1908; imprisoned more than once; in 1912 exiled to Ekaterinburg province; in 1916–17, member of the Irkutsk Party-Committee; in February 1917, fled from exile to Moscow and worked in the Moscow District-Bureau of the RSDRP; in October 1917, Chairman of the Military-Revolutionary Committee of Zamoskvorets district and then Chairman of the Zamoskvorets District-Soviet; during the Civil War, Commissar of a division, member of the Revolutionary War-Council of the army, and commander of a labour-army; from 1923 head of *Grozneft* (oil), Chairman of the board of *Yugostal* (steel), Deputy Chairman of the Supreme Council of the National Economy, Deputy Commissar of heavy industry, among other posts. Purged.

Kostomarov, Nikolai Ivanovich (1817–85), ethnographer, historian and writer; supporter of Ukrainian cultural-national autonomy.

Kotoshikhin, Grigory Karpovich (*circa* 1630–67), beaten by order of Tsar Aleksei Mikhailovich for mistakenly writing the Tsar's title in documents; fled abroad in 1664; in 1666, under the name of Ivan Selitsky, appointed to Swedish government-service and commissioned to write a study of 'Russia during the Reign of Aleksei Mikhailovich'; executed for murdering the owner of the house in which he lived.

Kovalenko, Petr Arsent'evich (1889–1936), Bolshevik, sentenced for participation in a student-movement and exiled to Irkutsk province; 1911, moved to Novonikolaevsk; in January 1918, Secretary of the Novonikolaevsk Committee of the RSDRP(B); underground-worker during the Civil War and subsequently at the Engineering Construction Institute in Moscow. Purged.

Kovalenko, Sof'ya L'vovna (1889–?), member of the Novonikolaevsk party-organisation and wife of Petr Kovalenko.

Kovalevsky, Maksim Maksimovich (1851–1916), historian, jurist, sociologist and professor at Moscow University; deputy to the First Duma and then member of the State-Council; one of the founders of the Party of Democratic Reforms; in 1906–7, published the newspaper *Strana*; from 1909, owned and edited the journal *Vestnik Evropy*.

Krasin, Leonid Borisovich (1870–1926), Social Democrat from 1890; exiled to Irkutsk for three years in 1895; a Bolshevik from 1903; in the first Russian Revolution, he headed a military-technical group under the Party's Central Committee and managed supply for fighting units; 1908, emigrated; abandoned political activity to work as an engineer; after October 1918, Chairman of the Extraordinary Commission for the supply of the Red Army, member of the Presidium of the Supreme Council of the National Economy, People's Commissar for Trade and Industry; in 1919, People's Commissar for Transportation; subsequently did diplomatic work in England and was, for a time, People's Commissar of Foreign Trade; in 1922, participated at the international conferences in Geneva and The Hague; from 1924, ambassador to France and then ambassador to England.

Krasnov, Petr Nikolaevich (1869–1947), lieutenant-general and one of the White leaders during the Civil War; in October 1917, together with A.F. Kerensky, attempted to suppress the Bolsheviks; in 1918–19 Ataman of the Don Army and commander of the White Cossack Army; emigrated to Germany in 1919; collaborated with Hitler's forces during WWII; executed after the British turned him over as a war-prisoner to Soviet authorities.

Krestinsky, Nikolai Nikolaevich (1883–1938), member of the RSDRP from 1903; arrested seven times; participated in founding *Pravda* and other Social-Democratic publications; member of the Social-Democratic fraction in the Third and Fourth State-Dumas; in 1905, arrested and exiled to the Urals; in March 1917, restored the Urals organisation of the RSDRP; in April led the First (free) Urals Social-Democratic Conference, which established a regional committee and elected him Chairman; 26 October (7 November) declared Soviet power in Ekaterinburg and headed a coalition revolutionary committee; deputy to the Constituent Assembly from Perm province; in Petrograd from December; 1918–22, People's Commissar of Finance for the RSFSR; following the death of Sverdlov, Secretary and then Lead-Secretary for the Central Committee of the RKP(B); from March 1919 to 1921, member of the Politburo of the Central Committee of the RKP(B); from 1921–30, ambassador to Germany, participating in the conferences at Genoa and The Hague; supported Trotsky in the struggle with Stalin; in 1930, Deputy People's Commissar of Foreign Affairs. Purged.

Krestovnikovs, a Russian family of industrialists and merchants; originally monastery-officials in the city of Pereslavl-Zalessky; the founder of the dynasty, Koz'ma Vasen'evich Krestovnikov, moved to Moscow in 1777 and opened a sugar-mill, bleaching factories and weaving mills; his sons and grandsons continued these businesses; Grigory Aleksandrovich Krestovnikov (1855–1918) was an Octobrist, director of the Moscow-Kursk Railway, Chairman of the Moscow Merchants' Bank and of the Moscow Stock-Exchange; from 1906, member of the State-Council representing the commercial-industrial bourgeoisie.

Krivov, Timofei Stepanovich (1886–1966), member of the RSDRP from 1905; participated in the Revolution of 1905–7 in Ufa and Zlatoust; organiser of terrorist-acts and 'expropriations'; arrested; emigrated 1910–11 and imprisoned upon return to Russia; after February 1917, member of the Ufa Provincial Executive Committee and worked in the political department of the Fifth Army; 1920–2, Secretary of the Urals Bureau of the

Central Committee of the RKP(B), then involved in party-, soviet- and trade-union work in Moscow; member of the Central Control-Commission, Deputy People's Commissar of the Worker-Peasant Inspectorate of the RSFSR, arbitrator for the RSFSR Council of the National Economy, Deputy People's Commissar of Finance for the RSFSR.

Krivoshein, Aleksandr Vasil'evich (1858–1923), State-Secretary and Chamberlain; responsible for implementing Stolypin's land-reforms; member of the Council of Ministers and the State Council, Deputy Minister of Finance; after October, one of the leaders of the counter-revolutionary 'centre-right'; in 1920, headed Wrangel's government in Crimea.

Kropotkin, Peter Alekseevich (1842–1921), prince, geographer, geologist, and theorist of revolutionary anarchism; 1872–4, member of the 'Tchaikovsky Circle' conducting revolutionary propaganda among St. Petersburg workers; in emigration from 1876 to early 1917; defencist during WWI; upon return to Russia, rejected a suggestion from A.F. Kerensky that he head the Provisional Government; acknowledged the socialist character of the October Revolution; from the summer of 1918, resided in Dmitrov; in July 1920 wrote a letter to Western workers calling upon them to prevent their governments from intervening in the Soviet Republic; in his works from 1918–20 dealt with questions involving Russia's economic growth and the cooperative-movement.

Krupskaya, Nadezhda Konstantinovna (1869–1939), a founding member of the RSDRP and wife of V.I. Lenin; from 1890, a revolutionary participant in Marxist student-circles in St. Petersburg; 1895, one of the organisers of the St. Petersburg 'Union of Struggle for the Emancipation of the Working Class'; arrested in 1896 and exiled for three years to Shushenskoe and then Ufa; 1901, emigrated and, as Secretary of *Iskra*, conducted correspondence with party-organisations in Russia; returned to Russia in 1917; member of the Secretariat of the Central Committee; participated in the October Revolution and afterwards became a member of the Collegium of the People's Commissariat of Education; from 1920 head of *Glavpolitprosvet* and, from 1929, Deputy People's Commissar of Education.

Krylenko, Nikolai Vasil'evich (1885–1938), member of the RSDRP from 1904; 1905–6, one of the leaders of the student-revolutionary movement in St. Petersburg; from 1911, contributing editor of the newspapers *Zvezda* and *Pravda*; seconded by the Central Committee to the Social-Democratic Duma-fraction; delegate to the First All-Russian Congress of Soviets; active participant in the October Revolution; led the Committee on Military and Naval Affairs of the first Soviet government and was later Commander-in-Chief; from 1918, worked in institutions concerned with Soviet justice; Chairman of the Revolutionary-Military Tribunal of the Republic, procurator of the Republic; from 1931, RSFSR People's Commissar of Justice; from 1936, People's Commissar of Justice for the USSR. Purged.

Krylov, Ivan Andreevich (1769–1844), Russian writer, fabulist, member of the St. Petersburg Academy of Sciences; published satirical journals and wrote tragedies, comedies and operatic libretti.

Kryukov, Fedor Dmitrievich (1870–1920), Russian writer from the family of a *stanitsa-ataman*; elected in 1906 as deputy to the First State-Duma from the region of the Don army; one of the founders of the Popular Socialists party (a neo-Narodnik group of urban intellectuals who repudiated terrorist-acts); in 1906, complained in the Duma and the press against using Cossack troops to suppress revolutionary demonstrations; his stories and fables dealt with the lives of Don Cossacks; contributed to *Russkoe bogatstvo*, which he edited from 1912; during the Civil-War years, edited the newspaper *Donskie vedemosti*.

Kryukov, Fedor Osipovich (1885–1950), member of the RSDRP from 1906; in February 1917, member of the Military Bureau of the Moscow Committee of the RSDRP(B); during October, fought against the Junkers; following October, Secretary of the Party-Committee in the

Alekseevsko-Rostokinsky district; May 1919, sent by the Central Committee of the RKP(B) to party-work in Ryazan province; 25 September 1919, injured in the explosion at Leontiev Lane organised by anarchists and Left S-Rs; 1918–24 member of the Moscow Soviet and subsequently involved in economic and soviet-work.

Krzhivitsky, Lyudvig (1859–1941), Polish public figure, sociologist, economist, ethnographer, pedagogue, publisher, and one of the first to translate Volume I of Marx's *Capital* into Polish; active in the Polish Marxist party '*Proletariat*' (1884–8); from the early 1890s, involved in scientific publications and pedagogical activities; 1921–36, professor at Warsaw University.

Krzhizhanovsky, Gleb Maksimilianovich (1872–1959), member of the RSDRP from 1893; one of the leaders of the St. Petersburg 'Union of Struggle for the Emancipation of the Working Class'; *Iskra* agent; in 1920, Chairman of the State-Commission for the Electrification of Russia (GOELRO); in 1921–23 and 1925–30, Chairman of *Gosplan*; in 1930–2, Chairman of *Glavenergo*; from 1930, leader of the Energy-Institute of the USSR Academy of Sciences.

Kühlmann, Richard von (1973–1948), State-Secretary of Foreign Affairs for Germany in 1917–18; headed the German delegation in negotiations for the Brest treaty.

Kun, Bela (1886–1939), one of the organisers and leaders of the Hungarian Communist Party; 1919 People's Commissar of Foreign Affairs and of Military Affairs in the Hungarian Soviet Republic; captured as a prisoner-of-war in Russia in 1916 and joined the RSDRP(B); returned to Russia after the fall of the Hungarian Soviet Republic. Purged.

Kurganov, CC Plenipotentiary in the Urals.

Kuropatkin, Aleksei Nikolaevich (1848–1925), infantry-general; in 1898–1904, War-Minister; commanded Russian forces in Manchuria during the Russo-Japanese War; during WWI, commanded the northern front; from July 1916 to February 1917, Governor-General of Turkestan; after February 1917, relieved of duty and arrested but later freed by the Provisional Government; resided at his former estate until his death.

Kursky, Dmitry Ivanovich (1874–1932), member of the RSDRP from 1904; active participant in the December armed uprising in Moscow; in October 1917, member of the Military-Revolutionary Committee in Odessa; 1919–20, Commissar of the main and field-staffs of the Red Army and member of the Revolutionary War-Council of the Republic; from 1918–28, People's Commissar of Justice for the RSFSR and first Soviet Procurator-General; 1924–7, Chairman of the Central Revision-Committee of the Communist Party; member of the Central Committee of the RKP(B); 1928–32, USSR ambassador to Italy.

Kuskova (*Esipova*) **Ekaterina Dmitrievna** (1869–1958), wife of S.N. Prokopovich; active in Social-Democratic circles in the 1890s; author of the programme-brochure for the 'Economists' and of the 'Credo'; in 1905–6, opposed a boycott of the First and Second Dumas, supporting a bloc of the Left that would include the Cadets; after October 1917, lived in Moscow and published the anti-Bolshevik newspaper *Vlast' naroda*; during the Civil War, supported a 'third-force' platform opposing both the Bolsheviks and the Whites; in 1921, helped to organise the Committee for Assistance to the Hungry; exiled abroad, together with Prokopovich, in 1922.

Kutler, Nikolai Nikolaevich (1859–1924), Cadet and department-director for the Ministry of Finance; in 1905–6, Minister of Agriculture; member of the Second and Third Dumas; one of the authors of the Cadet programme for agriculture; after February 1917, worked on various commissions for the Ministry of Trade and Industry representing the industrialists of southern Russia; after October, worked in the People's Commissariat of Finance.

Kuznetsov, Georgy Sergeevich (1881–?), Social-Democratic deputy to the Third Duma from Ekaterinburg province; sentenced to imprisonment for four years.

Kuzovkov, Dmitry Vasil'evich (1885–?), participated in the 1905–7 revolution in

Moscow; until October 1917, involved in teaching and scientific work; from 1917, Social-Democratic internationalist; in 1917–20, member of the Collegium of the financial, housing and land-departments of the Moscow Soviet; from 1918, active member of the Communist Academy; from 1921, director of the Institute of Red Professors; retired in 1937.

Kvitkin, Olympius Aristarkhovich (1874–1937), demographic statistician; arrested in 1898 for addressing workers at Bryansk factory in Bezhitsu; sentenced in 1901 to exile in Vologda province; joined the RSDRP in 1904, doing party-work in Orel, Bryansk and Kostroma; delegate to the Third to Fifth Congresses of the RSDRP (Bolshevik); in 1906, member of the Moscow Regional Bureau of the RSDRP; left political activity in 1908; 1911–15, lived in France; from 1919, served in the Central Statistical Department; from 1925, head of the USSR Census-Bureau; from 1926 to 1937, continued work on census-statistics. Purged.

Landezen (*Harting, Arkady Mikhailovich*), student; in the 1890s, began collaborating with the St. Petersburg secret police; suspected by other students, Harting went to Derpt and then settled in Paris under the name Landezen; from Paris, he provided the Russian government with intelligence concerning other Russians; 1890, together with a group of Russian *émigrés*, organised a workshop to prepare bombs for the assassination of Alexander III; the adventure was uncovered and followed by a sensational trial in Paris involving Harting, who had been hiding in Belgium and was sentenced to five years' imprisonment for incitement; escaped to Belgium, and in 1900–5 headed Russian political-intelligence work in Berlin; from August 1905, headed all Russian foreign-intelligence work; during WWI, worked in Russian counter-intelligence in France and continued this work for the Provisional Government.

Lapinsky, Pavel Lyudvigovich (*Levinson Ya.*) (1879–1937), Polish communist, economist and publicist; 1906–18, one of the leaders of the left wing of the Polish Socialist Party and then member of the Communist Party of Poland; during the 1920s, worked for the People's Commissariat of Foreign Affairs doing diplomatic work abroad; during the 1930s, involved in scientific and publicist-activities in the USSR; author of works on the world-economy and world-politics. Purged.

Larin, Yu. (*Lur'e, Mikhail Zal'manovich* (*Aleksandrovich*)) (1882–1932), economist, involved in the Social-Democratic movement from 1900; a liquidator after 1907; centrist during WWI; after February 1917, leader of the Menshevik-Internationalists; joined the RSDRP(B) in August 1917; following October, supported a coalition-government with Mensheviks and S-Rs; late 1917–early 1918, a member of the Presidium of the Supreme Council of the National Economy; subsequently worked in Soviet economic organisations.

Lashevich, Mikhail Mikhailovich (1884–1928), member of the RSDRP from 1901; after February 1917, Chairman of the Bolshevik group in the Petrograd Soviet; during October, member of the Petrograd Military-Revolutionary Committee; 1918–19, commanded the Third Army and was a member of the Revolutionary War-Council of the southern and eastern fronts; 1920–5, commanded the armed forces of the Siberian military region and was Chairman of the Siberian Revolutionary Committee; in 1925, Deputy People's Commissar for the Army and Navy, Deputy Chairman of the Revolutionary War-Council of the USSR, and a member of the Presidium of the Supreme Council of the National Economy; in 1925–6 a member of the Trotsky-Zinoviev opposition; expelled from the Party in 1927 but reinstated after repudiating his 'errors'; from 1926–8, vice-Chairman of the Chinese-Eastern railroad.

Latsis, Martin Ivanovich (*Subrabs, Yan Fridrikhovich*) (1888–1938), member of the RSDRP from 1905; actively participated in the Revolution of 1905–7; member of the Petrograd Military-Revolutionary Committee; following October, a member of the Collegium of the People's Commissariat of Internal Affairs; from

May 1918, member of the Collegium of the Cheka; July–November 1918, Chairman of the Cheka and the military tribunal of the Fifth Army of the eastern front; 1919–20, Chairman of the All-Ukrainian Cheka and then again of the Russian Cheka; from 1921, involved in administrative work; from 1932, Director of the G.V. Plekhanov Institute of the National Economy. Purged.

Lavrov, Petr Lavrovich (1823–1900), Russian philosopher, sociologist and publicist, one of the ideologists of the revolutionary Narodniks.

Legien, Karl (1861–1920), right-wing German Social Democrat and trade-union leader; from 1903, Secretary, and from 1913, Chairman of the International Secretariat of Trade-Unions; social-chauvinist during WWI; 1919–20, member of the National Assembly of the Weimar Republic.

Lenin (*Ul'yanov*) **Vladimir Il'ich** (*Il'in, V.; Lenin, N.; F.F.*) (1870–1924), leader of the Bolsheviks; in 1895, participated in founding the St. Petersburg 'Union of Struggle for the Emancipation of the Working Class'; arrested and exiled for three years to Yenisei province; from 1900, published *Iskra* abroad; from 1905, in St. Petersburg; from 1907, in emigration; arrived in Petrograd in 1917 and led the October Revolution; at the Second All-Russian Congress of Soviets, elected Chairman of the Council of People's Commissars.

Lenin, N., see Lenin, V.I.

Lermontov, Mikhail Yur'evich (1814–41), Russian poet.

Leroy-Beaulieu, Anatole (1842–1912), French publicist and professor of history; 1872–81, visited Russia four times; author of *L'empire des tsars et les Russes*, dealing with the state and social structure of Russia.

Leskov, Nikolai Semenovich (1831–95), Russian writer.

Lessing, Gotthold Ephraim (1729–81), German dramatist, philosopher, publicist and art- and literary critic.

Levi (*Gartshtein*) **Paul** (1883–1930), German Social Democrat and member of the 'Spartacist League'; elected to the Central Committee of the Communist Party of Germany at its founding congress; left the Central Committee in February 1921 and was expelled from the Party in April; subsequently rejoined the Social-Democratic Party.

Liebknecht, Karl (1871–1919); lawyer and a leader of the left wing of the German Social-Democratic Party from 1900; an internationalist during WWI; one of the leaders of the revolutionary 'Spartacist League'; leader of revolutionary workers in the German Revolution of November 1918; one of the founders of the Communist Party of Germany and leader of the Berlin uprising in January 1919; tortured and murdered after the uprising was crushed.

Litkens, Aleksandr Aleksandrovich, brother of Egraf Aleksandrovich; on 24 February 1938, *Pravda* reported that A.A. Likens, 'brigade-doctor, by instruction from the Supreme Soviet of the USSR in connection with the twentieth anniversary of the Red Army and Navy, is awarded the Order of the "Red Star" '.

Litkens, Egraf Aleksandrovich (1888–1922), member of the RSDRP from 1904; from 1917, member of the Central Committee of the Internationalists, and from 1919, member of the RKP(B); after February 1919, member of the Presidium of the Moscow Soviet; early 1919, Plenipotentiary of the People's Commissariat of Internal Affairs in the Crimea, then director of the party-school in the Fifth Army and head of the political department; from January 1921, Deputy People's Commissar of Education for the RSFSR; murdered by bandits in Yalta.

Litvinov, Maksim Maksimovich (*Vallakh, Maks*) (1876–1951), participant in the revolutionary movement from 1898 and a Bolshevik from 1903; from 1918, member of the Collegium of the People's Commissariat of Foreign Affairs; in 1921, political representative to Estonia; 1930–9, USSR People's Commissar of Foreign Affairs; 1941–3, Deputy People's Commissar of Foreign Affairs, and simultaneously USSR ambassador to the US.

Litvinov, Stepan Sergeevich (1888–?), member of the RSDRP from 1908; organiser of an underground printing works in Khar'kov; arrested in December 1909 and sentenced to exile in Irkutsk province.

Lloyd George, David (1863–1945), Prime Minister of Great Britain 1916–22; one of the organisers of foreign intervention in the Russian Civil War; subsequently favoured contacts with Soviet Russia.

Lobova, Bina, see Lobova, V.N.

Lobova, Valentina Nikolaevna (Bina) (1888–1924), member of the RSDRP from 1905; did revolutionary work in Rovno, Zhitomir, Perm, Motovilikha and Ekaterinburg; 1906–8, member of the Urals District-Committee of the RSDRP; in 1911, member of the Moscow Committee; in 1913, Secretary of the Bureau of the Central Committee of the RSDRP and of the Bolshevik group in the Fourth State-Duma; after October 1917, member of the Presidium of the Kiev Provincial Executive Committee; 1920–1, worked in Moscow, Perm, Samara and then in the Agitprop of the Central Committee of the RKP(B) (in 1922–3) and also in Siberia.

Lomonosov, Mikhail Vasil'evich (1711–65), first Russian natural-science writer of world-repute, also a poet who laid the foundations for modern Russian as a literary language, artist and historian.

London, Jack (*John Griffith*) (1876–1916), American author.

Loube, Émile François (1838–1929), head of the French government from January-November 1892 and President of France from 1899–1906.

Louis XVI (1754–93), King of France from 1774–92 from the Bourbon dynasty, overthrown in 1792 and executed.

Luchitsky, Ivan Vasil'evich (1845–1918), liberal-Narodnik historian; author of works on the history of religious wars and the French peasantry; deputy to the Third State-Duma; professor at St. Petersburg University.

Lunarcharsky, Anatoly Vasil'evich (1875–1933), joined the revolutionary movement in the early 1890s; involved in editing the Bolshevik newspapers *Vpered*, *Proletarii* and *Novaya zhizn'*; after 1907, proposed reconciling Marxism with religion; internationalist during WWI; during early 1917, a member of the *Mezhraiontsy* group; a Bolshevik from August 1917; from October 1917 until 1929, People's Commissar of Education and then Chairman of the Academic Committee under the Central Executive Committee of the USSR; in 1933, appointed Soviet ambassador to Spain; author of works on art and literature.

Luxemburg, Rosa (1871–1919), a leader of the left wing of the Second International; revolutionary figure from the beginning of the 1880s; participated in founding the Social-Democratic Party of Poland; from 1897, active in the German Social-Democratic movement; internationalist during WWI; initiator of the 'Spartacist League' in Germany; after the German Revolution of November 1918 participated in founding the Communist Party of Germany; in January 1919, arrested and killed by the German Freikorps.

Lykoshin, Aleksandr Ivanovich (1861–1918), Privy Councillor; 1882–1901, Deputy Chief-Prosecutor of the Governing Senate; in 1905, one of the organisers of the 'Union of the Russian People'; 1907–14, Deputy Minister of Internal Affairs; adviser to P.A. Stolypin; senator from 1911 and member of the State-Council from 1914.

Lyubosh, S. (*Lyuboshits, Semen Borisovich*) (1859–1929), journalist; editor of the newspaper *Obskaya zhizn'* and contributor to the journal *Sovremennoe slovo*.

L'vov, Nikolai Nikolaevich (1867–1944), large landowner and deputy to the First, Second, Third and Fourth State-Dumas; one of the founders of the 'Union of Emancipation', participant in the deputation to the Tsar of 6 June 1905; in 1906, member of the Cadet Central Committee and then one of the founders of the 'Party of Peaceful Renewal'; a Progressive from 1912; Deputy Chairman of the Fourth Duma; worked for the White-Guard press in 1918–20; after 1920, in emigration.

L'vov-Rogachevsky, Vasily L'vovich (*Rogachevsky*) (1873–1930), nobleman, literary critic and publicist; involved in the revolutionary movement from 1898; arrested and exiled more than once; follower of Maxim Gorky.

MacDonald, James Ramsay (1870–1957), one of the founders and leaders of the Independent Labour Party and the Labour Party in Britain; pacifist at the outbreak of WWI and then a chauvinist; in 1924 and 1930–1, Prime Minister; 1931–5, headed the National Government.

Mach, Ernst (1836–1916), Austrian physicist and philosopher; from 1895–1901, professor of philosophy at University of Vienna.

MacLean, John (1879–1923), one of the leaders of the left wing of the British Socialist Party; took an internationalist position during WWI.

Maisky, V. (*Lyakhovetsky, Ivan Mikahilovich* (1884–1975), Social Democrat and Menshevik; involved in the revolutionary movement from 1899 in Omsk; member of the RSDRP from 1902; wavered between Bolsheviks and Mensheviks after the party-split; arrested in 1906 and exiled to Tobolsk province whence he fled and emigrated to Germany in 1908; Menshevik-Internationalist during WWI; back in Russia from February 1917; worked in the Petrograd Soviet and the trade-unions; member of the Collegium of the Ministry of Labour in the Provisional Government; did not participate in the October Revolution; in August, headed the Labour-Department of the Komuch government in Samara; broke with the Mensheviks in 1919; from 1921, a member of the RKP(B); Chairman of the Siberian *Gosplan*; did diplomatic work from 1922; 1929–32, Soviet political representative to Finland; 1932–43, USSR ambassador to Great Britain; 1943–6, Deputy Minister of Foreign Affairs of the USSR; participated in the work of the Potsdam and Yalta Conferences.

Makarin, member of the Bolkhov organisation of the RKP(B); killed in August 1919.

Maklakov, Vasily Alekseevich (1870–1957), member of the Central Committee of the Cadet Party; deputy to the Second, Third and Fourth Dumas from Moscow; prominent lawyer and student of F.N. Plevako; in 1917, ambassador to France and then emigrated.

Maksimov, Konstantin Gordeevich (1894–1937), member of the RSDRP from 1914; did revolutionary work in Samara and Moscow; in April 1917, a member of the Moscow Committee of the RSDRP(B) and of the Moscow Soviet; during October, chief of intelligence for the Moscow Military-Revolutionary Committee; in 1918–20 Chairman of the food-department of the Moscow Soviet and then member of the Revolutionary War-Council and Plenipotentiary of Supply for the armies of the eastern front; in 1920–2, Deputy Chairman of the Industrial Bureau of the Urals Supreme Council of the National Economy and then deputy head of the Donbass coal-industry; later Chairman of the Supreme Council of the National Economy for Ukraine, member of the Presidium of the Supreme Council of the National Economy for the USSR and USSR Deputy People's Commissar of Trade. Purged.

Maksimovsky, Vladimir Nikolaevich (1887–1941), member of the RSDRP from 1903; did party-work in Kolomna, Moscow, Tula and elsewhere; arrested several times; after February 1917, member of the Moscow District-Bureau of the RSDRP(B); after October 1917, Secretary of the Moscow Committee of the Party and Deputy People's Commissar of Education; a Left-Communist during the spring of 1918; in 1920–1, member of the Democratic-Centralist group; in 1923, supported the Trotskyist opposition and then the 'New Opposition'; from 1925, Dean of the Timiryazev Agricultural Academy and member of the Presidium of the Communist Party.

Malatesta, Errico (1854–1932), one of the leaders of the anarchist movement in Italy and a supporter of Mikhail Bakunin in the first International.

Malyshev, Ivan Mikhailovich (1889–1918), member of the RSDRP from 1906; did revolutionary work in Verkhotur'e, Nadezhdinsk, Tyumen and Ekaterinburg; imprisoned in 1907 and in exile 1911–12; in 1915, member of the Ekaterinburg Committee of the RSDRP; after February 1917, Chairman of the Ekaterinburg Party-Committee; from April 1917, member of the Urals Regional Committee of the RSDRP(B), Deputy Chairman of the

City-Soviet and member of the Urals Regional Soviet; January 1918, Chairman of the Urals Regional Party-Committee and member of the Regional Executive Committee; March-April, served on the front against Dutov, leading operations during March-April on the Zlatoust-Chelyabinsk sector of the front; shot by White Guards on 23 June.

Malyutin, Chairman of the All-Russian Central Executive Committee in Bashkiria and member of the Bashkir Revolutionary Committee.

Mamed-Bekov, staff-captain of the Baku border-guards.

Mamontov (*Mamantov*) **Konstantin Konstantinovich** (1869–1920), lieutenant-general; fought in WWI, and during the Civil War commanded forces in Krasnov's army and the Fourth Don Cavalry-Corps in Denikin's army; in August-September 1919 led a raid of White-Guard cavalry behind Red-Army lines on the southern front; defeated in October-December 1919 by cavalry under S.M. Budenny; lost his command and died in Ekaterinburg from typhus on 14 February, 1920.

Markhlevsky, Yulian Yusefovich (1866–1925), from the 1880s, one of the leaders of Social Democracy in Poland and Lithuania; from 1909, did propaganda-work in Germany; one of the founders, together with Rosa Luxemburg and Karl Liebknecht, of the 'Spartacist League'; arrested in Germany but freed at the request of the Soviet government to go to Soviet Russia in 1918; elected to the All-Russian Central Executive Committee; in 1919, member of the CC of the Communist Party of Germany; participated in establishing the Communist International; from 1923, Chairman of the Central Committee of the International Society for the Relief of Revolutionaries.

Markov, Nikolai Evgen'evich (1876–1945), landlord and monarchist from Kursk; one of the leaders of the 'Union of the Russian People' and 'League of the Archangel Michael'; deputy to the Third and Fourth State-Dumas from Kursk province and leader of the extreme right-wing members; in 1918-20, served in the White army of General N.N. Yudenich; emigrated in 1920; died in Germany.

Martov, L. (*Tsedenbaum, Yuly Osipovich*) (1873–1923), one of the leaders of Menshevism; in the Social-Democratic movement from the 1890s; in 1895 one of the organisers of the St. Petersburg 'Union of Struggle for the Emancipation of the Working Class'; arrested in 1896 and exiled to Turukhansk for three years; in 1900, member of the *Iskra* editorial board; centrist during WWI; after February 1917, leader of the Menshevik-Internationalists; following October, opposed the Bolshevik dictatorship; in 1917, member of the Executive Committee of the Petrograd Soviet and member of the All-Russian Central Executive Committee; excluded along with other Mensheviks from the All-Russian Central Executive Committee in 1918; rejoined the All-Russian Central Executive Committee in 1919, and in 1919-20 was a deputy of the Moscow Soviet; 1920, emigrated to Germany.

Marx, Karl (1818–83), founder of scientific communism; organised the First International; author of *Capital* and numerous other works on scientific socialism.

Maslov, Petr Pavlovich (1867–1946), Social Democrat and economist; arrested in 1889 in the affair of the Fedoseev circle; emigrated in 1914; defencist during WWI; returned to Russia after February 1917 to work on economic issues for the Provisional Government; from July 1918, Commissar of Priuralie for the Provisional Siberian Government; participated in the State-Conference at Ufa and then left political activities for pedagogical and scientific work; member of the USSR Academy of Sciences.

Melent'ev, officer and member of the military staff that led the anti-Bolshevik Nev'yansk uprising in the Urals in June 1918; member of the Cadet Party.

Merkulov, Nikita Trofimovich (1879–1963), participated in all three revolutions in Moscow; joined the RSDRP after February 1917 and was a member of the Moscow Soviet; Chairman of the Moscow Military-Revolutionary Committee during the fighting in October and member of the staff of the Red Guards

824 • Biographical Notes

in Presnensky district; from July 1918, Commissar of the 123rd workers' regiment of the Eighth Army on the southern front; from late 1919, Chairman of the Presnensky District-Soviet, member of the Executive Committee of the Moscow Soviet and member of the Moscow Committee of the RKP(B); subsequently did economic work and retired in 1955.

Metternich, Klemens (1773–1859), Minister of Foreign Affairs and effectively head of the Austrian government from 1809–21; Chancellor from 1821–48; opponent of German unification and of Russian power in Europe; one of the organisers of the Holy Alliance; his career ended with the revolutions of 1848–9.

Meyendorff, Aleksandr Feliksovich (1869–1964), baron, major landowner and landlord; Octobrist from June 1907 and member of the Party's Central Committee in St. Petersburg; candidate in elections to the First Duma and deputy to the Third and Fourth Dumas from Livonia; emigrated in 1917.

Mikhail Fedorovich (1569–1645), Russian Tsar from 1613 and first ruler from the Romanov dynasty; elected by a *zemsky sobor*.

Mikhailovsky, Nikolai Konstantinovich (1842–1904), Russian sociologist, publicist, literary critic and Narodnik; one of the editors of *Otechestvennye zapiski* and *Russkoe bogatstvo*.

Mikhalych, see Sverdlov, Ya.M.

Mill, John Stuart (1806–73), English philosopher, sociologist and economist; author of *On Liberty* and *Considerations on Representative Government*.

Miller, Evgeny Karlovich (1867–1937), lieutenant-general and a leader of White forces during the Civil War; graduate of the General-Staff Academy and fought in WWI; in January 1919, member of the Provisional Government of the northern region; in May, appointed by Kolchak to command the forces of the northern region; from February 1920, War-Minister for the region; emigrated in 1920; from 1930–7, Chairman of the Russian All-Military Union; captured by NKVD agents in Paris, taken back to Moscow and executed.

Miller, V., pharmacist and member of the military staff that led the anti-Bolshevik Nev'yansk uprising in the Urals in June 1918; member of the Cadet Party.

Millerand, Alexandre (1859–1943), French social-reformist, lawyer and publicist; Minister of Public Works in the Briand cabinet and War-Minister in the cabinets of Raymond Poincaré and René Viviani; in 1920, Premier and Minister of Foreign Affairs; from 1920–4, President of France.

Milton, John (1608–74), English poet and political figure; supporter of the radical wing of the English Revolution in the seventeenth century; portrayed the spirit of the Revolution in his poems *Paradise Lost, Paradise Regained* and *Samson Agonistes*.

Milyukov, Pavel Nikolaevich (1859–1943), historian and publicist; from 1907, Chairman of the Central Committee of the Cadet Party and editor of its central organ, *Rech'*; during February 1917, advocated a constitutional monarchy; as Minister of Foreign Affairs in the Provisional Government, supported continuing the War until final victory; one of the organisers of the Kornilov affair; fled to the Don region after the Bolshevik Revolution and then emigrated.

Minkin, Aleksandr Eremeevich (1887–1955), member of the RSDRP from 1903; did party-work in Warsaw and the Urals; arrested several times; after February 1917, member of the Petrograd Committee of the RSDRP(B); following October, was, at various times, Secretary of provincial party-committees in Perm, Penza and Archangel, member of the Collegium of the People's Commissariat of Trade, USSR political representative in Uruguay, and Deputy Chairman of the RSFSR Supreme Court.

Minkov, Isaak Il'ich (1894–1935), emigrated to Canada in 1910 and in 1911 joined a group of Russian Social Democrats; from 1915, Secretary of the Russian department of the American Social-Democratic Party's Philadelphia Committee; returned to Russia following February 1917; member of the Moscow Regional Committee of the RSDRP(B) and member of the Provincial Executive Committee; Secretary of the Provincial Committee of the RKP(B) in Samara and member of the Provincial Executive Committee; 1923-7, candidate-member and then member of the Central Control-Commission of the Soviet Communist Party; retired in 1928.

Mirbach, Wilhelm von (1871–1918), count and envoy of Imperial Germany; from April 1918, ambassador in Moscow to the government of the RSFSR; assassinated by the Left S-R Ya.G. Blyumkin as the signal for a Left S-R insurrection in Moscow.

Missar, French nationalist and provocateur.

Moiseev, in 1912, head of the Odessa municipal administration and member of the 'Union of the Russian People'.

Mollov, Ruschu (*Gavrül*) **Georgievich** (1867–1925), a Bulgarian who took Russian citizenship; from 1889, served in the Ministry of Justice; in 1911, procurator of the Odessa court; in 1915, Director of Department of Police; in 1916, member of the Main Bureau of Factory- and Mining Affairs.

Moltke (*the younger*), **Helmuth Johann von** (1848–1916), from 1906–14, Chief of the German General Staff.

More, Thomas (1478–1535), English humanist, statesman and author; one of the founders of utopian socialism; his dialogue *Utopia* presents a vision of society where life and production are socialised.

Mostovenko, Pavel Nikolaevich (1881–1938), member of the RSDRP from 1901; several times arrested, imprisoned and exiled; member of the Petrograd Soviet and Chairman of the Moscow Soviet; in 1919, Secretary of the Ufa Provincial Committee of the RKP(B), Plenipotentiary of the Central Committee of the RKP(B) in Bashkirdistan; member and Secretary of the Bashkir Regional Committee of the RKP(B); member of the Bashkir Central Executive Committee; in 1921, RSFSR political representative in Lithuania; in 1922-3, Chairman of the trade-delegation in Czechoslovakia. Purged.

Mrachkovsky, Sergei Vital'evich (1888–1936), member of the RSDRP from 1905; arrested several times; in 1917, member of the Ekaterinburg Soviet and the Urals Regional Committee of the RSDRP(B); from February 1918, fought against Dutov, Commissar of the Ekaterinburg-Chelyabinsk front, Commissar of several divisions of the Red Army; from January 1919, commanded the special northern expeditionary force; in 1920, commanded the forces of the Priural'sk military region, those of western Siberia in 1922, those of the Privolga region in 1923, then Commandant of the Kronstadt Fortress; involved in economic work from 1925. Purged.

Muralov, Rodion Ivanovich (1884–1919), member of the RSDRP from 1904; did revolutionary work in the Serpukhovsky, Kolomensky and Bronnitsky districts; in 1906, member of the Moscow Regional Committee of the RSDRP; arrested several times; in October 1917, set up Soviet power in Ryazan; then worked in the Moscow Provincial Executive Committee and was a member of the Collegium of the Moscow Land-Department; died of typhus.

Murav'ev, Mikhail Nikolaevich (1796–1866), count and infantry-general; 1857-61 Minister of State-Domains; 1863-5, Governor-General of the north-western territory; participated in suppression of the Polish uprisings in 1830–1 and 1863–4, becoming known as the 'Hangman'.

Musset, Alfred de (1810–57), French romantic poet.

Mussi, an associate of Louis Pasteur.

Myasoedov, Sergei Nikolaevich (1865–1915), Colonel; from 1892, worked in the Department of the Gendarmerie and, from 1909, for War-Minister V.A. Sukhomlinov; in 1912, accused by A.I. Guchkov of spying for Germany and challenged Guchkov to a duel; sentenced to death by hanging in 1915.

Nakoryakov, Nikolai Nikandrovich (*Nazar*) (1881–1970), member of the RSDRP from 1902; did party-work in Kiev, Sevastopol, Samara and the Urals, where he edited party press-organs; arrested and exiled more than once up to 1911; sentenced to exile in Ekaterinburg province but fled to America; returned to Russia in 1917 and served in the First Army as Deputy Commissar of the Provisional Government; served in the White Army in 1919–20; in 1920–2, worked in the fuel-industry in Tobolsk; from 1922 worked for the State Publishing House *Gosizdat*; took part in publishing the *Soviet Encyclopaedia*; in 1930–7, head of OGIZ, the Association of State Book- and Journal Publishing Houses; retired in 1957.

Nansen, Fridtjof (1861–1930), Norwegian scholar, polar explorer and public figure; in 1913 Nansen travelled through the Barents Sea and the Kara Sea to the mouth of the Yenisei River and back through Siberia.

Napoleon I (*Napoleon Bonaparte*) (1769–1821), Emperor of France from 1804–14 and in March–June 1815.

Nazar, see Nakoryakov, N.N.

Neidgard, senator who headed a review of the municipal economy of St. Petersburg.

Nekrasov, Nikolai Alekseevich (1821–78), poet and dramatist.

Nekrasov, Nikolai Vissarionovich (1879–1940), member of the Central Committee of the Cadet Party and leader of its left wing; deputy in the Third and Fourth Dumas from Tomsk province; professor; one of the leaders of the United Committee of the Union of *Zemstvos* and the Union of Towns (*Zemgor*); in 1917, Minister of Transportation, Minister without Portfolio, and Finance-Minister of the Provisional Government; left the Cadet Party in the summer of 1917; worked in *Tsentrosoyuz* (the network of cooperatives).

Nevel'son, Roza Abramovna, first wife of E.A. Preobrazhensky.

Nicholas I (1796–1855), Emperor of Russia from 1825.

Nicholas II (1868–1918), from 1894, the last Russian Emperor.

Nietzsche, Friedrich (1844–1900), German philologist and philosopher.

Nikkeleva, an S-R from Orel.

Nikolaevsky, Boris Ivanovich (1887–1966), activist in the Russian Social-Democratic movement, historian, publicist, and collector of archival documents; in 1903–6, a Bolshevik; subsequently a Menshevik; worked in Samara, Ufa and Siberia; more than once arrested and exiled; worked for the Menshevik press.

Nikolai Mikhailovich (1859–1919), Grand Duke, military figure and historian, grandson of Nicholas I; graduated from the General-Staff Academy; Chairman of the Russian Historical Society; historian of the times of Alexander I; shot in Petropavlovsk prison in January 1919.

Nikolai Nikolaevich (*the younger*) (1856–1929), Grand Duke, adjutant-general and general of cavalry; graduated from the General-Staff Academy; Commander-in-Chief of Russian forces during WWI until August 1915, when the Tsar took personal command; re-appointed as Commander-in-Chief in 1917 as the last official act of Nicholas II, but then removed from command by the Provisional Government; 1919, emigrated to France.

Nikol'sky, Boris Vladimirovich (1870–1919), one of the founders of the nationalist club 'Russian Assembly' and of the 'Union of the Russian People'; accused by supporters of V.M. Purishkevich of embezzling public funds and left politics; 1913–17, lectured at the Yurevsky University and, from 1919, in Petrograd; taken hostage in 1919 and shot.

Nissen, brought greetings to the Third All-Russian Congress of Soviets from the left social democrats of Norway and Sweden.

Noske, Gustav (1866–1946), right-wing German Social Democrat; member of the Council of People's Representatives during the 1918 German Revolution; Defence-Minister from February 1919–March 1920; suppressed the political general strike by Berlin workers in 1919.

Novgorodtseva (*Sverdlova*) **Klavdiya Timofeevna** (1876–1960), member of the RSDRP from 1904 and wife of Ya.M. Sverdlov; member of Marxist circles in the Urals; in 1904, member of the Ekaterinburg Committee of the RSDRP and, from 1906, member of the Perm Committee; from 1906, in prison or exile almost without interruption; after February 1917, headed the *Priboi* press of the Central Committee of the RSDRP(B);

from 1917–20 headed the Secretariat of the Central Committee; from 1920, headed the Department of Children's Institutions of the All-Russian Central Executive Committee and the *Uchpedgiz* publishing house; from 1931–44, worked at *Glavlit*; author of several books; retired 1946.

Ogarev, Nikolai Platonovich (1813–77), Russian revolutionary, poet and publicist; friend and collaborator of A.I. Herzen; one of the organisers of a revolutionary circle at Moscow University in 1831; 1834–9 in exile; emigrated in 1856 and became one of the leaders of the Free Russian Press in London; one of the founders and co-editor of *Kolokol* ('The Bell'); propounded a socio-economic programme of peasant-revolution in the spirit of 'Russian socialism'; participated in creating the revolutionary society *Narodnaya Volya* ('The People's Will').

Oliger, Nikolai Fridrikhovich (*Fedorovich*) (1882–1919), prose-writer and dramatist; member of the RSDRP from 1900; arrested in 1901 and sent to Omsk prison; abandoned revolutionary activity and moved to St. Petersburg in the autumn of 1906 to devote himself to literature that reflected his personal revolutionary experiences; despite poor health, volunteered for the front in 1915 to serve in a medical and food-unit; in 1918, became head of the publicity-department with the staff of Ataman Semenov; from late 1918, in Chita as a member of the Territorial Bureau of the Cadet Party.

Olimpov (*Fofanov*) **Konstantin Konstantinovich** (1899–1940), 'ego-futurist' poet; enthusiastic supporter of the October Revolution and served for a period in the Red Army; during the 1920s founded the 'Academy of ego-poetry'; subsequently abandoned futurism.

Ol'nem, O.N. (*Tsekovskaya, Varvara Nikolaevna*) (1872–1941), prose-writer for the journals *Russkoe bogatstvo*, *Russkaya mysl'*, *Vestnik Evropy* and others; her work dealt with the lives of noble-families and state-officials; in 1918, worked for the People's Commissariat of Food- and Grain-Products.

Ortodoks (*Aksel'rod, Lyubov Isaakovna*) (1866–?), joined a revolutionary circle in Poltava in the 1880s; from 1887, lived abroad in Paris and Switzerland; involved in the Social-Democratic movement from the early 1890s, after 1903 as a Menshevik; author of several theoretical works.

Osinsky, N. (*Obolensky, Valerian Valerianovich*) (1887–1938), member of the RSDRP from 1907; during the Moscow uprising of December 1905 worked as reporter for the *Izvestiya* of the Moscow Soviet of Workers' Deputies; arrested in 1911 and exiled to Tver' where he served as correspondent for the newspapers *Zvezda* and *Pravda* and for the journal *Prosveshchenie* and others; in Moscow during 1913 as organiser and editor of the newspaper *Nash put'*; following October, manager of the State-Bank (*Gosbank*) of the RSFSR and Chairman of the Supreme Council of the National Economy; a Left-Communist in 1918; 1918–19, one of the editors of *Pravda* in the propaganda-department of the All-Russian Central Executive Committee; 1920–1, member of the Democratic-Centralists and later a Trotskyist; in 1921–3, Deputy People's Commissar of Agriculture; 1925, member of the Presidium of the USSR *Gosplan*; 1926–8, head of the Central Statistical Directorate of the USSR; 1929, Deputy Chairman of the Supreme Council of the National Economy; subsequently involved in economic administration. Purged.

Osipov, Plenipotentiary of the Central Committee of the RKP(B) for Red-Army mobilisation.

Ostrovskaya, Nadezhda Il'inichna (1881–1933), member of the RSDRP from 1903; Plenipotentiary of the Central Committee of the RKP(B) and the All-Russian Central Executive Committee in Orel province.

Ostwald, Friedrich Wilhelm (1853–1932), German chemist and philosophical idealist; from 1882, professor at the Riga Polytechnic-School; from 1887, professor at Leipzig University; Nobel laureate in 1909.

Ovsyannikov, Nikolai Nikolaevich (1884–1941), member of the RSDRP from 1903;

participant in the student-revolutionary movement from 1905–7; after February 1917, member of the Bureau of the Moscow Regional Committee of the RSDRP(B); propagandist and agitator; from 1922, served at the Supreme Courts of the RSFSR and the USSR and then as state-arbitrator for *Gosarbitrazh* under the USSR Council of People's Commissars; retired in 1938.

Pasteur, Louis (1822–1895), French chemist and microbiologist, founder of modern microbiology and immunology; in 1888, created and headed the Pasteur Institute for research in microbiology.

Pavlenkov, Florenty Fedorovich (1839–1900), book-publisher and revolutionary-democrat; published works by F. Engels, V.G. Belinsky, A.I. Herzen and others; more than once arrested and spent ten years in prison and exile.

Pelikan, Boris Aleksandrovich (?–1931), head of the Odessa municipal administration in 1913 and prominent member of the 'Union of the Russian People'; emigrated to Belgrade after 1917.

Pestkovsky, Stanislav Stanislavovich (1882–1937), member of the RSDRP from 1902; revolutionary activist in Poland and Lithuania; arrested more than once and exiled to Irkutsk province in 1907; 1914, fled from exile to London, returning to Russia after the February Revolution; after October, participated in seizing the Post and Telegraph in Petrograd; 1917–19 member of the Collegium of the People's Commissariat of Nationalities and Deputy People's Commissar; Plenipotentiary of the Council of People's Commissars on the western front for the creation of the Lithuanian–Belorussian Soviet Socialist Republic; 1919–20, Chairman of the Kirghiz Revolutionary Committee; in 1920–1, head of the Political Department on the western front; 1924–6, USSR political envoy to Mexico; from 1926, deputy chair of the International Society for the Relief of Revolutionaries; subsequently worked for the Comintern. Purged.

Petlyura, Simon Vasil'evich (1879–1926), Ukrainian-nationalist leader of the Ukrainian Social-Democratic Party; one of the organisers of the Central Rada in 1917; in November 1918, member, and later head, of the Directorate; in 1919, concluded a military alliance with Poland and supported bourgeois Poland in the Soviet-Polish War of 1920; emigrated in 1920 and was assassinated in Paris.

Peter I (*Peter the Great*) (1672–1725), Russian Tsar from 1682 (ruled independently from 1689); from 1721, first Emperor of Russia.

Peter III Fedorovich (1728–62), Russian Emperor in 1762; German prince Karl Peter Ulrich; grandson of Peter I; lived in Russia from 1742.

Petr, Petrukha, see Chugurin, I.D.

Petrov, Russian socialist emigrant; arrested in England together with G.V. Chicherin, Secretary of the 'Committee of Delegates', in a case involving the return of political emigrants to Russia (they were sent back to Russia in January 1918); greeted the Third All-Russian Congress of Soviets on behalf of the British Socialist Party.

Petrunkevich, Ivan Il'ich (1844–1928), landlord, *zemstvo*-figure and Cadet; in 1904, Chairman of the 'Union of Emancipation'; participant in *zemstvo*-congresses 1904–5; one of the founders and leaders of the Cadet Party and Chairman of its Central Committee; member of the First State-Duma and publisher of *Rech'*, the central organ of the Cadet Party; emigrated following October.

Pietry, Prefect of the Paris police in 1912.

Pisarev, Plenipotentiary of the Central Committee of the RKP(B) for mobilisation of the Red Army.

Pisarev, Dmitry Ivanovich (1840–1868), publicist, literary critic, materialist philosopher, utopian-socialist and revolutionary-democrat; principal organiser of the newspaper *Russkoe slovo*.

Plato (428/427–348/347 BC), ancient idealist philosopher and student of Socrates.

Platonov, Sergei Fedorovich (1860–1933), historian; 1918–29, Chairman of the Archival Commission and the commission for publishing the works of A.S. Pushkin; member of the Academy of Sciences of the USSR; in 1925–9, director of Pushkin House (the Institute of Russian

Literature under the USSR Academy of Sciences) and librarian for the Academy; arrested as a monarchist conspirator in 1930 and exiled to Samara.

Platten, Friedrich (*Fritz*) (1883–1942), Swiss left social democrat and one of the organisers of the Communist Party of Switzerland; in April 1917, helped V.I. Lenin to travel from Switzerland to Russia; wounded while protecting Lenin from an assassination-attempt in January 1918; in 1919, took part in establishing the Third International; member of the Bureau of the Comintern; 1921–3, Secretary of the Communist Party of Switzerland; after 1923, lived in Russia.

Plehve, Vyacheslav Konstantinovich (1846–1904), from 1881, Director of the Department of Police; 1884–94, senator and Deputy Minister of Internal Affairs; from 1899, State-Secretary of the Grand Duchy of Finland; from April 1902, Minister of Internal Affairs and head of the Gendarmerie; employed methods of police-terror and attempted to take control of the workers' movement (the *Zubatovshchina*); assassinated by the S-R Sazonov.

Plekhanov, Georgy Valentinovich (*Zhorzh*) (1856–1918), first propagandist of Marxism in Russia; involved in the revolutionary movement from 1875; from 1877, member of the Narodnik organisation 'The People's Will' and, after its split in 1879, headed 'Black Repartition'; in emigration from 1880 in Switzerland; 1883, created the first Russian Marxist organisation, the 'Emancipation of Labour' group; during the early 1890s, edited the newspaper *Iskra* and the journal *Zarya* with V.I. Lenin; participated in drafting the party-programme; a Menshevik after the Second Congress of the RSDRP; social-chauvinist during WWI; returned to Russia after February 1917 and supported the Provisional Government; opposed the October Revolution.

Pletnev, Valery Fedorovich (*Potapych*) (1886–1942), Menshevik from 1904–14 and internationalist during WWI; 1915–17, imprisoned in Siberia; 1918–19, member of the Presidium of the Moscow Provincial Council of the National Economy; 1919–20, Plenipotentiary of Supply for the First Turkestan Army and Chairman of the Council of the National Economy for the Turkestan Republic; 1921–32, Chairman of the Central Committee of *Proletkult* and subsequently worked at *Tsentrosoyuz* and *Soyuzkino*; from 1936, involved in editing literary works.

Pobedonostsev, Konstantin Petrovich (1827–1907), jurist and ultra-monarchist with exceptional influence over Alexander III; 1880–1905 Chief Procurator of the Holy Synod.

Podbel'sky, Vadim Nikolaevich (1887–1920), member of the RSDRP from 1905; party-worker in Tambov and then Moscow; more than once arrested and exiled; spent time in France and after February 1917 was a member of the Moscow Committee of the RSDRP(B) editing the newspaper *Sotsial-Demokrat*; participated in the October armed uprising in Moscow; member of the Moscow Military-Revolutionary Committee; in October 1917, Commissar of Post and Telegraph for Moscow and the Moscow region; from May 1918, People's Commissar of Post and Telegraph for the RSFSR.

Pod'yachev, Semen Pavlovich (1866–1934), Russian writer whose main theme was the tragedy of the Russian peasantry.

Poincaré, Raymond (1860–1934), from 1913–20, President of France; Premier in 1912–13, 1922–4 and 1926–9; one of the organisers of the anti-Soviet intervention.

Pokrovsky, Ivan Petrovich (1872–?), Social Democrat and physician; arrested in 1902 and, after two years of imprisonment, exiled to eastern Siberia; served as a physician in the Russo-Japanese War; deputy to the Third State-Duma from Kuban and Tersk regions and Chernomoriya province; supported the Bolsheviks in the Social-Democratic Duma-fraction; in 1910, Chairman of the Bolshevik fraction in the Third Duma and editor of the legal Bolshevik newspaper *Zvezda*.

Potap, see Ivanov.

Potapych, see Pletnev V.F.

Pouchet, Félix Archimède (1800–72), French physician and naturalist.

Pravdin, Aleksandr Georgievich (1879–1938), member of the RSDRP from 1899; party-worker in Odessa, St. Petersburg, Lugansk and elsewhere; 1912–14, contributor to *Pravda*; worked in the Urals in 1917; after October, Deputy People's Commissar of Internal Affairs; from 1923, member of the Central Executive Committee, Deputy Commissar of Transportation, Chairman of the management of Northern Railways, head of the transportation-group of the Worker-Peasant Inspectorate. Purged.

Predkal'n (*Priedkal'n*), **Andrei Yanovich** (1873–1923), Latvian Social Democrat and physician; in 1907, Bolshevik member of the Social-Democratic faction in the Third State-Duma; worked for the Bolshevik newspapers *Zvezda* and *Pravda*; after October, involved in scientific medical work.

Preobrazhenskaya, Aleksandra Alekseevna, sister of E.A. Preobrazhensky.

Preobrazhenskaya, Lyudmila Alekseevna, sister of E.A. Preobrazhensky.

Preobrazhenskaya, Ol'ga Alekseevna, sister of E.A. Preobrazhensky.

Preobrazhenskaya (*née Levitskaya*) **Varvara Alekseevna**, mother of E.A. Preobrazhensky

Preobrazhensky, Commissar of the Provisional Government.

Preobrazhensky, Aleksei Aleksandrovich (*Father Aleksei*), E.A. Preobrazhensky's father.

Preobrazhensky, Evgeny Alekseevich (*L-d; Leonid; L.; M. Leonov; M.L.; M.L-ev; E. Iduchansky*) (1886–1937).

Preobrazhensky, Leonid Evgen'evich, son of E.A. Preobrazhensky by his first wife.

Preobrazhensky, Viktor Alekseevich, brother of E.A. Preobrazhensky.

Prokopovich, Sergei Nikolaevich (1871–1955), ideologist of 'economism' and member of the 'Union of Emancipation'; in 1917, minister of the Provisional Government; after October, worked in famine-relief and was connected with the counter-revolutionary underground; exiled abroad in 1922.

Proudhon, Pierre-Joseph (1809–65), French petty-bourgeois socialist and anarchist theorist.

Purishkevich, Vladimir Mitrofanovich (1870–1920), landlord in Bessarabia; one of the founders of the 'Union of the Russian People' (the Black Hundreds) and, after its split, leader of the 'League of the Archangel Michael'; deputy to the Second, Third and Fourth State-Dumas; head of a hospital-train during WWI; participated in the assassination of Rasputin; opposed the Provisional Government after February 1917 and supported restoration of the monarchy; arrested in November 1917 by the Petrograd Cheka, condemned and then amnestied; died of typhus.

Purov, Plenipotentiary of the All-Russian Central Executive Committee and representative of the Central Committee of the RKP(B) in Orel province.

Pushkin, Alexander Sergeyevich (1799–1837), Russian poet.

Putilov, Aleksei Ivanovich (1866–sometime after 1926), industrialist and financier; nobleman; from 1906, managing director of the Russo-Chinese Bank and, from 1910, of the Russo-Asiatic Bank; shareholder in numerous companies; emigrated December 1917; supported the White movement financially during the Civil War.

Pythagoras of Samos (sixth century BC), ancient-Greek philosopher and mathematician.

Radek (*Sobel'son*) **Karl Berngardovich** (1885–1939), from early 1900, participated in the Social-Democratic movement in Galicia, Poland and Germany; internationalist during WWI; joined the RSDRP(B) in 1917; after October, worked in the People's Commissariat of Foreign Affairs, was Secretary of the Executive Committee of the Comintern, worked on *Pravda* and *Izvestiya*; a Left-Communist in 1918 and, from 1923–30, supported Trotsky. Purged.

Rafes, Moisei Grigor'evich (1883–1942), participated in the revolutionary movement from 1899; 1912–19, member of the Central Committee of the *Bund*; did revolutionary work in Vil'no, Gomel, Kiev and elsewhere; after February 1917, member of the Executive Committee of the Petrograd Soviet and then led the left wing of the *Bund* in Ukraine; joined the RKP(B) in the summer of 1919; Commissar in the Red Army and then worked for the Moscow Soviet; later worked in cinema-arts.

Rakovsky, Christian Georgievich (1873–1941), from the early 1890s, active in the Social-Democratic movements of Bulgaria, Romania, Switzerland and France; centrist during WWI; member of the RSDRP(B) from 1917; in 1918, Chairman of the Council of People's Commissars in Ukraine; from 1923, diplomatic representative in England and France; supporter of Trotsky. Purged.

Rasputin (*Novykh*) **Grigory Efimovich** (1872–1916), from a peasant-background in Tobolsk; enjoyed unlimited access to the Tsar and his wife as a 'visionary' and 'healer'; murdered by monarchists in Petrograd.

Ratner, Mark Borisovich (1871–1917), publicist, member of the *Bund*, lawyer; contributed to *Russkoe bogatstvo* and other publications; wrote articles on Marxism, the agrarian question and labour-legislation; critic of Marx's *Capital*; from 1903, one of the main publicists of the Socialist Jewish Workers' Party; social-chauvinist during WWI.

Reclus, Jean-Jacques Elisée (1830–1905), French geographer and sociologist; member of the first International and supporter of the Bakuninists.

Reinbot (*Rezvoi*) **Anatoly Anatol'evich** (1868–1918), major-general; in 1906–7, head of the Moscow municipal administration; brutally suppressed the revolutionary movement; engaged in bribery, extortion and embezzling of public money; removed from office and tried in court, but the sentence was not implemented; divisional commander during WWI; in 1914, with the permission of the Tsar, changed his family name to *Rezvoi*.

Richter, Eugen (1838–1906), one of the leaders of the German 'Free-minded People's Party' ('*Freisinnige Volkspartei*'), who thought the class-interests of the proletariat and bourgeoisie might be reconciled.

Robespierre, Maximilien (1758–94), Jacobin leader during the French Revolution; executed by the Thermidorians.

Rodichev, Fedor Izmailovich (1856–1933, other sources give 1853–1932), landlord in Tver', *zemstvo*-figure, jurist and member of the Central Committee of the Cadet Party; deputy to the First, Second, Third and Fourth Dumas and renowned orator; after February 1917, Commissar of the Provisional Government for Finnish affairs; after October, deputy to the Constituent Assembly; arrested in connection with the murder of M.S. Uritsky; fled to southern Russia in 1918 and emigrated; from early 1920, represented the Volunteer-Army in Poland.

Rodzyanko, Mikhail Vladimirovich (1859–1924), one of the leaders of the Octobrists and a major landlord; in 1911–17, Chairman of the Third and Fourth State-Dumas; in 1917, Chairman of the Provisional Committee of the State-Duma; emigrated with remnants of the Volunteer-Army after the Civil War.

Romanov, student at the Orel seminary.

Romanovs, a Russian *boyar*-family from the fourteenth to sixteenth century, descendants of Andrei Kobyla; until the early sixteenth century went by the name *Koshkin*, and until the end of the sixteenth century, *Zakhar'in*; the royal and imperial dynasty from 1613; the first Romanov tsar was Mikhail Fedorovich and the last was Nicholas II, deposed in 1917.

Romm, Nikolai Nikolaevich (1884–?), member of the RSDRP from 1904; more than once arrested; called to military service in 1906; arrested in September 1908 for revolutionary agitation among the soldiers and sentenced to exile in Karapchansky parish of Irkutsk province, where he remained until 1917.

Ropshin, V. (*Savinkov, Boris Viktorovich*) (1879–1925), one of the leaders of the S-R Party and head of its 'fighting organisation'; took part in the murder of V.K. Plehve in 1904 and of Grand Duke Sergei Aleksandrovich in 1905; arrested in 1906 and sentenced to death but fled abroad; volunteer in the French army during WWI; after February 1917, Commissar under the staff of the High Command, Commissar on the south-western front, Deputy Minister of War for the Provisional Government and then military Governor-General of Petrograd; after October, organised a number of counter-revolutionary actions in Yaroslavl', Rybinsk and Murom; subsequently represented Kolchak in Paris; in 1924, illegally returned to the USSR, was arrested and sentenced to ten years' imprisonment; officially reported to have committed suicide; under the pseudonym Ropshin, wrote the autobiographical *Memoirs of a Terrorist* and several other works.

Rothschilds, financial group in Western Europe that originated with the banking house of M.A. Rothschild in seventeenth-century France.

Rouget de Lisle, Claude Joseph (1760–1836), French military engineer, poet and composer whose *Marseillaise* became the anthem of the French Republic.

Rozental', member of the Presidium of the Urals Regional Committee of the RKP(B).

Rozhkov, Nikolai Aleksandrovich (1868–1927), historian and publicist; joined the RSDRP in 1905 as a Bolshevik; 1905–6, member of the Moscow Bolshevik Committee and, in 1906–7, member of the St. Petersburg Committee; involved with a number of Bolshevik publications; arrested in April 1908 and exiled to eastern Siberia in 1910; in exile, joined the Menshevik-liquidators; after February 1917, joined a group of Moscow Social Democrats favouring unification; Deputy Minister of Post and Telegraph for the Provisional Government; from August 1917, member of the Menshevik Central Committee; opposed the October Revolution; twice arrested at the beginning of the 1920s; broke with the Mensheviks in 1922 and worked as an instructor in Leningrad and Moscow schools and scientific institutions; author of more than three hundred publications on Russian history.

Rudnev, Vadim Viktorovich (1879–1940), from early 1905, one of the leaders of the S-R Party; more than once arrested and exiled; during the February Revolution, headed the Moscow committee of the S-Rs; in early July 1917, elected to head the Moscow city-administration; reacted to news of the Bolsheviks taking power in Petrograd by urging cities and *zemstvos* to support the Constituent Assembly; planned to make Moscow a centre for country-wide resistance to the Bolsheviks and to form a new provisional government; after dismissal of the Constituent Assembly, faced arrest and emigrated in 1919.

Rudzutak, Yan Ernestovich (1887–1938), member of the RSDRP from 1905; in 1906, member of the Riga Party-Committee; arrested in 1907 and sentenced to ten years of penal servitude; freed in 1917 by the February Revolution; instructor for the Moscow Soviet; member of the Presidium and Secretary for the Moscow Council of the Union of Textile-Workers; member of the Presidium of the Moscow City-Council of Trade Unions; then member of the Presidium of the Supreme Council of the National Economy and Chairman of *Tsentrotekstil'*; from 1920, member of the Central Committee of the RKP(B), and member of the Presidium and general Secretary of the All-Union Central Council of Trade-Unions; in 1921–4, Chairman of the Central-Asian Bureau of the RKP(B); 1923–4, Secretary of the Central Committee of the RKP(B); 1924–30, People's Commissar of Transportation; from 1926, Deputy Chairman of the Council of the National Economy and the USSR Council of Labour and Defence; from 1932, Chairman of the Central Control-Commission of the Communist Party and Commissar of the USSR Worker-Peasant Inspectorate; 1927–32, member of the Politburo of the Central Committee of the Communist Party. Purged.

Rukavishnikov, Ivan Sergeevich (1877–1930), Russian poet and prose-writer.

Ruskin, John (1819–1900), English writer, art-theorist and Christian-socialist who criticised the division of labour for causing poverty.

Ryabushinsky, Pavel Pavlovich (1871–1924), member of a family of bankers and industrialists; co-owner (with his brothers) of the Moscow Ryabushinsky Bank and of the newspaper *Utro Rossii*, expressing the interests of the big bourgeoisie; member of the Central Committee of the Octobrist Party; in 1906, joined the 'Party of Peaceful Renewal'; in 1916, member of the Moscow branch of the 'Progressive' Party; one of the inspirers and organisers of the putsch attempted by Kornilov; after October, emigrated to France.

Ryazanov (*Gol'dendakh*) **David Borisovich** (1870–1938), in the Social-Democratic movement from the 1890s; centrist during WWI and worked for Menshevik newspapers; from 1917, member of the RSDRP(B); worked in the trade-unions after October; in 1918, left the Party in protest against the Brest peace; one of Lenin's principal opponents during the trade-union debate of 1920–1 and was excluded from trade-union work; from May 1918–December 1920 head of *Glavarkhiv*; from 1921, Director of the Marx-Engels Institute; editor of the collected works of G.V. Plekhanov. Purged.

Rykov, Aleksei Ivanovich (1881–1938), member of the RSDRP from 1898; from 1905, member of the Central Committee of the RSDRP; participated in the armed uprising of December 1905 in Moscow; from 1906, in the underground, prison and emigration; from May 1917, member of the Presidium of the Moscow Soviet; in October 1917, Commissar of Internal Affairs and Justice in the first Soviet government; in the winter of 1917–18, worked to supply the city of Moscow with bread; from April 1918, Chairman of the Supreme Council of the National Economy; 1922–30, member of the Politburo of the Central Committee of the All-Union Communist Party; from 1921, Deputy Chairman of the Council of the National Economy and the Council of Labour and Defence for the USSR and for the RSFSR; 1924–30, Chairman of the Council of the National Economy of the USSR and simultaneously, until 1929, head of government for the RSFSR; one of the leaders of the 'Right-deviation'; 1931–6, USSR People's Commissar of Communications. Purged.

S., see Voitinsky, V.C.
S., see Shvarts, I.I.
Sadko, Mikhail, (*Sokolov, Vasilii Nikolaevich*) (1874–?), from 1893–6 a member of *Narodnaya Volya*; in 1897, joined the Northern Workers' Union and organised Marxist circles; from 1900 to 1903, did propaganda-work in Pskov; arrested three times; in 1905, wrote for the newspaper *Vpered*; as Secretary of the RSDRP participated in the December armed uprising in Moscow; arrested in 1906 and sentenced in 1909 to exile in Yenisei province; correspondent for *Irkutskoe slovo*, *Golos Sibiri*, *Nashe delo* and other publications.

Safarov (*Volodin*), **Georgy Ivanovich** (1891–1942), Bolshevik member of the RSDRP from 1908; party-worker in St. Petersburg, Samara, the Urals, Turkestan and abroad; after February 1917, returned to Russia and became a member of the Party's Petrograd Committee; worked at the newspaper *Pravda*; after October, did party-work in the Volga area and the Urals; a Left-Communist during the debate in 1918 over the Brest peace; from 1921, member of the Turkestan Bureau of the Central Committee of the RKP(B); in 1921–2, member of the Executive Committee of the Communist International and head of the Comintern's Eastern department; member of the 'New Opposition' and then joined the Trotsky-Zinoviev bloc; in 1926, First Secretary of the USSR's political mission in China. Purged.

Said-Galiev, Sakhib Garei (1894–1938), member of the RSDRP(B) from 1917; in 1919, Commissar for Nationality-Affairs in the Kazan Soviet; from 1920–4, Chairman of the Council of Ministers for the Tatar Republic and then for the Crimean Republic; 1924–6, in charge of financial and agricultural investigations for the Central Control-Commission and Worker-Peasant Inspectorate; from 1931, member of the Collegium of the USSR Commissariat of Labour; from 1933, head of the political department of the Saratov branch of the Ryazan-Urals railway. Purged.

Saint-Simon, Claude Henri de (1760–1825), French aristocrat and utopian-socialist.

Saltykov-Shchedrin (*Saltykov*), **Mikhail Evgrafovich** (1826–89), Russian satirist and one of the editors of the journal *Otechestvennye zapiski*.

Samoilov, Fedor Nikitich (1882–1952), member of the RSDRP from 1903; deputy to the Fourth State-Duma from Vladimir province and member of the Bolshevik fraction; 1919–20, Plenipotentiary of the Central Committee of the RKP(B) and the All-Russian Central Executive Committee attached to the Bashkir Military-Revolutionary Committee; member of the Bashkir Regional Committee of the RKP(B); author of the book *Malaya Bashkiriya v 1918–1920 gg*.

Samoilovna, R., see Zemlyachka, R.S.

Samsonov, Mikhail Borisovich (1881–?), member of the RSDRP from 1901; did revolutionary work in Saratov, Odessa, Sevastopol', Yalta and Ekaterinoslav; arrested in 1908 and exiled to Irkutsk province; lived in Irkutsk until 1917, and then in Chita.

Sanin, A.A. (1869–?), writer and Marxist from the 1890s; took part in publishing *Samarskii vestnik* and the collection *Proletarskaya bor'ba*.

Sapozhkov (?–1920), Left S-R and commander of the Second Turkestan Cavalry-Division; in July 1920, led an anti-Bolshevik rebellion in Samara province; died in battle on 6 September 1920.

Sazonov, Georgy Petrovich (1857–?), from 1899–1902, editor of the liberal newspaper *Rossiya*; after 17 October 1905, member of the 'Union of the Russian People' and had connections with Rasputin; wrote on the peasantry and the land-question.

Sazonov, Sergei Dmitrievich (1861–1927), diplomat and supporter of the Entente; from 1904, held several diplomatic posts in Europe; in 1909, Deputy Minister, and then from 1910–16, Minister of Foreign Affairs; from 1916, ambassador in London; supported the Provisional Government after February 1917; during 1918–19, a member of A.V. Kolchak's government and then of A.I. Denikin's; emigrated.

Scheidemann, Phillip (1865–1939), one of the right-wing leaders of the German Social-Democratic Party; proclaimed the Weimar Republic in 1918 and played a leading role in suppressing revolution in Germany.

Schelling, Friedrich Wilhelm Joseph (1775–1854), German-idealist philosopher.

Schiller, Johann Christoph Friedrich von (1759–1805), German poet, playwright and art-theorist.

Schopenhauer, Arthur (1788–1860), German philosopher.

Schreiner, Olive (1855–1920), South-African writer from a family of missionaries; concerned with women's issues, education, the racial problem and other subjects.

Sedoi (*Litvin, Zinovy Yakovlevich*) (1879–1947), member of the RSDRP from 1897; metal-worker; did party-work in St. Petersburg, Nizhny Novgorod, Moscow and Tiflis; one of the leaders of the December armed uprising in Moscow and leader of a fighting detachment in Presnensky district; when the uprising was suppressed, left for Finland and then Switzerland, Canada, the USA and France; returned to Russia in 1917 and was elected member of the Kiev City-Soviet; during the Civil War, fought against the White Guards at Tsaritsyn; from 1919, worked in military communications and then for the People's Commissariat of Communication; 1921–29, did administrative work; retired in 1939.

Sefarimovich (*Popov*), **Aleksandr** (1863–1949), writer and member of the RSDRP(B) from 1918; after October, worked for the *Izvestiya* of the Moscow Soviet of Workers' Deputies and, during the Civil War, as a correspondent for *Pravda*.

Semashko, Nikolai Aleksandrovich (1874–1949), nephew of G.V. Plekhanov and member of the RSDRP from 1893; physician; participated in the Moscow student-revolutionary movement; party-worker in Orel and Samara provinces and in Nizhny Novgorod; emigrated in 1906 to Switzerland; 1908–10, Secretary and Treasurer of the Foreign Bureau of the Central Committee of the RSDRP in Paris; returned to Russia in September 1917; provided medical assistance during the October Days and then became Commissar of the Moscow City-Duma and head of the medical department of the Moscow Soviet; from 1918–30, People's Commissar of Health; after 1930, involved in educational and scientific work.

Semen, see Shvarts, I.I.

Semenov, Grigory Mikhailovich (1890–1946), captain of the Transbaikal Cossack forces; fought in WWI; from July 1917, Commissar of the Provisional Government in the Transbaikal region responsible for forming volunteer-units; November-December 1917, led an unsuccessful rebellion against Soviet power and then fled to Manchuria; appointed by the Siberian Provisional Government as commander of a separate force with headquarters in Chita; appointed by A.V. Kolchak as commander of the Chita military region; early in 1919, with Japanese support, proclaimed himself Ataman of the Transbaikal Cossack troops; September 1921, emigrated; captured by Soviet forces in Manchuria in 1945 and executed in 1946.

Serebryakov, Leonid Petrovich (1888–1937), member of the RSDRP from 1905; more than once arrested; exiled to Narym in 1912; after the February Revolution, one of the organisers of the Kostroma Soviet and then went to Moscow; following October, member of the Presidium and Secretary of the Party's Moscow Regional Committee; 1919–1920, Secretary of the Central Committee of the RKP(B), Secretary of All-Russian Central Executive Committee, then member of the Revolutionary War-Council of the southern front and then head of the political directorate of the army and the navy; from 1921, Commissar of the Main Directorate of Transportation; from 1922, Deputy People's Commissar of Transportation; from 1924, Deputy Chairman of the Chinese Eastern Railway; in 1928, Plenipotentiary of the People's Commissariat of Communication in the USA; from 1923, active participant in the Trotskyist opposition. Purged.

Sergeev, Fedor Andreevich, see Artem.

Sergo (*Ordzhonikidze, Grigory Konstantinovich*) (1886–1937), member of the RSDRP from 1903; party-worker in western Georgia, Abkhazia and Baku; more than once imprisoned and exiled; after February 1917, organised revolutionary authority in Yakutia; June 1917, member of the Executive Committee of the St. Petersburg Committee of the RSDRP(B); in Petrograd during the October Revolution; subsequently, Extraordinary Commissar for Ukraine and southern Russia; during the Civil War, member of the Revolutionary War-Council of the Fourteenth and Sixteenth Armies on the Caucasus front; in 1921–6, Chairman of the Caucasus Bureau of the Central Committee and then Secretary of the Transcaucasus Territorial Committee of the Party, while simultaneously member of the Revolutionary War-Council of the USSR; from 1932, People's Commissar for Heavy Industry; ended his life by suicide.

Shakespeare, William (1564–1616), English playwright and poet.

Shamigulov, Gali K. (1890–1959), member of the RSDRP from 1910, Bolshevik; participated in the October Revolution in Orenburg; member of the Orenburg Military-Revolutionary Committee and Provincial Commissar for Nationalities in 1918; 1919–20, member of the Bashkir Regional Committee of the RKP(B) and Chairman of the Central Executive Committee and the Council of People's Commissars for Bashkiria; subsequently involved in party-, soviet- and economic work.

Shamshin, Ivan Dmitrievich, member of the RSDRP and father of Vasily Ivanovich Shamshin.

Shamshin, Ivan Ivanovich, member of the RSDRP and older brother of Vasily Ivanovich Shamshin; shot by Kolchak's forces in 1919.

Shamshin, Vasily Ivanovich (1885–1918), member of the RSDRP from 1904; one of the organisers of the Ob group of the RSDRP in Novonikolaevsk; more than once arrested; in 1909, sentenced to exile in Karapchansky in the Kirensky district; 1916, sent to Yakutsk; in Novonikolaevsk after February 1917; after October, Provincial Commissar of Labour and member of the Provincial Executive Committee of the Tomsk Soviet; June 1918, shot by Kolchak's forces.

Shamshina, Evdokiya Ivanovna, sister of Vasily Ivanovich Shamshin, arrested by gendarmes late in 1912.

Shilo, Andrei Ivanovich (1867–?), sentenced to prison in the case of the 'Peasants' Union'; deputy to the Third

State-Duma from Primorsk region; Trudovik; expelled from the Trudovik fraction on 9 June 1912, for being part of the audience given by the Tsar on 8 June to two hundred deputies of the State-Duma.

Shloss, author of liberal articles in the newspaper *Utro Rossii*.

Shmidt, Lyudvig Tomashevich (1875–?), Polish revolutionary in Dombrov; 1897, joined the Polish Socialist Party; more than once arrested; May 1916, condemned to exile in Irkutsk province.

Shmidt, Otto Yul'evich (1891–1956), academic, mathematician, astronomer, geophysicist and Arctic explorer; a Bolshevik from 1918; 1918–20, member of the Collegium of the People's Commissariat of Food, of the board of *Tsentrosoyuz* and of the Collegium of the Commissariat of Education and the Commissariat of Finance; from 1921–4, head of the state publisher *Gosizdat*; 1932–9, head of the Chief Directorate of the Northern Sea-Route; one of the organisers and chief editor of the *Bolshaya sovetskaya entsiklopediya*.

Shmidt, Valer'yan, member of the Orel Committee of the Social-Democratic Party and later a Menshevik.

Shtiber, head of the Prussian police under Bismarck.

Shumyatsky, Boris Zakharovich (1886–1938), member of the RSDRP from 1903; took part in the Krasnoyarsk armed uprising in December 1905; in 1917, Chairman of the Siberian Bureau of the Central Committee of the RKP(B) and Central-Committee Plenipotentiary in Siberia; delegate to the Sixth Party-Congress; member of the All-Russian Bureau of Military Organisations under the Central Committee of the RSDRP(B); November 1917–March 1918, Chairman of *Tsentrosibir'* and simultaneously, from December, Chairman of the east-Siberian region of the Military-Revolutionary Committee; supported the Left-Communists; a leader of the partisan-movement in western Siberia during the Civil War; 1919–20, Deputy Chairman of the Siberian Military-Revolutionary Committee; 1920-1, Chairman of the government of the Far-Eastern Republic; 1921–2, member of the Revolutionary War-Council of the Fifth Army; from 1923, political representative in Iran; 1926–8, Rector of the Communist University of the Toilers of the East and then member of the Central-Asian Bureau of the Central Committee of the All-Union Communist Party; from 1930, headed the cinema-industry. Purged.

Shuvalov, Ivan Ivanovich (1727–97), chamberlain, lieutenant-general, adjutant-general and senator; promoted the development of sciences and the arts in the court of Empress Elizavet Petrovna; supported M.V. Lomonosov and his plan to create the Moscow University.

Shvarts, Isaak Izrailevich (*S.; Semen*) (1879–1951), in the Social-Democratic movement from 1899, Bolshevik; seven times arrested, exiled, and fled from exile; exiled to Ekaterinburg in 1905; 1908–10 rebuilt party organisations in the Urals; arrested in 1911 and sentenced to permanent exile in Yenisei province where he remained until February 1917; after October a leading party-worker in Ukraine; 1918 member of the Central Committee of the RKP(B) in Ukraine; 1919–20 member of the Ukrainian Cheka and then Plenipotentiary of the Council of Labour and Defence in Odessa and Nikolaev; restored the Donbass; from 1921, Chairman of the Central Committee of the Miners' Union; from 1925, member of the Presidium of the All-Union Central Council of Trade-Unions; from 1930, Chairman of *Soyuzugol'* and then director of *Soyuzslantsa*; from 1938 to the end of his life, organised and led a scientific research institute investigating the medical use of herbal grasses.

Sibirsky, F. (*Lebedev, Fedor Nikolaevich*) (1879–?), journalist and Narodnik; worked for the journal *Golos Siberii* and also as a correspondent for the newspaper *Ural'skii rabochii*.

Simakov, member of the Bolkhov Committee of the RKP(B) in Orel province.

Sklyansky, Efraim Markovich (1892–1925), member of the RSDRP from 1913; military physician; after February 1917, member of the Dvinsk Committee of the RSDRP(B); delegate and member of the Presidium of the Second Congress of Soviets; member of the Petrograd Military-Revolutionary Committee; during the October Days, commanded the force that occupied the staff-headquarters of the Petrograd military district; Commissar of the General Staff for the Petrograd Military-Revolutionary Committee and then of General-Staff Headquarters in Mogilev; 1918–24, member of the Collegium of the People's Commissariat of War and Deputy Chairman of the Revolutionary War-Council of the Republic.

Skobelev, Matvei Ivanovich (1885–1938), in the Social-Democratic movement as a Menshevik from 1903; emigrated in 1906 and worked on Menshevik publications including Trotsky's *Pravda*; deputy to the Fourth State-Duma; centrist during WWI; after February 1917, Deputy Chairman of the Petrograd Soviet and of the Central Executive Committee; from May-August 1917, Minister of Labour in the Provisional Government; left the Mensheviks in October and worked for the co-operatives and in the Commissariat of Foreign Trade; a Bolshevik from 1922, involved mainly in economic work; in 1936–7, worked at the All-Union Radio Committee. Purged.

Skoropadsky, Pavel Petrovich (1873–1945), lieutenant-general and descendant of Hetman I.I. Skoropadsky; fought in the Russo-Japanese War and WWI; *aide-de-camp* of Nicholas II; supported the unification of 'Russian lands', including Poland, in a single federative state; in October 1917, became Ataman of Ukrainian Cossack forces and head of the army of the Central Rada; selected as Hetman with the approval of Wilhelm II, and declared a Ukrainian state; restored the rights of landlords and announced an All-Russian Federation with the objective of restoring Greater Russia; overthrown by Petlyura in November 1918 and fled to Berlin in December; in 1928, negotiated with representatives of the Russian All-Military Union (ROVS, a White military organisation founded by Wrangel in 1924) for the purpose of collaborating, but ended the discussions when M.A. Bulgakov's play *Days of the Turbins* was staged in Berlin and portrayed him badly; collaborated with Hitler.

Skrypnik, Nikolai Alekseevich (1872–1933), Social Democrat from 1897; as a Bolshevik, did party-work in the Urals in 1903; sentenced to death *in absentia* for his participation in the 1905 Revolution; in 1908–9 restored the Social-Democratic organisation in the Urals and formed the Urals Regional Bureau of the RSDRP; arrested 15 times and exiled seven times; from 1917, member of the Bolshevik Central Committee; one of the leaders of the October armed uprising in Petrograd; in Ukraine from December 1917, where he headed several commissariats, and was Deputy Chairman of Soviet Ukraine's Council of Ministers; in 1933, tried to protect Ukraine against the effects of the famine; denounced as a nationalist by Stalin and committed suicide.

Skvortsov-Stepanov, Ivan Ivanovich (1870–1928), in the revolutionary movement from 1892, member of the RSDRP from 1896, a Bolshevik from late 1904; more than once arrested, and exiled from 1901–4 to eastern Siberia; during 1905–7, worked for the literature- and lectures-group of the Moscow Committee; in 1907 and 1911, a Bolshevik candidate for the Third State-Duma; from February 1917, member of the Moscow Committee and editor of the *Izvestiya* of the Moscow Soviet of Workers' and Soldiers' Deputies; during the October Days, member of the Moscow Military-Revolutionary Committee; People's Commissar of Finance in the first Soviet government; 1919–20, in the leadership of the central cooperative-organisation *Tsentrosoyuz*; in 1920, political worker on the Soviet-Polish front; subsequently director of the Lenin Institute of the Central Committee of the RKP(B); author of works on the history of the revolutionary movement, political economy, atheism and the history of religion, and translator and editor of the three volumes of Marx's *Capital*.

Sleptsov, member of the Bolkhov Committee of the RKP(B) in Orel province.

Slutsksya, Vera, member of the Bryansk Social-Democratic organisation.

Smilga, Ivar Tenisovich (1892–1937), member of the RSDRP from 1907; 1914–15, member of the Bolshevik Committee in St. Petersburg; after February 1917, member of the Kronstadt Committee of the RSDRP(B), Chairman of the Regional Executive Committee of the Army, Navy and Workers of Finland; after October, Plenipotentiary of the Council of People's Commissars of the RSFSR in Finland; from the summer of 1918, at the fronts during the Civil War and member of the Revolutionary War-Councils on several fronts; from April 1919, member of the Revolutionary War-Council of the Republic and head of the political directorate of the Revolutionary War-Council of Russia; supported Trotsky during the trade-union discussions of 1920–1; 1921–8, Deputy Chairman of the Supreme Council of the National Economy; 1924–36, Deputy Chairman of the USSR *Gosplan*; 1925–7 rector of the G.V. Plekhanov Institute of National Economy; arrested in 1935. Purged.

Smirnov, E. (*Gurevich, Emmanuil L'vovich*) (1866–?), arrested in 1884 for participating in self-education circles and exiled to Ufa province; member of *Narodnaya Volya* until 1890; from 1901, a Social Democrat and, from 1903, a Menshevik; in 1905, an editor of the Menshevik newspaper *Nachalo*; liquidator in 1910; worked in the Social-Democratic fraction of the State-Duma; arrested in 1911 and banished from St. Petersburg; defencist during WWI; in 1917, editor of the newspaper *Vlast' naroda*; in 1930, worked at the Marx-Engels Institute in a non-party capacity.

Smirnov, Ivan Nikitich (1881–1936), member of the RSDRP from 1899; party-worker in Moscow and Vyshny Volochek; more than once arrested, imprisoned and exiled; from 1905, worked in Moscow, St. Petersburg, Rostov-on-Don and Khar'kov; in 1916, mobilised for service in the army; after February 1917, member of the Executive Committee of Tomsk Soviet; from August 1918 to April 1919, member of the Revolutionary War-Council of the eastern front; from April 1919 to May 1920, member of the Revolutionary War-Council of the Fifth Army; from December 1918 to October 1919, Chairman of the Siberian (Urals-Siberian) Bureau of the Central Committee of the RKP(B); from November, Chairman of the Siberian Regional Bureau of the RKP(B); From August 1919 to August 1921, Chairman of the Siberian Revolutionary Committee; organised and directed the revolutionary movement in the rear of Kolchak's forces; from October 1921, did party-work in Petrograd; 1923–7, People's Commissar of Post and Telegraph; from 1923, an active participant in the Trotskyist opposition. Purged.

Smirnov, Vladimir Mikhailovich (1887–1937), member of the RSDRP from 1907; after February 1917, worked in Moscow and was member of the editorial collective of the Bolshevik newspaper *Sotsial-demokrat* and the journal *Spartak*; from October, member of the Presidium of the Supreme Council of the National Economy; a Left-Communist in 1918; in 1919, one of the leaders of the 'military opposition'; in 1920–1, member of the Democratic-Centralist group; sided with the Trotskyist opposition in 1923. Purged.

Smol'nikov, member of the Bolkhov organisation of the RKP(B) in Orel province.

Sokolov, Aleksandr Nikolaevich (1889–?), not a member of a political party; arrested in 1907 for participation in a demonstration and strike and imprisoned in Poshekhon, Yaroslavl and Rybinsk; exiled to Irkutsk province in 1909.

Sokolov, Nikolai Dmitrievich (1870–1928), Social Democrat, lawyer; in 1909, candidate for the RSDRP in elections to the Third State-Duma; sympathised with the Bolsheviks; after February 1917, member of the Executive Committee of the Petrograd Soviet and supported a coalition with the bourgeoisie; after October, served as legal counsel in Soviet institutions.

Solov'ev, Vasily Ivanovich (1890–1939), member of the RSDRP from 1912; party-worker in Petrograd and Moscow; after February 1917, member of the Moscow Regional Committee and Bolshevik member of the City-Duma; in October 1917, member of a party fighting unit; in 1918, administrator for the Supreme Council of the National Economy and then member of the Revolutionary War-Council of the eastern front and the Revolutionary War-Council of the Second Army; from January 1920, deputy head of the Political Directorate of the Republic; then in the apparatus of the Central Committee of the RKP(B); in 1923–6, diplomat and Comintern worker; then head of the State Publishing House (*Gosizdat*) and director of the State Book-Chamber.

Sol'ts, Aron Aleksandrovich (1872–1945), member of the RSDRP from 1898, Bolshevik; participated in all three revolutions; in 1917, member of the editorial boards of the newspapers *Sotsial-demokrat* and *Pravda*; from 1921, member of the Presidium of the Central Control-Commission; then member of the Supreme Court of the RSFSR and the USSR.

Sorokin, member of the Perm Provincial Executive Committee.

Sosnovsky, Lev Semenovich (1886–1937), member of the RSDRP from 1904; active participant in the revolutionary movement in Ekaterinburg, Zlatoust, Samara, Odessa and St. Petersburg; worked for *Pravda* and other Social-Democratic publications; arrested in 1913 and exiled to Chelyabinsk; after February 1917, member of the Urals Regional Committee of the RSDRP(B); from August, Chairman of the Urals Regional Party-Committee and the Urals Regional Council of Trade-Unions; from October, Chairman of the Ekaterinburg Soviet; chief editor of the newspaper *Ural'skii rabochii*; in November 1917, deputy to the All-Russian Constituent Assembly from Perm province; in Petrograd from December 1917; 1918–24, member of the Presidium of the All-Russian Central Executive Committee; during the Civil War, Chairman of the Ekaterinoslav Provincial Executive Committee, of the Khar'kov Provincial Committee of the RKP(B) and of the Ekaterinburg Revolutionary Committee; took part in establishing the Bashkir ASSR; in 1921, head of a department in the Central Committee of the RKP(B); in 1922, member of the Soviet delegation to the Genoa Conference; in 1923, supported the Trotskyist opposition. Purged.

Spinoza, Benedict (*Baruch*) (1632–77) born to a Portuguese-Jewish family in Amsterdam; a materialist philosopher and atheist.

Spiridonova, Mariya Aleksandrovna (1884–1941), member of the S-R Party from 1905; in 1906, committed a terrorist-act against an officer of troops that were suppressing peasant-uprisings in Tambov province, was severely beaten and initially sentenced to death, but the sentence was changed to life-imprisonment in eastern Siberia; after February 1917, leader of the Left S-Rs and member of the S-R Central Committee; chaired the Second All-Russian congress of Soviets; supported by the Bolsheviks and Left S-Rs as candidate to chair the Constituent Assembly; opposed the Brest peace and the Bolshevik food-policy; arrested in June 1918 after an attempted insurrection by Left S-Rs but released; subsequently arrested and exiled several times up to 1937; then accused of plotting a peasant-uprising and sentenced to 25 years in prison; executed near Orel in September 1941.

Stakhovich, Aleksandr Aleksandrovich (1858–1915), landlord, horseman and Cadet; 1895–1904, leader of the nobility in Eletsk district; one of the founders of the 'Union of Emancipation'; deputy to the Second State-Duma from Orel province.

Stalin (*Dzhugashvili*), **Joseph Vissarionovich** (1878 (1879)–1953), joined the Georgian Social-Democratic organisation in 1898; from 1902–17, arrested and exiled six times, escaping four times; a Bolshevik after 1903; in 1906–7, participated in expropriations in the Caucasus; in 1907, one of the leaders of the Baku Committee of the RSDRP; in 1917, member of the editorial board of *Pravda*, member of the Politburo of the Central Committee of the RSDRP(B) and of the Military-Revolutionary Centre; in 1917–22, People's Commissar of Nationalities and, from 1919–22, Commissar of the Worker-Peasant Inspectorate; from 1918, member of the Revolutionary War-Council of the Republic; from 1922, General Secretary of the Central Committee; from 1941, Chairman of the Council of People's Commissars (Council of Ministers) of the USSR; during WWII, head of the State Defence-Committee (GKO), Commissar of Defence and Supreme Commander; in 1946–7, Minister of Armed Forces for the USSR.

Stankevich, Nikolai Vladimirovich (1813–40), philosopher and poet; in 1831, organised a literary-philosophical circle including K.S. Aksakov, V.P. Botkin, M.A. Bakunin, T.N. Granovsky and others; lived abroad from 1837.

Stefanovich, Yakov Vasil'evich (1854–1915), revolutionary Narodnik, member of the 'Tchaikovsky circle' in Kiev, participated in the movement 'to the people', member of *Zemlya i volya* and *Chernyi peredel*'; from 1891, member of the Executive Committee of *Narodnaya volya*; sentenced in 1883 to eight years of penal servitude.

Steklov (*Nakhamkis*) **Yury Mikhailovich** (1873–1941), in the Social-Democratic movement from 1893 and organiser of left Social-Democratic circles in Odessa; arrested in 1894 and exiled to Yakutsk province, then fled abroad; supported the Bolsheviks after 1903; after 1907, worked for *Sotsial-demokrat*, the central organ of the RSDRP and for the Bolshevik newspapers *Zvezda* and *Pravda*; member of the Social-Democratic group in the Third and Fourth State-Dumas; 'revolutionary-defencist' after 1917, member of the Executive Committee of the Petrograd Soviet, editor of the *Izvestiya* of the Petrograd Soviet and rejoined the Bolsheviks; after October, member of the All-Russian Central Executive Committee and the Central Executive Committee; editor of *Izvestiya*; during the Civil War, travelled the fronts with the propaganda-train *Izvestiya*; from 1928, headed the Committee for Educational and Scientific Institutions under the Central Executive Committee; author of works on the history of the revolutionary movement. Purged.

Stepnyak, C. (*Kravchinsky, Sergei Mikhailovich*) (1851–95), writer and publicist, revolutionary Narodnik in the 1870s; in 1872, member of the 'Tchaikovsky circle' and arrested during the movement 'to the people'; emigrated 1873; in 1875, fought against Turkey in Bosnia and Herzegovina; returned to Russia in 1878 and supported the Narodnik organisation *Zemlya i volya*; in 1878, assassinated N.V. Mezentsov, head of the Gendarmerie; emigrated to London; author of several works including *Andrei Kozhukov*.

Stolypin, Aleksandr Arkad'evich, journalist, director of the Literary-Artistic Society, head of the St. Petersburg City-Duma, Chairman of the 'Slavic Reciprocity' and 'Russian Grain' societies; member of the Central Committee of the 'Union of 17 October'; brother of P.A. Stolypin.

Stolypin, Petr Arkad'evich (1862–1911), Minister of Internal Affairs and Chairman of the Council of Ministers from 1906; suppressed the Revolution of 1905–7 and initiated agrarian reforms; fatally wounded by the S-R D.G. Bogrov.

Struve, Peter Berngardovich (1870–1944), economist, philosopher, historian and publicist; a 'Legal Marxist' in the 1890s; from October 1905, a member of the Central Committee of the Cadet Party and leader of its right wing; editor of the journal *Russkaya mysl*'; from 1917, worked as an academic in political economy and statistics; elected to the Academy of Sciences in 1917 but excluded in 1928; during the Civil War, was a member of A.I. Denikin's 'Special Council' and head of the Department of Foreign Relations under P.N. Wrangel; then emigrated.

Stukov, head of the agitation- and propaganda-department for the Ufa Provincial Committee of the RKP(B).

Sukhomlinov, Vladimir Aleksandrovich (1848–1926), adjutant-general of cavalry, general of cavalry and member of the State-Council; fought in the Russo-Turkish War of 1877–8; from 1905, Governor-General of Kiev, Volhynia, and Podolsk; from 1908, Chief of the General Staff; 1909–15, War-Minister; arrested in 1916 for not having prepared the Russian

Army for WWI, and imprisoned in the Petropavlovsk fortress; sentenced in 1917 to lifelong penal servitude; 1918, amnestied because of his age; emigrated to Finland and then to Germany.

Sverdlov, Jakov Mikhailovich (*Andrei, Mikhalych*) (1885–1919), member of the RSDRP from 1901; did revolutionary work in Nizhny Novgorod, Kostroma, Yaroslavl' and Kazan; in 1905, member of the Kazan Party-Committee; arrested several times; from July 1905, in the Urals (Perm, Ekaterinburg and other cities); February 1906, elected Chairman of the Urals Regional Party-Committee; June 1906, arrested in Perm, released in 1909; December 1909, arrested in Moscow and exiled to Siberia but fled; arrested in St. Petersburg and exiled to Narym but fled to St. Petersburg; in February 1913, betrayed to the police by the provocateur R.V. Malinovsky and exiled to Turukhansk region; freed by the February Revolution; in April 1917, led the First (free) Urals Conference of Bolsheviks called by the Urals Regional Committee of the Party; one of the leaders of the October Revolution in Petrograd, a member of the Petrograd Military-Revolutionary Committee, Chairman of the Bolshevik fraction at the second All-Russian Congress of Soviets; from November 1917, Chairman of All-Russian Central Executive Committee; from April 1918, Chairman of the commission to draft the RSFSR's Constitution; member and Secretary of the Central Committee and, from January, member of the *Orgburo* of the Central Committee of the RKP(B).

Tagiev, Zeinal Abdin (1842–?), millionaire banker and oil-industrialist; son of poor, undeducated parents; worked for thirty years as a stone-mason; became wealthy through commercial operations in the oil-industry; owner of textile-plants, 18 steamers on the Caspian, fishing enterprises, flour-mills and theatres; important landlord in Baku; from 1905, commercial consultant and state-councillor; funded *Leila and Majnun*, said to be the first opera in the Muslim world.

Tan, N.A. (*Bogoraz, Vladimir Germanovich*) (1865–1936), writer and publicist, ethnographer and linguist; a Narodnik during the early 1880s and an organiser of *Narodnaya volya* in southern Russia; involved in 1905 in founding the Peasant-Union; in 1906, one of the organisers of the party of Popular Socialists and worker with the newspaper *Rodnaya zemlya*; a defencist during WWI; after October, an instructor at several Leningrad higher-educational institutes, one of the first scholars to study the northern peoples, and Director of the Museum of the History of Religion under the USSR Academy of Sciences; author of numerous novels and stories.

Tchaikovsky, Petr Il'ich (1840–93), Russian composer.

Teslenko, Nikolai Vasil'evich (1870–?), attorney and trustee of the Moscow Ryabushinsky Bank; member of the Cadet Central Committee; supported war until victory during WWI; called for military dictatorship at a meeting of the Cadet Central Committee in August 1917; member of Denikin's 'Special Council'; emigrated in 1920.

Thiers, Adolphe (1797–1877), French politician, historian and attorney; following the July Revolution of 1830, minister and Premier of France; in 1834, organised suppression of the republican uprising in Lyon and Paris; during the Second Republic (1848–51) one of the leaders of the monarchist 'party of order'; left politics during the Second Empire (1851–70); headed a right-wing government after the fall of Napoleon III and brutally suppressed the Paris Commune.

Tikhomirov, Lev Aleksandrovich (1852–1923), revolutionary Narodnik and publicist; member of the 'Tchaikovsky circle', of *Zemlya i volya* and of the Executive Committee of *Narodnaya volya*; later left revolutionary politics and, from the 1890s, was a monarchist and theorist of autocracy (author of *On Monarchist Statehood*).

Tikhomirov, Viktor Aleksandrovich (1889–1919), Bolshevik member of the RSDRP from 1905; did party-work in Kazan, St. Petersburg and Moscow; arrested and exiled more than once; worked for *Pravda* in 1912; 1913 exiled to Olonestky district and then emigrated to Poland; participated in the February Revolution of 1917; an editor of *Pravda*' after the overthrow of the autocracy; in May, sent to Kazan to restore the provincial Bolshevik organisation; from July 1917, in Moscow as member of the Military Bureau under the Moscow Committee of the RSDRP(B); in October, member of the Moscow Military-Revolutionary Committee responsible for protecting the Moscow Soviet; then Secretary of the Bolshevik fraction of the Moscow Soviet and staff-member of the Moscow Military Museum (*Muzei Istorii Voisk*, or MVO); from March 1918, member of the Collegium of the People's Commissariat of Internal Affairs.

Tinyakov, Aleksandr, poet from Orel.

Titov, member of the Bolkhov Committee of the RKP(B) in Orel province.

Tizengauzen, Evgeny Evgen'evich (1860–?), baron, Octobrist, director of Serpukhov Manufacturing; deputy to the Third State-Duma from Moscow; as Chairman of the commission on labour-questions, defended the interests of industrialists.

Tolmachev, Ivan Nikolaevich (1863–sometime after 1929), lieutenant-general of the Russian Army and member of the 'Union of the Russian People'; oppressive prefect of Odessa from 1907–1911; removed from office in 1911; emigrated after October 1917.

Tolmachev, Nikolai Gur'evich (1895–1919), member of the RSDRP from 1913; February 1917, headed a detachment that liberated political prisoners from the Petropavlovsk fortress; March 1917, member of the St. Petersburg Committee of the RSDRP(B); then sent to Perm as organiser of the workers' militia and Red-Guard detachments, and member of the military organisation of the Perm Committee of the RSDRP(B); from spring 1918, Political Commissar of the Urals Regional Soviet on the Dutov front and commander of the Third Army of the eastern front; organiser of the first military-political educational institutions in the Red Army; in May 1919, Special Plenipotentiary of the Revolutionary War-Council on the Petrograd front; committed suicide to avoid capture.

Tolstoy, Lev Nikolaevich (1828–1910), count and Russian writer.

Trepov, Dmitry Fedorovich (1855–1906), nobleman and major-general; 1896–1905, head of police in Moscow; from 11 January 1905, Governor-General of St. Petersburg and then Deputy Minister of Internal Affairs and one of the organisers of the armed suppression of the revolution; dismissed from these duties in 1905 and appointed Commandant of the palace.

Treshchenkov, Nikolai Viktorovich (1875–1915), captain of a corps of gendarmes; from 1911, Assistant-Chief of the Irkutsk Provincial Gendarmerie for the Kirensky and Verkholensk parishes; in 1912, sent by the Department of Police to the Lena goldfields to suppress a strike and ordered the shooting of workers; following an investigation, removed from office and faced criminal charges, but the case was never completed; sent to the German front in 1914, and evidently perished there.

Tret'yakov, Pavel Mikhailovich (1832–98), entrepreneur, art-patron, collector and philanthropist; commercial adviser, honorary citizen of Moscow and member of the Moscow branch of the Council of Trade and Manufactures; elected to the Moscow stock-exchange company; member of the St. Petersburg Academy of Arts; member of the Russian Musical Society and of the Board of the Moscow Art-Society; in 1854, purchased a number of paintings that led to an impressive art-collection that he donated, along with the mansion that housed them, to the city of Moscow.

Troitsky, Aleksandr Georgievich (1877–?), statistician; in 1905 member of the left wing of the S-R 'Maximalists'; participated in the December 1905 armed uprising in Moscow as head of an S-R fighting brigade in the district of Sadovaya Ring; after February 1917, joined the 'Maximalists' again, but then joined the S-R Party; following October, joined the RKP(B); left the Party and political activity in 1921 and worked as a statistician in several Soviet institutions.

Trotsky (*Bronshtein*) Lev (*Leiba*) Davydovich (1879–1940), member of the RSDRP from 1897; in 1905, led the Petrograd Soviet, was arrested and exiled to Obdorsk; escaped *en route* and lived for ten years in emigration; occupied a middle-position between Bolsheviks and Mensheviks; returned to Russia after February 1917; member of the Petrograd Soviet and Chairman from September; after the Sixth Party-Congress (in August), joined the Bolsheviks; one of the leaders of the October armed uprising in Petrograd; from 1918, People's Commissar for the Army and later also for the Navy, and Chairman of the Supreme War-Council and the Revolutionary War-Council of the Republic (up to 1925); made several trips to the Urals during the Civil War; in September 1918, assisted local authorities in forming a partisan-movement in Ufa province; restored the left flank of the eastern front early in 1919 and changed the commander of the Third Army; from January 1920, Chairman of the Revolutionary War-Council of the First Revolutionary Labour-Army (in Ekaterinburg), created on the basis of the Third Army; visited several Urals cities; in 1923-7, leader of the (Trotskyist) Left Opposition in the RKP(B); 1925, removed from his posts as People's Commissar of War and Chairman of the Revolutionary War-Council of the USSR; expelled from the Party in 1927, exiled to Alma-Ata in 1928, exiled from the USSR in 1929; lived in Mexico; created the Fourth International; denounced the Stalinist régime for betraying the revolution; murdered by an NKVD agent.

Trubina, A.V., member of the RSDRP; one of the leaders of the Chelyabinsk and then the Ekaterinburg Social-Democratic organisation; arrested late 1911 (or early 1912) and exiled to Tomsk; wife of I.I. Shvarts.

Trusevich, Maksimilian Ivanovich (1863–?), nobleman; from 1889, assistant-prosecutor of the St. Petersburg Regional Court; from 1906, Director of the Department of Police; senator from 1909 and, from 1914, member of the State-Council.

Tsereteli, Irakly Georgievich (1881–1959), one of the leaders of Menshevism; 1902, exiled to eastern Siberia for participating in the student movement; deputy to the Second State-Duma from Kutaissi province; sentenced in 1907 to penal servitude and exile after 1912; returned to Petrograd after February 1917 and supported a coalition with the bourgeoisie to continue the war against Germany; Minister of Post and Telegraph for the Provisional Government and then Minister of Internal Affairs; after October, led the anti-Soviet bloc in the Constituent Assembly, and following the assembly's dissolution was one of the leaders of the Menshevik government in Georgia; emigrated to France and then to the USA.

Tugan-Baranovsky, Mikhail Ivanovich (1865–1919), Russian economist, historian and one of the representatives of 'Legal Marxism'; later an open exponent of capitalism; from late 1917–January 1918, Minister of Finance for the Central Rada.

Turgenev, Ivan Sergeevich (1818–83), Russian writer.

Tverskoi, P.A. (*Dement'ev, Petr Alekseevich*) (1850–1919 (1923)), businessman and publicist; under observation by political police (the Third Department) from 1878; emigrated to America in 1878; from the early 1880s, contributed to the periodicals *Russkoe bogatstvo*, *Mir bozhii*, *Russkaya mysl'* and others; in 1897, financed the journal *Sovremennik*.

Ul'yanov, Chairman of the Chernigov Provincial Cheka.

Urusov, Sergei Dmitrievich (1861–1937), prince and large landowner; in 1903–4, Governor-General of Bessarabia; in 1905, Deputy Minister of Internal Affairs in the cabinet of Witte; elected to the First State-Duma in 1906 from Kaluzhskaya region; member of the Party of Democratic Reform, standing to the right of the Cadets; from March-June 1917, Deputy Minister of Internal Affairs for the Provisional Government; deprived of civil rights after October (restored in 1929); in 1923, received the Order of the

Red Banner for his work in studying the Kursk magnetic anomaly with a special commission of the Presidium of the Supreme Council of the National Economy, and then retired.

Uspensky, Gleb Ivanovich (1843–1902), writer and Narodnik sympathiser.

Uspensky, Misha, childhood-friend of E.A. Preobrazhensky.

Vainer, Leonid Isaakovich (1878–1918), member of the RSDRP from 1905; did revolutionary work in Perm, Ekaterinburg and at factories and mines in the Urals; in 1917, member of the Ekaterinburg Committee of the RSDRP(B); after October, Secretary of the City-Duma and the Executive Committee of the Ekaterinburg Regional Soviet; member of the Urals Regional Committee of the RSDRP(B) and then Secretary; died at the front fighting White Guards in 1918.

Validov (Valid), Akhmed-Zaki (known in emigration as *Togan Akhmet Zaki Validi*) (1890–1970), historian, orientalist and journalist; prominent in the Muslim movement; member of the Presidium of the first All-Bashkir Congress, and in November declared the autonomy of Bashkiria; from December 1917, member of the Bashkir government; head of its military department and commander of Bashkir forces; cooperated with anti-Bolshevik forces, but in February 1919 joined the Soviet side, and the RKP(B) itself late in 1919; accused the Bolsheviks of destroying Bashkir autonomy and fled to Turkestan in 1920; ideologist and organiser of the Basmachi movement; emigrated in 1923 and became a professor at Istanbul University.

Varga, Evgeny Samuilovich (1879–1964), economist, member of the USSR Academy of Scinces, prominent figure in the international Communist movement; People's Commissar of Finance and then Chairman of the Supreme Soviet of the National Economy in the Hungarian Revolution; after the revolution's suppression in 1919, emigrated to Russia; 1927–42 headed the Institute of World-Economy and World-Politics.

Vasil'chenko, Semen Filippovich (1884–1937), member of the RSDRP from 1901; did revolutionary work in Rostov-on-Don and Siberia; more than once arrested; in 1905, exiled to hard labour and served this sentence until 1913 at the settlement of Verkholensk in Irkutsk province; escaped and lived in Irkutsk; internationalist during WWI; together with M.P. Zhakov, created the 'Union of Siberian Workers', which was disbanded in 1915; after February 1917, returned to Rostov-on-Don and headed the local Bolshevik organisation; in 1918, Commissar for the Donetsk-Krivoy Rog Republic and member of the Don Soviet government; returned to Moscow in 1920, organised publication of *Moskovskii rabochii* and later worked in publishing; author of literary works of an autobiographical character. Purged.

Veisman (*Tseitlin, L.S.*) (1877–?), from 1898, propagandist in Vitebsk Social-Democratic workers' circles; from 1901, in Moscow; delegate from Moscow to the Second Congress of the RSDRP and a centrist; then a Menshevik working in Odessa, Moscow and Vitebsk; left politics in 1907; after February 1917, in charge of editorial and publishing work for the Moscow Soviet; continued with editorial and publishing work after October.

Vel'man, Vladimir Ivanovich (1887–1937), member of the RSDRP from 1904; arrested in 1907 in the case of the Revel' Committee of the RSDRP, and sentenced to penal servitude in Irkutsk province; Secretary of the Irkutsk Committee of the RSDRP; from the beginning of the Revolution in 1917, Deputy Chairman of the Irkutsk Soviet and its Executive Committee; member of the Irkutsk organisation of the RSDRP, which united Bolsheviks and Mensheviks; from May, in Revel' as Deputy Chairman of the Soviet and Chairman of the Bolshevik fraction, and member of the Central Bureau of Bolshevik organisations in Estonia; in Moscow from the spring of 1918 as Deputy Chairman of the Main Committee of State-Construction; from 1921, member of the 'Small Council of Commissars'; from 1922–5, Deputy Chairman of the Council of People's Commissars; from 1925–8, Deputy Chairman and member of the Presidium of the RSFSR *Gosplan*; from 1928–30, Chairman of the Construction-Committee of the RSFSR Council of People's Commissars; from 1930, Plenipotentiary of the RSFSR Council of People's Commissars for capital-construction. Purged.

Verbov, Abram Aaronovich (1880–?), from 1906, agitator for the Ekaterinoslav organisation of the RSDRP, and did party-work, mostly in southern Russia; more than once arrested; member of a fighting committee; did propaganda-work in Gomel district and then in the Urals in 1906; arrested in 1907 and sent to the Nikolaevsk battalions; February 1909, sentenced to exile in Ekaterinburg province, but fled in the same year to Belgium and then to Bulgaria.

Vikman, P.M. (1890–?), member of the RSDRP from 1906; fought in the Civil War; 1918–20, Chairman of the Tver' Provincial Cheka; 1919–20, Chairman of the Bashkir Party-Committee and, in 1922–4, of the Smolensk Regional Party-Committee; later worked in All-Russian Central Executive Committee and the Central Committee of the All-Union Communist Party.

Vilonov, Nikifor Efimovich (1883–1910), member of the RSDRP; began revolutionary work in Kaluga in 1901 and then in Kiev and Ekaterinsolav; arrested several times; exiled to Yenisei province but fled in the summer of 1904; one of the founders of the RSDRP Committee in Kazan; from December 1904, in Ekaterinburg and organised several printing works in the Urals; twice arrested in 1905–6 and fled both times; emigrated in 1908; one of the organisers of the party-school on the island of Capri; died in Switzerland from consumption.

Vinogradov, F.V., imprisoned during 1910 in the Aleksandrovsk transit-prison at Irkutsk.

Vodovozov, Vasily Vasil'evich (1864–1933), liberal-Narodnik economist and publicist; from 1904 helped to edit *Nasha zhizn'*; 1906, worked on the Left-Cadet newspaper *Tovarishch*; supported the Trudoviks during elections to the Second State-Duma; 1912, contributed to the journal *Zaprosy zhizni*', working with Cadets, Popular Socialists and Menshevik-liquidators; opposed the Bolshevik Revolution; emigrated in 1926.

Voikov, Petr Lazarevich (1888–1927), Menshevik; in emigration from 1907 to February 1917; sent by the Provisional Government to resolve labour-conflicts in Ekaterinburg; a Bolshevik from August 1917; from January to July 1918, Supply-Commissar for the Urals Regional Soviet and member of the Extraordinary Investigative Commission; took part in shooting the Tsar's family, burying the remains, and shipping stocks of gold and platinum to Perm; 1918–24, Deputy Chairman of *Tsentrosoyuz*; from October 1924 to July 1927, Plenipotentiary representative of the USSR in Poland; 7 June, 1927, assassinated in Warsaw by the White Guard B. Koverda.

Voiloshnikov, Aviv Adrianovich (1877–1930), member of the Third State-Duma representing the Transbaikal Cossacks; member of the Social-Democratic fraction and supported the Bolsheviks; 1911–12, contributed to the Bolshevik newspapers *Zvezda* and *Pravda*; did economic work after October.

Voitinsky, Vladimir Savel'evich (S.) (1887–1962, other sources say 1885–1960), journalist and writer; contributed to the journals *Vestnik Evropy*, *Russkoe bogatstvo*, *Sovremennyi mir* and others; supported the Bolsheviks from early 1905; party-worker in St. Petersburg and Ekaterinoslav; sentenced to penal servitude in spring 1909; a Menshevik after February 1917; from June 1917, Assistant-Commissar of the Provisional Government on the northern front, and Commissar after the failure of Kornilov; in October 1917, participated in the Kerensky-Krasnov uprising and was arrested along with General P.N. Krasnov; imprisoned and then left for Georgia and eventual emigration.

Volin, Boris Mikhailovich (*Fradkin, Iosif Efimovich*) (1886–1957), member of the RSDRP from 1904; party-worker in Ekaterinoslav, Bryansk, the Urals and Moscow; editor of the Urals Bolshevik underground-newspaper *Ufimskii rabochii*; more than once arrested; emigrated 1910; returned to Russia in 1913 to resume party-work; in 1917, member of the Moscow Committee of the RSDRP(B); during October, Chairman of the Zamoskvorets Military-Revolutionary Committee; in 1918, one of the editors of *Pravda*' 1918-21, Chairman of the Bryansk Provincial Committee of the RKP(B) and Deputy People's Commissar of Internal Affairs for the Ukrainian Soviet Republic; 1921-4, editor of the newspaper *Rabochaya Moskva*; 1925-6, deputy editor of *Izvestiya*; 1927-9, headed the press-department of the People's Commissariat of Foreign Affairs; 1931-2, head of *Glavlit*; from 1932, director of the Institute of Red Professors; member of a partisan-unit during WWII; from 1945, scientific worker for the Institute of Marxism-Leninism; professor and author of several works on party-history.

Vorob'ev, A., Right S-R and member of the military staff of the anti-Bolshevik Nev'yansk uprising in the Urals in June 1918.

Votinov, worker at the Motovilikhinsk factory and provocateur.

Vovchinsky, Moisei Nikitich (1880-?), member of the RSDRP exiled to Nizhneilimsk.

Weitling, Wilhelm (1808-71), propagated the idea of egalitarian communism and regarded revolution as a spontaneous process led by declassed elements.

Wilhelm II Hohenzollern (1859-1941), German Emperor and Prussian King from 1888-1918; overthrown in the November Revolution of 1918.

Williams, member of the American Socialist Party.

Wilson, Thomas Woodrow (1856-1924), 28th President of the United States from 1913-21.

Witte, Sergei Yul'evich (1849-1915), count and member of the State-Council; Minister of Communications from February 1892, of Finance from August 1892, and Chairman of the Council of Ministers in 1905-6; introduced the spirits-monopoly in 1894, monetary reform on the basis of the gold-standard (1897), and construction of the Siberian railway; signed the Treaty of Portsmouth ending the Russo-Japanese War of 1904-5; made preparations for agrarian reform in 1903-4; author of the Manifesto of 17 October 1905; monarchist who proposed minor concessions to the liberal bourgeoisie and advocated severe repression of the people; dismissed from office in April 1906, and replaced by P.A. Stolypin.

Wrangel, Petr Nikolaevich (1878-1928), baron, lieutenant-general and one of the White leaders during the Civil War; 1918-19, in the Volunteer-Army and the Armed Forces of Southern Russia; in 1920, commander of the (so-called) Russian Army.

Yakovlev, Ivan Alekseevich, landlord and father of A.I. Herzen.

Yakubov, Arshak Stepanovich (1882-1923), member of the RSDRP from 1900; party-worker in Tiflis, Baku, Grozny, Sysran, Moscow and Siberia; in 1908, member of the Executive Bureau of the Moscow Committee of the RSDRP; at the beginning of 1909, First Secretary of the Moscow Committee; May 1909, sentenced to perpetual exile in Irkutsk; after February 1917, worked with the Irkutsk Soviet and the City-Duma; after October, member of the Collegium of the People's Commissariat of Food for the RSFSR; member of the Revolutionary War-Council of the Republic and the 'small Council of People's Commissars'; People's Commissar of the Worker-Peasant Inspectorate of Ukraine.

Yakubovich, Petr Filippovich (1860-1911), poet, writer and member of *Narodnaya Volya*; in 1887, sentenced to death in the 'Trial of the 21', changed to a sentence of penal servitude; later a member of the editorial board of the monthly *Russkoe bogatstvo* and author of several articles of literary criticism (under the pseudonym F.P. Grinevich).

Yakushkin, Pavel Ivanovich (1822-72), Russian writer, folklorist and ethnographer; arrested in the 1860s for distributing revolutionary propaganda in the countryside.

Yanson, Yakov Davydovich (1886-1938), member of the RSDRP from 1903; party-worker among soldiers in the Irkutsk military region; from September 1917, member of the Irkutsk Committee of the RSDRP(B); in October, Chairman of the Irkutsk Military-Revolutionary Committee, Commissar of Finance and Chairman of the Executive Committee of the Irkutsk Soviet; in 1918, Commissar of *Tsentrosibir'*; subsequently involved in party-work. Purged.

Yaroslavsky, Emel'yan Mikhailovich (*Gubel'man, Minei Izrailevich*) (1878–1943), member of the RSDRP from 1898; participant in the Revolution of 1905–7 and a military organiser for the RSDRP; in May 1917, Chairman of the Yakutsk Soviet; from July, worked for the Moscow military organisation of the RSDRP(B); editor of the newspaper *Derevenskaya pravda*; during the October Days, member of the Moscow Military-Revolutionary Committee and First Commissar of the Kremlin; then Commissar of the Moscow military region; supported the Left-Communists in 1918; 1918–19, Plenipotentiary of the Central Committee of the RKP(B) for mobilisation of the Red Army in several provinces; member of the Commission for the Struggle against Banditry under the Revolutionary War-Council of the Republic; 1919–20, Chairman of the Perm Provincial Party-Committee; from April 1920, member of the Siberian Bureau of the Central Committee of the RKP(B); from 1922, involved in party-work, journalism and scientific work; Academician of the USSR Academy of Sciences.

Yeltsin, Boris Mikhailovich (1871–1925), member of the RSDRP from 1897; Bolshevik party-worker in Ufa from 1910; in 1917, member of the Ufa City-Duma and the Ufa Party-Committee; in the autumn of 1917, party-candidate in Ufa province for elections to the Constituent Assembly; May-June 1918, supported withdrawal of Soviet forces from Ufa to allow the Czechoslovaks to cross Siberia 'peacefully'; in 1918–20, Chairman of the Ufa Provincial Council of Commissars and Chairman of the Provincial Party-Committee and the Provincial Executive Committee; in January 1919, Plenipotentiary of the Council of People's Commissars for the RSFSR in Ufa province; after 1920, worked in Moscow; joined the Trotskyist opposition. Purged.

Yudaev, member of the Bolkhov organisation of the RKP(B) in Orel province.

Yudenich, Nikolai Nikolaevich (1862–1933), infantry-general; in 1915–16, commander of the Caucasus Army and, in 1917, Chief-Commander of forces on the Caucasus front; 1919, commander of the north-western White-Guard army; emigrated following the collapse of his effort to take Petrograd in October-November 1919.

Yumagulov, Kharis Yumagulovich (1891–1937), ensign; member of the RSDRP(B) from 1918; after February 1917, member of the Military-Muslim Committee in Kazan, member of the Kazan Provincial Committee for Muslim Affairs and of the Provisional Proletarian Revolutionary Staff; Chairman of the All-Russian Central Executive Committee and of the Central Bureau of Communist Organisations of the Peoples of the East under the Bashkir Revolutionary Committee; expelled from the Party in 1922 for nationalist activities. Purged.

Yur'ev, Akim Aleksandrovich (1880–1957), member of the RSDRP from 1902; party-worker in the Kazan and Ufa organisations of the RSDRP; twice arrested, and in 1906 exiled to Yenisei province; after returning from exile, worked in the Ufa organisation of the RSDRP from 1911; after February 1917, member of the Urals Provincial Committee of the RSDRP(B) and of the Provincial Executive Committee; in 1918, member of the Urals Regional Committee of the RKP(B), Commissar of Labour for Ufa province and Chairman of the Ufa Provincial Council of the National Economy; from 1922, worked in the People's Commissariat of Foreign Trade and then in the Commissariat of Foreign Affairs of the USSR.

Zabelin, Ivan Egorovich (1820–1908), historian and archaeologist; honorary member of the Academy of Sciences and Chairman of the Society for History and Antiquities at Moscow University; one of the organisers of the Moscow Museum of History.

Zaikov, Arseny Ivanovich (1887–?), in the revolutionary movement from 1905; member of the Perm student-organisation of the RSDRP; in 1906, member of a Perm military-technical organisation;

more than once arrested; in 1909 sentenced to exile in Irkutsk province.

Zakhar'ina, Natal'ya Aleksandrovna, wife of A.I. Herzen from 1838–52.

Zalutsky, Petr Antonovich (1887–1937), S-R and, from 1907, a Bolshevik; from the end of 1916, member of the executive commission of the Petrograd Committee and the Russian Bureau of the Central Committee of the RSDRP(B); after February 1917, member of the Petrograd Soviet; member of the Petrograd Soviet during October and then Secretary of the Urals Bureau and of the Northwest Bureau of the Central Committee of the RKP(B); 1918–20, held responsible posts in the Red Army; 1921, member and Secretary of the All-Russian Central Executive Committee; subsequently did party- and economic work; from 1925 an active member of the Trotsky-Zinoviev opposition. Purged.

Zamyslovsky, Georgy Georgievich (1872–1920), nobleman, magistrate in the Baltic region and assistant prosecutor of the Grodno Regional Court; member of the Council of the 'Union of the Russian People' and of the 'League of the Archangel Michael'; gained notoriety for anti-Semitism in connection with the Beilis case; deputy to the Third and Fourth State-Dumas; in the Caucasus after 1917; died in Vladikavkaz from typhus.

Zarin (*Lengnik*) **Fridrikh Vil'gel'movich** (1873–1936), member of the RSDRP from 1893, Bolshevik; arrested in 1896 in the case of the 'Union of Struggle for the Emancipation of the Working Class' and exiled to eastern Siberia; subsequently did revolutionary work in Samara and Kiev; agent for *Iskra*; 1903–4, engaged in the struggle against Mensheviks abroad; returned to Russia in 1904 to do party-work in Moscow, Revel', Ekaterinoslav, Samara and St. Petersburg; after October 1917 member of the Collegium of the People's Commissariat of Education; involved in preparation of the GOELRO plan (State-Plan for the Electrification of Russia); then member of the Collegium of the Supreme Council of the National Economy, of the Commissariat of Foreign Trade and of the Red Army; from 1932, Deputy Chairman of the All-Union Society of Old Bolsheviks.

Zavadsky, Vikenty Petrovich (1884–1938), member of the RSDRP from 1904; party-worker until 1906 in Rybinsk; more than once arrested; in 1911, sentenced to exile in Verkholensk district in Irkutsk province. Purged.

Zdzyarsky, Miroslav Boleslavovich (1892–?), began his revolutionary activity in the student-organisations of Warsaw and Płock; several times arrested; in 1914 sentenced to exile in Irkutsk province; moved to Irkutsk city three months later and then to Novonikolaevsk.

Zelensky, Isaak Abramovich (1890–1938), member of the RSDRP from 1906; party-worker in Astrakhan, Penza, Orenburg, Saratov and Samara; in 1915, sent to permanent exile in Irkutsk province, but fled within a year; in Moscow from January 1917; after February 1917, party-organiser in the Basmanny district of Moscow; member of the Presidium of the Moscow Soviet; 1918–20, worked in food-procurement; 1920–4 Deputy Chairman of the Moscow Soviet and Secretary of the Moscow Committee of the RKP(B); 1925–31, Secretary of the Central-Asian Bureau of the Central Committee of the RKP(B); 1931–7, Chairman of *Tsentrosoyuz*. Purged.

Zemlyachka, (*née Zalkind, Samoilovna by marriage*), **Rosaliya Samoilovna** (1876–1947), member of the RSDRP from 1896; Bolshevik and agent of *Iskra*; during October, member of the Military-Revolutionary Committee of the Rogozhsko-Simonovsky district of Moscow; 1918–20, political worker in the Red Army; 1926–33, worked at the People's Commissariat of the Red Army and of Communication; 1939–43, deputy chair of the USSR Council of People's Commissars and then deputy chair of the Party's control-commission under the Central Committee of the All-Union Communist Party.

Zetkin, Klara (1857–1933), prominent figure in the German and international Communist movement and one of the founders of the Communist Party of Germany; one of the organisers of the Spartacist League; from 1920, a deputy in the German Reichstag; 1921–33, member of the Executive Committee of the Comintern.

Zhakov, Mikhail Petrovich (1893–1936), member of the RSDRP from 1911; party-worker in Kazan and Siberia; several arrests and periods of exile; with S.F. Vasil'chenko established the 'Union of Siberian Workers'; after February 1917, member of the Rostov Soviet and of the Rostovo-Nakhichevan and Don regional committees of the RSDRP(B); at the beginning of 1918, a member of the government of the Donetsk-Krivoy Rog Republic; 1921–2, member and Secretary of the Don Committee of the RKP(B); expelled from the Party in 1928 for supporting the Trotskyist opposition; from 1929, did educational and scientific work; retired in 1935. Purged.

Zhordaniya, Noi Nikolaevich (1869–1953), Social Democrat and a leader of Georgian Mensheviks; 1907–12, member of the Central Committee of the RSDRP; deputy to the First State-Duma from Tiflis; social-chauvinist during WWI; after February 1917, Chairman of the Tbilisi Soviet; 1918–21, head of the Menshevik government in Georgia; emigrated 1921.

Zinoviev, Secretary of the Bolkhov organisation of the RKP(B) in Orel province.

Zinoviev, Grigory Evseevich (*Radomysl'skii, Evsei Aronovich, 'G.Z.'*; 1883–1936), member of the RSDRP from 1901, doing revolutionary work from the late 1890s; 1908–April 1917, in emigration; as a member of the Central Committee of the RSDRP(B) opposed an armed uprising on the eve of the October Revolution; in November 1917, supported creation of a coalition-government with Mensheviks and S-Rs; after October, Chairman of the Petrograd Soviet, member of the Politburo of the Central Committee and Chairman of the Executive Committee of the Communist International; in 1925, one of the organisers of the 'New Opposition'; in 1926, co-leader of the Trotsky-Zinoviev bloc. Purged.

Zof, Vyacheslav Ivanovich (1889–1937), Bolshevik member of the RSDRP from 1913; in 1917, member of the Central Executive Committee and maintained contact between Lenin and the Central Committee; from the summer of 1918, Commissar of a brigade and of the 29th Rifle Division; Chief of Supply for the Third Army on the eastern front; March 1919–February 1920 member of the Revolutionary War-Council of the Baltic fleet and of the Petrograd Defence-Committee; from February 1920, Commissar of the Main Directorate of Water-Transportation and head of the Main Political Directorate of Water-Transportation; 1924–5, Commissar of USSR Naval Forces; member of the Revolutionary War-Council of the Republic; 1927–9, member of the Collegium of the People's Commissariat of Communication and Chairman of the Soviet commercial fleet; from 1930, Deputy People's Commissar of Transportation; from 1931, First Deputy People's Commissar of Water-Transportation. Purged.

Zolotov, Mikhail, district-superintendent of police.

Zolotov, Nikolai Mikhailovich, son of police-superintendent Zolotov, a Social Democrat, later emigrated.

Zuev, Nil Petrovich (1857–1918), nobleman; from 1903, Vice-Director and, from 1909, Director of the Department of Police.

References

Akademiya Nauk 1967, *Istoriya SSSR*, Vol. 7. Moscow: Nauka.

Bukharin, Nikolai and Evgeny Preobrazhensky 1920, *Azbukha kommunizma. Populyarnoe ob'yasnenie programmy Kommunisticheskoi partii Bol'shevikov*, Moscow: Gosizdat.

—— 1922, *The ABC of Communism*, translated by Eden and Cedar Paul, London: Communist Party of Great Britain.

Bukharin, Nikolai 1982 [1920], *Selected Writings on the State and the Transition to Socialism*, translated, edited and introduced by Richard B. Day, with forewords by Stephen F. Cohen and Ken Coates, Armonk, NY: M.E. Sharpe.

Bulgakov, Sergei Nikolaevich 1946, *Avtobiograficheskie zametki*, Paris: YMCA-Press.

—— 1996, *Moya Rodina. K 125-letiyu so dnya rozhdeniya. Izbrannoe*, Orel: Izd-vo Orlovskoi gosudarstvennoi-teleradioveshchatel'noi kompanii.

Bunin, Ivan Alekseyevich 1990 [1926], *Okayannye dni*, Moscow: Sovetskii pisatel'.

Deutscher, Isaac 1954, *The Prophet Armed: Trotsky 1879–1921*, Oxford: Oxford University Press.

—— 1959, *The Prophet Unarmed: Trotsky, 1921–1929*, Oxford: Oxford University Press.

—— 1963, *The Prophet Outcast: Trotsky, 1929–1940*, Oxford: Oxford University Press.

Day, Richard B. 1973, *Leon Trotsky and the Politics of Economic Isolation*, Cambridge: Cambridge University Press.

Day, Richard B. and Daniel Gaido 2009, *Witnesses to Permanent Revolution: The Documentary Record*, Leiden: Brill.

Dekrety sovetskoi vlasti, 1978, Vol. IX (June–July 1920), Moscow: Politizdat.

Dobrolyubov, Nikolai Alexandrovich 1984, *Izbrannoe*, Moscow: Sovremennik.

Engels, Friedrich 1990, *The Peasant Question in France and Germany*, in *Marx and Engels Collected Works*, Vol. 27, London: Lawrence & Wishart.

Erlich, Alexander 1960, *The Soviet Industrialization Debate, 1924–1928*, Cambridge, MA: Harvard University Press.

Fal'kner, Semen Anisimovich 1919, *Bumazhnye den'gi Frantsuzskoi revoliutsii*, Moscow: Vesenkha.

Figner, Vera Nikolayevna 1964, *Zapechatlennyi trud. Vospominaniya*, Vol. 1, Moscow: Mysl.

Fuller, William C. 2006, *The Foe Within: Fantasies of Treason and the End of Imperial Russia*. Ithaca, NY: Cornell University Press.

Goldenweiser, Emanuel Alexander 1914, 'The Russian Duma', *Political Science Quarterly*, 29, 3: 408–22.

Golikov, Georgii Nazarovich et al. 1970–1982, *V.I. Lenin. Biograficheskaya khronika. 1870–1924*, 12 Vols., Moscow: Politizdat.

Golubkov, A. 1931, 'O 1905 gode (Otryvki iz vospominanii)', *Katorga i ssylka*, 7, 80.

Gorinov, Mikhail M. and S.V. Tsakunov 1991, 'Life and Works of Evgeny Alekseevich Preobrazhensky', *Slavic Review*, 50, 2: 286–96.

—— 1992, 'Evgenii Preobrazhenskii: tragediya revolyutsionera', *Otechestvennaya istoriya*, 2: 79–95.

Haimson, Leopold 1995, 'Men'shevizm i evolyutsiya rossiiskoi intelligenttsii', *Rossiya XXI*, 5/6: 116–29.

Harper, Samuel N. 1908, *The New Electoral Law for the Russian Duma*, Chicago: University of Chicago Press.

Herzen, Alexander 1905, *Byloe i dumy*, St. Petersburg: Pavlenkov.

—— 1962, *Byloe i dumy*, Moscow: Gosizdat.
Hilferding, Rudolf 1918 [1910], *Finansovyi Kapital*, Petrograd: Izd-vo Kniga.
—— 1981 [1910], *Finance Capital*, London: Routledge and Kegan Paul.
Kautsky, Karl 1911, 'Finance Capital and Crises', *Social Democrat*, XV.
Kolb, Georg Friedrich 1872, *Istoriya chelovecheskoi kultury*, Vol. 1. St. Petersburg: S.V. Zvonarev.
KPSS 1983, *KPSS v resolyutsiyakh i resheniyakh s'ezdov, konferentsii i plenumov TsK*, Ninth edition, Vol. 1, 1898–1917, Moscow: Politizdat.
Krzhizhanovsky, Gleb Maximilianovich 1984, 'O Vladimir Il'iche', in *Vospominaniya o Vladimire Il'iche Lenine*, Vol. 2, Moscow: Politizdat.
Kuraev, Andrej 1997, 'Neterpimost' kak pravo na mysl'', in *Vyzov ekuminizma*, Moscow: Fond 'Blagovest'.
Lenin, Vladimir Ilich 1929, *Leninskii Sbornik*, Vol. XI, Gosizdat.
—— 1958–65, *Polnoe sobranie sochinenii*, 55 Vols., Moscow: Politizdat.
Lipkin, A. 1926, 'Provokator Krut (Po materialam proizvodstv Moskovskovo gubernskovo suda)', *Katorga i ssylka*, 6, 27.
—— 1927, 'Proval Soyuza sibirskikh rabochikh', *Katorga i ssylka*, 8.
London, Jack 2006 [1908], *The Iron Heel*, New York: Mondial.
Markov, Vladimir 1968, *Russian Futurism*, Berkeley, CA: University of California Press.
Marx, Karl 1907 [1867], *Kapital*, Volume I, translated by Ivan Ivanovich Skvortsov-Stepanov, Moscow: Moskovskoe Knigoizd-vo.
—— 1976 [1867], *Capital*, Volume I, Harmondsworth: Penguin.
Marx, Karl and Friedrich Engels 1962, *Selected Works*, Vol. 1, Moscow: Foreign Languages Publishing House.
Mill, John Stuart 1955 [1859], *On Liberty*, Chicago: Regnery.
Nikolaev, V. 1928, 'Sibirskaya periodicheskaya pechat' i politicheskaya ssylka', *Katorga i ssylka*, 6.
Osipova, Irina Ivanovna 1998, *Skvoz' ogn' muchenii i vodu slez…' Goneniya na Istinno-Pravoslavnuyu Tserkov'. Po materialam sledstvennykh i lagernykh del zaklyuchennykh*. Moscow: Serebryanye niti.

Perepiska Sekretariata TsK RKP(B) s mestnymi partiinymi organizatsiyami. (avgust-oktyabr' 1918g.): Sb. dokumentov, 1969, Vol. 4, Moscow: Politizdat.
Perepiska Sekretariata TsK RKP(B) s mestnymi partiinymi organizatsiyami. (noyabr'-dekabr' 1918 g.), 1970, Vol. 5, Moscow: Politizdat.
Pogonii, Yakov F., Vasilii Alexandrovich Sobolev et al 2001, *Lubyanka 2. Iz istorii otechestvennoi kontrrazvedki*, Moscow: Mosgorarkhiv.
Preobrazhensky, Evgeny Alekseevich 1917, *Chto nuzhno ural'skim rabochim*, Ekaterinburg.
—— 1918a, *Krest'yanskaya Rossiya i sotsializm (k peresmotru nashei agrarnoi programmy)*, Petrograd.
—— 1918b, *Anarkhizm i kommunizm*, Moscow: 'Kommunist'.
—— 1920, *Bumazhnye den'gi v epokhu proletarskoi diktatury*, Moscow: Gosudarstvennoe Izdatel'stvo.
—— 1923, *O morali i klassovykh normakh*, Moscow: Gosizdat.
—— 1926, 'Iz moikh vospominanii o Ya M. Sverdlove', in *Yakov Mikhailovich Sverdlov: Sbornik vospominanii i statei*, Leningrad: Gosizdat.
—— 1965, *The New Economics*, translated by Brian Pearce with an introduction by A. Nove, Oxford: Clarendon Press.
—— 1973, *From NEP to Socialism: A Glance into the Future of Russia and Europe*, translated by Brian Pearce, London: New Park Publications.
—— 1979, *The Crisis of Soviet Industrialization*, translated by Donald Filtzer, White Plains, NY: M.E. Sharpe.
—— 1985, *The Decline of Capitalism*, translated by Richard B. Day, Armonk, NY: M.E. Sharpe.
—— 1989 [1929] 'Avtobiografiya' in *Deyateli SSSR i revolyutsionnovo dvizheniya Rossii: Entsiklopedicheskii slovar' 'Granat'*, Moscow: Sovetskaya entsiklopediya.
Preobrazhensky, Leonid Evgenyevich n.d., *Vospominaniya*, Moscow: Main Archive.
Propokovich, S.N. 1918, *Opyt ischisleniya narodnovo dokhoda 50 gubernii Evropeiskoi Rossii*, Moscow.
Rakhmetov, V.N. (ed.) 1930, *Pervyi Vserossiiskii s'ezd Sovetov Rabochikh i Soldatskikh Deputatov*, Vol. 1, Moscow: Gosizdat.

Rakhmetov, V.N. and N.P. Miamalin (eds.) 1931, *Pervyi Vserossiiskii s'ezd Sovetov Rabochikh i Soldatskikh Deputatov*, Vol. 2, Moscow: Gosizdat.

Reznik, Genri Markovich et al. 1999, *Delo Mendelya Beilisa: Materialy sledstvennoi komissii Vremennovo pravitel'stva o sudebnom protsesse 1913 g. po obvineniyu v ritual'nom ubiistve*, St. Petersburg: Dmitrii Bulanin.

Shestoi s'ezd RSDRP (Bol'shevikov). Avgust 1917 goda: Protokoly, 1958, Moscow: Politizdat.

Schreiner, Olive 1911, *Woman and Labour*, New York: F.A. Stokes.

—— 1912, *Zhenshchina i trud*, Moscow: Izd. S. Dorovatovskago i I.A. Charushnikova.

Silin, Nikolai 1913, *Avstro-vengerskii bank*, Moscow: Universitet.

Smirnov, A.F. 1984, 'Borets za delo narodnoe' in Dobrolyubov 1984.

Stalin, Joseph 1951 [1924], 'Po povodu smerti Lenina. Rech' na II Vsesoyuznom s'ezde Sovetov, 26 April 1924', in *Sochineniya*, Vol. 6, Moscow: Gosizdat.

Stroev, E.S. et al. 1987, *Ocherki istorii Orlovskoi organizatsii KPSS*, Tula: Priokskoe knizhnoe izdatel'stvo.

Struchkov, Aleksei Alekseevich 1985, *Lenin i narod*, Moscow: 'Znanie'.

Terra, Victor (ed.) 1985, *Handbook of Russian Literature*, New Haven, CT: Yale University Press.

Tikhomirov, Lev Aleksandrovich 1997a, *Kritika demokratii*, Moscow: Red. zhurnala 'Moskva'.

—— 1997b, 'Nachala i kontsy. Liberaly i terroristy' in Tikhomirov 1997a.

—— 1997c [1888], 'Pochemu ya perestal byt' revolyutsionerom' in Tikhomirov 1997a.

—— 1997d, *Religiozno-filosofskie osnovy istorii*, Moscow: Red. zhurnala 'Moskva'.

Togan, Zaki Validi 1997, *Vospominaniya*, Moscow: Moskovskaya tipografiya No. 12.

Tretii Vserossiiskii s'ezd Sovetov rabochikh, soldatskikh i krest'yanskikh deputatov, 1918, St. Petersburg: Izdatel'stvo Priboi.

Varga, Eugen 1920, *Die wirtschaftspolitischen Probleme der proletarischen Diktatur*, Vienna: Genossenschaftsverlag der 'Neuen Erde'.

Vinogradov, F.G. 1925, 'V Aleksandrovskoi peresylke', *Katorga i ssylka*, 3, 16.

—— 1934, 'Bor'ba za kollektiv v Aleksandrovskoi peresylke v 1910 godu' in *Irkutskoe ssylka: Sbornik Irkutskovo zemlyachestva*, Moscow: Izdatel'stvo Vsesoyuznovo obshchestva politkatorzhan I ssysl'noposelentsev.

VKP(B) 1926, *1905 god v Orlovskom krae*, Orel: Izdatel'stvo istpartotdela Orlovskovo gubkoma VKP(B).

Zander, Lev 1989, 'Otets Sergii Bulgakov (kratkii ocherk evo zhizni i tvorchestva)' in Sergei Nikolaevich Bulgakov, *Pravoslavie. Ocherki ucheniya Pravoslavnoi tserkvi*, Third edition, Paris: YMCA-Press.

Index of Names

Abdul-Hamid II, 215
Abramov, 478
Adler, Friedrich, 314
Akhmadulin, 505
Akulov, Ivan Alekseevich, 377, 383
Aleksei Mikhailovich, 110
Aleksin, Sasha, xxxiv, xxxv, 5
Alexander I, 110, 122, 749
Alexander II, 137, 148, 362, 749
Amfiteatrov, Aleksandr Valentinovich, xxxii, 4, 223
Andreev, Leonid Nikolaevich, xxvii, 198, 205–7, 209, 213–14
Angarsky (*Klestov*), Nikolai Semenovich, 286
Anisimov, Ivan, xxxiv, xxxviii, 4, 5, 6–7
An-sky, Semen Akimovich, 110
Antonius Volynsky, 114
Antselovich, Naum Markovich, 534
Anuchin, Sergei Andreevich, 382
Aristotle, 221
Arosev, Aleksandr Yakovlevich, 311–12
Artem (*Sergeev, Fedor Andreevich*), 11, 19n5, 23, 24, 25, 61, 505, 506–7, 508n12, 522
Artsybashev, Mikhail, 109n2
Asquith, Herbert Henry, 196
Avenarius, Richard, 219
Avksent'ev, Nikolai Dmitrievich, 336, 364, 418
Azbukin, Dmitry Ivanovich, xliii
Azef, Evno Fishelevich, 87, 135

Babushkin, Ivan Vasil'evich, 32
Bakhtin, 356
Bakinovsky, Leon Vladislavovich, 32
Bakunin, Mikhail Aleksandrovich, 141, 615, 642
Bakunina, E., 110
Balakirev, Milii Alekseevich, 181
Barbe, Antonina Kazimirovna, 499
Baring, Maurice, 171

Barinov, 6–7
Bebel, August, 97, 655, 694
Bednyi, D., 694
Belinsky, Vissarion Grigor'evich, xx, xxvi, xxxi, li, 139–40, 157
Beloborodov, Aleksandr Georgievich, 377, 394
Belousov, Terentii Osipovich, 144–5, 153
Bentham, Jeremy, 218n4
Berdyaev, Nikolai Aleksandrovich, 114n2, 224
Berenshtam, Vladimir Vil'yamovich, 180–1
Berezovsky, Anton Iosifovich, 148
Bergman, (*Portnoi, K.*), 526
Berne, Ludwig, 140
Bethmann-Hollweg, Theobald, 125, 259
Bezrodnaya, Iulia Ivanovna, 109
Bismarck, Otto von, 125, 148, 237, 256, 654
Bissolati, Leonida, 454
Blank, Ruvim Mordkovich, 230
Blonsky, 685
Blücher, Vasilii Konstantinovich, 367
Blum, Oskar, 532–3
Bobrinsky, Vladimir Alekseevich, 114
Bobrovsky, Petr Semenovich, 6
Bogucharsky, V. (*Yakovlev, Vasily Yakovlevich*), 196–7
Borin, Ya. (*Borisov, Yakov Vasil'evich*), 240
Bosh, Evgeniya Bogdanovna (*Gotlibovna*), 12, 31, 288
Bramah, Ernest, 172
Brandes, Georg, 147
Briand, Aristide, 149, 454
Brichkina, Sof'ya Borisovna, 521
Brodovsky, 356
Bruno (*Pfaform-Bruno, Genrikh Ivanovich*), 32
Brusilov, Aleksei Alekseevich, 518
Bryukhanov, Nikolai Pavlovich, 10
Bryusov, Valery Yakovlevich, 90
Budenny, Semen Mikhailovich, 520

Bukharin, Nikolai Ivanovich, xviii, xlvi, xlix, l, lii, 265, 288, 291, 318n1, 349n4, 427n2, 519–25, 532, 540–5, 564, 646, 656, 694, 763, 786n5
Bulatsel', Pavel Fedorovich, 134
Bulgakov, Mikhail A., xvii
Bulgakov, Sergei Nikolaevich, xxi, xxiv–xxvi, xxvii, xxviii, xxx, xxxi, xxxvi, 114
Bulygin, Petr Pavlovich, 245
Bunin, Ivan Alekseevich, xxxv, 157
Burov, Ya., 694
Bustrem, Vladimir Vladimirovich, 32
Bykova (*born Proskuryakova*) Aleksandra Fedorovna, 168–9
Byron, George Gordon, 141, 213

Caillaux, Joseph, 149
Campanella, Tommaso (*Giovanni Domenico*), 217
Canning, George, 189
Catherine II Alekseevna, 110
Charushnikov, Akexander Petrovich, 97, 168, 240
Chekhov, Anton Pavlovich, 203, 211
Cherepanov, Sergei Aleksandrovich, 26, 31, 58, 60
Cherepanova, Mariya A., 26, 31
Chernov, Viktor Mikhailovich, 234–235, 287, 323, 335, 357, 364, 560, 564, 636
Chernyshevsky, Nikolai Gavrilovich, xx, xxvi, xxxi, li, 137
Chicherin, Georgy Vasil'evich, 521–2, 528n3
Chilikin, Feofilakt Nikolaevich, 145
Chlenov, Semen Borisovich, 540
Chugurin, Ivan Dmitrievich (*Petr*; *Petrukha*), 17, 18, 30
Clemenceau, Georges, 149, 454, 689
Curzon, George, 519

Dan (*Gurvich*), Fedor Il'ich, 225, 323
Danilov, S., 694
Danishevsky, Karl Khristianovich, 524
Danton, Georges Jacques, 48, 260, 313, 653
Dement'ev, E.A., 731
Demidov, Anatoly Nikolaevich, 296
Democritus, 219
Denikin, Anton Ivanovich, 418, 419, 426, 438, 454–7, 464, 468, 477, 483–4, 485, 487, 493, 541, 561–2, 563
Deutsch, Lev Grigor'evich, 149–50, 233
Deutscher, Isaac, xlix

Dioneo (*Shklovsky, Isaak Vladimirovich*), 172, 195–6, 226
Dmitriev, 427n2
Dmitrieva, Valentina Iovovna, 203
Dobrolyubov, Nikolai Aleksanderovich, xx, xxvi, xxxi, xxxii, 4, 137
Dorovatovsky, Sergei Pavlovich, 97, 168, 240
Dostoyevsky, Fedor Mikhailovich, 213
Dreiman, Rudolf Ansovich, 474, 475, 480
Dubasov, Fedor Vasil'evich, 79
Dudnik, Akim Minovich, 505
Dühring, Eugen Karl, 207
Durnovo, Petr Nikolaevich, 92
Dutov, Aleksandr Il'ich, 362, 446, 487n5, 607, 645
Dyun, 685
Dzhaparidze, Prokofy Aprasianovich, 289

Egor, see Kanatchikov, S.I.
Ekaterinoslavsky, Mikhail, xliv, 8–9
Eliseenko, A., 356
Elpat'evsky, Sergei Yakovlevich, 195
Emel'yanov, Vasily Antonovich, 427n2
Engels, Friedrich, xxxvi, 219, 341, 406, 607, 613–14, 642, 648, 671, 686, 713, 731
Epicurus, 219
Eremeev, Konstantin Stepanovich, 427n2
Erlich, Alexander, xlix, 6
Ermansky (*Kogan*) Osip Arkad'evich, 124, 225
Esinov, 427n2

Fal'kner, S.A., 750n25
Fedorov-Hartvig, 685
Fedorovich, 731
Fenomenov, Mikhail, xliii, 6
Fer'er, 685
Fet (*Shenshin*), Afanasy Afanas'evich, 142
Feuchtwanger, Lion, xvii
Feuerbach, Ludwig, li, 199, 206, 219
Fichte, Johann Gottlieb, 206, 219
Figner, Vera Nikolaevna, xxxiii n58, 149–50
Fokin, Ignatii Ivanovich, xlii, 8
Fourier, Charles, 217, 342
Frederick-William III, 125
Frolenko, Mikhail Fedorovich, 157
Frolov, 356
Fullarton, John, 744

Galkin, Anatolii M., 11, 24, 25
Galunov, Mikhail, 30

Ganetsky (*Fürstenberg*), Yakov Stanislavovich, 526
Gansberg, 685
Garibaldi, Giuseppe, 141
Geddes, Auckland, 489
Gegechkori, Evgeny Petrovich, 155
Gernet, 671
Gershenzon, M., 114
Goethe, Johann Wolfgang von, 197, 214
Gogol, Nikolai Vasilievich, 144n1, 424n4
Goikhbart, A., 671
Gololobov, Yakov Georgievich, 87, 185
Goloshchekin, Filipp (*Isai*) Isakovich, 377, 382, 388
Golubkov, A., xl
Gompers, Samuel, 330
Goncharov, Nikolai Kuz'mich, 312n3
Gorky, Maksim, 19, 147, 157, 180, 197, 198n2, 206, 233, 525
Gornfel'd, Arkady Georgievich, 123
Grave, Jean, 632
Gredeskul, Nikolai Andreevich, 544
Griboedov, Aleksandr Sergeevich, 123
Guchkov, Aleksandr Ivanovich, 82, 87, 164–5, 334
Guesde, Jules, 248, 259
Gurlitt, 685
Gusev-Orenburgsky (*Gusev*) Sergei Ivanovich, 193, 223, 394n8
Guzakov, Petr Vasil'evich, 497
Gyunter, Konrad, 125

Haimson, Leopold, xx
Hartman, Eduard, 206
Hegel, Georg Wilhelm Friedrich, li, 136, 140, 149, 206, 217–18, 219, 221
Heine, Heinrich, 89, 140, 145
Helvétius, Claude Adrien, 218n4
Henderson, Arthur, 345
Heraclitus of Ephesus, 219
Hertling, Georg Friedrich Graf von, 329–330
Herzen, Aleksandr Aleksandrovich, 136
Herzen, Aleksandr Ivanovich, xxxii, xxxiii, xlvi, li, liii, 111, 136–41, 149, 203–4, 250, 424
Hilferding, Rudolph, 741–5, 748
Hindenburg, Paul von, 337
Hoffmann, Max, 323, 325, 326, 327, 330
Homer, 171
Horvat, Dmitrii Leonidovich, 563
Hughes, William Morris, 25
Hurd, Dennis, 226
Hus, Jan, 218

Ignatovich, Nina Ivanovna, 245
Il'in, V., see V.I. Lenin
Iliodor (*Trufanov, Sergei Mikhailovich*), 195
Ilovaisky, Dmitry Ivanovich, 168
Ilyushin, Fedor Nikolaevich, 312n3, 427n2
Ioffe, Adolph Abramovich, 525
Ivanovich, St. (*Portugeis, S.I.*), 224
Ivinsky, Boleslav, 194
Izmailov, Abdrakhman Yu., 505
Izgoev, Aleksandr Solomonovich, 85, 114–16, 127, 149
Izvol'sky, A.P., 79n2

Kadomtsev, Erazm Samuilovich, 498
Kaledin, Aleksei Maksimovich, 312, 483n2, 487n5
Kalinin, Mikhail Ivanovich, 521
Kamenev (*Rozenfel'd*), Lev Borisovich, 518, 520–2, 524, 525
Kamensky, Anatoly Pavlovich, 109
Kanatchikov, Semen Ivanovich (*Egor*), 16, 427n2
Kant, Immanuel, 51, 206, 218, 220
Kapustin, Mikhail Yakovlevich, 185
Karakhan, Lev Mikhailovich, 33
Karavaev, Aleksandr L'vovich, 87
Kashirin, Nikolai Dmitrievich, 367
Kaskovich, see Kos'kovich S.F.
Kasso, Lev Aristidovich, 80, 115, 126
Katsura, Taro, 236
Kautsky, Karl, 40, 181, 560, 655, 671, 694, 745n21
Kerensky, Aleksandr Fedorovich, 12, 31n16, 309, 316, 331, 334, 336, 362, 363–4, 457, 464, 535, 597, 657, 680, 688, 720n19, 760n37, 760, 773, 775–7, 782, 783, 796n67
Kershenshteiner, G., 685
Kerzhentsov, V., 713
Kharitonov, Moisei Markovich, 394
Khionin, 356
Khokhryakov, Pavel Danilovich, 447
Khristich, 31
Khvostov, Aleksei Nikolaevich, 448
Kilchevsky, 693
Kil'ver, R., 694
Kin (*Orekhova*), Aleksandra Petrovna, 9, 14
Klyuchevsky, Vasily Osipovich, 168
Kokovtsov, Vladimir Nikolaevich, 92, 127
Kolb, Georg Friedrich, xxviii, xxxvi n68, 4
Kolchak, Aleksandr Vasil'evich, 264, 391n3, 409, 418, 454–7, 465, 466, 468, 471, 487, 541, 561–2, 563, 718

Kolegayev, Andrei Lukich, 589
Kolosov, Evgeny Evgen'evich, 234
Kolyubakin, Aleksandr Mikhailovich, 64
Komlev, 428
Kondurushkin, Stepan Semenovich, 148
Konovalov, Ivan Andreevich, 147, 170–2
Konteev, Dii Efimovich, 174
Konyukov, N., xlii
Kornilov, Lavr Georgievich, 307, 335, 336, 417, 607
Korolenko, Vladimir Galaktionovich, 110, 149–50, 225
Kosarev, Vladimir Mikhailovich, 376
Kosior, Iosif Viktent'evich, 32, 33
Kos'kovich S.F., 356
Kostomarov, Nikolai Ivanovich, 168
Kotina, E.M., 6
Kotoshikhin, Grigory Karpovich, 110
Kovalenko, Petr Arsent'evich, 11, 24, 25, 30, 32
Kovalenko, Sophia L'vovna, 30, 32
Kovalevsky, Maksim Maksimovich, 126–7, 157, 181, 203–204
Krasin, Leonid Borisovich, 518, 521
Krasnikova, Anna Pavlovna, xlii
Krasnikova, Ol'ga Pavlovna, xlii
Krasnov, Petr Nikolaevich, 409, 418, 419, 457, 464, 484, 487n5
Krestinsky, Nikolai Nikolaevich, 265n7, 506, 508n12, 525, 528n3, 546n2, 550n2, 554n10
Krivoshein, Aleksandr Vasil'evich, 107
Krivov, Timofei Stepanovich, 497
Kropotkin, Peter Alekseevich, 611–17, 632
Krupskaya, Nadezhda Konstantinovna, 11, 26, 31, 32, 685
Krut, David, 12, 32, 34
Krylenko, Nikolai Vasil'evich, 427n2
Krylov, Ivan Andreevich, 214n2
Kryukov, Fedor Dmitrievich, 109, 170, 193, 427n2
Krzhivitsky, Lyudvig, 223–4
Krzhizhanovsky, Gleb Maksimilianovich, xxxviii
Kühlmann, Richard von, 326
Kun, Bela, 556
Kunov, G., 694
Kurganov, 376
Kuropatkin, Aleksei Nikolaevich, 88
Kursky, Dmitry Ivanovich, 532–3
Kuskova (*Esipova*) Ekaterina Dmitrievna, 58
Kutler, Nikolai Nikolaevich, 64, 127

Kutuzov, 474, 478, 480
Kuzmenko, 12
Kuz'min, 377
Kuznetsov, Georgy Sergeevich, 87
Kuzovkov, Dmitry Vasil'evich, 6
Kvitkin, Olympii Aristarkovich, xliv, 8
Ky, 713

Lafargue, P., 694
Landezen (*Harting, Arkady Mikhailovich*), 149
Lapinsky, Pavel Lyudvigovich (*Levinson Ya.*), 528
Larin, Yu. (*Lur'e, Mikhail Zal'manovich (Aleksandrovich)*), 537–9, 713, 775n49, 787, 791, 796n67
Lashevich, Mikhail Mikhailovich, 400
Lassalle, Ferdinand Johann Gottlieb, 671
Latsis, Martin Ivanovich (*Subrabs, Yan Fridrikhovich*), 532–3
Lavrov, Petr Lavrovich, xxxviii
Lebedev (*Foma*), 9, 19, 19n6
Ledovsky, 6
Legien, Karl, 330
Lenin, Vladimir Il'ich, xxx, li, lii, 10, 11, 25–6, 30, 32, 33, 36, 225, 261n3, 265, 266–7, 269, 276n2, 289, 314, 318n1, 319, 322, 325, 326, 327, 329, 330, 348–349, 363, 367, 375, 376n2, 390, 391, 405–6, 430, 436, 465, 483, 493, 517–28, 530n8, 531n11–12, 540n2, 543, 546n2, 550n2, 553, 554n10, 564, 569–71, 575, 581, 655, 713
Lermontov, Mikhail Yur'evich, 89
Leroy-Beaulieu, Anatole, 69
Leskov, Nikolai Semenovich, xxvii
Lessing, Gotthold Ephraim, 140
Levi (*Gartshtein*) Paul, 525
Levitin, 685
Liebknecht, Karl, 314, 436, 643
Litkens, Aleksandr Aleksandrovich, xxxviii, 6
Litkens, Evgraf Aleksandrovich, 6
Litvinov, Maksim Maksimovich, 521
Litvinov, Stepan Sergeevich, 27
Lloyd George, David, 454, 520
Lobanov, 476, 478
Lobova, Valentina Nikolaevna (*Bina*), 9, 18
Lomonosov, Mikhail Vasil'evich, li, 92
London, Jack, xix
Loube, Émile François, 112
Louis XVI, 653
Luchitsky, Ivan Vasil'evich, 123
Lukin N.M. (*Antonov I.*), 693

Lunarcharsky, Anatoly Vasil'evich, 279, 410, 427n2
L'vov, Georgii Evgen'evich, 334
L'vov-Rogachevsky, Vasily L'vovich (*Rogachevsky*), 197
Lykoshin, Aleksandr Ivanovich, 107
Lyubosh, S., 126

MacDonald, James Ramsay, 454
Mach, Ernst, 219
MacLean, John, 314
Maisky, V. (*Lyakhovetsky, Ivan Mikahilovich*), 172
Makarin, 480–2
Makhno, Nestor Ivanovich, 547
Maklakov, Vasily Alekseevich, 85, 127, 133
Maksimov, Konstantin Gordeevich, 312n3
Maksimovsky, Vladimir Nikolaevich, 427n2
Malatesta, Errico, 611, 617, 632
Malyshev, Ivan Mikhailovich, 377, 378, 446–7
Malyutin, 508
Mamed-Bekov, 133
Mamontov (*Mamantov*) Konstantin Konstantinovich, 485–8
Markhlevsky, Yulian Yusefovich, 520
Markov, Nikolai Evgen'evich, 69–70, 648
Martov, L. (*Tsedenbaum, Yuly Osipovich*), 225, 315, 316, 410, 560
Marx, Karl, xviii, xxxvi, xxxvii, xxxviii, 95, 137–9, 159, 195, 203, 215, 217–18, 219, 226, 256, 341–5, 607, 610n3, 613–14, 642, 648, 671, 686, 734–9, 781
Maslov, Petr Pavlovich, 94–5, 162
Masterov, 480
Mazzini, Giuseppe, 141
Melent'ev, 356
Merkulov, Nikita Trofimovich, 427n2
Meshcheryakov, N., 713
Métivier, 149
Meyendorff, Aleksandr Feliksovich, 56, 185
Mikhailovsky, Nikolai Konstantinovich, xxxviii
Mikheev, N.M., xlv, 6, 9, 12, 31n16
Mill, John Stuart, li, 138
Miller, Evgeny Karlovich, 563
Miller, V., 356
Millerand, Alexandre, 520
Milton, John, 213
Milyukov, Pavel Nikolaevich, 82, 85, 126, 155–6, 204, 231, 275, 334
Minin, S., 693
Minkin, Aleksandr Eremeevich, 9

Minkov, Isaak Il'ich, 553
Mirbach, Wilhelm von, 363n4, 364
Missar, 149
Moiseev, 238
Mollov, Ruschu (*Gavriil*) Georgievich, 247
Moltke (*the younger*), Helmuth Johann, 654
More, Thomas, 217
Mostovenko, Pavel Nikolaevich, 508
Mrachkovsky, Sergei Vital'evich, 377
Muralov, Rodion Ivanovich, 312n3
Murav'ev, Mikhail Nikolaevich, 148
Musset, Alfred de, 90
Myasoedov, Sergei Nikolaevich, 164–5, 280
Myunkh, 685

Nakoryakov, Nikolai Nikandrovich (*Nazar*), 10, 19n5
Nansen, Fridtjof, 223
Napoleon I (*Napoleon Bonaparte*), 240, 653–4
Neidgard, 239
Nekrasov, Nikolai Alekseevich, 447
Nekrasov, Nikolai Vissarionovich, 107–8, 153
Nevel'son, Rosa Abramovna, xxii
Nicholas I, 90, 245, 389, 749
Nicholas II, 273, 409, 535, 655
Nietzsche, Friedrich Wilhelm, li, 134, 234–5
Nikkeleva, 6
Nikolai Mikhailovich, 122
Nikolai Nikolaevich (*the younger*), 249
Nikolaevsky, Boris Ivanovich, xx
Nikol'sky, 694
Nikol'sky, Boris Vladimirovich, 69
Nissen, 314
Noske, Gustav, 650, 665
Novgorodtseva (*Sverdlova*), Kalvdiya Timofeevna, 9, 14, 30

Osinsky, N. (*Obolensky, Valerian Valerianovich*), 349n4, 405–10, 542
Osipov, 547
Ogarev, Nikolai Platonovich, xxxiii
Oliger, Nikolai Fridrikhovich (*Fedorovich*), 203
Olimpov (*Fofanov*) Konstantin Konstantinovich, 130–2
Ol'nem, O.N. (*Tsekovskaya, Varvara Nikolaevna*), 193
Ortodoks (*Aksel'rod, Lyubov Isaakovna*), 224
Osipov, 427n2

Ostrovskaya, Nadezhda Il'inichna, 428
Ostwald, Friedrich Wilhelm, 219
Ovsyannikov, Nikolai Nikolaevich, 427n2

Paramonov, A.I., 12, 31
Pasmanik, D.S., 181
Pasteur, Louis, xxviii
Pavlovich, 666
Pelikan, Boris Aleksandrovich, 238n2
Pestkovsky, Santislav Stanislavovich, 32
Peter I (*Peter the Great*), 110
Peter III Fedorovich, 110
Petlyura, Simon Vasil'evich, 563
Petrov, 314
Petrov, S., 655
Petrunkevich, Ivan Il'ich, 197
Pietry, 148
Pisarev, 427n2
Pisarev, Dmitry Ivanovich, xxviii, xxxii, 4, 447
Plato, 141, 206, 219
Platonov, Sergei Fedorovich, 168
Platten, Friedrich, 314
Plehve, Vyacheslav Konstantinovich, 239
Plekhanov, Georgy Valentinovich, 40n6, 48, 149, 196–7, 248n4, 254–7, 259, 260
Pletnev, Valerii Fedorovich (*Potapych*), 21
Pobedonostsev, Konstantin Petrovich, 185, 672n6
Podbel'sky, Vadim Nikolaevich, 427n2
Podshchekoldin, 476, 479
Podtel'kov, F.G., 483n2
Pod'yachev, Semen Pavlovich, 148
Podvoisky, 666
Poincaré, Raymond, 259
Pokrovskaya, M., 731
Pokrovsky, 694
Pokrovsky, Ivan Petrovich, 87
Ponomarev, xliv, 8
Potyaev. A.I., 728
Pozner, V.M., 685
Pravdin, Aleksandr Georgievich, 427n2
Predkal'n (*Priedkal'n*), Andrei Yanovich, 64
Preobrazhenskaya, Aleksandra Alekseevna, xxii
Preobrazhenskaya, Lyudmila Alekssevna, xxii
Preobrazhenskaya, Ol'ga Alekseevna, xxii
Preobrazhenskaya, Varvara Alekseevna, xxii, xxiii, xxix
Preobrazhensky, Aleksei Aleksandrovich, xxi, xxii, xxiii, xxix

Preobrazhensky, Evgeny Alekseevich
Preobrazhensky, Leonid Evgen'evich, xxi, xxiv, xxix
Preobrazhensky, Viktor Alekseevich, xxii
Prokopovich, Sergei Nikolaevich, 56, 787n56, 791
Proudhon, Pierre-Joseph, 627
Purishkevich, Vladimir Mitrofanovich, 70, 82, 87, 115, 259, 648, 669, 773n46
Purov, 441
Pushkin, Aleksandr Sergeevich, xxviii, xlvi, li, 89–91, 136, 140
Pyatakov, Georgy (Yury) Leonidovich, 723
Pythagoras of Samos, 219

Radek (*Sobel'son*) Karl Berngardovich, 349n4, 518, 519, 521, 522, 526, 532
Rafes, Moisei Grigor'evich, 528n3
Rakovsky, Christian Georgievich, 314, 522
Rasputin (*Novykh*) Grigory Efimovich, 195
Ratner, Mark Borisovich, 196, 226
Reclus, Jean-Jacques Elisée, 632
Reinbot (*Rezvoi*) Anatoly Anatol'evich, 46
Richter, Eugen, 125
Robespierre, Maximilien, 313, 653
Rodichev, Fedor Izmailovich, 139, 204
Rodzyanko, Mikhail Vladimirovich, 77, 185
Romanov, 6
Romanov, Mikhail Fedorovich, 240
Romm, Nikolai Nikolaevich, 12, 32, 34
Ropshin, V. (*Savinkov, Boris Viktorovich*) i, 147, 233–4, 362, 364, 562, 564
Rouget de Lisle, Claude Joseph, 653
Rozental', 391
Rozhkov, Nikolai Aleksandrovich, 33, 178
Rudnev, Vadim Viktorovich, 588
Rudzutak, Yan Ernestovich, 520
Rukavishnikov, Ivan Sergeevich, 109, 193
Ryabushinsky, Pavel Pavlovich, 188–9, 639
Ryazanov (*Gol'dendakh*) David Borisovich, 427n2
Rykov, Aleksei Ivanovich, 9, 520–1, 523, 524

Sadko, Mikhail, 145
Safarov (*Volodin*), Georgy Ivanovich, 372, 377, 392, 394
Said-Galiev, Sakhib Garei, 505, 519
Saint-Simon, Claude Henri de, 217, 342
Saltykov-Schedrin, Mikhail Evgrafovich, xxxii, xxxvii, 4, 402n2
Samoilov, Fedor Nikitich, 507, 508n12
Samoilova, R., see Zemlyachka, R.S.
Samsonov, Mikhail Borisovich, 12, 32, 34

Sanin, A.A., 109
Sapozhkov, 547
Savinkov, Boris Viktorovich, see Ropshin, V.
Sazonov, Georgy Petrovich, 81
Sazonov, Sergei Dmitrievich, 155
Scheidemann, Phillip, 259, 344, 597, 599, 636, 651, 665
Schiller, Johann Christoph Friedrich von, 136, 654
Schmidt, Otto, 785n53
Schopenhauer, Arthur, li, 206
Schreiner, Olive, 97–8
Sedoi (*Litvin, Zinovii Yakovlevich*), 9
Sefarimovich (*Popov*), Aleksandr, 110, 147, 193–4, 223, 383
Semashko, Nikolai Aleksandrovich, 427n2
Sembat, Marcel, 636
Semenov, Grigorii Mikhailovich, 9, 563, 607
Serebryakov, Leonid Petrovich, 12, 265n7
Sereda, 430
Sergeev, Fedor Andreevich, see Artem
Sergo (*Ordzhonikidze, Grigory Konstantinovich*), 518
Shakespeare, William, 90, 123–4, 197
Shamigulov, Gali K., 499, 505, 508n12
Shamshin, Ivan Dmitrievich, 30
Shamshin, Ivan Ivanovich, 30
Shamshin, Vasily Ivanovich, 24, 30, 32
Shamshina, Evdokiya Ivanovna, 30
Sharrel'man, 685
Shatsky, 685
Shilo, Andrei Ivanovich, 145
Shkuro, 485n1
Shloss, 187–190
Shmidt, Valeryan, 6, 32
Shtampfer, 694
Shtiber, 148
Shul'ts, 685
Shumyatsky, Boris Zakharovich, 289–90
Shuvalov, Ivan Ivanovich, 92
Shvarts, Isaak Izrailevich (*S.; Semen*), 12, 31, 59, 247
Sibirsky, F. (*Lebedev, Fedor Nikolaevich*), 159–63
Silin, 751n13
Simakov, 474–5, 478, 480
Sklyansky, Efraim Markovich, 442, 506
Skobelev, Matvei Ivanovich, 335
Skoropadsky, Pavel Petrovich, 357, 607, 616, 639, 645
Skrypnik, Nikolai Alekseevich, 289

Skvortsov-Stepanov, Ivan Ivanovich, 64, 736n5
Sleptsov, 474, 478
Slutskaya, Vera, xlii
Smilga, Ivar Tenisovich, 521, 523–4
Smirnov, E. (*Gurevich, Emmanuil L'vovich*), 124
Smirnov, Ivan Nikitich, 522
Smirnov, Vladimir Mikhailovich, 349n4, 786
Smol'nikov, 475–6
Sokol'nikov, Grigorii Yakovlevich, 458, 723
Sokolov, Aleksandr Nikolaevich, 20
Sokolov, Nikolai Dmitrievich, 12, 31n16, 64
Solov'ev, Vasily Ivanovich, 290
Sol'ts, Aron Aleksandrovich, 312n5
Sorokin, 376
Sosnovsky, Lev Semenovich, 427n2, 522
Spinoza, Baruch, li, 219, 220
Spiridonova, Mariya Aleksandrovna, 363, 410
Stakhovich, Aleksandr Aleksandrovich, 448
Stalin (*Dzhugashvili*), Joseph Vissarionovich, xvii, xviii, xx, l, lii, liii, 286–7, 291, 430, 508n12, 518, 522, 525, 528n3, 655
Stankevich, Nikolai Vladimirovich, 136
Stefanovich, Yakov Vasil'evich, 233
Steklov (*Nakhamkis*) Yury Mikhailovich, 111, 149, 427n2, 655
Stepanov, I., 694
Stepnyak, C. (*Kravchinsky, Sergei Mikhailovich*), 147
Stogov, 398
Stolypin, Aleksandr Arkad'evich, xxvii
Stolypin, Petr Arkad'evich, xxvii, 36, 37, 79n2, 85, 107, 127, 157, 225, 590
Struve, Peter Berngardovich, 114–15, 127
Stuchka, Petr Ivanovich, 671
Stukov, 498
Sukhomlinov, Vladimir Aleksandrovich, 280
Sumatokhin, M., 713
Sverdlov, Yakov Mikhailovich (*Andrei, Mikhalych*), 9, 13–22, 30, 266–9
Svetlovsky, V., 731

Tagiev, Zeinal Abdin, 133–35
Tan, N.A. (*Bogoraz, Vladimir Germanovich*), 203, 232–3
Tchaikovsky, Petr Il'ich, 181, 437
Teslenko, Nikolai Vasil'evich, 64, 134

860 • Index of Names

Thiers, Adolphe, 535, 613
Tikhomirov, Lev Aleksandrovich, xxviii, xxxi, xxxvi, xxxvii n69
Tikhomirov, Viktor Aleksandrovich, 312n5
Tinyakov, Aleksandr, xxxiv, 5
Titov, 475, 480
Tizengausen, Evgeny Evgen'evich, 80
Tolmachev, Ivan Nikolaevich, 238n2
Tolmachev, Nikolai Gur'evich, 377, 392, 446–7
Tolstoy, Lev Nikolaevich, xxiii, 3, 109, 122, 140, 197, 206, 214, 222, 234, 417
Trepov, Dmitry Fedorovich, 79
Treshchenkov, Nikolai Viktorovich, 11, 25, 166n2
Tret'yakov, Pavel Mikhailovich, 683
Troitsky, Aleksandr Georgievich, 278
Trotsky (*Bronshtein*) Lev (*Leiba*) Davydovich, xvii, xlix, l, 314, 318n1, 319–20, 322, 326, 411, 414, 436, 458, 487n5, 506, 517–24, 555, 564, 666
Trubina, A.V., 12
Trusevich, Maksimilian Ivanovich, 54
Tsereteli, Irakly Georgievich, 33, 277–9, 335
Tugan-Baranovsky, Mikhail Ivanovich, 75
Turgenev, Ivan Sergeevich, 437
Tverskoi, P.A. (*Dement'ev, Petr Alekseevich*), 157

Ul'yanov, 427
Urusov, Sergei Dmitrievich, 127
Uspensky, Gleb Ivanovich, 149, 150n4
Uspensky, Mishka, xxvi, 3

Vainer, Leonid Isaakovich, 378, 447
Validov, Akhmed-Zaki, xxx, 505, 507
Vandervel'de, 694
Van-Kon, 671
Varga, Eugen Samuilovich (*Jenő*), 785n54
Vasil'chenko, Semen Filippovich, 32–4
Vedernikov, A.S., 312n4
Veisman (*Tseitlin, L.S.*), 429
Vel'man, Vladimir Ivanovich, 32
Verbov, Abram Aaronovich, 20
Vernikovsky, 10
Vetekamp, 685
Vikman, P.M., 508
Vilonov, Nikifor Efinmovich, 19
Vinninchenko, Vladimir, 316
Vinogradov, F.V., xxxv
Vipper, 694
Vodovozov, Vasily Vasil'evich, 230
Voikov, Petr Lazarevich, 377

Voiloshnikov, Aviv Adrianovich, 85
Volin, Boris Mikhailovich (*Fradkin, Iosif Efimovich*), 428, 429
Vorob'ev, A., 356
Votinov, 9
Vovchinsky, Moisie Nikitich, 32, 33

Weitling, Wilhelm, 342
Wilhelm II Hohenzollern, 125, 320, 330, 366, 563, 672
Williams, 314
Wilson, Thomas Woodrow, 329–30
Witte, Sergei Yul'evich, 79, 80, 92
Wrangel, Petr Nikolaevich, 522, 541–2, 562, 796

Yakovlev, Ivan Alekseevich, 136
Yakubov, Arshak Stepanovich, 17
Yakubovich, Petr Filippovich, 149–50
Yakushkin, Pavel Ivanovich, xxvii
Yanson, Yakov Davydovich, 32
Yanzhul, E.N., 685
Yaroslavsky, Emel'yan Mikhailovich (*Gubel'man, Minei Izrailevich*), 427n2, 666
Yeltsin, 506
Yudaev, 474
Yudenich, Nikolai Nikolaevich, 542, 563
Yumagulov, Kharis Yumagulovich, 495, 507–8
Yur'ev, Akim Aleksandrovich, 497
Yurovsky, A., 204

Zabelin, Ivan Egorovich, 168
Zaikov, Arsenii Ivanovich, 30
Zakhar'ina, Natal'ya Aleksandrovna, 136
Zalevsky, K., 655
Zalutsky, Petr Antonovich, 394
Zamyslovsky, Georgy Georgievich, 69–70, 134
Zarin (*Lengnik*) Fridrikh Vil'gel'movich, 373
Zavadsky, Vikentii Petrovich, 12, 32
Zdzyarsky, Miroslav Boleslavovich, 12, 32, 34
Zeidel', R., 685
Zelensky, Isaak Abramovich, 12
Zemlyachka (*née Zalkind, Samoilovna by marriage*), Rosaliya Samoilovna, 312
Zetkin, Clara, 97
Zhakov, Kallistrat Falaleevich, 205–7, 213–14, 217–19, 220–2
Zhakov, Mikhail Petrovich, 32–4
Zhegur, Ya., 713